PRACTICE-RELATED ISSUES

Chapter 11 ■ *Experimental Designs*

- This chapter is filled with practice examples throughout, such as evaluation of community organization intervention as well as services for battered women, nursing home residents, depressed clients, abusive parents, people suffering from trauma, children in residential treatment, hospice clients, case management clients, substance abusers, people with mental disabilities, people in rural areas, HIV/AIDS prevention, play therapy, family preservation, school social work, and others. Also included is coverage of practical pitfalls in conducting evaluations in social work practice settings and how to prevent or alleviate them. The chapter ends with a lengthy section that illustrates a social work experiment evaluating cognitive-behavioral interventions with parents at risk of child abuse.

Chapter 12 ■ *Single-Case Evaluation Designs*

- This entire chapter is devoted to practitioners' use of research to evaluate their own practice. Virtually every word in it deals directly with practice related issues.

Chapter 13 ■ *Program Evaluation*

- This chapter is filled with examples of issues and techniques for trying to conduct evaluations of practice in practice settings. Such examples include the following practice areas: managed care, family preservation, community mental health, family service agencies, case management, school social work, hospice, AIDS prevention, homelessness programs, assessing client or community needs, child abuse prevention programs, and services to people with developmental disabilities.

PART V: Data Collection Methods with Large Sources of Data

Chapter 14 ■ *Sampling*

- Client satisfaction survey example regarding sampling. Also, sampling social work students.

Chapter 15 ■ *Survey Research*

- Examples of surveys include one with welfare recipients and one regarding views about evidence-based practice

Chapter 16 ■ *Analyzing Available Records: Quantitative and Qualitative Methods*

- Impact of welfare reform
- Evaluating play therapy
- The core conditions of the helping relationship
- The practice of school social workers
- Community organization
- Self-image of social work
- Social work with adoptive families
- Care of the chronically mentally ill

PART VI: Qualitative Research Methods

Chapter 17 ■ *Qualitative Research: General Principles*

- Community-based services for the mentally ill
- Services for the homeless
- Client logs
- Social service agency volunteers
- Community organizing
- Fostering family involvement in nursing home care
- Case management

Chapter 18 ■ *Qualitative Research: Specific Methods*

- Residential treatment centers for children
- Evaluating in-service training
- Sexually abused girls
- Empowering battered women

PART VII: Analysis of Quantitative Data

Chapter 20 ■ *Quantitative Data Analysis*

- Assessing client satisfaction with services
- Assessing why clients drop out of treatment (coding example)
- Case management example regarding standard deviation
- Child welfare interventions regarding qualitative research and descriptive statistics

Chapter 21 ■ *Inferential Data Analysis: Part 1*

- Statistical significance explained with an example regarding intervention to prevent child abuse. (This example is returned to in various subsequent sections of this chapter.) Effect size is illustrated regarding the evaluation of interventions for male batterers.

Chapter 22 ■ *Inferential Data Analysis: Part 2*

- Examples include a school social work program in an inner-city high school, case management, psychotherapy, treating the chronically mentally ill, child abuse prevention, social service volunteers, caregiver burden, and support group intervention for people with AIDS

PART VIII: Writing Research Proposals and Reports

Chapter 23 ■ *Writing Research Proposals and Reports*

- Proposal writing examples regarding substance abuse treatment, child abuse prevention, and EMDR

Research Methods for Social Work

Sixth Edition

Allen Rubin
University of Texas at Austin

Earl R. Babbie
Chapman University

Australia • Brazil • Canada • Mexico • Singapore • Spain • United Kingdom • United States

Research Methods for Social Work, Sixth Edition
Allen Rubin and Earl R. Babbie

Social Work Editor: *Dan Alpert*
Development Editor: *Tangelique Williams*
Assistant Editor: *Alma Dea Michelena*
Editorial Assistant: *Ann Lee Richards*
Technology Project Manager: *Julie Aguilar*
Marketing Manager: *Terra Schultz*
Marketing Communications Manager: *Shemika Brett*
Project Manager, Editorial Production: *Tanya Nigh*
Creative Director: *Rob Hugel*
Art Director: *Vernon Boes*
Print Buyer: *Linda Hsu*
Permissions Editor: *Robert Kauser*
Production Service: *Katherine Bishop, Newgen–Austin*
Text Designer: *Newgen–Austin*
Copy Editor: *Anita Wagner*
Cover Designer: *Katherine Minerva*
Cover Images: *Royalty-Free/Corbis*
Cover Printer: *West Group*
Compositor: *Newgen*
Printer: *West Group*

Printed in the United States of America
1 2 3 4 5 6 7 11 10 09 08 07

For more information about our products, contact us at:
Thomson Learning Academic Resource Center
1-800-423-0563

For permission to use material from this text or product, submit a request online at **http://www.thomsonrights.com.**
Any additional questions about permissions can be submitted by e-mail to **thomsonrights@thomson.com.**

Library of Congress Control Number: 2006932556

Student Edition:
ISBN-13: 978-0-495-09515-6
ISBN-10: 0-495-09515-X

Thomson Higher Education
10 Davis Drive
Belmont, CA 94002-3098
USA

Dedication

In memory of

YETTA RUBIN

CORRINE RUBIN HARRIS

HERMAN OCTAVE BABBIE

Contents in Brief

Contents in Detail

PART 7
Analysis of Quantitative Data 477

PART 8 Writing Research Proposals and Reports 545

Preface

As with previous editions of this text, this sixth edition contains significant improvements to keep up with advances in the field and respond to the many excellent suggestions from colleagues who use this text in their teaching or who reviewed prior editions. Although we have aimed to streamline the text wherever possible, we also have added critical new material. Our most noteworthy changes to this edition are as follows.

• We have increased coverage of evidence-based practice, including a new chapter (2) on that topic as well as infusing more content about it into other chapters.

• We expanded and reorganized our coverage of qualitative methods. In addition to our coverage of qualitative methods as at least part of almost every chapter, we now have a three-chapter Part 6 devoted to qualitative methods.

• We moved our coverage of levels of measurement from our measurement chapter to our chapter on quantitative data analysis. Our rationale is that the prime relevance of levels of measurement is in terms of how it influences which data analysis procedures to use.

• We reorganized our coverage of causal inference, internal validity, and the elaboration model. In so doing, we added more material on the case-control design. In this connection, we created a new chapter (10) that covers these topics and precedes our chapter on experimental and quasi-experimental designs (which were separated into two chapters in the previous edition). By moving the elaboration model up into this new chapter, we show how correlational designs can improve their explanatory power through multivariate statistical control.

• With the elaboration model transferred from our quantitative data analysis section, we were able to reduce that section from four chapters to three.

• We added a section on logic models to our chapter on program evaluation.

• We moved our chapters on sampling and surveys back a bit. They now come after our chapters on designs for evaluating programs and practice.

• In response to feedback about the length of our sampling chapter and the difficulty many students have with the statistical material in it, we moved that statistical material to Appendix B, accompanying our table of random numbers. Instructors have the option of assigning Appendix B along with our chapter on sampling (14) if they want students to study the statistical content there.

• We added an illustration of an online survey about evidence-based practice to our chapter on surveys.

• We moved our coverage of secondary analysis to our chapter (16) on analyzing existing statistics. We also expanded our coverage of secondary analysis considerably.

• In response to recommendations from several reviewers, we moved our chapter on culturally competent research up so that it now immediately follows our chapter on research ethics.

Although the above changes are the most noteworthy ones, we also revised most chapters in additional ways that we hope instructors and students will find helpful. We believe and have been told by instructors that among this text's most important features have always been its comprehensive and deep coverage, and with each new edition we have sought to strengthen both. Research content can be difficult for students to grasp. We think student comprehension is not aided by a simplistic approach, so we explain things in depth and use multiple examples to illustrate the complex material and its relevance for practice. Moreover, taking this approach enhances the book's value to students in the long run. They seem to agree, and many students keep the book for their professional libraries rather than resell it at the end of the semester. This text's comprehensive coverage of the range of research methodologies and all phases in the research process—particularly expanded coverage of qualitative methods, culturally competent research, evidence-based practice, program and practice evaluation, illustrations of practice applications (including the practice-oriented study guide)—also represent our effort to help courses reflect current curriculum policy statements guiding the accreditation standards of the Council on Social Work Education.

We are excited about this new edition of *Research Methods for Social Work* and think the new material we've added, along with the other modifications, will meet the needs of instructors and students who seek to keep up with advances in the field. We hope you'll find this new edition useful. We would like to receive any suggestions you might have for improving this book even more. Please write to us in care of Thomson Brooks/Cole, 60 Garden Court, Suite 205, Monterey, CA 93940, or e-mail us at arubin@mail.utexas.edu.

ANCILLARY PACKAGE

Practice-Oriented Study Guide

This edition is accompanied by the sixth edition of a *Practice-Oriented Study Guide* that parallels the organization of the main text but emphasizes its application to practice. The guide is designed to enhance student comprehension of the text material and its application to the problems that students are likely to encounter in social work practice. Each chapter of the *Practice-Oriented Study Guide* lists behavioral objectives for applying the chapter content to practice, a summary that focuses on the chapter's practice applications, multiple-choice review questions that are generally asked in the context of practice applications (answers appear in an appendix along with cross-references to the relevant text material), exercises that involve practice applications that can be done in class (usually in small groups) or as homework, and practice-relevant discussion questions. A crossword puzzle appears at the end of each chapter of the *Study Guide* to provide students with an enjoyable way to test out and strengthen their mastery of the important terminology in each chapter. Solutions to each puzzle appear in an appendix.

In addition to enhancing student learning of research content, we hope that this *Study Guide* will significantly enhance the efforts we have made in the main text to foster student understanding of the relevance of research to practice and their consequent enthusiasm for research. We also expect that this *Study Guide* will be helpful to instructors by providing practice-relevant exercises that can be done in class or as homework.

WebTutor™ ToolBox on WebCT 0-534-66000-2

WebTutor™ ToolBox on Blackboard 0-534-69551-8

We have a supplemental web-based student- and course-management tool for our text called WebTutor ToolBox. WebTutor ToolBox's course-management tool gives you the ability to provide virtual office hours, post syllabi, set up threaded discussions, track student progress with the quizzing material, and much more. For students, WebTutor ToolBox offers real-time access to a full array of study tools, including experiential exercises and other materials from the print study guide, plus practice quizzes, flash cards, crossword puzzles, Microsoft® *PowerPoint*® slides, InfoTrac® College Edition exercises, and web links. WebTutor ToolBox also provides robust communication tools such as a course calendar, asynchronous discussion, real-time chat, a whiteboard, and an integrated e-mail system.

Instructor's Manual

As with previous editions, an *Instructor's Manual* mirrors the organization of the main text, offering our suggestions of teaching methods. Each chapter of the manual lists an outline of relevant discussion, behavioral objectives, teaching suggestions and resources, and test items. This *Instructor's Manual* is set up to allow instructors the freedom and flexibility needed to teach research methods courses.

The test questions for each chapter include approximately 15 to 20 multiple-choice items, 10 to 12 true/false items, and several essay questions that may be used for exams or to stimulate class discussion. Page references to the text are given for the multiple-choice and true/false questions. Test items are also available on disk in DOS, Macintosh, and Windows formats.

GSS Data

We have sought to provide up-to-date computer—and particularly microcomputer—support for students and instructors. Because many excellent programs are now available for analyzing data, we have provided data to be used with those programs. Specifically, we are providing data from the National Opinion Research Center's General Social Survey, thus offering students a variety of data gathered from respondents around the country in 1975, 1980, 1985, 1990, 1994 (no survey was done in 1995), and 2000. The data are accessible through our Book Companion Web Site, described below.

Book Companion Website

Accessible through http://info.wadsworth.com/rubbin_babbie/, the new text-specific Companion Site offers chapter-by-chapter online quizzes, chapter outlines, crossword puzzles, flash cards (from the text's glossary), web links, InfoTrac College Edition exercises, and review questions and exercises (from the ends of chapters in the text) that provide students with an opportunity to apply concepts presented in the text. The site also includes a learning guide to NViVO (a successor to NUD*IST), downloadable data analysis primers, and a *Social Work Research in Cyberspace* guide. Students can go to the Companion Site to access a primer for SPSS 11.0, as well as data from the GSS. The Instructor Companion Site features downloadable Microsoft® *PowerPoint*® slides.

ACKNOWLEDGMENTS

We owe special thanks to the following colleagues who reviewed this edition and made valuable suggestions for improving it: Julie Cooper Altman, Adelphi University; Elizabeth W. Lindsey, University of North Carolina, Greensboro; Edward J. Mullen, Columbia School of Social Work; David Schantz, University of Montana; Ce Shen, Boston College.

Another colleague, Esther Sales of the University of Pittsburgh, provided helpful feedback and suggestions in responding to a draft of our expanded coverage of secondary analysis. Two doctoral students at the University of Texas at Austin, Danielle Parrish and Kelly Gober, deserve special recognition for their valuable assistance.

Thanks also go to Dan Alpert, at Thomson Brooks/Cole, Thomson Higher Education's imprint for social work. We also appreciate the efforts of Sheila Walsh, editorial assistant; Alma Dea Michelena, assistant editor; and Katy German, project editor.

Allen Rubin
Earl Babbie

PART 1

An Introduction to Scientific Inquiry in Social Work

Science is a word everyone uses. Yet people's images of science vary greatly. For some, science is mathematics; for others, science is white coats and laboratories. The word is often confused with technology or equated with challenging high school or college courses.

If you tell strangers that you are taking a course dealing with scientific inquiry, and ask them to guess what department it's in, they are a lot more likely to guess something like biology or physics than social work. In fact, many social workers themselves often underestimate the important role that scientific inquiry can play in social work practice. But this is changing. More and more, social workers are learning how taking a scientific approach can enhance their practice effectiveness.

Although scholars can debate philosophical issues in science, for the purposes of this book we will look at it as a method of inquiry—that is, a way of learning and knowing things that can guide the decisions made in social work practice. When contrasted with other ways that social work practitioners can learn and know things, scientific inquiry has some special characteristics—most notably, a search for evidence.

In this opening set of chapters, we'll examine the nature of scientific inquiry and its relevance for social work. We'll explore the fundamental characteristics and issues that make scientific inquiry different from other ways of knowing things in social work.

In Chapter 1, we'll examine the value of scientific inquiry in social work practice and how it helps safeguard against some of the risks inherent in alternative sources of practice knowledge.

Chapter 2 will delve into evidence-based practice—a model of social work practice that emphasizes the use of the scientific method and scientific evidence in making practice decisions.

Chapter 3 will examine certain philosophical issues underlying the scientific method and how disagreements about philosophical issues can be connected to contrasting yet complementary approaches to scientific inquiry. It will also examine the structure and role of theory in social work research.

CHAPTER 1

Why Study Research?

What You'll Learn in This Chapter

Why require social work students to take a research course? We'll begin to answer that question in this chapter. We'll examine the way social workers learn things and the mistakes they make along the way. We'll also examine what makes scientific inquiry different from other ways of knowing things and its utility in social work practice.

INTRODUCTION

This book is about how social workers know things. Let's start by examining a few things you probably know already.

You know the world is round and that people speak Chinese in China. You probably also know it's cold on the planet Mars. How do you know? Unless you've been to Mars lately, you know it's cold there because somebody told you and you believed what you were told. Perhaps your physics or astronomy instructor told you it was cold on Mars, or maybe you read it in *Newsweek*. You may have read in *National Geographic* that people speak Chinese in China, and that made sense to you, so you didn't question it.

Some of the things you know seem absolutely obvious to you. If someone asked how you know the world is round, you'd probably say, "Everybody knows that." There are a lot of things everybody knows. Of course, at one time, everyone "knew" the world was flat.

Most of what we know is a matter of agreement and belief. Little of it is based on personal experience and discovery. A big part of growing up in any society, in fact, is the process of learning to accept what everybody around you "knows" is so. If you don't know the same things, then you can't really be part of the group. If you were to seriously question whether the world is round, then you'd quickly find yourself set apart from other people.

Although it's important to see that most of what we know is a matter of believing what we've been told, there's nothing wrong with us in that respect. That's simply the way we've structured human societies. The basis of knowledge is agreement. Because we can't learn all we need to know through personal experience and discovery alone, things are set up so we can simply believe what others tell us.

We can know things in other ways, however. In contrast to knowing things through agreement, we can also know things through direct experience and observation. If you dive into a glacial stream flowing down through the Canadian Rockies, you don't need anyone to tell you it's cold. You notice that all by yourself. The first time you stepped on a thorn, you knew it hurt before anyone told you.

When our experience conflicts with what everyone else knows, though, there's a good chance we'll surrender our experience in favor of the agreement.

Let's take an example. Imagine you're at a party. It's a high-class affair, and the drinks and food are excellent. You are particularly taken by one type of appetizer the host brings around on a tray. It's breaded, deep-fried, and especially tasty. You have a couple, and they are delicious! You have more. Soon you are subtly moving around the room to be wherever the host arrives with a tray of these nibbles.

Finally, you can't contain yourself any more. "What are they?" you ask. "How can I get the recipe?" The host lets you in on the secret: "You've been eating breaded, deep-fried worms!" Your response is dramatic: Your stomach rebels, and you promptly throw up all over the living room rug. Awful! What a terrible thing to serve guests!

The point of the story is that both feelings about the appetizer would be real. Your initial liking for them, based on your own direct experience, was certainly real, but so was the feeling of disgust you had when you found out that you'd been eating worms. It should be evident, however, that the feeling of disgust was strictly a product of the agreements you have with those around you that worms aren't fit to eat. That's an agreement you began the first time your parents found you sitting in a pile of dirt with half a wriggling worm dangling from your lips. When they pried your mouth open and reached down your throat to find the other half of the worm, you learned that worms are not acceptable food in our society.

Aside from the agreements we have, what's wrong with worms? They're probably high in protein and low in calories. Bite-sized and easily packaged, they're a distributor's dream. They are also a delicacy for some people who live in societies that lack our agreement that worms are disgusting. Other people might love the worms but be turned off by the deep-fried breadcrumb crust.

Reality, then, is a tricky business. You probably already suspect that some of the things you "know" may not be true, but how can you really know what's real? People have grappled with that question for thousands of years. Science is one of the strategies that have arisen from that grappling.

Science offers an approach to both agreement reality and experiential reality. Scientists have certain criteria that must be met before they will accept the reality of something they haven't personally experienced. In general, an assertion must have both logical and empirical support: It must make sense, and it must align with observations in the world. Why, for example, do Earth-bound scientists accept the assertion that it's cold on Mars? First, it makes sense: Mars is farther away from the sun than is Earth. Second, scientific measurements have confirmed the expectation.

So scientists accept the reality of things they don't personally experience: They accept an agreement reality, but with special standards for doing so.

More to our point, however, science offers a special approach to the discovery of reality through personal experience. It offers a special approach to the business of inquiry. *Epistemology* is the science of knowing; *methodology* (a subfield of epistemology) might be called "the science of finding out." This book is an examination and presentation of social science methodology applied to social work, and we will concern ourselves with how that methodology helps solve problems in social work and social welfare. Before addressing the more technical aspects of that methodology, let's explore why it's important for social work students to learn about it.

THE UTILITY OF SCIENTIFIC INQUIRY IN SOCIAL WORK

Some social work students wonder why research courses are required in a professional curriculum that is preparing them to become practitioners. They have so much to learn about helping people, and they are itching to learn it. Research methodology might be important for academic sociologists and psychologists, but these students might ask, "Why use up so much of social work education on research methods when my helping skills are still not fully developed?"

Some students expect research to be cold, aloof, and mechanistic: qualities that did not attract them to the social work field. Social work tends to be associated with such qualities as warmth, involvement, compassion, humanism, and commitment. These students see many social problems to tackle in the real world, and they are eager to take action. In fact, their unique background may have already led them to identify a problem area they want to deal with. They want to get on with it—but first they must clear this research hurdle.

You might be surprised at the proportion of social work *researchers* who started their careers feeling just that way. Many began their social work careers not as researchers, but as practitioners with a burning commitment to help disadvantaged people and to pursue social justice. With no initial inkling that someday they would become researchers, they discovered during their practice experience that their good intentions were not enough. They realized that our field needs more evidence to guide practitioners about what interventions and policies really help or hinder the attainment of their noble goals. Thus, it was their compassion and commitment to change that spurred them to redirect their efforts to research because it is through research that they could develop the evidence base for practice. Rather than continue to practice with interventions of unknown and untested effects, they decided that they could do more to help disadvantaged people and pursue social justice by conducting research that builds our profession's knowledge base and that consequently results in the delivery of more effective services to clients and the implementation of more effective social change efforts.

Most social work researchers do not fit the traditional stereotypes of academic researchers. They aim not to produce knowledge for knowledge's sake, but to provide the practical knowledge that social workers need to solve everyday practice problems. Ultimately, they aim to give the field the information it needs to alleviate human suffering and promote social welfare. Thus, social work research seeks to accomplish the same humanistic goals as social work practice; and like practice, social work research is a compassionate, problem-solving, and practical endeavor.

At this point you might think, "Okay, that's nice, but the odds that I am going to do research are still slim." But even if you never consider yourself a researcher, you are likely to encounter numerous situations in your career when you'll use your research expertise and perhaps wish you had more of it. For example, you may supervise a clinical program whose continued funding requires you to conduct a scientific evaluation of its effects on clients. You may provide direct services and want to use single-case design methodology to evaluate scientifically your own effectiveness or the effects certain interventions are having on your clients. You may be involved in community organizing or planning and want to conduct a scientific survey to assess a community's greatest needs. You may be administering a program and be required, in order to be accountable to the public, to document scientifically that your program truly is delivering its intended amounts and types of service. You may be engaged in social reform efforts and need scientific data to expose the harmful effects of current welfare policies and thus persuade legislators to enact more humanitarian welfare legislation.

Perhaps you remain skeptical. After all, this is a research text, and its authors may be expected to exaggerate the value of learning the methods of scientific inquiry. You might be thinking, "Even if I accept the notion that social work research is valuable, I still believe that the researchers should do their thing, and I'll do mine." But what will you do? The field remains quite uncertain as to what really works in many practice situations. Some agencies provide interventions that research has found to be ineffective. Some day you may even work in such an agency and be expected to provide such interventions. By understanding research and then reading studies that provide new evidence on what is and is not effective, you can increase your own practice effectiveness.

Reviews of Social Work Effectiveness

Since its inception, various leaders in the social work profession have sought ways to use science to guide social work practice. It was not until the last few decades of the 20th century, however, that a realization of the acute need to improve the evidence base of social work practice began to spread throughout the profession—especially among social work educators.

During the 1970s several authors jolted the social work profession with reviews of research indicating that direct social work practice was not effective (Fischer, 1973; Wood 1978; Mullen and Dumpson, 1972). Later studies, however, provided grounds for optimism about the emergence of effective interventions (Reid and Hanrahan, 1982; Rubin, 1985a; Gorey, 1996; Reid, 1997; Kirk and Reid, 2002). An important difference between the studies covered in the earlier reviews and those covered in the later reviews is whether the focus was on the effectiveness of specific, well-explicated interventions applied to specific problems or just the effectiveness of social workers in general.

Many of the earlier studies with negative outcomes did not evaluate specific, clearly described interventions. By evaluating the effectiveness of social workers in general, instead of evaluating specific interventions for specific problems, they were able to conclude that social workers in general were not being effective but were unable to identify which particular interventions were more or less effective than others. The early studies, therefore, provided little guidance to practitioners seeking ways to make their practice more effective. In contrast, the later studies evaluated interventions that were well explicated and highly specific about the problems they sought to resolve, the goals they sought to accomplish, and the procedures used to achieve those goals (Briar, 1987; Blythe and Briar, 1987).

The reviews discussed above imply that it is unsafe to assume that whatever a trained social worker does will be effective. If you approach your practice with that attitude, then much of what you do might be ineffective. The particular interventions and procedures you employ to achieve particular objectives with specific types of clientele or problems *do* matter. As the later reviews indicated, mounting scientific evidence supports the effectiveness of a variety of interventions.

Consider, for example, the box entitled "Contrasting Interventions: Helpful or Harmful?" Each intervention listed in Column A was at one time in vogue among mental health professionals and thought to be effective. Why did they think so? It seemed reasonable in light of the theories they embraced and their clinical intuitions. However, subsequent research found each to be ineffective and perhaps even harmful. In contrast, the interventions in Column B, which are geared to the same target populations as their counterparts in Column A, have consistently had their effectiveness supported by various research studies.

Research today is identifying more and more interventions that are being supported as effective—interventions that you can draw upon in your practice. Despite this progress, however, many social workers today continue to use some interventions and procedures that have not yet received adequate testing. Thyer (2002), for example, noted that some problems and fields of practice—such as child abuse and neglect, domestic violence, and political action—have a smaller evidence base than others, particularly when compared to interventions for mental disorders. And some interventions that have been evaluated and had positive outcomes need more testing before the evidence is sufficient to resolve any lingering doubt as to their effectiveness.

This doubt is not likely to be resolved soon. Moreover, new interventions continually emerge and are promoted without adequate scientific evidence as to their effectiveness. Some will have received no scientific testing whatsoever. Others will have been "tested" in a scientifically unsound manner in which the research design or measurement procedures were biased to produce desired results. Some will have been tested with certain ethnic groups but not with others. Professional social workers commonly are bombarded with fliers promoting expensive continuing education workshops for new interventions that are touted as being effective. Some claims are warranted, but some are not. In the face of this reality, understanding

CONTRASTING INTERVENTIONS: HELPFUL OR HARMFUL?

Column A **Once Popular but Not Supported by Research**	Column B **Supported by Research**
• Critical incident stress debriefing for trauma victims	• Prolonged exposure therapy for trauma victims
• In-depth, psychodynamic insight-oriented therapy for people suffering from severe and persistent schizophrenia	• Assertive case management/assertive community treatment for people suffering from severe and persistent schizophrenia
• Treating dysfunctional family dynamics as the cause of schizophrenia in a family therapy context	• Psychoeducational support groups for family caregivers of people suffering from severe and persistent schizophrenia

scientific inquiry and research methods becomes practice knowledge, too. If we cannot say with certainty that the actions of trained social workers have demonstrated effectiveness, then learning how to critically appraise whether adequate scientific evidence supports particular interventions in certain practice situations becomes at least as important as learning popular general practice methods that may not always be effective themselves.

The Need to Critique Research Quality

But, you might ask, why can't we just let the researchers produce the needed studies and then tell us practitioners the results? Practitioners would only have to focus on the practice aspects of those interventions that receive adequate scientific support. In an ideal world, that might not be a bad idea, but the real world is a lot messier.

There is a vast range in the quality of social work research—and of applied research in disciplines that are relevant to social work—that gets produced and published. Some of it is excellent, and some of it probably should never have been published. It is not hard to find studies that violate some of the fundamental principles that you will learn in this book. For example, you may encounter a study in which authors are evaluating a new intervention they have developed by rating client progress. Unfortunately, these ratings are frequently based on their own subjective judgments, which are highly vulnerable to being biased by their desire to see successful results. Or perhaps you will read an advocacy study that improperly defines things so as to exaggerate the need for the policy it is advocating. Sarnoff (1999), for example, criticizes a study by Goldberg and Tomlanovich (1984) that asked women in emergency rooms if they had ever experienced domestic violence. Twenty-two percent answered affirmatively, and the researchers misleadingly reported this as meaning "that 22% of emergency room visits were for injuries sustained by domestic violence" (Sarnoff, 1999:401). The fact that they *ever* experienced domestic violence does not mean that any or all of their emergency room visits were for that reason.

The unevenness in the quality of the studies in social work and allied fields has a variety of causes. Biases or varying degrees of competence among researchers are only partial explanations. Many weak studies are produced not because their authors were biased or did not know better, but because agency constraints kept them from conducting stronger studies. Later in this book, for example, you will learn the value of assigning clients to experimental and control conditions when the researcher is assessing the effectiveness of interventions. During control conditions, the interventions being tested are withheld from clients. Many agencies will not permit the use of control conditions in clinical research. (There are various practical reasons for this constraint—reasons we'll examine in this text.) Consequently, researchers are faced with a dilemma: Either do the study under conditions of weak scientific rigor or forgo the study. Having no better alternative and believing that limited evidence may be better than no evidence, researchers often opt to do the study.

This means that if social work practitioners are going to be guided by the findings of social work research studies, then they must understand social work research methods well enough to distinguish studies with adequate scientific methodologies and credible findings from those with weak methodologies and findings of little credibility. It also means that the quality of the social work research produced ultimately depends not just on the researchers' methodological expertise but also on their practice knowledge and practitioners' research knowledge. Without a partnership between practice-oriented researchers and methodologically informed practitioners, there is not likely to be a climate of support in agencies for the type of research our field desperately needs—research that is responsive to the real needs of agency practitioners under conditions that permit an adequate level of methodological rigor. Even if you never produce any research, an understanding of research methods will help you critically appraise and use research produced by others, communicate with researchers to help ensure that their work is responsive to the needs of practice, and ultimately help foster an agency environment conducive to carrying out good and relevant studies.

Earlier we discussed the value of understanding research methods so that you might determine which studies are sufficiently credible to guide your practice. Social workers also need to be able to critically appraise the methodologies of studies conducted by authors who attack the entire social work profession and social welfare enterprise. These authors are not necessarily politically inspired or out to harm the people we care about. They may care about the people just as much as we do and may sincerely believe that social workers and social welfare policies are hurting them. These authors and their research occasionally receive much attention in the popular media and are commonly cited by opponents of public welfare spending. A notable example is *Losing Ground* (1984), in which Charles Murray compiled masses of data to argue that public social welfare programs developed to help the poor have actually hurt rather than helped them. Another such critique is Christopher Lasch's *Haven in a Heartless World* (1977), which argued that social workers deliberately usurp parental functions and thus weaken families and exacerbate various social problems.

If critics like these are correct in their logic and conclusions, then we commonly hurt the people we are trying to help and exacerbate the problems we are trying to alleviate. And if these critics' logic or research methodology is faulty and their conclusions erroneous, then we are responsible to the people we serve (including the public) to point this out. Therefore, it is less from a concern for professional self-preservation than from a concern for our clients that we should be able to consider these critics' arguments and evidence on equal grounds. We should not be seen as a profession of antiscientific practitioners disregarding methodological principles, because this will lead others to decide for us whether our clients would be better off if we all went out of business. Indeed, if we are unable to do so, then we cannot call ourselves "professionals."

Compassion and Professional Ethics

Being professional involves several things. For one, we strive to make sure we provide our clients the most effective services available. How do we do that? Do we just ask our supervisors what they think is best? That may be a starting point, but practitioners who conform only to ongoing practices without keeping abreast of the latest research in their field are not doing everything possible to provide clients with the best possible service. Indeed, well-established, traditional social work services have often been found to be ineffective—as indicated by the aforementioned reviews of practice effectiveness.

Given how frequently social work services have been found ineffective and the recent emergence of studies that identify new and apparently effective interventions, one's failure to keep abreast of the research in the field is serious. With the absence of evidence for the notion that whatever trained social workers do is effective, we cannot justify disregarding research with the rationalization that we are too busy helping people. If our services have not been tested for their effects on clients, then chances are we are not really helping anyone. If so, then who benefits from our blind faith in conventional but untested practice wisdom? Not our clients. Not those who pay for our services. Not society. Do we? In one sense, perhaps. It is less work for us if we unquestioningly perpetuate ongoing practices. That way, we do not make waves. We do not have to think as much. There is one less task—reading research reports—in our daily grind. In the long run, however, practitioners who keep up on the research and know they are doing all they can to provide the best possible services to their clients might experience more job satisfaction and be less vulnerable to burnout.

The main reason to use research, however, is compassion for our clients. We care about helping them, and thus we seek scientific evidence about the effects of the services we are providing and of alternative services that might help them more. If the services we provide are not effective and others are, then we are harming our clients by perpetuating our current services. We are wasting their time (and perhaps money) by allowing their problems to go on without the best possible treatment. Because we are inattentive to the literature, we deny our clients a service opportunity that might better help them.

This point can be illustrated using an example of a highly regarded and often-cited piece of social work research in the field of mental health. During the 1970s, Gerard Hogarty (an MSW-level social worker) and his associates conducted a series of field experiments on the effectiveness of drug therapy and psychosocially oriented social casework in preventing relapse and enhancing community adjustment in the aftercare of formerly hospitalized patients suffering from schizophrenia (Hogarty, 1979). Hogarty and his associates found that drug therapy alone was highly effective in forestalling relapse but that it had no effect on community adjustment. Social casework by itself had no influence on relapse. The best results for community adjustment were found with patients who received drug therapy *and* social casework combined. However, the group of patients who only received social casework fared worse than the group who received no treatment whatsoever! Hogarty and his colleagues reasoned that this was because people suffering from schizophrenia tended to be unable to cope with the increased cognitive stimulation and expectations associated with psychosocial casework. Among its benefits, drug therapy's physiologic effects improved the patients' ability to handle and benefit from the stimulation of psychosocial casework. Without the drug therapy, they were better off without the casework!

Now suppose that when this research was published you were a practitioner or an administrator in an aftercare program whose caseload consisted primarily of persons diagnosed with schizophrenia. The program might have been traditionally oriented, emphasizing drug treatment without an intensive casework component like the one evaluated by Hogarty and associates. Perhaps there was no comprehensive social treatment effort, or perhaps there was an untested one that did not resemble the tested one above. If so, then your services may have been having no effect on your clients' levels of community adjustment. Had you used the research, you would be in a better position to realize and improve this situation. On the other hand, perhaps the emphasis in your program was on a psychosocial casework approach like the one Hogarty and his colleagues evaluated but with little or no systematic effort to ensure that patients were taking prescribed psychotropic drugs. In that case, the preceding findings would have suggested that your program may have been having a harmful effect on some clients, but one that could be turned into a beneficial effect if you had used the research and modified your services in keeping with its findings (that is, adding a systematic drug therapy component or monitoring medication compliance more persistently).

The preceding example illustrates that understanding research methods and using research discriminately has much to do with basic social work values such as caring and compassion. The practitioner who understands and uses such research shows more concern for the welfare of his or her clients and ultimately is more helpful to them than the one who justifies not taking that trouble on the basis of erroneous stereotypes about research. To better understand this point, sometimes it helps to put yourself in the shoes of the client system. Suppose a beloved member of your immediate family were to develop schizophrenia. Imagine the ensuing family trauma and concern. Now suppose the relative was being released to an aftercare program after hospitalization. Imagine the anxiety you and your family would have about your loved one's prospects in the community. Perhaps your relative has to be rehospitalized for failing to adjust in the community. Now imagine the outrage you would feel if you were to learn of Hogarty's research and discover that your relative received either social casework or drug therapy (but not both) because the program staff never bothered to use the research. How compassionate would those staff members seem to you? Chances are you might describe them as cold, uncaring, aloof, mechanistic, and dehumanized—or more like how the staff members would describe research.

The box entitled "4 Accused in 'Rebirthing' Death" provides another example to illustrate the value of research in social work practice. This one involves life and death and thus illustrates dramatically why practitioners who critically appraise and use research discriminately may be more compassionate—and

Here are excerpted highlights from an article by Carla Crowder and Peggy Lowe, *Rocky Mountain News*, May 19, 2000, p. 5A.

4 ACCUSED IN "REBIRTHING" DEATH AFFIDAVIT STATES GIRL, 10, SMOTHERED WHILE ADULTS PUSHED AND THERAPIST YELLED, "DIE RIGHT NOW"

A 10-year-old girl in "rebirthing" therapy smothered as she lay balled up and bound inside a blue flannel blanket with four adults pushing against her and a therapist yelling, "Go ahead, die right now."

Those details emerged Thursday in an arrest affidavit for four people who police say were involved in the April 18 videotaped asphyxiation of Candace Newmaker of Durham, N.C. An Evergreen psychotherapist and two assistants were arrested on allegations of child abuse resulting in death. . . .

Candace died April 19 at Children's Hospital in Denver, a day after she fell unconscious during a therapy session. . . .

Candace was lying in the fetal position and wrapped in the blanket like "a little ball" and then covered with pillows. The adults pushed against the pillows to simulate birth contractions.

The videotape shows that she was wrapped up for an hour and 10 minutes, and in the first 16 minutes, the child said six times that she was going to die. She begged to go to the bathroom and told them she was going to throw up.

"You want to die? OK, then die," [two therapists] responded. "Go ahead, die right now."

By the time they unbound her, Candace was "sleeping in her vomit.". . .

Rebirthing is a controversial procedure used on children who suffer from an attachment disorder in an attempt to help them connect with their parents.

Candace [was placed] in the blanket to simulate a womb, having her emerge in a "rebirth" to help her bond with her adoptive mother. . . .

[The adoptive mother] paid $7,000 for [the] two-week therapy, the last of several therapeutic approaches she had sought for Candace's "difficulties.". . . Her daughter was "frustrating and so emotionally laden," she told authorities.

Several . . . attachment disorder experts . . . were unfamiliar with rebirthing therapy, indicating the technique is not widespread and has even been rejected by some therapists.

"I don't know anything about rebirthing," said Forrest Lien, Director of Clinical Services at the Attachment Center at Evergreen, a pioneer agency for treating children with attachment disorder. "We really only want to use techniques that have been used and are researched and have proven outcomes."

ethical—than those who do not. On May 19, 2000, an article in the *Rocky Mountain News* reported the death of a 10-year-old girl who died as a result of an intervention delivered by a team of adults that included an MSW-level social worker. The intervention, called *rebirthing therapy,* does not have a base of evidence supported by research. As you read the excerpted quotes from this newspaper article in the box, keep in mind the link between compassion and the use of research to guide your practice.

ADDITIONAL REASONS WHY SOCIAL WORKERS SHOULD LEARN ABOUT RESEARCH

Studies on the effects of social work interventions are just one prominent example of useful social work research. A long list of other examples of completed research studies would also convey the value of research to social work and why students preparing to become practitioners should know research methods so they can use and contribute to such research. Many of these studies will be cited as illustrations of the methodological concepts addressed throughout this text.

We also could cite countless examples for additional topics on which you might someday want to see research findings related to policy or administration. Only a few will be cited here. For example, why do so many of your agency's clients terminate treatment prematurely? What types of clients stay with or drop out of treatment? What reasons do they give? What services did they receive? How satisfied were they with those services? What proportion of time do practitioners in your agency spend on different practice roles? Do they spend too much time performing functions that are more highly gratifying and too little time on functions that are less attractive but more needed by clients? What characteristics of social service volunteers best predict how long they will continue to volunteer? What can you do to orient, train, or reward them and reduce volunteer turnover? In what part of your target community or region should you locate your outreach efforts? Where are you most likely to engage hard-to-reach individuals such as the homeless or recent immigrants? Why do so many homeless individuals refuse to stay in shelters, sleeping instead on the streets? What are their experiences when they stay in a shelter, and what is staying in a shelter like from their point of view? What proportion of your target population does not understand English? Why are so few ethnic minorities being served by your agency? What does your agency mean to them? What is the agency atmosphere like from their viewpoint? What happens to the children of unskilled mothers whose welfare benefits have been severed? We could go on and on, but you get the idea: The possibilities are endless.

Learning research methods has value to practitioners beyond just using research studies. They will also be able to use research methods in face-to-face contact with people, especially for treatment planning. During assessment, for example, practitioners collect clinical data from various individuals. Research concepts about such topics as measurement error, reliability, validity, and the principles of sampling will help them evaluate the quality and meaning of the clinical data they collect and help them collect those data in ways that enhance their quality. Practitioners must examine the conditions and situations under which they collect information as part of their practice in the same way and for the same reasons as one systematically collects data for a formal research study.

Ethics is one of the most important concerns of social workers as they consider research, and it is a topic that is discussed throughout this book. The Code of Ethics of the National Association of Social Workers specifically requires social workers to keep current with and critically examine practice-related research in the professional literature and to include evidence-based knowledge as part of the knowledge base for their practice. When we use research discriminatingly, we help uphold and advance the values and mission of the profession and thus are more ethical in our practice. Still, social work students quite commonly approach research methodology with skepticism about the ethics of many research studies. We will address those ethical concerns in various chapters of the book, not just in the chapter devoted to ethics. We hope that by the time you finish reading this book, you will have a better understanding not only of the ethical dilemmas involved in social work research but also of the reasons why our professional Code of Ethics bears on our responsibility to understand, use, and contribute to research.

Perhaps more than ever before, social work research offers all social workers an opportunity to make a difference in the problems they confront. Whether you are a clinical practitioner seeking to maximize the effectiveness of your services, or a social activist seeking to promote more humane social welfare legislation, or perhaps both, the success of your efforts to help people is likely to be enhanced by your use of scientific inquiry and research.

Now that we've examined the value of scientific inquiry in social work, let's look at inquiry as an activity. We'll begin by examining the scientific method and then other ways of knowing, including inquiry as a natural human activity, as something we have engaged in every day of our lives. Next, we'll look at the kinds of errors we can make in normal inquiry and in unscientific sources of social work practice knowledge. We'll see some of the ways in which scientific inquiry guards against those errors.

THE SCIENTIFIC METHOD

When social workers question things and search for evidence as the basis for making practice decisions, they are applying the scientific method. A key feature of the **scientific method*** is that *everything is open to question.* That means that in our quest to understand things, we should strive to keep an *open mind* about everything that we think we know or that we want to

*Words in boldface are defined in the glossary at the end of the book.

believe. In other words, we should consider the things we call "knowledge" to be *provisional* and *subject to refutation*. This feature has no exceptions. No matter how long a particular tradition has been practiced, no matter how much power or esteem a particular authority figure may have, no matter how noble a cause may be, no matter how cherished it may be, we can question any belief.

Keeping an open mind is not always easy. Few of us enjoy facts that get in the way of our cherished beliefs. When we think about allowing everything to be open to question, we may think of old-fashioned notions that we ourselves have disputed and thus pat ourselves on the back for being so open-minded. If we have a liberal bent, for example, we may fancy ourselves as scientific for questioning stereotypes of gender roles, laws banning gay marriage, or papal decrees about abortion. But are we also prepared to have an open mind about our own cherished beliefs—to allow them to be questioned and refuted? Only when a belief you cherish is questioned do you face the tougher test of your commitment to scientific notions of the provisional nature of knowledge and keeping everything open to question and refutation.

Another key feature of the scientific method is the search for *evidence based on observation* as the basis for knowledge. The term *empirical* refers to this valuing of observation-based evidence. As we will see later, one can be empirical in different ways, depending on the nature of the evidence and the way we search for and observe it. For now, remember that the scientific method seeks truth through observed evidence—not through authority, tradition, or ideology—no matter how much social pressure or political correctness of either the right or the left may be connected to particular beliefs and no matter how many people cherish those beliefs or how long they've been proclaimed to be true. It took courage long ago to question fiercely held beliefs that the Earth is flat. Scientifically minded social workers today should find the same courage to inquire as to the observation-based evidence that supports interventions or policies that they are told or taught to believe in.

They should also examine the nature of that evidence. To be truly scientific, the observations that accumulated that evidence should have been *systematic* and *comprehensive*. To avoid overgeneralization and selective observation (errors we will be discussing shortly), the *sample* of observations should have been *large* and *diverse*. The observational *procedures should be specified* so that we can see the *basis for the conclusions* that were reached, assess whether overgeneralization and selective observation were truly avoided, and judge whether the conclusions are indeed warranted in light of the evidence and the ways in which it was observed.

The specified procedures also should be scrutinized for potential bias. The scientific method recognizes that we all have predilections and biases that can distort how we look for or perceive evidence. It therefore emphasizes the *pursuit of objectivity* in the way we seek and observe evidence. None of us may ever be purely objective, no matter how strongly committed we are to the scientific method. No matter how scientifically pristine their research may be, researchers want to discover something important—that is, to have findings that will make a significant contribution to improving human well-being or (less nobly) enhancing their professional stature. The scientific method does not require that researchers deceive themselves into thinking they lack these biases. Instead, recognizing that they may have these biases, they must find ways to gather observations that are not influenced by their own biases.

Suppose, for example, you devise a new intervention for improving the self-esteem of traumatized children. Naturally, you will be biased in wanting to observe improvements in the self-esteem of the children receiving your intervention. It's okay to have that bias and still scientifically inquire whether your intervention really does improve self-esteem. You would not want to base your inquiry solely on your own subjective clinical impressions. That approach would engender a great deal of skepticism about the objectivity of your judgments that the children's self-esteem improved. Thus, instead of relying exclusively on your clinical impressions, you would devise an observation procedure that was not influenced by your own biases. Perhaps you would ask colleagues who didn't know about your intervention or the nature of your inquiry to interview the children and rate their self-esteem. Or perhaps you would administer an existing paper-and-pencil test of self-esteem that social scientists regard as valid. Although neither alternative can guarantee complete objectivity, each would be more scientific in reflecting your effort to pursue objectivity.

Because there are no foolproof ways for social science to guarantee that evidence is purely objective, accurate, and generalizable, the scientific method also calls for the *replication* of studies. This is in keeping with the notion of refutability and the knowledge's provisional nature. *Replication* means duplicating a study to see if the same evidence and conclusions are produced. It also refers to modified replications in which the procedures are changed in certain ways that improve on previous studies or determine if findings hold up with different target populations or under different circumstances. The need to replicate implies that scientifically minded social workers should have the courage to question not only cherished beliefs that were not derived from scientific evidence but also the conclusions of scientific studies and the way those studies were carried out.

OTHER WAYS OF KNOWING

The scientific method is not the only way to learn about the world. As we mentioned earlier, for example, we all discover things through our personal experiences from birth on and from the agreed-on knowledge that others give us. Sometimes this knowledge can profoundly influence our lives. We learn that getting an education will affect how much money we earn later in life and that swimming beyond the reef may bring an unhappy encounter with a shark. Sharks, on the other hand, may learn that hanging around the reef may bring a happy encounter with unhappy swimmers. As students we learn that studying hard will result in better examination grades.

We also learn that such patterns of cause and effect are probabilistic in nature: The effects occur more often when the causes occur than when they are absent—but not always. Thus, students learn that studying hard produces good grades in most instances, but not every time. We recognize the danger of swimming beyond the reef without believing that every such swim will be fatal. Social workers learn that being abused as children makes people more likely to become abusive parents later on, but not all parents who were abused as children become abusive themselves. They also learn that severe mental illness makes one vulnerable to becoming homeless, but not all adults with severe mental illnesses become homeless. We will return to these concepts of causality and probability throughout the book. As we'll see, scientific inquiry makes them more explicit and provides techniques for dealing with them more rigorously than do other ways of learning about the world.

Tradition

One important secondhand way to attempt to learn things is through tradition. Each of us inherits a culture partly made of firmly accepted knowledge about the workings of the world. We may learn from others that planting corn in the spring will gain the greatest assistance from the gods, that sugar from too much candy will cause tooth decay, that the circumference of a circle is approximately twenty-two sevenths of its diameter, or that masturbation will blind us. We may test a few of these "truths" on our own, but we simply accept the great majority of them. These are the things that "everybody knows."

Tradition, in this sense of the term, has clear advantages for human inquiry. By accepting what everybody knows, you are spared the overwhelming task of starting from scratch in your search for regularities and understanding. Knowledge is cumulative, and an inherited body of information and understanding is the jumping-off point for the development of more knowledge. We often speak of "standing on the shoulders of giants"—that is, on the shoulders of previous generations.

At the same time, tradition may be detrimental to human inquiry. If you seek a fresh and different understanding of something that everybody already understands and has always understood, you may be seen as a fool. More to the point, it will probably never occur to you to seek a different understanding of something that is already understood and obvious.

When you enter your first job as a professional social worker, you may learn about your agency's preferred intervention approaches. (If you have begun the field placement component of your professional education, you may have already experienced this phenomenon.) Chances are you will feel good about receiving instructions about "how we do things in this agency." You may be anxious about beginning to work with real cases and relieved that you won't have to choose between competing theories to guide what you do with clients. In conforming to agency traditions you may feel that you have a head start, benefiting from the accumulated "practice wisdom" of previous generations of practitioners in your new work setting. Indeed you do. After all, how many recently graduated social workers are in a better position than experienced agency staff to determine the best intervention approaches in their agency?

But the downside of conforming to traditional practice wisdom is that you can become too comfortable doing it. You may never think to look for evidence that the traditional approaches are or are not as effective as everyone believes or for evidence concerning whether alternative approaches are more effective. And if you do seek and find such evidence, you may find that agency traditions make your colleagues unreceptive to the new information.

Authority

Despite the power of tradition, new knowledge appears every day. Aside from your personal inquiries, throughout your life you will benefit from others' new discoveries and understandings. Often, acceptance of these new acquisitions will depend on the status of the discoverer. You're more likely, for example, to believe the epidemiologist who declares that the common cold can be transmitted through kissing than to believe a layperson who says the same thing.

Like tradition, authority can both assist and hinder human inquiry. Inquiry is hindered when we depend on the authority of experts speaking outside their realm of expertise. The advertising industry plays heavily on this misuse of authority by having popular athletes discuss the nutritional value of breakfast cereals or movie actors evaluate the performance of automobiles, among similar tactics. It is better to trust the judgment of the person who has special training, expertise, and credentials in the matter, especially in the face of contradictory positions on a given question. At the same time, inquiry can be greatly hindered by the legitimate authority who errs within his or her own special province. Biologists, after all, can and do make mistakes in the field of biology. Biological knowledge changes over time. So does social work knowledge.

A social work–related example of how our knowledge changes over time and how traditional wisdom or authorities can be wrong was discussed by Angus M. Strachan (1986) and Cassandra E. Simon and her associates (1991). Before the 1980s, authorities in psychoanalysis and family therapy blamed faulty parenting as a prime cause of schizophrenia. They commonly portrayed the mothers of individuals who became afflicted with schizophrenia as "schizophrenigenic mothers" with cold, domineering, and overprotective behavior that did not permit their children to develop individual identities. Similar prominent ideas then in vogue blamed schizophrenia on such factors as parental discord, excessive familial interdependency, and mothers who give contradictory messages that repeatedly put their children in "double-bind" situations.

No compelling research evidence supported these concepts, but they were nonetheless widely accepted by mental health practitioners. As a result, clinicians often dealt with the family as a cause of the problem rather than develop treatment alliances with them. Instead of supporting families, clinicians often acted as the advocate of the client against the family's supposed harmful influences. Family therapists sought to help the parents see that the problem did not reside in the identified patients, but in dysfunctional family systems. Although family therapists did not intentionally seek to induce guilt or in other ways hurt these parents, many parents nonetheless reported feelings of self-recrimination for their offsprings' illnesses. As you can imagine, this was painful for many parents to "learn," particularly in view of the pain parents normally must live with knowing how ill their once-normal son or daughter has become and perhaps having to care for the child after he or she has reached adulthood.

If you have recently taken courses on psychopathology, then you probably know that current scientific evidence indicates that genetic and other biological factors play an important role in the causation of schizophrenia. Although environmental stress may be important, the evidence does not support the notion of treating schizophrenia as a result of bad parenting. Indeed, such treatment may be harmful. Inducing guilt among family members may exacerbate negative emotional intensity in the family. This, in turn, may make it more difficult for family members to provide the proper level of support and stimulation for their sick relatives, whose vulnerability to relapse seems to be worsened when they are exposed to high levels of environmental stress and overstimulation. Moreover, current theories recognize that undesirable family characteristics may be the result of the burden of living with a family member who has schizophrenia rather than the cause of the illness. Consequently, new treatment approaches were designed—usually called "psychoeducational approaches"—that sought to build alliances with families and be more supportive of them. During the 1980s and 1990s, these psychoeducational approaches consistently had their effectiveness supported by various research studies (as we alluded to earlier in this chapter, in the box that contrasts interventions).

Our point is that knowledge accepted on the authority of legitimate and highly regarded experts can be incorrect, and perhaps harmful. It is therefore important that social work practitioners be open to new discoveries that might challenge the cherished beliefs of their respected supervisors or favorite theorists. Also keep an open mind about the new knowledge that displaces the old. It, too, may be flawed no matter how prestigious its founders. Who knows? Perhaps some day we'll even find evidence that currently out-of-favor ideas about parental causation of schizophrenia had merit after all. That prospect may seem highly unlikely now given current evidence, but in taking a scientific approach to knowledge we try to remain objective and open to new discoveries, no matter how much they may conflict with the traditional wisdom or current authorities. Although complete objectivity may be an impossible ideal to attain, we try not to close our minds to new ideas that might conflict with tradition and authority.

Both tradition and authority, then, are two-edged swords in the search for knowledge about the world. They provide us with a starting point for our own inquiry. But they may also lead us to start at the wrong point or push us in the wrong direction.

Common Sense

The notion of *common sense* is often cited as another way to know about the world. Common sense can imply logical reasoning, such as when we reason that it makes no sense to think that rainbows cause rainfall, since rainbows appear only after the rain starts falling and only when the sun shines during the storm. Common sense can also imply widely shared beliefs based on tradition and authority. The problem with this sort of common sense is that what "everyone knows" can be wrong. Long ago everyone "knew" that the Earth was flat. It was just plain common sense, since you could see no curvature to the Earth's surface and since hell was below the surface. At one point in our history, a great many people thought that slavery made common sense. Terrorists think terrorism makes common sense. Many people think that laws against gays and lesbians marrying or adopting children make common sense. Most social workers think such laws make no common sense whatsoever. Although common sense often seems rational and accurate, it is an insufficient and highly risky alternative to science as a source of knowledge.

Popular Media

Much of what we know about the world is learned from the news media. We all know about the September 11, 2001, attack on the twin towers of the World Trade Center from watching coverage of that tragic event on television and reading about it in newspapers and magazines and on the Internet. The same sources informed us of the victims and heroes in New York City, Pennsylvania, and Washington, D.C. They provided information on the perpetrators of the attack and a great many related issues and events. We did not have to conduct a scientific study to know about the attack or have strong feelings about it. Neither did we need tradition or authority. We did not have to experience the attack firsthand (although we really did experience it—and probably were at least somewhat traumatized—by what we saw and heard on our television sets).

Although we can learn a lot from the popular media, we can also be misled by them. Witness, for example, disagreements between cable news networks such as CNN and the more politically conservative Fox as to which news network is really more trustworthy, fair, and balanced. Although most journalists might strive for accuracy and objectivity, some may be influenced by their own political biases. Some also might seek out the most sensational aspects of events and then report them in a biased manner to garner reader interest or appeal to their prejudices. (Ratings affect profits.) In 1965 and 1966, before the war in Vietnam became unpopular among the American public, news media coverage of demonstrations against the war typically focused on the most bizarrely dressed protestors engaging in the most provocative acts. You had to have been at the demonstrations to know that most of the protesters looked and acted like average American citizens. Those relying on media coverage were often misled into thinking that the only folks protesting the war at that time were unpatriotic left-wingers and deviant adolescents seeking attention via symbolically anti-American provocations.

Even when journalists strive for accuracy in their reportage, the nature of their business can impede their efforts. For example, they have deadlines to meet and word limits as to how much they can write. Thus, when covering testimony at city hall by neighborhood residents, some of whom support a proposed new economic development plan in their neighborhood and some of whom oppose it, their coverage might be dominated not by folks like the majority of residents, who may not be outspoken. Instead, they might unintentionally rely on the least representative but most outspoken and demonstrative supporters or opponents of the proposed development.

Then there are journalists whose jobs are to deliver editorials and opinion pieces, not to report stories factually. What we learn from them is colored by their predilections. The popular media also include fictional movies and television shows that can influence what we think we know about the world. Some fictional accounts of history are indeed educational; perhaps informing us for the first time about African Americans who fought for the Union during the Civil War or sensitizing us to the horrors of the Holocaust or of slavery. Others, however, can be misleading, such as when most mentally ill people are portrayed as violent or when most welfare recipients are portrayed as African Americans. In short, although we can learn many valuable things from the popular media, they do not provide an adequate alternative to scientific sources of knowledge.

RECOGNIZING FLAWS IN UNSCIENTIFIC SOURCES OF SOCIAL WORK PRACTICE KNOWLEDGE

Scientific inquiry safeguards against the potential dangers of relying exclusively on tradition, authority, common sense, or the popular media as the sources of knowledge to guide social work practice. It also helps safeguard against errors we might make when we attempt to build our practice wisdom primarily through our own practice experiences and unsystematic observations. Scientific inquiry also involves critical thinking so that we can spot fallacies in what others may tell us about their practice wisdom or the interventions they are touting. Let's now look at common errors and fallacies you should watch out for and at some of the ways science guards against those mistakes.

Inaccurate Observation

Imagine that you are providing play therapy to a group of eight hyperactive children with various emotional and behavioral problems. At the end of each one-hour group session, you write your progress notes. It is unlikely that you will have observed every clinically meaningful thing that transpired for each child in the session. Even if you did notice something meaningful in one child, you may not have realized it was meaningful at the time, especially if it happened while two children across the room went out of control and began fighting. Moreover, you may not remember certain observations later when it is time to record your progress notes—especially if something happens that keeps you from recording your observations until later that day. Recall, for example, the last person you talked to today. What kind of shoes was that person wearing? Are you even certain the person was wearing shoes? On the whole, we are pretty casual in observing things; as a result, we make mistakes. We fail to observe things right in front of us and mistakenly observe things that are not so.

In contrast to casual human inquiry, scientific observation is a conscious activity. Simply making observation more deliberate helps to reduce error. You probably don't recall, for example, what your instructor was wearing the first day of this class. If you had to guess now, you'd probably make a mistake. But if you had gone to the first class meeting with a conscious plan to observe and record what your instructor was wearing, then you'd have been more accurate.

In many cases, both simple and complex measurement devices help guard against inaccurate observations. Moreover, they add a degree of precision that is well beyond the capacity of the unassisted human senses. Suppose, for example, that you had taken color photographs of your instructor that day.

Overgeneralization

When we look for patterns among the specific things we observe around us, we often assume that a few similar events are evidence of a general pattern. Probably the tendency to overgeneralize is greatest when the pressure is highest to arrive at a general understanding. Yet overgeneralization also occurs casually in the absence of pressure. Whenever it does occur, it can misdirect or impede inquiry.

Imagine you are a community organizer and you just found out that a riot has started in your community. You have a meeting in two hours that you cannot miss, and you need to let others at the meeting know why citizens are rioting. Rushing to the scene, you start interviewing rioters, asking them for their reasons. If the first two rioters tell you they are doing it just to loot some stores, you would probably be wrong in assuming that the other 300 are rioting just for that reason.

To further illustrate overgeneralization, imagine your practice instructor brings in a guest lecturer to talk about a promising new intervention that she is excited about. Although she has a sizable caseload and has been providing the intervention to quite a few clients, suppose her lecture just focuses on an in-depth report of one or two clients who seemed to benefit enormously from the intervention. You might be wrong in assuming the intervention was equally effective—or even effective at all—with her other clients.

Scientists guard against overgeneralization by committing themselves in advance to a sufficiently large sample of observations (see Chapter 14). The replication of inquiry provides another safeguard. As we mentioned earlier, **replication** basically means repeating a study and then checking to see if the same results are produced each time. Then the study may be repeated under slightly varied conditions. Thus, when a social work researcher discovers that a particular program of service in a particular setting is effective, that is only the beginning. Is the program equally effective for all types of clients? For both men and women? For both old and young? Among all ethnic groups? Would it be just as effective in other agency settings? This extension of the inquiry seeks to find the breadth and the limits of the generalization about the program's effectiveness.

Totally independent replications by other researchers extend the safeguards. Suppose you read a study that shows an intervention to be effective. Later, you might conduct your own study of different clients, perhaps measuring effectiveness somewhat differently. If your independent study produced exactly the same conclusion as the one you first read, then you would feel more confident in the generalizability of the findings. If you obtained somewhat different results or found a subgroup of clients among whom the findings didn't hold at all, you'd have helped to save us from overgeneralizing.

Selective Observation

One danger of overgeneralization is that it may lead to selective observation. Once you have concluded that a particular pattern exists and developed a general understanding of why, then you will be tempted to pay attention to future events and situations that correspond with the pattern. You will most likely ignore those that don't correspond. Racial and ethnic prejudices depend heavily on this selective observation for their persistence.

Suppose you were once cheated by a shopkeeper you thought to be Jewish. You might conclude from that one event that Jewish shopkeepers are dishonest. Subsequently, you'd probably take special note of dishonest actions by other Jewish shopkeepers while ignoring honest Jews and dishonest non-Jews. Some people take special note of all the lazy African Americans they come across and ignore energetic African Americans and lazy whites. Others notice irrational and emotional women while overlooking stable women as well as unstable men.

The same goes for the way in which many people who are not on welfare perceive welfare recipients. Imagine what happens when people with a bias against welfare spending wait in the checkout line at the supermarket behind a mother with a fistful of food stamps. What do you think they are most likely to notice, remember, and discuss later at a cocktail party: the nutritious necessities in the mother's shopping cart or the unhealthy and unnecessary items? Likewise, if on their next trip to the supermarket they see another food stamp recipient purchasing nothing but nutritious items, are they as likely to remember and discuss that person at their next cocktail party?

Selective observation occurs among all of us, not just people with distasteful prejudices. Social work practitioners who have great compassion for their clients and who do the best they can to help their clients, for example, commonly engage in selective observation in ways that may limit their effectiveness. The practitioner trained to interpret problems in terms of family communication dynamics is apt to look vigilantly for signs of potential communication problems and then magnify the role those problems play in explaining the presenting problem. At the same time, that practitioner is likely to overlook other dynamics or perhaps underestimate their impact.

Recall the overgeneralization example of the practice instructor who brings in a guest lecturer to talk about a promising new intervention that she is excited about and who focuses her lecture on one or two clients who seemed to benefit enormously from the intervention. She may have selectively observed outcome only in those clients that seemed to be benefiting from her work. And even in those clients she may have selectively observed indicators of positive outcome and overlooked other indicators that might have cast doubt on how much the new intervention was really helping the clients.

Usually, a research design will specify in advance the number and kind of observations to be made as a basis for reaching a conclusion. If we wanted to learn whether women were more likely than men to support the pro-choice position on abortion, we'd commit ourselves to making a specified number of observations on that question in a research project. We might select a thousand people to be interviewed on the issue. Even if the first 10 women supported the pro-choice position and the first 10 men opposed it, we'd interview everyone selected for the study and recognize and record each observation. Then we'd base our conclusion on an analysis of all the observations.

A second safeguard against selective observation in scientific inquiry also works against most of the other pitfalls. If you overlook something that contradicts your conclusion about the way things are, then your colleagues will notice it and bring it to your attention. That's a service scientists provide to one another and to the enterprise of science itself.

Ex Post Facto Hypothesizing

Suppose you administer an outreach program for battered women still living with their batterers, and you have the idea that if your program is successful, soon after entering treatment a battered woman should start feeling more positive about herself as an individual and about her capacity to be less dependent on the batterer. You might test the program's effectiveness by conducting a brief structured interview with clients several times before and after they enter treatment. In the interview, you'd find out (1) how good they feel about themselves and (2) how capable they feel of living independently away from their batterers. You'd then examine whether they feel better or more capable after entering treatment than before entering it.

But suppose their answers are the opposite of what you expected—that is, suppose they express worse feelings after entering treatment than before. What a disappointment. "Aha!" you might say. "The reason for the negative findings is that before entering treatment the women were unconsciously protecting themselves with the psychological defense mechanism of denial. They expressed better feelings before treatment because they were refusing to face their dangerous and deplorable situations. Our treatment helped overcome some of this denial and helped them get more in touch with an unpleasant reality they need to face in order to begin trying to change. Therefore, the more 'negative' responses after entering treatment are really more 'positive'! It is good that they are beginning to recognize what bad shape they were in; that's the first step in trying to improve it."

The example we've just described is sometimes called *ex post facto hypothesizing*, and it's perfectly acceptable in science if it doesn't stop there. The argument you proposed clearly suggests that you need to test your hypothesis about the program's effectiveness in new ways among a broader spectrum of people. The line of reasoning doesn't prove your hypothesis is correct, only that there's still some hope for it. Later observations may prove its accuracy. Thus, scientists often engage in deducing information, and they follow up on their deductions by looking at the facts again.

Ego Involvement in Understanding

The search for regularities and generalized understanding is not a trivial intellectual exercise: It critically affects our personal lives. Our understanding of events and conditions, then, is often of special psychological significance to us. If you lose your job or fail to get a promotion, you may be tempted to conclude that your boss wants to get you out of the way to promote a personal friend. That explanation would save you from examining your own abilities and worth. Any challenge to that explanation is consequently also a challenge to your abilities and worth.

In countless ways, we link our understandings of how things are to the image of ourselves we present to others. Because of this linkage, any disproof of these understandings tends to make us look stupid, gullible, and generally not okay. So we commit ourselves all the more unshakably to our understanding of how things are and create a formidable barrier to further inquiry and more accurate understanding.

This *ego involvement* in understanding is commonly encountered in social work practice. Naturally, practitioners see it in some of their clients, who may blame others or external circumstances beyond their control for their difficulties rather than accept responsibility and face up to the way their own behavior contributes to their problems. Practitioners are less likely to see the way their own ego involvement may impede practice. Rather than scientifically reexamine the effectiveness of our own ways of practicing, which we may like because we are used to them and have special expertise in them, we may tenaciously engage in selective observation, ex post facto hypothesizing, and other efforts to explain away evidence that suggests our approach to practice may be ineffective.

Social workers who conduct evaluation research frequently confront this form of ego involvement when their evaluations fail to support the efficacy of the programs they are evaluating. Administrators and other practitioners affiliated with programs undergoing evaluation often don't want to be hassled with elegant evaluation research designs. They may prefer expediency to methodological rigor in the evaluations, and would rather leave the work of designing and conducting annoying evaluations to evaluators. The same folks who initially express disinterest and lack of expertise in evaluation design or say that they don't need a methodologically rigorous design, however, can become fanatical critics. They may challenge the methodology of any study whose findings question the efficacy of their program, no matter how rigorous that study might be. Influenced by their ego involvement and vested interests in the unsupported program, administrators and practitioners are capable of grasping at any straw or magnifying any trivial methodological imperfection in a study in order to undermine the study's methodological credibility. For these same reasons, they are unlikely to notice even glaring methodological imperfections in studies whose results they like; they are apt to tout those studies as proving the value of their programs. (Chapter 13, on program evaluation, will examine this phenomenon in more depth.)

Administrators and practitioners aren't the only social workers who are vulnerable to ego involvement in understanding. Program evaluators and other social work researchers are just as human. They also run the risk of becoming personally involved in and committed to the conclusions they reach in scientific inquiry. Sometimes it's worse than in nonscientific life. Imagine, for example, that you have discovered an apparent cure for cancer and have been awarded the Nobel Prize. How do you suppose you'd feel when somebody else published an article that argued your cure didn't really work? You might not be totally objective.

A firm commitment to the other norms of science we have examined works against too much ego involvement. But if you lack that commitment, you'll find that your colleagues can evaluate the critical article more objectively than you can. Ultimately, then, although ego involvement is sometimes a problem for individual scientists, it is less a problem for science in general.

Other Forms of Illogical Reasoning

Intelligent humans commonly engage in additional forms of illogical reasoning in their day-to-day lives. One illustration is what statisticians have called the *gambler's fallacy*. A consistent run of either good or bad luck is presumed to foreshadow its opposite. An evening of bad luck at poker may kindle the belief that a winning hand is just around the corner, and many a poker player has lost more money because of that mistaken belief. Or, conversely, an extended period of good weather may lead you to worry that it is certain to rain on the weekend picnic. Even the best of us get a little funny in our reasoning from time to time. Worse yet, we can get defensive when others point out the errors in our logic.

Social workers need to use critical thinking and be vigilant in looking for the flawed reasoning of individuals whose ego involvement or vested interests lead them to make fallacious claims or arguments. Gibbs and Gambrill (1999) have identified some common fallacies that you are likely to encounter in addition to the ones we've already mentioned. One is called the *straw person argument,* in which someone attacks a particular position by distorting it in a way that makes it easier to attack. For example, opponents of proposed health care reforms—such as national health insurance or a patients' bill of rights with managed care companies—might exaggerate the extent to which the proposed reforms contain features that will inflate costs or delays in obtaining medical care.

Another fallacy is the *ad hominem attack,* which tries to discredit the person making an argument rather than addressing the argument itself. In a recent debate between two psychologists who had vested interests in competing forms of psychotherapy, for example, one ridiculed the legitimacy of the school from which the other had obtained her professional degree. Another example would be when critics of the use of military force in a particular foreign policy imbroglio have their patriotism questioned by defenders of the policy or when proponents of using military force are automatically branded as *war lovers* by those who oppose using force.

Sometimes new interventions are promoted based merely on their *newness* or *promise*. This, too, is a fallacy. When you encounter colleagues making this argument, you might want to remind them that lobotomy was once considered to be a new and promising treatment for mental illness. A somewhat related fallacy is the *bandwagon appeal,* in which a relatively new intervention is touted on the basis of its growing popularity. The implicit assumption is that the sheer number of your professional colleagues jumping on the bandwagon must mean that the intervention is effective. A flier promoting expensive training workshops for a new therapy, for example, once highlighted the fact that more than 25,000 mental health practitioners around the world had already attended the workshops. When you encounter the bandwagon appeal, it may help to recall the various treatment approaches that we have mentioned earlier in this chapter, and others that we will discuss later, whose bandwagon wheels fell off when scientific evidence showed the treatments to be ineffective or harmful.

There are additional forms of illogical reasoning that you may encounter; you can find more examples in the Gibbs and Gambrill text. We are not implying that interventions or policies promoted with fallacious appeals are necessarily ineffective or undesirable. Some might eventually be supported or may have already been supported by sound scientific studies despite the unfortunate ways their proponents have chosen to promote them. The point is not to be swayed one way or the other by appeals based on illogical reasoning. Instead, look for and critically appraise the scientific evidence.

The Premature Closure of Inquiry

Overgeneralization, selective observation, and the defensive uses of illogical reasoning all conspire to close inquiry prematurely. This discussion began with our desire to understand the world around us, and the various errors we have detailed often lead us to stop inquiry too soon.

The bigot who says, "I already understand Mexicans, so don't confuse me with facts" has achieved a personal closure on the subject. Sometimes this closure of inquiry is a social rather than individual act. For example, the private foundation or government agency that refuses to support further research on an "already understood" topic effects closure as a social act, as does the denominational college that prohibits scholarship and research that might challenge traditional religious beliefs. Social workers may do this by refusing to consider evidence that their favored interventions, programs, or policies are not as effective as they believe. Feminist or minority group organizations may do this by ruling off-limits certain lines of inquiry that pose some risk of producing findings that sexists or bigots could use inappropriately to stigmatize or oppose the advancement of women and minorities. Chapter 4 will examine the ethics of this phenomenon in more depth, as well as the effects of politics and ideologies on inquiry.

The danger of premature closure of inquiry is obvious. It halts attempts to understand things before understanding is complete. If you review the history of human knowledge, however, you will reach a startling conclusion: We keep changing the things we know—even the things we know for certain. In an important sense, then, any closure of inquiry is premature.

Human social phenomena have a recursive quality that is less common in other scientific arenas. What we learn about ourselves affects what we are like and how we operate—often canceling out what we learned in the first place. This implies that social science inquiry will always be needed (making it a stable career choice).

At its base, science is an open-ended enterprise in which conclusions are constantly being modified. That is an explicit norm of science. Experienced scientists accept it as a fact of life and expect established theories to be overturned eventually. Even if one scientist considers a line of inquiry to be completed forever, others will not. Even if a whole generation of scientists closes inquiry on a given topic, a later generation is likely to set about testing the old ideas and changing many of them.

In part, the reward structure of science supports this openness. Although you may have to overcome a great deal of initial resistance and disparagement, imagine how famous you would be if you could demonstrate persuasively that something people have always believed simply isn't true. What if you could prove that carbon monoxide was really good for people? The potential rewards for astounding discoveries keep everything fair game for inquiry in science.

To Err Is Human

These, then, are some of the ways in which we go astray in our attempts to know and understand the world and some of the ways that science protects its inquiries from these pitfalls. For the most part, science differs from our casual, day-to-day inquiry in two important respects. First, scientific inquiry is a conscious activity. Although we engage in continuous observation in daily life, much of it is unconscious or semiconscious. In scientific inquiry, we make a conscious decision to observe, and we stay awake while we do it. Second, scientific inquiry is more careful than our casual efforts. In scientific inquiry, we are more wary of making mistakes and take special precautions to avoid error.

Nothing we've said should lead you to conclude that science offers total protection against the errors that nonscientists commit in day-to-day inquiry. Not only do individual scientists make every kind of error we've looked at, scientists as a group fall into the pitfalls and stay trapped for long periods. Although science attempts to protect its inquiries from the common pitfalls in ordinary inquiry, accurately observing and understanding reality is not an obvious or trivial matter, as we will see throughout this book.

Main Points

- Social work research seeks to provide the practical knowledge that social workers need to solve the problems they confront.
- Social work research seeks to give the field the information it needs to alleviate human suffering and promote social welfare.
- Social work research seeks to accomplish the same humanistic goals as social work practice. Like practice, social work research is a compassionate, problem-solving, and practical endeavor.
- Recognizing when particular interventions for particular practice situations have been supported by adequate scientific evidence is an important guide to social work practice.
- Social work practitioners should understand social work research methods well enough to discriminate between strong and weak studies.
- Compassion for our clients is the main reason for us to use research.
- Social workers have an ethical responsibility to utilize research and contribute to the development of the profession's knowledge base.
- Much of what we know is by agreement rather than by experience.
- Tradition and authority are important sources of understanding, but relying on them exclusively can be risky.
- When we understand through experience, we make observations and seek patterns of regularities in what we observe.
- In day-to-day inquiry, we often make mistakes. Science offers protection against such mistakes.
- When we use the scientific method, everything is open to question, and we should keep an open mind about everything we think we know or want to believe.
- When we use the scientific method, we should consider the things we call "knowledge" to be provisional and subject to refutation.
- When we use the scientific method, we should search for evidence that is based on observation as the basis for knowledge.
- Scientific observations should be systematic, comprehensive, and as objective as possible.
- Scientific observations should be specified in ways that show the basis for the conclusions that were reached and that allow others to judge whether the evidence warrants those conclusions.
- The scientific method calls for the replication of studies.
- People often observe inaccurately, but such errors are avoided in science by making observation a careful and deliberate activity.
- Sometimes we jump to general conclusions on the basis of only a few observations. Researchers and scientific practitioners avoid overgeneralization through replication, or the repeating of studies.
- Once a conclusion has been reached, we sometimes ignore evidence that contradicts the conclusion, only paying attention to evidence that confirms it. Researchers and scientific practitioners commit themselves in advance to a set of observations to be made regardless of whether a pattern seems to be emerging early.
- When confronted with contradictory evidence, all of us make up explanations to account for the contradictions, often making assumptions about facts not actually observed. Researchers and scientific practitioners, however, make further observations to test those assumptions.
- Sometimes people simply reason illogically. Researchers and scientific practitioners avoid this by being as careful and deliberate in their reasoning as in their observations. Moreover, the public nature of science means that scientists have colleagues looking over their shoulders.
- The same support of colleagues helps protect scientists from tying their ego to their conclusions.
- Whereas people often decide they understand something and stop looking for new answers, researchers and scientific practitioners—as a group—ultimately regard all issues as open.

Review Questions and Exercises

1. Review the common errors of human inquiry discussed in this chapter in the section "Recognizing Flaws in Unscientific Sources of Social Work Practice

Knowledge." Find a magazine or newspaper article, or perhaps a letter to the editor, that illustrates one of those errors. Discuss how a scientist would avoid making the error.

2. Examine a few recent issues of the journal *Research on Social Work Practice* or the journal *Social Work Research*. Find an article that reports evidence about the effectiveness of an intervention and thus illustrates the value of research in guiding social work practice. Discuss how a social worker might be guided by that article.

3. Examine several recent issues of a journal in an allied profession such as sociology or psychology. Discuss the similarities and differences you find between the articles in that journal and the ones you examined in Exercise 2.

Internet Exercises

1. Use InfoTrac® College Edition to find an example of a research study that offers useful implications for social work practice. After you find a useful research report, write down the bibliographical reference information for the report and briefly describe the report's implications for practice. For example, if you are interested in treatment for individuals suffering from mental disorders and substance abuse, then you might want to read "Analysis of Postdischarge Change in a Dual Diagnosis Population" by Carol T. Mowbray and colleagues, which appeared in *Health and Social Work* (May 1999). Toward the end of the article is a section with the subheading "Implications for Practice."

2. Go to the InfoTrac College Edition website and click on the "InfoWrite" bar at the left. Then click on "Critical Thinking." Discuss how the information you find there applies to becoming a more effective and compassionate practitioner.

3. Visit the Campbell Collaboration's website at www.campbellcollaboration.org. Find a review of research on the effectiveness of interventions for a problem that interests you. (You can find reviews there on domestic violence, sexual abuse, parent training, criminal offenders, juvenile delinquency, personality disorder, conduct disorder among youths, serious mental illness, substance abuse, welfare reform, housing, foster parent training, eating disorders, and many others.) Write a brief summary of its conclusions and discuss whether and why you think that review would or would not be helpful in guiding social work practice. (If you are more interested in health care interventions, you can use the Cochrane Collaboration's website at www.cochrane.org.)

Additional Readings

Gibbs, Leonard, and Eileen Gambrill. 1999. *Critical Thinking for Social Workers: Exercises for the Helping Professions*. Thousand Oaks, CA: Pine Forge Press. This enjoyable workbook is filled with useful exercises to help you reason more effectively about social work practice decisions as well as other decisions that you will encounter in life. The exercises will help you recognize propaganda in human services advertising and help you recognize and avoid fallacies and pitfalls in professional decision making.

Kirk, Stuart A., and William J. Reid. 2002. *Science and Social Work*. New York: Columbia University Press. This book presents a critical appraisal of past and present efforts to develop scientific knowledge for social work practice and to make social work practice more scientific. It identifies the conceptual and practical impediments these efforts have encountered, offers lessons to improve future efforts, and is optimistic about the progress being made. It is a must-read for students and others who want to learn about the enduring struggle to improve the scientific base of social work practice.

Lilienfeld, Scott O., Steven Jay Lynn, and Jeffrey M. Lohr. 2003. *Science and Pseudoscience in Clinical Psychology*. New York: Guilford Press. Although the title of this provocative text refers to psychology, it is highly relevant to social work. Reading it will enhance your understanding of the scientific method and help you recognize warning signs of pseudoscientific espousals touting the effectiveness of certain interventions—espousals that contain some features of scientific inquiry and thus have the surface appearance of being scientific, but which upon careful inspection can be seen to violate one or more principles of the scientific method or contain fallacies against which the scientific method attempts to guard.

CHAPTER 2

Evidence-Based Practice

What You'll Learn in This Chapter

In Chapter 1 we examined the value of research in social work as well as the risks of not taking a scientific approach in making decisions about social work practice or social policy. In this chapter, we'll examine in depth a comprehensive model to guide social workers in taking a scientific approach to practice. That model is called *evidence-based practice.*

INTRODUCTION

Throughout the history of social work, various practice models have emerged as guides to help practitioners synthesize theories and organize their views in deciding how to intervene with various practice situations. One of the earlier models, for example, was based largely on psychoanalytic theory and is commonly referred to as the *psychosocial model*. Over the years, many different models came into vogue, such as the problem-solving model, the task-centered model, and the cognitive-behavioral model—to mention just a few. Although some of these models had more research support than others, by and large the rationale for each model was based more on theoretical notions than on scientific evidence. Since the turn of the 21st century, however, a new model has emerged that is based primarily on the scientific method and scientific evidence. This new model, which is currently receiving a great deal of attention in social work and allied fields, is called *evidence-based practice*.

Evidence-based practice is a process in which practitioners make practice decisions in light of the best research evidence available. But rather than rigidly constrict practitioner options, the evidence-based practice model encourages practitioners to integrate scientific evidence with their practice expertise and knowledge of the idiosyncratic circumstances bearing on specific practice decisions. It also involves evaluating the outcomes of their decisions. Although evidence-based practice is most commonly discussed in regard to decisions about what interventions to provide clients, it also applies to decisions about how best to assess the practice problems and decisions practitioners make at other levels of practice—such as decisions about social policies, communities, and so on.

For example, a clinical practitioner following the evidence-based practice model with a newly referred client will attempt to find and use the most scientifically validated diagnostic tools in assessing client problems and treatment needs and then develop a treatment plan in light of the best research evidence available as to what interventions are most likely to be effective in light of that assessment, the practitioner's clinical expertise regarding the client, and the client's idiosyncratic attributes and circumstances. At the level of social policy, evidence-based practitioners will attempt to formulate and advocate policies that the best research available suggests are most likely to achieve their desired aims. Likewise, evidence-based practitioners working at the community level will make practice decisions at that level in light of community-level practice research. Moreover, evidence-based practitioners at each level will utilize research methods to evaluate the outcomes of their practice decisions to see if the chosen course of action is achieving its desired aim. If it is not, then the evidence-based practitioner will choose an alternative course of action—again in light of the best research evidence available and again evaluating its outcome.

HISTORICAL BACKGROUND

Although the evidence-based practice model in social work is new, its historical precedents are as old as the profession itself. Mary Richmond's seminal text on social work practice (*Social Diagnosis*, 1917), for example, discussed the use of research-generated facts to guide social reform efforts and to guide direct practice with individuals and groups. Throughout its early history, social work aspired to be a science-based helping art (Zimbalist, 1977). Despite this aspiration, most of the 20th century was marked by a gap between research and practice, as studies showed that social work practitioners rarely examined research studies or used them to guide their practice. Instead, they relied more on tradition (professional consensus) and authorities, such as consultants and supervisors (Mullen and Bacon, 2004; Kirk and Reid, 2002).

Concern about the gap between research and practice grew during the 1970s, as reviews of research (mentioned in Chapter 1) concluded that direct social work practice was not effective (Fischer, 1973; Wood 1978; Mullen and Dumpson, 1972). These reviews, combined with the studies on the lack of research utilization by social workers, spurred the convening of several national conferences throughout the decade. Their goal: to address and try to bridge the gap between research and practice and formulate recommendations to increase social workers' use of research to guide their practice—in short, to make social work practice more evidence-based.

One of the most significant developments that emerged out of those activities was the empirical clinical practice model (Jayaratne and Levy, 1979). The component of that model that received the most attention was the call for social work practitioners to employ single-case designs to evaluate their own practice effectiveness. (We will examine single-case designs in depth in Chapter 12.) The model also urged practitioners to base their practice decisions on scientific evidence and to use scientifically valid measurement instruments in the assessment phase of clinical practice. As we'll see in this chapter, that model was the prime forerunner of the evidence-based practice model and resembles it in various respects.

The term *evidence-based practice* is used in many of the helping professions, not just social work. It is an extension of the term *evidence-based medicine* (EBM), which was coined in the 1980s to describe a process in which medical professionals use the best evidence available in making clinical decisions about the medical care of individual patients (Rosenthal, 2006). A commonly cited text on evidence-based medicine laid the groundwork for applying its principles to other helping professions and replacing the word *medicine* with the more generic term *practice*. That book, *Evidence-Based Medicine: How to Practice and Teach EBM* (Sackett et al., 2000), defined EBM as "the integration of best research evidence with clinical expertise and patient values" (p. 1). The inclusion of clinical expertise and patient values in that definition is important. It signifies that evidence-based practice is *not* an unchanging list of interventions that—because they have the best scientific evidence—clinicians must use even when they seem contraindicated by the clinician's knowledge about a client's unique attributes and circumstances. Moreover, as we saw in Chapter 1, one tenet of the scientific method is that all knowledge is provisional and subject to refutation. Thus, to define EBM only in terms of a list of scientifically "approved" interventions that clinicians should employ in a mechanistic fashion would conflict with the scientific method's emphasis on the constantly evolving nature of knowledge.

Drawing upon the above developments, the first decade of the 21st century has witnessed a flurry of literature on evidence-based practice in the helping professions. The following books, for example, are on evidence-based practice specifically in social work and have been authored by social workers:

- Briggs, H. E., and T. L. Rzepnicki (eds.). 2004. *Using Evidence in Social Work Practice: Behavioral Perspectives*. Chicago: Lyceum Books.
- Corcoran, J. 2003. *Clinical Applications of Evidence-Based Family Interventions*. Oxford: Oxford University Press.
- O'Hare, T. 2005. *Evidence-Based Practices for Social Workers: An Interdisciplinary Approach*. Chicago, IL: Lyceum Books.
- Roberts, A. R., and K. R. Yeager (eds.). 2004. *Evidence-Based Practice Manual: Research and Outcome Measures in Health and Human Services*. New York: Oxford University Press.
- Roberts, A. R., and K. R. Yeager (eds.). 2006. *Foundations of Evidence-Based Social Work Practice Manual: Research and Outcome Measures in Health and Human Services*. New York: Oxford University Press.

In addition, a new journal recently emerged with the title *Journal of Evidence-Based Social Work*. Likewise, special issues of other social work journals have been devoted to articles on evidence-based practice per se, and many articles on the topic have also been appearing in the regular issues of social work journals. Accompanying these developments has been the convening of various social work conferences on evidence-based practice. In fact, one school of social work—the George Warren Brown School of Social Work at Washington University—has made evidence-based practice the guiding focus for its curriculum.

THE NATURE OF EVIDENCE-BASED PRACTICE

In applying the scientific method to practice decisions, evidence-based practice is unlike "authority-based practice" (Gambrill, 1999). Practitioners engaged in evidence-based practice will be critical thinkers. Rather than automatically accept everything others with more experience or authority tell them about practice, they will question things. They will recognize unfounded beliefs and assumptions and think for themselves about the logic and the evidence that supports what others may convey as practice wisdom. Rather than just conform blindly to tradition or authority, they will take into account the best scientific evidence available in deciding how to intervene at micro or macro levels of practice.

To use that evidence, such practitioners need to find it. They cannot be passive in this process, hoping or assuming that the evidence will somehow find its way to them. They need to "track down" that evidence as an ongoing, "lifelong" part of their practice. They need to know how to find relevant evidence and to understand research designs and methods so that they can "critically appraise" the validity of the evidence they find. Finally, they need to use research methods to evaluate whether the evidence-based actions they take actually result in the outcomes they seek to achieve (Gambrill, 2001).

The evidence-based practitioner will not always find evidence that automatically determines what actions to take. Sometimes the evidence will be inconclusive, with some valid studies implying one course of action, and other valid studies implying a different way to intervene. Sometimes the evidence will indicate what actions *not* to take, such as when studies show certain interventions or policies to be *ineffective*. Although evidence-based practitioners will not always find a clear answer on how best to proceed, the important thing is to *look* for those answers. You would not want to miss them if they exist. And even when the evidence is mixed, it will often indicate possibilities you had not considered that are supported by more evidence than another action you were considering. Moreover, you can test one possibility out, and if that doesn't appear to be working, you can try one of the other evidence-based alternatives.

Sometimes the evidence will point toward taking an action that the client does not want. One key step in the evidence-based practice process is considering the values and expectations of clients and involving them as informed participants in the decision-making process. Gambrill (2001) reminds us that evidence-based practice is primarily a compassionate, client-centered approach to practice. We care about finding the best evidence because we care about maximizing our helpfulness to the client. We should not, therefore, disregard the values and concerns of clients when deciding whether the evidence we find fits the particular client with whom we are working.

Also, even interventions supported by the best evidence are not necessarily effective with every client or situation. An intervention that works with clients of one ethnic group may be less effective with clients of a different ethnicity. An intervention that is effective in treating male batterers may not work with female batterers or vice versa. The evidence-based practitioner needs to consider whether the client or situation in question really matches the context in which the evidence-based intervention was tested. And even if things match, one should remember that evidence-based interventions are not guaranteed to work with every client or situation. Studies providing valid evidence that an intervention is effective typically find that the intervention is *more likely* to be effective than some alternative, not that it is effective with every case. (This pertains to the concept of *probabilistic knowledge*, which we will examine more closely in Chapter 3.) These considerations underscore the importance of the client-centered nature of evidence-based practice and of taking the final step in the evidence-based practice process: using research methods to evaluate whether the evidence-based actions you take with a particular case result in the outcomes you seek. Much of what you learn in this book will help you take this and other steps in the evidence-based practice process, which we mentioned earlier—such as finding relevant studies and critically appraising them.

STEPS IN EVIDENCE-BASED PRACTICE

Now that we've explored the nature of evidence-based practice, its value, and its historical underpinnings, let's examine more closely the steps that have been recommended in the evidence-based practice process. As we do, you may notice the need for practitioners to understand research methods throughout the process. Several authors have provided helpful overviews of the steps in evidence-based practice (Sackett et al., 1997; Cournoyer and Powers, 2002; and Gambrill, 2001). The steps we describe next are adapted from them.

Step 1. Formulate a Question to Answer Practice Needs

In the first step, the practitioner formulates a question based on what is known relevant to a practice decision that must be made and what additional information is needed to best inform that decision. Suppose, for example, you reside in Alaska and work in a residential treatment facility for girls with emotional and behavioral problems, most of whom are Native Alaskans who have been victims of physical or sexual abuse. Your first question might be, "What interventions have the most research evidence supporting their effectiveness with abused girls with emotional and behavioral problems who reside in residential treatment facilities?" As you search the literature for the answer to that question, you may quickly discover the need to incorporate into your question information about variations in the girls' characteristics.

Interventions that are effective in treating posttraumatic stress disorder (PTSD) may not be effective with borderline personality disorder. A particular intervention might be very effective with girls who have had a single trauma but ineffective with girls who have had multiple traumas. That same intervention might even be potentially harmful for girls with dissociative disorders. You might find that some interventions have been found to be effective with older girls but not younger ones. Consequently, you may have to revise your question and perhaps formulate a series of questions. Instead of just asking about abused girls with emotional and behavioral problems, you may need separate questions about the most effective interventions for girls with different diagnoses, different problem histories, different ages, and so on.

You'll also want to incorporate the Native Alaskan ethnicity of the girls into your question. If you do not, you are likely to find many studies relevant to your question, but perhaps none that included Native Alaskan participants. Consequently, the interventions you find that were effective with girls of other ethnicities might not be effective with the girls with whom you work. If you do incorporate the Native Alaskan ethnicity of the girls into your question, you will find numerous studies dealing with traumatized youths with substance abuse problems in combination with their other trauma-related disorders and few, if any, studies that focus exclusively on singular disorders that do not include substance abuse. You'll also find studies whose findings indicate that Native American youths with PTSD may not have a diagnosis of PTSD because cultural factors may influence them to mask their PTSD symptoms. Learning this might lead you to reconsider the diagnosis some of the girls have received and to consider evidence-based interventions for PTSD for some girls that had not previously had that diagnosis in their case record. Thus, including ethnicity in your question can make a huge difference in the evidence you find and the implications of that evidence for your practice.*

The questions we've discussed so far did not specify an intervention in advance. We took an open-ended approach in looking for evidence about whatever interventions have been studied and supported by the best scientific evidence. Sometimes, however, you'll have a good reason to narrow your question to one or more interventions that you specify in advance. Suppose, for example, the traumatized girls you work with are very young, and your agency tradition is to provide nondirective play therapy as the prime intervention for every girl. As a critically thinking, evidence-based practitioner you might inquire as to the scientific evidence base for this tradition. Suppose that esteemed consultants or supervisors ask you to just trust their authority—or "practice wisdom"—on the matter. As a truly evidence-based practitioner, you'll need the courage to proceed with a search for evidence anyway. If you do, you'd have good reason to formulate a question that specifies play therapy, such as the following: "Will nondirective play therapy be effective in reducing the trauma symptoms of sexually abused Native Alaskan girls aged 8 or less?"

Sometimes it is reasonable to specify one or more alternative interventions in your question, as well. Suppose, for example, a colleague who works in a similar setting, and with similar clients, informs you that in her agency they prefer directive play therapy approaches that incorporate components of exposure therapy and that a debate rages among play therapy luminaries as to whether her agency's approach or your agency's approach makes more sense on theoretical grounds. Seeking scientific evidence to guide your practice in light of this new information, you might formulate an evidence-based question that specifies both alternative interventions, such as: "If sexually abused Native Alaskan girls aged 8 or less receive nondirective play therapy or directive play therapy, which will result in fewer trauma symptoms?" You might also want to expand the question to include exposure therapy.

The following acronym might come in handy when you want to formulate a question that specifies one or more interventions in advance: CIAO. To help you remember this acronym, in Italy "ciao" means goodbye, so long, hasta la vista baby, or later dude. Here's what the acronym stands for:

- Client characteristics
- Intervention being considered
- Alternative intervention (if any)
- Outcome

Applying the acronym to our question illustrated above, we get:

- C: If sexually abused Native Alaskan girls aged 8 or less
- I: Receive nondirective play therapy

*We hope you are thinking critically and thus wondering what the evidence is for the assertions made in this paragraph on what you'll find if you incorporate the Native Alaskan ethnicity of the girls into your question. The assertions are based on what one of us (Rubin) found when he conducted a literature search on this question in preparation for a talk on evidence-based practice delivered on April 29, 2006 at the University of Alaska–Anchorage School of Social Work.

- **A**: Or directive play therapy incorporating exposure therapy techniques
- **O**: Which will result in fewer trauma symptoms?

Step 2. Search for the Evidence

Later in this book, we will examine in detail how to use the library and your computer to conduct literature reviews to guide research projects. The same principles that we will examine later apply to practitioners searching for evidence to guide their practice decisions. However, practitioners rarely have nearly as much time and other resources for conducting exhaustive literature reviews as researchers are likely to have. One option likely to appeal to busy practitioners is the use of computerized library searches or searches of professional literature databases.

To help you search for literature online, your libraries may provide a variety of Internet professional literature database services, such as FirstSearch, Cambridge Scientific Abstracts, Medline, and OVID. Within these services are choices as to which professional area you'd like to search. For example, Cambridge Scientific Abstracts offers *Social Service Abstracts* and *Sociological Abstracts.*

FirstSearch offers *Social Sciences Abstracts.* OVID offers *PsycINFO.* There is considerable overlap in what you'll find across different databases in related areas. For example, if you are looking for literature on child abuse, many of the references you'll find using *Social Service Abstracts* can also be found using *PsycINFO.* You can scan your library's list of online abstracting or indexing databases to find one (or perhaps a few) that seem most relevant to your topic.

After you enter some search terms these databases will instantly provide you with a list of relevant books, journal articles, dissertations, and other publications related to your search terms. You can click on the ones that seem most pertinent to view the abstract for that reference. You may even be able to download the entire journal article, book, or dissertation.

What search terms you enter will depend on what you are looking for. If you're interested in a particular book or journal, for example, you can click on *title* and then enter the title of that book or journal. To find the published works of a particular author, you can click on *author* and then enter the name of that author. To find references related to a particular subject area, you would follow the same procedure, typing in a search term connected to your subject of interest. Search terms that can be used in a search for evidence about the effectiveness of interventions include *treatment outcome, effectiveness, evaluation, intervention,* and similar terms. These terms can be used in conjunction with those that are descriptive of the client and situation, such as *residential treatment facility, post-traumatic stress disorder, dissociative disorders, borderline personality disorder, sexual abuse,* and *child abuse* for the example mentioned in Step 1.

Suppose, for example, you want to find literature on support groups for battered women. Then you might enter such search terms as *battered women, spouse abuse, domestic violence,* or *support groups.* You will have options as to how broad or narrow you'd like the search to be. If you want the search to be limited to evaluations of the effectiveness of support groups for battered women, then you could ask for only those references pertaining to an entire set of key words, such as *battered women and evaluation.* You might also be able to limit the search according to other criteria, such as certain years of publication or the English language. If you want a broader search, then you can enter more key words or more broadly worded key words (*domestic violence* will yield more references than *battered wives*), and you would ask for references pertaining to *any* of your key words instead of the entire set.

If you do not have online access to the professional literature through a specific library, an alternative is to access the Internet directly through your own personal computer's search engine. There are various websites through which you can search for the literature you need. One site is provided by the National Library of Medicine at www.nlm.nih.gov. There you can obtain free usage of Medline, a database containing many references relevant to social work and allied fields.

Perhaps the most expedient option, however, is to use a popular search engine, such as *Google.* Finding sources and links to relevant websites on Google has become so popular that many folks now use the word *google* as a verb. You might be amazed at how many things you can "google." Google our names, for example, and you can find links to websites about our books and other things, including our photos.

Google also provides a website called Google Scholar. The difference between the two sites is that Google is more likely to provide you with a list of links to websites pertinent to your search term, whereas Google Scholar will be geared to providing you with links to specific published scholarly articles and books

GOOGLING PTSD TREATMENT

When we recently entered the search term "PTSD treatment" on Google, the following useful website links appeared among our first two pages of results. (There were many more.)

- Treatment of PTSD // National Center for Post-Traumatic Stress . . .
This fact sheet describes elements common to many treatment modalities for PTSD, including education, exposure, exploration of feelings and beliefs, . . .

www.ncptsd.va.gov/facts/treatment/fs_treatment.html

- Running head: PROMISING PTSD TREATMENT APPROACHES
A recent review of current treatments of PTSD, Solomon, Gerrity, . . .

www.fsu.edu/~trauma/promising.html

- PTSD: Treatment Options
Information and articles about a variety of treatments for mental illness, covering everything from psychotherapy to herbal remedies.

www.mental-health-matters.com/articles/article.php?artID=34

- Post Traumatic Stress Disorder (PTSD) Treatment
There is a growing body of evidence about effective treatment of PTSD. . . . Treatment for PTSD typically begins with a detailed evaluation and development of . . .

www.omh.state.ny.us/omhweb/ebp/adult_ptsd.htm

- Amazon.com: Effective Treatments for PTSD: Practice Guidelines from the International Society for Traumatic Stress Studies: Books by Edna B. Foa, Terence M. . . .

www.amazon.com/exec/obidos/tg/detail/-/1572305843?v=glance

- Treatment of Posttraumatic Stress Disorder
Treatment of posttraumatic stress disorder (PTSD) involves psychotherapy and medication. EMDR may be used to treat PTSD. Read more about the treatment of PTSD.

www.healthyplace.com/Communities/anxiety/treatment/ptsd_3.asp

on the topic. The box titled "Googling PTSD Treatment," for example, displays six useful website links that appeared among our first two pages of results (there were many more) when we recently entered the search term "PTSD Treatment" in the Google search box. Likewise, the box titled "Google Scholar Results for Effective Treatments for PTSD" displays five useful references (there were many more) that appeared on our first page of results generated by entering the search term "Effective Treatments for PTSD" in the Google Scholar search box.

Top-Down and Bottom-Up Searches Two major approaches to searching for evidence have been defined by Mullen (2006) as the *top-down* and *bottom-up* strategies. Using the bottom-up strategy, you would search the literature looking for any and all sources that provide evidence pertaining to the practice question you formulated. You would then read and critically appraise the quality of the evidence in each source, judge whether it is applicable to your unique practice decision, and ultimately choose a course of action based on what you deem to be the best applicable evidence available. Using the top-down strategy, instead of starting from scratch to find and appraise all the relevant studies yourself, you would rely on the results of evidence-based searches that others have done. You can find these reports in such sources as books providing practice guidelines for intervening in specific problem areas or diagnostic categories, systematic reviews of the research in particular areas, or meta-analyses. A meta-analysis pools the statistical results across studies of particular interventions and generates conclusions about which interventions

GOOGLE SCHOLAR RESULTS FOR EFFECTIVE TREATMENTS FOR PTSD

When we recently entered the search term "Effective Treatments for PTSD" on Google Scholar, hundreds of references appeared. The first page of references included the following:

- [BOOK] Effective treatments for PTSD: practice guidelines from the International Society for Traumatic . . .
- Effects of Psychotherapeutic Treatments for PTSD: A Meta-Analysis of Controlled Clinical Trials, JJ Sherman—Journal of Traumatic Stress, 1998 . . . the magnitude of improvement due to psychotherapeutic treatments is moderate and that these treatments are effective in reducing PTSD symptoms, depression . . .
- PSYCHOSOCIAL TREATMENTS FOR POSTTRAUMATIC STRESS DISORDER: A Critical Review—EB Foa, EA Meadows—Annual Review of Psychology, 1997—psych.annualreviews.org . . . able to identify immediately following a trauma those who are likely to develop chronic PTSD and to develop efficacious and cost-effective treatments for these . . .
- Comparative Efficacy of Treatments for Posttraumatic Stress Disorder: A Meta-Analysis—ML Van Etten, S Taylor—Clinical Psychology & Psychotherapy, 1998—doi.wiley.com
- Cognitive-behavior therapy vs exposure therapy in the treatment of PTSD in refugees—N Paunovic, LG Ost—BEHAVIOUR RESEARCH AND THERAPY, 2001—psy.surrey.ac.uk . . . The conclusion that can be drawn is that both E and CBT can be effective treatments for PTSD in refugees. 2001 Elsevier Science Ltd. All rights reserved. . . .

have the strongest impacts on treatment outcome as indicated by meta-analytic statistics. (We'll examine meta-analysis in Chapter 22.)

The prime advantage of the top-down approach is its feasibility. The social work agency where you work may have limited computer access to Internet literature databases, which can be expensive. Universities typically provide their students and faculty with free access to Internet databases that save much time in searching the literature. If you have already used such databases to search the literature for term papers or other course assignments, you can imagine how much more time it would have taken to go to the library to look for the sources manually. Moreover, even with access to Internet databases, the bottom-up approach can be very time consuming if your search yields a large number of studies that need to be appraised as to the scientific quality of the evidence they provide and the applicability of that evidence to your unique practice decision. Some search terms—such as those looking for effective interventions for child maltreatment, domestic violence, or trauma—can yield more than a hundred studies that you'll need to examine. Reading and appraising those studies, even when you can download them electronically, can take a lot more time than is feasible for busy practitioners with large caseloads. How much easier it is to rely on others with advanced expertise in appraising research evidence in particular areas of practice.

The top-down approach, however, has one serious disadvantage—the fallibility of the experts who have conducted the reviews, appraised the evidence, and derived practice guidelines from them. To a certain extent, relying exclusively on a top-down search as an evidence-based way to answer your practice question requires relying on the authority of those experts. Because reliance on authority is inconsistent with the scientific method, using only a top-down approach is therefore paradoxical. Perhaps the "experts" missed many relevant studies in their search. Perhaps other experts with higher methodological standards would disagree with their appraisals as to the scientific quality of the evidence in particular studies and as to which interventions appear to be supported by the *best* evidence. Some "experts" may even be biased in their appraisals—especially if they have a vested interest in the intervention they claim has the best evidentiary support. If you conduct a top-down search

SOME USEFUL INTERNET SITES FOR REVIEWS AND PRACTICE GUIDELINES

- Campbell Collaboration: www.campbell collaboration.org/index.html
- Cochrane Collaboration: www.cochrane.org
- American Psychological Association's website on empirically supported treatments: www.apa .org/divisions/div12/rev_est/
- Center for Substance Abuse Prevention: modelprograms.samhsa.gov/template.cfm? page=default
- Crisis Intervention, Co-morbidity Assessment, Domestic Violence Intervention, and Suicide Prevention Network: www.crisisintervention network.com
- Expert Consensus Guideline Series: www .psychguides.com
- National Guideline Clearinghouse: www .guidelines.gov
- National Institute of Drug Abuse: www.nida .nih.gov/
- Substance Abuse and Mental Health Services Administration: www.samhsa.gov/index.aspx
- Additional sites for top-down reviews can be found by entering search terms into a search engine such as Google, Yahoo!, or others.

for effective interventions for PTSD, for example, you likely will find experts in exposure therapy and experts in eye-movement desensitization and processing (EMDR) therapy arguing over whose reviews are more biased and whose favored treatment approach has the better evidentiary support.

If feasibility obstacles to using the bottom-up approach require practitioners to rely solely on a top-down approach, therefore, they should do so as critical thinkers. They should not rely on just one or a few top-down sources that have been recommended to them or that they find at first. They should try to find and appraise all the top-down sources relevant to their practice decision and look for possible disagreements among them. They should try to ascertain whether the authors of the sources have a vested interest in the particular practice approach recommended. Finally, they should examine the evidentiary standards used in the appraisals of studies. Did the studies have to meet certain minimal methodological criteria to qualify for inclusion in the review? What methodological criteria were used to distinguish studies offering the best evidence from those offering weaker evidence? Were those criteria appropriate in light of the information in the rest of this book and in your research courses?

Fortunately, the top-down and bottom-up approaches are not mutually exclusive. Time and access permitting, you can search for and appraise individual studies as well as top-down sources that have already appraised individual studies and developed practice guidelines from them. In fact, a thorough bottom-up search implicitly would find and appraise top-down sources as well as individual studies. It can't hurt to augment your own review of individual studies with the reviews others have provided, as long as you critically appraise each source as recommended above. With that in mind, let's now look at two top-down resources that are regarded highly by researchers in social work and allied fields. The box titled "Some Useful Internet Sites for Reviews and Practice Guidelines" lists the websites for these two sources as well as some others that you might find useful.

The Cochrane Collaboration and the Campbell Collaboration The Cochrane Collaboration is an international nonprofit organization that recruits researchers, practitioners, and consumers into review groups that provide reviews of research on the effects of health care interventions. If you visit the Cochrane Collaboration's website at www.cochrane .org, you will find a link to its library, which contains its reviews, comments and criticisms, abstracts of other reviews, bibliographies of studies, reviews regarding methodology, and links that can help you conduct your own review. The Cochrane website also has information that will help you judge the quality of the Cochrane review system.

In 2000, shortly after the emergence of the Cochrane Collaboration, a sibling international nonprofit organization—the Campbell Collaboration—was formally established. Its mission and operations mirror those of its sibling but focus on social welfare, education, and criminal justice. Its reviews are written for use by practitioners, the public, policy makers, students, and researchers. If you go to its website at www.campbellcollaboration.org, you can find links that are like those of the Cochrane Collaboration but with a focus on topics not limited to health care. For example, you can find reviews of the effectiveness of interventions for domestic violence, sexual abuse, parent training, criminal offenders, juvenile delinquency, personality disorder, conduct disorder among youths, serious mental illness, substance abuse, welfare reform, housing, foster parent training, eating disorders, and many others.

Step 3. Critically Appraise the Relevant Studies You Find

As we noted in Chapter 1, there is a vast range in the quality of published studies evaluating the effectiveness of various interventions. Many are excellent, but many others violate some of the fundamental principles that you will learn in this book. It would be silly to attempt at this point to explain in depth all the research methods and research design concepts you'll need to know to critically appraise the studies you will find. That's what the rest of this book is for. However, a brief look at some highlights might help you better comprehend the evidence-based practice process.

Two of the main questions commonly asked in appraising the quality of the evidence reported in practice effectiveness studies are: (1) Was treatment outcome measured in a reliable, valid, and unbiased manner? (2) Was the research design strong enough to indicate conclusively whether the intervention or something else most plausibly explains the variations in client outcome? Studies can be ranked according to various evidence-based practice hierarchies developed to help guide appraisals of evidence. At the top of these evidentiary hierarchies are studies with the strongest designs in regard to the above two criteria for appraising the quality of evidence about whether the intervention, and not something else, most plausibly explains treatment outcome. Those designs are called *randomized clinical trials* (RCTs). Likewise, sources reviewing RCT studies would be at the top of an evidentiary ranking.

Randomized clinical trials are *experiments* that use random means (such as a coin toss) to assign clients who share similar problems or diagnoses into groups that receive different interventions. For example, one group might receive an intervention that is hypothesized to be more effective than treatment as usual, while another group receives treatment as usual. The random assignment procedure is used to avoid biases in the way clients are assigned to groups—biases such as assigning to one group the clients most motivated to change and assigning the least motivated clients to the other group. Then, if the predicted difference in outcome is found between the groups, it is not plausible to attribute the difference to a priori differences between incomparable groups.

Next on most evidentiary hierarchies are quasi-experiments that, although they differ from experiments by not using random procedures to assign clients to groups, use other means to reduce the plausibility of attributing differences in outcome to a priori differences between the groups. Although the alternative procedures used by quasi-experiments are less ideal than random assignment procedures, quasi-experiments that employ those procedures properly are considered to provide a strong source of evidence for guiding intervention decisions.

You should not automatically assume, however, that any study that employs an RCT or quasi-experimental design is a strong source of evidence. For example, perhaps outcome was measured in a biased manner. Maybe the clinician who invented the tested treatment subjectively rated whether the clients who received his treatment improved more than those who received treatment as usual. We'll examine these issues in more depth in Chapter 11, which is mainly devoted to experimental and quasi-experimental designs.

Next on most evidentiary hierarchies are single-case evaluation designs. These designs apply the logic of experiments and quasi-experiments in graphing the progress of individual cases with repeated measurements before and after the onset of treatment. Although these designs do not compare groups of clients, when their results are replicated and consistently support the effectiveness of an intervention they are considered to provide strong, albeit tentative, evidence about the potential effectiveness of that intervention. We'll examine single-case evaluation designs in depth in Chapter 12.

A variety of other sources generally appear closer to the bottom of most evidentiary hierarchies. One such source involves studies that show client improvement from one pretest to one posttest, with no controls for other plausible explanations for the improvement. (These alternative explanations usually are called threats to internal validity, which will be discussed in depth in Chapter 10.) Another involves correlational studies that lack sophisticated statistical controls and merely show that clients with different treatment histories have different attributes. For example, suppose a survey finds that clients who completed all twelve steps of a substance abuse treatment program had fewer relapses than clients who refused treatment, dropped out of treatment prematurely, or were dismissed from treatment for violating the treatment contract. Rather than supplying strong evidence in support of the effectiveness of the treatment, the results of that study could be attributed to a priori differences between the clients who were motivated to become rehabilitated and those who lacked such motivation.

At or near the bottom of most evidentiary hierarchies are such things as anecdotal case reports or opinions of respected clinical experts, based on their clinical experience. Although such sources may provide useful starting points as to what interventions to consider when no better sources of evidence are available, they do not provide the kind of objective evidence most highly valued in the scientific method. The experts might have vested interests in the intervention they tout, and their opinions or anecdotal case reports could be heavily influenced by the sorts of flaws discussed in Chapter 1, such as inaccurate observation, overgeneralization, selective observation, ego involvement in understanding, and so on.

Some scholars dislike evidentiary hierarchies that have been developed to guide evidence-based practice. Typically, those who have been most vocal in their criticism of these hierarchies are scholars who commonly employ forms of scientific inquiry that, in their view, are devalued by the evidence-based practice hierarchies. Although their concern is understandable, they may be reading more into the hierarchies than the creators of the hierarchies intended. An evidence-based practice evidentiary hierarchy is not intended to imply what kinds of research *in general* are better or worse irrespective of the *purpose* of the research. As we will see in Chapter 6, not all research purposes pertain to determining whether interventions really cause particular outcomes. For example, a well-done survey documenting the extent to which the homeless mentally ill are living in squalor, or the devastating impact of Hurricane Katrina on impoverished Gulf Coast residents, can be of great value in spurring an electorate to accept higher taxes to help these needy people. An RCT would probably be near the bottom of a hierarchy of research designs created for considering what kinds of studies will have the greatest impact on a nation that is not doing enough for people in need. Likewise, consider in-depth interviews of minority group clients on how they subjectively perceived the way they were treated in an agency that has made no effort to become culturally competent, and how those perceptions made them feel. Such interviews might not be high on a hierarchy designed to determine objectively the effects of an intervention, but would be high on a hierarchy designed for generating in-depth insights about clients' perceptions and feelings.

Step 4. Determine Which Evidence-Based Intervention Is Most Appropriate for Your Particular Client(s)

Even interventions supported by the best evidence are not necessarily effective with every client or situation. Strong studies providing valid evidence that an intervention is effective typically find that the intervention is *more likely* to be effective than some alternative, not that it is effective with every case. Interventions found to be effective with members of one ethnic group might not be effective with clients with other ethnicities. The intervention supported by the strongest studies might involve procedures that conflict with the values of certain cultures or individual clients. You might have to use your clinical expertise, your knowledge of the client, client feedback, and your cultural competence in making a judgment call.

Determining which of the interventions you find is the best fit for your particular client or group of clients involves several considerations. One consideration, of course, is the quality of the evidence that you appraise in Step 3. Students commonly ask, "How many good studies do I need to find that support a particular intervention before I can consider it evidence-based?"

There is no precise answer to that question. One or two strong studies supporting a particular intervention will probably suffice. An intervention supported by one very strong study probably has better evidence than an intervention supported only by many very weak studies.

More importantly, asking which intervention is evidence-based is not the right question. It has a ring of finality to it that is not consistent with the provisional nature and refutability of knowledge in the scientific method. Rather than ask whether to consider an intervention to be evidence-based, it's better to think in terms of which intervention has the best evidence for the time being. And if the evidence supporting that intervention emerged from research with clients unlike yours in clinically meaningful ways, it may not be as good as evidence from a study using a somewhat weaker design, but with clients who are just like yours.

But what if you find no intervention supported by any study involving clients just like yours even as you find an intervention supported by a strong study involving clients that are like yours in some important ways but unlike yours in other important ways? Unless the latter intervention is unacceptable for some clinical reason, it might be worth trying with your client. For example, suppose you found no intervention that appears to be effective with 12- and 13-year-old girls in a residential treatment facility who are diagnosed with borderline personality disorder. But maybe you found strong evidence supporting the effectiveness of an intervention for 14- to 16-year-old girls with that disorder but not in a residential facility. Since you found no better alternative, you might employ the latter intervention on a trial basis and evaluate (in Step 6) what happens.

If it is appropriate and possible to do so before finalizing the selection of any intervention and applying it, you should consider the values and expectations of your client, involve the client in the decision, inform the client about the intervention and the evidence about its potential effectiveness and any possible undesirable side effects, and obtain the client's informed consent to participate in the intervention. You'll probably want to avoid a lot of detail when you do this and thus merely say something like "This has the most evidence of effectiveness to date," "This has had a few promising results," or "We have some beginning evidence that this treatment may work well for people who have your kinds of concerns." That way, the client can make an informed decision regarding the treatment both in terms of what fits best (in terms of culture, personality, and other factors) and what is most likely to have positive outcomes. Beyond the ethical reasons for obtaining the client's informed consent regarding the choice of intervention, doing so might help the client feel a sense of ownership and responsibility in the treatment process. In turn, the client might be more likely to achieve a successful outcome.

Step 5. Apply the Evidence-Based Intervention

Once the selection of the intervention is finalized, several steps may be needed before applying it. To begin, you may need to obtain training in the intervention through a continuing education workshop or professional conference. Perhaps an elective course is offered on it at a nearby school of social work. You should also obtain readings on how to implement the intervention, including any treatment manuals for it. Try to locate a colleague who has experience providing the intervention and arrange for consultation or supervision. For some relatively new interventions, you may find a support group of professional colleagues who meet regularly to provide each other peer feedback about how they are implementing the new intervention with various cases. If you are unable to obtain sufficient training or supervision, you should try to refer the client to other practitioners who have the requisite training and experience in the intervention.

If you provide the intervention yourself, or if you continue working with the client after you've referred them for it, one more step should be taken before the intervention is introduced. As an evidence-based practitioner, you should formulate, in collaboration with the client, treatment goals that can be measured in evaluating whether the selected intervention really helps the client. Chapter 7 of this text will help you define treatment goals in measurable terms. Some of the studies you appraise in Step 2 might also identify useful ways to define and measure treatment goals.

Step 6. Evaluation and Feedback

During this phase, you and the client will measure and evaluate progress in achieving the treatment goals you have set. Chapters 8, 9, and 12 of this text will help you design the methods for doing that. You might, for example, have the client self-monitor certain behaviors, emotions, or cognitions daily for a while before you apply the intervention, during the course of treatment with the intervention, and perhaps during a follow-up period after you have completed the intervention protocol.

To assess whether the intervention appears to be effective for that particular client, you might graph the daily data and look for the pattern of the graphed data to improve significantly after intervention begins. You and the client should discuss the data in an ongoing fashion, including perhaps the need to modify the treatment plan if the intervention does not appear to be helpful or if treatment goals are achieved. Some clients may really like this process—seeing their progress and discussing why symptoms are getting worse or better. (Sometimes extraneous important events come up in their lives that affect their progress and that inform the treatment process.)

Once your work with the client has finished, you should communicate your findings to relevant colleagues. You might even want to write your work up as a single-case evaluation study for publication. (If you choose to do that, Chapter 12 of this text can help you, as can other parts of the text that discuss writing research reports.) Cournoyer and Powers (2002) even suggest that you might communicate your findings to the researchers whose studies provided the evidence base for choosing the intervention you applied and evaluated.

But perhaps you are wondering why Step 6 is needed in the first place. Why evaluate an intervention with your one client if published studies have already provided credible evidence of its effectiveness? There are two answers to this question. One, which we mentioned earlier, is that studies supporting the effectiveness of interventions typically do not find that the tested interventions are guaranteed to work with every client or situation. Instead, they merely find that it is more likely to be effective than some alternative. Your client may be one of the cases for whom the intervention does not work. The second answer involves the principle of replication. As we discussed in Chapter 1, the scientific method considers all knowledge to be provisional and subject to refutation. And as we will discuss in Chapter 12 and elsewhere, the more high-quality studies that replicate a particular outcome for a particular intervention, the more confidence we can have in the evidence about that intervention's effects.

CONTROVERSIES AND MISCONCEPTIONS ABOUT EVIDENCE-BASED PRACTICE

The emergence of evidence-based practice as a model being advocated for all practitioners to follow regardless of their practice roles and orientations stimulated controversy. Various objections were raised to the call for all practitioners to engage in evidence-based practice. Proponents of the model have characterized most of the objections as misconceptions. Let's now examine the most prominent objections to the model and why these criticisms have been deemed misconceptions.

A significant early event spurring interest in evidence-based practice was a 1995 report by the American Psychological Association's Division 12 Task Force on Promotion and Dissemination of Psychological Procedures (Task Force, 1995) and updates to that report (Chambless et al., 1996, 1998). According to that report, to have its effectiveness be considered "well-established" an intervention ideally should have a manual that provides step-by-step specific procedures that practitioners should follow in implementing the intervention. Such manuals are seen as increasing the likelihood that different practitioners will implement the intervention in the intended manner. Likewise, without such manuals, confidence in the effectiveness of the intervention would diminish in light of the increased potential for practitioners to implement it in ways that deviate from the manner in which it was found to be effective.

The impact of the Task Force report led many to equate its recommendations with evidence-based practice and to define evidence-based practice as the use of interventions that prestigious professional organizations or research reviews deemed to be effective. Moreover, some perceived the use of cookbook-like manualized procedures as a necessary feature of evidence-based practice. Based on this perception, a number of objections were raised, including those discussed next.

It is based on studies of clients unlike those typically encountered in everyday social work practice. One objection concerns the characteristics of clients that have participated in the type of experiments (RCTs) that reside at the top of the evidence-based practice research hierarchy. For example, RCTs typically have excluded clients with more than one diagnosis, and racial or ethnic minority clients have been underrepresented in most RCTs (Messer, 2006; Westen, 2006). This objection is particularly germane to social work, since social workers commonly work with ethnic minority clients or clients with multiple disorders or with unique concerns that don't fit the formal diagnostic categories required for participation in most RCTs. In light of the discrepancies between the kinds of clients participating in evaluations of manualized interventions and the kinds of clients practitioners are most likely to encounter in everyday practice, the perception of evidence-based practice as requiring practitioners to rigidly follow treatment manuals has been criticized as not allowing them the flexibility to use their expertise to respond to unique client attributes and circumstances.

It is an overly restrictive cookbook approach that denigrates professional expertise and ignores client values and preferences. A related objection portrays evidence-based practice as an overly restrictive approach that minimizes professional expertise and applies empirically supported interventions in the same way to all clients, and in doing so ignores client values and preferences. Proponents of evidence-based practice have dismissed this objection, as well as the one above, as being based on a misconception. They argue that these objections overlook the integration of clinical expertise in the evidence-based practice process, as mentioned in the most prominent definitions of evidence-based practice and as discussed earlier in this chapter (Gibbs and Gambrill, 2002; Mullen and Streiner, 2004). Recall that Step 4 in the evidence-based practice process, for example, calls for considering the values and expectations of the client and involving the client in the selection of an intervention.

The therapeutic alliance will be hindered. A related objection is based on research that has supported the notion that the quality of the practitioner–client relationship might be the most important aspect of effective treatment regardless of what type of intervention the practitioner employs. Some argue that rigid adherence to treatment manuals can inhibit practitioner flexibility in using professional experience and expertise in relationship building and that this consequently can harm the therapeutic alliance and result in poorer treatment outcomes (Reed, 2006; Messer, 2006; Westen, 2006; Zlotnik and Galambos, 2004). Moreover, RCTs typically have evaluated manualized interventions. Thus, they are seen as not only relating primarily to clients unlike the ones social workers typically encounter in everyday practice, but also involving cookbook-like procedures that don't fit—and perhaps hinder—everyday social work practice. Again, however, proponents of evidence-based practice dismiss this objection as ignoring the part of the definition of evidence-based practice that emphasizes the integration of clinical expertise in the evidence-based practice process.

It is merely a cost-cutting tool. Some critics of evidence-based practice have portrayed it as merely a cost-cutting tool that can be exploited by government agencies and managed care companies that pay for services. Their criticism is based on the notion that these third-party payers will only pay for the provision of interventions that have been supported by RCTs and only for the number of sessions that the RCT results indicate are needed. Proponents of evidence-based practice counter that this would not be a criticism of evidence-based practice, but rather a criticism of the way managed care companies might distort it. Moreover, they argue that some interventions supported by the best research evidence are more costly than the less supported alternatives (Gibbs and Gambrill, 2002; Mullen and Streiner, 2004). The aim of evidence-based practice is to find the most *effective* interventions, not to find the cheapest ones.

Evidence is in short supply. Another criticism of evidence-based practice is that there are not enough quality research studies to guide practice in many social work treatment areas and for many populations. Evidence-based practice proponents counter this criticism by asserting that a shortage of quality outcome studies is less of an argument against evidence-based practice than an argument for it. If practitioners are making decisions based on little or no evidence, all the more reason to "exercise caution and perhaps be even more vigilant in monitoring outcomes" (Mullen and Streiner, 2004:115).

Real-world obstacles prevent implementing it in everyday practice. Perhaps the most problematic controversy about evidence-based practice has nothing to do with its desirability, and is one that even its proponents find daunting. It has to do with obstacles to implementing it in real-world everyday practice. Social workers commonly work in settings where superiors do not understand or appreciate evidence-based practice and do not give practitioners enough time to carry out the evidence-based practice process—especially if they follow the bottom-up approach in searching for evidence (as discussed earlier in this chapter). Even in settings where evidence-based practice is valued, resources may be insufficient to provide staff with the time, training, publications, and access to Internet databases and search engines needed to carry out the evidence-based practice process efficiently and appropriately. Although some leaders in evidence-based practice are formulating and pilot testing strategies for overcoming these obstacles in agencies, the going is rough. One such leader is Edward Mullen, a social work professor at Columbia University. A recent e-mail message from him contained the following comments about a pilot project he is completing that addresses the above obstacles to implementing evidence-based practice (EBP) in three New York City agencies:

> I am struck by how difficult this is to pull off in real live agencies due to such things as time, limited access to computers and the internet (unlike universities where we have access to fee based databases, etc.). This says to me that a very major issue in the teaching of EBP is how to prepare students in EBP so that they will be prepared to function as EBP practitioners in real world agencies after graduation. A related issue is how to bring class and field work together in our efforts to teach students EBP. When I teach EBP to students they typically say it is an approach that they like and value but when they go into field work the approach can not be implemented because of agency barriers.

The evidence-based practice research hierarchy inappropriately devalues qualitative research and alternative philosophies. As we noted earlier in this chapter, the evidence-based practice research hierarchy bases the quality of the evidence reported in practice effectiveness studies largely on the following two questions: (1) Was treatment outcome measured in a reliable, valid, and unbiased manner? (2) Was the research design strong enough to indicate conclusively whether the intervention or something else most plausibly explains the variations in client outcome? RCTs are considered the strongest designs for obtaining affirmative answers to these questions, and well-controlled quasi-experiments are next in the hierarchy. Among the types of studies that are relatively low on the hierarchy are studies that rely on qualitative research methods—methods with a different set of priorities and that put more value on subjectively probing for deeper meanings than on trying to logically rule out alternative plausible explanations for treatment outcomes. We'll examine these methods closely in the next chapter and in many later chapters. Though their value is widely recognized by scholars in social work and allied fields with regard to many lines of inquiry other than evidence-based practice, many scholars who prefer qualitative methods feel that those methods are inappropriately devalued in the evidence-based practice research hierarchy.

Also objecting to the evidence-based practice research hierarchy are scholars who—on philosophical grounds—reject the emphasis on objectivity in the traditional scientific method that guides evidence-based practice research hierarchy. Some scholars argue that everything is subjective, that all we have are our subjective realities, and that no point of view about practice is therefore superior to any other. Proponents of evidence-based practice counter that if this is so, how can professionals claim to have special knowledge, and how do we avoid having elite authorities dictate what is and is not true (Gibbs and Gambrill, 2002)?

We will delve into these methodological and philosophical debates in more depth in the next chapter. Moreover, throughout the rest of this text you will be learning what you need to know about research methods in order to become an effective evidence-based practitioner.

Main Points

- Evidence-based practice is a process in which practitioners make practice decisions in light of the best research evidence available.

- The evidence-based practice model encourages practitioners to integrate scientific evidence with their practice expertise and knowledge of the idiosyncratic circumstances bearing on specific practice decisions.

- Although evidence-based practice is most commonly discussed in regard to decisions about what interventions to provide clients, it also applies to decisions about how best to assess the practice problems and decisions practitioners make at other levels of practice.

- Evidence-based practice involves critical thinking, questioning, recognizing unfounded beliefs and assumptions, thinking independently as to the logic and evidence supporting what others may convey as practice wisdom, and using the best scientific evidence available in deciding how to intervene with individuals, families, groups, or communities.

- Evidence-based practitioners need to track down evidence as an ongoing part of their practice. They need to know how to find relevant studies and understand research designs and methods so that they can critically appraise the validity of the studies they find. They need to base the actions they take on the best evidence they find and use research methods to evaluate whether the evidence-based actions they take result in the outcomes they seek to achieve.

- Steps in the evidence-based practice process include formulating a question, searching for evidence, critically appraising the studies you find, determining which evidence-based intervention is most appropriate for your particular client(s), applying the evidence-based intervention, and evaluating progress and providing feedback.

- Evidence-based practice questions may be open-ended regarding interventions or may specify one or more interventions in advance.

- Perhaps the most expedient way to search for evidence is to use a popular Internet search engine, such as *Google* or *Google Scholar.*

- Searching for evidence can employ *top-down* and *bottom-up* strategies.

- Using the bottom-up strategy, you would search the literature looking for any and all sources that provide evidence pertaining to the practice question you formulated. You would then read and critically appraise the quality of the evidence in each source, judge whether it is applicable to your unique practice decision, and ultimately choose a course of action based on what you deem to be the best applicable evidence available.

- Using the top-down strategy, instead of starting from scratch to find and appraise all the relevant studies yourself, you would rely on the results of evidence-based searches that others have done and that are reported in such sources as books providing practice guidelines, systematic reviews, or meta-analyses.

- Research hierarchies have been developed that can help guide appraisals of evidence. At the top of these hierarchies are sources reporting or reviewing studies with the strongest designs in regard to appraising whether an intervention, and not something else, most plausibly explains treatment outcome. Those designs are called *randomized clinical trials* (RCTs).

- Even interventions supported by the best evidence are not necessarily effective with every client or situation. Interventions found to be effective with members of one ethnic group might not be effective with clients of other ethnicities. Interventions supported by the strongest studies might involve procedures that conflict with the values of certain cultures or individual clients.

- Various objections have been raised to the call for all practitioners to engage in evidence-based practice. Proponents of the model have characterized most of the objections as misconceptions.

- Social workers commonly work in settings where resources might be insufficient to provide staff with the time, training, publications, and access to Internet databases and search engines needed to carry out the evidence-based practice process efficiently and appropriately.

Review Questions and Exercises

1. Formulate an evidence-based practice question to guide your decision about the most effective intervention to employ in the case of a 6-year-old African American boy who witnessed his father severely battering his mother and whose diagnosis includes both conduct disorder and post-traumatic stress disorder.

2. Suppose your search for evidence to answer your question in Exercise 1 yielded no study in which the characteristics of the participants matched those of your client. Discuss the various considerations that would guide your decision about which of several different empirically supported interventions is most likely to be effective for your client.

3. Discuss how your answer to Exercise 2 bears on several objections raised by critics of evidence-based practice.

Internet Exercises

1. To help you engage in the first two steps of the evidence-based practice (EBP) process and to find links to many other EBP-related sites, go to the following website: www.lib.umich.edu/socwork/rescue/ebsw.html. Discuss how what you found there can help you complete the first two steps of the EBP process.

2. Briefly describe how at least two of the links to additional EBP sites that you found at the site in Internet Exercise 1 can facilitate the EBP process.

3. Using an Internet search engine such as Google, enter a search term for a policy or intervention that interests you. In the search results, click on several links that look most interesting. Briefly describe what you find at those links and how helpful they appear to be in facilitating a search for evidence to guide practice decisions about the intervention or policy you specified in your search term.

4. If you have access to Google Scholar or one of the alternative database services specified in this chapter, go to that service and enter a search term for a policy or intervention that interests you. In the search results, click on several literature sources that look most relevant. Briefly summarize the type of evidence at each of those sources and how they would bear on practice decisions about the intervention or policy you specified in your search term.

5. As you may have done at the end of Chapter 1, visit the Campbell Collaboration's website at www.campbellcollaboration.org. Find a review of the effectiveness of interventions for a problem that interests you. Discuss how relying on reviews such as that one represents a top-down search strategy and why using such a strategy would be more expedient than using a bottom-up search strategy. (If you are more interested in health care interventions, you can use the Cochrane Collaboration's website at www.cochrane.org.)

Additional Readings

Corcoran, Jacqueline. 2000. *Evidence-Based Social Work Practice with Families: A Lifespan Approach.* New York: Springer. As its title suggests, this book describes family interventions whose effectiveness has been supported by some research studies. Social workers in the child welfare field, as well as in other fields dealing with families and children, may find this book particularly useful.

O'Hare, T. (2005). *Evidence-Based Practices for Social Workers: An Interdisciplinary Approach.* Chicago: Lyceum Books. This text contains chapters on defining evidence-based practice; describing its procedures, guiding principles, and evidence-based assessment procedures; and applying evidence-based practices to various types of clinical problems.

Roberts, A. R., and K. R. Yeager (eds.). (2004). *Evidence-Based Practice Manual: Research and Outcome Measures in Health and Human Services.* New York: Oxford University Press. This mammoth compendium contains 104 brief chapters on evidence-based practice. The first section contains 11 chapters that provide overviews of procedures and critical issues in evidence-based practice. The second section contains 6 chapters on getting funded and ethical issues in conducting research to guide evidence-based practice. The third section contains 25 chapters on a wide variety of concerns in evidence-based practice, especially regarding interventions that have the best evidence for being effective with various clinical problems. The remaining sections cover research on the prevalence of public health problems, evidence-based assessment principles and tools, program evaluation strategies, and other topics.

Roberts, A. R., and K. R. Yeager (eds.). (2006). *Foundations of Evidence-Based Social Work Practice.* New York: Oxford University Press. This is a more concise version of the above evidence-based practice manual by Roberts and Yeager, and it is focused more specifically on social work.

Williams, Janet, and Kathleen Ell. 1998. *Advances in Mental Health Research: Implications for Practice.* Washington, DC: NASW Press. This useful volume will help you learn about best practices in the mental health field. It presents a wide range of studies and mental health interventions that can guide mental health practitioners who want their practice to be evidence-based. Separate chapters deal with research on various areas of psychopathology, psychoeducation, cancer support groups, services for children and adolescents, community treatment models, substance abuse interventions, and case management.

CHAPTER 3

Philosophy and Theory in Social Work Research

What You'll Learn in This Chapter

We'll examine some underlying philosophical issues in social work research. You'll see how disagreements about these issues can be connected to contrasting, yet often complementary, approaches to scientific inquiry. We'll also examine the nature and creation of theory and the links between theory and research.

INTRODUCTION

In Chapter 1 we examined errors commonly made in our casual inquiries. We noted that scientists can make these same errors in their own inquiries and that science does not provide total protection against them. Not only is science fallible, but also its philosophical underpinnings are not universally agreed upon by scientists and philosophers of science.

Due to differing philosophical assumptions, not everyone agrees about how best to do science. Because one feature of scientific inquiry is that there should be no "sacred cows" and everything should be open to question, some scholars have been questioning and sometimes rejecting certain features of the scientific method that have been long cherished by most scientists. An ongoing debate rages over which argument makes more sense. A key issue in that debate concerns philosophical notions about the nature of reality and the pursuit of objectivity. On one side of the debate are those who emphasize the pursuit of objectivity in our quest to observe and understand reality. On the other side are those who believe that because it is impossible to be completely objective, it is not worth even trying to maximize objectivity. Some scholars go further and argue that an objective reality does not exist—that all we can do is examine each individual's own subjective reality. At the end of Chapter 2, for example, we noted that some scholars object to evidence-based practice because it emphasizes objectivity in the appraisal of evidence.

As we review the debate about objectivity in science, you may want to keep in mind that the scientific method would contradict itself if its features were depicted as "sacred cows" that themselves were not permitted to be questioned. If the scientific method were a closed system of beliefs that itself was not open to questioning, then it would be called an *ideology*. Let's therefore briefly examine the nature of ideologies as a basis for viewing philosophical debates about the scientific method.

IDEOLOGY

An ideology is a closed system of beliefs and values that shapes the understanding and behavior of those who believe in it. Its assumptions are fixed and strong and not open to questioning. To their believers, who may be called *ideologues,* ideologies offer absolute certainty and are immune to contradictory evidence. Ideologues "know" they are right and don't want to be confused with the facts. To protect their belief systems from contradictory evidence, they will commonly commit some of the errors we discussed in Chapter 1 such as overgeneralization, selective observation, ex post facto hypothesizing, and prematurely closing inquiry. You will have difficulty changing the closed mind of an ideologue, no matter how sharp your critical thinking and no matter how solid your evidence base.

Ideologies come in many different forms. If you watch some political talk shows on cable TV, for example, you might see political ideologues attempting to shout each other down with their opposing political ideologies. You might also see proponents or opponents of ethical issues such as abortion or stem cell research whose fixed and strong feminist or religious convictions leave no room for considering the possible correctness of opposing points of view. You can also observe ideologues in scholarly debates or in discussions of social work. If we were to tell you that the scientific method should never be questioned or modified, then we would be ideologues. If two social policy professors, one a Marxist and the other a conservative, fiercely criticized or espoused socially conservative welfare reform policies and did not permit students to cite evidence questioning their views on the issue (perhaps lowering the grades of students who did), then they might be ideologues. If a direct practice professor taught only a psychoanalytic approach to practice and refused to consider evidence showing that other approaches might be more effective for many of the problems social workers deal with, he might be an ideologue. If your classmate refuses on religious grounds to even question her convictions that homosexuality is a sin and that social workers should try to persuade gays and lesbians to become heterosexual, then she might be an ideologue.

We can be ideological in some of our beliefs, but not in others. The psychoanalytic professor and your evangelically conservative classmate might not be at all ideological in their open-minded approach to studying the beneficial or harmful effects of welfare reform. When scholars debate certain aspects of the scientific method or evidence-based practice, their positions can at times seem ideological, even though they tend not to be ideologues regarding other matters. Let's now examine that debate.

WHAT'S REALLY REAL?

Philosophers sometimes use the term *naive realism* to describe the way most of us operate in our day-to-day lives. When you sit down at a table to write, you probably don't spend a lot of time thinking about whether the table is "really" made up of atoms, which in turn are mostly empty space. When you step into the street and see a city bus hurtling down on you, that's not the best time to reflect on methods for testing whether the bus really exists. We all live our lives with a view that what's real is pretty obvious—and that view usually gets us through the day.

Some philosophical perspectives, however, view the nature of "reality" as perhaps more complex than we tend to assume in our everyday functioning. A postmodern view of reality, for example, rejects the notion of an objective reality and of objective standards of truth and logical reasoning associated with the scientific method. To postmodernists, there can be no objective standards of truth, because there is no distinction between the external world and what's in our minds. Everything is subjective; no points of view about reality are superior to others.

No matter how bizarre postmodernism may seem on first reflection, it has a certain ironic inevitability. Take a moment to notice the book you are reading; notice specifically what it looks like. Because you are reading these words, it probably looks something like Figure 3-1(a). But does Figure 3-1(a) represent the way your book "really" looks? Or does it merely represent what the book looks like from your current point of view? Surely, Figures 3-1(b), (c), and (d) are equally valid representations. But these views of the book are so different from one another. Which is the "reality"?

As this example illustrates, different people with different points of view of the book can offer different answers to the question "What does the book really look like?" Although traditional scientists would argue that we can find an objective answer to that question by specifying particular vantage points (for example, what does it look like when lying flat on the table and open to this page?), the postmodern view holds that there is no "book," only various images of it from different points of view. And all the different images are equally "true." Now let's apply these notions to a social situation.

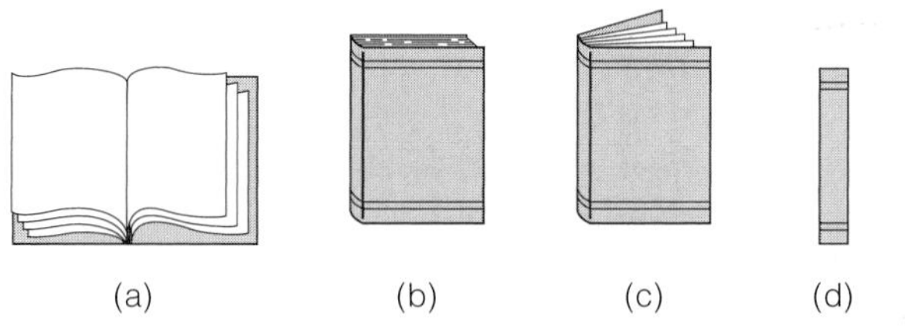

Figure 3-1 What Does the Book *Really* Look Like?

Imagine a husband and wife arguing. Figure 3-2(a) shows the wife's point of view about the quarrel. Take a minute to imagine how you would feel and what thoughts you would be having if you were the woman in this drawing. How would you explain later to an outsider—to your best friend, perhaps—what had happened in this situation? What solutions to the conflict would seem necessary or appropriate if you were the woman in this situation? Perhaps you have been in similar situations; maybe your memories of those events can help you answer these questions.

Now let's shift gears dramatically. What the woman's husband sees is another matter altogether [Figure 3-2(b)]. Imagine experiencing the situation from his point of view. What thoughts and feelings would you have? How would you tell your best friend what had happened? What solutions would seem appropriate for resolving the conflict?

Now consider a third point of view. Suppose you are an outside observer, watching the interaction between a wife and husband. What would it look like to you now? Unfortunately, we cannot easily show the third point of view without knowing something about the personal feelings, beliefs, past experiences, and so forth that you would bring to your task as an "outside" observer. (We might call you that, but you are, of course, observing from inside your own mental system.)

To take an extreme example, if you were a confirmed male chauvinist, you'd probably see the fight pretty much the same way the husband saw it. On the other hand, if you were committed to the view that men are generally unreasonable bums, then you'd see things the way the wife saw them in the earlier picture.

But consider this. Imagine that you look at this situation and see two unreasonable people quarreling irrationally with one another—neither acting in a way of which they should be proud. Can you get the feeling that they are both equally responsible for the conflict? Or imagine you see two people facing a difficult human situation, each doing the best he or she can to resolve it. Imagine feeling compassion for them; now

Figure 3-2 Two Subjective Views of Reality

notice the way each attempts at times to calm things down, to end the hostility, even though the gravity of the problem keeps them fighting.

Notice how different each new view is. Which is a "true" picture of what is happening between the wife and husband? You win the prize if you notice that the personal baggage you brought along to the observational task would again color your perception of what is happening.

This represents a critical dilemma for both science and scientists. Although our task is to observe and understand what is "really" happening, we are all human; as such, we bring along personal orientations that will color what we observe and how we explain it. Ultimately, there is no way you can totally step outside your humanness to see and understand the world as it "really" is. Whereas the traditional scientific (positivist) view acknowledges the inevitability of our human subjectivity, the postmodern view suggests no "objective" reality can be observed in the first place, only our different subjective views.

Applying this dilemma to social work practice, suppose you encounter a case in which wife battering has been reported, but the spouses now deny it. ("I/She just slipped and fell down the stairs. That's what caused all the facial and other bruises.") Perhaps each spouse fears the ramifications of incarceration. Perhaps the wife initially reported the abuse but now fears for her life since her husband threatened her with retaliation if she does not retract her accusation.

Taking the postmodern view, you might conclude that there is no objective answer to the question of what really happened. Nevertheless, you could function within agreed-upon standards of proof to reach a workable conclusion and course of action, such as moving the wife to a shelter. Taking the traditional scientific (positivist) view, however, you would acknowledge that although each spouse has his or her own subjective view of reality, although the wife changed her report of her view, and although your investigation into the situation might be influenced by your own prior experiences, it might be possible to ascertain objectively whether wife battering occurred and whether the wife needs to be protected—perhaps in a shelter. Taking the positivist view, you might agree with the postmodern view that it is virtually impossible to be completely objective and know for sure exactly what happened, but you would nevertheless believe that there is an objective answer to the question of what really happened and that it is worth trying to investigate things as objectively as possible to attempt to maximize the accuracy of your answer to the question. Thus, though the positivistic, scientific view and the postmodern one are fundamentally different in terms of ultimate reality, they do not necessarily produce different actions in immediate human affairs. The different philosophical stances one can take about the nature of reality and how to observe it are called paradigms. We will now examine specific scientific paradigms and how they can influence one's research.

PARADIGMS

Paradigms, like ideologies, organize our observations and make sense of them. Naturally, we can usually organize or make sense of things in more than one way. Different points of view are likely to yield different explanations. Imagine two people who begin working with emotionally abused wives: one a feminist and the other a firm believer in a right-wing conservative Christian view of traditional family values. The two are likely to develop different explanations or select different practice models in their work, particularly in regard to whether the wives should be encouraged to leave their husbands or participate with their husbands in a treatment approach that attempts to preserve the marriage while working on resolving the abuse.

No one ever starts with a completely clean slate to create a practice model or a theory. The concepts that are the building blocks of theory are not created out of nothing. If we suggest juvenile delinquency as an example of a topic to research, you may already have implicit ideas about it. If we ask you to list concepts that would be relevant to a theory of juvenile delinquency, you may be able to make suggestions. We might say that you already have a general point of view or frame of reference.

A **paradigm** is a fundamental model or scheme that organizes our view of something. Although it doesn't necessarily answer important questions, it can tell us where to look for the answers. As we'll see repeatedly, where you look largely determines the answers you'll find. Although paradigms share some similarities with ideologies, and although some folks can sound rather ideological about the particular paradigms they espouse, paradigms can be viewed as being more open to question and modification than ideologies.

Thomas Kuhn (1970) referred to paradigms as the fundamental points of view that characterize a science in its search for meaning. Although we sometimes think of science as developing gradually over time and marked by important discoveries and inventions, Kuhn said it is typical for one paradigm to become entrenched, resisting any substantial change. Eventually, however, as the shortcomings of that paradigm become obvious, a new paradigm would emerge to supplant the old one. Thus, the view that the sun revolved around the Earth was supplanted by the view that the Earth revolved around the sun. Kuhn's classic book on the subject is appropriately titled *The Structure of Scientific Revolutions.*

Social scientists have developed several paradigms for use in understanding social behavior. Supplanted paradigms in the social sciences, however, have had a different fate than what Kuhn observed for the natural sciences. Natural scientists generally believe that the succession from one paradigm to another represents progress from a false view to a true view. No modern astronomer, for example, believes that the sun revolves around the Earth.

In the social sciences, on the other hand, paradigms may gain or lose popularity but are seldom discarded altogether. Similar to social work practice models, the paradigms of the social sciences offer a variety of views, each with insights that others lack but also ignoring aspects of social life that other paradigms reveal.

The symbolic interactionist paradigm, for instance, sees social life as a process of interactions among individuals. Coming from this paradigm to address juvenile delinquency, you might focus on the ways in which young people interact as peers. How do they gain approval in the eyes of their friends? How do juvenile gangs recruit and initiate new members? Put differently, how do parents go about providing good or bad role models for their children? These are examples of the kinds of questions you might ask if you were approaching juvenile delinquency from the symbolic interactionist paradigm.

The functionalist or social systems paradigm, on the other hand, focuses on the organizational structure of social life. What are the components of society, and how are those components interrelated? From this paradigm, you might pay special attention to the impact of broad economic conditions on delinquency rates: Does delinquency increase during periods of high unemployment, for example? Or does the increased complexity of modern society make it harder for young people to understand what's right or wrong? Attention might be paid to the causes of failure in social control, or the breakdown of law and order.

The conflict paradigm describes social life as a struggle among competing individuals and groups. It is, for instance, a competition between the "haves" and the "have-nots" as in the Marxist "class struggle." From this paradigm, you might see juvenile delinquency as a response of the working class to their oppression by the rulers of society. Or, quite differently, you might see delinquency among young people as a way of competing for status.

The three paradigms we have just mentioned—the symbolic interactionist paradigm, the functionalist or social systems paradigm, and the conflict paradigm—are but a few of a larger list of social science paradigms. Three paradigms that have been debated over how best to conduct research in social work and the social sciences can be called *positivism, interpretivism,* and *critical social science*. Different authors use different labels for these paradigms, and not all authors are consistent in the way they define them. The inconsistent labeling of paradigms can confuse even the most experienced social scientists, and we would encourage you to keep this in mind if the labels we use differ from labels used in other writings you may have read. Let's now examine these paradigms and their research implications.

Positivism

When French philosopher Auguste Comte (1798–1857) coined the term *sociologie* in 1822, he launched an intellectual adventure that is still unfolding. Before Comte, society simply was. To the extent that people recognized different kinds of societies or changes in society over time, religious paradigms generally predominated to explain the differences. The state of social affairs was often seen as a reflection or expression of God's will. Alternately, people were challenged to create a "city of God" on Earth to replace sin and godlessness.

Comte separated his inquiry from religion. He thought that society could be studied scientifically, replacing religious belief with scientific objectivity—basing knowledge on observations through the five senses rather than on belief. He felt that society could be understood logically and rationally, and that it could be studied just as scientifically as biology or physics. Comte's view was to form the basic foundation for the subsequent development of the social sciences. In his optimism for the future, he coined the term **positivism** to describe this scientific approach—in contrast to what he regarded as negative elements in the Enlightenment.

Since Comte's time, the growth of science, the relative decline of superstition, and the rise of bureaucratic structures all seem to put rationality more and more in the center of social life. As fundamental as rationality is to most of us, however, some contemporary scholars have raised questions about it. Humans, for example, do not always act rationally. We're sure you can find ample evidence of this in your own experience. Many modern economic models, however, fundamentally assume that people will make rational choices in the economic sector: They will choose the highest-paying job, pay the lowest price, and so on. This ignores the power of such matters as tradition, loyalty, image, and many other qualities that compete with reason in determining human behavior.

A more sophisticated positivism asserts that we can rationally understand even "irrational" human behavior. Here's an example. In the famous Asch Experiment (Asch, 1958), a group of subjects were presented with a set of lines on a screen and asked to identify the two equal-length lines. If you were a subject in such an experiment, you would find the correct answer pretty obvious in each set of lines. To your surprise, however, you might find the other subjects all agreeing on a different answer!

As it turns out, you would be the only real subject in the experiment; all the others were working with the experimenter. The purpose of the experiment is to see whether you would be swayed by public pressure and go along with the incorrect answer. In one-third of the initial experiments, Asch found his subjects did just that.

Giving in to public pressure like this would be an example of nonrational behavior. Nonetheless, notice that such behavior can still be studied scientifically and rationally. Experimenters have examined the various circumstances that will lead more or fewer subjects to go along with the incorrect answer.

Contemporary positivists further recognize that scientists are not as objective as the ideal image of science assumes. Personal feelings can and do influence the problems scientists choose to study, what they choose to observe, and the conclusions they draw from those observations. Although contemporary positivists emphasize objectivity, precision, and generalizability in their inquiries, they recognize that observation and measurement cannot be as purely objective as implied by the ideal image of science. Nevertheless, they still attempt to anticipate and minimize the impact of potentially nonobjective influences. They also seek to verify causality and attempt to sort out what really causes what. They believe an objective external reality exists, although they recognize its elusive nature. Instead of attempting to verify universal laws, they examine the conditions under which particular ideas and hypotheses are and are not falsified.

Contemporary positivists commonly use highly structured research methods, but they are also likely to employ flexible methods, recognizing that we often are unable to determine in advance the best way to investigate some aspects of social reality. When they use flexible methods, they tend to see their findings as essentially tentative and exploratory in nature, generating new ideas for further testing. (Later we will examine the terms *quantitative methods* and *qualitative methods* and their connection with whether a research inquiry uses highly structured or flexible methods.)

Contemporary positivists are skeptical about the subjective impressions of researchers. Indeed, they tend to be skeptical of the conclusions of any individual research study. They see research as a never-ending and self-correcting quest for knowledge that requires the replication of findings by different investigators. Although contemporary positivists recognize that research is never entirely free from political and ideological values, they believe it is possible to use logical arrangements and observational techniques that reduce the influence of one's values on findings.

They also assume that others can judge the validity of one's findings in light of these mechanisms and can test them in later studies. Moreover, they assume that although social reality may remain elusive and that although no one study may be free of distortions, we can continue over the long haul to inch closer to understanding a true objective social reality if many researchers independently conduct rigorous studies using diverse approaches and then communicate about their findings and methodologies with open minds.

Interpretivism

One paradigm that contrasts with positivism but is not mutually exclusive with it can be called **interpretivism.** Interpretive researchers do not focus on isolating and objectively measuring causes or on developing generalizations. Instead, they attempt to gain an empathic understanding of how people feel inside, seeking to interpret individuals' everyday experiences, deeper meanings and feelings, and idiosyncratic reasons for their behaviors.

Interpretive researchers are likely to hang out with people and observe them in their natural settings, where they attempt to develop an in-depth subjective understanding of their lives. Rather than convey statistical probabilities for particular causal processes over a large number of people, interpretive researchers attempt to help readers of their reports sense what it is like to walk in the shoes of the small number of people they study.

Interpretive researchers believe that you cannot adequately learn about people by relying solely on objective measurement instruments that are used in the same standardized manner from person to person—instruments that attempt to remove the observer from the observee to pursue objectivity. Instead, interpretive researchers believe that the best way to learn about people is to be flexible and subjective in one's approach so that the subject's world can be "seen" through the subject's own eyes. It is not enough simply to measure the subject's external behaviors or questionnaire answers. The subjective meanings and social contexts of an individual's words or deeds must be examined more deeply.

Interpretive researchers may or may not agree with positivists that an objective, external social reality can be discovered. Regardless of their views on the existence of an objective external reality, however, interpretive researchers are more interested in discovering and understanding how people perceive and experience the world on an internal subjective basis. They further believe that no explanation of social reality will be complete without understanding how people's subjective interpretations of reality influence the creation of their social reality. A positivist researcher briefly observing each one of a large number of homeless women might note their neglect of personal hygiene and may therefore develop recommendations that are connected to emotional dysfunction or the need for social skills training. An interpretivist researcher, in contrast, would study a small group of homeless women more intensively, probe deeply into their subjective interpretations of their social reality, and conclude perhaps on this basis that their repugnant odor and appearance is a rational strategy for preventing sexual victimization in what they perceive to be a dangerous social context.

Critical Social Science

The final paradigm we consider here resembles the conflict paradigm mentioned earlier. Like the other paradigms, the **critical social science paradigm** has been labeled in various ways. Some have called it a "Marxist" paradigm. Others have called it a "feminist" paradigm. Labeling it an "empowerment" or "advocacy" paradigm might also make sense. Regardless of its name, its chief distinguishing feature is its focus on oppression and its commitment to use research procedures to empower oppressed groups. Toward that end, investigators committed to this paradigm might use highly structured or flexible research procedures or selected elements of other paradigms.

Researchers in this paradigm may use methods that are typically associated with positivists, but they are distinguished by their stance toward their findings. Positivist researchers attempt to minimize the influence of political or ideological values in interpreting their findings, as well as attempt to interpret those findings in a neutral and factual manner. Critical theorists, in contrast, set out to interpret findings through the filter of their empowerment and advocacy aims.

To illustrate this point, consider the difference between how a positivist researcher and a feminist researcher might interpret a finding that although male social workers tend to earn more than female social workers, this difference diminishes when we compare males and females with the same job responsibilities or years of experience. The positivist researcher, particularly one who is not well versed in women's issues, might conclude that this finding indicates that the influence of sexism on salaries in social work is less than many assume. The feminist researcher, however, might conclude from the same finding that sexism influences salaries through less pay for "women's work" or by the loss of annual increments during child-rearing years.

When critical theorists use interpretivist research methods, they are distinguished from interpretivists by going beyond the subjective meanings of the people they study and by their attempts to connect their observations to their a priori notion of an unjust, broader objective reality that they are seeking to change. Thus, a feminist researcher guided by the critical social science paradigm and taking an interpretive approach in the study of battered women would not stop at seeing reality through the eyes of the battered women but would also address aspects of the feminist's vision of reality that might not be shared by the women being studied. For example, if the battered women deny or minimize the severity of the battering, find excuses for the batterer, or think they cannot leave the batterer, a feminist researcher might note the discrepancy between the women's subjective views and the objective reality as seen by the researcher. A feminist researcher might also raise questions about the reasons for these undesirable discrepancies and attempt to derive recommendations for raising the women's feminist consciousness and empowering them.

As you read about these paradigms, perhaps you find yourself favoring one or disliking another, but you do not have to choose one over another. Individual researchers may find their investigations resemble one paradigm in one study and a different paradigm in another study—depending on what they seek to investigate. Moreover, they may find that sometimes they combine elements of more than one paradigm in the same study.

Each paradigm has its own advantages and disadvantages. We've discussed some of these advantages and disadvantages above. The disadvantages are most noticeable when an extremist view of a particular paradigm is championed. Positivists, for example, are particularly vulnerable to criticism when they fail to recognize the elusive nature of social reality and deny the role of subjectivity. At the other extreme are those who deny the existence of an external objective social reality, who say it is unknowable, and who argue that each individual's own subjective view of social reality is just as valid as any other's. Those who espouse this view—sometimes called *relativists, postmodernists,* or *radical social constructivists*—must contend with a different line of questioning. If an external objective social reality doesn't exist, they may be asked, then how have they observed this to be true? If an external reality is unknowable, then how do they know that?

Although we recognize serious problems in some extremist views of certain paradigms, we do not intend to advocate the choice of one paradigm or another. Perhaps you should think of them as though they were a bag of golf clubs. Different situations call for different clubs, although there is room for experimentation and choice. You may finally decide that some of the clubs are seldom if ever useful. However, it would not be useful to play the whole game with just the driver or the putter. No club is inherently superior; they are each just different.

As you read this book, you may notice that it reflects contributions from different paradigms. For example, in the chapters on surveys, experiments, and statistics, you will clearly detect elements of positivism. In the chapters on qualitative methods and measurement, you may find positivist and interpretivist ideas. Throughout the book you will see critical social science paradigm contributions, particularly where we discuss the use of social work research to alleviate human suffering and achieve social reform.

THEORY

Just as paradigms can influence how an investigation proceeds, so can theories. In fact, the distinction between the terms theory and paradigm is fuzzy, because some people can become so enamored of and entrenched in one particular theory that they tend to interpret a wide range of phenomena only in terms of that theory; they miss or dogmatically dismiss the alternative insights and perspectives that other theories might offer. Thus, some might depict certain theories—psychoanalytic theory, role theory, behavioral theory, and so on—as paradigms.

Although the terms are sometimes used interchangeably, there are important differences between paradigm and theory. Paradigms are general frameworks for looking at life. A **theory** is a systematic set of interrelated statements intended to explain some aspect of social life or enrich our sense of how people conduct and find meaning in their daily lives. Different people who share the same paradigm may or may not share the same theoretical orientations. For example, some positivist social work researchers might seek to verify the effectiveness of interventions that are rooted in cognitive or behavioral theory, while other positivist social work researchers might want to verify the effectiveness of interventions arising from psychoanalytic theory.

Social scientific theory has to do with what is, not with what should be. We point that out because social theory for many centuries has combined these two orientations. Social philosophers liberally mixed their observations of what happened around them, their speculations about why, and their ideas about how things ought to be. Although modern social scientists may do the same from time to time, it is important to realize that social science has to do with how things are and why.

This means that scientific theory—and, more broadly, science itself—cannot settle debates on value. Science cannot determine whether capitalism is better or worse than socialism except in terms of a specific set of agreed-on criteria. We could determine only scientifically whether capitalism or socialism most supported human dignity and freedom if we were able to agree on certain measures of dignity and freedom—and our conclusion would depend totally on the measures on which we had agreed. The conclusions would have no general meaning beyond that. By the same token, if we could agree that, say, suicide rates or giving to charity were good measures of a religion's quality, then we would be in a position to determine scientifically whether Buddhism or Christianity were the better religion. Again, however, our conclusion would be inextricably tied to the criteria on which we agreed. As a practical matter, people are seldom able to agree on criteria for determining issues of value, so science is seldom of any use in settling such debates. Moreover, people's convictions in matters of value are more nonrational than rational, making science, which deals in rational proofs, all the more inappropriate.

The distinction between theories and values can seem fuzzy when social scientists become involved in studying social programs that reflect ideological points of view. For example, one of the biggest problems social work researchers face is getting program staff and other stakeholders with varying ideologies to agree on criteria of success and failure. Suppose we want to evaluate a child welfare program that intervenes with parents referred for abuse or neglect in an effort to prevent future abuse and the consequent need to place the child in foster care. Such programs are often called "family preservation programs." Some funders and staff connected with these programs might ideologically value the preservation of the family as the chief criterion of program success. They would see the placement of an abused child in foster care as an indicator of program failure. Other funders and staff might value the protection of the child as the chief criterion of program success. They would disagree with those who see foster care placement as a sign of failure; instead, their chief indicators of success or failure would pertain to the child's well-being. Although achieving consensus on criteria of success and failure may be difficult, such criteria are essential if research is to tell us anything useful about matters of value.

Another example of this fuzzy distinction involves welfare reform policies. Some with more conservative ideologies might value getting people off welfare and into jobs as the chief criterion of successful social welfare policy. Those with more liberal ideologies might object to that criterion and be more concerned with how welfare reform affects a family's living conditions, their health insurance coverage, and parental ability to meet the needs of their children. Just as a stopwatch cannot tell us if one sprinter is better than another unless we can agree that speed is the critical criterion, research cannot tell us whether one social service program or social policy is better than another unless we agree on what program or policy outcomes we most value.

Theory plays an important role in social work research, as it does in social work practice. In both practice and research, theory helps us make sense of and see patterns in diverse observations. It helps direct our inquiry into those areas that seem more likely to show useful patterns and explanations. It also helps us distinguish between chance occurrences and observations that have value in anticipating future occurrences.

Imagine a colleague tells you that she allowed a young boy to play with small toys in a sandtray and nondirectively commented to him on the themes of his play. In this way, she tried to help the boy better cope with the tragic death of his mother and move on with his life. If you had not studied child development theory and learned about the importance of play, then you might respond with bewilderment, wondering how just letting a boy play and talking to him about it could be a powerful professional intervention. In fact, if you asked your colleague to explain why her intervention worked and she could not explain it, then you might be more skeptical about its likelihood of working with your clients than you would be if she could explain it theoretically. Without considering theory, you might flounder around in your practice trying anything and everything anyone told you in the hopes of stumbling on something that seemed to work. Then, if something did work with one client, you might continue to apply it indiscriminately with other clients for whom it might be inapplicable.

Suppose you decide to test your colleague's sandplay idea with one of your clients, a 6-year-old girl who has been depressed and withdrawn after witnessing the September 11, 2001, attack on and collapse of the World Trade Center towers that killed her father. After several sessions of sandplay, the girl's mother reports to you that the girl has begun to have angry outbursts and spells of intense sobbing in which she cries out for her father. Without theory, you might be inclined to stop the sandplay, fearing that it was having harmful effects. If, on the other hand, you were aware of theory on child development and grieving, then you might interpret the change in the girl's behavior as a necessary and therefore positive early step in the grieving process, and you would not stop the intervention.

Imagine you were conducting research on the effectiveness of the sandplay intervention in helping children of victims of the September 11, 2001, tragedy. If you were operating without theory, then you would be likely to encounter analogous problems. You might, for example, measure the impact of the intervention prematurely or look for the wrong indicators of success. Without theory, you might be clueless in designing your study. How long should the intervention last? What is the minimum and maximum age for subjects?

Some research studies are conducted in a less structured and more flexible fashion in an attempt to minimize the influence of theoretical expectations on what is being observed; that is, the researchers may not want their theoretical predilections to bias their outlook and narrow what they look for. Theory plays a role in these less structured studies as well. Although these studies may be less guided by theory, they typically seek to identify patterns that will help generate new theory. Also, it may be impossible for professionally trained researchers to put aside completely the theoretical frameworks they have learned. Their prior knowledge of child development theory, and theory on the grieving process, might help them see patterns in mounds of case record data—patterns suggesting that effective interventions with children who have lost a parent seem to involve a stage when the child acts out his or her anger over the loss. Moreover, the researchers' prior theoretical knowledge can help them make sense out of observations that paradoxically suggest that effective interventions involve a period during which the problem might appear (to a naive observer) to become exacerbated.

Theories also help researchers develop useful implications from their findings for practice and policy. Suppose a researcher finds that single-parent homes produce more delinquency than two-parent homes. Our understanding of why this is so and what we might do about it would be rather limited without the use of theory. Suppose, however, that we have a theoretical understanding of why single-parent homes produce more delinquency, and that lack of supervision and the absence of positive role models are two important reasons. This would improve our position to develop effective social programs, such as after-school mentoring programs.

Some valuable social work research studies, however, do not involve theory. For example, some studies focus exclusively on methodological issues, rather than attempt to explain something. Thus, they might survey published studies, perhaps seeking to identify what types of research methods are used most and least frequently, how often researchers use inappropriate research methods, or the frequency of particular types of findings. Other atheoretical studies might seek to describe something without attempting to explain it. For example, they might assess the average salaries of social workers in various areas, the needs for various services expressed by prospective or current service consumers, and so on.

Prediction and Explanation

In attempting to explain things, theories inescapably get involved in predicting things. A theory that views being a victim of abuse as a child as a prime factor in explaining later perpetration of child abuse as an adult, for example, would implicitly predict that people victimized as children are more likely than others to become perpetrators as adults. That prediction could be tested, and the credibility of the theory would be affected depending on whether we found that child victims are more likely to become perpetrators than others.

Although prediction is implicit in explanation, it is important to distinguish between the two. Often we are able to predict without understanding—for example, you may be able to predict rain when your trick knee aches. And often, even if we don't understand why, we are willing to act on the basis of a demonstrated predictive ability. Our ancient ancestors could predict sunrises and sunsets every day, and plan their activities accordingly, without understanding why the sun rose and set. And even if they thought they understood, with an explanation involving a stationary and flat Earth, they could predict accurately although their explanation was incorrect.

As we examine the components of theory, you will see that a set of predictions is an important part of theory. Consequently, it will be important to remember the distinction between prediction and explanation.

The Components of Theory

Earlier we defined theory as a systematic set of interrelated statements intended to explain some aspect of social life or enrich our sense of how people conduct and find meaning in their daily lives. The statements that attempt to explain things are called hypotheses. A **hypothesis** predicts something that ought to be observed in the real world if a theory is correct. It is a tentative and testable statement about how changes in one thing are expected to explain changes in something else. For example, a hypothesis in learning theory might be: The more children are praised, the more self-esteem they will have. The things that hypotheses predict are called **variables.** The foregoing hypothesis consists of two variables: (1) amount of praise and (2) level of self-esteem. The components of hypotheses are called variables because hypotheses predict how they *vary* together. Another term for this is that hypotheses predict *relationships* among variables. By **relationship,** we simply mean that a change in one variable is likely to be associated with a change in the other variable.

Most hypotheses predict which variable influences the other; in other words, which one is the cause and which one is the effect. A variable that explains or causes something is called the **independent variable.** It is called *independent* because it is doing the explaining or causing, and is not dependent on the other variable. Conversely, the variable being explained or caused—that is, the variable which is the effect—is called the **dependent variable.** In the foregoing hypothesis, for example, amount of praise is the independent variable, and level of self-esteem is the dependent variable.

A variable—regardless of whether it is independent or dependent—is a concept. A **concept** is a mental image that symbolizes an idea, an object, an event, or a person. The things that concepts symbolize might be relatively simple and relatively easy to observe, like gender, or more abstract and harder to observe, like level of self-esteem. Because variables vary, they are concepts that are themselves composed of other concepts. Gender, for example, is a concept that consists of the concepts male and female.

The concepts that make up a variable are called **attributes** of that variable. Attributes are characteristics or qualities that describe something or somebody. Additional examples include African American, intelligent, conservative, honest, physician, homeless, and so forth. Anything you might say to describe yourself or someone else involves an attribute. Variables, on the other hand, are logical groupings of attributes. Thus, for example, male and female are attributes, and gender is the variable composed of those two attributes. The variable *occupation* is composed of attributes such as farmer, professor, and truck driver. Social class is a variable composed of a set of attributes such as upper-class, middle-class, lower-class, or some similar set of divisions. The box "Illustration of a Hypothesis and its Components" graphically displays the connections and distinctions between the concepts, independent and dependent variables, and attributes that comprise hypotheses.

Thus, theories consist of hypotheses and two kinds of concepts: variables and the attributes that compose those variables. Theories also require observations. **Observations** are what we experience in the real world that help us build a theory or verify whether it is correct. When our observations are consistent with what we would expect to experience if a theory is correct, we call those observations **empirical support** for the theory. The credibility of a theory will depend on the extent to which: (1) our observations empirically support it, and (2) its components are systematically organized in a logical fashion that helps us better

ILLUSTRATION OF A HYPOTHESIS AND ITS COMPONENTS

Concepts	Hypothesis	Variables	Attributes
Student Teacher School Praise Confidence	Praise by teacher will ↓ increase Student confidence at school	Independent: Whether teacher praises student ↓ Dependent: Student's level of confidence at school	Praised Not praised ↑ High level of confidence ↓ Low level of confidence

COMPONENTS OF SCIENTIFIC THEORY

by Michael R. Leming, Department of Sociology, St. Olaf College

According to George Homans, scientific theory is an explanation of a phenomenon by the use of a deductive system of empirical propositions. The three basic components of scientific theory are (1) a conceptual scheme, (2) a set of propositions stating relationships between properties or variables, and (3) a context for verification.

The model of a suspension bridge serves as a good illustration of the relationship between scientific theory's three components. Bridges are constructed out of girders and rivets and tied into both banks of the river. In similar fashion, a theory consists of concepts ("rivets") and propositions ("girders") tied into an empirical base of support. It is the relationship between the components that makes for a bridge or theory. A disorganized pile of girders and rivets are not sufficient components for what we would call a bridge. Likewise concepts, propositions, and observations are not sufficient in themselves for scientific theory.

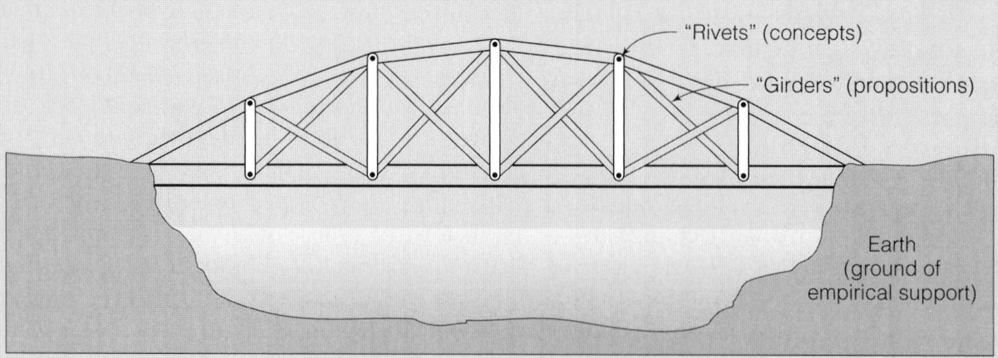

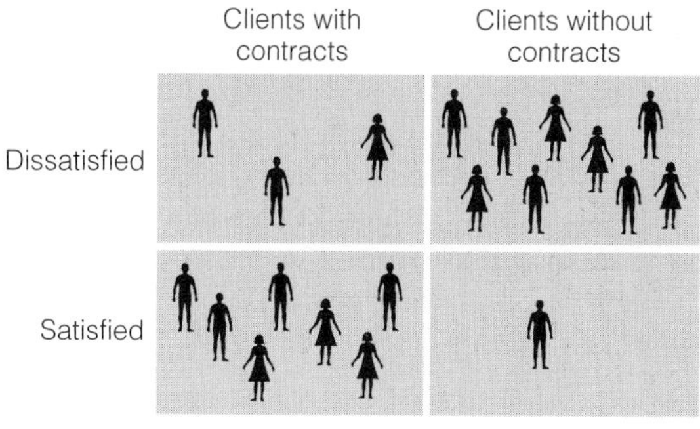

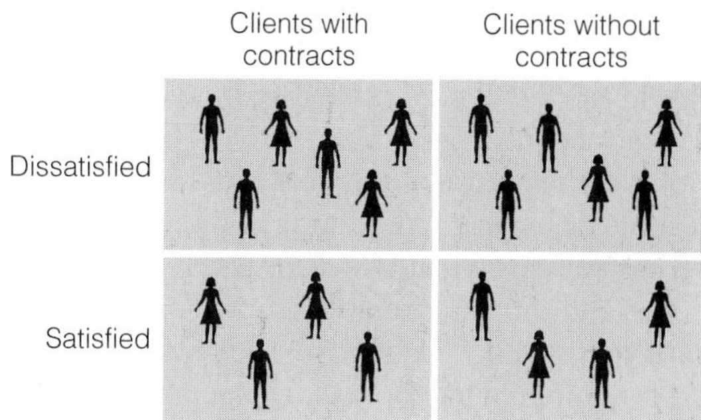

Figure 3-3 Relationships between Two Variables (Two Possibilities)

understand the world. As a gross generalization, scientific theory deals with the logical aspect of science; research methods deal with the observational aspect. A scientific theory describes the logical relationships that appear to exist among parts of the world, and research offers means for observing whether those relationships actually exist in the real world. The box titled "Components of Scientific Theory" graphically illustrates the bridge between theory and research.

The Relationship between Attributes and Variables

The relationship between attributes and variables lies at the heart of both description and explanation in science. For example, we might describe a social service agency's caseload in terms of the variable "gender" by reporting the observed frequencies of the attributes male and female: "The caseload is 60 percent men and 40 percent women." An unemployment rate can be thought of as a description of the variable employment status of a labor force in terms of the attributes "employed" and "unemployed." Even the report of family income for a city is a summary of attributes composing that variable: $3,124, $10,980, $35,000, and so forth.

The relationship between attributes and variables can be more complicated in the case of explanation. Here's a social work practice example, involving two variables: "use of contracting" and "level of client satisfaction." For the sake of simplicity, let's assume that the second variable has only two attributes: "satisfied" and "dissatisfied." Now suppose that 90 percent of the clients without contracts are dissatisfied, and the other 10 percent are satisfied. And suppose that 30 percent of the clients with contracts are dissatisfied, and the other 70 percent are satisfied. We graphically illustrate this in the first part of Figure 3-3. The relationship or association between the two variables can be seen in the pairings of their attributes. The two predominant pairings are: (1) those who have contracts and are satisfied and (2) those who have no contracts and are dissatisfied. Here are two other useful ways of seeing that relationship.

First, let's suppose that we play a game in which we bet on your ability to guess whether a client is satisfied or dissatisfied. We'll pick the clients one at a time (and will not tell you which one we've picked), and you guess whether the client is satisfied. We'll do it for all 20 clients in Part 1 of Figure 3-3. Your best strategy in that case would be to always guess dissatisfied, because 12 of the 20 are categorized that way. Thus, you'll get 12 right and 8 wrong, for a net success of 4.

Now suppose that when we pick a client from the figure, we have to tell you whether the practitioner engaged the client in contracting, and again you guess whether the client is satisfied. Your best strategy now would be to guess dissatisfied for each client without a contract and satisfied for each one with a contract. If you follow that strategy, you'll get 16 right and 4 wrong. Your improvement in guessing level of satisfaction by knowing whether contracting was used is an illustration of what is meant by the variables being related.

Second, by contrast, now consider how the 20 people would be distributed if use of contracting and level of satisfaction were unrelated to one another. This is illustrated in Part 2 of Figure 3-3. Notice that half the clients have contracts, half do not. Also notice that 12 of the 20 (60 percent) are dissatisfied. If 6 of the 10 people in each group were dissatisfied, then we would conclude that the two variables were unrelated to each other. Then, knowing whether contracting was used would not be of any value to you in guessing whether that client was satisfied.

We will look at the nature of relationships between variables in some depth in Part 7 of this book. In particular, we'll see some ways in which research analysis can discover and interpret relationships. For now, it is important that you have a general understanding of relationships to appreciate the logic of social scientific theories.

As we mentioned earlier, theories describe the relationships that might logically be expected among variables. Often, the expectation involves the notion of causation. A person's attributes on one variable are expected to cause, predispose, or encourage a particular attribute on another variable. In the example just given, the use of contracting seemed to possibly help cause clients to be more or less satisfied or dissatisfied. Something about participating in contracting seems to lead clients to be more satisfied than if they do not participate in contracting.

The discussion of Figure 3-3 has involved the interpretation of data. We looked at the distribution of the 20 clients in terms of the two variables. In the construction of a theory, we would derive an expectation about the relationship between the two variables based on what we know about each. We might postulate, for example, that clients with contracts are (1) more likely to agree with their practitioner about the problem to be worked on and (2) more likely to be motivated to work on that problem than are clients without contracts. Because they are more likely to agree with and be motivated to pursue the goals of the services, it follows that clients with contracts would be more likely to be satisfied with those services. We might further postulate that a prerequisite of effective treatment is to deal with problems and pursue objectives on which the client and practitioner agree.

Notice that the theory has to do with the two variables, "use of contracting" and "level of client satisfaction," not with people per se. People are, as we indicated before, the carriers of those two variables, so the relationship between the variables can only be seen by observing people. Ultimately, however, the theory is constructed of a variable language. It describes the associations that might logically be expected to exist between particular attributes of different variables.

In this example, "use of contracting" was the independent variable, and "level of client satisfaction" was the dependent variable. That is, we assume that levels of satisfaction are determined or caused by something; satisfaction depends on something, hence it is called the dependent variable. That on which the dependent variable depends is called the independent variable; in this case, satisfaction depends on use of contracting. Although the use of contracting with the clients being studied varies, that variation is independent of level of satisfaction.

TWO LOGICAL SYSTEMS

In Chapter 1, we referred to "the scientific method." Actually, it might be more accurate to refer to two scientific methods distinguished primarily by the ways in which they use theory in research. One method is based on deductive logic; we'll call it the deductive method. The other is based on inductive logic; we'll call it the inductive method. Let's now examine and contrast these two logical systems, beginning with the deductive method.

Comparing Deduction and Induction

In the deductive method, the researcher begins with a theory and then derives one or more hypotheses from it for testing. Next, the researcher defines the variables in each hypothesis and the operations to be used to measure them in specific, observable terms. In the final step, the researcher implements the specified measurements, thus observing the way things really are and seeing if those observations confirm or fail to confirm the hypotheses. Sometimes this final step involves conducting experiments, or interviewing people, or visiting and watching the subject of interest.

Figure 3-4 schematically diagrams the deductive model of scientific inquiry, moving from theory to operationalization to observation. We see the researcher beginning with an interest in some problem or an idea about it—say, the problem of adolescent runaways. Next comes the development of a theoretical understanding. The theoretical considerations result in a hypothesis, or an expectation about the way things ought to be in the world if the theoretical expectations are correct.

For example, the researcher might see family dysfunctioning as explaining why adolescents run away,

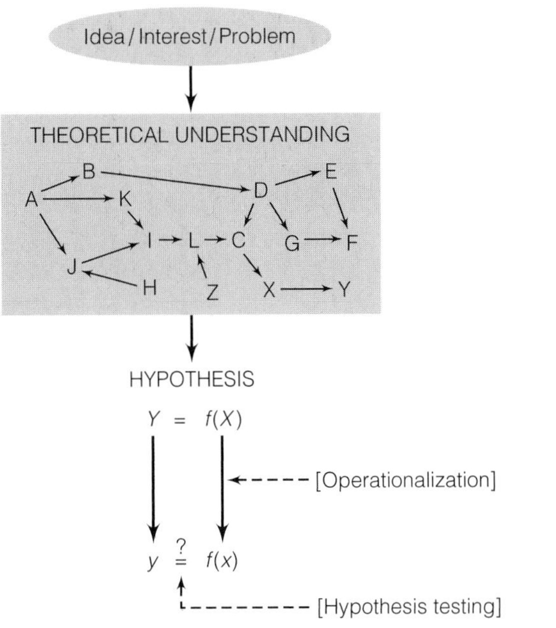

Figure 3-4 The Deductive Image of Science

and perhaps use family systems theory to understand family dysfunctioning and what to do about it. In Figure 3-4, this broadly conceived hypothesis is represented by the notation $Y = f(X)$. This is a conventional way of saying that Y (for example, runaway episodes) is a *function of* (is in some way affected by) X (for example, family dysfunctioning). At that level, however, X and Y have general rather than specific meanings. From this theoretical understanding, the researcher derives one or more specific hypotheses—for example, that providing family systems therapy will reduce the likelihood of future runaway episodes. Next, those two general concepts must be translated into specific, observable indicators to make the hypothesis testable. This is done in the operationalization process. The lowercase y and lowercase x, for instance, represent concrete, observable indicators of capital Y and capital X. In the runaway example, y (lowercase) refers to the need to spell out in observable terms exactly what constitutes a runaway episode, and x (lowercase) refers to the need to describe in specific terms the substance and processes that constitute the type of family systems theory being tested. Finally, observations are made to test the hypothesis.

As we already noted, the deductive method uses what is called deductive logic (see *deduction* in the Glossary), which is in contrast to inductive logic (see *induction* in the Glossary). W. I. B. Beveridge, a philosopher of science, describes these two systems of logic as follows:

> Logicians distinguish between inductive reasoning (from particular instances to general principles, from facts to theories) and deductive reasoning (from the general to the particular, applying a theory to a particular case). In induction one starts from observed data and develops a generalization which explains the relationships between the objects observed. On the other hand, in deductive reasoning one starts from some general law and applies it to a particular instance.
>
> (1950:113)

The classic illustration of deductive logic is the familiar syllogism "All men are mortal; Socrates is a man; therefore Socrates is mortal." This syllogism presents a theory and its operationalization. To prove it, you might perform an empirical test of Socrates' mortality. That is essentially the approach discussed as the deductive model. Using inductive logic, you might begin by noting that Socrates is mortal and observe other men as well. You might then note that all of the observed men were mortals, thereby arriving at the tentative conclusion that all men are mortal.

Figure 3-5 shows a graphic comparison of the deductive and inductive methods. In both cases, we are interested in the relationship between the number of hours spent studying for an exam and the grade earned on that exam. Using the deductive method, we would begin by examining the matter logically. Doing well on an exam reflects a student's ability to recall and manipulate information. Both abilities should be increased by exposure to the information before the exam. In this fashion, we would arrive at a hypothesis that suggests a positive relationship between the number of hours spent studying and the grade earned on the exam. We say "positive" because we expect grades to increase as the hours of studying increase. If increased hours produced decreased grades, then that would be called a "negative" relationship. The hypothesis is represented by the line in Part I(a) of Figure 3-5.

Our next step, using the deductive method, would be to make observations that are relevant to testing our hypothesis. The shaded area in Part I(b) of the figure represents perhaps hundreds of observations of different students, noting how many hours they studied and what grades they got. Finally, in Part I(c), we compare the hypothesis and the observations. Because observations in the real world seldom if ever match

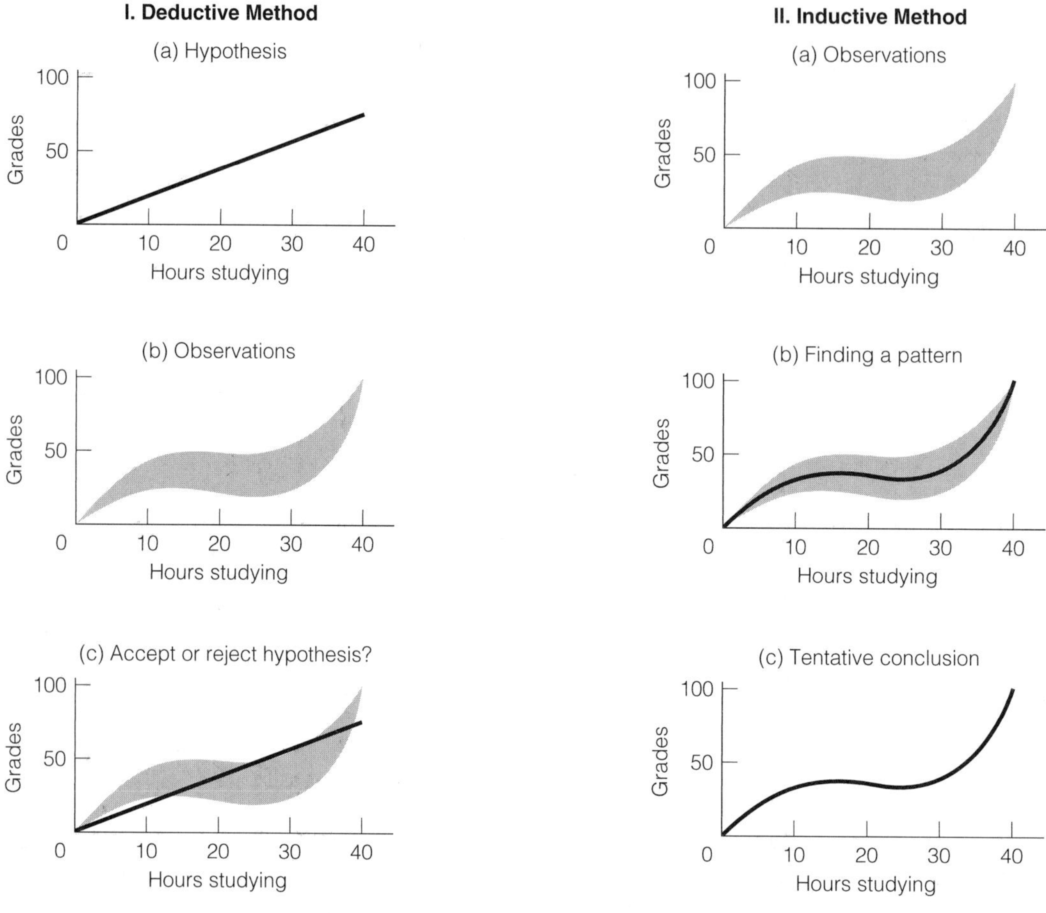

Figure 3-5 Deductive and Inductive Methods

our expectations perfectly, we must decide whether the match is close enough to consider the hypothesis confirmed. Put differently, can we conclude that the hypothesis describes the general pattern that exists, granting some variations in real life?

Let's turn to addressing the same research question but now using the inductive method. In this case, we would begin—as in Part II(a) of the figure—with a set of observations. Curious about the relationship between hours spent studying and grades earned, we might simply arrange to collect relevant data. Then we'd look for a pattern that best represented or summarized our observations. In Part II(b) of the figure, the pattern is shown as a curved line that runs through the center of the curving mass of points.

The pattern found among the points in this case suggests that with 1 to 15 hours of studying, each additional hour generally produces a higher grade on the exam. With 15 to approximately 25 hours, however, more study seems to slightly lower the grade. Studying more than 25 hours, on the other hand, results in a return to the initial pattern: More hours produce higher grades. Using the inductive method, then, we end up with a tentative conclusion about the pattern of the relationship between the two variables. The conclusion is tentative because the observations we have made cannot be taken as a test of the pattern—those observations are the source of the pattern we've created.

What do you suppose would happen next in an actual research project? We'd try to find a logical explanation for the pattern discovered in the data, just as Hogarty tried to find a logical explanation for the discovery that the people with schizophrenia who

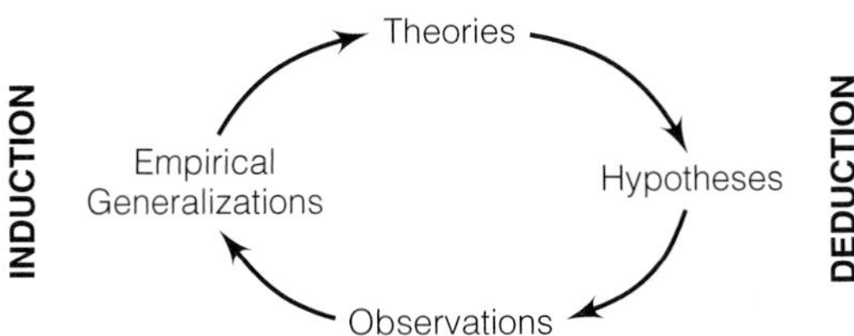

SOURCE: Adapted from Walter Wallace's *The Logic of Science in Sociology*, Copyright © 1971 by Walter Wallace. Reprinted by permission of the current publisher, Aldine de Gruyter, Hawthorne, NY.

Figure 3-6 The Wheel of Science

received social casework without drug therapy fared worse than those who received neither drugs nor casework. Eventually, we'd arrive at an explanation—one that would generate further expectations about what should be observed in the real world. Then, we'd look again.

In actual practice, then, theory and research interact through a never-ending alternation of deduction, induction, deduction, and so forth. Walter Wallace (1971) has represented this process nicely as a circle, which is presented in modified form in Figure 3-6. In the Wallace model, theories generate hypotheses, hypotheses suggest observations, observations produce generalizations, and those generalizations result in modifications of the theory. The modified theory then suggests somewhat modified hypotheses and a new set of observations that produce somewhat revised generalizations, further modifying the theory. In this model there is clearly no beginning or ending point. You can begin anywhere in examining what interests you. Thus, if we seek to understand and do something about the problem of adolescent runaways, we can begin by deriving hypotheses from family systems theory (or some other theory) and then making observations to test those hypotheses; or we can begin by immersing ourselves in observations of runaways until we are struck by certain consistent patterns that seem to point us in a particular theoretical direction that in turn will lead to hypotheses and observations.

In summary, the scientific norm of logical reasoning provides a bridge between theory and research—a two-way bridge. Scientific inquiry in practice typically involves an alternation between deduction and induction. During the deductive phase, we reason toward observations; during the inductive phase, we reason from observations. Both logic and observation are essential. In practice, both deduction and induction are routes to the construction of social theories.

The Links between Theory and Research

The contrast between induction and deduction illustrates two models for linking theory and research in social scientific inquiry. Actual research studies have developed many variations on these themes. Sometimes, theoretical issues are introduced merely as a background for empirical analyses. Other studies cite selected empirical data to bolster theoretical arguments. In neither type of case is there really an interaction between theory and research for the purpose of developing new explanations.

Some studies make no use of theory at all. For example, suppose that social workers in a particular agency need to give a funding source evidence that clients received the types of services the funders intended them to receive, that the clients felt highly satisfied with those services, and that treatment dropout rates were low. The social workers could get that evidence by surveying clients and agency records. They would conduct that study not to test or develop theory, but merely to meet the pragmatic purpose of program maintenance. This type of atheoretical study, despite lacking linkages to theory, would have some immediate practical value. Depending on its results, for example, the study could determine whether funding was continued (and perhaps even expanded) or discontinued (or perhaps just reduced).

Although social work research studies can have value without any linkages to theory, their value might be enhanced by such linkages. The above study, for example, might contribute more to the profession's knowledge base if it aimed to go beyond the agency's immediate funding concerns and attempted to build social work practice theory about factors that influence client satisfaction and treatment completion and the consequent implications for what social workers in other agencies can do to improve service delivery. (This is not to suggest that atheoretical studies have no potential value for theory advancement. Related findings in an otherwise unconnected batch of atheoretical studies could, for example, be synthesized and connected to theory in a review of studies.)

There is no simple cookbook recipe for conducting social scientific research. It is far more open-ended than the traditional view of science would suggest. Ultimately, science rests on three pillars: logic, observation, and theory. As we'll see throughout this book, they can be fit together in many patterns.

SOCIAL WORK PRACTICE MODELS

In social work, we may apply existing social science theories in an effort to alleviate problems in social welfare. But texts on social work practice are less likely to cite social science theories as guides to social work practice than they are to cite something called *practice models*. These models help us organize our views about social work practice and may or may not reflect a synthesis of existing theories.

The social work literature is diverse in which practice models are identified and how they are labeled. If you have taken other social work courses, then you may have encountered the following terms for practice models: psychosocial, functionalist, problem-solving, cognitive-behavioral, task-centered, case management, crisis intervention, ecological perspective, life model, generalist, evidence-based practice, and eclectic, among many others. Social work practice models tend not to be mutually exclusive. Many of them, for example, stress the importance of the worker–client relationship and the need to forge a therapeutic alliance.

If interpreted narrowly, any of these models can appear to omit important aspects of practice or perhaps overemphasize things that are not applicable to many types of problems or clients. Certain models, for example, have been portrayed as more applicable to voluntary clients than to involuntary clients, or more applicable to clients who want and can afford long-term treatment geared toward personality change than to those who need immediate, concrete, and short-term help with socioeconomic crises and who are unable or unlikely to utilize long-term treatment. Certain models are sometimes criticized for dealing only with superficial aspects of client problems—for dealing only with symptoms without resolving underlying issues that will perpetuate the problem in other forms. Other models, in contrast, are criticized for overemphasizing unrealistically lofty long-term psychological and curative goals that are not relevant to many clients who need social care, economic assistance, or protective environments.

Over time, partly in response to criticism, particular models tend to expand, encompassing important new areas of research findings and theory. As this happens, distinctions between the models become increasingly blurred. This process is evident in Eda Goldstein's description of the psychosocial model in the *Encyclopedia of Social Work* (1995). Goldstein describes how the psychosocial model expanded after it came under increasing criticism in the 1960s for being too narrowly psychoanalytic and insufficiently attuned to the needs and strengths of oppressed populations and other diverse target groups. In response to these criticisms, emerging new theories, and the changing landscape of social work practice, the psychosocial model broadened to encompass a social systems and ecological perspective, factors in cultural diversity, crisis theory and crisis intervention, cognitive theory, biological forces, communications theory, role theory, and the impact of community, organizational, and societal forces. Despite this expansion, however, Goldstein acknowledges that the psychosocial model still emphasizes personality factors more than do other models, and therefore may be more congenial to psychotherapists than are some other models.

We won't delve into the characteristics of all the various models of social work practice or into the subtleties of how they are similar and different. You can study that in courses on practice or in courses that introduce you to the profession of social work. Instead, we'll simply illustrate how certain themes can influence the way we choose to research social work problems.

Let's begin by considering the evaluation of an outreach program for battered women who still live with their batterers. In researching the effectiveness of the program, a key question is, what do we measure as an indicator of successful program outcome? As its name implies, one theme of the functionalist model of practice is to use the function of the agency as a basis for identifying successful outcomes. Those who take a functionalist approach, therefore, might be guided by the agency's mission in choosing an outcome indicator and in formulating a hypothesis.

Suppose the stated objective of the program is to help the women realize the danger they are in and to leave their batterers. This might imply testing the hypothesis that participation in the program increases the likelihood that battered women will leave their abusers. Researchers might be even more likely to pursue this line of inquiry if they or their agency were further identified with a feminist model that tended to see women's problems in terms of male oppression. How do you suppose individuals who follow an older and narrower version of the psychosocial model might view this approach? Chances are some would call it shortsighted and superficial. The psychosocial model gives more emphasis to the intrapsychic bases of client problems and to the notion that clients carry problems from previous relationships—dating back to childhood—into current relationships. Proponents of this model might wonder whether battered women, having left one batterer, would soon find themselves in a relationship with another batterer (or perhaps return someday to the original abuser). If so, then simply leaving the current batterer might not be a sufficient indicator of successful intervention.

Instead, psychosocially oriented investigators might want to measure change in certain personality characteristics and follow clients over a long period to see if they stay out of battering relationships. A possible hypothesis here might be: Participation in the program reduces depression and dependency and increases the likelihood of avoiding being battered in the future.

Some practitioners who have worked with battered women might find some aspects of that particular psychosocial perspective unacceptable, perceiving that it seems at least in part to "blame the victim" for her plight. They might therefore undertake research to assess whether the prevalence of dysfunctional personality characteristics among battered women, or their difficulties in staying out of a battering relationship, can be seen as normal reactions to having been victimized, rather than part of the explanation for the original victimization. Of course, some psychosocial proponents might be equally likely to pursue this line of research, although they might expect to find the opposite type of results.

Let's consider another illustration, this time looking at the psychosocial model and the cognitive-behavioral model. We'll apply this illustration to the treatment of parents at risk of child abuse. The cognitive-behavioral model looks at problems such as child abuse in terms of dysfunctional emotions connected to irrational beliefs and the need to restructure cognitions and learn better coping skills and parenting skills. Rather than focusing on long-term personality change and dealing with unresolved issues stemming from the parents' own childhoods, this model deals in the present with specific skills, cognitions, and behaviors that can be changed in the short term through behavior modification and cognitive therapy techniques.

When researching the outcome of the treatment of at-risk parents, individuals influenced by this model might do the following: administer paper-and-pencil tests that attempt to gauge whether parents have become less angry, have changed their attitudes about normal childhood behaviors that they first perceived as provocative, and have learned new child-rearing techniques (such as using time-outs). These researchers might also directly observe the parents with their children in situations that require parenting skills and count the number of times the parents exhibit desirable (praise, encouragement, and so forth) and undesirable (slapping, threatening, and so forth) parenting behaviors.

Those who are influenced by the psychosocial model might be somewhat skeptical of the adequacy of the preceding approach to researching treatment outcome. In particular, they might doubt whether any observed improvements would last long after treatment ended and whether the parents' ability to give desired test answers or act in an acceptable manner while being observed would really reflect the normal home environment when observers aren't present. They might suggest that a better indicator of outcome would be whether parents were actually court-reported for abusive behavior over the longer haul.

Although the foregoing illustration is essentially hypothetical, note that the bulk of actual research with favorable outcomes has evaluated interventions that are associated with the cognitive or behavioral models of practice. Most other models have received less research, and their outcomes have not been as consistently favorable. Proponents of some other models often attribute this to the "superficiality" of outcome indicators used in cognitive-behavioral evaluations and the difficulty of assessing the more complex, longer-range goals of their models. We won't resolve this debate here, and we expect it to continue for quite a while. Before we leave this section, let's look at one more hypothetical illustration of how practice models, theory, and research are interconnected.

Suppose a social service agency is concerned about the high incidence of premature termination of treatment in its caseload. How might different practice models influence different hypotheses about the possible causes of this problem?

Those who take a psychosocial approach might hypothesize that staff members with more extensive training in clinical diagnosis and psychotherapy have fewer premature terminations. Those taking a cognitive-behavioral approach might hypothesize that cases with specific, observable target behaviors entered in the case records as treatment goals are less likely to terminate prematurely. Those taking a functionalist approach—which, among other things, emphasizes the primacy of the therapeutic relationship—might hypothesize that clients who terminate treatment prematurely will rate the quality of the worker–client relationship lower than clients who do not terminate prematurely.

Finally, let's consider the implications of two related models, the problem-solving and task-centered models, in this illustration. Both models recommend partializing clients' multiple and long-range problems into a series of steps, first treating the target problem that is both most pressing to the client and has the potential for some quick success. More target problems are then addressed, one at a time, in order of their tractability and relevance to the client—saving the most intractable and least relevant in the client's view for the later stages of treatment. Both models also emphasize the importance of working on objectives that both worker and client agree are important and developing a contract with the client on those objectives, rather than just dealing with the deeper psychodynamic problems that (even if diagnostically sound) may have no relevance to the client.

If you were influenced by these models, then what hypotheses about premature terminations might you formulate? Our guess is that you'd hypothesize that cases in which the practitioner partialized target problems and contracted with clients about mutually agreed-on treatment objectives were less likely to terminate prematurely than those in which practitioners did not take these steps.

PROBABILISTIC KNOWLEDGE

Few things in human behavior can be explained entirely by factors we can identify. Many factors contribute to the explanation of particular phenomena even if we have not yet discovered all of them. Being poor, for example, is a factor that contributes to homelessness, but being poor alone does not cause homelessness. Other factors also come into play, such as the lack of low-income housing, alcoholism or mental disorders, the sudden loss of a job, and so on. We can say with great certainty that being poor makes one more likely to be homeless, but on the other hand we recognize that although poverty contributes to the causation of homelessness, most poor people are not homeless. Thus, when explaining or predicting human behavior, we speak in terms of probability, not certainty.

Knowledge based on probability enables us to say that if A occurs, then B is more likely to occur. It does not enable us to say that B *will* occur, or even that B will *probably* occur. For example, a research study that finds that Intervention A is more likely to be effective than Intervention B does not guarantee that Intervention A will be effective with your client. Likewise, research into the causation of mental illness has suggested that the offspring of mentally ill parents are about 10 times more likely than the rest of the population to become mentally ill. But most children of mentally ill parents never become mentally ill; only about 10 percent of them do. Because only some 1 percent of the rest of the population ever become mentally ill, we can say that having mentally ill parents appears to be one factor that can contribute to mental illness (perhaps through the transmission of certain genetic combinations that make one biologically more vulnerable to other factors that can contribute to mental illness). Our ability to say that parental mental illness is a "cause" of mental illness in their offspring is further restricted by the observation that the parents of many mentally ill people were never mentally ill themselves. (Again, genetics offers a possible explanation here.)

Many "causes" that help "determine" human behavior, therefore, are neither necessary nor sufficient for the "effect" they help to cause. Among many of the homeless, alcoholism may have played a role in causing their homelessness. Yet one can be homeless without ever having been an alcoholic. Alcoholism therefore is not a necessary condition for homelessness to occur. Neither is it a sufficient condition, because alcoholism alone does not produce homelessness.

People who crave certainty may be uneasy with probabilistic knowledge and therefore may spurn the findings of social research. They may prefer the comfort of less complex, nonscientific routes to "understanding," such as freewill notions that we simply choose to do what we do. Alternatively, they may prefer narrow explanations proffered with certainty by supervisors and other authorities. In your social work practice, you may find that dealing with uncertainty can be a constant source of uneasiness and anxiety. You may find more relief from this discomfort by latching onto and following unquestioningly the "certain" pronouncements of a guru of a practice dogma than you find in the probabilistic findings of scientific research. In Chapter 1 we discussed the risks associated with such reliance on authority. Although escaping from the discomfort of uncertainty may make you feel better, it might lead you further from the truth, which ultimately is not in your clients' best interests. But be forewarned (and therefore hopefully forearmed to be better utilizers of research): Most research studies will not give you the kinds of answers that will bring certainty to your practice.

TWO CAUSAL MODELS OF EXPLANATION

As we've seen, a multiplicity of reasons can account for a specific behavior. When we try to explain a person's behavior by enumerating the many reasons for it, reasons that might be unique to that individual, we are using the **idiographic model** of explanation. Of course, we never totally exhaust those reasons in practice. Nevertheless, we must realize that the idiographic model is used frequently in many different contexts.

As an example, let's say we are interested in understanding why a particular young man has become delinquent. If you were his practitioner, you would want to learn everything you could about his family situation, neighborhood, school environment, peers, and anything else that might account for his delinquent behavior. Does he live in a single-parent or dysfunctional family? Does he have delinquent brothers or sisters? Does he belong to a gang? How is he doing in school? Is his family poor? Does he have physical or psychological problems that might contribute to his behavior and your understanding of it? In this instance, your purpose would be to understand this one person as fully as possible, in all his idiosyncratic peculiarities. This is the idiographic model of explanation.

Whereas the idiographic model is often used in daily life and in social work practice, other situations and purposes call for a different approach, one called the **nomothetic model** of explanation. Rather than seeking to understand a particular person as fully as possible, we try to understand a general phenomenon partially. Following up on the previous example, you might be interested in learning about the causes of juvenile delinquency in general. What factors are most important for explaining delinquency among many young people? Let's consider the role of single-parent homes in causing delinquency.

If you were to study a large number of young people, you would discover a higher incidence of delinquency among those who live in single-parent homes than among those who live with two-parent families. This certainly does not mean that single-parent homes always produce juvenile delinquency or that two-parent homes always prevent it. As a general rule, however, single-parent homes are more likely than two-parent homes to produce delinquency.

Actually, social scientists have discovered the single factor about single-parent homes that increases the likelihood of juvenile delinquency: the lack of adult supervision. Specifically, two-parent families are more likely to have an adult at home when the young person gets home from school; it's the presence of adult supervision that decreases the likelihood of delinquent behavior. In the case of single-parent homes, young people are more likely to be unsupervised after school and thus are more likely to get into trouble.

Whereas the idiographic model seeks to understand everything about a particular case by using as many causative factors as possible, the nomothetic model seeks a partial understanding of a general phenomenon using relatively few variables. The young delinquent we described at the beginning of this discussion may or may not live in a single-parent home; even if he does, that fact may or may not help account for his delinquency. Taking an idiographic tack, we would want to discover all of the particular factors that led that one young man astray. From a nomothetic point of view, we would want to discover those factors, such as lack of adult supervision, that account for many instances of delinquency in general.

The nomothetic model of explanation is inevitably probabilistic in its approach to causation. Being able to name a few causal factors seldom if ever provides a complete explanation. In the best of all practical worlds, the nomothetic model indicates a very high (or very low) probability or likelihood that a given action will occur whenever a limited number of specified considerations are present. Identifying more considerations typically increases the degree of explanation, but the model's basic simplicity calls for balancing more explanation with fewer identified causal factors.

To further illustrate the use of the nomothetic and idiographic models in social work practice, imagine you are a clinical practitioner living in New York City. You have volunteered to treat survivors who are experiencing symptoms of post-traumatic stress disorder (PTSD) in the wake of the September 11, 2001, attack on the World Trade Center. In your practice, you regularly keep up with the emerging research literature to make sure you provide the most effective services to your clients, and you recently learned of a promising new intervention for people with PTSD. The intervention has received support in several nomothetic research articles. It seems particularly relevant to a 9/11 survivor you are treating.

The nomothetic research articles show that the new intervention appears more likely to be effective than alternative treatment approaches with people in general who suffer from PTSD. With the new intervention, 70 percent of clients have their PTSD symptoms disappear within a few weeks, as compared to only 30 percent of those receiving alternative approaches. The new intervention, however, tends to involve more temporary emotional discomfort than alternative approaches, because it requires that clients call up vivid images of the traumatic incident. You would not want to keep providing the new intervention to your client if it's not working.

The research gives you a nomothetic basis for considering the new intervention; that is, it tells you in probabilistic terms that the new intervention is effective in general, but it cannot guarantee that it will be effective for your particular client. Perhaps your client is like the 30 percent who were not helped by the new intervention. The research you've read may give no indication of the variables that make the intervention more or less successful: gender, age, social class, family situation, and so on. Moreover, the research was not done with survivors of the September 11 attack.

As a social work practitioner, you will be interested in one particular case, and you will want to consider the range of particular characteristics that might influence the intervention's effectiveness. Imagine that your particular case involves a family of two preschool children and their mother, a young woman who immigrated to New York from Puerto Rico and does not speak English fluently. Suppose her husband was a custodian killed in the 9/11 attack and that she also worked as a custodian in the same tower as her husband but was on a lower floor at the time of the attack and feels guilty that she escaped but her husband didn't. One of her two preschool children has a serious learning disability. The mother is exhibiting PTSD symptoms. So are both of her children, having viewed televised images of the World Trade Center towers being struck and then collapsing. Suppose the mother was abused as a child. To what extent might that be influencing her PTSD symptoms or the likelihood that the new intervention will succeed with her? Will the likelihood of success also be influenced by her minority and immigrant status, language factors, or socioeconomic stressors? Will it also work with children as young as hers? Will it work with children who have serious learning disabilities? Note, too, that the intervention may not work as well with survivors of the 9/11 attack as it does with other kinds of traumas. This is an example of the idiographic model of causation.

Clearly, all of the contextual variables just discussed in this idiographic example could be and often are examined in nomothetic analyses. Thus, we could study whether the new intervention is effective with a large sample of 9/11 survivors, We also could study whether it is more likely to be effective with adults than with children, with children without learning disabilities, or with people who have not previously been victims of other traumas. The key difference is that the nomothetic approach looks for causal patterns that occur in general, whereas the idiographic approach aims at fully explaining a single case.

You could take an idiographic approach in finding out if the intervention is effective with your particular client by conducting a single-case design evaluation. That approach would entail measuring your client's PTSD symptoms each day for a week or two and graphing the results before implementing the new intervention. Then you would continue to graph the symptoms after the new intervention begins. Whether the graphed data show a clear amelioration in PTSD symptoms that coincides with the onset of the intervention will indicate whether the intervention appears to be effective for your particular client. In Chapter 12 of this book, on single-case designs, you will learn more about how to design and conduct idiographic studies like this in your own practice.

The box "Illustration of Idiographic and Nomothetic Tests of a Hypothesis" graphically illustrates the difference between an idiographic and a nomothetic test of a hypothesis regarding a therapy that studies have shown to be effective in alleviating PTSD symptoms. The bottom of the box illustrates a nomothetic test involving 200 research participants. Its results provide probabilistic grounds for deeming the intervention to be effective. At the top of the box, however, an idiographic test shows that the intervention is effective with one client (Jill) but ineffective with another client (Jack). Jack and Jill were not in the nomothetic experiment. But had they received the therapy as part of the nomothetic experiment, Jill would have been among the 70 percent of recipients whose symptoms were alleviated, and Jack would have been among the 30 percent of recipients whose symptoms were not alleviated.

ILLUSTRATION OF IDIOGRAPHIC AND NOMOTHETIC TESTS OF A HYPOTHESIS

HYPOTHESIS: Exposure therapy is effective in alleviating PTSD symptoms

IDIOGRAPHIC

(Therapy is effective with Jill, but not with Jack)

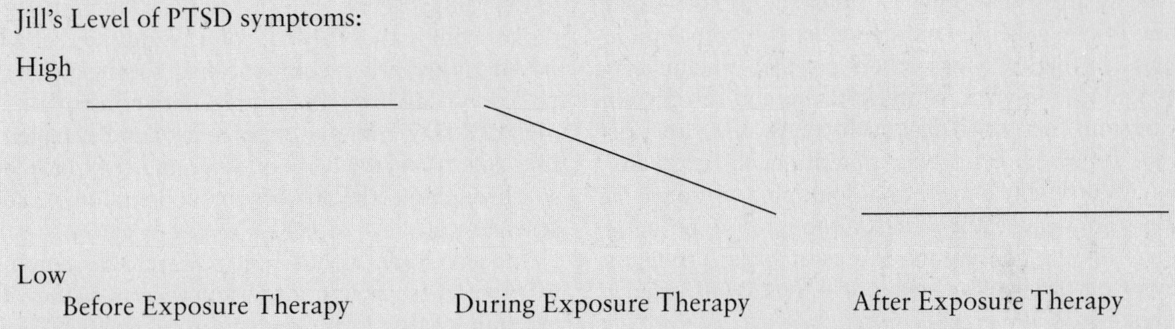

Jill's Level of PTSD symptoms:

High

Low

Before Exposure Therapy | During Exposure Therapy | After Exposure Therapy

Jack's Level of PTSD symptoms:

High

Low

Before Exposure Therapy | During Exposure Therapy | After Exposure Therapy

NOMOTHETIC

(Therapy is effective on **probabilistic** grounds based on results with 200 participants)

	Number of Participants by Treatment Condition	
PTSD Symptoms	Exposure Therapy	No Treatment Control Group
Alleviated	70 (Jill would be in this group)	30
Not Alleviated	30 (Jack would be in this group)	70

QUANTITATIVE AND QUALITATIVE METHODS OF INQUIRY

The foregoing discussions of reality and different models for understanding illustrate how complex things can get when we examine the philosophical underpinnings of social work research. As we indicated earlier, not all social scientists or social work researchers share the same philosophical assumptions. Some accept a postmodern view of reality, whereas others dismiss that view as nonsense. Some social scientists are generally more interested in idiographic understanding, whereas others are more inclined to the nomothetic view. Moreover, the nature of your professional activities may push you in one direction or the other. Direct-service practitioners, for example, will probably choose an idiographic approach to understanding specific clients, although a nomothetic understanding of common causes of social problems may suggest variables to explore in the case of specific clients.

Different research purposes, and perhaps different philosophical assumptions, can lead researchers to choose between two contrasting, yet often complementary, overarching approaches to scientific inquiry. These two approaches are called *quantitative methods* and *qualitative methods*. **Quantitative methods** emphasize the production of precise and generalizable statistical findings and are generally more appropriate to nomothetic aims. When we want to verify whether a cause produces an effect in general, we are likely to use quantitative methods. (Sometimes quantitative methods are also used in studies with idiographic aims—especially in idiographic studies employing single-case designs, as will be discussed in Chapter 12.)

Qualitative research methods emphasize the depth of understanding associated with idiographic concerns. They attempt to tap the deeper meanings of particular human experiences and are intended to generate theoretically richer observations that are not easily reduced to numbers.

During the first half of the 20th century, sociologists commonly used qualitative methods. Social work research during that period often involved social surveys—a quantitative method. Of course, direct-service practitioners typically have always relied heavily on a qualitative approach when looking at all the idiosyncratic aspects of a particular client's case. Around the middle of the 20th century, however, the potential for quantitative methods to yield more generalizable conclusions became appealing to social scientists in general. Gradually, quantitative studies were regarded as superior—that is, as more "scientific"—and began to squeeze out qualitative studies.

Toward the end of the 20th century, qualitative methods enjoyed a rebirth of support in the social sciences generally, including social work. In a new swing of the professional pendulum, some scholars even called quantitative methods obsolete and implored the profession to concentrate on qualitative methods (De Maria, 1981; Heineman, 1981; Ruckdeschel and Faris, 1981; Taylor, 1977). Many scholars, however, do not believe that the two contrasting types of methods are inherently incompatible. In their view, despite philosophical differences, quantitative and qualitative methods play an equally important and complementary role in knowledge building, and they have done so throughout the history of contemporary social science.

Indeed, some of our best research has combined the two types of methods within the same study. One example of this is an inquiry by McRoy (1981) into the self-esteem of transracial and inracial adoptees. Quantitative measurement used two standardized scales. One scale revealed no differences in levels of self-esteem between the two groups of adoptees, but the other scale revealed differences in the use of racial self-referents. In light of her inconsistent quantitative findings, McRoy used the qualitative approach of open-ended, probing interviews to generate hypotheses on how families were handling issues of racial identity with their adopted children. Her qualitative analysis of the interview data suggested the following tentative factors that might influence how adoptees adjust to racial identity problems: parental attitudes, sibling and peer relationships, role-model availability, extended family factors, racial composition of school and community, and experience with racism and discrimination.

Thus, whether we should emphasize qualitative or quantitative research methods may depend on the conditions and purposes of our inquiry. Qualitative methods may be more suitable when flexibility is required to study a new phenomenon about which we know very little, or when we seek to gain insight into the subjective meanings of complex phenomena to advance our conceptualization of them and build theory that can be tested in future studies. Qualitative research thus can sometimes pave the way for quantitative studies of the same subject. Other times, qualitative methods produce results that are sufficient in themselves.

In sum, you do not need to choose one camp or the other. Each approach is useful and legitimate. Each makes its unique contribution to inquiry. Each has its own advantages and disadvantages. Each is a set of tools, not an ideology. Researchers need to match the tools they use with the research questions and conditions they face—using quantitative methods for some studies, qualitative methods for others, and both methods in combination for still others.

OBJECTIVITY AND SUBJECTIVITY IN SCIENTIFIC INQUIRY

A recurrent theme implicit in much of what we have discussed throughout this chapter is the pursuit of objectivity in scientific inquiry. Both quantitative and qualitative methods try to be objective, although they do it in different ways (as we will see in later chapters).

When researchers try to be objective, they are trying to observe reality without being influenced by the contents of their own minds. Likewise, when they observe what other people do, they attempt to conduct their observations in ways that will avoid influencing people to do things that they ordinarily would not do when not being observed. When they ask people questions, they attempt to ask the questions in ways that will tap how people really think or feel, not some false impression that people want to convey. It would be misleading, however, to give you the impression that objectivity is easy to achieve or even that its meaning is obvious. As we've seen, even contemporary positivists agree that being completely objective is impossible.

In contrast, some researchers—typically using qualitative methods—recognize the advantages of subjective inquiry. For example, they might experience something directly themselves (such as being homeless or sleeping in a homeless shelter) and record what that does to the contents of their own minds. Thus, they learn what it feels like to walk in the shoes of the people they seek to understand.

But even when researchers emphasize subjective modes of inquiry, they might paradoxically wonder whether their subjective observations are objective. That is, they might wonder whether other people who observe or experience what they observed or experienced would come up with similar thoughts or feelings. Or did the prior mental and emotional baggage they brought to their experiences and observations influence them to interpret things in ways that yield an inaccurate portrayal of the phenomenon they are trying to understand?

Ultimately, we have no way of proving whether we are observing reality objectively and accurately at any given moment. Nonetheless, scientists do have a standard to use in lieu of a direct pipeline to objective reality: agreement. As you'll recall from the earlier discussion, we all use agreement as a standard in everyday life; scientists, however, have established conscious grounds for such agreements.

In a sense, this whole book is devoted to a discussion of the criteria for reaching scientific agreements. Whereas many of the agreements of everyday life are based in tradition, for example, scientists use standards of rigorous logic and careful observation. When several scientists use the established techniques of scientific inquiry and arrive at the same conclusion, then we judge them all to have been objective and to have discovered objective reality.

This is not to suggest that social workers or other social investigators always proceed objectively. Being human, they often fall into the errors of human inquiry discussed earlier.

When social workers devise and test a new intervention approach, for instance, the value of their efforts and the recognition they will receive will be far greater when their findings show that their intervention is effective than when it is shown to be ineffective. Sure, a study about an ineffective intervention may be worth publishing so that others can learn from and avoid repeating the "failure," but it is much more gratifying to be able to show the field that you have discovered something that works than it is to discuss why things went wrong.

Because of their vested interests in finding certain results, researchers often devise ways of observing phenomena that attempt to prevent their biases from influencing what is observed. They can do this in many ways, as we will see in later sections of this book. For example, they might employ observers who are not given potentially biasing information about the research. They might use paper-and-pencil self-report scales that respondents complete outside the researcher's presence. Perhaps they'll look at existing information, such as school records, that were collected by others who know nothing of their research. These are just a few examples; we'll examine many more in later chapters. When we do examine these alternatives, we will see that none is foolproof. Every way of observing a phenomenon has some potential for error.

Although we may not know whether one particular observer or observation method is really objective, we assume that objectivity has been achieved when different observers with different vested interests agree on what is observed, or when different observational strategies yield essentially the same findings.

We'll close this chapter with an example that illustrates some of the issues we have been discussing about objectivity and subjectivity and qualitative and quantitative methods. Suppose a medical social worker wants to assess the psychosocial aspects of hospice care versus standard hospital care for terminally ill patients. Put simply, standard hospital care emphasizes using medical technology to fight disease at all costs, even if the technology entails undesirable costs in quality of life and patient discomfort. Hospice care emphasizes minimizing patients' discomfort and maximizing their quality of life during their final days, even if that means eschewing certain technologies that prolong life but hinder its quality.

Suppose the social worker's prime focus in the study is whether and how quality of life differs for patients depending on the form of care they receive. In a quantitative study, the social worker might ask the closest family member of each patient to complete a standardized list of interview questions about the degree of pain the patient expressed feeling, the frequency of undesirable side effects associated with medical technology (loss of hair due to chemotherapy, for example), the patient's mood, the patient's activities, and so on. An effort would probably be made to find an instrument that scored each question—scores that could be summed to produce an overall quality-of-life score. Ideally, it would be an instrument that had been tested elsewhere and seemed to produce consistent data over repeated administrations and with different interviewers. Thus, it would appear to be a measure that seems unaffected by the investigator's predilections or vested interests. If the scores of the hospice-treated patients turn out to be higher than the scores for patients receiving standard medical care, then the social worker might conclude that hospice care better affects quality of life than does standard medical care.

Perhaps, however, the social worker is skeptical as to whether the instrument really taps all of the complex dimensions of quality of life. The instrument only gives a numerical score—perhaps this is superficial; it tells us little about the ways the two forms of care may differentially affect quality of life, and it provides little understanding of what patients experience and what those experiences mean to them.

As an alternative, the social worker may choose to take a more subjective and qualitative approach to the inquiry. This might entail spending a great deal of time on the standard and hospice wards that care for terminally ill patients in the hospital. There the social worker might simply observe what goes on and keep a detailed log of the observations. The information in the logs can be analyzed to see what patterns emerge. In Chapter 4 we will examine in depth a study that took this approach (Buckingham and associates, 1976), one in which the investigator actually posed as a terminally ill patient and observed how he was treated differently in the two wards and how this made him feel. Rather than rely on indirect quantitative measures that attempt to avoid his own subjectivity, he decided to experience the phenomenon directly. Based on his direct observations and subjective experiences, he was able to discuss in depth how the medical staff members on the hospice ward seemed much more sensitive and empathic than those on the other ward, how family members seemed encouraged to be more involved on the hospice ward and the implications this had for personalized care, and how all of this made the patient feel. By subjectively entering the role of the patient, the investigator was able to propose a deep, empathic understanding of how the two forms of care had different implications for quality of life.

But what are the potential pitfalls of the preceding approach? Some might question whether the investigator's previous ties to hospice care, his predilections, and his desire to obtain important findings may have predisposed him to make observations that would reflect favorably on the relative advantages of hospice care. In short, they would be concerned about whether his observations were sufficiently objective. Which of the two studies is preferable, the quantitative or qualitative? Actually, both are valuable. Each provides useful information, and each has its own set of advantages and disadvantages in its quest for truth and understanding.

Main Points

- An ideology is a closed system of beliefs and values that shapes the understanding and behavior of those who believe in it.
- Scholars are debating some aspects of the scientific method, particularly philosophical notions about the nature of reality and the pursuit of objectivity.
- A paradigm is a fundamental model or scheme that organizes our view of something.

- The social sciences use a variety of paradigms that influence the ways in which research can be done.

- Positivist paradigms emphasize objectivity, precision, and generalizability in research. Contemporary positivist researchers recognize that observation and measurement cannot be as purely objective as the ideal image of science implies, but they still attempt to anticipate and minimize the impact of potential nonobjective influences.

- The interpretivist paradigm emphasizes gaining an empathic understanding of how people feel inside, how they interpret their everyday experiences, and what idiosyncratic reasons they may have for their behaviors.

- The critical social science paradigm focuses on oppression and uses research procedures to empower oppressed groups.

- Objectivity is an important objective of scientific inquiry, but not all scholars agree on how best to attain it.

- A theory is a systematic set of interrelated statements intended to explain some aspect of social life or enrich our sense of how people conduct and find meaning in their daily lives.

- The distinction between theories and values can seem fuzzy when social scientists become involved in studying social programs that reflect ideological points of view.

- In attempting to explain things, theories inescapably get involved in predicting things. Although prediction is implicit in explanation, it is important to distinguish between the two. Often, we are able to predict without understanding.

- Observations that we experience in the real world help us build a theory or verify whether it is correct. When our observations are consistent with what we would expect to experience if a theory is correct we call those observations empirical support for the theory. The credibility of a theory will depend on the extent to which: (1) our observations empirically support it, and (2) its components are systematically organized in a logical fashion that helps us better understand the world.

- A hypothesis predicts something that ought to be observed in the real world if a theory is correct. It is a tentative and testable statement about how changes in one thing are expected to explain changes in something else.

- Hypotheses predict relationships among variables—that a change in one variable is likely to be associated with a change in the other variable.

- A variable is a concept, which means it is a mental image that symbolizes an idea, an object, an event, or a person.

- A variable that explains or causes something is called the independent variable. The variable being explained or caused is called the dependent variable.

- The concepts that make up a variable are called attributes of that variable.

- In the deductive method, the researcher begins with a theory and then derives one or more hypotheses from it for testing. In induction one starts from observed data and develops a hypothesis to explain the specific observations.

- Science is a process that involves an alternating use of deduction and induction.

- Most explanatory social research uses a probabilistic model of causation. X may be said to cause Y if it is seen to have some influence on Y.

- The idiographic model of explanation aims to explain through the enumeration of the many and perhaps unique considerations that lie behind a given action.

- The nomothetic model seeks to understand a general phenomenon partially.

- Quantitative research methods attempt to produce findings that are precise and generalizable.

- Qualitative research methods emphasize depth of understanding, attempt to subjectively tap the deeper meanings of human experience, and are intended to generate theoretically rich observations.

Review Questions and Exercises

1. Think about a social work practice approach or a social justice issue or cause to which you are strongly committed and about which you fiercely hold certain beliefs. Rate yourself on a scale from 1 to 10 on how scientific you are willing to be about those beliefs. How willing are you to allow them to be questioned

and refuted by scientific evidence? How much do you seek scientific evidence as a basis for maintaining or changing those beliefs? Find a classmate whose beliefs differ from yours. Discuss your contrasting views. Then rate each other on the same 10-point scale. Compare and discuss the degree to which your self-rating matches the rating your classmate gave you. If you are not willing to be scientific about any of those beliefs, discuss your reasons in class and encourage your classmates to share their reactions to your point of view.

2. Examine several recent issues of a social work research journal (such as *Research on Social Work Practice* or *Social Work Research*). Find one article illustrating the idiographic model of explanation and one illustrating the nomothetic model. Discuss the value of each and how they illustrate the contrasting models.

3. Suppose you have been asked to design a research study that evaluates the degree of success of a family preservation program that seeks to prevent out-of-home placements of children who are at risk of child abuse or neglect by providing intensive in-home social work services. Under what conditions might you opt to emphasize quantitative methods or qualitative methods in your design? What would be the advantages and disadvantages of each approach? How and why might you choose to combine both types of methods in the design?

Internet Exercises

1. Use InfoTrac College Edition to find an article that discusses the scientific method. Read an article that sounds useful. Write down the bibliographical reference information for the article and summarize the article in a few sentences.

2. Use InfoTrac College Edition to find an article in *Policy Studies Journal* (Spring 1998) by Ann Chih Linn entitled "Bridging Positivist and Interpretivist Approaches to Qualitative Methods." Briefly describe Linn's thesis that these two approaches can be combined and are not mutually exclusive.

3. Using a search engine such as Google, Yahoo, or Lycos, find information on the web for at least two of the following paradigms. Give the web addresses and report on main themes you find in the discussions.

Critical social science	Feminism
Interpretivism	Positivism
Postmodernism	Social constructivism

Additional Readings

Babbie, Earl. 1986. *Observing Ourselves: Essays in Social Research.* Belmont, CA: Wadsworth. This collection of essays expands some of the philosophical issues raised in this book, including objectivity, paradigms, concepts, reality, causation, and values.

Denzin, Norman K., and Yvonna S. Lincoln. 1994. *Handbook of Qualitative Research.* Thousand Oaks, CA: Sage. In this work, various authors discuss the conduct of qualitative research from the perspective of various paradigms, showing how the nature of inquiry is influenced by one's paradigm. The editors also critique positivism from a postmodernist perspective.

Kaplan, Abraham. 1964. *The Conduct of Inquiry.* San Francisco: Chandler. This is a standard reference volume on the logic and philosophy of science and social science. Though rigorous and scholarly, it is eminently readable and continually related to the real world of inquiry.

Kuhn, Thomas. 1970. *The Structure of Scientific Revolution.* Chicago: University of Chicago Press. In an exciting and innovative recasting of the nature of scientific development, Kuhn disputes the notion of gradual change and modification in science, arguing instead that established paradigms tend to persist until the weight of contradictory evidence brings their rejection and replacement by new paradigms. This short book is both stimulating and informative.

Lofland, John, and Lyn H. Lofland. 1995. *Analyzing Social Settings: A Guide to Qualitative Observation and Analysis.* Belmont, CA: Wadsworth. This excellent text discusses how to conduct qualitative inquiry without rejecting the positivist paradigm. It also includes a critique of postmodernism.

Reinharz, Shulamit. 1992. *Feminist Methods in Social Research.* New York: Oxford University Press. This book explores several social research techniques—for example, interviewing, experiments, and content analysis—from a feminist perspective.

PART 2

The Ethical, Political, and Cultural Context of Social Work Research

Social work research—like social work practice—is about people. Moreover, it usually involves them as research participants. Consequently, it helps to learn about ethical issues in social work before studying specific research methods and designs. The decisions we can and do make about how we structure and conduct our research are influenced by ethical considerations, as we will see.

Research involving people often has political implications as well. For example, the researcher's own politics and ideology can influence what is studied and how research is carried out. Also, the results of social work research sometimes influence how agency stakeholders view their prospects for securing more funds for their programs. Sometimes its results can influence social policies, perhaps to the like or dislike of people at different ends of the political spectrum.

Moreover, sometimes research results are reported in ways that offend members of certain cultures, such as when studies of the prevalence of alcohol abuse among the members of that culture are disseminated in ways that reinforce stereotypes about that culture. In addition, research studies can fail to be completed or can produce misleading findings if they are implemented in a culturally incompetent manner.

In Chapter 4, we'll examine special ethical and political considerations that arise in social work research. This chapter will establish an ethical and political context for the discussions of research methods in the remaining chapters.

Chapter 5 will explore how social work researchers can use qualitative and quantitative methods to improve the cultural competence of all phases of the research. We'll see how cultural competence can help researchers obtain and provide information that is relevant and valid for minority and oppressed populations and thus improve practice and policy with those populations.

CHAPTER 4

The Ethics and Politics of Social Work Research

What You'll Learn in This Chapter

In this chapter, you'll see something of the social context in which social work research is conducted. As you'll see, ethical and political considerations must be taken into account alongside scientific ones in the design and execution of research.

INTRODUCTION

Before they can implement their studies, social workers and other professionals who conduct research that involves human subjects confront questions about the ethics of their proposed investigations. They must resolve these questions not only to meet their own ethical standards, but also to meet the standards of committees that have been set up to review the ethics of proposed studies and to approve or disapprove the studies' implementation from an ethical standpoint.

Concern about the ethics of research that involves human subjects has not always been as intense as it is today. The roots of this concern date back many decades to an era in which studies on human subjects could be conducted with little scrutiny of their ethics, an era in which some research became notorious for its inhumane violations of basic ethical standards. The most flagrant examples were the Nazi atrocities in medical experimentation that were conducted during the Holocaust.

Another notorious example was the Tuskegee syphilis study that started in 1932 in Alabama. In that study, medical researchers diagnosed several hundred poor African American male sharecroppers as suffering from syphilis, but did not tell them they had syphilis. Instead, they told the men that they were being treated for "bad blood." The researchers merely studied the disease's progress and had no intentions of treating it. Even after penicillin had been discovered as a cure for syphilis, the study continued without providing penicillin or telling the subjects about it. Thirteen journal articles reported the study during this time, but it continued uninterrupted. As reported by James Jones in his book on the Tuskegee experiment, *Bad Blood: The Tuskegee Syphilis Experiment* (1981:190), "none of the health officers connected with the Tuskegee Study expressed any ethical concern until critics started asking questions." In fact, when a member of the medical profession first objected to the study (in 1965), he got no reply to his letter to the Centers for Disease Control, which read:

> I am utterly astounded by the fact that physicians allow patients with a potentially fatal disease to remain untreated when effective therapy is available. I assume you feel that the information which is extracted from observations of this untreated group is worth their sacrifice. If this is the case, then I suggest that the United States Public Health Service and those physicians associated with it need to reevaluate their moral judgments in this regard.
>
> (Jones, 1981:190)

Jones reported that this letter was simply filed away with the following note stapled to it by one of the authors of one of the articles that reported the study: "This is the first letter of this type we have received. I do not plan to answer this letter." In December 1965, Peter Buxtun, who was trained as a social worker while in the U.S. Army, was hired by the Public Health Service as a venereal disease interviewer. Buxtun soon learned of the Tuskegee study from co-workers, and after studying published articles on it, he became relentless in his efforts to intervene. A series of letters to, and difficult meetings with, high-ranking officials ultimately prompted them to convene a committee to review the experiment, but that committee decided against treating the study's subjects.

Buxtun then went to the press, which exposed the study to the public in 1972. This exposure prompted U.S. Senate hearings on the study. Subsequently, in the mid-1970s, the men were treated with antibiotics, as were their wives, who had contracted the disease; and their children, who had it congenitally (Royse, 1991). According to Jones (1981:203), it was the social worker Peter Buxtun—aided by the press—who deserves the ultimate responsibility for stopping the Tuskegee study.

ETHICAL ISSUES IN SOCIAL WORK RESEARCH

When we consider research such as the Tuskegee study, it is not hard to find the ethical violations and to agree that the research was blatantly unethical. However, some ethical violations in social work research can be subtle, ambiguous, and arguable. Sometimes there is no "correct" answer to the situation, and people of goodwill can disagree.

In most dictionaries and in common usage, *ethics* is typically associated with morality, and both deal with matters of right and wrong. But what is right and what wrong? What is the source of the distinction? For individuals, the sources vary. They may be religions, political ideologies, or the pragmatic observation of what seems to work and what doesn't.

Webster's New World Dictionary is typical among dictionaries in defining *ethical* as "conforming to the standards of conduct of a given profession or group." Although the idea may frustrate readers in search of moral absolutes, what we regard as morality and ethics in day-to-day life is a matter of agreement among members of a group. And it is not a surprise that different groups have agreed on different codes of conduct.

If you are going to live in a particular society, then it is extremely useful for you to know what that society considers ethical and unethical. The same holds true for the social work research "community." If you are going to do social work research, then you should be aware of the general agreements that are shared by researchers about what's proper and improper in the conduct of scientific inquiry. The section that follows summarizes some of the more important ethical agreements that prevail in social work research, as well as in research in allied fields.

Voluntary Participation and Informed Consent

Social work research often, though not always, represents an intrusion into people's lives. The interviewer's knock on the door or the arrival of a questionnaire in the mail signals the beginning of an activity that the respondent has not requested and that may require a significant portion of his or her time and energy. Participation in research disrupts the subject's regular activities.

Social work research, moreover, often requires that people reveal personal information about themselves—information that may be unknown to their friends and associates. And social work research often requires that such information be revealed to strangers. Social work practitioners also require such information. But their requests may be justified on the grounds that the information is required for them to serve the respondent's personal interests. Social work researchers cannot necessarily make this claim, perhaps only being able to argue that their efforts will ultimately help the entire target population of people in need.

A major tenet of medical research ethics is that experimental participation must be voluntary. The same norm applies to most social work research studies. No one should be forced to participate. All participants must be aware that they are participating in a study, be informed of all the consequences of the study, and consent to participate in it. This norm might not apply to certain studies. For example, if a community organization measures the amount and speed of automobile traffic at a busy intersection near a school as part of an effort to convince the city to erect a traffic light, it would not need to obtain informed consent from the drivers of every automobile it observes passing through the intersection.

The norm of voluntary participation is far easier to accept in theory than to apply in practice. Again, medical research provides a useful parallel. Many experimental drugs are tested on prisoners. In the most rigorously ethical cases, the prisoners are told the nature—and the possible dangers—of an experiment; that participation is completely voluntary; and, further, that they can expect no special rewards, such as early parole, for participation. Even under these conditions, some volunteers clearly are motivated by the belief that they will personally benefit from their cooperation.

When the instructor in a social work class asks students to fill out a questionnaire that he or she hopes to analyze and publish, students should always be told that their participation in the survey is completely voluntary. Even so, most students will fear that nonparticipation will somehow affect their grade. The instructor should be especially sensitive to such beliefs in implied sanctions and make special provisions to obviate them. For example, the instructor could leave the room while the questionnaires are being completed. Or students could be asked to return the questionnaires by mail or drop them in a box near the door just before the next course meeting.

You should be clear that this norm of voluntary participation goes directly against several scientific concerns we'll be discussing later in this text. One such concern involves the scientific goal of *generalizability,* which is threatened to the extent that the kinds of people who would willingly participate in a particular research study are unlike the people for whom the study seeks generalizations. Suppose the questionnaire assesses student attitudes about the feminization of poverty, and only a minority of students voluntarily participate—those who care the most deeply about feminism and the poor. With such a small group of respondents, the instructor would have no basis for describing student attitudes in general, and if he or she did generalize the findings to the entire student population, then the generalizations might be seriously misleading.

The need, in some studies, to conceal the nature of the study from those being observed is another scientific concern that is compromised by the norm of voluntary participation and informed consent. This need stems from the fear that participants' knowledge about the study might significantly affect the social processes being studied among those participants. Often the researcher cannot reveal that a study is even being done. Rosenhan (1973), for example, reported a study in which the research investigators posed as patients in psychiatric hospitals to assess whether hospital clinical staff members, who were unaware of the study, could recognize "normal" individuals (presumably the investigators) who (presumably) did not require continued hospitalization. (The results suggested that they could not.) Had the subjects of that study—that is, the clinical staff members—been given the opportunity to volunteer or refuse to participate, then the study would have been so severely compromised that it would probably not have been worth doing. What point would there be to such a study if the clinical staff was aware that the investigators were posing as patients?

But the fact that the norm of voluntary participation and informed consent may be impossible to follow does not alone justify conducting a study that violates it. Was the study reported by Rosenhan justified? Would it have been more ethical not to conduct the study at all? That depends on whether the long-term good derived from that study—that is, observations and data on the identification, understanding, and possible amelioration of problems in psychiatric diagnosis and care—outweighs the harm done in denying clinical staff the opportunity to volunteer or refuse to participate in the study. The need to judge whether a study's long-term benefits will outweigh its harm from ethically questionable practices also applies to ethical norms beyond voluntary participation, and thus we will return to it later. The norm of voluntary participation and informed consent is important. In cases where you feel ultimately justified in violating it, it is all the more important that you observe the other ethical norms of scientific research, such as bringing no harm to the people under study.

Regardless of how you may feel about the norm of voluntary participation and informed consent, if your study involves human subjects then you will probably have to obtain the approval of its ethics from an independent panel of professionals called an **institutional review board (IRB)**. IRBs became widespread during the 1970s as a result of federal legislation and increased public concern about the ethics of biomedical and behavioral research. Today, all organizations that engage in research and receive federal money are required to have an IRB that reviews the ethics of proposed studies that involve human subjects. Investigators in organizations that wish to conduct such studies must get the advance approval of their organization's IRB. This applies to all studies that use human subjects, not just those that receive government funding. IRBs may continue to oversee studies after they are implemented, and they may decide to suspend or terminate their approval of a study.

A later section of this chapter will focus on IRBs. For now—in regard to informed consent—we want to point out that your IRB will probably require participants to sign a **consent form** before they participate in your study. The consent form should provide full information about the features of the study that might affect their decision to participate, particularly regarding the procedures of the study, potential harm, and anonymity and confidentiality. IRB consent forms can be quite detailed. Separate forms are required if children are research participants. If you conduct a study involving parents and children, for example, you will probably have to use one consent form for parents that might be several pages long, another form for parents to consent to their child's participation, and a third form for the child to sign. The latter form usually is called an **assent form** and will be briefer and use simpler language that a child can understand. Likewise, to obtain truly informed consent, you should consider the reading level of prospective research participants and have a translated version if they do not speak English. Figure 4-1 displays (in condensed fashion) excerpts from the sample consent forms used by the University of Texas at Austin's Institutional Review Board. (We have not reproduced the entire forms because of their length.)

No Harm to the Participants

Social work research should never injure the people being studied, regardless of whether they volunteer for the study. Perhaps the clearest instance of this norm in practice concerns the revealing of information that would embarrass them or endanger their home lives, friendships, jobs, and so forth. This norm is discussed more fully in the next section.

Research participants can be harmed psychologically in the course of a study, and the researcher must be aware of the often subtle dangers and guard against them. Research participants are often asked to reveal deviant behavior, attitudes they feel are unpopular, or personal characteristics they may feel are demeaning such as low income, the receipt of welfare payments,

Condensed Excerpts from Sample Consent Forms Used by the University of Texas at Austin's Institutional Review Board

You are being asked to participate in a research study. This form provides you with information about the study. The Principal Investigator (the person in charge of this research) or his/her representative will also describe this study to you and answer all of your questions. Please read the information below and ask questions about anything you don't understand before deciding whether or not to take part. Your participation is entirely voluntary and you can refuse to participate without penalty or loss of benefits to which you are otherwise entitled.

Title of Research Study:

Principal Investigator(s) (include faculty sponsor), UT affiliation, and Telephone Number(s):
[Do not use "Dr." as it might imply medical supervision. Instead, use "Professor or Ph.D. or Pharm.D, etc."]

Funding source:

What is the purpose of this study? *[Please include the number of subjects]*

What will be done if you take part in this research study?

What are the possible discomforts and risks?
[Studies that involve psychological risk . . .

The principles that apply to studies that involve psychological risk or mental stress are similar to those that involve physical risk. Participants should be informed of the risk and told that treatment will not be provided. They should be given the names and telephone numbers of agencies that may alleviate their mental concerns, such as a crisis hot line. If the principal investigator or the faculty sponsor of a student investigator is qualified to treat mental health problems, that person may be listed as a resource.]

What are the possible benefits to you or to others?

If you choose to take part in this study, will it cost you anything?

Will you receive compensation for your participation in this study?

What if you are injured because of the study?

If you do not want to take part in this study, what other options are available to you?

Participation in this study is entirely voluntary. You are free to refuse to be in the study, and your refusal will not influence current or future relationships with The University of Texas at Austin *[and or participating sites such as AISD or any other organization]*.

How can you withdraw from this research study and who should I call if I have questions?

If you wish to stop your participation in this research study for any reason, you should contact: at (512) . You are free to withdraw your consent and stop participation in this research study at any time without penalty or loss of benefits for which you may be entitled. Throughout the study, the researchers will notify you of new information that may become available and that might affect your decision to remain in the study.

In addition, if you have questions about your rights as a research participant, please contact *[name]* Chair, The University of Texas at Austin Institutional Review Board for the Protection of Human Subjects, *[phone number]*.

How will your privacy and the confidentiality of your research records be protected?

Authorized persons from The University of Texas at Austin and the Institutional Review Board have the legal right to review your research records and will protect the confidentiality of those records to the extent permitted by law. If the research project is sponsored

SOURCE: Reprinted with permission of the University of Texas at Austin Institutional Review Board.

Figure 4-1 Condensed Excerpts from Sample Consent Forms Used by the University of Texas at Austin's Institutional Review Board

then the sponsor also has the legal right to review your research records. Otherwise, your research records will not be released without your consent unless required by law or a court order.

If the results of this research are published or presented at scientific meetings, your identity will not be disclosed.

[Please note that for studies with audio or video recordings, participants must be told: (a) that the interviews or sessions will be audio or videotaped; (b) that the cassettes will be coded so that no personally identifying information is visible on them; (c) that they will be kept in a secure place (e.g., a locked file cabinet in the investigator's office); (d) that they will be heard or viewed only for research purposes by the investigator and his or her associates; and (e) that they will be erased after they are transcribed or coded. If you wish to keep the recordings because of the requirements of your professional organization with respect to data or because you may wish to review them for additional analyses at a later time, the statement about erasing them should be omitted and you should state that they will be retained for possible future analysis.

If you wish to present the recordings at a convention or to use them for other educational purposes, you should get special permission to do so by adding, after the signature lines on the consent form, the following statement,

"We may wish to present some of the tapes from this study at scientific conventions or as demonstrations in classrooms. Please sign below if you are willing to allow us to do so with the tape of your performance."

And add another signature line prefaced by, "I hereby give permission for the video (audio) tape made for this research study to be also used for educational purposes." This procedure makes it possible for a participant to agree to being taped for research purposes and to maintain the confidentiality of the information on that tape.]

Will the researchers benefit from your participation in this study *[beyond publishing or presenting the results]***?**

Signatures:

Other circumstances in which addenda may need to be included:

1. (For your information only. This explanatory section should NOT be placed into the consent form.)

[When informed consent cannot be obtained from the subject because the subject is an adult who does not have the ability to read and understand the consent form (for example, the subject has advanced Alzheimer's Disease or another cognitive problem), then the study should be explained verbally using language the subject can understand. The Subject should then be asked if she/he agrees to participate. If the subject does not want to participate, she/he should not be enrolled unless it is determined by the person legally responsible that it is in the subject's best interest.

When appropriate, the following text should be added as an addendum to the Informed Consent Form before the Signature section:]

If you cannot give legal consent to take part in this study because you may have trouble reading or understanding this consent form, then the researcher will ask for your assent. Assent is your agreement to be in the study. The researcher will explain the study to you in words that you can understand. You should ask questions about anything you don't understand. Then you should decide if you want to be in the research study. If you want to participate, you or someone who can sign a legal document for you must also give their permission and sign this form before you take part.

You agree to participate:

____

Subject's signature **Date**

____

Signature of Principal Investigator or Representative **Date**

____

Witness (if available) **Date**

Figure 4-1 *(continued)*

If you are not the subject, please print your name:

______________________________ and indicate one of the following:

________ **The subject's guardian**

________ **A surrogate**

________ **A durable power of attorney**

________ **A proxy**

________ **Other, please explain:**

If the child is between 13 and 17, a child signature line may be added to the consent form. If the child is between 7 and 12, the child should sign a separate assent form.

Sample Parental Consent Form for the Participation of Minors: Selected Elements
(Use this in conjunction with the consent form template for adults.)

CONSENT FORM
TITLE of STUDY

Your (son/daughter/child/infant/adolescent youth) is invited to participate in a study of (describe the study). My name is ________ and I am a ________ at The University of Texas at Austin, Department of ________. This study is (state how study relates to your program of work or your supervisor's program of work). I am asking for permission to include your (son/daughter/child/infant/adolescent youth) in this study because ________. I expect to have (number) participants in the study.

If you allow your child to participate, (state who will actually conduct the research) will (describe the procedures to be followed. If the study will take place in a school setting refer to the material under the subheadings in the consent form for minors section of *Procedures and Forms* for examples of information that should be included about the specific activities for which consent is being sought, the time when the study will be conducted, arrangements for students who do not participate, and access to school records.)

Any information that is obtained in connection with this study and that can be identified with your (son/daughter/child/infant/adolescent youth) will remain confidential and will be disclosed only with your permission. His or her responses will not be linked to his or her name or your name in any written or verbal report of this research project.

Your decision to allow your (son/daughter/child/infant/adolescent youth) to participate will not affect your or his or her present or future relationship with The University of Texas at Austin or (include the name of any other institution connected with this project). If you have any questions about the study, please ask me. If you have any questions later, call me at xxx-yyyy. If you have any questions or concerns about your (son/daughter/child/infant/adolescent youth)'s participation in this study, call *[name]*, Chair of the University of Texas at Austin Institutional Review Board for the Protection of Human Research Participants at *[number]*.

You may keep the copy of this consent form.

You are making a decision about allowing your (son/daughter/child/infant/adolescent youth) to participate in this study. Your signature below indicates that you have read the information provided above and have decided to allow him or her to participate in the study. If you later decide that you wish to withdraw your permission for your (son/daughter/child/infant/adolescent youth) to participate in the study, simply tell me. You may discontinue his or her participation at any time.

____
Printed Name of (son/daughter/child/infant/adolescent youth)

______________________________ __________
Signature of Parent(s) or Legal Guardian Date

______________________________ __________
Signature of Investigator Date

Figure 4-1 *(continued)*

Assent for Minors
If the minor is between 7 and 17, his or her assent to participate in the study should be obtained by one of two ways. If the minor is old enough to read and comprehend the parental consent form (more or less between 13 and 17) use the assent signature line method shown at the top of the page titled "Sample Assent Forms for Minors . . ." If the minor is not old enough to comprehend the parental consent form, but is old enough to realize that he or she is participating in a research project (more or less from 7 to 12) use a separate assent form. A sample assent form is at the bottom of the page with the sample forms.

Sample Assent Forms for Minors

Assent Signature Line
If the minor is between the ages of 13 and 17 and capable of understanding the consent form signed by the parents(s), add the following paragraph to the end of that form, underneath the line for the signature of the investigator.

I have read the description of the study titled (give title) that is printed above, and I understand what the procedures are and what will happen to me in the study. I have received permission from my parent(s) to participate in the study, and I agree to participate in it. I know that I can quit the study at any time.

____________________________ __________
Signature of Minor Date

Assent Form
If a research participant is a minor between the ages of 7 and 12, use an assent form. A sample assent form is printed below. Modify it for your study. The title may be a simplified version of the title on the parental consent form.

ASSENT FORM
(Title of Study)

I agree to be in a study about (give general topic of study). This study was explained to my (mother/father/parents/guardian) and (she/he/they) said that I could be in it. The only people who will know about what I say and do in the study will be the people in charge of the study (modify if information will be given to parents, teachers, doctors, etc.).

(Provide here an overview, from the child's perspective, of what he or she will do in the study. Write this so that a child of seven can understand it, e.g., "In the study I will be asked questions about how I solve problems. I will also be asked how I feel about my family and myself."

Writing my name on this page means that the page was read (by me/to me) and that I agree to be in the study. I know what will happen to me. If I decide to quit the study, all I have to do is tell the person in charge.

____________________________ __________
Child's Signature Date

____________________________ __________
Signature of Researcher Date

Figure 4-1 (*continued*)

and the like. Revealing such information is likely to make them feel at least uncomfortable.

Social research projects may also force participants to face aspects of themselves that they do not normally consider. That can happen even when the information is not revealed directly to the researcher. In retrospect, a certain past behavior may appear unjust or immoral. The project, then, can be the source of a continuing, personal agony for the subject. If the study concerns codes of ethical conduct, for example, the subject may begin questioning his or her own morality, and that personal concern may last long after the research has been completed and reported.

By now, you should have realized that just about any research you might conduct runs the risk of injuring other people somehow. There is no way for the researcher to guard against all these possible injuries; however, some study designs make them more likely than others. If a particular research procedure seems likely to produce unpleasant effects for participants—asking survey respondents to report deviant behavior, for example—the researcher should have the firmest of scientific grounds for doing it. If the research design is essential and also likely to be unpleasant for participants, then you will find yourself in an ethical netherworld and may find yourself forced to do some personal agonizing. Although agonizing has little value in itself, it may be a healthy sign that you have become sensitive to the problem.

Although the fact often goes unrecognized, participants can be harmed by data analysis and reporting. Every now and then, research participants read the books published about the studies in which they have participated. Reasonably sophisticated participants will be able to locate themselves in the various indexes and tables. Having done so, they may find themselves characterized—though not identified by name—as bigoted, abusive, and so forth. At the very least, such characterizations are likely to trouble them and threaten their self-images. Yet the whole purpose of the research project may be to explain why some people are prejudiced and others are not.

Like voluntary participation, not harming people is an easy norm to accept in theory but often difficult to ensure in practice. Sensitivity to the issue and experience with its applications, however, should improve the researcher's tact in delicate areas of research.

Increasingly in recent years, social researchers have been getting support for abiding by this norm. Federal and other funding agencies typically require an independent evaluation of the treatment of human subjects for research proposals, and most universities now have human subject committees to serve that evaluative function. Although sometimes troublesome and inappropriately applied, such requirements not only guard against unethical research but also can reveal ethical issues that have been overlooked by even the most scrupulous of researchers.

Anonymity and Confidentiality

The protection of subjects' identities is the clearest concern in the protection of their interests and well-being in survey research. If revealing their survey responses would injure them in any way, adherence to this norm becomes all the more important. Two techniques—*anonymity* and *confidentiality*—will assist you in this regard, although the two are often confused.

Anonymity A respondent has **anonymity** when the researcher cannot identify a given response with a given respondent. This means that an interview survey respondent can never be considered anonymous, because an interviewer collects the information from an identifiable respondent. (We assume here that standard sampling methods are followed.) An example of anonymity would be a mail survey in which no identification numbers are put on the questionnaires before their return to the research office.

As we will see in Chapter 15 (on survey research), ensuring anonymity makes it difficult to keep track of who has or has not returned the questionnaires. Despite this problem, you may be advised to pay the necessary price in some situations. If you study drug abuse, for example, assuring anonymity may increase the likelihood and accuracy of responses. Also, you can avoid the position of being asked by authorities for the names of drug offenders. When respondents volunteer their names, such information can be immediately obliterated on the questionnaires.

Confidentiality In a survey that provides **confidentiality**, the researcher is able to identify a given person's responses but essentially promises not to do so publicly. In an interview survey, for instance, the researcher would be in a position to make public the income reported by a given respondent, but the respondent is assured that this will not be done.

You can use several techniques to ensure better performance on this guarantee. To begin, interviewers and others with access to respondent identifications should be trained in their ethical responsibilities. As soon as possible, all names and addresses should be removed from questionnaires and replaced with identification numbers. A master identification file should be created that links numbers to names to permit the later correction of missing or contradictory information, but this file should not be available to anyone else except for legitimate purposes. Whenever a survey is confidential rather than anonymous, it is the researcher's responsibility to make that fact clear to respondents. Never use the term *anonymous* to mean confidential.

As in social work practice, situations can arise in social work research in which ethical considerations dictate that confidentiality not be maintained. Suppose in the course of conducting your interviews you learn children are being abused or respondents are at imminent risk of seriously harming themselves or others. It would be your professional (and perhaps legal) obligation to report this to the proper agency. Participants need to be informed of this possibility as part of the informed consent process before they agree to participate in a study.

There may be other situations in which government agents take legal action to acquire research data that you believe should remain confidential. For example, they may subpoena data on participants' drug use and thus legally force you to report this information. To protect research participants from such efforts, in 1989 the U.S. National Institutes of Health began issuing certificates of confidentiality. Researchers can submit proposals to apply for these certificates. By obtaining a certificate of confidentiality, researchers eliminate the risk of having their data subpoenaed.

Deceiving Participants

We've seen that handling participants' identities is an important ethical consideration. Handling your own identity as a researcher can be tricky also. Sometimes it's useful and even necessary to identify yourself as a researcher to those you want to study. You'd have to be a master con artist to get people to complete a lengthy questionnaire without letting on that you were conducting research.

Even when it's possible and important to conceal your research identity, there is an important ethical dimension to consider. Deceiving people is unethical, and within social research, deception needs to be justified by compelling scientific or administrative concerns. Even then, the justification will be arguable.

Sometimes, researchers admit they are doing research but fudge about why they are doing it or for whom. Suppose you've been asked by a public welfare agency to conduct a study of living standards among aid recipients. Even if the agency is looking for ways of improving conditions, the recipient participants are likely to fear a witch hunt for "cheaters." They might be tempted, therefore, to give answers that make themselves seem more destitute than they really are. Unless they provide truthful answers, however, the study will not produce accurate data that will contribute to an effective improvement of living conditions. What do you do? One solution would be to tell participants that you are conducting the study as part of a university research program—concealing your affiliation with the welfare agency. Doing that improves the scientific quality of the study but raises a serious ethical issue in the process.

Analysis and Reporting

As a social work researcher, then, you have several ethical obligations to the participants in your study. At the same time, you have ethical obligations to your professional colleagues. A few comments on those latter obligations are in order.

In any rigorous study, the researcher should be more familiar than anyone else with the study's technical shortcomings and failures. You have an obligation to make them known to your readers. Even though you may feel foolish admitting mistakes, you should do it anyway. Negative findings should be reported if they are at all related to your analysis. There is an unfortunate myth in scientific reporting that only positive discoveries are worth reporting (and journal editors are sometimes guilty of believing that as well). In science, however, it is often just as important to know that two variables are not related as to know that they are. If, for example, an experiment finds no difference in outcome between clients treated and not treated with a tested intervention, then it is important for practitioners to know that they may need to consider alternative interventions—particularly if the same null finding is replicated in other studies. And replication would not be possible if the original experiment were not reported.

The ethical importance of reporting negative findings in studies evaluating the effectiveness of interventions, programs, or policies is particularly apparent in the evidence-based practice process (as discussed in Chapter 2). Suppose you are conducting an evidence-based practice search looking for interventions with the best evidence supporting their effectiveness for the problem presented by your client and you find a well-designed study supporting the effectiveness of a relevant intervention that we'll call Intervention A. If you find no other studies with contradictory findings, you might be tempted to deem Intervention A the one with the best evidence base for your client's problem. But suppose several other studies found Intervention A to be ineffective for that problem but were not reported because the investigators believed that no one is interested in hearing about interventions that don't work. In reality, then, interventions other than Intervention A might have better, more consistent evidence supporting their effectiveness, and if you knew of the studies with negative findings about Intervention A you might propose one of those other interventions to your client. Moreover, suppose your client is African American or Hispanic, and that the one study supporting Intervention A involved only Caucasian clients whereas the other studies—the ones with negative results—involved African American or Hispanic clients. The ethical implications of not reporting those other studies should be apparent to you; not reporting them would mislead you into proposing the wrong, unhelpful intervention to your client.

Researchers should also avoid the temptation to save face by describing their findings as the product of a carefully preplanned analytic strategy when that is not the case. Many findings arrive unexpectedly—even though they may seem obvious in retrospect. So they uncovered an interesting relationship by accident—so what? Embroidering such situations with descriptions of fictitious hypotheses is dishonest and tends to mislead inexperienced researchers into thinking that all scientific inquiry is rigorously preplanned and organized.

In general, science progresses through honesty and openness, and it is retarded by ego defenses and deception. Researchers can serve their fellow researchers—and scientific discovery as a whole—by telling the truth about all the pitfalls and problems they have experienced in a particular line of inquiry. Perhaps that candor will save their colleagues from the same problems.

WEIGHING BENEFITS AND COSTS

We have noted that ethical considerations in the conduct of social work research often pose a dilemma. The most ethical course of action for researchers to take is not always clear-cut. Sometimes it is difficult to judge whether the long-term good to be derived from a study will outweigh the harm done by the ethically questionable practices that may be required for adequate scientific validity. Consider, for example, the study in which a team of researchers deceptively posed as hospitalized mental patients, concealing their identity from direct care staff members to study whether the staff could recognize their normalcy.

Earlier we asked whether the potential benefits of the study—regarding psychiatric diagnosis and care—justified violating the norm of voluntary participation by direct staff. What if the purpose of that study had been to verify whether suspected physical abuse of patients by staff was taking place? Suppose an appalling amount of staff neglect and abuse of patients really was occurring and that the researchers uncovered it. Would the potential benefits to current and future patients to be derived from exposing and perhaps reforming the quality of care outweigh using deception in the research?

If alternative ways to conduct the research are available—that is, ways that can provide equally valid and useful answers to the research question without engaging in ethically questionable research practices—then the dilemma will be resolved and an alternate methodology can be chosen. But sometimes no such alternatives appear. If not, then how researchers resolve this dilemma will depend on the values they attach to the various costs and benefits of the research and whether they believe that some ends ever justify some means. No objective formula can be applied to this decision; it is inherently subjective. Some individuals would argue that the end never justifies the means. Others might disagree about which particular ends justify which particular means.

An Illustration: Living with the Dying—Use of Participant Observation

A study by Robert Buckingham and his colleagues (1976) provides one example of how the long-term good to be derived from a study may have justified violating ethical guidelines. This study, which involved deceiving participants and not obtaining their informed consent to participate, might be of special interest to students who are interested in practicing social work in a medical or hospice setting. (We briefly discussed this study in Chapter 3, and we reexamine it here, particularly in regard to its ethical ramifications.)

Buckingham and his colleagues wanted to compare the value of routine hospital care with hospice care for the terminally ill. (As we mentioned in Chapter 3, the emphasis in hospice care is on minimizing discomfort and maximizing quality of life, and this might entail eschewing medical procedures that prolong life but hinder its quality. Routine hospital care, in contrast, is more likely to emphasize prolonging life at all costs, even if that requires a lower quality of life for the dying patient. The routine approach is less attentive to the psychosocial and other nonmedical needs of the patient and family.)

Buckingham wanted to observe and experience the treatment of a terminally ill patient in two wards of a hospital: the surgical-care (non-hospice) ward and the palliative-care (hospice) ward. For his observations to be useful, it was necessary that staff members and other patients on his ward not know what he was doing. The steps that he took to carry out his deception are quite remarkable. Before entering the hospital, he lost 22 pounds on a six-month diet. (He was naturally thin before starting his diet.) He submitted himself to ultraviolet radiation so he would look as if he had undergone radiation therapy. He had puncture marks from intravenous needles put on his hands and arms so he would look as if he had undergone chemotherapy. He underwent minor surgery for the sole purpose of producing biopsy scars. He learned how to imitate the behavior of patients dying with pancreatic cancer by reviewing their medical charts and maintaining close contact with them. Finally, for several days before entering the hospital, he grew a patchy beard and abstained from washing.

Buckingham stayed in the hospital 10 days, including two days in a holding unit, four days in the surgical-care unit, and four days in the hospice unit. His findings there supported the advantages of hospice care for the terminally ill. For example, on the surgical-care ward he observed staff communication practices that were insufficient, impersonal, and insensitive. Physicians did not communicate with patients. Staff members in general avoided greeting patients, made little eye contact with them, and often referred to them by the names of their diseases rather than by their personal names. Complacent patients did not receive affection. The negative aspects of the patients' conditions were emphasized.

Buckingham's observations on the hospice ward, however, were quite different. Staff maintained eye contact with patients. They asked questions about what the patients liked to eat and about other preferences. They asked patients how they could be more helpful. They listened to patients accurately, unhurriedly, and empathically. Physicians spent more time communicating with patients and their families. Staff encouraged family involvement in the care process. It is not difficult to see the value of Buckingham's findings in regard to enhancing the care of the terminally ill and their families. In considering whether the benefits of those findings justify Buckingham's particular use of deception, several other aspects of the study might interest you.

Before entering the hospital, Buckingham engaged the hospital's top medical, administrative, and legal staff members in planning and approving the study. The heads of both the surgery ward and the hospice ward also participated in the planning and approved the study. In addition, the personnel of the hospice ward were informed in advance that their unit was going to be evaluated, although the nature of the evaluation was not revealed. Finally, an ad hoc committee was formed to consider the ethics of the study, and the committee approved the study. In light of these procedures and this study's benefits, it may not surprise you to learn that no ethical controversy emerged in response to this study.

Right to Receive Services versus Responsibility to Evaluate Service Effectiveness

Perhaps the most critical ethical dilemma in social work research pertains to the right of clients in need to receive services and whether the benefit of improving the welfare of clients in the long run ever justifies delaying the provision of services to some clients in the short run. Practitioners engaged in the evidence-based practice process will search for the best available evidence about the effectiveness of services. As mentioned in Chapter 2, at the top of the evidence-based practice research hierarchy for evaluating service effectiveness are studies with the strongest designs for making inferences about whether the service provided or something else most plausibly explains variations in client outcome. Those designs involve experiments that evaluate the effectiveness of services by comparing the fates of clients who receive the service being evaluated and those from whom we withhold the service. (We will examine experiments in depth in Chapter 11.) Two values are in conflict here: doing something to try to provide immediate help to people in need, and the professional's responsibility to ensure that the services clients receive have had their effects—either beneficial or harmful—scientifically tested.

Some researchers argue that individuals in need should never be denied service for any period or for any research purposes. Others counter that the service being delayed is one whose effects, if any, have not yet been scientifically verified—otherwise, there would be no need to test it. How ethical, they ask, is it to provide the same services perennially without ever scientifically verifying whether those services are really helping anyone or are perhaps harmful? And if they are potentially harmful, are those who receive them actually taking a greater risk than those who are temporarily denied them until their effects are gauged? Using another medical parallel, would you think your physician was ethical if he or she treated you with a drug knowing that the beneficial or harmful effects of that drug were as yet untested? If you were being paid to participate in a medical experiment to test the effectiveness of a drug whose benefits and negative side effects were as yet unknown, which group would you feel safer in: the group receiving the drug or the group not receiving it?

The seriousness of the client's problem is one factor that bears on this dilemma. It would be much harder to justify the delay of service to individuals who are experiencing a dangerous crisis or are at risk of seriously harming themselves—suicidal clients, for example—than to those in less critical need. Another factor is the availability of alternative interventions to which the tested intervention can be compared. Perhaps those who are denied the tested service can receive another one that might prove to be no less beneficial.

If alternative interventions are available, then the conflict between the right to service and the responsibility to evaluate can be alleviated. Instead of comparing clients who receive a new service being tested to those who receive no service, we can compare them to those who receive a routine set of services that was in place before the new one was developed. This is a particularly ethical way to proceed when insufficient resources are available to provide the new service to all or most clients who seek service. This way, no one is denied service, and the maximum number that resources permit receive the new service.

Another way to reduce the ethical dilemma when resources don't permit every client to receive the new service is to assign some clients to a waiting list for the new service. As they wait their turn for the new service, they can be compared to the clients currently receiving the new service. Ultimately, everyone is served, and the waiting list clients should be free to refuse participation in the study without being denied services eventually.

NASW CODE OF ETHICS

If decisions about the ethics of research involve subjective value judgments in which we must weigh the potential benefits of the research against its potential costs to research participants, and if we must make those decisions in light of various idiosyncratic factors, then those decisions pose dilemmas for which there may be no right or wrong answers. But researchers can do some things to be as ethical as possible. They can obtain collegial feedback as to the ethics of their proposed research. As mentioned earlier, they can (and perhaps must) obtain approval from an institutional review board (IRB), which we'll discuss later in this chapter. They should carefully consider whether there are ethically superior alternatives and strive to ensure that their research proposal is the most ethical one that they can conceive.

To guide them in this endeavor, various professional associations have created and published formal codes of conduct to cover research ethics. Figure 4-2 shows the codes from the "Evaluation and Research" section of the Code of Ethics of the National Association of Social Workers. Although those codes provide ethical guidelines for conducting research, another section—on social workers' ethical responsibilities as professionals—reminds us that we can violate our ethical responsibilities as professionals not only when we conduct research, but also when we refrain from using it to guide our practice. It is worded as follows:

> Social workers should critically examine and keep current with emerging knowledge relevant to social work. Social workers should routinely review the professional literature. . . . Social workers should base practice on recognized knowledge, including empirically based knowledge, relevant to social work and social work ethics.
>
> (NASW, 1999, SECTION 4.01)

FOUR ETHICAL CONTROVERSIES

As you may already have guessed, the adoption and publication of professional codes of conduct have not totally resolved the issue of research ethics. Social scientists still disagree on some general principles, and those who seem to agree in principle still debate specifics. In this section, we will describe briefly four research projects that have provoked ethical controversy and discussion. These are not the only controversial projects that have been done, but they illustrate ethical issues in the real world, and we thought you'd find them interesting and perhaps provocative.

Of the four illustrations of controversial research projects we examine here, the first two are from social psychology and sociology, and the last two are from social work. The first project examined obedience in a laboratory setting. The second studied homosexual behavior. The third was designed to withhold welfare benefits from 800 poor Texans in order to evaluate the effectiveness of a new program that was intended to

Section 5.02 Evaluation and Research

(a) Social workers should monitor and evaluate policies, the implementation of programs, and practice interventions.

(b) Social workers should promote and facilitate evaluation and research to contribute to the development of knowledge.

(c) Social workers should critically examine and keep current with emerging knowledge relevant to social work and fully use evaluation and research evidence in their professional practice.

(d) Social workers engaged in evaluation or research should carefully consider possible consequences and should follow guidelines developed for the protection of evaluation and research participants. Appropriate institutional review boards should be consulted.

(e) Social workers engaged in evaluation or research should obtain voluntary and written informed consent from participants, when appropriate, without any implied or actual deprivation or penalty for refusal to participate; without undue inducement to participate; and with due regard for participants' well-being, privacy, and dignity. Informed consent should include information about the nature, extent, and duration of the participation requested and disclosure of the risks and benefits of participation in the research.

(f) When evaluation or research participants are incapable of giving informed consent, social workers should provide an appropriate explanation to the participants, obtain the participants' assent to the extent they are able, and obtain written consent from an appropriate proxy.

(g) Social workers should never design or conduct evaluation or research that does not use consent procedures, such as certain forms of naturalistic observation and archival research, unless rigorous and responsible review of the research has found it to be justified because of its prospective scientific, educational, or applied value and unless equally effective alternative procedures that do not involve waiver of consent are not feasible.

(h) Social workers should inform participants of their right to withdraw from evaluation and research at any time without penalty.

(i) Social workers should take appropriate steps to ensure that participants in evaluation and research have access to appropriate supportive services.

(j) Social workers engaged in evaluation or research should protect participants from unwarranted physical or mental distress, harm, danger, or deprivation.

(k) Social workers engaged in the evaluation of services should discuss collected information only for professional purposes and only with people professionally concerned with this information.

(l) Social workers engaged in evaluation or research should ensure the anonymity or confidentiality of participants and of the data obtained from them. Social workers should inform participants of any limits of confidentiality, the measures that will be taken to ensure confidentiality, and when any records containing research data will be destroyed.

(m) Social workers who report evaluation and research results should protect participants' confidentiality by omitting identifying information unless proper consent has been obtained authorizing disclosure.

(n) Social workers should report evaluation and research findings accurately. They should not fabricate or falsify results and should take steps to correct any errors later found in published data using standard publication methods.

(o) Social workers engaged in evaluation or research should be alert to and avoid conflicts of interest and dual relationships with participants, should inform participants when a real or potential conflict of interest arises, and should take steps to resolve the issue in a manner that makes participants' interests primary.

(p) Social workers should educate themselves, their students, and their colleagues about responsible research practices.

Figure 4-2 NASW Code of Ethics

wean people from welfare. The fourth tested whether the decisions made by journal editors about whether or not to publish submitted research papers were biased in favor of publishing studies in which positive findings supported the effectiveness of social work interventions.

Observing Human Obedience

One of the more unsettling rationalizations to come out of World War II was the German soldier's common excuse for atrocities: "I was only following orders." From the point of view that gave rise to this comment, any behavior—no matter how reprehensible—could be justified if someone else could be assigned responsibility for it. If a superior officer ordered a soldier to kill a baby, then the fact of the order was said to exempt the soldier from personal responsibility for the action.

Although the military tribunals that tried the war crime cases did not accept the excuse, social scientists and others have recognized the extent to which this point of view pervades social life. Often people seem willing to do things they know would be considered wrong by others—if they can cite some higher authority as ordering them to do it. Such was the pattern of justification in the My Lai tragedy of Vietnam, when U.S. soldiers killed more than 300 unarmed civilians—some of them young children—simply because their village, My Lai, was believed to be a Vietcong stronghold. This sort of justification appears less dramatically in day-to-day civilian life. Few would disagree that this reliance on authority exists, yet Stanley Milgram's study (1963, 1965) of the topic provoked considerable controversy.

To observe people's willingness to harm others when following orders, Milgram brought 40 adult men—from many different walks of life—into a laboratory setting that he designed to create the phenomenon under study. If you had been a subject in the experiment, you would have had something like the following experience.

You would have been informed that you and another subject were about to participate in a learning experiment. As the result of drawing lots, you would have been assigned the job of "teacher" and your fellow subject the job of "pupil." Your pupil then would have been led into another room, strapped into a chair, and had an electrode attached to his wrist. As the teacher, you would have been seated in front of an impressive electrical control panel covered with dials, gauges, and switches. You would have noticed that each switch had a label giving a different number of volts, ranging from 15 to 315. The switches would have had other labels, too, some with the ominous phrases "Extreme-Intensity Shock," "Danger—Severe Shock," and "XXX."

The experiment would run like this. You would read a list of word pairs to the learner and then test his ability to match them. You couldn't see him, but a light on your control panel would indicate his answer. Whenever the learner made a mistake, you would be instructed by the experimenter to throw one of the switches—beginning with the mildest—and administer a shock to your pupil. Through an open door between the two rooms, you'd hear your pupil's response to the shock. Then you'd read another list of word pairs and test him again.

As the experiment progressed, you'd be administering ever more intense shocks until your pupil was screaming for mercy and begging for the experiment to end. You'd be instructed to administer the next shock anyway. After a while, your pupil would begin kicking the wall between the two rooms and screaming. You'd be told to give the next shock. Finally, you'd read a list and ask for the pupil's answer—and there would only be silence from the other room. The experimenter would inform you that no answer was considered an error and instruct you to administer the next higher shock. This process would continue up to the "XXX" shock at the end of the series.

What do you suppose you really would have done when the pupil first began screaming? When he began kicking on the wall? Or when he became totally silent and gave no indication of life? You'd refuse to continue giving shocks, right? And surely the same would be true of most people.

So we might think—but Milgram found out otherwise. Of the first 40 adult men Milgram tested, nobody refused to continue administering the shocks until they heard the pupil begin kicking the wall between the two rooms. Of the 40, five did so then. Two-thirds of the subjects, 26 of the 40, continued doing as they were told through the entire series—up to and including the administration of the highest shock.

As you've probably guessed, the shocks were phony, and the "pupil" was another experimenter. Only the "teacher" was a real subject in the experiment. You wouldn't have been hurting another person, even though you would have been led to think you were. The experiment was designed to test your willingness to follow orders—presumably to the point of killing someone.

Milgram's experiments have been criticized both methodologically and ethically. On the ethical side, critics particularly cited the effects of the experiment on the subjects. Many seem to have personally experienced about as much pain as they thought they were administering to someone else. They pleaded with the experimenter to let them stop giving the shocks. They became extremely upset and nervous. Some had uncontrollable seizures.

How do you feel about this research? Do you think the topic was important enough to justify such measures? Can you think of other ways in which the researcher might have examined obedience? There is a wealth of discussion regarding the Milgram experiments on the web. Search for *Milgram experiments*, *human obedience experiments*, or *Stanley Milgram*.

Trouble in the Tearoom

The second illustration was conducted by a graduate student and published in a 1970 book called *Tearoom Trade: Impersonal Sex in Public Places*. Researcher

Laud Humphreys wanted to study homosexual acts between strangers meeting in public restrooms in parks; the restrooms are called "tearooms" by those who used them for this purpose. Typically, the tearoom encounter involved three people: the two men actually engaged in the homosexual act and a lookout.

To gather observations for his study, Humphreys began showing up at public restrooms and offering to serve as a lookout whenever it seemed appropriate. Humphreys wanted to go beyond his observations as lookout and learn more about the people he was observing. Many of the participants were married men who wanted to keep their homosexuality secret and thus avoid being stigmatized and losing their status in their communities. They probably would not have consented to being interviewed. Instead of asking them for an interview, Humphreys tried to note the license plate numbers of their vehicles and then track down their names and addresses through the police. Then disguising himself enough to avoid recognition, he visited the men at their homes and announced that he was conducting a survey. In that fashion, he collected the personal information he was unable to get in the restrooms.

Humphreys' research provoked considerable controversy both within and outside the social scientific community. Some critics charged Humphreys with a gross invasion of privacy in the name of science. What men did in public restrooms was their own business and not his. Others were mostly concerned about the deceit involved: Humphreys had lied to the participants by leading them to believe he was only participating as a voyeur. Some were more concerned with Humphreys' follow-up survey than with what he did in public facilities. They felt it was unethical for him to trace the participants to their houses and interview them under false pretenses. Still others justified Humphreys' research. The topic, they said, was worth study and could not be studied any other way. They considered the deceit to be essentially harmless, noting that Humphreys was careful not to harm his subjects by disclosing their tearoom activities.

The tearoom trade controversy, as you might imagine, has never been resolved. It is still debated, and probably will be for a long time, because it stirs emotions and contains ethical issues about which people disagree. What do you think? Was Humphreys ethical in doing what he did? Are there parts of the research you feel were acceptable and other parts that were not? Whatever you feel in the matter, you are sure to find others who disagree with you.

"Welfare Study Withholds Benefits from 800 Texans"

That was the front-page headline that greeted readers of the Sunday, February 11, 1990, edition of the *Dallas Morning News*. Then they read the following: "Thousands of poor people in Texas and several other states are unwitting subjects in a federal experiment that denies some government help to a portion of them to see how well they live without it."

This was pretty strong stuff, and soon the story was covered on one of the national TV networks. Let's examine it further for our third illustration.

The Texas Department of Human Services received federal money to test the effectiveness of a pilot program that had been designed to wean people from the state's welfare rolls. The program was targeted to welfare recipients who found jobs or job training. Before the new program was implemented, these recipients received four months of free medical care and some child care after they left the welfare rolls. The new program extended these benefits to one year of Medicaid coverage and subsidized child care. The rationale was that extending the duration of the benefits would encourage recipients to accept and keep entry-level jobs that were unlikely to offer immediate medical insurance or child care.

The federal agency that granted the money attached an important condition: Receiving states were required to conduct a scientifically rigorous experiment to measure the program's effectiveness in attaining its goal of weaning people from welfare. Some federal officials insisted that this requirement entailed randomly assigning some people to a control group that would be denied the new (extended) program and would instead be kept on the old program (just four months of benefits). The point of this was to maximize the likelihood that the recipient group (the experimental group) and the nonrecipient (control) group were equivalent in all relevant ways except for the receipt of the new program. If they were, and if the recipient group was weaned from welfare to a greater extent than the nonrecipient group, then it could be safely inferred that the new program, and not something else, caused the successful outcome. (We will examine this logic further in Chapters 10 and 11.)

If you have read many journal articles reporting on experimental studies, you are probably aware that many of them randomly assign about one-half of their subjects to the experimental group and the other half to the control group. This routine procedure denies the experimental condition to approximately one-half of the subjects. The Texas experiment was designed to include all eligible welfare recipients statewide, assigning 90 percent of them to the experimental group and 10 percent to the control group. Thus, only 10 percent of the subjects, which in this study amounted to 800 people, would be denied the new benefits if they found jobs. Although this seems more humane than denying benefits to 50 percent of the subjects, the newspaper account characterized the 800 people in the control group as "unlucky Texans" who seemed to be unfairly left out of a program that was extending benefits to everyone else who was eligible statewide and who numbered in the many thousands. Moreover, the newspaper report noted that the 800 control subjects would be denied the new program for two years to provide ample time to compare outcomes between the two groups. To boot, these 800 "unlucky Texans" were not to be informed of the new program or of the experiment. They were to be told of only the normal four-month coverage.

Advocates of the experiment defended this design, arguing that the control group would not be denied benefits. They would receive routine benefits, and the new benefits would not have been available for anyone in the first place unless a small group was randomly assigned to the routine policy. In other words, the whole point of the new benefits was to test a new welfare policy, not merely to implement one. The defenders further argued that the design was justified by the need to test for unintended negative effects of the new program, such as the possibility that some businesses might drop their child care or insurance coverage for employees, knowing that the new program was extending these benefits. That, in turn, they argued, could impel low-paid employees in those businesses to quit their jobs and go on welfare. By going on welfare and then getting new jobs, they would become eligible for the government's extended benefits, and this would make the welfare program more expensive.

Critics of the study, on the other hand, argued that it violated federal ethics standards such as voluntary participation and informed consent. Anyone in the study must be informed about it and all its consequences and must have the option to refuse to participate. One national "think tank" expert on ethics likened the experiment to the Tuskegee syphilis study (which we discussed earlier), saying, "It's really not that different." He further asserted, "People ought not to be treated like things, even if what you get is good information."

In the aftermath of such criticism, Texas state officials decided to try to convince the federal government to rescind the control group requirement so that the state could extend the new benefits to the 800 people in the control group. Instead of using a control group design, they wanted to extend benefits to everyone and find statistical procedures that would help ferret out program defects (a design that might have value, but which would be less conclusive as to what really causes what, as we will see in later chapters). They also decided to send a letter to the control group members that explained their special status.

Two days after the *Dallas Morning News* broke this story, it published a follow-up article reporting that the secretary of the U.S. Department of Health and Human Services, in response to the first news accounts, instructed his staff to cooperate with Texas welfare officials so that the project design would no longer deny the new program to the 800 control group members. Do you agree with his decision? Did the potential benefits of this experiment justify its controversial ethical practices?

A control group probably could not have been formed had recipients been given the right to refuse to participate. Who would want to be denied extended free medical and child care benefits? Assuming it were possible, however, would that influence your opinion of the justification for denying them the new program? Do you agree with the expert who claimed that this study, in its original design, was not that different from the Tuskegee syphilis study? Instead of assigning 90 percent of the subjects to the experimental group, what if the study assigned only 10 percent to it? That way, the 800 assigned to the experimental group may have been deemed "lucky Texans," and the rest might not have been perceived as a small group of unlucky souls who were being discriminated against. In other words, perhaps there would have been fewer objections if the state had merely a small amount of funds to test out a new program on a lucky few. Do you think that would have changed the reaction? Would that influence your own perception of the ethical justification for the experiment?

Social Worker Submits Bogus Article to Test Journal Bias

Our final illustration is the first well-publicized ethical controversy to involve a social worker's research. National news media ran several stories on it, including two stories in the *New York Times* (September 27, 1988, pp. 21, 25; and April 4, 1989, p. 21) and one in the *Chronicle of Higher Education* (November 2, 1988, pp. A1, A7). The information for this illustration was drawn primarily from those three news articles.

The social worker, William Epstein, started with the hypothesis that journal editors were biased in favor of publishing research articles whose findings confirmed the effectiveness of evaluated social work interventions and biased against publishing research articles whose findings failed to support the effectiveness of tested interventions. To test his hypothesis, Epstein fabricated a fictitious study that pretended to evaluate the effectiveness of a social work intervention designed to alleviate the symptoms of asthmatic children. (Some might deem asthma to be a psychosomatic illness.) Epstein concocted two versions of the bogus study. In one version, he fabricated findings that supported the effectiveness of the intervention; in the other version, he fabricated data that found the intervention to be ineffective.

Epstein submitted the fictitious article to 146 journals, including 33 social work journals and 113 journals in allied fields. Half of the journals received the version that supported the effectiveness of the intervention, and half received the other version. Epstein did not enter his own name as author of his fabricated article, instead using a pair of fictitious names.

In his real study, Epstein interpreted his findings as providing some support for his hypothesis: Journal editors were biased in favor of publishing the version of the bogus article with positive findings and against publishing the version with negative findings. Among the social work journals, for example, eight accepted the positive version and only four accepted the negative version. Nine journals rejected the positive version, and 12 rejected the negative version. Among the journals in allied fields, 53 percent accepted the positive version, and only 14 percent accepted the negative version. A statistical analysis indicated that the degree of support these data provided for Epstein's hypothesis was "tentative" and not statistically significant.

After being notified of the acceptance or rejection of his fictitious article, Epstein informed each journal of the real nature of his study. Later, he submitted a true article under his own name that reported his real study to the *Social Service Review*, a prestigious social work journal. That journal rejected publication of his real study, and its editor, John Schuerman, led a small group of editors who filed a formal complaint against Epstein with the National Association of Social Workers. The complaint charged Epstein with unethical conduct on two counts: (1) deceiving the journal editors who reviewed the bogus article, and (2) failing to obtain their informed consent to participate voluntarily in the study.

Schuerman, a social work professor at the University of Chicago and an author of some highly regarded research articles, recognized that sometimes the benefits of a study may warrant deceiving subjects and not obtaining their informed consent to participate. But he argued that in Epstein's (real) study, the benefits did not outweigh the time and money costs incurred for many editors and reviewers to read and critique the bogus article and staff members to process it.

When an article is submitted for publication in a professional social work journal, it is usually assigned to several volunteer reviewers, usually social work faculty members who do not get reimbursed for their review work. The reviewers do not know who the author is so that the review will be fair and unbiased. Each reviewer is expected to read each article carefully, perhaps two or three times, recommend to the journal editor whether the article should be published, and develop specific suggestions to the author for improving the article. The journal editor also is usually a faculty member volunteering his or her own time as an expected part of one's professional duties as an academician. Schuerman noted that, in addition to the time and money costs mentioned, Epstein's experiment had exacted an emotional cost: "the chagrin and embarrassment of those editors who accepted the [bogus] article" (*New York Times*, September 27, 1988, p. 25).

Epstein countered that journal editors are not the ones to judge whether the benefits of his (real) study justified its costs. In his view, the editors are predisposed to value their own costs dearly. Thus, they are unlikely to judge any study that would deceive them as being worth those costs. Epstein argued that the journals are public entities with public responsibilities. Testing whether they are biased in deciding what to publish warranted his deception and the lack of informed consent to participate, actions that were necessary to test for their bias.

One might argue that if journal editors and reviewers are biased against publishing studies that fail to confirm the effectiveness of tested interventions, then the field may not learn that certain worthless interventions in vogue are not helping clients. Moreover, if several studies disagree about the effectiveness of an intervention, and only those that confirm its effectiveness get published, then an imbalanced and selective set of replications conceivably might be disseminated to the field. This would mislead the field into believing that an intervention is yielding consistently favorable outcomes when, in fact, it is not. This could hinder the efforts of social workers to provide the most effective services to their clients—and therefore ultimately reduce the degree to which we enhance clients' well-being.

One could argue that Epstein's study could have been done ethically if he had forewarned editors that they might be receiving a bogus paper within a year and obtained their consent to participate in the study without knowing the specifics of the paper. An opposing viewpoint is that such a warning might affect the phenomenon being studied, tipping off the reviewers in a manner that predisposes them to be on guard not to reveal a real bias that actually does influence their publication decisions.

Some scholars who have expressed views somewhat sympathetic of Epstein's thesis have argued that journal editors and reviewers exert great influence on our scientific and professional knowledge base and therefore need to have their policies and procedures investigated. Schuerman, who filed the charges against Epstein, agreed with this view, but he argued that Epstein's study was not an ethical way to conduct such an investigation.

In an editorial in the March 1989 issue of the *Social Service Review*, Schuerman elaborated his position. He noted that journals have low budgets and small staffs and depend heavily on volunteer reviewers "who see their efforts as a professional responsibility" and receive little personal or professional benefit for their work (p. 3). He also portrayed Epstein's research as "badly conducted," citing several design flaws that he deemed to be so serious that they render the anticipated benefits of the Epstein study as minimal, and not worth its aforementioned costs. Schuerman also cited Epstein as admitting to serious statistical limitations in his study and to characterizing his research as only exploratory. "It is at this point that issues of research design and research ethics come together," Schuerman argued (p. 3). In other words, Schuerman's point is that the methodological quality of a study's research design can bear on its justification for violating ethical principles. If the study is so poorly designed that its findings have little value, it becomes more difficult to justify the ethical violations of the study on the grounds that its findings are so beneficial.

The initial ruling of the ethics board of the National Association of Social Workers was that Epstein had indeed violated research rules associated with deception and failure to get informed consent. It could have invoked serious sanctions against Epstein, including permanent revocation of his membership in the professional association and referral of the case to a state licensing board for additional sanctions. But Epstein was permitted to appeal the decision before any disciplinary action was taken. His appeal was upheld by the executive committee of the association, which concluded that his research did not violate its ethical rules. The committee exonerated Epstein, ruling that the case was a "disagreement about proper research methodology," not a breach of ethics. It did not publicize additional details of its rationale for upholding Epstein's appeal and reversing the initial ruling. Epstein speculated that the reversal may have been influenced by the publicity the case received in the press.

If Epstein's speculation is valid, then one might wonder whether the reversal was prompted by the executive committee's sincere judgment that the research really did not violate ethical rules or by expediency considerations, perhaps connected to concerns about potential future publicity or other costs. What do you think? What ideas do you have about the two rulings and about the ethical justification for Epstein's study? Which ruling do you agree with? Do you agree with Schuerman's contention that methodological flaws in the research design can bear on research ethics? Is it possible to agree with Schuerman on that issue and still agree with the executive committee that this case was a disagreement about methodology and not a breach of ethics? If, just for the sake of discussion, you assume that Epstein's study had serious design flaws that prevented the possibility of obtaining conclusive findings, then how would that assumption affect your position on the ethical justification for Epstein's study?

INSTITUTIONAL REVIEW BOARDS

The foregoing examples illustrate that reasonable people might disagree about the ethics of some research projects. Determining whether a particular study is ethical can be difficult and should not be based solely on the judgment of the individuals proposing the research. Researchers can try to ensure that their studies are ethical by obtaining the consent of an independent panel of professionals, called an institutional review board (IRB).

As we mentioned earlier in this chapter, IRB reviews are mandatory for research in agencies receiving federal money. IRB panelists review research proposals involving human subjects and rule on their ethics. Although there is no guarantee that every IRB decision will be the "correct" or best decision about the ethics of a proposed project, at least that decision is being made by an independent panel of professionals who—unlike the investigator proposing the study—have no vested interests or ego involvement in the proposed study.

Suppose Epstein had obtained the advance approval of an IRB at his university for his study using a bogus article to test for journal bias. (Epstein told us that his university had no IRB at that time, but that he did obtain informal feedback from some of his colleagues, who agreed that his study was ethical.) Had Epstein been able to obtain an IRB approval, even those who later depicted his study as unethical would have had no basis for charging him with unethical conduct. Instead, their complaint would have been with the IRB if it had approved his study. By not making the decision himself—and thus avoiding the chances that his own vested interests or ego involvement, if any, could have influenced his decision—Epstein would have been operating responsibly, regardless of how some might later judge the ethics of the research method. Even if we deem Epstein's study to have been ethical, we can say that obtaining IRB approval (had it been possible for him to do so) would have protected Epstein from any ensuing ethical controversy. The case has an epilogue: Epstein completed a replication of his earlier study (Epstein, 2004). This time he obtained permission from his university's IRB to waive informed consent.

IRBs vary in the amount and format of materials they require to describe the proposed research. In the process of deciding whether to approve a research proposal, an IRB may require certain modifications to make the research acceptable, such as providing additional information to subjects before their consent to participate is obtained. For example, some social work research studies might involve situations in which ethical considerations dictate that confidentiality not be maintained, such as when child abuse is unexpectedly encountered or when respondents are at imminent risk of seriously harming themselves or others. You may need to add this contingency to your own consent form and IRB application form. You may also need to assure your participants and your IRB that you will arrange for services to be offered to any subject you encounter who needs them. Because they vary so much, we suggest that you examine your university's IRB forms and procedures, which may be accessible online. Alternatively, you can examine Figure 4-3, which presents condensed and partial excerpts from the template used by the University of Texas at Austin to guide investigators as to what materials to submit in their applications for IRB approval. It will give you an idea of the kinds of things that are commonly required by other IRBs.

If you are fortunate enough to have a research instructor who requires that you design and carry out a research project, then you may find that you have to get your study approved by your university's IRB before you can begin collecting data. Moreover, if your research project is to be carried out in an agency that receives federal money, you may have to obtain approval from both your school's IRB and the agency's IRB. Just what you needed, right? Don't panic. Perhaps your study will qualify for an exemption from a full review and you'll be able to obtain approval within a few days. Federal regulations allow IRBs to grant exemptions to certain kinds of studies, although institutions vary considerably in interpreting the federal regulations. Exempt studies receive an expedited review. Studies may qualify for an exemption from a full review if they:

1. Are conducted as part of normal educational practices, including research on the effectiveness of alternative educational approaches

2. Use educational tests with adequate protection of confidentiality

3. Use survey or interview procedures or observe public behavior while protecting confidentiality

4. Use existing data without violating confidentiality

5. Are federal demonstration projects

6. Survey or interview elected or appointed public officials or candidates for public office, without violating confidentiality

The actual and precise wording of the exemptions is much more complicated and ought to be available from your IRB. Most student research (with the exception of doctoral dissertations) qualifies for at least one exemption, particularly the first, third, or fourth. Note that studies that appear to meet one or more exemptions might still require a full review if subjects can be identified, if knowledge of their responses could place them at risk of some sort of harm, or if the data are sensitive. Of course, if your study involves some controversial procedures—such as pretending to faint every time your instructor mentions statistics so you can see whether research instructors are capable of exhibiting compassion or whether this

I. Title
II. Investigators (co-investigators)
III. Hypothesis, Research Questions, or Goals of the Project
IV. Background and Significance
V. Research Method, Design, and Proposed Statistical Analysis
VI. Human Subject Interactions

A. Identify the **sources of potential participants,** derived materials, or date. Describe the characteristics of the subject population such as their anticipated number, age, sex, ethnic background, and state of health. Identify the criteria for inclusion and/or exclusion. Explain the rationale for the use of special classes of participants whose ability to give voluntary informed consent may be in question. Such participants include students in one's class, people currently undergoing treatment for an illness or problem that is the topic of the research study, people who are mentally retarded, people with a mental illness, people who are institutionalized, prisoners, etc. When do you expect human subject involvement in this project to begin and when do you expect it to end?

If the participants are prisoners or residents of correction facilities, the composition of the IRB must be augmented by a prisoner's advocate. Please inform the IRB if this applies to your project.

If some of the potential participants or the parents of child participants are likely to be more fluent in a language other than English, the consent forms should be translated into that language. Both English and the other language versions of the form should be provided, with one language on one side of a page and the other on the other side of the page. This translation may be completed after IRB approval of the study and consent forms. Specify here your intentions with respect to the languages of the consent forms. (If you plan to conduct your study with students from the Austin Independent School District, you will be required to provide a Spanish language version of your parental consent form.)

B. Describe the **procedures for the recruitment of the participants.** Append copies of fliers and the content of newspaper or radio advertisements. If potential participants will be screened by an interview (either telephone or face-to-face) provide a script of the screening interview.

If the potential participants are members of a group that may be construed as stigmatized (e.g., spousal abusers, members of support groups, people with AIDS, etc.) your initial contact with the potential participants should be through advertisements or fliers or through people who interact with the potential participants because of their job duties. These people may describe your study to the potential participants and ask them to contact you if they are interested in talking to you about the study.

C. Describe the **procedure for obtaining informed consent.**

D. Research Protocol. What will you ask your participants to do? When and where will they do it? How long will it take them to do it? Describe the type of research information that you will be gathering from your subjects, i.e., the data that you will collect. *Append copies of all surveys, testing materials, questionnaires, and assessment devices. Append copies of topics and sample questions for non-structured interviews and focus group discussions.*

VII. Describe any **potential risks** (physical, psychological, social, legal, or other) and assess their likelihood and seriousness.

Describe the procedures for protecting against (or minimizing) any potential risks and include an assessment of their effectiveness. Discuss the procedures that will be used to maintain the confidentiality of the research data.

If your study involves deception, describe the procedures for debriefing the participants.

VIII. Describe and assess the **potential benefits** to be gained by participants (if any) and the benefits that may accrue to society in general as a result of the planned work. Discuss the risks in relation to the anticipated benefits to the participants and to society.

IX. Indicate the specific **sites or agencies involved in the research project** besides The University of Texas at Austin. These agencies may include school districts, day care centers, nursing homes, etc. Include, as an attachment, approval letters from these institutions or agencies on their letterhead. The letter should grant you permission to use the agency's facilities or resources; it should indicate knowledge of the study that will be conducted at the site. If these letters are not available at the time of IRB review, approval will be contingent upon their receipt.

SOURCE: Reprinted with permission of the University of Texas at Austin Institutional Review Board.

Figure 4-3 Excerpts from the Template to Guide Research Proposals Used by the University of Texas at Austin's Institutional Review Board

is an effective way to influence exam content—then obtaining IRB approval may be problematic (not to mention what it will do to your grade when the instructor reads your report). Other (more realistic) problematic examples include surveys on sensitive topics such as drug abuse or sexual practices or on traumatic events that may be painful for respondents to remember.

BIAS AND INSENSITIVITY REGARDING GENDER AND CULTURE

In several chapters of this book, you will encounter examples of how gender and cultural bias and insensitivity can hinder the methodological quality of a study and therefore the validity of its findings. Much has been written about these problems in recent years, and some theorists have suggested that when researchers conduct studies in a sexist or a culturally insensitive manner, they are not just committing methodological errors but also going awry ethically.

The question of ethics arises because some studies are perceived to perpetuate harm to women and minorities. Feminist and minority scholars have suggested a number of ways that such harm can be done. Interviewers who are culturally insensitive can offend minority respondents. If they conduct their studies in culturally insensitive ways, then their findings may yield implications for action that ignore the needs and realities of minorities, may incorrectly (and perhaps stereotypically) portray minorities, or may inappropriately generalize in an unhelpful way. By the same token, studies with gender bias or insensitivity may be seen as perpetuating a male-dominated world or failing to consider the potentially different implications for men and women in one's research.

Various authors have recommended ways to avoid cultural and gender bias and insensitivity in one's research. We will cover these recommendations in greater depth in later chapters on methodology—especially Chapter 5 on culturally competent research—but we'll also mention them here in light of their potential ethical relevance. Among the more commonly recommended guidelines regarding research on minorities are the following:

- Spend some time immersing yourself directly in the culture of the minority group(s) that will be included in your study (for example, using qualitative research methods described in Chapters 17 and 18) before finalizing your research design.
- Engage minority scholars and community representatives in the formulation of the research problem and in all the stages of the research to ensure that the research is responsive to the needs and perspectives of minorities.
- Involve representatives of minority groups who will be studied in the development of the research design and measurement instruments.
- Do not automatically assume that instruments successfully used in prior studies of one ethnic group can yield valid information when applied to other ethnic groups.
- Use culturally sensitive language in your measures, perhaps including a non-English translation.
- Use in-depth pretesting of your measures to correct problematic language and flaws in translation.
- Use bilingual interviewers when necessary.
- Be attuned to the potential need to use minority interviewers instead of nonminorities to interview minority respondents.
- In analyzing your data, look for ways in which the findings may differ among different categories of ethnicity.
- Avoid an unwarranted focus exclusively on the deficits of minorities; perhaps focus primarily on their strengths.
- In addition to looking for differences among different ethnic groups, look for differences among varying levels of acculturation within specific minority groups.
- Assess your own cross-cultural competence.
- Look for cross-cultural studies in your literature review.
- Use specialized sampling strategies (discussed in Chapters 5 and 14) that are geared toward adequately representing minority groups.

In her book *Nonsexist Research Methods*, Margrit Eichler (1988) recommended the following feminist guidelines to avoid gender bias and insensitivity in one's research:

- If a study is done on only one gender, make that clear in the title and the narrative and don't generalize the findings to the other gender.

• Don't use sexist language or concepts (for example, males referred to as "head of household," and females referred to as "spouses").

• Don't use a double standard in framing the research question (such as looking at the work–parenthood conflict for mothers but not for fathers).

• Don't overemphasize male-dominated activities in research instruments (such as by assessing social functioning primarily in terms of career activities and neglecting activities in homemaking and child rearing).

• In analyzing your data, look for ways in which the findings might differ for men and women.

• Don't assume that measurement instruments used successfully with males are automatically valid for women.

• Be sure to report the proportion of males and females in your study sample.

THE POLITICS OF SOCIAL WORK RESEARCH

At this point, you may have gleaned that a fine line can be found between ethical and political issues in social work research. Both ethics and politics hinge on ideological points of view. What is unacceptable from one point of view may be acceptable from another. Thus, we will see that people disagree on political aspects of research just as they disagree on ethical ones. As we change topics now, we will distinguish ethical from political issues in two ways.

First, although ethics and politics are often closely intertwined, the ethics of social work research deals more with the methods employed, whereas political issues are more concerned with the practical costs and use of research. Thus, for example, some social workers raise ethical objections to experiments that evaluate the effectiveness of social work services by providing those services to one group of clients while delaying their provision to another group of clients. Those who voice these objections say that the harm done to clients in delaying service provision outweighs the benefits to be derived from evaluating the effectiveness of those services.

A political objection, on the other hand, might be that if the results of the evaluation were to suggest that the services were not effective, then those negative results might hurt agency funding. Another political objection might be that withholding services would reduce the amount of fees for service or third-party payments received, not to mention the bad publicity that would be risked regarding agency "neglect" of people in need.

Second, ethical aspects can be distinguished from political aspects of social work research because there are no formal codes of accepted political conduct that are comparable to the codes of ethical conduct we discussed earlier. Although some ethical norms have political aspects—for example, not harming subjects clearly relates to our protection of civil liberties—no one has developed a set of political norms that can be agreed on by social work researchers. The only partial exception to the lack of political norms is in the generally accepted view that a researcher's personal political orientation should not interfere with or unduly influence his or her scientific research. It would be considered improper for you to use shoddy techniques or lie about your research as a way to further your political views. As you can imagine, however, studies are often enough attacked for allegedly violating this norm.

Objectivity and Ideology

In Chapter 3, we suggested that social research can never be totally objective, because researchers are humanly subjective. Science attempts to achieve objectivity by using accepted research techniques that are intended to arrive at the same results, regardless of the subjective views of the scientists who use them. Social scientists are further urged to seek facts, regardless of how those facts accord with their cherished beliefs or personal politics.

But many scholars do not believe that social research is ever entirely value-free. They argue that values can influence any phase of the research process, such as the selection of a research question or sample or the definition of a variable. For example, when investigators are evaluating the effectiveness of a program to help battered women, values about family stability or women's welfare can influence what outcome indicators of program effectiveness are chosen.

Those researchers who cherish maintaining family stability may define effectiveness in terms of whether the batterer was reformed, thus enabling the family to stay together safely. Those who are more concerned about women's rights and safety than about family stability might choose an opposite indicator of program effectiveness, such as whether it empowers the battered woman to divorce her husband.

In another example, planners working for a state bureaucracy that is researching the effectiveness of a new state program or policy may focus the research on whether the new approach saves the state money, such as when a new case management program reduces state hospitalization costs for its mentally ill citizens. In their zeal to meet budget-balancing priorities, planners may not think to study indicators of client well-being. Perhaps many people in need of hospitalization are worse off under the new program, for example. Clinical researchers, on the other hand, may evaluate the effectiveness of the new program in terms of its effects on the symptomatology or quality of life of the mentally ill individuals, perhaps believing that those concerns are more important than saving taxpayer money on services that are already underfunded and inadequate. In their zeal to maximize client well-being, they may not think to examine the program costs that are required to produce specific increments of benefit to clients.

Here is one more example. Researchers of homelessness may be influenced by their values in the way they define homelessness, which in turn influences whom they include in their sample of homeless individuals. Do the homeless include only people living in the streets? Or do they also include people "doubling up" with friends or relatives or living in squalid, temporary quarters who cannot find a decent place they can afford? It is difficult to make such decisions independently of our values. Researchers who have been active in social action efforts to alleviate homelessness may be predisposed to choose the broader definition, which will indicate a greater number of the homeless; researchers who believe social welfare spending is wasteful and incurs too much dependency among the poor may be predisposed to choose the narrower definition.

Scholars who believe that social research is never really value-free typically recommend that we should be aware of and describe our values upfront rather than kid ourselves or others that we are completely objective. Indeed, not all social scientists agree that researchers should try to separate their values from their research activities. Some have argued that social science and social action cannot and should not be separated. Explanations of the status quo in society, they contend, shade subtly into defenses of that same status quo. Simple explanations of the social functions of, say, discrimination can easily become justifications for its continuance. By the same token, merely studying society and its ills without a commitment to making society more humane has been called irresponsible.

Social work has a long tradition of using research as a tool to try to make society more humane. Zimbalist (1977), for example, describes how the profession embraced the social survey movement at the turn of the 20th century as a way to convince society to enact environmental reform to alleviate a host of urban problems. In its overriding concern to spur social reform, the social survey movement was frequently selective in what facts it would present, attempting to "make a case" rather than providing a scientifically disciplined and balanced presentation and interpretation of data.

Social work researchers today may attempt to be more objective than they were a century ago, but their efforts still commonly carry on the tradition of using research findings to spur social action. For example, surveys on homelessness may be conducted in the hope that their findings will influence legislators and their tax-averse constituents to spend more public funds to alleviate homelessness. A social service agency might survey a community to learn of unmet needs that it can try to meet. Survey results might imply the need for new types of agency services and might be used to convince funding sources to grant new money to the agency to help it better address the unmet needs that its research uncovers.

There is nothing wrong with viewing research as a tool that can be used to alleviate human suffering and promote social welfare. Indeed, in the social work profession, that is what research is all about. From a scientific standpoint, however, it is one thing to let our values spur us to undertake specific research projects in the hope that the truth we discover will foster the achievement of humanitarian aims. It is quite another to let our values or ideological beliefs spur us to hide from or distort the truth by biasing the way we conduct our research or interpret its findings. Attempting to be completely objective and value-free in the way we conduct research is an impossible ideal, and it is risky to kid ourselves into thinking that we are completely neutral. This does not mean, however, that we shouldn't try to keep our beliefs from distorting our pursuit of truth. Being aware of our biases throughout all phases of our research helps us minimize their impact on our work. And being up-front in describing our predilections to others better prepares them to evaluate the validity of our findings.

You may find this a bit unsettling. How will we ever know what's true if the goal of being completely objective is so hard to attain and if we are constantly producing new research that disagrees with previous research? In Chapter 1, we noted that science is an open-ended enterprise in which conclusions are constantly being modified. Inquiry on a given topic is never completed, and the eventual overturning of established theories is an accepted fact of life. In light of this, many social work practitioners may simply opt to be guided exclusively by tradition and authority. Rather than use research findings to help guide their practice (in keeping with the evidence-based practice process), they merely attempt to conform to the traditional ways of operating in their particular agency or to the ordinations of prestigious, experienced practitioners whom they respect. However, according to NASW's Code of Ethics, refusing to utilize research to guide their practice is unethical. Moreover, they should realize that various practice authorities themselves are unlikely to be completely objective.

Social Research and Race

In light of the foregoing discussion, you may not be surprised to learn that some social science research studies have stimulated considerable controversy about whether their findings were merely intrusions of a researcher's own political values. Nowhere have social research and politics been more controversially intertwined than in the area of race relations.

For the most part, social scientists during the 20th century supported the cause of African American equality in the United States. Many were actively involved in the civil rights movement, some more radically than others. Thus, social scientists were able to draw research conclusions that support the cause of equality without fear of criticism from colleagues. To recognize the solidity of the general social science position in the matter of equality, we need to examine only a few research projects that have produced conclusions that disagree with the predominant ideological position.

Most social scientists—overtly, at least—supported the end of even de facto school segregation. Thus, an immediate and heated controversy was provoked in 1966 when James Coleman, a respected sociologist, published the results of a major national study of race and education. Contrary to general agreement, Coleman found little difference in academic performance between African American students attending integrated schools and those attending segregated ones. Indeed, such obvious things as libraries, laboratory facilities, and high expenditures per student made little difference. Instead, Coleman reported that family and neighborhood factors had the most influence on academic achievement. Coleman's findings were not well received by many of the social scientists who had been active in the civil rights movement. Some scholars criticized Coleman's work on methodological grounds, but many others objected hotly on the grounds that the findings would have segregationist political consequences.

Another example of political controversy surrounding social research in connection with race concerns the issue of IQ scores of black and white people. In 1969, Arthur Jensen, a Harvard psychologist, was asked to prepare an article for the *Harvard Educational Review* that would examine the data on racial differences in IQ test results (Jensen, 1969). In the article, Jensen concluded that genetic differences between African Americans and whites accounted for the lower average IQ scores of African Americans. He became so identified with that position that he appeared on college campuses across the country discussing it.

Jensen's position was attacked on numerous methodological bases. It was charged that many of the data on which Jensen's conclusion was based were inadequate and sloppy—there are many IQ tests, some worse than others. Similarly, critics argued that Jensen had not sufficiently accounted for social-environment factors. Other social scientists raised other appropriate methodological objections.

Beyond the scientific critique, however, Jensen was condemned by many as a racist. He was booed, and his public presentations were drowned out by hostile crowds. Jensen's reception by several university audiences was not significantly different from the reception received by abolitionists a century before, when the prevailing opinion favored leaving the institution of slavery intact.

A similar reaction erupted in response to a book titled *The Bell Curve*, published in 1994 and coauthored by Charles Murray, a sociologist known as a leading thinker on the political right, and the late Richard J. Herrnstein, a psychologist and distinguished professor at Harvard University. A small portion of the lengthy book argues that ethnic differences in intelligence can be attributed in part (but not exclusively) to genetic factors.

In their book, Murray and Herrnstein see intelligence as a crucial factor that influences whether Americans will prosper or wind up in an underclass culture of poverty and other social ills. Based on the thesis that intelligence is so hard to change, the book recommends against spending money on a variety of social programs, including those aimed at improving the intellectual performance of disadvantaged youths.

Critics have pointed to serious methodological shortcomings in the procedures and conclusions in the Murray and Herrnstein study. But as with the earlier controversy involving Jensen, what is most germane to this chapter is not the methodological critique of *The Bell Curve,* but its political condemnation. When the book first appeared, its early critics gave more attention to political objections than to the study's serious methodological shortcomings. It was attacked in a *Boston Globe* editorial before it was even published. The *Washington Post* reported that former Education Secretary William Bennett, a conservative supporter and friend of Murray, strongly praised the book but was made nervous by the section on race and intelligence. Because of that section, Bennett reportedly characterized Murray as a "marked man."

New Republic magazine devoted its October 31, 1994, issue to the book. The issue contains a 10-page article by Murray and Herrnstein, based on the section of their book that dealt with intelligence and genetics. Preceding that article are 17 pages of editorials by 20 different authors about both *The Bell Curve* and Murray and Herrnstein's *New Republic* article. Some of the editorials debate whether the magazine was ethical in even considering publishing the article, and most sharply attack the article or criticize the magazine's decision to publish it. One editorial depicts Murray and Herrnstein as dishonest. Another portrays them as seeking to justify oppression. Others liken them to racists trying to justify their racism or to bigots practicing pseudoscientific racism. One harsher editorial, titled "Neo-Nazis," implies that the relevant chapter from Murray and Herrnstein's book is "a chilly synthesis" of the findings of previous works published by neo-Nazis.

In an editorial that justified the decision to publish the Murray and Herrnstein article on grounds of free inquiry, the magazine's editor argued that the burden of proof for suppressing debate on the topic rests with those who seek to suppress the debate. The editorial argues for judging the issue on scientific and logical grounds, not tarring and feathering the authors by impugning their motives or by associating them with Nazis. The editorial also responds to critics who claim that *The Bell Curve* hurts the feelings of African Americans, especially African American children, who don't want to be called genetically inferior. The editor depicts the view that African Americans are vulnerable people who must be shielded from free and open intellectual exchange as itself inherently racist.

Many social scientists limited their objections to the Coleman, Jensen, and Murray and Herrnstein research to scientific, methodological grounds. The purpose of our account, however, is to point out that political ideology often gets involved in matters of social research. Although the abstract model of science is divorced from ideology, the practice of science is not.

When political and ideological forces restrict scientific inquiry in one area, this can have unfortunate spin-off effects that restrict needed inquiry in related areas. For example, in 1991 Lovell Jones, director of Experimental Gynecology–Endocrinology at the University of Texas's M. D. Anderson Cancer Center, expressed concern regarding the dearth of health research about the higher rate of mortality seen in African American women with breast cancer as compared to white women with breast cancer. Jones postulated that one plausible factor that might contribute to the higher mortality rate among African American women is that they have more breast tumors that are "estrogen receptor negative," which means that those tumors tend to be more "aggressive." Jones found it striking that there had been no concrete studies to investigate this possibility; based on feedback he had received from white research colleagues, he thought he knew why. His colleagues told him that they did not want to pursue this line of inquiry because it would be too controversial politically. They said the research would have to delve into racial differences in genetic predispositions to breast tumors. They feared that they would therefore be accused, like Jensen was, of racial bias—if not for their own findings on breast tumors, then for making it easier for other investigators to study more politically sensitive differences in genetic predispositions between African Americans and whites (differences connected to intelligence, for example).

Jones also observed that for 10 years (as of 1991) we had known that white women with a family history of breast cancer have a higher risk of developing breast cancer than do white women with no family history. Jones reasoned that the field should have quickly followed up this research by investigating whether the same holds true for African American women with and without family histories of breast cancer. But not until 10 years after the research on white women first appeared did the first study on African American women come out. Jones attributed this time lapse to the political risk that faced researchers in conducting such an investigation; the researchers feared that if they were to find that the risk of African American women getting breast cancer is higher than that of white women, they would be attacked as racists.

Jones further recounted how he was once told by a staff member of a national news program that a spokesperson for the National Cancer Institute suggested that they would prefer that the word *genetics* not be used in commenting on cancer among African Americans. In a somewhat related incident, Jones recalled how he once wrote an editorial for a prominent newspaper, an editorial that discussed cancer among minority populations. The paper's editor called him to say that the paper could not run the editorial because it would be accused of racial bias if it did. But when the editor learned that Jones was African American, he said, "Well then, we can use it."

Jones's comments* illustrate how politically rooted taboos against certain lines of inquiry may do a disservice to the very people they seek to protect. What is your opinion about such taboos? Are some or all of them justified? Or is the benefit of ensuring that some research findings will not be misused for harmful purposes outweighed by the risk that such taboos will keep others from conducting much needed research in related areas?

Main Points

- Social work research projects are likely to be shaped not only by technical, scientific considerations but also by administrative, ethical, and political considerations.

- What's ethically "right" and "wrong" in research is ultimately a matter of what people agree is right and wrong.

- Scientists agree that participation in research should, as a general norm, be voluntary. This norm, however, can conflict with the scientific need for generalizability.

- Probably all scientists agree that research should not harm those who participate in it, unless the participants willingly and knowingly accept the risks of harm.

- *Anonymity* refers to the situation in which even the researcher cannot identify an individual by the specific information that has been supplied.

- *Confidentiality* refers to the situation in which the researcher—although knowing which data describe which subjects—agrees to keep that information confidential.

- In some instances, the long-term benefits of a study are thought to outweigh the violation of certain ethical norms. But determining whether a study's ends justify its means is a difficult and often highly subjective process. Nowadays, institutional review boards make such determinations in approving studies.

- Bias and insensitivity about gender and culture have become ethical issues for many social scientists.

- Guidelines have been proposed by feminist and other scholars.

- Although science is neutral on political matters, scientists are not.

- Even though the norms of science cannot force individual scientists to give up their personal values, the use of accepted scientific practices provides a safeguard against "scientific" findings being the product of bias alone.

- Ideological priorities can restrict inquiry out of a fear that certain truths can be misperceived or misused in a manner that will harm certain vulnerable groups; this restriction can lead to incomplete or distorted knowledge building that risks harming the people it seeks to protect.

Review Questions and Exercises

1. Suppose a social work researcher decides to interview children who were placed for adoption in infancy by their biological parents. The interviewer will focus on their feelings about someday meeting their biological parents. Discuss the ethical problems the researcher would face and how those might be avoided.

*Lovell Jones's comments were presented in part at the Texas Minority Health Strategic Planning Conference, Austin, Texas, July 18, 1991, in his presentation titled "The Impact of Cancer on the Health Status of Minorities in Texas." Jones elaborated on his conference remarks in a telephone conversation with Allen Rubin on July 25, 1991. Some of the material included in his comments is covered in Jerome Wilson, "Cancer Incidence and Mortality Differences of Black and White Americans: A Role for Biomarkers," in Lovell Jones (ed.), *Minorities and Cancer,* 1989, Springer Verlag, pp. 5–20.

2. Suppose a researcher personally opposed to transracial adoption wants to conduct an interview survey to explore the impact of transracial adoption on the self-images of adoptees. Discuss the personal involvement problems he or she would face and how those might be avoided.

3. Consider the following real and hypothetical research situations. Identify the ethical component in each. How do you feel about it? Do you feel the procedures described are ultimately acceptable or unacceptable? It might be useful to discuss some of these with classmates.

a. A social work professor asks students in a social policy class to complete questionnaires that the instructor will analyze and use in preparing a journal article for publication.

b. After a field study of a demonstration of civil disobedience, law enforcement officials demand that the researcher identify those people who were observed breaking the law. Rather than risk arrest as an accomplice after the fact, the researcher complies.

c. After completing the final draft of a book reporting a research project, the researcher and author discovers that 25 of the 2,000 survey interviews were falsified by interviewers, but the author chooses to ignore that fact and publishes the book anyway.

d. Researchers obtain a list of abusive parents they wish to study. They contact the parents with the explanation that each has been selected "at random" from among the general population to take a sampling of "public opinion."

e. A social work doctoral student is conducting dissertation research on the disciplinary styles of abusive parents with toddlers. Each parent and his or her child enter a room with toys scattered around it, and the parent is asked to have the child straighten up the toys before playing with them. The parent is told that the researcher will observe the parent–child interactions from behind a one-way mirror.

f. In a study of sexual behavior, the investigator wants to overcome subjects' reluctance to report what they might regard as deviant behavior. To get past their reluctance, subjects are asked the following question: "Everyone masturbates now and then. About how much do you masturbate?"

g. A researcher discovers that 85 percent of the students in a particular university smoke marijuana regularly. Publication of this finding will probably create a furor in the community. Because no extensive analysis of drug use is planned, the researcher decides to ignore the finding and keep it quiet.

h. To test the extent to which social work practitioners may try to save face by expressing clinical views on matters about which they are wholly uninformed, the researcher asks for their clinical opinion about a fictitious practice model.

i. A research questionnaire is circulated among clients as part of their agency's intake forms. Although clients are not told they must complete the questionnaire, the hope is that they will believe they must—thus ensuring a higher completion rate.

j. A participant-observer pretends to join a group that opposes family planning services so she can study it, and she is successfully accepted as a member of the inner planning circle. What should the researcher do if the group makes plans for: (1) a peaceful, though illegal, demonstration against family planning services? (2) the bombing of an abortion clinic during a time when it is sure to be unoccupied?

Internet Exercises

1. Use InfoTrac College Edition to find an article that discusses ethical issues in social research. Click the "Key Words" icon and then enter one of the following terms: *research ethics, informed consent,* or *institutional review boards.* Then click on "Submit Search." Read an article that piques your interest. Write down the bibliographical reference information for the article and summarize the article in a few sentences.

2. Repeat Internet Exercise 1, this time entering the term *research politics* as the key words.

3. Using InfoTrac College Edition, search for *informed consent* and then narrow your search to *research.* Skim the resulting articles and begin to identify groups of people for whom informed consent may be problematic—people who may not be able to give it. Suggest some ways in which the problem might be overcome.

4. Visit the National Institutes of Health (NIH) Human Subjects/Research Ethics Tutorial site at http://cme.nci.nih.gov/. www.cancer.gov/clinicaltrials/learning/page3. Click on the prompt for "Human Participant Protections Education for Research Teams." If you take the online tutorial at this site, you will receive a certificate of completion that some IRBs now require of principal investigators and their research assistants working on studies involving human subjects. This certificate might therefore come in handy later on if you become a research assistant or need IRB approval for your research. You might also ask your instructor if extra credit could be granted for obtaining this certificate.

5. Visit http://hsc.virginia.edu/hs-library/historical/apology/ for more information on the Tuskegee syphilis study and additional Web links on that topic. Alternatively, you can use a search engine to search for the key word *Tuskegee.*

Additional Readings

Jones, James H. 1981. *Bad Blood: The Tuskegee Syphilis Experiment.* New York: The Free Press. This remarkable book provides a fascinating account of the Tuskegee study we discussed in this chapter. Its account of the history of that study may astound you, and you may be inspired by the tale of a social worker whose relentless battles over several years with public health authorities and ultimately his willingness to use the press got the study stopped.

Lee, Raymond. 1993. *Doing Research on Sensitive Topics.* Newbury Park, CA: Sage. This book examines the conflicts between scientific research needs and the rights of the people involved—with guidelines for dealing with such conflicts.

Potocky, Miriam, and Antoinette Y. Rodgers-Farmer (eds.). 1998. *Social Work Research with Minority and Oppressed Populations.* New York: Haworth Press. This collection of articles contains innovative ideas for avoiding cultural bias and insensitivity in research with minority and oppressed populations; these groups include people living with HIV or AIDS, low-income urban adolescents, women of color, nonwhite ethnic elders, and African American children.

Sweet, Stephen. 1999. "Using a Mock Institutional Review Board to Teach Ethics in Sociological Research," *Teaching Sociology* 27 (January), 55–59. Though written for professors, this article provides some research examples that challenge your ethical instincts.

CHAPTER 5

Culturally Competent Research

What You'll Learn in This Chapter

In Chapter 4 we noted that cultural bias and insensitivity is an ethical issue. Avoiding them requires cultural competence. In this chapter we will go beyond ethics and examine how cultural competence can influence the success of social work research studies and the validity of their findings. You'll see how researchers can formulate and conceptualize research problems in ways that are responsive to the concerns of minority populations, improve the cultural sensitivity of the measurement procedures they use, interpret their findings in a culturally competent manner, and improve the recruitment and retention of minority and oppressed populations as participants in their research.

INTRODUCTION

Much of social work practice—at the macro as well as micro levels—involves minority and oppressed populations. Consequently, in social work education a heavy emphasis is placed on helping students learn more about cultural diversity and become more culturally competent practitioners. Cultural competence is also important in the research curriculum. In research, the term **cultural competence** means being aware of and appropriately responding to the ways in which cultural factors and cultural differences should influence what we investigate, how we investigate, and how we interpret our findings.

Research Participants

Culturally competent researchers will attempt to include a sufficient and representative number of research participants from minority and oppressed populations. Moreover, they will learn how to maximize the likelihood of obtaining such participation. Studies that do not include adequate representation from specific minority and oppressed populations in their samples—no matter how rigorously the studies are designed in other respects—are not generalizable to those populations.

In reviewing this problem, Hohmann and Parron (1996) discussed several studies showing that different cultural groups utilize services differently, have different expectations of services, and interpret and react differently to the problems for which they seek services. Thus, if members of particular minority groups are underrepresented in studies evaluating the effectiveness of interventions, how do we know whether they would benefit from those interventions?

In light of the emphasis on cultural competence in the social work curriculum, you may be surprised to learn that an emphasis on cultural competence in research in social work and allied fields is a relatively recent development. Acknowledging that minority participants historically have not been adequately represented in clinical research, the National Institutes of Health (NIH) in 1994 issued a new policy mandating that all research projects funded by NIH that involve human subjects must include adequate representation of women and members of ethnic minority groups in their samples. Exceptions to this requirement could be justified only with a "clear and compelling" rationale (Miranda, 1996). Moreover, the new policy stipulated that research proposals must include detailed plans for how women and minority participants would be recruited and retained in the study. Investigators are now required to describe their prior experience in recruiting and retaining such participants, report collaborations with other researchers who have this experience, and provide letters of support for their study from relevant community groups (Hohmann and Parron, 1996).

As implied in the NIH stipulations, just seeking representation of minorities in your study does not guarantee that you will get it. Successfully recruiting and retaining minority participants in research requires special, culturally sensitive knowledge and efforts, which we will discuss in this chapter. One such requirement involves being responsive to the concerns of minority communities in the way research problems are formulated. Insensitivity to those concerns can lead not only to problems in recruitment and retention of participants, but also to findings that are not relevant to the needs perceived by members of those communities.

Measurement

An additional feature of culturally competent research is the use of measurement procedures that have been shown to be reliable and valid for the minority and oppressed populations participating in the research. (We'll examine the concepts of reliability and validity in measurement in Chapter 8.) If we measure the outcome of our interventions with instruments that are not reliable or valid for some ethnic minority participants, even interventions that are very effective will yield misleading results for those participants. For example, if we ask questions that respondents don't understand, their answers will be unreliable. If the questions mean something to them other than what we intend them to mean, our information will not be valid. Thus, even if our intervention is helping them attain their goal, our measures may not indicate that attainment because they are not really measuring that goal.

Data Analysis and Interpretation

Cultural competence can also affect how data are analyzed and interpreted. Culturally competent researchers will not just be interested in whether minority groups differ from the majority group. If they have a sufficiently diverse sample of research participants, rather than combine all minority groups together as one category to compare to the majority group in the data analysis, they will compare the various minority groups to each other. There are two reasons for this. First, it would be culturally insensitive to be concerned only with how minority groups as a whole compare to the majority group and not with each other. Second, different minority groups differ from the majority group in different ways. For example, Asian Americans on average currently have higher levels of academic achievement than American Caucasians, whereas some other minority groups in the United States on average currently have lower levels of academic achievement than Caucasians. Thus, if the Asian Americans' achievement levels were combined with the levels of one or more of the minority groups with lower levels, their combined (average) level might be close to that of Caucasians. This would mask the real differences as compared to Caucasians, and would overlook important differences between the minority groups.

Cultural insensitivity in the data analysis and reporting phases of research can also result in interpreting ethnic differences in a prejudicial manner, focusing too much on the deficits of minorities and too little on their strengths. Miranda (1996), for example, cites studies that interpreted the lower likelihood to delay gratification among inner-city minority children, as compared to middle-class white children, as innate deficits. Miranda depicts this as a racist interpretation because it overlooked the possibility that the inner-city minority children were merely responding in an adaptive manner to their disadvantaged environment.

Cultural insensitivity in interpreting data can also occur when ethnic minorities are not even included in a study and yet its findings are generalized as if they had been included. Likewise, studies whose research participants include only one gender should clarify that its results do not generalize to the other gender.

Because minority groups are more likely to be poor than majority populations, culturally competent researchers will include *socioeconomic factors* in their analyses when they are studying other ways in which minority and majority populations differ. For example, if their findings show that African Americans are less likely than whites to be interested in long-term psychodynamic forms of treatment, rather than considering only cultural factors as the explanation, they will examine whether the difference can be explained by the fact that African Americans are more likely to be poor and therefore more in need of the crisis services to deal with the pressing day-to-day problems confronting poor people of any ethnicity—such as services for problems in finances, unemployment, and housing.

Acculturation

Culturally competent researchers will also consider the *immigration experience* and *acculturation* as factors to include in their research as they study differences between minority and majority populations. Sensitivity to these factors will also alert researchers to study differences within a particular minority group. For example, Latinos or Asians who recently immigrated to the United States are likely to have different needs and problems, have different attitudes about child rearing or marital roles, and respond to social services differently than Latinos or Asians whose parents or grandparents have lived in the United States for several decades or longer. The longer a member of a minority culture has lived amidst a majority culture, the more likely that person is to be acculturated to the majority culture. **Acculturation** is the process in which a group or individual changes after coming into contact with a majority culture, taking on the language, values, attitudes, and lifestyle preferences of the majority culture. If you want to study factors influencing service utilization patterns or child-rearing attitudes among Korean Americans, for example, degree of acculturation is one of the factors you should examine.

Impact of Cultural Insensitivity on Research Climate

Misleading results are not the only harm that can come from culturally insensitive research. In Chapter 4, on ethics, we noted that culturally insensitive interviewers can offend minority respondents. Moreover, studies that use culturally insensitive procedures, or which are not responsive to the concerns of minority populations, can poison the climate for future research among those populations. For example, Norton and Manson (1996) discussed the harmful impact of news headlines resulting from press releases put out by investigators in a 1979 study of alcohol use among the Inupiat tribe in Alaska. One headline read,

"Alcohol Plagues Eskimos." Another read, "Sudden Wealth Sparks Epidemic of Alcoholism." Overnight, Standard & Poor's dramatically reduced the bond rating of the Inupiat community, which meant that some important municipal projects could no longer be funded. Consequently, some Alaska Native tribes no longer are receptive to research on alcoholism, despite the importance of that problem in their communities.

Now that we see the importance of cultural competence in social work research, let's look at how researchers can attempt to make their studies more culturally competent. We'll start with the process of problem formulation.

DEVELOPING CULTURAL COMPETENCE

If you want to conduct research on an ethnic minority population, it would behoove you to know quite a bit about that population's culture. Thus, before you begin any investigation it is crucial that you are well read in the literature on the culture of minority or oppressed populations relevant to your study. This should include readings that describe the culture and its values as well as research studies dealing with issues bearing on the participation of its members in your study.

In other words, you should develop **cultural competence** regarding the population you want to include in your study. As discussed by Vonk (2001), cultural competence involves knowledge, attitudes, and skills. You should understand the minority culture's historical experiences—including the effects of prejudice and oppression—and how those experiences influence the ways in which its members live and view members of the dominant culture. You should also understand its traditions, values, family systems, socioeconomic issues, and attitudes about social services and social policies. You should be aware of how your own attitudes are connected to your own cultural background and how they may differ from the worldview of members of the minority culture. You should be aware of and try to avoid **ethnocentrism,** which is the belief in the superiority of your own culture. You should develop skills in communicating effectively both verbally and nonverbally with members of the minority culture and establishing rapport with them.

Norton and Manson (1996), for example, identified some of the important things you should know to enhance the cultural competence of your research on Native Americans. You should know how Native Americans feel about the loss of their ancestral lands. You should know about the important role played by tribes in their lives and in influencing their participation in research. You should realize that in addition to obtaining the individual's consent to participate in your research, you may have to seek the tribe's permission. You should also be aware of the diversity among tribal cultures and the diversity in where Native Americans reside. You should know that a large minority of Native Americans live on reservations and how they feel about that. You should know that many of them previously living on reservations were forced after World War II to resettle in urban areas. You should know how they feel about that. You might be surprised to learn that according to the 1990 U.S. census the city with the largest number of Native American residents is New York City. Yet Native Americans who dwell in urban areas are less likely than other ethnic minority populations to concentrate in the same neighborhoods.

Thompson and her associates (1996) identified some important things you should know before implementing studies of mental health services with African Americans. You should know that prior studies that fostered negative images of African Americans or that have been insensitive in other ways have led many African Americans to distrust research, especially research conducted by whites. As is the case with Native Americans, African Americans may see researchers as taking from their community but not giving anything in return. You should be aware of the relatively high degree of stigma that some African Americans attach to the concept of mental illness, and how this, coupled with their distrust of research, makes it difficult to obtain their participation in research.

Miranda and her associates (Miranda, 1996; Alvidrez, Azocar, and Miranda, 1996) discuss how misconceptions about Latino attitudes and Latino utilization of mental health services can impede the efforts of psychotherapy researchers to recruit and retain Latinos in their studies. Although the underutilization of mental health services by Latinos has been attributed to their negative attitudes about treatment, many studies have found that Latinos view mental health services positively and often hold more positive views than whites. Another common misconception is that American Latinos prefer family members or *curanderos* (traditional folk healers who dispose herbal medicines and potions for emotional problems) to professional mental health services. But Miranda and associates cite several studies which indicate that the use of traditional folk healers accounts for only a small portion of Latino underutilization of professional mental health services in the United States. If you plan to conduct a study evaluating mental health services in an area where many Latinos reside, it is important that you have accurate knowledge about what influences service utilization among Latinos. Otherwise, you might not undertake appropriate efforts to recruit and retain the participation of Latinos in your study, and you might too readily attribute their lack of participation to negative attitudes rather than to your inadequate efforts to recruit and retain Latinos. For example, Miranda and associates discuss how the individual is valued less among many traditional Latinos than is the family, including extended as well as nuclear family members. Consequently, researchers may need to interact with family members before individuals are permitted or willing to participate in treatment outcome studies.

The above are just some examples of things researchers need to learn about the cultures of ethnic minority groups relevant to their studies and why they need to know those things. Many other examples could be cited, as could the cultures of groups that are disadvantaged or oppressed for reasons other than ethnicity, such as individuals who are homeless or in need of intervention for HIV and AIDS. We will discuss additional examples and additional groups throughout this chapter.

Of course, you may already have accumulated considerable experience, knowledge, and sensitivity regarding the culture of interest before even contemplating your research. If so, this might reduce the extent of your basic readings. Nevertheless, you should review the recent literature—especially the research literature—to enhance your assessment of your own cultural competence and to make sure your conceptions are accurate and consistent with the latest findings. Moreover, cultures are not monolithic. They contain diverse subcultures that might be related to differences in factors such as geographic origin, socioeconomic status, and acculturation. In assessing your own cultural competence, therefore, be sure not to overlook the cultural diversity within the culture in which you already have expertise. In this connection, we have observed in-class dialogues between some of our Korean doctoral students in which, despite their own ethnic heritage and expertise in the culture of Korean Americans, they have suggested helpful ways to improve the cultural sensitivity of each other's plans for dissertation research on Korean Americans.

What you learn in other parts of this book can help you learn more about cultures with which you are not already familiar. Chapter 2, for example, provided tips for facilitating literature reviews. Additional tips can be found in Chapter 6 and Appendix A. In addition to the literature review, another helpful early step in seeking to improve the cultural competence of your research involves using the *participant observation* methods described in Chapter 18. These methods will help you immerse yourself more directly in the culture of interest and enhance your assessment of your own cultural competence.

You should also seek the advice of professional colleagues who are members of the culture or who have a great deal of experience in working with its members. These colleagues should include practitioners as well as scholars whose works have dealt with the culture of interest. Your colleagues can help you not only to learn more about the culture, but also to formulate research questions that are responsive to the needs and perspectives of its members. So too can the input of community members and their leaders. In fact, it is essential that representatives of the minority cultures be included in the formulation of the research questions and in all subsequent stages of the research. Not only will this help you formulate research questions that are responsive to minority group concerns, it also can help you prevent or deal with culturally related problems that might arise in later stages of the research design and implementation—problems that you might not otherwise have anticipated. Likewise, it can foster a sense of community commitment to the research and more receptivity to future studies.

Using *focus groups*, which we'll discuss in Chapter 18, can aid in learning how community representatives view issues relevant to your study. Alvidrez, Azocar, and Miranda (1996), for example, mention how conducting a focus group made up of young African American women before initiating investigations about parenting interventions can help researchers. By better understanding attitudes about child rearing among this population, the researchers can be more prepared to develop culturally specific hypotheses about how young African American women might respond to the parenting interventions of concern. Focus groups can also help you to anticipate barriers to recruiting and retaining participants in your study and to identify steps you can take that might enhance recruitment and retention. Let's look now at some of those barriers and steps.

RECRUITING AND RETAINING THE PARTICIPATION OF MINORITY AND OPPRESSED POPULATIONS IN RESEARCH STUDIES

Recruiting a sufficient and representative sample of research participants from minority and oppressed populations can be a daunting challenge. So can retaining their participation throughout the study after they have been recruited. Many reasons have been postulated to explain difficulties in the recruitment and retention of participants from minority and oppressed populations. Earlier in this chapter we discussed how the recruitment efforts of current studies can be hampered by the poisoned climate of previous studies that were conducted in a culturally insensitive manner. A related barrier is the perception that the research question may have value for the larger society but little value to a particular minority group. Perhaps members of a particular minority group are likely to distrust research in general or members of the majority culture in general.

Some prospective participants can get turned off by *culturally insensitive informed consent procedures.* For example, Norton and Manson (1996) observe, "The sophisticated language required by IRB protocols may be intimidating to American Indians and Alaska Natives, particularly those for whom English is a second language" (p. 858). They cite an example in which some American Indian Vietnam veterans misinterpreted a consent form, thinking that the words "Clinical Research" in the title meant that they were being asked to participate in a medical procedure rather than an interview.

Another barrier pertains to *not knowing where to look for participants.* Suppose you want to study the impact of parental depression on the child-rearing practices of parents who recently immigrated to the United States from Korea or from Latin America. Because such immigrants have extremely low rates of utilization of traditional mental health services, you may have meager success if you try to recruit participants only through referral sources or advertisements at traditional mental health service providers, where you think they may be in treatment for depression. Locating or identifying prospective participants can be a special challenge when dealing with populations who lack a known residence—such as homeless individuals, migrant workers, or undocumented immigrants. Other hard-to-locate populations consist of people who have some characteristic that is stigmatized by society and therefore risky for them to disclose. People in need of intervention for HIV or AIDS, for example, comprise one such "hidden" population (Roffman et al., 1998).

In light of the many barriers to the recruitment and retention of participants from minority and oppressed populations, what can be done to alleviate or overcome those barriers? The literature on this issue is still emerging. A number of potentially useful approaches have been recommended; future inquiries are likely to develop additional recommendations. Not all of the existing recommendations have received adequate empirical testing. Some are based on what various investigators believe they have learned from their experiences in conducting research among certain minority or oppressed populations. With the understanding that some of these recommendations can be viewed more as practice wisdom than as evidence-based procedures, let's look now at what some culturally competent investigators recommend as culturally sensitive approaches for overcoming barriers to the recruitment and retention of participants from minority and oppressed populations.

Obtain Endorsement from Community Leaders

If prospective participants in your study see that it has been endorsed by community leaders whom they respect, their distrust of the researchers or their skepticism about the value of the research to their community may be alleviated. Norton and Manson (1996), for example, discuss the need for investigators who seek to recruit American Indian or Alaskan Natives to obtain permission first from the prospective participant's tribe. They note that the Navajo Nation now has a board staffed by tribal representatives who review, approve, and monitor all health-related research proposed for their community. Tribal governments aggressively evaluate the value of proposed research projects to the tribe. One tribal council even asserted that it had the authority to grant collective consent to participate on behalf of its members.

Seeking consent from community leaders can be a major undertaking. When done in a thorough and careful manner, it involves obtaining their input into the formulation of the research questions as well as into how the study is to be designed and implemented and how its results are to be presented and disseminated. But the effort can pay off not only by enhancing recruitment and retention of participants, but also by improving the design of your study or the interpretation of its results. Norton and Manson (1996) cite an example in which their dialogue with a tribal government alerted them to the greater reluctance of study participants in one of their research sites to disclose alcohol consumption to local staff than to clinicians from external communities. Learning this led them to change their plans to use local interviewers, and thus they could obtain responses that were less biased.

Use Culturally Sensitive Approaches Regarding Confidentiality

For those minority groups that value collective identity, it may not be enough to assure individual confidentiality. They might also require community confidentiality. Norton and Manson advise that when undertaking research in American Indian and Alaska Native communities investigators should not identify specific communities when publishing their studies. Press releases should not come from the investigators; instead, they should be initiated by the tribal government. Research findings should be in the form of generalizations; readers should not be able to ascertain the identity of the local communities associated with those findings.

Employ Local Community Members as Research Staff

If you have adequate funding, you can hire local community members to help locate and recruit prospective participants and obtain their informed consent. If the folks you hire also happen to be community leaders, all the better, since they can enhance your efforts to publicize your research and express their enthusiastic support for it. Employing community members to obtain informed consent also might help overcome any problems in understanding the consent forms or in being intimidated by them, since the members can explain the study verbally and answer questions about it in ways that prospective participants may be more likely to understand. Another benefit of employing local community members in your research is that in doing so your study benefits the community just by providing more jobs. One drawback of employing local community members as research staff is its implications regarding confidentiality. Prospective participants may not want members of their own community interviewing them or knowing of their participation.

Provide Adequate Compensation

People from all backgrounds can be reimbursed for their time and effort in participating in research studies. Compensation for participating in research is particularly applicable to studies of minority and oppressed populations. In light of the high poverty rates in some minority communities, compensation might provide a strong inducement for members to participate. Those same high poverty rates, however, may lead some to view high levels of compensation as coercive and thus unethical. Although you do not want to pay too much, an appropriate level of compensation can be another way your study benefits the local community. Payment should be large enough to provide an incentive yet not so large that it becomes coercive. Norton and Manson (1996) add that compensation need not be limited to individual participants. They cite a request by a Pueblo community that compensation be provided to the tribe as a whole, in keeping with the tribe's emphasis on collective identity.

Money is not the only form of compensation that you can use. If you are studying the homeless, for example, responding quickly to their need for some food or clothing can build trust and reward their participation. A sandwich, some cigarettes, or a cup of coffee can be significant to them. Perhaps you can accompany them to an agency that will give them some shelter, financial assistance, or health care. Food vouchers are a commonly used noncash way researchers can reward homeless or other low-income individuals for their research participation. Perhaps a fast-food chain will be willing to donate vouchers worth about $5 each to your study.

Alleviate Transportation and Child-Care Barriers

Because of the high poverty rates in some minority communities, some barriers to recruitment and retention pertain not to cultural issues per se, but to economic difficulties. For example, suppose you work in a child guidance center and want to evaluate a new, culturally sensitive intervention for an economically disadvantaged minority group in which the parent and child are treated together. Many of the parents you seek to recruit might experience transportation or child-care barriers to coming to your child guidance center for the treatment sessions. A culturally competent approach to your research, therefore, might include the provision of free transportation and child care (for their other young children). An alternative to providing free transportation would be to conduct the treatment and data collection sessions at their homes, although many families might still need child care during those sessions.

Choose a Sensitive and Accessible Setting

If your treatment or data collection sessions are not conducted in the participants' homes, you should make sure that the choice of the setting in which they are conducted is sensitive to participant needs, resources, and concerns. Areán and Gallagher-Thompson (1996) have provided some useful insights concerning the culturally sensitive choice of a setting. For example, even if minority group members have transportation and are not dissuaded from participating by economic barriers, some might be reluctant to travel to a particular setting in a different neighborhood out of fear of a racially motivated crime. Or perhaps the setting is in a dangerous section of their own neighborhood. These fears might be particularly salient to elderly minority individuals.

The site you choose, therefore, should be located somewhere that participants will perceive as convenient as well as safe. You should also consider whether some participants might be uncomfortable with the nature of the building you choose. If you choose a community church, for example, some prospective participants who don't belong to that church might be uncomfortable entering it. Others might not want their neighbors to see them receiving services or participating in a research study. Perhaps a nearby university site, where friends won't know of their participation, would be preferable. If you can implement some of the recommendations we've already mentioned—such as conducting focus groups, involving community leaders in planning your study, and employing local community members as research staff—you should try to ascertain which possible settings are and are not accessible to your prospective participants and be sensitive to their concerns.

Use and Train Culturally Competent Interviewers

It may seem obvious to you that one of the most important ways to enhance the recruitment and retention of minority group participants in your research is to make sure that the research staff who will come into contact with prospective participants are culturally competent. One way to do this, of course, is to employ members of the local community as your research staff, as we mentioned earlier. We also mentioned that in some cases employing local community members may conflict with confidentiality concerns. What other steps can you take to maximize cultural competence when employing local community members is deemed undesirable or infeasible?

One recommendation commonly found in the literature on culturally competent research is to use interviewers who are of the same ethnicity as the members of the minority population whom you seek to recruit. Thus, if you seek to recruit and retain African American participants in a particular community, you might employ African American interviewers from a different community.

Note, however, that although matching interviewer and participant ethnicity probably won't impede your recruitment efforts, several studies have suggested that successful interviewing depends more on interviewer competence than on racial matching (Jackson and Ivanoff, 1999). In a study by Thompson and colleagues (1996), for example, racial matching had no effect on the likelihood of African American psychiatric inpatients agreeing to be interviewed. According to the researchers, more important than racial matching is whether the interviewer has adequate previous experience or training in working with members of the target population. Their interviewer training consisted of practicing how to approach participants, practicing how to give them an overview of the study, practicing how best to discuss confidentiality and voluntary participation, and thoroughly learning the intricacies of the survey instruments they were to use. The interviewers had to review every line on every page of the interviewing protocols and of the instructions for introducing the study. Using a script prepared by the research staff, they had to rehearse introducing and explaining the study. They also had to role-play practice interviews with each other and complete two practice interviews with real patients. These practice interviews were reviewed and critiqued.

Although the Thompson study illustrates that with ample interviewer training, interviewer–participant matching may not be necessary, we should not overgeneralize their results. They may have had different findings had their subjects not been psychiatric inpatients. What if they had been unable to find interviewers who had ample previous experience working with members of the target population? What if they lacked the resources to train their interviewers so extensively? Under those conditions, matching the ethnicity of interviewers and participants may have made a huge difference.

Use Bilingual Staff

If you are trying to recruit participants from communities where many members have difficulty speaking English, your recruitment staff should be able to communicate in the language with which prospective participants are most comfortable. For example, if your study is to take place in a heavily Latino community, your interviewers should be able to converse in Spanish. If they cannot, your recruitment efforts are unlikely to succeed. Likewise, after recruiting participants, your data collection efforts will need to be conducted in Spanish. And if you are evaluating a treatment, that treatment should be conducted in Spanish. Otherwise, even successful recruitment efforts are likely to be wasted because you will retain so few non-English-speaking participants in the study.

Understand Cultural Factors Influencing Participation

Earlier in this chapter we discussed the important role played by tribes in the lives of Native Americans and how many Latinos value the family more than the individual. We noted that researchers might need to interact with tribal leaders or family members before individuals are permitted or willing to participate in a study. Miranda and her associates (Miranda, 1996; Alvidrez, Azocar, and Miranda, 1996) have identified other cultural factors bearing upon recruitment and retention of low-income traditional Latinos in research on mental health services. *Familismo* refers to strong, traditional family values among traditional Latinos. *Machismo* refers to the power of the father in decision making, economic and emotional stability, and protecting the family from danger. *Marianismo* refers to the mother's spiritual superiority as she is capable of suffering and self-sacrifice to help her husband and children. *Personalismo* refers to the preferences of many traditional Latinos for a dignified approach when you associate with them, such as by using formal language and formal greetings that convey respect. At the same time, however, recruitment efforts should not be too formal. *Simpatía* refers to the expectation of traditional Latinos that the person treating them with respect will also interact in a warm and friendly manner. To illustrate how sensitivity to these cultural factors can enhance recruitment and retention, Miranda and her associates cite studies whose research staff experienced success in recruiting and retaining Latinos by being warm and personable while using such touches as formal titles (such as *senor* or *señora*), the polite forms of words (such as *usted* for "you"), and remembering the names of participants' children and asking about the children during each interview.

Use Anonymous Enrollment with Stigmatized Populations

Locating and recruiting prospective participants can be a special challenge if your study concerns people who have some characteristic that is stigmatized by society and therefore risky for them to disclose. People in need of intervention for HIV and AIDS constitute one such population. University of Washington social work professor Roger A. Roffman and four associates (1997, 1998) were honored with an Outstanding Research Award presented by the Society for Social Work and Research for their study of the effectiveness of a telephone group approach to AIDS prevention counseling with gay and bisexual men who had recently engaged in unprotected anal or oral sex with men.

It was not easy for the researchers to find prospective participants for their study. Their recruitment period lasted almost two years and included "advertising in the gay press, news coverage in the mainstream press, distributing materials to HIV testing centers and gay/lesbian/bisexual health and social service agencies, and mailing posters to gay bars and baths" (Roffman et al., 1998:9). By implementing both the study and the intervention by telephone, Roffman and his associates were able to assure prospective participants of anonymity if they desired it. Publicizing **anonymous enrollment** in their recruitment materials enabled prospective participants to feel safer in responding to the recruitment effort and thus helped the research team find a larger pool of prospective participants, many of whom normally would remain hidden because of the societal risk involved in being identified. Beyond making it possible to contact more prospective participants, anonymous enrollment further helped secure their willingness to engage in the study.

Roffman and his associates were creative in their efforts to ensure anonymity and make the prospective applicants feel safe participating in the study. Anonymously enrolled clients were reimbursed (with no name entered on the payee line of the mailed check) for the cost of renting postal boxes in nearby post offices. They used pseudonyms to receive mailed materials from the research staff. The research team succeeded in engaging 548 participants in the study and therefore concluded that anonymous enrollment is an effective way to facilitate participation in research by hidden groups who might otherwise remain unreached. The team also acknowledged, however, that its approach applied only to prospective participants who had telephones and to interventions that can be delivered by telephone. The researchers also acknowledged that although anonymous enrollment appeared to be an important component of identifying and engaging prospective participants in the study, maintaining their participation was facilitated by having a staff that was culturally competent for this population.

Utilize Special Sampling Techniques

Anonymous enrollment is just one way to identify, engage, and maintain hidden groups in your study. The literature on this issue is in its infancy, and future inquiries are likely to identify alternative innovative approaches. Some approaches involve specialized sampling techniques that we'll be discussing in Chapter 14. One sampling approach commonly associated with this challenge is *snowball sampling,* which involves asking each research participant you find to help you locate other potential participants. For example, in studying the homeless you begin by going to certain areas of town where the homeless are thought most likely to be found. Once you find homeless individuals, you would attempt to expand your snowball sample by asking them for information to help you locate other homeless people whom they know. Another technique would be to recruit relatively large proportions of participants from relatively small minority groups. This is done to ensure that enough cases of certain minority groups are selected to allow for subgroup comparisons within each of those minority groups.

Learn Where to Look

Culturally competent researchers have learned not to rely exclusively on traditional agencies as referral sources in seeking to recruit certain minority group participants or members of hidden and stigmatized populations. But what are the alternatives? The answer to this question will vary depending on your target population. In their study of people in need of intervention for HIV and AIDS, for example, Roffman and his associates advertised in the gay press, distributed materials at HIV testing centers and gay/lesbian/bisexual health and social service agencies, and mailed posters to gay bars and baths. Homeless participants might be recruited in such places as steam tunnels, loading docks, park benches, bus terminals, missions and flophouses, and abandoned buildings. Culturally competent researchers studying African Americans who have emotional problems have learned that many such individuals do not seek help from traditional mental health services. These researchers therefore seek help in recruiting participants for their studies from ministers, primary care physicians, and informal support networks in addition to traditional service agencies (Thompson et al., 1996). We do not mean to imply that traditional agencies should be ignored, however—just that they should not be relied on *exclusively.*

Rather than try to identify all the diverse places where you might look to find participants, which will vary greatly depending on the target population of your study, our advice here is that you learn where to look by following some of the other recommendations that we've already discussed. Your literature review on the culture of the target population might offer some important insights. So will advice from key community members or colleagues with expertise about the population of interest. Focus groups (to be discussed in Chapter 18) might offer some additional tips. Of particular value might be what you learn from the involvement of community leaders in the planning of your study or the use of indigenous community members as research staff. As you are learning about the community, you might find it useful to develop a profile of the community. Your profile might list the various organizations and other potential referral sources as well as additional key community members who can assist in your recruitment efforts (Areán and Gallagher-Thompson, 1996).

Connect with and Nurture Referral Sources

Whether you are relying on traditional or nontraditional organizations for referrals to your study, your success in securing sufficient referrals from those sources will be enhanced if you have established rapport with the individuals working in them. For example, you might attend their meetings and see whether you can volunteer your assistance to them. The more extensive your earlier interactions with key individuals upon whom you will rely for referrals, and the better your already established relationship with them, the more helpful they are likely to be when you seek their assistance in recruiting participants for your research. After establishing rapport with referral sources, you should inform them of the benefits your study can provide to the field as well as to individual participants. For example, perhaps the participants will receive a promising new service as well as compensation and other rewards for participating. Perhaps the field will learn whether the promising new service is really effective. Discuss their questions about your study and attempt to assuage their fears about it. You should also nurture your relationship with your referral sources throughout your study. Continue to attend their meetings and assist them. Keep them apprised of how your study is going. Let them know incrementally of any preliminary findings as they emerge.

Use Frequent and Individualized Contacts and Personal Touches

Although many of the techniques we've been discussing so far bear on retention as well as recruitment, much of our discussion has emphasized recruitment more than retention. In studies that involve multiple sessions with participants, however, successful recruitment efforts will be in vain if they are not followed by successful retention efforts. Studies assessing treatment outcome, for example, will need to undertake special efforts to retain clients in treatment. If a no-treatment control group is involved, its members will need to be reminded and motivated to participate in pretesting, posttesting, and perhaps several administrations of follow-up testing.

Miranda and her associates (Miranda, 1996; Alvidrez, Azocar, and Miranda, 1996) recommended some approaches to enhance retention that have been successful in several treatment outcome studies involving low-income Latino participants. We believe that their recommendations might apply to some other low-income minority groups, as well. For example, Miranda and her associates advocate the telephoning of no-treatment control group participants regularly, perhaps monthly, by research assistants who are warm and friendly and who ask about the well-being of the participants and their families. The same research assistant should call each time, and should remember and discuss the details of the participant's situation and his or her family's situation. This builds rapport and continuity between phone calls. They even recommend sending birthday cards to participants and their children. As we mentioned earlier, transportation to and from each assessment session along with modest cash or food voucher reimbursements to participants after each assessment session will also help. Providing coffee, cold drinks, and perhaps some sandwiches or snacks is also a nice touch. When possible, Miranda and her associates recommend scheduling assessment sessions that coincide with special occasions. For example, you can schedule an assessment during the week of a child's birthday, so that you can celebrate at the end of the session with a birthday cake and a small gift. Perhaps you can videotape the celebrations and give the tape to participants as a memento of their participation in the study.

In addition to the regular contacts and personal touches that we've just mentioned, there is something else you should always do—something of great importance. Be sure to make **reminder calls** to participants before their scheduled treatment or assessment sessions. In fact, in addition to calling them a day or two in advance, you should try calling them a week or two in advance. If they are poor, they may not own an answering machine. Perhaps they've moved, and you will need time to track them down.

Use Anchor Points

Making reminder calls and other contacts is not easy if your participants are homeless or residentially transient. Hough and his associates (1996), based on their review of the research on homeless mentally ill people, recommend using **anchor points**, which are pieces of information about the various places you may be able to find a particular participant. The more anchor points you identify when you first engage an individual in your study, the more likely you will be to find them later. If your participant is a homeless woman, for example, some anchor points might include where she usually sleeps, eats, or hangs out. You might also ask if she has any nearby family or friends and how you can contact them. Are there any social service workers, landlords, or other individuals in the community who might know how to locate her? Is there an address where she goes to pick up her mail, her messages, or Supplemental Security Income checks? What, if any, nicknames or aliases does she use? All this information should be recorded systematically on a tracking form. In your subsequent contacts with the participant or others who know of her whereabouts you should continually update your anchor point information.

Use Tracking Methods

Using your anchor points, Hough and his associates recommend additional techniques for tracking and contacting your participants. If your anchor points include a telephone number, you can use **phone tracking.** As we mentioned above, you should start calling a week or two in advance of an interview. With a homeless individual, expect to make quite a few calls to the anchor points just to arrange one interview. You should also give homeless participants a toll-free number where they can leave messages about appointment changes, changes in how to locate them, or other relevant information. You might even offer incentives, such as food vouchers, for leaving such messages. To help participants remember appointments and how to contact the research project, you should give them a card that lists useful information on one side, such as key community resources. On the other side, the card should show appointment times and the research project's address and telephone number.

In addition to phone tracking, you can use **mail tracking,** in which you mail reminder notices about impending interviews or ask participants to call in to update any changes in how to contact them. Mail tracking might also include sending birthday cards, holiday greetings, and certificates of appreciation for participation. All correspondence should be signed by the research staff member whom the participant knows.

You can also use **agency tracking,** in which you ask service providers or other community agencies whether they have been in recent contact with participants whom you are unable to locate. Some of these agencies may have been identified in your anchor points. If they are unable to tell you where to locate the participant, you can contact additional agencies, such as social service agencies, hospitals, police, probation and parole officers, substance abuse programs, shelters, public housing staff, Social Security offices, or even the coroner's office. The cooperation you get from these agencies will be enhanced if you follow some of the other recommendations we've mentioned earlier in this chapter, such as obtaining endorsement for your study from community leaders and connecting with and nurturing your relationships with community agencies relevant to your study.

If your efforts at phone tracking and agency tracking fail to locate a participant, you can resort to **field tracking.** Field tracking is particularly relevant to research on the homeless, and involves talking with people on the streets about where to find the participant. You might go where other homeless people who know the participant hang out and ask them. Offering them small gifts such as coffee or cigarettes might help. You can also use your anchor points to identify neighbors, friends, family, or previous hangout spots that might help you find the participant.

Regardless of which tracking methods you use, Hough and his associates argue that your persistence is probably the most important factor in obtaining satisfactory retention rates. With some homeless mentally ill participants, for example, you may need to seek out 10 anchor points several times each, make 15 attempts to contact the participant, or show up for a fifth scheduled interview with a participant who has not shown up for the previous four.

These tracking techniques can conflict with the ethical guideline of protecting anonymity and privacy, discussed in Chapter 4. Consequently, before you can use them, you will be required to anticipate them in your informed consent procedures. Participants will need to give you advance permission to seek their whereabouts from the various sources we've been discussing. In addition, you will need to make sure that you do not inadvertently reveal sensitive information about your participant to these sources. The sources should *not,* for example, be informed that your study is on mental illness or AIDS. If these sources are given an address or phone number for the research study, neither should contain anything that would hint at the sensitive nature of the research topic.

CULTURALLY COMPETENT MEASUREMENT

Earlier in this chapter we mentioned that culturally insensitive measurement can create problems beyond producing unreliable or invalid information. It can also offend participants, dissuade them from participating in your study or in future studies, and lead to results that they perceive as harmful to their communities. We also discussed how you can attempt to minimize those problems. At this point, we'll look more closely at how culturally competent measurement procedures attempt to avoid the problem of producing unreliable or invalid information.

There are three main threats to culturally competent measurement in social work research. One, which we've mentioned above, involves the use of interviewers whose personal characteristics or interviewing styles offend or intimidate minority respondents or in other ways make them reluctant to divulge relevant and valid information. Another involves the use of language, either in self- or interviewer-administered instruments, that minority respondents do not understand. The third involves cultural bias. Let's begin with interviewer characteristics.

Culturally Competent Interviewing

As we've noted, using and training culturally competent interviewers is one of the most important ways to enhance the recruitment and retention of minority group participants in research. If interviewing is being used not just to obtain participation in your study, but also as one of your data collection methods, whether your interviewers are culturally competent can have a profound impact on the quality of the data you obtain from minority participants. Three key factors influencing the degree of cultural competence in data collection by interviewers are whether (1) the interviewers speak the same language as the respondent, (2) they are of the same ethnicity as the respondent, and (3) they have had adequate training and experience in interviewing the people of the same ethnicity as the respondent.

The need for your interviewers to speak the language of the people they are interviewing should be self-evident and not require elaboration. If you are an American of European descent who speaks only English, imagine how you would respond to an interview conducted only in Chinese! The influence of matching interviewer and interviewee ethnicity, however, can be more complicated. When people are interviewed by "outsiders," they may have a tendency to exaggerate their views in one direction, in an effort to give socially desirable answers. When they are interviewed by someone of their own ethnicity, however, their wish to appear socially desirable may influence them to exaggerate in the other direction. For example, African Americans or Native Americans might deny their true feelings of anger or resentment about racism to a white interviewer. But if they are interviewed by members of their own ethnicity, they might exaggerate their feelings of anger or resentment about racism, in an analogous attempt to give answers that they think the interviewer wants to hear.

Although matching interviewer and interviewee ethnicity is not a foolproof guarantee, it is a good rule of thumb to follow whenever possible. Imagine how you would feel, for example, going into a poverty-stricken ethnic neighborhood to interview residents who deem people of your ethnicity as outsiders and perhaps resent them. How much training and experience would it take for you to be as comfortable in the interview as an interviewer who grew up in a neighborhood like that? Even if both of you read the same interview questions verbatim, chances are you would show more discomfort in your posture, eye contact, physical distance from the interviewee, and the naturalness of your tone of voice.

If matching interviewer and interviewee ethnicity is not feasible, you should at least try to use interviewers who have had previous experience in working with members of the target population. Of course, this, too, may not be feasible. But even if you are able to match interviewer and interviewee ethnicity and use interviewers with the desired previous experience, the need to train them is crucial. Their training should go beyond the general principles for training interviewers, as will be discussed in Chapter 15, and should include a focus on cultural competence through the provision of information and the use of supervised rehearsals, role-playing, and practice interviews. The box titled "Further Notes on Methodology: Interviewing Asians" further illustrates measurement problems related to cultural competence in interviewing and how to avoid them.

Language Problems

Regardless of whether we collect data using interviews or alternative techniques, we need to modify our procedures when some of our research participants are not fluent in the majority language. Three rather obvious steps to be taken under these circumstances are the use of bilingual interviewers, the translating of the measures into the language of the respondents, and pretesting the measures in dry runs to see if they are understood as intended. But even these steps will not guarantee success in attaining reliable and valid measurement, or what can be called **translation validity.** The translation process, for example, is by no means simple.

One problem pertains to the fluency of the bilingual interviewers or translators. Perhaps they are not as fluent in the minority language as we think they are. For example, there may be language differences

FURTHER NOTES ON METHODOLOGY: INTERVIEWING ASIANS

If the successive goals of any scientific inquiry are to describe, explain, and predict, much Asian American research will come under the category of description. An important means of securing this information in its full depth is the intensive face-to-face interview. We ruled out the use of mailed questionnaires for this study because of an astonishingly high rate of nonresponse in other studies of Asian Americans.

It was not an easy task to secure interviews from some of the Asian groups. While Indians and Pakistanis were eager to be interviewed and had a lot to say, members of the Chinese, Korean, and Filipino groups were reluctant to participate. Some of them not only refused to grant interviews but also refused to give names of potential respondents in their ethnic groups. Since we had adopted a snowball approach [Chapter 14] in identifying members of different ethnic groups and the potential respondents in each group, such refusal inordinately delayed completion of the fieldwork. In the interviews we found that the high value of modesty in Asian cultural backgrounds, the gratefulness to America for homes and jobs, a vague fear of losing both in case something went wrong, and the consequent unwillingness to speak ill of the host country, made the Asian American response to any question about life and work likely to be positive, especially if the interviewer was white. We found that the only way to resolve this critical dilemma was in establishing rapport and checking and rechecking each response. For example, after an extensive account of how satisfying his job was, a male Filipino respondent almost reversed his account as soon as the tape recorder was turned off. In another case, a male respondent from India admitted off-record that life in America was not a bed of roses, even though he had earlier painted a rosy picture.

Aggressive interviewing is not likely to produce the desired results, but may make a respondent timid and constrained. We found that a white male interviewer is unsuitable for interviewing Asian women, not because he is aggressive but because he is likely to be defined as such in terms of cultural norms. Lack of empathy and cultural appreciation on the part of the interviewer, or a chance comment or exclamation which is defined negatively by the respondent may shut off the flow of response. For example, during an interview between a Filipino female respondent and a white female interviewer, the respondent mentioned that her brother was living with her along with her husband and children. The interviewer exclaimed, wondering aloud if her husband and children did not mind such an arrangement. Thinking that she had probably committed some cultural "goof," the Filipino respondent just dried up. All her later responses were cut and dried and "correct."

We found that it was most expedient to match a female respondent with a female interviewer from another Asian national background. Sameness of nationality may constrain responses, as respondents may be afraid that confidential information may be divulged. However, it may not be wise for a female Asian to interview an Asian man; the strong patriarchal feeling of Asian men may play a confounding role in their responses. Thus, it would seem that only men would be appropriate interviewers for Asian men.

We recognize, however, that there is no foolproof formula for conducting an interview which would assure its complete integrity. A white man interviewing an Asian man will insure confidentiality, objectivity, and impartiality, but there may be a lack of the cultural appreciation and sensitivity so important for handling sensitive cultural data. On the other hand, an Asian or white female interviewer may provoke boastful responses from an Asian man.

Finally, the most intriguing aspects of in-depth interview situations with Asian Americans is the seeming inconsistency of responses, which may, at times, border on contradiction. It is not uncommon to find Asians simultaneously attracted to and repulsed by some aspect of a person, symbol, value, or system. This way of thought has to be understood in the context of Chinese, Japanese, or Indian philosophic values which view an absolute system of value with uneasiness. This is very different from the typical Western mind which abhors paradoxes and contradictions, or anything that is not clear, well-defined, and determined [Mehta, Asoka, *Perception of Asian Personality*. Calcutta: S. Chand, 1978; Nandi, Proshanta K., "The Quality of Life of Asian Americans in Middle Size Cities: A Neglected Area of Research," in *Bridge* 5(4): 51–53, 59]. This dualism among Asian Americans is likely to pose a major challenge to conventional research techniques in both gathering and interpretation of data.

Source: Nandi, Proshanta K., 1982, "Surveying Asian Minorities in the Middle-Sized City," in William T. Liu (ed.), *Methodological Problems in Minority Research* (Chicago: Pacific/Asian American Mental Health Research).

regarding a particular foreign language between those who can speak only in that language and those who are bilingual. United States residents who are bilingual in English and Spanish, for example, might use some English words with a Spanish sound when speaking Spanish—words that might be unintelligible to recent immigrants from Latin America who speak only in Spanish (Grinnell, 1997).

But even if words are accurately translated, that does not guarantee that you have accurately translated the concept being conveyed by those words. Consider North American terms such as "feeling blue" or "downhearted" that are commonly used in instruments that measure depression. It is difficult to translate these terms into other languages. For example, if you ask Latino or Asian respondents in their own language if they are "feeling blue" they may think you are asking them if they literally have blue skin.

Yu, Zhang, and associates (1987) provide the following illustration of some of the complexities involved in translating instruments. They were trying to translate items on self-esteem from English to Chinese for a study being conducted in Shanghai. Their first problem involved whether to translate the instrument into Shanghainese, an unstandardized and unwritten language, or into a standard Chinese language. Another difficulty involved a set of questions that began with the words, "Think of a person who . . . ," such as "Think of a person who feels that he is a failure generally in life" or "Think of a person who feels he has much to be proud of." They would then ask, "Is this person very much like you, much like you, somewhat like you, very little like you, or not at all like you during the past year?" (1987:78). In their pretesting, Yu and Zhang discovered that most respondents did not understand this form of questioning and frequently asked questions like, "Who is this person?" "What did you say his name is?" (1987:79).

Yu and Zhang consequently modified the questions but still encountered problems in their continued pretesting. One problematic revised item read, "Have you ever felt that you had something to be proud of?" Yu and Zhang discovered that in the culture they were studying humility is an important virtue, and therefore they could not use a negative answer to this question as an indicator of self-esteem. Another revised item read, "Have you ever thought that you were a failure in life?" Many poor housewives responded with a blank look, asking, "What is a failure in life?" Living in a society where the communist government then assigned jobs and salaries, and where almost no one was ever fired and where income variations were minimal, they previously had not thought of life in terms of competitiveness and success or failure. Yu and Zhang also reported culturally related suspicions that interviewers were part of a surveillance system; such suspicions could impede the validity of the information respondents provide.

One procedure that has been developed to deal with complexities in translating instruments from one language into another is called **back-translation.** This method begins with a bilingual person translating the instrument and its instructions to a target language. Then another bilingual person translates from the target language back to the original language (not seeing the original version of the instrument). The original instrument is then compared to the back-translated version, and items with discrepancies are modified further. But back-translation is by no means foolproof. It does not guarantee translation validity or the avoidance of *cultural bias*.

Cultural Bias

A measurement procedure has a **cultural bias** when it is administered to a minority culture without adjusting for the ways in which the minority culture's unique values, attitudes, lifestyles, or limited opportunities alter the accuracy or meaning of what is really being measured. Avoiding cultural bias goes beyond resolving language difficulties. For example, the reluctance among Chinese respondents to acknowledge pride is not a translation problem, but one of understanding unique cultural values and their implications for social desirability. As another example, asking about sexual issues is extremely taboo in some cultures.

Cultural bias applies not only when administering measurement procedures with people who don't speak the dominant language or who are not assimilated to the dominant culture, but also to minorities who are well assimilated to the majority culture. Some may be alienated or perplexed by certain phrases that don't apply to them. Ortega and Richey (1998), for example, discuss how cultural consultants suggested altering some standardized measures to make them more culturally sensitive to African American and Filipino American parents. "I feel like a wallflower when I go out" was changed to "I feel like people don't notice me when I go out." Another change altered "My family gets on my nerves" to "My family upsets me." In a third instance, "My family gives me the moral support I need" was changed to "My family helps me to feel hopeful" (pp. 57–58).

Cultural bias can also occur when the phrases in an instrument are perfectly clear to respondents. Consider, for example, a true/false item on a scale measuring different types of psychopathology worded as follows, "When I leave home I worry about whether the door is locked and the windows are closed." African American youths may be more likely than whites to answer "true," even when they have no more psychopathology than whites. This is because the African American youths are more likely than whites to live in high-crime neighborhoods where an unlocked door is an invitation to burglars (Nichols, Padilla, and Gomez-Maqueo, 2000).

Rogler (1989) provided several additional examples of the influence of cultural bias in connection to research in mental health. One study that Rogler and Hollingshead (1985) conducted in Puerto Rico, for example, examined how one spouse's schizophrenia influences marital decision making. Questions commonly used to evaluate such decision making in the United States—"where to go on vacation, which school the children should attend, the purchasing of insurance policies, and so on"—did not apply to impoverished Puerto Rican families who were "struggling to satisfy their most elementary needs for food, clothing, and housing" (1989:297).

In another example, Rogler discussed findings that indicate that Puerto Ricans who live in the Washington Heights section of Manhattan reported more psychiatric symptoms than did their counterparts in other ethnic groups who share the same social class. Rogler cites other findings that show that the psychiatric symptom statements on the measuring scales were evaluated as less socially undesirable by Puerto Rican respondents than by respondents from other ethnic groups. In other words, the social desirability bias against admitting to psychiatric symptoms seemed to be influencing Puerto Rican respondents less than other respondents. Therefore, the finding of higher rates of psychiatric symptomatology among Puerto Ricans may have been invalid, a measurement error resulting from cultural differences in the social undesirability of particular scale responses.

To anticipate and avoid problems like these, Rogler recommended that researchers spend a period of direct immersion in the culture of the population to be studied before administering measures that were developed on other populations. To assess potential problems in the applicability of the measures, researchers should use various methods that we discussed earlier, such as interviewing knowledgeable informants in the study population and using participant observation methods. When Rogler and his associates did this, for example, they observed spiritualist mediums attempting to control the spirits of patients in a psychiatric hospital in Puerto Rico. This helped sensitize the researchers to the importance of spiritualism in that culture and influenced how they interpreted patient reports of evil spirits in their psychiatric measures.

Rogler's work also illustrates the importance of **pretesting** your measurement instrument in a dry run to see if your target population will understand it and not find it too unwieldy. We think you can see from this discussion that such pretesting is particularly important when applying an instrument to a population other than the one for whom it was initially developed.

It was through pretesting, for example, that Rogler learned of the inapplicability of questions about vacations and insurance policies when studying decision making among impoverished Puerto Rican families.

As the literature on culturally competent measurement grows, some traditional concepts for avoiding measurement error are being expanded, questioned, or modified. Ortega and Richey (1998), for example, question the "common practice of rewording or repeating the same questions in an instrument," which is sometimes done to enable researchers to assess an instrument's reliability. Doing this, Ortega and Richey argue, "may be perceived as coercive, cumbersome, and rude by respondents whose culture values reticence and courteousness." Likewise, mixing positively and negatively worded items can present translation and interpretation problems in some cultures that have difficulties with negatively worded items (pp. 59–60). (In Chapter 8 we'll discuss the reasons why researchers like to mix positively and negatively worded items, such as by asking whether a person loves their mother in one item and then asking if they hate her in a later item.)

So far, we have been discussing cultural bias primarily in the context of interviews and measurement instruments. Before leaving this topic, we should point out that cultural bias can also mar data collected using direct observation. Cauce, Coronado, and Watson (1998), for example, cite research showing that when viewing videotaped interactions of African American mothers and daughters, African American observers rated the interactions as having less conflict than did the other observers. The African American raters also rated the mothers as less controlling. Thus, if your study uses observers or raters, it is critical that they be culturally competent.

Measurement Equivalence

All of the steps that we've been recommending for developing culturally competent measurement won't guarantee that a measurement instrument that appeared to be valid when tested with one culture will be valid when used with another culture. (We'll be discussing measurement validity in depth in Chapter 8.) In the United States, this issue is particularly relevant to the use of instruments that have been tested with whites and then used in research on members of minority groups. Allen and Walsh (2000) point out that most of the validated personality tests currently used in the United States were validated with samples consisting mainly of Euro-Americans. When we modify such instruments, we should assess whether the modified instrument used with the minority culture is really equivalent to the version validated with the dominant culture. We need to do the same when a measure is validated in one country, but then applied in another country.

The term **measurement equivalence** means that a measurement procedure developed in one culture will have the same value and meaning when administered to people in another culture (Burnette, 1998; Moreland, 1996). Three types of measurement equivalence that tend to be of greatest concern are *linguistic equivalence, conceptual equivalence,* and *metric equivalence.*

Linguistic equivalence, also known as **translation equivalence,** is attained when an instrument has been translated and back-translated successfully. **Conceptual equivalence** means that instruments and observed behaviors have the same meanings across cultures. For example, Moreland (1996) notes that some cultures consider a belch to be a compliment, whereas others consider it to be an insult. If you are observing antisocial behaviors among children, you will not have conceptual equivalence if you count belching as an antisocial behavior among participants from a culture that considers it to be a compliment. **Metric equivalence,** also known as **psychometric equivalence** or **scalar equivalence,** means that scores on a measure are comparable across cultures.

To illustrate the difference between conceptual equivalence and metric equivalence, suppose that you devise an instrument that intends to measure the degree of burden experienced by caregivers of frail elderly parents. Some items on the instrument might refer to "objective" burden, such as how much time is spent on caregiving. Other items might refer to "subjective" burden, such as how depressed the caregiver feels about caregiving. At the level of conceptual equivalence, you might be concerned that items about depression, such as "I feel blue," might not have the same meaning across two or more different cultures. At the level of metric equivalence, you might wonder whether in some cultures the amount of time spent in caregiving is really an indicator of burden, because some cultures may so esteem their elderly and the caregiving role that the act of caregiving is not seen or experienced as a burden.

An instrument cannot have metric equivalence unless it has linguistic and conceptual equivalence. However, as we have illustrated above, linguistic and conceptual equivalence do not guarantee metric equivalence. Accurately understanding the intended meaning of a question about how much time one spends in caregiving does not guarantee that a higher score on time spent indicates more of the concept "burden." Eight hours a day may be perceived in one culture as spending a moderate amount of time on caregiving, whereas in another it may seem huge and more burdensome.

Stanley Sue (1996) offers an illustration of problems in metric equivalence in which a study used a scale measuring psychopathology that is widely esteemed for its validity among whites. The scale was administered to whites and to Asian Americans at varying levels of acculturation. The least acculturated Asian Americans had scale scores supposedly indicating the greatest degree of psychopathology, and the whites had scores supposedly indicating the lowest degree of psychopathology. The more acculturated Asian Americans had scores in the middle. Did these findings indicate that Asian Americans really had more psychopathology than whites and that the least acculturated Asian Americans had the most psychopathology? Possibly. Perhaps the stresses associated with immigration, culture conflict, adjusting to a new environment, language difficulties, prejudice, and so on contributed to higher levels of psychopathology. An alternative possibility, however, is that ethnic differences in the tendency to agree with whatever is being asked makes the scores from the two cultures metrically nonequivalent. Instead of having more psychopathology, perhaps the Asian Americans simply are more likely to agree with statements about psychopathological symptoms in connection with their culture's emphasis on being polite and the notion that disagreeing is impolite.

Suppose the latter explanation in the above illustration is the correct one. Would that mean that the scale should not be used to measure psychopathology among Asian Americans because it lacks metric equivalence between the two cultures? Not necessarily. Although the lack of metric equivalence indicates the possibility that the scale is not equally valid for Asian Americans, perhaps some modifications connected to cultural differences can resolve the problem. The problem might also be alleviated by developing unique norms and cutoff scores for Asian Americans. Perhaps a higher score by Asian Americans should be considered indicative of the same level of psychopathology as a lower score by whites. For example, suppose a score of 60 on the scale is considered to indicate the need for mental health treatment, based on studies of the scale with whites. Perhaps analogous studies of the scale with Asian Americans will indicate that a higher score, perhaps around 70 or so, should be considered to indicate the need for mental health treatment by Asian Americans. The foregoing example illustrates the risks you take when you use the same instrument to compare the attributes of two cultural groups. Different scores on the measure indicate only that the two groups *may* differ. Lack of measurement equivalency is the alternative explanation (Sue, 1996).

In the box titled "Methodological Problems in the Study of Korean Immigrants: Linguistic and Conceptual Problems," two researchers further illustrate some of the problems in measurement equivalence that we have been discussing.

Assessing Measurement Equivalence

Several procedures can be used to assess the measurement equivalence of an instrument. One approach involves using statistical procedures that we'll examine in Chapter 8 to see if items that are answered in similar ways in one culture are answered in similar ways in another culture.

For example, suppose you want to assess caregiver burden among Mexican Americans who are the primary caregivers for their relatives suffering from Alzheimer's disease. Let's assume that you want to use a scale measuring caregiver burden that has been validated with samples comprised almost exclusively of Euro-Americans. Suppose the scale was found to measure three aspects of caregiver burden among Euro-American caregivers: objective burden (in which items asking about things like hours spent caregiving and other sacrifices correlated the most with each other); depression (in which items asking about different aspects of depression correlated the most with each other); and physical health (in which items asking about various indicators of the caregiver's physical well-being correlated the most with each other). To assess measurement equivalence with Mexican American caregivers you would see whether the same items correlate with each other on the same three aspects of caregiver burden. The correspondence need not be perfect. If the discrepancies are small, the results would suggest that the instrument measures the same aspects in both cultures.

Another procedure for assessing measurement equivalence involves assessing whether individuals at

METHODOLOGICAL PROBLEMS IN THE STUDY OF KOREAN IMMIGRANTS: LINGUISTIC AND CONCEPTUAL PROBLEMS

In most research with non-Westerners, the first obstacle is the language barrier. Since some of our interviewers and the majority of our respondents had difficulty using either spoken or written English, our interview schedules were translated into Korean by the investigators themselves, all of whom are native-born Koreans and bilingual. This translated version was administered to 30 or 40 immigrants as a pretest. On the basis of suggestions and comments given by the respondents, a number of questions were reworded, added, or eliminated. Pretest interviewers also participated in the preparation of the final version.

The difficulties of translation between Western and non-Western languages are well known. Many words are just not translatable even literally; for instance, *full-time* or *part-time, random sampling,* or even *community.* As in other Oriental languages, one must also pay a great deal of attention to honorifics when translating from English to Korean.

The most difficult problem, however, was conceptual ambiguity. In our first study, social invitations were used as an index of social assimilation. Our respondents were asked, "How often have you been invited by Americans to their homes in the past year (excluding business-related ones)?" Another question was, "How often have you invited Americans to your home in the past year?" Invitation was translated into Korean as *cho dae.* While the English invitation is used to request the presence of a person at a variety of occasions, the Korean *cho dae* means to request the presence of a person at a formal dinner or occasion, usually for a well-prepared entertainment. Thus, *cho dae* has a more restricted meaning than *invitation.*

Certainly the problem of conceptual equivalence is paramount. In another study, we investigated marital roles in Korean immigrant families. For our study, we used the instrument which Blood and Wolfe (1960) had developed for their study of American families in the Detroit area. The Korean translation of some terms resulted in negative connotations which could stiffen a Korean man's resistance to the sharing of marital roles (for example, *grocery shopping* or *dish washing*).

The following examples are not necessarily unique to non-Western research. Many respondents reported their family incomes instead of individual incomes. When they were asked, "How often have you changed your residence since you arrived in the Chicago area?" a number of unanticipated questions were raised. Does the frequency of moving include the changes of address before marriage? If so, are we asking for the frequency of the husband's or the wife's moves? Does a move include a change of apartment in the same building? In addition, some of our respondents did not recall how often they moved, and often a husband and wife disagreed.

Our respondents were supposed to answer the question, "How well do you speak English?" with one of the following: (a) fluent; (b) good; (c) fair; (d) poor; (e) not at all. Since this is a self-evaluation of English ability, it is debatable how many of our respondents would actually choose the first or the last category.

They would probably exaggerate or underestimate a little to avoid these extremes because this is "normal, polite, and intelligent" Korean behavior. Only six percent of our respondents said they spoke English fluently, while two percent replied that they spoke no English, although many respondents in our first study indicated that English language was their most important problem. The fact that 75 percent of our respondents reported their English speaking ability was "fair" to "good" might be reliable but certainly not valid information.

In our first study we wanted to know if our respondents would like to return to Korea after their retirement. However, the Korean version of the question did not specifically refer to retirement. We did not use the Korean term *twae jik*

(*continued*)

because the connotation is much narrower than the English word *retirement*. Normally, *twae jik* means disengagement from an official or public position accompanied by a pension or retirement benefit. Disengagement from self-employment is not *twae jik*. The conceptual equivalence of the English retirement, we thought, would be a composite of the following: "When you get old, you won't have to work and can take things easy for the rest of your life." Our question was, "When you get old, would you like to return to Korea and wish to spend the rest of your life there?" No wonder the overwhelming majority (82 percent) of our respondents wanted to go back to their native country and take things easy for the rest of their lives! It turned out that we had asked about their dreams, rather than their plans.

Source: Won Moo Hurh and Kwang Chung Kim, "Methodological Problems in the Study of Korean Immigrants: Conceptual, Interactional, Sampling and Interviewer Training Difficulties," in William T. Liu (ed.), *Methodological Problems in Minority Research* (Chicago: Pacific/Asian American Mental Health Research Center, 1982), pp. 61–80. Used by permission.

different levels of acculturation tend to respond differently to the instrument. Using the above example, in addition to administering the caregiver burden scale, you might assess the Mexican American caregivers' degree of acculturation and whether they recently immigrated from Mexico. If recent immigrants and others who are less acculturated tend to have the same average burden scores as their more acculturated counterparts, that would support the notion that the scale might be equivalent. If, on the other hand, their average scores are different, that might suggest possible problems in measurement equivalence, since scale scores seem to be influenced by cultural differences.

You should be cautious in making this inference, however. Perhaps the immigration experience and being new and less acculturated in a foreign land actually do make the caregiving role more burdensome. If so, then the differences in average scores would not mean the scale lacked equivalence. To get a better handle on this issue, you might want to explore whether several individual items on the scale each correlated highly with the culture-related factors and whether deleting or modifying those items would sufficiently reduce the differences in average scale scores.

If the foregoing analyses have not convinced you that your scale lacks measurement equivalence, your next step would be to test its validity separately in the different cultures in which you plan to use it, using the various techniques for assessing validity that we'll discuss in Chapter 8. Assessing the scale's validity is the ultimate test of its measurement equivalence. For example, you might see if a sample of Mexican American caregivers score much higher on the scale than a demographically equivalent sample of Mexican Americans who are not caregivers.

Figure 5-1 depicts the three types of measurement equivalence that we have been discussing. It shows how assessing linguistic equivalence is a prerequisite for assessing conceptual equivalence and how metric equivalence may be assessed once linguistic and conceptual equivalence have been established.

PROBLEMATIC ISSUES IN MAKING RESEARCH MORE CULTURALLY COMPETENT

Several knotty issues complicate efforts to make research more culturally competent. One involves complexities in defining who qualifies as a member of a specific ethnic minority group. For example, Norton and Manson (1996) suggest that it is not always easy to answer the question, "Who is American Indian or Alaskan Native?" What about individuals who seek the benefits of affirmative action as Native Americans merely because their great-great-grandmother was a Cherokee? Beutler and his associates (1996) point to vagaries and inconsistencies regarding who to classify as Hispanic. Cubans, for example, qualify as Hispanic for "special affirmative action considerations, whereas Spaniards (the original Hispanics) do not" (p. 893).

A related problem involves the labels we communicate to our research participants to classify their eth-

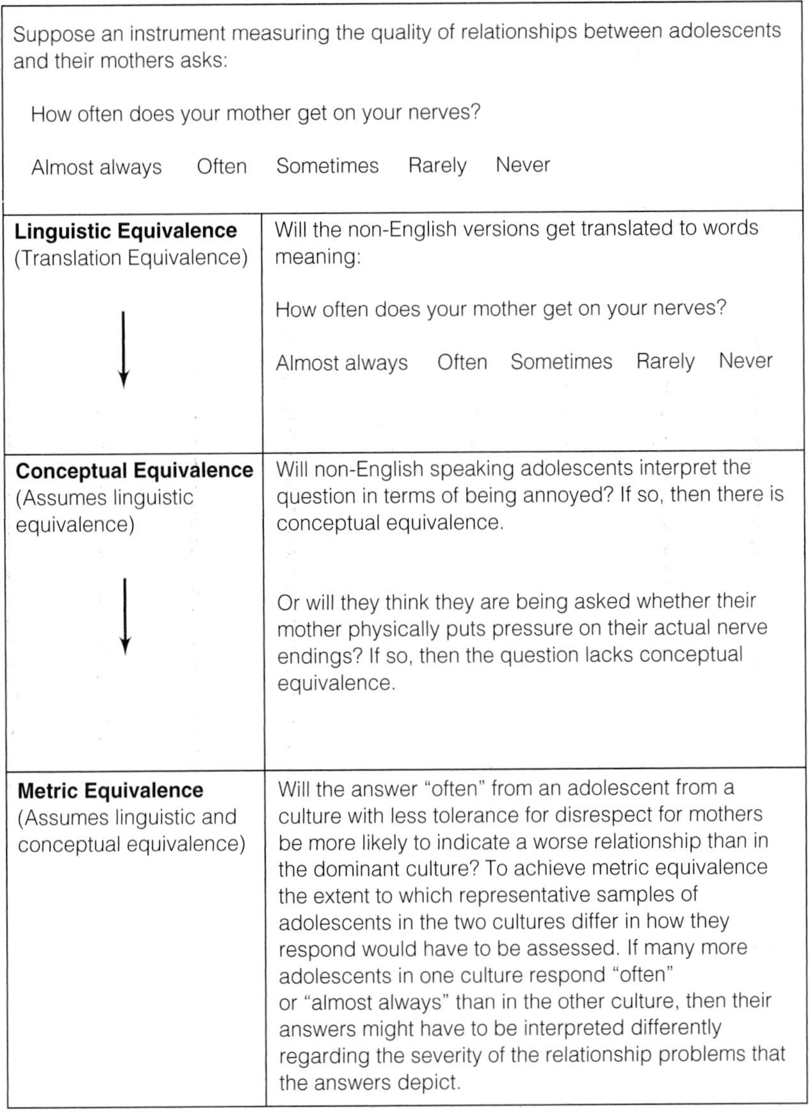

Suppose an instrument measuring the quality of relationships between adolescents and their mothers asks:

How often does your mother get on your nerves?

Almost always Often Sometimes Rarely Never

Linguistic Equivalence (Translation Equivalence) ↓	Will the non-English versions get translated to words meaning: How often does your mother get on your nerves? Almost always Often Sometimes Rarely Never
Conceptual Equivalence (Assumes linguistic equivalence) ↓	Will non-English speaking adolescents interpret the question in terms of being annoyed? If so, then there is conceptual equivalence. Or will they think they are being asked whether their mother physically puts pressure on their actual nerve endings? If so, then the question lacks conceptual equivalence.
Metric Equivalence (Assumes linguistic and conceptual equivalence)	Will the answer "often" from an adolescent from a culture with less tolerance for disrespect for mothers be more likely to indicate a worse relationship than in the dominant culture? To achieve metric equivalence the extent to which representative samples of adolescents in the two cultures differ in how they respond would have to be assessed. If many more adolescents in one culture respond "often" or "almost always" than in the other culture, then their answers might have to be interpreted differently regarding the severity of the relationship problems that the answers depict.

Figure 5-1 Types of Measurement Equivalence

nicity. Some less acculturated Hispanic Americans, for example, might prefer the term *Latino*. Many of those who are more acculturated might prefer the term *Hispanic*. Others might resent either term, and prefer to be classified according to their nationality, such as *Mexican American*. If you are planning a study in a particular geographical area where one term is more commonly preferred, and another term is likely to be resented, it would behoove you to find this out in advance and make sure you use the preferred term when communicating with participants to whom that term applies.

Another issue pertains to important subgroup differences within specific ethnic minority groups. No ethnic minority group is homogeneous. Each is heterogeneous with regard to such characteristics as culture of origin, socioeconomic status, level of acculturation, whether and how recently individuals or their prior generations immigrated, whether individuals speak the language of the dominant culture, and whether they had traumatic political refugee experiences (Alvidrez, Azocar, and Miranda, 1996). Failing to consider this heterogeneity can result in misleading research conclusions. When we use the term

"Hispanic," it makes a difference whether we are referring to people whose roots are in Mexico, Cuba, Puerto Rico, or elsewhere in Latin America. When we use the term "American Indian" or "Native American," it makes a difference whether we are referring to people who live in Alaska, on a reservation in New Mexico, or in an apartment in the Bronx. If a study evaluating treatment effectiveness includes only low-income African American participants and only middle-class whites, and fails to consider socioeconomic factors, it might end up attributing differences in treatment outcome between the whites and African Americans to ethnicity even if those differences in outcome were really due to socioeconomic differences. To be truly culturally competent, therefore, merely including ample numbers of minority group participants is not enough. One also has to assess and analyze additional characteristics so as to avoid the following two problems: (1) attributing to ethnicity differences that are really due to other factors, and (2) overgeneralizing to an entire minority group conclusions that apply only to subgroups within that minority group.

We'll end this chapter by noting that there is no foolproof recipe for ensuring that your research will be culturally competent in all respects. Researchers in social work and allied fields are still learning how to make our studies more culturally competent. They also are empirically testing some of the recommendations that are emerging through the practice wisdom of researchers conducting cross-cultural studies. Nevertheless, if you follow the recommendations made in this chapter, we think you will significantly enhance the cultural competence of your research. As with other aspects of research methodology, how much you can do will be influenced by the extent of your resources. Within your feasibility constraints we hope you will do all you can to maximize the cultural competence of your research, which includes maximizing your cultural competence in general.

Main Points

- Cultural competence means being aware of and appropriately responding to the ways in which cultural factors and cultural differences should influence what we investigate, how we investigate, and how we interpret our findings.

- Studies that do not include adequate representation from specific minority and oppressed populations in their samples are not generalizable to those populations.

- Cultural insensitivity can result in interpreting research findings on ethnic differences in a prejudicial manner, focusing too much on the deficits of minorities and too little on their strengths.

- Culturally competent researchers will include socioeconomic factors in their analyses when they are studying other ways in which minority and majority populations differ.

- Culturally competent researchers will also consider the immigration experience and acculturation as factors to include in their research as they study differences between minority and majority populations.

- Acculturation is the process in which a group or individual changes after coming into contact with a majority culture, taking on the language, values, attitudes, and lifestyle preferences of the majority culture.

- Studies that use culturally insensitive procedures, or which are not responsive to the concerns of minority populations, can poison the climate for future research among those populations.

- Before you begin any investigation with minority or oppressed populations, it is crucial that you develop cultural competence regarding those populations, including being well read in the literature on their cultures.

- Representatives of the minority cultures being studied should be included in the formulation of the research questions and in all subsequent stages of the research.

- To alleviate barriers to the recruitment and retention of research participants from minority and oppressed populations, you should: obtain endorsement from community leaders; use culturally sensitive approaches regarding confidentiality; employ local community members as research staff; provide adequate compensation; alleviate transportation and child-care barriers; choose a sensitive and accessible setting; use and train culturally competent interviewers; use bilingual staff; understand cultural factors influencing participation; use anonymous enrollment with stigmatized populations; utilize special sampling techniques; learn where to look; connect with and nurture referral sources; use frequent and individualized contacts and personal touches; use anchor points; and use tracking methods.

• Three main threats to culturally competent measurement include (1) the use of interviewers whose personal characteristics or interviewing styles offend or intimidate minority respondents or in other ways make them reluctant to divulge relevant and valid information, (2) the use of language that minority respondents do not understand, and (3) cultural bias.

• When some of your research participants are not fluent in the majority language, you should use bilingual interviewers, translate measures into the language of the respondents, and pretest the measures to see if they are understood as intended.

• Back-translation is one step to be taken to try to attain translation validity. It begins with a bilingual person translating the instrument and its instructions to a target language. Then another bilingual person translates from the target language back to the original language. The original instrument is then compared to the back-translated version, and items with discrepancies are modified further.

• Measurement equivalence means that a measurement procedure developed in one culture will have the same value and meaning when administered to people in another culture.

• Linguistic equivalence is attained when an instrument has been translated and back-translated successfully.

• Conceptual equivalence means that instruments and observed behaviors have the same meanings across cultures.

• Metric equivalence means that scores on a measure are comparable across cultures.

• Ways to assess measurement equivalence include assessing whether scores on an instrument are correlated with measures of acculturation and testing the measure's validity separately in the different cultures in which you plan to use it.

• Three issues complicating efforts to make research more culturally competent are (1) complexities in defining who qualifies as a member of a specific ethnic minority group, (2) preferences and resentments regarding the labels communicated to research participants to classify their ethnicity, and (3) important subgroup differences within specific ethnic minority groups (no ethnic minority group is homogeneous).

Review Questions and Exercises

1. Suppose you wanted to conduct research whose findings might help improve services or policies affecting migrant farmworkers who recently immigrated from Mexico to the United States.

a. Contrast how taking a culturally competent approach would differ from a culturally insensitive approach in each of the following phases of the research process: (1) formulating a research question; (2) measurement; (3) recruiting participants; and (4) interpreting findings.
b. Discuss the steps you would take to recruit and retain the participation of the migrant farmworkers in your study.

2. Suppose, in the Exercise 1 study, you wanted to use the "Child's Attitude toward Mother (CAM)" scale to assess mother–child relationship problems. (You'll find that scale in Figure 8-2 of Chapter 8.)

a. Examine that scale and identify at least two items that might be problematic from the standpoint of conceptual equivalence or metric equivalence. Discuss why.
b. Briefly describe the steps you would take to maximize the linguistic equivalence and conceptual equivalence of a revised version of the scale.
c. Briefly describe how you would assess the measurement equivalence of your revised scale.

3. Examine the tables of contents and abstracts of recent issues of the journal *Research on Social Work Practice* until you find an article reporting on a study assessing the measurement equivalence of a scale. Briefly summarize how that study assessed measurement equivalence and its findings.

Internet Exercises

1. Using Google or an alternative search engine, enter the search term *culturally sensitive research* to find at least one report of an effort to conduct culturally sensitive research or to improve the cultural sensitivity of a measurement instrument. Briefly summarize and critically appraise what you find.

2. Go to www.Treatment.org/Documents/documents .html. There you will find a report entitled, "Increasing Cultural Sensitivity of the Addiction Severity Index (ASI): An Example with Native Americans in

North Dakota." Read the first two chapters of that report, with an emphasis on Chapter 2. Critically appraise the steps that were or were not taken to try to improve and assess the cultural sensitivity of the ASI.

3. Use InfoTrac College Edition to find an article titled, "Translation of the Rosenberg Self-Esteem Scale into American Sign Language: A Principal Components Analysis," by Teresa V. Crowe, which appeared in the March 2002 issue of *Social Work Research*. Briefly describe and critically appraise the steps taken in the reported study to achieve and assess measurement equivalence.

4. Use InfoTrac College Edition to find an article titled, "Korean Social Work Students' Attitudes Toward Homosexuals," by Sung Lim Hyun and Miriam McNown Johnson, which appeared in the Fall 2001 issue of the *Journal of Social Work Education*. Briefly describe how the study reported in this article illustrates the concept of *metric equivalence*.

5. Use InfoTrac College Edition to find an article titled, "Ethnic Pride, Biculturalism, and Drug Use Norms of Urban American Indian Adolescents" by Stephen Kulis, Maria Napoli, and Flavio Francisco Marsiglia, which appeared in the June 2002 issue of *Social Work Research*. Briefly describe and critically appraise how that study illustrates research that is culturally sensitive.

6. Go to the website developed and operated by Dr. Marianne Yoshioka, a social work professor at Columbia University, called "Psychosocial Measures for Asian-American Populations," and located at www.columbia.edu/cu/ssw/projects/pmap. Download some of the abstracts of measures you find at that site, and briefly describe how they illustrate at least two main points about culturally sensitive measurement discussed in this chapter.

Additional Readings

Cuéllar, Israel, and Freddy A. Paniagua (eds.). 2000. *Handbook of Multicultural Mental Health: Assessment and Treatment of Diverse Populations*. San Diego, CA: Academic Press. This edited volume contains chapters covering material that can enhance your cultural competence in practice as well as research. Among the research concepts covered are cultural bias in sampling and interpreting psychological test scores and how to assess measurement equivalence. Several chapters also focus on specific minority groups in discussing culturally competent practice and research with each group.

Fong, Rowena, and Sharlene Furuto (eds.). 2001. *Culturally Competent Practice: Skills, Interventions, and Evaluations*. Boston: Allyn & Bacon. As its title implies, most of the chapters in this book focus on culturally competent social work practice. Developing that cultural competence is important in its own right, and it will also help you become more culturally competent in your research. In addition, Part 4 of this five-part book focuses on applying culturally competent practice concepts and skills in the evaluation of programs and practice. Key concepts addressed include applying culturally competent evaluation skills, the strengths perspective, and the empowerment process in designing evaluations and in interacting with African American, Mexican American and Latino, Native American, Asian American, and Hawaiian and Pacific Islander individuals, families, organizations, and communities.

Hernandez, Mario, and Mareesa R. Isaacs (eds.). 1998. *Promoting Cultural Competence in Children's Mental Health Services*. Baltimore, MD: Paul H. Brookes. In addition to offering a useful perspective on various dimensions of cultural competence in children's mental health services, this book provides three chapters focusing specifically on cultural competence in evaluation and research.

Journal of Consulting and Clinical Psychology, 64(5), 1996. This psychology journal often contains excellent research articles relevant to clinical social work practice and research. This issue has a special section on recruiting and retaining minorities in psychotherapy research. Among the articles in this special section are ones focusing on Native Americans, African Americans, Latinos, elderly minorities, and homeless mentally ill people.

Potocky, Miriam, and Antoinette Y. Rodgers-Farmer (eds.). 1998. *Social Work Research with Minority and Oppressed Populations*. New York: Haworth Press. As we mentioned in Chapter 4, this handy collection of articles contains innovative ideas for avoiding cultural bias and insensitivity in research with minority and oppressed populations. Most pertinent to this chapter are two articles that describe issues in the construction of instruments to measure depression among women of color and gerontological social work concerns among nonwhite ethnic elders.

Suzuki, Lisa A., Paul J. Meller, and Joseph G. Ponterotto (eds.). 1996. *Handbook of Multicultural Assessment*. San Francisco, CA: Jossey-Bass. This handbook begins by covering various issues regarding cultural sensitivity in the usage of psychological assessment instruments across cultures. Then it reviews cultural sensitivity issues pertaining to specific instruments for assessing social, emotional, and cognitive functioning. Its final section examines emerging issues in multicultural assessment.

PART 3

Problem Formulation and Measurement

Posing problems properly is often more difficult than answering them. Indeed, a properly phrased question often seems to answer itself. You may have discovered the answer to a question just in the process of making the question clear to someone else. Part 3 considers the structuring of inquiry, which involves posing research questions that are proper from a scientific standpoint and useful from the social work and social welfare standpoint.

After providing an overview of the research process, Chapter 6 addresses the beginnings of research. It examines some of the purposes of inquiry; sources and criteria for selecting a research problem; common issues and processes to be considered in sharpening the research question and planning a research study; and the units of analysis in social work research. After reading this chapter, you should see how social work research follows the same problem-solving process as does social work practice.

Chapter 7 deals with specifying what you want to study and the steps or operations for observing the concepts you seek to investigate—a process called *conceptualization* and *operationalization.* We're going to look at some of the terms we use quite casually in social work practice—such as self-esteem, social adjustment, and compassion—and see how essential it is to be clear about what we really mean by such terms. Once we have gotten clear on what we mean when we use certain terms, we are then in a position to create measurements to which those terms refer.

Chapter 8 looks at common sources of measurement error and steps we can take to avoid measurement error and assess the quality of our measurement procedures. Finally, we'll look at the process of constructing some measurement instruments that are frequently used in social work research. Chapter 9 will discuss guidelines for asking questions and for the construction of questionnaires and scales.

What you learn in Part 3 will bring you to the verge of making controlled, scientific observations. Learning how to make such observations should enhance your work as a social worker even if you never conduct a research study. Practitioners are constantly engaged in making observations that guide their decision making. The more scientific and valid their observations, the better will be the decisions they make based on those observations.

CHAPTER 6

Problem Formulation

What You'll Learn in This Chapter

Here you'll learn about the beginnings of the research process, the phases of that process, how to plan a research study, and the wide variety of choices to be made concerning who or what is to be studied when, how, and for what purpose.

INTRODUCTION

Social work research has much in common with evidence-based social work practice. Both endeavors follow essentially the same problem-solving process in seeking to resolve social welfare problems. Both begin with the formulation of the problem, which includes recognizing a difficulty, defining it, and specifying it. Researchers and evidence-based practitioners then generate, explore, and select alternative strategies for solving the problem. Finally, they implement the chosen approach, evaluate it, and disseminate their findings. In both practice and research, these phases are contingent on one another. Although the logical order is to go from one phase to the next, insurmountable obstacles encountered in any particular phase will prevent you from moving to the next phase and require you to return to a previous phase.

For example, in evidence-based practice if an intervention with the best evidence is unacceptable to your client, you might need to resume your search to find an alternative intervention without as much evidence but which fits your client's values and preferences. Likewise, you would have to do the same if after implementing and evaluating an intervention you find it to be ineffective with your client. As we consider the research process, keep in mind that these same returns to earlier phases apply. Thus, if after designing an elegant research study we realize that its implementation costs would exceed our resources, we would need to return to earlier phases and come up with a study that would be more feasible to implement.

OVERVIEW OF THE RESEARCH PROCESS

• Phase 1: Problem Formulation. In the first phase, a difficulty is recognized for which more knowledge is needed. A question—the research question—is posed. The question and its inherent concepts are progressively sharpened to become more specific, relevant, and meaningful to the field. As this is done, the question of feasibility of implementation is always considered. Ultimately, the purpose of the research is finalized and the elements of the research, including units of analysis, hypotheses, variables, and operational definitions, are explicated. The literature review is one critical step in this phase.

• Phase 2: Designing the Study. The second phase considers alternative logical arrangements and data collection methods. Which arrangements and methods are selected will depend on the issues addressed in the problem formulation phase. Feasibility is one such issue; the purpose of the research is another. Studies that inquire about causation will require logical arrangements that meet the three criteria for establishing causality; these criteria will be discussed in Chapter 10. Other arrangements might suffice for studies that seek to explore or describe certain phenomena.

The term *research design* can have two connotations. One refers to alternative logical arrangements to be selected. This connotes experimental research designs, correlational research designs, and so forth. The other connotation deals with the act of designing the study in its broadest sense. This refers to all of the decisions we make in planning the study—decisions not only about what overarching type of design to use, but also about sampling, sources and procedures for collecting data, measurement issues, data analysis plans, and so on.

• Phase 3: Data Collection. In Phase 3, the study designed in the second phase is implemented. The study's purpose and design direct to what degree this implementation is rigidly structured in advance or is more flexible and open to modification as new insights are discovered. Deductive studies that seek to verify hypotheses or descriptive studies that emphasize accuracy and objectivity will require more rigidly structured data-collection procedures than will studies that use qualitative methods to better understand the meanings of certain phenomena or to generate hypotheses about them.

• Phase 4: Data Processing. Depending on the research methods chosen, a volume of observations will have been amassed in a form that is probably difficult to interpret. Whether the data are quantitative or qualitative, the data processing in the fourth phase typically involves the classification, or coding, of observations in order to make them more interpretable. The coded information commonly is entered in some computer format. However, small-scale studies carried out by social work practitioners, particularly studies involving single-case designs, may not require computerization. Subsequent chapters will describe some of the ways in which quantitative, qualitative, and single-case data are processed or transformed for analysis.

• Phase 5: Data Analysis. In this phase, the processed data are manipulated to help answer the research question. Conceivably, the analysis will also yield unanticipated findings that reflect on the research problem but go beyond the specific question that guided the research. The results of the analysis will feed back into the initial problem formulation and may initiate another cycle of inquiry. Subsequent chapters will describe a few of the many options available in analyzing data.

• Phase 6: Interpreting the Findings. It will become apparent throughout the rest of this book that there is no one correct way to plan a study and no way to ensure that the outcome of the data analysis will provide the correct answer to the research question. Certain statistical procedures may be essential to provide the best possible interpretation of the data, but no mathematical formula or computer will obviate the need to make some judgments about the meaning of the findings. Inevitably, we encounter rival explanations of the findings and must consider various methodological limitations that influence the degree to which the findings can be generalized.

Consequently, research reports do not end with a presentation of the data analysis results. Instead, the results are followed by or included in a thorough discussion of alternative ways to interpret those results, of what generalizations can and cannot be made based on them, and of methodological limitations bearing on the meaning and validity of the results. Finally, implications are drawn for social welfare policy and program development, social work practice and theory, and future research.

• Phase 7: Writing the Research Report. Although writing up our research logically comes in the last phase of the research process, in practice we write pieces of it as we go along. The components of the research report follow in large part the above phases of the research process. Although the specific terminology of the headings will vary from study to study, typically the report begins with an *introduction* that provides a background to the research problem, informs the reader of the rationale and significance of the study, and reviews relevant theory and research. This introduction is followed by an explication of the conceptual elements of the study, including units of analysis, variables, hypotheses, assumptions, and operational definitions. A *methodology* section delineates in precise terms the design of the study, including the logical arrangements, sampling and data-collection procedures, and the measurement approach used. Next come the *results* of the data analysis, which identify the statistical procedures employed; display data in tables, graphs, or other visual devices; and provide a narrative that reports in a technical, factual sense what specific data mean. This is followed by a *discussion* section, which includes the issues identified in Phase 6. Depending on the length of the report or its discussion section (or both) and whether an abstract was developed, the report might end with a brief summary of the foregoing components that highlights the major findings and conclusions. Chapter 23 of this book provides further information on writing research reports.

Diagramming the Research Process

Ultimately, the research process needs to be seen as a whole for an effective research design to be created. Unfortunately, both textbooks and human cognition operate on the basis of sequential parts. Figure 6-1 presents a schematic view of the social work research process. We present this view reluctantly, because it suggests more of a "cookbook" approach to research than is the case in practice. Nonetheless, it should help you picture the whole process before we launch into the specific details of particular components of research.

At the top of the diagram are problems, ideas, and theories, the possible beginning points for a line of research. The capital letters (A, B, X, Y, and so on) represent variables or concepts such as sexism, social functioning, or a particular intervention. Thus, the problem might be finding out whether certain interventions are more effective than others in improving social functioning. Alternatively, your inquiry might begin with a specific idea about the way things are. You might have the idea that men in your agency are promoted to supervisory or administrative positions sooner than women and that administrative practices therefore reflect the problem of sexism. We have put question marks in the diagram to indicate that you aren't sure things are the way you suspect they are. Finally, we have represented a *theory* as a complex set of relationships among several variables.

Notice, moreover, that there is often a movement back and forth across these several possible beginnings. An initial problem may lead to the formulation of an idea, which may fit into a larger theory. The theory may produce new ideas and facilitate the perception of new problems.

Any or all of these three elements may suggest the need for empirical research. The purpose of such

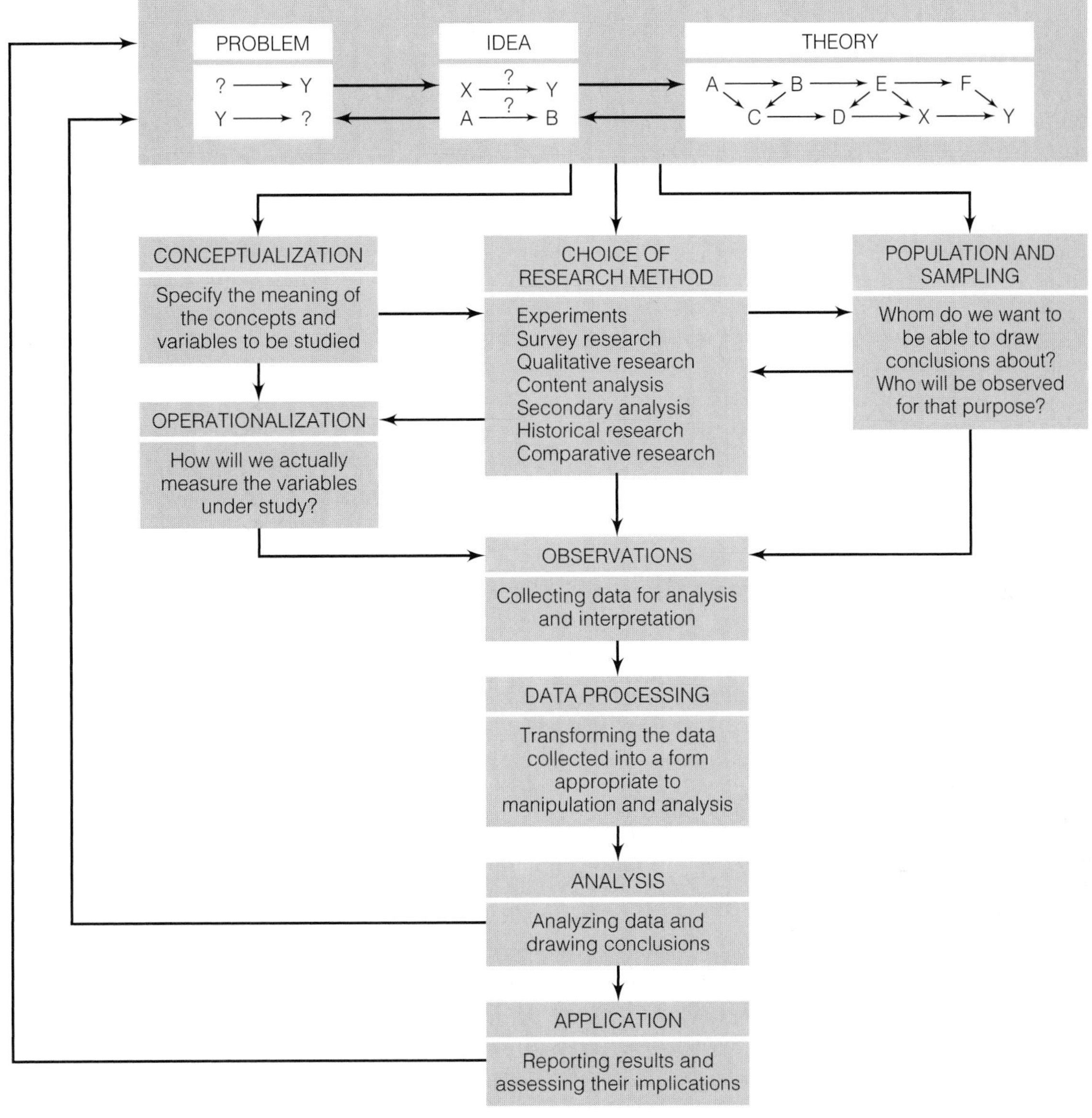

Figure 6-1 The Social Work Research Process

research can be to explore a problem, test a specific idea, or validate a complex theory. Whatever the purpose, a variety of decisions need to be made, as the remainder of the diagram shows.

To make this discussion more concrete, let's take a specific research example. Suppose you are working in a group residential facility for children who have behavioral or emotional disorders. A problem is perceived about the amount of antisocial behavior that is occurring in the cottages (residential units). You have the idea that some cottages may have more antisocial behavior than others and that this might have something to do with different styles of behavioral management used by parents in different cottages. You find a framework to pursue your idea further in learning theory. Based on that theory, you postulate that the cottage parents who use behavioral reinforcement contingencies—such as tokens for good behavior that can be accumulated and cashed in for certain special privileges—are the ones whose cottages experience the fewest antisocial behaviors. Or your initial expertise in learning theory may have stimulated the idea, which in turn may have led you to notice the problem.

Your next step would be to conceptualize what you mean by "styles" of behavioral management, reinforcement contingencies, and antisocial behavior. Then you would need to specify the concrete steps or operations that will be used to measure the concepts. Decisions must be made about whom to study. Will you study all of the residents or cottages in the facility—that is, its population? If not, then how will you go about selecting a sample of them? Or do you wish to draw conclusions about group-care facilities in general and thus conceive of your entire facility as a sample that represents a larger population of facilities?

Additional decisions must be made about the choice of a research method. Will you conduct an experiment, randomly assigning children to cottages using different behavioral management styles? Will you conduct a survey, simply interviewing parents about how they attempt to manage behavior and their perception of the frequency of antisocial behaviors in their cottages? Will you do a content analysis of case records to try sorting out the answer to your question? Perhaps you will opt for qualitative methods, observing and discussing in an open-ended manner what goes on in the cottages, rather than attempt to test some precisely defined hypothesis.

Whatever you decide, your next step is to implement that decision, which means conducting your observations. The data you collect will then be processed and analyzed. Suppose in the process of conducting your study you learned that your facility systematically obtains follow-up information from the community about how well discharged youths adjust to the postdischarge community environment. This information includes data on juvenile court contacts, school attendance, and school academic performance and conduct. Suppose further that you get a new idea after finding empirical support for your initial idea that different behavioral management styles are associated with different levels of antisocial behavior, and after finding that the above postdischarge data are available. You wonder whether the differences you found continue after the child is discharged; that is, you wonder whether the children who are exposed to the most effective behavioral management styles while they are residents will continue to exhibit less antisocial behavior after they return to the community.

The completion of one research study will then have looped back to generate the research process all over again, this time in connection to social adjustment in the community. Suppose you conduct the new study. If your results are like those of similar research that has been conducted in this problem area, you will find that the type of treatment children received or the gains they make in your program have little or no bearing on their postdischarge adjustment. In other words, you find no difference in postdischarge adjustment between children who received certain types of behavior management in your program and those who received other types, or between those who exhibited little antisocial behavior prior to discharge and those who exhibited a lot (Whittaker, 1987).

Once again, you will return to the beginning of the research process. You have a new problem, one that has been identified in the research you just completed: What happens in your facility seems to have no bearing on postdischarge outcome. Is your program therefore ineffective? Perhaps; if so, that would be a whopper of a problem to begin dealing with. But in thinking about this, you get another idea. Perhaps your program is effective as far as it goes and given the resources it has; the problem may be that you need to go further—to intervene in the postdischarge environment. Perhaps it is not reasonable to expect your program to do more than demonstrate its ability to enhance the functioning of children while they are in residence and provide them with a healthy environment for as long as they are there. If society expects you to influence their behavior in the community, then it needs to provide your program with the mandate and the resources to intervene in the postdischarge community environment.

Your new idea may be thoughtful and quite plausible, but is it valid? Or is it just a convenient rationalization for the dismal results of your last study? To find out, you begin working on another study. This time your focus will be not on predischarge factors that are associated with adjustment, but on factors in the postdischarge environment associated with it. To what extent are there harmful and beneficial environmental conditions associated with community adjustment—conditions that perhaps can be influenced by postdischarge social work intervention? Suppose the results of your new study confirm such an association. Stop reading for a moment at the end of this sentence and ask yourself whether those results would again return you to the start of a new research process and what the next problem or idea might be.

Okay, have you thought about it? If so, then you probably came up with several new problems or ideas. Chances are that one of them was to test whether certain postdischarge interventions can be implemented effectively to influence environmental conditions—and whether those interventions ultimately promote improved community adjustment. Perhaps this could be done on a small, pilot basis if you have funding restraints.

The Research Proposal

Quite often in the design of a research project you will have to lay out the details of your plan for someone else's review or approval or both. In the case of a course project, for example, your instructor might very well want to see a "proposal" before you set off to work. Later in your career, if you wanted to undertake a major project, you might need to obtain funding from a foundation or government agency, and it would most definitely want a detailed proposal that described how you were going to spend its money.

In Chapter 23, we'll discuss how to develop and write research proposals. Different funding agencies may have different requirements for the elements or structure of a research proposal. Commonly required elements include (1) problem or objective, (2) conceptual framework, (3) literature review, (4) sampling procedures, (5) measurement, (6) design and data-collection methods, (7) data analysis plans, (8) schedule, and (9) budget.

Now that you've had a broad overview of social research, let's move on and learn exactly how to design and execute each specific step. If you have found a research topic that really interests you, keep that topic in mind as we see how you might go about studying it.

SELECTING TOPICS AND RESEARCH QUESTIONS

Throughout this book we will discuss the issues involved in all phases of the research process in much greater depth. Let's begin with a closer examination of the first phase: problem formulation. This phase commences with the selection of a topic or problem.

Impetus for Topic Selection

Because social work is such a diverse profession, the possible research topics in the field are virtually endless. They can be in one problem area or cut across different problem areas, such as health or mental health, child welfare, gerontology, substance abuse, poverty, mental retardation, crime and delinquency, family violence, and many others. Within one or more problem areas, research might focus on individuals, families, groups, communities, organizations, or broader social systems. It might deal with the characteristics of a target population, the services social workers provide, the way social workers are supervised or trained, issues in the administration of social welfare agencies, issues in social policy, assessment of client and community needs for purposes of guiding program development or treatment planning, the reasons prospective clients don't use services, the dynamics of the problems social workers deal with and their implications for service delivery, how adequately social agencies are responding to certain problems and whether they are reaching the target population in the intended manner, attitudes practitioners have about certain types of clients or services, factors bearing on citizen participation strategies and their outcomes—and a host of other topics.

In social work research, as distinguished from social scientific research in other disciplines, the impetus for selecting a topic should come from decisions that confront social service agencies or the information needed to solve practical problems in social welfare. The researcher's intellectual curiosity and personal interests certainly come into play, as they do in all research, but a study is more likely to have value to the social work field (and to be considered social work research) if the topic is selected because it addresses information needed to guide policy, planning, or practice decisions in social welfare. The value of social work research depends on its applicability to practical social work and social welfare concerns, not on whether it builds or tests general social science theories. Some useful social work research studies can be carried out without any explicit linkages to general social science theories. Other useful studies do have such linkages. Sometimes, by relating the problem formulation to existing theory, we might enhance the study's potential utility, particularly if that theory provides a framework that helps other researchers comprehend the rationale for and significance of framing the question as we did.

When we say that social work research sets out to solve practical problems in social welfare, the connotation of an "applied" research focus is inescapable. This is in contrast to "pure" research, which connotes the attempt to advance knowledge for its own sake. But this distinction is not as clear as it first may seem. Although social work research may not aim to advance general social science theory, its findings may still have that effect. Polansky (1975), for example, discusses how a social work research study in which he participated—on "behavioral contagion in children's groups"—was cited more frequently in the social psychology literature than in the social work literature (Polansky, Lippitt, and Redl, 1950). By the same token, an applied aim is not necessary in an investigation for it to produce knowledge that is relevant to solving social welfare problems. Social work has always "borrowed" basic social scientific knowledge advanced by "pure" social research and applied it to practical social welfare concerns.

Is It Social Work Research?

Some important studies can transcend disciplinary boundaries and still be valuable as social work research. A study to assess the impact of socioenvironmental family stress on whether children drop out of school, for example, could be done by educational psychologists or sociologists. But if the practical need that provided the impetus for selecting that research problem had to do with informing policy makers about the need to employ school social workers to help alleviate family stress as one way to fight the dropout problem, then the study would be of great interest to social workers. The same would apply if the study's main implication was about guiding the practice of school social workers, such as pointing to the need for intensifying interventions to alleviate socioenvironmental sources of family stress or helping families better cope with that stress (as opposed to focusing intervention exclusively on counseling the student).

A study by Royse (1988) exemplifies the sometimes fuzzy distinction between social work research and research associated with other social scientific disciplines. Royse was interested in the degree of predictability of voting precincts with regard to voter support or nonsupport of referenda to continue or approve new taxes to support the provision of human services. His analysis of precinct-by-precinct election returns on such referenda identified certain patterns from which he developed implications for social service administrators and members of planning committees who conduct campaigns to influence the outcome of similar future elections. Would you consider Royse's study to be social work research? Or would you be more likely to associate it with another field—political science, perhaps?

Although Royse's study appears to overlap with political science, and perhaps will be cited by political scientists, we can also call it social work research for three reasons. One reason is that Royse was a social work faculty member at the time he reported his study. Also, his study was published in a social work journal, *ARETE*. But perhaps the most important reason to consider the study as social work research is that its prime purpose was to develop knowledge to guide the practice of social service administrators. What if the same study, with the same implications, were done by a political scientist? Some might still consider it social work research, whereas others might argue that although its findings are relevant to social workers, it is not social work research. We know of no "correct" answer to this question, and you might understandably feel that it matters little what we call the research. Our point is merely to illustrate the difficulty that can arise when we try to distinguish social work research from social research, a difficulty connected to the fact that social work traditionally has taken social scientific knowledge from a variety of disciplines and applied it to social welfare problems.

NARROWING RESEARCH TOPICS INTO RESEARCH QUESTIONS

Research topics are broad starting points that need to be narrowed down into a research question or research problem. (Because the research question typically deals with needed information to solve practical problems in social welfare, the terms *research question* and *research problem* are often used interchangeably.) Suppose, for example, you want to conduct research on the topic *welfare reform* in the United States. What specific question about welfare reform do you want to research? Do you want to study the similarities and differences among states in the features of their welfare reform legislation? How about factors influencing the legislative process? Perhaps you can compare differential rates of "success" that alternative welfare reform policies have had in removing people from welfare rolls. In contrast, you might want to assess the ways in which policies that aim to remove people from welfare by increasing recipient work requirements have impacted the lives of the people who have been moved off of welfare. How do they manage to survive? What happens to their health insurance coverage when they no longer are eligible for Medicaid? Do their young children receive adequate supervision, nutrition, and medical care?

As you can see from the above example, research topics can contain a vast number of diverse alternative research questions, and until you narrow your topic down into a specific research question, you can become immobilized, not knowing where to begin. Several criteria can guide you in the narrowing down process. Some of these criteria may have already guided your choice of the broader topic. *Personal interest,* for example, may have guided you to choose the topic *sexual abuse of children.* Perhaps you are interested in that topic because you worked for a child welfare agency investigating reported sexual abuse. That experience may have you particularly interested in a research question regarding the validity of a certain investigative procedure for determining whether or not sexual abuse really occurred. Or perhaps you have worked in a treatment center for sexually abused girls and want to study which of several alternative treatment approaches are most effective in alleviating their trauma symptoms. Perhaps you have worked with perpetrators and want to test out the effectiveness of a new treatment for them. Maybe your professional or personal experiences have piqued your curiosity as to whether a close nurturing relationship with a positive adult role model helps prevent the development of severe emotional and behavioral disorders among sexually abused children.

Another criterion for narrowing your topic might be the *information needs of the agency* in which you work or with whom you consult. If you want to conduct your research in a residential treatment center that treats many sexually abused girls who have developed severe impulse control problems, for example, the center staff might advise you that they have a more urgent need to answer the question, "Which is more effective, Intervention A or Intervention B, in helping these girls develop better impulse control?" than to answer the question, "Does a close nurturing relationship with a positive adult role model help prevent the development of severe emotional and behavioral disorders among sexually abused children?"

When you narrow your topic into a specific research question, you will have to consider the *feasibility* of actually investigating that question. Various resource and other barriers might force you to come up with an alternative question that is more feasible to study. We'll say more about such barriers shortly.

Ultimately, the most important criterion that should guide you in narrowing down your research topic into a research question is that its answer should have significant potential *relevance for guiding social welfare policy or social work practice.* One way to gauge the general utility of a research question is to discuss it with key people who work in the area to which your research question pertains. Another is to conduct a thorough review of the literature relevant to your research question. The *literature review* is perhaps the most important step in this process. It not only will help you assess the general utility of your research question; it will also provide you with an excellent basis for selecting a research question to begin with. Consequently, we'll say more about the literature review a bit later. First, though, let's review the attributes of good research questions.

Attributes of Good Research Questions

In discussing the process of narrowing down broad topics into research questions, we have already identified some of the attributes that distinguish good from bad research questions. To begin, we have observed that *a topic is not a research question.* Topics are broad, and are not worded as questions. Research questions need to be narrow and worded as questions. Thus, the treatment of sexually abused girls is a topic, and not a research question. In contrast, a good research question might be, "Is play therapy effective in alleviating trauma symptoms among sexually abused girls aged six to eight?"

Just wording a broad topic in question form does not guarantee that you will have a *good* research question. The question needs to be *narrow and specific.* Thus, "Is childhood sexual abuse an important issue in the treatment of depression among women?" would be a better research question if it were worded as follows, "What proportion of women currently in treatment for major depression report having been sexually abused as a child?"

Research questions need to be *posed in a way that can be answered by observable evidence.* Asking whether criminal sentences for perpetrators of sexual abuse should be stiffer is not a research question. Its answer will depend not on observable evidence, but on arguments based largely on value judgments. Of course, it is conceivable that people could marshal known evidence to support their argument in this debate. Perhaps they could mention the high recidivism rate among perpetrators or studies documenting the failure of rehabilitation programs. But that would not make the question being debated a research question. The studies being cited in the debate, however, might have investigated good research questions, such as "What are the recidivism rates for certain kinds of juvenile sex offenders who have and have not received certain kinds of treatment?"

Above we noted that the most important criterion that should guide you in narrowing down your research topic into a research question is that its answer should have significant potential *relevance for guiding social welfare policy or social work practice*. By the same token, a crucial attribute of a good research question is whether it addresses the decision-making needs of agencies or practical problems in social welfare. This does not mean that researchers must ask planners, practitioners, administrators, or other significant social welfare figures to select research questions for them (although getting feedback from those individuals about their needs and priorities is a valuable step in the process). Inspiration for useful research questions can come from many sources. Sometimes it's something you read, something you observe in an agency, or something a colleague says to you. Sometimes a good idea pops into your head from out of the blue.

Whatever the question's source, it's important that before you get carried away—before you invest much of your resources in planning to study the question, before you let your initial enthusiasm or idiosyncratic personal interests wed you too firmly to that question—you take steps to ensure that it passes the "So what?" test. This means that the study you propose to conduct has clear significance and utility for social work practice or social welfare. Assessing in advance whether your study is likely to be useful and significant means skeptically asking what difference the answer to your research question would make to others who are concerned about social work practice or social welfare. For example, a proposed study of the social service needs of family caregivers of relatives with HIV or AIDS might have obvious significance for practice or policy. If you asked your professional colleagues for their reactions about the likely value of such a study, they would probably be enthusiastic immediately. On the other hand, if you were to ask the same colleagues about a study that would assess the leisure-time activities of social service agency directors, they might actually respond by asking "So what?" and wondering whether you might better use your time by studying a question of greater significance for people in need.

Finally, it is essential that there be more than one possible acceptable answer to the research question. This last requirement can be violated in various ways. One would be by posing a tautological research question: a truism in which the answer is a foregone conclusion. Here's an example of a truism: "Would increasing the proportion of time practitioners spend on certain activities be associated with a decrease in the proportion of time they have left for other activities?

Another way in which only one answer might be acceptable would be when feasibility constraints or a system of values make it impossible to implement any changes based on the answer to the research question. Thus, in a fledgling voluntary agency that is constantly struggling to raise enough funds to meet its payroll obligations, there might be little practical value in studying whether increasing the staff–client ratio or travel budget for attending professional conferences would improve staff morale. Feasibility is an attribute of a good research question even when more than one possible answer would be acceptable. If you lack the means or cooperation to conduct the sort of study needed to answer the research question you have posed, then that question won't work for you. You'll need to change it to a question for which you have adequate resources to investigate fully. In light of the great influence it can have on formulating a good research question, let's now look at some of the issues bearing on the feasibility of research.

Feasibility

Experienced and inexperienced researchers alike find it much easier to conceive of rigorous, valuable studies than to figure out how they can actually implement them. One of the most difficult problems that confronts researchers is how to make a study feasible without making the research question so narrow that it is no longer worth investigating or without sacrificing too much methodological rigor or inferential capacity. Inexperienced researchers commonly formulate idealistic, far-reaching studies and then become immobilized when they find out how much they must scale down their plans if their study is to be feasible. With seasoning, we learn how to strike a happy medium—that is, we learn to formulate and appreciate research questions that are not so narrow that they are no longer worth doing, yet are not so grandiose that they are not feasible to investigate.

Common issues in determining the feasibility of a study are its scope, the time it will require, its fiscal costs, ethical considerations, and the cooperation it will require from others. The larger the scope of the study, the more it will cost in time, money, and cooperation. Sometimes, the scope is too large because the study seeks to assess more variables than can be handled statistically given the available sample size. Ethical issues were examined at length in Chapter 4. A paramount ethical issue that bears on feasibility is whether the value and quality of the research will outweigh any potential discomfort, inconvenience, or risk experienced by those who participate in the study.

The fiscal costs of a study are easily underestimated. Common expenses are personnel costs, travel to collect data, long-distance telephone calls to track down survey nonrespondents who have left town, printing and copying expenses, data-collection instruments, and postage. Postage costs are easily underestimated. Bulky questionnaires may require more stamps than expected, and nonresponse problems may necessitate multiple mailings. In each mailing, we may also need to enclose a stamped return envelope. Personnel costs commonly involve the hiring of interviewers, coders, and data-entry personnel for computer processing.

Time constraints may also turn out to be much worse than anticipated. Inexperienced researchers in particular may underestimate the time required to recruit participants for the study or to make multiple follow-up contacts to urge survey nonrespondents to complete and mail in their questionnaires. Scheduled interviews are often missed or canceled, requiring the scheduling of additional ones. Time may be needed to develop and test data collection instruments, perhaps through several dry runs, before actual data collection takes place. A great deal of unanticipated time may be needed to reformulate the problem and revise the study based on unexpected obstacles encountered in trying to implement the research. And, of course, time is needed for each additional phase of the research process: data processing and analysis, writing the report, and so forth.

One time constraint that can be extremely frustrating is obtaining advance authorization for the study. Approval may need to be secured from a variety of sources, such as agency administrators and practitioners, the agency board, and a human subjects review committee that assesses the ethics of the research. Political squabbles in an agency can delay obtaining approval for a study simply because the battling forces will suspect almost anything that its adversaries support. Administrative turnover can also cause frustrating delays. You may have to delay implementing a study when, for example, an executive director moves on to another agency after you have spent considerable time involving him or her in the formulation of your research.

Sometimes, lack of cooperation in one setting forces the researcher to seek a different setting in which to implement a study. Agency members in the original setting may be skeptical about research and refuse to authorize it at all. Perhaps they fear that the research findings will embarrass the agency or certain units or staff. Perhaps in the past they have had bad experiences with other researchers who were insensitive to agency needs and procedures. A common complaint is that researchers exploit agencies so they can get the data they need for their own intellectual interests and career needs (doctoral dissertations, for example) and then give nothing back to the agency in useful findings that can help solve agency problems. Some of these agency resistances to research are quite rational, and it is a mistake to treat them lightly or to assume that they result from the insecurity or ignorance of agency members.

Involving Others in Problem Formulation

Several activities in the problem formulation phase aim to ensure that we ultimately identify an important research problem and articulate a useful research question that is feasible for us to investigate. By engaging in these activities, we progressively sharpen the original research question and its conceptual elements in line with the above criteria. Or we may reject the original question and formulate a new one that better meets these criteria.

Obtaining critical feedback from colleagues and others is an important step in this process, one that helps us more rigorously appraise the study's utility, the clarity of our ideas, alternative ways of looking at the problem, and pragmatic or ethical considerations that pose potential obstacles to the study's feasibility. You must stress to these individuals that you are *not* looking for their approval and that you want them to be critical or skeptical. Otherwise, it may be expedient for them to think they are currying favor with you by patting you on the back, complimenting you for your initiative and fine mind, and then letting you fall on your face at no cost to themselves.

In Chapter 13 (on program evaluation), we will discuss some of the steps researchers can take to try to overcome or prevent agency resistances to research. One important step is to involve all relevant agency figures as early as possible in all phases of problem formulation and research design planning. Interact with them and their ideas about what needs to be done. Don't pretend to involve them solely to get their support. Be responsive to what they say, not only in the interaction but also in how you actually formulate the study. If you are responsive to their needs, and if they feel they have made a meaningful contribution to the study's design, then chances are better that they will find the study useful and will support it. The dialogue may also build a better, more trusting relationship that can dispel some anxieties about a researcher investigating something in their agency. Moreover, it may help them better understand the purpose and necessity for some of the inconveniences your methodology creates.

One last note before we leave this topic: Lack of cooperation can come not only from agency staff and board members, but also from clients or other individuals we hope will be the participants in our research. Perhaps they will refuse to be observed or interviewed or to respond to a mailed questionnaire (particularly when the data-collection procedure is cumbersome or threatening). Even if they are willing to participate, will we be able to find them? Suppose you were trying to carry out a longitudinal study of the homeless mentally ill; that is, a study that collects data over a period of years. Imagine how difficult it would be to keep track of them and find them for follow-up interviews (not to mention locating them in the first place for initial interviews). To ensure that your study is sensitive to the needs, lifestyles, and concerns of service consumers, do not overlook representatives of service consumers' groups when involving relevant agency figures in the research planning.

We'll turn now to another important step in the problem formulation phase that will help us identify an important research problem and articulate a useful research question: compiling the literature review.

Literature Review

One of the most important steps, not only in the problem formulation phase but also in the entire process of designing a study, is the literature review. Although we are discussing this step after discussing feasibility issues, the literature review is completed at no one point in the research process. As the research design evolves, new issues will emerge that require additional investigation of the literature. Be that as it may, usually it is important to initiate a thorough literature review as early as possible in the research process.

Why and When to Review the Literature Novice researchers commonly make the mistake of putting off their literature reviews until they have sharpened their research question and come up with a design to investigate it. Research can be done that way, but it is not the most efficient use of time. The result may be reinventing the wheel or failing to benefit from the mistakes and experiences of others. Until we review the literature, we have no way of knowing whether the research question has already been adequately answered, of identifying the conceptual and practical obstacles that others have already encountered in this line of research, of learning how those obstacles have been overcome, and of deciding what lines of research can best build on the work that has already been done in a particular problem area.

Another reason to review the literature early: It is a prime source for selecting a research question to begin with. What better way to reduce the chances of selecting an irrelevant or outdated research question than by knowing what has already been done in a particular problem area and the implications of that work for future research? What better way to ensure that your study will be valued as part of a cumulative knowledge-building effort regarding that problem, as opposed to being seen as an obscure study that does not seem to address anything that anyone else is addressing or cares about?

Building on prior research does not necessarily imply that your study should never depart radically from previous work or that it should never duplicate a previous study. There may be sound reasons for both. The point is that you make that decision not in ignorance of the prior research, but in light of it and what your judgment tells you to do. You may wish to repeat a previous study if you think replication is warranted and would be the best contribution you can make. Perhaps your research question has already been answered but the limitations of the methodologies used to investigate it make you skeptical of the validity of the answer currently in vogue. So you might decide to study the same question with a better methodology.

On the other hand, you may be inspired to look at the problem in a way no one else ever has. You would do this not just to satisfy your own curiosity, but also because careful consideration of what's been done before has convinced you that this radical departure is precisely what the field now needs.

There are countless examples of how an early search of the literature can enrich your study and save you from later headaches. Identifying valid measurement instruments, for example, lets you adapt existing measures instead of spending endless hours constructing and testing your own instruments. Another benefit of the literature search is that you can identify alternative conceptions of the problem or variables that had not occurred to you.

Suppose you plan to evaluate the effectiveness of a case management program in helping clients recently discharged from psychiatric hospitals adjust to living in the community. It might seem eminently reasonable to select a reduction in the number of days spent in rehospitalization as the indicator of program effectiveness. But a review of the previous research in this area would inform you that some case management programs paradoxically result in an increase in days of rehospitalization. You would learn that in the face of a woefully inadequate system of community-based resources for the chronically mentally ill, clients commonly may need rehospitalization, and effective case managers see that they get what they need.

Had you not done the literature review before implementing your study, you would not have arranged to handle this unforeseen paradox in your design. If your data did indeed show an increase in days of rehospitalization, then you would not be able to conclude that this meant your program was effective because you selected the opposite outcome as the indicator of effectiveness in your problem formulation. But having done the literature review early, you were able to avoid this quandary. You did this by selecting alternative indicators of effectiveness, such as the amount of services (other than case management) clients received while in the community, the quality of their living arrangements, whether they received adequate financial support while in the community, and how well they performed basic activities of daily living in the community. In short, the focus was not on whether the program reduced the amount of time clients spent in the hospital, but whether it improved their quality of life while in the community.

Some researchers who are using the grounded theory method to construct theory in an inductive fashion (as discussed in Chapter 3) might opt to delay the literature review until they near the end of the research process. Their reason for doing so would be to avoid being influenced by other people's theories in what they observe or how they interpret what they observe. In Chapter 17, we will discuss some logical pitfalls in conducting this kind of research (along with its advantages). We will see that it requires the researcher to make subjective judgments about what is being observed, and this means that what researchers perceive may be influenced in various ways by the orientations they bring to the research. Not everyone agrees with this point of view, and you should know that it is an issue about which reasonable people can disagree. Gilgun (1991) points out that although some grounded theorists delay the literature review, most of them do a thorough literature review before beginning their research. Although they want to conduct their observations with minds as open as possible, they want to start out with an understanding of the current knowledge base and its gaps.

How to Review the Literature Now that we have established the utility of the literature review, let's briefly examine some common sources for finding the literature that social work researchers typically seek. Appendix A—on using the library—will provide additional information germane to this task. Because so many articles and books are always being published, the best way to begin your review is usually by examining guides to the literature. These guides include abstracts, bibliographies, and indexes.

Abstracts in various fields provide short summaries of published work and indicate where to find the complete publication. You might find relevant material in *Social Work Abstracts* (previously called *Social Work Research & Abstracts*) or abstracts in allied fields such as psychology, sociology, urban studies, or public administration.

Your library's subject guide is another good place to start. Look under several subjects related to your general field of interest. If you're looking for literature pertaining to the problem of child sexual abuse, for example, don't just look under child sexual abuse. Look also at child abuse, child welfare, and so on. While examining the various references, be on the lookout for any bibliographies, particularly those that are annotated, that others have already compiled on your topic; if you find a good one, your search can be expedited a great deal. Also watch for special handbooks that review the literature in an entire field of study.

As we discussed in Chapter 2 in connection with searching for evidence in the evidence-based practice process, your best bet might be to conduct an online computerized search. Your libraries may provide a variety of Internet professional literature database services, such as PsycINFO, PubMed, or Medline. These services include complete references and abstracts to thousands of journals. With these services, you identify a list of key words related to your topic and then receive a computer printout that abstracts published references associated with those key words. You also may be able to conduct an online literature search using a publicly available search engine, such as Google or Yahoo!. Likewise, if you go to the website provided by the National Library of Medicine at www.nlm.nih.gov, you can obtain free usage of Medline.

But don't rely too much on the "magic" of the computer. Some computerized systems will not have some of the references you need, and even if they do have them, there is no guarantee that the key words you select will match theirs. When using these systems, therefore, be sure to use a broad list of key words and to use the noncomputerized guides to the literature as well.

Reference libraries can help you identify the proper computerized abstracting services for your particular research project and compile lists of key words. Keep in mind, however, that such services are not always free. Their use might add to the fiscal costs of your study. (Appendix A provides more detail about these services.)

No matter how thorough you are in using guides to the literature, you should remember that there may be a time lapse between the publication of a study and its appearance in one of the literature guides, so it is wise to review routinely the tables of contents of recent issues of every professional journal closely related to your topic. This does not take long, assuming these journals are easily accessible in your library. When you spot a promising title in the table of contents, read the abstract on the first page of the article; it will tell you what you need to know and whether a particular article is sufficiently relevant to your particular focus to warrant reading more. As you read the specific references you have found, make a list of additional relevant references they cite. This way your bibliography accumulates like a snowball.

Don't just examine journals associated exclusively with social work. Many cross-disciplinary, problem-focused journals are filled with studies that are relevant to the problems dealt with by social workers. For example, if you're interested in studies on the effectiveness of social workers in administering mental health and mental retardation programs, then look also at journals such as *Administration in Mental Health, American Journal of Mental Deficiency, Mental Retardation*, and *Community Mental Health Journal*. Students tend to be unaware of many of these journals, but that problem is easily remedied by examining the issues of *Social Work Abstracts* from any recent year. Each issue will include a list of the periodicals abstracted for that issue. (The list changes somewhat in each issue.)

How will you know when you have completed your literature review—that you have found all the literature that you need to find? The question has no foolproof answer, one that will guarantee you have not missed any significant work (such as a very recent study in an obscure journal your library doesn't carry). The best answer to this question is that you have probably reviewed enough literature when, having gone through all of the steps delineated here—including the scanning of the recent issues of all relevant journals—you find that you are already familiar with the references cited in the most recently published articles.

PURPOSES OF RESEARCH

What is learned in the literature review influences another early decision in the research process—determining the purpose of the research. Social work research, of course, serves many purposes. Although a given study can have more than one purpose—and most do—we will examine some of the more common purposes separately because each has different implications for other aspects of research design.

Exploration

Much of social work research is conducted to explore a topic—to provide a beginning familiarity with it. This purpose is typical when a researcher is examining a new interest, when the subject of study is relatively new and unstudied, or when a researcher seeks to test the feasibility of undertaking a more careful study or wants to develop the methods to be used in a more careful study.

As an example, let's consider the deinstitutionalization movement in mental health policy. This movement began after drugs that facilitate the control of the symptomatology of mental illness were discovered in 1955. It grew during the 1960s, spurred on by additional pharmacological discoveries, litigation that protected patients' civil rights against involuntary commitment and institutionalization, and emerging community mental health programs. During the 1970s, state governments, faced with fiscal crises and taxpayer unrest, developed the rationale that federal funding for Medicaid, Medicare, and community mental health centers would permit massive discharges from state-funded psychiatric institutions. Although many people applauded this movement as restoring the civil liberties of mental patients and letting them live in the least restrictive environment, others feared that this massive "dumping" was premature because community facilities were inadequate for the proper care of many discharged patients and many patients would thus be significantly harmed by it.

Suppose that you were practicing at that time as a social worker in a mental health planning agency. Or suppose you were a generalist practitioner for a community mental health program. In either case, when your nearby state hospital began discharging patients en masse to the community, you might have sought answers to critical questions you had about the impact of the new policy and what those answers implied for trying to modify the policy or for program development. You might have wanted to learn about the living conditions of the newly discharged patients. What types of neighborhoods were they living in? Were they living in boarding homes? In halfway houses? With their families? In the streets? Were their living facilities in decent shape? Were the ex-patients getting proper nutrition and medication? Were their finances adequate to meet their subsistence needs? How were they spending their time? What burden did the new policy seem to be imposing on their families? How was the community responding? Were neighbors ridiculing or victimizing the ex-patients?

Even if you had never considered yourself a researcher, you might have undertaken an exploratory study to obtain at least approximate answers to some of your questions. Or, in order to devise a questionnaire for a more careful, large-scale survey, you might have conducted relatively unstructured interviews with a small number of ex-patients to provide insights into what questions should be included on the questionnaire and how they should be worded. Exploratory studies are valuable in social work research. They are essential whenever a researcher is breaking new ground, and they can almost always yield new insights into a topic for research. Exploratory studies are also a source of grounded theory, as Chapter 17 discusses.

The chief shortcoming of exploratory studies is that they seldom provide satisfactory answers to research questions. They can only hint at the answers and give insights into the research methods that could provide definitive answers. The reason exploratory studies are seldom definitive in themselves is the issue of representativeness, which is discussed at length in Chapter 14 in connection with sampling. Once you understand sampling and representativeness, you will be able to determine whether a given exploratory study actually answered its research problem or merely pointed the way toward an answer.

Description

Many social work studies seek a second purpose: to describe situations and events. The researcher observes and then describes what was observed. Because scientific observation is careful and deliberate, scientific descriptions are typically more accurate and precise than casual descriptions.

In the preceding example on the deinstitutionalization movement, an example of a descriptive study would be a careful, large-scale survey of a representative sample of ex-patients; the sampling would be conducted to describe the precise proportion of the discharged population living under certain kinds of arrangements, the proportion properly taking their medications, the frequency with which they were robbed, their average finances, and so on. The U.S. census is an excellent example of a descriptive social scientific research project. Its goal is to describe accurately and precisely a wide variety of characteristics of the U.S. population, as well as the populations of smaller areas such as states and counties.

A Gallup Poll conducted during a political election campaign has the purpose of describing the electorate's voting intentions. A researcher who computes and reports the number of times individual legislators voted for or against social welfare legislation also has or serves a descriptive purpose. In social work, one of the best-known descriptive studies is the annual canvass of schools of social work conducted by the Council on Social Work Education that identifies a wide variety of characteristics of students and faculty in every school. By following the report of each annual canvass, one can see important trends in social work education, such as increases or decreases in the number of applicants and enrollments at various degree levels, the proportion of women or ethnic minorities enrolled or teaching, and so on.

The preceding examples of descriptive studies are all quantitative in nature. However, descriptive studies also can be qualitative. The term *description* is used differently in qualitative and quantitative studies. In quantitative studies, *description* typically refers to the characteristics of a population; it is based on quantitative data obtained from a sample of people that is thought to be representative of that population. The data being described in quantitative studies are likely to refer to surface attributes that can be easily quantified such as age, income, size of family, and so on. In quantitative descriptive studies, the objectivity, precision, and generalizability of the description are paramount concerns. We will be examining these considerations in depth in Chapters 8 through 12.

In qualitative studies, *description* is more likely to refer to a thicker examination of phenomena and their deeper meanings. Qualitative descriptions tend to be more concerned with conveying a sense of what it's like to walk in the shoes of the people being described—providing rich details about their environments, interactions, meanings, and everyday lives—than with generalizing with precision to a larger population. A qualitative descriptive study of mothers receiving welfare in states where the levels of such support are lowest, for example, might describe the effects that the inadequate payments have on the daily lives of a small sample of mothers and their children, how they struggle to survive, how their neighbors and welfare workers interact with them, how that makes them feel, and what things they must do to provide for their families. A quantitative descriptive study of mothers receiving welfare, in contrast, would be likely to select a large, representative sample of these mothers and assess things like how long they require public assistance, their ages and educational levels, and so on. We will examine methods for qualitative description in more depth in Chapters 9, 17, and 18.

Explanation

A third general purpose of social work research is to explain things. Reporting the voting intentions of an electorate is a descriptive activity, but reporting why some people plan to vote for or against a tax initiative to fund human services is an explanatory activity. Reporting why some cities have higher child abuse rates than others is a case of explanation, but simply reporting the different child abuse rates is description. A researcher has an explanatory purpose if he or she wishes to know why battered women repeatedly return to live with their batterers, rather than simply describing how often they do. In the preceding example on deinstitutionalization, an explanatory study might look at why some clients have better living conditions than others. Perhaps variations in discharge planning would explain some of the differences. Or the study might look at why some neighborhoods express more opposition to the discharge policy than others. Perhaps more resistance is found in the more residential neighborhoods.

Evaluation

A fourth purpose of social work research is to evaluate social policies, programs, and interventions. The evaluative purpose of social work research actually encompasses all three of the preceding purposes: exploration, description, and explanation. For example, we might conduct open-ended exploratory interviews with community residents as a first step toward evaluating what services they need. We might conduct a descriptive community survey to evaluate the problems residents report having and the services they say they need. A descriptive study might also evaluate whether services are being implemented as intended. We might conduct an explanatory analysis to evaluate whether factors such as ethnicity or acculturation explain why some residents are more likely than others to utilize services.

Evaluative studies also might ask whether social policies, programs, or services are effective in achieving their stated goals. Evaluations of goal achievement can be done in an exploratory, descriptive, or explanatory way. For example, if we simply ask practitioners in an open-ended fashion to recall techniques they've employed that seemed to be the most or least effective in achieving treatment goals, we would be conducting an exploratory evaluation to generate tentative insights as to what ways of intervening might be worth evaluating further. Suppose we evaluate the proportion of service recipients who achieve treatment goals, such as whether they graduate from high school as opposed to dropping out. That would be a descriptive evaluation. We should not call it *explanatory* unless our study design enables us to determine whether it was really our service, and not some other factor, that explained why the goal was achieved. Perhaps the students who were the most motivated to succeed were more likely to seek our services than those who were least motivated. If, however, we assess such alternative factors, then we will have an explanatory evaluation—one which enables us to determine whether it was really our services that caused the desired outcome. Part 4 of this text will cover the evaluation of program and practice effectiveness in much greater depth.

Constructing Measurement Instruments

Some studies aim to develop and test out measurement instruments that can be used by other researchers or by practitioners as part of the assessment or evaluation aspects of their practice. The research questions implicit in these studies contrast with the types of research questions we've discussed so far. Rather than attempt to develop implications for practice, they ask whether a particular measurement instrument is a useful and valid tool that can be applied in practice or research. Thus, they may assess whether a 40-item family risk scale accurately predicts whether parents in treatment for child abuse or neglect are likely to be abusive or neglectful again in the future. Or they may assess whether such an instrument that has been accurate with clients from a dominant culture in one country is valid when used with clients of minority ethnicity in that country or with clients residing in other countries. Chapters 8 and 9 of this text will examine the key concepts and methods pertaining to studies that develop and test out measurement instruments.

Multiple Purposes

Although it is useful to distinguish the purposes of social work research, we emphasize again that most social work studies have elements of several of these purposes. Because studies can have more than one purpose, sometimes it is difficult to judge how best to characterize a particular study's purpose. This is complicated further by the sometimes fuzzy distinction between exploratory and explanatory purposes. Suppose, for example, that you develop a program of social support services for family caregivers of persons with HIV or AIDS. Early in this endeavor you learn that some caregivers are heterosexual spouses who knew that their spouses had HIV or AIDS before marrying them. In planning support services for this subgroup of caregivers, you believe it is important to understand why they married in light of the potential burden of caregiving and grief that lay ahead.

Because this topic is new and unstudied, because you can obtain only a very small and potentially atypical sample, and because you are seeking only to garner tentative beginning insights into this phenomenon, you may choose to conduct an exploratory study. In your exploratory study, perhaps you will conduct open-ended interviews with five or ten caregivers about their decision to marry their spouses, seeking primarily to understand why they married them and what that might imply for their social support needs. Although your study is partly exploratory, it also has an explanatory purpose. You are exploring a new phenomenon with the long-range aim of explaining it. Thus, if someone asked you whether your study was exploratory or explanatory, you might have to ponder a while before correctly answering, "Both."

In attempting to differentiate exploratory and explanatory purposes you might also consider two additional research purposes: *understanding* and *predicting*. If your study is seeking to develop a beginning understanding of a phenomenon, it is more likely to be exploratory than explanatory, even though it might include questions asking respondents to explain why they did something. On the other hand, your study is more likely to be explanatory to the extent that it seeks to rigorously test out predictions (hypotheses) implied by tentative explanations derived from previous work on the topic. You will see these several research purposes at work in the following discussions of other aspects of research design. One issue closely related to the purpose of your research involves the time period during which your research observations will be conducted. Let's turn now to a consideration of that issue.

THE TIME DIMENSION

Research observations may be made more or less at one time, or they may be deliberately stretched over a long period. If, for example, the purpose of your study is to describe the living arrangements of mentally ill patients immediately after their hospital discharge, then you might decide to observe each patient's living arrangements at a predetermined point after their discharge. If, on the other hand, the purpose of your study is to describe how these living arrangements change over time, then you would need to conduct repeated observations of these individuals and their living arrangements over an extended period.

Cross-Sectional Studies

Research studies that examine some phenomenon by taking a cross section of it at one time and analyzing that cross section carefully are called *cross-sectional studies*. Such a study may have an exploratory, descriptive, or explanatory purpose. A single U.S. census, for example, exemplifies a cross-sectional study for descriptive purposes. If you conducted one open-ended, unstructured interview with each client who prematurely terminated treatment in your agency during a specified period—to generate insights about why your agency's treatment termination rate is so high—you would be conducting a cross-sectional study for exploratory purposes. If you conducted one structured interview with both these clients and those who completed their planned treatment—to test the hypothesis that practitioner–client disagreement about treatment goals is related to whether treatment is completed—then you would be conducting a cross-sectional study for explanatory purposes.

Explanatory cross-sectional studies have an inherent problem. They typically aim to understand causal processes that occur over time, yet their conclusions are based on observations made at only one time. For example, if your cross-sectional study of patients recently discharged from a psychiatric hospital found that those who were living with their families were functioning better and had less symptomatology than those who were not living with their families, then you would not know whether the differences in functioning or symptomatology between the two groups commenced before or after they entered their current living arrangements. In other words, you wouldn't know whether different living arrangements helped cause differences in functioning and symptomatology or whether the latter differences helped to explain placement in particular living arrangements. Although merely finding in a cross-sectional study that such a relationship existed might have significant value, obtaining a better understanding of the causal processes involved in that relationship would require methodological arrangements that we will discuss later in chapters on research designs and statistical analysis.

Longitudinal Studies

Studies that are intended to describe processes occurring over time and thus conduct their observations over an extended period are called **longitudinal studies.** An example is a researcher who participates in and observes the activities of a support group for battered women or an advocacy group for families of the mentally ill from its beginnings to the present. Analyses of newspaper editorials or U.S. Supreme Court decisions over time on a subject such as abortion or psychiatric commitment are other examples. In the latter instances, the researcher may conduct observations and analyses at one point in time, but because the study's data correspond to events that occur at different chronological points, the study would still be considered longitudinal.

Longitudinal studies can be of great value in assessing whether a particular attribute increases one's risk of developing a later problem. To do this, longitudinal studies might follow over time individuals with and without a particular attribute that might increase their risk of developing that problem. At a later time, the incidence of the problem between the two groups can be compared. For example, children who do and do not have a parent diagnosed with schizophrenia might be followed and compared over many years to see if they become afflicted with schizophrenia. If the incidence of schizophrenia among the children of parents with schizophrenia is significantly higher than it is among the other children, then having a parent with schizophrenia would be deemed a risk factor for developing schizophrenia. Similar longitudinal studies could be conducted to assess the relative risk of contracting HIV or AIDS between groups with and without particular risk factors. By comparing the incidence rates of a problem between two groups, longitudinal studies can calculate the likelihood that individuals with a particular risk factor will develop the problem.

Many qualitative studies that directly observe people over time are naturally longitudinal in nature. Longitudinal studies can be more difficult for quantitative studies such as large-scale surveys. Nonetheless, they are often undertaken. Three special types of longitudinal studies should be noted here. **Trend studies** are those that study changes within some general population over time. One example would be a comparison of U.S. censuses over time to show growth in the national population or in specific minority groups. Another example would be an examination of the data generated over the years in the Council on Social Work Education's annual canvasses of schools of social work, perhaps to identify fluctuations over time in the number of social work students who specialize in various methods or fields of practice. At the level of a local agency, one could assess whether the types of clients or problems that make up an agency's caseload are changing over time, and perhaps use that analysis to make projections as to what these trends imply for future staffing patterns or in-service training needs.

Cohort studies examine more specific subpopulations (cohorts) as they change over time. Typically, a cohort is an age group, such as the post–World War II baby boom generation, but it can also be based on some other time grouping, such as people whose first episode of schizophrenia occurred during a particular time period after deinstitutionalization policies were implemented. For example, we might be interested in what happens to the incidence of substance abuse among young adults with schizophrenia as they age, since such abuse is particularly dangerous for this group due to the nature of their illness and the prescribed medications they take. In 1990 we might survey a sample of such persons 20–25 years of age and ask them about their use of alcohol or drugs. In 2000 we might survey another sample of such persons 30–35 years of age, and another sample of those 40–45 years of age in 2010. Although the specific set of people would be different, each sample would represent the survivors of the cohort with schizophrenia at the age of 20–25 in 1990.

Panel studies examine the same set of people each time. One example would be a follow-up study of people who graduated with a master's degree in social work during a particular year. We might want to see, for example, whether their attitudes about the value of the required research, policy, or administration courses change over time. If appreciation of those courses begins to increase dramatically several years after graduation as the alumni move into supervisory and administrative positions, then this information would be useful to both students and faculty as they discuss whether the curriculum should be revised to make it more relevant to the priorities of current students. Or suppose you wanted to learn how teenage mothers from different ethnic groups adapted to their child-rearing responsibilities. You might arrange to observe and interview a sample of such young mothers over time. You'd be in a position to see what they learned from other family members, the role played by their children's fathers, and so on. By getting to know a specific set of young mothers in depth, you'd be able to understand a wide range of changes occurring in their lives.

Because the distinctions among trend, cohort, and panel studies are sometimes difficult to grasp at first, we'll contrast the three study designs using the same variable: social work practitioner attitudes about cognitive-behavioral interventions. A trend study might look at shifts over time among direct-service practitioners in their propensity to use cognitive-behavioral interventions. For example, every five or ten years, a new national sample of practitioners could be surveyed.

A cohort study might follow shifts in attitudes among practitioners who earned their social work degrees during a particular era, perhaps between 2000 and 2002. We could study a sample of them in 2003, a new sample of them in 2008 or 2013, and so forth.

A panel study could start with the same sample as the cohort study but return to the same individuals in subsequent surveys, rather than draw new samples of practitioners who graduated between 2000 and 2002. Only the panel study would give a full picture of the shifts in attitudes among specific individuals. Cohort and trend studies would only uncover net changes.

Longitudinal studies have an obvious advantage over cross-sectional studies in providing information that describes processes over time. But often this advantage comes at a heavy cost in both time and money, especially in a large-scale survey. Observations may have to be made at the time events are occurring, and the method of observation may require many research workers.

Because panel studies observe the same set of people each time, they offer the most comprehensive data on changes over time and are generally considered the most powerful and accurate of the three longitudinal approaches. Their chief disadvantage is that they are the most formidable of the three approaches to carry out, because of the costs and other difficulties involved in tracking the same individuals over time. A related disadvantage that only affects panel studies is *panel attrition*: Some respondents who are studied in the first wave of the survey may not participate later. The reasons for this are many. Some respondents move away and cannot be found. Some die. Some lose interest and simply refuse to participate anymore. The danger of such attrition is that those who drop

THE TIME DIMENSION AND AGING

by Joseph J. Leon, Behavioral Science Department, California State Polytechnic University, Pomona

One way to identify the type of time dimension used in a study is to imagine a number of different research projects on growing older in American society. If we studied a sample of individuals in 1990 and compared the different age groups, the design would be termed cross-sectional. If we drew another sample of individuals using the same study instrument in the year 2000 and compared the new data with the 1990 data, the design would be termed trend.

Suppose we wished to study only those individuals who were 51 to 60 in the year 2000 and compare them with the 1990 sample of 41- to 50-year-old persons (the 41 to 50 age cohort); this study design would be termed cohort. The comparison could be made for the 51 to 60 and 61 to 70 age cohorts as well. Now, if we desired to do a panel study on growing older in America, we would draw a sample in the year 1990 and, using the same sampled individuals in the year 2000, do the study again. Remember, there would be fewer people in the year 2000 study because all the 41- to 50-year-old people in 1990 are 51 to 60 and there would be no 41- to 50-year-old individuals in the year 2000 study. Furthermore, some of the individuals sampled in 1990 would no longer be alive in the year 2000.

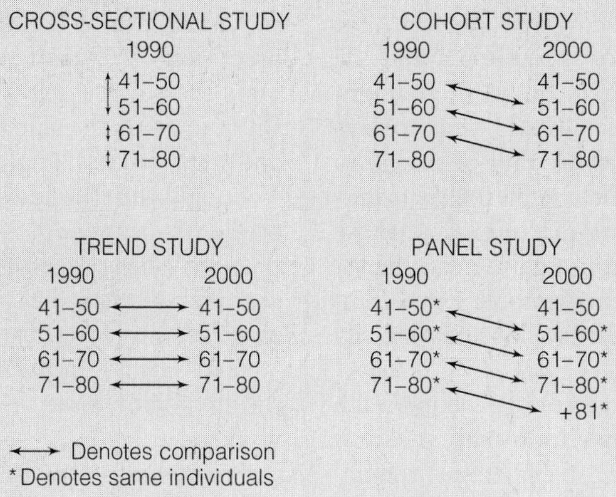

CROSS-SECTIONAL STUDY

1990
41–50
51–60
61–70
71–80

COHORT STUDY

1990	2000
41–50	41–50
51–60	51–60
61–70	61–70
71–80	71–80

TREND STUDY

1990		2000
41–50	⟷	41–50
51–60	⟷	51–60
61–70	⟷	61–70
71–80	⟷	71–80

PANEL STUDY

1990	2000
41–50*	41–50
51–60*	51–60*
61–70*	61–70*
71–80*	71–80*
	+81*

⟷ Denotes comparison
*Denotes same individuals

out of the study may not be typical, thereby distorting the study's results. When Carol S. Aneshenshel and her colleagues conducted a panel study of Hispanic and non-Hispanic adolescent girls, for example, they looked for and found differences in characteristics of survey dropouts among Hispanics born in the United States and those born in Mexico. Those differences needed to be considered to avoid misleading conclusions about differences between Hispanics and non-Hispanics (Aneshenshel et al., 1989).

Another potential disadvantage of panel studies is that observing people at an early point may influence what they say or do later. For instance, a teenage gang member who earlier expressed intense enthusiasm for gang membership but who now is having second thoughts about it may not admit to such thoughts to avoid appearing inconsistent and unsure of himself and thus lose face.

You've now seen several purposes that guide social work research and how they relate to the time dimension. To get further clarification of this dimension, we suggest you examine the box titled "The Time Dimension and Aging." We turn now to a consideration of whom or what you want to study.

UNITS OF ANALYSIS

In all social scientific research, including that done for social work, there is a wide range of variation in what or who is studied. We don't mean the *topics* of research but what are technically called the **units of analysis.** Most typically, social scientists use individual people as their units of analysis. You can make observations to describe the characteristics of a large number of individual people, such as their genders, ages, regions of birth, attitudes, and so forth. You then aggregate or total the descriptions of the many individuals to provide a descriptive picture of the population made up of those individuals.

For example, you might note the age and gender of each individual client in your agency and then characterize the caseload as a whole as being 53 percent women and 47 percent men and having a mean age of 34 years. This is a descriptive analysis of your agency's caseload. Although the final description would be of the agency as a whole, the individual characteristics are aggregated for purposes of describing some larger group. Units of analysis, then, are units that we initially describe for the ultimate purpose of aggregating their characteristics in order to describe some larger group or explain some abstract phenomenon.

It is important to understand the concept *units of analysis* because some studies don't use individual people as the units of analysis. Suppose a study uses *neighborhoods* as the units of analysis and finds that neighborhoods with the highest proportion of recently arrived immigrants also have the highest crime rates. Without examining the study's units of analysis, we might conclude that certain *individuals*—in this case, recently arrived immigrants—have the highest crime rates. But what if the immigrants have low crime rates but are too poor to live in safer neighborhoods? Then we would make a serious mistake to infer that they have the highest crime rates. That mistake would be called the *ecological fallacy*, which we will be examining in more depth shortly. Unless you consider a study's units of analysis, you risk committing the ecological fallacy. These concepts will become clearer when we consider some possible alternative units of analysis.

Individuals

As mentioned above, individual human beings are perhaps the most typical units of analysis in social work research. We tend to describe and understand phenomena among groups with different attributes by aggregating and manipulating information about individuals in those groups.

Examples of circumscribed groups whose members may be units of analysis—at the individual level—include clients, practitioners, students, residents, workers, voters, parents, and faculty members. Note that each term implies some population of individual people. The term *population* will be considered in some detail in Chapter 14. At this point, it is enough to realize that studies that have individuals as their units of analysis typically refer to the population made up of those individuals.

As the units of analysis, individuals may be characterized in terms of their membership in social groupings. Thus, an individual may be described as belonging to a rich or a poor family, or a person may be described as having parents who did or did not graduate from high school. We might examine in a research project whether people whose parents never completed high school were more likely to become school dropouts than those whose parents did complete high school, or whether dropouts from rich families are more likely to have emotional disorders than dropouts from poor families. In each case, the individual would be the unit of analysis—not the parents or the family.

Groups

Social groups themselves also may be the units of analysis. This case is not the same as studying the individuals within a group. If you were to study the members of a street gang to learn about gang members, the individual (gang member) would be the unit of analysis. But if you studied all of the gangs in a city in order to learn the differences, say, between big and small gangs, between "uptown" and "downtown" gangs, and so forth, the unit of analysis would be the *gang*, a social group.

Families also could be the units of analysis in a study. You might describe each family in terms of its total annual income and whether or not it had a mentally ill member. You could aggregate families and describe the mean income of families and the percentage with mentally ill members. You would then be in a position to determine whether families with higher incomes were more likely to have mentally ill members than those with lower incomes. The individual *family* in such a case would be the unit of analysis.

Other units of analysis at the group level might be friendship cliques, married couples, parent–child dyads, census blocks, cities, or geographic regions. Each term also implies a population. *Street gangs* implies some population that includes all street gangs. The population of street gangs could be described, say, in terms of its geographical distribution throughout a city, and an explanatory study of street gangs might discover whether large gangs were more likely than small ones to engage in intergang warfare.

Formal social organizations may also be the units of analysis. An example would be social service agencies, which implies a population of all social service agencies. Individual agencies might be characterized in terms of the number of employees, annual budgets, number of clients, percentage of practitioners or clients who are from ethnic minority groups, and so forth. We might determine whether privately funded agencies hire a larger or smaller percentage of minority group employees than do publicly funded agencies. Other examples of formal social organizations that are suitable as units of analysis are churches, colleges, army divisions, academic departments, and shelters for battered women or the homeless.

When social groups are the units of analysis, their characteristics may be derived from those of their individual members. Thus, a family might be described in terms of the age, race, or education of its head. In a descriptive study, then, we might find the percentage of all families that have a college-educated head. In an explanatory study, we might determine whether families with a college-educated head have, on the average, more or fewer children than do families with heads who have not graduated from college. In each example, however, the family would be the unit of analysis. (Had we asked whether college graduates—college-educated *individuals*—have more or fewer children than their less educated counterparts, then the individual person would have been the unit of analysis.)

Social groups (and also individuals) may be characterized in other ways—for instance, according to their environments or their membership in larger groupings. Families, for example, might be described in terms of the type of dwelling unit in which they reside, and we might want to determine whether rich families are more likely than poor families to reside in single-family houses (as opposed, say, to apartments). The unit of analysis would still be the family.

If all of this seems unduly complicated, be assured that in most research projects you are likely to undertake, the unit of analysis will be relatively clear to you. When the unit of analysis is not so clear, however, it is absolutely essential to determine what it is—otherwise, you will be unable to determine what observations are to be made about whom or what.

Some studies have the purpose of making descriptions or explanations that pertain to more than one unit of analysis. In these cases, the researcher must anticipate what conclusions he or she wishes to draw with regard to what units of analysis.

Social Artifacts

Another large group of possible units of analysis may be referred to generally as social artifacts, or the products of social beings or their behavior. One class of artifacts would include social objects such as books, poems, paintings, automobiles, buildings, songs, pottery, jokes, and scientific discoveries.

Each object implies a population of all such objects: all books, all novels, all biographies, all introductory social work textbooks, all cookbooks. An individual book might be characterized by its size, weight, length, price, content, number of pictures, volume of sale, or description of its author. The population of all books or of a particular kind of book could be analyzed for the purpose of description or explanation. For example, you could analyze changes in the contents of social work practice textbooks over time to assess possible trends regarding increases or decreases in the extent to which research evidence is cited to support the effectiveness of the practice principles or interventions being espoused. Or, you might compare British and American texts to see which are more likely to emphasize linkages between policy and practice.

Social interactions form another class of social artifacts that are suitable for social work research. Faith-based counseling sessions could be examined to assess the extent to which religious proselytizing occurs. Aspects of gay and lesbian weddings could be compared to aspects of heterosexual weddings. Realize that when a researcher reports that weddings between same-sex partners differ in certain ways from other weddings, the weddings are the units of analysis, not the individuals being married.

Some other possible examples of social interactions that might be the units of analysis in social work research are friendship choices, divorces, domestic violence incidents, agency board meetings, gang fights, and protest demonstrations.

Units of Analysis in Review

The concept of the unit of analysis may seem very complicated. It need not be. It is irrelevant whether you classify a given unit of analysis as a group, a formal organization, or a social artifact. It is essential, however, that you be able to identify your unit of analysis. You must decide whether you are studying marriages or marriage partners, crimes or criminals, agencies or agency executives. Unless you keep this point constantly in mind, you risk making assertions about one unit of analysis based on the examination of another.

To test your grasp of the concept of units of analysis, we present statements from actual research projects. See if you can determine the unit of analysis in each. (The answers are at the end of this chapter.)

1. Women watch TV more than men because they are likely to work fewer hours outside the home than men. . . . Black people watch an average of approximately three-quarters of an hour more television per day than white people. (Hughes, 1980:290)

2. Of the 130 incorporated U.S. cities with more than 100,000 inhabitants in 1960, 126 had at least two short-term nonproprietary general hospitals accredited by the American Hospital Association. (Turk, 1980:317)

3. The early Transcendental Meditation organizations were small and informal. The Los Angeles group, begun in June 1959, met at a member's house where, incidentally, Maharishi was living. (Johnston, 1980:337)

4. However, it appears that the nursing staffs exercise strong influence over . . . a decision to change the nursing care system. . . . Conversely, among those decisions dominated by the administration and the medical staffs . . . . (Comstock, 1980:77)

5. In 1958, there were 13 establishments with 1,000 employees or more, accounting for 60 percent of the industry's value added. In 1977, the number of this type of establishment dropped to 11, but their share of industry value added had fallen to about 46 percent. (York and Persigehl, 1981:41)

6. Though 667,000 out of 2 million farmers in the United States are women, women historically have not been viewed as farmers, but rather, as the farmer's wife. (Votaw, 1979:8)

7. The analysis of community opposition to group homes for the mentally handicapped . . . indicates that deteriorating neighborhoods are most likely to organize in opposition, but that upper-middle-class neighborhoods are most likely to enjoy private access to local officials . . . . (Graham and Hogan, 1990:513)

8. This study explores the key dimensions of social work practice position vacancy descriptions and seeks to reflect the changing self-image of modern social work. . . . Which of the major conceptualized dimensions of practice are being emphasized most in position vacancy descriptions published in the profession? Are these position vacancy descriptions and the most emphasized dimensions changing over time? If so, in which directions and to what degree are the position vacancy descriptions and dimensions changing? (Billups and Julia, 1987:17)

Figure 6-2 graphically illustrates different units of analysis and the statements that might be made about them.

The Ecological Fallacy

At this point it is appropriate to reexamine the **ecological fallacy.** As we noted earlier, the ecological fallacy means the just-mentioned danger of making assertions about individuals as the unit of analysis based on the examination of groups or other aggregations. Let's consider another hypothetical illustration of this fallacy.

Suppose, like Royse (1988), that we are interested in learning something about the nature of electoral support for tax initiatives to fund new human service programs in countywide elections. Assume we have the vote tally for each precinct so that we can tell which precincts gave the referendum the greatest and the least support. Assume also that we have census data that describes some characteristics of those precincts.

Our analysis of such data might show that precincts whose voters were relatively old gave the referendum a greater proportion of their votes than did

Figure 6-2 Illustrations of Units of Analysis

precincts whose voters were younger on average. We might be tempted to conclude from these findings that older voters were more likely to vote for the referendum than younger voters—that age affected support for the referendum. In reaching such a conclusion, we run the risk of committing the ecological fallacy because it may have been the younger voters in those "old" precincts who voted for the referendum. Our problem is that we have examined *precincts* as our units of analysis and wish to draw conclusions about *voters.*

The same problem would arise if we discovered that crime rates were higher in cities having large African American populations than in those with few

Units of Analysis	Sample Statements
 Households	20% of the households are occupied by more than one family
	30% of the households have holes in their roofs
	10% of the households are occupied by aliens
	Notice also that 33%, or 4 of the 12 families, live in multiple-family households with family as the unit of analysis

Figure 6-2 *(continued)*

African Americans. We would not know if the crimes were actually committed by African Americans. Or if we found suicide rates higher in Protestant countries than in Catholic ones, we still could not know for sure that more Protestants than Catholics committed suicide.

Notice that the researcher very often must address a particular research question through an ecological analysis. Perhaps the most appropriate data are simply not available. For example, the precinct vote tallies and the precinct characteristics mentioned in our initial example might be easy to obtain, but we may not have the resources to conduct a postelection survey of individual voters. In such cases, we may reach a tentative conclusion, recognizing and noting the risk of committing the ecological fallacy.

Don't let these warnings against the ecological fallacy, however, lead you to commit what we might call an *individualistic fallacy*. Some students who are new to research have trouble reconciling general patterns of attitudes and actions with individual exceptions. If you know a rich Democrat, for example, that doesn't deny the fact that most rich people vote for Republican candidates—as individuals. The ecological fallacy deals with something else altogether—drawing conclusions about individuals based solely on the observation of groups.

Reductionism

Another concept related to units of analysis is **reductionism.** Basically, reductionism is an overly strict limitation on the kinds of concepts and variables to be considered as causes in explaining a broad range of human behavior. Sociologists may tend to consider only sociological variables (values, norms, roles); economists may consider only economic variables (supply and demand, marginal value); or psychologists may consider only psychological variables (personality types, traumas). For example, what causes child abuse? The psychopathology of the perpetrator? Pathological dynamics in family interaction patterns? Socioeconomic stress? Cultural norms? Abnormalities in the child? Scientists from different disciplines tend to look at different types of answers and ignore the others. Explaining all or most human behavior in terms of economic factors is called *economic reductionism;* explaining all or most human behavior in terms of psychological factors is called *psychological reductionism;* and so forth. Note how this issue relates to the discussion of paradigms in Chapter 3.

Reductionism of any type tends to suggest that particular units of analysis or variables are more relevant than others. A psychologist or psychiatrist might choose perpetrator psychopathology as the cause of child abuse, and thus the unit of analysis would be the individual perpetrator. A family therapist, though, might choose families as units of analysis and examine the interactional dynamics of family systems. A sociologist might also choose families as the unit of analysis to examine the degree of socioenvironmental stress they experience.

Once the foregoing aspects of problem formulation have been handled, you are ready to specify and operationally define the variables in your study and, if the study is not purely descriptive, to postulate relationships among those variables (that is, to develop hypotheses). This phase of the research process sets the stage for preparing a measurement strategy and for designing other aspects of the study. Although it is generally considered part of the problem formulation phase, it is a bridge to subsequent phases. The amount and importance of the material involved in this phase merit examination in a separate chapter, which we will take up next.

Main Points

- Social work research follows essentially the same problem-solving process as does social work practice. Each follows similar phases, and each requires that moving to the next phase depends on successfully completing earlier phases. At any point in the process, unanticipated obstacles may necessitate looping back to earlier phases.
- A good research topic should pass the "So what?" test. Also, it should be specific, capable of being answered by observable evidence, feasible to study, and open to doubt and thus answerable in more than one possible way.
- Conducting the literature review is an important step in the problem formulation process. Usually, a thorough grounding in the literature should precede, and provide a foundation for, the selection of an important topic.
- Anticipating issues in the feasibility of a study is also an important part of problem formulation. Time constraints, fiscal costs, lack of cooperation, and ethical dilemmas are essential things to consider when planning a study.
- Exploration is the attempt to develop an initial, rough understanding of some phenomenon.
- Description is the precise measurement and reporting of the characteristics of some population or phenomenon under study.
- Explanation is the discovery and reporting of relationships among different aspects of the phenomenon under study.
- Evaluation studies can be conducted with exploratory, descriptive, and explanatory purposes.
- Cross-sectional studies are those based on observations made at one time.
- Longitudinal studies are those in which observations are made at many times. Such observations may

be made of samples drawn from general populations (trend studies), samples drawn from more specific subpopulations (cohort studies), or the same sample of people each time (panel studies).

• Units of analysis are the people or things whose characteristics social researchers observe, describe, and explain. Typically, the unit of analysis in social research is the individual person, but it may also be a group or a social artifact.

Review Questions and Exercises

1. Consider a problem in social welfare in which you have a special interest (such as child abuse, mental illness, the frail elderly, and so on). Formulate three different research questions about that problem, each of which would be important for the field to answer and might, in your opinion, be of interest to a funding agency. Formulate each question to deal with a different research purpose—one for exploration, one for description, and one for explanation.

2. Look through a social work research journal and find examples of at least three different units of analysis. Identify each unit of analysis and present a quotation from the journal in which that unit of analysis was discussed.

Internet Exercises

1. Use InfoTrac College Edition to find an article that reports a research study that illustrates exploration, description, or explanation. Identify which of these three purposes that study illustrates and briefly justify your judgment in that regard.

2. Use InfoTrac College Edition to locate the following longitudinal study from the July 2002 issue of the journal *Social Work:* "Welfare Use as a Life Course Event: Toward a New Understanding of the U.S. Safety Net," by M. R. Rank and T. A. Hirschl. Describe the nature of the study design, its primary findings, and the implications of those findings for social work practice and social welfare policy.

Additional Readings

Alexander, Leslie B., and Phyllis Solomon (eds.). 2006. *The Research Process in the Human Services: Behind the Scenes.* Belmont, CA: Thomson Brooks/Cole. The chapters in this excellent and unique book report research studies completed by esteemed researchers. The studies are followed by commentaries by the investigators regarding the real-world agency feasibility obstacles they encountered in carrying out their research and how they modified their research plans in light of those obstacles.

Maxwell, Joseph A. 1996. *Qualitative Research Design: An Interactive Approach.* Thousand Oaks, CA: Sage. Maxwell covers many of the same topics as this chapter does but with its attention devoted specifically to qualitative research projects.

Menard, Scott. 1991. *Longitudinal Research.* Newbury Park, CA: Sage. Beginning by explaining why researchers conduct longitudinal research, the author goes on to detail a variety of study designs as well as suggestions for the analysis of longitudinal data.

Answers to Units of Analysis Exercise (page 145)

1. individuals
2. cities
3. groups: organizations
4. groups
5. companies
6. individuals
7. neighborhoods
8. artifacts: position vacancy descriptions

CHAPTER 7

Conceptualization and Operationalization

What You'll Learn in This Chapter

In this chapter, you'll discover that many social work terms communicate vague, unspecified meanings. In research, we must specify exactly what we mean (and don't mean) by the terms we use to describe the elements of our study.

INTRODUCTION

The preceding chapter described various aspects of the problem formulation phase. If you are doing quantitative research, explicating the conceptual elements of the research comes at the end of that phase. Chapter 7 deals with that end stage of problem formulation—the process of moving from vague ideas about what you want to study to being able to recognize and measure what you want to study. This is the *conceptualization and operationalization* process. It involves refining and specifying abstract concepts (**conceptualization**) and developing specific research procedures (**operationalization**) that will result in empirical observations of things that represent those concepts in the real world. This process gets closer to concrete measurements, because operationalization sets the stage for actual data collection. Thus, this chapter provides the final steps of problem formulation and previews what will come in the next chapter on measurement.

As you read this chapter, keep in mind that it applies primarily to quantitative research. In purely qualitative studies, we do not predetermine specific, precise, objective variables and indicators to measure. Instead, we emphasize methodological freedom and flexibility so that the most salient variables, and their deeper meanings, will emerge as we immerse ourselves in the phenomena we are studying. In fact, the term *operationalization* is virtually absent from most texts that deal exclusively with qualitative research methods. Despite their greater flexibility, however, even qualitative studies begin with an initial set of anticipated meanings that can be refined during data collection and interpretation.

CONCEPTUAL EXPLICATION

Once the foregoing aspects of problem formulation (discussed in Chapter 6) have been handled, you are ready to specify and operationally define the variables in your study and, if the study is not purely descriptive, to postulate relationships among those variables (that is, to develop hypotheses). As we discussed in Chapter 3, a *variable* is a concept we are investigating. We defined a *concept* as a mental image that symbolizes an idea, an object, an event, a behavior, a person, and so on. We can also think of concepts as words that people agree upon to symbolize something. The words can represent something relatively easy to observe such as gender, height, residence, ethnicity, or age. Or they can represent something more difficult to observe such as level of self-esteem, morale of residents in long-term care, level of social functioning, staff burnout, racism, sexism, ageism, homophobia, and so on.

Some concepts are composed of other concepts. Gender, for example, is a concept that consists of the concepts *male* and *female*. As we discussed in Chapter 3, the concepts that make up a broader concept are called **attributes.** Thus, male and female are the attributes of the concept *gender*.

You may wonder why we use the term *variables* in research. Why don't we just stick with the term *concepts*? One reason is that we investigate things that we think will *vary*. Male, for example, is a concept but can't be a variable. It can only take on one value, and therefore is only an *attribute*. Gender, on the other hand, is a concept that can take on *more* than one value and therefore be a variable. We could, for example, investigate the relationship between gender and salary. Do men earn more than women? It would make no sense, however, to investigate the relationship between male and salary. Male and salary are both concepts, but only the concept salary conveys variation and therefore can qualify as a variable.

A concept is a variable if it: (1) comprises more than one attribute, or value, and thus is capable of varying; and (2) is chosen for investigation in a research study. In quantitative research studies, a third condition must be met before a concept can be called a variable: It must be translated into observable terms. The term *operational definition* refers to that translation: the operations, or indicators, we will use to determine the attribute we observe about a particular concept. Thus, a family's risk of child abuse can be operationally defined as the variable: score on the Family Risk Scale (a scale completed by child welfare workers based on their observations of the family). We will discuss operational definitions in much greater length later in this chapter. First, however, let's examine the development of hypotheses.

Developing a Proper Hypothesis

You may recall from Chapter 3 that a variable that is postulated to explain another variable is called the independent variable. The variable being explained is called the dependent variable. The statement that postulates the relationship between the independent and dependent variables is called the hypothesis. In other words, hypotheses are tentative statements that predict what we expect to find about the way our variables co-vary together. A good hypothesis has some of the attributes of a good research question. It should be clear and specific. It should have more than one possible outcome—that is, it should not be a truism. As discussed in Chapter 6, an example of a truism would be to postulate that if the proportion of time practitioners spend filling out administrative forms increases, then the proportion of time left for their remaining activities decreases.

Hypotheses also should be value-free and testable. For example, the statement "Welfare reform legislation should be repealed" is not a hypothesis. It is a judgmental recommendation, not a predicted relationship between two variables that is stated in terms that can be verified or refuted. If we modify the statement to read, "Welfare reform is harmful to the children of welfare recipients," we have made it sound more like a hypothesis. But it would still not qualify as a good hypothesis statement. Although it is predicting that a concept, welfare reform, is harming children, it is not clear and specific regarding the nature of the harm—that is, the specific nature of the concept that is meant to be the dependent variable. Moreover, the concept intended as the independent variable, "welfare reform," is also vague. What specific aspect of welfare reform are we referring to? We could change the statement into a good hypothesis by being more clear and specific about both concepts or variables. One way to do so would be to postulate "Welfare reform policies that move parents off welfare by increasing recipient work requirements will increase the number of children who lack health insurance coverage." The latter statement predicts a relationship between two clearly stated variables that can be verified or refuted by examining whether increases in the number of children who lack health insurance coverage occur after such policies are implemented or by examining whether states that implement such policies have greater increases in the number of children who lack health insurance coverage than do states not implementing them.

Extraneous Variables

A third category of variables is termed **extraneous variables.** These variables represent alternative explanations for relationships that are observed between independent and dependent variables. Suppose, for example, that the economy improves at the same time that a new welfare policy is implemented. If the living standards or employment rates of poor people improve after the policy is implemented, how do we determine whether the improvement is due to the independent variable (the change in policy) or an extraneous variable (the change in the economy)? Suppose that a study finds that the more social services received by hospital patients, the shorter the patients' life span. That relationship would probably be explained away by the fact that the cases involving the most serious illnesses—particularly terminal illnesses—need to receive more social services. Thus, *severity of illness* might be conceptualized as an extraneous variable that might explain the relationship between life span and amount of social services received.

Sometimes our studies check on the possibility that the relationship between our independent and dependent variables, or the apparent lack thereof, is misleading—that it is explained away by other variables. When we do that, the variables that we seek to control in our design are no longer extraneous variables, but **control variables.** In the above example, we could still conceive of *severity of illness* as an extraneous variable, but because we are controlling for it, we can call it a *control variable* in our study.

Sometimes control variables are called *moderating variables.* **Moderating variables** can affect the strength or direction of the relationship between the independent and dependent variable. Thus, if we predict that an intervention will be effective only among females, and not among males, "gender" would be a moderating variable. Likewise, if we predict that an intervention will be effective only among criminal offenders who committed nonviolent crimes, then "type of crime" would be a moderating variable.

Suppose we want to check on this possibility: The relationship between *life span* and *amount of social services received* is explained by the fact that cases involving the most serious illnesses need to receive more social services. To check this out, we would do the following. First, we would separate all cases into subgroups according to seriousness of illness. For the sake of simplicity, assume we would divide them into only two groups: (1) those with life-threatening illnesses and (2) those whose illnesses are not life-threatening. Next, we would assess the relationship between life span and amount of social services received just for those cases with life-threatening illnesses. Then we would do the same just for those cases whose illnesses are not life-threatening. Thus, we would be *controlling* for seriousness of illness by examining whether the original relationship between our independent and dependent variables changes or stays the same for each level of serious illness. The term *control* in this

Table 7-1 Hypothetical Illustration of a Spurious Relationship

WAS PATIENT'S ILLNESS CURED?	DID PATIENT RECEIVE SOCIAL SERVICES IN HOSPITAL? YES	NO
Cured		
Number	10	90
(percent)	(10)	(10)
Not Cured		
Number	90	10
(percent)	(90)	(10)
Total	100	100

context does not mean that the researcher has control over the nature of the illness. It simply means that the researcher examines the hypothesized relationship separately for each category of the control variable.

Tables 7-1 and 7-2 illustrate this sort of control with a simplified hypothetical example that uses numbers and percentages of hospitalized patients whose illnesses are and are not cured in the hospital. Table 7-1 shows that only 10 percent of the patients receiving social services while in the hospital were cured, whereas 90 percent of those not receiving social services were cured. Table 7-2, however, shows that when we control for type of illness upon hospital admission, there is no difference in cure rates between the patients receiving and not receiving social services. All of the patients with acute illnesses were cured, regardless of whether they received social services. All of the patients with chronic or terminal illnesses were not cured, regardless of whether they received social services. How did this happen? As you can glean from Table 7-2, it happened because 90 percent of the patients with chronic or terminal illnesses received social services, whereas only 10 percent of those with acute illnesses did so. Thus, the original relationship shown in Table 7-1 was *spurious*. A **spurious relationship** is one that no longer exists when a third variable is controlled.

We will return to the concept of spurious relationships in later chapters of this text, when we discuss designs and statistical approaches for ferreting out whether an apparent relationship between two variables really means that one variable causes the other.

Table 7-2 Illustration of How Controlling for a Third Variable Shows That an Original Relationship Is Spurious

	TYPE OF ILLNESS UPON HOSPITAL ADMISSION			
	ACUTE		CHRONIC OR TERMINAL	
	RECEIVED SOCIAL SERVICES	DID NOT RECEIVE SOCIAL SERVICES	RECEIVED SOCIAL SERVICES	DID NOT RECEIVE SOCIAL SERVICES
Cured				
Number	10	90	0	0
(percent)	(100)	(100)	(0)	(0)
Not Cured				
Number	0	0	90	10
(percent)	(0)	(0)	(100)	(100)
Total	10	90	90	10

But to enhance your understanding of the concept of controlling for extraneous variables let's consider a few more examples before moving on.

Here's another example. The proportion of reported AIDS cases in the United States is higher among certain ethnic groups than among others. A study that reported that finding might have conceptualized ethnicity as the independent variable and AIDS rate as the dependent variable. But would its finding mean that certain ethnic groups were biologically more susceptible to AIDS or that some other explanation was operating? We might note that the ethnic groups with the higher rates of AIDS are those that also have higher rates of poverty, school dropout, substance abuse, and related social problems. We might therefore suppose that the higher AIDS rates among certain groups are explained not by biological variables, but by socioeconomic variables that result in greater intravenous drug abuse and less awareness of AIDS prevention methods among those ethnic groups. To test this, we might examine what happens to the AIDS rate in each ethnic group when we control for the effects of socioeconomic status. In doing this, we would compare the rates of each ethnic group only for particular levels of socioeconomic status. For example, we would compare the poor people in each ethnic group, the middle-class people in each ethnic group, and so on, rather than comparing the groups as a whole. We would thus be using socioeconomic status as a control variable, because we would be factoring out its effects in looking at the relationship between ethnicity and AIDS rate. In other words, controlling for a variable means taking each level of that control variable separately and looking at how the original relationship between the independent and dependent variables changes or remains the same within each level of the control variable.

Suppose we wish to conduct an explanatory study to test the hypothesis that case management intervention increases the level of social adjustment of discharged psychiatric patients in the community. Our independent variable would be whether the patient received case management intervention, and our dependent variable would be level of social adjustment. Also suppose that we suspect that patients referred to case managers are those whose disabilities are the most chronic and whose social adjustment therefore may be most difficult to improve. If that were the case, the effects of the case management services might be masked by the lower capacities for improvement in the case management clients. We would then seek to control for the extraneous variable of degree of chronicity, which we might operationally define as the number of times the individual was admitted as an inpatient to a psychiatric hospital or the total amount of time the individual was an inpatient during all psychiatric hospitalizations. We would test the hypothesis by comparing the social adjustment outcome of patients with the same particular degree of chronicity who did and did not receive case management services. We would do this for each degree of chronicity (high, medium, low, and so on) that was included in chronicity's operational definition.

Suppose we wish to conduct a different explanatory study, this time testing the hypothesis that the amount of citizen participation of neighborhood residents in the early planning of community-based residential facilities for discharged psychiatric patients is associated with the amount of community opposition those facilities ultimately encounter. Amount of citizen participation in early planning would be our independent variable. Our dependent variable would be amount of community opposition encountered. Suppose we thought that the results of our study might vary according to type of community. Perhaps we expect that more citizen participation leads to less opposition in nonresidential sections of town, but that it backfires in more affluent, residential neighborhoods, leading to more opposition. Then we would control for this variable: type of community. We would look separately at the relationship between amount of citizen participation and amount of opposition in each type of community.

Notice that our original hypothesis did not identify the cause or the effect. Conceivably, the amount of citizen participation that takes place might be less a cause of the amount of opposition than a result of it. For example, some planners might not be inclined to promote citizen participation unless they are compelled to deal with stiff preliminary opposition to their plans. Thus, when they encounter little opposition, they may feel that promoting significant citizen participation is unnecessary or perhaps too risky in the sense that it might stir up resistance among those who are currently uninvolved and perhaps unaware of the plans. On the other hand, when they encounter stiff opposition to their plans, they might have no choice but to promote citizen participation activities that they had hoped to avoid and that are aimed at overcoming an initially high level of opposition.

In the same sense, there is nothing inherent in a particular concept that makes it an independent, dependent, or moderating variable in every study in which it is observed. For example, if one study postulates that amount of citizen participation is the cause of the amount of opposition, then amount of citizen participation is the independent variable, and amount of opposition is the dependent variable. But another study could reverse the hypothesis, making amount of citizen participation the dependent variable and amount of community opposition the independent variable. You should also realize that whether a variable is independent or dependent does not depend on the sequence in which it is specified in the hypothesis. For example, if we postulate that amount of community opposition will be lowered if we involve citizens in planning, then amount of community opposition is the dependent variable even though it is specified first in the hypothesis. This can be confusing, because even though the cause must happen before the effect, putting the effect first in the hypothesis does not mean you are saying that it will happen first.

Mediating Variables

Another type of variable that can affect the relationship between the independent and dependent variables is a *mediating variable*. A **mediating variable** is the mechanism by which an independent variable affects a dependent variable. If we think an intervention reduces recidivism among criminal offenders by first

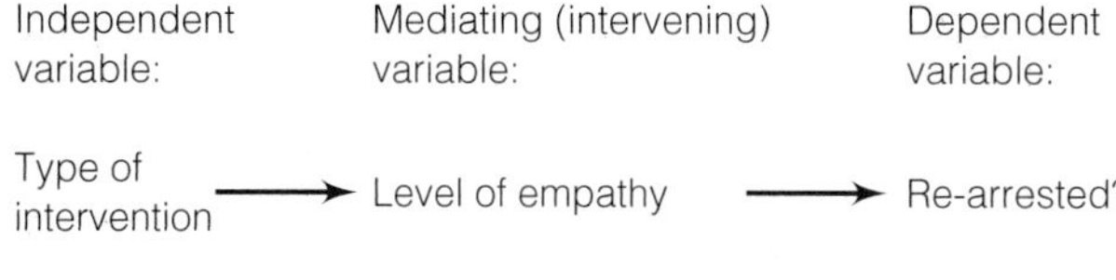

Figure 7-1 Illustration of a Mediating Variable

increasing prisoner empathy for crime victims, then "level of empathy for crime victims" would be our mediating variable. It would come between our independent variable (whether prisoners receive the intervention) and our dependent variable (whether they get re-arrested for another crime). In other words, we would be conceptualizing a causal chain in which the independent variable affects the mediating variable, which in turn affects the dependent variable, as illustrated in Figure 7-1. Because mediating variables come between independent and dependent variables, they can also be called **intervening variables.**

Students sometimes confuse the terms *mediating variables* and *moderating variables*. It might help to keep in mind that one definition for the verb *mediate* is to act as a *medium* that occurs between stages and moves something from one stage (the independent variable) to another stage (the dependent variable). In contrast, one definition for the verb *moderate* is to change the extent or severity of something. Thus, moderating variables reside outside the causal chain between the independent and dependent variables but can influence the degree of the relationship between the two. Mediating variables, however, reside in the middle of the causal chain and have no impact on independent variables. In a sense they are sort of an intermediary dependent variable in that they can be influenced by the independent variable and then in turn affect the ultimate and actual dependent variable. Gender, for example, cannot be influenced by an intervention to increase prisoner empathy and thus could not be a mediating variable. It could, however, be a moderating variable in that (as noted above) it might influence the extent of the relationship between an intervention and recidivism.

Types of Relationships between Variables

Some hypotheses predict positive or negative (inverse) and curvilinear relationships between variables. In a **positive relationship,** the dependent variable increases as the independent variable increases (or decreases as the independent variable decreases)—that is, both variables move in the same direction. Thus, we might postulate a positive relationship between the amount of symbolic rewards citizens receive for participating in community organizations and the extent to which they participate. We might also postulate a positive relationship between level of client satisfaction with social services and the extent to which the delivered service focused on the problem or goal for which the client originally sought help (as opposed to a problem or goal that the practitioner chose to work on without involving the client in the decision). The top graph in Figure 7-2 pictorially represents this hypothesized positive relationship.

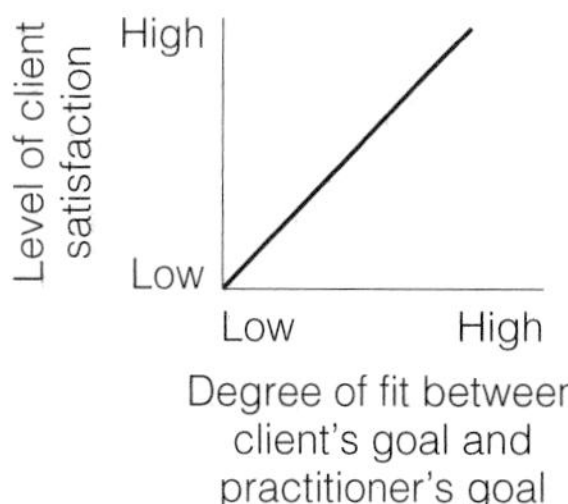

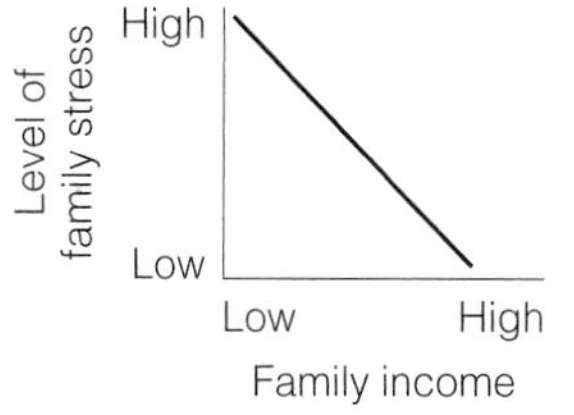

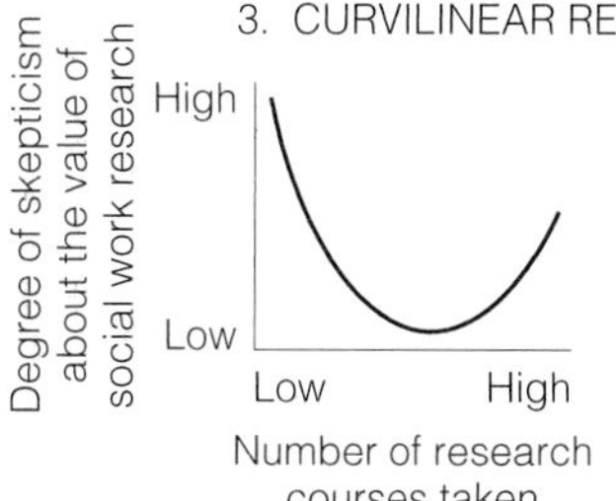

Figure 7-2 Graphic Display of Types of Hypothetical Relationships between Variables

A **negative, or inverse, relationship** means that the two variables move in opposite directions—that is, as one increases, the other decreases. We might postulate a negative relationship between the caseload size of direct-service practitioners and their degree of effectiveness because those whose caseloads are too large might be expected to have less time to provide quality services. A negative relationship might also be postulated between family income and level of family stress. The middle graph in Figure 7-2 pictorially represents this hypothesized negative relationship.

A **curvilinear relationship** is one in which the nature of the relationship changes at certain levels of the variables. For example, some social work educators believe that the students who are most skeptical about the value of published social work research are those who have either taken many research courses or none at all. Those who have never had a research course may not yet have learned to appreciate research's potential utility. Those with a great deal of knowledge about research might be disillusioned by the many serious methodological flaws they detect in much of the published research. Consequently, those with the least skepticism may be the ones in the middle—those who have enough knowledge to appreciate the value of good research but who have not yet critically scrutinized enough of the literature to realize how many published studies are seriously flawed. Educators who believe this notion might hypothesize a U-curve that begins with a negative relationship between the number of courses taken and the degree of skepticism about research and ends with a positive relationship between them. In other words, skepticism decreases as more courses are taken up to a certain number of courses, and then it increases as more courses are taken beyond that. The bottom graph in Figure 7-2 pictorially represents this hypothesized curvilinear relationship.

OPERATIONAL DEFINITIONS

In quantitative research, as we noted earlier in this chapter, before we can implement a study to collect data on our variables, we must first translate those variables into observable terms. The term **operational definition** refers to that translation: the operations, or indicators, we will use to determine the quantity or attribute we observe about a particular variable. Operational definitions differ from nominal definitions. *Nominal* definitions, like dictionary definitions, use a set of words to help us understand what a term means, but they do not tell us what indicators to use in observing the term in a research study. For example, a nominal definition of social adjustment might be appropriate performance of one's major roles in life—as parent, student, employee, spouse, and so on. This definition may give us clues about how we might develop an operational definition, but it does not specify precisely what indicators we will observe and the exact categories of social adjustment we will note in our research on social adjustment.

We can operationally define abstract variables in many ways. One operational definition of social adjustment might be a score on a scale that measures level of social adjustment. Another operational definition might be whether an individual is receiving social services aimed at restoring social functioning. Those who receive such services might be categorized as having lower levels of social adjustment than others who do not receive such services. Here's a contrasting example: In an institutional facility for the severely developmentally disabled, our operational definition might identify individuals with higher levels of social adjustment as those whose case records indicate that they were deemed ready to be placed in a sheltered workshop. Operational definitions point the way to how a variable will be measured.

Operationally Defining Anything That Exists

You may have reservations about science's ability to operationally define some abstract variables of concern to social workers such as *love, hate, empathy, feminism, racism, homophobia,* and *spirituality.* You may have read research reports that dealt with something like *spirituality,* and you may have been dissatisfied with the way the researchers measured whatever they were studying. You may have felt they were too superficial, that they missed the aspects that really matter most. Maybe they measured *spirituality* as the number of times a person went to church, or maybe they measured *liberalism* by how people voted in a single election. Your dissatisfaction would surely have been increased if you found yourself being misclassified by the measurement system.

Skepticism about our ability to operationally define some abstract variables is understandable. Most of the variables in social work research don't actually exist in the way that rocks exist. Indeed, they are made up. Moreover, they seldom have a single, unambiguous meaning. Consider *feminism,* for example. We are not able to observe a feminist in the way we observe a rock. We could attempt to observe whether individuals are feminists by simply asking them if they are. Or we could ask them if they belong to a feminist organization or agree with the position statements of such organizations.

Notice that each of these operational definitions might produce different results. When asked, some people may say that they are a feminist even though they disagree with the positions favored by feminist organizations. They may even think that they really are a feminist, according to their own idiosyncratic notion of what that term means. In fact, abstract variables such as *feminism, spirituality,* and the like do not exist in nature like rocks do. They are merely terms that we have made up and assigned specific meanings to for some purpose such as doing research. Yet these terms have *some* reality. After all, there are feminist models of social work practice and research.

Perhaps you've read a research study assessing the proportion of social workers who use spirituality in their practice. If these things don't exist in reality, then what is it that we are observing and talking about? What indeed? Let's take a closer look by considering two variables of interest to social workers—racism and homophobia.

Throughout our lives, we've observed a lot of things that we connect to racism and homophobia and known they were real through our observations. We've also read or heard reports from other people that seemed real. For example, we heard people say nasty things about people who are gay, lesbian, or members of particular ethnic minority groups. We read about hate crimes against such people. We read about discrimination against them in employment or in other matters. We've heard some people call them ugly names. At some point, some folks made up shorthand terms—such as *racists* and *homophobics*—to portray people who did or approved of some of these things. Even though people cannot directly observe racism and homophobia in the way they observe a rock, and even though racism and homophobia don't exist in nature the way rocks exist, we agree to use those made-up terms to represent a collection of apparently related phenomena that we've each observed in the course of life.

Yet each of these terms does not exist apart from our rough agreements to use them in a certain way. Each of us develops our own mental image of real phenomena that we've observed as represented by terms like *racism* and *homophobia.* Some may consider it racist to oppose having lower college admission standards—for affirmative action purposes—for members of minority groups that historically have been discriminated against. Others may hold the opposite view, arguing that the notion that members of those groups need lower standards is racist because it implies that they are somehow inferior.

When we hear or read abstract terms such as *racism,* the mental images we have of those terms are evoked in our minds. It's as though we have file drawers in our minds containing thousands of sheets of paper, and each sheet of paper has a label in the upper right-hand corner. One sheet of paper in your file drawer has the term *racism* on it. On your sheet are all the things you were told about racism and everything you've observed that seemed to be an example of it. Someone else's sheet has what they were told about racism plus all the things they've observed that seemed to be examples of it.

The technical term for those mental images, those sheets of paper in our mental file drawers, is *conception.* Each sheet of paper is a conception. In the big picture, language and communication only work to the extent that we have considerable overlap in the kinds of entries we have on our corresponding mental file sheets. The similarities we have on those sheets represent the agreements existing in the society we occupy. When we were growing up, we were told approximately the same thing when we were first introduced to a particular term. Dictionaries formalize the agreements our society has about such terms. Each of us, then, shapes his or her mental images to correspond with those agreements, but because all of us have different experiences and observations, no two people end up with exactly the same set of entries on any sheet in their file systems.

How can we operationally define variables that do not really exist apart from our idiosyncratic conceptions of them? Suppose we want to measure whether a boy doing poorly at school is depressed. We can observe, for example, how often he says he dislikes himself and has no hope for the future. We can ask his parents how often he isolates himself at home or plays with friends. Perhaps his teacher will tell us he can't concentrate in school and is a loner in the school yard. All of those things exist, so we can observe them. But are we really observing *depression*? We can't answer that question. We can't observe depression in that sense, because depression doesn't exist the way those things we just described exist. Perhaps his negative self-statements and social isolation are due to low self-esteem, not depression. Perhaps he also has attention deficit hyperactivity disorder, which would explain his inability to concentrate in school. Depression as a *term* exists. We can observe the number of letters it contains and agree that there are 10. We can agree that it has three syllables and that it begins with the letter "D." In short, we can observe the aspects of it that are real.

In this context, Abraham Kaplan (1964) distinguishes three classes of things that scientists measure. The first class is *direct observables:* those things we can observe rather simply and directly, like the color of an apple or the check mark made in a questionnaire. The second class is *indirect observables.* If someone puts a check mark beside female in our questionnaire, then we can indirectly observe that person's gender. Minutes of agency board meetings provide indirect observations of past agency actions. Finally, *constructs* are theoretical creations based on observations but which themselves cannot be observed directly or indirectly.

Depression, then, is an abstraction—a construct that consists of a "family of conceptions" (Kaplan, 1964:49) that includes your concepts that constitute depression, our concepts that make it up, and the conceptions of all those who have ever used the term. It cannot be observed directly or indirectly, because it doesn't exist. We made it up. All we can measure are the direct observables and indirect observables that we think the term *depression* implies. IQ is another example. It is constructed mathematically from observations of the answers given to a large number of questions on an IQ test. Later in this chapter we'll discuss sources of existing scales that measure such things as social adjustment, marital satisfaction, and family risk of child abuse. These are further examples of constructs.

Conceptualization

Day-to-day communication usually occurs through a system of vague and general agreements about the use of terms. Usually, people do not understand exactly what we wish to communicate, but they get the general drift of our meaning. *Conceptualization* is the process through which we specify precisely what we will mean when we use particular terms. Suppose we want to find out, for example, whether women are more compassionate than men. We can't meaningfully study the question, let alone agree on the answer, without some precise working agreements about the meaning of the term *compassion.* They are working agreements in the sense that they allow us to work on the question. We don't need to agree or even pretend to agree that a particular specification might be worth using.

Indicators and Dimensions

The end product of this conceptualization process is the specification of a set of *indicators* of what we have in mind, markers that indicate the presence or absence of the concept we are studying. Thus, we may agree to use visiting children's hospitals at Christmas as an indicator of compassion. Putting little birds back in their nests may be agreed on as another indicator, and so forth. If the unit of analysis for our study were the individual person, we could then observe the presence or absence of each indicator for each person under study. Going beyond that, we could add the number of indicators of compassion observed for each individual. We might agree on 10 specific indicators, for example, and find six present in Peter, three in Paul, nine for Mary, and so forth.

Returning to our original question, we might calculate that the women we studied had an average of 6.5 indicators of compassion, and the men studied had an average of 3.2. On the basis of that group difference, we might therefore conclude that women are, on the whole, more compassionate than men. Usually, though, it's not that simple.

Let's imagine that you are interested in studying the attitudes of different religious groups about the term *social justice.* To most social work professors and students, a belief in social justice implies politically liberal views about such issues as redistributing wealth, women's reproductive rights, gay and lesbian rights, and not imposing the prayers or symbols of a particular religion on students in public schools, among many others. Let's say that one of the groups you study are members of a fundamentalist, evangelical Christian church.

In the course of your conversations with church members and perhaps in attending religious services, you would have put yourself in a situation where you could come to understand what the members mean by "social justice." You might learn, for example, that members of the group firmly believe aborted fetuses are murdered humans and that gays and lesbians, women and doctors who engage in abortions, and non-Christians are sinners who will burn eternally in Hell unless they are converted. In fact, they may be so deeply concerned about sinners burning in Hell that they are willing to be aggressive, even violent, in making people change their sinful ways. Within this paradigm, then, opposing gay and lesbian rights, imposing Christian prayers in public institutions, and perhaps even blockading abortion clinics might be seen by church members as acts that promote social justice.

Social scientists often focus their attention on the meanings given to words and actions by the people under study. Although this can clarify the behaviors observed, it almost always complicates the concepts in which we are interested.

Whenever we take our concepts seriously and set about specifying what we mean by them, we discover disagreements and inconsistencies. Not only do we disagree, but also each of us is likely to find a good deal of muddiness within our own individual mental images. If you take a moment to look at what *you* mean by *social justice*, you'll probably find that your image contains several kinds of social justice. The entries on your file sheet can be combined into groups and subgroups, and you'll even find several different strategies for making the combinations. For example, you might group the entries into economic justice and civil rights.

The technical term for such a grouping is *dimension:* a specifiable aspect or facet of a concept. Thus, we might speak of the "economic dimension" and the "civil rights dimension" of social justice. Or social justice might be concerned with helping people be and have what we want for them or what they want for themselves. Thus, we could subdivide the concept of social justice according to several sets of dimensions. Specifying dimensions and identifying the various indicators for each dimension are both parts of conceptualization. Specifying the different dimensions of a concept often paves the way for a more sophisticated understanding of what we are studying. We might observe, for example, that law students are more committed to the civil rights dimension of social justice, whereas economics majors are more concerned with the redistribution of wealth.

Conceptions and Reality

Reviewing briefly, our concepts are derived from the mental images (conceptions) that summarize collections of seemingly related observations and experiences. Although the observations and experiences are real, our concepts are only mental creations. The terms associated with concepts are merely devices created for purposes of filing and communication. The word *homophobia* is an example.

Ultimately, the word is only a collection of letters and has no intrinsic meaning. We could have as easily and meaningfully created the word *anti-homosexualism* to serve the same purpose. Often, however, we fall into the trap of believing that terms have real meanings. That danger seems to grow stronger when we begin to take terms seriously and attempt to use them precisely. And the danger is all the greater in the presence of experts who appear to know more than you do about what the terms really mean. It's easy to yield to the authority of experts in such a situation.

Once we have assumed that terms have real meanings, we begin the tortured task of discovering what those real meanings are and what constitutes a genuine measurement of them. We make up conceptual summaries of real observations because the summaries are convenient. They prove so convenient, however, that we begin to think they are real. The process of regarding unreal things as real is called *reification*, and the reification of concepts in day-to-day life is very common.

Creating Conceptual Order

The clarification of concepts is a continuing process in social research. In rigorously structured research designs such as surveys and experiments, operationally defining variables is vital at the beginning of study design. In a survey, for example, it results in a commitment to a specific set of questionnaire items that will represent the concepts under study. Without that commitment, the study could not proceed. However, investigators may find themselves still refining the meanings of concepts as they attempt to communicate their findings to others in a final report.

In some forms of qualitative research, concept clarification is an ongoing element in data collection. Suppose you were conducting interviews and observations of a radical political group that is devoted to combating oppression in American society. Imagine how the concept of "oppression" would shift meaning as you delved more and more deeply into the members' experiences and worldviews. In the analysis of textual materials, social researchers sometimes speak of the "hermeneutic circle," a cyclical process of ever-deeper understanding.

> The understanding of a text takes place through a process in which the meaning of the separate parts is determined by the global meaning of the text as it is anticipated. The closer determination of the meaning of the separate parts may eventually change the originally anticipated meaning of the totality, which again influences the meaning of the separate parts, and so on.
>
> (Kvale, 1996:47)

Even in less structured forms of qualitative research, however, you must also begin with an initial set of anticipated meanings that can be refined during data collection and interpretation. No one seriously believes it is possible to observe life with no preconceptions; thus, the scientific observer is conscious and explicit about those starting points.

Let's continue the discussion of initial conceptualization as it applies most to structured inquiries such as surveys and experiments. The specification of nominal definitions focuses our observational strategy, but it does not allow us to observe. As a next step, we must specify exactly what we are going to observe, how we will do it, and what interpretations we will place on various possible observations. As we discussed earlier, all of these further specifications make up the operational definition of the concept—a definition that spells out precisely how the concept will be measured. Strictly speaking, an operational definition is a description of the "operations" that will be undertaken in measuring a concept, as we discussed earlier in this chapter.

Wishing to examine socioeconomic status (SES) in a study, for example, we might decide to ask the people we are studying two questions:

1. What was your total family income during the past 12 months?

2. What is the highest level of school you completed?

Here, we would probably want to specify a system for categorizing the answers people give us. For income, we might use categories such as "less than $5,000" or "$5,000 to $10,000." Educational attainment might be similarly grouped in categories. Finally, we would specify the way a person's responses to these two questions would be combined in creating a measure of SES. Chapter 9, on constructing measurement instruments, will present some of the methods for doing that.

Ultimately, we would have created a working and workable definition of SES. Others might disagree with our conceptualization and operationalization, but the definition would have one essential scientific virtue: It would be absolutely specific and unambiguous. Even if someone disagreed with our definition, that person would have a good idea how to interpret our research results, because what we meant by the term SES—reflected in our analyses and conclusions—would be clear.

Here is a diagram that shows the progression of measurement steps from our vague sense of what a term means to specific measurements in a scientific study:

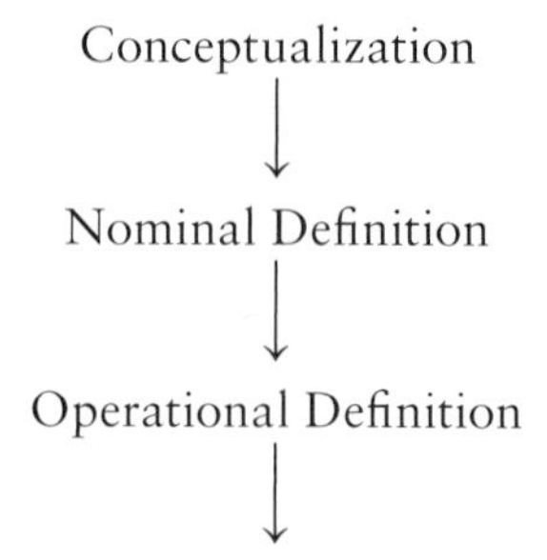

Measurements in the Real World

Thus, social scientists can measure anything that's real, and they can even do a pretty good job of measuring things that aren't. Granting that such concepts as socioeconomic status, racism, and compassion aren't ultimately real in the sense that a rock is real, we've now seen that social scientists can create order in handling them, albeit an order based on utility rather than on ultimate truth.

The Influence of Operational Definitions

How we choose to operationally define a variable can greatly influence our research findings. If our task is to describe and report the unemployment rate in a city, for example, our definition of *being unemployed* is critical. That definition will depend on our definition of another term: the *labor force*. If it seems patently absurd to regard a 3-year-old child as being unemployed, then it is because such a child is not considered a member of the labor force. Thus, we might follow the U.S. Bureau of the Census in its convention and exclude all persons younger than 14 from the labor force.

This convention alone, however, would not give us a satisfactory definition, because it would count school students, the retired, the disabled, and homemakers among the unemployed. We might follow the census convention further by defining the labor force as "all persons 14 years of age and over who are employed, looking for work, or waiting to be called back to a job from which they have been laid off or furloughed." Unemployed persons, then, would be members of the labor force who are not employed. If a student, homemaker, or retired person is not looking for work, then such a person would not be included in the labor force.

But what does "looking for work" mean? Must a person register with the state employment service or go from door to door asking for employment? Or would it be sufficient to want a job or be open to an offer of employment? Conventionally, in survey research "looking for work" is defined operationally as saying "yes" in response to an interviewer's asking "Have you been looking for a job during the past seven days?" (Seven days is the time period most often specified, but for some research purposes it might make more sense to shorten or lengthen it.)

We have spelled out these considerations in some detail so that you will realize that the conclusion of a descriptive study about the unemployment rate, for example, depends directly on how each issue is resolved. Increasing the period of time during which people are counted as looking for work would have the effect of adding more unemployed persons to the labor force as defined, thereby increasing the reported unemployment rate. If we follow another convention and speak of the *civilian* labor force and the *civilian* unemployment rate, then we are excluding military personnel; that, too, increases the reported unemployment rate, because military personnel would be employed—*by definition.*

Thus, the descriptive statement that the unemployment rate in a city is 3 percent, or 9 percent, or whatever it might be, depends directly on the operational definitions used. Let's consider some additional examples of the ways operational definition choices can influence our findings.

Suppose a community organizer wants to study factors that influence citizen participation in a barrio in Los Angeles. Her results may vary, depending on whether she operationally defines *citizen participation* as attendance by barrio residents at meetings of a social action organization, their attendance at city government meetings where issues of concern to the barrio are being discussed, contacts they make with governmental officials, or participation in protest demonstrations. The factors that motivate people to attend a protest demonstration might be different than those that motivate them to attend a meeting or write their city council member.

Suppose we want to evaluate a child welfare program aimed at preventing child abuse and preserving families. If we operationally define *child abuse rates* in terms of the number of children placed in foster care and the program reduces that number, the program would be deemed successful. However, what if the rate of abuse actually increases because so many children at great risk for abuse were *not* placed in foster care? Had the operational definition of *child abuse rates* included other indicators of abuse, the same program with the same results might have been deemed a failure.

Suppose we want to study trends over time in the incidence of rape on college campuses. In the past, if a person did not resist sexual intercourse after heavy drinking, generally it was not defined as rape, even if he or she regretted it later and would have resisted had he or she been sober. Today, many would define the same situation as rape if the person later reports regretting the intercourse and feels manipulated through the pressure to drink. The number of rapes that we would find in our study would vary quite a bit depending on whether or not our operational definition of rape included a person saying later that he or she regretted and would have resisted intercourse instead of "consenting" after drinking. Suppose we did include that in our operational definition and then reported our findings to the media. Chances are the media would not consider the difference between our (broader) operational definition of rape and the narrower definitions used in the past. Consequently, a headline might inaccurately portray a shocking jump in the incidence of rape on college campuses.

Gender and Cultural Bias in Operational Definitions

Special care is needed to avoid gender and cultural bias in choosing operational definitions. Suppose we attempt to operationally define family dysfunction by including observable indicators of "excessive" contact and dependence between grown children and their parents. What may be considered excessive or pathological dependence in an individualistic culture that emphasizes independence might be quite normal in a culture that values group welfare over individual welfare and that emphasizes the healthy aspects of using the family as a natural support system (Grinnell, 1997).

As to gender bias, suppose we are studying whether the quality of attachment to a parent during childhood influences the resilience of children who had been sexually abused by someone other than a parent. Suppose we develop a questionnaire to send to adults who had been sexually abused as children; in asking about early childhood parental attachments, we refer only to the mother and not the father, reflecting a gender bias that only mothers are nurturers of young children. Or maybe we want to study the extent and causes of spouse abuse, but inadvertently—because of *gender bias*—refer to it only as *wife abuse.* Some might argue that asking whether a person remains calm and unemotional in stressful situations as an indicator of social functioning might involve a gender bias. The idea here would be that women might be more inclined to express their emotions and might find that doing so helps them cope.

Another example of gender bias would involve excluding unpaid forms of work that women are more likely than men to do—such as child rearing—in operationally defining concepts such as *occupation* or *work*. Finally, perhaps we want to study whether certain social policies or organizational procedures are effective in alleviating the conflict that employees with young children experience between their roles as parents and as employees. Our operational definition would involve a gender bias if we specified only mothers and not fathers in operationally defining such role conflict, such as by asking whether an agency allows mothers to have flexible work schedules to care for their young children (and not mentioning fathers in the question).

The above examples do *not* mean that every time we refer to only one gender our operational definition automatically is biased. If only one gender is relevant to our study, and if our findings are going to be reported in reference to that gender only, then it may be appropriate to include only that gender in our operational definition. Male batterers, for example, may need a separate intervention program than female batterers. If we are assessing the men in a group being treated for wife battering, then it would be acceptable to refer to wife abuse instead of spouse abuse. The key here is to be aware of whether defining things in terms of only one gender is appropriate or not, rather than let our definition refer to only one gender inadvertently.

OPERATIONALIZATION CHOICES

As we've indicated, the social work researcher has a wide variety of options available when it comes to measuring a concept. Although the choices are intimately interconnected, we've separated them for purposes of discussion. Please realize, however, that operationalization does not proceed through a systematic checklist.

Range of Variation

In operationalizing any concept, you must be clear about the range of variation that interests you in your research. To what extent are you willing to combine attributes in fairly gross categories?

Let's suppose you want to measure people's incomes in a study—collecting the information either from records or in interviews. The highest annual incomes people receive run into the millions of dollars, but not many people get that much. Unless you are studying the very rich, it probably wouldn't be worth much to allow for and track such extremely high categories. Depending on whom you are studying, you'll probably want to establish a highest income category with a much lower floor—maybe $200,000 or more. Although this decision will lead you to throw together people who earn a trillion dollars a year with "paupers" earning only $200,000, they'll survive it, and that mixing probably won't hurt your research any. The same decision faces you at the other end of the income spectrum. In studies of the general American population, a cutoff of $10,000 or less might work just fine.

In the study of attitudes and orientations, the question of range of variation has another dimension. Unless you're careful, you may unintentionally end up measuring only "half an attitude." Here's an example of what we mean.

Suppose you're interested in the views of social work practitioners about transracial adoptions—that is, adoptions of a child, usually of minority ethnicity, by parents of a different ethnicity. You'd anticipate in advance that some practitioners consider it a great way to find foster parents for children who otherwise would have little chance of being adopted, whereas other practitioners have never heard of and have no interest in the concept. Given that anticipation, it would seem to make sense to ask people how much they favor expanding the use of transracial adoptions. You might give them answer categories ranging from "Favor it very much" to "Don't favor it at all."

This operationalization, however, conceals half of the spectrum of attitudes toward transracial adoptions. Many practitioners, including minority practitioners concerned about the self-image and stigmatization of minority children raised by white parents in a predominantly white community, have feelings that go beyond simply not favoring it: They are *opposed* to it. In this instance, there is considerable variation on the left side of zero. Some oppose it a little, some quite a bit, and others a great deal. To measure the full range of variation, then, you'd want to operationalize attitudes toward transracial adoptions with a range from favoring it very much, through no feelings one way or the other, to opposing it very much.

This consideration applies to many of the variables we study in social science. Virtually any public issue involves both support and opposition, each in varying degrees. Political orientations range from ultraliberal to ultraconservative, and depending on the people you are studying, you may want to allow for radicals on one or both ends. People are not just more or less religious—some are antireligious.

We do not mean that you must measure the full range of variation in any given case. You should, however, consider whether such measurement is needed in the light of your research purpose. If the difference between *not religious* and *antireligious* isn't relevant to your research, then forget it. Someone has defined *pragmatism* by saying "any difference that makes no difference is no difference." Be pragmatic.

Finally, your decision on the range of variation should also be governed by the expected distribution of attributes among your subjects of study. That is what we meant earlier when we said range depends on whom you are studying. In a study of college professors' attitudes toward the value of higher education, you could probably stop at *no value* and not worry about those who might consider higher education dangerous to students' health. (If you were studying students, however. . . .)

Variations between the Extremes

Precision is a consideration in operationalizing variables. (As we will see in Chapter 8, it also is a criterion of quality in measurement.) What it boils down to is how fine you will make distinctions among the various possible attributes composing a given variable. Does it really matter whether a person is 17 or 18 years old, or could you conduct your inquiry by throwing them together in a group labeled "15 to 19 years old"? Don't answer too quickly. If you wanted to study rates of voter registration and participation, you'd definitely want to know whether the people you studied were old enough to vote.

If you are going to measure age, then, you must look at the purpose and procedures of your study and decide whether fine or gross differences in age are important to you. If you measure political affiliation, will it matter to your inquiry whether a person is a conservative Democrat rather than a liberal Democrat, or is it sufficient to know the party? In measuring religious affiliation, is it enough to know that a person is a Protestant, or do you need to know the denomination? Do you simply need to know whether a person is married or not, or will it make a difference to know if he or she has never married or is separated, widowed, or divorced?

Of course, there are no general answers to questions like these. They come out of the purpose of your study—the purpose you have in making a particular measurement. We can mention a useful guideline, however. Whenever you're not sure how much detail to get in a measurement, get too much rather than too little. During the analysis of data, it will always be possible to combine precise attributes into more general categories, but it will never be possible to separate out the variations that were lumped together during observation and measurement.

A Note on Dimensions

When people get down to the business of creating operational measures of variables, they often discover—or worse, never notice—that they are not exactly clear about which dimensions of a variable are of real interest. Here's one example to illustrate what we mean.

Let's suppose we are doing in-depth qualitative interviews to determine the attitudes of families toward the long-term care of relatives in nursing homes. Here are just a few of the different dimensions we might examine:

- Do family members think their relative receives adequate care?
- How adequate or inadequate do they think the care is?
- How certain are they in their judgment of the adequacy of care?
- How do they feel about the inadequacy of nursing home care as a problem in society?
- What do they think causes it?
- Do they think it's inevitable?
- What do they feel should be done about it?
- What are they willing to do personally to improve nursing home care?
- How certain are they that they would be willing to do what they say they would do?

The list could go on and on. How people feel about the adequacy of care in nursing homes has many dimensions. *It's essential that you be clear about which ones are important in your inquiry and direct the interviews appropriately.* Otherwise, you may measure how people feel about it when you really wanted to know how much they think there is, or vice versa.

EXAMPLES OF OPERATIONALIZATION IN SOCIAL WORK

Throughout this chapter, we have discussed how some terms might be operationally defined as well as some complexities involved in operationalization choices. Typically, we have three broad categories of choices for operationalizing variables: **self-reports, direct observation**, and the examination of **available records.**

Let's consider the construct *marital satisfaction*. Suppose you are conducting a research study, and marital satisfaction is one of your variables. Perhaps you want to see if family therapy increases marital satisfaction, in which case it would be your dependent variable. Or maybe you want to see if higher levels of marital satisfaction among foster parents contribute to successful foster placement, in which case marital satisfaction would be your independent variable. In either study, what are some of the ways in which you might operationally define marital satisfaction? Would you simply define it as the amount of happiness in a marriage? That *nominal* definition won't do as an *operational* definition because it won't bring you any closer to the *observable* indicators of marital satisfaction. You would merely have substituted one unobservable construct (*happiness*) for another. Here are a few options that would be operational.

In the study on foster placement, you might simply ask the couples if they have recently sought help for marital problems. Thus, you would be using *self-reports*. You might consider those who answer "Yes" to have less marital satisfaction than those who say "No." Similarly, you might just ask the couples whether they consider themselves to have high, medium, or low degrees of marital satisfaction. You might understandably have some qualms as to whether the answers you'll get are sufficiently accurate and objective indicators of marital satisfaction, and we are not necessarily recommending either approach. But you should see that either one would be an *operational* definition.

A more thorough *self-report* option would be an *existing scale* previously devised to measure marital satisfaction. You would ask each person in your study to complete the scale. The higher the score on the scale, the more marital satisfaction. (If both spouses respond, perhaps you will add both scores to get a combined score per couple.) Existing scales that have been constructed to measure certain constructs build the indicators of the construct into the scale. For example, a scale to measure marital satisfaction might ask either spouse how often he or she is annoyed with the spouse, has fun with the spouse, feels he or she can rely on the spouse, wants to be with the spouse, is proud of the spouse, feels controlled by the spouse, resents the spouse, and so on. Each scale item gets a score, and the item scores are summed for a total score of marital satisfaction. For instance, an individual might get a score of 5 for each positive item (such as feeling proud of spouse) to which he or she responds "always" and for each negative item (such as resenting the spouse) to which the response is "never." If there are 20 items on the scale and the individual responds "always" to every positive item and "never" to every negative item, then the total scale score would be 100. That score would indicate that this person had more marital satisfaction than another person who responded "sometimes" to every item, receiving a score of, say, 3 for every item and therefore a total score of 60.

Alternatively, you might interview each couple about their marriage and count the number of times that either partner makes a derogatory statement about the marriage or the spouse. This option would be using *direct observation*. If you go this route, you'll have to grapple with the ground rules for considering a statement derogatory. Perhaps you'll just have to leave that to the judgment of the interviewer, and see if an independent observer (perhaps viewing a videotape of the interview) tends to agree with the interviewer's counts. We'll say more about this when we discuss *reliability* in the next chapter.

Another way to use direct observation would be to ask the spouses to conduct a typical 15-minute conversation while you observe and count the number of times they interrupt one another, raise their voices, or make various physical gestures that seem to indicate frustration or dissatisfaction with the other. This can be tricky. If the couple is disagreeing about an intellectual or political issue (such as foreign policy, for example), perhaps the partners actually enjoy having heated, animated debates. Although you have an observable definition, you might wonder whether it is really measuring marital satisfaction. We'll get into that issue as well in the next chapter when we discuss *validity*.

Of course, we might attempt to operationally define marital satisfaction in many other ways. For example, if we are doing cross-cultural research, we might compare divorce rates in different geographic areas as one operational indicator of marital satisfaction. This illustrates the use of *available records*.

Again, this does not mean that such rates would be a true indicator of the construct, just that they would be operational. Perhaps the culture with the lower divorce rates has no more marital satisfaction, just stricter taboos against divorce.

We'll conclude this section with an example that concerns many social work students: the concept of *social work interviewing skill*. Perhaps you will someday conduct a study to see whether your agency's inservice training program is effective in improving the interviewing skills of the recently graduated social workers it hires. Or perhaps you will want to see whether there is any difference in interviewing skills among recently hired social workers who have only MSW degrees, those who have only BSW degrees, and those who have both BSW and MSW degrees. How will you operationally define interviewing skill?

One option would be to have the social workers conduct initial intake interviews with new clients entering the agency (or, alternatively, social workers role-playing clients) and then, on completion of each interview, have the clients (or role players) rate how at ease they felt during the interview, how interested the interviewer seemed in them, whether the interviewer seemed to ask the right questions and to understand how they felt, and so on.

Another option would be to list specific behaviors associated with good and bad interviewing, videotape each interview, and then count the behaviors. Desirable behaviors might include maintaining eye contact, giving intermittent positive gestures (smiles, nods, and so on), and paraphrasing answers to prompt elaboration, among many others. Undesirable behaviors might include slouching, yawning, looking at one's watch, and passing judgment on answers. You might add the desirable behaviors and subtract the undesirable behaviors to get a score that would operationalize interviewing skills.

A simpler option might be to have two agency colleagues who are both highly experienced interviewers and supervisors independently view the videotapes and then give an overall rating to each interview (not knowing how the other rated it): for example, from "poor" to "excellent," from 1 to 10, or some such. This option would rely heavily on the judgment of the expert observers, and it may or may not prove as useful as the previous option, which used indicators that were more behaviorally specific. In either case, you would want to see if different raters agreed in their ratings; that is, to see if their ratings are reliable—an issue we will discuss in the next chapter.

As another alternative, we return to the option of using existing paper-and-pencil self-report scales to obtain the operational definition. An assortment of such scales are available to measure interviewing skill. Typically, they present the subject with a case situation and various client statements. The subject then writes down how he or she would respond or selects a response from multiple choices. The responses are scored, and the subject receives a summated score for interviewing skills, certain components of interviewing skill (such as empathy, questioning, and so on), or both. The box titled "Operationally Defining Level of Positive Parenting: Illustration of Three Categories of Operationalization Choices" further illustrates alternative ways to operationally define variables and some of the advantages and disadvantages of each alternative.

EXISTING SCALES

In the foregoing examples, you can see why the use of existing scales can be a popular way to operationally define variables. They spare researchers the costs in time and money of devising their own measures and provide an option that has been used successfully to measure the concept in previous studies. Therefore, let's examine how you find relevant scales and salient information about them.

The most thorough procedure would be to conduct a literature review on the construct you seek to measure. For example, you might review the literature on marital satisfaction to locate materials that report measures of marital satisfaction. We refer you to Chapter 6 and Appendix A for information on how to conduct a literature review. Of course, this would be a relatively quick literature review, because the purpose is to locate measures of a construct, not review all the research on the construct.

One way to expedite the search for measures is to consult reference volumes that list and describe many existing measures. Figure 7-3 lists volumes that might be useful. Some of them reprint the actual measurement instrument; others describe it and provide additional references. Usually, they will discuss the quality of the instrument (such as its reliability and validity) and tell you how to obtain it and more information about it. You will also be told whether it's copyrighted, which will indicate whether you must purchase it or use it with the author's permission.

Despite the practical advantages of using existing self-report scales to operationally define variables,

OPERATIONALLY DEFINING LEVEL OF POSITIVE PARENTING: ILLUSTRATION OF THREE CATEGORIES OF OPERATIONALIZATION CHOICES

Suppose you work in a state child welfare agency that is evaluating an innovative new intervention program to improve positive parenting for parents referred to the agency because of child abuse or neglect. The agency assumes that by improving positive parenting skills it will reduce the incidence of child neglect and abuse. Several similar counties have been selected for the evaluation. Some counties will implement the new program, and some comparable counties will receive the traditional program. The *hypothesis* for the evaluation is that parents referred for child abuse or neglect in the counties receiving the innovative program will improve their parenting more than their counterparts in the counties receiving the traditional program.

An important task in designing the evaluation is developing an *operational definition* of the *dependent variable: level of positive parenting.* You have been given that task. Three broad categories of choices for the operational definition are illustrated below, along with how each could be used in testing the hypothesis. The illustrations are just some of the ways in which you could operationally define level of positive parenting. You may be able to conceive of superior alternatives.

Category	Operational Definition	Testing the Hypothesis	Some Advantages and Disadvantages
Direct observation	You might begin by making a list of positive parenting behaviors—praising, encouraging, modeling, consistency, use of time-outs, and so on. Another list might specify undesirable parenting behaviors—threatening, slapping, screaming, criticizing, bribing, belittling, and so on. Then you might directly observe the parents or foster parents in a challenging parenting situation (such as getting children to put away their toys) and count the number of times the parents show positive and negative behaviors. Perhaps you will give them +1 for every positive behavior and −1 for every negative behavior and tally the points to get a parenting skill score.	See if the average scores of parents in the counties receiving the innovative program are higher (better) than the average scores of parents in the counties receiving the traditional program.	Advantages: 1. Behaviors are observed firsthand. Disadvantages: 1. Time-consuming 2. Parents will know they are being observed and may not behave the same as when they are not being observed. 3. Possibility of observer bias
Self-report	Ask the parents to complete an *existing self-report scale* that purports to measure knowledge or attitudes about parenting. Such a scale might ask parents questions about what they would do in various child-rearing situations or how	See if the average scale scores of parents in the counties receiving the innovative program are better than the average scale scores of parents in the counties receiving the traditional program.	Advantages: 1. Less costly and less time-consuming than direct observation 2. If scales are completed anonymously, parents might be more likely to reveal undesirable attitudes.

Category	Operational Definition	Testing the Hypothesis	Some Advantages and Disadvantages
	they perceive various normal childhood behaviors that some parents misperceive as provocative.		Disadvantages: 1. Parents might distort their true attitudes to convey a more socially desirable impression. 2. The scale may not be valid. 3. Knowledge and attitudes may not always reflect actual behaviors.
Examination of available records	Examine county records of the number of documented incidents of child abuse and neglect.	See if the number of documented incidents of child abuse and neglect in the counties receiving the innovative program is lower than the number in the counties receiving the traditional program.	Advantages: 1. Less costly and time-consuming than either direct observation or self-report 2. You don't have to assume that positive parenting knowledge and skills translate into less abuse; you measure abuse per se. Disadvantages: 1. Reliance on adequacy of county records 2. Won't show whether the parents who received your intervention improved their parenting 3. Possibility of biased reporting

not everyone would agree that they are the best way to operationalize a particular variable in a particular study, and there can be difficulties in using them. Consider the preceding example on interviewing skill. Which measurement approach would give you more confidence that your data adequately reflected practitioners' interviewing skill: their answers to a paper-and-pencil test or their actual performance in a real face-to-face interview with a client? Many of you, we suspect, would prefer the latter as a more realistic test of the interviewer's skill. At the same time, however, you might opt to use an existing self-report scale in an actual study of interviewing skill, not because you think it is the best measure of that concept, but because you lack the resources needed to use a preferable measure.

We will further discuss the advantages and disadvantages of using self-report scales in Chapters 8 and 12, and how to construct them in Chapter 9. We'll end this section by identifying some of the issues to consider in choosing an existing scale as an operational definition.

Let's begin on a practical note: How lengthy is the scale? Will it take too long for the subjects in your study to complete? Suppose, for example, a lengthy scale that takes more than an hour to complete was tested on people who were paid $20 to complete the scale. Its success under those circumstances would not be relevant to a study of busy people who were mailed the scale and asked to volunteer that much time—without pay—to complete and mail back the scale.

American Psychiatric Association. 2000. *Handbook of Psychiatric Measures.* Washington, DC: American Psychiatric Association.

Anastasi, A. 1988. *Psychological Testing.* New York: Macmillan.

Beere, C. A. 1990. *Sex and Gender Issues: A Handbook of Tests and Measures.* New York: Greenwood Press.

Conoley, J. C., and J. J. Kramer. 1995. *The 12th Mental Measurements Yearbook.* Lincoln, NE: Buros Institute of Mental Measurements.

Corcoran, K. J., and J. Fischer. 2000a. *Measures for Clinical Practice: Vol. 1. Couples, Families, Children* (3rd ed.). New York: Free Press.

Corcoran, K. J., and J. Fischer. 2000b. *Measures for Clinical Practice: Vol. 2. Adults* (3rd ed.). New York: Free Press.

Fredman, N., and R. Sherman. 1987. *Handbook of Measurements for Marriage and Family Therapy.* New York: Brunner/Mazel.

Grotevant, H. D., and D. I. Carlson (eds.). 1989. *Family Assessment: A Guide to Methods and Measures.* New York: Guilford Press.

Hersen, M., and A. S. Bellack (eds.). 1988. *Dictionary of Behavioral Assessment Techniques.* Elmsford, NY: Pergamon Press.

Hudson, W. W. 1992. *The WALMYR Assessment Scales Scoring Manual.* Tempe, AZ: WALMYR.

Hudson, W. W. 1982. *The Clinical Measurement Package: A Field Manual.* Homewood, IL: Dorsey Press.

Jacob, T., and D. L. Tennebaum. 1988. *Family Assessment: Rationale, Methods, and Future Directions.* New York: Plenum Press.

LaGreca, A. M. 1990. *Through the Eyes of the Child: Obtaining Self-Reports from Children and Adolescents.* Boston: Allyn & Bacon.

Magura, S., and B. S. Moses. 1987. *Outcome Measures for Child Welfare Services.* Washington, DC: Child Welfare League of America.

Martin, R. P. 1988. *Assessment of Personality and Behavior Problems: Infancy through Adolescence.* New York: Guilford Press.

Maruish, M. E. (ed.). 2002. *Psychological Testing in the Age of Managed Behavioral Health Care.* Mahwah, NJ: Lawrence Erlbaum Associates.

Maruish, M. E. (ed.). 2000. *Handbook of Psychological Assessment in Primary Care Settings.* Mahwah, NJ: Lawrence Erlbaum Associates.

Mash, E. J., and L. G. Terdal. 1988. *Behavioral Assessment of Childhood Disorders.* New York: Guilford Press.

McCubbin, H. I., and A. I. Thompson (eds.). 1987. *Family Assessment Inventories for Research and Practice.* Madison: University of Wisconsin–Madison.

Mullen, E. J., and J. L. Magnabosco (eds.). 1997. *Outcomes Measurement in the Human Services.* Washington, DC: NASW Press.

Ogles, B. M., and K. S. Masters. 1996. *Assessing Outcome in Clinical Practice.* Boston: Allyn & Bacon.

Ollendick, T. H., and M. Hersen. 1992. *Handbook of Child and Adolescent Assessment.* Des Moines, IA: Allyn & Bacon.

Reynolds, C. R., and R. W. Kamphaus (eds.). 1990. *Handbook of Psychological and Educational Assessment of Children.* New York: Guilford Press.

Rutter, M., H. H. Tuma, and I. S. Lann (eds.). 1988. *Assessment and Diagnosis in Child Psychopathology.* New York: Guilford Press.

Sawin, K. J., M. P. Harrigan, and P. Woog (eds.). 1995. *Measures of Family Functioning for Research and Practice.* New York: Springer.

Suzuki, L., P. J. Meller, and J. G. Ponterotto (eds.). 1996. *Handbook of Multicultural Assessment.* San Francisco: Jossey-Bass.

Touliatos, J., B. F. Perlmutter, and M. A. Straus (eds.). 1990. *Handbook of Family Measurement Techniques.* Newbury Park, CA: Sage.

Wetzler, S. (ed.). 1989. *Measuring Mental Illness: Psychometric Assessment for Clinicians.* Washington, DC: American Psychiatric Press.

Figure 7-3 Reference Volumes for Existing Scales That Can Operationally Define Variables in Social Work

Another practical question is whether the scale will be too difficult for your participants to complete. For example, will it be too cumbersome or too complexly worded for them? Suppose you want to study depression among undocumented immigrants from Mexico. Chances are you would not be able to use a scale that was developed to assess depression among American college students, no matter how successful it proved to be with the latter population.

If your study seeks to measure change over time, perhaps before and after receiving a social work intervention, you will need a scale that is sensitive to small changes over relatively short periods. Some clients, after being treated for low self-esteem, for example, might still have lower self-esteem compared to the rest of the population but still higher self-esteem than they did before the intervention. Some self-esteem scales might be able to detect this movement, while others might not, still simply indicating that these people have much lower self-esteem than the rest of the population.

Two critical issues to consider in choosing a scale are its reliability and validity. In the next chapter we'll discuss in depth these two terms, which deal with statistical information on the measurement consistency of instruments and whether they really measure what they intend to measure. For now, we'll just note that the reference literature on existing scales will usually report whatever reliability and validity figures have been established for a particular scale. But interpret those figures with caution. If they are based on studies that tested the instrument on a population dissimilar to yours or under study conditions unlike those of your study, then they may have no bearing on the instrument's suitability for your particular study. No matter how reliable and valid the reference literature says a scale may be, you may find that you have to modify it for your particular study or that you cannot use it at all. Moreover, the way an instrument's reliability and validity were assessed may have been seriously flawed from a methodological standpoint, thus limiting the value of those figures, no matter how impressively high they may be. Therefore, you may want to go beyond the reference sourcebook that gives an overview of an existing scale and examine firsthand the studies that reported the development and testing of the scale.

OPERATIONALIZATION GOES ON AND ON

Although we've discussed conceptualization and operationalization in quantitative studies as activities that precede data collection and analysis—you design your operational measures before you observe—you should realize that these two processes continue throughout a research project, even after data have been collected and analyzed. Here's what we mean by that.

We have suggested that you measure a given variable in several different ways in your research. That is essential if the concept lying in the background is at all ambiguous and open to different interpretations and definitions. By measuring the variable in several different ways, you will be in a position to examine alternative operational definitions during your analysis. You will have several single indicators to choose from and many ways to create different composite measures. Thus, you'll be able to experiment with different measures—each representing a somewhat different conceptualization and operationalization—to decide which gives the clearest and most useful answers to your research questions.

This doesn't mean you should select the measurement that confirms your expectations or proves your point. That's clearly not appropriate and doesn't do much to advance our profession's knowledge base. Instead, operationalization is a continuing process, not a blind commitment to a particular measure that may turn out to have been poorly chosen. Suppose, for example, that you decide to measure compassion by asking people whether they give money to charity, and everybody answers "Yes." Where does that leave you? Nowhere. Your study of why some people are more compassionate than others would be in deep trouble unless you had included other possible measures in designing your observations.

The validity and utility of what you learn in your research doesn't depend on when you first figured out how to look at things any more than it matters whether you got the idea from a learned textbook, a dream, or your brother-in-law.

A QUALITATIVE PERSPECTIVE ON OPERATIONAL DEFINITIONS

Recognizing the risks inherent in trying to predetermine how to operationally define abstract constructs, we should remember that researchers conducting purely qualitative studies do not restrict their observations to predetermined operational indicators. Instead, they prefer to let the meanings of little-understood phenomena emerge from their observations. How they do this will be discussed in more detail later in this book, but we will elaborate a bit on this issue now.

In qualitative studies, the problem of operationally defining variables in advance is threefold. First, we may not know in advance what all the most salient variables are. Second, limitations in our understanding of the variables we think are important may keep us from anticipating the best way to operationally define those variables. Third, even the best operational definitions are necessarily superficial, because they are specified only in terms of observable indicators. Although operational definitions are necessary in quantitative studies, they do not pertain to probing into the deeper meanings of what is observed. These deeper meanings are the purview of qualitative studies.

In a purely quantitative study, we assume that we know enough in advance about a phenomenon to

ILLUSTRATIONS OF THE QUALITATIVE PERSPECTIVE ON OPERATIONALIZATION AND ITS COMPLEMENTARITY WITH A QUANTITATIVE PERSPECTIVE

To further illustrate the qualitative perspective on operationalization, as well as its complementarity with a quantitative perspective, let's examine two research questions.

1. *Is burnout among social workers more likely to occur when they work in public welfare agencies or in private family service agencies?*
A qualitative study would not pose this research question. Instead of defining burnout operationally in terms of one or two observable indicators and then looking at it in relationship to a predetermined independent variable (or set of such variables), it might examine the experiences of a small group of social workers in depth and attempt to portray in a richer and deeper sense what it feels like to be burned out and what it means to the social worker. The study might, for example, be in the form of a biography of the career of one or more social workers who are burned out, perhaps contrasted with a biography of one or more who are not burned out. Conceivably, the qualitative study could be done in conjunction with a quantitative study—that is, the quantitative component could look at which of the two types of agencies had more burnout, whereas the qualitative component could try to discover the underlying reasons for the quantitative differences.

2. *Who are the most popular social work instructors: those who teach practice, research, or policy?*
A qualitative study would not pose this research question either. Instead of using an operational definition of *popularity* and then seeing if it's related to type of course taught, it might involve observations of all aspects of instructor interactions with students in and out of the classroom, analysis of course materials, and in-depth, open-ended interviews with instructors and students to try to identify what makes instructors popular and what it means to be popular (perhaps popularity does not necessarily imply the most effective instruction).

Identifying instructors who appear to be the most popular could be part of a qualitative study, but the point of the study would be to probe more deeply into the meaning and experience of their popularity, not to see if a particular operational indicator of popularity is quantitatively related to another predetermined variable. Rather than report numbers on how popular one group of instructors is compared to another group, a qualitative study might begin by identifying instructors who students generally agree are the most and least popular. It might then provide a wealth of information about each of those instructors, attempting to discern themes and patterns that appear to distinguish popular from unpopular instructors or to provide the field with ideal or undesirable case study types of instructional patterns to emulate or avoid emulating. As with the previous question, the qualitative component of a study could be done in conjunction with a quantitative component. There is no reason why the hypothesis that popularity will be related to curriculum area taught could not be tested as part of a larger study that looks qualitatively at the deeper meaning of other aspects of popularity.

pose a narrow research question about a limited set of variables and to develop precise, objective, observable indicators of those variables that can be counted to answer the research question. In a purely qualitative study, we assume that we need to develop a deeper understanding of some phenomenon and its subjective meanings as it occurs in its natural environment. We take it for granted that we will not be able to develop that richer understanding if we limit ourselves to observable indicators that can be anticipated in advance and counted. In qualitative research, we immerse ourselves in a more subjective fashion in open-ended, flexible observations of phenomena as they occur naturally, and then we try to discern patterns and themes from an immense and relatively unstructured set of observations. Also, in qualitative research, the social context of our observations is emphasized.

To illustrate the importance of social context, as well as the qualitative perspective, imagine a quantitative study that tests the hypothesis that increasing the number of home visits by child welfare practitioners will improve parental functioning and therefore preserve families. Studies like this have been done, and the dependent variable is often operationally defined in quantifiable terms of whether or not (or for how long) children are placed in foster care. A problem with many of these studies is that the increased home visitation might also increase the practitioner's awareness of neglectful or abusive acts by parents. If so, then it is conceivable that any reductions in foster care placement because of improved parental functioning are canceled out by increases in foster care placement because of increased practitioner monitoring. Thus, the hypothesis might not be supported even though the increased home visits are improving service outcomes.

A qualitative inquiry, in contrast, would probe into the deeper meaning and social context of the processes and outcomes in each case. Instead of merely counting the number of placements, it would learn that a foster care placement in one case, and the avoidance of a placement in another case, could both mean that the practitioner has achieved a valuable outcome. Moreover, a qualitative study would observe in detail what practitioners and clients did, probe into the deeper meanings of what was observed, and attempt to discern patterns that indicated the conditions under which practitioners appear to be more or less effective.

In describing this qualitative perspective on operational definitions we are not implying that it's a superior perspective (although many qualitatively oriented researchers think so). It's neither superior nor inferior. Neither is it mutually exclusive with a quantitative perspective (although some researchers believe the two perspectives are in conflict). In the foregoing family preservation illustration, for example, a qualitative inquiry could be conducted simultaneously with the quantitative inquiry, and both could be part of the same study. The qualitative component could shed light on why the quantitative hypothesis was not supported. The box titled "Illustrations of the Qualitative Perspective on Operationalization and Its Complementarity with a Quantitative Perspective" provides two additional examples of this issue.

Main Points

- Hypotheses consist of independent variables (the postulated explanatory variable) and dependent variables (the variable being explained).
- Relationships between variables can be positive, negative, or curvilinear.
- Extraneous, or control, variables may be examined to see if the observed relationship is misleading.
- A spurious relationship is one that no longer exists when a third variable is controlled.
- Mediating variables are intervening mechanisms by which independent variables affect dependent variables.
- Moderating variables influence the strength or direction of relationships between independent and dependent variables.
- Concepts are mental images we use as summary devices for bringing together observations and experiences that seem to have something in common.
- It is possible to measure the things that our concepts summarize.
- Conceptualization is the process of specifying the vague mental imagery of our concepts, sorting out the kinds of observations and measurements that will be appropriate for our research.
- Operationalization is an extension of the conceptualization process.
- In operationalization, concrete empirical procedures that will result in measurements of variables are specified.
- Operationalization is the final specification of how we would recognize the different attributes of a given variable in the real world.
- In determining the range of variation for a variable, be sure to consider the opposite of the concept. Will it be sufficient to measure religiosity from "very

much" to "none," or should you go past "none" to measure "antireligiosity" as well?

• Operationalization begins in study design and continues throughout the research project, including the analysis of data.

• Existing self-report scales are a popular way to operationally define many social work variables, largely because they have been used successfully by others and provide cost advantages in terms of time and money, but scales need to be selected carefully and are not always the best way to operationally define a variable.

• Additional ways to operationalize variables involve the use of direct behavioral observation, interviews, and available records.

• Qualitative studies, rather than predetermining specific, precise, objective variables and indicators to measure, begin with an initial set of anticipated meanings that can be refined during data collection and interpretation.

Review Questions and Exercises

1. Pick a social work concept—such as child neglect or abuse, quality of life, or level of informal social support—and specify that concept so that it could be studied in a research project. Be sure to specify the indicators and dimensions you wish to include (and exclude) in your conceptualization.

2. Specify two hypotheses in which a particular concept is the independent variable in one hypothesis and the dependent variable in the other. Try to hypothesize one positive relationship and one negative, or inverse, relationship.

Internet Exercises

1. Use InfoTrac College Edition to find several research articles in the journal *Health and Social Work*. For each study, write down how the main variables in the study were operationally defined. Notice how often existing scales were used as the operational definitions.

2. Using a search engine such as Google or Yahoo!, enter the key word *empathy*. Browse through several of the websites on empathy that will appear on your screen. Make a list of the various dimensions of empathy that are described.

3. Use InfoTrac College Edition to find the article titled "Social Justice and the Research Curriculum" by John F. Longres and Edward Scanlon in the Fall 2001 issue of the journal *Health and Social Work*. Also examine the reactions to that article in that same issue. Based on what you read, discuss difficulties in operationally defining the term *social justice*. Also discuss how the article illustrates concept clarification as an ongoing element in data collection.

4. Go to a website developed and operated by Dr. Marianne Yoshioka, a social work professor at Columbia University. The site is called "Psychosocial Measures for Asian-American Populations," and is located at www.columbia.edu/cu/ssw/projects/pmap. Download three of the abstracts of existing scales you find at that site that operationally define three different concepts. Identify the concepts that are operationally defined by the scales. Also briefly describe how the scales you find attempt to avoid or alleviate cultural bias in operational definitions.

Additional Readings

American Psychiatric Association. 2000. *Handbook of Psychiatric Measures*. Washington, DC: American Psychiatric Association. This comprehensive reference volume provides information on a great many scales that can be used in assessment as part of clinical practice or in operationally defining variables for research and evaluation.

Miller, Delbert. 1991. *Handbook of Research Design and Social Measurement*. Newbury Park, CA: Sage. This useful reference work, especially Part 6, cites and describes a wide variety of operational measures used in earlier social research. Several cases present the questionnaire formats that were used. Though the quality of these illustrations is uneven, they provide excellent examples of the variations possible.

CHAPTER 8

Measurement

What You'll Learn in This Chapter

Now we'll go from conceptualization and operationalization, the first steps in measurement, to a consideration of broader issues in the measurement process. The emphasis in this chapter will be on measurement error, how to avoid it, and assessing how well we are avoiding it.

INTRODUCTION

We have come some distance. After asserting that social workers can measure anything that exists, we discovered that many of the things we might want to measure and study really don't exist. Next we learned that it's possible to measure them anyway. We learned that the first step toward doing that is by operationally defining them—that is, we identify the operations, or indicators, that we will use to indicate the presence, absence, amount, or type of the concept we are studying.

We also learned that researchers have a wide variety of options available when they want to operationally define a concept, and that it's possible to choose indicators that are imprecise or that represent something other than what they really seek to measure. In presenting so many alternatives and choices for you to make in measurement, we realize that we may create a sense of uncertainty and insecurity. You may find yourself worrying about whether you will make the right choices. To counterbalance this feeling, let's add a momentary dash of certainty and stability.

Many variables have rather obvious, straightforward measures. No matter how you cut it, gender usually turns out to be a matter of male or female: a variable that can be measured by a single observation, either looking or asking a question. It's usually fairly easy to find out how many children a family has, although you'll want to think about adopted and foster children. And although some fine-tuning is possible, for most research purposes the resident population of a country is the resident population of that country—you can find the answer in an almanac. A great many variables, then, have obvious single indicators. If you can get just one piece of information, you have what you need.

Sometimes, however, no single indicator will give you the measure that you really want for a variable. As discussed in Chapter 7, many concepts are subject to varying interpretations, each with several possible indicators. In these cases, you will want to make several observations for a given variable. You can then combine the several pieces of information you've collected to create a *composite* measurement of the variable in question. Chapter 9, on constructing measurement instruments, discusses ways to do that, so we'll give you only a simple illustration at this point.

Consider the concept *school performance.* Some young clients do well in school, and others don't perform well in their courses. It might be useful to study that, perhaps asking what characteristics and experiences are related to high levels of performance, and many researchers have done so. How should we measure overall performance? Each grade in any single course is a potential indicator of school performance, but in using any single grade we run a risk that the one used will not be typical of the student's general performance. The solution to this problem is so firmly established that it is, of course, obvious to you: the *grade point average.* We assign numerical scores to each letter grade, total the points a student earns, and divide by the number of courses taken to obtain a composite measure. (If the courses vary in number of credits, adjustments are made in that regard.) Creating such composite measures in social research is often appropriate.

No matter how we operationally define abstract concepts we need to be mindful of the extreme vulnerability of the measurement process to sources of measurement error. This is so whether we use single or composite indicators and no matter how we go about collecting data on the indicators we select—whether we use self-report scales, available records, interviews, or direct observation. We must carefully plan to minimize the likelihood that those errors will occur and then take certain steps to check on the adequacy of our measures. How to do that is the focus of this chapter.

COMMON SOURCES OF MEASUREMENT ERROR

Measurement error occurs when we obtain data that do not accurately portray the concept we are attempting to measure. Some inaccuracies may be minor, such as when parents forget about one of the eleven temper tantrums their son had last week, and report that he had ten. Other inaccuracies may be serious, such as when a measure portrays an abusive parent as nonabusive. Common sources of measurement error come in two types: systematic error and random error. Let's begin with systematic error.

Systematic Error

Systematic error occurs when the information we collect consistently reflects a false picture of the concept we seek to measure, either because of the way we collect the data or the dynamics of those who are providing the data. Sometimes our measures really don't measure what we think they do. For example, measuring what people think is the right thing to do will not necessarily reflect what they themselves usually do. When we try to measure likely behavior by collecting data on attitudes or views, we may be making a big mistake. Words don't always match deeds. Some folks who espouse "liberal" views on issues like school busing end up moving to the suburbs or enrolling their children in private schools when it's their own kids who will be bused. Many people who support the idea of locating residences for the mentally disabled in residential areas would fight efforts to locate one on their block.

Biases Even when measures tap someone's true views, systematic error may occur in thinking that something else (that is, likely behavior) is being measured. Perhaps the most common way our measures systematically measure something other than what we think they do is when **biases** are involved in the data collection. Biases can come in various forms. We may ask questions in a way that predisposes individuals to answer the way we want them to, or we may smile excessively or nod our heads in agreement when we get the answers that support our hypotheses. Or individuals may be biased to answer our questions in ways that distort their true views or behaviors. For instance, they may be biased to agree with whatever we say, or they may do or say things that will convey a favorable impression of themselves.

The former bias, agreeing or disagreeing with most or all statements regardless of their content, is called the **acquiescent response set.** The latter bias, the tendency of people to say or do things that will make them or their reference group look good, is called the **social desirability bias.** Most researchers recognize the likely effect of a question that begins "Don't you agree with the Bible that . . . ," and no reputable researcher would use such an item. Unhappily, the biasing effect of items and terms is far subtler than this example suggests.

The mere identification of an attitude or position with a prestigious person or agency can bias responses. An item such as "Do you agree or disagree with the statement in our professional code of ethics that . . ." would have a similar effect. We should make it clear that we are not suggesting that such wording will necessarily produce consensus or even a majority in support of the position identified with the prestigious person or agency, only that support would probably be increased over the support that would have been obtained without such identification. Questionnaire items can be biased negatively as well as positively. "Do you agree or disagree with the position of Adolf Hitler when he stated that . . ." is an example.

To further illustrate the ways in which different forms of wording questions can have relatively subtle biasing effects, we may consider Kenneth Rasinski's analysis of the results of several General Social Survey Studies of attitudes toward government spending (1989). He found that the way programs were identified affected how much public support they received. Here are some comparisons:

MORE SUPPORT	LESS SUPPORT
"Halting rising crime rate"	"Law enforcement"
"Dealing with drug addiction"	"Drug rehabilitation"
"Assistance to the poor"	"Welfare"
"Solving problems of big cities"	"Assistance to big cities"

Asking practitioners about their treatment orientations can involve some subtle biases. Suppose you asked them if they agreed that they should try to motivate people with psychotic disorders who resist taking their psychiatric medications to do so. The practitioners might be predisposed to agree. It sounds right that patients should take the medicine that their physicians have prescribed for them and that social workers ought to help motivate severely ill people to take better care of themselves. But suppose you asked whether they agreed that the principle of self-determination means that they should respect the right of these patients to refuse treatment and should therefore not urge them to take their medications if they don't want to.

As another example of bias, consider the following. In 1989, more than 20 national magazines simultaneously published a questionnaire as part of a survey of opinions on child care and family issues. (We first saw the questionnaire in the February 27, 1989, issue of the *New Republic*.) Readers were encouraged to tear out and complete the questionnaire and return it to "Your Family Matters" at a New York City address. At the top of the questionnaire, readers were informed that the survey was being sponsored by the "nonpartisan advocates Child Care Action Campaign and the Great American Family Tour" and that a national cable television channel underwriting the survey would be airing a special documentary, *Hush*

Little Baby: The Challenge of Child Care. Also at the top, in large bold letters, was the heading, "TELL THE PRESIDENT YOUR FAMILY MATTERS." Under this buildup were the questionnaire items, beginning with the following two yes-or-no items:

1. Do you think the federal government pays enough attention to child care and other family concerns?

2. Do you think family issues should be a top priority for the president and Congress?

Some of the subsequent items asked for opinions about whether various levels of government should develop policies to make child care more available and affordable and should set minimum standards for child-care centers.

You may note at least three levels of bias in this survey. At one level, it is not hard for readers to discern that the questionnaire's heading shows that the opinions desired by the surveyors are those that call for more government attention to child-care and family issues. Indeed, the heading instructs the reader to "tell the president your family matters." The second level of bias concerns the issue of who would bother to complete and mail in the questionnaire. People who care deeply about the issue of child care, especially those who strongly believe that more government attention to it is needed, were probably much more likely to respond than those who feel otherwise. (We will examine the latter level of bias—response rate bias—more closely in Chapter 15, on survey research.) The third level of bias has to do with what segments of the population are likely to see the questionnaire in the first place. Chances are that people who subscribe to and read the selected magazines are not representative of the rest of the population in regard to views on child-care and family issues, and perhaps are more likely to share the views of the survey sponsors than are the rest of the population. (We will examine that type of bias in Chapter 14, on sampling.)

Social Desirability Bias Earlier we noted the potential for the *social desirability bias*. Be especially wary of this bias. Whenever you ask people for information, they answer through a filter of concern about what will make them look good. This is especially true if they are being interviewed in a face-to-face situation. Thus, for example, a particular man may feel that things would be a lot better if women were kept in the kitchen, not allowed to vote, forced to be quiet in public, and so forth. Asked whether he supports equal rights for women, however, he may want to avoid looking like a male chauvinist pig. Recognizing that his views might have been progressive in the 15th century but are out of step with current thinking, he may choose to say "yes." The main guidance we can offer you in relation to this problem is to suggest that you imagine how you would feel in giving each of the answers you offered to respondents. If you'd feel embarrassed, perverted, inhumane, stupid, irresponsible, or anything like that, then you should give serious thought to whether others will be willing to give those answers. We will have more to say about the social desirability bias later in this chapter and in forthcoming chapters on data-collection methods and on designs for evaluating programs and practice.

Cultural Bias As we discussed in Chapter 5, another common source of bias stems from cultural disparities. Intelligence tests, for example, have been cited as biased against certain ethnic minority groups. The argument is posed that children growing up in economically disadvantaged environments with different values, opportunities, and speaking patterns are at a disadvantage when they take IQ tests geared to a white, middle-class environment. It is argued, for example, that a minority child may score lower than a white child of equal or lower intelligence simply because the language of the questions is less familiar or because the questions refer to material things that white, middle-class children take for granted but that are unknown to disadvantaged children.

This argument is controversial, but the potential for cultural bias in measurement is not. Suppose, for example, that you are conducting a survey to see whether recent immigrants to the United States from Asia are less likely to utilize social services than are second- or third-generation Asian Americans. If the recent immigrants, because of language difficulties, don't understand your questions as meaning the same as do the other groups, then differences in the data between the groups may have less to do with differences in their views on social service use than with the systematic language bias in your questions.

Monette, Sullivan, and DeJong (1994) illustrated a similar phenomenon in regard to a study of the mental health of Native Americans. In that study, the word *blue* had to be dropped from an instrument that measured depression because *blue* did not mean "sad" among Native Americans. The same study found that to avoid cultural bias in assessing the use of mental health services, traditional healers (what you may call "faith healers" or "spiritualists") had to be added to the list of professionals from whom Native Americans might seek help.

Random Error

Unlike systematic errors, **random errors** have no consistent pattern of effects. Random errors do not bias our measures; they make them inconsistent from one measurement to the next. This does not mean that whenever data change over time we have random error. Sometimes things really do change—and when they do, our measures should detect that change. What it does mean is that if the things we are measuring do not change over time but our measures keep coming up with different results, then we have inconsistencies in measurement, or random error.

Random errors can take various forms. Perhaps our measurement procedures are so cumbersome, complex, boring, or fatiguing that our subjects say or do things at random just to get the measurement over with as quickly as possible. For example, halfway through a lengthy questionnaire full of complicated questions, respondents may stop giving much thought to what the questions really mean or how they truly feel about them.

Another example might be when two raters are recording the number of times a social worker gives an empathic response in a videotaped interview with a client. If the raters are not really sure how to recognize an empathic response when they see one, they may disagree substantially about how many empathic responses they observed in the same videotape. Note the difference between this sort of error and systematic error. If one rater was the videotaped social worker's mentor or fiancée and the other rater was the social worker's rival for a promotion, then the differences in the ratings would probably result from systematic error.

For yet another example of random error, suppose clients who have no familiarity with social service jargon are asked whether they have received brokerage, advocacy, or linkage services. Odds are they would have no idea what those terms meant. Not understanding what they were being asked but not wishing to appear ignorant or uncooperative, they might answer "yes" or "no" at random, and they might change their answers the next time they were asked, even though the situation had not changed. That would represent random error. But suppose that even though they had no earthly idea what they were being asked, they suspected that an affirmative response would make them or their social worker look better. If they then responded affirmatively to every question just so they would not appear negativistic or get practitioners in trouble, that would represent systematic error associated with a social desirability bias or acquiescent response set.

Although the term *bias* may sound more insidious than "random error" or "inconsistency in measurement," random error can be a serious problem. Suppose, for example, that an extremely effective school social work intervention to improve the self-esteem of underachieving third graders is being evaluated. Suppose further that the measurement instrument selected for the evaluation was constructed for use with well-educated adults and that the researchers evaluating the intervention were unaware of the fact that underachieving third graders would not understand many of the items on the instrument. This lack of understanding would mean that the children's responses would be largely random and have little to do with their level of self-esteem. Consequently, the likelihood that the instrument would detect significant increases in self-esteem, even after an effective intervention, would be slim. Random error in measurement, therefore, can make a highly effective intervention look ineffective.

Errors in Alternate Forms of Measurement

Earlier we mentioned four alternative options that are commonly used to measure variables in social work research: written self-reports, interviews, direct behavioral observation, and examining available records. We also noted that each option is vulnerable to measurement error. Let's now look at the four options separately and see some of the similarities and differences in the ways each is vulnerable to measurement errors.

Written Self-Reports Having people complete questionnaires or scales is a relatively inexpensive and expedient way to collect data. Consequently, it is perhaps the most commonly used measurement option in social work research. Written self-reports can be used to gather background information about people (their age, gender, ethnicity, and so on) or to measure their knowledge, attitudes, skills, or behavior. Regardless of which of these things we seek to measure, we would want to avoid random errors associated with the difficulty some people may have in understanding how we have worded our items or in the length and complexity of our instrument. We would also want to avoid systematic errors resulting from bias in the way we have worded our items or in respondents' propensity to convey a socially desirable image of themselves.

Even if we completely avoid problems in the way we construct our instruments, however, we should remember that people's *words* don't necessarily match their *deeds*. For example, parents referred for abuse or neglect who have completed a mandatory parent education program can learn and check off the desired answers to a written test of their knowledge of, attitudes about, and skills in child rearing without becoming any less likely to neglect or abuse their children. Their written responses about their behavior may be grossly inaccurate because they may want to portray themselves in a socially desirable light. Having them complete the instruments anonymously might alleviate some of this bias, but it does not guarantee the avoidance of such gross inaccuracies because people tend to see themselves in a socially desirable manner.

But even if you were to avoid all of the errors we have mentioned, that would not guarantee that the written answers really measure what you think they measure. Suppose, for example, you develop a self-report scale that you think will measure social workers' orientations about practice. Suppose you are particularly interested in measuring the extent to which they are more oriented toward providing office-based psychotherapy exclusively versus a case management approach that emphasizes—in addition to the therapeutic relationship—such services as home visits, brokerage, advocacy, and helping clients learn social skills and how to manage concrete basic living tasks. Let's further suppose that you word each item by asking how important is it to provide each of these things to clients. It is conceivable that many respondents who provide office-based psychotherapy exclusively, and who see the other services as beneath their level of expertise, might nevertheless endorse each service as very important because they think that practitioners who are at lower levels than they are would deliver the services other than psychotherapy. Those respondents might be answering in a completely accurate and unbiased manner. They might really believe that those services are very important; they just might not believe that they themselves are the ones who should deliver them. If you interpreted their scale scores as a measure of the way they conduct their own practice, however, your measure would be in error. It would not be measuring what you intend it to measure. The technical term used to convey whether a self-report measure really measures what it is intended to measure is **validity.** We will discuss *validity* in much greater depth later in this chapter.

Interviews Another way to collect self-reported information is through interviews. Although interviews are a more time-consuming and costly way to collect data than by using written self-reports, they have several advantages. If a respondent doesn't understand how a question is worded, the interviewer can clarify it. The interviewer can also ensure that the respondent does not skip any items. In addition, interviewers can observe things about the respondent and probe for more information about vague responses to open-ended questions. In qualitative studies that attempt to develop a deeper and more subjective understanding of how people experience things, the use of such open-ended probes can be vital.

Despite their advantages, interviews are susceptible to most of the same sources of error as are written self-reports, particularly regarding social desirability bias. As we noted earlier, the tendency to answer questions in ways that convey a favorable impression of oneself can be greater in an interview than when completing a written instrument. This tendency can be exacerbated when interviewers introduce their own subtle biases, such as by smiling or nodding when respondents answer in ways that support a study's hypothesis. Sometimes interviews can involve biases that are less subtle, such as when a therapist interviews her clients upon termination of therapy to ask them how much her therapy has helped them. It's much harder to tell her face-to-face that her therapy did not help than it is to report the same thing by completing a written instrument, especially if the instrument can be completed without the therapist knowing which clients completed which instrument.

Interviews also involve additional sources of random error. Different interviewers, for example, might be inconsistent in the way they ask questions and record answers. Different interviewer characteristics might affect how respondents answer questions. A white interviewer might get different responses than an African American interviewer when interviewing people about their views on race issues. A female interviewer might get different responses than a male interviewer when asking people how they feel about equal rights for women.

Direct Behavioral Observation Rather than rely on what people say as the way to assess their attitudes, skills, or behavior, we can observe their behavior directly. For example, if we want to assess the effects of an intervention program on the parenting behaviors of parents who were referred for abuse or neglect, then we could make home visits and observe how they interact with their children. Or we could have their children play with a bunch of toys in a playroom and then observe through a one-way mirror how the parents handle the challenging task of getting the children to put away their toys.

Although direct behavioral observation can be more time-consuming and costly, it has the advantage of seeing behavior for ourselves and not having to wonder whether the way people answer questions reflects how they actually behave. Yet direct observation, too, can be highly vulnerable to systematic error, such as social desirability biases. As we noted earlier, people who know they are being observed may act in a much more socially desirable manner than when they are not being observed or when they do not know they are being observed. In addition, the observers themselves might be biased to perceive behaviors that support their study's hypothesis. Random errors can result from inconsistencies in the way different observers observe and record things, perhaps stemming from differences in how well they understand the phenomena they are looking for and recording.

Examining Available Records Perhaps the least time-consuming and costly measurement option is the examination of available records. Returning to the example of assessing practitioner orientations about their practice, we might want to examine their process notes in their case records, looking to see how often they employ different techniques or provide different services. But some practitioners might exaggerate their records regarding the amount of time they spend on certain activities in the belief that someone might use those records to evaluate their performance. That would be a source of *systematic error.* Maybe they resent all the record keeping that is expected of them and thus aren't careful in documenting their tasks. That would create *random errors.*

AVOIDING MEASUREMENT ERROR

At this juncture, you may be wondering, "Egad, is the measurement process so fraught with error that research is hardly worth doing?" We do not intend to imply that. But we are saying that the measurement process is extremely vulnerable to errors, that we need to be aware of the potential for these errors to occur, and that we must take steps to deal with them.

It is virtually impossible to avoid all possible sources of measurement error. Even if all we do is canvass an agency's caseload to describe the proportions of male and female clients of different ages and ethnic groups, chances are we will have some measurement error. For instance, there may be clerical oversights in recording data, coding them, or typing them for computer input. Even relatively concrete concepts such as ethnicity can be misunderstood by respondents to surveys. During the 1970s, for example, the Council on Social Work Education was asked by some of its Native American constituents to change one item on the questionnaire the council used in its annual canvass of schools of social work. The item pertained to the ethnicity of faculty members, and so the council changed the category that previously read *American Indian* to *Native American.* In the first year after that change, there was a large jump in the number of Native American faculty members reported. In fact, some schools that reported having only white faculty members the year before now reported having only Native American faculty members. Fortunately, by comparing the data to the previous year's report from each school, the measurement error was easy to detect and correct. The clerical staff members who had completed the questionnaire in certain schools thought that the term Native American referred to anyone born in the United States, regardless of their ethnicity.

No one should be dissuaded from pursuing research simply because of the inevitability of measurement errors. No one expects a study to have perfect measurement, at least not in the field of social scientific research. What matters is that you try to minimize any major measurement errors that would destroy the credibility and utility of your findings and that you assess how well your measures appear to have kept those errors from exceeding a reasonable level.

Because measurement errors can occur in a myriad of ways, it's not easy to tell you how to avoid them. The steps you can take depend in large part on your data-collection methods. We will discuss some of those steps in Chapter 9, on constructing measurement instruments, and other steps in later chapters. But here is a brief preview of a few of those steps, just to give you an idea of the sorts of things that can be done.

If you are constructing a questionnaire or self-report scale, try to use unbiased wording (to minimize systematic error) and terms that respondents will understand (to minimize random error). Obtain collegial feedback to help spot biases or ambiguities that you may have overlooked. (Because we know what we mean by what we write, it's easy for us to be unaware of ambiguities in our wording.) And be sure to test the questionnaire in a dry run to see if your target population will understand it and not find it too unwieldy.

If you're using people to conduct interviews or rate behaviors they observe, be sure to train them carefully, and make sure that they are consistent in how they perform their tasks. Also attempt to minimize the extent to which they can be influenced by biases. For example, if they are collecting information on how well clients function before and after an intervention as compared to individuals who receive no intervention, try to keep your data collectors blind as to whether any particular measure is being taken before or after the intervention or on whether or not any specific individual received the intervention.

If your measurement involves direct observation of behaviors, then try to arrange the situation so that the client is not keenly aware that observations are occurring and is therefore less likely to act out of character in order to look good. This *unobtrusive observation* is used to minimize the social desirability bias. We will return to the concept of unobtrusive observation in several forthcoming chapters.

If your measurement relies on the use of available records, don't assume that they are sufficiently free of error because an agency values them or because they're "official." Talk to agency practitioners and others "in the know" about how carefully or haphazardly records are kept. Probe about any possible reasons why those who enter the data might be influenced by certain biases that reduce your confidence in the validity of what they record.

Several other data-collection steps are rather generic in nature, and their use cuts across the many data-collection alternatives. One such step involves the principle of **triangulation.** Triangulation deals with systematic error by using several different research methods to collect the same information. Because there is no one foolproof method for avoiding systematic measurement error, we can use several imperfect measurement alternatives and see if they tend to produce the same findings. If they do, then we can have more confidence (but no guarantee) that measurement error is at an acceptable level. If one method yields data that sharply conflict with the data provided by alternative measures, then we have reason to suspect serious errors somewhere and have clues as to where they may have occurred. Triangulation requires that the different measures have different potential sources of error. If we expect each measure to be vulnerable to the same sources of error, then consistency among the measures would not really tell us whether that source of systematic error was being avoided.

For instance, suppose we assess practitioner responsiveness to chronically mentally disabled clients in three ways, as follows: (1) We assess their self-reported attitudes about treating the disabled, (2) we ask disabled clients about the amount of contact they had with the practitioners and how satisfied they were with the help they received, and (3) we survey case records to tabulate the amount of services practitioners provided to disabled clients. Suppose the practitioners all say that they derive great satisfaction from treating disabled clients but that the case records show that disabled clients usually receive less than three contacts from them and then are no longer followed. Suppose further that the large majority of disabled clients corroborate the case records in terms of the amount of service they received and add that the practitioner seemed impatient with their slowness and disinterested in the problems that they felt were most important. Having triangulated your measures, you would be in a far better position to judge the credibility of your data than if you had used only one of the preceding measures. Moreover, you would be able to avoid the apparent errors inherent in relying on self-reports in measuring practitioner attitudes, errors that seem to be associated with a social desirability bias, which you would not have been able to avoid had you not triangulated your measures.

The other generic steps you can take to minimize measurement error are closely related to triangulation. They involve making sure, before you implement the study, that the measurement procedures you will use have acceptable levels of reliability and validity. Reliability and validity are two of the most important concepts you can learn about research methods. Both concepts will be discussed thoroughly throughout the remainder of this chapter.

RELIABILITY

In the abstract sense, **reliability** is a matter of whether a particular technique, applied repeatedly to the same object, would yield the same result each time. Thus, reliability has to do with the amount of random error in a measurement. The more reliable the measure, the less random error in it.

Suppose a large classmate—a tackle on your school's football team—asks you and another classmate to guesstimate how much he weighs. You look him over carefully and guess that he weighs 260 pounds. Your classmate guesstimates 360 pounds. This would suggest that the technique of having people estimate how much other people weigh is not very reliable. Suppose, however, that each of you had used his bathroom scale to measure his weight. The scale would have indicated virtually the same weight each time, indicating that the scale provided a more reliable measure of weight than did your guesstimates.

Reliability, however, does not ensure accuracy. Suppose he set his bathroom scale to shave 10 pounds off his weight just to make him feel better. Although the scale would (reliably) report the same weight for him each time, the weighings you and your classmate performed would both be wrong due to systematic error (that is, a biased scale).

Here's another hypothetical example. Let's suppose we are interested in studying morale among social workers in two different kinds of agencies. One set is composed of public assistance agencies; the other is composed of family service agencies. How should we measure morale? Following one strategy, we could spend some time observing the workers in each agency, noticing such things as whether they joke with one another, whether they smile and laugh a lot, and so forth. We could ask them how they like their work and even ask them whether they think they would prefer their current setting or the other one being studied. By comparing what we observed in the different agencies, we might reach a conclusion about which setting produced the higher morale.

Now let's look at some of the possible reliability problems inherent in this method. First, how we feel when we do the observing is likely to color what we see. We may misinterpret what we see. We may see workers kidding each other and think they are having an argument. Or maybe we'll catch them on an off day. If we were to observe the same group of workers several days in a row, we might arrive at different evaluations on each day. And if several observers evaluated the same behavior, they too might arrive at different conclusions about the workers' morale.

Here's another strategy for assessing morale. Suppose we check the agency records to see how many worker resignations occurred during some fixed period of time. Presumably that would be an indicator of morale: the more resignations, the lower the morale. This measurement strategy would appear to be more reliable; we could count up the resignations over and over and we should continue to arrive at the same number.

If you find yourself thinking that the number of resignations doesn't necessarily measure morale, you're worrying about validity, not reliability. We'll discuss validity in a moment. First, let's complete the discussion of reliability.

Reliability problems crop up in many forms in social research. Survey researchers have known for a long time that different interviewers get different answers from respondents as a result of their own attitudes and demeanors. If we were to conduct a study of editorial positions on some public issue, we might assemble a team of coders to take on the job of reading hundreds of editorials and classifying them in terms of the position each takes on the issue. Different coders would code the same editorial differently. Or we might want to classify a few hundred specific occupations in terms of some standard coding scheme—say, a set of categories created by the Department of Labor or by the Bureau of the Census. Not all of us would code those occupations into the same categories.

Each of these examples illustrates problems of reliability. Similar problems arise whenever we ask people to give us information about themselves. Sometimes we ask questions for which people don't know the answers. (How many times have you been to church?) Sometimes we ask people about things that are totally irrelevant to them. (Are you satisfied with China's current relationship with Albania?) Sometimes people don't understand what our questions mean, such as when we use words that children have not yet learned or terms that have different meanings in different cultures. And sometimes we ask questions that are so complicated that a person who had a clear opinion on the matter might arrive at a different interpretation on being asked the question a second time.

How do you create reliable measures? There are several techniques. First, in asking people for information—if your research design calls for that—be careful to ask only about things the respondents are likely to be able to answer. Ask about things relevant to them and be clear in what you're asking. The danger in these instances is that people will give you answers—reliable or not. People will tell you what they think about China's relationship with Albania even if they haven't the foggiest idea what that relationship is.

Another way to handle the problem of reliability in getting information from people is to use measures that have proven their reliability in previous research. In the case of unreliability generated by research workers, there are several solutions. To guard against interviewer unreliability, it is common practice in surveys to have a supervisor call a subsample of the respondents on the telephone and verify selected pieces of information. Replication works in other situations as well. If you are worried that newspaper editorials or occupations may not be classified reliably, then why not have each editorial or occupation independently coded by several coders? Those editorials or occupations that generate disagreement should be evaluated more carefully and resolved.

Finally, clarity, specificity, training, and practice will avoid a great deal of unreliability and grief. If we were to spend time with you reaching a clear agreement on how we were going to evaluate editorial positions on an issue—discussing the various positions that might be represented and reading through several together—we'd probably be able to do a good job of classifying them in the same way independently.

Types of Reliability

The type of measurement reliability that is most relevant to a particular study varies according to the study's purpose and design. If the study involves judgments made by observers or raters, for example, then we need to assess the extent of agreement, or consistency, between or among observers or raters. If the study involves using a written self-report scale that respondents complete to measure certain constructs such as self-esteem, depression, job satisfaction, and so on, then reliability is usually measured in one or two ways. If the self-report scale is being used to measure changes in people over time, then we need to assess the *stability* of the scale in providing consistent measurements from one administration to the next. A particularly expedient alternative way to assess a scale's reliability, without concern as to stability over time, is to measure its *internal consistency*. Let's now look at each of these alternatives in more detail.

Interobserver and Interrater Reliability

The term for the degree of agreement or consistency between or among observers or raters is **interobserver reliability** or **interrater reliability.** Suppose you are studying whether an in-service training program for paraprofessionals or volunteers increases the level of empathy they express in videotaped role-play situations. To assess interrater reliability you would train two raters; then you would have them view the same videotapes and independently rate the level of empathy they observed in each. If they agree approximately 80 percent or more of the time in their ratings, then you can assume that the amount of random error in measurement is not excessive. Some researchers would argue that even 70 percent agreement would be acceptable.

Instead of calculating the percentage of agreement, you might want to calculate the correlation between the two sets of ratings. For example, suppose the ratings are on a scale from 1 to 10 and that although the two raters rarely choose the exact same rating, they both tend to give high or low ratings in a consistent fashion; that is, one pair of ratings might be a 9 and an 8, and another pair might be a 2 and a 3. As one rater goes up, the other rater goes up. As one goes down, the other goes down. Although they rarely agree on the exact number, they move up and down together. If so, although the percentage of agreement might be low, the correlation might be high, perhaps above .80. We will discuss correlation later in Part 7. At this point, it is sufficient to know that correlations can range from zero (meaning no relationship—no correlation) to 1.0 (meaning a perfect relationship with no random error). Later we will also discuss how correlations can be negative, ranging from zero to −1.0.

Test–Retest Reliability

In studies that seek to assess changes in scale scores over time, it is important to use a stable measure—that is, a scale that provides consistency in measurement over time. If the measurement is not stable over time, then changes that you observe in your study may have less to do with real changes in the phenomenon being observed than with changes in the measurement process. The term for assessing a measure's stability over time is **test–retest reliability.**

To assess test–retest reliability, simply administer the same measurement instrument to the same individuals on two separate occasions. If the correlation between the two sets of responses to the instrument is above .70 or .80 (the higher the better), then the instrument may be deemed to have acceptable stability. But assessing test–retest reliability can be tricky. What if the individual actually changes between testing and retesting? What if the conditions (time of day and so forth) of the test are different from those of the retest? In assessing test–retest reliability, you must be certain that both tests occur under identical conditions, and the time lapse between test and retest should be long enough that the individuals will not recall their an-

AN EXAMPLE OF TEST–RETEST RELIABILITY

In their research on Health Hazard Appraisal, a part of preventive medicine, Jeffrey Sacks, W. Mark Krushat, and Jeffrey Newman (1980) wanted to determine the risks associated with various background and lifestyle factors, making it possible for physicians to counsel their patients appropriately. By knowing patients' life situations, physicians could advise them on their potential for survival and on how to improve it. This purpose, of course, depended heavily on the accuracy of the information gathered about each subject in the study.

To test the reliability of their information, Sacks and his colleagues had all 207 subjects complete a baseline questionnaire that asked about their characteristics and behavior. Three months later, a follow-up questionnaire asked the same subjects for the same information, and the results of the two surveys were compared. Overall, only 15 percent of the subjects reported the same information in both studies.

Sacks and his colleagues report the following:

> Almost 10 percent of subjects reported a different height at follow-up examination. Parental age was changed by over one in three subjects. One parent reportedly aged 20 chronologic years in three months. One in five ex-smokers and ex-drinkers have apparent difficulty in reliably recalling their previous consumption pattern.
>
> (1980:730)

Some subjects erased all trace of previously reported heart murmur, diabetes, emphysema, arrest record, and thoughts of suicide. One subject's mother, deceased in the first questionnaire, was apparently alive and well in time for the second. One subject had one ovary missing in the first study but present in the second. In another case, an ovary present in the first study was missing in the second study—and had been for ten years! One subject was reportedly 55 years old in the first study and 50 years old three months later. (You have to wonder whether the physician-counselors could ever have nearly the impact on their patients that their patients' memories did.) Thus, test–retest revealed that this data collection method was not especially reliable.

swers from the first testing and yet be short enough to minimize the likelihood that individuals will change significantly between the two testings. Approximately two weeks is a common interval between the test and the retest. The box titled "An Example of Test–Retest Reliability" further illustrates the importance of assessing this form of reliability and how to do it.

Internal Consistency Reliability

Whether or not we plan to assess changes on a measure over time, it is important to assess whether the various items that make up the measure are *internally consistent*. This method, called **internal consistency reliability,** assumes that the instrument contains multiple items, each of which is scored and combined with the scores of the other items to produce an overall score. Using this method, we simply assess the correlation of the scores on each item with the scores on the rest of the items. Or we might compute the total scores of different subsets of items and then assess the correlations of those subset totals. Using the *split-halves method*, for example, we would assess the correlations of subscores among different subsets of half of the items. Because this method only requires administering the measure one time to a group of respondents, it is the most practical and most commonly used method for assessing reliability.

Before the advent of computers made it easy to calculate internal consistency correlations, research texts commonly mentioned a more time-consuming and more difficult and impractical method for measuring a scale's reliability that was akin to internal consistency reliability. It was called **parallel-forms reliability.** That method requires constructing a second measuring instrument that is thought to be equivalent to the first. It might be a shorter series of questions, and it always attempts to measure the same thing as the other instrument. Both forms are administered to the same set of individuals, and then we assess whether the two sets of responses are adequately correlated. This reliability assessment method is extremely rare in social work research because constructing a second instrument and ensuring its equivalence to the first is both cumbersome and risky. Inconsistent results on the two "parallel" forms might not mean that the main measure is unreliable. The inconsistency may merely result from shortcomings in the effort to make the second instrument truly equivalent to the first.

The most common and powerful method used today for calculating internal consistency reliability is **coefficient alpha.** The calculation of coefficient alpha is easily done using available computer software. To calculate coefficient alpha, the computer subdivides all the items of an instrument into all possible split halves (subsets of half of the items), calculates the total subscore of each possible split half for each subject, and then calculates the correlations of all possible pairs of split half subscores. Coefficient alpha equals the average of all of these correlations. When coefficient alpha is at about .90 or above, internal consistency reliability is considered to be excellent. Alphas at around .80 to .89 are considered good, and somewhat lower alphas can be considered acceptable for relatively short instruments. (For statistical reasons that we won't go into, when instruments contain relatively few items, it is harder to get high correlations among the subset scores.) The box titled "A Hypothetical Illustration of Coefficient Alpha" attempts to clarify this procedure.

We'll return to the issue of reliability more than once in the chapters ahead. For now, however, let's recall that even perfect reliability doesn't ensure that our measures measure what we think they measure. Now let's plunge into the question of validity.

VALIDITY

In conventional usage, the term *validity* refers to the extent to which an empirical measure adequately reflects the *real meaning* of the concept under consideration. Whoops! We've already committed to the view that concepts don't have any real meaning. Then how can we ever say whether a particular measure adequately reflects the concept's meaning? Ultimately, of course, we can't. At the same time, as we've already seen, all of social life, including social research, operates on *agreements* about the terms we use and the concepts they represent. There are several criteria regarding our success in making measurements that are appropriate to those agreements.

Face Validity

To begin, there's something called **face validity.** Particular empirical measures may or may not jibe with our common agreements and our individual mental images associated with a particular concept. We might quarrel about the adequacy of measuring worker morale by counting the number of resignations that occurred, but we'd surely agree that the number of resignations has *something* to do with morale. If we were to suggest that we measure morale by finding out how many books the workers took out of the library during their off-duty hours, then you'd undoubtedly raise a more serious objection: That measure wouldn't have any face validity.

Face validity is necessary if a measurement is to be deemed worth pursuing—but it is far from sufficient. In fact, some researchers might argue that it is technically misleading to call it a type of validity at all. Whether a measure has face validity is determined by subjective assessments made by the researcher or perhaps by other experts. Having face validity does not mean that a measure really measures what the researcher intends to measure, only that it *appears* to measure what the researcher intended.

To illustrate the limited value of face validity, let's consider the development of the paranoia scale in the Minnesota Multiphasic Personality Inventory (MMPI). The MMPI has long been one of the most widely used and highly regarded personality measures. When it was originally developed for clinical assessment purposes, it contained nine scales. Each scale had items to which one can respond either "true" or "false." One scale measured paranoia. For each item on this scale, a particular answer (either true or false) was scored higher or lower for paranoia. To validate the scale, it was administered to large numbers of people who were and were not diagnosed as paranoid. Items were deemed valid if individuals who were diagnosed as paranoid tended to answer those items differently than did individuals not diagnosed as paranoid.

Below are several of those items on the paranoia scale. Each item differentiated those with paranoia from those not so diagnosed. Examine each item

A HYPOTHETICAL ILLUSTRATION OF COEFFICIENT ALPHA

Suppose you develop a four-item scale to measure depression among elementary school children as follows:

	Often	Sometimes	Almost Never
1. I feel sad.	2	1	0
2. I cry.	2	1	0
3. I'm unhappy.	2	1	0
4. I can't sleep.	2	1	0

Suppose you administer the scale to 200 children to test its internal consistency reliability. If the scale is internally consistent, then children who circle 0 on some items should be more likely than other children to circle 0 on the other items as well. Likewise, children who circle 2 on some items should be more likely than other children to circle 2 on the other items. If the scale has excellent internal consistency reliability, then the correlation of each item with each of the other items might look something like this:

Interitem correlation matrix:

	Item 1	Item 2	Item 3	Item 4
Item 1	1.0			
Item 2	.6	1.0		
Item 3	.5	.5	1.0	
Item 4	.4	.5	.6	1.0

In an instant, computer software such as SPSS (described in Appendix D or refer to the Wadsworth website) can produce the above correlation matrix and calculate coefficient alpha. You can see in the above matrix that the four items are strongly correlating with each other. (You can ignore the 1.0 correlations, which simply mean that each item is perfectly correlated with itself.) Let's suppose the coefficient alpha for this scale is .80 (good). Here's how your computer might have arrived at that figure, which is the average of the correlations of the total scores of all possible split halves of the items:

Correlation of the sum of item 1 + item 2 with the sum of item 3 + item 4	= .85
Correlation of the sum of item 1 + item 3 with the sum of item 2 + item 4	= .80
Correlation of the sum of item 1 + item 4 with the sum of item 2 + item 3	= .75
Sum of the correlations of all three possible split halves of the items	= 2.40

Coefficient Alpha = Average (mean) of the three correlations = 2.40/3 = .80

It may be helpful to note that the above three split halves exhaust all the possible ways you can divide the four-item scale into two halves. For example, item 1 can be paired with item 2, with item 3, or with item 4. There are no other possible ways to subdivide the scale into two halves, each containing two items. Your computer won't show you any of the split halves or their correlations. It will only tell you the bottom line—that coefficient alpha equals .80 (or whatever else it happens to be for your actual data). We have presented these split halves and their hypothetical correlations just to help take the mystery out of how coefficient alpha gets calculated and what it means.

and see if you can determine which answer, "true" or "false," those with paranoia were more likely to select.

"Most people will use somewhat unfair means to gain profit or an advantage rather than lose it."

"I tend to be on my guard with people who are somewhat more friendly than I had expected."

"I think most people would lie to get ahead."

From a face validity standpoint, we expect that you probably chose "true" as the response more likely to be selected by those with paranoia. Indeed, it seems reasonable to suppose that those with paranoia would be more suspicious of the tendencies of others to cheat them, deceive them, or lie to them. But the opposite was the case! Those with paranoia were more likely than normals to answer "false" to the above items (Dahlstrom and Welsh, 1960). In light of this fact, and with 20/20 hindsight, we might be able to construct a rational explanation of why this occurred, perhaps noting that paranoids have unrealistically high expectations of what other people are like and that such overly idealistic expectations lead them to feel betrayed and persecuted when people act less nobly. But without the benefit of hindsight, there is a good chance that we would link the face validity of the preceding items to the likelihood that paranoids would more frequently respond "true." If this were the case, and if we relied solely on face validity to determine the scale's quality and its scoring system, then on these items we would be more likely to give a worse (higher) paranoia score to those without paranoia and a better (lower) paranoia score to those with paranoia.

Content Validity

A technically more legitimate type of validity, one that includes elements of face validity, is known as **content validity.** The term refers to the degree to which a measure covers the range of meanings included within the concept. For example, a test of mathematical ability, Carmines and Zeller (1979) point out, cannot be limited to addition alone but would also need to cover subtraction, multiplication, division, and so forth. Like face validity, however, content validity is established on the basis of judgments; that is, researchers or other experts make judgments about whether the measure covers the universe of facets that make up the concept. Although we must make judgments about face and content validity when we construct a particular measure, it is important to conduct an empirical assessment of the adequacy of those judgments. For no matter how much confidence we may have in those judgments, we need empirical evidence to ascertain whether the measure indeed measures what it's intended to measure. For example, how strongly does the measure correlate with other indicators of the concept it intends to measure? The two most common ways of empirically assessing whether a measure really measures what it's intended to measure are called *criterion-related validity* and *construct validity.*

Criterion-Related Validity

Criterion-related validity is based on some external criterion. When we assess the **criterion validity** of an instrument, we select an external criterion that we believe is another indicator or measure of the same variable that our instrument intends to measure. For instance, the validity of the college board exam is shown in its ability to predict the students' success in college. The validity of a written driver's test is determined, in this sense, by the relationship between the scores people get on the test and how well they drive. In these examples, success in college and driving ability are the *criteria.* In the MMPI example just cited, the criterion was whether an individual was diagnosed as having paranoia. The validity of the MMPI was determined by its ability, on the basis of its scores, to distinguish those diagnosed as paranoid from those without that diagnosis.

Two subtypes of criterion-related validity are **predictive validity** and **concurrent validity.** The difference between them has to do with whether the measure is being tested according to (1) its ability to predict a criterion that will occur in the future (such as later success in college) or (2) its correspondence to a criterion that is known concurrently. Suppose your introductory practice course instructor devises a multiple-choice test to measure your interviewing skills before you enter your field placement. To assess the concurrent validity of the test, she may see if scores on it correspond to ratings students received on their interviewing skills in videotapes in which they role-played interviewing situations. To assess the predictive validity of the test, she may see if scores on it correspond to field instructor evaluations of their interviewing skills after the students complete their field work. The predictive validity might also be assessed by comparing the test scores to client satisfaction ratings of the students' interviews after they graduate.

If you read studies that assess the criterion validity of various instruments, then you'll find many that ascertain whether an instrument accurately differentiates between groups that differ in respect to the variable being measured. For example, the MMPI study discussed above examined whether the test accurately differentiated between groups known to be diagnosed and not diagnosed with paranoia. When the criterion validity of a measure is assessed according to its ability to differentiate between "known groups," the type of validity being assessed may be called **known groups validity,** which is simply a subtype of criterion-related validity. Thus, to test the known groups validity of a scale designed to measure racial prejudice, you might see whether the scores of social work students differ markedly from the scores of Ku Klux Klan members.

Here's another example of known groups validity. Suppose you devised an instrument to measure the degree of empathy that juvenile sex offenders you were treating developed for their victims while in treatment. To assess the known groups validity of your instrument, you might compare the scores on it of juvenile sex offenders who haven't been treated with the scores of students attending a nearby high school. If the measure is valid, you would expect the average scores of the offenders to show much less empathy for victims of sex offenses than the average scores of the nonadjudicated students. This would be a reasonable approach to assessing known groups validity. But what if the purpose for which you developed your instrument was to measure subtle improvements that offenders made in their empathy during the course of their treatment?

Knowing that an instrument can detect extreme differences between groups does not necessarily mean that it will detect more subtle differences between groups with less extreme differences. An ability to detect subtle differences is termed the **sensitivity** of an instrument. Showing that an instrument can differentiate two extremely different groups that do and do not require treatment for a particular problem does not mean that the instrument will show that the treated group improved somewhat after treatment. Thus, when we select instruments to measure progress in treatment, we need to be mindful of the issue of sensitivity and of whether the instrument's known groups validity is based on groups whose differences are more extreme than the differences we expect to detect in our own study.

Recognizing that the concept of criterion validity can be somewhat tricky, you may want to test your understanding of it. To begin, see if you can think of behaviors that might be used to validate each of the following attitudinal qualities:

Is very religious

Supports the rights of gays and lesbians to marry

Is concerned about global warming

Now let's see if you can think of ways in which you would assess the concurrent and predictive validity of measures of the following constructs among social work students or practitioners:

Attitude about evidence-based practice

Willingness to engage in social action to advocate for improvements in social justice

Finally, imagine you wanted to assess the known groups validity of an instrument that intends to measure a sense of hopelessness and despair among the elderly. How might you do so? What would that approach imply about the instrument's potential sensitivity in measuring subtle improvements in hopelessness and despair among extremely frail nursing home residents?

Construct Validity

Assuming you are comfortable with the issue of criterion-related validity, let's turn to a more complex form of validity, **construct validity.** This form is based on the way a measure relates to other variables within a system of theoretical relationships. Let's suppose, for example, that you are interested in studying "marital satisfaction"—its sources and consequences. As part of your research, you develop a measure of marital satisfaction, and you want to assess its validity. In addition to developing your measure, you will also have developed certain theoretical expectations about the way marital satisfaction "behaves" in relation to other variables. For example, you may have concluded that family violence is more likely to occur at lower levels of marital satisfaction. If your measure of marital satisfaction relates to family violence in the expected fashion, then that constitutes evidence of your measure's construct validity. If "satisfied" and "dissatisfied" couples were equally likely to engage in family violence, however, that would challenge the validity of your measure.

In addition to testing whether a measure fits theoretical expectations, construct validation can involve assessing whether the measure has *both* convergent validity and discriminant validity.

A measure has **convergent validity** when its results correspond to the results of other methods of measuring the same construct. Thus, if the clients whom clinicians identify as having low levels of marital satisfaction tend to score lower on your scale of marital satisfaction than clients who clinicians say have higher levels of marital satisfaction, then your scale would have convergent validity.

A measure has **discriminant validity** when its results do not correspond as highly with measures of other constructs as they do with other measures of the same construct. Suppose, for example, that the results of a measure of depression or self-esteem correspond more closely to clinician assessments of maritally satisfied and dissatisfied clients than do the results of your marital satisfaction scale. Then your scale would not have construct validity even if it had established convergent validity. The idea here is that if your scale were really measuring the construct of marital satisfaction, it should correspond more highly to other measures of marital satisfaction than do measures of conceptually distinct concepts. Likewise, if your scale is really measuring marital satisfaction, it should not correspond more highly with measures of self-esteem or depression than it does with measures of marital satisfaction.

It is possible that a scale that intends to measure marital satisfaction will correspond to another measure of marital satisfaction, and yet not really be a very good measure of the construct of marital satisfaction. If we assume, for example, that people who have low self-esteem or who are depressed are less likely to be maritally satisfied than other people, then a scale that really has more to do with depression or self-esteem than with marital satisfaction will still probably correspond to a measure of marital satisfaction. The process of assessing discriminant validity checks for that possibility and thus enables us to determine whether a measure really measures the construct it intends to measure, and not some other construct that happens to be related to the construct in question.

Let's consider another hypothetical example regarding construct validity. Suppose you conceptualized a construct that you termed "battered women's syndrome" and developed a scale to measure it. Let's further suppose that your scale had items about how often the women felt sad, hopeless, helpless, undeserving of a better fate, and similar items that, although you didn't realize it, all had a lot to do with depression and self-esteem.

You administered your scale to women residing in a battered women's shelter and to those with no reported history of battering and found that the two groups' scores differed as you predicted. Thus, you established the scale's criterion-related validity. Then you administered it to battered women before and after they had completed a long period of intensive intervention in a battered women's program and found that, as you predicted, their scores on your scale improved. This gave you theoretically based confidence in the construct validity of your scale.

At that point, however, you realized that depression and low self-esteem were a big part of what you were conceptualizing as a battered women's syndrome. You began to wonder whether improvement on your scale had more to do with becoming less depressed or having more self-esteem than it did with overcoming your notion of a syndrome. So you decided to test your scale's discriminant validity. You repeated the same studies, but this time also had the women complete the best scale that you could find on depression and the best scale you could find on self-esteem. Your results showed that battered women improved more on those scales after treatment than they improved on your scale. Moreover, the differences between battered women and women with no history of battering were greater on those scales than on your scale. In addition, you found that the scores on your scale corresponded more highly with the scales on depression and self-esteem than they did with the women's status regarding battering or treatment. In light of this, you appropriately concluded that although your scale had criterion-related validity, it had more to do with measuring other constructs such as self-esteem and depression than it had to do with measuring your conception of a battered women's syndrome. Therefore, it lacked construct validity.

Factorial Validity

One more type of validity that you are likely to encounter in articles reporting social work research studies is called *factorial validity*. This type of validity can be statistically more complex than the types we have discussed so far, but you don't need to master its statistics to comprehend what it means. **Factorial validity** refers to how many different constructs a scale measures and whether the number of constructs and the items that make up those constructs are what the researcher intends.

Let's say that you develop a scale to measure the severity of trauma symptoms in abused children. Keeping it simple, let's suppose that you intend the scale to contain an overall symptom severity score as well as subscores for each of the following three constructs: (1) internalizing symptoms (such as depression, withdrawal, anxiety, and so on), (2) externalizing symptoms (such as antisocial behaviors), and (3) somatic symptoms (such as digestive problems, headaches, and so on). When discussing factorial validity, the subscore constructs are most commonly called *factors* or *dimensions*.

Let's say that your scale contains a total of 15 items, with three sets of five items designed to measure each of the three factors. To assess your scale's factorial validity, you would use a statistical procedure called **factor analysis**. The results of the factor analysis would indicate which subsets of items correlate more strongly with each other than with the other subsets. Each subset would constitute a factor or dimension. Suppose your factor analysis shows that instead of three factors, you have six factors. Or suppose it shows that you have three factors, but that the items making up those three factors are not even close to the ones you intended to correlate most highly with each other. In either case, your scale would lack factorial validity. In contrast, if your results showed that you had three factors, and that the items making up each factor were for the most part the ones you intended to correlate most highly with each other, then your scale would have factorial validity.

A scale need not be multidimensional to have factorial validity—that is, it need not contain subscores measuring multiple factors. Perhaps you intend it to be unidimensional; that is, to contain only one overall score measuring one overarching construct. If you intend your scale to be unidimensional, and the results of your factor analysis reveal only one factor, then your scale has factorial validity.

As you may have surmised, factorial validity is similar to construct validity. In fact, some researchers consider it to be another way to depict construct validity. To illustrate this point, let's reexamine the items in the box titled "A Hypothetical Illustration of Coefficient Alpha." The hypothetical scale in that box was intended to be a unidimensional measure of depression with four items: sadness, crying, being unhappy, and not sleeping. Chances are that a factor analysis would confirm that it indeed is unidimensional. However, suppose the scale consisted of the following four additional items:

"I lack confidence."

"I dislike myself."

"I don't like the way I look."

"Other kids are smarter than I am."

Notice that although kids who are depressed may have lower self-esteem than kids who are not depressed, the four additional items appear to have more to do with self-esteem than with depression. A factor analysis would probably show that those four items correlate much more strongly with each other than with the first four items. Likewise, it would probably show that the scale is not a unidimensional measure of depression as intended, but rather a multidimensional scale in which half of the items are measuring depression and half are measuring a different construct. The fact that half the items are measuring a construct other than depression would suggest that the scale lacks factorial validity as a unidimensional measure of depression and that, for the same reasons, it lacks construct validity in that it appears to be measuring a different (albeit related) construct as much as it is measuring its intended construct.

Students often find these differences among the types of validity a bit overwhelming. To get a better grasp on factorial validity and its similarity to construct validity we recommend that you study Figure 8-1. The figure also illustrates the other types of validity we've been discussing. You might also find the following real illustration helpful. It is intended to further clarify the assessment of reliability and validity.

AN ILLUSTRATION OF RELIABLE AND VALID MEASUREMENT IN SOCIAL WORK: THE CLINICAL MEASUREMENT PACKAGE

During the mid-1970s, Walter Hudson and his associates began to develop and validate a package of nine short, standardized scales that they designed for repeated use by clinical social workers to assess client problems and monitor and evaluate progress in treatment. The nine scales were collectively referred to as The Clinical Measurement Package (Hudson, 1982). Each scale was found to have test–retest reliability and an internal consistency reliability of at least .90, which is quite high. Each scale also was reported to be valid.

Although each scale measures a different construct, the nine scales are similar in format. Each lists 25 statements that refer to how the client feels about things, and the client enters a number from 1

Face validity:

Dork Depression Scale

	Strongly Agree				Strongly Disagree
1. I feel sad	5	4	3	2	1
2. I cry a lot	5	4	3	2	1
3. I worry a lot	5	4	3	2	1
4. I am anxious	5	4	3	2	1
5. I lack confidence	5	4	3	2	1
6. I dislike myself	5	4	3	2	1

Scale developer Dr. Donald Dork thinks, "Hmm; on the face of it, my scale items sure seem to be measuring depression."

Content validity:

A group of experts on depression examines Dr. Dork's 6-item scale and tells him, "We think you need more items on additional indicators of depression; you haven't covered the entire domain of depression yet. In fact, you seem to have as much content on anxiety and self-esteem as on depression."

Criterion validity (known groups):

People in treatment for depression score higher (worse) on Dork Depression Scale

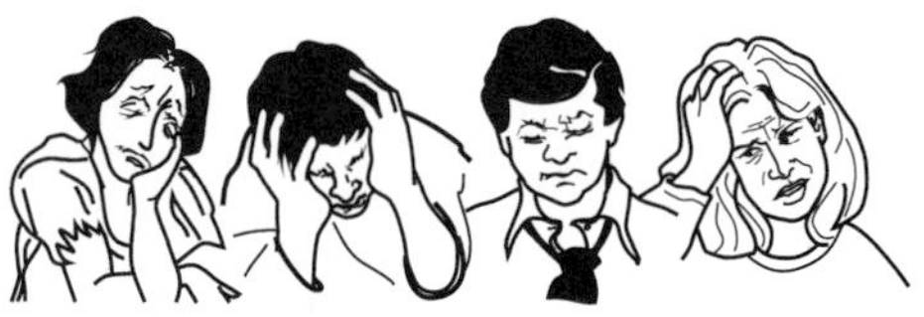

Individual total scale scores:
22 21 19 18
Group mean score: 20

People not in treatment for depression score lower (better) on Dork Depression Scale

Individual total scale scores:
12 11 9 8
Group mean score: 10

Ignoring the expert feedback on content validity, Dr. Dork administers his scale to two known groups. The results encourage him that perhaps his scale really is measuring depression. He publishes his results.

Construct validity:

Drs. Rubin and Babbie read Dr. Dork's study and were unimpressed with his criterion validity results. Reasoning that the constructs of depression, anxiety, and self-esteem share some overlapping indicators, they questioned whether Dork's findings were due to such overlap and consequently whether the Dork scale really measures the construct of depression more than it measures the related

Figure 8-1 Types of Validity, Using a Hypothetical Scale as an Illustration

constructs of anxiety and self-esteem. To find out, they administered Dork's scale along with other existing scales measuring depression, anxiety, and self-esteem to a large sample of social service recipients. For their first analysis, they analyzed the **factorial validity** of Dork's scale, and found that instead of containing just one factor—depression—it contained three factors: depression, anxiety, and self-esteem. Items 1 and 2 comprised the depression factor. Items 3 and 4 comprised the anxiety factor. And items 5 and 6 comprised the self-esteem factor. These factors are evident in the correlation matrix and the factor analysis results below (as well as in the wording of the items).

Factorial validity?

	Interitem correlation matrix:						*Factor loadings:*		
							Factor 1	Factor 2	Factor 3
	Item 1	Item 2	Item 3	Item 4	Item 5	Item 6	Depression	Anxiety	Self-esteem
Item 1	1.0						.7	.2	.2
Item 2	.6	1.0					.7	.2	.2
Item 3	.2	.2	1.0				.2	.7	.2
Item 4	.2	.2	.6	1.0			.2	.7	.2
Item 5	.2	.2	.2	.2	1.0		.2	.2	.7
Item 6	.2	.2	.2	.2	.6	1.0	.2	.2	.7

For their next analysis, Rubin and Babbie assessed the Dork scale's convergent and discriminant validity by examining the correlations between the total scores on the Dork scale and the total scores on the other scales. The results that appear below show that although Dork's scale had convergent validity, it lacked discriminant validity because its correlation was higher with the scales measuring anxiety (r = .50) and self-esteem (r = .50) than with the existing scale measuring depression (r = .40). In their published article they cautioned practitioners against using Dork's scale to diagnose depression—and that a high score on his scale appears to be at least as likely to indicate problems in anxiety or self-esteem as it is to indicate a diagnosis of depression. In that connection, they noted that although depressed people may be more anxious and have less self-esteem than most other people, items 3 and 4 on the Dork scale appear to have more to do with anxiety than with depression, and items 5 and 6 appear to have more to do with self-esteem. In light of their factor analysis results and discriminant validity results, Rubin and Babbie concluded that Dork's scale lacked construct validity; it was not really measuring the construct of depression more than it was measuring other, related constructs.

Convergent validity?

Dork Depression Scale ⟵ r = .40 ⟶ An existing depression scale

Discriminant validity?

Dork Depression Scale ⟵ r = .50 ⟶ An existing anxiety scale

Dork Depression Scale ⟵ r = .50 ⟶ An existing self-esteem scale

Figure 8-1 *(continued)*

to 5 beside each statement to indicate how often he or she feels that way. The 25 responses are summed (with reverse scoring for positively worded items) to get the client's total score on the scale (the higher the score, the greater the problem with the construct being measured). The nine constructs that the nine scales were designed to measure are: (1) depression, (2) self-esteem, (3) marital discord, (4) sexual discord, (5) parental attitudes about child, (6) child's attitude toward father, (7) child's attitude toward mother, (8) intrafamilial stress, and (9) peer relationships.

For a discussion of the entire measurement package, readers are referred to the preceding reference (Hudson, 1982). For our purposes in this text, however, let's examine the characteristics of one scale and how its reliability and validity were assessed empirically. The scale we will examine is the Child's Attitude toward Mother (CAM) scale, whose reliability and validity were reported by Giuli and Hudson (1977). The CAM scale is reproduced in Figure 8-2 with permission from W. W. Hudson, The Clinical Measurement Package, Chicago, Illinois, The Dorsey Press © 1982.

What sources of measurement error would most concern you if you were considering using this scale? Notice that you might not be too concerned about the acquiescent response set because some of the items are worded positively and others are worded negatively. But what about a social desirability bias? Look at items 13 and 20. Would children who hate their mothers or feel violent toward them admit to such feelings? Will differences in scale scores really measure differences in these feelings, or will they instead just measure differences in the propensity of children to admit to their socially undesirable feelings? We can resolve these questions by assessing the scale's criterion-related validity or its construct validity, and we will shortly examine how Giuli and Hudson did so.

But before we consider the validity of the scale, what about its reliability? How vulnerable does the scale appear to be to random error? Will having to select a number from 1 to 5 for each of the 25 items be too cumbersome for children? Are there any words or phrases that they might not understand such as *embarrasses* in item 5, *too demanding* in item 6, or *puts too many limits on me* in item 9? If the scale is too cumbersome, or if it's too difficult to understand, then it will contain too many random errors, which means that measurement will lack consistency and therefore be unreliable.

Giuli and Hudson administered the scale to 664 high school students. To assess its internal consistency reliability, they computed coefficient alpha, which, as noted earlier in this chapter, is the average of all possible split-half reliabilities. They found a very high *internal consistency reliability,* with a coefficient alpha of .94. To assess the scale's stability over time, they assessed its test–retest reliability. This was done with a sample of adults enrolled in a graduate-level psychology statistics course. The students completed the scale twice, with one week between tests. The *test–retest reliability* was .95, which is very high.

To assess the scale's criterion validity, they asked the 664 high school students to indicate whether they were having problems with their mothers. Those who said "yes" had a mean CAM score of 49.9. Those who said they were not had a mean CAM score of 20.8. This large and significant difference was interpreted by Giuli and Hudson to mean that the scale has excellent *criterion validity* because it does so well at differentiating those who acknowledge a problem with their mother from those who deny having such a problem.

But was the scale really measuring the construct of child's attitude toward mother? Perhaps it was really measuring something else, such as level of depression or self-esteem, that was related to having problems with parents. To assess the scale's *construct validity,* each of the 664 high school students also completed scales (from The Clinical Measurement Package) that measured depression and self-esteem. The strength of the relationship between each measure and whether the student admitted to having problems with his or her mother was then assessed. The CAM score turned out to be much more strongly related to the latter criterion than was either the depression score or the self-esteem score. Giuli and Hudson concluded that these findings supported the construct validity of the CAM scale.

No study in social research is ever perfectly flawless. Even the best ones have some (perhaps unavoidable) limitations. This is just as true for studies assessing measurement reliability and validity as it is for other sorts of studies. Let's consider some possible limitations in the Giuli and Hudson study, for example. Note that reliability was not assessed for children younger than high school age. We cannot fault Giuli and Hudson for that; it's unreasonable to expect them to study every conceivable age group. Finding the resources to do that is extremely difficult. Nevertheless, it would be inappropriate to assume that the same

Today's Date ____________

CHILD'S ATTITUDE TOWARD MOTHER (CAM)

Name ____________________

This questionnaire is designed to measure the degree of contentment you have in your relationship with your mother. It is not a test, so there are no right or wrong answers. Answer each item as carefully and accurately as you can by placing a number beside each one as follows:

1 Rarely or none of the time
2 A little of the time
3 Some of the time
4 A good part of the time
5 Most or all of the time

Please begin.

1. My mother gets on my nerves. ____
2. I get along well with my mother. ____
3. I feel that I can really trust my mother. ____
4. I dislike my mother. ____
5. My mother's behavior embarrasses me. ____
6. My mother is too demanding. ____
7. I wish I had a different mother. ____
8. I really enjoy my mother. ____
9. My mother puts too many limits on me. ____
10. My mother interferes with my activities. ____
11. I resent my mother. ____
12. I think my mother is terrific. ____
13. I hate my mother. ____
14. My mother is very patient with me. ____
15. I really like my mother. ____
16. I like being with my mother. ____
17. I feel like I do not love my mother. ____
18. My mother is very irritating. ____
19. I feel very angry toward my mother. ____
20. I feel violent toward my mother. ____
21. I feel proud of my mother. ____
22. I wish my mother was more like others I know. ____
23. My mother does not understand me. ____
24. I can really depend on my mother. ____
25. I feel ashamed of my mother. ____

Figure 8-2 Sample Scale from *The Clinical Measurement Package:* Child's Attitude toward Mother

high level of reliability applies to elementary school students, especially those in the lower grades. Perhaps children that young would find the instrument much more difficult to understand or much more cumbersome than did the high school students and therefore would be much less consistent in their responses to it.

Note also the debatable criterion that Giuli and Hudson used to separate the students having problems with their mothers from those not having such problems. Like the CAM scale itself, that criterion was vulnerable to a social desirability bias because it relied on students' willingness to acknowledge that they were having problems with their mothers. It is conceivable that those not willing to acknowledge such problems on the CAM scale, because of a social desirability bias, were also unwilling to acknowledge having problems in a general sense when asked, because of the same bias. If so, then the construct actually being measured might have less to do with real attitudes toward one's mother than with a willingness

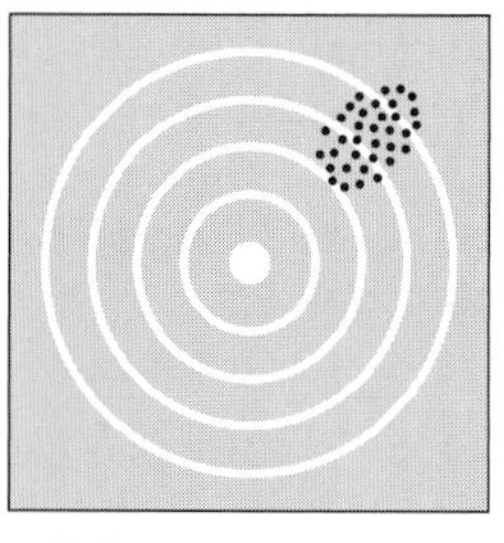
Reliable but not valid

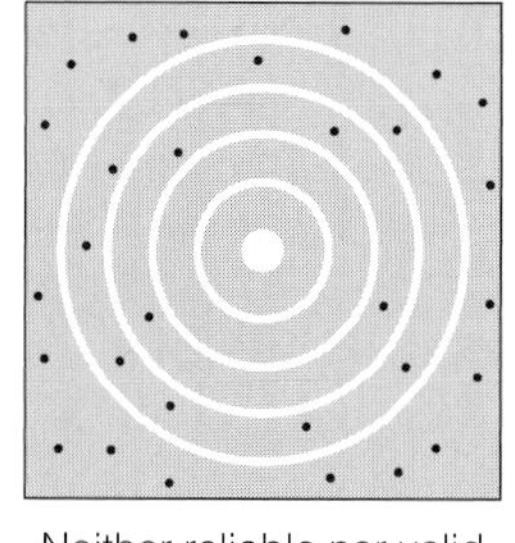
Neither reliable nor valid

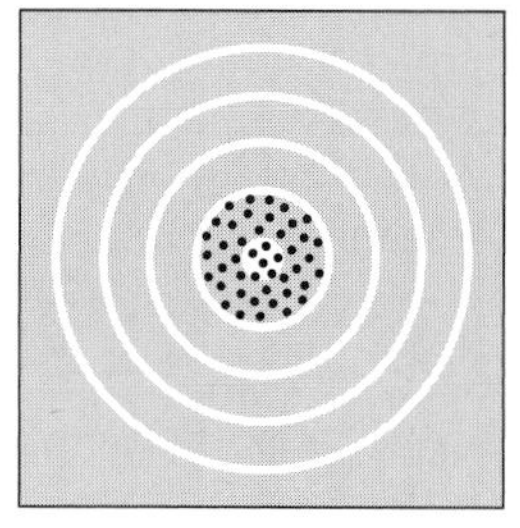
Valid *and* reliable

Figure 8-3 An Analogy to Validity and Reliability

to acknowledge socially undesirable attitudes. When selecting a criterion measure of the construct in question, it is essential that the criterion be an *independent* measure of the construct, not just a parallel form of the same measure whose validity you are assessing. If it is not—that is, if it seems just as vulnerable in the same way to the same biases as is the measure in question—then you are really measuring parallel-forms reliability instead of validity.

Giuli and Hudson recognized this problem and conducted a further assessment of the CAM scale's validity. This time they assessed its *known groups* validity. To do this, they obtained a sample of 38 children who were receiving therapy for a variety of problems. They divided the children into two groups: those known by the therapist to have behaviorally identifiable problems with their mother and those for whom no such problem could be established. The average CAM score for the first group was 54.82, as compared to 14.73 for the latter group. Because the therapists' observations were not vulnerable to the same biases as the CAM scale, the large and significant differences in CAM scores provided stronger grounds for claiming the validity of the CAM scale—that is, for claiming that it really measures attitudes, not just some systematic bias bearing on a person's willingness to acknowledge those attitudes.

RELATIONSHIP BETWEEN RELIABILITY AND VALIDITY

As we noted earlier, although it is desirable that a measure be reliable, its reliability does not ensure that it's valid. Suppose an abusive mother and father were referred by the courts to family therapy as a precondition for keeping their child. As involuntary clients, they might be reluctant to admit abusive behaviors to the therapist, believing that such admissions would imperil maintaining custody of their child. Even if they continued to abuse their child, they might deny it every time the therapist asked them about it. Thus, the therapist would be getting highly reliable (that is, consistent) data. No matter how many times and ways the therapist asked about abusive behaviors, the answer would always be the same.

But the data would not be valid: The answer would not really measure the construct in question—the amount of child abuse that was occurring. Instead, what was really being measured was the reluctance of the parents to convey a socially undesirable image to the therapist.

Figure 8-3 graphically portrays the difference between validity and reliability. If you can think of measurement as analogous to hitting the bull's-eye on a target, you'll see that reliability looks like a "tight pattern," regardless of where it hits, because reliability is a function of consistency. Validity, on the other hand, is a function of shots being arranged around the bull's-eye. The failure of reliability in the figure can be seen as random error, whereas the failure of validity is a systematic error. Notice that neither an unreliable nor an invalid measure is likely to be useful. Notice also that you can't have validity without also having reliability.

A certain tension often exists between the criteria of reliability and validity. Often we seem to face a trade-off between the two. If you'll recall for a moment the earlier example of measuring morale in different work settings, you'll probably see that the strategy of immersing yourself in the day-to-day routine of the agency, observing what went on, and talking to the workers seems to provide a more valid measure of morale than counting resignations. It just seems obvious that we'd be able to get a clearer sense of whether the morale was high or low in that fashion than we would from counting the number of resignations.

However, the counting strategy would be more reliable. This situation reflects a more general strain in research measurement. Most of the really interesting concepts that we want to study have many subtle nuances, and it's difficult to specify precisely what we mean by them. Researchers sometimes speak of such concepts as having a "richness of meaning." Scores of books and articles have been written on topics such as depression, self-esteem, and social support, and all of the interesting aspects of those concepts still haven't been exhausted.

Yet science needs to be specific to generate reliable measurements. Very often, then, the specification of reliable operational definitions and measurements seems to rob such concepts of their richness of meaning. For example, morale is much more than a lack of resignations; depression is much more than five items on a depression scale.

Developing measures that are reliable and still capable of tapping the richness of meaning of concepts is a persistent and inevitable dilemma for the social researcher, and you will be effectively forearmed against it by being forewarned. Be prepared for it and deal with it. If there is no clear agreement on how to measure a concept, then measure it several different ways. If the concept has several different dimensions, then measure them all. And above all, know that the concept does not have any meaning other than what we give it. The only justification we have for giving any concept a particular meaning is utility; measure concepts in ways that help us understand the world around us.

RELIABILITY AND VALIDITY IN QUALITATIVE RESEARCH

We began our comments on validity by reminding you that we depend on agreements to determine what's real, and we've seen some of the ways in which social scientists can agree among themselves that they have made valid measurements. There is still another way to look at validity.

Who Decides What's Valid?

Social researchers sometimes criticize themselves and each other for implicitly assuming they are somewhat superior to those they study. Indeed, we often seek to uncover motivations of which the social actors themselves are unaware. You think you bought that new BurpoBlaster because of its high performance and good looks, but we know you are really trying to establish a higher social status for yourself.

This implicit sense of superiority would fit comfortably with a totally positivistic approach (the biologist feels superior to the frog on the lab table), but it clashes with the more humanistic, and typically qualitative, approach taken by many social scientists. Thus, for example, Silverman (1993:94–95) says this of validity in the context of in-depth interviews:

> If interviewees are to be viewed as subjects who actively construct the features of their cognitive world, then one should try to obtain intersubjective depth between both sides so that a deep mutual understanding can be achieved.

Ethnomethodologists, in seeking to understand the way ordinary people conceptualize and make sense of their worlds, have urged all social scientists to pay more respect to those natural, social processes. At the very least, behavior that may seem irrational from the scientist's paradigm will make logical sense if it is seen through the actor's paradigm.

Ultimately, social researchers should look both to their colleagues and their subjects as sources of agreement on the most useful meanings and measurements of the concepts we study. Sometimes one will be more useful, sometimes the other. Neither should be dismissed, however. Keeping this in mind, and noting that much of our discussion of reliability and validity so far applies most clearly to quantitative research, let's now give more attention to the use of these terms in qualitative research.

Qualitative Approaches to Reliability and Validity

Although much of the basic logic about reliability and validity is the same in qualitative and quantitative research, qualitative researchers may approach the issues somewhat differently than quantitative researchers. Let's see what some of those differences might be.

In a quantitative study of adolescent depression, the researcher would conceivably administer a standardized depression scale to a sizable sample of adolescents, perhaps to assess the extent of depression among adolescents or perhaps to see if the extent of depression was related to other variables. In planning the study, or in reading about it, a critical issue would be the depression scale's reliability and validity. But we would know that even the best depression scale is not 100 percent reliable and valid. Even using the best scale, the study would be dealing with probabilistic knowledge—that is, specific scores would indicate a higher or lower probability that the adolescent is depressed. A good clinical scale would be correct about 90 percent of the time in depicting an adolescent as depressed or not depressed, and it would be important to know how often the scale is accurate and how often it's mistaken. But if all we have on each adolescent is quantitative data from a scale score, then we will not know which adolescents are being accurately depicted and which are among the 10 percent or so who are not.

In a qualitative study of adolescent depression, the researcher would not rely on a standardized instrument. The researcher would be more likely to study a much smaller sample of adolescents and conduct extensive and varied direct observations and in-depth interviews with each one of them and their significant others. Perhaps the scope would be limited to a biographical case study of the impact of adolescent depression on one family. Or perhaps the sample would include several families. In either case, the sample would be small enough to permit the researcher to describe the everyday lives of the subjects in such rich detail that the reader would not question the existence of depression or simply would not care what construct was used to label the observed phenomenon.

Suppose the qualitative report described an adolescent girl whose academic and social functioning began to deteriorate gradually after the onset of puberty. After achieving high grades throughout her previous schooling, she began staying awake all night, sleeping all day, and refusing to go to school. On the days when she did attend school, she was unable to concentrate. Her grades began to fall precipitously. She began to isolate herself from family and friends and refused to leave her room. She began to express feelings of hopelessness about the future and negative thoughts about her looks, intelligence, likability, and worthiness. She no longer had the energy to do things she once did well, and started to neglect basic daily tasks associated with cleanliness and grooming. She began to wear the same black clothes every day, refusing to wear any other color. When family or friends reached out to her, she became unresponsive or irritable. She displayed no signs of substance abuse but began to wonder if that might make her feel better. She began to have thoughts of suicide and started to cut herself. She showed no signs of schizophrenia such as delusions or hallucinations.

A good qualitative report would depict the above clinical deterioration in a format replete with detailed observations and quotations that would be many pages long and would leave the reader with a sense of having walked in the shoes of the girl and her family, sensing the girl's depression and agony as well as the burden placed on the family. The detail of the study and its report would be so rich that if the girl did not score in the depressed range of a standardized scale, the reader would be likely to conclude that this was one of the 10 percent or so of cases in which the scale got it wrong. The reader might not even care whether the phenomenon described fit best under the rubric of depression or under some other label. Rather than verifying a label for it that could be generalized to others, the study would be geared more to giving the reader a deeper sense of the situation that the girl and her family were struggling with, the ways in which the various family members experienced the situation and the subjective meanings it had for them, and what they felt they needed.

The point of qualitative studies, in other words, is to study and describe things in such depth and detail, and from such multiple perspectives and meanings, that there is less need to worry about whether one particular measure is really measuring what it's intended to measure. In quantitative studies, on the other hand, we are more likely to rely heavily on one indicator, or a few indicators, administered perhaps in a matter of minutes, to determine the degree to which a hypothetical construct applies to a large number of people, and with an eye toward generalizing what we find to an even larger number of people. In such studies, it is critical to assess the reliability and validity of the indicators we use. It is thus possible to recognize the critical role of reliability and validity in quantitative studies while at the same time appreciating the need to take a different perspective on the role of reliability and validity in qualitative studies. In fact, without even attempting to quantitatively assess the validity of in-depth qualitative measurement, one could argue that the directness, depth, and detail of its observations often gives it better validity than quantitative measurement.

We are not, however, saying that the concepts of reliability and validity have no role in qualitative studies. Qualitative researchers disagree on the nature and extent of the role of reliability and validity in their work, and their disagreement is connected to the epistemological assumptions they make. At one extreme are the researchers who conduct qualitative research without buying into a postmodern rejection of the notion of an objective reality or of our ability to improve or assess our objectivity. These researchers use varied criteria to judge whether the evidence reported in qualitative studies is to be trusted as accurate and unbiased. One way they may do this is by using triangulation, which—as we noted earlier—involves using several measurement alternatives and seeing if they tend to produce the same findings. For example, they might see if different interviewers or observers generate the same findings. They might even compare the qualitative interpretations with data from quantitative measures. To the degree that the quantitative data support the qualitative interpretations, the qualitative material may be seen as more credible (or reliable).

Some researchers judge the reliability of qualitative interpretations according to criteria that aren't really quantitative but that resemble the underlying logic of quantitative approaches to reliability. Akin to interobserver reliability in quantitative studies, for example, one might assess whether two independent raters arrive at the same interpretation from the same mass of written qualitative field notes. What distinguishes this from a quantitative approach is that the consistency between the two raters would not be calculated through quantitative indicators such as percentages of agreement or correlations. Instead, one would merely ask whether the two arrived at the same particular overarching interpretation. (Some researchers might argue that this is still a quantitative indicator—that is, agreement is either 100 percent or zero percent.) Akin to internal consistency reliability, one might examine whether different sources of data fit consistently with the researcher's observations and interpretations. Rather than calculate quantitative reliability coefficients, however, one would attempt to illustrate how, on an overall basis, the different sources were in qualitative agreement.

Some researchers use indicators of reliability of a more distinctly qualitative nature. They might, for example, ask the research participants to confirm the accuracy of the researcher's observations. Or the participants might be asked whether the researcher's interpretations ring true and are meaningful to them. Some researchers judge reliability according to whether the report indicates ways in which the researcher searched thoroughly for disconfirming evidence, such as by looking for other cases or informants whose data might not fit the researcher's interpretation. They might also ask whether the researcher sufficiently varied the time, place, and context of the observations, and whether the interpretations fit consistently across the observations taken at different times, places, and contexts.

Jane Kronick (1989) has proposed four criteria for evaluating the validity of qualitative interpretations of written texts. The first is analogous to internal consistency reliability in quantitative research—that is, the interpretation of parts of the text should be consistent with other parts or with the whole text. Likewise, the "developing argument" should be "internally consistent." Second, Kronick proposes that the interpretation should be complete, taking all of the evidence into account. Her third criterion involves "conviction." This means that the interpretation should be the most compelling one in light of the evidence within the text. Fourth, the interpretation should be meaningful. It should make sense of the text and extend our understanding of it.

As in quantitative research, limitations inhere in some of the qualitative approaches to reliability and validity. For instance, the research participants may not confirm the accuracy of a researcher's observations or interpretations because they do not like the way they are portrayed, may not understand the researcher's theoretical perspective, or may not be aware of patterns that are true but which only emerge from the mass of data. A second rater may not confirm the interpretations of the principal investigator because certain insights might require having conducted the observations or interviews and might not emerge from the written notes alone.

While some qualitative researchers disagree about which of the above types of approaches to reliability and validity to use and how to use them, others reject the whole idea of reliability and validity in keeping with their postmodern epistemological rejection of assumptions connected to objectivity. Or they define reliability and validity in terms that are worlds apart from what other researchers mean by those two words. Sometimes, they define reliability and validity in terms that researchers who do not share their epistemological assumptions would perceive as nonscientific or even antiscientific. For instance, some would deem a study valid if a particular group deemed as oppressed or powerless experienced it as liberating or empowering. Thus, rather than define validity in terms of objectivity and accuracy, some define it according to whether findings can be applied toward some political or ideological purpose (Altheide and

Johnson, 1994). Others point to writing style as a validity criterion, deeming a study valid if the report is written in a gripping manner that draws the reader into the subjects' worlds so closely that readers feel as though they are walking in the subjects' shoes, recognize what they read to correspond to their own prior experiences, and perceive the report to be internally coherent and plausible (Adler and Adler, 1994). In this connection, some have depicted postmodern qualitative research as blurring the distinction between social science and the arts and humanities (Neuman, 1994). In fact, one qualitative study used fictional novels and plays as sources of data for developing insights about the experience of family caregiving of relatives with Alzheimer's disease (England, 1994).

As you encounter the terms *reliability* and *validity* throughout the remainder of this book, they will be used primarily in reference to their quantitative meanings, because these terms are more commonly used in quantitative research. But we will also be discussing qualitative research in the remaining chapters, and we hope you'll keep in mind the distinctive ways in which reliability and validity are considered in qualitative research as you read that material.

Main Points

- Measurement error can be systematic or random. Common systematic errors pertain to social desirability biases and cultural biases. Random errors have no consistent pattern of effects, make measurement inconsistent, and are likely to result from difficulties in understanding or administering measures.

- Alternative forms of measurement include written self-reports, interviews, direct behavioral observation, and examining available records. Each of these options is vulnerable to measurement error.

- Because no form of measurement is foolproof, applying the principle of triangulation—by using several different research methods to collect the same information—we can use several imperfect measurement alternatives and see if they tend to produce the same findings.

- Reliability concerns the amount of random error in a measure and measurement consistency. It refers to the likelihood that a given measurement procedure will yield the same description of a given phenomenon if that measurement is repeated. For instance, estimating a person's age by asking his or her friends would be less reliable than asking the person or checking the birth certificate.

- Different types of reliability include interobserver reliability or interrater reliability, test–retest reliability, parallel-forms reliability, and internal consistency reliability.

- Validity refers to the extent of systematic error in measurement—the extent to which a specific measurement provides data that relate to commonly accepted meanings of a particular concept. There are numerous yardsticks for determining validity: *face validity, content validity, criterion-related validity,* and *construct validity.* The latter two are empirical forms of validity, whereas the former are based on expert judgments.

- Two subtypes of criterion-related validity are *predictive validity* and *concurrent validity.* The difference between these subtypes has to do with whether the measure is being tested according to ability to predict a criterion that will occur in the future or its correspondence to a criterion that is known concurrently.

- *Known groups validity* is another subtype of criterion-related validity. It assesses whether an instrument accurately differentiates between groups known to differ in respect to the variable being measured.

- The ability to detect subtle differences between groups or subtle changes over time within a group is termed the sensitivity of an instrument.

- Construct validation involves testing whether a measure relates to other variables according to theoretical expectations. It also involves testing the measure's convergent validity and discriminant validity.

- A measure has *convergent validity* when its results correspond to the results of other methods of measuring the same construct.

- A measure has *discriminant validity* when its results do not correspond as highly with measures of other constructs as they do with other measures of the same construct and when its results correspond more highly with the other measures of the same construct than do measures of alternative constructs.

- *Factorial validity* refers to how many different constructs a scale measures and whether the number of constructs and the items making up those constructs are what the researcher intends.

• The creation of specific, reliable measures often seems to diminish the richness of meaning that our general concepts have. This problem is inevitable. The best solution is to use several different measures to tap the different aspects of the concept.

• Studies that assess the reliability and validity of a measure, just like any other type of study, can be seriously flawed. Ultimately, the degree to which we can call a measure reliable or valid depends not just on the size of its reliability or validity coefficient, but also on the methodological credibility of the way those coefficients were assessed. For example, was an appropriate sample selected? Was the criterion of the construct truly independent of the measure being assessed and not vulnerable to the same sources of error as that measure?

• Reliability and validity are defined and handled differently in qualitative research than they are in quantitative research. Qualitative researchers disagree about definitions and criteria for reliability and validity, and some argue that they are not applicable at all to qualitative research. These disagreements tend to be connected to differing epistemological assumptions about the nature of reality and objectivity.

Review Questions and Exercises

1. In a newspaper or magazine, find an instance of invalid or unreliable measurement. Justify your choice.

2. Suppose a geriatric social worker assesses whether a life history review intervention improves the level of depression among frail nursing home residents by administering a depression measure to them before and after the intervention. Suppose the measure had its validity assessed by comparing scores of frail nursing home residents on it to the scores of healthy elderly folks living independently.

a. What type (and subtype) of validity was assessed?

b. Why should the social worker be concerned about the measure's sensitivity?

c. What more would be needed to establish the measure's construct validity?

d. If the measure is valid, can we assume it is also reliable? Why?

Internet Exercises

1. Use InfoTrac College Edition to find several research articles in the journal *Health and Social Work* that utilized existing scales to measure variables. How adequately do the articles report the reliability and validity of the scales they used? What type of reliability and validity do they report? What types of reliability and validity tend to get reported more and less often than others?

2. Using a search engine, enter the search term *cultural bias in IQ tests*. Then go to one of the listed websites that intrigues you. (Some of the sites are humorous.) Summarize what you find there and how it illustrates cultural bias in measurement.

3. Return to the website mentioned in Chapter 5, "Psychosocial Measures for Asian-American Populations," at www.columbia.edu/cu/ssw/projects/pmap. Find two abstracts at that site that assessed different forms of reliability and validity. Briefly describe and contrast how each assessed reliability and validity and their results.

Additional Readings

Denzin, Norman K., and Yvonna S. Lincoln. 1994. *Handbook of Qualitative Research*. Thousand Oaks, CA: Sage. This edited volume of informative and provocative papers discusses the various nonpositivist epistemologies that influence qualitative inquiry and their implications for how qualitative research is conceptualized, carried out, interpreted, and reported. Many of the chapters discuss alternative ways that reliability and validity are viewed and handled in qualitative research.

Hudson, Walter. 1982. *The Clinical Measurement Package*. Chicago: Dorsey Press. This field manual describes in detail the nine scales discussed in this chapter that are used by clinical social workers.

Silverman, David. 1993. *Interpreting Qualitative Data: Methods for Analyzing Talk, Text, and Interaction*. Thousand Oaks, CA: Sage. Chapter 7 deals with the issues of validity and reliability specifically in regard to qualitative research.

CHAPTER 9

Constructing Measurement Instruments

What You'll Learn in This Chapter

Now that you understand measurement error, its common sources, and the concepts of reliability and validity, let's examine the process of constructing some measurement instruments that are commonly used in social work research.

INTRODUCTION

The preceding chapter focused on levels of measurement and the broad issue of measurement error. In this chapter, we will delve further into measurement methodology by examining the construction of measurement instruments widely used in social work research: questionnaires, interview schedules, and scales. Later in this book, we will look at alternative research designs and modes of collecting data. Some of these methodologies will not require the application of the instruments just mentioned, so we will be discussing ways to measure social work variables that don't involve asking people questions or administering written instruments to them. But despite the value of those alternative methodologies, instruments designed to gather data by communicating with people orally or in writing (with questionnaires, interview schedules, and scales) are among the most prominent techniques that social work researchers use to collect data. As we examine the construction of these types of instruments, bear in mind that the principles guiding their design will vary, depending on whether the research is primarily qualitative or quantitative. Among the most important objectives in designing quantitative instruments is the avoidance of measurement error. Thus, we seek to construct instruments that are reliable and valid. Among the most important objectives in designing qualitative instruments is probing for depth of meaning from the respondent's perspective. We'll begin our consideration of instrument construction by examining some broad guidelines for asking people questions.

GUIDELINES FOR ASKING QUESTIONS

As we implied above, one of the most common ways that social work researchers operationalize their variables is by asking people questions as a way to get data for analysis and interpretation. Asking people questions is most commonly associated with survey research, which will be discussed in Chapter 15, but it is also used often in experiments (to be discussed in Chapter 11) and in qualitative research (Chapters 17 and 18). Sometimes the questions are asked by an interviewer, and the list of questions is referred to as an *interview schedule*. Instead of using an interview schedule, some qualitative studies utilize an *interview guide*, which lists topics to be asked about but not the exact sequence and wording of the questions. Sometimes the questions are written down and given to respondents for completion. In that case, we refer to the sets of questions as *questionnaires*, or perhaps as *self-administered questionnaires*.

As we'll see, several general guidelines can assist you in framing and asking questions that serve as excellent operationalizations of variables. There are also pitfalls that can result in useless and even misleading information. This section should assist you in differentiating the two. Let's begin with some of the options available to you in creating questionnaires.

Questions and Statements

The term *questionnaire* suggests a collection of questions, but an examination of a typical questionnaire will probably reveal as many statements as questions. That is not without reason. Often, the researcher is interested in determining the extent to which respondents hold a particular attitude or perspective. If you are able to summarize the attitude in a fairly brief statement, then you will often present that statement and ask respondents whether they agree or disagree with it. Rensis Likert formalized this procedure through the creation of the Likert scale, a format in which respondents are asked to strongly agree, agree, disagree, or strongly disagree, or perhaps strongly approve, approve, and so forth. Both questions and statements may be used profitably. Using both in a given questionnaire gives you more flexibility in the design of items and can make the questionnaire more interesting as well.

Open-Ended and Closed-Ended Questions

In asking questions, researchers have two options. We may ask **open-ended questions,** in which the respondent is asked to provide his or her own answer to the question. Open-ended questions can be used in interview schedules as well as in self-administered questionnaires. For example, the respondent may be asked, "What do you feel is the most important problem facing your community today?" and be provided with a space to write in the answer or be asked to report it orally to an interviewer.

In an *interview schedule,* the interviewer may be instructed to probe for more information as needed. For instance, if the respondent replies that the most important problem facing the community is "urban decay," the interviewer may probe for more clarification by saying, "Could you tell me some more about that problem?" (We'll discuss this process in greater depth in Chapter 15, on survey research.) Because of the opportunity to probe for more information, open-ended questions are used more frequently on interview schedules than on self-administered questionnaires, although they commonly appear in both formats.

With **closed-ended questions**, the respondent is asked to select an answer from among a list provided by the researcher. Closed-ended questions can be used in self-administered questionnaires as well as interview schedules and are popular because they provide a greater uniformity of responses and are more easily processed. Open-ended responses must be coded before they can be processed for computer analysis, as will be discussed in several later chapters. This coding process often requires that the researcher interpret the meaning of responses, opening the possibility of misunderstanding and researcher bias. There is also a danger that some respondents will give answers that are essentially irrelevant to the researcher's intent. Closed-ended responses, on the other hand, can often be transferred directly into a computer format.

The chief shortcoming of closed-ended questions lies in the researcher's structuring of responses. When the relevant answers to a given question are relatively clear, there should be no problem. In other cases, however, the researcher's structuring of responses may overlook some important responses. In asking about "the most important problem facing your community," for example, your checklist of problems might omit certain ones that respondents would have said were important.

In the construction of closed-ended questions, you should be guided by two structural requirements. The response categories provided should be *exhaustive:* They should include all of the possible responses that might be expected. Often, researchers ensure this by adding a category labeled something like "Other (Please specify: ___________)."

Second, the answer categories must be *mutually exclusive:* The respondent should not feel compelled to select more than one. (In some cases, you may wish to solicit multiple answers, but these may create difficulties in data processing and analysis later on.) To ensure that your categories are mutually exclusive, you should carefully consider each combination of categories, asking yourself whether a person could reasonably choose more than one answer. In addition, it is useful to add an instruction to the question that asks the respondent to select the *one best* answer, but this technique is not a satisfactory substitute for a carefully constructed set of responses.

Make Items Clear

It should go without saying that questionnaire items should be clear and unambiguous, but the broad proliferation of unclear and ambiguous questions in surveys makes the point worth stressing here. Often you can become so deeply involved in the topic under examination that opinions and perspectives are clear to you but will not be clear to your respondents—many of whom have given little or no attention to the topic. Or if you have only a superficial understanding of the topic, you may fail to specify the intent of your question sufficiently. The question "What do you think about the proposed residential facility for the developmentally disabled in the community?" may evoke in the respondent a counterquestion: "*Which* residential facility?" Questionnaire items should be precise so that the respondent knows exactly what question the researcher wants answered.

Avoid Double-Barreled Questions

Frequently, researchers ask respondents for a single answer to a combination of questions. That seems to happen most often when the researcher has personally identified with a complex question. For example, you might ask respondents to agree or disagree with the statement "The state should abandon its community-based services and spend the money on improving institutional care." Although many people would unequivocally agree with the statement and others would unequivocally disagree, still others would be unable to answer. Some would want to abandon community-based services and give the money back to the taxpayers. Others would want to continue community-based services but also put more money into institutions. These latter respondents could neither agree nor disagree without misleading you.

As a general rule, whenever the word *and* appears in a question or questionnaire statement, you should check whether you are asking a **double-barreled question.** See the box titled "Double-Barreled and Beyond" for imaginative variations on this theme.

DOUBLE-BARRELED AND BEYOND

Even established, professional researchers sometimes create double-barreled questions and worse. Consider this question, asked of Americans in April 1986, at a time when America's relationship with Libya was at an especially low point. Some observers suggested the U.S. might end up in a shooting war with the North African nation. The Harris Poll sought to find out what American public opinion was.

> If Libya now increases its terrorist acts against the U.S. and we keep inflicting more damage on Libya, then inevitably it will all end in the U.S. going to war and finally invading that country, which would be wrong.

Respondents were given the opportunity of answering "Agree," "Disagree," or "Not sure." Notice the elements contained in the complex statement:

1. Will Libya increase its terrorist acts against the U.S.?

2. Will the U.S. inflict more damage on Libya?

3. Will the U.S. inevitably or otherwise go to war against Libya?

4. Would the U.S. invade Libya?

5. Would that be right or wrong?

These several elements offer the possibility of numerous points of view—far more than the three alternatives offered respondents to the survey. Even if we were to assume hypothetically that Libya would "increase its terrorist attacks" and the U.S. would "keep inflicting more damage" in return, you might have any one of at least seven distinct expectations about the outcome:

	U.S. will not go to war	War is probable but not inevitable	War is inevitable
U.S. will not invade Libya	1	2	3
U.S. will invade Libya, but it would be wrong	—	4	5
U.S. will invade Libya, and it would be right	—	6	7

The examination of prognoses about the Libyan situation is not the only example of double-barreled questions sneaking into public opinion research. Here are some statements the Harris Poll presented in an attempt to gauge American public opinion about Soviet General Secretary Gorbachev:

> He looks like the kind of Russian leader who will recognize that both the Soviets and the Americans can destroy each other with nuclear missiles so it is better to come to verifiable arms control agreements.
>
> He seems to be more modern, enlightened, and attractive, which is a good sign for the peace of the world.
>
> Even though he looks much more modern and attractive, it would be a mistake to think he will be much different from other Russian leaders.

How many elements can you identify in each of the statements? How many possible opinions could people have in each case? What does a simple "agree" or "disagree" really mean in such cases?

Source: Reported in *World Opinion Update*, October 1985 and May 1986.

Respondents Must Be Competent to Answer

In asking respondents to provide information, you should continually ask yourself whether they are able to do so reliably. In a study of child rearing, you might ask respondents to report the age at which they first talked back to their parents. Aside from the problem of defining *talking back to parents,* it is doubtful whether most respondents would remember with any degree of accuracy.

As another example, student government leaders occasionally ask their constituents to indicate the way students' fees ought to be spent. Typically, respondents are asked to indicate the percentage of available funds that should be devoted to a long list of activities. Without a fairly good knowledge of the nature of those activities and the costs involved, the respondents cannot provide meaningful answers. (Administrative costs will receive little support although they may be essential to the program as a whole.)

One group of researchers who examined the driving experience of teenagers insisted on asking an open-ended question about the number of miles driven since they received licenses. Although consultants argued that few drivers would be able to estimate such information with any accuracy, the question was asked nonetheless. In response, some teenagers reported driving hundreds of thousands of miles.

Respondents Must Be Willing to Answer

Often, we would like to learn things from people that they are unwilling to share with us. For example, Yanjie Bian indicates that it has often been difficult to get candid answers from people in China "where people are generally careful about what they say on nonprivate occasions in order to survive under authoritarianism. During the Cultural Revolution between 1966 and 1976, for example, because of the radical political agenda and political intensity throughout the country, it was almost impossible to use survey techniques to collect valid and reliable data inside China about the Chinese people's life experiences, characteristics, and attitudes towards the Communist regime" (1994:19–20).

Sometimes, American respondents may say they are undecided when, in fact, they have an opinion but think they are in a minority. Under that condition, they may be reluctant to tell a stranger (the interviewer) what that opinion is. Given this problem, the Gallup Organization, for example, has utilized a "secret ballot" format that simulates actual election conditions by giving the "voter" complete anonymity. In an analysis of the Gallup Poll election data from 1944 to 1988, Smith and Bishop (1992) found that this technique substantially reduced the percentage of respondents who said they were undecided about how they would vote.

This problem is not limited to survey research, however. Richard G. Mitchell, Jr., (1991:100) faced a similar problem in his qualitative research among American survivalists:

> Survivalists, for example, are ambivalent about concealing their identities and inclinations. They realize that secrecy protects them from the ridicule of a disbelieving majority, but enforced separatism diminishes opportunities for recruitment and information exchange. . . . "Secretive" survivalists eschew telephones, launder their mail through letter exchanges, use nicknames and aliases, and carefully conceal their addresses from strangers. Yet once I was invited to group meetings, I found them cooperative respondents.

Questions Should Be Relevant

Similarly, questions asked in a questionnaire should be relevant to most respondents. When attitudes are requested on a topic that few respondents have thought about or really care about, the results are not likely to be useful. Of course, the respondents may express attitudes even though they have never given any thought to the issue and pose the risk of misleading the researcher.

This point is illustrated occasionally when you ask for responses relating to fictitious persons and issues. In a political poll, one of your authors (Babbie) asked respondents whether they were familiar with each of 15 political figures in the community. As a methodological exercise, he made up a name: Tom Sakumoto. In response, 9 percent of the respondents said they were familiar with him. Of those respondents familiar with him, about half reported seeing him on television and reading about him in the newspapers.

When you obtain responses to fictitious issues, you can disregard those responses. But when the issue is real, you may have no way of telling which responses genuinely reflect attitudes and which reflect meaningless answers to an irrelevant question.

Short Items Are Best

In the interest of being unambiguous and precise and pointing to the relevance of an issue, the researcher is often led into long and complicated items. That should be avoided. Respondents are often unwilling to study an item to understand it. The respondent should be able to read an item quickly, understand its intent, and select or provide an answer without difficulty. In general, you should assume that respondents will read items quickly and give quick answers; therefore, you should provide clear, short items that will not be misinterpreted under those conditions.

Avoid Negative Items

The appearance of a negation in a questionnaire item paves the way for easy misinterpretation. Asked to agree or disagree with the statement "The community should not have a residential facility for the developmentally disabled," a sizable portion of the respondents will read over the word *not* and answer on that basis. Thus, some will agree with the statement when they are in favor of the facility, and others will agree when they oppose it. And you may never know which is which.

In a study of civil liberties support, respondents were asked whether they felt "the following kinds of people should be prohibited from teaching in public schools," and were presented with a list including such items as a communist, a Ku Klux Klansman, and so forth. The response categories "yes" and "no" were given beside each entry. A comparison of the responses to this item with other items that reflected support for civil liberties strongly suggested that many respondents answered "yes" to indicate willingness for such a person to teach rather than indicate that such a person should be prohibited from teaching. (A later study in the series that gave "permit" and "prohibit" as answer categories produced much clearer results.)

Avoid Biased Items and Terms

Recall from the earlier discussion of conceptualization and operationalization that none of the concepts we typically study in social science ultimately have true meaning. *Prejudice* has no ultimately correct definition, and whether a given person is prejudiced depends on our definition of that term. This same general principle applies to the responses we get from persons who complete a questionnaire.

The meaning of someone's response to a question depends in large part on the wording of the question that was asked. That is true of every question and answer. Some questions seem to encourage particular responses more than other questions. Questions that encourage respondents to answer in a particular way are called **biased.** In our discussion of the social desirability bias in Chapter 8, we noted that we need to be especially wary of this bias whenever we ask people for information. This applies to the way questionnaire items are worded. Thus, for example, in assessing the attitudes of community residents about a halfway house proposed for their neighborhood, we would not ask if residents agreed with prominent clergy in supporting the facility. Likewise, we would not ask whether they endorsed "humanitarian" proposals to care for the needy in the community.

Questions Should Be Culturally Sensitive

Some of the illustrations above about problems in asking questions pertain to issues of cultural bias and insensitivity. For example, items that are clear in one culture may not be clear in another. Respondents living in totalitarian societies might be unwilling to answer some questions that respondents in freer societies are willing to answer. Consequently, even if we find that our measurement instruments are reliable and valid when tested with one culture, we cannot assume that they will be reliable and valid when used with other cultures. Chapter 5 discussed the issue of culture competence in measurement extensively, so we won't repeat that material here. The importance of that material, however, bears reminding you of it as we discuss the topics in this chapter. Before moving on to the topic of formatting questionnaires, we'd like to call your attention to the box "Learning from Bad Examples," which illustrates problems in asking questions that we've just discussed.

QUESTIONNAIRE CONSTRUCTION

General Questionnaire Format

The format of a questionnaire is just as important as the nature and wording of the questions asked. An improperly laid out questionnaire can lead respondents to miss questions, confuse them about the nature of the data desired, and, in the worst case, lead them to

LEARNING FROM BAD EXAMPLES

by Charles Bonney, Department of Sociology, Eastern Michigan University

Here's a questionnaire I've used to train my students in some of the problems of question construction. These are questions that might be asked in order to test the hypothesis "College students from high-status family backgrounds are more tolerant toward persons suffering mental or emotional stress" (where *status* has been operationally defined as the combined relative ranking on family income, parents' educational level, and father's occupational prestige—or mother's, *if* father not present or employed). Each question has one or more flaws in it. See if you can identify these problems. (A critique of the questionnaire appears at the end of the box.)

Questionnaire

1. What is your reaction to crazy people?

____

____

2. What is your father's income?

____

3. As you were growing up, with whom were you living?

__________ both parents

__________ mother only

__________ father only

__________ other (please specify)

4. What is your father's occupation?

____

(If father is deceased, not living at home, or unemployed or retired, is your mother employed?

__________ yes __________ no)

5. Did your parents attend college?

__________ yes __________ no

6. Wouldn't you agree that people with problems should be sympathized with?

__________ yes __________ no

7. The primary etiology of heterophilic blockage is unmet dependency gratification.

__________ agree

__________ undecided

__________ disagree

8. If a friend of yours began to exhibit strange and erratic behavior, what do you think your response would be?

____

throw the questionnaire away. Both general and specific guidelines are suggested here.

As a general rule, the questionnaire should be spread out and uncluttered. Inexperienced researchers tend to fear that their questionnaire will look too long and thus squeeze several questions onto a single line, abbreviate questions, and use as few pages as possible. All these efforts are ill advised and even dangerous. Putting more than one question on a line will lead some respondents to miss the second question altogether. Some respondents will misinterpret abbreviated questions. And, more generally, respondents who find they have spent considerable time on the first page of what seemed a short questionnaire will be more demoralized than respondents who quickly completed the first several pages of what initially seemed a long form. Moreover, the latter will have made fewer errors and will not have been forced to reread confusing, abbreviated questions. Nor will they have been forced to write a long answer in a tiny space.

The desirability of spreading questions out in the questionnaire cannot be overemphasized. Squeezed-

9. Has *anyone* in your immediate family ever been institutionalized?

_________ yes _________ no

Critique

The most fundamental critique of any questionnaire is simply, "Does it get the information necessary to test the hypothesis?" While questions can be bad in and of themselves, they can be good only when seen in terms of the needs of the researcher. Good questionnaire construction is probably about as much an art as a science, and even "good" questions may contain hidden pitfalls or be made even better when the overall context is considered, but the following flaws definitely exist:

1. Derogatory and vague use of a slang term. Because it's the first question it's even worse: it may contaminate your results either by turning off some people enough to affect your response rate or it may have a "funneling effect" on later responses.

2. The operational definition of status calls for *family* income, not just father's. Also, it's been found that people are more likely to answer a question as personal as income if categories are provided for check-off, rather than this open-ended format.

3. "As you were growing up" is a vague time period. Also, the question is of dubious relevance or utility in the current format, although it *could* have been used to organize questions 2, 4, and 5.

4. The format (asking about mother's employment only if there's no employed father) may well be sexist. Although it follows the operational definition, the operational definition itself may well be sexist. There are two additional problems. First, a checklist nearly always works better for occupation—open-ended questions often get answers that are too vague to be categorized. Also, in cases where status *will* be measured by mother's occupation, the question only elicits whether or not she's employed at all.

5. Limited measure of educational levels. Also, it's double-barreled: what if one parent attended college and the other didn't?

6. "Wouldn't you agree" is leading the respondent. Also, "sympathized" and "problems" are vague.

7. Technical jargon. No one will know what it means. (In fact, *I'm* not even sure what it means, and I wrote it! As close as I can translate it, it says, "the main reason you can't get a date is because your folks ignored you.")

8. Asks for speculation regarding a vague, hypothetical situation—which is not always bad, but there's usually a better way. Note, however, that the question is not double-barreled as many have said: it asks only about behavior that is *both* "strange" and "erratic."

9. "Institutionalized" is a vague term. Many types of institutionalization would clearly be irrelevant.

together questionnaires are disastrous whether they are to be completed by the respondents themselves or administered by trained interviewers. And the processing of such questionnaires is another nightmare. We'll have more to say about this in Chapter 20.

Formats for Respondents

In one of the most common types of questionnaire items, the respondent is expected to check one response from a series. For this purpose, our experience has been that boxes adequately spaced apart are the best format. Modern word processing makes the use of boxes a practical technique these days; setting boxes in type can also be accomplished easily and neatly. You can approximate boxes by using brackets: [ ], but if you're creating a questionnaire on a computer, you should take the few extra minutes to use genuine boxes that will give your questionnaire a more professional look. Here are some easy examples:

□ ❍ ❑

1. Yes
2. No
3. Don't know

Figure 9-1 Circling the Answer

Rather than providing boxes to be checked, you might print a code number beside each response and ask the respondent to circle the appropriate number (see Figure 9-1). This method has the added advantage of specifying the code number to be entered later in the processing stage (see Chapter 20). If numbers are to be circled, however, provide clear and prominent instructions to respondents because many will be tempted to cross out the appropriate number, which makes data processing even more difficult. (Note that the technique can be used more safely when interviewers administer the questionnaires because the interviewers themselves record the responses.)

Contingency Questions

Quite often in questionnaires, certain questions will be clearly relevant only to some respondents and irrelevant to others. In a study of birth control methods, for instance, you would probably not want to ask men if they take birth control pills.

Frequently, this situation—in which the topic is relevant only to some respondents—arises when the researcher wishes to ask a series of questions about a certain topic. You may want to ask whether your respondents belong to a particular organization and, if so, how often they attend meetings, whether they have held office in the organization, and so forth. Or you might want to ask whether respondents have heard anything about a certain community issue and then learn the attitudes of those who have heard of it.

The subsequent questions in series such as these are called **contingency questions:** Whether they are to be asked and answered is contingent on responses to the first question in the series. The proper use of contingency questions can facilitate the respondents' task in completing the questionnaire because they are not faced with trying to answer questions that are irrelevant to them.

There are several formats for contingency questions. The one shown in Figure 9-2 is probably the clearest and most effective. Note two key elements in this format: (1) The contingency question is set off to the

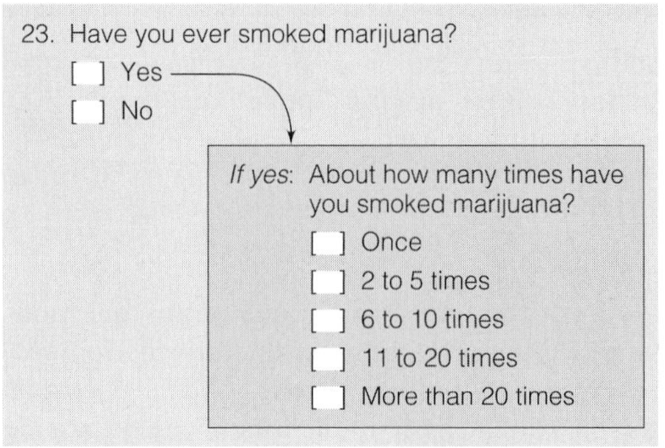

Figure 9-2 Contingency Question Format

side and enclosed in a box and thus isolated from the other questions; (2) an arrow connects the contingency question to the answer on which it is contingent. In the illustration, only respondents who answer "yes" are expected to answer the contingency question. The rest of the respondents should simply skip it.

Note that the questions in Figure 9-2 could have been dealt with by a single question: "How many times, if any, have you smoked marijuana?" The response categories, then, might have read: "Never," "Once," "2 to 5 times," and so forth. Such a single question would apply to all respondents, and each would find an appropriate answer category. Such a question, however, might put some pressure on respondents to report having smoked marijuana, because the main question asks how many times they have done so, even though it allows for those who have *never smoked marijuana even once.* (The emphasis used in the previous sentence gives a fair indication of how respondents might read the question.) The contingency question format in Figure 9-2 should reduce the subtle pressure on respondents to report having smoked marijuana.

The foregoing discussion shows how seemingly theoretical issues of *validity* and *reliability* are involved in so mundane a matter as putting questions on a piece of paper. Used properly, this technique allows you to construct some rather complex sets of contingency questions without confusing the respondent. Figure 9-3 illustrates a more complicated example.

Sometimes a set of contingency questions is long enough to extend over several pages. Suppose you are studying the voting behaviors of poor people, and you wish to ask a large number of questions of individuals who had voted in a national, state, or local election. You could separate out the relevant respondents

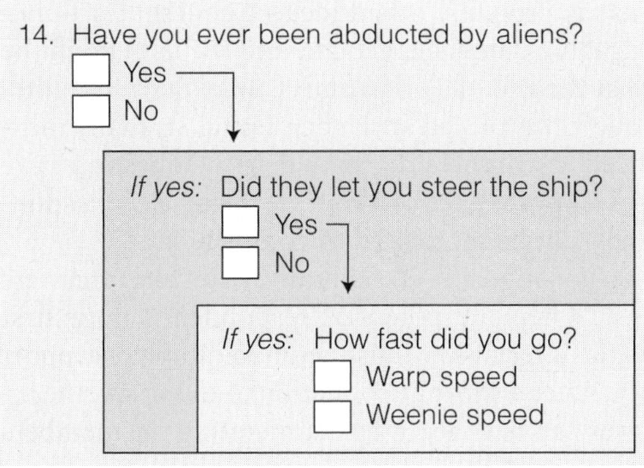

14. Have you ever been abducted by aliens?
☐ Yes
☐ No

If yes: Did they let you steer the ship?
☐ Yes
☐ No

If yes: How fast did you go?
☐ Warp speed
☐ Weenie speed

Figure 9-3 Contingency Table

13. Have you ever voted in a national, state, or local election?
[ ] Yes (Please answer questions 14–25.)
[ ] No (Please skip questions 14–25. Go directly to question 26 on page 8.)

Figure 9-4 Instructions to Skip

with an initial question such as "Have you ever voted in a national, state, or local election?" but it would be confusing to place the contingency questions in a box that stretched over several pages. It would make more sense to enter instructions in parentheses after each answer, telling respondents to answer or skip the contingency questions. Figure 9-4 illustrates this method.

In addition to these instructions, it would be worthwhile to place an instruction at the top of each page that contains only the contingency questions. For example, you might say, "This page is only for respondents who have voted in a national, state, or local election." Clear instructions such as these spare respondents the frustration of reading and puzzling over questions that are irrelevant to them and also decrease the chance of getting responses from those for whom the questions are not relevant.

Matrix Questions

Quite often, you'll want to ask several questions that have the same set of answer categories. This is typically the case whenever the Likert response categories are used. In such cases, it's often possible to construct a matrix of items and answers as illustrated in Figure 9-5.

17. Beside *each* of the statements presented below, please indicate whether you Strongly Agree (SA), Agree (A), Disagree (D), Strongly Disagree (SD), or are Undecided (U).

	SA	A	D	SD	U
a. What this country needs is more law and order.	[ ]	[ ]	[ ]	[ ]	[ ]
b. The police should be disarmed in America.	[ ]	[ ]	[ ]	[ ]	[ ]
c. During riots, looters should be shot on sight.	[ ]	[ ]	[ ]	[ ]	[ ]
etc.					

Figure 9-5 Matrix Question Format

This format has at least three advantages. First, it uses space efficiently. Second, respondents will probably be able to complete a set of questions presented this way more quickly. Third, the format may increase the comparability of responses given to different questions for the respondent as well as for the researcher. Because respondents can quickly review their answers to earlier items in the set, they might choose between, say, "strongly agree" and "agree" on a given statement by comparing their strength of agreement with their earlier responses in the set.

The format also presents some dangers, however. Its advantages may encourage you to structure an item so that the responses fit into the matrix format when a different, more idiosyncratic, set of responses might be more appropriate. Also, the matrix question format can foster a response set among some respondents: They may develop a pattern, for example, of agreeing with all of the statements. That would be especially likely if the set of statements began with several that indicated a particular orientation (for example, a liberal political perspective) with only a few later statements representing a different orientation. Respondents might assume that all the statements represented the same orientation and, reading quickly, misread some of them, thereby giving the wrong answers. In Chapter 8 we referred briefly to this problem as the *acquiescent response set*. This problem can be reduced somewhat by interspersing positively and negatively worded statements to represent different orientations and by making all statements short and clear. For instance, in Chapter 8 we noted that the CAM scale handled this problem by interspersing items such as "I resent my mother" and "I hate my mother" with items such as "I really enjoy my mother" and "I feel proud of my mother."

Ordering Questions in a Questionnaire

The *order* in which questions are asked can also affect the answers given. First, the appearance of one question can affect the answers given to later ones. For example, if several questions have been asked about the dangers of terrorism to the United States and then a question asks respondents to volunteer (open-ended) what they believe to represent problems facing the United States, terrorism will receive more citations than would otherwise be the case. In this situation, it is preferable to ask the open-ended question first.

If respondents are asked to assess their overall religiosity ("How important is your religion to you in general?"), their responses to later questions about specific aspects of religiosity will be aimed at consistency with the prior assessment. The converse would be true as well. If respondents are first asked specific questions about different aspects of their religiosity, their subsequent overall assessment will reflect the earlier answers.

Some researchers attempt to overcome this effect by randomizing the order of questions. This is usually a futile effort. To begin, a randomized set of questions will probably strike respondents as chaotic and worthless. It will be difficult to answer, moreover, because they must continually switch their attention from one topic to another. And, finally, even in a randomized ordering of questions the appearance of one question can affect the answers given to later ones—except that you will have no control over this effect.

The safest solution is sensitivity to the problem. Although you cannot avoid the effect of question order, you should attempt to estimate the resulting effect and thus be able to interpret results in a meaningful fashion. If the question order seems especially important in a given study, then you might construct more than one version of the questionnaire with different possible ordering of questions. You would then be able to determine the effects. At the very least, you should pretest the different forms of your questionnaire.

The desired ordering of questions differs somewhat between self-administered questionnaires and interviews. In the former, it might be best to begin the questionnaire with the most interesting set of questions. The potential respondents who glance casually over the first few questions should want to answer them. Perhaps the questions will ask for attitudes that they are aching to express. At the same time, however, the initial questions should not be threatening. (Beginning with questions about sexual behavior or drug use is probably a bad idea.) Requests for duller demographic data (age, gender, and the like) might be placed at the end of a self-administered questionnaire. Such questions placed at the beginning, as many inexperienced researchers do, may give the questionnaire the initial appearance of a routine form, and a respondent may not be motivated to complete it.

Just the opposite is generally true for interview surveys. When the potential respondent's door first opens, the interviewer must begin to establish rapport quickly. After a short introduction to the study, the interviewer can best begin by enumerating the members of the household, getting demographic data about each. Such questions are easily answered and are generally nonthreatening. Once the initial rapport has been established, the interviewer can move into the area of attitudes and more sensitive matters. An interview that began with the question "Do you believe in God?" would probably end rather quickly.

The impact of item order is not uniform. When J. Edwin Benton and John Daly (1991) conducted a local government survey, they found that respondents with less education were more influenced by the order of questionnaire items than were those with more education. In another study, Robert Greene, Katrina Murphy, and Shelita Snyder (2000) tested alternate versions of a mailed questionnaire: one with items requesting demographic data at the end, and another with those items at the beginning. Their results questioned the conventional wisdom, which we mentioned above, that such items are best placed at the end of self-administered questionnaires.

Questionnaire Instructions

Every questionnaire, whether it is to be completed by respondents or administered by interviewers, should contain clear instructions and introductory comments where appropriate.

It is useful to begin every self-administered questionnaire with basic instructions to be followed in completing it. Although many people these days are familiar with forms and questionnaires, you should begin by telling them exactly what you want: that they are to indicate their answers to certain questions by placing a check mark or an X in the box beside the appropriate answer or by writing in their answer when asked to do so. If many open-ended questions are used, respondents should be given some guidance about whether brief or lengthy answers are expected. If you wish to encourage your respondents to elaborate on their responses to closed-ended questions, that should be noted.

If a questionnaire is arranged into content subsections—political attitudes, religious attitudes, background data—introduce each section with a short statement about its content and purpose. For example, "In this section, we would like to know what people around here consider the most important community problems." Demographic items at the end of a self-administered questionnaire might be introduced thusly: "Finally, we would like to know just a little about you so we can see how different types of people feel about the issues we have been examining."

Short introductions such as these help make sense out of the questionnaire for the respondent. They make the questionnaire seem less chaotic, especially when it taps a variety of data. And they help put the respondent in the proper frame of mind for answering the questions.

Some questions may require special instructions to facilitate proper answering. That is especially true if a given question varies from the general instructions that pertain to the whole questionnaire. Specific examples will illustrate this situation.

Despite the desirability of mutually exclusive answer categories in closed-ended questions, more than one answer may often apply for respondents. If you want a single answer, then make this clear in the question. An example would be, "From the list below, please check the *primary reason* for your decision to attend college." Often the main question can be followed by a parenthetical note: "Please check the one best answer." If, on the other hand, you want the respondent to check as many answers as apply, that should be made clear as well.

When a set of answer categories are to be rank-ordered by the respondent, then the instructions should indicate as much, and a different type of answer format should be used (for example, blank spaces instead of boxes). These instructions should indicate how many answers are to be ranked (for example, all, first and second, first and last, most important and least important) and the order of ranking (for instance, "Place a 1 beside the most important, a 2 beside the next most important, and so forth"). Rank-ordering their responses is often difficult for respondents, however, because they may have to read and reread the list several times, so this technique should only be used when no other method will produce the desired result. And if it is used, the list of answer categories to be ranked should be relatively short. Ranking approximately 10 or more categories, for example, may be too difficult for many respondents.

In multiple-part matrix questions, it is helpful to give special instructions unless the same format is used throughout the questionnaire. Sometimes respondents will be expected to check one answer in each *column* of the matrix, and in other questionnaires they will be expected to check one answer in each *row*. Whenever the questionnaire contains both types, add an instruction to clarify which is expected in each case.

Pretesting the Questionnaire

No matter how carefully researchers design a data-collection instrument such as a questionnaire, there is always the possibility—indeed the certainty—of error. They will always make some mistake: an ambiguous question, a question that people cannot answer, or some other violation of the rules just discussed.

To guard against such errors, pretest the questionnaire in a dry run (as we mentioned in Chapter 8). The pretest sample can be small—perhaps 10 people or less. They should be like the people you intend to include in your study. They need not be a randomly selected sample; you can use your judgment in selecting people whom you think are like those who will participate in your actual study. The ones who participate in the pretest, however, should *not* later participate in the actual study.

When pretesting your instrument, by and large it's better to ask people to complete the questionnaire than to read through it looking for errors. All too often, a question seems to make sense on a first reading but proves impossible to answer.

Stanley Presser and Johnny Blair (1994) describe several different pretesting strategies and report on the effectiveness of each. They also provide data on the cost of the various methods. There are many more tips and guidelines for questionnaire construction, but covering them all would take a book in itself. Now we'll complete this discussion with an illustration of a real questionnaire, showing how some of these comments find substance in practice.

Before turning to the illustration, however, we want to mention a critical aspect of questionnaire design that we discuss in Chapter 20: precoding. Because the information collected by questionnaires is typically transformed into some type of computer format, it's usually appropriate to include data-processing instructions on the questionnaire itself. These instructions indicate where specific pieces of information will be stored in the machine-readable data files. In Chapter 20, we'll discuss the nature of such storage and point out appropriate questionnaire notations. As a preview, however, notice that the following illustration has been precoded with the mysterious numbers that appear near questions and answer categories.

A Composite Illustration

Figure 9-6 is part of a questionnaire used by the University of Chicago's National Opinion Research Center in its General Social Survey. The questionnaire deals with people's attitudes toward the government and is designed to be self-administered.

10. Here are some things the government might do for the economy. Circle one number for each action to show whether you are in favor of it or against it.

1. Strongly in favor of
2. In favor of
3. Neither in favor of nor against
4. Against
5. Strongly against

	PLEASE CIRCLE A NUMBER					
a. Control of wages by legislation	1	2	3	4	5	28/
b. Control of prices by legislation	1	2	3	4	5	29/
c. Cuts in government spending	1	2	3	4	5	30/
d. Government financing of projects to create new jobs	1	2	3	4	5	31/
e. Less government regulation of business	1	2	3	4	5	32/
f. Support for industry to develop new products and technology	1	2	3	4	5	33/
g. Supporting declining industries to protect jobs	1	2	3	4	5	34/
h. Reducing the work week to create more jobs	1	2	3	4	5	35/

11. Listed below are various areas of government spending. Please indicate whether you would like to see more or less government spending in each area. Remember that if you say "much more," it might require a tax increase to pay for it.

1. Spend much more
2. Spend more
3. Spend the same as now
4. Spend less
5. Spend much less
8. Can't choose

	PLEASE CIRCLE A NUMBER						
a. The environment	1	2	3	4	5	8	36/
b. Health	1	2	3	4	5	8	37/
c. The police and law enforcement	1	2	3	4	5	8	38/
d. Education	1	2	3	4	5	8	39/
e. The military and defense	1	2	3	4	5	8	40/
f. Retirement benefits	1	2	3	4	5	8	41/
g. Unemployment benefits	1	2	3	4	5	8	42/
h. Culture and the arts	1	2	3	4	5	8	43/

12. If the government *had* to choose between keeping down inflation or keeping down unemployment, to which do you think it should give highest priority?

Keeping down inflation	1	44/
Keeping down unemployment	2	
Can't choose	8	

Figure 9-6 A Sample Questionnaire

13. Do you think that labor unions in this country have too much power or too little power?

Far too much power	1	45/
Too much power	2	
About the right amount of power	3	
Too little power	4	
Far too little power	5	
Can't choose	8	

14. How about business and industry, do they have too much power or too little power?

Far too much power	1	46/
Too much power	2	
About the right amount of power	3	
Too little power	4	
Far too little power	5	
Can't choose	8	

15. And what about the federal government, does it have too much power or too little power?

Far too much power	1	47/
Too much power	2	
About the right amount of power	3	
Too little power	4	
Far too little power	5	
Can't choose	8	

16. In general, how good would you say labor unions are for the country as a whole?

Excellent	1	48/
Very good	2	
Fairly good	3	
Not very good	4	
Not good at all	5	
Can't choose	8	

17. What do you think the government's role in each of these industries should be?

1. Own it
2. Control prices and profits but not own it
3. Neither own it nor control its prices and profits
8. Can't choose

	PLEASE CIRCLE A NUMBER					
a. Electric power	1	2	3	4	8	49/
b. The steel industry	1	2	3	4	8	50/
c. Banking and insurance	1	2	3	4	8	51/

18. On the whole, do you think it should or should not be the government's responsibility to . . .

1. Definitely should be
2. Probably should be
3. Probably should not be
4. Definitely should not be
8. Can't choose

	PLEASE CIRCLE A NUMBER					
a. Provide a job for everyone who wants one	1	2	3	4	8	52/
b. Keep prices under control	1	2	3	4	8	53/
c. Provide health care for the sick	1	2	3	4	8	54/
d. Provide a decent standard of living for the old	1	2	3	4	8	55/
e. Provide industry with the help it needs to grow	1	2	3	4	8	56/

Figure 9-6 *(continued)*

f.	Provide a decent standard of living for the unemployed	1	2	3	4	8	57/
g.	Reduce income differences between the rich and poor	1	2	3	4	8	58/
h.	Give financial assistance to college students from low-income families	1	2	3	4	8	59/
i.	Provide decent housing for those who can't afford it	1	2	3	4	8	60/

19. How interested would you say you personally are in politics?

Very interested	1	61/
Fairly interested	2	
Somewhat interested	3	
Not very interested	4	
Not at all interested	5	
Can't choose	8	

20. Here are some other areas of government spending. Please indicate whether you would like to see more or less government spending in each area. Remember that if you say "much more," it might require a tax increase to pay for it.

> 1. Spend much more
> 2. Spend more
> 3. Spend the same as now
> 4. Spend less
> 5. Spend much less
> 8. Can't choose

PLEASE CIRCLE A NUMBER

a.	Prenatal care for pregnant mothers who can't afford it	1	2	3	4	5	8	62/
b.	Health care for children whose families don't have insurance	1	2	3	4	5	8	63/
c.	Preschool programs like Head Start for poor children	1	2	3	4	5	8	64/
d.	Child care for poor children	1	2	3	4	5	8	65/
e.	Child care for all children with working parents	1	2	3	4	5	8	66/
f.	Housing for poor families with children	1	2	3	4	5	8	67/
g.	Services for disabled and chronically ill children	1	2	3	4	5	8	68/
h.	Drug abuse prevention and treatment for children and youth	1	2	3	4	5	8	69/
i.	Nutrition programs for poor children and families, such as food stamps and school lunches	1	2	3	4	5	8	70/
j.	Contraceptive services for teenagers	1	2	3	4	5	8	71/

THANK YOU VERY MUCH FOR COMPLETING THE QUESTIONNAIRE

Figure 9-6 *(continued)*

CONSTRUCTING COMPOSITE MEASURES

Some variables are too complex or multifaceted to be measured with just one item on a questionnaire. These variables are composites of various indicators, and accordingly they require composite or cumulative measures that combine several empirical indicators of the referent variable into a single measure. Examples of complex variables that social work researchers may find difficult to tap adequately with a single questionnaire item are marital satisfaction, level of social functioning, level of client satisfaction with services, practitioner attitudes about working with various target populations, quality of life, and attitudes about women or minorities. (In Chapter 7 we discussed how you might go about locating existing composite measures, and information about their reliability and validity, from published material.)

The composite or cumulative measures of complex variables are called **scales** or *indexes*. These two terms typically are used interchangeably in social research literature, although the construction of scales ideally is supposed to involve more rigor. For the purposes of this text, we'll use the terms interchangeably, and we'll refer mainly to scales, since that term is more commonly used in social work research. Indexes and scales allow us to represent complex variables with scores that provide greater potential for variance than would a single item. Analyzing one score derived from multiple items is also more efficient than analyzing each item separately.

Consider, for example, the CAM scale we examined in Chapter 8. Instead of analyzing 25 responses of 1 to 5 that deal with different facets of children's attitudes toward their mothers, we are able to sum all 25 responses and obtain one score that ranges from 25 to 125 to represent that multifaceted variable.

Indexes and scales typically provide ordinal measures of variables. In other words, they rank-order people (or other units of analysis) in terms of specific variables such as attitude toward mother, social functioning, and the like. That rank order is determined by the overall score that combines all of the scale's items.

Item Selection

The first step in constructing a scale is *item selection*. To begin, naturally, items should have *face validity*. If you want to measure self-esteem, for example, each item should appear *on its face* to indicate some aspect of self-esteem. You might conceive of concepts related to self-esteem, such as depression, but your self-esteem scale should include items that only reflect self-esteem, not items that reflect depression. Thus, if you are measuring self-esteem, you would not ask people if they feel lonely or blue just because you think that depression is related to self-esteem. Instead, you would reserve that question for a scale that measures depression and restrict the self-esteem scale to items that pertain to the favorability of one's self-image. (You might have items that ask people whether they feel they are smart, attractive, likable, competent, trustworthy, and so on.) This is known as *unidimensionality* in scale construction.

Items should also have adequate *variance*. If everyone gives the same response to a particular item, then that item would have no use in constructing a scale. Suppose, for example, that on a scale that attempts to measure parental child-rearing attitudes, no parents admitted to wanting to sexually abuse their children. That item would not be useful in distinguishing parents who are more likely to be abusive from those who are less likely. To find out whether items have adequate variance, you would pretest the scale and then examine the range of responses to each item.

Ultimately, which items you select for a scale should depend on how those items influence the scale's *reliability* and *validity*, which are determined by using procedures discussed in the last chapter. Items that have no relationship with other items on the same scale, or with an external criterion of the validity of the scale, should be discarded or modified.

Handling Missing Data

In virtually every study that uses indexes and scales, some respondents fail to respond to some items. Sometimes they may just leave the item blank; at other times they may choose a "don't know" response. There are several ways to deal with this problem of missing data.

First, if all but a few respondents respond to every item, you may decide to exclude from the analysis the data from those few respondents whose index or scale contains some missing data. But this should not be done if it looks as if it might bias your remaining sample, such as by excluding most of the people who share a particular characteristic.

Second, you may sometimes have grounds for treating missing data as one available response. For instance, if a questionnaire has asked respondents to indicate their participation in a number of activities by checking "yes" or "no" for each, many respondents may have checked some of the activities "yes" and left the remainder blank. In such a case, you might decide that a failure to answer meant "no" and score missing data in this case as though the respondents had checked the "no" space.

Third, a careful analysis of missing data may yield an interpretation of their meaning. In constructing a measure of political conservatism, for example, you may discover that respondents who failed to answer a given question were generally as conservative on other items as those who gave the conservative answer. As another example, a study that measured religious beliefs found that people who answered "don't know" about a given belief were almost identical to the "disbelievers" in their answers about other beliefs. (*Note*: You should not take these examples as empirical guides in your own studies; they only suggest ways you might analyze your own data.) Whenever the analysis of missing data yields such interpretations, then, you may decide to score such cases accordingly.

You can handle this problem in other ways. If an item has several possible values, you might assign the middle value to cases with missing data—for example, you could assign a 2 if the values are 0, 1, 2, 3, and 4. For a continuous variable such as age, you could similarly assign the mean to cases with missing data. Or missing data can be supplied by assigning values at random. All of these are conservative solutions: They work against any relationships you may expect to find.

If you're creating an index out of several items, it sometimes works to handle missing data by using proportions based on what is observed. Suppose your index is composed of six indicators of an agency's cultural competence, in which each agency is given one point for each of six culturally competent features that it has. Suppose that for one agency you have information on only four of the indicators and do not know whether or not it has the other two features of cultural competence. If the agency has earned 4 points out of a possible 4 on the other 4 indicators, then you might assign that agency an index score of 6; if the agency has 2 points (half the possible score on four indicators), you could assign a score of 3 (half the possible score on six indicators).

The choice of a particular method to use depends so much on the research situation as to preclude the suggestion of a single "best" method or a ranking of the several we have described. Excluding all cases with missing data can bias the representativeness of the findings, but including such cases by assigning scores to missing data can influence the nature of the findings. The safest and best method would be to construct the scale or index using alternative methods and see whether the same findings follow from each. Understanding your data is the final goal of analysis anyway.

SOME PROMINENT SCALING PROCEDURES

As you might imagine from the lengthy list of reference volumes for existing scales we presented in Figure 7-3, scales can come in a seemingly endless variety of formats. Some scaling procedures are highly complex and require a tremendous expenditure of labor to develop. Because of the time and expense involved, some scaling formats that historically have been highly regarded by social scientists, such as Guttman scaling and Thurstone scaling, are rarely used these days by social work researchers who must operate within the constraints of more limited budgets and time restrictions. Less complex scales can be as simple as one-item scales that may have minimal wording and can be administered in a conversational format. For example, if you want to assess the moods of very young children (perhaps before and after receiving some form of treatment such as play therapy), you might present them with a handful of simple cartoonish faces, with a smiley face at one end of the continuum and a frowning, sad face at the other end. You would then ask them to select the face that best fit how they were feeling. Or you might assess how well your adult clients were responding to your intervention for anxiety by asking them to rate their anxiety on a scale from 1 to 10, with 1 representing no anxiety and 10 representing the worst anxiety imaginable.

Likert Scaling

Not all highly regarded scaling formats are extraordinarily expensive. The term **Likert scale**, for example, is associated with a question format that is frequently used in contemporary survey questionnaires. Basically, the respondent is presented with a *statement* in the questionnaire and then asked to indicate whether he or she "strongly agrees," "agrees," "disagrees," "strongly disagrees," or is "undecided." Modifications of the wording of the response categories (for example, "approve") may be used, of course.

The particular value of this format is the unambiguous *ordinality* of response categories. If respondents were permitted to volunteer or select such answers as "sort of agree," "pretty much agree," "really agree," and so forth, the researcher would find it impossible to judge the relative strength of agreement intended by the various respondents. The Likert format resolves this dilemma.

The Likert format also lends itself to a straightforward method of scale or index construction. Because identical response categories are used for several items that intend to measure a given variable, each such item can be scored in a uniform manner. With five response categories, scores of 0 to 4 or 1 to 5 might be assigned, taking the direction of the items into account (for instance, assign a score of 5 to "strongly agree" for positive items and to "strongly disagree"

	Very Much	Somewhat	Neither	Somewhat	Very Much	
Interesting	☐	☐	☐	☐	☐	Boring
Simple	☐	☐	☐	☐	☐	Complex
Uncaring	☐	☐	☐	☐	☐	Caring
Useful	☐	☐	☐	☐	☐	Useless
			etc.			

Figure 9-7 Semantic Differential

for negative items). Each respondent would then be assigned an overall score that represents the summation of the scores he or she received for responses to the individual items.

The Likert method is based on this assumption: An overall score based on responses to the many items that reflect a particular variable under consideration provides a reasonably good measure of the variable. These overall scores are not the final product of index or scale construction; rather, they are used in an *item analysis* to select the *best* items. Essentially, each item is correlated with the large, composite measure. Items that correlate most highly with the composite measure are assumed to provide the best indicators of the variable, and only those items would be included in the scale that is ultimately used for analyses of the variable.

Note that the uniform scoring allowed by Likert-type response categories assumes that each item has about the same *intensity* as the rest. You should also realize that the Likert format can be used in a variety of ways (such as by having fewer or more response categories or by using continuums from strongly approve to strongly disapprove, very satisfied to very dissatisfied, and so on instead of strongly agree to strongly disagree) and that you are not bound to the method described. Such items can be combined with other types of items in the construction of simple scales. However, if all of the items being considered for inclusion in a composite measure are in the Likert format, then you should consider the method we have described.

Semantic Differential

As we've seen, Likert-type items ask respondents to agree or disagree with a particular position. The **semantic differential** format asks them to choose between two opposite positions. Here's how it works.

Suppose we are conducting an experiment to evaluate the effectiveness of this book on readers' appreciation of social work research. Let's say that we have created experimental and control groups as will be described in Chapter 11. Now we have the study participants report their feelings about social work research. A good way to tap those feelings would be to use a semantic differential format.

To begin, you must determine the *dimensions* along which each selection should be judged by participants. Then you need to find two *opposite* terms to represent the polar extremes along each dimension. Let's suppose one dimension that interests you is simply whether participants are interested in research. Two opposite terms in this case could be "interesting" and "boring." Similarly, we might want to know whether they regarded research as "complex" or "simple," "caring" or "uncaring," and so forth.

Once we have determined the relevant dimensions and have found terms to represent the extremes of each, we might prepare a rating sheet to be completed by each participant. Figure 9-7 shows an example of what it might look like.

On each line of the rating sheet, the participant would indicate how he or she felt about social work research: whether it was interesting or boring, for instance, and whether it was "somewhat" that way or "very much" so. To avoid creating a biased pattern of responses to such items, it's a good idea to vary the placement of terms that are likely to be related to each other. Notice, for example, that "uncaring" and "useful" are on the left side of the sheet and "caring" and "useless" are on the right side. It's highly likely that those who select "uncaring" would also choose "useless" as opposed to "useful."

CONSTRUCTING QUALITATIVE MEASURES

Although much of the material in this chapter so far has been about quantitative measurement instruments, such as self-administered questionnaires and scales, constructing measurement instruments is also relevant to qualitative research methods. For example, earlier in this chapter, we discussed guidelines for asking questions that are just as applicable to gathering information from respondents in qualitative studies as they are in quantitative studies. In either type of study, for instance, one should avoid wording that is biased, too complex, or irrelevant to respondents.

At this point, however, we will examine some of the ways that instrument construction is different in qualitative measurement than in quantitative measurement. Let's begin by noting that, like quantitative research, qualitative research often involves gathering data by directly observing people in addition to asking them questions. In this chapter, we are limiting the discussion to measures for asking people questions, not instruments used for recording direct observations. The latter types of instruments will be discussed in later chapters.

The chief difference between quantitative and qualitative measures for asking people questions is that quantitative measures are always highly structured, tend to use closed-ended questions primarily, and may be administered in either an interview or questionnaire format, whereas qualitative measures rely on interviews that are often unstructured and that mainly contain open-ended questions with in-depth probes. In Chapter 18, we will discuss qualitative interviewing in greater detail; here we merely want to illustrate how its measures contrast with quantitative measures.

Qualitative interviews can range from completely unstructured, informal conversational interviews that use no measurement instruments to highly structured, standardized interviews in which interviewers must ask questions in the exact order and with the exact wording in which they are written in advance. Between these two extremes are semistructured interviews that use interview guides that list in outline form the topics and issues the interview should ask about, but which allow the interviewer to be flexible, informal, and conversational and to adapt the style of the interview and the sequencing and wording of questions to each particular interviewee.

Figure 9-8 presents excerpts from an exemplary, highly structured, standardized open-ended interview schedule that has been used in a qualitative study of openness in adoption conducted by Ruth McRoy and Harold Grotevant. Their entire schedule consists of 179 items. We think that the 46 items we have excerpted for Figure 9-8 sufficiently illustrate a superbly crafted standardized interview schedule and some of the points we made about constructing measurement instruments that apply to both quantitative and qualitative research. Notice, for example, the openendedness, neutrality, and logical arrangement and sequencing of the questions. Notice also where and how the schedule systematically instructs interviewers to probe for detail and clarification and how it provides parenthetical details to help interviewers clarify the point of the question for respondents who may initially have difficulty in answering. We'd also like you to notice its use of contingency questions. Finally, we suggest you compare this schedule with the questionnaire presented in Figure 9-6 to see the contrast between quantitative and qualitative inquiry in the way questions are asked and the much greater opportunity afforded by qualitative inquiry to probe for in-depth meanings and subjective perspectives.

How might the McRoy–Grotevant instrument have appeared had it been in the form of an interview guide for a semistructured interview? Perhaps it would have been a brief outline of questions to ask about, such as the following one, which we have imagined based on some of the excerpts in Figure 9-8:

I. Background regarding adoption
   A. Prior expectations? Counseling?
   B. Adoption process? How it felt?
   C. Discussions with child? Relatives?
   D. Characteristics of child? Similarities and dissimilarities with parents?
   E. Anticipation of life changes and how prepared for?

II. Knowledge about degrees of openness in adoption
   A. Understandings of meanings and options before adoption?
   B. Advantages and disadvantages of each option anticipated?

III. Type of adoption chosen and issues
   A. How discussed and dealt with in family?
   B. Problems? Discomfort discussing? Manipulation? Other siblings?

IV. Issues involving birth parents
   A. Impact of communications on child? On parents? On birth parents? On other children?

McRoy/Grotevant Adoption Research
School of Social Work
2609 University Ave.
University of Texas at Austin
Austin, TX 78712

Code #: __ __ __ __ - __ - __ __
Interviewer: ______________
Date: ______________

ADOPTIVE PARENT INTERVIEW

Begin the interview process by reviewing with the parent the number of adopted children s/he has, their names and ages.

BACKGROUND REGARDING ADOPTION

1. Could you begin by telling me a little bit about why you decided to adopt?

2. Whom did you talk to about adoption before you reached your decision?
   What advice did you receive?

3. What did you expect the adoption process to be like?

4. Please explain the process you went through to adopt ______________.

5. How did you feel going through the process?

.
.
.

11. Do any of your friends have adopted children?
    (Probe: How have they and their experiences influenced your feelings?)

.
.
.

32. When did you tell ______________ (child) s/he was adopted?

33. Have you had any problems since your adoption?

34. How old were you when ______________ (child) was adopted?

35. How did your relatives react to your decision to adopt?

36. In what ways is ______________ (child) like you (temperament, appearance)?

37. In what ways is ______________ (child) dissimilar to you (temperament, appearance)?

38. Did you anticipate that the arrival of ______________ (child) would mean making changes in your life style?
    If so, what changes did you anticipate?

Figure 9-8 Standardized Open-Ended Interview Schedule

39. How did you and your spouse prepare for the arrival of ______________________ (child)? (e.g., reading, talking with each other or to others, preparing siblings, etc.)

40. Did you and your spouse talk about how your relationship might change?
    How did you plan to handle the changes?
    How did your relationship *actually* change after the adoption of your child?

41. Please describe the time around the arrival of ______________________ in your family.
    How would you describe ______________________'s early behavior (Probe: pleasant, easy, fussy, difficult, etc.)?
    What were some of the satisfactions and problems you encountered in the first 3 years?
    What was your relationship like with ______________________ during those early years? (Probe for specific events and behaviors rather than global evaluations.)

KNOWLEDGE ABOUT DEGREES OF OPENNESS IN ADOPTION

42. What options did your adoption agency offer regarding open or closed adoptions (non-identifying information, photos of birthparents, continued sharing of information, meeting parents, ongoing contact, etc.)?

43. Had you heard of open adoptions before you came to ______________________ (agency)?

44. If so, what did you think the term meant?

45. What does the term "semi-open adoption" mean to you?

46. What does the term "traditional or closed adoption" mean to you?

47. Describe the process you went through before deciding what form of openness you would choose.

48. What option did you choose?

49. Why did you choose this option?

50. What do you see as the advantages and the disadvantages of:
    a. traditional "closed" adoption

    b. semi-open adoption

    c. open adoption

IF FAMILY CHOSE A TRADITIONAL (CLOSED) ADOPTION, CONTINUE DIRECTLY ON TO THE *PINK* SECTION, PAGES *6–7*.

Figure 9-8 *(continued)*

IF FAMILY CHOSE TO SHARE INFORMATION ONLY, NOW GO TO THE *GREEN* SECTION, PAGES *8–9.*

IF FAMILY CHOSE TO MEET THE BIRTHPARENTS, NOW GO TO THE *YELLOW* SECTION, PAGES *10–11.*

IF FAMILY RESPONDENT CHOSE TO HAVE ONGOING FACE TO FACE CONTACT, NOW GO TO THE *BLUE* SECTION, PAGES *12–14.*

IF FAMILY INITIALLY CHOSE SEMI-OPEN AND LATER CHANGED TO FULLY DISCLOSED, NOW GO TO THE *ORANGE* SECTION, PAGES *15–18.*

IF FAMILY CHOSE CONFIDENTIAL (CLOSED) ADOPTION [This section appears on pink paper]

51. How do you plan to talk with your child about adoption? (Or, for older children, How have you talked with your child about adoption?)
    a. Now?
    b. In middle childhood?
    c. In adolescence?

52. Does ________________ (child) know what "birthmother" means?

53. What does ________________ (child) call his/her birthmother?

54. What does ________________ (child) call his/her birthfather?

55. How do you feel about this?

56. Does ________________ (child) like to talk about his/her adoption?
    Does s/he initiate conversations with you about it?

57. Does ________________________ (child) ever try to use his/her adoption as a lever to get his/her way? If so, please describe.

58. If there are other siblings in the household, do they ever try to use ________________ (child's) adoption against him/her? If so, please describe.

.
.
.

IF FAMILY CHOSE TO SHARE INFORMATION ONLY. . . . [This section appears on green paper]

.
.
.

Figure 9-8 *(continued)*

72. How do you feel after you have received a letter, picture, gift, etc. from the birthparents?

.
.
.

75. What impact do you think sharing information will have on:
    a. your child?

    b. you and your spouse?

    c. on birthparents?

    d. on other children in the family (if applicable)?

.
.
.

IF FAMILY CHOSE TO MEET BIRTHPARENTS . . . . [This section appears on yellow paper]

82. Describe the circumstances of your *FIRST* meeting. Did it occur at placement or later?

.
.
.

84. How did you feel about the birthparents? Has that feeling changed since then? If so how?

.
.
.

87. How do you think the birthparents felt about you?

.
.
.

IF FAMILY CHOSE TO HAVE ONGOING CONTACT . . . . [This section appears on blue paper]

.
.
.

106. Do you plan to have continued contact? (Why or why not?)

.
.
.

111. How would you describe your relationship with the birthparent(s)? (Probe: as a relative, friend, etc.)

.
.
.

117. How do you feel after a visit? Have your feelings changed over time?

.
.
.

IF FAMILY INITIALLY CHOSE A LESS OPEN OPTION AND LATER CHANGED TO A MORE OPEN OPTION . . . . [This section appears on orange paper]

.
.
.

Figure 9-8 *(continued)*

```
136. Describe the changes that took place.

137. How did you feel about the decision to change?
     .
     .
     .
166. What is the most satisfying aspect of your relationship with
     your child's birthmother?

167. What is the most difficult aspect of your relationship with your
     child's birthmother?
     .
     .
     .
179. We've talked about quite a few things, but I wonder if there
     might be something that we have skipped which you might feel to
     be important to understanding you and your family. Is there any-
     thing that you would like to add to what we have discussed?
```

Figure 9-8 (*continued*)

A COMPARISON OF QUANTITATIVE AND QUALITATIVE APPROACHES TO ASKING PEOPLE QUESTIONS

	Quantitative Approaches	Qualitative Approaches
Similarities in Measurement Principles		
Try to use language that respondents will understand	always	always
Ask one question at a time; avoid double-barreled questions	always	always
Only ask questions that respondents are capable of answering and that are relevant to them	always	always
Avoid biased items and terms	always	always
Stylistic Differences		
Questionnaires or scales	often	rarely
Interviews	sometimes	usually
Same wording and sequence of questions for all respondents	always	rarely
Interviewer flexibility regarding wording, sequencing, and conversational style	never	very often
Open-ended questions	rarely	usually

(*continued*)

	Quantitative Approaches	Qualitative Approaches
Probes	rare and brief	frequent and in-depth
Closed-ended questions	usually	sometimes
Formality of interview	Relaxed, friendly demeanor, but professional tone and not overly casual	More likely to resemble a spontaneous, informal, friendly conversation
Complementary Functions		
Objectivity and consistency versus flexibility and subjective meanings	Develop measures to be administered to many respondents in ways that attempt to minimize random and systematic measurement error, but that may be at a superficial level, requiring an investigation of their validity	Develop measures that allow for researcher flexibility and subjectivity in order to pursue deeper, more valid levels of understanding of subjective meanings among fewer respondents
Generalizability versus in-depth, theoretical understanding	Verify, in a precise, statistical fashion, whether understandings emerging from qualitative measurement are generalizable	Develop a deeper theoretical understanding of the meanings of statistical findings emerging from quantitative measurement
Test hypotheses versus generating hypotheses and deeper understandings	Test hypotheses, perhaps generated from qualitative studies, generating new findings that might require further qualitative study to be sufficiently understood	Study phenomena whose meanings are not sufficiently understood, perhaps generating hypotheses for quantitative study

B. Impact of face-to-face meetings? Feelings each set of parents has about the other?

C. Degree of ongoing contact? Why?

V. Any changes in degree of openness over time?

A. What type of changes?

B. Impact?

As we end this chapter, we remind you that, despite pointing out the differences between quantitative and qualitative measures for asking people questions, we've identified commonalities shared by the two approaches. We'd also like to reiterate that the same study can use both approaches; they need not be seen as mutually exclusive or in conflict. We summarize these points in the box "A Comparison of Quantitative and Qualitative Approaches to Asking People Questions."

Main Points

• Questionnaires provide a method of collecting data by (1) asking people questions or (2) asking them to agree or disagree with statements that represent different points of view.

• Questions may be open-ended (respondents supply their own answers) or closed-ended (they select from a list of answers provided them).

• Usually, short items in a questionnaire are better than long ones.

• Negative items and terms should be avoided in questionnaires because they may confuse respondents.

• In questionnaire items, bias is the quality that encourages respondents to answer in a particular way to avoid or support a particular point of view. Avoid it.

• Contingency questions are questions that should be answered only by people giving a particular response to some preceding question. The contingency question format is highly useful because it doesn't ask people questions that have no meaning for them. For example, a question about the number of times a person has been pregnant should be asked only of women.

• Matrix questions are those in which a standardized set of closed-ended response categories are used in answering several questionnaire items. This format can facilitate the presentation and completion of items.

• Single indicators of variables may not have sufficiently clear validity to warrant their use.

• Composite measures, such as scales and indexes, solve this problem by including several indicators of a variable in one summary measure.

• Face validity is the first criterion for the selection of indicators to be included in a composite measure; the term means that an indicator seems at face value to provide some measure of the variable.

• If different items are indeed indicators of the same variable, then they should be related empirically to one another. If, for example, frequency of church attendance and frequency of prayer are both indicators of religiosity, then people who attend church frequently should be found to pray more than those who attend church less frequently.

• Once an index or a scale has been constructed, it is essential that it be validated.

• Likert scaling is a measurement technique that is based on the use of standardized response categories (for instance, strongly agree, agree, disagree, strongly disagree) for several questionnaire items. The Likert format for questionnaire items is popular and extremely useful.

• Scales and indexes that appear to be reliable and valid when tested with one culture may not be reliable and valid when used with other cultures.

• Although qualitative and quantitative measurement approaches share certain principles, quantitative measures are always highly structured, tend to use closed-ended questions primarily, and may be administered in either an interview or questionnaire format, whereas qualitative measures rely on interviews that are often unstructured and mainly contain open-ended questions and in-depth probes.

Review Questions and Exercises

1. Find a questionnaire in a magazine or newspaper (a reader survey, for example). Bring it to class and critique it.

2. For each of the open-ended questions listed below, construct a closed-ended question that could be used in a questionnaire.

a. What was your family's total income last year?

b. How do you feel about increasing public spending on social welfare?

c. How important is learning theory in your approach to social work practice?

d. What was your main reason for studying to be a social worker?

e. What do you feel is the biggest problem that faces this community?

3. Construct a set of contingency questions for use in a self-administered questionnaire that would solicit the following information:

a. Is the respondent employed?

b. If unemployed, is the respondent looking for work?

c. If the unemployed respondent is not looking for work, is he or she retired, a student, or a homemaker?

d. If the respondent is looking for work, how long has he or she been looking?

4. Using the Likert format, construct a brief scale to measure client satisfaction with service delivery.

Internet Exercises

1. Using InfoTrac College Edition, enter the term *scaling* to find an article that discusses scale development. Write down the bibliographical reference information for the article and summarize the article in a few sentences. If the article reports the development of a particular scale, critique the scale, its development, or both—either positively or negatively.

2. Find a questionnaire on the web. (Hint: Search for "questionnaire.") Critique at least five of the questions contained in it—either positively or negatively. Be sure to give the web address for the questionnaire and the exact wording of the questions you critique.

3. Using InfoTrac College Edition, find the article by Robert Greene, Katrina Murphy, and Shelita Snyder, "Should Demographics Be Placed at the End or at the Beginning of Mailed Questionnaires? An Empirical Answer to a Persistent Methodological Question," which appeared in the December 2000 issue of *Social Work Research*. Briefly summarize the main points of the article and give a brief critical appraisal.

Additional Readings

Fowler, Floyd J., Jr. 1995. *Improving Survey Questions: Design and Evaluation*. Thousand Oaks, CA: Sage. A comprehensive discussion of questionnaire construction, including a number of suggestions for pretesting questions.

Miller, Delbert. 1991. *Handbook of Research Design and Social Measurement*. Newbury Park, CA: Sage. An excellent compilation of frequently used and semistandardized scales, its many illustrations reported in Part 4 may be directly adaptable to studies or at least suggestive of modified measures. Studying the illustrations, moreover, may give a better understanding of the logic of composite measures in general.

Moore, David W. 2002. "Measuring New Types of Question-Order Effects: Additive and Subtractive," *Public Opinion Quarterly, 66,* 80–91. This work offers an extensive examination of the various ways in which question wording can affect responses.

Potocky, Miriam, and Antoinette Y. Rodgers-Farmer (eds.). 1998. *Social Work Research with Minority and Oppressed Populations*. New York: Haworth Press. As we mentioned in Chapters 4 and 5, this handy collection of articles contains innovative ideas for avoiding cultural bias and insensitivity in research with minority and oppressed populations. Most pertinent to this chapter are two articles that describe issues in the construction of instruments to measure depression among women of color and gerontological social work concerns among nonwhite ethnic elders.

Smith, Eric R. A. N., and Peverill Squire. 1990. "The Effects of Prestige Names in Question Wording." *Public Opinion Quarterly, 5,* 97–116. Prestigious names not only affect the overall responses given to survey questionnaires, but also such things as the correlation between education and the number of "don't know" answers.

PART 4

Designs for Evaluating Programs and Practice

Whereas the previous two chapters dealt with the validity of measurement, we now turn to a different form of validity. In this section we'll examine the validity of inferences made about the effectiveness of interventions, policies, and programs. In Chapter 1, we discussed the need to assess the effectiveness of social work practice and programs. We noted that this need stems from such forces as public skepticism about our effectiveness, increasing demands for accountability, and our own professional and humanitarian concerns for the welfare of clients. Implicit in the term *effectiveness* is the notion of causality. Thus, when we discussed evidence-based practice in Chapter 2, we noted that a key question in appraising the quality of the evidence reported in practice effectiveness studies pertains to whether the research design is strong enough to indicate conclusively whether the intervention or something else most plausibly caused the variations we observe in client outcome.

The next four chapters will examine the logic of causal inference and show how different design arrangements bear on our ability to infer cause and effect. They will address these issues primarily from the standpoint of evaluating the effectiveness of social work services.

Chapter 10 will begin by discussing criteria necessary for inferring causality and some common sources of error in causal inference. Then it will look at some correlational research designs with explanatory purposes, their limitations regarding causal inference, and how they can use statistical controls to improve the plausibility of the explanations they posit.

Chapter 11 focuses on group experiments, quasi-experiments, and pre-experimental pilot studies for evaluating the effectiveness of interventions, programs, and policies. It examines the reasons for using each type of design, the strengths and weaknesses of each, and how each design does or does not enhance our ability to make causal inferences.

Chapter 12 discusses single-case evaluation designs. It shows how causal inferences can be made about the effects of a particular intervention on a particular case. Although the generalizability of this approach is limited, Chapter 12 will examine why single-case evaluation designs have great potential utility to practitioners as the final stage in the evidence-based practice process.

Chapter 13 will examine some practical pitfalls in carrying out experiments and quasi-experiments in social work agencies and some mechanisms for dealing with those pitfalls. It will also discuss the politicized atmosphere influencing efforts to evaluate programs and practice, how vested interests can influence the ways in which evaluations are conducted and utilized, and how evaluators can deal with those political forces.

What you learn in these chapters should help you appreciate the paradoxical complexities that are involved in selecting a research design and in appraising the evidence you find when engaging in evidence-based practice. On the one hand, using an acute skepticism, you should be prepared to swiftly spot logical arrangements that do not permit sweeping generalizations or causal inferences to be made. On the other hand, you should be aware of the practical obstacles that make ideal logical arrangements infeasible and thus be able to appreciate the utility of findings that may have to be interpreted cautiously.

CHAPTER 10

Causal Inference and Correlational Designs

What You'll Learn in This Chapter

This chapter examines the criteria for drawing causal inferences from research findings and some common sources of error in causal inference. We'll see how some research designs are vulnerable to these sources of error and how they can use statistical controls to improve their value.

INTRODUCTION

In this chapter we'll look at issues in causal inference and their relationship to various research designs. Let's begin by defining what we mean by the terms *inference, causal inference,* and *research design.*

In social work research studies, an **inference** is a conclusion that can be logically drawn in light of our research design and our findings. A **causal inference** is one derived from a research design and findings that logically imply that the independent variable really has a *causal* impact on the dependent variable. The term **research design** can refer to all the decisions made in planning and conducting research, including decisions about measurement, sampling, how to collect data, and logical arrangements designed to permit certain kinds of inferences. Because we'll be focusing on the connection between research design and inference in this chapter, we'll use the term *research design* primarily in connection with logical arrangements.

The kinds of inferences that we seek to make—and legitimately can make—will vary depending on the purpose of our research. Likewise, the kinds of research designs that are most and least appropriate will depend upon our research purposes and the types of inference we seek to make. For example, if our purpose is limited to *description*—such as describing the proportion of homeless people who have severe and persistent mental illnesses—then we don't need a design that will permit us to explain what's *causing* something. Neither would we need such a design if our purpose is limited to *exploring* or *describing* in a pilot study what types of interventions or client problems appear to be associated with what types of service outcomes. That is, we would not be seeking to infer whether certain types of practices or interventions really are the *explanations* or *causes* of differences in outcome. However, if our purpose is causal in nature—such as to ascertain whether a particular intervention is effective—then we'll need a design that enables us to determine what really is the cause of variations we observe in client outcomes.

Shortly we'll examine some specific types of designs, their strengths and weaknesses regarding causal inference, and how they can use statistical controls to improve the plausibility of the explanations they posit. But first we'll need to examine the criteria that are necessary for inferring causality.

CRITERIA FOR INFERRING CAUSALITY

There are three specific criteria for inferring causality. *The first requirement in a causal relationship between two variables is that the cause precedes the effect in time.* It makes no sense in science to imagine something being caused by something else that happened later on. A bullet leaving the muzzle of a gun does not cause the gunpowder to explode; it works the other way around.

As simple and obvious as this criterion may seem, we will discover endless problems in this regard in the analysis of social work research findings. Often, the time order that connects two variables is simply unclear. Suppose, for example, that a study finds that nuclear families containing a member suffering from schizophrenia are much more likely to be at lower levels of socioeconomic status than are families without such members. Which comes first—the schizophrenia or the lower socioeconomic status? Does socioeconomic stress contribute to the onset of schizophrenia? Or does having a schizophrenic member reduce a family's ability to advance socioeconomically? Even when the time order seems essentially clear, exceptions can often be found. For instance, we would normally assume that the educational level of parents would be a cause of the educational level of their children, yet some parents may return to school as a result of the advanced education of their own children.

Another example of this ambiguity can be found in a study by Rubin (1991) that evaluated the effectiveness of a support group intervention for battered women. One of the group's intervention goals was to help women still living with their batterers to leave them. One of the six women who participated in the study left her abusive husband the day before she attended her first support group meeting. Because the intended effect (leaving the batterer) preceded the hypothesized cause (attending the support group meetings), it would seem at first glance that the intervention could not have caused the intended effect. Indeed, it would seem more logical to suppose that attending the group meeting, rather than being the cause of the separation, was merely one of a variety of ways in which the woman was implementing a decision to separate—a decision that resulted from other forces.

On the other hand, one could argue that this woman's awareness of the support group, and her anticipation of being part of it, emboldened her to leave.

Perhaps she also anticipated being embarrassed by admitting to the group that she continued to live with her batterer, and wanting to make a good impression on the group may have contributed in some way to her decision to leave when she did. If either explanation seems plausible, it follows that without the intervention (that is, without the presence of the support group) the woman may not have left the batterer, even though she left him before attending the support group.

Because people sometimes change their behavior or cognitions in anticipation of events, such as when our moods improve in anticipation of a joyful event or when our spending increases in anticipation of a bonus or a tax rebate, we must consider potential anticipatory effects when we think about time order and causality.

The second requirement in a causal relationship is that the two variables be empirically correlated with one another. Being correlated means that changes in one variable are associated with changes in another variable. (See our discussion of types of relationships between variables in Chapter 7.) It would make no sense to say that a support group helped women leave their batterers if women in the support group were no more likely to leave their batterers than women receiving no support.

The third requirement for a causal relationship is that the observed empirical correlation between two variables cannot be explained away as the result of the influence of some third variable that causes the two under consideration. For instance, you may observe that your left knee generally aches just before it rains, but this does not mean that your joints affect

CORRELATION AND CAUSALITY

by Charles Bonney, Department of Sociology, Eastern Michigan University

Having demonstrated a statistical relationship between a hypothesized "cause" and its presumed "effect," many people (sometimes including researchers who should know better) are only too eager to proclaim "proof" of causation. Let's take an example to see why "it ain't necessarily so."

Imagine you have conducted a study on college students and have found an inverse correlation between marijuana smoking (variable M) and grade point average (variable G)—that is, those who smoke tend to have lower GPAs than those who do not, and the more smoked, the lower the GPA. You might therefore claim that smoking marijuana lowers one's grades (in symbolic form, $M \rightarrow G$), giving as an explanation, perhaps, that marijuana adversely affects memory, which would naturally have detrimental consequences on grades.

However, if an inverse correlation is all the evidence you have, a second possibility exists. Getting poor grades is frustrating; frustration often leads to escapist behavior; getting stoned is a popular means of escape; ergo, low grades cause marijuana smoking ($G \rightarrow M$)!

Unless you can establish which came first, smoking or low grades, this explanation is supported by the correlation just as plausibly as the first.

Let's introduce another variable into the picture: the existence and/or extent of emotional problems (variable E). It could certainly be plausibly argued that having emotional problems may lead to escapist behavior, including marijuana smoking. Likewise it seems reasonable to suggest that emotional problems are likely to adversely affect grades. That correlation of marijuana smoking and low grades may exist for the same reason that runny noses and sore throats tend to go together—neither is the cause of the other, but rather, both are the consequences of some third variable ($E \rightrightarrows \genfrac{}{}{0pt}{}{M}{G}$). Unless you can rule out such third variables, this explanation too is just as well supported by the data as is the first (or the second).

(*continued*)

Then again, perhaps students smoke marijuana primarily because they have friends who smoke, and get low grades because they are simply not as bright or well prepared or industrious as their classmates, and the fact that it's the same students in each case in your sample is purely coincidental. Unless your correlation is so strong and so consistent that mere coincidence becomes highly unlikely, this last possibility, while not supported by your data, is not precluded either.

Incidentally, this particular example was selected for two reasons. First of all, *every* one of the above explanations for such an inverse correlation has appeared in a national magazine at one time or another. And second, every one of them is probably doomed to failure because it turns out that, among college students, most studies indicate a *direct* correlation, i.e., it is those with higher GPAs who are more likely to be marijuana smokers! Thus, with tongue firmly in cheek, we may reanalyze this particular finding:

1. Marijuana relaxes a person, clearing away other stresses, thus allowing more effective study; hence, $M \rightarrow G$.

or

2. Marijuana is used as a reward for really hitting the books or doing well ("Wow, man! An 'A'! Let's go get high!"); hence, $G \rightarrow M$.

or

3. A high level of curiosity (E) is definitely an asset to learning and achieving high grades and may also lead one to investigate "taboo" substances; hence, $E \rightrightarrows {}^{M}_{G}$.

or

4. Again coincidence, but this time the samples just happened to contain a lot of brighter, more industrious students whose friends smoke marijuana!

The obvious conclusion is this: if *all* of these are possible explanations for a relationship between two variables, then no *one* of them should be too readily singled out. Establishing that two variables tend to occur together is a *necessary* condition for demonstrating a causal relationship, but it is not by itself a *sufficient* condition. It is a fact, for example, that human birthrates are higher in areas of Europe where there are lots of storks, but as to the meaning of that relationship . . . !

the weather. A third variable, relative humidity, is the cause of both your aching knee and the rain. Likewise, a third variable, preexisting readiness to change, might explain why the women who leave their batterers are more likely to join the support group and leave their batterers. Perhaps the support group really didn't make them any more likely to leave than they were when they joined the group. The box titled "Correlation and Causality" illustrates the point that correlation does not necessarily point to a particular causal relationship.

To review, most social work researchers consider two variables to be causally related—that is, one causes the other—if (1) the cause precedes the effect in time, (2) there is an empirical correlation between them, and (3) the relationship between the two is not found to result from the effects of some third variable. Any relationship that satisfies all of these criteria is causal, and these are the only criteria.

INTERNAL VALIDITY

When we consider the extent to which a research study permits causal inferences to be made about relationships between variables, we again encounter the term *validity*. You may recall that when we were discussing measurement validity in Chapter 8, we referred to validity as the extent to which a measure really measures what it intends to measure. When discussing causal inference, however, the term is used differently. Two forms of validity that are important when considering causality are *internal validity* and *external validity*.

Internal validity refers to the confidence we have that the results of a study accurately depict whether one variable is or is not a cause of another. To the extent that the preceding three criteria for inferring causality are met, a study has internal validity. Conversely, to the extent that we have not met these criteria, we are limited in our grounds for concluding that the independent variable does or does not play a causal role in explaining the dependent variable. *External validity* refers to the extent to which we can *generalize* the findings of a study to settings and populations beyond the study conditions. We will examine external validity later in this chapter, after we examine internal validity in some depth. Let's begin that examination by discussing various threats to internal validity.

A threat to internal validity is present whenever anything other than the independent variable can affect the dependent variable. When evaluating the effectiveness of programs or practice, for example, the problem of **internal invalidity** refers to the possibility that investigators might erroneously conclude that differences in outcome were caused by the evaluated intervention when, in fact, something else really caused the differences. Campbell and Stanley (1963:5–6) and Cook and Campbell (1979:51–55) have identified various threats to internal validity. Here are seven prominent ones:

1. *History.* During the course of the research, extraneous events may occur that will confound the results. The term **history** is tricky. The extraneous events need not be major news events that one would read about in a history book, but simply extraneous events that coincide in time with the manipulation of the independent variable. For example, suppose a study evaluates the effectiveness of social services in improving resident morale in a nursing home merely by measuring the morale of a group of residents before and after they receive social services. Perhaps some extraneous improvement in the nursing home environment—an improvement independent of the social services—was introduced between the before and after measures. That possibility threatens the internal validity of the research because it, rather than the independent variable (social services), might cause the hypothesized improvement in the dependent variable (morale).

2. *Maturation or the passage of time.* People continuously grow and change, whether they are a part of a research study or not, and those changes affect the results of the research. In the above nursing home illustration, for example, it would be silly to infer that the greater physical frailty of residents several years after receiving social services was caused by the social services. Maturation, through the aging process, would represent a severe threat to the internal validity of such a conclusion. But this threat to internal validity does not require that basic developmental changes occur; it can also refer simply to the effects of the passage of time. Suppose, for example, that a study to evaluate the effectiveness of a crisis counseling program for victims of rape merely assessed the mood state or social functioning of the victims before and after treatment. We might expect the rape victims' emotional moods or social functioning levels to be at their worst in the immediate aftermath of the trauma. With or without crisis counseling at that point, we might expect the mere passage of time to alleviate some portion of the terrible impact of the trauma, even if we assume that the long-term effects will still be devastating. Likewise, consider bereavement counseling: It would be silly also to conclude that, just because the functioning level or mood of clients whose loved one died immediately before counseling was somewhat better after counseling, the bereavement counseling must have caused the improvement.

3. *Testing.* Often the process of testing by itself will enhance performance on a test without any corresponding improvement in the real construct that the test attempts to measure. Suppose we want to see if a workshop helps social workers perform better on their state licensure exam. We might construct a test that we think will measure the same sorts of things measured on the licensure exam and then administer that test to social workers before and after they take our workshop. If their scores on the exam improve, then we might wish to attribute the improvement to the effects of our workshop. But suppose the social workers, after taking the first test, looked up answers to test items before our workshop began and remembered those answers the next time they took the same test. They would then score higher on the posttest without even attending our workshop, and we could not claim therefore that taking our workshop caused their scores to improve.

4. *Instrumentation changes.* If we use different measures of the dependent variable at posttest than we did at pretest, how can we be sure that they are comparable to each other? Suppose in evaluating the workshop to help social workers perform better on their state licensure exam we do not want workshop participants to take the same test twice (to avoid testing effects). We might therefore construct two versions of the outcome test—one for the pretest and one for the posttest—that we think are equivalent. Although we would like to conclude that our workshop caused any improvement in scores, it is conceivable that the real reason may have been that, despite our best efforts,

the posttest version was an easier exam than the pretest version. And if their scores worsened, rather than indicating that our workshop made them less well prepared for the exam, perhaps the posttest version was more difficult.

Analogous possibilities can occur when the measurement instruments involve ratings made by researchers or practitioners based on interviews with participants or observations of their behavior. Perhaps the researchers or practitioners who provided the posttest ratings were not the same ones who provided the pretest ratings. Perhaps one set of raters had different standards or abilities than the other set. Even if the same raters are used at both pretest and posttest, their standards or their abilities may have changed over the course of the study. Perhaps their skill in observing and recording behaviors improved as they gained more experience in doing so over the course of the study, enabling them to observe and record more behaviors at posttest than at pretest.

A more subtle type of change in instrumentation can occur in experimental studies of children. If a long time passes from pretest to posttest, the child may have outgrown some of the pretest items. For example, if a scale devised to measure the self-esteem of children aged 6 to 12 is administered to children aged 12 at pretest and then aged 15 three years later, the scale items may not have the same meaning to the participants as teenagers as they did to them as 12-year-olds.

5. *Statistical regression.* Sometimes it's appropriate to evaluate the effectiveness of services for clients who were referred because of their extreme scores on the dependent variable. Suppose, for example, that a new social work intervention to alleviate depression among the elderly is being pilot tested in a nursing home among residents whose scores on a depression inventory indicate the most severe levels of depression. From a clinical standpoint, it would be quite appropriate to provide the service to the residents who appear most in need of the service. But consider from a methodological standpoint what is likely to happen to the depression scores of the referred residents even without intervention. In considering this, we should consider that, with repeated testing on almost any assessment inventory, an individual's scores on the inventory are likely to fluctuate somewhat from one administration to the next—not because the individual really changed, but because of the random testing factors that prevent instruments from having perfect reliability. For example, some residents who were referred because they had the poorest pretest scores may have had atypically bad days at pretest and may score better on the inventory on an average day. Perhaps they didn't sleep well the night before the pretest, perhaps a chronic illness flared up that day, or perhaps a close friend or relative passed away that week.

When we provide services to only those people with the most extremely problematic pretest scores, the odds are that the proportion of service recipients with atypically bad pretest scores will be higher than the proportion of nonrecipients with atypically bad pretest scores. Conversely, those who were not referred because their pretest scores were better probably include some whose pretest scores were atypically high (that is, people who were having an unusually good day at pretest). Consequently, even without any intervention, the group of service recipients is more likely to show some improvement in its average depression score over time than is the group that was not referred. There is a danger, then, that changes occurring because subjects started out in extreme positions will be attributed erroneously to the effects of the independent variable.

Statistical regression is a difficult concept to grasp. It might aid your understanding of this term to imagine or actually carry out the following amusing experiment, which we have adapted from Posavac and Carey (1985). Grab a bunch of coins—15 to 20 will suffice. Flip each coin six times and record the number of heads and tails you get for each coin. That number will be the pretest score for each coin. Now, refer each coin that had no more than two heads on the pretest to a social work intervention that combines task-centered and behavioral practice methods. Tell each referred coin (yes, go ahead and speak to it—but first make sure you are truly alone) that tails is an unacceptable behavior and that therefore its task is to try to come up heads more often. After you give each its task, flip it six more times, praising it every time it comes up heads. If it comes up tails, say nothing because you don't want to reward undesirable behavior.

Record, as a posttest, the number of heads and tails each gets. Compare the total number of posttest heads with the total number of pretest heads for the referred coins. The odds are that the posttest is higher. Now flip the nonreferred coins six times and record their posttest scores, but say nothing at all to them. We do not want them to receive the intervention; that way we can compare the pretest–posttest change of the coins that received the intervention to what happened among those coins that did not receive the intervention. The odds are that the untreated coins did not show nearly as much of an increase in the number of heads as did the treated coins.

This experiment works almost every time. If you got results other than those described here, odds are that if you replicated the experiment you would get such results the next time. What do these results mean? Is task-centered and behavioral casework an effective intervention with coins? According to the scientific method, our minds should be open to this possibility—but we doubt it. Rather, we believe these results illustrate that if we introduce the independent variable only to those referred on the basis of extreme scores, we can expect some improvement in the group solely because those scores will statistically regress to (which means they will move toward) their true score. In this case, the coins tend to regress to their true score of three (50 percent) heads and three (50 percent) tails. When the assessment is done on people, we can imagine their true score as being the mean score they would get if tested many times on many different days.

Of course, human behavior is more complex than that of coins. But this illustration represents a common problem in the evaluation of human services. Because we are most likely to begin interventions for human problems that are inherently variable when those problems are at their most severe levels, we can expect some amelioration of the problem to occur solely because of the natural peaks and valleys in the problem and not necessarily because of the interventions.

6. *Selection biases.* Comparisons don't have any meaning unless the groups being compared are really *comparable*. Suppose we sought to evaluate the effectiveness of an intervention to promote positive parenting skills by comparing the level of improvement in parenting skills of parents who voluntarily agreed to participate in the intervention program with the level of improvement of parents who refused to participate. We would not be able to attribute the greater improvement among program participants to the effects of the intervention—at least not with a great deal of confidence about the internal validity of our conclusion—because other differences between the two groups might explain away the difference in improvement. For example, the participants may have been more motivated than program refusers to improve and thus may have been trying harder, reading more, and doing any number of things unrelated to the intervention that may really explain why they showed greater improvement. **Selection biases** are a common threat to the internal validity of social service evaluations because groups of service recipients and nonrecipients are often compared on outcome variables in the absence of prior efforts to see that the groups being compared were initially truly equivalent. Perhaps this most typically occurs when individuals who choose to use services are compared with individuals who were not referred to those services or who chose not to utilize them.

7. *Ambiguity about the direction of causal influence.* As we discussed earlier in this chapter, there is a possibility of ambiguity concerning the time order of the independent and dependent variables. Whenever this occurs, the research conclusion that the independent variable caused the changes in the dependent variable can be challenged with the explanation that the "dependent" variable actually caused changes in the independent variable.

Suppose, for example, a study finds that clients who completed a substance abuse treatment program are less likely to be abusing substances than those who dropped out of the program. There would be ambiguity as to whether the program influenced participants not to abuse substances or whether the abstinence from substance abuse helped people complete the program.

EXTERNAL VALIDITY

When a study has a high degree of internal validity, it allows causal inferences to be made about the sample and setting that were studied. But what about other settings and larger populations? Can we generalize the same causal inferences to them?

As we mentioned earlier, **external validity** refers to the extent to which we can *generalize* the findings of a study to settings and populations beyond the study conditions. Internal validity is a necessary but not sufficient condition for external validity. Before we can generalize a causal inference beyond the conditions of a particular study, we must have adequate grounds for making the causal inference under conditions of that study in the first place. But even when internal validity in a particular study is high, several problems may limit its external validity.

A major factor that influences external validity is the representativeness of the study sample, setting, and procedures. Suppose a deinstitutionalization program is implemented in an urban community. Suppose that community residents strongly support the program, that it's well funded, and that there is a comprehensive range of noninstitutional community support resources accessible to the mentally disabled clients residing in the community. Suppose, in turn, that the well-funded program can afford to hire high-caliber staff members, give them small caseloads, and reward them amply for good work. Finally, suppose that an evaluation with high internal validity finds that the program improves the clients' quality of life.

Would those findings imply that legislators or mental health planners in other localities could logically conclude that a similar deinstitutionalization program would improve the quality of life of mentally disabled individuals in their settings? Not necessarily. It would depend on the degree to which their settings, populations, and procedures matched those of the studied program.

Suppose their community is rural, has fewer or more geographically dispersed community-based resources for the mentally disabled, or has more neighborhood opposition to residences being located in the community. Suppose legislators view deinstitutionalization primarily as a cost-saving device and therefore do not allocate enough funds to enable the program to hire or keep high-caliber staff members or give them caseload sizes that are small enough to manage adequately. And what about differences in the characteristics of the mentally disabled target population? Notice that we have said nothing about the attributes of the clients in the tested program. Perhaps they were different in age, diagnosis, ethnicity, average length of previous institutionalization, and degree of social impairment than the intended target population in the communities generalizing from the study findings. To the extent that such differences apply, similar programs implemented in other settings might not have the same effects as did the program in the tested setting.

Would such differences mean that this study had low external validity? Not necessarily. On the one hand, we could say that a study has low external validity if its conditions are far removed from conditions that could reasonably be expected to be replicated in the "real" world. On the other hand, a study's external validity could be adequate even if it cannot be generalized to many other settings. A study must be generalizable to some real-world settings, and it must represent that which it intends to represent. It does not have to represent every conceivable population or setting.

For example, a study that evaluates a program of care for the profoundly and chronically disabled in rural settings does not need to be generalizable to the mildly or acutely disabled or to the disabled residing in urban settings in order to have external validity. It just has to be representative of those attributes that it intends to represent, no matter how narrowly it defines them.

Problems in external validity abound in the literature that evaluates social work practice and programs. One common problem that limits external validity is ambiguity or brevity in reportage. Many studies do not adequately articulate the specific attributes of the clients who participated in the evaluated service. Many are vague about the practitioners' attributes. Some studies generalize about the effectiveness of *professional* social work practitioners based on findings about the effectiveness of *student* practitioners. Some studies leave out important details about the evaluated clinical setting, such as caseload size and the like. Consequently, although it may be clear that the evaluated intervention did or did not cause the desired change among the studied clients—that is, that the study had high *internal validity*—it is often not clear to whom those findings can be *generalized*. Thus, some studies find services to be effective but do not permit the generalization that those services would be effective beyond the study conditions. Likewise, other studies find no support for the effectiveness of services, but do not permit the generalization that those services would be ineffective when implemented under other conditions.

CORRELATIONAL DESIGNS

Although investigators conducting explanatory studies typically would like to have as much internal and external validity as possible, some designs they use are stronger than others from the standpoint of internal validity, whereas other designs they use are stronger from the standpoint of external validity. The strongest designs from an internal validity standpoint are experiments. They have the strongest controls for threats to internal validity because they can manipulate the independent variable. For example, in evaluating the effectiveness of a new intervention, they will use some random procedure like a coin toss to determine which clients receive the new intervention and which ones do not. We'll see how they do this—and how they use other features to maximize internal validity—in the next chapter, which will be devoted to experimental and quasi-experimental designs.

In the next chapter we'll also see why experimental designs often are not feasible in the real world of agency practice. Moreover, they may be impossible to implement when the causal focus of our inquiry is something other than whether an intervention is effective. For example, suppose we are interested in testing a hypothesis that having been abused as a child causes a greater likelihood of child abuse among teenage parents. We could not randomly assign people to having been abused as a child or not.

Let's turn now to three correlational designs that can be used to examine the plausibility of causal inferences when experimental designs are not feasible. First we'll look at cross-sectional studies. After that we'll examine case-control studies and then longitudinal studies. Although these designs are weaker than well-designed experiments from the standpoint of internal validity, they are often stronger from the standpoint of external validity. Their external validity is enhanced by studying people in the real world—not under conditions manipulated in an experiment.

Cross-Sectional Studies

A **cross-sectional study** examines a phenomenon by taking a cross section of it at one point in time. Cross-sectional studies may have exploratory, descriptive, or explanatory purposes. A single U.S. census, for example, exemplifies a cross-sectional study for descriptive purposes. If you conducted one open-ended, unstructured interview with each client who prematurely terminated treatment in your agency during a specified period—to generate insights about why your agency's treatment termination rate is so high—you would be conducting a cross-sectional study for exploratory purposes. If you conducted one structured interview with both these clients and those who completed their planned treatment—to test the hypothesis that practitioner–client disagreement about treatment goals is related to whether treatment is completed—then you would be conducting a cross-sectional study for explanatory purposes.

From the standpoint of internal validity, explanatory cross-sectional studies have an inherent problem. They typically aim to understand causal processes that occur over time, yet their conclusions are based on observations made at only one time. For example, if your cross-sectional study of patients recently discharged from a psychiatric hospital found that those who were living with their families were functioning better and had less symptomatology than those who were not living with their families, then you would not know whether the differences in functioning or symptomatology between the two groups commenced before or after they entered their current living arrangements. In other words, you wouldn't know whether different living arrangements helped cause differences in functioning and symptomatology or whether the latter differences helped to explain placement in particular living arrangements.

Although cross-sectional studies don't permit definitive, conclusive inferences about what is really causing what, they can have value in building our profession's scientific knowledge base. For example, by showing that two variables are related, cross-sectional studies can support the plausibility of the notion that one might be the cause of the other. Likewise, if they show no relationship between the two variables, then the notion of a causal relationship is less plausible. Suppose that a cross-sectional study examines the plausibility of parent–child discord as a cause of childhood behavioral disorders by administering two measures to children at the same point: One assesses the degree of parent–child discord and one assesses whether the child has a behavioral disorder. If the two measures are highly and positively correlated—that is, if the probability of behavioral disorder is higher when the amount of parent–child discord is greater—then the results support the *plausibility* of the supposition that the discord contributes to the causation of behavioral disorders.

Although the results are consistent with the notion that discord helps cause the disorder, they do not themselves demonstrate that the nature of the relationship is indeed causal. For instance, time order is not taken into account. Perhaps the causal order of the relationship is the other way around—that is, perhaps parent–child discord, rather than causing the behavioral disorder, increases as a result of the disorder. Also, the preceding correlation by itself does not rule out alternative variables that might cause both the discord and the behavioral disorder. For example, perhaps stressful life events produce both problems simultaneously.

Recognizing that simple correlations at one point in time do not permit causal inferences, researchers using cross-sectional designs may attempt to rule out the plausibility of rival hypotheses by controlling for alternative variables through multivariate statistical procedures. They do that by collecting data on as many plausible alternative explanatory variables as they can and then analyzing all of the variables simultaneously. Later in this chapter we will see how they can do that.

Case-Control Studies

A type of design that shares some of the internal validity weaknesses and external validity strengths of cross-sectional studies—and which also relies on multivariate statistical procedures to improve the plausibility of its inferences—is called the *case-control design*. The case-control design is popular because of its feasibility. As in cross-sectional designs, data can be collected at just one point in time. The **case-control design** compares groups of cases that have had contrasting outcomes and then collects *retrospective* data about past differences that might explain the difference in outcomes.

Suppose we want to learn what interventions may be effective in preventing children who are victims of child abuse from becoming perpetrators of abuse as adults. As will be discussed in the next chapter, we might conduct an experiment that tested one or more particular interventions. But experiments in general are often not feasible, and in this case an additional obstacle to feasibility would be the need to follow and measure the participating children over many years, even after they reach parenthood. Using the case-control design as an alternative, we could find a sample of two groups of parents who had been victims of child abuse: one group that had been referred at least once as adults to public child welfare agencies as perpetrators of child abuse, and another group that had never been so referred.

We could then collect retrospective data from the adults in each group, asking about their past experiences, seeking to find some intervention that the nonperpetrators were much more likely than the perpetrators to have received earlier in life. (Or perhaps we'll find something harmful that the perpetrators were more likely to have experienced.) Suppose we find that after controlling statistically for a variety of relevant personal attributes and experiences, the main past experience that distinguishes the two groups is whether a volunteer from a Big Brother or Big Sister agency or some similar program provided them with a long-term positive, caring relationship that commenced soon after they had been abused as children. That finding would suggest that practitioners intervening with abused children might want to do all they can to secure such a relationship for the children.

But despite their popularity, case-control designs can be fraught with problems that limit what can be inferred or generalized from their findings. Cases may need to be selected using sampling procedures that create doubt about how *representative* they are of the population of people with their outcomes or past experiences. For example, advertisements may be needed to find adults who were abused as children and who did and did not become perpetrators. The people recruited in that fashion may be quite unlike those who cannot be found or who are unwilling to participate in such a study. (We'll examine sampling procedures in Chapter 14.)

Also, perhaps the good relationships children had with caring volunteers is explained more by their preexisting childhood resilience than by the effect of the relationships on the children's resilience. In other words, perhaps the children who were already more resilient were more motivated and better able to utilize and connect with the adult volunteers.

In addition, perhaps adult *memories* of childhood experiences may be *faulty*. Forgetting is only one way in which their memories could be faulty. Another way is termed **recall bias.** Maybe the perpetrators had relationships with adult volunteers that were just as good as the relationships that the nonperpetrators had, but their current recollections of the quality and value of those relationships are tainted by knowing that things didn't work out for them later in life. Likewise, perhaps the adults who are leading happier and more successful lives are more predisposed to attribute their well-being to happy childhood memories, while perhaps blocking out the negative ones.

The above are just a few of the problems with the case-control design; Shadish, Cook, and Campbell (2001) list many more. Despite these problems, studies using case-control designs—like cross-sectional designs—can be used in an exploratory fashion to generate hypotheses about the possible effects of interventions. If they use multivariate statistical procedures, the plausibility of the explanations they postulate becomes more tenable. Consequently, they can provide a valuable basis for designing studies using more valid designs to test the effectiveness of those interventions. An example of a valuable case-control study is summarized in the box "A Case-Control Study of Adverse Childhood Experiences as Risk Factors for Homelessness."

Longitudinal Studies

As you may recall from our discussion of them in Chapter 6, longitudinal studies describe processes occurring over time and thus conduct their observations

A CASE-CONTROL STUDY OF ADVERSE CHILDHOOD EXPERIENCES AS RISK FACTORS FOR HOMELESSNESS

Along with three associates, Daniel Herman, a social work professor at Columbia University, conducted a case-control study to ascertain whether adult homelessness could be explained in part by certain adverse childhood experiences (Herman, Susser, Struening, and Link, 1997). They began by analyzing available data from an earlier survey of 1,507 adults that was conducted in 1990. They then reinterviewed respondents to that survey, including all 169 who reported having been homeless at some time in their adult lives and a comparable group who had never been homeless but who had attributes typically associated with a higher risk of homelessness (being poor, mentally ill, and so on).

In their follow-up interviews they used a scale designed to assess respondents' recollections of the quality of parental care during childhood. The answers to various items on the scale enabled the researchers to determine whether the respondent recalled the following types of adverse childhood experiences: lack of parental care, physical abuse, sexual abuse, lack of care plus either type of abuse, and any childhood adversity.

Their initial results indicated that lack of care and physical abuse were each strongly correlated with a greater likelihood of homelessness. The combination of lack of care plus either physical or sexual abuse during childhood was even more strongly correlated with a greater likelihood of adult homelessness.

What made this study particularly valuable, however, was its use of multivariate statistical procedures to control for extraneous variables that might explain away the above findings. Using these procedures, the researchers were able to control for the respondent's gender, age, ethnicity, current residence (urban versus rural), parental socioeconomic status, whether the family was on welfare during childhood, and the extent of current depressive symptoms. It was important to control for these variables. For example, growing up in poverty might be the real explanation for an increased likelihood of homelessness as an adult, and also explain adverse childhood experiences. Parents living in poverty are less likely to be able to care well for their children. Thus, the relationship between adverse parental care and adult homelessness might be spurious—with both attributes being explained by poverty.

A noteworthy strength of this study was its control for the respondent's current emotional well-being. Herman and his colleagues astutely reasoned that a current depressed mood among some respondents might bias them toward recalling more adverse aspects of their childhood experiences. Likewise, respondents who were currently better off emotionally might be biased against recalling adverse childhood experiences.

After controlling for all these variables in their multivariate analyses, Herman and his colleagues found that their initial results changed somewhat. Lack of care and physical abuse continued to be strongly correlated with homelessness, and so did the combination of the two. But the combination of lack of care and sexual abuse was no longer a significant correlate of adult homelessness.

Another nice feature of this study was the way its authors discussed the strengths and limitations of their case-control design. It's easy for authors to point out their study's strengths, and indeed there were many in this study. Not so easy, yet more impressive, is when authors correctly discuss their study's limitations. Thus, Herman and his colleagues point out that people with particularly lengthy homelessness experiences were probably underrepresented in their sample and that despite their control for current level of depression, recall bias is still a potential threat to the validity of their findings because respondents who had been homeless might be predisposed toward recalling more adverse childhood experiences. But recall bias comes with the territory when conducting even the best case-control studies, and this one certainly deserves recognition as among the best in social work.

Source: Herman, Daniel B., Ezra S. Susser, Elmer L. Struening, and Bruce L. Link. 1997. "Adverse Childhood Experiences: Are They Risk Factors for Adult Homelessness?" *American Journal of Public Health, 87,* 249–255.

over an extended period. Let's return to the example discussed above regarding what interventions may be effective in preventing children who are victims of child abuse from becoming perpetrators of abuse as adults. Unlike cross-sectional and case-control designs, longitudinal studies follow people prospectively over time and so are better able to ascertain the time order of events. Thus, a longitudinal study would be able to determine whether recipients and nonrecipients of the preventive intervention had or had not been perpetrators of abuse before receiving the intervention. If the difference between the groups only appeared after the intervention, knowing that would strengthen the plausibility of the notion that the intervention might explain the difference. Consequently, a well-designed longitudinal study will have increased internal validity by establishing time order in addition to correlation. However, a longitudinal study would need to control for various other threats to internal validity before it could claim to have a strong basis for making causal inferences. Perhaps, for example, those who received the intervention were less impaired and more resilient than the others, and those differences in impairment and resilience explained both their decision to participate in the intervention and their ability to avoid becoming perpetrators. The researchers could control for that by using certain features of experimental design, which we'll examine in the next chapter.

An alternative way to strengthen the internal validity of longitudinal studies—as was the case with cross-sectional and case-control studies—is to employ multivariate statistical procedures that control for the possible influences of extraneous variables. The term *multivariate statistical procedures* might seem daunting, and perhaps it would be were we to delve into the mathematical aspects of it. But we can examine the concept in a manner that is not too difficult to grasp. In fact, we already did—back in Chapter 7. You may recall that Tables 7-1 and 7-2 used a hypothetical illustration involving social services and hospital cure of illnesses to show how controlling for a third variable can reveal that an original relationship was really spurious. The fact that a third variable was involved made the analysis multivariate. Being able to show whether an original relationship is spurious is only one way that the use of multivariate procedures helps ferret out alternative explanatory variables in data generated by cross-sectional, case-control, and longitudinal studies. Let's look at these ways now.

THE ELABORATION MODEL

The multivariate statistical procedures involved in calculating whether the relationships we observe between two variables change or do not change when we control for additional variables go way beyond the scope of this text. But we can use a process called the **elaboration model** to understand the logic of how multivariate procedures enable us to evaluate whether a relationship that we observe between two variables (a *bivariate* relationship) really appears to be explanatory or causal in nature. This is done by studying the effects on the original relationship that are produced by introducing other variables. This process can lead to the various types of interpretations (elaborations) of the original relationship that we observed, which we will examine in the following subsections.

As we do so, we will use hypothetical illustrations involving the term *case management.* Case management is commonly provided by social workers, and social work roles such as linkage and advocacy (among others) typically constitute the case manager's efforts to help discharged psychiatric patients get the services they need in a timely and appropriate fashion.

Replication

Whenever an original bivariate relationship appears to be essentially the same in the multivariate analysis as it was in the bivariate analysis, the term **replication** is assigned to the result. For example, suppose you wonder whether the effectiveness of your case management services for discharged psychiatric patients is due to the fact that former patients abusing alcohol or drugs were less likely to utilize your services than those not abusing substances. If you examine outcome separately for the two types of ex-patients and still find that—for each type of ex-patient—those receiving your services did better than those not receiving your services, your original relationship was *replicated.*

Explanation

An original relationship might be *explained away as spurious*—that is, two variables that were related in a bivariate analysis are no longer related when one or more *extraneous variables* are controlled for in a multivariate analysis. For example, suppose it turned out that the effectiveness of your case management services for discharged psychiatric patients really was because the former patients abusing alcohol or drugs were less likely to utilize your services than those not abusing substances. Suppose when you examined outcome separately for the two types of ex-patients you found no difference in outcome between service users and nonusers. Then your original relationship would be a **spurious relationship** because it was *explained away* by the fact that the ex-patients not abusing substances were more likely to utilize your services than the substance abusers (whose abuse presumably was the real reason for their poorer outcomes).

Interpretation

An original relationship might be *interpreted* based on multivariate control—that is, additional variables might help explain why the independent variable is related to the dependent variable. For example, suppose the prime reason your case management services are effective is because they motivate most service recipients to take their medications in the manner prescribed. Suppose those recipients not taking their medications have no better outcomes than their nonrecipient counterparts who don't take their medications. Then whether or not recipients take their medications would be a *mediating variable* (also called an *intervening variable,* as discussed in Chapter 7) that helps interpret the mechanism through which the original relationship occurs. Thus, interpretation is like explanation, but the difference is that an intervening variable doesn't explain away the original relationship—instead, it identifies a *mechanism* through which the independent variable really did have an effect on the dependent variable.

Specification

The multivariate analysis might *specify* the conditions under which the original relationship tends to diminish or increase—that is, the original relationship might hold for some but not all categories of the additional variable(s) being controlled. For example, suppose your case management services are effective for women but not for men. In other words, female recipients of your services are more likely than female nonrecipients to have successful outcomes, whereas there is no difference in outcome between men who do and don't utilize your services. If so, then you have *specified* a condition under which the original relationship occurs. (As you may recall from our discussion of different kinds of variables in Chapter 7, in this instance gender would be a *moderating variable.*)

Suppressor Variables

Two variables that were not related in the bivariate analysis, or that were weakly related in it, might be strongly related after additional variables, called **suppressor variables,** are controlled in the multivariate analysis. Suppose, for example, that you originally find no relationship between whether or not someone receives your case management services and their treatment outcome. Suppose further that for some reason (perhaps they were ordered by the court to receive treatment after being arrested) ex-patients with the worst prognoses are much more likely to utilize your services than those with better prognoses. Then, even if your services are effective with both types of ex-patients, your program might seem ineffective in a bivariate analysis merely because those whose prognoses make them more likely to succeed are also less likely to use your services, whereas those less likely to succeed are more likely to use your services: Those two factors cancel each other out and thus conceal the real impact of your case management services. Thus, prognosis would be a suppressor variable. (Table 10-6, which we'll present and discuss later in this chapter, illustrates this further.)

Distorter Variables

Sometimes the *direction* of a bivariate relationship reverses when a third variable is controlled in a multivariate analysis. For example, a relationship that originally was negative might become positive or vice versa. When this happens, the variable being controlled is called a **distorter variable.** To illustrate how this could happen, let's again suppose that ex-patients with the worst prognoses are much more likely to utilize your services than ex-patients with better prognoses. This time, however, let's also suppose that—despite the effectiveness of your services—the pretreatment differences in prognosis between the two groups of ex-patients is so extreme that it actually makes it look as though your services made people worse. In other words, the impact of prognosis could be so strong as to not only suppress but even reverse the apparent impact of your case management services. If this possibility seems far-fetched, then consider the experience of Michel de Seve. When de Seve set out to examine the starting salaries of men and women in the same organization, she was surprised to find that the women received higher starting salaries, on the average, than their male counterparts. The distorter variable was time of first hire. Many of the women had been hired relatively recently when salaries were higher overall than in the earlier years when many of the men had been hired (reported in Cook, 1995).

Table 10-1 Hypothetical Relationship between Case Management Provision and Rehospitalization

REHOSPITALIZED?	CASE-MANAGED	NOT CASE-MANAGED
Yes	50%	40%
No	50	60
	100%	100%
	(200)	(200)

HYPOTHETICAL ILLUSTRATION OF THE ELABORATION PROCESS: CASE MANAGEMENT EVALUATION

To clarify the elaboration model further and to get some more practice at interpreting multivariate tables, let's look at some more hypothetical examples regarding the evaluation of case management services for discharged psychiatric patients. In the following hypothetical examples, case management effectiveness will be indicated by rehospitalization rates. This is a controversial and probably inadequate indicator of case management effectiveness, for reasons we shall discuss shortly, but its problems make it a useful indicator to use in our example.

Suppose you assess the effectiveness of a case management program that serves psychiatric patients who are being discharged to diverse communities. You decide to use rehospitalization rates as the indicator of case management effectiveness, comparing the rehospitalization rate of the first 200 discharged patients who receive case management services to the rehospitalization rate of the first 200 discharged patients who receive other, more traditional forms of service. Suppose you find that 50 percent of the 200 case-managed patients are rehospitalized, whereas only 40 percent (80 patients) of the patients who are not case-managed are rehospitalized. In other words, the case-managed patients seem to fare worse in avoiding rehospitalization than do the others, making case management look not only ineffective but perhaps somewhat harmful. This hypothetical result is illustrated in Table 10-1.

You might wonder whether these results are misleading. Perhaps case management really is beneficial, but discovering its true relationship to rehospitalization rates requires controlling for some extraneous variable. You might begin to search for that extraneous variable by supposing that case managers with a master's degree might be more effective than those with a baccalaureate degree. Perhaps the poor bivariate results you obtained can be attributed to the large number of case managers who lack graduate-level professional training. If so, then the rehospitalization rates for patients assigned to practitioners with a master's degree should be lower.

You could test this supposition in a multivariate analysis like the one in Table 10-2. First, you would divide your sample into subsets on the basis of the extraneous variable being controlled (which, in this illustration, is the degree level of the practitioner—baccalaureate or master's). Then you would recompute the relationship between your independent and dependent variables (that is, between case management provision and rehospitalization rate) separately for each subset (each category) of the variable being controlled. If, as a result of this elaboration process, your findings were like those in Table 10-2, you would conclude that the original relationship was replicated—that the higher rehospitalization rate of case-managed patients was not affected by controlling for practitioner degree level.

But suppose you then realize that you have overlooked another, possibly more relevant extraneous variable. You wonder whether the bivariate relationship between case management provision and rehospitalization rate can be explained by the fact that the patients with the most chronic impairments are both more likely to be rehospitalized and to be referred for case management. In other words, you suppose that the extraneous variable—type of impairment—accounts for the variation in both the independent and dependent variables, and that without their relationship to the extraneous variable, the original bivariate

Table 10-2 Original Relationship Replicated: Hypothetical Data Relating Case Management Provision to Rehospitalization, Controlling for Practitioner's Degree

	BACCALAUREATE DEGREE		MASTER'S DEGREE	
REHOSPITALIZED?	CASE-MANAGED	NOT CASE-MANAGED	CASE-MANAGED	NOT CASE-MANAGED
Yes	50%	40%	50%	40%
No	50	60	50	60
	100%	100%	100%	100%
	(100)	(100)	(100)	(100)

Table 10-3 Original Relationship Spurious: Hypothetical Data Relating Case Management Provision to Rehospitalization, Controlling for Type of Impairment

	ACUTE IMPAIRMENT		CHRONIC IMPAIRMENT	
REHOSPITALIZED?	CASE-MANAGED	NOT CASE-MANAGED	CASE-MANAGED	NOT CASE-MANAGED
Yes	38%	36%	53%	55%
No	62	64	47	45
	100%	100%	100%	100%
	(40)	(160)	(160)	(40)

relationship would disappear. For the sake of simplicity, assume that you operationally define type of impairment in terms of the number of times patients have been hospitalized for psychiatric reasons—if more than once, you might call them chronic; otherwise, you might call them acute.

You would test this supposition by constructing a multivariate table in the same manner as we did in Table 10-2, but this time controlling for a different extraneous variable—type of impairment. This process is illustrated in Table 10-3. Unlike the outcome in Table 10-2, if your results resembled those in Table 10-3, you would conclude that the original bivariate relationship was *spurious*—that the type of impairment, which preceded both your independent and dependent variables, *explains away* the original relationship between case management provision and rehospitalization rate.

The basis for this conclusion is the observation that for patients with the same type of impairment, virtually no difference in rehospitalization rates can be found between those who do and do not receive case management. For the acute subset, those patients who were and were not case-managed had rehospitalization rates of between 36 and 38 percent. For the subset whose impairments were deemed chronic, both groups of patients had a rehospitalization rate of between 53 and 55 percent.

Also notice how the acute subset of patients had both a lower rate of case management and a lower rehospitalization rate, whereas the chronic subset of patients had both a higher rate of case management

Table 10-4 Original Relationship Specified: Hypothetical Data Relating Case Management Provision to Rehospitalization, Controlling for Adequacy of Community-Based Care

	ADEQUATE CARE		INADEQUATE CARE	
REHOSPITALIZED?	CASE-MANAGED	NOT CASE-MANAGED	CASE-MANAGED	NOT CASE-MANAGED
Yes	10%	30%	90%	50%
No	90	70	10	50
	100%	100%	100%	100%
	(100)	(100)	(100)	(100)

and a higher rehospitalization rate. Thus, this table shows that the chronically impaired patients simply were much more likely to receive case management and that their greater impairment, not the impact of case management, accounts for the higher rehospitalization rate among case-managed patients.

To better understand the logic of this analysis, reexamine Table 10-1 and compare it to Table 10-3. Try to see how Table 10-1 could be constructed from the data in Table 10-3 simply by removing the extraneous variable (type of impairment) controlled for in Table 10-3. For example, to get the total number of case-managed patients who were rehospitalized, multiply 38 percent (.38) times 40 (it equals 15), and 53 percent (.53) times 160 (it equals 85). Add them together: 15 plus 85 equals 100. Total the number of case-managed patients: 40 plus 160 equals 200. Thus, 100 of the 200 case-managed patients, or 50 percent, were rehospitalized, just as indicated in Table 10-1. You can use the same process to see how the data for patients who were not case-managed in the two tables are in agreement.

So far in our hypothetical example, we have shown how the original relationship, in the direction of higher rehospitalization rates for case-managed patients, was explained away as spurious when we controlled type of impairment. But what if you suspect that there really is a relationship between case management provision and rehospitalization rates—and that the true impact of case management on rehospitalization rates is being affected by an uncontrolled variable?

Suppose, then, that you decide to control for one more variable: adequacy of community-based care. Your rationale is that perhaps case-managed patients ought to have higher rehospitalization rates when they are discharged to communities that are unwilling or inadequately prepared to care for them humanely. You might therefore suppose that case management effectiveness is indicated by higher rehospitalization rates in unreceptive or inadequately prepared communities where patients are more likely to require rehospitalization and by lower rehospitalization rates in communities that are willing and able to provide humane care. (You might operationally define adequacy of community-based care in terms of resident attitudes, the availability of various essential services, and so on.) In other words, because case managers are responsible for seeing that client needs are met, they might be effecting higher rehospitalization rates for clients who need rehospitalization and lower rates in communities where humane care does not require rehospitalization.

Table 10-4 illustrates hypothetical data that would support your supposition. This table illustrates how multivariate analyses might *specify* the conditions under which the original bivariate relationship might diminish or increase. According to this hypothetical table, when community-based care is adequate, case-managed clients have only one-third the rehospitalization rate of clients who were not case-managed. But when community-based care is inadequate, case-managed clients are almost twice as likely to be rehospitalized as are clients who are not case-managed.

Again, see how the data in Table 10-4 are consistent with the data in Table 10-1? For example, for the case-managed clients, 10 percent (.10) times 100 (in

Table 10-5 Hypothetical Relationship between Case Management Provision and Rehospitalization

REHOSPITALIZED?	NUMBER CASE-MANAGED	NUMBER NOT CASE-MANAGED
Yes	100	100
No	100	100
Total	200	200

the adequate care subset) plus 90 percent (.90) times 100 (in the inadequate care subset) equals 100 rehospitalized patients, or 50 percent (.50) times the total of 200 case-managed clients.

So far, we have used the same bivariate table to illustrate *replicating* the bivariate relationship, explaining it away as *spurious,* and *specifying* the conditions under which the original relationship holds for some but not all categories of a distorter variable. To illustrate two additional functions in the elaboration process—those that involve *interpretation (mediating variables)* and *suppressor variables*—we'll need to change the numbers a bit in the hypothetical bivariate relationship.

To illustrate *suppressor variables,* we'll begin by examining the hypothetical data in Table 10-5, a different set of outcomes in which case-managed patients are no less likely to be rehospitalized than patients who are not case-managed. Specifically, the rehospitalization rate is 50 percent for both groups of patients. But suppose you suspect that type of impairment is operating as a suppressor variable; that is, it is suppressing the true effectiveness of case management. You could control for type of impairment in the same way that we illustrated in Table 10-3. Last time, though, we were controlling it to explain away as spurious the relationship in which receiving case management was associated with a greater rehospitalization rate. Now we are controlling it to see if receiving case management is more strongly associated with lower rehospitalization rates than is indicated in the bivariate table.

Essentially, then, we are going through the same process as in Table 10-3, using the same variables, except now we are showing how multivariate control can find a relationship where there originally was none, whereas in Table 10-3 we were showing how multivariate control can find no relationship where there originally was one.

Looking at Table 10-6, you can see that 75 percent of the case-managed patients had a chronic impairment (150 of 200), and 60 percent of them were rehospitalized (90 of 150). Only 25 percent of the patients not receiving case management had a chronic impairment (50 of 200), and 80 percent of them were rehospitalized (40 of 50). Thus, for patients with chronic impairments, the case management rehospitalization rate of 60 percent was better than the 80 percent rate for those who were not receiving case management. Looking at the patients with acute impairments, we see that again the 20 percent rehospitalization rate for those who received case management (10 of 50) was better than the 40 percent rehospitalization rate for those who did not receive case management (60 of 150). In sum, because case-managed patients were more likely to have chronic impairments, and because people with chronic impairments were more likely to need rehospitalization, type of impairment was operating as a suppressor variable, causing the bivariate relationship to be less than the true relationship between receiving case management and rehospitalization rate.

We have thus shown how multivariate control can change the original bivariate relationship between independent and dependent variables. But so far our interest in the controlled variables has not gone beyond seeing what their control does to the relationship between the independent and dependent variables. We have looked to the controlled variables to see if the bivariate relationship changes, but we have not looked to them to help us *interpret* why or how the bivariate relationship exists. When we control variables for the purpose of **interpretation,** we look at how the bivariate relationship changes—not for the purpose of concluding that the original bivariate data were misleading, but to understand the basis for the relationship and the mechanisms through which it occurs.

For example, imagine that a bivariate table shows that 300 case-managed patients have a 30 percent rehospitalization rate, versus a 60 percent rehospitalization rate for 300 patients not receiving case management. Suppose we want to better understand why and how case management practitioners achieve lower rehospitalization rates, and identify the processes that account for the difference. Perhaps we think the chief factor that influences case management's superior outcome might be the case manager's better success in getting patients to take their psychotropic medica-

Table 10-6 Original Relationship Strengthened When Suppressor Variable Controlled: Hypothetical Data Relating Case Management Provision to Rehospitalization, Controlling for Type of Impairment

	ACUTE IMPAIRMENT		CHRONIC IMPAIRMENT	
REHOSPITALIZED?	CASE-MANAGED	NOT CASE-MANAGED	CASE-MANAGED	NOT CASE-MANAGED
Yes	10	60	90	40
No	40	90	60	10
	50	150	150	50

Table 10-7 Interpretation of Original Relationship: Hypothetical Data Relating Case Management Provision to Rehospitalization, Controlling for Medication Compliance

	MEDICATIONS TAKEN		MEDICATIONS NOT TAKEN	
REHOSPITALIZED?	CASE-MANAGED	NOT CASE-MANAGED	CASE-MANAGED	NOT CASE-MANAGED
Yes	20	30	70	150
No	180	70	30	50
	200	100	100	200

tions consistently as prescribed by their psychiatrist. To test this possibility, we might obtain data like the hypothetical set in Table 10-7.

In Table 10-7 we see that two-thirds (200 of the 300) of case-managed patients took their medications, whereas only one-third of the other patients did so. We also see that among the patients who took their medications the rehospitalization rate was 10 percent for case-managed patients (20 of 200) and 30 percent for the others (30 of 100). Among the patients who did not take their medications, however, the rehospitalization rate was 70 percent for case-managed patients (70 out of 100) and 75 percent for the others (150 out of 200). Thus, we can see that the superior effectiveness of case management was influenced by how successful the case managers were in getting their patients to take their medication. When the medications were taken, the case management rehospitalization rate was only 10 percent, which was one-third of the 30 percent rate for the others. But when medications were not taken, the case management rehospitalization rate shot up to 70 percent, and was only slightly better than the 75 percent rate for the others.

At this point, you may be wondering whether the results in Table 10-7 are merely another illustration of **specification,** in which the original relationship diminishes or increases when we control for a third variable. Why, you may wonder, are we calling this something else; specifically, why are we calling this *interpretation*? The answer is in the way we are conceptualizing the causal ordering—or time sequence—of the variables. In this hypothetical example, we are not conceptualizing medication taking as something that occurs before and influences the occurrence of case management. When we show that case management effectiveness changes according to medication taking, we are not saying that the original relationship is wrong or misleading. Instead, we are conceptualizing medication taking as something that case managers influence, as something that helps us understand why the original relationship exists. We are saying that a chief way in which case managers achieve lower rehospitalization rates is by achieving medication taking. We can look at the hypothetical results and see that 200 of the 300 case-managed patients (two-thirds) were taking their medications, whereas only one-third of the other patients were doing so.

We are not, however, saying that everyone doing a study like this or looking at these results would conceptualize things in the same way that we have. Suppose the decision to refer patients to a case manager was influenced by a preexisting assessment of whether or not they were taking their medications before referral, perhaps with the strange idea that case management services should only be provided to patients who are already at higher levels of motivation and functioning. Under those circumstances, medication taking would be seen as an extraneous variable whose control changed the meaning or meaningfulness of the original relationship, not as a variable that helps us understand why the original relationship exists and is meaningful and the mechanisms by which case managers achieve their lower rates.

Students often experience difficulty with this type of distinction in the elaboration model, commonly finding the terminology to be fuzzy and confusing. If that's how you are experiencing it, then we would encourage you not to worry too much about such terminology as *specification* versus *interpretation* or whether or not to call a particular variable a *distorter variable,* an *extraneous variable,* or a "whatchamacallit" variable. Although we think the terminology is useful and important, we think it's far more important that you see the need to conceptualize variables that might change or help you better understand bivariate relationships, regardless of how you classify them.

Now that we've covered the criteria for inferring causality and the concepts of internal and external validity, we are ready to examine in the next chapter the ways in which experimental and quasi-experimental designs attempt to meet all three criteria for inferring causality and thus maximize their internal validity (sometimes at the cost of having less external validity). These designs attempt to provide the most conclusive causal inferences for guiding evidence-based practice decisions about the effectiveness of interventions.

Main Points

- An inference is a conclusion that can be logically drawn in light of our research design and our findings.
- A causal inference is one derived from a research design and findings that logically imply that the independent variable really has a *causal* impact on the dependent variable.
- The term *research design* can refer to all the decisions made in planning and conducting research, including decisions about measurement, sampling, how to collect data, and logical arrangements designed to permit certain kinds of inferences.
- There are three basic criteria for the determination of causation in scientific research: (1) The independent (cause) and dependent (effect) variables must be empirically related to each other, (2) the independent variable must occur earlier in time than the dependent variable, and (3) the observed relationship between these two variables cannot be explained away as being due to the influence of some third variable that causes both of them.
- Internal validity refers to the confidence we have that the results of a study accurately depict whether one variable is or is not a cause of another.
- Common threats to internal validity are history, maturation, testing, instrumentation changes, statistical regression, selection bias, and causal time order.
- External validity refers to the extent to which we can *generalize* the findings of a study to settings and populations beyond the study conditions.
- Correlational designs can be used to examine the plausibility of causal inferences when experimental designs are not feasible.
- Cross-sectional studies are those based on observations made at one time.
- The case-control design compares groups of cases that have had contrasting outcomes and then collects *retrospective* data about past differences that might explain the difference in outcomes.
- A common limitation in case-control designs is recall bias. This occurs when a person's current recollections of the quality and value of past experiences are tainted by knowing that things didn't work out for them later in life.

• Although cross-sectional studies, case-control studies, and longitudinal studies do not control for all threats to internal validity, by employing multivariate statistical controls they can strengthen the plausibility of the notion that the relationships they find are explanatory in nature.

• The basic steps in elaboration are as follows: (1) A relationship is observed to exist between two variables, (2) a third variable is held constant in the sense that the cases under study are subdivided according to the attributes of that third variable, (3) the original two-variable relationship is recomputed within each subgroup, and (4) the comparison of the original relationship with the relationships found within each subgroup provides a fuller understanding of the original relationship itself.

• The outcome of an elaboration analysis may be replication (whereby an original relationship is essentially the same after controlling for additional variables), explanation (whereby an original spurious relationship is reduced essentially to zero when an extraneous variable is held constant), interpretation (whereby controlling for a moderating variable helps interpret the mechanism through which the original relationship occurs), or specification (whereby controlling for an additional variable specifies the conditions under which the original relationship tends to diminish or increase—that is, the original relationship might hold for some but not all categories of the additional variable(s) being controlled).

• A suppressor variable conceals the relationship between two other variables; a distorter variable causes an apparent reversal in the relationship between two other variables (from negative to positive or vice versa).

Review Questions and Exercises

1. Pick three of the threats to internal validity discussed in this chapter and make up examples (other than those discussed in the chapter) to illustrate each.

2. Briefly sketch a case-control design to generate hypotheses about interventions that may be the most helpful in preventing teens from running away.

a. What are the background variables that would be important to control for?
b. Explain and illustrate with a table how multivariate statistical control via the elaboration model could control for at least one of those background variables.
c. Identify and explain three uncontrolled threats to the validity of your study that would represent major reasons why the results would be only exploratory.

3. A director of a prison Bible studies program claims that his program prevents recidivism. His claim is based on data showing that only 14 percent of the inmates who complete his Bible studies program recidivate, as compared to 41 percent of the inmates who choose not to participate in his program. Based on what you read in this chapter, explain why his claim is not warranted.

4. A study with an exceptionally high degree of internal validity conducted with Native Alaskan female adolescents who have recently been sexually abused concludes that an intervention is effective in preventing substance abuse among its participants. Explain how this study can have little external validity from one perspective, yet a good deal of external validity from another perspective—depending upon the target population of the practitioners who are utilizing the study as a potential guide to their evidence-based practice.

5. A newspaper article (Perlman, 1982) discussed arguments that linked fluoridation to acquired immune deficiency syndrome (AIDS), citing this evidence: "While half the country's communities have fluoridated water supplies, and half do not, 90% of AIDS cases are coming from fluoridated areas and only 10% are coming from nonfluoridated areas." Discuss this in terms of what you have learned about the criteria of causation, indicating what other variables might be involved.

Internet Exercises

1. On the web, find a study that used a case-control design. Critically appraise the appropriateness of its conclusions in light of what you've read in this chapter. Include in your appraisal an identification of the study's major strengths and weaknesses. Does the study have value despite its limitations? Explain.

2. On the web, find a study that used a cross-sectional design. Critically appraise the appropriateness of its conclusions in light of what you've read in this chapter. Include in your appraisal an identification of the

study's major strengths and weaknesses. Does the study have value despite its limitations? Explain.

3. On the web, find a study that used a longitudinal design. Critically appraise the appropriateness of its conclusions in light of what you've read in this chapter. Include in your appraisal an identification of the study's major strengths and weaknesses. Does the study have value despite its limitations? Explain.

Additional Readings

Alexander, Leslie B., and Phyllis Solomon (eds.). [illegible] *[illegible]cess in the Human Services:* [illegible]mont, CA: Thomson Brooks/ [illegible] this valuable compendium of [illegible]rs, and we repeat our recommendation here—this time for its chapter illustrating a cross-sectional study, two chapters illustrating longitudinal studies, and two chapters illustrating case-control studies. As we mentioned earlier, each study is followed by commentaries by the investigators regarding the real-world agency feasibility obstacles they encountered in carrying out their research and how they modified their research plans in light of those obstacles.

Rosenberg, Morris. 1968. *The Logic of Survey Analysis.* New York: Basic Books. In the most comprehensive statement of elaboration available, Rosenberg presents the basic paradigm and then suggests logical extensions. It's difficult to decide which is more important—this aspect of the book or its voluminous illustrations. Both are simply excellent, and this book serves an important instructional purpose.

CHAPTER **11**

Experimental Designs

What You'll Learn in This Chapter

This chapter examines the ways in which experimental designs and quasi-experimental designs attempt to maximize internal validity. It also examines both the limitations and utility of pre-experimental pilot studies. Understanding the strengths and weaknesses of these various design arrangements is essential in appraising the studies you find in the evidence-based practice process.

INTRODUCTION

Social work researchers often want to make inferences about cause and effect. So do social work practitioners engaged in evidence-based practice, who search and appraise the literature seeking to ascertain the effectiveness of interventions. As discussed in Chapter 10, the best causal evidence comes from designs that control for threats to internal validity. In so doing, they permit inferences as to whether change in the dependent variable was really caused by the independent variable and not something else. In this chapter we'll see why and how *experimental designs* are thought to have the most internal validity, and why they are thus considered to reside at the top of the evidence-based practice research hierarchy for questions about intervention effectiveness.

EXPERIMENTAL DESIGNS

Experimental designs attempt to provide maximum control for threats to internal validity by first randomly assigning research participants to *experimental* and *control groups*. Next, they introduce one category of the independent variable (such as a new program or intervention method) to the **experimental group** while withholding it from the **control group.** Then they compare the extent to which the experimental and control groups differ on the dependent variable. The latter comparison, though coming at the end of the sequence, usually involves assessing the experimental and control groups before and after introducing the independent variable.

For example, suppose we wanted to assess the effectiveness of an intervention used by gerontological social workers in nursing home facilities, an intervention that engages clients in a review of their life history in order to alleviate depression and improve morale. Rather than just compare residents who requested the intervention with those who did not—which would be vulnerable to a *selection bias* because we could not assume the two groups were equivalent to begin with—our experimental approach would use a random assignment procedure (such as coin tosses). Thus, each resident who agrees to participate and for whom the intervention is deemed appropriate would be randomly assigned to either an experimental group (which would receive the intervention) or a control group (which would not receive it). Observations on one or more indicators of depression and morale (the dependent variables) would be taken before and after the intervention is delivered. To the extent that the experimental group's mood improves more than that of the control group, the findings would support the hypothesis that the intervention causes the improvement.

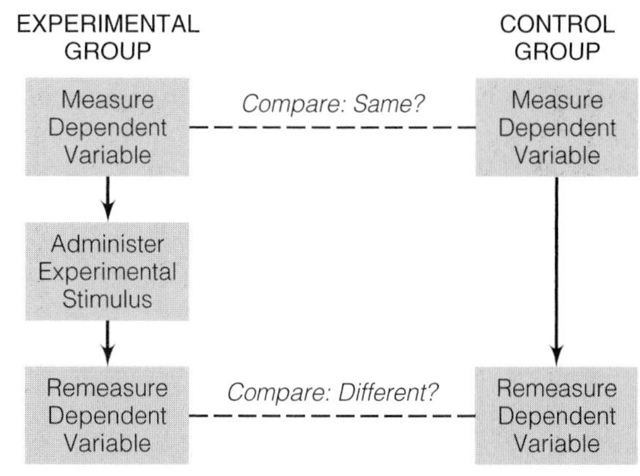

Figure 11-1 Diagram of Basic Experimental Design

The preceding example illustrates the *classic experimental design,* also called the **pretest–posttest control group design.** This design is diagrammed in Figure 11-1. The shorthand notation for this design is

$$\begin{array}{llll} R & O_1 & X & O_2 \\ R & O_1 & & O_2 \end{array}$$

The R in this design stands for random assignment of research participants to either the experimental group or the control group. The O_1's represent pretests, and the O_2's represent posttests. The X represents the tested intervention.

Notice how this design controls for many threats to internal validity. If the improvement in mood were caused by history or maturation, then there would be no reason the experimental group should improve any more than the control group. Likewise, because the residents were assigned on a randomized basis, there is no reason to suppose that the experimental group was any more likely to statistically regress to less extreme scores than was the control group. Random assignment also removes any reason for supposing that the two groups were different initially with respect to the dependent variable or to other relevant factors such as motivation or psychosocial functioning.

Notice also, however, that the pretest–posttest control group design does not control for the possible effects of testing and retesting. If we think that taking a pretest might have an impact on treatment effects, or if we think that it might bias their posttest responses, then we might opt for an experimental design called the **posttest-only control group design.** Another, more common, reason for choosing the posttest-only control group design is that pretesting may not be possible or practical, such as in the evaluation of the effectiveness programs to prevent incidents of child abuse. The shorthand notation for this design is

R	X	O
R		O

This design assumes that the process of random assignment removes any significant initial differences between experimental and control groups. This assumption of initial group equivalence permits the inference that any differences between the two groups at posttest reflect the causal impact of the independent variable.

If we would like to know the amount of pretest–posttest change but are worried about testing effects, then we could use a fancy design called the **Solomon four-group design.** The shorthand notation for this design is

R	O_1	X	O_2
R	O_1		O_2
R		X	O_2
R			O_2

This design, which is highly regarded by research methodologists but rarely used in social work studies, combines the classical experimental design with the posttest-only control group design. It does this simply by randomly assigning research participants to four groups instead of two. Two of the groups are control groups, and two are experimental groups. One control group and one experimental group are pretested and posttested. The other experimental and control group are posttested only. If special effects are caused by pretesting, then they can be discerned by comparing the two experimental group results with each other and the two control group results with each other.

Sometimes experiments are used to compare the effectiveness of two alternative treatments. Pretests are recommended in such experiments so that the comparative amounts of change produced by each treatment can be assessed. This design is called the **alternative treatment design with pretest** (Shadish, Cook, and Campbell, 2001). The shorthand notation for this design is

R	O_1	X_A	O_2
R	O_1	X_B	O_2
R	O_1		O_2

The first row above represents the participants randomly assigned to Treatment A. The second row represents the participants randomly assigned to Treatment B. The third row represents the participants randomly assigned to a control group. To show that Treatment A is more effective than Treatment B, the first row would need to show more improvement from O_1 to O_2 than both of the other rows. If the first two rows both show approximately the same amounts of improvement, and both amounts are more than in the third row, that would indicate that both treatments are approximately equally effective. But if the third row shows the same degree of improvement as in the first two rows, then neither treatment would appear to be effective. Instead, we would attribute the improvement in all three rows to an alternative explanation such as history or the passage of time.

Some experiments use the first two rows of this design but not the third row. In other words, they compare the two treatments to each other but not to a control group. Such experiments can have conclusive, valid findings if one group improves significantly more than the other. But suppose they both have roughly the same amount of improvement. The temptation would be to call them equally effective. However, with no control group, we cannot rule out threats to internal validity, such as history or the passage of time, as alternative explanations of the improvement in both groups.

A similar type of design can be used to see not only whether an intervention is effective, but also which components of the intervention may or may not be necessary to achieve its effects. Experiments using this design are called **dismantling studies.** The shorthand notation for this design is

R	O_1	X_{AB}	O_2
R	O_1	X_A	O_2
R	O_1	X_B	O_2
R	O_1		O_2

The first row above represents the participants randomly assigned to a treatment that contains components A and B. The second row represents the participants randomly assigned to receive the A component only. The third row represents the participants randomly assigned to receive the B component only. The fourth row represents the participants randomly assigned to a control group. If the first row shows more improvement from O_1 to O_2 than all of the other rows, then that would indicate that the treatment is effective and that both components (A and B) are needed. If either of the next two rows shows as much improvement as the first row shows, then that would indicate that the component signified in that row is all that is needed to achieve the effects shown in the first row, and that the other component may not be needed.

Dismantling studies have received considerable attention in recent debates about the effectiveness of a relatively new intervention for *post-traumatic stress disorder* (PTSD). You may have heard about this controversial intervention, which is called *eye movement desensitization and reprocessing* (EMDR). Briefly put, this intervention combines various cognitive-behavioral intervention techniques with a technique involving the stimulation of rapid eye movements. Many experiments using the pretest–posttest control group design have found it to be effective. However, most (but not all) dismantling studies found that the same effects could be achieved using the cognitive-behavioral components of the intervention without the eye movements. Some reviewers of the dismantling studies have argued that their results indicate that EMDR is nothing more than traditional cognitive-behavioral intervention with an unnecessary eye movement gimmick. Leaders in the EMDR field have fiercely criticized the dismantling studies, and argue that their intervention really does represent a major new breakthrough in the treatment of PTSD. Perhaps vested interests and ego involvement influence those on both sides of this debate (Rubin, 2002).

Randomization

It should be clear at this point that the cardinal rule of experimental design is that the experimental and control groups must be comparable. Ideally, the control group represents what the experimental group would have been like had it not been exposed to the intervention or other experimental stimulus being evaluated. There is no way to guarantee that the experimental and control groups will be equivalent in all relevant respects. There is no way to guarantee that they will share exactly the same history and maturational processes or will not have relevant differences before the evaluated intervention is introduced. But there is a way to avoid biases in the assignment of clients to groups and to guarantee a high mathematical likelihood that their initial, pretreatment group differences will be insignificant: through random assignment to experimental and control groups, a process also known as *randomization.*

Randomization, or random assignment, is not the same as random sampling. The research participants to be randomly assigned are rarely randomly selected from a population. Instead, they are individuals who voluntarily agreed to participate in the experiment, a fact that limits the external validity of the experiment. Unlike random sampling, which pertains to *generalizability,* randomization is a device for increasing internal validity. It does not seek to ensure that the research participants are representative of a population; instead, it seeks to reduce the risks that experimental group participants are not representative of control group participants.

The principal technique of randomization simply entails using procedures based on probability theory to assign research participants to experimental and control groups. Having recruited, by whatever means, the group of all participants, the researchers might flip a coin to determine to which group each participant is assigned; or researchers may number all of the participants serially and assign them by selecting numbers from a random numbers table (such as the one in Appendix B); or researchers may put the odd-numbered participants in one group and put the even-numbered ones in the other.

In randomization the research participants are our study population that we randomly divide into two samples, with each group consisting of one-half of our study population. As we will see in Chapter 14, on sampling, if the number of research participants involved is large enough it is reasonable to expect that the various characteristics of the participants will be distributed in an approximately even manner between the two groups, thus making the two groups comparable.

Matching

Although randomization is the best way to avoid bias in assigning research participants to groups and increasing the likelihood that the two groups will be comparable, it does not guarantee full comparability. One way to further improve the chances of obtaining comparable groups is to combine randomization with **matching,** in which pairs of participants are matched on the basis of their similarities on one or more variables, and one member of the pair is then

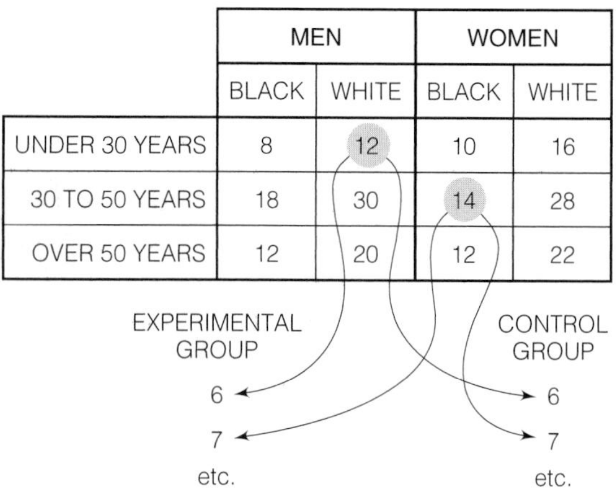

Figure 11-2 Quota Matrix Illustration

randomly assigned to the experimental group and the other to the control group. Matching can also be done without randomization, as we will see soon when we discuss quasi-experiments, but we only have a true experiment when matching is combined with randomization. Matching without randomization does not control for all possible biases in who gets assigned to which group.

To illustrate matching with randomization, suppose 12 of your research participants are young white men. You might assign 6 of those at random to the experimental group and the other 6 to the control group. If 14 research participants are middle-aged African American women, you might randomly assign 7 to each group. The overall matching process could be most efficiently achieved through the creation of a *quota matrix* constructed of all the most relevant characteristics. (Figure 11-2 provides a simplified illustration of such a matrix.) Ideally, the quota matrix would be constructed to result in an even number of research participants in each cell of the matrix. Then, half of the research participants in each cell would randomly go into the experimental group and half into the control group.

Alternatively, you might recruit more research participants than are required by your experimental design. You might then examine many characteristics of the large initial group of research participants. Whenever you discover a pair of highly similar participants, you might assign one at random to the experimental group and the other to the control group. Potential participants who were unlike anyone else in the initial group might be left out of the experiment altogether.

Whatever method is used, the desired result is the same. The overall average description of the experimental group should be the same as that of the control group. For instance, they should have about the same average age, the same gender composition, the same racial composition, and so forth. As a general rule, the two groups should be comparable in terms of those variables that are likely to be related to the dependent variable under study. In a study of gerontological social work, for example, the two groups should be alike in terms of age, gender, ethnicity, and physical and mental health, among other variables. In some cases, moreover, you may delay assigning research participants to experimental and control groups until you have initially measured the dependent variable. Thus, for instance, you might administer a questionnaire that measures participants' psychosocial functioning and then match the experimental and control groups to assure yourself that the two groups exhibited the same overall level of functioning before intervention.

Providing Services to Control Groups

You may recall reading in Chapter 4 that the withholding of services from people in need raises ethical concerns. It may also be unacceptable to agency administrators, who fear bad publicity or the loss of revenues based on service delivery hours. We must therefore point out that when we discuss withholding the intervention being tested from the control group, we do not mean that people in the control group should be denied services. We simply mean that they should not receive the *experimental* intervention that is being tested during the period of the test.

When experiments are feasible to carry out in social work settings, control group participants are likely to receive the usual, routine services provided by an agency. Experimental group participants will receive the new, experimental intervention being tested, perhaps in addition to the usual, routine services. Thus, the experiment may determine whether services that include the new intervention are more effective than routine services, rather than attempt to ascertain whether the new intervention is better than no service. Moreover, control group participants may be put at the top of a waiting list to receive the new intervention once the experiment is over. If the results of the experiment show that the tested intervention is effective, or at least is not harmful, it can then be offered to control group participants. The researcher may also want to measure whether control group participants change in the desired direction after they receive the intervention. The findings of this measurement can buttress the main findings of the experiment.

QUASI-EXPERIMENTAL DESIGNS

In many social work agencies, obtaining a control group is not feasible. And when we can obtain a control group, it is often not feasible to use randomization to determine which participants are assigned to it versus the experimental group.

Agency administrators and practitioners may cite various reasons why it's not acceptable to withhold interventions from clients or prospective clients: Withholding services may seem unethical, it may have unwanted fiscal implications, or it may lead to complaints from consumers who feel deprived. As we discussed above, the ethical concerns are not always warranted. But agency administrators and practitioners who strongly believe in the value of the service being evaluated may not be persuaded of that. They may not agree that perpetually providing untested services may be more questionable ethically than withholding services that might be ineffectual or harmful. No matter how strong a case we may make for random assignment to experimental and control groups, our chances of getting it are usually quite slim. Even if we were able to convince an agency director of the merits of using an experimental design, chances are we also would have to convince the board members to whom the director reports. It might also be necessary to convince agency practitioners, whom the administrator does not want to alienate and who will refer participants to the experiment.

Rather than forgo any evaluation in such instances, alternative research designs sometimes can be created and executed that have less internal validity than randomized experiments but still provide more support for causal inferences than do pre-experimental designs. These designs are called **quasi-experimental designs** and are distinguished from "true" experiments primarily because they do not randomly assign participants to experimental and control groups.

Despite the lack of random assignment, well-designed quasi-experiments can have a high degree of internal validity. Consequently, they reside high on the evidence-based practice research hierarchy—just below well-designed experiments. Let's now examine three commonly used quasi-experimental designs that, when designed and conducted properly, can attain a reasonable degree of internal validity.

Nonequivalent Comparison Groups Design

The **nonequivalent comparison groups design** can be used when we are unable to randomly assign participants to groups but can find an existing group that appears similar to the experimental group and thus can be compared to it.

Suppose, for example, that we want to evaluate the effects on depression of an intervention that gives pets to nursing home residents. It's unlikely that you would be permitted to select randomly in any nursing home the residents who will and will not receive pets. You can probably imagine the administrative hassles that might erupt because some residents or their relatives feel they are being deprived. As an alternative to a true experimental design, then, you may be able to find two nursing homes that agree to participate in your research and that appear very similar in all of the respects that are relevant to internal validity: for example, the same numbers and types of residents and staff, the same level of care, and so on. In particular, you would want to make sure that the resident populations of the two homes were quite similar in terms of age, socioeconomic status, mental and physical disabilities, psychosocial functioning, ethnicity, and so on. You could then introduce the intervention in one home, and use the other as a comparison group. (The term *comparison group* is used instead of *control group* when participants are not assigned randomly.)

The two homes could be compared in a pretest to make sure that they really are equivalent on the dependent variable before introducing the independent variable. If their average depression scores are about the same, then it would be reasonable to suppose that differences at posttest represent the effects of the intervention. Of course, such a causal inference would be even more credible had the participants been randomly assigned. But to the extent that you could provide convincing data as to the comparability of the two homes on plausible extraneous variables, and if the differences on their average pretest scores are trivial, then your causal inference would be credible and your study would have value. The shorthand notation for this design is

$$O_1 \quad X \quad O_2$$
$$O_1 \qquad\quad O_2$$

You may note that the preceding notation is the same as the pretest–posttest control group design except that it lacks the *R* for random assignment.

Here's another example of this design, using an excerpt from an actual study in which two junior high schools were selected to evaluate a program that sought to discourage the use of tobacco, alcohol, and drugs.

> The pairing of the two schools and their assignment to "experimental" and "control" conditions was not random. The local Lung Association had identified the school where we delivered the program as one in which administrators were seeking a solution to admitted problems of smoking, alcohol, and drug abuse. The "control" school was chosen as a convenient and nearby demographic match where administrators were willing to allow our surveying and breath-testing procedures. The principal of that school considered the existing program of health education effective and believed that the onset of smoking was relatively uncommon among his students.
>
> The communities served by the two schools were very similar. The rate of parental smoking reported by the students was just above 40 percent in both schools.
>
> (McAlister et al., 1980:720)

Without the participants having been randomly assigned to experimental and control groups, we might wonder if the two schools are comparable. It helps to know, however, that in the initial set of observations, the experimental and comparison (control) groups reported virtually the same (low) frequency of smoking. Over the 21 months of the study, smoking increased in both groups, but less so in the experimental group than in the control group, suggesting that the program did affect students' behavior.

When you read a report of a study that used a nonequivalent comparison groups design, it is important to remember that if selection biases seem highly plausible in that study, then the notion that the groups are really comparable is severely undermined. Unless the researcher can present compelling evidence to document the comparability of the groups on relevant extraneous variables and on pretest scores, then any differences in outcome between the two groups are highly suspect. In other words, depending on how well the researcher documents the comparability of the groups, studies using this design can be strong enough to guide practice or can be very weak.

Even when much evidence is supplied supporting the notion that the groups are comparable, nagging doubts often remain. Rarely can researchers obtain evidence about every possible extraneous variable that might account for differences in outcome between the groups. For example, the fact that two groups are comparable in their pretest scores and in various background characteristics does not ensure that they are equally motivated to change. Suppose an evaluation is being conducted to see whether a prison Bible studies program reduces re-arrest rates after prisoners are released. Suppose further that the prisoners who attend the Bible studies program do so voluntarily and that the study compares the re-arrest rates of those prisoners to a matched group of prisoners who share the same background characteristics as the Bible studies group but who chose not to attend the Bible studies program. No matter how many data are provided documenting the background similarities of the two groups, we might remain quite skeptical about their comparability regarding the prisoners' notions of morality, sense of remorse, and motivation to go straight—extraneous variables that might have a greater influence on re-arrest rates than many of the background variables on which the groups have been shown to be comparable.

Ways to Strengthen the Internal Validity of the Nonequivalent Comparison Groups Design

Shadish, Cook, and Campbell (2001) propose several design features that can help offset some of the doubts about the comparability of nonequivalent comparison groups in the nonequivalent comparison groups design. Here are two features that may be feasible when evaluating services in social service agencies.

1. *Use multiple pretests.* One key concern regarding selectivity biases is that the experimental group might be more motivated to change than the control group and therefore was probably already in the process of change before treatment began. By administering the same pretest at different time points before intervention begins, we can detect whether one group is already engaged in a change process and the other is not. It can also help us detect whether statistical regression is occurring in one group but not the other. The shorthand notation for adding this design feature to the nonequivalent comparison groups design is

$$
\begin{array}{llll}
O_1 & O_2 & X & O_3 \\
O_1 & O_2 & & O_3
\end{array}
$$

In the top row in this diagram the experimental group gets the treatment (X). The bottom row represents the comparison group. In each row, O_1 and O_2 signify the first and second pretests. O_3 signifies the posttest. Suppose two groups of substance abusers have the same mean score of 10 at O_1, indicating how many days during the past month they used illegal substances. Suppose at O_2 the experimental group mean drops to 6, and the comparison group mean stays at 10. Suppose at O_3 the experimental group mean drops further, to 4, and the comparison group mean stays at 10. Without the second pretest, the difference between 10 and 4 at posttest would appear to indicate that the treatment (X) was effective—that it caused the reduction in substance abuse. But with the second pretest, we can see that the treatment did not cause the drop—that the two groups of abusers were not really comparable because the experimental group was already engaged in a change process before treatment began (perhaps due to greater motivation to change), and the comparison group was not. Conversely, if the O_2 scores of both groups had remained at 10, we would have more confidence that the drop to 4 at posttest really indicated that the treatment was effective—that it caused the reduction in substance abuse.

2. *Use switching replications.* Another way to detect whether a desired outcome might be due to a selection bias is by administering the treatment to the comparison group after the first posttest. If we replicate in that group—in a second posttest—the improvement made by the experimental group in the first posttest, then we reduce doubt as to whether the improvement at the first posttest was merely a function of a selection bias. If our second posttest results do not replicate the improvement made by the experimental group in the first posttest, then the difference between the groups at the first posttest can be attributed to the lack of comparability between the two groups. The shorthand notation for adding this design feature is

$$O_1 \quad X \quad O_2 \quad O_3$$
$$O_1 \quad O_2 \quad X \quad O_3$$

The top row in this diagram represents the experimental group. The bottom row represents the comparison group. In each row, O_1 signifies the pretest. O_2 and O_3 represent the posttests. The treatment is signified by X.

Returning to our substance abuse example, suppose the two groups of substance abusers have the same mean score of 10 at O_1, indicating how many days during the past month they used illegal substances. Suppose at O_2 the experimental group (in the top row) mean drops to 4, and the comparison group mean stays at 10. Suppose at O_3 the experimental group mean stays at 4, and the comparison group mean drops to 4. That would suggest that the treatment was effective, and that the difference between the O_2 scores of 10 and 4 was not merely due to a selection bias. In contrast, suppose at O_3 the comparison group mean does *not* improve; that is, despite receiving the intervention, it stays at 10. That would suggest that the treatment was *not* effective, and that the difference in improvement between the two groups *was* merely due to a selection bias.

Simple Time-Series Designs

Another commonly used set of quasi-experimental designs are called **time-series designs.** These designs go beyond the *use of multiple pretests* by additionally emphasizing the *use of multiple posttests.* A particularly feasible time-series design—feasible because it does not require a comparison group—is called the **simple interrupted time-series design.** The shorthand notation for this design is

$$O_1\ O_2\ O_3\ O_4\ O_5\ X\ O_6\ O_7\ O_8\ O_9\ O_{10}$$

Each O in the notation represents a different observation point for measuring the dependent variable over time. No particular number of measurements is required, although the more the better. The notation above indicates that the dependent variable was measured at five points in time before the intervention (X) was introduced and another five times after that.

To illustrate the time-series design, we will begin by asking you to assess the meaning of some hypothetical data. Suppose your colleague—a child therapist working in a child guidance center—tells you that she has come up with an effective new technique for reducing hostile antisocial behaviors by children with behavioral disorders during their sessions of group play therapy. To prove her assertion, she tells you about a play therapy group that has had four sessions. During the first two sessions, she noticed that there seemed to be an unusually high number of time-outs required in response to hostile antisocial behaviors, but she did not count them. After the second session, she developed her new technique and decided to test it out. To test it, she counted the number of time-outs in each of the next two sessions, not employing her new

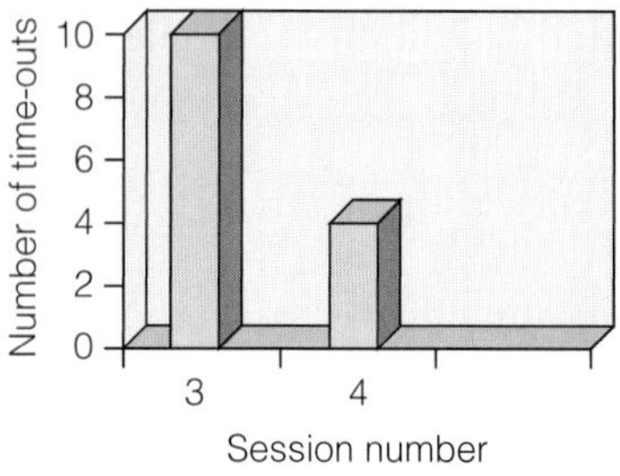

Figure 11-3 Two Observations of Time-outs: Before and After Using New Technique

technique in the third session, and then employing it in the fourth session.

She tells you that during the third session, when she did not employ her technique, there were 10 time-outs, whereas the number of time-outs fell to 4 during the fourth session. In other words, she contends, her new technique cut the number of time-outs in half. This simple set of data is presented graphically in Figure 11-3.

Are you persuaded that the new technique employed during session 4 was the cause of the drop in time-outs? You'd probably object that her data don't prove the case. Two observations aren't really enough to prove anything. The improvement in time-outs could have resulted from history, maturation, or statistical regression—not to mention the possibility of instrumentation; that is, a change in her own inclination to administer time-outs. Ideally, she should have had two separate play therapy groups with children assigned randomly to each, employed the intervention in only one group after one or more pretest sessions, and then compared the two groups in later sessions. But she doesn't have two classes of randomly assigned students. Neither does she have a nonequivalent comparison group. All she has is the one group.

Suppose, however, that instead of counting the time-outs only in sessions 3 and 4, she had been counting them in every session throughout a 10-session treatment period and recording each number in a running log. Suppose further that instead of introducing her new technique during session 4, she introduced it during session 6 and then continued employing it through session 10. Her log would allow you to conduct a time-series evaluation.

Figure 11-4 presents three possible patterns of time-outs over time. In each pattern, the new technique is introduced after the fifth session (that is, during the sixth session). In each pattern, the vertical line between the fifth and sixth sessions separates the five sessions before the new technique was used and the five sessions during which it was used. Which of these patterns would give you confidence that the new technique had the impact she contends it did?

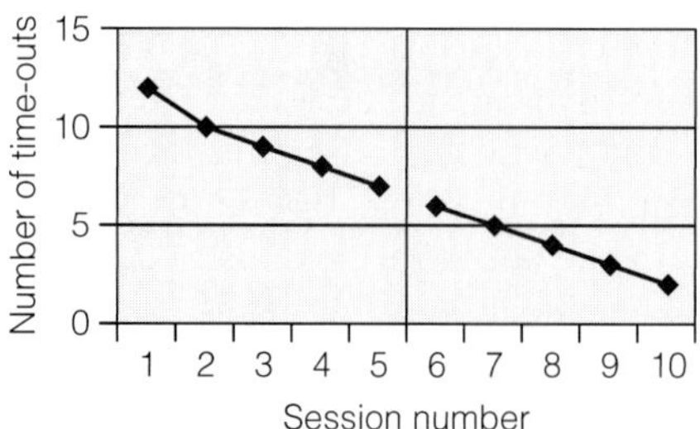

Pattern 2

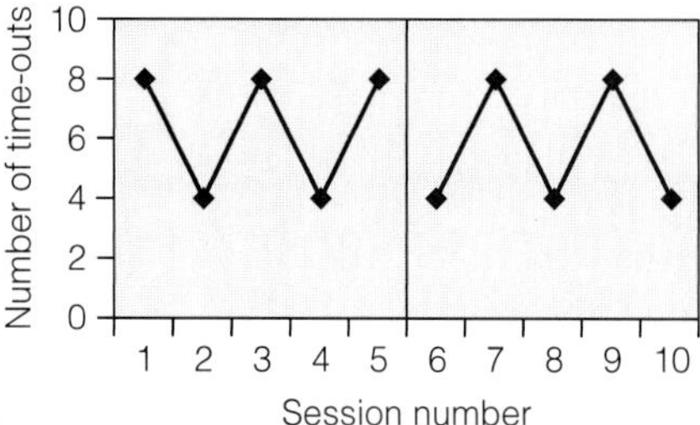

Pattern 3

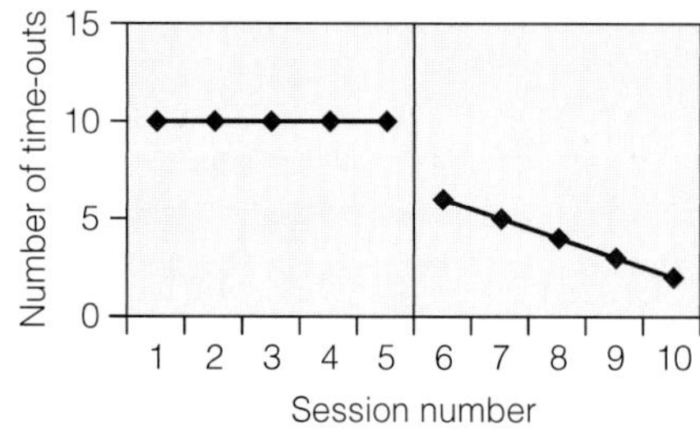

Figure 11-4 Time-Series Perspective: Three Patterns of Time-outs

If the time-series results looked like pattern 1 in Figure 11-4, you'd probably conclude that a trend of fewer time-outs with each session had begun well before the new technique was introduced and had continued unaffected after the new technique was introduced. The long-term data suggest that the trend would have occurred even without the new technique.

Pattern 1, then, contradicts the assertion that the new technique decreased the number of time-outs.

Pattern 2 contradicts her assertion also. It indicates that the number of time-outs had been bouncing up and down in a regular pattern throughout the 10 sessions. Sometimes it increases from one session to the next, and sometimes it decreases; the new technique simply was introduced at a point where there would have been a decrease in time-outs anyway. More to the point, we note that during the five sessions when the new technique was used, the number of time-outs kept fluctuating cyclically between increases and decreases in the same way it fluctuated during the first through fifth sessions, or before the new technique was introduced.

Only pattern 3 in Figure 11-4 supports her contention that the new technique mattered. As we see, the number of time-outs before the new technique was introduced had been steady at 10 time-outs per session. Then, beginning immediately with session 6, when the new technique was introduced, the number of time-outs fell to six and continued dropping with each successive session. The data in pattern 3 therefore exclude the possibility that the decrease in time-outs results from a process of maturation indicated in pattern 1 or from regular fluctuations indicated in pattern 2. They also rule out the possibility of statistical regression because the improvement was not based on movement from one extreme and atypical pretest score.

The pattern 3 data do not, however, rule out history as a possible explanation. In other words, it is conceivable that some extraneous event may have caused the change. Perhaps the child guidance center's new psychiatrist started prescribing a new medication for attention deficit hyperactivity disorder at the same time the new play therapy technique was introduced. Or perhaps a family therapy service for the same children commenced at that time. Nevertheless, the data in pattern 3 do reduce somewhat the *plausibility* of the explanation that history caused the change because the extraneous event would have had to occur at the same time that the new technique was introduced—in a way that could be portrayed as an unlikely coincidence.

One way to further reduce the plausibility of history as an explanation for time-series data like those in pattern 3 would be to find another play therapy group that could serve as a nonequivalent comparison group, and assess it at the same points in time as the play therapy group receiving the new technique. If your colleague did that, she would be using a third type of quasi-experimental design—the multiple time-series design. Let's now take a close look at that type of design.

Multiple Time-Series Designs

Multiple time-series designs are a stronger form of time-series analysis than simple time-series designs (that is, they have greater internal validity) because they add time-series analysis to the nonequivalent comparison groups design. Probably the most applicable multiple time-series design for social workers is the **interrupted time-series with a nonequivalent comparison group time-series design.** The shorthand notation for this design is

$$O_1\ O_2\ O_3\ O_4\ O_5\ X\ O_6\ O_7\ O_8\ O_9\ O_{10}$$

$$O_1\ O_2\ O_3\ O_4\ O_5\quad\ O_6\ O_7\ O_8\ O_9\ O_{10}$$

In this design, both an experimental group and a nonequivalent comparison group (neither assigned randomly) are measured at multiple points in time before and after an intervention is introduced to the experimental group.

Carol Weiss presented a useful example of this design, one that compared time-series data from an "experimental" state to time-series data from four "control" states:

> An interesting example of multiple time series was the evaluation of the Connecticut crackdown on highway speeding. Evaluators collected reports of traffic fatalities for several periods before and after the new program went into effect. They found that fatalities went down after the crackdown, but since the series had had an unstable up-and-down pattern for many years, it was not certain that the drop was due to the program. They then compared the statistics with time-series data from four neighboring states where there had been no changes in traffic enforcement. Those states registered no equivalent drop in fatalities. The comparison lent credence to the conclusion that the crackdown had had some effect.
>
> (1972:69)

Although this study design is not as good as one in which participants are assigned randomly, it is nonetheless an improvement over assessing the experimental group's time-series performance without comparison to a control group. It is also an improvement over comparing an experimental and a nonequivalent comparison group without the added benefit of time-series data. The key in assessing this aspect of evaluation studies is *comparability*, as the following example illustrates.

Rural development is a growing concern in the poor countries of the world and one that has captured the attention and support of many rich countries. Through national foreign assistance programs and international agencies such as the World Bank, the developed countries are in the process of sharing their technological knowledge and skills with the developing countries. Such programs have had mixed results, however. Often, modern techniques do not produce the intended results when applied in traditional societies.

Rajesh Tandon and L. Dave Brown (1981) undertook an experiment in which technological training would be accompanied by instruction in village organization. They felt it was important for poor farmers to learn how to organize and exert collective influence within their villages—to get needed action from government officials, for example. Only then would their new technological skills bear fruit.

Both intervention and evaluation were attached to an ongoing program in which 25 villages had been selected for technological training. Two poor farmers from each village had been trained in new agricultural technologies and then sent home to share their new knowledge with their fellow villagers and to organize other farmers into "peer groups" that would help spread that knowledge. Two years later, the authors randomly selected two of the 25 villages (subsequently called Group A and Group B) for special training and 11 others as comparison groups. A careful comparison of demographic characteristics showed the experimental and comparison groups to be strikingly similar to each other, suggesting they were sufficiently comparable for the study.

The peer groups from the two experimental villages were brought together for special training in organization building. The participants were given information about organizing and making demands on the government, as well as opportunities to act out dramas that were similar to the situations they faced at home. The training took three days.

The outcome variables considered in the evaluation were all concerned with the extent to which members of the peer groups initiated group activities that were designed to improve their situation. Six types were studied. "Active initiative," for example, was defined as "active effort to influence persons or events affecting group members versus passive response or withdrawal" (Tandon and Brown, 1981:180). The data for evaluation came from the journals that the peer group

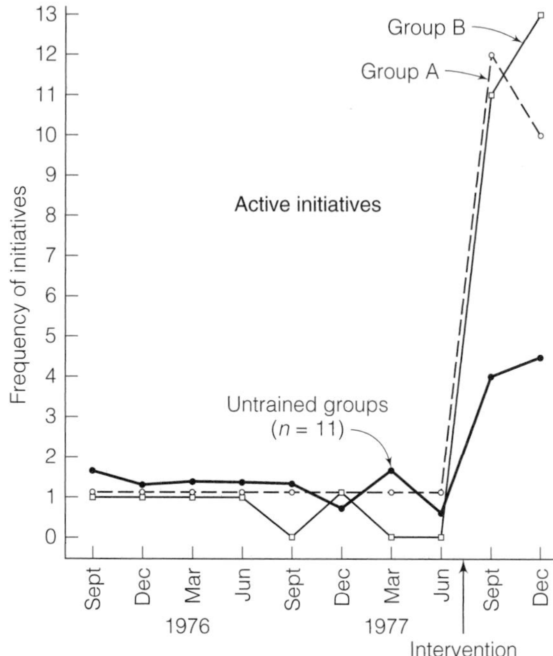

SOURCE: Rajesh Tandon and L. Dave Brown, "Organization-Building for Rural Development: An Experiment in India," *Journal of Applied Behavioral Science* (April–June 1981):182.

Figure 11-5 Multiple Time-Series Design: Active Initiatives over Time

leaders had been keeping since their initial technological training. The researchers read through the journals and counted the number of initiatives taken by members of the peer groups. Two researchers coded the journals independently and compared their work to test the reliability of the coding process. Figure 11-5 compares the number of active initiatives by members of the two experimental groups with those coming from the comparison villages. Similar results were found for the other outcome measures.

Notice two things about the graph. First, there is a dramatic difference in the number of initiatives by the two experimental groups as compared with the eleven comparison villages, which seems to confirm the effectiveness of the special training program. Second, notice that the number of initiatives also increased among the comparison villages. The researchers explain this latter pattern as a result of contagion. Because all the villages were near each other, the lessons learned by peer group members in the experimental groups were communicated in part to members of the comparison villages.

This example illustrates the strengths of multiple time-series designs when true experiments are inap-

AN ILLUSTRATION OF A QUASI-EXPERIMENT IN SOCIAL WORK

One of this book's authors (Rubin) contracted with a county child protective service agency to evaluate the effectiveness of one of the agency's programs. The three-year, federally funded demonstration program aimed to prevent foster care placement—and thus preserve families—of children of substance-abusing parents who had been referred for child abuse or neglect. The program sought to achieve its family preservation aims by having its staff provide both intensive case management intervention and direct child welfare services that emphasized things such as role-modeling, behavioral techniques, and the use of the relationship between worker and parents.

Although the routine child protective services provided by other agency units were similar to the services in the demonstration program, two things set the demonstration program apart from the routine services: (1) Federal funding enabled the demonstration program practitioners to have much lower caseloads and thus see their clients much more frequently than the practitioners in the other units, and (2) contracts with other agencies were established to improve the prospects that families in the demonstration program would receive a comprehensive spectrum of services to meet their multiple needs. Because random assignment to experimental and control groups was not acceptable to the agency, Rubin devised a quasi-experimental design. One component of the overall evaluation design was called the *overflow design.* The overflow design was a nonequivalent comparison group design because it sought to achieve comparability between groups of clients treated and not treated by the demonstration program without using random assignment to achieve that comparability. Instead of random assignment, the basis for determining which treatment condition each family received was whether the demonstration program's caseloads were full at the time of case assignment.

The demonstration program had far fewer practitioners than the rest of the agency, and could only serve 42 active cases at any particular time. Consequently, practitioners expected that many substance-abusing parents would be referred to the demonstration program when its caseloads were full and therefore would have to be referred back to the other units where they would receive the same routine services that all clients received before the demonstration program began.

Despite lacking random assignment, this design would probably possess adequate internal validity, because it seemed unlikely that families that happen to be referred when caseloads are full would not be comparable to families that happen to be referred when caseloads are not full. It seemed reasonable to suppose that if demonstration program families had fewer placements of children out of the home than did comparison group families (in the overflow group) that received the routine services, the difference could be attributable to the effects of the program rather than to extraneous differences between the two groups.

Although it seemed unlikely that the two groups would not be comparable, Rubin recognized that this was not the same degree of unlikelihood provided by random assignment. He wondered, for example, whether those practitioners who refer the families would eventually become predisposed to referring only those cases in greater need to the demonstration program. This did not seem to be a far-fetched possibility, because the referring practitioners might want to see that the cases with the most need get the most intensive, most comprehensive services. Also, they might tire of having cases referred to the demonstration program referred back to them during overflow periods and therefore might become predisposed to not refer cases to the demonstration program unless those cases were in unusually great need. Another concern was that practitioners in the routine units, who knew about the family preservation aims and methods of the demonstration program, might resent the extra resources and lower caseloads of the demonstration program workers and consequently might copy some of the demonstration program methods to prove that they could be just as effective at preserving families.

(*continued*)

In light of these concerns, Rubin added a simple time-series component to the design. It examined agency-wide out-of-home placements of children of referred substance-abusing parents during the four six-month intervals immediately preceding the demonstration program and four six-month intervals after it began. He reasoned that if routine unit practitioners were copying the demonstration program's methods, it would be reflected in a countywide (combining both the demonstration program cases and the routine service unit cases) reduction in out-of-home placements after the onset of the program, and thus no differences might appear in the overflow design. He also reasoned that the same reduction might occur if the demonstration program was effective but its cases were in greater need than the cases in the other units. The results of the nonequivalent comparison group component (overflow design) provided relatively little support for the effectiveness of the demonstration program. Still, the results of the simple time-series design component partially supported the program's effectiveness (Rubin, 1997).

propriate for the program being evaluated. The box "An Illustration of a Quasi-Experiment in Social Work" describes another example of an actual quasi-experiment—one that combined aspects of nonequivalent comparison groups designs and simple time-series designs.

PRE-EXPERIMENTAL PILOT STUDIES

Not all evaluations of social work interventions strive to produce conclusive, causal inferences. Some have an exploratory or descriptive purpose and thus can have considerable value despite having a low degree of internal validity. Thus, when we say that a particular design has low internal validity, we are not saying that you should never use that design or that studies that do so never have value.

Suppose, for example, that your agency has initiated a new, innovative intervention for a small target group about which little is known. It might be quite useful to find out whether clients' posttest scores are better (or perhaps worse!) than their pretest scores in a **pre-experimental design** that lacks the features that give experiments and quasi-experiments their internal validity. You might implement that design on a pilot study basis, purely for the purpose of generating tentative exploratory or descriptive information.

Pilot studies such as this are commonly produced in practice settings where experimental and quasi-experimental designs are not feasible and are often reported in practice-oriented journals. If the posttest scores are much better than at pretest, then you might be encouraged to view the hypothesis that the intervention is effective as more plausible, even though you cannot claim you verified conclusively that the intervention caused the desired effects. Although you haven't controlled for history, passage of time, and various other threats to internal validity, such results would establish correlation and time order. Therefore, they might provide a basis for continued testing of the intervention. Moreover, if you do seek funding for a more ambitious experiment or quasi-experiment, your credibility to potential funding sources will be enhanced if you can include in your proposal for funding evidence that you were able to successfully carry out a pilot study and that its results were promising.

Sometimes, however, investigators report pre-experimental studies as if they were valid tests of the effectiveness of an intervention. Although they usually acknowledge the limitations of their pre-experimental designs, they sometimes draw conclusions that suggest to the unwary reader that the evaluated intervention is effective and should be considered evidence-based. This is unfortunate, because—despite their value as pilot studies—pre-experimental designs rank low on the evidence-based practice research hierarchy due to their negligible degree of internal validity. Let's now examine some common pre-experimental designs and consider why they have low internal validity.

One-Shot Case Study

One particularly weak pre-experimental design, the **one-shot case study**, doesn't even establish correlation. The shorthand notation for this design is

X O

The *X* in this notation represents the introduction of a stimulus, such as an intervention. The *O* represents observation, which yields the measurement of the dependent variable. In this design, a single group of research participants is measured on a dependent variable after the introduction of an intervention (or some other stimulus) without comparing the obtained results to anything else.

For instance, a service might be delivered and then the service recipients' social functioning measured. This design offers no way for us to ascertain whether the observed level of social functioning is any higher (or lower!) than it was to begin with, or any higher (or lower!) than it is among comparable individuals who received no service. Thus, this design—in addition to failing to assess correlation—fails to control for any of the threats to internal validity.

One-Group Pretest–Posttest Design

A pre-experimental design that establishes both correlation and time-order—and which therefore has more value as a pilot study—is the **one-group pretest–posttest design.** This design assesses the dependent variable before and after the stimulus (intervention) is introduced. Thus, in the evaluation of the effectiveness of social services, the design would assess the outcome variable before and after services are delivered. The shorthand notation for this design is

$$O_1 \quad X \quad O_2$$

The subscripts 1 and 2 in this notation refer to the sequential order of the observations; thus, O_1 is the pretest before the intervention, and O_2 is the posttest after the intervention.

Despite its value as a pilot study, this design does not account for factors other than the independent variable that might have caused the change between pretest and posttest results—factors usually associated with the following threats to internal validity: history, maturation, testing, and statistical regression.

Suppose, for example, that we assess the attitudes of social work students about social action strategies of community organization—strategies that emphasize tactics of confrontation and conflict (protests, boycotts, and so on)—before and at the end of their social work education. Suppose we find that over this time they became less committed to confrontational social action strategies and more in favor of consensual community development approaches.

Would such a finding permit us to infer that the change in their attitude was *caused* by their social work education? No, it would not. Other factors could have been operating during the same period and caused the change. For instance, perhaps the students matured and became more tolerant of slower, more incremental strategies for change (the threat to internal validity posed by **maturation** or the **passage of time**). Or perhaps certain events extraneous to their social work education transpired during that period and accounted for their change (the threat of *history*). For example, perhaps a series of protest demonstrations seemed to backfire and contribute to the election of a presidential candidate they abhorred, and their perception of the negative effects of these demonstrations made them more skeptical of social action strategies.

In another example of the one-group pretest–posttest design, suppose we assess whether a cognitive-behavioral intervention with abusive parents results in higher scores on a paper-and-pencil test of parenting skills and cognitions about childhood behaviors. In addition to wondering whether history and maturation might account for the improvement in scores, we would wonder about statistical regression. Perhaps the parents were referred for treatment at a time when their parental functioning and attitudes about their children were at their worst. Even if the parenting skills and cognitions of these parents were quite unacceptable when they were at their best, improvement from pretest to posttest might simply reflect the fact that they were referred for treatment when they were at their worst and that their scores therefore couldn't help but increase somewhat because of regression toward their true average value before intervention.

Posttest-Only Design with Nonequivalent Groups (Static-Group Comparison Design)

A third pre-experimental design is the **posttest-only design with nonequivalent groups.** The shorthand notation for this design, which has also been termed the **static-group comparison design,** is

$$\begin{array}{cc} X & O \\ & O \end{array}$$

This design assesses the dependent variable after the stimulus (intervention) is introduced for one group, while also assessing the dependent variable for a second group that may not be comparable to the first group and that was not exposed to the independent variable. In the evaluation of the effectiveness of social services, this design would entail assessing clients on an outcome variable only after (not before) they receive the service being evaluated and comparing their performance with a group of clients who did not receive the service and who plausibly may be unlike the treated clients in some meaningful way.

Let's return, for example, to the preceding hypothetical illustration about evaluating the effectiveness of a cognitive-behavioral intervention with abusive parents. Using the posttest-only design with nonequivalent groups rather than comparing the pretest and posttest scores of parents who received the intervention, we might compare their posttest scores to the scores of abusive parents who were not referred or who declined the intervention. We would hope to show that the treated parents scored better than the untreated parents, because this would indicate a desired correlation between the independent variable (treatment status) and the dependent variable (test score). But this correlation would not permit us to infer that the difference between the two groups was caused by the intervention. The most important reason for this is the design's failure to control for the threat of *selection biases*. Without pretests, we have no way of knowing whether the scores of the two groups would have differed as much to begin with—that is, before the treated parents began treatment. Moreover, these two groups may not really have been equivalent in certain important respects. The parents who were referred or who chose to participate may have been more motivated to improve or may have had more supportive resources than those who were not referred or who refused treatment.

It is not at all uncommon to encounter program providers who, after their program has been implemented, belatedly realize that it might be useful to get evaluative data on its effectiveness and are therefore attracted to the posttest-only design with nonequivalent groups. In light of the expedience of this type of design, and in anticipation of the practical administrative benefits to be derived from positive outcome findings, the providers may not want to hear about selection biases and low internal validity. But we nevertheless hope you will remember the importance of these issues and tactfully discuss them with others when the situation calls for it.

Figure 11-6 graphically illustrates the three pre-experimental research designs just discussed. See if you can visualize where the potentially confounding and misleading factors could intrude into each design.

1. THE ONE-SHOT CASE STUDY

Administer the experimental stimulus to a single group and measure the dependent variable in that group afterward. Make an intuitive judgment as to whether the posttest result is "high" or "low."

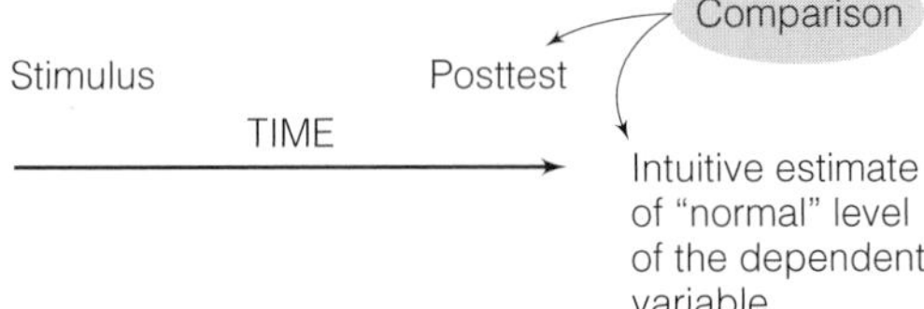

2. THE ONE-GROUP PRETEST–POSTTEST DESIGN

Measure the dependent variable in a single group, administer the experimental stimulus, and then remeasure the dependent variable. Compare pretest and posttest results.

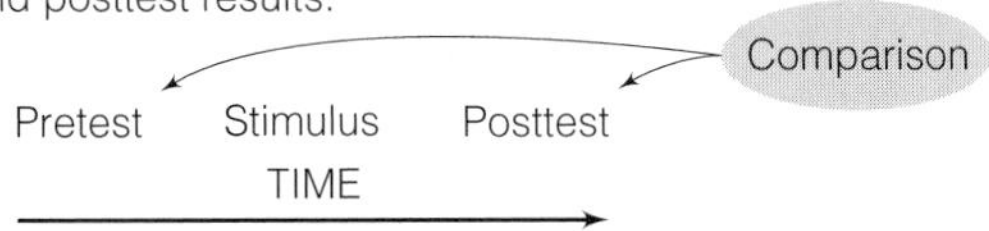

3. THE STATIC-GROUP COMPARISON

Administer the experimental stimulus to one group (the experimental group), then measure the dependent variable in both the experimental group and a comparison group.

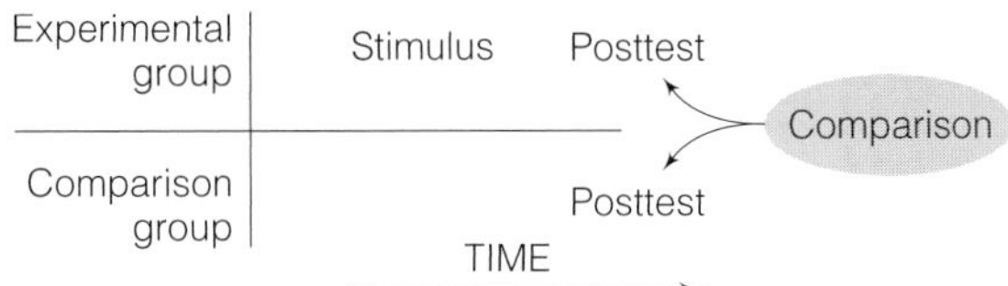

SOURCE: Adapted from Donald Campbell and Julian Stanley, *Experimental and Quasi-Experimental Designs for Research* (Chicago: Rand McNally, 1963), pp. 6–13. Copyright 1963 American Educational Research Association, Washington, D.C. Used by permission.

Figure 11-6 Three Pre-experimental Research Designs

ADDITIONAL THREATS TO THE VALIDITY OF EXPERIMENTAL AND QUASI-EXPERIMENTAL FINDINGS

So far, we have seen how the logic of experimental and quasi-experimental designs can control for most threats to internal validity. Additional threats to the validity of the conclusions we draw from such designs require methodological efforts that go beyond their design logic. Let's now look at each of these additional threats and the steps that can be taken to alleviate them.

Measurement Bias

No matter how well an experiment or quasi-experiment controls for other threats to internal validity, the credibility of its conclusions can be damaged severely if its measurement procedures appear to have been biased. Suppose, for example, that a clinician develops a new therapy for depression that promises to make her rich and famous and then evaluates her invention in an experiment by using her own subjective clinical judgment to rate improvement among the experimental and control group participants, knowing which group each participant is in. Her own ego involvement and vested interest in wanting the experimental group participants to show more improvement would make her study so vulnerable to *measurement bias* that her "findings" would have virtually no credibility. Although this example may seem extreme, serious measurement bias is not as rare in experimental evaluations as you might imagine. It is not difficult to find reports of otherwise well-designed experiments in which outcome measures were administered or completed by research assistants who knew the study hypothesis, were aware of the hopes that it would be confirmed, and knew which group each participant was in.

Whenever measurement of the dependent variable involves using research staff to supply ratings (either through direct observation or interviews), the individuals who supply the ratings should not know the experimental status of the participants they are rating. The same principle applies when the people supplying the ratings are practitioners who are not part of the research staff but who still might be biased toward a particular outcome. In other words, they should be "blind" as to whether any given rating refers to someone who has received the experimental stimulus (or service) or someone who has not.

The term *blind ratings* or *blind raters* means that the study has controlled for the potential—and perhaps unconscious—bias of raters toward perceiving results that would confirm the hypothesis. Likewise, whenever researchers fail to inform you that such ratings were blind, you should be skeptical about the study's validity. No matter how elegant the rest of a study's design might be, its conclusions are suspect if results favoring the experimental group were provided by raters who might have been biased.

The use of blind raters, unfortunately, is often not feasible in social work research studies. When we are unable to use them, we should look for alternative ways to avoid rater bias. For example, we might use validated self-report scales to measure the dependent variable rather than rely on raters who may be biased. But even when such scales are used, those administering them can bias the outcome. For example, if participants ask questions about scale items that confuse them, biased testers might consciously or unconsciously respond in ways that predispose participants to answer scale items in ways that are consistent with the desired outcome. We have even heard of situations where biased testers—in providing posttest "instructions"—encouraged experimental group participants to answer "valid" scales in ways that would show how much they improved since the pretest. The term **research reactivity** refers to changes in outcome data that are caused by researchers or research procedures rather than the independent variable. Let's now look at the various ways in which research reactivity can threaten the validity of experimental findings.

Research Reactivity

Biasing comments by researchers in data collection is just one of many forms of research reactivity. Two related terms that are used to refer to that sort of reactivity are **experimental demand characteristics** and **experimenter expectancies.** Research participants learn what experimenters want them to say or do, and then they cooperate with those "demands" or expectations.

Demand characteristics and experimenter expectancies can appear in more subtle ways as well. Some therapists who treat traumatized clients, for example, will repeatedly ask the client at different points during therapy sessions to rate on a scale from 0 to 10 how much distress they are feeling during therapy when they call up a mental image of the traumatic event. Through the therapist's verbal communication as well as nonverbal communication (smiles or looks of concern, for example), the client can learn that the therapist hopes the rating number will diminish over the course of therapy. Some studies evaluating trauma therapy administer the same 0–10 rating scale at pretest and posttest that the therapist administers throughout treatment. Even if the pretests and posttests are administered by research assistants who are unaware of clients' experimental group status, clients will have learned from the therapist that they are expected to report lower distress scores at posttest than at pretest. Worse yet, in some studies it is the therapist herself who administers the same 0–10 scale at posttest that she has been using repeatedly as part of the therapy.

One way to alleviate the influence of experimenter expectancies and demand characteristics is to separate the measurement procedures from the treatment procedures. Another way is to use measurement procedures that are hard for practitioners or researchers to influence. Instead of using the above 0–10 scale at pretest and posttest, for example, a research assistant could administer physiological measures of distress (such as pulse rate) while the client thinks of the traumatic event. It would also help if the assistants administering pretest and posttest scales were blind as to the study's hypothesis or the experimental status of the participants, to avoid giving cues about expected outcomes (Shadish, Cook, and Campbell, 2001).

Sometimes we can use raters or scale administrators who are not blind but do not seem likely to be biased. We may, for instance, ask teachers to rate the classroom conduct of children who receive two different forms of social work intervention. The teachers may know which intervention each student is receiving but not have much technical understanding of the interventions or any reason to favor one intervention over another.

A related option is to directly observe and quantify the actual behavior of participants in their natural setting rather than rely on their answers to self-report scales or on someone's ratings. It matters a great deal, however, whether that observation is conducted in an *obtrusive* or *unobtrusive* manner. **Obtrusive observation** occurs when the participant is keenly aware of being observed and thus may be predisposed to behave in ways that meet experimenter expectancies. In contrast, **unobtrusive observation** means that the participant does not notice the observation.

Suppose an experiment is evaluating the effectiveness of a new form of therapy in reducing the frequency of antisocial behaviors among children in a residential treatment center. If the child's therapist or the researcher starts showing up with a pad and pencil to observe the goings-on in the child's classroom or cottage, he or she might stick out like a sore thumb and make the child keenly aware of being observed. That form of observation would be obtrusive, and the child might exhibit atypically good behavior during that observation.

A more unobtrusive option would be to have teachers or cottage parents tabulate the number of antisocial behaviors of the child each day. Their observation would be less noticeable to the child because they are part of the natural setting and being observed by a teacher or cottage parent is part of the daily routine and not obviously connected to the expectations of a research study.

Whenever we are conducting experimental research (or any other type of research), and we are unable to use blind raters, blind scale administrators, unobtrusive observation, or some other measurement alternative that we think is relatively free of bias, we should try to use more than one measurement alternative, relying on the principle of *triangulation,* as discussed in Chapter 8. If two or more measurement strategies, each vulnerable to different biases, produce the same results, then we can have more confidence in the validity of those results.

Another form of research reactivity can occur when the research procedures don't just influence participants to tell us what they think we want to hear in response to our measures, but when the measures themselves produce desired changes. For instance, suppose as part of the research data-collection procedures to measure outcome, participants in a parent education intervention self-monitor how much time they spend playing with or holding a friendly conversation with their children. That means that they will keep a running log, recording the duration of every instance that they play with or hold a conversation with their child. Keeping such a log might make some parents realize that they are spending much less quality time with their children than they had previously thought. This realization might influence them to spend more quality time with their children; in fact, it might influence them to do so more than the parent education intervention did.

It is conceivable that desired changes might occur among experimental group participants simply because they sense they are getting special attention or special treatment. To illustrate this form of reactivity, suppose a residential treatment center for children conducts an experiment to see if a new recreational program will reduce the frequency of antisocial behaviors among the children. Being assigned to the experimental group might make some children feel better about themselves and about the center. If this feeling—and not the recreational program per se—

causes the desired change in their behavior, then a form of research reactivity will have occurred. This form of reactivity has been termed **novelty and disruption effects** because introducing an innovation in a setting where little innovation has previously occurred can stimulate excitement, energy, and enthusiasm among recipients of the intervention (Shadish, Cook, and Campbell, 2001).

A similar form of reactivity is termed *placebo effects*. **Placebo effects** can be induced by experimenter expectancies. If experimental group participants get the sense that they are about to receive a special new treatment that researchers or practitioners expect to be very effective, then the mere power of suggestion—and not the treatment itself—can bring about the desired improvement.

If we are concerned about potential placebo effects or novelty and disruption effects and wish to control for them, then we could employ an experimental design called the **placebo control group design.** The shorthand notation for this design is

$$R \quad O_1 \quad X \quad O_2$$
$$R \quad O_1 \quad \quad \quad O_2$$
$$R \quad O_1 \quad P \quad O_2$$

This design randomly assigns clients to three groups: an experimental group and two different control groups. One control group receives no experimental stimulus, but the other receives a placebo (represented by the *P* in the preceding notation). Placebo group subjects would receive special attention of some sort other than the tested stimulus or intervention. Perhaps practitioners would meet regularly to show special interest in them and listen to them but without applying any of the tested intervention procedures.

Placebo control group designs pose complexities from both a planning and interpretation standpoint, particularly when experimental interventions contain elements that resemble placebo effects. For example, in some interventions that emphasize constructs such as "empathy" and "unconditional positive regard," intervention effects are difficult to sort from placebo effects. But when they are feasible to use, placebo control group designs provide greater control for threats to the validity of experimental findings than do designs that use only one control group.

We do not want to convey the impression that an experiment's findings lack credibility unless it can guarantee the complete absence of any possible research reactivity or measurement bias. It is virtually impossible for experiments in social work or allied fields to meet that unrealistic standard. Instead, the key issue should be whether reasonable efforts were taken to avoid or minimize those problems and whether or not the potential degree of bias or reactivity seems to be at an egregious level. That said, let's move on to a different type of threat to the validity of experimental findings.

Diffusion or Imitation of Treatments

Sometimes, service providers or service recipients are influenced unexpectedly in ways that tend to diminish the planned differences in the way a tested intervention is implemented among the groups being compared. This phenomenon is termed **diffusion,** or **imitation, of treatments.** For instance, suppose the effects of hospice services that emphasize palliative care and psychosocial support for the terminally ill are being compared to the effects of more traditional health care providers, who historically have been more attuned to prolonging life and thus less concerned with the unpleasant physical and emotional side effects of certain treatments. Over time, traditional health care providers have been learning more about hospice care concepts, accepting them, and attempting to implement them in traditional health care facilities. With all of this diffusion and imitation of hospice care by traditional health care providers, failure to find differences in outcome between hospice and traditional care providers may have more to do with unanticipated similarities between hospice and traditional providers than with the ineffectiveness of hospice concepts.

A similar problem complicates research that evaluates the effectiveness of case management services. Many social workers who are not called case managers nevertheless conceptualize and routinely provide case management functions—such as outreach, brokerage, linkage, and advocacy—as an integral part of what they learned to be good and comprehensive direct social work practice. Consequently, when outcomes for clients referred to case managers are compared to the outcomes of clients who receive "traditional" social services, the true effects of case management as a treatment approach may be blurred by the diffusion of that approach among practitioners who are not called case managers. In other words, despite their different labels, the two treatment groups may not be as different in the independent variable as we think they are.

Preventing the diffusion or imitation of treatments can be difficult. Shadish, Cook, and Campbell (2001) suggest separating the two treatment conditions as much as possible, either geographically or by using different practitioners in each. Another possibility is to provide ongoing reminders to practitioners about the need not to imitate the experimental group intervention when seeing control group clients. To monitor the extent to which the imitation of treatment is occurring or has occurred, researchers can utilize qualitative methods (see Chapters 17 and 18) to observe staff meetings, conduct informal conversational interviews with practitioners and clients, and ask them to keep logs summarizing what happened in each treatment session. If these efforts detect imitation while the experiment is still under way, then further communication with practitioners may help alleviate the problem and prevent it from reaching a level that seriously undermines the validity of the experiment.

Compensatory Equalization, Compensatory Rivalry, or Resentful Demoralization

Suppose you conduct an experiment to see if increasing the involvement of families in the treatment of substance abusers improves treatment effectiveness. Suppose the therapists in one unit receive special training in working with families and are instructed to increase the treatment involvement of families of clients in their unit, while the therapists in another unit receive no such training or instructions. Assuming that the staff in the latter unit—and perhaps even their clients and the families of their clients—are aware of the treatment differences, they may seek to offset what they perceive as an inequity in service provision. The staff in the latter unit therefore might decide to compensate for the inequity by providing enhanced services that go beyond the routine treatment regimen for their clients. This is termed **compensatory equalization.** If compensatory equalization happens, the true effects of increasing family involvement could be blurred, as described above with diffusion or imitation of treatments.

What if the therapists not receiving family therapy training in the above example decide to compete with the therapists in the other unit who do receive the training? Perhaps they feel their job security or prestige is threatened by not receiving the special training and try to show that they can be just as effective without the special training. They may start reading more, attending more continuing education workshops, and increasing their therapeutic contact with clients. This is called **compensatory rivalry.** The control group therapists' extra efforts might increase their effectiveness as much as the increased family involvement might have increased the effectiveness of the experimental group therapists. If so, this could lead to the erroneous impression that the lack of difference in treatment outcome between the two groups means that increasing family involvement did not improve treatment effectiveness. The same problem could occur if the clients in one group become more motivated to improve because of the rivalry engendered by their awareness that they are not receiving the same treatment benefits as another group.

The converse of *compensatory rivalry* is **resentful demoralization.** This occurs when staff or clients become resentful and demoralized because they did not receive the special training or the special treatment. Consequently, their confidence or motivation may decline and may explain their inferior performance on outcome measures. To detect whether compensatory equalization, compensatory rivalry, or resentful demoralization is occurring—and perhaps intervene to try to minimize the problem—you can use qualitative methods, such as participant observation of staff meetings and informal conversational interviews with clients and practitioners.

Attrition (or Experimental Mortality)

Let's now look at one more threat to the validity of experimental and quasi-experimental findings: **attrition,** which is sometimes referred to as **experimental mortality.** Often participants will drop out of an experiment before it is completed, and the statistical comparisons and conclusions that are drawn can be affected by that. In a pretest–posttest control group design evaluating the effectiveness of an intervention to alleviate a distressing problem, for example, suppose that experimental group participants who perceive no improvement in their target problem prematurely drop out of treatment and refuse to be posttested. At posttest, the only experimental group participants left would be those who felt they were improving. Suppose the overall group rate of perceived improvement among control group participants is exactly the same as the overall rate among those assigned to the experimental group (including the dropouts), but all of the nonrecipients agree to be posttested because none had been disappointed. The experimental group's average posttest score is likely to be higher than the control group's—even if the intervention was ineffective—

merely because of the attrition (experimental mortality) of experimental group participants who perceived no improvement.

As another example, consider an evaluation that compares the effectiveness of family therapy and discussion groups in the treatment of drug addiction. Shadish, Cook, and Campbell (2001) point out that addicts with the worst prognoses are more likely to drop out of discussion groups than they are to drop out of family therapy. Consequently, the family therapy intervention may have poorer results at posttest not because it is less effective than discussion groups, but because the different attrition rates left more difficult cases in the family therapy group at posttest. Even if the dropouts agreed to be posttested, that would not resolve the attrition problem. The dilemma in that instance would be that the experimental group's overall average outcome score will not be an accurate depiction of intervention effects because it will have been influenced by the scores of people who did not complete the family therapy intervention. Consequently, the family therapy intervention still may have poorer results at posttest not because it is less effective than discussion groups, but because it had more cases that failed to complete the course of therapy.

Researchers conducting experimental or quasi-experimental evaluations of the effectiveness of practice or programs should strive to minimize attrition. Here are ways to do that:

1. *Reimbursement.* Reimbursing participants for their participation in research might not only alleviate attrition but also enhance your ability to recruit people to participate in your study at the outset. The level of reimbursement should be sensitive to the time and efforts of participants in pretesting and posttesting. The payment should be large enough to work as an incentive without being so great that it becomes coercive. The amount should fit the difficulties that clients experience in participating as well as fit their income levels and emotional states. With low-income participants, for example, you should anticipate difficulties in child care and transportation to and from pretesting and posttesting (and perhaps follow-up testing). If feasible, an alternative to extra payments for transportation and child-care costs might be to provide the transportation to the testing site, as well as a small child-care service there. Alternatively, it might make sense to conduct the testing at the participant's residence (if doing so did not introduce serious measurement biases).

After pretesting, you might want to increase the amount of reimbursement over time at each subsequent measurement point and give a bonus to participants who stay the distance and complete all of the measurements throughout the study. The amount should go beyond the transportation and other costs to the participant and should be enough to acknowledge to participants that their time is valued and that the measurement can be an imposition. The amount should also fit within your research budget. If you can afford it, paying participants $15 to complete pretests, $20 to complete posttests, and perhaps another $15 bonus to stay the distance might be reasonable amounts, but they might have to be adjusted upward depending on factors such as child-care costs and inflation. (Discount department-store gift certificates in the above amounts are commonly used instead of cash payments.)

2. *Avoid intervention or research procedures that disappoint or frustrate participants.* Participants are more likely to drop out of an experiment or quasi-experiment if they are disappointed or frustrated with the intervention they are receiving as part of the study. Of course, there's not much you can do to prevent disappointment over the fact that the intervention simply is not effective. But you can try to have the intervention delivered by the most experienced, competent professionals possible. Of particular importance is their experience and ability in developing supportive professional relationships with clients. In contrast, if your intervention is delivered by inexperienced practitioners who are not yet comfortable or confident in building and maintaining treatment alliances with clients, then participants receiving the intervention are more likely to become put off and drop out.

Another way to prevent disappointment and frustration with the intervention is to make sure during the recruitment and orientation of participants that they have accurate expectations of the intervention and that the intervention is a good fit with their treatment objectives and expectations. It also helps if the intervention itself does not contain noxious procedures, such as having participants recall repressed traumatic memories in ways that are like reexperiencing the trauma, and then ending sessions without resolving the intense distress that the recalled memory has stimulated. Finally, minimizing the amount of time that elapses between recruitment of participants and the onset of treatment can help avoid attrition because participants assigned to a particular treatment group may become disappointed and frustrated if the wait is much longer than they had expected.

Annoying research procedures can also influence participants to drop out. Common examples are overwhelming participants with measurement procedures that exceed their expectations, stamina, or resources. Researchers should not mislead prospective participants by underestimating the extent of the measurement procedures to which they will be subjected. Neither should researchers mislead participants about issues such as child-care requirements or resources, scheduling difficulties, providing feedback about measurement scores, or protecting confidentiality. Shadish, Cook, and Campbell (2001) encourage researchers to conduct preliminary pilot studies to identify causes of attrition that can be anticipated and alleviated when the main experiment begins. For example, research assistants who are not involved in other parts of the pilot study could interview dropouts to ascertain how they experienced the study and why they dropped out.

3. *Utilize tracking methods.* Many recipients of social work interventions are transient or secretive about where they live. Many are unemployed. Some lack telephones. The poor, the homeless, substance abusers, and battered women are prominent examples. Shadish, Cook, and Campbell (2001) review the tracking strategies that have been used to find such participants and retain their participation in treatment and measurement. One of their recommendations is to obtain as much location information as possible at the outset of their participation, not only from the participants themselves, but also from their friends, relatives, and other agencies with which they are involved. (You will need to get the participant's signed permission to contact these sources.) Another recommendation is to develop relationships with staff members at agencies who may later be able to help you find participants. You can also give participants a business card that shows treatment and measurement appointment times and a toll-free number where they can leave messages about appointment changes or changes in how to locate them. If participants have telephones, then research assistants can call them to remind them of each appointment. If they have mailing addresses, you can augment your telephone tracking by mailing them reminder notices of upcoming appointments. (You may recall that we discussed these tracking methods in more depth in Chapter 5, on culturally competent research.)

PRACTICAL PITFALLS IN CARRYING OUT EXPERIMENTS AND QUASI-EXPERIMENTS IN SOCIAL WORK AGENCIES

As our discussion of attrition illustrates, carrying out valid, useful experimental or quasi-experimental research in social work takes more than developing a rigorous research design. Unlike such studies carried out in other disciplines, which tend to take place in laboratory settings or research clinics controlled by researchers, social work experiments tend to take place in agency settings that are controlled by people who are not researchers, who may not understand the requisites of experimental and quasi-experimental designs, and who may even resent and attempt to undermine the demands of the research design. Consequently, if you try to do this kind of research, it won't take you long to learn that in this business the various adages and two-word bumper sticker warnings about best-laid plans going awry are particularly applicable. Let's now look at four practical pitfalls that are commonly encountered in implementing experimental and quasi-experimental research in service-oriented agencies.

Fidelity of the Intervention

The term **intervention fidelity** refers to the degree to which the intervention actually delivered to clients was delivered as intended. We often evaluate social work interventions that cannot be spelled out in step-by-step manuals. Instead, we rely on social work practitioners to implement general guidelines in skillful, creative, and idiosyncratic ways with each client. Some practitioners, however, might have better judgment than others. Some might misunderstand or misinterpret the intervention's intent. This means that the intervention we think we are evaluating may not be the one intended for experimental group participants, or that the services received by experimental and control group participants may be more similar than we intended. Related reasons why interventions (the independent variables of experimental and quasi-experimental research) may not be implemented as intended include delays and start-up problems in implementing new programs, the use of staff members who are inexperienced with or untrained in the new intervention, high initial staff turnover in new programs, organizational changes that affect the program, loss of staff enthusiasm over time, and ongoing supervision provided by agency supervisors who may not follow the research protocol.

A good way to assess intervention fidelity is to videotape several randomly selected treatment sessions from each of your practitioners. Have two experts in the intervention independently view each taped session and then complete a rating scale assessing their judgment of the degree to which the intervention in the session was implemented appropriately. Calculate the correlation of the two independent sets of ratings. If it is high—say around .80—then you have good interrater reliability. Hopefully, the raters' scale scores will also indicate that the intervention fidelity was at least adequate. For example, suppose the rating scale categories, with the corresponding score in parentheses, were *unacceptable* (1), *minimally acceptable* (2), *almost acceptable* (3), *acceptable* (4), and *excellent* (5). If your study's intervention fidelity ratings were consistently at or above a score of 4 (acceptable) but your main findings showed that the intervention was not effective, then it would be difficult for critics to attribute your main findings to a lack of intervention fidelity.

But you do not have to wait until the end of your study to have the tapes rated and utilize the ratings. You could have that done incrementally throughout your study. If you find early in your study that the tapes are receiving low ratings, then you can take steps to try to improve the way the practitioners in your study are implementing the intervention. Better yet, have some ratings done on a pilot basis before your study begins. If there are intervention fidelity problems, then delay the onset of the study until you correct the problem and begin to consistently achieve acceptable ratings. This would not, however, remove the need to assess fidelity during your study as well.

Contamination of the Control Condition

Even if the experimental group receives the intended intervention at an acceptable level of intervention fidelity, the control condition can be contaminated if control group and experimental group members interact. Suppose, for example, an experiment in a school social work intervention assigns students in the same school to either an experimental group that receives the new intervention being tested or a control group that receives the routine services. The students in each group will interact in the school setting, and the improvements among the experimental group students may therefore have a beneficial spillover effect on the behavior of the control group students. If this happens, the two groups will not be as different on outcome measures (dependent variables) as was predicted, and we may therefore erroneously conclude that the new intervention did not make a difference. Solomon and Paulson (1995) suggest that contamination of the control condition can even occur if experimental and control group clients share the same agency waiting room.

Resistance to the Case Assignment Protocol

Some practitioners may resent having to assign cases to treatment conditions on the basis of research requirements rather than on the basis of their own professional judgment about the best service match for each client. Practitioners tend to believe that the services they provide are effective, so they may not be committed to adhering to the research protocol in case assignment, because they think they already "know" the answer to the research question. Believing they already know what services work best for what clients, they may feel compelled to violate—perhaps in a covert fashion—the research protocol to make sure that the client receives the service they think that client should receive. Even if they are unsure as to what service works best for what client, they may pressure to enroll clients in the greatest need into the experimental condition because it's new and innovative or offers more services than does the control condition.

Shadish, Cook, and Campbell (2001) reviewed studies that had the following findings about unsuccessful implementation of case assignment protocols: (1) Implementation is less likely to be successful when agency staff implement the case assignment decisions than when outside researchers control them; (2) practitioners seek loopholes to exempt some clients from the case assignment protocol, and when such exemptions are allowed the successful implementation of the protocol is less likely; (3) implementation is less likely to be successful when several people, rather than one person, control the case assignment process; and (4) covert manipulation of random assignment occurred often in 30 reviewed criminal justice experiments.

Shadish and his associates offer a number of recommendations to alleviate the above case assignment problems. The following are based on their recommendations and are most relevant to social work evaluations in service-oriented agencies: (1) Carefully explain the purpose and nature of the case assignment protocol to agency staff; (2) provide incentives to them for implementing the protocol properly; (3) pilot test the randomization procedure in the agency; (4) make sure that you develop clearly worded procedures—in operational terms—for implementing, controlling, and monitoring the case assignment protocol throughout the entire study; (5) have the case assignment protocol controlled by only one person, who is part of the research team, and not an agency staff member; (6) keep the master list of case assignments in a secure place and a backup copy of it in a different secure place; (7) do not show the master assignment list to agency staff; (8) hold ongoing meetings with agency staff to discuss the case assignment process; (9) have a research staff member continually monitor the implementation of the case assignment protocol throughout the entire study; and (10) keep a log throughout the study of each case assignment and any violations of the case assignment protocol.

Client Recruitment and Retention

Recruiting a sufficient number of clients to participate in the study can be difficult when the research must rely on referrals of clients from outside agencies. This can be particularly problematic when the research design precludes joint involvement by referred clients in the services provided by the referring agencies. This can result in "dumping" by those agencies of cases they do not want to serve, perhaps because the dumped clients resist services or seem less likely to benefit from services. Moreover, the agencies may be reluctant to refer any clients, because that might adversely affect the referring agency's reimbursement when it is based on the amount of services provided directly by the referring agency. Referring agencies also might not understand and even resent having their referrals assigned to a control condition, particularly if that assignment means referring control clients back to the referral agency.

Moreover, difficulties in client recruitment and retention can arise from the clients' own reactions to case assignment procedures and measurement requirements. Clients may resent the use of randomized procedures to determine which service they receive, and they may therefore not participate. Some clients might first agree to participate and then change their minds after learning that they have not been assigned to the new, innovative, experimental condition. Other clients might take longer to drop out of the control or comparison condition; perhaps after being inconvenienced by completing the pretesting they will refuse to participate in the posttesting. (Problems in retention are the same as the problems of attrition, discussed earlier in this chapter.)

Failing to recruit a sufficient number of clients can also result from overly optimistic estimates or promises by the staff in agencies where a study takes place. Relying on such estimates or promises can be particularly risky when that agency never before served as a site for an experiment or quasi-experiment. For example, a while back the staff at a child guidance center estimated that it could provide more than 100 clients for a one-year experiment evaluating the effectiveness of a new intervention being delivered by its child therapists. It ended up providing less than 20 clients during the first year of the study, and the study had to be extended to three years just to obtain 39 participants (Rubin et al., 2001).

If you plan to conduct an experiment or a quasi-experiment in an agency that never before served as the main site for such a study, you should be skeptical about staff estimates regarding the number of participants it can provide in a specific time frame. Minimally, you should look for evidence that would assure you that the agency really can deliver the estimated number of participants who would meet your study's eligibility requirements and who would agree to participate. If you cannot obtain that evidence based on the agency's prior experiences or existing data, you probably should conduct a brief pilot test before starting your study in that agency, to see if the number of participants provided during that brief time span is consistent with the rate of participation projected for the entire study. For example, if an agency estimates that in one year it will provide 100 participants, but provides only 3 during your one-month pilot test, you'll probably want to revise your plans for obtaining a sufficient number of participants before implementing your study.

The foregoing possibilities do not exhaust all of the pitfalls you are likely to encounter if you attempt to carry out experimental or quasi-experimental research. They're simply among the more common ones in a seemingly endless list. The point here is twofold: (1) Be prepared to encounter pitfalls like these, and (2) build mechanisms into your design to prevent, detect, and deal with these pitfalls before they ruin your study.

Mechanisms for Avoiding or Alleviating Practical Pitfalls

Solomon and Paulson (1995) recommend several additional mechanisms to help you avoid or alleviate the pitfalls discussed above. One important suggestion is to engage agency staff members in the design of the research and enlist their support from its inception. Although this may help reduce the likelihood or degree of their resistance to the research, it will not guarantee that their resistance is eliminated. You should not assume that agency staff members' support for the research protocol will endure as they begin to encounter daily practice concerns. Instead, you should build into the study ongoing mechanisms in which some research staff members are on site throughout the project to interact with program staff members and monitor whether they are complying with the research protocol and implementing the experimental and control conditions as intended.

Another suggestion is to locate experimental and control conditions in separate buildings or agencies. This may help avoid contaminating the control condition. You might promote the fidelity of the intervention by developing a treatment manual that clearly and specifically defines the components and steps of both experimental and control interventions. You might anticipate and alleviate client recruitment and retention problems by planning to recruit clients assertively on an ongoing basis throughout your study, rather than assume that your initial cohort will be large enough and will remain intact. As we discussed in the section above on attrition, client recruitment and retention might also be enhanced by reimbursing clients for their participation, particularly for their time and efforts in pretesting and posttesting.

Another good idea is to conduct a *pilot study* before implementing your main study. Above we mentioned conducting a brief pilot test just to see if the agency estimate about the projected number of study participants is accurate. A pilot study can also help you detect additional problems. Do you have intervention fidelity? Is imitation of treatments occurring in the control condition? Are there unanticipated problems in the way instruments are being administered or completed? Are there any other unanticipated data-collection problems? Do staff who initially agreed to your protocol for assigning cases to experimental and comparison groups—perhaps because they really didn't understand the protocol and its implications, or perhaps because they just weren't paying that much attention and wanted to appear agreeable—start objecting to the protocol and perhaps trying to undermine it when they realize that clients they think should receive the new intervention are being assigned to the control group?

Another good reason for conducting a pilot study is that if you submit a grant application to obtain funding for an experiment or quasi-experiment, then showing that you completed a successful pilot study is likely to reassure the funding source that you have detected and resolved any of the above pitfalls likely to undermine your study. In light of all the foregoing reasons, some consider conducting a pilot study not just a good idea, but essential!

QUALITATIVE TECHNIQUES FOR AVOIDING OR ALLEVIATING PRACTICAL PITFALLS

Detecting and alleviating practical pitfalls is one place in which techniques commonly employed in qualitative studies can come in handy as a valuable part of a quantitative research study. We've been mentioning qualitative methods throughout this book, and will give them much more attention when we get to Chapters 17 through 19. Qualitative methods offer a number of techniques that on-site research staff members can use in attempting to observe research implementation pitfalls.

For example, they can interact formally or informally with agency staff members to identify compliance problems or learn how they are implementing the interventions. They can use videotapes or practitioner activity logs to assess intervention fidelity. They can also identify implementation problems by following along with (shadowing) practitioners in their daily activities. They can participate in in-service trainings or group supervision to identify discrepancies between the intended intervention and what agency trainers or supervisors are prescribing. The box titled "Qualitative Techniques for Experimental or Quasi-Experimental Research" summarizes the ways techniques commonly employed in qualitative studies can be used to help avoid or alleviate the many practical pitfalls that can be encountered in trying to carry out quantitative research studies.

As we leave this chapter, we hope you can begin to sense how difficult it may be to carry out successfully a well-controlled experiment or quasi-experiment in

QUALITATIVE TECHNIQUES FOR EXPERIMENTAL OR QUASI-EXPERIMENTAL RESEARCH

It is not uncommon to hear researchers known primarily for their experimental or quasi-experimental quantitative findings say that almost all of their "quantitative" studies have included components that relied on qualitative methods. In this box we will list some prominent qualitative techniques and the important functions they can serve in experimental and quasi-experimental studies. You can read more about these techniques in Chapters 17 and 18. Many of the ideas for this box were derived from a presentation by Phyllis Solomon (University of Pennsylvania School of Social Work) and Robert I. Paulson (Portland State University School of Social Work) at the first annual conference of the Society for Social Work and Research, in Washington, D.C., April 11, 1995. Their presentation was titled "Issues in Designing and Conducting Randomized Human Service Trials."

Qualitative Technique	Functions in Experimental and Quasi-Experimental Studies
Ethnographic shadowing (follow along and observe practitioners in their daily activities)	• Learn how they actually implement the intervention • Learn if the interventions and other aspects of the research protocol are being implemented as intended
Participant observation during training or group supervision	• Identify discrepancies between the intended intervention and what agency trainers or supervisors are actually prescribing
Participant observation during agency staff meetings	• Determine whether agency staff are complying with the research protocol and identify difficulties they are having with compliance
Informal conversational interviews with agency staff	• Identify compliance problems with the research protocol • Learn how they are actually implementing the interventions
Videotaping or audiotaping practitioner–client sessions	• Assess the fidelity of the intervention (Is it being implemented in a skillful manner, as intended?)
Practitioner activity logs	• Assess the fidelity of the intervention • Are the proper amounts and types of services being delivered to the clients for whom they were intended?
Event logs	• Identify major organizational and systems changes that may impede continued compliance with the research protocol
Focus groups	• Document the process of implementing the research design and interventions, and identify implementation problems • Develop possible explanations for unexpected, puzzling findings
Snowball sampling	• Recruit subjects from vulnerable or hard-to-find target populations
Semistructured, open-ended interviews (using interview guides) with prospective clients who refuse services or clients who prematurely terminate services	• Learn why they are unwilling to participate or why they dropped out so as to figure out ways to improve client recruitment and retention
Content analysis of agency documents and service delivery manuals	• Identify potential practical pitfalls that need to be planned for in developing the research design • Develop specificity about the services being evaluated • Did the proper amounts and types of services get delivered to the clients for whom they were intended?
Semistructured, open-ended interviews with practitioners or their clients following data analysis	• Develop possible explanations for unexpected, puzzling findings

a real social work setting. You will need to plan carefully and obtain substantial resources to do it well; otherwise the practical pitfalls we have been discussing are likely to ruin carefully constructed designs that seem to have impeccable internal validity on paper. But even the best-laid plans can encounter practical obstacles that are impossible to foresee. Because of these obstacles, no experiments or quasi-experiments in social work agencies are flawless. Even the best ones at the top of the evidence-based practice research hierarchy are imperfect. As an evidence-based practitioner, you should not feel compelled to search for—and be guided by—only those studies that have no flaws. No such studies exist. If you require that a study be flawless before you let it guide your practice, you'll wind up without any evidence to guide you. The critical challenge is to be able to recognize and be guided by those imperfect studies that offer the best evidence, recognize and perhaps be guided by weaker studies whose flaws are more serious but not fatal, and distinguish the foregoing imperfect studies from those whose egregious and fatal flaws render their findings virtually worthless from the standpoint of internal validity and causal inference. We'll end this chapter with the box "An Illustration of a Social Work Experiment." The study described in that box illustrates how experiments in social work agencies often have to deviate from conventional design arrangements, can be imperfect, and yet can still be considered "true" experiments worthy of guiding evidence-based practice.

AN ILLUSTRATION OF A SOCIAL WORK EXPERIMENT

The design described in the following illustration is patterned after the classical pretest–posttest control group design, but it uses four experimental groups and one control group instead of just one experimental group. Each experimental group receives a different intervention, and the experimental groups are compared with each other as well as with the control group. Another interesting aspect of this example is that the control group is not denied service; it receives the routine service instead of the experimental one.

Experiment on Cognitive-Behavioral Interventions with Parents at Risk of Child Abuse

Whiteman, Fanshel, and Grundy (1987) were interested in the effectiveness of different aspects of a cognitive-behavioral intervention aimed at reducing parental anger in the face of perceived provocation by children in families in which child abuse had been committed or in families at risk for child abuse. Underlying their inquiry were prior research findings that suggested that although child abuse is caused by complex multiple factors and stressors, a common stressor that situationally may more immediately trigger the abusive act is the parent's anger resulting from perceived provocation by the child. Whiteman and associates postulated that abusive parents cognitively appraise the perceived provocation as a threat to their needs, values, or interests. Attaching this negative meaning to the situation, they become angry and physiologically tense. The ultimate abusive act, then, is an impulsive, maladaptive attempt to cope with stress.

The foregoing conceptual framework suggested testing a composite package of cognitive-behavioral interventions that attempt to develop three coping skills: (1) giving a less negative meaning to the situation—seeing the child's behavior as resulting from factors other than malicious intent; (2) relaxation techniques to attenuate the intense pressure that results in impulsive, abusive behavior; and (3) problem-solving techniques to provide acceptable ways to prevent and ameliorate perceived provocations.

Fifty-five clients participated in their experiment. Fifteen were identified child abusers then being treated by a public agency in New York City. Forty were being treated by a private agency whose social workers had some indication that a child was in danger of parental maltreatment. The participants were randomly assigned to four inter-

(*continued*)

vention groups and a control group that received no experimental intervention but instead continued to receive services from the referral agency.

The first intervention group received cognitive restructuring interventions that dealt with the parents' perceptions, expectations, appraisals, and stresses. The second intervention group was trained in relaxation procedures. The third intervention group worked on problem-solving skills. The fourth intervention group received a treatment package comprising the three interventional modalities delivered separately to the first three intervention groups. Despite these variations, each intervention group stressed the same cognitive-behavioral intervention techniques and principles such as gradual skill acquisition, behavioral rehearsal, and recognition and reinforcement of progress. Also, each intervention was delivered over a brief treatment span of six sessions that took place in the clients' homes. The practitioners delivering the interventions were all social work doctoral students who had master's degrees in social work. Three were experienced clinicians.

The dependent variables in the experiment—the indicators of the effectiveness of the intervention—were measured by an assessment instrument that contained sections on parental anger and parental child-rearing attitudes and styles. This instrument was administered in tape-recorded pretest and posttest sessions in the clients' homes. The authors reported that the internal consistency reliability of the sections of the measurement instrument ranged from .66 to .90, but they did not report the instrument's validity.

The results revealed no significant differences among the experimental and control groups at pretest. At posttest, however, the treated (experimental group) participants had significantly greater reductions in anger than the untreated (control group) participants. The intervention group with the greatest reduction in anger was the one that received the composite package of interventions delivered separately to the other three intervention groups.

The posttest results on child-rearing attitudes and styles were less clear-cut. Some intervention groups improved more than the control groups on some sections of the instrument, but the results were inconsistent across the different sections of the instrument. Analysis of the data on all intervention participants as one overall experimental group, however, revealed significant improvements on two of the four sections of the instrument—those measuring parental empathy and responses to irritating behavior. (No significant improvement was found on sections that measured affection and discipline.)

In light of their findings, Whiteman and associates recommended that social workers use the composite intervention package to attempt to reduce anger and promote positive child-rearing attitudes among abusive or potentially abusive parents. Their results also indicated the importance of the problem-solving skills component in reducing anger, the importance of the cognitive restructuring component in improving child-rearing attitudes, and the relative unimportance of including the relaxation component in the intervention package.

The study by Whiteman and his colleagues demonstrates nicely the applicability of experimental design to social work practice. Among other things, it shows how clients can be randomly assigned to experimental and control groups without denying services to the control group participants (who continued to receive the services provided by the referral agency). The preceding study also illustrates how experimental designs can control for many, but not necessarily all, threats to internal validity. Take a moment to review the threats we discussed earlier in this chapter and in the preceding chapter. Consider which were and were not controlled in this experiment. You should be able to see that history, maturation, statistical regression, selection biases, and causal time order were controlled.

But what about testing? Did taking the pretest sensitize clients to figuring out the socially acceptable answers at posttest? What about experimenter expectancies? Did the treated clients improve in their anger, attitudes, and behavior when confronted with real-life stressful situations, or did they just learn during the six sessions what instrument answers were more acceptable to the clinicians or researchers? Remember, the authors reported the reliability of the instrument, but not its validity. Did it really assess their anger and attitudes, or did it assess their propensity to give socially desirable answers? Random assignment to experimental and control conditions won't resolve the preceding measurement questions, particularly when measurement is obtrusive, as is interviewing subjects in tape-recorded sessions.

Apparently, attrition was not a problem in the study under discussion, for the authors reported none. But what about diffusion or imitation of treatments? Little was said about the nature of the services provided by the referral agencies. Did any of those services incorporate cognitive-behavioral treatment ideas that resembled the tested intervention package? If so, might their use have blurred the true effects of the tested intervention?

The study by Whiteman and associates also illustrates problems regarding the artificiality and potentially limited generalizability of some experiments—problems associated with *external validity*. (We discussed external validity in Chapter 10.) For example, can we generalize from the effects of doctoral students in a special, experimental setting to the likely effects of practitioners with lesser training working under less ideal circumstances, such as with larger caseloads? And would the intervention be as effective with clients who would refuse to participate in the experiment? You might also wonder about client attributes. Whiteman and his colleagues reported various statistics to describe those attributes, which we omitted from our synopsis for the sake of brevity. Finally, you might wonder about research reactivity in connection to novelty and placebo effects. To what extent do the special research procedures used, or experimental clients' awareness that they were receiving a special treatment, limit our ability to assume that the same effects would be attained under routine service delivery conditions outside of a research context?

In posing these questions, we are not attempting to denigrate the study. Indeed, it is one of the best examples of experimental research available in the social work literature! The purpose of these questions is to illustrate that not even the best study can control for all threats to validity. No single study ever "proves" anything. No matter how strong a study may be in some, or even most respects, we must remain vigilant in considering potential limitations and in understanding the need for replication in the scientific method.

Main Points

- Experiments are an excellent vehicle for the controlled testing of causal processes.

- The classical experiment tests the effect of an experimental stimulus on some dependent variable through the pretesting and posttesting of experimental and control groups.

- The Solomon four-group design and the posttest-only control group design are variations on the classical experiment that attempt to safeguard against problems associated with testing effects.

- Randomization is the generally preferred method for achieving comparability in the experimental and control groups.

- It is generally less important that a group of experimental subjects be representative of some larger population than that experimental and control groups be similar to one another.

- Control group participants in experiments in social work settings need not be denied services. They can receive alternate, routine services, or be put on a waiting list to receive the experimental intervention.

- When random assignment to experimental and control groups isn't possible, a nonequivalent comparison groups design can be used, in which the experimental group is compared to an existing group that appears similar to it.

- Ways to strengthen the internal validity of nonequivalent comparison groups designs include selecting a comparison group as similar as possible to the experimental group, administering multiple pretests, and switching replications.

- Time-series designs can be used as an alternative to the nonequivalent comparison groups design.

- Time-series designs attempt to attain internal validity through the use of repeated measures before and after the introduction of an intervention.

• Three forms of pre-experiments are: the one-shot case study, the one-group pretest–posttest design, and the posttest-only design with nonequivalent groups.

• Although the classical experiment with random assignment of subjects guards against most threats to internal validity, additional methodological efforts may be needed to prevent or alleviate the following problems: (a) measurement bias, (b) research reactivity, (c) diffusion or imitation of treatments, (d) compensatory equalization, (e) compensatory rivalry, (f) resentful demoralization, and (g) attrition.

• Many practical pitfalls are likely to be encountered in attempting to implement experiments or quasi-experiments in service-oriented agencies. These pitfalls may compromise the fidelity of the interventions being evaluated, contaminate the control condition or the case assignment protocol, or hinder client recruitment and retention.

• Another way to detect and alleviate practical pitfalls is by conducting a pilot study of your experiment or quasi-experiment before implementing it in full.

• A good way to assess intervention fidelity is to videotape several randomly selected treatment sessions from each of your practitioners. Have two experts in the intervention independently view each taped session and then complete a rating scale assessing their judgment of the degree to which the intervention in the session was implemented appropriately.

• The inclusion of various qualitative research methods as part of an experiment can aid in detecting and alleviating many of the above problems.

• Techniques for minimizing attrition include reimbursing participants for their participation, avoiding intervention or research procedures that disappoint or frustrate them, and tracking participants.

• Many experimental studies fail to include measurement procedures, such as blind raters, to control for researcher or practitioner bias toward perceiving results that would confirm the hypothesis.

• Experimental demand characteristics and experimenter expectancies can hinder the validity of experimental findings if they influence research participants to cooperate with what experimenters want them to say or do.

• Obtrusive observation occurs when the participant is keenly aware of being observed and thus may be predisposed to behave in ways that meet experimenter expectancies. In contrast, unobtrusive observation means that the participant does not notice the observation.

Review Questions and Exercises

1. Briefly sketch an experimental design for testing a new intervention in your fieldwork agency or in another social work agency with which you are familiar. Then conduct a qualitative (open-ended, semistructured) interview with one or two direct-service practitioners and an administrator in that agency, asking them how feasible it would be to carry out your study in their agency.

2. What potential threats to the validity of the findings can you detect in the following hypothetical design? In a residential treatment center containing four cottages, the clinical director develops a new intervention to alleviate behavior problems among the children residing in the four cottages. The center has four therapists, each assigned to a separate cottage. The clinical director selects two cottages to receive the new intervention. The other two will receive the routine treatment. To measure outcome, the clinical director assigns a social work student whose field placement is at the center to spend an equal amount of time at each cottage observing and recording the number of antisocial behaviors each child exhibits and the number of antisocial statements each makes.

3. Briefly sketch a nonequivalent comparison groups design for evaluating the effectiveness of a parent education program for parents at high risk for child abuse. What would you do to assure the readers of your study that the threat of a selectivity bias seems remote? Include in your sketch a description of the dependent variable and when and how it would be measured.

4. Identify six things you would do to avoid or alleviate practical pitfalls in carrying out the above study.

5. Briefly sketch a multiple time-series design to evaluate the effectiveness of a statewide job-training program for welfare recipients. Explain how it provides adequate control for history, passage of time, statistical regression, and selection biases.

6. Briefly sketch a case-control design to generate hypotheses about interventions that may be the most helpful in preventing teen runaways. What are the background variables that would be most important to control for? Identify and explain three uncontrolled

threats to the validity of your study that would represent major reasons why the results would be exploratory only.

Internet Exercises

1. Use InfoTrac College Edition to find an experiment that evaluated the effectiveness of a social work intervention. How well did it control for the additional threats to validity discussed in this chapter? What efforts did it make to alleviate attrition? Were its measurement procedures obtrusive or unobtrusive? Do they appear to be free from serious bias? Also critique the study's external validity—either positively or negatively.

2. Use InfoTrac College Edition to find a study that used a pre-experimental design to evaluate the outcome of a social work intervention. Critique the study's internal validity—and discuss whether it had value despite its pre-experimental nature.

3. In this chapter, we looked briefly at the problem of "placebo effects." On the web, find a study in which the placebo effect figured importantly. Briefly summarize the study, including the source of your information. (Hint: You might want to do a search using the term *placebo* as a key word.)

4. Use InfoTrac College Edition to find a study that used a nonequivalent comparison groups design to evaluate the effectiveness of a social work intervention. How well did it control for selection biases?

5. Use InfoTrac College Edition to find a study that used a simple or multiple time-series design to evaluate the effectiveness of a social work intervention. How well did it control for history, maturation or passage of time, statistical regression, and selection biases?

6. Use InfoTrac College Edition to find a study that used a case-control design to test or generate hypotheses about effective social work intervention with some problem. Critique the validity of the study, identifying its strengths as well as weaknesses.

7. Use InfoTrac College Edition to find a study that used a cross-sectional design to test or generate hypotheses about effective social work intervention with some problem. Critique the validity of the study, identifying its strengths as well as weaknesses.

Additional Readings

Alexander, Leslie B., and Phyllis Solomon (eds.). 2006. *The Research Process in the Human Services: Behind the Scenes*. Belmont, CA: Thomson Brooks/Cole. We are recommending this compendium of readings in several chapters. Its first five chapters are relevant to this chapter in that they illustrate real-world obstacles confronting researchers who try to implement well-designed experiments and quasi-experiments in agency settings. Each chapter includes a commentary by the investigators regarding the feasibility obstacles they encountered in carrying out their research and how they modified their research plans in light of those obstacles.

Campbell, Donald, and Julian Stanley. 1963. *Experimental and Quasi-Experimental Designs for Research*. Chicago: Rand McNally. An excellent analysis of the logic and methods of experimentation in social research, this book is especially useful in its application of the logic of experiments to other social research methods. Though fairly old, this book has attained the status of a classic and is still cited frequently.

Cook, Thomas D., and Donald T. Campbell. 1979. *Quasi-Experimentation: Design and Analysis Issues for Field Settings*. Chicago: Rand McNally, 1979. This work is an expanded and updated version of Campbell and Stanley.

Shadish, William R., Thomas D. Cook, and Donald T. Campbell. 2001. *Experimental and Quasi-Experimental Designs for Generalized Causal Inference*. New York: Houghton Mifflin. This excellent book is a successor to the books mentioned above by Campbell and Stanley and by Cook and Campbell. One primary difference from the earlier books is its increased attention to external validity, epistemology (refuting philosophical attacks on the possibility of objectivity), and designs without random assignment.

CHAPTER 12

Single-Case Evaluation Designs

What You'll Learn in This Chapter

Here you'll see how direct-service practitioners can use the logic of time-series designs with an individual client or client system in order to evaluate their own effectiveness and the effectiveness of particular interventions. These designs, then, are particularly applicable to the final stage of the evidence-based practice process.

INTRODUCTION

In Chapter 11, we saw that when people cannot be assigned to control groups, time-series designs can help evaluate the impact of programs or interventions on groups of individuals. By taking repeated measures of the dependent variable (the service or policy goal, or target problem that one seeks to change), treated groups can serve as their own controls. These repeated measures attempt to identify stable trends in the target problem. Marked deviations in these trends that coincide with the introduction or withdrawal of the service or intervention can support the plausibility of the hypothesis that changes in the dependent variable were caused by variation in the service or intervention (the independent variable).

Key concepts here are multiple measurement points and unlikely coincidences. The more measurement points one has and the more stable the trends identified in that measurement, the easier it is to infer whether any changes in the target problem can be attributed to changes in the independent variable or to rival sources of change, such as maturation, history, or statistical regression. In other words, identifying stable trends through many repeated measures enhances the internal validity of evaluations that cannot utilize control groups by enabling the researcher to pinpoint precisely where change in the dependent variable occurs and whether those points coincide with changes in the independent variable. To the extent that changes in the dependent variable consistently occur only after the independent variable is introduced or withdrawn (and not at other times), a pattern of coincidences has been established that makes rival explanations such as maturation and history seem unlikely.

OVERVIEW OF THE LOGIC OF SINGLE-CASE DESIGNS

Single-case evaluation designs apply the logic of time-series designs to the evaluation of the effect of interventions or policy changes on individual cases or systems. Such designs involve obtaining repeated measures of a client system with regard to particular outcome indicators of a target problem. Repeated measures of the trend in the target problem are obtained before a particular intervention is introduced, and these repeated measures are continued after intervention is introduced to see if a sustained pattern of improvement in the target problem commences shortly after the onset of intervention.

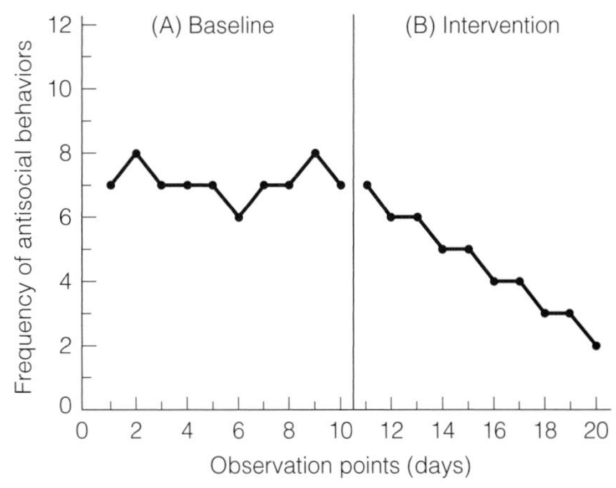

Figure 12-1 Graph of Hypothetical Single-Case Design Outcome Supporting Effectiveness of Intervention (Basic AB Design)

The phase of repeated measures that occurs before intervention is introduced is called the *baseline.* A **baseline** is a control phase—that is, it serves the same function as a control group does in group experiments. The data patterns collected during the baseline (control) phases are compared to the data patterns collected during the *intervention* (experimental) phases. To infer that an intervention is effective—that is, that improvements in the dependent variable can be attributed to the intervention and not to some rival explanation such as history or maturation—we look for shifts in the trend or pattern of the data that coincide with shifts between baseline and intervention phases.

Consider the graph in Figure 12-1, for example. We see a shift from a stable pattern of no consistent change in the target problem during baseline to a sustained trend of improvement in the target problem at the start of and throughout the intervention phase. Something other than the intervention may have caused that change, but that would be a big coincidence given the large number of repeated measures and the absence of any marked shift in the data pattern at any time other than after intervention begins.

Now, for the sake of contrast, consider the graph in Figure 12-2. Here we see virtually the same intervention data as in Figure 12-1, but after a trend during baseline that shows that the target problem was already improving during baseline at the same rate at which it continued to improve during intervention. Here we would conclude that something other than the intervention, such as maturation or the mere

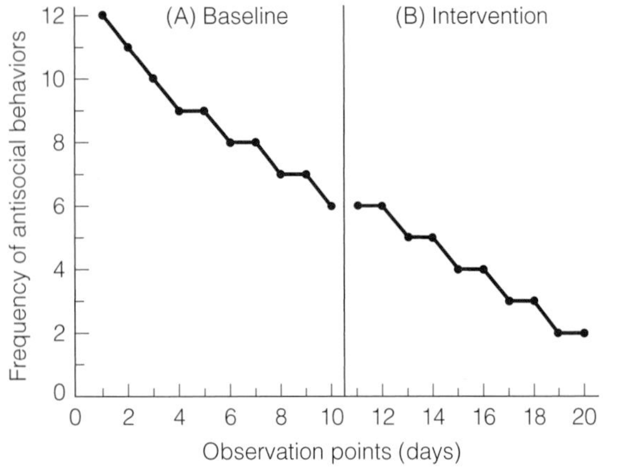

Figure 12-2 Graph of Hypothetical Single-Case Design Outcome Not Supporting Effectiveness of Intervention (Basic AB Design)

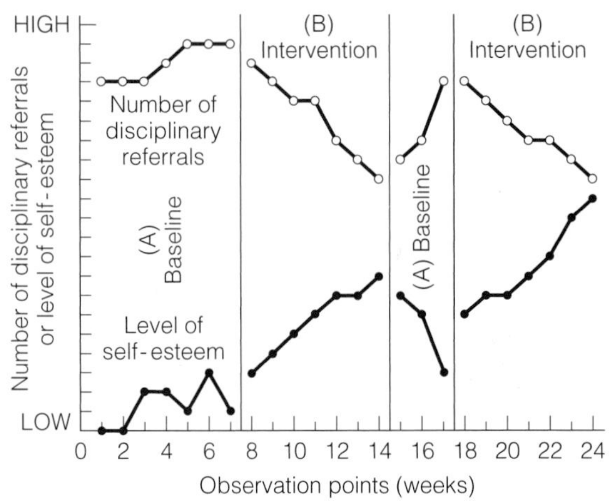

Figure 12-3 Graph of Hypothetical Single-Case Design Outcome Supporting Effectiveness of Intervention (ABAB Design)

passage of time, was probably causing the improvement. This example illustrates how repeated measures during the baseline and intervention phases enable us to control for threats to internal validity that refer to processes that were under way before treatment begins. Without repeated measures in each phase—that is, with only one preintervention measure and one postintervention measure—we would have no way to detect such ongoing processes (for example, maturation, reactivity, regression toward the mean) and thus would need experimental and control groups.

But what about history? Perhaps a big coincidence really did occur regarding the illustration depicted in Figure 12-1. Perhaps a dramatic and helpful change took place in the client's social environment precisely when intervention began. History cannot be ruled out with results like those in Figure 12-1, but note how history seems less plausible than in simple pretest–posttest group designs that contain only two data points (one before intervention and one after) and in which longer periods of time usually separate the two data points. In single-case designs, we can pinpoint the day or the week when the stable pattern of improvement begins, and we can discuss with the client what significant events or changes occurred at that point (other than the onset of intervention) to get a fairly good idea of whether history seems like a plausible explanation.

Single-case designs can increase their control for history by having more than one baseline and intervention phase. We will examine in depth how that is done later in this chapter. For now, let us consider the following illustration. Suppose a school social worker who seeks to enhance the self-esteem and social functioning of an acting-out adolescent at high risk of dropping out of school monitors the student's disciplinary referrals and administers a standardized self-esteem scale on a weekly basis. Suppose further that the social worker decides to interrupt the intervention phase for a few weeks, to see whether the student could maintain the improvement without being dependent on lengthy treatment. If a graph of the student's repeated measures resembles the data patterns displayed in Figure 12-3, then the social worker would have reasonable grounds for inferring that it is probably the intervention, and not history, that accounts for the student's improved functioning. Such an inference is reasonable because the shifts in the data patterns, or trends, occur on three successive occasions that coincide with the introduction or interruption of intervention and at no other time. With this many successive trend shifts, the odds become extremely slim that other events are producing the desired change in the target problem and simply happen to coincide with variation in the independent variable. Thus, the history hypothesis becomes far-fetched.

SINGLE-CASE DESIGNS IN SOCIAL WORK

When the preceding logic of time-series analysis is applied to the evaluation of outcome with individual cases, the research designs can be termed *single-*

subject designs, single-case designs, or *single-system designs.* The latter two terms are favored by those who seek to remind us that client systems need not be individual subjects, but can include a family unit, a community, and so on. The term *single-case designs* has become the more commonly used term in social work. Regardless of what we call them, a distinguishing feature of these designs is that the sample size is one. Whether our unit of analysis is one individual, one family, one community, or one organization, the number of sampling elements is one. Consequently, one of the chief limitations of these designs is their dubious external validity. In Chapter 14 we'll discuss the precariousness of generalizing from samples that lack adequate size or selection procedures. What, then, are we to think of a sampling approach that contains only one element? Although some researchers dismiss these designs as little more than idiosyncratic case studies that cannot be generalized, a case can be made for their increased usage in social work.

Those who pooh-pooh single-case designs because of their small sample size perhaps overlook the important role they have played in the history of behavioral research, beginning early in the 20th century with laboratory research on animal behavior. Who, for example, would want to dismiss the importance of Pavlov's dog as a single case in the development of learning theory? As for research on human behavior, single-case designs began to proliferate during the 1960s, when behavior modification studies burgeoned.

Eventually, recognition grew that single-case designs could be used not only in behavioral modification studies, but also in the evaluation of any social service intervention for which target problems could be operationally defined in terms that were conducive to multiple, repeated measures. By the late 1970s, a growing cadre of social work researchers and educators was advocating an increased emphasis on these designs as a way to integrate research and practice, increase the amount of practice-oriented research being produced, and ultimately advance the empirical base of social work practice. Today, single-case design evaluations are recognized as the most rigorous way that practitioners can implement the final stage of the evidence-based practice process (as discussed in Chapter 2): assessing whether the intervention they have provided to an individual client appears to be effective in helping that client achieve his or her treatment goals.

As discussed earlier in this book, significant scientific advances do not necessarily require the use of large-scale studies that attempt to verify hypotheses. Important contributions can also be made by exploratory studies that use more flexible methods, including smaller samples, in efforts to discover new insights and generate hypotheses and theories for which generalizability can be tested later in more tightly controlled studies using larger samples.

With a high degree of internal validity, single-case experiments can identify interventions that seem to work in one, perhaps idiosyncratic, context and that can be tested for generalizability in subsequent studies. These later studies might include larger-scale experiments that use control groups, or they might be additional single-case experiments that attempt to replicate the original single-case experiment in other contexts. For example, suppose a gerontological social worker finds, based on his or her results in a single-case design, that reviewing life history with a particular client in a long-term care facility significantly improved the client's morale and diminished the client's depression. Gerontological social workers in similar facilities with similar clients could attempt to replicate the intervention and study. To the extent that they also replicate the results, evidence would then accumulate that supported the generalizability of the findings. Ultimately, this evidence may be sufficient to secure the more extensive degree of support needed to make feasible a larger-scale experiment utilizing a control group. But even if a larger, control group experiment is never conducted, the accumulation of single-case evidence will advance the scientific basis for continuing to deliver the tested intervention.

Accumulating findings of single-case experiments has value not only in advancing the scientific basis of particular interventions or of a particular practitioner's effectiveness, but also in evaluating an entire agency or program. Suppose, for example, that a funding source calls for a program evaluation to determine whether a family service agency is providing effective services and thus merits continued or perhaps increased levels of support. Suppose further that administrative and ethical considerations rule out the possibility of using a control group in the evaluation. One option might be to conduct a time-series design. But suppose target problems and service objectives vary substantially from case to case. The objective might be to reduce a child's antisocial behavior in one case, decrease marital conflict in another, prevent abusive parental behavior in a third, and so on. One option would be to conduct a separate single-case experiment on each case or on a representative subset of cases and to use the idiosyncratic case objectives or target problems as the dependent variable in each experiment. The agency could then report not only the proportion of its cases that attain successful outcomes but also, and more important, the proportion of those outcomes that the logic of time-series analysis shows to have been caused specifically by receiving agency services.

A reverse process also illustrates the value of single-case designs—that is, individual practitioners or agencies may wonder whether interventions supported initially by group experiments in other settings will work as well in their particular, and perhaps idiosyncratic, context. For instance, suppose a few gerontological social workers first learned about reviewing life histories from an experiment reported in a gerontological social work journal, and they wondered whether they were capable of implementing the reported intervention as effectively and whether their particular clients would be able to benefit from it as much as those in the reported study, whose characteristics may have been inadequately specified or may have differed slightly from those of their clients. They could conduct single-case experiments with one or more clients to answer these questions for themselves. Such experiments would reduce their doubt not only about the effectiveness of particular interventions with particular clients, but also about their own effectiveness as clinical practitioners.

USE OF SINGLE-CASE DESIGNS AS PART OF EVIDENCE-BASED PRACTICE

As we noted above and in Chapter 2, single-case designs can be implemented by some practitioners as part of their own clinical practice with individual clients—in the final phase of the evidence-based practice process. Because these designs require only one case, the practitioner need not worry about amassing large samples or assigning clients to control groups. Each experiment contains idiosyncratic objectives that are applicable to an individual case—objectives that the practitioner would be helping the client attain as a routine part of practice were no experiment to take place. Likewise, in evidence-based practice the practitioner would routinely want to monitor the client's progress in attaining those objectives. By taking repeated measures of changes in the target problem, the practitioner both monitors client progress (or lack thereof) and acquires a tool for a more systematic understanding of events or circumstances that may exacerbate or ameliorate the target problem.

For example, suppose a child in a joint-custody arrangement is being treated for explosive and antisocial behaviors. Suppose further that the problematic behaviors tend to occur shortly before the child is about to go into the custody of one or the other parent. Repeated measures of the target behavior might help the practitioner chronologically identify this coincidence during the initial stages of service delivery, which in turn would help the practitioner better understand the causes of the target problem and develop an appropriate strategy to deal with it. Practitioners who spend considerable amounts of time unsystematically attempting to record and evaluate their practices might find conducting single-case designs to be one way to make that effort more systematic and valid.

There are, however, practical obstacles to integrating single-case designs as part of direct practice. These constraints make it unrealistic for many practitioners to utilize these designs, particularly when they are working in certain kinds of agency settings or with certain types of target problems. Client crises often do not allow practitioners enough time to take repeated measures to identify baseline trends before implementing the intervention. In some settings, heavy caseloads reduce the amount of time practitioners have to plan or conduct repeated measures during any phase. The practitioner's peers and supervisors in an agency may not recognize the value of researching one's own practice effectiveness and therefore may not support it. Clients may resent the extensive self-monitoring procedures that these designs may require.

Despite these obstacles, practitioners should strive to implement single-case designs whenever they can. Some interventions or services have not yet received adequate scientific testing concerning their beneficial or harmful effects on clients. Some others that have been tested and found to be *relatively* effective are not effective with all clients who receive them. In light of this, the question may not be whether each of us can afford the time needed to use single-case methodology as part of our practices, but whether our profession can afford not to allocate the time. Given our commitment to the social welfare of our clients and our aspiration to call our work truly professional, we can conduct single-case experiments when implementing untested interventions to see whether they are helping clients, harming them, or merely wasting scarce resources that could be put to better use. Likewise, concern for a particular client should prompt us to conduct a single-case evaluation, if feasible, to assess whether even an intervention whose probable effectiveness is supported by prior research is effective for that particular client.

Wasting scarce resources in the social welfare arena is not just a question of efficiency or public accountability, but also one of compassion and professional concern for clients. If we are wasting our own and the client's time on ineffectual services, then we are not ameliorating suffering. Neither are we able to use that time to implement alternative services that might really help that client. By conducting single-case designs as part of their practice, social work practitioners can obtain immediate feedback that will indicate whether they should modify the service program to better help (or perhaps stop hindering) specific clients.

Our point is not that practitioners would necessarily become researchers intent on publishing their findings, but that the use of scientific measurement procedures and single-case design logic can be an important part of evidence-based practice—simply in being a more compassionate, conscientious, and professional practitioner—and requires no aspirations to be a researcher or to publish scientific findings. Suppose, for example, a new technique is developed for the treatment of trauma symptoms among rape victims, a technique that requires clients to engage in emotionally painful treatment sessions in which they repeatedly recall and retell the details of the rape. Suppose further that although the technique's effectiveness has not yet been adequately tested with well-controlled experiments or quasi-experiments, clinical practitioners worldwide are excited about it and using it. Among the practitioners who use this technique and have sufficient time to use single-case methodology, which are the more compassionate and professional—those who use single-case design logic and scientific measurement procedures to monitor whether this intervention is helping clients, harming them, or wasting their time or those who are less systematic about monitoring the technique's effects?

Along the same lines, suppose you had a rare illness that required the use of one or more alternative medical treatments that had not yet been adequately tested. Which physician would you find more humane and want to treat you—one who used single-case principles to monitor the positive and negative effects of each alternative treatment on you or one who simply applied the treatment with which he or she was most comfortable and then didn't burden you with a bunch of scientific testing?

But readers should not be misled by an overly rosy portrayal of the feasibility of conducting single-case designs as part of their own practices; nor should they think that single-case designs offer a panacea for resolving long-standing doubts about the effectiveness of social work practice. As we will see shortly, conducting repeated measures of target problems in a way that provides data that are credible from the standpoint of reliability and validity can be a difficult and complex task. And delaying treatment until a stable trend of baseline measurements has been established (even when it's possible to do so) is a lot easier to recommend in a textbook or classroom lecture than to do when confronted by individuals who are suffering. Also, many client problems do not lend themselves to any sort of repeated measures. It is silly, for example, to conduct repeated measures to see whether a crisis intervention succeeded in helping a family whose house burned down find an emergency shelter. It either did or did not; one need not monitor variation in the degree of goal attainment to find out.

Their limitations notwithstanding, single-case designs can be valuable tools for social work researchers, administrators, planners, and practitioners. Because most readers of this text are preparing for careers as social work practitioners, the rest of this chapter will treat the topic of single-case designs primarily from the standpoint of conducting them as part of one's own evidence-based practice. But this treatment will also provide information needed by researchers who seek to conduct single-case designs or by administrators who will use them for agency evaluation, planning, and accountability.

MEASUREMENT ISSUES

Early decisions in planning a single-case experiment involve identifying the target problem and goals and defining them in operational terms. These decisions influence the next phase of the research plan: developing a measurement and data collection plan.

Operationally Defining Target Problems and Goals

Identifying target problems is chiefly a practice consideration and is treated in depth in various texts on practice and assessment. It might involve gathering information from a broad spectrum of individuals who are connected to the client system and carefully considering the reliability and validity of information provided by alternative sources. It might involve the use of standardized assessment instruments, such as self-report scales. It might involve a process of partialization in which problems are prioritized: The most urgent yet easily resolved problems are addressed first and the thornier, longer-term ones are tackled later. It might also involve establishing a contract in which client and practitioner agree on the problems to be tackled and how they will be monitored. Readers are referred to practice texts (Compton and Galaway, 1994; Hepworth, Rooney, and Larsen, 2002; Reid and Epstein, 1972) for a thorough treatment of this topic from a practice standpoint.

From a research standpoint, the critical issue is defining the target problems in operational terms (that is, in precise and observable terms). Operational definitions were discussed at length in Chapter 7, and the same issues discussed there apply to single-case designs. For some reason, however, practitioners seem more likely to dispute the applicability of operational definitions when thinking about individual cases than when thinking about research in general. Some argue that it is impossible to define certain clinical constructs, such as level of social functioning, in specific and observable terms. However, most skeptics ultimately realize that clinicians or clients would never have selected a target problem in the first place if they had no way to observe, at least indirectly, its indicators—that is, they would never choose to work toward improving client functioning in one area or another unless they already had some basis for observing certain indicators that convinced them that the level of functioning was unacceptably low.

Any problem that we would have reason to work on, therefore, could be operationally defined if we simply considered the specific indicators that led us to decide that it needed our attention. Consider the alternative. If it were possible to identify a problem that could not be defined in operational terms, then on what grounds would the practitioner or client have decided that it required intervention? And how in the world would they ever decide whether the problem was or was not adequately resolved? Here we are dealing not just with a research issue, but also with a practice issue. Imagine, for example, trying to learn how to do clinical assessment or when to terminate interventions from a practice instructor who taught exclusively via presentations of his or her own cases and was unable to identify for students what he or she observed in each case that led him or her to work on one particular target problem in one case and a different problem in another, or what the instructor observed that led him or her to terminate the intervention in each case.

In considering operational definitions, some students note that practitioners might rely on the client's complaint that a particular problem requires attention. But even here practitioners are using an operational definition; that is, they are persuaded to work on a problem based on their observation of the extent of the client's expressed difficulty or dissatisfaction with that problem. Thus, they could take repeated measures simply by having clients indicate daily on a brief scale the degree of difficulty they felt they experienced with the problem that day.

But saying that all identified target problems can be operationally defined does not mean that the selection of observable indicators is always a routine or easy decision. We often are confronted with knotty target problems that cannot be observed directly (for example, anxiety, depression, or self-esteem issues) and that require us to select and observe indirect indicators of the problem. There may be an extensive array of potential indicators, and selecting the wrong one might lead to incorrect conclusions later. Take self-esteem, for example. Some self-report measures of self-esteem treat level of self-esteem as a fairly permanent personality trait, and consequently these measures are not sensitive to small, short-term changes. If the operational definition of the target problem were a score on such a scale, then it might be exceedingly difficult to detect changes in self-esteem that represented meaningful improvements from a clinical standpoint.

Among the array of potential observable indicators of a target problem there may be positive indicators that represent the problem's absence or negative indicators that signify its presence. For instance, if the target problem concerned a client's depression, an operational definition might involve negative indicators such as the frequency of crying spells or the frequency of self-derogatory remarks. The goal then would be a reduction in the observed indicators. The operational definition might also include positive indicators such as the amount of time spent in social interaction with friends. If so, then the goal would be to increase those indicators. Practitioners might want to restrict their definition to positive indicators for clinical reasons, so that they and the client are not always thinking in negative terms about the problem. They might also choose to monitor several indicators of the problem or goal, perhaps including some that are positive as well as some that are negative.

What to Measure

Because of the need to obtain many repeated observations in single-case experiments, the operational indicators should occur frequently enough to be measured on a regular basis. Direct-service practitioners working in a suicide prevention program, for example, might want to monitor the amount of sleep a client gets each day, the daily number of positive client self-cognitions, or weekly scores on a self-report depression inventory. The practitioners probably would not record an infrequent event such as the number of suicide attempts each day or week because it would take too long to establish enough variation in the data pattern. On the other hand, a planner or administrator who uses single-case methodology to evaluate the effectiveness of an entire suicide prevention program could appropriately monitor the number of reported suicides or suicide attempts each week in a populous area served by the program. Likewise, a practitioner who works with an abusive parent might want to monitor the amount of time the parent plays with the child each day or the number of positive statements (praise, encouragement, and so on) from parent to child during weekly observation sessions, rather than record the daily or weekly incidence of serious abuse by the parent. But an administrator of a countywide program to prevent child abuse appropriately could monitor the countywide incidence of serious child abuse each week.

No strict rule determines how many operational indicators we should measure. The fewer we measure, the greater the risk that we fail to detect client improvement on indicators other than those being measured. For example, a case manager might be effective in motivating a chronically mentally ill client to take medication as prescribed and in securing more community support services. But if the case manager only measured the client's degree of psychopathology or the client's job-seeking behavior, then he or she might get negative results and erroneously conclude that the intervention was not working. On the other hand, it is unwise to try to measure so many indicators that the data-gathering process becomes unwieldy and overwhelms the client, practitioner, or both. Moreover, the greater the number of indicators that are monitored, the greater the risk that the data pattern of one or more of them will show improvement after intervention solely on the basis of chance fluctuations.

Triangulation

As a rule of thumb, two or three indicators are generally considered appropriate. This is usually a feasible approach on the one hand, and it meets the criterion of triangulation on the other. As discussed in Chapter 8, triangulation is a principle that applies to all types of research designs, not just single-case experiments. It refers to situations in which researchers are confronted with a multiplicity of imperfect measurement options, each having advantages and disadvantages. To maximize the chances that the hypothesized variation in the dependent variable will be detected, the researcher triangulates measures: More than one measurement option is used. Despite its connotation of a triangle, triangulation does not require using three options, only more than one.

In single-case designs, triangulation does not necessarily mean that more than one target problem is to be measured. It means that more than one indicator of the same target problem is to be measured. For instance, a school social worker whose client is underachieving might want to monitor the amount of time the client spends on homework each night and teacher ratings of his or her class attentiveness and participation. Triangulation does not require that the social worker also monitor indicators of other problems, such as antisocial behaviors (fighting, disciplinary referrals, and so on). The practitioner may choose to monitor more than one problem, but the principle of triangulation does not require it. The principle of triangulation applies to all measurement options—not just what to measure—and we will consider it again in our discussion of data gathering.

DATA GATHERING

The options and decisions to be made in planning measurement and data collection in single-case experiments are not unlike those that confront researchers who are designing other types of studies. Researchers must decide whether the data sources should be available records, interviews, self-report scales, or direct observations of behavior. The advantages and disadvantages of these sources are largely the same in single-case experiments as those in other types of research.

Who Should Measure?

One issue involves who should do the measuring. When practitioners make measurements to evaluate their own practice, the risk of observer bias might be heightened, for it is only human to want to obtain findings that support our practice effectiveness and indicate that client suffering is being ameliorated. Perhaps even riskier is relying exclusively on clients to do the measuring themselves. Clients may be biased to perceive positive results not only to please themselves or to project a socially desirable image to the practitioner, but also to avoid disappointing the practitioner. Significant others (teachers, cottage parents, and so on) might be asked to monitor certain behaviors in the hope that they have less invested than the client or practitioner in seeing a positive outcome. But neither their objectivity nor their commitment to the study can be guaranteed. This is particularly important in light of the large amount of time and dedication that might be required to monitor the client's behavior carefully and systematically on a continuous basis. In light of the repeated measures required by single-case designs and the strong potential for bias, there is no easy answer about who should do the measuring. Here, then, we return to the principle of triangulation and perhaps use all three of the preceding options to gather the data. In this context, we see another advantage of triangulation—the opportunity it provides for assessing measurement reliability. To the extent that different data gatherers agree in their measures, we can have more confidence that the data are accurate.

Sources of Data

In considering alternative sources of data (available records, interviews, self-report scales, or direct behavioral observations), several issues are particularly salient in single-case designs. Available records, for example, might enable the researcher or practitioner to obtain a retrospective baseline of pretreatment trends and therefore not have to delay treatment while collecting baseline data. This, of course, can occur only when we are fortunate enough to have access to existing records that contain carefully gathered, reliable data that happen to correspond to the way the target problem has been operationally defined in the single-case experiment.

Self-report scales also merit special consideration in single-case designs. On the one hand, they can be quite convenient; repeated measures can be expedited by simply having clients complete a brief self-report scale each day where they reside or each time the practitioner sees them. Self-report scales also ensure that the repeated measures are administered and scored in a uniform fashion.

On the other hand, the use of these scales carries special risks in single-case experiments. For one thing, clients might lose interest in completing them carefully over and over again. Perhaps a more serious risk, however, is the potential for the client to be biased to complete these scales with responses that convey a socially desirable impression. This risk would be greatest when the single-case experiment is being conducted by practitioners to evaluate their own practice, because clients might be particularly predisposed to give inaccurate responses in order to please the clinicians about their helpfulness or favorably impress them.

Reliability and Validity

Readers might wonder at this point whether these risks could be avoided by using standardized self-report scales with established high levels of reliability and validity. All other things being equal (such as relevance to the problem or client, sensitivity to change, and instrument length and complexity), of course it is better to use scales whose reliability and validity have been empirically supported, if such scales are available for the particular variable one seeks to measure. But the conditions under which the validity of standardized instruments is tested tend to contrast with single-case experimental conditions in critical ways. Standardized instruments tend to be validated in large-scale assessment studies in which (1) the respondent is part of a large group of individuals who have no special, ongoing relationship with the researcher and who are by and large anonymous; (2) the instrument will not be completed more than one or two times by each respondent; and (3) a respondent's score on the instrument has no bearing on whether he or she is benefiting from some service.

In contrast, when clients complete these instruments as part of single-case experiments, they are not anonymous and have a special relationship with a service provider. They may therefore be sensitive about the impression they are conveying and more intent on conveying a favorable impression than in a more anonymous situation. With each repeated completion of the instrument, their answers may become less valid, perhaps due to carelessness or because they remember their previous answers. Finally, and perhaps most important, they may be keenly aware of the difference between nontreatment (baseline) phases and treatment phases; they may know that if the service is being effective, then their scores should improve during the treatment phases. This awareness may predispose them to convey a more positive impression during the treatment phases. In light of these differences, we cannot assume that a particular self-report instrument will adequately avoid social desirability biases in a single-case experiment just because it has empirically been shown in other contexts not to have serious validity problems.

Direct Behavioral Observation

The large number of repeated measures in single-case experiments also complicates the decision to use direct behavioral observations as the data source. This is particularly problematic when the experiment is conducted as part of one's own practice, because busy practitioners may lack the time needed to conduct the observations themselves or the resources needed to induce someone else to observe the client. To the extent that observation of the target problem can be limited to office or home visits, the difficulty of practitioner observation is reduced. But many target problems need to be observed on a more continuous basis.

Barring the availability of a significant other (such as a teacher, relative, or cottage parent) who is willing to observe on a regular basis, we are commonly forced to rely on our clients to observe themselves. The term for client self-observation is *self-monitoring.* If the dependent variable is the number of a certain type of thoughts or feelings that a client has during a particular period—phenomena that only the client could observe—then self-monitoring would be the only direct observation option.

The problem with self-monitoring is that, in addition to its vulnerability to measurement bias (as discussed earlier), it is highly vulnerable to the problem of research reactivity. As we discussed in Chapter 11, one way in which **reactivity** can occur is when the process of observing or recording the data—that is, the self-measurement process itself—brings about change in the target problem. For example, suppose a practitioner encourages a mother who has a conflictual relationship with her son to record each time she praises him and each time she scolds him. Regardless of what else the practitioner does, the mere act of recording may sensitize the mother to her tendency to scold her son too often and praise him too rarely, and this in turn may bring her to praise him more and scold him less.

From a clinical standpoint, of course, reactivity might not be such a bad idea—that is, self-monitoring can be used as a clinical tool to help bring about the desired change. Indeed, it's often used that way. But when it's used as the only measurement procedure in research, it clouds the process of inferring whether the intervention alone brought about the change. This problem can be offset somewhat by the realization that if self-monitoring alone is bringing about the desired change, then the change might be detected by noticing an improving trend in a graph of the pretreatment (baseline) data.

You might ask, then, what's the best way to avoid the above problems without sacrificing the use of direct observation? Answering this question is easy; the problem is getting the resources needed to do things the best way. First, we would again use the principle of triangulation; that is, we would have more than one person conduct the observations. Second, we would seek to include at least one observer who did not have a vested interest in the outcome of the study or the impression conveyed by the data and who therefore might be relatively unbiased. Third, we would assess the interrater reliability of the observers (how much their observations agree). And fourth, we would arrange for at least one observer to conduct the observations in a relatively unobtrusive manner.

Unobtrusive versus Obtrusive Observation

As we discussed in Chapter 11, unobtrusively observing behavior means that the observer blends into the observation setting in such a way that the act of observing and recording is by and large not noticeable to those who are being observed. For example, a group worker who is attempting to reduce the amount of antisocial behavior by boys in a residential facility might ask a colleague who supervises their recreational activities to observe the number of fights, arguments, and so on the targeted boys get into and to record the numbers in the notebook that he or she always carries while supervising the boys.

The opposite of unobtrusive observation is obtrusive observation. Measurement is obtrusive to the extent that the subject is aware of the observation and therefore vulnerable to research reactivity or to acting in an atypical manner in order to convey a socially desirable impression. Self-monitoring is perhaps the most obtrusive form of observation because the subject is both observee and observer. But many other forms of observation can be so obtrusive that the credibility of the entire study is imperiled. Some of these examples can be deceptive because researchers or practitioners may take steps that at first glance seem to provide some degree of unobtrusiveness.

For example, the researcher or practitioner may observe the client through a one-way mirror, thinking that because the client cannot see him or her, the client is less aware of the observation. To a certain extent this is true. But consider the following wrinkle. After taking pretreatment (baseline) measures through a one-way mirror of a conflictual mother–son dyad interacting, the practitioner introduces a task-centered intervention in which the practitioner and the mother agree that the mother's task will be to try to praise her son more when he acts appropriately. The practitioner continues to monitor the interactions through a one-way mirror to see if the intervention will be effective in increasing the number of statements of praise as compared to the pretreatment baseline.

Although it is commendable that the practitioner made observations while not visible by the clients, it is wrong to suppose that the observations were truly unobtrusive or that the baseline and intervention phases were really comparable in their degree of obtrusiveness. In both phases, the mother has some degree of awareness that the practitioner is watching from the other side of the mirror. And in the intervention phase, she knows precisely which behavior—praise—the practitioner is watching for, knowledge she did not have in the earlier, baseline phase.

Thus, the degree of obtrusiveness in both phases is compounded by the increased vulnerability to a social desirability bias during the intervention phase. And because the client is more inclined to provide the socially desirable response during the intervention phase, the problem of obtrusiveness becomes a bigger threat to the credibility of the findings. In other words, the desired increase in praise could easily have nothing to do with the efficacy of the intervention, but instead merely reflect the fact that after the intervention was introduced the client became more predisposed to put on a socially desirable performance—one that might have no correlation whatsoever to the way the mother interacts with her child in a natural setting or when the practitioner is not watching. You might think this example is far-fetched, that no one would conduct single-case research with such obvious potential measurement bias, but studies like this have not only been conducted, but also published in our professional literature!

Data Quantification Procedures

Data gathered through direct observation in single-case experiments can be quantified in terms of their *frequency, duration,* or *magnitude.* For example, the target problem of temper tantrums could be recorded in terms of the number of temper tantrums observed in a specified period (frequency), how long each tantrum lasted (duration), or how loud or violent it was (magnitude). Using the principle of triangulation, all three quantification procedures could be used simultaneously.

Another procedure—*interval recording*—combines both frequency and duration and may be used when it is impractical to record either frequency or duration alone. This method involves dividing an observation period into equal blocks of short time intervals and then recording whether or not the target behavior occurred at all during each interval. Suppose, for example, that a target problem of an intervention with conflictual spouses was operationally defined as the degree to which they interrupt each other when conversing. Suppose further that the observer was recording interruptions during a 30-minute period in which the couple was instructed to engage in a typical conversation. (Let's put obtrusiveness aside for now.) The interruptions might occur so rapidly that the observer would be overwhelmed trying to record each one in a frequency count. The interruptions might last so long that duration recording would be too fatiguing. With interval recording, the observer would break the 30-minute session into equal intervals of perhaps one minute each. Then all that would be required would be to enter a check mark for each interval that contained at least one interruption.

But the direct observation of behavior does not always require continuous observation during lengthy sessions. *Spot-check recording* can be used to observe target behaviors that occur frequently, last a long time, or are expected to occur during specified periods. For instance, suppose a social worker in a residential treatment facility for distressed adolescents introduces a behavioral modification intervention that seeks to increase the amount of school homework

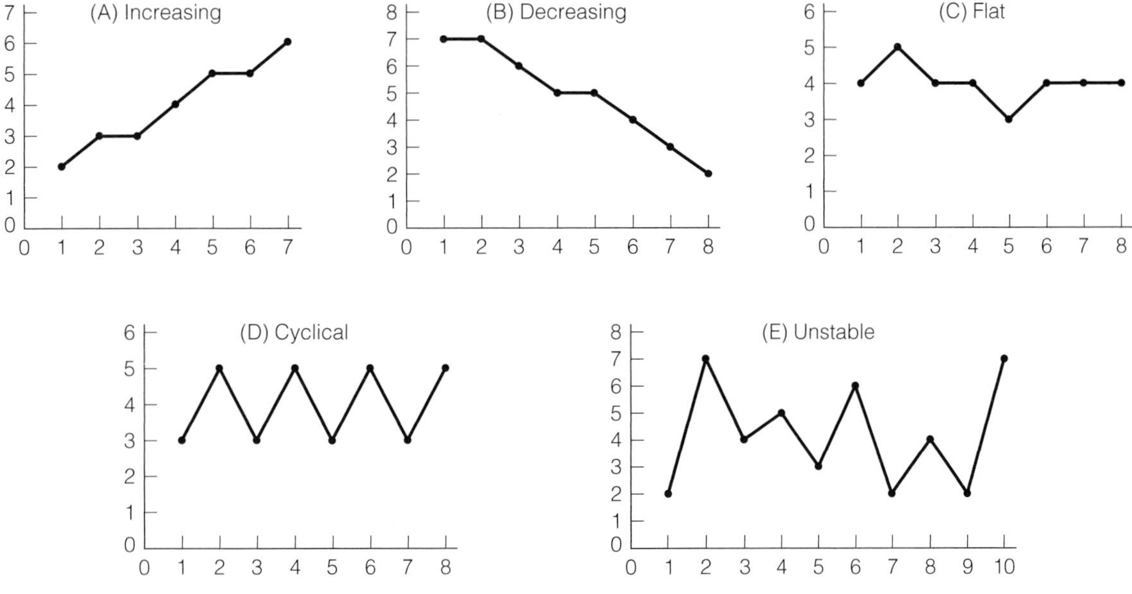

Figure 12-4 Alternative Baseline Trends

that residents do during specified study periods each evening. The social worker or a cottage parent could briefly glance at the study area each evening, varying the precise time of the observation from day to day, and quickly record whether or not specified individuals were studying (yes or no) or simply count how many were studying at that particular moment. Spot checks thus have the advantage of being not only less time-consuming but also less obtrusive than continuous observation because the observer appears only briefly and at unexpected, intermittent times.

The Baseline Phase

The logic of single-case designs requires taking enough repeated measures to make it unlikely that extraneous factors (such as changes in the client's environment) would account for improvements that take place in the target problem with the onset of intervention. The logic also relies on comparing trends that are identified in the repeated measures to control for factors such as maturation or statistical regression. Based on this logic, the internal validity of single-case designs is enhanced when the baseline period has enough measurement points to show a stable trend in the target problem and enough points to establish the unlikelihood that extraneous events that affect the target problem will coincide only with the onset of intervention. Although the ideal number of baseline measurement points needed will vary depending on how soon a stable trend appears, it is reasonable to plan for somewhere between five and ten baseline measures. With some stable baselines, one can begin to see trends with as few as three to five data points. But the more data points we have, the more confidence we can have in the stability of the observed trend and in the unlikelihood that extraneous events will coincide only with the onset of intervention.

The realities of practice do not always permit us to take an ideal number of baseline measures, however. For example, the client's problem might be too urgent to delay intervention any longer, even though the baseline trend appears unstable or is unclear. When an ideal baseline length is not feasible, we simply come as close to the ideal as the clinical and administrative realities permit.

A stable trend is one that shows the target problem to be occurring in a predictable and orderly fashion. The trend is identified by plotting the data points chronologically on a graph, drawing a line between each data point, and then observing whether the overall pattern is clearly increasing, as in part A of Figure 12-4, decreasing (part B), relatively flat (part C), or cyclical (part D). By contrast, part E of Figure 12-4 illustrates an unstable baseline without an obvious trend.

The meaning of increasing or decreasing baselines depends on the operational definition of the target

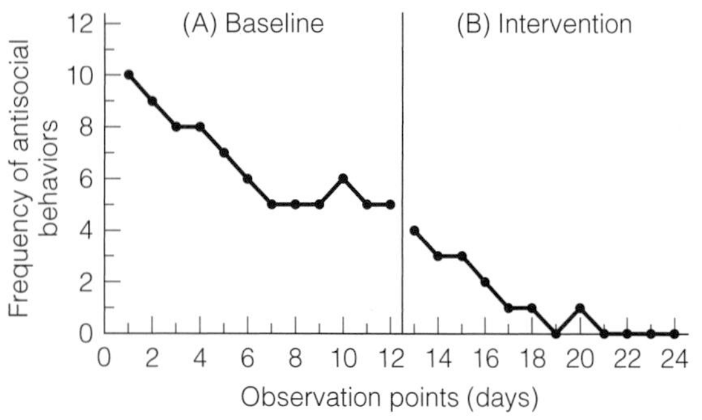

Figure 12-5 Graph of Hypothetical Outcome after Extending a Baseline with an Improving Trend (AB Design)

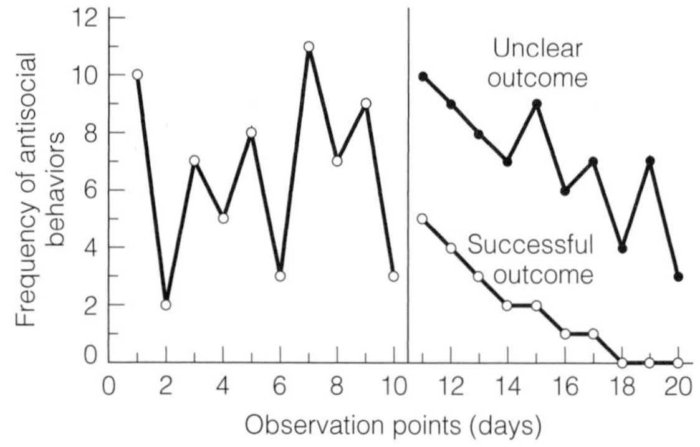

Figure 12-6 Graph of Two Hypothetical Outcomes with an Unstable Baseline (AB Design)

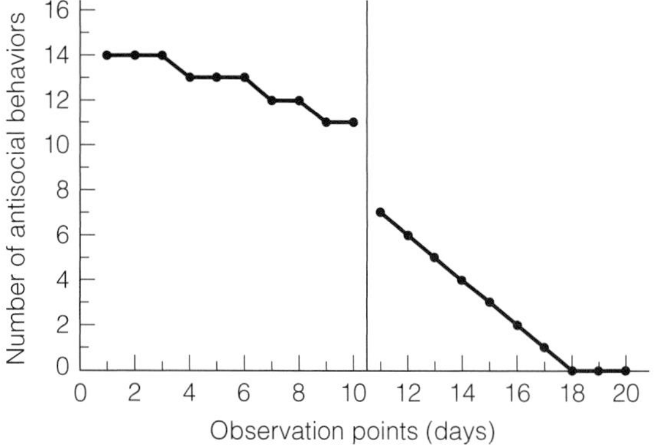

Figure 12-7 Graph of a Hypothetical Outcome Supporting Intervention Efficacy with an Improving Baseline (AB Design)

problem. If it involves undesirable phenomena such as temper tantrums, then an increasing baseline trend would mean the problem is worsening, and a decreasing baseline would indicate improvement. If the operational definition involves desirable indicators such as doing homework, then an increasing baseline would signify improvement and a decreasing baseline would signify deterioration.

When the baseline trend signifies improvement, even if it is stable, it may be advisable to continue collecting baseline measures until the improving trend levels off, as illustrated in Figure 12-5. If intervention is introduced at the peak of an improving baseline trend (before it levels off), it will be difficult to achieve a dramatic improvement in the trend. In other words, the baseline trend would mean that the client was improving so steadily without any intervention that (1) even an effective intervention might not affect the rate of improvement, and (2) perhaps no intervention on that particular indicator was needed in the first place. Introducing an intervention on the heels of an improving baseline introduces the risk of erroneously concluding that an intervention made no difference simply because the ongoing improvement process was already so steady.

We would also want to extend baseline measures beyond the point at which we initially planned to introduce the intervention if the baseline data collected up to that point were unstable (that is, if they failed to yield a predictable trend). As noted earlier, when we observe an unstable baseline, we ideally would extend the baseline measures until a stable pattern appears. However, it was also noted that the constraints of practice do not always permit us to extend the baseline until a desirable trend is obtained. Other priorities, such as client suffering or endangerment, may take precedence over the internal validity of the research design. If so, then we simply do the best we can with what we have. Perhaps the intervention is so effective that even an unstable or improving baseline pattern will prove to be clearly worse than the intervention data pattern. Figure 12-6 shows an unstable baseline juxtaposed with two alternative intervention data patterns. One pattern illustrates the difficulty of interpreting outcome with an unstable baseline; the other pattern shows that it is not necessarily impossible to do so.

In a similar vein, Figure 12-7 illustrates that even with an improving baseline it may be possible to obtain results that support the efficacy of the intervention.

We also might want to deviate from the planned time of completion of the baseline phase when, after the design is implemented, we learn that extraneous environmental changes that may have a potentially important effect on the target problem will coincide with the beginning of the intervention period. For example, if the client has a severe hay fever problem and the target behavior is something like interpersonal irritability or school performance, then we would not want to introduce the intervention at the beginning or end of the hay fever season. If we learn of such a situation after the baseline phase has begun, then we might extend the baseline longer than initially planned so that it includes enough data points to identify a stable trend after the relevant environmental conditions have changed. Another option would be to withdraw the intervention for a short time later and then reintroduce it, hoping that the hiatus from treatment would provide a second baseline whose beginning or end would not coincide with important environmental changes. (This latter option is called an ABAB design, and it will be examined in more depth shortly.)

Practitioners can employ single-case practice evaluation procedures even when an adequate baseline is impossible, such as when they cannot obtain more than one or two baseline data points. They can even use these procedures when it is impossible to obtain any baseline data whatsoever. The rationale is that although the lack of an adequate baseline impedes the drawing of causal inferences, the rest of the data collected can enhance practice by providing a more scientific process for monitoring client progress. In light of the aforementioned practical difficulties in taking repeated measures, especially regarding the practitioner's ability to obtain measures that are not highly vulnerable to various sources of measurement error, you may question whether the likely benefit of these procedures justifies their costs in those instances when it is impossible to obtain an adequate baseline. If you do not think they are justified in such instances, remember that we are referring only to instances when obtaining an adequate baseline is impossible. When you can obtain an adequate baseline, the argument for not using these procedures is much weaker.

Remember also that if you do use these procedures even when you cannot obtain more than a couple of baseline data points, your data do not provide a suitable basis for inferring anything about your efficacy. You may find that these procedures are quite valuable in enhancing your monitoring of client progress, but you should resist the temptation to claim that your data verify the effectiveness of your intervention.

We also remind you that when you cannot delay intervention in order to take baseline measures, you should consider whether it is possible to obtain a useful *retrospective baseline.* Also called a *reconstructed baseline,* a retrospective baseline is constructed from past data. The two primary sources of data for a retrospective baseline are available records or the memory of the client (or significant others). An example of using available records would be obtaining school records on attendance, grades, detentions, and so on for a child who has behavioral problems in school. An example of using memory, provided in a study by Nugent (1991), would be asking clients with anger control problems to recall how many blowups they had during the previous week or two, and perhaps triangulating their data with spouse or parent recollections. Bloom, Fischer, and Orme (2006) offer the following two guidelines when relying on memory to reconstruct a baseline: (1) Use specific, identifiable events that are easy to recall (such as angry blowups, detention referrals, and so on) and therefore less vulnerable to distortion than things that are harder to recall (such as feelings of inadequacy, anxiety, and so on); and (2) for the same reason, use only the immediate past, such as the past week or two, and do not go back more than one month.

ALTERNATIVE SINGLE-CASE DESIGNS

AB: The Basic Single-Case Design

As illustrated in Figures 12-1, 12-2, 12-5, 12-6, and 12-7, the simplest single-case design includes one baseline phase (A) and one intervention phase (B): the **AB design.** This is a popular design among practitioner-researchers because it involves only one baseline phase and therefore poses the least conflict with service delivery priorities. But this design is weaker than single-case designs with more baselines. With only one baseline, there is only one point at which the independent variable shifts from baseline to intervention. Consequently, only one unlikely coincidence can occur. Although taking many repeated measures reduces the plausibility that some extraneous event and not the intervention would explain a major shift in the data pattern of the dependent variable that occurs only after the onset of intervention, extraneous events are controlled much better when there are several shifts between baseline and intervention phases.

Despite its *relative* weakness, the AB design is still quite useful. More rigorous designs may not be feasible in many practice situations, and with enough repeated measures the AB design can provide some logical and empirical evidence about the effectiveness of interventions for which the impact on clients has not yet received enough scientific testing. Also, AB designs can be replicated, and if the results of various AB studies on the same intervention are consistent, then the evidence about the effectiveness of the intervention is strengthened. For instance, suppose several AB studies at different times and with different clients all find that the same type of target problem only begins to improve shortly after the same intervention is introduced. How credible is the argument that with every client an extraneous event could have coincided only with the onset of intervention and caused the improvement? AB designs are also useful in that they provide immediate feedback to practitioners that enables them to monitor variations in the target problem, explore with the client alternative explanations of changes, and modify service delivery if the need for modification is indicated by this information. Thus, AB designs—when feasible—are an excellent way to implement the final stage of the evidence-based practice process.

ABAB: Withdrawal/Reversal Design

To better control for extraneous events, the **ABAB withdrawal/reversal design** adds a second baseline phase (A) and a second intervention phase (B). The second baseline phase is established by withdrawing the intervention for a while. After a stable trend is identified in the second baseline, the intervention is reintroduced. This design assumes that if the intervention caused the improvement in the target problem during the first intervention period, then the target problem will reverse toward its original baseline level during the second baseline (after the intervention is withdrawn). When the intervention is reintroduced, the target problem should start improving again. The basic inferential principle here is that if shifts in the trend or level of the target problem occur successively each time the intervention is introduced or withdrawn, then it is not plausible that some extraneous event and not the intervention is causing the change. Because the independent variable is changed three times, there is more causal evidence than in the AB design. In other words, the number of unlikely successive coincidences that would have to occur in an ABAB design is three, rather than one in the AB design.

The ABAB design has two major problems, although both often can be resolved. One is a practical or ethical problem. Practitioners may feel that withdrawing an intervention that appears to be working is indefensible in light of the suffering or other costs the client may bear if conditions revert to baseline. These concerns would be intensified with clients who had dangerous problems or who were particularly sensitive to setbacks. Practitioners may fear that withdrawal of the intervention would confuse or alienate the client and perhaps hurt the practitioner–client relationship or in other ways impede future efforts when the intervention is reintroduced. These are important and valid concerns, and researchers should not fault practitioners who resist implementing ABAB designs because of these concerns.

Practitioners, however, should not underestimate the opportunities they have for implementing ABAB designs without compromising intervention priorities. Occasionally, there are natural breaks in the intervention phase when the practitioner attends a conference or takes a vacation, and these periods can be exploited to establish a second baseline (provided that the practitioner is not the only one observing and recording the extent of the target problem). Also, it is often consistent with good practice to withdraw an intervention temporarily at a point at which the target problem appears to have been overcome and then monitor whether the client can sustain his or her gains during the hiatus of treatment.

The second major, but potentially resolvable, problem with ABAB designs is that the assumption that the target problem can revert to baseline conditions may not be valid in many practice situations. Perhaps an intervention has had irreversible effects during the first intervention period. For instance, suppose the intervention involved social skills training, perhaps training individuals with mild developmental disabilities to interact at social gatherings or in the workplace. Once these skills are learned and the individuals are rewarded in the natural environment for using them, they may not need training to be reintroduced in order to sustain the gains they have made. Or suppose the intervention was to help an elderly woman become less isolated, lonely, and depressed. Suppose further that the intervention was environmentally oriented and focused on securing a better residence for her, one where she would be among peers with whom she could easily interact and become friends. If this intervention succeeded during the first B period, is it reasonable to suppose that she would lose her new

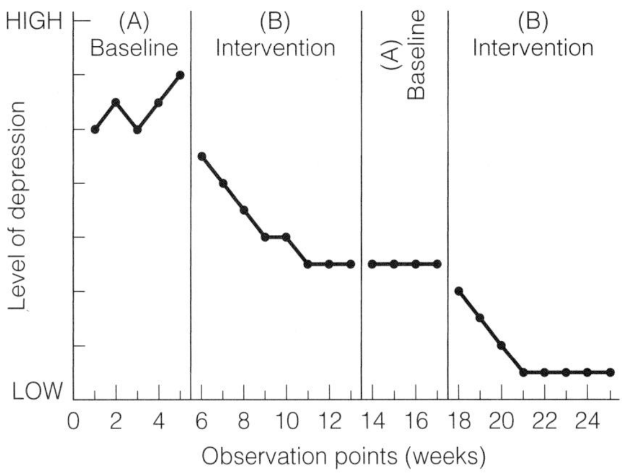

Figure 12-8 Graph of Hypothetical Outcome of ABAB Design Supporting Intervention Efficacy despite Failure to Obtain a Reversal during Second Baseline

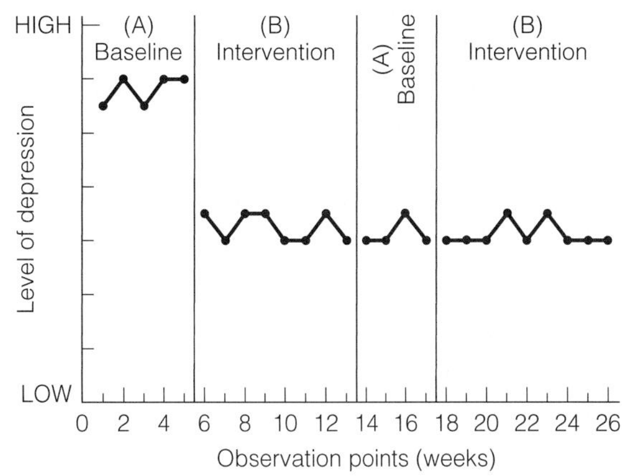

Figure 12-9 Graph of Hypothetical Outcome of ABAB Design with Unclear Results

friends or become depressed again because the practitioner withdrew the intervention (that is, efforts to change her environment, not the new residence)?

To reduce the chances that effects will be irreversible, in some situations we might want to keep the first intervention period relatively short. Then, as soon as the second baseline shows a trend toward reversal, we could reintroduce the intervention and hope to reestablish the improving trend that was briefly interrupted during the second baseline. Irreversible effects also may be less problematic if, despite the failure to obtain a reversal during the second baseline, we observed a new, improving trend during the second intervention period. Suppose, for example, that in the case of the depressed and lonely elderly woman we reintroduce the environmentally oriented intervention by getting her a pet and that this further alleviates her depression. This possibility is illustrated in Figure 12-8, in which we see a shift in the dependent variable each time the intervention is introduced, but gains made during the first intervention phase are maintained during the second baseline. Despite the absence of a reversal during the second baseline, the data's overall pattern would support the conclusion that it is the intervention and not some extraneous variable that accounts for the improvement and that the intervention's effects simply do not tend to reverse when the intervention is withdrawn.

So what do we conclude when the results of the ABAB design resemble those in Figure 12-9? Was the improvement that occurred only after the first introduction of the intervention caused by some extraneous event that happened to coincide with that introduction? In other words, should we refrain from attributing the improvement to the effects of the intervention because no other changes occurred in the target problem the next two times the intervention was introduced or withdrawn? Or can we speculate that perhaps the intervention was so effective, or the nature of the target problem so irreversible, that only one shift in the trend or level of the target problem (that is, the shift at the onset of the first intervention phase) was possible? Depending on the nature of the target problem and what we learn from the client about extraneous events that coincide with changes in the design phases, it may be possible in some cases to decide which of these rival explanations seems more plausible. Perhaps an even better way to resolve this dilemma is through **replication.** If results like those depicted in Figure 12-9 tend to be obtained consistently in future ABAB experiments on the same intervention, then the case for powerful or irreversible effects would be strengthened because there is no rational reason why extraneous events that cause shifts in the target problem should occur with every client only at those points at which intervention is first introduced.

Multiple-Baseline Designs

Multiple-baseline designs also attempt to control for extraneous variables by having more than one baseline and intervention phase. But instead of withdrawing the intervention to establish more than one baseline, multiple-baseline designs begin two or more baselines simultaneously. This is done by measuring different target behaviors in each baseline or by measuring the same target behavior in two different settings or across two different individuals. Although each baseline starts simultaneously, the intervention is introduced at a different point for each one. Thus, as the intervention is introduced for the first behavior, setting, or individual, the others are still in their baseline phases. Likewise, when the intervention is introduced for the second behavior, setting, or individual, the third (if there are more than two) is still in its baseline phase.

The main logical principle here is that if some extraneous event, such as a significant improvement in the environment, coincides with the onset of intervention and causes the client's improved functioning, then that improvement will show up in the graph of each behavior, setting, or individual at the same time, even though some might still be in baseline. On the other hand, if the intervention is accountable for the improvement, then that improvement will occur on each graph at a different point that corresponds to the introduction of the intervention.

Figure 12-10 illustrates a hypothetical multiple-baseline design across three nursing home residents who feel an extreme sense of hopelessness. In this hypothetical illustration, the practitioner read a report of a group experiment by Mercer and Kane (1979), the findings of which supported the efficacy of reducing hopelessness in residents like these by having them care for a houseplant. The practitioner begins taking baseline measures of hopelessness via a self-report scale for each resident at the same time. But he or she gives each resident a houseplant, along with instructions about caring for it, at three different times. Each resident's level of hopelessness, as reflected in the self-report scores, begins to decrease steadily only after the intervention is introduced. Therefore, it is not reasonable to suppose that some extraneous event, such as some other improvement in the overall environment of the nursing home, really caused the change.

But suppose the results looked like those in Figure 12-11. There we see that the steady improvement in hopelessness commenced for each resident at the same time that the first intervention (houseplant) was introduced. It is not plausible to infer that the plant was causing the improvement because two of the residents had not yet received theirs. Instead, it is more plausible to suppose that some extraneous improvement in the broader nursing home environment coincided with the onset of the intervention with the first resident and caused the improvement in all three. This illustrates how an AB design (with the first resident) could yield misleading findings because of its weaker control for history than occurs in multiple-baseline designs.

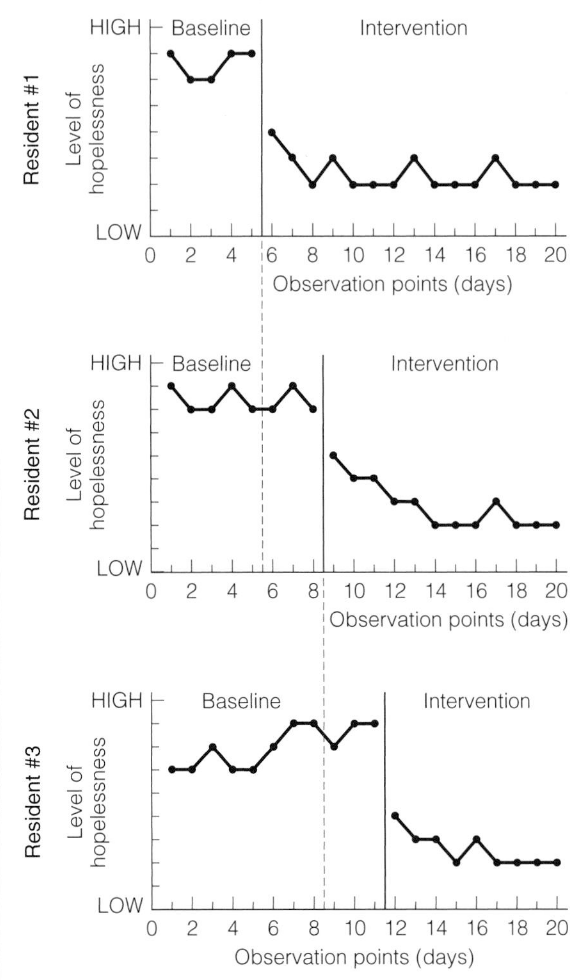

Figure 12-10 Graph of Hypothetical Outcome of Multiple-Baseline Design across Subjects Supporting Efficacy of Intervention

Figures 12-12 and 12-13 illustrate the same logical principles with multiple-baseline designs across target behaviors or settings. Both figures refer to a hypothetical case that involves a boy referred to a residential treatment center because of his antisocial behaviors. There he participates in a cognitive-behavior modification intervention like the one reported by Taber (1981) that includes teaching him how to say things to himself to help stop him from committing

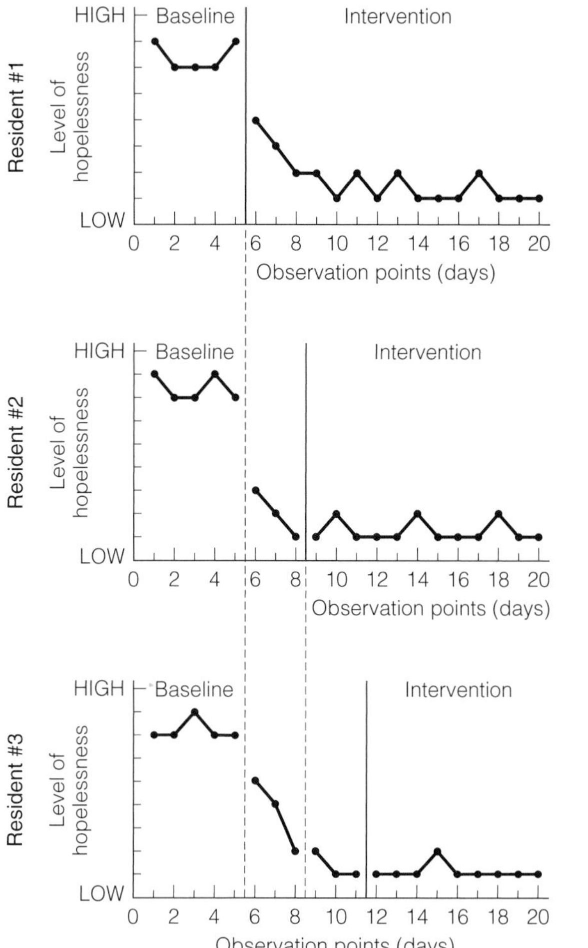

Figure 12-11 Graph of Hypothetical Outcome of Multiple-Baseline Design across Subjects Illustrating Extraneous Variable as Plausible Cause of Improvement

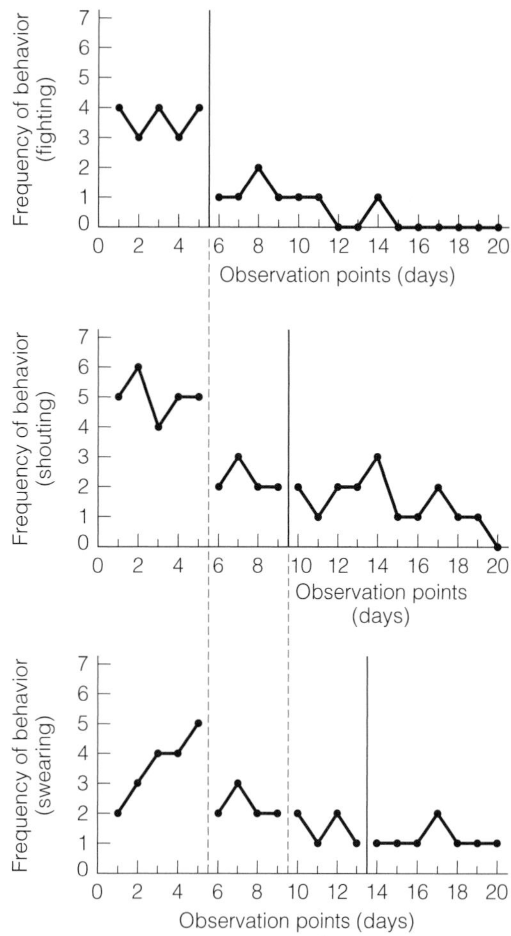

Figure 12-12 Graph of Hypothetical Outcome of Multiple-Baseline Design across Target Behaviors, with Unclear Results

explosive, antisocial behaviors in situations in which he has been most vulnerable to losing control. In Figure 12-12, the first baseline ends and intervention begins as the client starts to rehearse the verbal self-instructions in connection to fighting. One week later, he begins to rehearse in connection to impulsive, inappropriate shouting. The following week he starts rehearsing in connection to swearing.

The graphs in Figure 12-12 show that once the client begins rehearsing for fighting, a dramatic shift in the data pattern occurs for all three target behaviors at the same time. What caused this? Was it an extraneous event in the residential facility that happened to coincide with the end of the first baseline? Perhaps. But when multiple baselines are applied across different behaviors, a data pattern like this could also be caused by a rival explanation, one termed *generalization of effects*. **Generalization of effects** occurs when an intervention, although intended to apply to only one behavior or setting at a time, affects other target behaviors or settings that are still in the baseline phase as soon as it is applied to the first behavior or setting. In the current illustration, for instance, the rehearsals regarding fighting perhaps helped the boy simultaneously apply the verbal self-instructions to other behaviors that he knew got him into trouble.

Another way that generalization of effects could occur is when the intervention affects only one target behavior but the change in that behavior changes the other behaviors in turn. In the preceding illus-

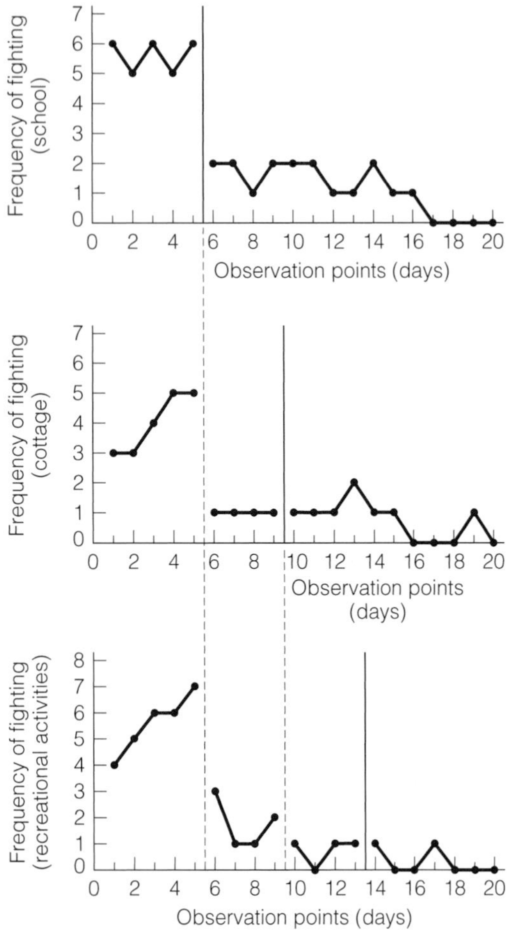

Figure 12-13 Graph of Hypothetical Outcome of Multiple-Baseline Design across Settings, with Unclear Results

tration, for example, the reduction in fighting conceivably gave the boy less to shout and swear about. The reduction in fighting also could have led to more positive feedback from peers and adults, and this improvement in his interpersonal relations (or the rewarding nature of the feedback) could have reduced his need to swear and shout or increased his desire to act appropriately.

The same sort of ambiguity in the data pattern appears in Figure 12-13. Here the three baselines end as the boy rehearses the verbal self-instructions across three different settings. At the end of the first baseline, he rehearses in connection to school. At the end of the second, he rehearses in connection to the cottage. At the end of the third, he rehearses in connection to recreational activities. As in Figure 12-12, we do not know whether the simultaneous improvement in all three settings at the end of the first baseline resulted from an extraneous event or from generalization of effects.

How do we decide which rival explanation—history or generalization of effects—is the more plausible? We may be unable to do so. But, if it is feasible, we might try to replicate the experiment with other clients. If we continue to get results like those in Figures 12-12 and 12-13, then the generalization of effects hypothesis becomes more plausible, because it is not reasonable to suppose that some extraneous event would cause improvement in the target problem only at the point where the first baseline ends when clients were treated at different times.

With some interventions, it is difficult to conceive how they could possibly be applied to different behaviors or settings at different times. Suppose, for example, that the intervention involves family systems therapy in a case in which a child's poor functioning in various areas is theoretically thought to stem from problems in the parents' relationship with each other. If the practitioner seeks to resolve the target problem in the child by focusing intervention on the parental relationship, then it may not be realistic to try applying the intervention to different behaviors or settings regarding the child. Moreover, to do so might be deemed clinically inappropriate because it would continue to focus the intervention on the child.

Multiple-Component Designs

Several designs can be used to analyze the impact of changes in the intervention. These designs are appropriate when we decide to modify an intervention that does not appear to be helping the client or when we seek to determine which parts of an intervention package really account for the change in the target problem. One such design is called the *changing intensity design*. It includes several phases of the same intervention, but in each phase either the amount of intervention or the level of performance expected of the client is increased. The symbol for this design is $AB^1B^2B^3$. As a hypothetical illustration of this design, suppose a chronically mentally disabled individual is unable to maintain steady employment. The intervention might be social skills training to prepare him for job interviews and appropriate on-the-job behavior. If during B^1 (the first intervention phase) an inadequate degree of improvement is observed, then the amount of time the client spends in social skills training might be increased. Implementing this change marks the beginning of the second intervention phase (B^2). Suppose B^2 results in increased improvement, but at a level that still is not acceptable. A third intervention phase, B^3, might be initiated and might involve further increasing the amount of time the client spends in social skills training.

Consider a different approach with this case: When the social skills training yields no improvement in the first intervention phase, it is replaced by a different intervention. Instead of increasing the amount of time the client spends in social skills training, a different behavioral reinforcement intervention is introduced—one that offers a reward for each real job interview the client undergoes or each week he keeps his job. So far, we would have an ABC design, in which B was the social skills training phase and C was the reinforcement phase. Suppose there still is no improvement, so a case advocacy phase is initiated to investigate the possibility that we may need to convince prospective employers to consider hiring or be more tolerant of individuals whose illnesses impede their job-seeking skills or on-the-job behavior. The case advocacy phase, then, would add a fourth component to the design, and we would have an ABCD design.

The preceding two designs are flexible; they allow practitioners to change intervention plans as warranted by the data patterns that are observed in each successive phase. But they must be used cautiously because of limitations associated with *carryover effects, order effects,* and *history.*

In the ABCD illustration, suppose that a sustained pattern of improvement was obtained only during the D phase (case advocacy) as illustrated in Figure 12-14. It would be risky to conclude that for future clients like this one all we need to do is provide the case advocacy and not the other two interventions. It is plausible that had we changed the D phase to the B phase for this client, we may not have had the same positive results. Perhaps the client's social skills improved during the original B phase but those skills were insufficient to help him stay employed because employers were either unwilling to risk hiring someone with a history of mental illness or unwilling to tolerate any deviance whatsoever from any employee. Conceivably, only with the addition of the case advocacy during the D phase did the improvement in social skills matter. Perhaps the case advocacy would have had no impact had it not been preceded by helping the client attain a level of social functioning that prospective employers could be convinced to tolerate. In other words, the

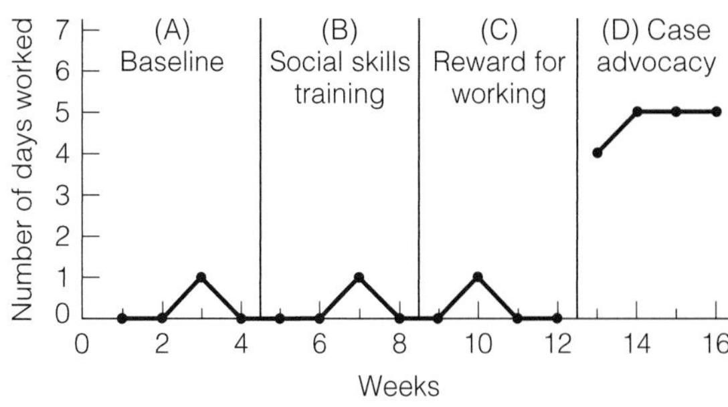

Figure 12-14 Graph of Hypothetical Outcome of Multiple-Component (ABCD) Design, with Unclear Results

case advocacy might not have worked without the order effects (that is, in coming after the social skills training, not before it) and the carryover effects of the social skills training on the case advocacy efforts.

History is also a limitation: We must recognize that as we continue to substitute new interventions for those whose data patterns do not adequately differ from baseline, we increase the odds that one of those substitutions eventually will coincide with an extraneous improvement in the client's environment.

One way to sort out the above possibilities would be to replicate the interventions with future clients, introducing them in a different sequence while measuring outcome in the same way. Ultimately, we might find that the intervention that was originally in the D phase produced the desired results only when it was introduced after the interventions in the original B or C phase.

Another option would be to start out with a more complex **multiple-component design** that attempts, in advance, to control for the above limitations. There are a variety of such designs. Because their complexity limits their applicability to real social work practice settings, they will be mentioned only briefly here. One is the "construction design," A-B-A-C-A-BC-( ), in which the A phases represent baselines and the BC phase combines the B and C interventions. The phase indicated by the parentheses refers to the intervention or combination of interventions that appears to be most effective and is ultimately chosen. Another is the "strip design," A-BC-A-B-A-C-( ), which is like the construction design but in which the combined intervention (BC) is introduced first. Other possibilities include the "alternating intervention design," A-Randomized Alternation of B & C-(B or C), and the "interaction design," A-B-A-B-BC-B-BC. We recommend the following texts that deal exclusively with single-case designs to readers who wish to pursue these complex designs in depth: Barlow and Hersen (1984), Bloom, Fischer, and Orme (2006), and Jayaratne and Levy (1979).

DATA ANALYSIS

In analyzing the results of single-case experiments, we ask the following three questions:

1. Is there a *visual* pattern in the graph(s) that depicts a series of coincidences in which the frequency, level, or trend of the target problem changes only after the intervention is introduced or withdrawn?

2. What is the *statistical* probability that the data observed during the intervention phase(s) are merely part of the normal, chance fluctuations in the target problem, fluctuations that we could have expected to occur had the baseline been extended and intervention not introduced?

3. If change in the target problem is associated with the tested intervention, is the amount of change important from a *substantive,* or *clinical,* standpoint?

These three questions refer to the visual, statistical, and substantive significance of the findings.

When we analyzed the meanings of each graph in Figures 12-1 through 12-14, we dealt with *visual significance.* Visual significance is ascertained not through the use of fancy statistics but merely by "eyeballing" the data pattern, as the term *visual* implies. To the extent that shifts in the target problem either do not occur when intervention is introduced or occur just as often at other times, there is less visual significance; that is, in those instances there is less visual evidence for supposing that the intervention is affecting the target problem. To the extent that shifts in the frequency, level, or trend of the target problem tend to coincide only with shifts in the independent variable as it moves from one phase to another, there is more visual significance and thus more logical support for supposing that the intervention is affecting the target problem.

Sometimes our visual analysis of the data will obviate the need for statistical analysis, particularly when the degree of visual significance (or lack thereof) is dramatic. Indeed, some single-case methodologists cite evidence that suggests that when experienced researchers judge whether an outcome is visually significant, their conclusions are usually supported by subsequent statistical analyses (Jayaratne, Tripodi, and Talsma, 1988). Practitioners who tend to be immobilized by their anxiety about statistics, therefore, can implement single-case designs in the hope that their visual analysis of the data will be sufficient.

Sometimes, however, the changes in the level or trend of the target problem from one phase to the next are subtle or we are not sure whether our visual analysis of the data is being influenced by our desire to see a favorable outcome. At these times, it is helpful to augment our visual analysis with a statistical one.

Statistical and substantive significance mean the same thing in single-case designs as they do in other sorts of research, and they will be discussed in depth, in connection to group designs, in Chapters 21 and 22. If you'd like to learn when and how to calculate alternative procedures for estimating statistical significance in single-case design research, we recommend the chapter on that topic in Rubin, *Statistics for Evidence-Based Practice and Evaluation* (2007).

Interpreting Ambiguous Results

Most of this chapter has used illustrations involving clear-cut hypothetical data patterns to simplify conveying the logic of single-case research regarding the differentiation of results that are visually significant from results that are not visually significant. Unfortunately, however, single-case studies in the real world often obtain ambiguous results that are more difficult to interpret. Consider, for example, Figure 12-15, which shows the results from a study by Rubin (1991).

The data in Figure 12-15 were collected from a battered woman who was participating in an intervention geared to helping battered women live independently

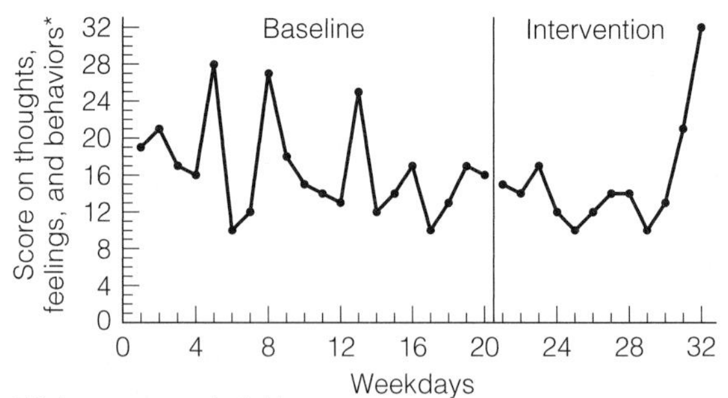

SOURCE: Allen Rubin, "The Effectiveness of Outreach Counseling and Support Groups for Battered Women: A Preliminary Evaluation," Research on *Social Work Practice*, 1(4), October 1991, p. 349. Reprinted by permission of Sage Publications, Inc.

Figure 12-15 Graph of Outcome of Group Treatment of a Battered Woman

from their batterers. The data refer to thoughts, feelings, and behaviors associated with feeling better about oneself and doing things to become more independent. An increase in scores during the intervention phase, therefore, would indicate a desirable outcome.

As you can see, the data in the graph reveal a somewhat unstable baseline, followed by 11 days of intervention without any improvement in scores, and then two days of dramatic improvement at the end of the study. (This case was part of a larger study involving more clients, and feasibility constraints required that the data collection for this woman end after her 32nd data point.)

How would you interpret this graph? Do you think it reflects visual significance? One can be tempted to perceive visual significance in this graph, particularly if one is affiliated with the agency and wants the intervention to succeed. One might focus on the dramatic improvement toward the end of the intervention phase and argue that, although it took awhile before the intervention started having an effect, it eventually worked. One might further argue that this woman may have been denying her situation and that it therefore stands to reason that the intervention effects would not occur immediately at the onset of treatment. This argument is not unreasonable. Indeed, those who take a psychosocial approach to practice might not expect most clients to begin showing improvement on outcome indicators until intervention has been ongoing for quite a long time because of such factors as resistance, denial, and so on.

We believe, however, that a more compelling argument can be made against perceiving visual significance in this graph, based on two major points. First, the increase in the scores at the end of the intervention period could be nothing more than a random, or perhaps cyclical, temporary blip—just as there were a few upward blips during the unstable baseline. We do not know how short-lived the improvement will be. Second, even if the improvement is permanent, the fact that it did not occur sooner during intervention increases the plausibility that it could be the result of history.

When we argue that this graph is not visually significant, we do not mean to imply that it shows that the intervention could not have caused the improvement. We merely mean that this graph does not provide enough evidence to deem alternative explanations (such as history) much less plausible than the conclusion that the intervention did cause the improvement. We believe it is possible that it simply took awhile before the effects of the intervention began to be reflected in the outcome scores. However, saying that this is possible is a far cry from saying that the graph reflects in a visually significant way that this indeed is the most plausible explanation. In other words, saying that a graph is not visually significant does not mean that its interpretation is unambiguously negative. In this case, we believe the interpretation is ambiguous, and that the graph lacks visual significance in light of that ambiguity.

The foregoing example illustrates the ambiguity that can occur when intervention goes on for quite a while before any noticeable improvement occurs in the target problem. Sometimes, however, improvement in the target problem coincides nicely with the onset of the intervention, but then reverses sharply during the last data point or two. If the intervention and monitoring cannot be continued, then it may be difficult to determine whether the intervention was effective.

Perhaps the undesirable data points at the end of the intervention period indicate that the temporary improvement was merely the result of a honeymoon period or extraneous factors that coincided with the onset of the intervention. On the other hand, perhaps the undesirable data points at the end of the intervention period are themselves merely a result of extraneous forces causing a temporary blip in the context of meaningful, sustainable intervention effects. Ambiguous results can occur in many other ways as well, particularly when there is instability in the data during baseline, the intervention phase, or both.

Aggregating the Results of Single-Case Research Studies

At several points in this chapter, we noted that the interpretation of ambiguous data patterns in single-case research can be enhanced through the replication process. If, for example, improvement occurs late in the intervention phase of one study, then we cannot rule out history as a plausible explanation. But if improvement occurs roughly at the same late point consistently across studies, then it seems more plausible to argue that the intervention takes awhile before showing desired effects than to argue that extraneous events are causing the improvement across different clients who begin intervention at different times. The same logic holds when we don't know whether the data pattern reflects irreversible intervention effects in an ABAB study or the generalization of effects in a multiple-baseline study.

Above and beyond facilitating the interpretation of ambiguous data, replication can serve two additional important purposes in single-case research. One purpose is to reduce doubt about the external validity of our findings. The more we can replicate a particular type of outcome across different clients, settings, and practitioners, the more confidence we develop (inductively) in our ability to generalize that outcome. The other purpose is to evaluate an entire service program. If, for example, an agency conducts a single-case evaluation on a reasonably representative sample of its clients (such as every fifth client entering treatment during a particular time period), then it can assess its overall agency effectiveness by aggregating the results of each individual evaluation.

When we want to aggregate the results of various individual studies, either to deal with ambiguous findings or to generalize about the effectiveness of an intervention or an agency, we need a mechanism for making sense out of the variations in outcome from study to study. One such mechanism is to report the proportion of studies that had each type of outcome in which we are interested. For example, we would want to know the proportion of outcomes that were and were not visually significant, and we might want to know the proportion of studies with the same type of ambiguous data pattern. Thus, we might be able to say that an effective intervention was delivered in, say, 60 percent of our agency's cases. Or we might be able to say that in, say, 70 percent of our replications, a data pattern was found that suggests delayed intervention effects.

One problem here is the absence of systematic guidelines as to what specific percentages represent cutoff points regarding alternative interpretations. Should an agency, for example, be happy with a 50 percent effectiveness rate? A lower rate? Or is a higher effectiveness rate needed before it can claim to be effective in an overall, aggregated sense as a program? If a practitioner replicates an AB study across 10 clients and obtains visually significant results three times, should he or she conclude that the intervention was effective with three cases, or should the practitioner wonder whether some other factor (such as history) accounts for the data pattern in those three cases, because the visual significance was not replicated in the remaining seven cases? As the field of single-case research matures, perhaps such guidelines will be developed. For now, however, there may be some value in merely describing the proportion of various outcomes being obtained in connection to a particular intervention, practitioner, or agency. As those outcomes accumulate, one can inductively look for patterns that might suggest hypotheses as to the conditions under which a particular practitioner, intervention, or agency is successful. This accumulation might also establish effectiveness rate norms to which the results of future aggregated evaluations can be compared.

The process of aggregating the results of single-case studies illustrates how this type of research has the potential to go well beyond idiosyncratically evaluating intervention with a "single subject." Although we have identified a variety of feasibility problems in carrying out single-case research, and we certainly do not see it as a panacea that everyone can use when other designs are not feasible, we hope that you will consider applying what you have learned in this chapter throughout your career as a professional social worker.

The Role of Qualitative Research Methods in Single-Case Evaluation

In Chapter 11 we saw that some techniques commonly used in qualitative studies can make valuable contributions when incorporated with quantitative methods in experimental and quasi-experimental designs. The same is true of single-case evaluation designs, which are generally considered quantitative. One way these techniques can be helpful is in interpreting ambiguous quantitative results. When instability occurs at a particular point in the data pattern, for instance, we can employ open-ended interviews with the client and significant others to try to learn whether important extraneous events in the client's social environment coincided with the instability. If they did, we might be more inclined to attribute certain changes in the graphed data to extraneous forces, rather than consider them reflections of the effectiveness or ineffectiveness of the intervention. If interviewing fails to identify any extraneous forces that may explain the changes observed in the graph, the notion that those changes represent intervention effects becomes more plausible.

Another important role for interviewing in single-case evaluation is in assessment. Open-ended interviews with the client and with significant others can improve our understanding of the target problem, how to measure it, and how best to intervene. Interviews with significant others can be used to corroborate the improvement (or lack thereof) self-reported or self-monitored by the client. Interviews can also assess what parts of the intervention clients perceive to be most helpful and why. In Chapter 17, we will

QUALITATIVE TECHNIQUES FOR SINGLE-CASE EVALUATION

As we did for group designs in the previous chapter, in this box we will list some prominent qualitative techniques and the important functions they can serve in single-case design evaluation studies. You can read more about these techniques in Chapters 17 and 18.

Qualitative Technique	Functions in Single-Case Evaluation
Informal conversational interviews with clients or significant others	• Identify extraneous events or forces connected with changes in the graphed data • Assess target problem and develop measurement and intervention plan • Assess what parts of the intervention client perceives to be most helpful and why • Corroborate the improvement (or lack thereof) self-reported or self-monitored by the client or by the significant other
Videotaping or audiotaping practitioner–client sessions	• Assess the fidelity of the intervention (Is it being implemented in a skillful manner, as intended?)
Event logs completed by client or significant others	• Assess where and when target problems occur and the circumstances that mediate them • Identify extraneous events occurring during baseline or intervention phases that might be helpful in interpreting whether changes that occur in the quantitative data are attributable to the intervention

examine additional techniques that are commonly used in qualitative studies and useful in single-case evaluation. Event logs completed by clients or their significant others can also be quite helpful in assessing where and when target problems occur and the circumstances that mediate them. Event logs can also help identify extraneous events occurring during baseline or intervention phases that might be helpful in interpreting whether changes that occur in the quantitative data are attributable to the intervention. The utility of qualitative techniques as part of single-case designs is summarized in the box titled "Qualitative Techniques for Single-Case Evaluation."

Main Points

• Any target problem on which a practitioner would choose to focus can be defined in operational terms and then measured. If it could not be, then the practitioner would have had no basis for observing that it was an important problem in the first place.

• Taking many repeated measures and identifying stable trends in the data enhances the internal validity of single-case designs by facilitating control for extraneous factors that affect the target problem.

• Baselines are control phases of repeated measures taken before an intervention is introduced. Baselines ideally should be extended until a stable trend in the data is evident.

• Single-case designs can be used by practitioners to monitor client progress or their own effectiveness more scientifically and systematically.

• Single-case designs have special measurement problems. Triangulating measures is therefore recommended. This means simultaneously using more than one imperfect measurement option.

• Special caution must be exercised in single-case designs with regard to the measurement problems of reactivity, obtrusiveness, and social desirability bias.

• Including more than one baseline and intervention phase in a single-case experiment strengthens the control of history through the principle of unlikely successive coincidences. This is done in ABAB designs and multiple-baseline designs.

• AB designs have the weakest control for history, but they are the most feasible designs, can provide useful information, and are an excellent way to implement the final stage of the evidence-based practice process.

• When we use designs with more phases than the AB design, we must exercise caution regarding possible carryover effects, order effects, generalization of effects, and the irreversibility of effects.

• The prime weakness of single-case designs is their limited external validity. With a sample of one, we are dealing with idiosyncratic conditions that cannot be generalized to other clients, practitioners, or settings. But this problem can be alleviated through replication.

• Single-case design data should always be analyzed for their visual and practical significance.

• The visual as well as statistical results of single-case research can be ambiguous; the replication process can help resolve this ambiguity.

• The results of various single-case studies can be aggregated by calculating the proportion of studies with specific types of outcomes.

Review Questions and Exercises

1. Select some aspect of your own behavior that you would like to improve (for example, smoke less, eat less, exercise more, study more, and so on) and develop a plan to improve it. Conduct a single-case experiment and analyze the data to see if your plan is effective. Try to be aware of the degree to which you experience the measurement problems of reactivity and bias.

2. Think of a particular case or intervention that has piqued your curiosity about practice effectiveness. Design a single-case experiment that is relevant to that case or intervention. Try to design it in a way that would be feasible to implement.

Internet Exercises

1. Use InfoTrac College Edition to find a study that used a single-case evaluation AB design. Critique the study's design—either positively or negatively—and discuss whether you agree with the way its data were interpreted.

2. Use InfoTrac College Edition to find a study that used a single-case evaluation ABAB design or a multiple-baseline design. Critique the study's design—either positively or negatively—and discuss whether you agree with the way its data were interpreted.

Additional Readings

Barlow, David H., and Michael Hersen. 1984. *Single-Case Experimental Designs: Strategies for Studying Behavioral Change*. New York: Pergamon Press. This is an excellent and thorough text that is written from a more technical perspective than the Bloom text listed above. It is one of the most widely cited texts on single-case designs.

Bloom, Martin, Joel Fischer, and John G. Orme. 2006. *Evaluating Practice: Guidelines for the Accountable Professional*, 5th ed. Boston: Allyn & Bacon. This excellent, comprehensive text is an invaluable reference guide for social workers who plan to implement single-case designs as a regular part of their practice. All important aspects of single-case designs and ways to combine the roles of practitioner and researcher are covered in depth, and students often report that they learn a great deal about practice per se in this unique book.

Jayaratne, Srinika, and Rona L. Levy. 1979. *Empirical Clinical Practice*. New York: Columbia University Press. Here is a user-friendly introduction to scientifically based practice. It covers single-case designs from the perspective of clinical practice and provides a step-by-step outline for incorporating them in practice. Reprints and critiques of published single-case research studies help readers integrate the text.

Rubin, Allen. 2007. *Statistics for Evidence-Based Practice and Evaluation*. Belmont, CA: Thomson Brooks/Cole. Chapter 18 of this practitioner-friendly text discusses when and how to use various procedures for calculating the statistical significance and effect size of single-case design findings. One of the coauthors of the text you are reading recommends this book highly. Can you guess which one?

CHAPTER **13**

Program Evaluation

What You'll Learn in This Chapter

Whereas the previous three chapters emphasized the logic of research designs in evaluating the effectiveness of interventions, this chapter focuses on the broader picture of evaluating entire programs. It will examine the use of program evaluation not only to assess program effects, but also for the purposes of program planning and monitoring processes in program implementation. In addition, you'll see the practical and political obstacles that program evaluators encounter and how evaluators try to deal with them.

INTRODUCTION

The previous three chapters focused on the logic of methods of different experimental and quasi-experimental designs for evaluating the effectiveness of interventions at various levels of practice. When it comes to evaluating entire programs, however, other research questions arise in addition to whether the program is effective. Experiments and quasi-experiments, therefore, are not the only designs used in program evaluation. Many other types of quantitative and qualitative designs and methods can be used. *Program evaluation* refers to the purpose of research rather than to any specific research methods. Its purpose is to assess and improve the conceptualization, design, planning, administration, implementation, effectiveness, efficiency, and utility of social interventions and human service programs (Rossi and Freeman, 1993).

At the start of this book, we distinguished social work research from basic social scientific research by its purpose, citing the former's focus on practical knowledge that social workers need so they can solve the problems they confront in their practice and that agencies need to guide their efforts to alleviate human suffering and promote social welfare. In light of that focus, program evaluation—when applied to social welfare settings and issues—is conceptually very similar to social work research, and many of the research studies conducted by social workers have a program evaluation purpose. Because program evaluation has more to do with the purposes of research than with specific research methods, this chapter will focus more on the implications of those purposes for carrying out research than on particular methodologies or designs.

PURPOSES OF PROGRAM EVALUATION

A program evaluation might have one or more of the following three broad purposes: (1) to assess the ultimate *success* of programs, (2) to assess problems in how programs are being *implemented*, or (3) to obtain information needed in program *planning* and *development*. Program evaluations can be further classified as *summative* or *formative*. **Summative evaluations** are concerned with the first of the three purposes: involving the ultimate success of a program and decisions about whether it should be continued or chosen in the first place from among alternative options. The results of a summative evaluation convey a sense of finality. Depending on whether the results imply that the program succeeded, the program may or may not survive. **Formative evaluations,** on the other hand, are not concerned with testing the success of a program. They focus instead on obtaining information that is helpful in planning the program and in improving its implementation and performance.

Summative evaluations will generally be quantitative in approach. Formative evaluations may use quantitative methods, qualitative methods, or both. As you will see, these types or purposes of program evaluation are not mutually exclusive. Rather, they complement one another, and some comprehensive evaluations include summative and process components that involve a host of different research methods. Before we examine in depth the various types of program evaluation, let's begin with a historical overview.

HISTORICAL OVERVIEW

Although the growth of program evaluation is a fairly recent phenomenon, planned social evaluation is really quite old. Some authors have traced it back to 2200 B.C. in China and connected it with personnel selection (Shadish, Cook, and Leviton, 1991). Whenever people have instituted a social reform for a specific purpose, they have paid attention to its actual consequences, even if they have not always done so in a conscious, deliberate, or systematic fashion or called what they were doing program evaluation.

In the mid-19th century, for example, the reform movement for more humane care of the mentally ill, led by Dorothea Dix, succeeded in getting states to build more public mental hospitals. Some superintendents of state mental hospitals contributed to such hospitals' growth by citing data that, they contended, indicated that state hospitals were succeeding in curing mental illness (Grob, 1973). Those superintendents were discharging 90 percent or more of their patients and claiming that this meant that they were achieving 90 percent to 100 percent cure rates! At that time, notions of rehospitalization, relapse, and chronicity were not in vogue, and the superintendents therefore temporarily got away with using discharge from the state hospital as an operational definition of recovery from mental illness, although they didn't use the term *operational definition*. (Here we begin to see the importance of the political context of program evaluation, a theme we'll examine in depth later in this chapter.)

More systematic approaches to program evaluation can be traced back to the beginning of the 20th century. Early efforts evaluated schools that used different teaching approaches, comparing educational outcomes by examining student scores on standardized tests. Several decades later, experimental program evaluation studies examined the effects of worker morale on industrial productivity and the impact of public health education programs on hygienic practices. In the 1940s, after New Deal social welfare programs were implemented, studies examined the effects of work relief versus direct relief, the effects of public housing, and the impact of treatment programs on juvenile delinquency. Program evaluation received additional impetus during World War II, with studies on soldier morale and the impact of personnel and propaganda policies on morale.

After the war, large public expenditures were committed to programs that attempted to improve housing, public health, attitudes toward minorities, and international problems in health, family planning, and community development. As expenditures grew, so did interest in data on the results of these programs.

Program evaluation became widespread by the late 1950s as efforts increased to alleviate or prevent social problems such as juvenile delinquency and to test innovations in psychotherapy and new psychopharmacological discoveries. By the late 1960s textbooks, professional journals, national conferences, and a professional association on evaluation research emerged. This explosion of interest in program evaluation continued during the 1970s, as the public increasingly demanded evidence for a return on its investment in various programs to combat poverty, child abuse, substance abuse, crime and delinquency, mental illness, and so on. But by the late 1970s, after public funding for these programs waned, declines began in the funding of studies to evaluate them. This trend toward reduced funding of program evaluation accelerated during the 1980s, as federal evaluation offices were hit hard by the budget cuts of the Reagan administration (Shadish, Cook, and Leviton, 1991).

The "age of accountability" continued through the 1980s and 1990s, even though the government provided less funding for program evaluation than it did before the 1980s. Liberals and conservatives alike demanded that programs be more accountable to the public and show whether they were really delivering what they promised to deliver. In fact, the need to evaluate may be greater when program funding is scarce than when it is abundant, because the scarcity of funds may intensify concerns that meager funding not be wasted on ineffectual programs. In this connection, it is a mistake to assume that only fiscal conservatives—those who are reluctant to spend money on social programs—are the ones who have been expressing skepticism about what "bang the public is getting for its buck." Individuals of all political persuasions have this interest, including human service professionals who fiercely support increased social welfare spending but who are dedicated to finding better ways to help people and who do not want to see scarce welfare resources squandered on programs that don't really help their intended target populations. In fact, a major group that has historically been a force in favor of greater accountability consists of consumer rights advocates who are concerned about whether clients—the consumers of our services—are being served properly.

As a result of these forces, and despite governmental funding cuts, by the 1990s program evaluation had become ubiquitous in the planning and administration of social welfare policies and programs. In fact, instead of having a program evaluator position, an agency might assign responsibility for program evaluation activities to personnel called *planners* or *program analysts* (Posavac and Carey, 1985). Funding sources still required both a program evaluation component as a prerequisite for approving grant applications and supportive evaluative data as a basis for renewing funding. But this requirement became a mixed blessing. On the one hand, the requirement that programs evaluate their efforts induced agency personnel to support more research that could help us improve policies and programs and find better ways to help people. On the other hand, this requirement came to mean that agency personnel and others have had vested interests in the findings of that research.

THE IMPACT OF MANAGED CARE

The emphasis on program evaluation in health and human service agencies continues to grow because of the impact of "managed care." The term **managed care** has been defined in various ways and refers to a variety of arrangements that try to control the costs of health and human services. These arrangements vary in the range of their components and proposed benefits, but the basic idea of managed care is to have a large organization contract with care providers who agree to provide services at reduced costs. Care providers are willing to reduce the costs because the organizations pay for the cost of services for a great number of people. The large organization paying for the care typically is the service recipient's employer or health insurance company. Providers are willing to meet the reduced cost demands of the large organizations so they will be eligible to have the cost of their services covered and thus get more referrals of clients covered under managed care plans. Some common types of managed care organizations are health maintenance organizations (HMOs), preferred provider organizations (PPOs), and employee assistance programs (EAPs). Public social service agencies also may employ managed care techniques to reduce the costs and inefficiencies of service provision.

In simple terms, here's how managed care works. Suppose Jane Doe is employed by a large state agency or a large corporation that provides EAP coverage for employees who have mental health or substance abuse problems. Suppose Jane has developed a drinking problem that is impeding her work and she is advised to get treatment for it in order to keep her job. Her employer will give her a list of substance abuse service providers covered by its EAP program—providers who have agreed to the EAP's service cost specifications. If Jane uses services from one of those approved providers, then most or all of the service costs will be covered by the EAP. If she goes to a nonapproved provider for the services, however, the EAP will cover either a lower proportion of or perhaps none of the costs. Thus, in all likelihood, Jane will choose a provider from the approved list. As more and more people become covered by a managed care plan of some sort, providers who don't agree to the reduced cost demands of managed care organizations greatly risk having too few referrals to sustain their practices.

Another way in which managed care companies attempt to reduce costs is by reviewing requests for services by those they cover and approving—that is, agreeing to pay for—only those services that they deem to be necessary and effective. This refers to both the type of service as well as the amount of service. This puts pressure on service providers to come up with brief treatment plans as well as evidence as to how many sessions are needed to achieve what effects. Suppose two alcohol abuse programs have two markedly different approaches to treating alcohol abuse. Suppose one program does not bother to evaluate the outcomes of treatment for its clients whereas the other measures outcome from each client and shows that 90 percent of its clients never again evidence alcohol-related problems while at work after 10 treatment sessions. The latter program is more likely to be approved by Jane Doe's EAP.

Managed care is controversial. For-profit managed care organizations have been criticized for caring more about their own shareholders' profits than about whether clients are really getting all the care they need. Having insurance companies decide how much care is needed may result in horror stories about clients who commit suicide or suffer in other ways because managed care companies denied requests for services that they deemed unnecessary but which really were necessary. Practitioners complain about pressures to provide less service than is really needed or about increased paperwork that leaves less time for client care. This controversy is outside the scope of our research methods text, but what is pertinent here is the effect that managed care is having on the way service providers use research methods to evaluate their services. This impact should also be pertinent to you, the reader of this text, because in your social work practice you are likely to experience pressures to use these methods to measure the outcomes of the services you provide.

As we already mentioned, one major impact of managed care is an increased emphasis on program evaluation, particularly regarding measuring what outcomes are achieved by specific amounts and types of services. But, as we've discussed in earlier chapters, there are many ways to attempt to measure the outcomes of social work services. For example, choices must be made among measurement approaches that may or may not be valid, and which may vary in regard to objectivity and bias. Pressures to measure outcomes immediately with whatever instruments one has available may conflict with the desire to use the best instruments or with the need to have uniform instruments across practitioners or agencies (Abramovitz et al., 1997). Choices must also be made as to what design to use, ranging from pre-experimental designs that lack internal validity to randomized experiments that have high amounts of internal validity.

Are any of these options more or less likely to be chosen by service providers in response to managed care pressures? No definitive study has yet been done to answer this question. But the emerging literature on managed care and our discussions with service providers seem to suggest that while there is increasing pressure on service providers to operationally specify treatment goals in quantifiable terms for each client and then measure whether those goals have been achieved, little or no pressure is being exerted by managed care companies to ensure that an internally valid design is being used that would permit scientifically logical causal inferences as to whether any improvements observed are really the result of treatment rather than the product of history, maturation, or other threats to internal validity (Mullen and Magnabosco, 1997).

In addition, concern has been expressed about flaws in the databases being created in response to managed care pressures. Depicting many of them as fraudulent, Hudson (1997) noted that practitioners often enter client diagnoses into the databases according to what diagnoses managed care companies will cover, rather than the diagnosis that best fits the client's problem. The consequence of this practice, Hudson argued, is that statistical analyses of these databases will yield misleading findings about the nature, incidence, and correlates of various diagnoses.

Managed care organizations vary in the documentation they require. One common expectation is that clients complete forms that assess their degree of satisfaction with the care they've received. For example, they may be asked to rate how difficult it was to get an appointment or to get to the agency, how comfortable the agency staff made them feel, and how much they think the services helped them (Todd, 1998). Assessing customer satisfaction may be a desirable thing for any organization to do. Indeed, consumers' responses may imply useful guidelines for improving service delivery. However, consumer satisfaction surveys are a far cry from the kinds of internally valid experiments and quasi-experiments that we discussed in Chapter 11. They may be highly vulnerable to social desirability biases, and even if clients really feel satisfied, that does not necessarily mean that services caused significant improvements in target problems. Perhaps clients are satisfied merely because service providers were very nice to them, regardless of improvements in target problems.

Another way to meet managed care expectations might be to have direct-service providers specify, probably in collaboration with clients, operational treatment goals for each client and then ask clients whether those goals were met. Thus, Jane Doe's goal might be to abstain from consuming any alcoholic beverages during work hours or over lunch, and if she reports success in achieving this goal, the treatment is considered effective for her. Investigating the validity of her report (here we again encounter the possibility of social desirability bias), or using single-case design experimental procedures to rule out the plausibility of alternative explanations for the change in her behavior, is typically not a requirement. Likewise, there is no uniform standard for longer-term follow-up. How long must she continue her abstinence for the treatment to be deemed successful?

Managed care companies are increasingly requiring the completion of standardized outcome instruments that have been shown to be reliable and valid. In addition, they may require that the same instruments be completed in different settings so that comparisons can be made (Mullen and Magnabosco, 1997). Consequently, a vast range of outcomes measurement instruments is available and growing. In one chapter in a book by Cynthia Franklin and Paula Nurius, *Constructivism in Practice: Methods and Challenges* (1998), Tracy Todd lists companies that can help in the identification of outcome measures. Todd also lists some reference guides for finding outcome measurement tools. Another useful reference for identifying outcome measures that can be used to meet managed care expectations in social work is *Outcomes Measurement in the Human Services: Cross-Cutting Issues and Methods,* edited by Edward Mullen and Jennifer Magnabosco (1997).

But even when standardized instruments are used, outcome still tends to be measured in the context of simple pretest–posttest designs without comparison or control groups. In the future, perhaps stronger designs will be required. Single-case evaluation designs have been proposed by Corcoran and Gingerich (1994) as one way to strengthen the assessment of client outcomes that fits well both with the expectations of managed care companies as well as the resource and time constraints of direct-service practitioners. Just how much these designs will be used remains to be seen. And if they are used extensively, it also remains to be seen how well they will be used. For example, will practitioners make sufficient efforts to obtain unbiased (and perhaps triangulated) outcome measures? Will they utilize replication and a sufficient number of measurement points to warrant the causal inferences they will be predisposed to make about their effectiveness? Time will tell. For now, however, it seems reasonable to predict that regardless of what designs direct-service providers use to document their effectiveness to managed care companies, those providers will have intense vested interests in reporting results that make their services look effective. Because funding for their services will hang in the balance, their willingness or ability to conduct scientifically valid assessments of their effectiveness may be limited. With that in mind, let's move now to a discussion of the politics of program evaluation.

THE POLITICS OF PROGRAM EVALUATION

Because the findings of evaluation research can provide ammunition to a program's supporters or opponents, intense political pressure is introduced into the program evaluation process. Vested interests can impede the atmosphere for free, scientific inquiry. Instead of pursuing truth as scientifically as possible to improve human well-being, program evaluation efforts may be implemented in ways that fit perceived program maintenance needs. Sometimes, this means that there will be intense pressure to design the research or interpret its findings in ways that are likely to make the program look good. Other times, it may simply mean that the program evaluation is conducted in the cheapest, most convenient way possible, guided by the belief that funding sources don't pay much attention to the quality of the research and just want to be able to say that the programs they fund have been evaluated. Consequently, it is naive to suppose that when administrators hire someone to be responsible for program evaluation activities or to conduct a specific evaluation, they will pick the person most qualified from a scientific, research methodology standpoint.

Political considerations—that the evaluation will be done to favor vested interests—may be a much higher priority. Indeed, it probably is not overly cynical to suppose that commitment to conducting the most scientific study possible sometimes will threaten administrators and be perceived as a problem. They are unlikely to admit as much; rather, they may call individuals with a devotion to methodological rigor "too ivory towerish and out of touch with the real world." (And sometimes they are correct—if zeal for methodological rigor blinds researchers and makes them insensitive to realistic feasibility constraints that make some methodological compromises appropriate and unavoidable.)

Consequently, it's not unusual to see agencies fill program evaluation positions with people who lack any special proficiency in or dedication to research design, but who instead are good computer jocks—high-tech bureaucrats who can grind out evaluative data that will put the program in a favorable light and who will not make waves about academic issues such as the evaluation's internal or external validity.

When you're in a position in your career to participate in, conduct, or use program evaluations, you should not be naive about the potential influence of vested interests on the integrity or quality of evaluations. We will spend much of this chapter discussing that influence, because it is, in large part, what distinguishes program evaluation from other forms of social research. Nevertheless, it would be misleading to imply that all program evaluation is corrupt. Agency administrators and others who have vested interests often have sufficient integrity and professional concern for learning the best ways to help clients that they are able to put their vested interests aside and act in a manner that fosters the most objective, scientific evaluation possible. Although it may be naive to assume that all (or even most) evaluations will be immune from the political pressures applied by those who have vested interests, it would be too cynical to assume that all evaluations are politically biased.

After you finish this chapter, we hope that your view of the politics of program evaluation is a savvy one—that you will be vigilant about the potential for the corrupting influence of vested interests and yet aware that despite this potential many objective and useful program evaluation studies have been done in the past and are likely to be done in the future.

In-House versus External Evaluators

When program evaluators work for the agency being evaluated, they are called **in-house evaluators.** Program evaluators who work for external agencies such as government or regulating agencies and private research consultation firms (which often bid for government grants to evaluate programs that receive public funds) are **external evaluators.** This group also includes university faculty members who have secured research grants to evaluate programs or simply wish to conduct applied research as part of their scholarly duties.

In-house evaluators are often thought to have certain advantages over external evaluators. They may have greater access to program information and personnel, more knowledge about program processes that might bear on the design of an evaluation or the meaning of findings, and more sensitivity to the program's research needs and the realistic obstacles to the feasibility of certain research designs or methods. They might also be more likely to be trusted by program personnel and consequently receive better cooperation and feedback from them. But the flip side of the coin is that their commitment to the program, their superiors, or the advancement of their own careers might make them less objective and independent than external evaluators.

But it would be naive to suppose that external evaluators are never subjected to the same kinds of political considerations as are in-house evaluators. External evaluators may have strong incentives to get and stay in the good graces of the personnel of the program being evaluated. If they alienate those personnel, then the quality of their evaluation may be imperiled by the lack of cooperation with the research agenda. In fact, one criterion for choosing the recipient of a program evaluation grant might be the quality of the relationship the evaluator has with the program and that relationship's potential for securing cooperation from program participants.

Also, it's incorrect to assume that external sponsors of the evaluation are always more objective than in-house personnel. Perhaps the sponsors of the evaluation want to stop funding the program and need negative evaluation results to justify the cessation of funding to their own constituents. On the other hand, the sponsors might fret that negative results would make them (the sponsors) look bad and in turn threaten their own fundraising efforts.

One of the authors of this text (Rubin) has worked on several program evaluations that illustrate these points. In one, the U.S. Congress allocated funds for demonstration programs with the stipulation that the funded programs be evaluated by external evaluators. But Congress did not stipulate anything further about the nature of the evaluation designs or how the external evaluators were to be selected. At a meeting in Washington, the federal bureaucrats—who perhaps were primarily concerned with having Congress continue to fund their programs in the future—encouraged recipients of their funding to use simple pre-experimental designs and simplistic measures of program effects that are likely to generate favorable results. For example, they advocated simply assessing whether there was a 10 percent reduction in out-of-home placements of children from the year before the funded project started to the year after its implementation. They dismissed the need for design controls for threats to internal validity or for statistical controls for chance fluctuations. (Chapter 21 will examine this statistical issue in depth.)

In an informal conversation at the meeting, one external program evaluator, whose job security at an agency in the private sector depended on securing contracts from programs to be their external evaluator, confided that he would not propose rigorous designs because he believed that such designs would scare off programs whose contracts he needed. Instead, he would propose uncontrolled, pre-experimental designs that would use outcome measures that were vulnerable to practitioner bias and easy for programs to administer to their practitioners. He seemed to be having great success at the meeting, claiming to have secured "external" evaluation contracts from four program administrators who went to the meeting before selecting an evaluator.

Fiscal concerns not only can affect the evaluation designs employed, but also can lead to attempts to influence the way findings are interpreted, because administrators may believe that the prospects for future funding are enhanced by obtaining favorable evaluation outcomes. This influence can be exerted in various ways, some more subtle than others. Evaluators can be told, for example, that if the program has a successful outcome, then spinoff programs are likely to be funded, and the evaluator can receive the contract to be the "external" evaluator in those spinoff programs. Assuming additional program development further down the road, external evaluators may realize that staying in the good graces of the folks whose programs are being evaluated, and producing desired conclusions for those programs, can have significant long-term benefits for the evaluator's own job security, income, and career.

Another way to influence evaluators is by creating headaches for them when their evaluations are written in a manner that program administrators do not like. External evaluators quickly learn, for example, that if they produce reports that reflect favorably on the evaluated program, then program staff members are extremely unlikely to mobilize efforts to discredit the evaluation's credibility or the evaluator's competence.

They also learn that if their reports are not as positive as program staff members desire, especially if those members are worried about the impact of the evaluation findings on future funding, such mobilization efforts are likely to ensue, and the evaluator's standing with his or her employing agency might be seriously tarnished. A weak study with positive findings is unlikely to be attacked by program staff members who stand to benefit by those findings. However, a strong study with a few relatively minor flaws is likely to be vilified by staff members who see the findings as a threat to their funding prospects.

These things happen not just because there are good guys and bad guys. They happen because many program staff members work hard to secure scarce funding for programs that they believe are helping people. These program staff members may believe that even if we are unsure of the effectiveness of their programs, we should continue investing funds in and working to improve them. Negative findings, they may fear, will simply lead to funding cutbacks with no opportunity to improve on current efforts. Some might argue, from a more cynical perspective, that some staff members are also concerned with enhancing the fiscal well-being of their own agency and the status of their own jobs. There probably is a good deal of truth in both points of view, keeping individual differences in mind.

Another illustration of these points occurred during the mid-1970s, when the Council on Social Work Education (CSWE) was awarded a research grant by the social work training unit of the National Institute of Mental Health (NIMH) to evaluate the community mental health curricula of schools of social work. A prime purpose of the evaluation was to describe the different ways in which graduate schools of social work were implementing their NIMH training grants. At that time, almost every master's degree program in social work was receiving many thousands of dollars annually to prepare students for practice in the field of community mental health, and the research project sought to identify community mental health curriculum innovations fostered by the NIMH grants.

The researchers were able to identify innovative community mental health curricula in some schools. But based on data gathered over a two-year period during multiple site visits to participating schools, they concluded that most schools of social work had initiated no curriculum innovations associated specifically with community mental health. Instead, their NIMH grant funds enabled them to expand their traditional curriculum, and they justified that practice on the grounds that everything that has always been taught in a school of social work is related to community mental health.

We might anticipate that faculty members and administrators in schools of social work would be upset with the preceding conclusion, which was included in the report of the evaluation (Rubin, 1979), because school personnel might fear that it would threaten continuation of NIMH funding for programs that used the funds to expand their regular programs without developing any special mental health curriculum. At the same time, we might also anticipate that the NIMH social work training staff would appreciate the candor of the report, thinking that they then could use the report to distinguish schools that appropriately used NIMH funding from those that did not and to influence the latter schools to be more accountable to them. But as it turned out, according to CSWE administrators, the NIMH staff expressed more consternation about the findings than did anyone else.

Their fear was that bureaucrats in other units of NIMH—units that were competing with social work for federal funds—could use the report as ammunition in their efforts to secure a bigger slice of the funding pie for their units at the expense of social work training. If that were to happen, not only would schools of social work receive less funding, but also the staff members of the social work training unit would lose status in the bureaucracy and see their own budget reduced.

So, you see, the web of politics in program evaluation can be extensive, and sometimes the external groups that sponsor an evaluation are not as independent and objective as we might suppose. In the foregoing example, the NIMH social work training staff were quite eager to get a report that would portray schools of social work as doing wonderfully innovative things with their NIMH funds, a report that they could then use to justify their own performance in allocating funds and monitoring their usage and in order to argue for more funding for their unit. In choosing CSWE to conduct the evaluation, it is reasonable to suppose that they fully expected that a glowing report would be forthcoming because CSWE is funded and governed by representatives of schools of social work and because one of CSWE's main goals is to lobby for greater funding for social work education. In fact, some CSWE administrative staff expressed displeasure with the report and tried to influence its author, a CSWE staff member, to modify the interpretation of the findings in order to depict more favorably the public benefits of NIMH funding for schools of social work.

Utilization of Program Evaluation Findings

As the preceding discussion illustrates, the findings of program evaluation studies can affect jobs, programs, and investments. But beliefs and values also are at stake. Consequently, political and ideological forces can influence whether and how program evaluation findings are used.

As president, Richard Nixon appointed a blue-ribbon national commission to study the consequences of pornography. After a diligent, multifaceted evaluation, the commission reported that pornography didn't appear to have any of the negative social consequences often attributed to it. Exposure to pornographic materials, for example, didn't increase the likelihood of sex crimes. You might have expected liberalized legislation to follow from the research. Instead, the president said the commission was wrong.

Less dramatic examples of the failure to follow the implications of evaluation research could be listed almost endlessly. Undoubtedly, every evaluation researcher can point to studies that he or she has conducted that were ignored—studies providing clear research results and obvious policy implications.

There are three important reasons why the implications of evaluation research results are not always put into practice. First, the implications may not always be presented in a way that nonresearchers can understand. Second, evaluation results sometimes contradict deeply held beliefs. That was certainly the case with the pornography commission just mentioned. If everybody knows that pornography is bad, that it causes all manner of sexual deviance, then it is likely that research results to the contrary will have little immediate impact. By the same token, people thought Copernicus was crazy when he said the Earth revolved around the sun. Anybody could tell the Earth was standing still.

The third barrier to the use of evaluation results is vested interests. Suppose a group of practitioners in a family service agency, after receiving extensive training (and indoctrination) in a new model of therapy, succeeds in convincing agency colleagues and superiors to let them form a new unit that specializes in service delivery based on that model of therapy. They are convinced that their services will be effective, and forming the new unit has significantly enhanced their prestige and autonomy in the agency. How do you think they are going to feel when your evaluation suggests that their program doesn't work? It is unlikely that they'll fold up their tent, apologize for misleading people, and return willingly to their old routines. It's more likely that they'll point out inescapable limitations in your research, call it misleading or worthless, and begin intense lobbying with colleagues and superiors to have the program continue.

Logistical and Administrative Problems

The social context of program evaluation affects not only the utilization of the outcomes of evaluative studies but also the logistics involved in their implementation. *Logistics* refers to getting research participants to do what they're supposed to do, getting research instruments distributed and returned, and other seemingly unchallenging tasks. In Chapter 11, we discussed common logistical problems that can plague experimental and quasi-experimental program evaluations. Sometimes practitioners or their supervisors are not exactly thrilled with the research requirements of the program evaluation. Not surprisingly, they may resist implementing them in a careful manner. At other times, logistical problems are unintentional, resulting from the uncontrollable context of daily life. For example, busy practitioners who are committed to the program evaluation, but whose main priority is service delivery, can simply forget to comply with research protocols. On several occasions, for example, we've observed practitioners in evaluations sometimes forget about experimental and control conditions. In their zeal to help clients, they provided an intervention to control group clients that was supposed to be provided to experimental group clients only.

Sometimes, you may find the best-laid plans go awry when unforeseen circumstances influence program personnel to make unanticipated changes that can wreak havoc on an evaluation. If you're lucky, they will discuss in advance the changes they are considering, which will enable you to learn about these changes in a timely way and interact with program personnel in a way that helps protect the evaluation's viability and utility. This is most likely to occur if you have been allocated enough resources to be on-site at the program on a daily basis. If, however, your resources are insufficient to have a frequent on-site presence and ongoing interaction with program personnel, then you may find out about program changes that wreak havoc on the planned evaluation too late to salvage the evaluation. Do not presume that evaluation plans made months earlier will remain at the forefront of the minds of program personnel as they encounter unexpected difficulties in operating their programs. Moreover, even if they do remember the evaluation plans, they may not realize that the program changes they are considering will impact the evaluation.

For instance, in a family preservation program that one of us (Rubin) evaluated, the program administrator became concerned during the study that clients served by the program did not appear to be improving rapidly enough. Consequently, she decided to extend the treatment duration for each client from three months to one year, not realizing that this would reduce the evaluation's sample size by 75 percent. (Instead of having four cohorts each receiving a three-month treatment during the year, there would be only one twelve-month cohort.) Neither did she think to inform the evaluation staff of this decision, which was made several months after the evaluation began and which additionally bore on the timing of the posttests.

Later in the midst of the evaluation the same administrator decided to start referring comparison group clients who seemed to show the most promise for improving their parenting to a comparable family preservation intervention program, not realizing (or perhaps not caring) that this would affect the study design's internal validity. And to make matters worse, the program administrator, who after a lengthy planning discussion had agreed to a careful, detailed plan for ensuring the equivalence of the family preservation group and the comparison group, decided to assign all of the clients with the most serious problems to her program, and the clients with the least serious problems to the comparison group. She assigned clients on that basis for three years and did not inform the evaluator of that until she saw undesirable outcome results at the completion of the evaluation.

Planning an Evaluation and Fostering Its Utilization

Posavac and Carey (1985) propose several steps that they postulate will help program evaluators anticipate and deal with potential logistical problems and potential resistance to an evaluation and its utilization. As a first step, they recommend learning as much as possible about the *stakeholders*—those with vested interests in the evaluation whose beliefs, income, status or careers, and workload might be affected by the evaluation. To promote their identification with the evaluation and their support of it during the data-collection phase, it is essential that they be involved in a meaningful way in planning the evaluation. Service recipients are also stakeholders and therefore should be included in the planning.

It also is important at the outset to find out who wants the evaluation, why they want it, and who doesn't want it. For example, if program sponsors want the evaluation but program personnel either don't know about it or don't want it, then the evaluator should try to make the program personnel more comfortable with the evaluation to foster their cooperation in collecting and interpreting data. One way to do this, of course, is by involving them as stakeholders, and by sharing mutual incremental feedback throughout all phases of the evaluation. Then, involvement should begin early in the planning of the evaluation, not after the research design is ready to be implemented. In addition to fostering cooperation with the evaluation, involving personnel in the planning is thought to improve the chances for identifying those daily organizational realities that might pose logistical obstacles to alternative research designs or data-collection methodologies.

Planning an evaluation is a two-way street. It should consider not only potential problems posed by stakeholders, but also potential problems stemming from mistakes the evaluator might make in designing the evaluation. For example, involving decision makers who are likely to use the research helps ensure that evaluators will address questions that are relevant to their decision-making needs rather than questions that are trivial or of interest only to audiences who are not in a position to act on the research findings. Also, without adequate input from program personnel, evaluators might choose or develop the wrong data-collection instruments, such as self-report scales that clients might not understand or be willing to complete. Conceivably, the attainment of program objectives might need to be measured idiosyncratically for each client because each client has unique needs and target problems. If so, practitioners might convince evaluators to assess goal attainment through an aggregation of single-case designs rather than through a group experiment that assesses all clients with the same outcome measures. Evaluators also might not understand the unrealistic burden that their data-collection procedures might place on practitioners who already strain to meet heavy paperwork requirements without sacrificing the quality of service they are providing to their many clients.

The cooperation of program personnel might be fostered further by assuring them that they will get to see and respond to a confidential draft of the evaluation report before it's finalized and disseminated to other stakeholders. They should not be led to think that they will be able to censor the report, but they should be assured that their suggestions will be taken seriously. By meeting with key personnel to discuss the report, evaluators can point out and clarify implications of the findings that personnel might find particularly useful for improving the program. And this should be done in a timely fashion—not after it's too late for certain decisions to be made.

The evaluator can foster the evaluation report's utilization by tailoring its form and style to the needs and preferences of those who are in a position to use it. Clear, succinct, and cohesive composition always helps, as does careful typing and a neat, uncluttered layout. The briefer and neater the report, the more likely that busy administrators and practitioners will read it carefully. When adapting the report to an audience of program personnel, do not present every peripheral finding. And do not present negative findings bluntly and tactlessly. If program objectives are not being attained, couch the findings in language that recognizes the yeoman efforts and skills of program personnel and that does not portray them as inadequate. Try not to convey a message of success or failure, but provide suggestions for developing new programs or improving existing ones. Alert program personnel in the planning stage that all reports bring both good and bad news and that the focus will be less on judging the program's value than on identifying feasible ways to improve it. And make sure that sufficient attention is given to realistic, practical implications of the findings.

As a final step in engaging program personnel in planning the evaluation, Posavac and Carey recommend obtaining their feedback regarding a written proposal that reflects their input. The purpose of presenting them with the proposal is to make certain that they agree with evaluators about the components of the evaluation and the nature of the program being evaluated. In addition, by reconsidering everything in a final, written package, they might see logistical problems that were not apparent in earlier discussions.

The evaluation proposal should include a graphic picture depicting essential program components, their linkage to short-term process objectives, indicators of success in achieving short-term objectives, how those short-term objectives lead to long-term program outcomes, and indicators of success in achieving long-term outcomes. The graphic portrayal is called a *logic model*. We will examine logic models more closely soon, after we discuss various types of program evaluation regarding program planning, processes, and outcomes—all of which get portrayed in a logic model.

But before moving on, a note of caution is in order. We are not implying that if you follow all the steps we have proposed you are certain to avoid problems in the way program personnel respond to a proposed evaluation or its findings. These steps are recommended as ways to reduce the likelihood of encountering those problems or the severity of those problems if they do arise. But even if you follow all of the proposed steps, under certain circumstances you may still encounter serious problems with program personnel. If, for example, they feel their funding is threatened by your findings, then they may still seek to discredit your evaluation, even if you went by the book in dealing with them.

TYPES OF PROGRAM EVALUATION

So far in this chapter we have been discussing the politics of program evaluation primarily in connection to assessing the effectiveness of programs in attaining their formal goals. Asking whether a program is achieving a successful outcome is perhaps the most significant evaluative question we might ask and probably the question that immediately comes to mind when we think about program evaluation. It may also be the most politically charged question because it bears so directly on key vested interests, such as those associated with funding. But as we noted above, program evaluation can have other purposes and other research questions that, although they may ultimately have some bearing on program outcome, focus on issues in the conceptualization, design, planning, administration, and implementation of interventions and programs.

At this point, then, we are going to look at the different types of program evaluation. We will do so with particular attention to methodological issues, but you will see that political considerations keep cropping up. We'll begin by looking at the evaluation of program outcome and efficiency. You'll see that even within this one type of program evaluation there are competing views about how to proceed.

Evaluating Outcome and Efficiency

Evaluations of program outcome and efficiency may assess whether the program is effectively attaining its goals, whether it has any unintended harmful effects, whether its success (if any) is being achieved at a reasonable cost, and how the ratio of its benefits to its cost compares with the benefits and costs of other programs with similar objectives.

This approach to evaluation, sometimes called the *goal attainment model* of evaluation, refers to the formal goals and mission of the program—whether it's achieving what its funders or the general public want it to achieve. Typically, in designing goal attainment evaluations, the program's formal goals will be specified as dependent variables and operationally defined in terms of measurable indicators of program success.

The focus is on maximizing the internal validity of the evaluation design to rule out bias and other plausible rival explanations of outcome and to be able to determine whether the particular outcomes observed were really caused by the program. Thus, evaluations of goal attainment ideally should strive to use the most internally valid experimental or quasi-experimental design possible and to use rigorous, objective, quantitative measures. In short, this approach to program evaluation primarily attempts to assess causal connections between program efforts and indicators of program outcome.

No matter how rigorous the assessment of outcome, the evaluation may be deemed incomplete unless it also assesses the costs of obtaining the outcome. In other words, how efficient is the program in achieving its outcome? Suppose, for example, that an evaluation of a case management program to prevent rehospitalization of the chronically mentally ill concludes that the program successfully reduces the number of days patients are hospitalized. Suppose further that the total number of days hospitalized for 50 case-managed patients during the course of the evaluation is 400, as compared to 500 for 50 controls. In other words, the case management program made a difference of 100 fewer hospitalized days.

So far, so good. But suppose the extra cost of providing the case management services during the study period was $50,000. Thus, each day of hospitalization saved by providing case management was costing $500 (which we get by dividing $50,000 by 100). If the cost of hospital care was less than $500 per day per patient, then some might conclude that despite the program's effectiveness, it was not an efficient way to care for the mentally ill.

Such questions of efficiency tend to be purely economic and may not account for important value judgments, such as those dealing with the worth of humanistic benefits reaped by service recipients. The costs of the preceding hypothetical program to the public at large may seem high, but some supporters might believe that those costs are justified by the improved quality of life experienced by patients when they reside in the community.

Thus, once again we see the social and political context of program evaluation. Different stakeholders might disagree about whether a particular benefit of a program is worth the extra cost, depending on which stakeholder is bearing the cost and which is reaping the benefit. And many benefits, such as improved health or an individual's self-esteem, cannot be valued in dollars.

Nevertheless, it's useful to assess program efficiency. Even if humanistic considerations lead us to believe that a less efficient program is still the most desirable option, at least we could make that decision in light of the ratio of costs to benefits. And sometimes assessing efficiency helps us to determine which alternative program provides more humanistic benefits. Suppose, for example, that an alternative type of case management program that costs $25,000 for 50 cases results in 425 hospitalized days for the same study period as the case management program that resulted in 400 hospitalized days. Although the $25,000 program had a slightly worse outcome, its costs were only half that of the $50,000 program. That means that an allocation of $50,000 would enable us to provide the cheaper program to twice as many cases as the more expensive program. Therefore, assuming that a finite level of funding does not permit us to provide the more expensive program to most of the target population, the slightly less effective but much more efficient program might yield greater humanistic benefits.

Cost-Effectiveness and Cost–Benefit Analyses

The two major approaches to assessing the efficiency of a program are called *cost-effectiveness analysis* and *cost–benefit analysis*. In **cost-effectiveness analysis,** the only monetary considerations are the costs of the program itself; the monetary benefits of the program's effects are not assessed. In **cost–benefit analysis**, an effort is made to monetize the program's outcome in addition to its costs.

In the foregoing case management example, we would be conducting a cost-effectiveness analysis if we limited our focus to the program-cost-per-day of hospitalization prevented. Thus, if we report that one program costs $500 per hospitalized day prevented, and another program costs $300 per hospitalized day prevented, we have reported the findings of a cost-effectiveness analysis. If, on the other hand, we had attempted to monetize outcome by assessing the societal benefits of the program in terms such as the increased economic productivity of the individuals who receive case management, we would have been conducting a cost–benefit analysis. Borrowing from White (1988), we can illustrate the difference between cost–benefit and cost-effectiveness analyses with the following example.

Suppose two alternative school social work interventions are evaluated, each of which aims to reduce the dropout rate of youths at inner-city high schools. Existing data reported before the study have shown that the graduation rate in the targeted high schools is only 50 percent. Intervention A costs $50,000 and is used by 100 students; 75 of the 100 students graduate from high school. Intervention B costs $40,000 and is utilized by 100 students; 60 of them graduate from high school. Based on the previously established 50 percent graduation rate, one would expect 50 of every 100 students to graduate. Because 75 of 100 (75 percent) who participated in Intervention A graduated, a cost-effectiveness analysis would find that Intervention A had the effect of adding 25 graduates at a cost of $50,000, or $2,000 per additional graduate. Intervention B was $10,000 cheaper to implement ($40,000 is $10,000 less than the $50,000 cost of Intervention A) but had the effect of adding only 10 graduates for the $40,000, which comes to $4,000 per additional graduate. Thus, Intervention A is more cost-effective, because $2,000 per additional graduate is a better cost-effectiveness ratio than $4,000 per additional graduate.

Notice that so far we have not estimated the monetary value of graduating from high school, an estimate that would be required if we were conducting a cost–benefit analysis. Suppose we did conduct such an analysis and found that the projected increased career earnings of the high school graduates was $50,000 per graduate and that the government would have to spend $10,000 less on social services and welfare benefits to each high school graduate, as compared to each dropout. Adding those two figures, we could estimate that the monetary benefit per additional graduate is $60,000. Because Intervention B had the effect of adding 10 graduates, we could conclude that its monetized outcome was 10 times $60,000, or $600,000. That figure would be far in excess of the intervention's $40,000 cost, so we could argue that the intervention is worth funding—that it is cost-beneficial because the dollar value of benefits resulting from the intervention exceed its dollar value costs.

Note that we could draw this conclusion without ever comparing Intervention B to Intervention A. Of course, were we to estimate the cost–benefit of Intervention A, we would find that Intervention A's monetized outcome would be even more cost-beneficial (with benefits equaling 25 times $60,000, or $1,500,000) than Intervention B's. Cost–benefit analyses need not ask whether one program's benefits-to-costs ratio is better than another program's. They may just look at one program and ask whether its monetized benefits exceed its monetary costs.

Assessing the costs of a program can be highly complex. It requires technical expertise in cost accounting and deals with such accounting concepts as variable versus fixed costs, incremental versus sunk costs, recurring versus nonrecurring costs, hidden versus obvious costs, direct versus indirect costs, future costs, opportunity costs, and so forth (Posavac and Carey, 1985). Because program evaluators often lack that expertise, they often do not include cost-effectiveness or cost–benefit analyses as part of their evaluations.

The cost-accounting concepts just mentioned go beyond the scope of this text. Because cost-effectiveness analysis attempts to monetize only program costs and not program outcomes, it involves fewer cost-accounting complexities and fewer questionable monetizing assumptions than does cost–benefit analysis. When we attempt to monetize the outcome of health and welfare programs, we get into difficult value issues, such as attaching a dollar figure to the value of human lives. White (1988) offers the example of neonatal intensive care units to illustrate this point.

Although intensive care units for very low birthweight babies are not cost-beneficial, every major hospital in this country spends hundreds of thousands of dollars providing them. The same point applies to the frail elderly. No matter what the costs are for nursing homes or other programs of care for the frail elderly, the monetized benefits of those programs—such as through increased earning capacity—are not going to exceed the program costs. We do not put a dollar value on the quality-of-life benefits that we seek to provide the frail elderly.

Likewise, when hospice programs attempt to alleviate the pain and suffering of terminally ill people, they cannot monetize that benefit in terms of dollars that the outcome of their care generates through patients' increased earning capacity. Because of the values problem in attempting to analyze benefits in monetary terms, as well as the difficulty in foreseeing and monetizing all of the costs and benefits that might be attributable to a program's outcome, cost-effectiveness analyses are generally considered less controversial and more doable than are cost–benefit analyses. Still, excellent cost–benefit analyses can be found.

Table 13-1 Cost and Benefits per Patient in Experimental (E) and Control (C) Groups for 12 Months after Admission

CATEGORY	GROUP C	GROUP E	GROUP E − C
COSTS			
I. Direct treatment costs			
A. Mendota Mental Health Institute (MMHI)			
Inpatient	$3096	$ 94	$−3002*
Outpatient	42	0	−42*
B. Experimental Center Program	0	4704	4704†
Total	$3138	$4798	$ 1660†
II. Indirect treatment costs			
A. Social service agencies			
1. Other hospitals (not MMHI)			
University hospitals	$ 147	$ 239	$ 92*
Madison General Hospital	417	87	−330*
St. Mary's Hospital	152	17	−135
Methodist Hospital	220	39	−181
Out-of-town hospitals	808	264	−544*‡
Total	$1744	$ 646	$−1098
2. Sheltered workshops (Madison Opportunity Center Inc. and Goodwill Industries)	$ 91	$ 870	$ 779*‡
3. Other community agencies			
Dane County Medical Health Center	55	50	−5
Dane County Social Services	41	25	−16*
State Department of Vocational Rehabilitation	185	209	24§
Visiting Nurse Service	0	23	23*
State Employment Service	4	3	−1‖
B. Private medical providers	22	12	−10‡¶
Total	$2142	$1838	$ −304†
III. Law enforcement costs			
A. Overnights in jail	$ 159	$ 152	$ −7‡
B. Court contacts	17	12	−5‡
C. Probation and parole	189	143	−46
D. Police contacts	44	43	−1‡
Total	$ 409	$ 350	$ −59†
IV. Maintenance costs			
A. Cash payments			
1. Governmental (including administration)			
Social Security (supplemental security income, retirement, survivors and disability)	$ 557	$269	$ −288*
Aid for Dependent Children	446	167	−279*
Unemployment Compensation	19	55	36#
Welfare	33	43	10
Other costs (including supervised residences)	43	0	−43*
Total	$1098	$534	$ −564†

Table 13-1 *(continued)*

CATEGORY	GROUP C	E	E − C
COSTS			
2. Private	102	197	95#
3. Experimental Center payments	0	202	202†
4. Patient payments	. . .	. . .	. . .
B. In kind food and lodging costs, by source			
1. Private (from family, Salvation Army, etc.)	287	102	−185
2. Government and Experimental Center	0	0	0
Total Measured Maintenance Costs	$1487	$1035	$−452†
V. Family burden costs			
A. Lost earnings due to patient	$ 120	$ 72	−48**††
B. Other costs (see VI, physical illness and emotional strain)	. . .	. . .	. . .
Total Costs for Which Monetary Estimates Have Been Made	$7296	$8083	$−797†
VI. Other family burden costs			
A. See V, lost earnings	. . .	. . .	. . .
B. No. of families reporting physical illness due to patient	25	14	−11**
C. Percent of family members experiencing emotional strain due to patient	48	25	−23**‡‡
VII. Burdens on other people (eg, neighbors, co-workers)	. . .	. . .	. . .
VIII. Illegal activity costs, average			
A. No. of arrests	1.0	0.8	−0.2#
B. No. of arrests for felony	0.2	0.2	0.0#
IX. Patient mortality costs (% of group dying during year)			
A. Suicide	1.5	1.5	0.0
B. Natural causes	0.0	4.6	4.6
BENEFITS			
I. Earnings§§			
A. From competitive employment	$1136	$2169	$1033*#
B. From sheltered workshops	32	195	163*#
Total Benefits for Which Monetary Estimates Have Been Made	$1168	$ 2364	$1196†
II. Labor market behavior			
A. Days of competitive employment per year	77	127	50#
B. Days of sheltered employment per year	10	89	79#
C. Percent of days missed from job	3	7	4#
D. No. of beneficial job changes	2	3	1‖‖
E. No. of detrimental job changes	2	2	0‖‖

(continued)

Table 13-1 *(continued)*

CATEGORY	GROUP C	GROUP E	GROUP E − C
BENEFITS			
III. Improved consumer decision making			
A. Insurance expenditures	$33	$56	$−23[#]
B. Percent of group having a savings account	27	34	7
IV. Patient mental health (see Table 2)	. . .	. . .	. . .
VALUED BENEFITS MINUS VALUED COSTS			
Valued benefits	$−1168	$−2364	$−1196
Valued costs	7296	8093	797
Net (Benefits Minus Costs)	$−6128	$−5729	$ −399[†]

*Significant at the $P < .05$ level.

†Significance not tested because the number is a sum of means.

‡These data are derived from agency or patient reports on the number of contacts. Patient reports were used only when it was not possible or was excessively costly to obtain the relevant information from the agency. Estimates of the cost per contact were obtained from the agency.

§Data from the Department of Vocational Rehabilitation (DVR) were available only for the 28-month study period as a whole, a period that included the follow-up period after the experiment. The per-patient costs are 12/28, or 43% of the 28-month cost and reflect the average cost for one year. The figures reflect some double counting because much of the DVR expenditures went for payments to other agencies that are included in the Cost section (category II). However, we have been able to account for and to exclude DVR payments to the sheltered workshops, which comprise by far the major source of double counting.

‖Significant at the $P < .10$ level.

¶These figures include fees for physicians, psychologists, and nurses but exclude any associated laboratory fees.

#These data are derived from patient reports and as such are subject to misreporting. In some cases, individual spot-checks were made with the agency in question; agencies that were not able to provide us with information on all patients were sometimes able to provide it on the spot-check basis.

**These figures are derived from interviews conducted four months after admission with 22 families (34%) of E-group patients and 18 families (27%) of C-group patients. The other families were not interviewed because: they lived outside of Dane County (23%), the subject or the family refused consent (18%), the relative could not be contacted (21%), or miscellaneous reasons (8%). The questionnaire examined the families' experience in the two weeks preceding the interview only, and these figures were projected to an annual average. The reduced sample size and the single interview yielded data that must be interpreted with caution.

††These figures were derived by multiplying the number of days family members missed work because of the patient by a daily wage of $24 (or $3 an hour).

‡‡This figure is based on interviewers' assessments.

§§The earnings do not include the value of fringe benefits, if there were any.

‖‖These figures reflect our judgments, which were based on examination of patient reports.

Source: Weisbrod, Burton A.; Test, Mary Ann; and Stein, Leonard I. "Alternative to Mental Hospital Treatment: II. Economic Benefit-Cost Analysis," *Archives of General Psychiatry,* vol. 37, April 1980, 400–405. (Table appears on pp. 401–402.)

An illustration of one done in an evaluation of a community support program for the mentally ill (Weisbrod, Test, and Stein, 1980) is presented in Table 13-1. It should give you a better sense of the complexities involved in monetizing program costs and outcomes.

Problems and Issues in Evaluating Goal Attainment

When people don't like a message they receive, they often blame the messenger. In the same vein, when they don't like the findings of an outcome evaluation, they often blame the evaluation's methodology. It is commonly perceived that over the years evaluations of program outcomes have had far more negative findings, indicating program failure, than positive findings. It is also widely believed that studies with negative findings tend not to be used because of the vested interests at stake. And expectations that rigorous, experimental outcome studies tend to produce negative findings have made administrators wary of such studies and reluctant to authorize them. One common complaint is that all these studies do is tell us that we are failing; they don't show us how to do things better.

One important criticism of the traditional approach to evaluating goal attainment correctly points out that the determination of program goals and their measurable indicators can be hazardous. Sometimes the mission of a program is stated in grandiose terms that no one really takes seriously—terms articulated for political reasons or to convince legislators or others that a program should be funded. Consequently, it's argued that finding negative outcomes in evaluations of the attainment of those goals is a foregone conclusion—that evaluations are doomed to keep coming up with negative findings if they keep taking formally stated goals seriously.

In addition to their grandiosity, formal goals are often stated so vaguely that different evaluators may find it impossible to agree on what they really mean in terms of specific, observable indicators of success. The Head Start program in the War on Poverty is often cited as a case in point. Its formal mission was to offset the effects of poverty and enhance children's opportunities. That's a noble mission, but what are its operational indicators? Evaluative researchers have disagreed over whether the focus of the outcome measures should be on indicators of learning readiness, academic achievement, emotional development and self-esteem, classroom conduct, delinquency later in life, physical health and nutrition, resource redistribution, or something else. The possibilities seem endless, and often program personnel themselves cannot agree on what specific indicators of success are implied by their program's mission statement.

Consequently, when evaluators choose a few operational indicators of success, they risk missing areas in which the program really is succeeding. If so, then their negative findings may be misleading and may endanger the continuation of programs that are succeeding in other, equally important ways. In light of these problems, some argue that the evaluation of outcome ought to be abandoned altogether and replaced by evaluations of program processes. Others argue that, even with these problems, outcome studies at least tell us some things about what is and is not being attained—which is better than having no information at all about program outcomes, particularly if appropriate caution is exercised in acting on the findings.

Some program evaluators suggest keeping the goal attainment model, but with some adjustments. One idea has been to ignore the formal goals or mission statement of a program and simply measure every conceivable indicator of outcome that the evaluators think has some potential of being affected by the program. But the feasibility of such undisciplined fishing expeditions for endless potential indicators may be dubious. Also, there is a statistical problem when a large number of dependent variables are assessed independently of one another—a problem we'll discuss in Chapter 22. An alternative suggestion, therefore, has been to assess official program goals as well as a limited number of additional goals that seem to be the most plausible in light of the social science theories on which the program is based. But this suggestion, too, may be somewhat (albeit less) vulnerable to the same statistical problem, and it offers no guarantee that the most important effects of the program will be detected.

Monitoring Program Implementation

Some programs have unsuccessful outcomes simply because they are not being implemented properly. Suppose an AIDS prevention program develops a public education leaflet and decides to evaluate its effectiveness in a small pilot distribution in a particular high school. Suppose the program personnel deliver the leaflets to the school's vice principal, who agrees to disseminate them to all students. Suppose that for some reason—unanticipated opposition by the principal or the PTA, mere oversight, or whatever—the leaflets never get disseminated. Or perhaps they get disseminated in an undesirable way. Maybe instead of handing them out to every student in a school assembly, the vice principal merely deposits them in teachers' mailboxes with a vague message encouraging them to distribute the leaflets to their students. Maybe some teachers distribute the leaflets but most do not.

Suppose further that the program personnel never learn that the leaflets were not disseminated as intended. The implications of this turn of events would be quite serious. Because few or no students would have received the leaflet in the first place, the intervention was never implemented as planned and had no chance to succeed. No matter what indicators of outcome were chosen, the leaflet dissemination effort would be doomed to fail. But it would fail not because it was a bad idea or an ineffectual leaflet but because it was never really tried. If the evaluators had merely conducted an outcome study and had not assessed whether and how the program got implemented, they would be in danger of abandoning a public education intervention that, if only implemented properly, might effectively prevent the spread of AIDS.

This example illustrates that no matter how well an outcome evaluation is designed, if it's not supplemented by an evaluation of program implementation, then it risks not identifying or misinterpreting the meaning of negative results. In turn, no matter how highly we value outcome studies, there is a clear need for the evaluation of program implementation. And familiarity with organizational goal theory helps us realize the true importance of implementation evaluations.

Even when we can be sure that we have properly identified the formal, official goals of a program and their operational indicators, we cannot assume that those goals are the real priority of the program personnel who are responsible for attaining them. Program personnel at all levels tend over time to become preoccupied with daily routines and with their own agendas—that is, with unofficial goals pertaining to organizational maintenance, personal prestige and career advancement, bureaucratic rules and procedures, and the like. As these unofficial goals displace official, formal goals, they may result in activities that are either irrelevant to or at odds with the attainment of the official goals.

Thus, for example, administrators of family service agencies may secure federal poverty funds not because they are devoted to fighting poverty, but because those funds will help balance agency budgets and enhance the agency board evaluation of the administrators' performance. Suppose the administrators propose to use the funds so that the agencies can reach out to more poverty-stricken individuals and thus try to engage them in receiving the agencies' direct services. Once they've received the funds, however, there is no guarantee that the agencies will try to reach poor clients as diligently as they promised in their grant applications. Even if the administrators sincerely sought to do so, they might run into unanticipated resistance by direct-service practitioners who think that such efforts would be an unrewarding and improper use of their therapeutic talents and who prefer to continue serving the kind of clientele with whom they are familiar and comfortable.

Consider the implications for program evaluation in the foregoing hypothetical example. Suppose a nationwide outcome study were done to see if the federal funding of direct social services to the poor resulted in a reduction in poverty or a reduction in various psychosocial problems among the poor. If the family service agencies never really tried very hard to serve poor clients because of their own internally directed objectives, then the outcome would in all likelihood be negative. But it would be wrong to conclude from such results that the provision of direct services to the poor is an ineffective way to help them deal with the problems of poverty, because the services never reached enough poor people in the first place.

For the same reasons, one can see from this example the importance of evaluating program implementation even without any evaluation of program outcome. If an evaluation of agency caseload attributes found that the agencies never implemented the program as planned—that poor people were not being served—then who needs an outcome evaluation? And those results would be quite useful. Instead of just depicting the program as a success or failure, it would identify what went wrong and could help policy makers consider ways to improve the program's implementation. In addition, simply monitoring program implementation would help keep the agency accountable to its funders. Ultimately, of course, they would want to know the program's outcome. But, in the meantime, just knowing how the program is being implemented is invaluable.

Evaluations of program implementation are not necessarily concerned only with the question of whether a program is being implemented as planned. Many other possible questions might examine how best to implement and maintain the program. Here are just a few of the important questions that can be researched without getting into questions of outcome:

- Which fundraising strategy yields the most funds?
- What proportion of the target population is being served?
- What types of individuals are not being reached?
- Why are so many targeted individuals refusing services?
- What satellite clinic locations are reaching the most clients?
- What types of practitioners seem to have the best attitudes about working with certain underserved target populations?
- Do practitioners in specialized units have better attitudes than those in multipurpose units?
- How skillful are various types of practitioners in their clinical interventions?
- In what areas do they seem least prepared and in need of continuing education?
- How are staff members reacting to new agency procedures? What difficulties are they experiencing with the procedures?
- Are clients satisfied with services? Why or why not?
- Why do so many clients drop out of treatment prematurely?

Process Evaluation

A term closely aligned with monitoring program implementation is called *process evaluation*. Process evaluations (which are an example of *formative evaluations*, mentioned at the beginning of this chapter) ask many of the same questions as indicated above in connection with monitoring program implementation, and they focus on identifying strengths and weaknesses in program processes and recommending needed improvements.

Often agency administrators will ask evaluators to conduct outcome evaluations of their programs while those programs are still in their infancy and have not yet had enough time to identify and resolve start-up bugs and other problematic processes in implementation. These administrators may be in a hurry for outcome data because they are under intense pressure from funding sources to prove their success at goal attainment. Seasoned evaluators, however, may try to persuade them to table any outcome evaluation until a process evaluation has been completed so that outcome data are collected only after the program has been debugged. The administrators may or may not have the time or resources to conduct a process evaluation first and then an outcome evaluation. In contrast, other administrators, perhaps under less external pressure, may be content just to have the process evaluation, asking not whether their program works, but how to make it work better.

All of the methodologies covered in this book can be applied to evaluate program implementation. The most appropriate methodology to use depends on the nature of the research question. Surveys that use questionnaires or scales might assess staff, client, or community attitudes that affect program implementation decisions. Available records might be analyzed to assess whether the attributes of clients being served match program priorities regarding the intended target population. Experimental or quasi-experimental designs might be used to assess the effectiveness of alternative fundraising strategies, to measure the impact of different organizational arrangements on staff attitudes, to determine which outreach strategies are most successful in engaging hard-to-reach prospective clients in treatment, and so on.

Process evaluations, however, tend to rely heavily on qualitative methods, which we'll discuss at length in the three chapters of Part 6 of this text. Open-ended qualitative interviewing, for instance, might be the best way to learn how staff members are reacting to new agency procedures and the unanticipated difficulties they might be experiencing with them. Qualitative interviewing might also work best for discovering the reasons clients cite for service dissatisfaction or for refusing or prematurely terminating service delivery. Participant observation might be used to assess how staff members relate to clients or to one another. In some studies, evaluators have posed as clients and observed how staff members behaved and the ways in which their behavior affected clients.

Evaluation for Program Planning: Needs Assessment

Thus far, we have been discussing the evaluation of programs that have already been implemented. But the term *program evaluation* also connotes diagnostic evaluation. Just as clinical practitioners evaluate client problems and needs during a preintervention assessment period to develop the best treatment plan, program evaluators may assess a program's target population in order to enhance program planning. They might assess the extent and location of the problems the program seeks to ameliorate, as well as the target population's characteristics, problems, expressed needs, and desires. This information is then used to guide program planning and development concerning such issues as what services to offer, how to maximize service utilization by targeted subgroups, where to locate services, and so on.

For example, suppose you are planning a new statewide program to help the homeless. What would you need to know to guide your planning? You might want to find out how many homeless people there are in the state. How many are there in specific locations in the state? What are the reasons for each individual's homelessness, and how many people are there for each reason? How many choose to be homeless? How many seem to be homeless because of mental illness or substance abuse? How many are homeless because they lost their jobs and cannot find work? How long have they been homeless? How many of the homeless are in different ethnic groups, and how many are recent immigrants or do not speak English? What proportion of the homeless consists of children and entire family units? What special problems do the children experience in such matters as education, health, nutrition, self-esteem, and so on? What special problems and needs are expressed by the adult homeless, those with emotional disorders, and others? These are just a few of the diagnostic questions you might ask; the answers will help you suggest what interventions to develop, where to locate them, how to staff them, and so on.

The process of systematically researching diagnostic questions like those just mentioned is called *needs assessment*. The term **needs assessment** is widely used to cover all sorts of techniques for collecting data for program planning purposes, and it has become essentially synonymous with evaluation for program planning.

Before we examine specific alternative techniques of needs assessment, it's important to address a thorny conceptual issue that complicates the definition of needs: whether they're defined in normative terms or in terms of demand. If needs are defined normatively, then a needs assessment would focus on comparing the objective living conditions of the target population with what society, or at least that segment of society that is concerned with helping the target population, deems acceptable or desirable from a humanitarian standpoint. Normatively defining the needs of the homeless, for instance, might lead you to conclude that certain housing or shelter programs need to be developed for individuals who are living in deplorable conditions on the streets, even if those individuals don't express any dissatisfaction with their current homelessness.

If needs are defined in terms of demand, however, only those individuals who indicate that they feel or perceive the need themselves would be considered to be in need of a particular program or intervention. Thus, in this homelessness example, individuals who prefer to be homeless might not be counted as in need of the program. Defining needs in terms of demand can be tricky. Perhaps individuals express no need for a planned program because they don't understand how the planned program will help them or because they have come to expect that every time a social program is provided to them it is stigmatizing or unacceptable to them in some other way. Thus, in assessing whether the homeless need a new shelter program, many homeless individuals might express no need for the program and might even disdain the idea because they have no reason to believe that the new program really will be more acceptable to them than the filthy, crowded, dangerous shelters they already refuse to use.

How we define *needs* affects the choice of specific techniques to assess them. For example, if we define needs normatively, we might be able to establish the need for a particular program by analyzing existing statistics. Thus, if census data showed a relatively high number of unmarried teenage mothers in a particular area, then we might be predisposed to conclude that more family planning or child-rearing education services are needed in that area. But if we take demand into account, then we might want to supplement the census information by conducting a survey of teenage mothers to determine under what conditions they would actually use the particular services that we are contemplating.

The specific techniques for conducting a needs assessment are usually classified in five categories: (1) the key informants approach, (2) the community forum approach, (3) the rates under treatment approach, (4) the social indicators approach, and (5) the community survey approach. Let's look at each one.

Key Informants The key informant approach utilizes questionnaires or interviews to obtain expert opinions from individuals who are presumed to have special knowledge about the target population's problems and needs, as well as about current gaps in service delivery to that population. The **key informants** selected to be surveyed might include leaders of groups or organizations that are in close contact with the target population and that have special knowledge of its problems. It might also include practitioners who work closely with the target population.

In assessing the needs of the homeless, for instance, key informants might include professionals who work in public shelters or soup kitchens; researchers or other personnel who address homelessness as part of their work for local planning agencies; neighborhood leaders who live in communities where the homeless tend to congregate; administrators and case managers who work in community mental health programs; public officials who advocate legislation to help deal with the problem of homelessness; leaders of citizen advocacy groups who work on behalf of the poor, homeless, or mentally ill; and law enforcement officials who have been dealing with the problem.

The prime advantage of the key informants approach is that a sample can be obtained and surveyed quickly, easily, and inexpensively. Also, conducting the survey can provide the fringe benefits of building connections with key community resources that are concerned about the problem and of giving your program some visibility. The chief disadvantage of this method, however, is that your information is not coming directly from the target population; that information's quality depends on the objectivity and depth of knowledge underlying the expressed opinions.

To illustrate this disadvantage, consider the following possible pitfalls in an assessment of homelessness. Perhaps key informants who are affiliated with public shelters are unaware of those individuals who refuse to use the shelters, their reasons for doing so, and the unique problems they have. Perhaps advocates for poverty legislation will be likely to downplay needs associated with the mentally ill homeless because they see homelessness primarily as an economic problem and do not want to foster the notion that people are homeless because of either defects in character or voluntary preferences. Perhaps mental health officials will be biased toward exaggerating mental illness as the cause of homelessness, or perhaps their bias will be to downplay the problem of homelessness among the mentally ill because that problem may reflect negatively on the mental health policies they have implemented. Perhaps neighborhood leaders where the homeless tend to congregate will be biased toward perceiving the need for services that get the homeless out of their neighborhood. In light of pitfalls like these, it is important that the representativeness of the key informant sample be maximized by using sampling procedures that are as scientific as possible. (We'll discuss such procedures in the next chapter.) But even that is no guarantee that these pitfalls will be sufficiently minimized.

Community Forum The **community forum** approach involves holding a meeting in which concerned members of the community can express their views and interact freely about their needs. This approach offers several nonscientific advantages, including its feasibility, its ability to build support and visibility for the sponsoring agency, and its ability to provide an atmosphere in which individuals can consider the problem in depth and be stimulated by what others have said to consider things they might otherwise have overlooked. Still, from a scientific standpoint this approach is risky.

Those who attend such meetings might not be representative of the people in the best position to know about the needs of the target population and of those whose views are relatively unbiased. Instead, those who have vested interests or particular axes to grind are likely to be overrepresented. The views expressed at such meetings are expressed publicly, and therefore strong social pressures might inhibit certain individuals from speaking at all or from expressing minority viewpoints. In light of these problems, rather than hold an open meeting for anyone to attend, it may be advisable to hold a series of closed meetings, each for a different, preselected, homogeneous group.

Rates under Treatment The **rates under treatment** approach attempts to estimate the need for a service and the characteristics of its potential clients, based on the number and characteristics of clients who already use that service. This method makes the most sense when the rates under treatment are examined in a community other than, but similar to, a target community that does not yet provide the service in question. The assumption is that if the two communities really are comparable, then the size and characteristics of the target population in the community without the service will parallel the size and characteristics of those already being treated in the comparison community.

A prime data-collection method in this approach is the secondary analysis of case records from the comparison community. The prime advantages of the rates under treatment approach are its quickness, easiness, inexpensiveness, and unobtrusiveness. Its prime disadvantage is that it assesses only that portion of the target population that is already using services, and thus it pertains primarily to demand and may underestimate normative need. In fact, it may even underestimate demand because the number of individuals who want to utilize the service may exceed the caseload capacity in the comparison community. Moreover, many who want to use that type of service may choose not to use the one offered in the comparison community because of something undesirable in the way it is being provided.

Another disadvantage of this approach is that the records and data in the comparison community may be unreliable or biased. Accurate record keeping may be a low priority in many agencies in the comparison community, particularly if service delivery demands leave little time for it. Also, agencies may exaggerate the number of clients served or their needs for services so that they will look good to funding sources or others to whom they are accountable. One way this can happen is by multiple counting of the same individual across different agencies serving the target population. Another way is by recording one unit of service delivered to a family of four in such a manner that others might think that four units of service were provided to four different members of the target population. These inaccuracies often are not intentional.

Social Indicators Another type of needs assessment that makes use of existing statistics is the **social indicators** approach. This approach does not look just at treatment statistics; it examines aggregated statistics that reflect conditions of an entire population. For example, infant mortality rates (the number of infants who die during their first year of life) can be an indicator of the need for prenatal services in a particular community. Such rates could also be examined to identify communities that have the greatest need for these services. Likewise, rates of reported child abuse in a community can be used as an indicator of that community's need for a newly developed abuse prevention program. School dropout rates can indicate the need for a school district to hire school social workers. Using social indicators is unobtrusive and can be done quickly and inexpensively. But those advantages need to be weighed against potential problems in the reliability of a particular existing database. Also, this approach's utility depends on the degree to which the existing indicators can be assumed to reflect future service use patterns accurately.

As we noted, the social indicators approach to needs assessment relies on the utilization of existing statistics. In Chapter 16, we'll discuss the methodological issues involved in using existing statistics as well as prominent sources for finding existing statistics. You may find that material particularly useful if you plan to conduct a needs assessment using the social indicators approach.

Surveys of Communities or Target Groups The most direct way to assess the characteristics and perceived problems and needs of the target group is to survey its members. This usually involves surveying a sample drawn from the population, although sometimes it's feasible to undertake a census of the entire target group.

Surveying members of target groups to assess their needs involves applying the principles and techniques of sampling and survey research that we'll be discussing in the next two chapters. Ideally, random sampling techniques should be used when we want to maximize the representativeness of the sample. But exceptions to this can be made—for instance, when it's impossible to obtain in advance a list of people from whom to sample, as when attempting to survey the homeless. In such cases, qualitative sampling approaches, which we'll discuss in Chapter 17, may be more appropriate than quantitative ones.

Data-collection methods might use highly structured, quantitative questionnaires or semistructured, qualitative interviews, depending on the nature of the target group and what is already known or not known about its possible needs. For example, in assessing the need for additional day care facilities for low-income parents, the needs assessment might include questions about the number of preschool-aged children living with respondents, current child-care arrangements, whether and when respondents would use a new day care facility, what respondents expect it to provide, what respondents would do differently to further their own education or careers were a day care facility provided, and respondents' demographic attributes.

The advantages and disadvantages of the direct survey approach parallel those of surveys in general. Evaluators ought to be particularly mindful of the potential biases associated with low response rates, social desirability, and acquiescent response sets.

Suppose, for example, that the survey is conducted by mail. Those who bother to respond cannot be assumed to represent those who do not respond. In all likelihood, the respondents will feel a greater need for the program than the nonrespondents, and they are likely to differ in other ways as well. Suppose the questions are phrased only in general terms concerning whether a particular service ought to be available. Respondents might be predisposed to agree. Why not agree with the provision of a new service if no mention is made about its costs or whether the respondent would actually use it? But if respondents who agree that a service sounds nice are asked if they think it's worth specific costs or whether they intend to use it, they might respond negatively.

Thus, the advantages of this method—its directness and its potential for ascertaining how prospective service consumers perceive their need for and likely use of programs—need to be weighed against potential biases in measurement or in response rates. Of course, what you will have learned in this book about sampling, measurement, and surveys might enable you to design a needs assessment survey that adequately minimizes those biases. But doing so would be time-consuming and expensive, and feasibility constraints might instead require that you use one or more of the foregoing four approaches to needs assessment.

Like research methods in general, each of the five approaches to needs assessment has its own advantages and disadvantages. Ideally, then, we should combine two or more approaches to needs assessment to get a more complete picture of normative needs, felt needs, and demand for prospective services.

Focus Groups

A relatively speedy and inexpensive qualitative research method often used for needs assessment, or for collecting other forms of program evaluation data, involves the use of **focus groups.** We'll give more attention to the use of focus groups in Chapter 18, on qualitative methods. We'll see the advantages and disadvantages of bringing together in the same room a small group of key informants, referral sources, service consumers or potential consumers, or community residents to engage in a guided discussion of community needs or the need to provide a specific program to a particular target population of clients or prospective clients. We'll also see how group dynamics can bring out needs assessment information that might not have emerged in a community survey.

LOGIC MODELS

Some program evaluations have a comprehensive scope that covers methods and purposes associated with program planning, program processes, and program outcomes. Such evaluations are enhanced by the development and use of logic models. As we mentioned earlier in this chapter, a **logic model** is a graphic portrayal that depicts the essential components of a program, shows how those components are linked to short-term process objectives, specifies measurable indicators of success in achieving short-term objectives, conveys how those short-term objectives lead to long-term program outcomes, and identifies measurable indicators of success in achieving long-term outcomes.

Logic models are seen not only as useful tools in guiding evaluations and as a way to help agency administrators and practitioners remain apprised of the program evaluation protocol, but also as tools that will help program planners and administrators in conceptualizing, developing, and managing their programs. Conrad and colleagues put it this way:

> From a program manager's perspective, the logic model becomes a management tool that helps the program manager keep the program from deviating from its ideal implementation. For the evaluator, the logic model provides a framework for understanding the extent to which the program as implemented is consistent with the program as intended.
>
> (1999:21)

Some federal and private funding sources now require grant applications to include a logic model. The rationale, in part, is that such models help in reviewing the appropriateness of both the evaluation design and the proposed program. Moreover, a good logic model is seen as enhancing the prospects that the program will be managed well, monitored incrementally to assess whether it is being implemented properly, and have its short- and long-range objectives evaluated as planned.

There is no one way to construct a logic model. The W. K. Kellogg Foundation (2004), for example, identifies three different approaches for doing so. One approach emphasizes the underlying theory that influenced decisions about program components and thus explains the reasons for those decisions. Rather than focus on specific program "nuts and bolts," a *theory-based logic model* will begin graphically with boxes identifying underlying program assumptions. It will then show how those assumptions lead to boxes

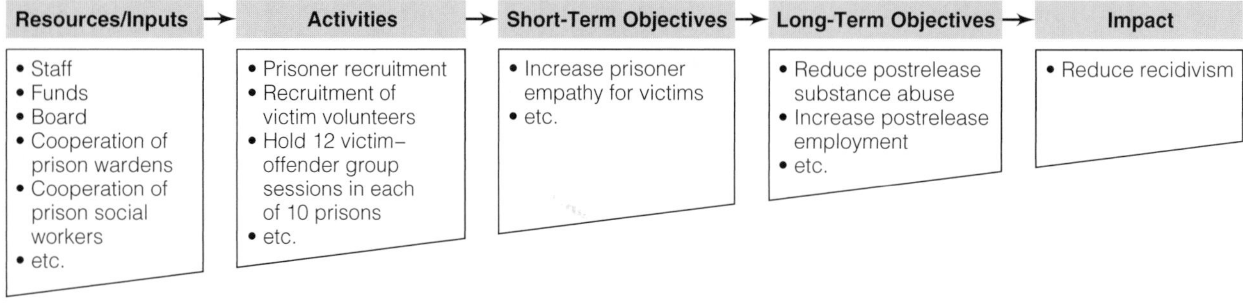

Figure 13-1 Template for Constructing an Outcomes Approach Logic Model for an In-Prison Pre-release Restorative Justice Program in Which Victims and Offenders Interact in Groups

depicting program resources (inputs), how the inputs lead to boxes displaying program processes and activities, how the activities aim to achieve short-term outcomes, how the short-term outcomes intend to lead to longer-term outcomes, and how the longer-term outcomes intend to lead to the ultimate program impact. Unlike other approaches to logic models, the intended short- and long-term program outcomes in the theory approach might be worded in broad terms rather than measurable indicators. Like the other approaches, the columns of boxes will be followed by arrows depicting how they lead to the next column. Thus, the column of boxes depicting assumptions will be followed by arrows pointing to resources, the resource boxes will be followed by arrows pointing to processes and activities, and so on.

Another logic model approach emphasizes outcomes. The boxes in this approach will contain more detail than in the theory approach. Also, the *outcomes approach logic model* is less likely to begin with underlying program assumptions and more likely to begin with program inputs (resources).

A third logic model approach emphasizes the details of the implementation process. It is less likely to include columns of boxes displaying assumptions and inputs and displays less detail regarding outcomes. Instead, the activities approach logic model is likely to contain more boxes providing great detail about each activity that must be implemented to keep the program on track.

Which logic model to choose will vary depending upon program needs and what seems to be most helpful for those involved in program management and evaluation. Regardless of which approach you might choose, you should try to find a happy medium between making your logic model so skimpy that it fails to adequately convey the various model components and their logical connections versus packing it with so much detail that the essence is hard to see. Figure 13-1 displays a basic, skeletal format of what an outcomes approach logic model might look like. The program involved is an in-prison pre-release restorative justice program in which victims and offenders interact in groups. Figure 13-2 presents a logic model that is more theory based and which was used in the evaluation of a federally funded homeless prevention program.

AN ILLUSTRATION OF A QUALITATIVE APPROACH TO EVALUATION RESEARCH

In several places throughout this text we have reiterated the view that quantitative and qualitative approaches to empirical inquiry are equally important. In this chapter we have noted that program evaluations can use both quantitative and qualitative methods. This point is reinforced in the box titled "Combining Quantitative and Qualitative Methods in Program Evaluation."

Because the emphasis in the previous two chapters was on the use of quantitative methods to evaluate the effectiveness of interventions, we'll end this chapter with an illustration of a program evaluation that emphasized qualitative methods. The illustration we'll use was reported by Robert Bogdan and Steven Taylor (1990), two qualitatively oriented researchers who had been conducting evaluation research since the early 1970s on policy issues connected to the institutionalization and deinstitutionalization of people with developmental disabilities (people who are often labeled "mentally retarded"). Their work led them to question the policy of institutionalization and to

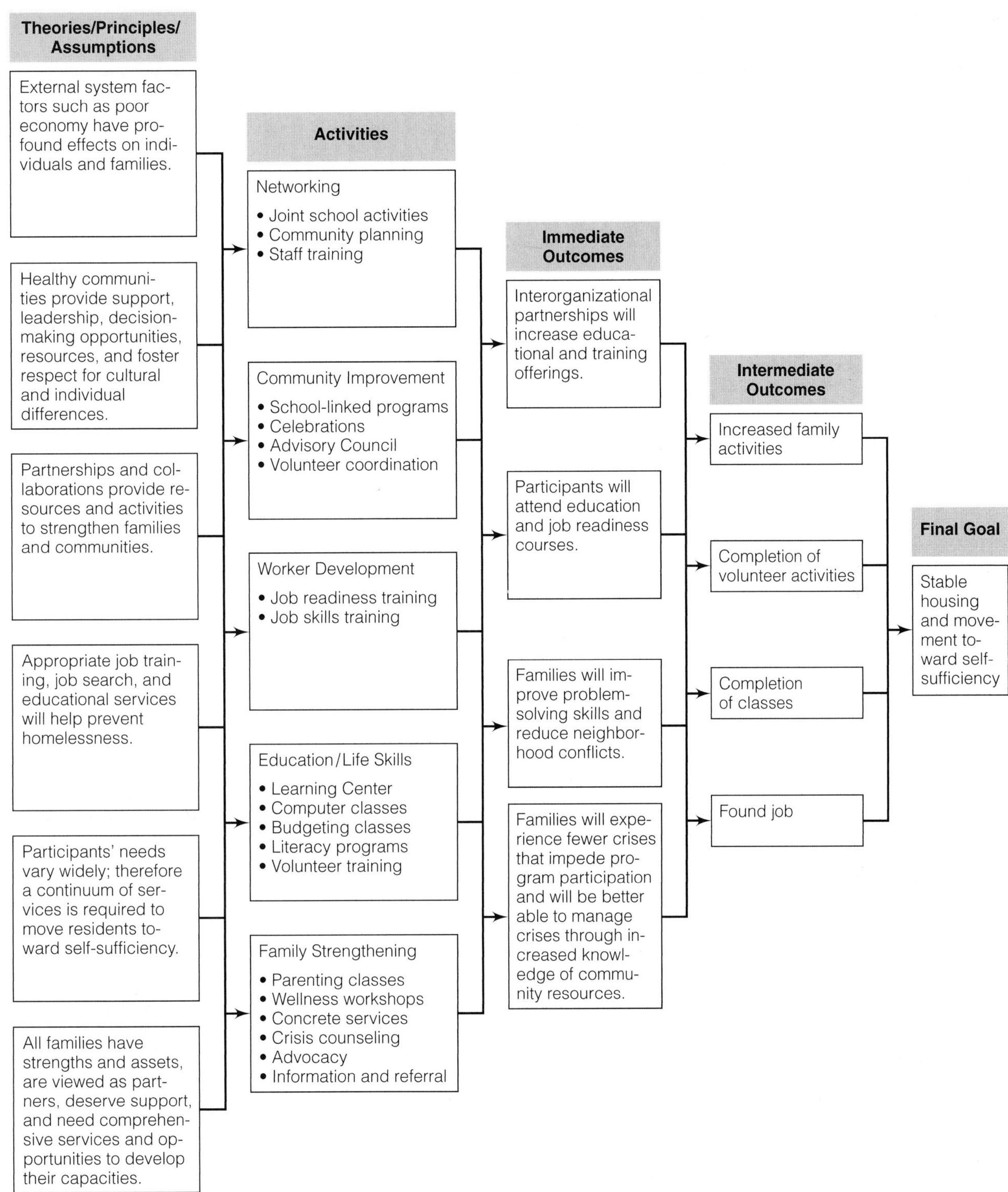

SOURCE: Mulroy, Elizabeth A., and Helenann Lauber. 2004. "A User-Friendly Approach to Program Evaluation and Effective Community Interventions for Families at Risk of Homelessness," Social Work, 49 (4), 573–586. (Figure appears on p. 578.)

Figure 13-2 Theory-Based Logic Model Used in a Federally Funded Homeless Prevention Program

COMBINING QUANTITATIVE AND QUALITATIVE METHODS IN PROGRAM EVALUATION

Evaluative Function	Quantitative Methods	Qualitative Methods
Planning an evaluation		Open-ended interviews with stakeholders
		Content analysis of program documents
		Participant observation of program activities
Needs assessment	Survey of key informants, target group, or community	Community forum
	Rates under treatment	Focus groups
	Social indicators	
Process evaluation (Monitoring program implementation and identifying needed improvements)	Staff and client surveys	Case studies of model programs
	Analysis of agency records on amounts of various types of service delivery and to whom	Focus groups of program staff and service consumers
		Open-ended interviews with staff about unofficial goals and implementation problems
		Participant observation of service provision, staff training, and staff meetings
		Open-ended interviews with service consumers
		Content analysis of staff meeting documents or practitioner entries in client records
		Videotaping or audiotaping service provision to assess practitioner skill or compliance with recommended procedures
Evaluating goal attainment	Experimental and quasi-experimental designs, combined with process evaluation to determine the nature of the program that did or did not attain its goals	Supplement outcome evaluation with foregoing process evaluation methods to ascertain the nature of the successful program or to learn whether the unsuccessful program was really implemented as intended
Evaluating efficiency	Cost-effectiveness analysis	
	Cost–benefit analysis	

become strong advocates for deinstitutionalization and the integration of people with disabilities into the community. However, their review of qualitative studies that documented the plight of disabled people who have been transferred from dehumanized institutions to dehumanized conditions in the community raised questions about how to improve this target population's integration into the community.

Bogdan and Taylor believed that many quantitatively oriented outcome evaluations on the effects of deinstitutionalization asked the wrong question, what they called the "Does it work?" question. In their apparent orientation to the stakeholder service model of evaluation practice, Bogdan and Taylor noted that community-based practitioners, like human service practitioners in general, believe in their work. They are not skeptical about what they do and therefore find no value in evaluative studies that merely tell whether a particular program was or was not effective. When "Does it work?" studies produce pessimistic results, they attribute the findings to the unfortunate prevalence of poorly funded, poor-quality community-based programs.

Moreover, they tend to see community integration as a moral question similar to the issue of slavery. Bogdan and Taylor drew an analogy between asking about the effectiveness of policies and programs that free people from institutions and asking about the effectiveness of policies that freed slaves in the Civil War era, pointing out that slavery would not be justified were outcome studies to find that freed slaves were encountering difficulties in community integration. We find this analogy debatable, but we share it with you so that you can see how Bogdan and Taylor's values influenced their work. Even if you disagree with their analogy, you might admire their candor about their values and about how values influenced the questions they asked. (Do you recall our discussion way back in Chapter 3 on the issue of whether research is ever truly value-free?)

Rather than study whether community integration works, Bogdan and Taylor asked, "What does integration mean?" (notice the qualitative orientation to meanings) and "How can integration be accomplished?" Bogdan and Taylor saw these questions as more optimistic ones than asking whether community integration works. They also saw these questions as more responsive to practitioner or stakeholder needs, not only because practitioners are optimistic about what they do, but also because they are more interested in formative information about how better to accomplish their aims than they are in summative outcome conclusions.

Their focus on discovering insights about what community integration means and how better to achieve it led them to eschew random sampling and to use instead qualitative sampling strategies (which will be discussed in Part 6). Bogdan and Taylor were not interested in studying typical, or average, programs. They were not interested in representativeness. Instead, they sought to identify exemplary programs that were reputed to be doing well in achieving community integration. Their sampling efforts toward identifying exemplary programs used a variety of techniques, "including announcements in professional newsletters, national mailings, and reviews of the professional literature" (1990:187). They also contacted various key informants who could tell them which agencies they felt were doing a good job and who could identify other key informants who might know of other exemplary programs. The key informants included disability rights activists, university-based researchers, and leaders of parent and professional groups.

Bogdan and Taylor conducted in-depth, open-ended phone interviews with officials in each program that was identified in their snowball sample. The purpose of these interviews was to obtain information that would help them whittle the sample down to eight agencies that promised to yield the most comprehensive understanding of what community integration means and how best to achieve it. Their interview questions attempted to probe into what the programs were doing, how well they seemed to be doing it, and how sincere they seemed to be in their efforts. These questions, as well as routine questions about agency characteristics, enabled the researchers to select a sample of agencies that all seemed exemplary, but which varied in geographic location, services offered, and administrative arrangements.

The reason for the small sample size was that each agency in the sample was studied intensively, including a series of visits by the researchers over a three-year period. To gain entry into the agencies, and to foster their enthusiastic cooperation with the study, the researchers honestly told agency staff members that their agency had been nominated as innovative or exemplary. This not only flattered administrators but helped them realize that their participation provided an opportunity to gain national visibility as a model program. Bogdan and Taylor reported that this ironically seemed to lead many officials and staff to talk more openly about their problems than they otherwise might have done.

Each agency site visit lasted several days, during which the researchers employed an approach that involved triangulated qualitative data-collection methods such as direct observation, intensive interviewing, and document analysis. The interviews were conducted with staff members, clients and their family members, and representatives of other local agencies. The site visits yielded thousands of pages of field notes and interview transcripts (and probably none of the inferential statistics that we'll try to fascinate you with in later chapters).

Bogdan and Taylor's prime approach to data presentation was through *case studies*. The case studies were prepared after each agency visit. They provided an agency overview, described the innovative agency policies that seemed to be fostering community integration, and provided illustrative case examples of how agency innovations are perceived to be affecting people's lives. When applicable, they also reported agency problems and dilemmas. The case study "stories" of the agencies were then disseminated to the field as a whole through short articles in relevant newsletters, articles that focused on the positive aspects of the visited agencies. The articles attempted to disseminate state-of-the-art descriptions to provide readers with new ideas that they might be able to adapt in their efforts to improve community integration in their own agencies.

With this positive, "optimistic," qualitative approach that focuses on process, Bogdan and Taylor believed they were producing research that would have greater utility to the field, and ultimately do more to improve the well-being of disabled individuals, than producing quantitative studies of outcome. Although some researchers may disagree as to whether their particular approach is more valuable than other particular approaches to research and evaluation, we think few will fail to appreciate the value of their approach as one of a variety of valuable ways to use research in our efforts to improve practice, alleviate human suffering, and promote social welfare.

Main Points

- Program evaluation applies different research methods and designs in order to assess and improve the conceptualization, design, planning, administration, implementation, effectiveness, efficiency, and utility of social interventions and human service programs.

- Although people have always in some way evaluated the reforms they have instituted, systematic and scientific approaches to program evaluation during the latter half of the 20th century burgeoned as increased social welfare spending spawned an "age of accountability."

- The advent of managed care has intensified pressures on service providers to evaluate the outcomes of their services. But it has also intensified vested interests in obtaining findings that make their services look effective.

- The importance of program evaluation in funding decisions creates a highly political atmosphere in which stakeholders with vested interests can impede free scientific inquiry.

- Political considerations can affect not only in-house evaluators but also external evaluators who seem to be more independent. Even funding sources and other external sponsors of an evaluation can have a stake in its outcome and may try to influence it for political reasons.

- Political and ideological forces can influence not only the methodology and interpretation of evaluative research, but also whether and how its findings are used. We cannot assume that the implications of evaluation research will necessarily be put into practice, especially if they conflict with official interests or points of view.

- The social context of program evaluation studies also affects the logistics involved in implementing them.

- Several steps have been proposed to help evaluators alleviate potential problems in the logistics of their studies, as well as to alleviate resistance to them and their utilization. These steps involve learning as much as possible about the stakeholders and their vested interests in the evaluation, involving them in a meaningful way in all phases of planning and performing the evaluation, maintaining ongoing mutual feedback between them and the evaluator, and tailoring the evaluation and its reportage to their needs and preferences as much as possible without sacrificing scientific objectivity.

- Although the evaluation of program outcome is one of the first things that comes to mind when people think of program evaluation, other important foci of evaluation research address research questions that are concerned with planning new programs and monitoring their implementation.

• Evaluations of program outcome should strive to enhance causal inference by using the most internally valid experimental or quasi-experimental design possible.

• The assessment of efficiency asks whether program outcomes are being achieved at a reasonable cost and applies the principles of cost accounting to calculate the ratio of program benefits to costs. But deciding whether the benefits of a program justify its costs ultimately means going beyond purely economic considerations and involves making value judgments about humanistic benefits.

• Evaluating program outcome, or goal attainment, is complicated by ambiguities in determining the specific outcome indicators implied by official organizational goals, by the intentionally grandiose nature of some statements of organizational missions, and by the displacement of official goals by unofficial ones.

• Some programs have unsuccessful outcomes not because they are wrong in theory, but because they were never implemented as intended.

• Outcome evaluations ought to be supplemented by evaluations that monitor program implementation. Monitoring implementation can help resolve problems early on, keep agencies accountable, and identify the best ways to implement and maintain programs.

• The most common focus in evaluation for program planning is the assessment of need. Needs can be defined normatively or in terms of demand.

• Five approaches to needs assessment are (1) surveying key informants, (2) holding a community forum, (3) examining rates under treatment, (4) analyzing social indicators, and (5) conducting a direct survey of the community or target group. Each approach is imperfect but offers its own unique advantages and disadvantages. Ideally, a needs assessment will combine more than one approach.

• Evaluation proposals should include a logic model, which is a graphic picture depicting essential program components, their linkage to short-term process objectives, indicators of success in achieving short-term objectives, how those short-term objectives lead to long-term program outcomes, and indicators of success in achieving long-term outcomes.

• Different logic models might emphasize program theory, program activities, or program outcomes. Which logic model to choose will vary depending on program needs and what seems to be most helpful for those involved in program management and evaluation.

• Various qualitative methods can be useful in program evaluation. One such method useful in needs assessment involves the use of focus groups, which involve people in a guided discussion.

Review Questions and Exercises

1. Interview an administrator and some practitioners at a social welfare agency, perhaps the one in which you have your field placement. What evaluations, if any, have been conducted at the agency and with what outcomes? Were the findings used? Why or why not? Try to identify the stakeholders and their vested interests about those evaluations and findings. If no evaluation has ever been conducted, why not? Are politically or ideologically based resistances involved?

2. In the same or another agency, construct skeletal plans for evaluating program implementation and outcome. What resistances or logistical problems to the evaluation might be anticipated? How would the evaluation be useful to decision makers? What difficulties did you encounter in translating the agency's formal mission statement into observable indicators of outcome?

3. Consider a social problem that is currently receiving a lot of media attention in your community. Design a needs assessment study regarding that problem or a specific service you have in mind for alleviating it. Assume a data-collection budget of $5,000 and a six-month deadline for designing and completing the assessment.

4. Find a research article in a social work journal that describes a study conducted for the purpose of evaluating program outcome. See if you can identify the stakeholders in the research, and critique the article from the standpoint of whether it showed how it controlled for potential biases associated with vested interests. Although it is dated, a good example for critiquing purposes would be the study by Boone, Coulton, and Keller, "The Impact of Early and Comprehensive Social Work Services on Length of Stay," *Social Work in Health Care,* Fall 1981, pp. 1–9.

Internet Exercises

1. Using InfoTrac College Edition, enter the key words *program evaluation* to find two articles: one that reports a program evaluation study and one that discusses the politics of program evaluation. Write down the bibliographical reference information for each article. For the one reporting a study, briefly identify the strengths and weaknesses of that study. For the other article, summarize its main points about the politics of program evaluation.

2. Using a search engine such as Google or Yahoo!, enter the search term *program evaluation reports*. Click on a report that piques your interest. Write down the bibliographical reference information for the report, identify the type of evaluation it illustrates, and briefly identify its methodological strengths and weaknesses.

3. Using a search engine such as Google or Yahoo!, enter the search term *logic models*. Browse several of the websites that come up. Write down the most useful sites you examined and briefly summarize at least one thing at each site that you learned about logic models. Also briefly describe any differences you noticed in the examples of logic models displayed at the different sites.

Additional Readings

Alexander, Leslie B., and Phyllis Solomon (eds.). 2006. *The Research Process in the Human Services: Behind the Scenes*. Belmont, CA: Thomson Brooks/Cole. Here again we recommend this valuable book. It is a must-read for students who anticipate conducting program evaluation research in social work agencies. The chapters discuss efforts by esteemed researchers to implement different research methods and how those investigators grappled with the real-world agency challenges they encountered. The investigators discuss how they had to negotiate with agency stakeholders and modify their research designs in light of the obstacles they encountered. They also discuss the consequent strengths and weaknesses of the research methods they ultimately employed.

Evaluation Studies Review Annual. Sage Publications puts out a new review annually; each year has different editors and contains some of the best articles on program evaluation that have been published. This is an excellent source for examples of exemplary program evaluation studies, debates on methodological issues, and analyses of the political context of program evaluation. The contents vary in level of difficulty; some are more relevant to experienced program evaluators, but many are relevant to all students interested in this topic.

Mullen, Edward J., and Jennifer L. Magnabosco (eds.). 1997. *Outcomes Measurement in the Human Services: Cross-Cutting Issues and Methods*. Washington, DC: NASW Press. This is a compendium of 30 chapters written by different authors. It provides useful perspectives on emerging developments and issues in alternative ways to measure outcome in various types of human service settings. Included in these perspectives are critical analyses of the implications of managed care for outcome evaluations. You will also find references for some specific outcome measurement instruments that you might want to use.

Roberts, Michael C., and Linda K. Hurley. 1997. *Managing Managed Care*. New York: Plenum Press. This introduction to managed care focuses on psychological services for children and families. In addition to discussing the basics of managed care, problematic service implications, legal and ethical implications, and implications for practitioners who deal with managed care, it includes useful coverage of evaluation issues and techniques.

Shadish, William R., Thomas D. Cook, and Laura C. Leviton. 1991. *Foundations of Program Evaluation: Theories of Practice*. Newbury Park, CA: Sage. This unique book develops a typology of program evaluation models and a conceptual framework to critically analyze theories of program evaluation. Using that framework, it compares the work of seven of the field's foremost theorists and develops recommendations for a new theory of program evaluation.

PART 5

Data-Collection Methods with Large Sources of Data

In earlier chapters, we have discussed qualitative and quantitative approaches to inquiry and have indicated that social work research studies can have various purposes. The degree to which researchers need to build certain logical arrangements into their studies depends on which purposes guide their work.

For example, if we conduct a nomothetic, quantitative study seeking to describe with precision the characteristics of a population, then it is important to use logical procedures in selecting participants for our study that will maximize the likelihood that the chosen participants are representative of the population to whom we seek to generalize. It is also important that data are collected from those participants in a standardized manner that attempts to maximize objectivity. In contrast, if we are conducting a qualitative study seeking to explore a new area about which little is known, or perhaps seeking to develop a tentative, in-depth understanding of a phenomenon, procedures for selecting study participants, as well as the way data are obtained from them, can be more flexible. Trying to structure exploratory studies tightly in order to permit conclusive logical inferences and allow precise generalizations to be made from the findings would be not only unnecessary but also undesirable. An inflexible methodology in an exploratory or qualitative study would not permit researchers the latitude they need to probe creatively into unanticipated observations or into areas about which they lack the information needed to construct a design that would be logically conclusive.

Although the next three chapters will describe procedures used in both quantitative and qualitative studies, the emphasis will be on quantitative procedures geared toward obtaining findings from large sources of data. For example, we will look at how to select a sample of study participants and collect data from them that can be generalized with accuracy to a larger population. We will also look at how to obtain and analyze data that are already available.

Chapter 14, on sampling, deals with generalizability. As we'll see, it is possible for us to select a few people or things for observation and then apply what we observe to a much larger group of people or things. We'll also look briefly at some of the more flexible methods for obtaining study participants, but we'll save the more in-depth coverage of those more flexible methods for Chapter 17, which focuses exclusively on qualitative research methods.

Chapter 15 will describe survey research, which involves collecting data by asking people questions. Like Chapter 14, Chapter 15 will discuss some flexible methods for obtaining data but will emphasize methods that attempt to maximize the objectivity, accuracy, and generalizability of the information provided by respondents in self-administered questionnaires or through interviews.

Chapter 16 will examine methods for obtaining and analyzing data in available records. We'll look at both quantitative and qualitative methods for doing so, and we'll see that which method to use depends on the nature of the data and the purpose of our inquiry.

CHAPTER **14**

Sampling

What You'll Learn in This Chapter

Now we'll see how social scientists can select a few hundred or thousand people for study—and discover things that apply to hundreds of millions of people not studied.

INTRODUCTION

One of the most visible uses of survey sampling lies in the political polling that is subsequently tested by the election results. Although some people doubt the accuracy of sample surveys, others complain that political polls take all the suspense out of campaigns by foretelling the result.

Going into the 2000 presidential elections, however, pollsters generally agreed that the election was "too close to call." Robert Worcester has compiled the national polls completed during the two days before the election. Despite some variations, the overall picture they present is amazingly consistent (see Table 14-1).

As we now know, the election was so close that even the election officials were unable to declare the result unambiguously, and the matter had to be settled in the U.S. Supreme Court. That cliffhanger proved once and for all that the accuracy of modern polling doesn't have to take all the suspense out of elections.

Now, how many interviews do you suppose it took each of these pollsters to come within a couple of percentage points in estimating the behavior of approximately 100 million voters? Often fewer than 2,000! In this chapter, we're going to find out how social researchers can pull off such wizardry.

For another powerful illustration of the potency of sampling, look at this graphic portrayal of President George W. Bush's approval ratings prior to and following the September 11, 2001, terrorist attack on the United States (see Figure 14-1). The data reported by several different polling agencies describe the same pattern.

Sampling is the process of selecting observations. In this chapter, we'll see how **probability sampling** techniques—which involve random sampling—allow a researcher to make relatively few observations and generalize from those observations to a much wider population. We'll examine the requirements for generalizability.

As you'll discover, random selection is a precise, scientific procedure; there is nothing haphazard about it. Specific sampling techniques can allow us to determine or control the likelihood of specific individuals being selected for study. In the simplest example, flipping a coin to choose between two individuals gives each person exactly the same probability of selection: 50 percent. More complex techniques guarantee an equal probability of selection when substantial samples are selected from large populations.

Although probability sampling is precise, it's not always feasible to use probability sampling techniques. Consequently, social work research studies often use *non*probability sampling. Therefore, we'll take some time to examine a variety of nonprobability methods as well. Although not based on random selection, these methods have their own logic and can provide useful samples for social inquiry. We'll examine both the advantages and the shortcomings of such methods, and we'll see where they fit within the social scientific enterprise.

THE HISTORY OF SAMPLING

Sampling in social research has developed hand in hand with political polling, largely because political polling is one of the few opportunities social researchers have to discover the accuracy of their estimates. Election day gives them specific results, and they find out how well or how poorly they did.

President Alf Landon

You may have heard about the *Literary Digest* in connection with political polling. The *Digest* was a popular newsmagazine published in the United States between 1890 and 1938. In 1920, *Digest* editors mailed postcards to people in six states, asking them who they were planning to vote for in that year's presidential contest between Warren Harding and James Cox. Names were selected for the poll from telephone directories and automobile registration lists. Based on the postcards that people sent back, the *Digest* correctly predicted that Harding would be elected. In elections that followed, the *Literary Digest* expanded the size of its poll and made correct predictions in 1924, 1928, and 1932.

In 1936, the *Digest* conducted its most ambitious poll: Ten million ballots were sent to people listed in telephone directories and to automobile registration lists. More than 2 million responded, giving Republican contender Alf Landon a stunning 57 to 43 percent landslide over the incumbent, President Franklin Roosevelt. The editors modestly cautioned:

> We make no claim to infallibility. We did not coin the phrase "uncanny accuracy" which has been so freely applied to our Polls. We know only too well the limitations of every straw vote, however enormous the sample

Table 14-1 Election Eve Polls Reporting Percentage of Population Voting for U.S. Presidential Candidates, 2000

	PERCENTAGE			
POLL	GORE	BUSH	NADER	BUCHANAN*
11/5: Hotline [Polling Co/GSG]	43	51	4	1
11/5: Marist College	46	51	2	1
11/5: Fox [Opinion Dynamics]	47	47	3	2
11/5: *Newsweek* [PRSA]	46	49	6	0
11/5: NBC/*Wall St. Journal* [Hart/Teeter]	45	48	4	2
11/5: Pew	46	49	3	1
11/5: ICR	44	46	7	2
11/5: Harris	47	47	5	1
11/5: Harris (online)	47	47	4	2
11/5: ABC/*Washington Post* [TNSI]	46	49	3	1
11/6: IDB/CSM [TIPP]	47	49	4	0
11/6: CBS	48	47	4	1
11/6: Portrait of America [Rasmussen]	43	52	4	1
11/6: CNN/*USA Today* [Gallup]	46	48	4	1
11/6: Reuters/MSNBC [Zogby]	48	46	5	1
11/6: Voter.com [Lake/Goeas]	45	51	4	0
11/7: Election Results	**48**	**48**	**3**	**1**

Source: Adapted from Robert Worcester, *WAPOR Newsletter,* Winter 2001.

*"Don't knows" have been apportioned so the totals equal 100%. (Rounding error may result in totals of 99% or 101%.)

> gathered, however scientific the method. It would be a miracle if every State of the forty-eight behaved on Election Day exactly as forecast by the Poll.
>
> (LITERARY DIGEST, 1936A:6)

Two weeks later, the *Digest* editors knew the limitations of straw polls even better: Voters gave Roosevelt a third term in office by the largest landslide in history, with 61 percent of the vote. Landon won only 8 electoral votes to Roosevelt's 523. The editors were puzzled by their unfortunate turn of luck.

A part of the problem surely lay in the poll's 22 percent return rate. The editors asked:

> Why did only one in five voters in Chicago to whom the *Digest* sent ballots take the trouble to reply? And why was there a preponderance of Republicans in the one-fifth that did reply? . . . We were getting better cooperation in what we have always regarded as a public service from Republicans than we were getting from Democrats. Do Republicans live nearer to mailboxes? Do Democrats generally disapprove of straw polls?
>
> (LITERARY DIGEST, 1936B:7)

A part of the answer to these questions lay in the *sampling frame* used by the *Digest*: telephone subscribers and automobile owners. Such a sampling

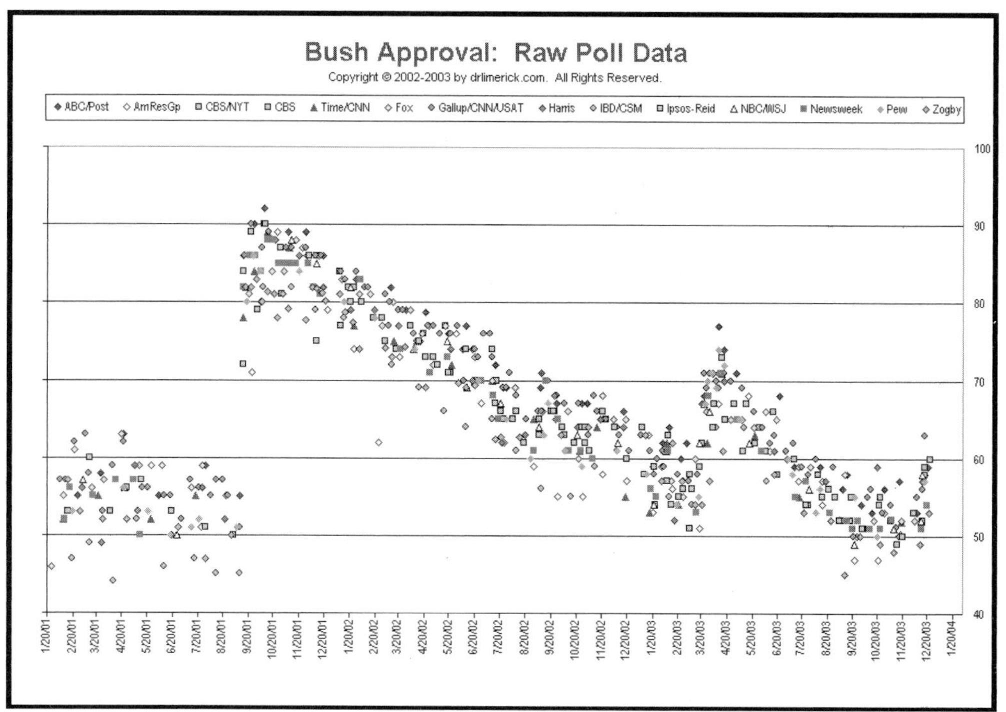

Figure 14-1 Bush Approval: Raw Poll Data

design selected a disproportionately wealthy sample, especially coming on the tail end of the worst economic depression in the nation's history. The sample effectively excluded poor people—who predominantly voted for Roosevelt's New Deal recovery program.

President Thomas E. Dewey

The 1936 election also saw the emergence of a young pollster whose name was to become synonymous with public opinion. In contrast to the *Literary Digest,* George Gallup correctly predicted that Roosevelt would beat Landon. Gallup's success in 1936 hinged on his use of quota sampling, which we'll have more to say about later in the chapter. For now, you need only know that **quota sampling** is based on a knowledge of the characteristics of the population being sampled: what proportions are men and women, and what proportions are of various incomes, ages, and so on. People are selected to match the population characteristics: the right number of poor, white, rural men; the right number of rich, black, urban women; and so on. The quotas are based on those variables that are most relevant to the study. By knowing the numbers of people with various incomes in the nation, Gallup selected his sample to ensure the right proportion of respondents at each income level.

Gallup and his American Institute of Public Opinion used quota sampling to good effect in 1936, 1940, and 1944—correctly picking presidential winners in each year. Then, in 1948, Gallup and most political pollsters suffered the embarrassment of picking New York Governor Thomas Dewey over incumbent President Harry Truman. Several factors accounted for the 1948 failure. First, most of the pollsters stopped polling in early October despite a steady trend toward Truman during the campaign. In addition, many voters were undecided throughout the campaign but went disproportionately for Truman when they stepped into the voting booth. More important for our present purposes, however, Gallup's failure rested on the unrepresentativeness of his samples.

Quota sampling—which had been effective in earlier years—was Gallup's undoing in 1948. This technique requires that the researcher know something about the total population (of voters in this instance). For national political polls, such information came primarily from census data. By 1948, however, a world war had already produced a massive movement from country to city and radically changed the character of the U.S. population as described by the 1940 census—whose data Gallup used. City dwellers, moreover, were more likely to vote Democratic, hence the overrepresentation of rural voters also underestimated the number of Democratic votes.

President John Kerry

Improvements made in political polling enabled election eve polls to accurately predict the outcomes of presidential elections in the decades that followed. Today, probability sampling is the primary method for selecting large, representative samples for social science research. Basically, this technique selects a "random sample" from a list that contains the names of everyone in the population of study interest. By and large, current probability sampling methods are far more accurate than earlier (nonprobability) sampling techniques.

The value of probability sampling techniques was underscored in the presidential election of 2004. Most election eve polls conducted with probability samples accurately predicted that George Bush would be reelected, beating John Kerry by a small margin. But on election day various news media and political groups attempted to get an early scoop on the outcome by conducting exit polls, asking voters whom they voted for as the voters left the voting sites. The exit polls did not use rigorous probability sampling. Instead, they were most likely to interview those voters who happened to be near and willing (and perhaps eager) to reveal whom they voted for. As it turned out, Kerry voters were more likely to participate in the exit polls than were Bush voters. Knowing the results of the exit polls, various conservative TV pundits looked gloomy throughout the day before the actual results came in, as they anticipated a Kerry presidency and speculated about what went wrong in the Bush campaign. Likewise, various Kerry supporters looked exuberant. Their moods reversed as the actual vote counts came in showing Bush leading in key states predicted in the Kerry column in the exit polls.

NONPROBABILITY SAMPLING

Despite its advantages, probability sampling is impossible or inappropriate in many of the research situations faced by social workers. Consequently, social work research is often conducted using *nonprobability sampling techniques.* Suppose you wanted to study homelessness: No list of all homeless individuals is available from which to draw a random sample, and you're not likely to create such a list yourself. Moreover, as we'll see, there are times when probability sampling wouldn't be appropriate even if it were possible. We'll begin now with a discussion of some nonprobability sampling techniques used in social work, and then we'll examine the logic and techniques of probability sampling. We'll examine four types of **nonprobability sampling** procedures in this section: (1) reliance on available subjects, (2) purposive or judgmental sampling, (3) quota sampling, and (4) snowball sampling. Then, we'll examine techniques for selecting *informants.*

Reliance on Available Subjects

Relying on available subjects—sometimes called **availability sampling,** *accidental sampling,* or *convenience sampling*—is a frequently used sampling method in social work because it is usually less expensive than other methods and because other methods may not be feasible for a particular type of study or population. As one indicator of the popularity of this sampling method in social work, some form of availability sampling was reported in the majority of research articles published from 1994 through 1999 in the journal *Social Work Research* (Monette et al., 2002).

Availability sampling can be an extremely risky sampling method. For example, stopping people at a street corner or some other location would be a risky way to assess public opinion about a social issue. Suppose the location was near a suburban shopping mall and you were polling opinions about proposals to change Social Security or health care policies for the elderly. Your findings would represent the opinions only of people with the characteristics of those passing the sampling point at the specified times. In all likelihood, elderly people and poor people would be underrepresented in your sample. Younger and more affluent people—folks who are likely to disagree with the older or poorer folks about the policies in question—are likely to be overrepresented in your sample. Even when the use of this method is justified on grounds of feasibility, the researcher must exercise great caution in generalizing from the resulting data and should alert readers to the risks associated with this method.

Suppose several students in a social work research course chose to do a team research project by interviewing students in the course about their attitudes about private practice. The representativeness of the sample would be dubious. Perhaps that research class was the only one whose scheduling did not conflict with an elective on psychotherapy, so students who aspired to become private practitioners of psychotherapy would be more likely to take that research class. It is virtually impossible to anticipate all of the possible biases that might render a particular accidental sample atypical.

University researchers frequently conduct surveys among the students enrolled in large lecture classes. The ease and inexpense of such a method explains its popularity, but it seldom produces data of any general value. Surveys may be useful to pretest a questionnaire, but such a sampling method should not be used for a study that purports to describe students as a whole.

Consider this report on the sampling design in an examination of knowledge and opinions about nutrition and cancer among medical students and family physicians:

> The fourth-year medical students of the University of Minnesota Medical School in Minneapolis comprised the student population in this study. The physician population consisted of all physicians attending a "Family Practice Review and Update" course sponsored by the University of Minnesota Department of Continuing Medical Education.
>
> (COOPER-STEPHENSON AND THEOLOGIDES, 1981:472)

After all is said and done, what will the results of this study represent? They do not meaningfully compare medical students and family physicians in the United States or even in Minnesota. Who were the physicians who attended the course? We can guess that they were probably more concerned about their continuing education than other physicians—and we can't say that for sure. Although such studies can be the source of useful insights, care must be taken not to overgeneralize from them.

Despite their risks, however, some studies using availability sampling can provide useful tentative findings, especially when no egregious forms of bias can be detected in the sampling approach taken and when care is taken not to overgeneralize their findings. Suppose, for example, that a local foundation is concerned about a dangerous new drug that recently caused several deaths among teens in the United States. It wants to find out how widely the drug is used among high school students in your Midwestern city. The foundation gives you a small grant to survey high school students in your city about whether and how much they've experimented with the new drug. There are 10 high schools in your city, but you manage to obtain permission to conduct your survey in only two of them. One of the high schools is in a poor neighborhood and has a relatively large proportion of African American students. The other high school is in a middle-class neighborhood and has relatively few ethnic minority students.

You conduct your survey by having teachers disseminate your questionnaire about drug use to all the students in each of the two schools. A cover letter asks each student to voluntarily participate in the study by completing the questionnaire and returning it anonymously in a sealed envelope into a large drop box located at the school. Suppose that 50 percent of the students at each school participate, and the other 50 percent do not. Suppose further that your findings indicate that exactly 30 percent of the survey respondents in each school report having experimented with the new drug, and that exactly 20 percent of them say they will continue using it on occasion.

What would be the value of your findings? In considering the answer to this question, we should note that yours is an availability sample because it does not include the 50 percent of those students who were either unwilling to answer questions about drug use or not motivated to take the time and effort to respond to your survey. Perhaps the students experimenting with drugs were more interested in a drug survey than those not into drugs and thus much more motivated to respond than the other students. Another possibility is that the students experimenting with drugs were more likely to be threatened by your survey and therefore *less* likely to respond. Moreover, not only did your survey not include the nonrespondents in the two schools, but also it did not include the other eight high schools that refused to participate in your survey. Perhaps drug experimentation in those eight schools is greater than or less than it is in the two schools that agreed to participate.

Should the community disregard your findings because they were based on an availability sample? In answering this question, you might note that even if all of the students in the two participating schools who had experimented with the new drug were included among your respondents, your findings would nevertheless mean that 15 percent of all the students in the two schools say they had experimented with the drug. (Thirty percent of *half* of the students is 15 percent of *all* the students.) Likewise, the findings would mean that 10 percent of all the students (half of the 20 percent) in those two schools say they will continue using it on occasion. Moreover, your findings would mean that these figures are minimum estimates because it is conceivable that students experimenting with the new drug were less likely than others to respond to your survey.

Assuming that the students were not lying about experimenting with the dangerous new drug, we think your findings would have significant value. We think your findings would spur the community to implement a program to educate students about the dangers of the new drug and to try in other ways to prevent its usage. Moreover, we think that the community would be concerned not only about the students in the two schools that participated in your survey, but also about the remaining schools. In fact, we think your findings would spur the remaining schools to replicate your survey among their students. Although your findings should not be generalized to other schools, they certainly would provide a tentative—but still valuable—basis for concern about the scope of the problem elsewhere, even including other cities.

Another type of research that typically relies on availability samples—and which has immense value to the social work profession and to the public—involves the use of experimental or quasi-experimental designs in evaluating the effectiveness of social work practice or programs, as discussed in Chapter 11. When you want to evaluate whether or how much your services are helping a particular client or group of clients, it's not like asking people at random to respond to a poll predicting the outcome of a presidential election. You usually must rely on an availability sample of clients who need your services and come to your agency for those services. That's one of the reasons that experimental designs are often characterized as having a relatively low degree of external validity.

Purposive or Judgmental Sampling

Sometimes you may appropriately select your sample on the basis of your own knowledge of the population, its elements, and the nature of your research aims: in short, based on your judgment and the purpose of the study. Especially in the initial design of a questionnaire, you might wish to select the widest variety of respondents to test the broad applicability of questions. Although the study findings would not represent any meaningful population, the test run might effectively uncover any peculiar defects in your questionnaire. This situation would be considered a pretest, however, rather than a final study.

In some instances, you may wish to study a small subset of a larger population in which many members of the subset are easily identified, but enumerating all of them would be nearly impossible. For example, you might want to study the homeless. Many homeless people might be visible in certain areas of town, such as near shelters, a Salvation Army facility, or other social welfare facilities. But it would not be feasible to define and sample all of them. In studying all or a sample of the most visible homeless individuals, you might collect data sufficient for your purposes, particularly if your study is exploratory. Thus, you might ask personnel in those facilities to use their judgment in handpicking cases that they think represent those segments of the homeless population with which they are familiar.

Suppose you are writing a grant proposal to secure funding for new social services to be targeted to the homeless, and the funding source requires that your proposal include an assessment of the social service needs of the homeless in your community. Suppose, given your agency's meager resources and the nearness of the proposal submission deadline, you have neither the time nor money to conduct a community-wide survey of the homeless using probability sampling. One option would be to select a **purposive,** or **judgmental, sample** of community leaders, experts, and professionals known for their work with and expertise on the problem of homelessness in your locality. You could use your knowledge of the community to handpick key people who, in your judgment, best represent the range of persons who would best know the needs of the homeless in your community and then survey them as to their estimates of those needs.

Sometimes **purposive sampling** is used to select not typical cases but atypical ones. This is commonly done when we seek to compare opposite extremes of a phenomenon in order to generate hypotheses about it. For example, in seeking to generate hypotheses about the etiology of mental illness, we might want to study certain children of mentally ill parents, contrasting the life experiences and other attributes of children who became diagnosably mentally ill and those who became extraordinarily healthy. Or, in seeking to gain insights into the attributes of effective practice, we might handpick for intensive study those cases with whom practitioners felt extremely successful and those cases with whom they felt extremely ineffectual.

Researchers conducting qualitative studies are often particularly interested in studying deviant cases—cases that don't fit into fairly regular patterns of attitudes and behaviors—in order to improve their understanding of the more regular pattern. This is called **deviant case sampling,** and it is another form of purposive sampling. For example, you might gain important tentative insights into the processes of a support group for battered women by interviewing women who remain relatively quiet during support group meetings or by interviewing group members who only rarely attend the meetings. We will discuss deviant case sampling further in Chapter 17, on qualitative research methods.

Quota Sampling

Quota sampling, mentioned earlier, is the method that helped George Gallup avoid disaster in 1936—and set up the disaster of 1948. Like probability sampling, quota sampling addresses the issue of representativeness, although the two methods approach the issue quite differently.

Quota sampling begins with a matrix that describes the target population's characteristics: what proportion of the population is male and female, for example; and, for each sex, what proportions fall into various age categories, educational levels, ethnic groups, and so forth. In establishing a national quota sample, we would need to know what proportion of the national population is urban, Eastern, male, under 25, white, working class, and the like, and all the other permutations of such a matrix.

Once we have created such a matrix and assigned a relative proportion to each cell in the matrix, we would collect data from people who had all of the characteristics of a given cell. All the people in a given cell are then assigned a weight that is appropriate to their portion of the total population (a process called **weighting**). When all of the sample elements are so weighted, the overall data should provide a reasonable representation of the total population.

Quota sampling has several inherent problems. First, the quota frame (the proportions that different cells represent) must be accurate, and getting up-to-date information for this purpose is often difficult. The Gallup failure to predict Truman as the presidential victor in 1948 was due partly to this problem. Second, biases may exist in the selection of sample elements within a given cell—even though its proportion of the population is accurately estimated. An interviewer instructed to interview five persons meeting a given, complex set of characteristics may still avoid people living at the top of seven-story walkups, occupying particularly rundown homes, or owning vicious dogs. Researchers using quota sampling should be aware of potential problems like this and work to prevent them. For example, they should do all they can to obtain an accurate count of the number and characteristics of individuals who make up a particular cell. They should make sure that interviewers are properly trained and supervised to minimize the chances that the interviewers will violate the sampling protocol in order to skip certain undesirable interviews. But there is no guarantee that all potential problems like these will be anticipated or prevented. Therefore, you would be advised to treat quota sampling warily if your purpose is statistical description.

Snowball Sampling

Another nonprobability sampling technique, one that some researchers consider a form of accidental sampling, is called **snowball sampling.** Snowball sampling is appropriate when the members of a special population are difficult to locate. It might be appropriate, for example, to find a sample of homeless individuals, migrant workers, or undocumented immigrants. This procedure is implemented by collecting data on the few members of the target population whom one is able to locate, and then asking those individuals to provide the information needed to locate other members of that population they happen to know. The term *snowball* refers to the process of accumulation as each located subject suggests other subjects. This sampling procedure also results in samples that have questionable representativeness, so it is used primarily for exploratory purposes. Nevertheless, snowball sampling is an important and commonly used technique in qualitative research (as we'll discuss in Chapter 17), and in research on minority and oppressed populations it is often necessary (as we mentioned in Chapter 5).

SELECTING INFORMANTS IN QUALITATIVE RESEARCH

When qualitative research involves the researcher's attempt to understand some social setting—a juvenile gang or local neighborhood, for example—much of that understanding will come from a collaboration with one or more members of the group being studied. Whereas social researchers speak of "respondents" as people who provide information about themselves and thus allow the researcher to construct a composite picture of the group those respondents represent, **informants** are members of the group or other people knowledgeable about it who are willing to talk about the group per se.

Potential informants should be evaluated on several criteria. Are they in positions of regular interaction with other members of the group or setting, for example, or are they isolated? Is their information fairly limited to their specific roles or does it cover many aspects of the group or setting? These and other criteria affect how useful different potential informants might be.

Usually, we want to select informants who are somewhat typical of the groups we are studying; otherwise their observations and opinions may be misleading. Interviewing administrators alone will not give us a well-rounded view of how a welfare program is working, for example. Along the same lines, we would get a biased view of homelessness if we only interviewed those homeless individuals staying in shelters, or those who speak English, and not those who refuse to use shelters or who don't speak English.

Because of their willingness to work with outside investigators, it is probably inevitable that informants will be somewhat "marginal" or atypical within their group. Sometimes, however, you will only learn about their marginality in the course of your research. The marginal status of informants may not only bias the view you get but also limit their access (and hence yours) to the different sectors of the community you wish to study.

These comments should provide some sense of the concerns involved in selecting people to observe and interview in qualitative research projects. Let's shift gears now and look at sampling in large-scale surveys—sampling that aims to produce precise, statistical descriptions of large populations.

THE LOGIC OF PROBABILITY SAMPLING

If all members of a population were identical in all respects—demographic characteristics, attitudes, experiences, behaviors, and so on—we wouldn't need careful sampling procedures. Any sample would be sufficient. In this extreme case of homogeneity, in fact, one case would be enough as a sample to study the whole population's characteristics.

Of course, the human beings who compose any real population are quite heterogeneous, varying in many ways from one another. Figure 14-2 shows a simplified heterogeneous population: The 100 members of this small population differ by sex and race. We'll use

Figure 14-2 A Sample of Convenience: Easy but Not Representative

this hypothetical micropopulation to illustrate various aspects of sampling through the chapter.

If a sample of individuals from a population is to provide useful descriptions of the total population, then it must contain essentially the same variations that exist in the population. This is not as simple as it might seem, however.

Let's look at some of the ways in which researchers might go astray. This will help us see how probability sampling provides an efficient method for selecting a sample that should adequately reflect variations in the population.

Conscious and Unconscious Sampling Bias

At first glance, it may look as though sampling is a pretty straightforward matter. To select a sample of 100 university students, you might simply go to campus and interview the first 100 students you find walking around campus. This kind of sampling method is often used by untrained researchers, but it has serious problems.

Figure 14-2 shows what can happen when you simply select people who are convenient for study. Although women are only 50 percent of our micropopulation, those closest to the researcher (in the upper-right corner) happen to be 70 percent women; and although the population is 12 percent African American, not one black individual was selected into the sample.

Beyond the risks inherent in simply studying people who are convenient, we find other potential problems. To begin, our own personal leanings or biases may affect the sample selected in this manner; hence the sample would not truly represent the student population. Suppose you're intimidated by students who look particularly "cool," feeling they might ridicule your research effort. You might consciously or unconsciously avoid interviewing such people. Or you might feel that the attitudes of "super-straight-looking" students would be irrelevant to your research purposes, and you avoid interviewing them.

Even if you sought to interview a "balanced" group of students, you wouldn't know the exact proportions of different types of students who make up such a balance, and you wouldn't always be able to identify the different types just by watching them walk by.

Even if you made a conscientious effort to interview every 10th student who entered the university library, you could not be sure of getting a representative sample, because different types of students visit the library with different frequencies. Your sample would overrepresent students who visit the library more often.

When we speak of "bias" in connection with sampling, this simply means those selected are not "typical" or "representative" of the larger populations from which they have been chosen. This kind of bias is virtually inevitable when people are picked by a seat-of-the-pants approach.

Similarly, public-opinion call-in polls—in which radio or TV stations or newspapers ask people to call specified telephone numbers or use the Internet to register their opinions—cannot be trusted to represent general populations. At the very least, not everyone in the population will be aware of the poll or have Internet access. This problem also invalidates polls by magazines and newspapers that publish coupons for readers to complete and return. Even among readers or viewers who are aware of such polls, not all of them will express opinions, especially if it will cost a stamp, an envelope, or a telephone charge. The possibilities for inadvertent sampling bias are endless and not always obvious. Fortunately techniques are available that let us avoid bias.

Representativeness and Probability of Selection

Although the term **representativeness** has no precise, scientific meaning, its commonsense meaning makes it a useful concept in our discussion of sampling. As we'll use the term here, a sample will be representative of its population if the sample's aggregate characteristics closely approximate those same aggregate characteristics in the population. (Samples need not be representative in all respects; representativeness is limited to those characteristics that are relevant to the substantive interests of the study, although you may not know which ones are relevant.) If the population, for example, contains 50 percent women, then a representative sample would also contain "close to" 50 percent women.

A basic principle of probability sampling is that a sample will be representative of its population if all members of that population have an equal chance of being selected in the sample. (We'll see shortly that the size of the sample selected also affects the degree of representativeness.) Samples that have this quality are often labeled **EPSEM** samples (**equal probability of selection method**). We'll discuss variations of this principle later, but it is primary and forms the basis of probability sampling.

Moving beyond this basic principle, we must realize that samples—even carefully selected EPSEM samples—seldom, if ever, perfectly represent the populations from which they are drawn. Nevertheless, probability sampling offers two special advantages.

First, probability samples, even if never perfectly representative, are typically more representative than other types of samples because the biases discussed in the preceding section are avoided. In practice, there is a greater likelihood that a probability sample will be representative of the population from which it is drawn than will a nonprobability sample.

Second, and more important, probability theory permits us to estimate the sample's accuracy or representativeness. Conceivably, an uninformed researcher might, through wholly haphazard means, select a sample that nearly perfectly represents the larger population. The odds are against doing so, however, and we would be unable to estimate the likelihood that he or she has achieved representativeness. The probability sampler, on the other hand, can provide an accurate estimate of success or failure.

We've said that probability sampling ensures that samples are representative of the population we wish to study. As we'll see in a moment, probability sampling rests on the use of a random selection procedure. To develop this idea, though, we need to give more precise meaning to two important terms: *element* and *population*.

An **element** is that unit about which information is collected and that provides the basis of analysis. Typically, in survey research, elements are people or certain types of people. However, other kinds of units can constitute the elements for social work research—for example, families, social clubs, or corporations might be the elements of a study. (Note: Elements and units of analysis are often the same in a given study, though the former refers to sample selection and the latter to data analysis.)

Up to now we've used the term *population* to mean the group or collection that we're interested in generalizing about. More formally, **population** is the theoretically specified aggregation of study elements. Whereas the vague term Americans might be the target for a study, the delineation of the population would include the definition of the element Americans (for example, citizenship, residence) and the time referent for the study (Americans as of when?). Translating the abstract "adult New Yorkers" into a workable population would require a specification of the age that defines adult and the boundaries of New York. Specifying the term "college student" would include a consideration of full- and part-time students, degree and nondegree candidates, and undergraduate and graduate students, among other issues.

A **study population** is that aggregation of elements from which the sample is actually selected. As a practical matter, you are seldom in a position to guarantee that every element that meets established theoretical definitions actually has a chance of being selected in the sample. Even where lists of elements exist for sampling purposes, the lists are usually somewhat incomplete. Some students are always omitted, inadvertently, from student rosters. Some telephone subscribers request that their names and numbers be unlisted. Thus, the study population from which the sample is taken is likely to be only a part of the population of interest.

Researchers often decide to limit their study populations more severely than indicated in the preceding examples. National polling firms may limit their national samples to the 48 contiguous states, omitting Alaska and Hawaii for practical reasons. A researcher who wishes to sample social work practitioners may limit the study population to those whose names appear on the membership list of the National Association of Social Workers or on a list of those licensed by a particular state. (In a sense, we might say that these researchers have redefined their universes and populations, in which case they must make the revisions clear to their readers.)

Random Selection

With these definitions in hand, we can define the ultimate purpose of sampling: to select a set of elements from a population in such a way that descriptions of those elements accurately portray the total population from which the elements are selected. Probability sampling enhances the likelihood of accomplishing this aim and also provides methods for estimating the degree of probable success.

Random selection is the key to this process. In **random selection,** each element has an equal chance of selection that is independent of any other event in the selection process. Flipping a coin is the most frequently cited example: Provided that the coin is perfect (that is, not biased in terms of coming up heads or tails), the "selection" of a head or a tail is independent of previous selections of heads or tails. No matter how many heads turn up in a row, the chance that the next flip will produce "heads" is exactly 50:50. Rolling a perfect set of dice is another example.

Such images of random selection, although useful, seldom apply directly to sampling methods in social research. More typically, social researchers use tables of random numbers or computer programs that provide a random selection of sampling units. A **sampling unit** is that element or set of elements considered for selection in some stage of sampling. In Chapter 15, on survey research, we'll see how computers are used to select random telephone numbers for interviewing, a technique called *random-digit dialing.*

The reasons for using random selection methods are twofold. First, this procedure serves as a check on conscious or unconscious bias on the part of the researcher. The researcher who selects cases on an intuitive basis might very well select cases that would support his or her research expectations or hypotheses. Random selection erases this danger. More important, random selection offers access to the body of probability theory, which provides the basis for estimating the characteristics of the population as well as estimates of the accuracy of samples.

CAN SOME RANDOMLY SELECTED SAMPLES BE BIASED?

When discussing probability sampling, students commonly make two mistakes. One mistake is to equate the population with any list of elements from which a sample is selected. Another is to assume that if the intended sample has been randomly selected then the sample is random regardless of the nonprobability reasons why many randomly selected elements refuse to participate in the ultimate sample. Both of these mistakes involve the concept of *sampling frames.* Before examining these mistakes further, let's first define the term *sampling frame* and distinguish it from the term *population.*

Sampling Frames and Populations

Simply put, a **sampling frame** is the list or quasi-list of elements from which a sample is selected. If a sample of students is selected from a student roster, the roster is the sampling frame. If the primary sampling unit for a complex population sample is the census block, the list of census blocks composes the sampling frame—in the form of a printed booklet, a magnetic tape file, or some other computerized record. Here are some reports of sampling frames appearing in research journals:

> The data for this research were obtained from a random sample of *parents of children in the third grade in public and parochial schools in Yakima County, Washington.*
>
> (Petersen and Maynard, 1981:92)

> The sample at Time 1 consisted of 160 names drawn randomly from the *telephone directory of Lubbock, Texas.*
>
> (Tan, 1980:242)

> The data reported in this paper . . . were gathered from a probability sample of *adults aged 18 and over residing in households in the 48 contiguous United States.* Personal interviews with 1,914 respondents were conducted by the Survey Research Center of the University of Michigan during the fall of 1975.
>
> (Jackman and Senter, 1980:345)

In each example, we've italicized the actual sampling frames.

Properly drawn samples provide information appropriate for describing the population of elements composing the sampling frame—nothing more. It is necessary to make this point in view of the all-too-common tendency for researchers to select samples from a given sampling frame and then make assertions about a population similar to, but not identical to, the study population defined by the sampling frame.

For an example of an overgeneralized sampling frame, take a look at this report, which discusses the drugs most frequently prescribed by American physicians:

> Information on prescription drug sales is not easy to obtain. But Rinaldo V. DeNuzzo, a professor of pharmacy at the Albany College of Pharmacy, Union University, Albany, NY, has been tracking prescription drug sales for 25 years by polling nearby drugstores. He publishes the results in an industry trade magazine, MM&M. DeNuzzo's latest survey, covering 1980, is based on reports from 66 pharmacies in 48 communities in New York and New Jersey. Unless there is something peculiar about that part of the country, his findings can be taken as representative of what happens across the country.
>
> (Moskowitz, 1981:33)

The main thing that should strike you is the casual comment about whether there is anything peculiar about New York and New Jersey. There is. The lifestyle in these two states is hardly typical of the other 48. We cannot assume that residents in these large, urbanized, Eastern seaboard states necessarily have the same drug-use patterns as residents of Mississippi, Utah, New Mexico, and Vermont.

Does the survey even represent prescription patterns in New York and New Jersey? To determine that, we would have to know something about the manner in which the 48 communities and the 66 pharmacies were selected. We should be wary in this regard, in view of the reference to "polling nearby drugstores." As we'll see, there are several methods for selecting samples that ensure representativeness, and unless they are used, we should not generalize from the study findings.

A sampling frame, then, must be consonant with the population we wish to study. In the simplest sample design, the sampling frame is a list of the elements composing the study population. In practice, though, existing sampling frames often define the study population rather than the other way around. In other words, we often begin with a population in mind for our study; then we search for possible sampling frames. Having examined and evaluated the frames available for our use, we decide which frame presents a study population most appropriate to our needs.

Studies of organizations are often the simplest from a sampling standpoint because organizations typically have membership lists. In such cases, the list of members constitutes an excellent sampling frame. If a random sample is selected from a membership list, the data collected from that sample may be taken as representative of all members—if all members are included in the list.

Populations that can be sampled from good organizational lists include elementary school, high school, and university students and faculty; church members; factory workers; fraternity or sorority members; members of social, service, or political clubs; and members of professional associations.

The preceding comments apply primarily to local organizations. Often statewide or national organizations do not have a single, easily available membership list. There is, for example, no single list of Episcopalian church members. However, a slightly more complex sample design could take advantage of local church membership lists by first sampling churches and then subsampling the membership lists of those churches selected. (More about that later.)

Other lists of individuals may be especially relevant to the research needs of a particular study. Government agencies maintain lists of registered voters, for example, that might be used if you wanted to conduct a pre-election poll or an in-depth examination of voting behavior—but you must ensure that the list is up-to-date. Similar lists contain the names of automobile owners, welfare recipients, taxpayers, business permit holders, licensed professionals, and so forth. Although it may be difficult to gain access to some of these lists, they provide excellent sampling frames for specialized research purposes.

Realizing that the sampling elements in a study need not be individual persons, we may note that the lists of other types of elements also exist: universities, businesses of various types, cities, academic journals, newspapers, unions, political clubs, professional associations, and so forth.

Telephone directories are frequently used for "quick and dirty" public opinion polls. Undeniably they are easy and inexpensive to use, and that is no doubt the reason for their popularity. And, if you want to make assertions about telephone subscribers, the directory is a fairly good sampling frame. (Realize, of course, that a given directory will not include new subscribers or those who have requested unlisted numbers. Sampling is further complicated by the inclusion in directories of nonresidential listings.) Unfortunately, telephone directories are all too often taken to be a listing of a city's population or of its voters. There are many defects in this reasoning, but the chief one involves a social-class bias. Poor people are less likely to have telephones; more affluent people may have more than one line. A telephone directory sample, therefore, is likely to have a middle- or upper-class bias.

The class bias inherent in telephone directory samples is often hidden. Pre-election polls conducted in this fashion are sometimes quite accurate, perhaps because of the class bias evident in voting itself: Poor people are less likely to vote. Frequently, then, these two biases nearly coincide, and the results of a telephone poll may come very close to the final election outcome. Unhappily, the pollster never knows for sure until after the election. And sometimes, as in the case of the 1936 *Literary Digest* poll, you may discover that the voters have not acted according to the expected class biases. The ultimate disadvantage of this method, then, is the researcher's inability to estimate the degree of error to be expected in the sample findings.

Street directories and tax maps are often used for easily obtained samples, but they may also suffer from incompleteness and possible bias. For example, in strictly zoned urban regions, illegal housing units are unlikely to appear on official records. As a result, such units would have no chance for selection, and sample findings could not be representative of those units, which are often poorer and more crowded than the average.

Most of the above comments apply to the United States; the situation is quite different in some other countries. In Japan, for example, the government maintains quite accurate population registration lists. Moreover, citizens are required by law to keep their information up-to-date, as it may change by a residential move or births and deaths in the household. As a consequence, it is possible to select *simple random samples* of the Japanese population, by the process described later in this chapter. Such a registration list in the United States would conflict directly with American norms regarding individual privacy.

Nonresponse Bias

We have just discussed errors in overgeneralization that can occur when sampling frames are not consonant with the population to which we seek to generalize. As we mentioned earlier, another common error occurs when a substantial proportion of people in the randomly selected sample choose not to participate in the study.

Suppose, for example, you want to survey the social workers in your state regarding their views of evidence-based practice and how often they engage in it. You plan to conduct the survey by mailing (through the postal service) each social worker a questionnaire for them to complete and return in the stamped, self-addressed envelope that you enclose with the questionnaire. Your first step would be to obtain a list of all the social workers and their addresses. Let's assume that the only list available to you is the membership roster of your state's chapter of NASW. Let's further suppose that there are 10,000 social worker names on that list and that your limited research budget has only $1,000 for postage. Obviously, you cannot afford to survey all 10,000 members. Let's say you can afford the postage for a sample of 500 social workers, which you randomly select from the list of 10,000.

Your sampling frame is the list of 10,000 names, and you *hope* your sample will be the 500 social workers whose names you randomly selected from that list. We emphasize the word *hope* because many of the 500 randomly selected social workers may choose not to respond to your survey. Suppose only 200 respond. That would not be a probability sample. Why not? Because the reasons for inclusion ultimately were not random. Perhaps most of the 200 who responded are familiar with evidence-based practice and engage in it frequently. Perhaps most of the 300 who did not respond chose not to because they either never heard of evidence-based practice, don't care about it, or dislike it. Perhaps many of them don't engage in it and feel embarrassed about admitting that. Clearly then, despite choosing the 500 names randomly, your 200 respondents would comprise a nonprobability sample—moreover, a quite biased and unrepresentative one!

Although you used random procedures to generate what you hoped would be your sample, what you really wound up with was a nonprobability sample of 200 available subjects—those who for whatever reasons took the trouble to participate. It also bears noting that even if you had 100 percent participation from all 500 social workers, you might have had some bias in your sample. That's because many social workers in your state might not be current members of NASW. This refers back to our discussion above, regarding the distinction between sampling frames and populations. (We used the term *sampling frame* in this illustration, and not *study population,* because your aim is to generalize to all social workers in your state, not just NASW members.)

In light of the refusal to participate by some randomly selected individuals, many samples that are considered to be random may not be from a technically pure standpoint. That is, when one or more randomly selected individuals opt not to participate in a study, the randomly selected sample only represents those elements in the population who agree to participate. There might be important differences between those who so choose and those who refuse regarding the variables being assessed. However, when the proportion of the selected elements who refuse to participate is trivial, it is usually reasonable—from a practical standpoint—to call the participants a probability sample. Suppose, for example, that 490 (98%) of the 500 social workers respond to your survey, and that 343 (70%) of them express favorable views about evidence-based practice. Even if all 10 of the nonrespondents dislike evidence-based practice, your estimate of the proportion favoring evidence-based practice would be off by less than 2 percentage points. That is, the true percentage favoring evidence-based practice out of the 500 would be 343 divided by 500, or 68.6 percent—only 1.4 percentage points less than your finding of 70 percent. But this raises the question of where the cutoff point is for deeming the refusal rate to be too high to still interpret your findings as if they were based on probability sampling. There is no scientific or mathematical answer to this question. Our best guidance on this is to examine whether the proportion of refusals is large enough that their numbers could have changed your findings to a meaningful extent had they participated and been unlike the actual participants in regard to the variables of your study.

Review of Populations and Sampling Frames

Surprisingly little attention has been given to the issues of populations and sampling frames in social research literature. With this in mind, we've devoted special attention to them here. To further emphasize the point, here is a summary of the main guidelines to remember:

1. Findings based on a sample can be taken as representative only of the aggregation of elements that compose the sampling frame.

2. Often, sampling frames do not truly include all the elements that their names might imply. Omissions are almost inevitable. Thus a first concern of the researcher must be to assess the extent of the omissions and to correct them if possible. (Realize, of course, that the researcher may feel he or she can safely ignore a small number of omissions that cannot easily be corrected.)

3. Even to generalize to the population composing the sampling frame, it is necessary for all elements to have equal representation in the frame: Typically, each element should appear only once. Elements that appear more than once will have a greater probability of selection, and the sample will, overall, overrepresent those elements.

SAMPLE SIZE AND SAMPLING ERROR

Probability theory is a branch of statistics that provides the basis for estimating the parameters of a population. A **parameter** is the summary description of a given variable in a population. The mean income of all families in a city is a parameter; so is the age distribution of the city's population. When researchers generalize from a sample, they're using sample observations to estimate population parameters. Probability theory enables them both to make these estimates and to arrive at a judgment of how likely it is that the estimates will accurately represent the actual parameters in the population. So, for example, probability theory allows pollsters to infer from a sample of 2,000 voters how a population of 100 million voters is likely to vote—and to specify exactly what the probable margin of error in the estimates is.

Estimating the Margin of Sampling Error

Although some complex statistical concepts and formulas are required to specify the exact probable margin of error in probability sampling, we can understand the logic involved without getting into the heavy math. (The mathematical material can be found in Appendix B.) Let's start by imagining that we are tossing a coin to see if it is more likely to come up heads or tails. Suppose we flip it twice and it comes up heads both times. We would not conclude that the coin always comes up heads or even that it is predisposed to come up heads. We don't need math to recognize that a coin that comes up heads half the time and tails half the time easily can come up heads twice in a row or tails twice in a row. If, based on our two coin flips, we concluded that the coin comes up heads 100 percent of the time, our estimate of the population of flips of that coin would be off by 50 percentage points. That is, our estimate of 100 percent heads and zero percent tails would be 50 percentage points away from the true population parameter of 50 percent heads and 50 percent tails. The difference between the true population parameter (50%) and our estimate (100%) is called **sampling error.** Thus, our sampling error would be 50 percentage points.

Now imagine that instead of tossing the coin twice we tossed it 20 times. The likelihood that we would get 100 percent heads (or 100 percent tails) would be quite tiny. Thus, because we increased our sample size, we reduced the likelihood that we would have a sampling error of 50 percentage points. And the larger the number of coin tosses, the lower that likelihood becomes. Thus, as sample size increases, the likelihood of random error in sampling decreases. Conversely, the larger the sample size, the greater the likelihood that our estimate will be close to the true population parameter.

To further illustrate this logic, suppose we had the name of every person in the United States written on a tiny piece of paper, had all the pieces crumpled up so that the names were not visible, and put them all in an enormous container. Suppose we shook up the container vigorously and then with eyes closed drew names out of the container at random. Suppose the first two names we drew were female, and we therefore concluded that the percentage of females in the population is 100 percent. Just like with the coins, our sampling error would be close to 50 percentage points. The proportion of females in the United States population is 50.8 percent according to the U.S. Census Bureau's *Statistical Abstract* (2006). Next, suppose we had randomly drawn 1,000 slips of paper. The odds are quite high that we would get very close to having 508 (50.8 percent) females and 492 (49.2 percent) males. It probably wouldn't be exactly those numbers. We might, for example, get 518 (51.8 percent) females and 482 (48.2 percent) males. If we did, our sampling error would be one percentage point.

When political polls predict the outcomes of presidential elections, the same logic is involved, and that's why their predictions quite often are so accurate. If you've noticed the results of such polls in the newspaper or on TV, you may recall that they come with an estimate of the margin of sampling error. For example, a poll predicting that the vote will be 51 percent for candidate x and 49 percent for candidate y might say that the margin of error is plus or minus 3 percent. That means that there is a very high probability that the true population parameters are between 48 percent and 54 percent for candidate x and 46 percent and 52 percent for candidate y. (That is, 3 percent is added to and subtracted from the estimates for each candidate to identify the range of likely outcomes in the larger population.) That is why sometimes news reporters will characterize such poll results as a "statistical dead heat." In other words, if the margin of sampling error is 3 percent, but the poll results show only a two percent difference between the two candidates, then it is quite conceivable that the candidate with 49 percent in the poll might really be favored by 50 percent or more people in the larger population, and the candidate with 51 percent in the poll might really be favored by 50 percent or fewer people in the population.

The same logic applies when we are trying to generalize from a sample to a population about other attributes, such as age, income, ethnicity, educational level, and so on. If a sufficiently large sample is selected randomly, we can estimate those parameters with a small margin of sampling error. When we say "sufficiently large" we do not mean large in the sense of percentage of the population. Accurate presidential polls are conducted with less than 2,000 people, much less than 1 percent of the population of voters.

Probability theory gives us a formula for estimating how closely sample statistics are clustered around a true population value. To put it another way, probability theory enables us to estimate the degree of sampling error to be expected for a given sample design. (This statistical formula is presented in Appendix B.) The formula enables us to be confident (at some level) of being within a certain range of a population parameter, and to estimate the expected degree of error on the basis of one sample drawn from a population. Using this formula, for example, a presidential pollster might report that she is 95 percent confident that between 48 and 54 percent of the population of voters will vote for candidate x.

The formula also provides a basis for determining the appropriate sample size for a study. Once you have decided on the degree of sampling error you can tolerate, you'll be able to calculate the number of cases needed in your sample. Thus, for example, if a pollster assumes that the election will be close, and wants to be 95 percent confident of predicting the election results within plus or minus 5 percentage points of the actual votes, then she'll need to select a sample of at least 400 people. Although you may not use the formula in any of your own research, Table 14-2 is a convenient guide for estimating the sample size you'll need for the degree of sampling error you can tolerate. It also illustrates how, as sample sizes reach a certain point, further increases in sample size would yield diminishing returns in reducing sampling error and perhaps not be worth the additional data-collection costs.

To use Table 14-2, find the intersection between the sample size and the approximate percentage distribution that you anticipate in the population. For example, suppose we assume that roughly 50 percent of the population intends to vote for candidate x, and 50 percent intend to vote for candidate y. Table 14-2 shows that increasing the sample size from 100 to 1100 will reduce the estimated sampling error by 7 percentage points. But increasing it from 1100 to 2000 will reduce it by only another eight-tenths of 1 point.

This, then, is the basic logic of probability sampling. Random selection permits the researcher to link findings from a sample to the body of probability theory so as to estimate the accuracy of those findings. The

Table 14-2 Estimated Sampling Error

SAMPLE SIZE	ESTIMATED PERCENTAGE DISTRIBUTION				
	50/50	60/40	70/30	80/20	90/10
100	10	9.8	9.2	8	6
200	7.1	6.9	6.5	5.7	4.2
300	5.8	5.7	5.3	4.6	3.5
400	5	4.9	4.6	4	3
500	4.5	4.4	4.1	3.6	2.7
600	4.1	4	3.7	3.3	2.4
700	3.8	3.7	3.5	3	2.3
800	3.5	3.5	3.2	2.8	2.1
900	3.3	3.3	3.1	2.7	2
1000	3.2	3.1	2.9	2.5	1.9
1100	3	3	2.8	2.4	1.8
1200	2.9	2.8	2.6	2.3	1.7
1300	2.8	2.7	2.5	2.2	1.7
1400	2.7	2.6	2.4	2.1	1.6
1500	2.6	2.5	2.4	2.1	1.5
1600	2.5	2.4	2.3	2	1.5
1700	2.4	2.4	2.2	1.9	1.5
1800	2.4	2.3	2.2	1.9	1.4
1900	2.3	2.2	2.1	1.8	1.4
2000	2.2	2.2	2	1.8	1.3

researcher may report that he or she is x percent confident that the population parameter is between two specific values.

Other Considerations in Determining Sample Size

The importance of the foregoing material notwithstanding, decisions about sample size in social work research rarely involve estimating sampling error. Often, this is due to practical limitations. It may not be possible to obtain an adequate sampling frame for some populations of concern to social workers, such as homeless people or undocumented recent immigrants. Meager budgets for conducting research or time constraints may preclude conducting preliminary surveys to estimate population parameters. Inadequate resources may also force researchers to simply select the largest sample the budget will permit, knowing in advance that sample size will fall short of the number needed for a desired estimated sampling error.

In studies that have meager resources but seek to conduct complex statistical analyses, the selected sample size will often be determined by multiplying the number of variables to be simultaneously analyzed by the minimum number of cases per variable required by the appropriate statistical procedure. A related consideration involves statistical power analysis, which we will address in Chapter 22. At this point, for the sake of simplicity, we can say that statistical power analysis deals with determining how large a sample needs to be in order for researchers to have an adequate probability of obtaining statistically significant findings.

Because of the complexities and various factors involved in determining the desired sample size for many studies, you may want to use a statistical software program to help you make this determination. One of the more popular programs available is the Statistical Package for the Social Sciences (SPSS). SPSS offers a feature called SamplePower, which can help you determine your desired sample size based on various aspects of your research design and data analysis plans. (A guide for using SPSS is presented in Appendix D.)

TYPES OF PROBABILITY SAMPLING DESIGNS

Up to this point, we have focused on simple random sampling (SRS). And, indeed, the body of statistics typically used by social researchers assumes such a sample. As we shall see shortly, however, we have several choices of sampling method, and you will seldom, if ever, choose simple random sampling, for two reasons. First, with all but the simplest sampling frame, simple random sampling is not feasible. Second, and probably surprisingly, simple random sampling may not be the most accurate method available. Let's turn

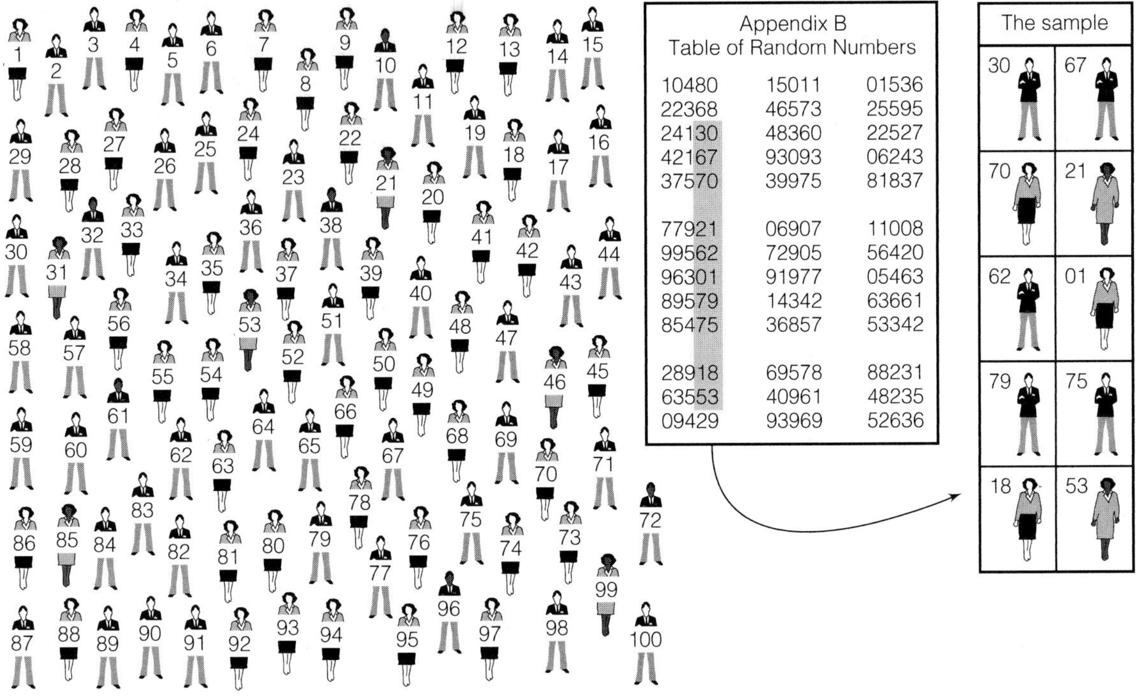

Figure 14-3 A Simple Random Sample

now to a discussion of simple random sampling and the other options available.

Simple Random Sampling

Once a sampling frame has been established in accord with the preceding discussion, to use **simple random sampling (SRS)** the researcher assigns a single number to each element in the sampling frame without skipping any number in the process. A table of random numbers is then used to select elements for the sample. Appendix B displays such a table, along with a box explaining its use.

If your sampling frame is in machine-readable form—for example, on computer disk or magnetic tape—a simple random sample can be selected automatically by computer. (In effect, the computer program numbers the elements in the sampling frame, generates its own series of random numbers, and prints out the list of elements selected.)

Figure 14-3 illustrates simple random sampling. Note that the members of our hypothetical micropopulation have been numbered from 1 to 100. Based on the procedures explained in Appendix B, we decide to use the last two digits of the first column and to begin with the third number from the top. This yields person number 30 as the first one selected into the sample. Number 67 is next, and so forth. (Person 100 would have been selected if "00" had come up in the list.)

Systematic Sampling

Simple random sampling is seldom used in practice. As we shall see, it is not usually the most efficient sampling method, and it can be rather laborious if done manually. SRS typically requires a list of elements. When such a list is available, researchers usually employ systematic sampling rather than simple random sampling.

In systematic sampling, every *k*th element in the total list is chosen (systematically) for inclusion in the sample. If the list contains 10,000 elements and you want a sample of 1,000, you select every 10th element for your sample. To guard against any possible human bias in using this method, you should select the first element at random. Thus, in the preceding example, you would begin by selecting a random number between 1 and 10. The element having that number is included in the sample, plus every 10th element following it. This method is technically referred to as a

systematic sample with a random start. Two terms are frequently used in connection with systematic sampling. The **sampling interval** is the standard distance between elements selected in the sample: 10 in the preceding sample. The **sampling ratio** is the proportion of elements in the population that are selected: 1/10 in the example.

$$\text{Sampling interval} = \frac{\text{population size}}{\text{sample size}}$$

$$\text{Sampling ratio} = \frac{\text{sample size}}{\text{population size}}$$

In practice, systematic sampling is virtually identical to simple random sampling. If the list of elements is indeed randomized before sampling, one might argue that a systematic sample drawn from that list is, in fact, a simple random sample. By now, debates over the relative merits of simple random sampling and systematic sampling have been resolved largely in favor of the simpler method: systematic sampling. Empirically, the results are virtually identical. And, as we shall see in a later section, systematic sampling is slightly more accurate than simple random sampling in some instances.

There is one danger involved in systematic sampling. The arrangement of elements in the list can make systematic sampling unwise. Such an arrangement is usually called periodicity. If the list of elements is arranged in a cyclical pattern that coincides with the sampling interval, then a grossly biased sample may be drawn. Two examples will illustrate.

In one study of soldiers during World War II, the researchers selected a systematic sample from unit rosters. Every 10th soldier on the roster was selected for the study. The rosters, however, were arranged in a table of organizations: sergeants first, then corporals and privates, squad by squad. Each squad had 10 members. As a result, every 10th person on the roster was a squad sergeant. The systematic sample selected contained only sergeants. It could, of course, have been the case that no sergeants were selected for the same reason.

As another example, suppose we select a sample of apartments in an apartment building. If the sample is drawn from a list of apartments arranged in numerical order (for example, 101, 102, 103, 104, 201, 202, and so on), there is a danger of the sampling interval coinciding with the number of apartments on a floor or some multiple thereof. Then the samples might include only northwest-corner apartments or only apartments near the elevator. If these types of apartments have some other particular characteristic in common (for example, higher rent), the sample will be biased. The same danger would appear in a systematic sample of houses in a subdivision arranged with the same number of houses on a block.

In considering a systematic sample from a list, then, you should carefully examine the nature of that list. If the elements are arranged in any particular order, you should figure out whether that order will bias the sample to be selected and take steps to counteract any possible bias (for example, take a simple random sample from cyclical portions).

In summary, systematic sampling is usually superior to simple random sampling, in convenience if nothing else. Problems in the ordering of elements in the sampling frame can usually be remedied quite easily.

Stratified Sampling

In the two preceding sections, we discussed two methods of sample selection from a list: random and systematic. *Stratification* is not an alternative to these methods, but it represents a possible modification in their use.

Simple random sampling and systematic sampling both ensure a degree of representativeness and permit an estimate of the error present. *Stratified sampling* is a method for obtaining a greater degree of representativeness—for decreasing the probable sampling error. To understand why that is the case, we must return briefly to the basic theory of sampling distribution.

We recall that sampling error is reduced by two factors in the sample design. First, a large sample produces a smaller sampling error than a small sample. Second, a homogeneous population produces samples with smaller sampling errors than does a heterogeneous population. If 99 percent of the population agrees with a certain statement, then it is extremely unlikely that any probability sample will greatly misrepresent the extent of agreement. If the population is split 50:50 on the statement, then the sampling error will be much greater.

Stratified sampling is based on this second factor in sampling theory. Rather than selecting a sample from the total population at large, we ensure that appropriate numbers of elements are drawn from homogeneous subsets of that population.

Suppose you seek to obtain a stratified sample of clients in a large social service agency in order to assess client satisfaction with the services they received. You suspect that ethnic minority clients might be relatively dissatisfied with services, and you want to ensure that they are adequately represented in the sample. Consequently, you might first organize your list of cases so that clients of the same ethnicity are grouped together. Then you would draw appropriate numbers from each ethnic group. In a nonstratified sample, representation by ethnicity would be subjected to the same sampling error as other variables. In a sample stratified by ethnicity, the sampling error on this variable is reduced to zero.

Even more complex stratification methods are possible. In addition to stratifying by ethnicity, you might also stratify by age group, type of presenting problem, and so forth. In this fashion, you might be able to ensure that your sample would contain the proper numbers of Hispanic children with behavior disorders, black families experiencing marital discord, elderly Asian American clients, and so forth.

The ultimate function of **stratification,** then, is to organize the population into homogeneous subsets (with heterogeneity between subsets) and to select the appropriate number of elements from each. To the extent that the subsets are homogeneous on the stratification variables, they may be homogeneous on other variables as well. If age group is related to type of presenting problem, then a sample stratified by age group will be more representative in terms of presenting problem as well. If socioeconomic status is related to ethnicity, then a sample stratified by ethnicity will be more representative in terms of socioeconomic status.

The choice of stratification variables typically depends on what variables are available. Gender can often be determined in a list of names. University lists are typically arranged by class. Lists of faculty members may indicate their departmental affiliation. Government agency files may be arranged by geographical region. Voter registration lists are arranged according to precinct.

In selecting stratification variables from among those available, however, you should be concerned primarily with those that are presumably related to variables that you want to represent accurately. Because gender is related to many variables and is often available for stratification, it is often used. Education is related to many variables, but it is often not available for stratification. Geographical location within a city, state, or nation is related to many things. Within a city, stratification by geographical location usually increases representativeness in social class, ethnic group, and so forth. Within a nation, stratification increases representativeness in a broad range of attitudes as well as in social class and ethnicity.

Methods of stratification in sampling vary. When you are working with a simple list of all elements in the population, two are predominant. One method is to sort the population elements into discrete groups based on whatever stratification variables are being used. On the basis of the relative proportion of the population represented by a given group, you select—randomly or systematically—a number of elements from that group that constitutes the same proportion of your desired sample size. For example, if elderly Hispanics compose 1 percent of the client population and you desire a sample of 1,000 clients, then you would select 10 elderly Hispanic clients.

The other method is to group cases as just described and then put those groups together in a continuous list. You would then select a systematic sample, with a random start, from the entire list. Given the arrangement of the list, a systematic sample would select proper numbers (within an error range of 1 or 2) from each subgroup. (Note: A simple random sample drawn from such a composite list would cancel out the stratification.)

Figure 14-4 offers a graphic illustration of stratified, systematic sampling. As you can see, we lined up our micropopulation according to sex and race. Then, beginning with a random start of "3," we've taken every 10th person thereafter: 3, 13, 23, . . . , 93.

Stratified sampling ensures the proper representation of the stratification variables to enhance the representation of other variables related to them. Taken as a whole, then, a stratified sample is likely to be more representative on several variables than a simple random sample. Although the simple random sample is still regarded as somewhat sacred, we often can do better.

Implicit Stratification in Systematic Sampling

It was mentioned earlier that systematic sampling can, under certain conditions, be more accurate than simple random sampling. That is the case whenever the arrangement of the list creates an implicit stratification. As already noted, if a list of agency cases is arranged by ethnicity, then a systematic sample provides a stratification by ethnicity whereas a simple random sample would not.

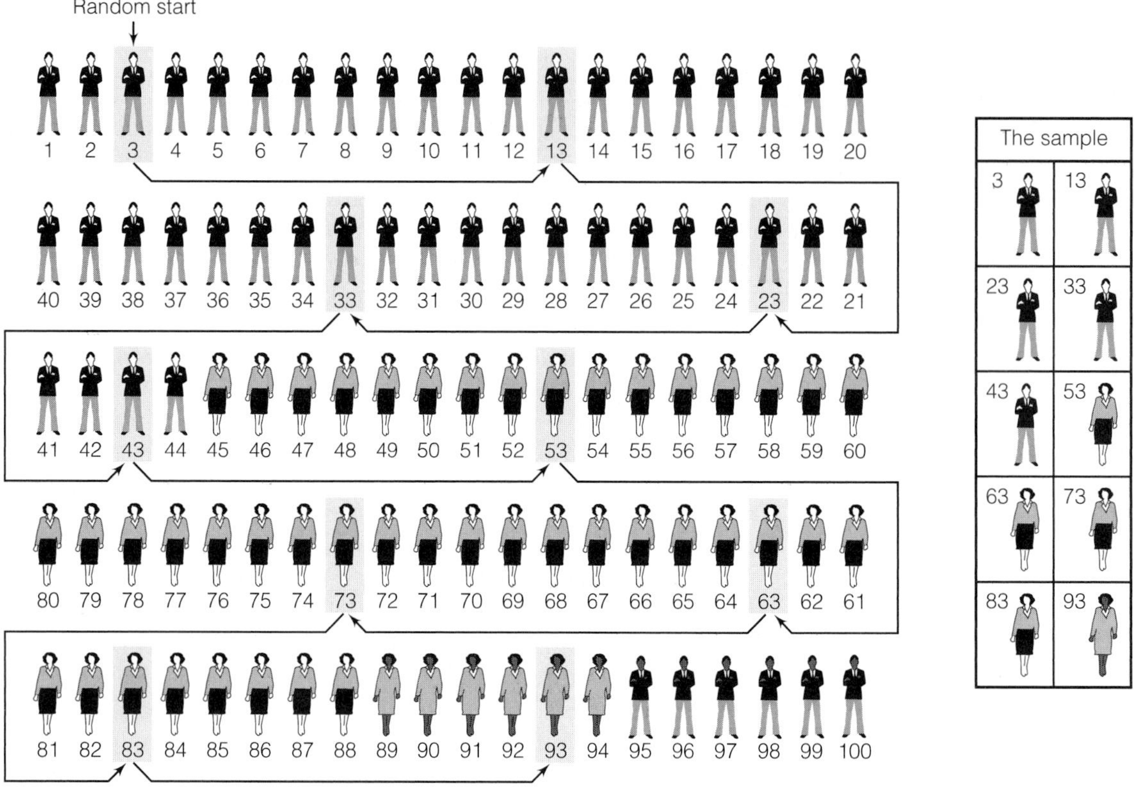

Figure 14-4 A Stratified, Systematic Sample with a Random Start

In a study of students at the University of Hawaii, after stratification by school class, the students were arranged by their student identification numbers. These numbers, however, were their Social Security numbers. The first three digits of the Social Security number indicate the state in which the number was issued. As a result, within a class, students were arranged by the state in which they were issued a Social Security number, providing a rough stratification by geographical origins. You should realize, therefore, that an ordered list of elements may be more useful to you than an unordered, randomized list. This point has been stressed here in view of an unfortunate belief that lists should be randomized before systematic sampling. Only if the arrangement presents the problems discussed earlier should the list be rearranged.

Proportionate and Disproportionate Stratified Samples

So far we have been illustrating stratified random sampling with a uniform proportion of cases drawn from each homogeneous grouping. This is called *proportionate stratified sampling*. For example, if our overall sample is to be 10 percent of the population, then we would draw 10 percent of each homogeneous group. In some studies, however, it may be advisable to select a larger proportion of cases from some groups than from others. Suppose, for example, that the preceding client satisfaction survey is being conducted in an agency whose 1,000 clients include 600 white clients, 300 African American clients, 40 Hispanic clients, 30 Asian American clients, 20 Native American clients, and 10 clients whose ethnicity falls in a catchall "other" category. We could select 10 percent of the white and African American clients and have 60 and 30 cases in each group. But if we selected 10 percent of the clients in the other groups, we would have only four Hispanics, three Asian Americans, two Native Americans, and one "other." There would be nothing wrong with this if all we sought to do was to come up with an overall satisfaction rating for the entire agency.

But what if we sought a detailed analysis about each ethnic group or sought to generalize about which ethnic groups were more satisfied or dissatisfied than

Table 14-3 Illustration of Disproportionate Stratified Sampling

ETHNIC GROUP	NUMBER OF CASES	AVERAGE RATING
White	60	4.0
Black	30	2.0
Hispanic	20	1.0
Asian American	15	3.0
Native American	10	1.0
Other	5	2.0

others? Such an analysis would not be possible for groups represented by only a handful of cases. Therefore, we would have to take a larger proportion of the very small homogeneous groupings than of the larger ones. This is called **disproportionate stratified sampling.** This sampling procedure gives cases from specified small subgroups a disproportionately better chance of being selected than cases from larger subgroups.

For example, we might select 10 percent of the white and African American clients and 50 percent from each of the remaining groups. That would give us 20 Hispanics, 15 Asian Americans, 10 Native Americans, and 5 "other." This would permit us to undertake our detailed analyses. But if we also wanted to portray an overall agency composite of client satisfaction, then we would have to weight the average satisfaction level of each ethnic group in accordance with its overall proportion in the agency population.

Suppose on a scale of 1 to 5 (very dissatisfied to very satisfied) the average rating of each group was as shown in Table 14-3. If the influence on the overall mean of the ratings in the 50-percent-selection groups was not adjusted in accordance with the groups' true proportion in the population, then the overall agency average satisfaction rating would be calculated as shown in Equation (1) in Figure 14-5.

But the average rating of 2.75 would underestimate the true overall level of client satisfaction because of the disproportionate influence of the ethnic groups represented by 50 percent of their cases. To correct for this, we would weight the two 10 percent groups by multiples (weights) of 5 (to raise their influence to an equivalent 50 percent representation), as shown in Equation (2) in Figure 14-5.

Thus, the true overall average rating of client satisfaction of 3.17 would be above the midpoint of 3.0 on the 1-to-5 rating scale, not below it as implied by the misleading 2.75 calculation. This would not negate the accuracy or importance of calculations that show that ethnic minority clientele tend to be far less satisfied with services than is depicted by the overall rating.

MULTISTAGE CLUSTER SAMPLING

The preceding sections have dealt with reasonably simple procedures for sampling from lists of elements. Such a situation is ideal. Unfortunately, however, much interesting social research requires the selection of samples from populations that cannot be easily listed for sampling purposes. Examples would be the population of a city, state, or nation; all university students in the United States; and so forth. In such cases, the sample design must be much more complex and typically involves the initial sampling of groups of elements—*clusters*—followed by the selection of elements within each selected cluster, a multistage design called **cluster sampling.**

Cluster sampling may be used when it's either impossible or impractical to compile an exhaustive list of the elements that compose the target population. All church members in the United States would be an example of such a population. It is often the case, however, that the population elements are already grouped into subpopulations, and a list of those subpopulations either exists or can be created practically. Thus, church members in the United States belong to discrete churches, and it would be possible to discover or create a list of those churches. Following a cluster sample format, then, the list of churches would be sampled in some manner as discussed previously (for example, a stratified, systematic sample). Next, you would obtain lists of members from each selected church. Each list would then be sampled to provide samples of church members for study. (For an example, see Glock, Ringer, and Babbie, 1967.)

Another typical situation concerns sampling among population areas such as a city. Although there is no single list of a city's population, citizens reside on discrete city blocks or census blocks. We might, therefore, select a sample of blocks initially, create a list of people living on each selected block, and subsample the people on each block.

$$\frac{(60 \times 4) + (30 \times 2) + (20 \times 1) + (15 \times 3) + (10 \times 1) + (5 \times 2)}{60 + 30 + 20 + 15 + 10 + 5} = \frac{240 + 60 + 20 + 45 + 10 + 10}{140} = \frac{385}{140} = 2.75 \tag{1}$$

$$\frac{(60 \times 4 \times 5) + (30 \times 2 \times 5) + (20 \times 1) + (15 \times 3) + (10 \times 1) + (5 \times 2)}{(60 \times 5) + (30 \times 5) + 20 + 15 + 10 + 5} = \frac{1200 + 300 + 20 + 45 + 10 + 10}{300 + 150 + 20 + 15 + 10 + 5} = \frac{1585}{500} = 3.17 \tag{2}$$

Figure 14-5 Equations for Table 14-3

In a more complex design, you might sample blocks, list the households on each selected block, sample the households, list the persons residing in each household, and, finally, sample persons within each selected household. This multistage sample design would lead to the ultimate selection of a sample of individuals but would not require the initial listing of all individuals in the city's population.

Multistage cluster sampling, then, involves the repetition of two basic steps: listing and sampling. The list of primary sampling units (churches, blocks) is compiled and, perhaps, stratified for sampling. Then a sample of those units is selected. The selected primary sampling units are then listed and perhaps stratified. The list of secondary sampling units is then sampled, and so forth.

Multistage Designs and Sampling Error

Although cluster sampling is highly efficient, the price of that efficiency is a less accurate sample. A simple random sample drawn from a population list is subject to a single sampling error, but a two-stage cluster sample is subject to two sampling errors. First, the initial sample of clusters will represent the population of clusters only within a range of sampling error. Second, the sample of elements selected within a given cluster will represent all of the elements in that cluster only within a range of sampling error. Thus, for example, you run a certain risk of selecting a sample of disproportionately wealthy city blocks, plus a sample of disproportionately wealthy households within those blocks. The best solution to this problem lies in the number of clusters initially selected and the number of elements selected within each.

You'll typically be restricted to a total sample size; for example, you may be limited to conducting 2,000 interviews in a city. Given this broad limitation, however, you have several options in designing your cluster sample. At the extremes, you might choose one cluster and select 2,000 elements within that cluster; or you might choose 2,000 clusters and select one element within each. Of course, neither extreme is advisable, but a broad range of choices lies between them. Fortunately, the logic of sampling distributions provides a general guideline to follow.

Recall that sampling error is reduced by two factors: an increase in the sample size and increased homogeneity of the elements being sampled. These factors operate at each level of a multistage sample design. A sample of clusters will best represent all clusters if a large number are selected and if all clusters are very much alike. A sample of elements will best represent all elements in a given cluster if a large number are selected from the cluster and if all elements in the cluster are very similar.

With a given total sample size, however, if the number of clusters is increased, the number of elements within a cluster must be decreased. In this respect, the representativeness of the clusters is increased at the expense of more poorly representing the elements that compose each cluster, or vice versa. Fortunately, the factor of homogeneity can be used to ease this dilemma.

Typically, the elements that compose a given natural cluster within a population are more homogeneous than are all elements that compose the total population. The members of a given church are more alike than are all church members; the residents of a given city block are more alike than are all the residents of a whole city. As a result, relatively fewer elements may be needed to adequately represent a given natural cluster, although a larger number of clusters may be needed to adequately represent the diversity found among the clusters. This fact is most clearly seen in the extreme case of very different clusters that are composed of identical elements within each. In such a situation, a large number of clusters would adequately represent all their members. Although this extreme situation never exists in reality, it is closer to the truth in most cases than its opposite: identical clusters composed of grossly divergent elements.

The general guideline for cluster design, then, is to maximize the number of clusters selected while decreasing the number of elements within each cluster. Note, however, that this scientific guideline must be balanced against an administrative constraint. The efficiency of cluster sampling is based on the ability to minimize the listing of population elements. By initially selecting clusters, you need list only the elements that compose the selected clusters, not all of the elements in the entire population. Increasing the number of clusters, however, goes directly against this efficiency factor in cluster sampling. A small number of clusters may be listed more quickly and more cheaply than a large number. (Remember that all of the elements in a selected cluster must be listed even if only a few are to be chosen in the sample.)

The final sample design will reflect these two constraints. In effect, you will probably select as many clusters as you can afford. Lest this issue be left too open-ended at this point, we present one rule of thumb. Population researchers conventionally aim for the selection of 5 households per census block. If a total of 2,000 households is to be interviewed, then you would aim at 400 blocks with 5 household interviews on each. Figure 14-6 graphically portrays this process.

Before turning to more detailed procedures that are available to cluster sampling, we repeat that this method almost inevitably involves a loss of accuracy. The manner in which this appears, however, is somewhat complex. First, as noted earlier, a multistage sample design is subject to a sampling error at each stage. Because the sample size is necessarily smaller at each stage than the total sample size, each stage's sampling error will be greater than would be the case for a single-stage random sample of elements. Second, sampling error is estimated on the basis of observed variance among the sample elements. When those elements are drawn from among relatively homogeneous clusters, the estimated sampling error will be too optimistic and must be corrected in light of the cluster sample design.

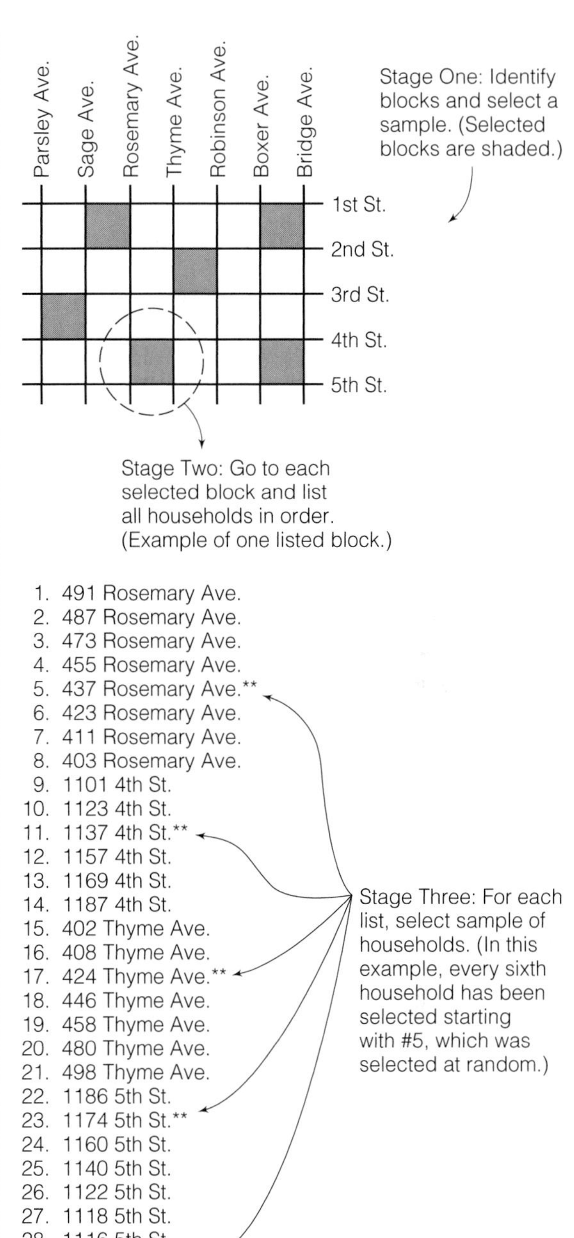

Figure 14-6 Multistage Cluster Sampling

Stratification in Multistage Cluster Sampling

Thus far, we have looked at cluster sampling as though a simple random sample were selected at each stage of the design. In fact, stratification techniques can be used to refine and improve the sample being selected.

The basic options available are essentially the same as those possible in single-stage sampling from a list. In selecting a national sample of churches, for example, you might initially stratify your list of churches by denomination, geographical region, size, rural or urban location, and perhaps by some measure of social class.

Once the primary sampling units (churches, blocks) have been grouped according to the relevant and available stratification variables, either simple random or systematic sampling techniques can be used to select the sample. You might select a specified number of units from each group or stratum, or you might arrange the stratified clusters in a continuous list and systematically sample that list. To the extent that clusters are combined into homogeneous strata, the sampling error at this stage will be reduced. The primary goal of stratification, as before, is homogeneity.

There is no reason why stratification could not take place at each level of sampling. The elements listed within a selected cluster might be stratified before the next stage of sampling. Typically, however, that is not done. (Recall the assumption of relative homogeneity within clusters.)

Probability Proportionate to Size (PPS) Sampling

This section introduces a more sophisticated form of cluster sampling that is used in many large-scale survey sampling projects. In the preceding discussion, we talked about selecting a random or systematic sample of clusters and then a random or systematic sample of elements within each cluster selected. Notice that this produces an overall sampling scheme in which every element in the whole population has the same probability of selection.

Let's say we're selecting households within a city. If there are 1,000 city blocks and we initially select a sample of 100, then each block has a 100/1,000 or .1 chance of being selected. If we next select 1 household in 10 from those residing on the selected blocks, then each household has a .1 chance of selection within its block. To calculate the overall probability of a household being selected, we simply multiply the probabilities at the individual steps in sampling. In other words, each household has a 1/10 chance of its block being selected and a 1/10 chance of that specific household being selected if the block is chosen. In this case, each household has a 1/10 × 1/10 = 1/100 chance of selection overall. Because each household would have the same chance of selection, the sample so selected should be representative of all households in the city.

There are dangers in this procedure, however. In particular, the variation in the size of blocks (measured in numbers of households) presents a problem. Let's suppose that half the city's population resides in 10 densely packed blocks filled with high-rise apartment buildings, and suppose that the rest of the population lives in single-family dwellings spread out over the remaining 900 blocks. When we first select our sample of 1/10 of the blocks, it's quite possible that we'll miss all of the 10 densely packed high-rise blocks. No matter what happens in the second stage of sampling, our final sample of households will be grossly unrepresentative of the city, comprising only single-family dwellings.

Whenever the clusters sampled are of greatly differing sizes, it's appropriate to use a modified sampling design called **probability proportionate to size (PPS)**. This design guards against the problem we've just described and still produces a final sample in which each element has the same chance of selection.

As the name suggests, each cluster is given a chance of selection proportionate to its size. Thus, a city block with 200 households has twice the chance of selection as one with only 100 households. Within each cluster, however, a fixed number of elements is selected, say, 5 households per block. Notice how this procedure results in each household having the same probability of selection overall.

Let's look at households of two different city blocks. Block A has 100 households, Block B has only 10. In PPS sampling, we would give Block A 10 times as good a chance of being selected as Block B. So if, in the overall sample design, Block A has a 1/20 chance of being selected, that means Block B would only have a 1/200 chance. Notice that this means that all the households on Block A would have a 1/20 chance of having their block selected; Block B households have only a 1/200 chance.

If Block A is selected and we're taking 5 households from each selected block, then the households on Block A have a 5/100 chance of being selected into the block's sample. Because we can multiply probabilities in a case such as this, we see that every household on Block A had an overall chance of selection equal to 1/20 × 5/100 = 5/2,000 = 1/400.

If Block B happens to be selected, on the other hand, then its households stand a much better chance of being among the 5 chosen there: 5/10. When this is combined with the households' relatively poorer chance of having their block selected in the first place, however, they end up with the same chance of selection as those on block A: 1/200 × 5/10 = 5/2,000 = 1/400.

Further refinements to this design make it a very efficient and effective method for selecting large cluster samples. For now, however, it's enough to understand the basic logic involved.

ILLUSTRATION: SAMPLING SOCIAL WORK STUDENTS

Now let's use a hypothetical example to see what cluster sampling looks like in practice. The illustration that follows is less complex than the area probability samples that are employed in studies of geographic areas such as cities, states, or the nation. It is hypothetical because the recent social work research literature is devoid of studies that use probability cluster sampling. Nonetheless, this example illustrates the applicability of cluster sampling to social work research and the various principles of this sampling approach.

Suppose you obtained a large research grant to conduct a longitudinal study of how social work students change their attitudes about cultural diversity during their social work education. Suppose there are 100 graduate programs of social work and 300 undergraduate programs in the United States. You will need to make several repeated site visits to each program selected for the study to collect longitudinal data from the students there. You desire a nationally representative sample of students, but your travel budget limits your site visits to 40 programs.

There is no national list of social work students, so a multistage sampling design is created. In the initial stage of sampling, programs are selected with probability proportionate to size (PPS), and then students are selected from each.

Selecting the Programs

The Council on Social Work Education publishes an annual report that lists each social work education program and its enrollment size. This list constitutes the sampling frame for the first stage of sampling. Suppose it shows a nationwide total of approximately 50,000 students, including 25,000 each at both the graduate and undergraduate levels. Consequently, you decide to select 20 programs from each level for your study.

Table 14-4 Form Used in Listing Social Work Education Programs

PROGRAM	ENROLLMENT SIZE	CUMULATIVE ENROLLMENT
School A	200	200
School B	400	600
School C	100	700

For your data analysis, you desire a sample size of 1,000 students, so you decide to select 25 students from each of the 40 participating programs. To accomplish this, you make two lists of programs: one for graduate programs and one for undergraduate programs. Each list identifies the enrollment size of each program and the cumulative enrollment of the programs on the list, as illustrated in Table 14-4.

The object at this point is to select a sample of 20 programs from each list in a way such that each program would have a chance of selection proportionate to its enrollment size. To accomplish this, the cumulative totals are used to create ranges of numbers for each program that equal the number of students enrolled in that program. School A in Table 14-4 is assigned the numbers 1 through 200, School B is assigned 201 through 600, School C is assigned 601 through 700, and so forth.

By selecting 20 numbers between 1 and 25,000 for each list, we can select 40 programs for the study. The 20 numbers could be selected in a systematic sample as follows. Set the sampling interval at 1,250 (25,000/20). Select a random start at between 1 and 1,250. Let's say the starting number randomly selected is 563. Because that number falls within the range of numbers assigned to School B (201 through 600), School B is selected.

Increments of 1,250 (the sampling interval) are then added to the random starting number, and every school within whose range one of the resultant numbers appears is selected to participate in the study. In this fashion, each school has a chance of selection that is directly proportionate to its enrollment size. A school that enrolls 400 students has twice the chance of selection as a school with 200 and 10 times the chance of selection as one with only 40 students.

Selecting the Students

Once the sample of programs is selected, a list of the students enrolled is obtained from each selected program. A sampling interval is then computed for each program based on its enrollment size and the number of students desired from each program (25). If a program enrolled 250 students, then the sample interval would be set at 10. A random number is selected and incremented by the sampling interval to select the sample of students from that school. This procedure is repeated for each school.

PROBABILITY SAMPLING IN REVIEW

The preceding discussions have been devoted to the key sampling method used in controlled survey research: probability sampling. In each examined variation, we have seen that elements are chosen for study from a population on a basis of random selection with known nonzero probabilities. Depending on the field situation, probability sampling can be extremely simple or extremely difficult, time-consuming, and expensive. Whatever the situation, however, it remains the most effective method for selecting study elements. There are two reasons for this.

First, probability sampling avoids conscious or unconscious biases in element selection on the part of the researcher. If all elements in the population have an equal (or unequal and subsequently weighted) chance of selection, then there is an excellent chance that the selected sample will closely represent the population of all elements.

Second, probability sampling permits estimates of sampling error. Although no probability sample will be perfectly representative in all respects, controlled selection methods permit the researcher to estimate the degree of expected error.

AVOIDING GENDER BIAS IN SAMPLING

Before leaving this chapter, however, let's look at another form of bias to be avoided in sampling: *gender bias*. Like cultural bias (discussed in Chapter 5), all aspects of the research process can be affected by gender bias, and sampling is one area in which it can be particularly problematic. It can even affect probability sampling; for example, when we inappropriately decide to exclude a particular gender from our sampling frame. Perhaps the most commonly encountered **gender bias** problem in sampling is the unwarranted generalization of research findings to the population as a whole when one gender is not adequately represented in the research sample. Campbell (1983) reviewed the occurrence of gender biases in the sex-role research literature and identified several illustrations of this problem. For example, she cited studies on achievement motivation and on management and careers whose samples included only white, middle-class male subjects but which did not specify in their conclusions that their generalizations were limited to individuals with those attributes. She was particularly critical of life-cycle research, as follows:

> Nowhere is the effect of bias on sampling more evident than in the popular and growing field of the life cycle or stages. Beginning with Erikson's . . . work on the "Eight Stages of Man" to Levinson's Seasons of a Man's Life . . . the study of life cycles has focused on male subjects. When women are examined, it is in terms of how they fit or don't fit the male model. Without empirical verification, women are said to go through the same cycles as men . . . or are said to go through cycles that are antithetical to men's. . . . Based on a survey of the literature on life cycles, Sangiuliano . . . concluded that "Mostly we (researchers) persist in seeing her (woman) in the reflected light of men." . . .
>
> (1983:206)

The inadequate representation of a particular gender in a sample can be much subtler than just excluding them entirely or including an insufficient proportion of them. It could also occur because of biased data-collection procedures, even when the number of individuals of a particular gender is not the issue. For example, Campbell notes that the Gallup Poll interviews male subjects beginning at 6 P.M., and conducts most interviews with females between 4 and 6 P.M. Thus, Campbell argues that most professional women would not be home before 6 P.M. and cannot be adequately represented in the sample. If she is correct, then even if the overall proportion of women in the Gallup Poll seems to be sufficient, the views expressed by the women in the sample are not adequately representative of the views of the population of women.

As another example, if we wanted to generalize about gender-related differences in job satisfaction, we would not want to select our sample only from those work settings where professional or managerial positions go predominantly to men and where semiprofessional clerical jobs go predominantly to women.

There may be instances, however, when the exclusion of a particular gender from a study's sample is warranted or inescapable—instances where only one gender is relevant and where generalizations will be restricted to that gender. Thus, only one gender would be included in the sample of a survey of client satisfaction in a program whose clientele all happen to be of the same gender—for example, a group support program for battered women or for female rape victims.

We must be on guard not to let sex-role biases improperly influence us so that we deem a particular gender irrelevant for a given study. For example, we should not be predisposed to restrict our samples to men when we study topics such as aggression, management, unemployment, or criminal behavior and to women when we study things such as parenting, nurturing, or housekeeping.

In this chapter, we've taken on a basic issue in much social work research: selecting observations that will tell us something more general than the specifics we've actually observed. As we proceed through the rest of this book, we'll see how this issue bears upon various designs for collecting and analyzing research data. In the next chapter, for example, we'll examine how different survey methods are vulnerable to sampling bias and how survey researchers can try to avoid it.

Main Points

- A sample is a special subset of a population that is observed for purposes of making inferences about the nature of the total population itself.

- Purposive sampling is a type of nonprobability sampling method in which the researcher uses his or her own judgment in selecting sample members. It is sometimes called a judgmental sample.

- When informants are used, they should be selected in such a fashion as to provide a broad, diverse view of the group under study.

- In general, nonprobability sampling methods are regarded as less reliable than probability sampling methods. However, they are often easier and cheaper to use.

- The chief criterion of the quality of a sample is the degree to which it is representative—the extent to which the characteristics of the sample are the same as those of the population from which it was selected.

- Probability sampling methods provide one excellent way to select samples that will be quite representative.

- The chief principle of probability sampling is that every member of the total population must have the same known, nonzero probability of being selected into the sample.

- The most carefully selected sample will almost never perfectly represent the population from which it was selected. There will always be some degree of sampling error.

- Probability sampling methods allow us to estimate the amount of sampling error that should be expected in a given sample.

- A sampling frame is a list or quasi-list of the members of a population. It is the resource used in the selection of a sample. A sample's representativeness depends directly on the extent to which a sampling frame contains all the members of the total population that the sample is intended to represent.

- Simple random sampling is logically the most fundamental technique in probability sampling.

- Systematic sampling involves the selection of every *k*th member from a sampling frame. This method is functionally equivalent to simple random sampling, with a few exceptions.

- Stratification is the process of grouping the members of a population into relatively homogeneous strata before sampling. This practice improves the representativeness of a sample by reducing the degree of sampling error.

- Multistage cluster sampling is a more complex sampling technique that is frequently used in those cases in which a list of all the members of a population does not exist. An initial sample of groups of members (clusters) is selected first, and then all members of the selected cluster are listed, often through direct observation in the field. Finally, the members listed in each selected cluster are subsampled, thereby providing the final sample of members.

- Probability proportionate to size (PPS) is a special, efficient method for multistage cluster sampling.

- If the members of a population have unequal probabilities of selection into the sample, it is necessary to assign weights to the different observations made in order to provide a representative picture of the total population. Basically, the weight assigned to a particular sample member should be the inverse of its probability of selection.

- Gender bias should be avoided in sampling.

Review Questions and Exercises

1. Review the discussion of the 1948 Gallup Poll that predicted that Thomas Dewey would defeat Harry Truman for president. Discuss ways in which Gallup could have modified his quota sample design to have avoided the error.

2. Using Appendix B of this book, select a simple random sample of 10 numbers in the range from 1 to 9,876. Describe each step in the process.

3. In a paragraph or two, describe the steps involved in selecting a multistage cluster sample of nursing home residents throughout the nation.

Internet Exercises

1. Use InfoTrac College Edition to find two research articles in the journal *Health and Social Work*—one that used probability sampling and one that used nonprobability sampling. Critique the sampling procedures used in each—either positively or negatively.

2. Use InfoTrac College Edition to examine briefly four additional research articles in the journal *Health and Social Work*. How many used probability sampling methods? How many relied exclusively on nonprobability methods?

3. Browse some of your favorite sites on the Internet until you find one conducting a survey of visitors to that site. For example, certain news media sites typically conduct daily polls about political issues. Discuss the sampling problems connected to the survey you find, addressing issues such as the sampling frame, the representativeness of the sample, and so on.

4. Go to the website for the Crime Victimization Survey of the Bureau of Justice Statistics at www.ojp.usdoj.gov/bjs/abstract/cvusst.htm. Download and then examine the "Methodology" file for the most recent year. Summarize and critique the multistage sampling procedures used in the survey and described in the downloaded file.

5. Go to the website for the General Social Survey (GSS) at www.icpsr.umich.edu/GSS/. Click "Search" and then enter the term *sampling*. Then click on "Appendix A Sampling Design and Weighting." Summarize the GSS sampling procedures and how and why they changed over time. Include in your summary a discussion of the procedures for sampling African Americans.

6. Use InfoTrac College Edition to find the following article in the July 2002 issue of the journal *Social Work*: "Living on the Edge: Examination of People Attending Food Pantries and Soup Kitchens," by M. A. Biggerstaff, P. M. Morris, and A. Nichols-Casebolt. Critically appraise the multistage cluster-sampling procedure used in that study.

Additional Readings

Frankfort-Nachmias, Chava, and Anna Leon-Guerrero. 1997. *Social Statistics for a Diverse Society*. Thousand Oaks, CA: Pine Forge Press. See Chapter 11 especially. This statistics textbook covers many of the topics we've discussed in this chapter but in a more statistical context. It demonstrates the links between probability sampling and statistical analyses.

Kish, Leslie. 1965. *Survey Sampling*. New York: Wiley. Unquestionably, this is the definitive work on sampling in social research. If you need to know something more about sampling than you found in this chapter, this is the only place to go. Kish's coverage ranges from the simplest matters to the most complex and mathematical. He is both highly theoretical and downright practical. Easily readable and difficult passages intermingle as Kish exhausts everything you could want to know about each aspect of sampling.

Sudman, Seymour. 1983. "Applied Sampling," pp. 145–194 in Peter H. Rossi, James D. Wright, and Andy B. Anderson (eds.), *Handbook of Survey Research*. New York: Academic Press. An excellent, practical guide to survey sampling.

CHAPTER 15

Survey Research

What You'll Learn in This Chapter

Researchers have many methods for collecting data through surveys—from mail questionnaires to personal interviews to online surveys conducted over the Internet. Survey data that have been collected by others are also available for analysis. Social work researchers should know how to select an appropriate method and how to implement it effectively.

INTRODUCTION

Survey research is a very old research technique. In the Old Testament, for example, we find:

> After the plague the Lord said to Moses and to Eleazar the son of Aaron, the priest, "Take a census of all the congregation of the people of Israel, from twenty years old and upward. . . ."
>
> (NUMBERS 26:1–2)

Ancient Egyptian rulers conducted censuses for the purpose of administering their domains. Jesus was born away from home because Joseph and Mary were journeying to Joseph's ancestral home for a Roman **census.**

A little-known survey was attempted among French workers in 1880. A German political sociologist mailed some 25,000 questionnaires to workers to determine how much they were exploited by employers. The lengthy questionnaire included items such as these:

> Does your employer or his representative resort to trickery in order to defraud you of a part of your earnings?
>
> If you are paid piece rates, is the quality of the article made a pretext for fraudulent deductions from your wages?

The survey researcher in this case was Karl Marx (1880:208). Though 25,000 questionnaires were mailed out, there is no record of any being returned.

The precursors to surveys in social work were conducted in Europe in the mid-19th century. They focused on the earnings and expenditures of the working poor. Some were conducted to determine appropriate levels of relief grants; others were done to provide evidence for social reform. A prominent influence on the early use of surveys in social work was Charles Booth, a wealthy and politically conservative London ship owner who set out in 1886 to disprove claims by Marxists that one-fourth of the working class lived in severe poverty. Using his own money to fund the research, Booth and his assistants surveyed East London residents about many socioeconomic forces that affected their lives. It took 17 volumes of *The Life and Labour of the People of London* (1891–1903) to report the study. Ironically, instead of disproving the Marxists' claims, Booth concluded that they had underestimated the proportion of people living in poverty. Booth even recommended social welfare measures that he termed *limited socialism.*

Booth's work coincided with the emergence of early social reform efforts in the social work profession. As the 20th century began, muckraking journalists and novelists spurred public interest in surveys such as Booth's, surveys that would document the muckraker's depictions of urban squalor and exploitation. The most famous of the social surveys to follow was the *Pittsburgh Survey,* which was conducted from 1909 to 1914 by social workers and civic leaders to assess social conditions in that city. Published in several volumes, the Pittsburgh survey exposed the city's deplorable social conditions and stimulated major social reforms.

The Pittsburgh Survey's success demonstrated how survey methods can be used for social reform purposes, and it helped spark what was called the "Social Survey Movement" by social workers in cities throughout the United States. The surveys that were conducted as part of this "movement" were broad in scope, reporting vast amounts of data on industrial, economic, political, and social factors in one city at a time. The data were amassed to arouse communities to the need for social reform. The surveys thus were often reported in a biased manner and were soon being seen as propagandistic. By the 1920s, their credibility was tarnished, and their popularity waned as the social reform era ended. But the movement had a lasting impact on the use of surveys in social work. Its early successes prompted social agencies to adopt narrower surveys that focused on specialized agency concerns as a regular function. Eventually, the utility of survey methods for a wide range of research purposes was recognized.

Today, survey research is perhaps the most frequently used mode of observation in the social sciences. You probably have been a **respondent** in a survey more than once, and quite possibly you have done a survey of your own. In a typical survey, the researcher selects a sample of respondents and administers a standardized **questionnaire** to them.

Several of the fundamental elements of survey research have already been covered in detail in this book, so you are already partially trained in this important research method. We examined the logic and techniques of questionnaire construction in Chapter 9, so we won't repeat that here. Also, Chapter 14 covered the topic of sampling, referring most often to survey situations.

Given that you already know how to prepare a questionnaire and select a sample of people to answer it, this chapter will focus on the options available to you for administering the questionnaire. How do you go about getting questionnaires answered?

As you'll see, sometimes it's appropriate to have respondents complete questionnaires themselves, and other times it's more appropriate to have interviewers ask the questions and record the answers. This latter technique can be used in face-to-face interviews or over the telephone. We'll examine each possibility and then compare their relative advantages and disadvantages.

The use of survey results has become an important aspect of survey research in recent years, and it's especially useful for students and others with scarce research funds. Let's begin by looking at the kinds of topics you could study using survey research.

TOPICS APPROPRIATE TO SURVEY RESEARCH

Although survey research can be used for exploratory or explanatory purposes, it is probably the best method for describing a population that is too large to observe directly. Careful probability sampling provides a group of respondents whose characteristics may be taken to reflect those of the larger population, and carefully constructed standardized questionnaires provide data in the same form from all respondents.

For example, surveys can be excellent vehicles for measuring attitudes and orientations in a large population. Public opinion polls are well-known examples of this use. Indeed, polls have become so prevalent that at times the public seems unsure what to think of them. Pollsters are criticized by those who don't think (or don't want to believe) that polls are accurate (candidates who are "losing" in polls often tell voters not to trust the polls).

The general attitude toward public opinion research is further complicated by scientifically unsound "surveys" that nonetheless capture our attention because of their topics or "findings." For example, cable news programs commonly ask viewers to respond online with their opinion on some controversial political issue. Whom do the respondents represent? Only those people who have the time and inclination to watch the program, have online access, and care enough about the issue to get out of their seats and go to their computers to participate in the poll. Moreover, if the cable news network is reputed to have a political bias, its viewers probably underrepresent people who don't share that bias. And if the broadcasters are biased, their bias may be reflected in the way they word their polling question. "Do you support the pro-abortion view that it's ethical to destroy the lives of unborn, unwanted children?"

Sometimes, people use the pretense of survey research for other, decidedly nonscientific purposes. For example, you may have received a telephone call indicating you've been selected for a survey only to find the first question was "How would you like to make thousands of dollars a week right there in your own home?" Or you may have been told you could win a prize if you could name the president whose picture is on the penny. (Tell them it's Elvis.) Unfortunately, a few unscrupulous telemarketers will try to prey on the general cooperation people have given to survey researchers.

By the same token, some political parties and charitable organizations conduct phony "surveys." Often under the guise of collecting public opinion about some issue, respondents are ultimately asked to contribute money to support the sender's positions. Some political campaigns have produced another form of bogus survey, called the "push poll." Here's what the American Association for Public Opinion Polling had to say in condemning push polls (Bednarz, 1996):

> A "push poll" is a telemarketing technique in which telephone calls are used to canvass potential voters, feeding them false or misleading "information" about a candidate under the pretense of taking a poll to see how this "information" affects voter preferences. In fact, the intent is not to measure public opinion but to manipulate it—to "push" voters away from one candidate and toward the opposing candidate. Such polls defame selected candidates by spreading false or misleading information about them. The intent is to disseminate campaign propaganda under the guise of conducting a legitimate public opinion poll.

In short, the labels *survey* and *poll* are sometimes misused. Done properly, however, survey research can be a useful tool of social inquiry. The key task for you is separating the wheat from the chaff. We trust this chapter will help you in that task. Let's turn now to the three major methods for getting responses to questionnaires.

SELF-ADMINISTERED QUESTIONNAIRES

There are three main methods of administering survey questionnaires to a sample of respondents. This section will deal with the method in which respondents are asked to complete the questionnaires themselves—*self-administered questionnaires*—and the following sections will deal with surveys that are administered by staff interviewers in face-to-face encounters or by telephone.

Although the mail survey is the typical method used in self-administered studies, there are several other common methods. In some cases, it may be appropriate to administer the questionnaire to a group of respondents who have gathered at the same place at the same time. A survey of students taking an introductory social work course, for example, might be conducted in this manner during class. High school students might be surveyed during homeroom period.

Some experimentation has been conducted on the home delivery of questionnaires. A research worker delivers the questionnaire to the home of sample respondents and explains the study. The questionnaire is left for the respondent to complete and the researcher to pick up later.

Home delivery and the mail can be used in combination as well. Questionnaires can be mailed to families, and then research workers visit homes to pick up the questionnaires and check them for completeness. In just the opposite method, questionnaires have been hand delivered by research workers with a request that the respondents mail the completed questionnaires to the research office.

On the whole, when a research worker delivers the questionnaire, picks it up, or does both, the completion rate seems higher than for straightforward mail surveys. Additional experimentation with this method is likely to point to other techniques for improving completion while reducing costs.

Mail Distribution and Return

The basic method for collecting data through the mail has been to send a questionnaire accompanied by a letter of explanation and a self-addressed, stamped envelope for returning the questionnaire. The respondent is expected to complete the questionnaire, put it in the envelope, and return it. If, by any chance, you've received such a questionnaire and failed to return it, it would be valuable to recall the reasons you had for not returning it and keep them in mind any time you plan to send questionnaires to others.

A common reason for not returning questionnaires is that it's too much trouble. To overcome this problem, researchers have developed several ways to make returning them easier. For instance, a **self-mailing questionnaire** requires no return envelope: When the questionnaire is folded a particular way, the return address appears on the outside. The respondent therefore doesn't have to worry about losing the envelope.

More elaborate designs are available also. The university student questionnaire described later in this chapter was bound in a booklet with a special, two-panel back cover. Once the questionnaire was completed, the respondent needed only to fold out the extra panel, wrap it around the booklet, and seal the whole thing with the adhesive strip running along the edge of the panel. The foldout panel contained the return address and postage. The design was improved when the study was repeated a couple of years later. Both the front and back covers had foldout panels: one for sending the questionnaire out and the other for getting it back—thus avoiding the use of envelopes altogether.

The point here is that anything you can do to make the job of completing and returning the questionnaire easier will improve your study. Imagine receiving a questionnaire that made no provisions for its return to the researcher. Suppose you had to (1) find an envelope, (2) write the address on it, (3) figure out how much postage was required, and (4) put stamps on the envelope. How likely is it that you would return the questionnaire?

A few brief comments are in order here on the postal options available to you. You have choices for mailing questionnaires and getting them returned. For outgoing mail, your choices are essentially between first-class postage and bulk rate. First-class is more certain, but bulk rate is far cheaper. (Consult your local post office for rates and procedures.) On return mail, your choice is between postage stamps and business-reply permits. Here, the cost differential is more complicated. If you use stamps, you pay for them whether or not people return their questionnaires. With the business-reply permit, you pay for only those that are used, but you pay an additional surcharge of approximately a nickel per returned piece. This means that stamps are cheaper if a lot of questionnaires are returned, but business-reply permits are cheaper if fewer are returned—and you won't know in advance how many will be.

You will have many other considerations when choosing from among the postal options. Some researchers, for example, feel that stamps communicate more "humanness" and sincerity than bulk rate and business-reply permits. Other surveyors worry that respondents will steam off the stamps and use them for some purpose other than returning the questionnaires. Because both bulk rate and business-reply permits require establishing accounts at the post office, you'll probably find stamps much easier in small surveys.

Cover Letter

An important factor influencing response rates to mailed surveys is the quality of the cover letter that accompanies the questionnaire. The cover letter is usually what prospective respondents read first, so it should be constructed in a way that will motivate them to respond and alleviate any resistance they may have about participating in the survey.

To motivate individuals to respond, explain the purpose and importance of the survey in terms that the prospective respondent can understand. Obtain an endorsement of or sponsorship for the study from organizations or people who are esteemed by prospective respondents and then identify those organizations or people in the cover letter. Explain why each individual's response is important to the success of the study and to solving a problem that respondents care about.

To alleviate resistance to participating, assure potential participants of the anonymity of their responses, explain how the sample was selected, and indicate how long it takes to complete the questionnaire (the quicker, the better).

Figure 15-1 is a cover letter that accompanied a 1995 survey of social workers. It illustrates the elements just discussed for motivating participation and reducing resistance.

Monitoring Returns

The mailing of questionnaires sets up a new research question that may prove valuable to the study. As questionnaires are returned, don't sit idly by; instead, undertake a careful recording of the varying rates of return among respondents.

An invaluable tool in this activity is a return rate graph. The day on which questionnaires were mailed is labeled "Day 1" on the graph, and every day thereafter the number of returned questionnaires is logged on the graph. It's usually best to compile two graphs. One shows the number returned each day—rising, then dropping. The second reports the cumulative number or percentage. In part, this activity is gratifying to the researchers as they get to draw a picture of their successful data collection. More important, however, it is their guide to how the data collection is going. If follow-up mailings are planned, the graph provides a clue about when such mailings should be launched. (The dates of subsequent mailings should be noted on the graph.)

As completed questionnaires are returned, each should be opened, quickly looked over, and assigned an identification (ID) number. These numbers should be assigned serially as the questionnaires are returned—even if other ID numbers have already been assigned. Two examples should illustrate the important advantages of this procedure.

First, let's assume you're studying attitudes toward day care programs for preschool children. In the middle of your data collection, the news media begins to cover accusations of sexual abuse in day care programs. By knowing the date of that public disclosure and the dates when questionnaires have been received, you will be able to determine the effects of the disclosure.

Second, in a less sensational way, serialized ID numbers can be valuable in estimating nonresponse biases in the survey. Barring more direct tests of bias, you may wish to assume that those who failed to answer the questionnaire will be more like respondents who delayed answering than like those who answered right away. An analysis of questionnaires received at different points in the data collection might then be used to estimate sampling bias. For instance, if the level of client satisfaction with agency services decreases steadily through the data collection, with those replying right away reporting higher satisfaction and those replying later reporting lower satisfaction, you might tentatively conclude that those who failed to answer at all have even lower satisfaction. Although it would not be advisable to make statistical estimates of bias in this fashion, you could take advantage of approximate estimates.

If respondents have been identified for purposes of follow-up mailing, then such mailings should be prepared for as the questionnaires are returned. The case study later in this chapter will discuss this process in greater detail.

Follow-up Mailings

Follow-up mailings may be administered in several ways. In the simplest, nonrespondents are sent a letter of additional encouragement to participate. A better method, however, is to send a new copy of the survey questionnaire with the follow-up letter. If potential

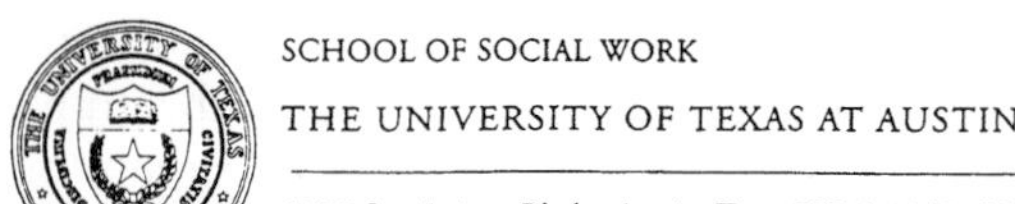

SCHOOL OF SOCIAL WORK
THE UNIVERSITY OF TEXAS AT AUSTIN

1925 San Jacinto Blvd. • Austin, Texas 78712-1203 • MC D3500 • Fax (512) 471-9600 • email utssw@utxvms.cc.utexas.edu

Practitioner Views About
Parenting and Mental Illness

Dear Colleague:

Enclosed is a brief questionnaire that attempts to measure your views about the role of parenting problems in the development and treatment of severe and persistent mental illness. Most of the items refer to severe and persistent forms of mental illness, such as schizophrenia, bipolar disorder or severe forms of depression.

All Austin area Licensed Master Social Workers recognized as Advanced Clinical Practitioners by the Texas State Board of Social Worker Examiners as of September 18, 1995, have been selected for this survey. Your response is very important to the study because it will add to the generalizability of the study and thus increase the value of the study. Your participation is voluntary and your responses are anonymous. No one will be able to identify your returned questionnaire. Please note that your present or future association with the University of Texas at Austin will not be affected whether you choose to participate or not.

Your experience and knowledge are important aspects of clinical social work practice and your contribution to the knowledge base through participation in this study will be of great value to our profession. Please take 5 minutes out of your busy schedule to complete the questionnaire and return it in the self-addressed stamped envelope. You do not have to answer every question, but we do encourage you to do so.

Please return your completed questionnaire as soon as possible. If you have any questions, please do not hesitate to contact me, Allen Rubin, Ph. D., LMSW-ACP at 512-471-9218, or my research assistant Jose G. Cardenas, LMSW-ACP 512-331-5100. Thank you for your attention and time.

Respectfully,

Allen Rubin, Ph.D., LMSW-ACP

Admissions and Academic Programs (512) 471-5457 • Dean's Office (512) 471-1937 • General Information (512) 471-5456

Figure 15-1 A Sample Cover Letter

respondents have not returned their questionnaires after two or three weeks, the questionnaires probably have been lost or misplaced. Receiving a follow-up letter might encourage them to look for the original questionnaire, but if they can't find it easily, the letter may go for naught.

The methodological literature on follow-up mailings strongly suggests that it is an effective method for increasing return rates in mail surveys. In general, the longer a potential respondent delays replying, the less likely he or she is to do so at all. Properly timed follow-up mailings thus stimulate more responses.

The effects of follow-up mailings will be seen in the response rate curves that are recorded during data collection. The initial mailings will be followed by a rise and subsequent subsiding of returns, the follow-up mailings will spur a resurgence of returns, and more follow-ups will do the same. In practice, three mailings (an original and two follow-ups) seem the most efficient.

The timing of follow-up mailings is also important. Here the methodological literature offers less precise guides, but in our experience two or three weeks is a reasonable interval between mailings. (This period might be increased by a few days if the mailing time—out and in—is more than two or three days.)

When researchers conduct several surveys of the same population over time, they will be able to develop more specific guidelines in this regard. The Survey Research Office at the University of Hawaii conducts frequent student surveys and has been able to refine the mailing and remailing procedure considerably. Indeed, a consistent pattern of returns has been found that appears to transcend differences of survey content, quality of instrument, and so forth. Within two weeks after the first mailing, approximately 40 percent of the questionnaires are returned; within two weeks after the first follow-up, an additional 20 percent are received; and within two weeks after the final follow-up, another 10 percent are received. (These response rates all involved the sending of additional questionnaires, not just letters.) Do not assume, however, that a similar pattern would appear in surveys of different populations. This illustration only indicates the value of carefully tabulating return rates for every survey conducted.

If the individuals in the survey sample are not identified on the questionnaires, it may not be possible to remail only to nonrespondents. In such a case, you should send your follow-up mailing to all members of the sample, thanking those who may have already participated and encouraging the participation of those who have not. (The case study reported in a later section of this chapter describes another method that may be used in an anonymous mail survey.)

Acceptable Response Rates

A question that new survey researchers frequently ask concerns the percentage return rate that should be achieved in a mail survey. The body of inferential statistics used in connection with survey analysis assumes that all members of the initial sample complete and return their questionnaires. Because this almost never happens, however, response bias becomes a concern, with the researcher testing (and hoping for) the possibility that the respondents look essentially like a random sample of the initial sample, and thus a somewhat smaller random sample of the total population.

Nevertheless, overall **response rate** is one guide to the representativeness of the sample respondents. If a high response rate is achieved, then there is less chance of significant response bias than if a low rate is achieved. But what is a high response rate? A quick review of the survey literature will uncover a wide range of response rates. Each may be accompanied by a statement like "This is regarded as a relatively high response rate for a survey of this type." (A U.S. senator made this statement about a poll of constituents that achieved a 4 percent return rate.) Even so, we can still state three rules of thumb about return rates. First, a response rate of at least 50 percent is usually considered adequate for analysis and reporting. Second, a response of at least 60 percent is *good*. Third, a response rate of 70 percent is *very good*. You should bear in mind, however, that these are only rough guides; they have no statistical basis, and a demonstrated lack of response bias is far more important than a high response rate.

As you can imagine, one of the more persistent discussions among survey researchers concerns ways to increase response rates. You'll recall that this was a chief concern in the earlier discussion of options for mailing out and receiving questionnaires. Survey researchers have developed many ingenious techniques to address this problem. Some have experimented with novel formats. Others have paid respondents to participate. The problem with paying, of course, is that it's expensive to make meaningfully high payments to hundreds or thousands of respondents, but some imaginative alternatives have been used. Some researchers have said, "We want to get your two-cents worth on some issues, and we're willing to pay"—enclosing two pennies. Another enclosed a quarter, suggesting that the respondent make some little child happy. Still others have enclosed paper money.

Don Dillman (1978) provides an excellent review of the various techniques that survey researchers have used to increase return rates on mail surveys, and he evaluates the impact of each. More important, he stresses the necessity of paying attention to all aspects of the study—what he calls the "Total Design Method"—rather than one or two special gimmicks.

A Case Study

The steps involved in the administration of a mail survey are many and can best be appreciated by examining an actual study. We'll thus conclude this section with a detailed description of a student survey conducted by the students in a graduate seminar in survey research methods at the University of Hawaii taught by one of us (Babbie). As you'll see shortly, the study does not represent the theoretical ideal for such studies, but in that regard it serves our purposes here all the better.

Approximately 1,100 students were selected from the computerized university registration list through a stratified, systematic sampling procedure. For each student selected, six self-adhesive mailing labels were printed by a computer.

By the time the questionnaires were ready for distribution, it became apparent that the research funds were inadequate to cover several mailings to the entire sample of 1,100 students (questionnaire printing costs were higher than anticipated). As a result, a systematic two-thirds sample of the mailing labels was chosen.

Earlier, it was decided to keep the survey anonymous to encourage more candid responses to some sensitive questions. (Later surveys of the same issues among the same population indicated that such anonymity was unnecessary.) Thus, the questionnaires would carry no identification of students on them. At the same time, the surveyors hoped to reduce the follow-up mailing costs by mailing only to nonrespondents.

To achieve both aims, a special postcard method was devised. Each student was mailed a questionnaire that carried no identifying marks, plus a postcard that was addressed to the research office—with one of the student's mailing labels affixed to the reverse side of the card. The introductory letter asked the student to complete and return the questionnaire—assuring anonymity—and to return the postcard simultaneously. Receiving the postcard would reveal that the student had returned his or her questionnaire—without indicating *which* questionnaire it was. This procedure would then facilitate follow-up mailings.

The 32-page questionnaire was printed in booklet form (photo-offset and saddle-stitched). A three-panel cover permitted the questionnaire to be returned without an additional envelope.

A letter that introduced the study and its purposes was printed on the front cover of the booklet. It explained why the study was being conducted (to learn how students feel about a variety of issues), how students had been selected for the study, the importance of each student's responding, and the mechanics of returning the questionnaire.

Students were assured that their responses to the survey would be anonymous, and the postcard method was explained. A statement followed about the auspices under which the study was being conducted, and a telephone number was provided for those who might want more information about the study, although just five students called for such information.

By printing the introductory letter on the questionnaire, the surveyors avoided having to enclose a separate letter in the outgoing envelope, thereby simplifying the task of assembling mailing pieces.

The materials for the initial mailing were assembled in the following steps: (1) One mailing label for each student was stuck on a postcard; (2) another label was stuck on an outgoing manila envelope; and (3) one postcard and one questionnaire were placed in each envelope—with the name on the postcard double-checked with the name on the envelope.

These steps were accomplished with an assembly line procedure that involved several members of the research team. Although the procedure was organized in advance, actual practice determined the best allocation of tasks and people. The entire process was delayed several days while the first manila envelopes were exchanged for larger ones, a delay that could have been avoided if the surveyors had walked through the assembly process in advance.

The distribution of the survey questionnaires had been set up for a bulk rate mailing. Once the questionnaires had been stuffed into envelopes, they were grouped by zip codes, tied in bundles, and delivered to the post office.

Shortly after the initial mailing, questionnaires and postcards began arriving at the research office. Questionnaires were opened, looked over, and assigned identification numbers as described earlier in this chapter. For every postcard received, the remaining labels for that student were destroyed.

After two or three weeks, all of the remaining mailing labels were used to organize a follow-up mailing. The assembly procedures described previously were repeated with one exception: A special, separate letter of appeal was included in the mailing piece. The new letter indicated that many students had returned their questionnaires already, but that it was very important for everyone to do so.

As expected, the follow-up mailing stimulated more returns, and the logging procedures were continued. The returned postcards told the researchers which additional mailing labels to destroy. Unfortunately, time and financial pressures disallowed a third planned mailing, but the first two mailings had resulted in an overall return rate of 62 percent.

We trust this illustration will give you a fairly good sense of what's involved in the execution of mailed self-administered questionnaires—a very popular survey method. Let's turn now to another method of conducting surveys.

INTERVIEW SURVEYS

The **interview** is an alternative method of collecting survey data. Rather than ask respondents to read questionnaires and enter their own answers, researchers send interviewers to ask the questions orally and record respondents' answers. Interviewing is typically done in a face-to-face encounter, but telephone interviewing, as we'll see, follows most of the same guidelines. Also, most interview surveys require more than one interviewer, although you might undertake a small-scale interview survey yourself. Portions of this section will discuss methods for training and supervising a staff of interviewers who will assist you on a survey.

This section deals specifically with survey interviewing. In Chapter 18 we'll talk about the less structured, in-depth interviews often conducted in qualitative research.

The Role of the Survey Interviewer

Having a questionnaire administered by an interviewer rather than the respondent has several advantages. To begin, interview surveys typically attain higher response rates than mail surveys. A properly designed and executed interview survey ought to achieve a completion rate of at least 80 to 85 percent. (Federally funded surveys often require one of these response rates.) Respondents seem more reluctant to turn down an interviewer who is standing on their doorsteps than they are to throw away mail questionnaires.

Within the context of the questionnaire, the presence of an interviewer generally decreases the number of "Don't knows" and "No answers." If minimizing such responses is important to the study, then the interviewer can be instructed to probe for answers—for example, "If you had to pick one of the answers, which do you think would come closest to your feelings?" Interviewers can also provide a guard against confusing questionnaire items. If the respondent clearly misunderstands the intent of a question or indicates that he or she does not understand it, then the interviewer can clarify matters, thereby obtaining relevant responses. (Such clarifications must be strictly controlled, however, through formal *specifications*. See "Coordination and Control" at the end of the "Interview Surveys" section.)

Finally, the interviewer can observe as well as ask questions. For example, the interviewer can note the respondent's race if this is considered too delicate a question to ask. Similar observations can be made about the quality of the dwelling, the presence of various possessions, the respondent's ability to speak English, the respondent's general reactions to the study, and so forth. In one survey of students, respondents were given a short, self-administered questionnaire to complete—on sexual attitudes and behavior—during the course of the interview. While a student completed the questionnaire, the interviewer made detailed notes on the respondent's dress and grooming.

Before leaving this example, we raise an important ethical issue. Some researchers have objected that such practices violate the spirit of the agreement by which the respondent has allowed the interview. Although ethical issues seldom are open and shut in social research, you should be sensitive to that aspect of research. We have examined ethical issues in detail in Chapter 4.

By necessity, survey research is based on an unrealistic *stimulus–response* theory of cognition and behavior. We must assume that a questionnaire item will mean the same thing to every respondent, and every given response must mean the same when given by different respondents. Although this is an impossible goal, survey questions are drafted to approximate the ideal as closely as possible.

The interviewer also must fit into this ideal situation. The interviewer's presence should not affect a respondent's perception of a question or the answer given. The interviewer, then, should be a neutral medium through which questions and answers are transmitted.

If this goal is successfully accomplished, then different interviewers will obtain exactly the same responses from a given respondent. (Recall earlier discussions of reliability.) This neutrality has a special importance in area samples. To save time and money, a given interviewer is typically assigned to complete all of the interviews in a particular geographic area—a city block or a group of nearby blocks. If the interviewer does anything to affect the responses obtained, then the bias thus interjected might be interpreted as a characteristic of that area.

Let's suppose that a survey is being done to determine attitudes toward low-cost housing to help in the selection of a site for a new government-sponsored development. An interviewer who is assigned to a given neighborhood might—through word or gesture—communicate his or her own distaste for low-cost housing developments. Respondents might therefore tend to give responses that generally agree with the interviewer's own position. The survey results would indicate that the neighborhood in question strongly resisted construction of the development in its area, although the apparent resistance might only reflect the interviewer's attitudes.

General Guidelines for Survey Interviewing

The manner in which interviews ought to be conducted will vary somewhat by survey population and also be affected somewhat by the nature of the survey content. Nevertheless, we can provide general guidelines that apply to most if not all interviewing situations.

Appearance and Demeanor As a general rule, the interviewer should dress in a fashion that is similar to that of the people who will be interviewed. A richly dressed interviewer will probably have difficulty getting good cooperation and responses from poorer respondents. And a poorly dressed interviewer will have similar difficulties with richer respondents.

To the extent that the interviewer's dress and grooming differ from those of the respondents, it should be in the direction of cleanliness and neatness in modest apparel. If cleanliness is not next to godliness, then it appears to be next to neutrality. Although middle-class neatness and cleanliness may not be accepted by all sectors of American society, they remain the primary norm and are more likely to be acceptable to the largest number of respondents.

Dress and grooming are typically regarded as signals of a person's attitudes and orientations. At the time this is being written, wearing torn jeans, green hair, and a razor-blade earring may communicate—correctly or incorrectly—that you are politically radical, sexually permissive, in favor of drug use, and so forth. Any of these impressions could bias responses or affect the willingness of people to be interviewed.

In demeanor, interviewers should be pleasant if nothing else. Because they will be prying into the respondents' personal lives and attitudes, they must communicate a genuine interest in getting to know each respondent without appearing to spy. They must be relaxed and friendly without being too casual or clinging. Good interviewers also are able to determine quickly the kind of person the respondent will feel most comfortable with and the kind of person with whom the respondent would most enjoy talking. There are two aspects of this. Clearly, the interview will be more successful if the interviewer can become that kind of person. Further, because respondents are asked to volunteer a portion of their time and to divulge personal information about themselves, they deserve the most enjoyable experience the researcher and interviewer can provide.

Familiarity with Questionnaire If an interviewer is unfamiliar with the questionnaire, then the study suffers and an unfair burden is placed on the respondent. The interview is likely to take more time than necessary and be generally unpleasant. Moreover, the interviewer cannot acquire familiarity by skimming through the questionnaire two or three times. It must be studied carefully, question by question, and the interviewer must practice reading it aloud.

Ultimately, the interviewer must be able to read the questionnaire items to respondents without error, without stumbling over words and phrases. A good model for interviewers is the actor who is reading lines in a play or motion picture. The lines must be read as naturally as though they constituted a natural conversation, but that conversation must follow exactly the language set down in the questionnaire.

By the same token, the interviewer must be familiar with the specifications prepared in conjunction with the questionnaire. Inevitably, some questions will not exactly fit a given respondent's situation, and the interviewer must determine how the question should be interpreted in that situation. The specifications provided to the interviewer should give adequate guidance in such cases, but the interviewer must know the organization and contents of the specifications well enough to refer to them efficiently. It would be better for the interviewer to leave a given question unanswered than spend five minutes searching through the specifications for clarification or trying to interpret the relevant instructions.

Following Question Wording Exactly Earlier we discussed the significance of question wording for the responses obtained. A slight change in the wording of a given question may lead a respondent to answer "Yes" rather than "No." Even though you have very carefully phrased your questionnaire items to obtain the information you need and to ensure that respondents will interpret items precisely as you intend, all this effort will be wasted if interviewers rephrase questions in their own words.

Recording Responses Exactly Whenever the questionnaire contains open-ended questions—that is, those that solicit the respondent's answer—it is critical that the interviewer record that answer exactly as given. No attempt should be made to summarize, paraphrase, or correct bad grammar.

This exactness is especially important because the interviewer will not know how the responses are to be coded before processing. Indeed, the researchers may not know the coding until they have read a hundred or so responses. For instance, the questionnaire might ask respondents how they feel about the traffic situation in their community. One respondent might answer that there are too many cars on the roads and that something should be done to limit their numbers. Another might say that more roads are needed. If the interviewer recorded these two responses with the same summary—"congested traffic"—the researchers would be unable to take advantage of the important differences in the original responses.

Sometimes, the respondent may be so inarticulate that the verbal response is too ambiguous to permit interpretation. However, the interviewer may be able to understand the respondent's intention through his or her gestures or tone. In such a situation, the exact verbal response should still be recorded, but the interviewer should add marginal comments that give both the interpretation and the reasons for arriving at it.

More generally, researchers can use marginal comments to explain aspects of the response that are not conveyed in the verbal recording, such as the respondent's apparent uncertainty in answering, anger, embarrassment, and so forth. In each case, however, the exact verbal response should also be recorded.

Probing for Responses Sometimes, respondents will answer a question inappropriately. For example, the question may present an attitudinal statement and ask the respondent to strongly agree, agree somewhat, disagree somewhat, or strongly disagree. The respondent, however, may reply: "I think that's true." The interviewer should follow this reply with a **probe,** a nondirective phrase or question to solicit a more complete answer. An effective one in this example would be: "Would you say you strongly agree or agree somewhat?" If necessary, interviewers can explain that they must check one or the other of the categories provided. If the respondent adamantly refuses to choose, the interviewer should write in the exact response given by the respondent.

Probes are more frequently required in eliciting responses to open-ended questions. For instance, in response to a question about traffic conditions, the respondent might simply reply, "Pretty bad." The interviewer could obtain an elaboration on this response through a variety of probes. Sometimes the best probe is silence; if the interviewer sits quietly with pencil poised, the respondent will probably fill the pause with additional comments. (This technique is used effectively by journalists.) Appropriate verbal probes might be "How is that?" or "In what ways?" Perhaps the most generally useful probe is "Anything else?"

Frequently, it is necessary to probe for answers that will be sufficiently informative for analytic purposes. In every case, however, such probes *must* be completely neutral. The probe cannot affect the nature of the subsequent response in any way. Whenever you anticipate that a given question may require probing for appropriate responses, you should present one or more useful probes next to the question in the questionnaire. This practice has two important advantages. First, you will have more time to devise the best, most neutral probes. Second, all interviewers will use the same probes whenever they are needed. Thus, even if the probe is not perfectly neutral, all respondents will be presented with the same probe. This is the same logical guideline discussed for question wording. Although a question should not be loaded or biased, it is essential that every respondent be presented with the same question, even a biased one.

Coordination and Control

Most interview surveys require the assistance of several interviewers. In the large-scale surveys, of course, such interviewers are hired and paid for their work. As a student researcher, you might find yourself recruiting friends to assist you. Whenever more than one interviewer is involved in a survey, their efforts must be carefully controlled. There are two aspects of this control: training interviewers and supervising them after they begin work.

The interviewer training session should begin with a description of the study. Even though the interviewers may be involved only in the project's data-collection phase, they will find it useful to understand what will be done with the interviews they conduct and what purpose will be served. Morale and motivation are usually low when interviewers don't know what's going on.

The training on how to interview should begin with a discussion of general guidelines and procedures, such as those discussed earlier in this chapter. Then you should turn to the questionnaire itself. The whole group should go through the questionnaire together—question by question. Do not simply ask if anyone has questions about the first page of the questionnaire. Read the first question aloud, explain its purpose, and then answer or address the interviewers' questions or comments. Once all of their questions and comments have been handled, go on to the next question in the questionnaire.

It's always a good idea to prepare what are called **specifications** to accompany an interview questionnaire. Specifications are explanatory and clarifying comments about how to handle difficult or confusing situations that may occur with specific questions in the questionnaire. When you are drafting the questionnaire, try to think of all the problem cases that might arise—the bizarre circumstances that might make a question difficult to answer. The survey specifications should provide detailed guidelines on how to handle such situations. As an example, such a simple matter as age might present problems. Suppose a respondent says he or she will be 25 next week. The interviewer might not be sure whether to take the respondent's current age or the nearest one. The specifications for that question should explain what should be done. (Probably, you would specify that age as of last birthday should be recorded in all cases.)

If you have prepared a set of specifications, go over them with the interviewers when you go over the individual questions in the questionnaire. Make sure your interviewers fully understand the specifications as well as the questions themselves and the reasons for them.

This portion of the interviewer training is likely to generate many troublesome questions from your interviewers: "What should I do if . . . ?" Never give a quick answer. If you have specifications, be sure to show how the solution to the problem could be determined from the specifications. If you do not have them prepared, then show how the preferred handling of the situation fits within the general logic of the question and the purpose of the study. Giving offhand, unexplained answers to such questions will only confuse the interviewers, and they will probably not take their work seriously. If you don't know the answer to a question, admit it and ask for time to decide on the best answer. Then think out the situation carefully and be sure to give all of the interviewers your answer and explain your reasons.

Once you have gone through the whole questionnaire, conduct one or two demonstration interviews in front of everyone. Preferably, you should interview someone else. Realize that your interview will be a model for those you are training, so make it good. It would be best, moreover, if the demonstration interview were done as realistically as possible. Do not pause during the demonstration to point out how you have handled a complicated situation: Handle it and then explain later. It's irrelevant if the person you are interviewing gives real answers or takes on some hypothetical identity for the purpose, as long as the answers are consistent.

After the demonstration interviews, pair off your interviewers and have them practice on each other. When they have completed the questionnaire, have them reverse roles and do it over again. Interviewing is the best training for interviewing. As your interviewers practice on each other, wander around and listen in on the practices so that you'll know how well they are doing. Once the practice is completed, everyone in the group should discuss their experiences and ask any other questions they may have.

The final stage of the training for interviewers should involve "real" interviews. Have your interviewers conduct questioning under actual final survey conditions. You may want to assign them people to interview or perhaps allow them to pick people themselves. Do not have them practice on people you have selected in your sample, however. After each interviewer has completed three to five interviews, have him or her check back with you. Look over the completed questionnaires to see if there is any evidence of misunderstanding. Again, answer any questions that individual interviewers may have. Once you are convinced that a given interviewer knows what to do, assign actual interviews—using the sample you have selected for the study.

You must continue to supervise the work of interviewers over the course of the study. Don't let them conduct more than 20 or 30 interviews without seeing you. You might assign an interviewer 20 interviews, have him or her bring back those questionnaires when they are completed, look them over, and assign another 20 or so. Although that may seem overly cautious, you must continually protect yourself against misunderstandings that may not be evident early in the study.

If you are the only interviewer in your study, then these comments may not seem relevant to you—but that's not wholly the case. You would be advised, for example, to prepare specifications for potentially troublesome questions in your questionnaire. Otherwise, you run the risk of making ad hoc decisions during the course of the study that you will later regret or forget. Also, the emphasis that has been placed on practice applies just as much to the one-person project as to the complex, funded survey with a large interviewing staff.

TELEPHONE SURVEYS

For years, telephone surveys had a bad reputation among professional researchers. These surveys are limited by definition to people who have telephones. Years ago, then, this method produced a substantial social class bias by excluding poor people from the surveys. This was vividly demonstrated by the *Literary Digest* fiasco of 1936. Even though voters were contacted by mail, the sample was partially selected from telephone subscribers—who were hardly typical in a nation that was still in the midst of the Great Depression.

Over time, however, the telephone has become a standard fixture in almost all American homes. By 2003, the U.S. Bureau of the Census (2006:737, Table 1117) estimated that 95.5 percent of all housing units had telephones, so the earlier form of class bias has substantially diminished.

A related sampling problem involves unlisted numbers. If the survey sample is selected from the pages of a local telephone directory, then it would omit all of those people—typically folks who only have cell phones and richer people who request that their numbers not be published. This potential bias has been erased through a technique that has advanced telephone sampling substantially: *random-digit dialing*, which we'll examine later.

Telephone surveys have many advantages that underlie the method's popularity. Probably the greatest advantages are money and time, in that order. In a face-to-face, household interview, you may drive several miles to a respondent's home, find no one there, return to the research office, and drive back the next day—possibly finding no one there again. It's cheaper and quicker to let your fingers make the trips.

When interviewing by telephone, you can dress any way you please without affecting the answers respondents give. And sometimes respondents will be more honest in giving socially disapproved answers if they don't have to look you in the eye. Similarly, it may be possible to probe into more sensitive areas, though that is not necessarily the case. (People are, to some extent, more suspicious when they can't see the person asking them questions—perhaps a consequence of "surveys" aimed at selling magazine subscriptions and time-share condominiums.)

Realize, however, that people can communicate a lot about themselves over the phone, even though they can't be seen. For example, researchers worry about the impact of an interviewer's name (particularly if ethnicity is relevant to the study) and debate the ethics of having all interviewers use vanilla "stage names" such as Smith or Jones. (Female interviewers sometimes ask permission to do this to avoid subsequent harassment from men they interview.)

Telephone surveys can give you greater control over data collection if several interviewers are engaged in the project. If all of the interviewers are calling from the research office, then they can get clarification from the person in charge whenever the inevitable problems occur. Alone in the boondocks, an interviewer may have to wing it between weekly visits with the interviewing supervisor.

Another important factor involved in the use of telephone surveys has to do with personal safety. Don Dillman (1978:4) describes the situation this way:

> Interviewers must be able to operate comfortably in a climate in which strangers are viewed with distrust and must successfully counter respondents' objections to being interviewed. Increasingly, interviewers must be willing to work at night to contact residents in many households. In some cases, this necessitates providing protection for interviewers working in areas of a city in which a definite threat to the safety of individuals exists.

Concerns for safety thus hamper face-to-face interviews in two ways. First, potential respondents may refuse to be interviewed, fearing the stranger interviewer. Second, the interviewers themselves may be in danger. All this is made even worse by the possibility of the researchers being sued for huge sums if anything goes wrong.

Telephone interviewing still has problems. As we've already mentioned, the method is hampered by the proliferation of bogus "surveys," which are actually sales campaigns disguised as research. If you have any questions about any such call you receive, by the way, ask the interviewer directly whether you've been selected for a survey only or if a sales "opportunity" is involved. It's also a good idea, if you have any doubts, to get the interviewer's name, phone number, and company. Hang up if they refuse to provide that information.

The ease with which people can hang up, of course, is another shortcoming of telephone surveys. Once you've been let inside someone's home for an interview, they are unlikely to order you out of the house in midinterview. It's much easier to terminate a telephone interview abruptly, saying something like, "Whoops! Someone's at the door. I gotta go." or "OMIGOD! The pigs are eating my Volvo!" (That sort of thing is much harder to fake when you're sitting in their living room.)

Another potential problem for telephone interviewing is the prevalence of answering machines. A study conducted by Walker Research (1988) found that half of the owners of answering machines acknowledged using their machines to "screen" calls at least some of the time. Research by Tuckel and Feinberg (1991), however, showed that answering machines had not yet significantly affected the ability of telephone researchers to contact prospective respondents. Nevertheless, the researchers concluded that as answering machines continued to proliferate, "the sociodemographic characteristics of owners will change." This fact made it likely that "different behavior patterns associated with the utilization of the answering machine" could emerge (1991:216).

The growth in popularity of cell phones has become a new source of concern for survey researchers, since cell phone numbers are typically not included in phone surveys. Those who use cell phones exclusively, moreover, tend to be younger, and in 2004 they were more likely to vote for John Kerry than older voters were. Scott Keeter (2006) found, however, that researchers who weighted their results in terms of age avoided bias in this respect.

Computer-Assisted Telephone Interviewing

Computers are also changing the nature of telephone interviewing. One innovation is **computer-assisted telephone interviewing (CATI).** This method has been in use for more than 10 years and is often used by academic, government, and commercial survey researchers. Though there are variations in practice, here's what CATI can look like.

Imagine an interviewer wearing a telephone-operator headset, sitting in front of a computer screen. The central computer randomly selects a telephone number and dials it. (This avoids the problem of unlisted telephone numbers.) The video screen shows an introduction ("Hello, my name is . . .") and the first question to be asked ("Could you tell me how many people live at this address?").

When the respondent answers the phone, the interviewer says hello, introduces the study, and asks the first question displayed on the screen. When the respondent answers, the interviewer types it into the computer terminal—either the verbatim response to an open-ended question or the code category for the appropriate answer to a closed-ended question. The answer is immediately stored in the central computer. The second question appears on the video screen, is asked, and the answer is entered into the computer. Thus, the interview continues.

In addition to the obvious advantages in terms of data collection, CATI automatically prepares the data for analysis; in fact, the researcher can begin analyzing the data before the interviewing is complete, thereby gaining a preview of how the analysis will turn out. Still another innovation that computer technology makes possible is described in the box entitled "Voice Capture™."

NEW TECHNOLOGIES AND SURVEY RESEARCH

As we have already seen in the case of computer-assisted telephone interviewing (CATI), many of the new technologies affecting people's lives also open new possibilities for survey research. For example, recent innovations in self-administered questionnaires make use of the computer. Among the techniques being tested are these (Nicholls, Baker, and Martin, 1996):

Computer-assisted personal interviewing (CAPI): Similar to CATI but used in face-to-face interviews rather than over the phone.

Computer-assisted self-interviewing (CASI): A research worker brings a computer to the respondent's home, and the respondent reads questions

VOICE CAPTURE™

by James E. Dannemiller, SMS Research, Honolulu

The development of various CATI techniques has been a boon to survey and marketing research, though mostly it has supported the collection, coding, and analysis of "data as usual." The Voice Capture™ technique developed by Survey Systems, however, offers quite unusual possibilities, which we are only beginning to explore.

In the course of a CATI-based telephone interview, the interviewer can trigger the computer to begin digitally recording the conversation with the respondent. Having determined that the respondent has recently changed his or her favorite TV news show, for example, the interviewer can ask, "Why did you change?" and begin recording the verbatim response. (Early in the interview, the interviewer has asked permission to record parts of the interview.)

Later on, coders can play back the responses and code them—much as they would do with the interviewer's typescript of the responses. This offers an easier and more accurate way of accomplishing a conventional task. But that's a tame use of the new capability.

It's also possible to incorporate such oral data as parts of a cross-tabulation during analysis. We may create a table of gender by age by reasons for switching TV news shows. Thus, we can hear, in turn, the responses of the young men, young women, middle-aged men, and so forth. In one such study we found the younger and older men tending to watch one TV news show, while the middle-aged men watched something else. Listening to the responses of the middle-aged men, one after another, we heard a common comment: "Well, now that I'm older . . ." This kind of aside might have been lost in the notes hastily typed by interviewers, but such comments stood out dramatically in the oral data. The middle-aged men seemed to be telling us they felt "maturity" required them to watch a particular show, while more years under their belts let them drift back to what they liked in the first place.

These kinds of data are especially compelling to clients, particularly in customer satisfaction studies. Rather than summarize what we feel a client's customers like and don't like, we can let the respondents speak directly to the client in their own words. It's like a focus group on demand. Going one step further, we have found that letting line employees (bank tellers, for example) listen to the responses has more impact than having their supervisors tell them what they are doing right or wrong.

As exciting as these experiences are, I have the strong feeling that we have scarcely begun to tap into the possibilities for such unconventional forms of data.

on the computer screen and enters his or her own answers.

Computerized self-administered questionnaire (CSAQ): The respondent receives the questionnaire via floppy disk, bulletin board, or other means and runs the software, which asks questions and accepts the respondent's answers. The respondent then returns the data file.

Touch-tone data entry (TDE): The respondent initiates the process by calling a number at the research organization. This prompts a series of computerized questions, which the respondent answers by pressing keys on the telephone keypad.

Voice recognition (VR): Instead of asking the respondent to use the telephone keypad, as in TDE, this system accepts spoken responses.

Nicholls and colleagues report that such techniques are more efficient than conventional techniques, and they do not appear to result in a reduction of data quality.

Jeffery Walker (1994) has explored the possibility of conducting surveys by fax machine. Questionnaires are faxed to respondents, who are asked to fax their answers back. Of course, such surveys can only represent that part of the population that has fax machines. Walker reports that fax surveys don't achieve as high a response rate as do face-to-face interviews, but because of the perceived urgency, they do produce higher response rates than do mail or telephone surveys. In one test case, all those who had ignored a mail questionnaire were sent a fax follow-up, and 83 percent responded.

We've already noted that, as a consumer of social research, you should be wary of "surveys" whose apparent purpose is to raise money for the sponsor. This practice has already invaded the realm of "fax surveys," evidenced by a fax entitled, "Should Hand Guns Be Outlawed?" Two fax numbers were provided for expressing either a "Yes" or "No" opinion. The smaller print noted, "Calls to these numbers cost $2.95 per minute, a small price for greater democracy. Calls take approx. 1 or 2 minutes." You can imagine where the $2.95 went.

Online Surveys

The new technology of survey research includes the use of the Internet and the World Wide Web—two of the most far-reaching developments of the last couple of decades—to conduct **online surveys.** One way to conduct an online survey is via e-mail. Your questionnaire can be part of the e-mail message or an attached file. Another way to conduct an online survey is through a website. Using the latter option, you would use web design software to design your questionnaire at a website for online use by respondents who would be directed to go to that site.

The main advantage of online surveys is that they can quickly and inexpensively be sent to very large numbers of prospective respondents anywhere in the world. The main disadvantage concerns the representativeness of the respondents.

People who use the Internet and are most apt to respond to online surveys are likely to be younger, more affluent, and more highly educated than the rest of your target population. Mick Couper (2001) provides an excellent overview of the issues concerning the present and prospective state of online surveys.

The rapid development of surveys on the World Wide Web is leading some researchers to argue that soon Internet surveys (especially web surveys) will replace traditional methods of survey data collection. Others are urging caution or even voicing skepticism about the future role web surveys will play. Clearly, we stand at the threshold of a new era for survey research, but how this will play out is not yet clear (Couper, 2001:464).

One immediate objection that many social researchers make to online surveys concerns *representativeness:* Will the people who are surveyed online be representative of meaningful populations such as all U.S. adults, all voters, and so on? This is the criticism raised with regard to surveys via fax, and with regard to telephone surveys before most U.S. households had them.

Camilo Wilson (1999), founder of Cogix (www.cogix.com), points out that some populations are ideally suited to online surveys: specifically, those who visit a particular website. For example, Wilson indicates that market research for online companies *should* be conducted online, and his firm has developed software, ViewsFlash, for precisely that purpose. Although website surveys could easily collect data from all who visit a particular site, Wilson suggests that survey sampling techniques can provide sufficient consumer data without irritating thousands or millions of potential customers.

But how about general population surveys? Humphrey Taylor and George Terhanian (1999:20) prompted part of the debate currently brewing within the survey research community with an article, "Heady Days Are Here Again." Acknowledging the need for caution, they urged that online polling be given a fair hearing:

> One test of the credibility of any new data collection method hinges on its ability to reliably and accurately forecast voting behavior. For this reason, last fall we attempted to estimate the 1998 election outcomes for governor and US Senate in 14 states on four separate occasions using internet surveys.

The researchers compared their results with 52 telephone polls that addressed the same races. Online polling correctly picked 21 of the 22 winners, or 95 percent. However, simply picking the winner is not a sufficient test of effectiveness: How close did the polls come to the actual percentages received by the various candidates? Taylor and Terhanian report their online polls missed the actual vote by an average of 6.8 percentage points. The 52 telephone polls missed the same votes by an average of 6.2 percentage points.

Warren Mitofsky (1999) is a critic of online polling. In addition to disagreeing with the way Taylor and Terhanian calculated the ranges of error just reported, he has called for a sounder, theoretical basis on which to ground the new technique.

One key to online polling is the proper assessment and use of weights for different kinds of respondents—as was discussed in the context of quota sampling in Chapter 14. Taylor and Terhanian are aware of the criticisms of quota sampling, but their initial experiences with online polling suggest to them that the technique should be pursued. Indeed, they conclude by saying "This is an unstoppable train, and it is accelerating. Those who don't get on board run the risk of being left far behind" (1999:23).

Many of the cautions urged in relation to online surveys today are similar to those urged years ago in relation to telephone surveys. Mick Couper (2001:466) observes:

> Several years ago, I predicted that the rapid spread of electronic data collection methods such as the Internet would produce a bifurcation in the survey industry between high-quality surveys based on probability samples and using traditional data collection methods, on the one hand, and surveys focused more on low cost and rapid turnaround than on representativeness and accuracy on the other. In hindsight, I was wrong, and I underestimated the impact of the Web on the survey industry. It has become much more of a fragmentation than a bifurcation (in terms of Web surveys at least), with vendors trying to find or create a niche for their particular approach or product. No longer is it just "quick and dirty" in one corner and "expensive but high quality" in the other; rather, there is a wide array of approaches representing varying levels of quality and cost.

Whether online surveys will gain the respect and extensive use enjoyed by telephone surveys today remains to be seen. Students who consider using this technique should do so in full recognition of its potential shortcomings. The box "Online Survey of Views about Evidence-Based Practice" presents an illustration of an online survey in social work.

Researchers are amassing a body of experience with this new technique, yielding lessons for increasing success. For example, Survey Sampling International suggests the following do's and don'ts for conducting online surveys:

> *Do* use consistent wording between the invitation and the survey. *Don't* use terms such as "unique ID number" in the invitation, then ask respondents to type their "password" when they get to the survey. Changing terminology can be confusing.
>
> *Do* use plain, simple language.
>
> *Don't* force the respondent to scroll down the screen for the URL for the study location.
>
> *Do* offer to share selected results from the study with everyone who completes the survey. Respondents will often welcome information as a reward for taking the study, especially when they are young adults and teens.
>
> *Do* plan the time of day and day of week to mail, depending on the subject of the study and type of respondent. Send the invitation late afternoon, evening, or weekend, when respondents are most likely to be reading mail at home, especially if the study requests respondents to check an item in the kitchen or other area in the home. If a parent–child questionnaire is planned, send the invitation late afternoon when children are home, not early in the day, when respondents can't complete the study because children are at school.
>
> *Do* be aware of technical limitations. For example, WebTV users currently cannot access surveys using Java. If respondents' systems need to be Java-enabled or require access to streaming video, alert panelists at the beginning of the study, not midway through.
>
> *Do* test incentives, rewards, and prize drawings to determine the optimal offer for best response. Longer surveys usually require larger incentives.
>
> *Do* limit studies to 15 minutes or less.
>
> WWW.WORLDOPINION.COM/THE_FRAME/FRAME4.HTML, REPRINTED WITH PERMISSION

The World Wide Web is already seeing extensive use as a marketplace for surveys and other research techniques. As only a few illustrative examples, see:

The Gallup Organization (www.gallup.com/)

Harris Poll Online (www.harrisinteractive.com/)

SMS Research (www.smshawaii.com/)

The Survey/Marketing Research e-Store (www.streamlinesurveys.com/Streamline/estore/index.htm)

Zogby International (www.zogby.com/)

ONLINE SURVEY OF VIEWS ABOUT EVIDENCE-BASED PRACTICE

In 2005 the *Journal of Social Work Education* disseminated a call for papers, encouraging prospective authors to submit manuscripts that would be reviewed for possible publication in a special issue on the topic of evidence-based practice (EBP) in social work education. Upon seeing this call for papers Allen Rubin asked his doctoral student research assistant, Danielle Parrish, if she'd like to collaborate with him in writing a conceptual article on that topic to be submitted for the special issue. She agreed, and they began reviewing the literature and developing ideas. As things progressed, they realized that the value of their work might be enhanced if they could augment their conceptual ideas with evidence from a national survey about how social work faculty members were viewing EBP.

At first, the idea of such a survey seemed impractical for two reasons: (1) The deadline for submitting their manuscript for the special issue was in about six months; and (2) they had no special funding for such an ambitious survey. Upon further reflection, however, Rubin thought it just might be doable if done online, and Parrish agreed. They estimated that it would take only about 30–40 hours for a team of MSW student assistants to go to the website of every graduate school of social work and download the e-mail addresses listed there for each program's faculty members. They estimated that the labor costs for this would be about $500. Rubin knew that he could cover those costs with the small amount of funds left over in his annual professorship endowment, but nevertheless was successful in procuring with a quick turnaround the funds in a special research grant from his university. Six MSW students were hired, and they were able to download the e-mail addresses of all faculty (N = 3,061) from 170 of the 181 accredited graduate schools of social work with accessible websites as listed on the website of the Council on Social Work Education.

While their assistants were downloading the e-mail addresses, Rubin and Parrish developed an online survey instrument consisting of 10 items that they estimated would take faculty member respondents only about five minutes to complete. The survey items were posted on a university website, and a link to the website was created and inserted into the e-mails sent to potential respondents. Whereas an e-mail reply to the survey would have shown the respondent's e-mail address, the website survey ensured the anonymity of each participant's response, and the link made it convenient to use. In addition, the e-mail that went out to faculty members detailed the purpose of the research, the importance of each recipient's participation, the anonymous and voluntary nature of the study, and Rubin's contact information. (It was not terribly time-consuming to send out 3,061 e-mail messages because, by cutting and pasting the addresses into 10 groups with a different e-mail nickname for each group, only 10 messages had to be sent, with each automatically going to about 300 recipients.)

Immediately after sending the e-mail, technological problems emerged. First Rubin's e-mail system was deluged with 135 undeliverable e-mails, due primarily to obsolete addresses. Some folks sent e-mails to Rubin indicating that his e-mail message had been delivered to their school's "spam jam," decreasing the likelihood that their colleagues received it. Others informed Rubin by e-mail that the survey website link somehow was deleted from his e-mail message by their university's e-mail system. Still others responded by e-mail to say that they could not access the survey website.

To address these technical difficulties, the researchers corresponded by e-mail with those who had reported difficulties to improve access to the survey. In addition, the researchers consulted with university technology support, and created a new university-hosted website address that was sent out in subsequent follow-up mailings. However, it is likely that technical problems precluded the response of many potential participants who did not take the time to obtain assistance in accessing the website or to respond to later e-mails.

In all, there were three follow-up e-mails to the potential respondents. The final mailing asked respondents to either complete the survey by accessing the website link or respond to Rubin by e-mail with the reason why they did not complete the survey (for example, perhaps they could not access the website). This was done to assess how representative or biased the respondent sample might be.

All of these efforts yielded a final sample of 973 respondents, which was 32 percent of the original list of 3,061 e-mail addresses. Due to the various technical problems there was no way to know the exact response rate among those who actually received the e-mail messages and were able to access the survey website. With various adjustments for the technical problems, Rubin and Parrish *estimated* that the response rate was at least 47 percent among those who actually received their e-mails and were able to access the survey website. Moreover, the e-mailed responses to the final follow-up message suggested that decisions about responding to the survey generally were not influenced by views about EBP.

Despite the tech-related nonresponse problems encountered, the findings of the survey proved to be quite valuable. A surprisingly large proportion of respondents reported teaching students that certain interventions deserved special recognition as being "evidence-based" even if the types of "evidence" supporting those interventions are generally considered weak sources of evidence—sources that reside at or near the bottom of the EBP research hierarchy. The proportion was so large that even if every nonrespondent did not teach about EBP in the problematic way, the adjusted proportion of faculty members saying that they teach about EBP this way would still be troubling. For example, even if the proportion fell from 50 percent (in the sample) to 20 percent (in the population), the prospects of one out of five faculty members teaching about EBP this way would be unsettling.

Based on feedback received after e-mailing the survey findings to all potential respondents, the findings appeared to have created quite a stir among many faculty members and spurred some schools to hold faculty meetings to discuss how faculty members were viewing and teaching about evidence-based practice. The reactions to the survey findings spurred the convening of a national symposium on improving the teaching of evidence practice.

The Rubin and Parrish survey illustrates how an online survey can be conducted with a limited amount of time and money, and how it might have value even with nonresponse problems. Yet it also illustrates some of the potential technical difficulties you should anticipate if you plan to conduct an online survey—difficulties that can make such surveys a lot more time-consuming than some might imagine them to be. Finally, it illustrates that despite these technical difficulties, when done well, online surveys can produce useful information that otherwise could only have been obtained with survey methods beyond the means of investigators with limited time and funds.

COMPARISON OF DIFFERENT SURVEY METHODS

Now that we've seen several ways to collect survey data, let's take a moment to compare them directly.

Self-administered questionnaires are generally cheaper and quicker than face-to-face interview surveys. These considerations are likely to be important for an unfunded student wishing to undertake a survey for a term paper or thesis. Moreover, if you use the self-administered mail format, it costs no more to conduct a national survey than a local one of the same sample size. In contrast, a national interview survey (either face-to-face or by telephone) would cost far more than a local one. Also, mail surveys typically require a small staff: One person can conduct a reasonable mail survey alone, although you shouldn't underestimate the work involved. Further, respondents are sometimes reluctant to report controversial or deviant attitudes or behaviors in interviews but are willing to respond to an anonymous self-administered questionnaire.

Interview surveys also have many advantages. For instance, they generally produce fewer incomplete questionnaires. Although respondents may skip questions in a self-administered questionnaire, interviewers are trained not to do so. Computers offer a further check on this in CATI surveys. Interview surveys, moreover, have typically achieved higher completion rates than self-administered ones.

Although self-administered questionnaires may deal with sensitive issues more effectively, interview surveys are definitely more effective in dealing with complicated ones. Prime examples would be the enumeration of household members and the determination of whether a given household address contains more than one housing unit. Although the concept of housing unit has been refined and standardized by the Bureau of the Census and interviewers can be trained to deal with the concept, it's extremely difficult to communicate in a self-administered questionnaire. This advantage of interview surveys pertains more generally to all complicated contingency questions.

With interviewers, it is possible to conduct a survey based on a sample of addresses or phone numbers rather than on names. An interviewer can arrive at an assigned address or call the assigned number, introduce the survey, and even—following instructions—choose the appropriate person at that address to respond to the survey. By contrast, self-administered questionnaires addressed to "occupant" receive a notoriously low response.

Finally, interviewers who question respondents face-to-face are able to make important observations aside from responses to questions asked in the interview. In a household interview, they may note the characteristics of the neighborhood, the dwelling unit, and so forth. They may also note characteristics of the respondents or the quality of their interaction with the respondents—whether the respondent had difficulty communicating, was hostile, seemed to be lying, and so forth.

The chief advantages of telephone surveys over those conducted face-to-face are primarily a matter of time and money. Telephone interviews are much cheaper and can be mounted and executed quickly. Also, interviewers are safer when interviewing residents in high-crime areas. Moreover, we've seen that the impact of the interviewers on responses is somewhat lessened when they can't be seen by the respondents. As only one indicator of the popularity of telephone interviewing, when Johnny Blair and colleagues (1995) compiled a bibliography on sample designs for telephone interviews, they listed more than 200 items.

Online surveys have many of the strengths and weaknesses of mail surveys. Once the available software has been further developed, they are likely to be substantially cheaper. An important weakness, however, lies in the difficulty of assuring that respondents to an online survey will be representative of some more general population.

Clearly, each survey method has its place in social research. Ultimately, you must balance the advantages and disadvantages of the different methods in relation to your research needs and resources.

STRENGTHS AND WEAKNESSES OF SURVEY RESEARCH

Like other modes of observation in social scientific research, surveys have special strengths and weaknesses. It is important to know these in determining whether the survey format is appropriate to your research goals.

Surveys are particularly useful when we describe the characteristics of a large population. A carefully selected probability sample in combination with a standardized questionnaire offers the possibility of making refined descriptive assertions about a student body, a city, a nation, or other large population. Surveys determine unemployment rates, voting intentions, and the like with uncanny accuracy. Although examining official documents such as marriage, birth, and death records can provide equal accuracy for a few topics, no other method of observation can provide this general capability.

Surveys—especially the self-administered variety—make very large samples feasible. Surveys of 2,000 people are not unusual. A large number of cases is important for both descriptive and explanatory analyses. Whenever several variables are to be analyzed simultaneously, it is essential to have a large number of cases.

Because surveys make large samples feasible, their findings may be more generalizable than the findings of experiments. (As we mentioned earlier, experiments in social work typically are unable to obtain probability samples.) This advantage in generalizability, however, is offset by the limited ability of surveys to show causality. For example, a survey of the moods of thousands of elderly people can tell us in general whether elderly people with pets have better moods than elderly people without pets. It wouldn't, however, be able to sort out whether having pets caused their moods to improve or whether being less depressed in the first place is what leads to getting a pet.

The survey would also enable us to analyze multiple variables simultaneously; thus, we could see whether the relationship between mood and pets applied to elderly people of different ethnicities, different income levels, different living arrangements, different levels of dependency, and so on. But we'd still be uncertain as to causality. By conducting a longitudinal survey—for example, assessing the same elderly folks' moods and pet situations over time—we'd be in a better position to speculate about causality. In other words, we could ascertain whether the moods were changing before or after the pets were obtained, although we'd still have less confidence regarding causal inferences than in an experiment. Despite the uncertainty about causality, the high level of generalizability of the findings to the population as a whole, as well as to various subgroups of the population in their natural settings, is an advantage of surveys that few experiments can offer.

In one sense, surveys are flexible. Many questions may be asked on a given topic, giving you considerable flexibility in your analyses. Although experimental design may require you to commit yourself in advance to a particular operational definition of a concept, surveys let you develop operational definitions from actual observations.

Finally, standardized questionnaires have an important strength in regard to measurement generally. Earlier chapters have discussed the ambiguous nature of most concepts: They have no ultimately real meanings. One person's religiosity is quite different from another's. Although you must be able to define concepts in ways that are most relevant to your research goals, you may not find it easy to apply the same definitions uniformly to all respondents. The survey researcher is bound to this requirement by having to ask exactly the same questions of all respondents and having to impute the same intent to all respondents giving a particular response.

Survey research has weaknesses, though. First, the requirement for standardization just mentioned often seems to result in the fitting of round pegs into square holes. Standardized questionnaire items often represent the least common denominator in assessing people's attitudes, orientations, circumstances, and experiences. By designing questions that will be at least minimally appropriate to all respondents, you may miss what is most appropriate to many respondents. In this sense, surveys often appear superficial in their coverage of complex topics. Although this problem can be partly offset through sophisticated analyses, it is inherent in survey research.

Similarly, survey research can seldom deal with the *context* of social life. Although questionnaires can provide information in this area, the survey researcher can seldom develop the feel for the total life situation in which respondents are thinking and acting that, say, the participant observer can (see Chapter 18).

Although surveys are flexible in the sense mentioned earlier, they are inflexible in other ways. Studies that use direct observation can be modified as field conditions warrant, but surveys typically require that an initial study design remain unchanged throughout. As a qualitative field researcher, for example, you can become aware of an important new variable operating in the phenomenon you are studying and begin to observe it carefully. The survey researcher would likely be unaware of the new variable's importance and could do nothing about it in any event.

Finally, surveys are subject to artificiality. Finding out that a person gives liberal answers to a questionnaire does not necessarily mean the person is liberal. This shortcoming is especially salient in the realm of action. Surveys cannot measure social action; they can only collect self-reports of recalled past action or of prospective or hypothetical action. This problem has two aspects. First, the topic of study may not be amenable to measurement through questionnaires. Second, the act of studying that topic—an attitude, for instance—may affect it. A survey respondent may have given no thought to whether the governor should be impeached until asked for his or her opinion by an interviewer. He or she may, at that point, form an opinion on the matter.

Survey research is generally weak on validity and strong on reliability. In comparison with qualitative research, for example, the artificiality of the survey format strains validity. As an illustration, people's opinions on issues seldom take the form of strongly agreeing, agreeing, disagreeing, or strongly disagreeing with a specific statement. Their survey responses in such cases, then, must be regarded as approximate indicators of what we first have in mind in framing the questions. This comment, however, needs to be held in the context of earlier discussions of the ambiguity of validity itself. To say something is a valid or an invalid measure assumes the existence of a "real" definition of what is being measured, and many scholars now reject that assumption.

COMBINING SURVEY RESEARCH METHODS AND QUALITATIVE RESEARCH METHODS

By combining qualitative research methods with survey research methods, we can benefit from the strengths of survey research while we offset its weaknesses regarding superficiality, missing social context, inflexibility, artificiality, and questionable validity. The book *Qualitative Methods in Family Research,* edited by Jane Gilgun, Kerry Daly, and Gerald Handel (1992), includes a chapter by Mark Rank that advocates for the blending of qualitative and quantitative methods and shows the benefits of it in a study of childbearing among welfare recipients.

Rank was interested in the debate over whether welfare programs like Aid to Families with Dependent Children (AFDC) encouraged women to have more children by increasing the payments when additional children are born. He began his study with qualitative interviews and fieldwork observations (like the ones to be described in Chapters 17 and 18) at various agencies serving welfare recipients and in neighborhoods where many recipients lived. The people he observed and talked to in these settings did not agree with the stereotype of women choosing to bear more children so their public assistance payments would increase. Instead, they believed that most women receiving welfare wanted to get off welfare and did not want any more children.

Were their beliefs accurate? To find out, Rank conducted a secondary analysis of survey data from the databases of the Wisconsin (Rank's state) Department of Health and Social Services and the U.S. Bureau of the Census. His quantitative analysis supported his preliminary qualitative findings. Women on welfare had a "substantially lower fertility rate than women in the general population" (1992:289). Even when Rank controlled for various demographic variables, women on welfare still had a much lower fertility rate.

Rank then wondered what accounted for his dramatic findings. To find out, he and his assistant conducted in-depth qualitative interviews with 50 families on welfare. The open-ended, semistructured interviews were conducted face-to-face in the respondents' homes, were tape-recorded, and lasted up to three hours. None of the nonpregnant women they interviewed wanted to have another child in the near future. They consistently cited financial and social forces that are not conducive to having more children. Virtually all of them expressed wanting to get off of welfare, and they appeared to recognize that the meager increase in payments for having more children was far outweighed by the increase in economic, social, and psychological costs that would come with having more children. Rank concluded that his quantitative and qualitative data reinforced each other and enhanced the validity of his findings, findings that challenged the assumption of conservative and neoliberal policy analysts that welfare payments encourage women to have more children.

Whereas Rank's work *began* with qualitative observations, a study in which one of us (Rubin) was involved illustrates the value of employing qualitative methods *after* survey methods yield enigmatic findings. Students in a doctoral research seminar in 1982 conducted a class project involving the secondary analysis of survey data from the Council on Social Work Education in an effort to identify variables that might explain why some schools of social work were experiencing much larger declines in applications to their master's degree programs than were others during that era of nationwide declines in applications to MSW programs. Their main finding was highly unexpected and puzzling. The schools with the worst declines in applications were more likely to have doctoral programs and greater prestige.

To try to figure out what accounted for these surprising findings the students conducted semi-structured, open-ended qualitative telephone interviews with administrators in those schools with the most severe and the least severe declines. What they learned was that the schools with the least severe declines tended to have initiated aggressive recruitment efforts to people who ordinarily would not have applied to their programs due to pragmatic obstacles (geographic distance, jobs, and so on) and had developed nontraditional outreach programs that often involved modifications in their curriculum standards. Administrators in the more prestigious schools experiencing the most severe declines expressed an unwillingness to alter their curriculum standards in order to keep up enrollments. Thus, the qualitative data uncovered a different meaning to the more superficial, and perplexing, survey data that seemed to portray the more prestigious schools as somehow losing their attractiveness to prospective applicants.

Reliability is a clearer matter. By presenting all subjects with standardized wording, survey research goes a long way toward eliminating unreliability in observations made by the researcher. Moreover, careful wording of the questions can also reduce significantly the respondent's own unreliability.

As with all methods of observation, a full awareness of the inherent or probable weaknesses of survey research can partially resolve them in some cases. Ultimately, though, you are on the safest ground when you can use a number of different research methods in studying a given topic. The box titled "Combining Survey Research Methods and Qualitative Research Methods" illustrates this point. In so doing, it also illustrates the point we've been repeating throughout this text regarding the complementarity of quantitative and qualitative methods.

Main Points

- Survey research, a popular social research method, is the administration of questionnaires to a sample of respondents selected from some population.

- Survey research is especially appropriate for making descriptive studies of large populations; survey data may also be used for explanatory purposes.

- Questionnaires may be administered in three basically different ways: (1) Self-administered questionnaires can be completed by the respondents themselves; (2) interviewers can administer questionnaires in face-to-face encounters, reading the items to respondents and recording the answers; and (3) interviewers can conduct telephone surveys.

- Follow-up mailings for self-administered questionnaires should be sent to potential respondents who fail to respond to the initial appeal.

- Properly monitoring questionnaire returns will provide a good guide to determining when a follow-up mailing is appropriate.

- The essential characteristic of interviewers is that they be neutral; their presence in the data-collection process must not have any effect on the responses given to questionnaire items.

- Interviewers must be carefully trained to be familiar with the questionnaire, to follow the question wording and question order exactly, and to record responses exactly as they are given.

- A probe is a neutral, nondirective question that is designed to elicit an elaboration on an incomplete or ambiguous response given in an interview in response to an open-ended question. Examples include: "Anything else?" "How is that?" "In what ways?"

- The advantages of a self-administered questionnaire over an interview survey are economy, speed, lack of interviewer bias, and the possibility of anonymity and privacy to encourage more candid responses on sensitive issues.

- Surveys conducted over the telephone have become more common and more effective in recent years, and computer-assisted telephone interviewing (CATI) techniques are especially promising.

- The advantages of an interview survey over a self-administered questionnaire are fewer incomplete questionnaires and fewer misunderstood questions, generally higher return rates, and greater flexibility in terms of sampling and special observations.

- Survey research in general has advantages in terms of economy and the amount of data that can be collected. The standardization of the data collected represents another special strength of survey research.

- Survey research has the weaknesses of being somewhat artificial and potentially superficial. It is not good at fully revealing social processes in their natural settings.

• New technologies offer additional opportunities for social researchers. They include various kinds of computer-assisted data collection and analysis as well as the chance to conduct surveys by fax or over the Internet. The latter two methods, however, must be used with caution because respondents may not be representative of the intended population.

• Online surveys have many of the strengths and weaknesses of mail surveys. Although they are cheaper to conduct, it can be difficult to ensure that the respondents represent a more general population.

Review Questions and Exercises

1. Which survey method (mailed, face-to-face interview, telephone interview, or e-mail) would you choose to administer a structured questionnaire for each of the following scenarios? State the reasons for your choice and identify any additional information that would make it easier to choose among these four options.

a. National survey of parents of children in treatment for psychotic disorders. The parents are members of the National Association for the Mentally Ill. The purpose of the survey is to assess the way the mental health professionals have related to the parents and the parents' satisfaction with the services provided to their children.

b. National survey of licensed mental health professionals who treat children with psychotic disorders. The purpose of the survey is to assess how the mental health professionals view the causes of childhood psychoses and working with parents.

c. Survey of the students in your school of social work to assess how they view the causes of childhood psychoses and working with parents of children in treatment for psychosis.

2. If you were to conduct a mail survey for each of the above scenarios, what would you do to maximize the response rate?

3. Locate a survey being conducted on the web. Briefly describe the survey and discuss its strengths and weaknesses.

4. Look at your appearance right now. Identify aspects of your appearance that might create a problem if you were interviewing a general cross section of the public.

Internet Exercises

1. Use InfoTrac College Edition to find a study in a social work journal (such as *Social Work* or *Health and Social Work*) that used a survey design. Identify the strengths and weaknesses of the survey methods used in the study.

2. Go to the following site that deals with online survey methodology: www.websm.org/. Briefly describe something you find there that makes you more optimistic or more skeptical about the likelihood of obtaining representative samples of respondents when using online surveys in social work research

3. Go to the following site on the Gallup Poll: www.gallup.com/. Once there, look for information on how Gallup Polling is conducted. (As of this writing, the information can be found in the FAQs under "How does Gallup Polling work?" which links to a 6-page document, "How Polls Are Conducted.") Briefly summarize what you learn there and why you think the Gallup survey methodology is or is not likely to yield accurate, representative findings.

4. Go to the following United States Bureau of the Census website: www.census.gov, and select QuickFacts. Once there, select your state. Click on the map of your state that appears on your screen. A map with county names will then appear. Click on your county. Find the estimated percentage of all people and of children in your county who live in poverty.

Additional Readings

Babbie, Earl. 1990. *Survey Research Methods*. Belmont, CA: Wadsworth. This is a comprehensive overview of survey methods. (You thought we'd say it was lousy?) Although it overlaps this one to some degree, the text also covers aspects of survey techniques that are omitted here.

Bradburn, Norman M., and Seymour Sudman. 1988. *Polls and Surveys: Understanding What They Tell Us*. San Francisco: Jossey-Bass. These veteran survey researchers answer questions about their craft that are commonly asked by the general public.

Dillman, Don A. 2000. *Mail and Internet Surveys: The Tailored Design Method,* 2nd ed. New York: Wiley. This book provides an excellent review of survey methodology in general. It discusses the various ways to conduct surveys, including Internet surveys, and makes many good suggestions for improving response rates.

Feick, Lawrence F. 1989. "Latent Class Analysis of Survey Questions That Include Don't Know Responses." *Public Opinion Quarterly* 53:525–47. "Don't know" can mean a variety of things, as this analysis indicates.

Groves, Robert M. 1990. "Theories and Methods of Telephone Surveys," pp. 221–240 in W. Richard Scott and Judith Blake (eds.), *Annual Review of Sociology* (vol. 16). Palo Alto, CA: Annual Reviews. An attempt to place telephone surveys in the context of sociological and psychological theories and to address the various kinds of errors common to this research method.

CHAPTER **16**

Analyzing Existing Data: Quantitative and Qualitative Methods

What You'll Learn in This Chapter

This chapter will present overviews of three methods for analyzing existing data: secondary analysis, content analysis, and historical and comparative analysis. Each method allows researchers to study things from afar without influencing them in the process.

INTRODUCTION

In examining the advantages and disadvantages of alternative modes of measurement, we have confronted problems that are associated with some degree of intrusion by researchers into whatever they are studying. We have discussed, for example, social desirability biases that may influence what people tell us or how they behave when they know we are observing them. Observation is called *obtrusive* when people know we are observing them. Conversely, observation is *unobtrusive* to the extent that those being observed are unaware of it.

The one mode of observation that best avoids being obtrusive is the use of existing data. By *existing data,* we do not mean just compilations of statistical data, although such compilations would be included as a prime example of existing data. The term has a much broader meaning and includes an almost endless array of possible data sources, such as agency case records and practitioner process notes, reports or editorials in newspapers or on TV, minutes of board meetings, agency memoranda and annual reports, books or professional journal articles, legal opinions or laws relevant to social welfare, and administrative rulings.

Three major advantages associated with the method of using existing data are its unobtrusiveness, its expedience (it usually costs less and takes less time than do other methods of data collection), and our ability to study phenomena that have occurred in the past. In light of these advantages, this chapter will examine three methods of analyzing existing data: secondary analysis, content analysis, and historical and comparative analysis.

To set the stage for our examination of these three research methods, we want to draw your attention to an excellent book that should sharpen your senses about the potential for unobtrusive measures in general. It is, among other things, the book from which we take the term *unobtrusive measures.*

A COMMENT ON UNOBTRUSIVE MEASURES

In 1966, Eugene J. Webb and three colleagues published an ingenious little book on social research (revised in 1981) that has become a classic. It focuses on the idea of *unobtrusive* or *nonreactive* research. Webb and his colleagues have played freely with the task of learning about human behavior by observing what people inadvertently leave behind them. Want to know what exhibits are the most popular at a museum? You could conduct a poll, but people might tell you what they thought you wanted to hear or what might make them look more intellectual and serious. You could stand by different exhibits and count the viewers that came by, but people might come over to see what you were doing. Webb and his colleagues suggest you check the wear and tear on the floor in front of various exhibits. Those where the tiles have been worn down the most are probably the most popular. Want to know which exhibits are popular with little kids? Look for mucus on the glass cases. To get a sense of the most popular radio stations, you could arrange with an auto mechanic to check the radio dial settings for cars brought in for repair.

The possibilities are limitless. Like an investigative detective, the social researcher looks for clues, and clues of social behavior are all around you. In a sense, everything you see represents the answer to some important social scientific question—all you have to do is think of the question. Although problems of validity and reliability crop up in unobtrusive measures, a little ingenuity can either handle them or put them in perspective. We encourage you to look at Webb's book. It's enjoyable reading and should be a source of stimulation and insight for you in taking on social inquiry through the use of the data that already exist. For now, let's turn our attention to three unobtrusive methods often used by social scientists.

SECONDARY ANALYSIS

As was evident in Chapter 15, surveys are usually major undertakings. A large-scale survey may take several months or even more than a year to progress from conceptualization to having data in hand. (Smaller-scale surveys, of course, can be done more quickly.) At the same time, however, you can pursue your particular social research interests—analyzing survey data from, say, a national sample of 2,000 respondents—while avoiding the enormous expenditure of time and money that such a survey entails. *Secondary analysis* makes such work possible.

Secondary analysis is a form of research in which the data collected and processed in one study are reanalyzed in a subsequent study. Often, the subsequent study is conducted by a different researcher, and often for a different purpose. Sometimes, however, a different researcher will reanalyze the data for the same purpose, stemming perhaps from doubts about the conclusions derived from the original analysis in the first study. Secondary analyses might also be conducted by the original researcher, perhaps to answer different research questions that require examining different relationships among variables or perhaps to re-examine a modified version of the original research question by controlling for additional variables in the analysis. Moreover, some data sets are so large that not all of their variables (or the vast range of research questions that might pertain to those variables) can feasibly be analyzed in the original study.

The use of secondary analysis is growing among social researchers as more and more data archives become available from agencies and governmental and research sources. Also, technological advances have made it easier to access and analyze these archived data sets. Technological advances also have made it easier for social researchers to *share* their data with one another.

Suppose, for example, that you are concerned about and want to research a potential problem in social work education. Perhaps you have noticed that female faculty members tend to occupy the lower ranks in your school or that they are unlikely to have administrative positions. You might want to assess, on a national basis, whether women and men of equivalent backgrounds differ in regard to such variables as rank, academic responsibilities, salary, and scholarly productivity.

Conducting a nationwide survey of social work faculty members would be quite costly and time-consuming. Even if you could get the resources to conduct the survey, you would have to worry about the potential problem of nonresponse. As an alternative to conducting the survey yourself, you could purchase—for far less money than the cost of conducting a survey—a copy of all the data for a given year on the population of social work faculty members already collected by the Council on Social Work Education in its annual statistical canvass, which includes the information you seek to analyze.

The Growth of Secondary Analysis

Beginning in the 1960s, survey researchers became aware of the potential value that lay in archiving survey data for analysis by scholars who had nothing to do with the survey design and data collection. Even when one researcher had conducted a survey and analyzed the data, those same data could be further analyzed by others, who had slightly different interests. Thus, if you were interested in the relationship between political views and attitudes toward gender equality, you could examine that research question through the analysis of any data set that happened to contain questions relating to those two variables.

The initial data archives were very much like book libraries, with a couple of differences. First, instead of books, the data archives contained data sets: initially as punched cards, then as magnetic tapes. Today they're typically contained on computer disks, CD-ROMs, or online servers. Second, whereas you're expected to return books to a conventional library, you can keep the data obtained from a data archive.

Esther Sales, Sara Lichtenwalter, and Antonio Fevola (2006) depict the growth in the use of secondary analysis as follows:

> Research data have always held the potential for later revisits. The more ambitious the study and the better the quality of the database, the greater the potential for further exploration. Most researchers engaging in large-scale studies, often heavily funded by the federal government, recognized that they have barely skimmed the surface of their data set's potential before the project ends. Funding sources also have become concerned about the limited informational yield compared to the dollar investment that many large-scale research studies entail. In recent years, several federal agencies funding behavioral research have developed new policies to counter this shortfall in study findings. An expanding number of federal agencies, including the National Science Foundation, the National Institute on Alcohol and Alcoholism, and the National Institute of Child Health and Human Development, have issued calls for secondary analyses of existing data sets. More notably, the National Institutes of Health (NIH) now has moved beyond its long-standing general policy of encouraging data sharing . . . mandating that data from studies they fund be placed in a repository that others may access. It now requires that large-budget research proposals include in their application a plan for data access, storage, and sharing. In addition, several professional organizations . . . as well as some scientific journals, encourage or require researchers to archive data used for publications or presentations. . . . These organizations have created pressures on researchers that are rapidly expanding data availability and retrieval options.
>
> (2006, PP. 545–546)

Types and Sources of Data Archives

Varied sources collect and provide data to social work researchers. These sources include university research organizations, government and human service agencies, the United Nations, and professional associations. It would take a whole book just to list the sources of data available for analysis. In this section, we'll mention a few and point you in the direction of finding others that are relevant to your research interest.

One type of data archive provides continuing time-series surveys of different samples drawn from the same population. A well-known current example of this type is the General Social Survey (GSS). Every year or two, the federal government commissions the National Opinion Research Center (NORC) at the University of Chicago to conduct a major national survey to collect data on a large number of social science variables. These surveys are conducted precisely for the purpose of making data available to scholars at little or no cost. You can learn more about the GSS at www.icpsr.umich.edu/gss/. Another type of archive contains data collected in a national census of an entire population. Data collected in cross-sectional surveys and longitudinal surveys comprise two additional types of archives. Some archives contain more than one of the foregoing types of data sources.

Numerous resources are available for identifying and acquiring existing data for secondary analysis. Here are a few. The National Data Archive on Child Abuse and Neglect (www.ndacan.cornell.edu/) has data sets on child abuse and neglect. Another source with child welfare data is the Annie E. Casey Foundation (www.aecf.org/), which has a data set called KIDS COUNT that contains variables relating to the well-being of children. The National Archive of Criminal Justice Data (www.icpsr.umich.edu/NACJD/) has a data set from a domestic violence research project.

Esther Sales and her associates (2006) recommend several additional sources of data. The largest data repository they mention is at the Inter-university Consortium of Political and Social Research (ICPSR) at the University of Michigan. It is available to researchers working at member institutions worldwide. Its archives, which can be accessed at www.icpsr.umich.edu, contain social work–related data on aging, substance abuse, mental health, criminal justice, health and medical care, and education. Another useful source mentioned by Sales and her associates is the Sociometrics' Social Science Electronic Data Library (www.socio.com/edl.htm). Its archive contains more than 200 studies on social work–related topics. For a website that provides links to a broad array of social science data, Sales and her associates recommend the University of California–San Diego Social Science Data on the Internet (http://odwin.ucsd.edu/idata).

Sources of Existing Statistics

Data sets also can be derived from **existing statistics** in administrative and public records. This type of data is often in aggregate form in agency records. Suppose you wanted to assess the impact of a new statewide program to prevent child abuse. You could examine the existing statistics in the records compiled by the state's human services agency to see whether changes occurred in annual rates of removing children from their homes due to abuse after the program was implemented. When the data are in aggregate form, only, they cannot be re-analyzed using the individual as the unit of analysis, Instead, they can be analyzed only in the form of statistics that apply to the aggregate, such as the prevalence of child abuse in different geographic areas, the proportions of different types of services provided in different agencies, and so on.

One valuable book you can buy is the annual *Statistical Abstract of the United States,* which is published by the U.S. Department of Commerce through its Bureau of the Census. It includes statistics on the individual states and (less extensively) cities as well as on the nation as a whole. You can learn the number of work stoppages in the country year by year, residential property taxes of major cities, the number of water-pollution discharges reported around the country, the number of business proprietorships in the nation, and hundreds of other such handy bits of information. You can buy the *Statistical Abstract* on a CD-ROM, making the search for and transfer of data quite easy.

Federal agencies—the Departments of Labor, Agriculture, Transportation, and so forth—publish countless data series. To find out what's available, go to your library, find the government documents section, and spend a few hours browsing through the shelves. You can also visit the U.S. Government Printing Office site on the World Wide Web (www.access.gpo.gov) and look around.

The web is the latest development in access to existing statistics. Table 16-1 illustrates the richness of this resource.

Table 16-1 Website Sources for Existing Statistics

United States Government Websites	
Bureau of the Census	www.census.gov/
Bureau of Labor Statistics	www.bls.gov/
Central Intelligence Agency (CIA)	www.cia.gov/
Department of Education	www.ed.gov/
Dept. of Health and Human Services	www.os.dhhs.gov/
Dept. of Housing and Urban Development	www.hud.gov/
Federal Agency Statistics Directory (links)	www.fedstats.gov/
Federal Bureau of Investigation	www.fbi.gov/
Federal Interagency Forum on Child and Family Statistics	www.childstats.gov
Government Printing Office	www.access.gpo.gov
U.S. House of Representatives	www.house.gov/
U.S. Senate	www.senate.gov
White House	www.whitehouse.gov/
Other Websites for Existing Statistics	
Child Welfare League of America	http://ndas.cwla.org/
Crime Statistics	www.crime.org/
National Archive of Computerized Data on Aging	www.icpsr.umich.edu/NACDA/index.html
National Assoc. for Welfare Research and Statistics	www.nawrs.org/
National Data Archive on Child Abuse and Neglect	www.ndacan.cornell.edu
United Nations Databases	www.un.org/databases/index.html
World Bank	www.worldbank.org/

World statistics are available through the United Nations. Its *Demographic Yearbook* presents annual vital statistics (births, deaths, and other data relevant to populations) for the individual nations of the world. The website for the United Nations databases is listed in Table 16-1. Organizations such as the Population Reference Bureau publish a variety of demographic data, U.S. and international, that a secondary analyst could use. Its *World Population Data Sheet* and *Population Bulletin* are resources heavily used by social scientists. Social indicator data can be found in the journal *SINET: A Quarterly Review of Social Reports and Research on Social Indicators, Social Trends, and the Quality of Life.* Other publications report a variety of other kinds of data. Again, a trip to your library, along with a web search, is the best introduction to what's available.

The amount of data provided by nongovernment agencies is as staggering as the amount your taxes buy. Chambers of commerce often publish data reports on business, as do private consumer groups. Ralph Nader has information on automobile safety, and Common Cause covers politics and government. And, as mentioned earlier, George Gallup publishes reference volumes on public opinion as tapped by Gallup Polls since 1935.

We're tempted to continue listing data sources, but you probably have already gotten the idea. We suggest you visit the government documents section the next time you're at your college library. You'll be amazed by the data waiting for your analysis. The lack of funds to support expensive data collection is no reason for not doing good and useful research.

Advantages of Secondary Analysis

The advantages of secondary analysis are obvious and enormous: It is cheaper and faster than doing an original survey (or most other types of research). Moreover, the cost savings of this approach enable you to conduct research on very large samples—much larger samples than you would be able to study with typical levels of funding.

Another advantage is that—depending on who did the original study—you may benefit from the work of top-flight professionals. In addition, the archived data may have been generated by studies that received well-funded federal research grants that made it feasible to implement rigorous sampling approaches and obtain high response rates. Thus, as Sales and her associates (2006) point out:

> The samples for such studies are therefore likely to be highly representative of the populations from which they are drawn. Inferences from such studies are likely to have high external validity . . . which makes them a powerful and persuasive base for discussions of social needs and social policy. Because social work researchers have only infrequently been recipients of major federal grants, the ability to access high-quality data that inform on key social problems may have special advantage for our field.
>
> (P. 549)

Well-funded, large-scale studies are also likely to have assessed a much larger number of variables than most original social work research studies can assess. Secondary analysis thus provides the advantage of gathering information on a much larger number of variables. Moreover, in addition to examining information separately for many more variables, a very large sample size makes it possible to employ sophisticated multivariate statistical techniques for analyzing relationships among many variables simultaneously and thus ferreting out the relative explanatory power of each variable when the other variables are controlled. (Recall our discussion of the elaboration model in Chapter 10. We'll revisit this issue when we discuss multivariate analysis in Chapter 22.)

Another advantage of conducting a secondary analysis of a well-funded study is the likelihood that the original study was methodologically strong in general, not just in the size and representativeness of its sample. For example, to be successful in securing major funding for very large-scale studies, research proposals had better reflect well-controlled designs and very strong measurement procedures. Chances are, no matter how well you understand the design and measurement concepts that we've discussed in this book, it will be difficult for you to obtain the level of funding needed to enable you to obtain the resources required to actually implement a study that is as rigorous as you'd like it to be.

Sales and her associates (2006) also identify the following additional advantages of secondary analysis:

- **Human Subject Concerns.** Proposing to use previously collected data is likely to expedite IRB approval. [Recall our discussion of IRBs in Chapter 4.] Because you are not collecting the data, you avoid ethical concerns regarding data collection (assuming ample safeguards for protecting identities of respondents).

- **Access Hard-to-Identify Populations.** Finding and gathering data from members of hidden or hard to locate populations [such as those discussed in Chapter 5] can be expensive and beyond the means of most social work researchers. This pertains not only to stigmatized populations, but also to people with low-incidence problems (such as same-sex adoptive parents). Accessing a data set from a well-funded study whose sample was large enough to include sufficient members from such populations may make more sense than trying to collect original data from those members yourself.

- **Monitoring Trends Over Time.** As we mentioned above, some data archives contain data gathered in time-series studies or longitudinal studies. Completing such studies probably will require more time and years than you can or want to spend on your research.

- **Comparative Studies.** Comparing social problems across different nations is another example of a type of study that—due to its expense—can be conducted much more feasibly in a secondary analysis than in an original study.

- **Technical Support.** The federal government encourages the secondary analysis of data archives by providing detailed manuals to help researchers access and analyze the data. In addition, some popular data archives provide workshops offering hands-on training. Some government agencies even reimburse attendee expenses associated with attending their workshops.

Limitations of Secondary Analysis

Secondary analysis can also involve some limitations. If you conduct a secondary analysis or analyze existing statistics in your research (or your practice), you should not assume that the data are free of problems just because they are "official" or because a prestigious agency published them. The data may be outdated by the time they are released. In addition, a key problem is the recurrent question of validity. When one researcher collects data for one particular purpose, you have no assurance that those data will be appropriate to your research interests. Typically, you'll find that the original researcher asked a question that "comes close" to measuring what you are interested in, but you'll wish the question had been asked just a little differently—or that another, related question had also been asked. Your question, then, is whether the question that was asked provides a valid measure of the variable you want to analyze. Let's look now at some of the special problems that you might encounter when using this method.

Missing Data Whenever you base your research on an analysis of data that already exist, you are obviously limited to what exists. Before investing a great deal of time in planning a study that will use existing data, you should check the data source to see if the data you need are there at all. If they are there, then you should check to see whether large chunks of the data on certain key variables are missing. If you conduct a national research study using existing data on ethnicity and poverty among retirees in the United States, for example, and states with relatively large numbers of relatively affluent white retirees (such as Florida and Arizona) are missing from the database—or in the database but without reporting ethnicity—then your results might be seriously inaccurate.

Sometimes a variable may have data entered on it, but the lack of variation in the data renders it missing in the sense of being a variable. You may recall from our discussion of variables in Chapters 3 and 7 that to be a variable, a concept must *vary*. Suppose you want to evaluate the effectiveness of a play therapy intervention for traumatized 6-year-olds by examining its impact on their grades in first grade, using school grade records. You should first check the school records to see if sufficient variation exists in grades at that level. Suppose first grade teachers give virtually every student an A to avoid discouraging the students or lowering their self-esteem. If that is the case, grades will be missing as a variable in the records because they will not sufficiently vary.

Problems of Validity You will encounter validity problems if the agency that collected the existing statistics you are analyzing defined your variables in ways that don't match your definitions of those variables. Suppose, for example, that a state welfare agency—perhaps seeking to show that its recent welfare reform policy succeeded in getting welfare recipients back to work—defines participation in a government job training program as being employed. Suppose you, however, are skeptical about how often such training leads to actual paid employment and therefore do not want to count such training in your definition of being employed. Maybe the government data do not distinguish between part-time and full-time employment, and you have defined success in getting welfare recipients back to work to mean full-time employment with wages that match or exceed welfare benefits. If you must rely on the government's existing statistics for your research, you would have a serious validity problem.

Another type of validity problem occurs when existing statistics deal with phenomena that often go unreported but include only reported incidents in the records. Thus, existing statistics may underestimate the number of individuals who have been physically abused by a spouse or a partner or the number of coeds who have been sexually abused on dates because many such incidents go unreported. The actual incidence of these problems can be underestimated even further if the existing statistics include only incidents involving the filing of criminal charges, omitting incidents that were unreported as well as those that were reported but did not lead to criminal charges.

Improper data-collection methods can also cause validity problems, such as when survey interviewers make up information so they can avoid dangerous neighborhoods. Likewise, direct-service practitioners who resent having to spend so much time completing forms on their cases can become careless and sloppy in rushing to complete those forms.

Problems of Reliability The analysis of existing data depends heavily on the quality of the data themselves: Are they accurate reports of what they claim to report? That can be a substantial problem sometimes because the weighty tables of government statistics are sometimes grossly inaccurate.

Because a great deal of the research into crime depends on official crime statistics, this body of data has come under critical evaluation. The results have not been encouraging. Suppose, for purposes of illustration, that you were interested in tracing the long-term trends in marijuana use in the United States. Official statistics on the numbers of people arrested for selling or possessing it would seem to be a reasonable measure of use. Right? Not necessarily.

To begin, you face a hefty problem of validity. Before the passage of the Marijuana Tax Act in 1937, marijuana was legal in the United States, so arrest records would not give you a valid measure of use. But even if you limited your inquiry to the post-1937 era, you would still have problems of reliability that stem from the nature of law enforcement and crime record keeping.

Law enforcement, for example, is subject to various pressures. Crime reports may rise or fall depending on increases or decreases in the budget for hiring police. A public outcry against marijuana, led perhaps by a vocal citizens' group, can result in a police "crackdown on drug trafficking"—especially during an election or budget year. A sensational story in the press can have a similar effect. In addition, the volume of other business that faces police affects marijuana arrests.

Lois DeFleur (1975) has traced the pattern of drug arrests in Chicago between 1942 and 1970 and has demonstrated that the official records present a far more accurate history of police practices and political pressure on police than a history of drug use. On a different level of analysis, Donald Black (1970) and others have analyzed the factors that influence whether an offender is actually arrested by police or let off with a warning. Ultimately, official crime statistics are influenced by whether specific offenders are well or poorly dressed, whether they are polite or abusive to police officers, and so forth. Consider unreported crimes, which are sometimes estimated to be as much as 10 times the number of crimes known to police, and the reliability of crime statistics gets even shakier.

These comments concern crime statistics at a local level. Often it's useful to analyze national crime statistics, such as those reported in the FBI's annual *Uniform Crime Reports.* Additional problems are introduced at the national level. Different local jurisdictions define crimes differently. Also, participation in the FBI program is voluntary, so the data are incomplete.

Finally, the process of record keeping affects the records that are kept and reported. Whenever a law enforcement unit improves its record-keeping system—computerizing it, for example—the apparent crime rates always increase dramatically. That can happen even if the number of crimes committed, reported, and investigated does not actually increase.

Similar problems of reliability can occur in existing statistics on many other variables of interest to social work researchers whose definitions or record-keeping methods change over time. Consider child abuse, for example. Some methods of corporal punishment that were deemed acceptable several decades ago are now considered to constitute child abuse. Likewise, statistics on rape may now include incidents of intercourse with a date who did not want it but who was too inebriated to resist, whereas in the past narrower definitions were used to count the incidence of rape.

Awareness is your first protection against the problems of validity and reliability in the analysis of existing data—knowing that the problems may exist. Investigating the nature of the data collection and tabulation may help you assess the nature and degree of these problems so that you can judge their potential impact on your research interest. Replication can also help alleviate the problem.

Inadequate Documentation Often, however, you may not be able to ascertain the nature or appraise the quality of the procedures used to collect and process data in the study that supplied the data for your secondary analysis. For example, information may not be available on such concerns as how well interviewers were trained, whether bias was somehow introduced in data gathering, or how carefully the data were coded (Sales et al., 2006).

Feasibility Issues Although secondary analysis usually is less costly than collecting original data yourself, we should not understate how time consuming this method sometimes is. Some huge data sets, for example, can overwhelm researchers who are not yet accustomed to handling data sets with that many variables or with multiple waves of data collection. When you first encounter such data sets, you may need to make the data sets manageable by extracting only some variables and some waves. You are likely to find this to be necessary despite the vastly expanded capacity of current computers. You also should consider seeking technical assistance if such technical support is available.

Other common feasibility issues pertain to changes in the existing data over time, gaining access to those data, and then maintaining access. As Alexander and Solomon (2006:418) observe:

> Accessing [government] data sets frequently takes a good deal of negotiation with agencies for permission for use, and often requires compromises and contractual agreements. Generally, it is necessary to work with the producers of the data in order to truly understand the meaning of the existing information.

To illustrate these problems, Alexander and Solomon include in their book a commentary by Diane DePanfilis (2006) on the challenges that DePanfilis and Zuravin (2002) had to deal with in their study that analyzed existing statistics to assess the effect of services on the recurrence of child maltreatment. They used two sources of available records in Baltimore's public agency for child protective services: case records and a statewide management information system.

One problem involved policy changes over time that resulted in changes in the way the data were formatted. This difficulty was particularly germane because of the longitudinal nature of their study. Other problems involved difficulties in gaining access to the existing data and then not losing that access over time due to administrative or policy changes. DePanfilis (in Alexander and Solomon, 2006:435–437) recommends the following steps for gaining and maintaining access to existing data:

> **1. Prepare a short prospectus about the proposed study.**
>
> **2. Schedule face-to-face meetings with agency administrators . . . .** [A]dministrators at state and local levels must approve the study. Approvals must occur prior to submitting a proposal for funding, as a letter that confirms access to the data is required in order to convince a funding source that conducting the study will be feasible in a particular jurisdiction. The researcher is advised to thoroughly understand the state laws about who may have access to existing child welfare data for research purposes *before* developing the prospectus or planning these meetings.
>
> **3. Gain human research protection approval for the use of archival records in research.**
>
> **4. Develop procedures for access to electronic files.**
>
> **5. Develop procedures for access to case records.** The specific methods for access to hard copies of case records will vary by jurisdiction. It is likely that the researcher must request office space within the local agency for reviewing and coding case records, as the need to protect the confidentiality of the participants' information would usually forbid taking records or copies of records out of the public agency office.
>
> **6. Overcome unanticipated barriers when gaining access to existing records . . . .** It is not uncommon for the agency administrator who wrote the letter of support at the time a proposal was written to be unavailable at the time a study is implemented. . . . About a third of the way into our study, a new administrator at the state level was concerned about the number of research studies being undertaken regarding child welfare policies and practices. . . . The administrator asked for a new Attorney General position about the legality of providing access to child welfare data for research purposes. [This] resulted in our stopping our case-level data collection for nine months.

DePanfilis adds that the prospects for gaining and maintaining access to agency records will be significantly enhanced by developing relationships with agency staff members in charge of operations. For example, she and Zuravin "went out of our way to give people fruit baskets, to participate in local agency programs, and to touch base with administrators on a regular basis" (p. 437).

DePanfilis also discusses problems in the databases they were analyzing—problems that take considerable time to reconcile. For example, it took them a year to plan the data-collection process. One problem was that they wanted to use both the children and the family as the units of analysis, and the case record data had to be transformed accordingly. In conducting a pilot test, they found discrepancies in 50 percent of the records between the data self-reported by the client, the statewide management information system data, and the case record data.

Despite the foregoing feasibility issues, analyzing existing statistics is usually less costly and less time-consuming than collecting original data. And despite the potential problems that often need to be resolved in the data, the analysis of existing statistics can provide valuable findings for guiding policy and practice.

Illustrations of the Secondary Analysis of Existing Statistics in Research on Social Welfare Policy

Two studies of social welfare policy illustrate the applicability to social work of analyzing existing statistics. They also illustrate some of the problems that have already been discussed in using this method.

In one study, Martha Ozawa (1989) investigated whether the (no longer existing) Aid to Families with Dependent Children (AFDC) welfare program contributed to the dramatic increase in illegitimate births among adolescents. Ozawa hypothesized that a high AFDC payment and a high AFDC acceptance rate increased that birthrate because more generous payments and higher acceptance rates made it easier for the childbearing adolescent to establish her own household and avoid an unwanted marriage. In this connection, Ozawa envisioned positive aspects of the adolescent's decision to raise a child alone rather than to marry. She emphasized that she was not studying the impact of AFDC on the decision to bear a child (she cited prior research showing that adolescents do not bear infants out of wedlock to receive AFDC payments). Instead, she was studying the impact of AFDC on the adolescent's decision whether to marry or raise the child alone.

Ozawa's unit of analysis was the state. Her dependent variable was the state's rate of illegitimacy among women aged 19 and under. Her independent variables included the state AFDC benefit level and the state AFDC acceptance rate. (These were not the only independent variables she studied, but to keep this illustration simple we'll focus on the two primary ones.)

Analyzing data from the U.S. National Center for Health Statistics, Ozawa showed that the national adolescent illegitimacy rate rose 70 percent between 1970 and 1982. To assess the impact of AFDC on those rates, she obtained government data published by the Bureau of the Census, the House Committee on Ways and Means, and the Social Security Administration. Her results supported her hypothesis: Pregnant adolescents in states with higher AFDC payments and higher acceptance rates were less likely to marry than those in states with lower AFDC payments and lower acceptance rates.

In developing policy implications from her findings, Ozawa urged policy makers to understand the positive aspects of the decision not to marry and to consider "granting AFDC payments to low-income, unmarried adolescent mothers regardless of the economic backgrounds of their parents" (1989:11).

In another study, Claudia Coulton, Shanta Pandey, and Julia Chow (1990) were concerned that economic forces in the United States during the 1980s were concentrating poor people in deteriorating central urban neighborhoods where they were becoming further isolated from economic opportunities and increasingly exposed to adverse social and physical conditions associated with extreme poverty. Coulton and her associates postulated that published research that had already documented this trend was based primarily on national census data that might have underestimated the problem, because income estimates from the 1980 census were for income earned in 1979 and thus did not reflect the impact of the recession that began late in 1979 and continued into the early 1980s.

To study this phenomenon in depth, as well as several related statistical phenomena that we won't go into here, Coulton and her associates decided to limit their study to one urban area: Cleveland, Ohio. They recognized that this decision would limit the generalizability of their findings but believed that others could replicate their study in other cities to see if the same patterns could be observed.

Coulton and her associates prefaced their study by noting that poverty rates rose sharply in the 1980s and that to the extent that poverty was becoming more geographically concentrated, it was becoming more difficult for poor people to reach jobs located in the suburbs. Workers who could afford to move closer to suburban jobs were induced to do so, and this further concentrated the poverty of the inner city neighborhood they left behind and reduced the opportunity of those who were left behind to find jobs close to home (to which they could travel). As the neighborhood deteriorated, the worsening social environment conceivably might have had harmful effects on the individuals left behind—particularly the youths—as they became increasingly exposed to such problems as teen pregnancy, delinquency, school dropout, and so on.

The research team used a variety of sources of existing statistics for Cleveland, including data from the Center for Regional Economic Issues located at Case Western Reserve University, birth and death information reported by the Ohio Department of Health (which provided data on low birth weight, infant death rate, teen birthrate, and illegitimacy rates), crime rate data from the Federal Bureau of Investigation, juvenile delinquency data from the Cuyahoga County

Juvenile Court, drug arrest rates from the Cleveland Police Department, and housing value data from the Housing Policy Research Program of Cleveland State University.

The existing statistics analyzed by Coulton and her associates showed that by 1988 nearly 50 percent of Cleveland's poor people lived in neighborhoods of concentrated poverty, compared with 21 percent in 1970. (The researchers defined high-poverty areas as census tracts where more than 40 percent of the population lives in a household below the poverty threshold.) Thus, poor people were becoming more spatially isolated from the rest of society and less likely to encounter nonpoor people in their neighborhoods. The statistics on poverty-related physical and social problems that Coulton and her associates analyzed indicated that as poor people were becoming more concentrated in high-poverty areas, the social and physical problems to which they were being exposed were deteriorating rapidly, particularly for people who were living in "emerging poverty areas" that lost many blue-collar workers in the early 1980s and consequently became poverty areas after 1980. Noting the importance of the person-in-environment framework for social work practice and the special vulnerability of poor children living in high-poverty neighborhoods, Coulton and her associates recommended that social workers consider interventions at the environmental level:

> Social workers need practice models that combine their traditional approaches to service delivery with economic redevelopment of distressed parts of the city and mechanisms that reestablish connections between central city residents and distant, suburban job locations. Barriers to these connections are geographic but also involve social networks, information channels, and psychological distance. As poor neighborhoods become increasingly adverse environments due to economic and social decline, programs and interventions are needed that will disrupt their growing isolation from the mainstream.
>
> (1990:15)

In addition to providing an excellent illustration of the creative analysis of a variety of sources of existing statistics, the study by Coulton and her associates offers a splendid example of the relevance of research (and policy!) to social work practice. Now that you see the advantages and problems of secondary analysis, let's turn to another method for analyzing existing data, this time focusing on available data that are more qualitative in nature.

CONTENT ANALYSIS

Content analysis is a way of transforming qualitative material into quantitative data. It may be applied to virtually any form of communication, not just available records. It consists primarily of coding and tabulating the occurrences of certain forms of content that are being communicated.

For example, we might analyze social work course syllabi to see if certain types of faculty members or schools have more content on ethnic minorities than do others. Or we might examine presentations at social work conferences at different times in our profession's history, perhaps counting the number of references to psychoanalytic concepts or to ecological or social reform concepts to see if the popularity of different professional orientations or conceptual frameworks has shifted over time. Or we might tabulate how often various types of issues are mentioned in the minutes of community organization meetings. Is the amount of citizen participation reflected in the minutes related to how frequently certain types of issues appear in the minutes?

Content analysis research can have great applicability to direct social work practice. In his text *Effective Casework Practice,* Joel Fischer (1978) calls the practitioner–client relationship the keystone of casework practice and identifies practitioner empathy, warmth, and genuineness as the three core conditions of an effective helping relationship. The field first learned of the importance of these conditions from an extensive body of content analysis research studies, which were reviewed by Marsden (1971). In these studies, written and taped excerpts from therapy sessions were rated according to the degree to which the core relationship conditions were observed. The findings tended to indicate that the more these three conditions were present, the better the clinical process and outcome.

Some topics are more appropriately addressed by content analysis than by any other method of inquiry. Suppose for a moment that you're interested in how mentally ill individuals are portrayed on television. Perhaps the National Alliance for the Mentally Ill plans to mount a campaign to educate the public about the nature of mental illness, alleviate fears about the mentally ill, and offset stereotypes about them. Suppose one facet of the campaign is aimed at the television medium and seeks to reduce the extent to which TV programs portray mentally ill individuals as violent or dangerous. Suppose further that you seek to evaluate the impact of that facet of the campaign on TV programming, and you will use a time-series design to assess whether the campaign seems to be reducing the extent to which mentally ill individuals are portrayed as violent or dangerous. Content analysis would be the best mode of observation for your time-series study.

Briefly, here's what you would do. First, you'd develop an operational definition of your dependent variable: the extent to which mentally ill individuals are portrayed as violent or dangerous. The section on coding later in this chapter will help you do that. Next you'd have to decide what to watch. Probably you would decide (1) what stations to watch, (2) for what days or period, and (3) at what hours. Then, you'd stock in some snacks and start watching, classifying, and recording. Once you had completed your observations, you'd be able to analyze the data you collected and determine whether mentally ill individuals were being portrayed less violently after than before the campaign.

Content analysis, then, is particularly well suited to the study of communications and to answering the classic question of communications research: "Who says what, to whom, why, how, and with what effect?" As a mode of observation, content analysis requires a considered handling of the *what,* and the analysis of data collected in this mode, as in others, addresses the *why* and *with what effect.*

Sampling in Content Analysis

In the study of communications, as in the study of people, it is often impossible to observe directly everything in which you are interested. In your study of television portrayals of the mentally ill, for example, we'd advise against attempting to watch everything that's broadcast. It wouldn't be possible, and your brain would probably short-circuit before you got close to discovering that for yourself. Usually, then, it's appropriate to sample.

Your first decision would be to decide whether each TV show was to be given one overall score, whether each mentally ill person in it would be given a separate score, or perhaps some other option. Next, you would need to establish the universe to be sampled from. In this case, what TV stations will you observe? What will be the period of the study—which days and what hours of those days will you observe? Then, how many programs do you want to observe and code for analysis?

Now you're ready to design the sample selection. As a practical matter, you wouldn't have to sample among the different stations if you had assistants—each of you could watch a different channel during the same time period. But let's suppose you are working alone. Your final sampling frame, from which a sample will be selected and watched, might look something like this:

- Jan. 7, Channel 2, 7–9 P.M.
- Jan. 7, Channel 4, 7–9 P.M.
- Jan. 7, Channel 9, 7–9 P.M.
- Jan. 7, Channel 2, 9–11 P.M.
- Jan. 7, Channel 4, 9–11 P.M.
- Jan. 7, Channel 9, 9–11 P.M.
- Jan. 8, Channel 2, 7–9 P.M.
- Jan. 8, Channel 4, 7–9 P.M.
- Jan. 8, Channel 9, 7–9 P.M.
- Jan. 8, Channel 2, 9–11 P.M.
- Jan. 8, Channel 4, 9–11 P.M.
- Jan. 8, Channel 9, 9–11 P.M.
- Jan. 9, Channel 2, 7–9 P.M.
- Jan. 9, Channel 4, 7–9 P.M.
- and so on.

Notice that we've made several decisions for you in the illustration. First, we have assumed that channels 2, 4, and 9 are the ones appropriate to your study. We've assumed that you found the 7 to 11 P.M. prime-time hours to be the most relevant and that two-hour periods would do the job. We picked January 7 out of the hat for a starting date. In practice, of course, all of these decisions should be based on your careful consideration of what would be appropriate to your particular study.

Sampling is simple and straightforward once you have become clear about your units of analysis and the observations that are appropriate to those units and have created a sampling frame like the one we've illustrated. The alternative procedures available to you are the same ones described in Chapter 14: random, systematic, stratified, and so on.

Sampling Techniques

In content analysis of written prose, sampling may occur at any or all of the following levels: words, phrases, sentences, paragraphs, sections, chapters, books, writers, or the contexts relevant to the works. Other forms of communication may also be sampled at any of the conceptual levels appropriate to them.

Any of the conventional sampling techniques discussed in Chapter 14 may be used in content analysis. We might select a *random* or *systematic* sample of agency memoranda, of state laws passed regarding the rights of mental patients, or of the minutes of community organization meetings. We might number all course syllabi in a school of social work and then select a random sample of 25.

Stratified sampling is also appropriate to content analysis. To analyze the editorial policies of American newspapers, for example, we might first group all newspapers by region of the country, size of the community in which they are published, frequency of publication, or average circulation. We might then select a stratified random or systematic sample of newspapers for analysis. Having done so, we might select a sample of editorials from each selected newspaper, perhaps stratified chronologically.

Cluster sampling is equally appropriate to content analysis. Indeed, if individual editorials were to be the unit of analysis in the previous example, then the selection of newspapers at the first stage of sampling would be a cluster sample. In an analysis of political speeches, we might begin by selecting a sample of politicians; each politician would represent a cluster of political speeches. The study of TV portrayal of the mentally ill described previously is another example of cluster sampling.

We repeat: Sampling need not end when we reach the unit of analysis. If novels are the unit of analysis in a study, then we might select a sample of novelists, subsamples of novels written by each selected author, and a sample of paragraphs within each novel. We would then analyze the content of the paragraphs to describe the novels themselves.

Let's turn now to a more direct examination of analysis that has been mentioned frequently in the previous discussions. At this point, *content analysis* will refer to the coding or classification of material being observed. Part 7 will deal with the manipulation of those classifications to draw descriptive and explanatory conclusions.

Coding in Content Analysis

Content analysis is essentially a coding operation. Communications—oral, written, or other—are coded or classified according to some conceptual framework. Newspaper editorials, for example, may be coded as liberal or conservative. Radio broadcasts might be coded as propagandistic or not. Novels might be coded as pro–social welfare or not. Political speeches might be coded as to whether or not they impugn the character of welfare recipients or the homeless. Recall that terms such as these are subject to many interpretations, and the researcher must specify definitions clearly.

Coding in content analysis involves the logic of conceptualization and operationalization as discussed in Chapter 7. In content analysis, as in other research methods, you must refine your conceptual framework and develop specific methods for observing in relation to that framework.

Manifest and Latent Content

Content analysis, like other forms of research, involves choices between *depth* and *specificity* of understanding. Often, this represents a choice between *validity* and *reliability,* respectively. Typically, qualitative researchers opt for depth, preferring to base their judgments on a broad range of observations and information, even at the risk that another observer might reach a different judgment of the situation. The choice in content analysis is between coding *manifest content* versus coding *latent content.*

Coding the **manifest content**—the visible, surface content—of a communication more closely approximates the use of a standardized questionnaire. To determine, for example, how sexist certain books are, you might simply count the number of times male pronouns are used in conjunction with generalized prestigious roles (such as referring to the role of some nonspecified physician as "his" role) or the average number of such uses per page. This strictly quantitative method would have the advantage of ease and *reliability* in coding and of letting the reader of the research report know precisely how sexist language was measured. It would have a disadvantage, on the other hand, in terms of *validity.* Surely the term *sexist book* conveys a richer and deeper meaning than the number of times male pronouns are used.

Alternatively, you may take a more qualitative approach by coding the **latent content** of the communication: its underlying meaning. In the current example, you might read an entire book or a sample of paragraphs or pages and make an overall assessment of how sexist the book is. Although your total assessment might well be influenced by the inappropriate appearance of male pronouns, it would not depend fully on the frequency with which such words appeared.

Clearly, this second method seems better designed for tapping the underlying meaning of communications, but its advantage comes at a cost of reliability and specificity. Somewhat different definitions or standards may be used, especially if more than one person is coding the novel. A passage—perhaps depicting boys as heroes and girls as being rescued—might be deemed sexist by one coder but not another. Even if you do all of the coding yourself, there is no guarantee that your definitions and standards will remain constant throughout the enterprise. Moreover, the reader of your research report would be generally uncertain about the definitions you have used.

Wherever possible, the best solution to this dilemma is to use *both* methods. A given unit of observation should receive the same characterization from both methods to the extent that your coding of manifest and latent content has been reasonably valid and reliable. If the agreement achieved by the two methods is fairly close, though imperfect, then the final score might reflect the scores assigned in the two independent methods. If, on the other hand, coding manifest and latent content produces gross disagreement, then you would be well advised to reconsider your theoretical conceptualization.

Conceptualization and the Creation of Code Categories

For all research methods, conceptualization and operationalization typically involve the interaction of theoretical concerns and empirical observations. If, for example, you believe some newspaper editorials to be liberal and others to be conservative, then ask yourself why you think so. Read some editorials, asking yourself which are liberal and which are conservative. Was the political orientation of a particular editorial most clearly indicated by its manifest content or by its tone? Was your decision based on the use of certain terms (for example, *leftist, fascist,* and so on) or on the support or opposition given to a particular issue or political personality?

Both inductive and deductive methods should be used in this activity. If you are testing theoretical propositions, then your theories should suggest empirical indicators of concepts. If you have begun with specific empirical observations, then you should attempt to derive general principles relating to them and then apply those principles to the other empirical observations.

Throughout this activity, you should remember that the operational definition of any variable is composed of the attributes included in it. Such attributes, moreover, should be mutually exclusive and exhaustive. A newspaper editorial, for instance, should not be described as both liberal and conservative, though you should probably allow for some to be middle-of-the-road. It may be sufficient for your purposes to code novels as being erotic or nonerotic, but you may also want to consider that some could be antierotic. Paintings might be classified as representational or not, if that satisfied your research purpose, or you might wish to further classify them as impressionistic, abstract, allegorical, and so forth.

Realize further that different levels of measurement may be used in content analysis. You may, for example, simply characterize newspaper editorials as liberal or conservative, or you might wish to use a more refined ranking, ranging from extremely liberal to extremely conservative. Bear in mind, however, that the level of measurement implicit in your coding methods does not necessarily reflect the nature of your variables. If the word *love* appeared 100 times in Novel A and 50 times in Novel B, then you would be justified in saying that the word *love* appeared twice as often in Novel A, but not that Novel A was twice as erotic as Novel B. Similarly, if Person A agrees with twice as many anti-Semitic questionnaire statements as Person B, that does not make Person A twice as anti-Semitic.

No coding scheme should be used in content analysis until it has been carefully pretested. You should decide what manifest or latent contents of communications will be regarded as indicators of the different attributes that compose your research variables and then write down these operational definitions and use them in the actual coding of several units of observation. If you plan to use more than one coder in the final project, each should independently code the same set of observations so that you can determine the extent of agreement produced. In any event, you should take special note of any difficult cases: observations not easily classified using the operational definition. Finally, you should review the overall results of the pretest to ensure they will be appropriate to your analytic concerns. If, for example, all of the pretest newspaper editorials have been coded as liberal, then you may want to reconsider your definition of that attribute.

As with other types of research, it is not essential that you commit yourself in advance to a specific definition of each concept. Often you will do better to devise the most appropriate definition of a concept on the basis of your subsequent analyses. In the cases of erotic novels, for example, you might count separately the frequency with which different erotic words appear. This procedure would allow you to determine, during your later analysis, which words or combinations of words provided the most useful indication of your variable.

Counting and Record Keeping

If you plan to evaluate your content analysis data quantitatively, then your coding operation must be amenable to data processing.

First, the end product of your coding must be *numerical*. If you are counting the frequency of certain words, phrases, or other manifest content, then that will necessarily be the case. Even if you are coding latent content on the basis of overall judgments, you will need to represent your coding decision numerically: 1 = very liberal, 2 = moderately liberal, 3 = moderately conservative, and so on.

Second, it is essential that your record keeping clearly distinguishes between your units of analysis and your units of observation, especially if they are different. The initial coding, of course, must relate to your units of observation. If novelists are your units of analysis, for instance, and you wish to characterize them through a content analysis of their novels, then your primary records will represent novels. You may then combine your scoring of individual novels to characterize each novelist.

Third, when counting, it normally is important to record the base from which the counting is done. It would tell us little that inappropriate male pronouns appeared 87 times in a book if we did not know about how many words were in the book altogether. The issue of observation base is most easily resolved if every observation is coded in terms of one of the attributes making up a variable. Rather than simply counting the number of liberal editorials in a given collection, for example, code each editorial by its political orientation, even if it must be coded "no apparent orientation."

Let's suppose that we want to study the practice of school social workers. More specifically, suppose we seek to learn whether school social workers today are more likely to intervene with family members and school personnel than in the past and whether in the past they were more likely to restrict their intervention to counseling the troubled student.

One possible approach would be to use school social workers as the units of analysis and to rank the practice orientation reflected in the assessment and process notes in a sample of case records for each social worker sampled. Table 16-2 illustrates a portion of a tally sheet that might utilize a four-point scale to code the orientation of each social worker. In the first column, each social worker in the sample has been assigned an identification number to facilitate mechanized data processing. The second column identifies the number of case records coded for each social worker, important information because it is necessary to calculate the percentage of case records with particular attributes.

The next column in Table 16-2 is for assigning a subjective overall assessment of the social worker's orientation. (Such assignments might later be compared with the several objective measures.) Other columns provide space for recording the number of case records that reflect specific interventions, target problems, or assessment notions. In a real content analysis, there would be spaces for recording additional information in the case records, such as client attributes, dates of service, social worker attributes, and so on.

Qualitative Data Analysis

Not all content analysis results in counting. Sometimes a qualitative assessment of the materials is most appropriate. Bruce Berg (1989:123–125) discusses "negative case testing" as a technique for qualitative hypothesis testing. First, in the grounded theory tradition, you begin with an examination of the data, which may yield a general hypothesis. Let's say that you're examining the leadership of a new community association by reviewing the minutes of meetings to see who made motions that were subsequently passed. Your initial examination of the data suggests that the wealthier members are the most likely to assume this leadership role.

The second stage in the analysis is to search your data to find all the cases that would contradict the initial hypothesis. In this instance, you would look for poorer members who made successful motions and wealthy members who never did. Third, you must

Table 16-2 An Abbreviated Sample Tally Sheet

SOCIAL WORKER ID	NUMBER OF CASE RECORDS EVALUATED	SUBJECTIVE EVALUATION*	NUMBER OF CASE RECORDS WITH ENVIRONMENTAL TARGET PROBLEMS	NUMBER OF CASE RECORDS WITH ENVIRONMENTAL INTERVENTIONS	NUMBER OF CASE RECORDS WITH ASSESSMENTS FOCUSING ON STUDENT PSYCHOPATHOLOGY
001	37	2	10	6	25
002	26	4	25	24	2
003	44	3	30	23	14
004	30	1	0	0	30

*1—Counseling only; 2—Slightly environmental; 3—Moderately environmental; 4—Very environmental.

review each of the disconfirming cases and either (1) give up the hypothesis or (2) see how it needs to be fine-tuned.

Let's say that in your analysis of disconfirming cases, you notice that each of the unwealthy leaders has a graduate degree, whereas each of the wealthy nonleaders has little formal education. You may revise your hypothesis to consider both education and wealth as routes to leadership in the association. Perhaps you'll discover some threshold for leadership (a white-collar job, a level of income, and a college degree) beyond which those with the most money, education, or both are the most active leaders.

This process is an example of what Barney Glaser and Anselm Strauss (1967) called *analytic induction*. It is inductive in that it primarily begins with observations, and it is analytic because it goes beyond description to find patterns and relationships among variables.

There are, of course, dangers in this form of analysis, as in all others. The chief risk is misclassifying observations to support an emerging hypothesis. For example, you may erroneously conclude that a nonleader didn't graduate from college or you may decide that the job of factory foreman is "close enough" to being white-collar.

Berg (1989:124) offers techniques for avoiding these errors:

1. If there are sufficient cases, select some at random from each category in order to avoid merely picking those that best support the hypothesis.

2. Give at least three examples in support of every assertion you make about the data.

3. Have your analytic interpretations carefully reviewed by others uninvolved in the research project to see whether they agree.

4. Report whatever inconsistencies you do discover—any cases that simply do not fit your hypotheses.

Realize that few social patterns are 100 percent consistent, so you may have discovered something important even if it doesn't apply to absolutely all of social life. However, you should be honest with your readers in that regard.

Quantitative and Qualitative Examples of Content Analysis

Let's look at two examples of content analysis in action in social work. Both involve qualitative material. The first will illustrate the transformation of qualitative material into quantitative data. The second keeps a qualitative focus throughout.

A Quantitative Illustration: The Changing Self-Image of Social Work Two social workers, James Billups and Maria Julia (1987), wanted to see whether and how the self-image of modern social work has been changing since the formation of the National Association of Social Workers (NASW) in 1955. They decided to study this issue by conducting a content analysis of social work practice position vacancy descriptions that appeared in 1960, 1970, and 1980.

An early task that confronted Billups and Julia was choosing the sources of vacancy descriptions that they would analyze. They thought it would make the most sense to use the publication put out by NASW that carries the most position vacancy descriptions in social work. For the years 1960 and 1970, that source was the journal *Social Casework*. Subsequently, NASW made its *NASW News* the prime source for position vacancy announcements. Accordingly, Billups and Julia decided to use *Social Casework* as their source for 1960 and 1970 and *NASW News* as their source for 1980.

Both publications were issued ten times per year, and each issue contained a very large number of position vacancy descriptions. Because of their resource constraints, Billups and Julia did not want to analyze every one of the thousands of descriptions that had been published over the three years of interest. As explained in Chapter 14, with such a large population it is not necessary to study the entire population of descriptions in order to describe them accurately. Probability sampling techniques enable us to obtain accurate descriptions of a population based on a small fraction of that population. Billups and Julia selected a systematic random sample of 506 position vacancy descriptions, which accounted for 10 percent of the population of descriptions published in 1960, 1970, and 1980.

Next Billups and Julia had to formulate a standard definition of dimensions of practice that they would look for in the position vacancy descriptions. They decided that they would examine manifest content only (not latent content). They defined dimensions of practice according to the following four major components: (1) position title (such as administrator, caseworker, clinical social worker, and therapist), (2) principal field of practice where the work would take place (such as family and child welfare, and mental health), (3) major practice responsibilities (such as casework, group work, and direct or indirect practice), and (4) required or preferred education and experience. These four components were broken down into mutually exclusive and exhaustive subcategories. Standardized coding instructions were developed that were used by two coders. The intercoder reliability was assessed and found to be acceptable.

Billups and Julia found marked changes in the position vacancy announcements over the years. There was a dramatic drop in the mention of method-specific titles and responsibilities, for example. Whereas almost half of the announcements in 1960 mentioned the term *casework* or *caseworkers*, almost none did in 1980. Replacing the method-specific terms were terms such as *social worker, direct practice, clinical social workers*, and *therapists*.

Other sizable changes were observed in the fields of practice mentioned in the announcements. Whereas the family and child welfare field was mentioned by almost 60 percent of the announcements in 1960, in 1980 it was only 21 percent. The largest growth was observed in the fields of mental health, aging, corrections, rehabilitation, industrial social work, and substance abuse.

In interpreting these changes, Billups and Julia call attention to two possible contrasting trends. On the one hand, the reduction in the use of method-specific titles such as *casework* and *group work* might signify "a growing expectation that more social work practitioners will need to assume both a holistic view of problems and a broader repertoire of approaches to practice" than in the past (1987:21). On the other hand, decreases in public welfare fields and increases in the use of terms such as *therapist* might signify abandonment of the very poor and a narrower approach to practice imitating the roles of other clinical professions.

A Qualitative Illustration: Adoption Revelation and Communication The foregoing Billups and Julia study illustrates a quantitative approach to content analysis in that it transformed manifest qualitative material into quantitative categories. But some approaches to content analysis keep a strict qualitative focus throughout, reporting qualitative material only in qualitative terms and without transforming the material into quantitative data. An example of this approach in social work is a study by Ruth McRoy and her associates (1990) on adoption revelation.

The researchers thought that the relatively high frequency of psychiatric treatment referrals of adopted children might indicate problems in the process of revealing to children that they were adopted. They decided to explore this issue by looking for patterns among case illustrations of problematic and nonproblematic revelations of adoption. Their nonprobability sample (an availability sample) consisted of 50 adoptive families whose adopted child was in residential treatment facilities and who had been adopted before the age of two.

Intensive, open-ended interviews were conducted with the parents, adopted child, and caseworker for each family. The interviews were tape-recorded and transcribed verbatim. A content analysis was then performed on the information on the tapes. (Thus, this study did not use an unobtrusive content analysis as a way of collecting data; it used intensive interviews for that purpose. The content analysis was applied after the data were collected.)

Like many qualitative research reports, this one did not provide much detail as to methodological procedures—details that would enable the reader to assess the validity of its conclusions. As we will discuss in the next two chapters, qualitative approaches eschew such structure in favor of more flexible approaches that permit deeper probing into subjective meanings—probes that usually seek to generate new insights more than they seek to test hypotheses.

McRoy and her associates presented the results of their content analysis of their interview data primarily in the form of lengthy quotes that they incorporated into composite case illustrations. In one case illustration, for example, a girl was not told by her parents that she was adopted until she was 10 years old. The quotation shows that she refused to believe them and was traumatized by the revelation. In two other case illustrations, boys who learned of being adopted when they were 5 years old reacted with anger or mistrust.

One theme that seemed to cut across the case illustrations was the need for social workers who worked with adoptive families to deal with issues concerning how, when, and by whom children are informed of their adoption. Social workers need to encourage adoptive parents to be the first to inform the child of the adoption.

Another recurrent theme was the need for ongoing communication between parents and the child about the adoption and the need to express empathy and understanding regarding the child's ongoing questions about his or her background and the reasons for being placed for adoption. The evidence for this conclusion is presented in several quotes that illustrate how learning of being adopted seemed to trigger problems in some families but not in others. In one, a daughter describes how she became rebellious against her parents when she found out at age 10 what adoption really means. The problem became exacerbated, in her view, when her parents seemed to have difficulty discussing the adoption with her and were not always truthful with her about aspects of the adoption. Other quotes are provided from cases that involved better communication where the children reported less discomfort with the adoption issue.

These illustrations of content analysis in action should give you a clearer picture of the procedures and potential that characterize this research method. Let's conclude the discussion of content analysis with an overview of its particular strengths and weaknesses.

Strengths and Weaknesses of Content Analysis

Probably the greatest advantage of content analysis is its economy in terms of both time and money. A single college student could undertake a content analysis, whereas undertaking a survey, for example, might not be feasible. There is no requirement for a large research staff; no special equipment is required. As long as you have access to the material to be coded, you can undertake content analysis.

Ease of correcting mistakes is another advantage of content analysis. If you discover you have botched a survey, you may be forced to repeat the whole research project with all its attendant costs in time and money. If you botch your qualitative research, it may be impossible to redo the project; the event under study may no longer exist. In content analysis, it's usually easier to repeat a portion of the study than it is for other research methods. You might be required, moreover, to recode only a portion of your data rather than repeat the entire enterprise.

Importantly, content analysis permits you to study processes that occur over long periods of time. You might focus on the imagery of blacks conveyed in American novels of 1850 to 1860, for example, or you might examine changing imagery from 1850 to the present.

Finally, content analysis has the advantage, mentioned at the outset of the chapter, of being *unobtrusive*—that is, the content analyst seldom affects the subject *being studied*. Because the books have already been written, the case records already recorded, the speeches already presented, content analyses can have no effect on them. Not all research methods have this advantage.

Content analysis has disadvantages as well. For one thing, it's limited to the examination of *recorded* communications. Such communications may be oral, written, or graphic, but they must be recorded in some fashion to permit analysis.

Content analysis, as we have seen, has both advantages and disadvantages in terms of validity and reliability. For validity, problems are likely unless you happen to be studying communication processes per se. For instance, did the drop in the mention of terms such as *casework* in the Billups and Julia study necessarily mean that practitioners were becoming more holistic in their practice and using a broader repertoire of intervention approaches? Conceivably, the only thing that changed was the labels being used to describe the same forms of practice—that the field was merely using more fashionable terminology for the same old practices.

Although validity is a common problem with content analysis, the concreteness of materials studied in quantitative approaches to content analysis strengthens the likelihood of reliability. You can always code and recode and even recode again if you want, making certain that the coding is consistent. In qualitative research, by contrast, there's probably nothing you can do after the fact to ensure greater reliability in observation and categorization.

HISTORICAL AND COMPARATIVE ANALYSIS

In this final section of the chapter, we examine historical and comparative research, a method that differs substantially from those previously discussed, though it overlaps somewhat with qualitative research, content analysis, and the analysis of existing statistics.

Our examination of research methods to date has focused primarily on studies anchored in one point in time and in one locale, whether a particular small group or a nation. This focus, although accurately portraying the main emphasis of contemporary social work research, conceals the fact that social scientists are also interested in tracing the development of social forms over time and comparing those developmental processes across cultures.

Historical and comparative analysis is usually considered a qualitative method, one in which the researcher attempts to master many subtle details. The main resources for observation and analysis are historical records. Although a historical and comparative analysis might include content analysis, it is not limited to communications. The method's name includes the word *comparative* because most social scientists—in contrast to historians, who may simply describe a particular set of events—seek to discover common patterns that recur in different times and places.

Many historical writings can be found in the social work literature. Biographies of social work pioneers constitute a large segment of these writings. Another segment contains case studies that trace the development of social welfare policies and programs. Less common, but perhaps more useful for informing current practice, are studies that are more comparative in their efforts to seek recurring patterns that help explain the past and imply possible lessons for the present. An excellent example of the latter type of study, one with particular relevance to social work research, is Sidney Zimbalist's book *Historic Themes and Landmarks in Social Welfare Research* (1977).

Based on his analysis of social work research studies published between the late 19th century and the mid-1960s, Zimbalist identified a recurring cycle in which social work researchers exhibited an excessive tendency to go overboard in embracing the latest wave of research. Rather than take a balanced and critical outlook regarding the range of research approaches available, considering both their strengths and weaknesses and the conditions under which each is most appropriate, social work researchers tended to faddishly embrace promising new approaches as a panacea for the profession's research needs.

Zimbalist detected this cycle in early research on the causes of poverty and the measurement of its prevalence, in the embracing of the social survey movement at the beginning of the 20th century, and in the study of the multiproblem family in the mid-1960s. By describing the past, Zimbalist's work gives us a framework for understanding fads in social work research that may emerge today or in the future.

Another excellent example of historical and comparative research that offers lessons for the present is a study by Morrissey and Goldman (1984) on recurrent cycles of reform in the care of the chronic mentally ill. Morrissey and Goldman identify parallels between the recent deinstitutionalization movement and Dorothea Dix's 19th-century crusade to build state hospitals to provide asylum and sanctuary to individuals too sick to fend for themselves in communities that did not want them. In Dix's era, the reform intended to make care more humane by shifting its locus from the community to the hospital. In today's era of deinstitutionalization, the reform intended to make care more humane by shifting its locus from the hospital to the community. But today we hear of large numbers of mentally ill individuals who are homeless or in jails and who are living in squalor—many of the same conditions that prompted Dix's crusade more than a century ago.

Morrissey and Goldman show how both reforms failed for the same reason: Each merely shifted the locus of care without garnering enough public fiscal support to ensure that the new locus of care would ultimately be any more humane than the old one. Without adequate financing, Dix's intended humane sanctuaries for the mentally ill too often became overcrowded, inhumane "snake-pits" where sick individuals who could not afford expensive private care could be warehoused and forgotten. Without adequate financing, the noble intentions of the deinstitutionalization movement have for too many individuals led to community-based conditions as bad as in the back wards of state hospitals.

One lesson for today from this research is that if we seek to ensure more humane care for the long-term mentally ill, we must go beyond conceptualizing idealized programs or notions about where to provide care; the real issue is convincing the public to allocate adequate fiscal support for that care. Without the latter, our reformist efforts may be doomed to repeat the unintended consequences of previous reforms.

Sources of Historical and Comparative Data

As we saw in the case of existing statistics, there is no end of data available for analysis in historical research. To begin, historians may have already reported on whatever it is you want to examine, and their analyses can give you an initial grounding in the subject, a jumping-off point for more in-depth research. Ultimately, you will usually want to go beyond others' conclusions and examine "raw data" and draw your own conclusions. These vary, of course, according to the topic under study. Raw data might, for example, include old letters or diaries, sermons or lectures, and so forth.

In discussing procedures for studying the history of family life, Ellen Rothman (1981) points to the following sources:

> In addition to personal sources, there are public records which are also revealing of family history. Newspapers are especially rich in evidence on the educational, legal, and recreational aspects of family life in the past as seen from a local point of view. Magazines reflect more general patterns of family life; students often find them interesting to explore for data on perceptions and expectations of mainstream family values. Magazines offer several different kinds of sources at once: visual materials (illustrations and advertisements), commentary (editorial and advice columns), and fiction. Popular periodicals are particularly rich in the last two. Advice on many questions of concern to families—from the proper way to discipline children to the economics of wallpaper—fills magazine columns from the early nineteenth century to the present. Stories that suggest common experiences or perceptions of family life appear with the same continuity.
>
> (1981:53)

Organizations generally document themselves, so if you are studying the development of some organization you should examine its official documents: charters, policy statements, speeches by leaders, and so on.

Often, official government documents provide the data needed for analysis. To better appreciate the history of race relations in the United States, A. Leon Higginbotham, Jr. (1978) examined 200 years of laws and court cases involving race. Himself the first African American appointed to a federal judgeship, Higginbotham found that the law, rather than protecting blacks, was the embodiment of bigotry and oppression. In the earliest court cases, there was considerable ambiguity over whether blacks were indentured servants or, in fact, slaves. Later court cases and laws clarified the matter—holding blacks to be something less than human.

Many of the source materials for historical research can be found in academic libraries. Specialized librarians may be available to help you locate obscure documents. Skills in using the library, therefore, are essential if you wish to conduct historical research. (We discuss using the library in Appendix A.)

Two broad types of source materials are *primary* sources and *secondary* sources. Primary sources provide firsthand accounts by someone who was present at an event—for example, diaries, letters, organizational bylaws, the minutes of a meeting, the orally reported memory of an eyewitness, and so on. Secondary sources describe past phenomena based on primary sources. Thus, if you cite a book on the history of Lyndon Johnson's Great Society social welfare programs, you are using a secondary source. But if you go to the LBJ Presidential Library in Austin, Texas, and cite letters, laws, and official documents from that period that you find there, then you are using primary sources.

A danger in working exclusively with secondary sources is that you may merely repeat the mistakes contained in those sources and fail to give yourself the opportunity to provide a new, independent perspective on past events. But primary sources can be flawed as well. For example, an eyewitness could have been biased or may experience faulty memory.

Stuart (1981) argues that people who produce or write primary sources based on events they witnessed probably had a vested interest in those events. He cites an example of bias in the statistical reports of the populations of Native Americans on reservations by Indian agents in the late 19th century. Some agents exaggerated the population size in order to obtain more supplies for their reservations from the federal government's Office of Indian Affairs.

A television biography of Lyndon Johnson, aired by the Public Broadcasting System, relied heavily on primary sources such as people who worked on Johnson's White House staff. His decision not to run for reelection in 1968 was portrayed largely in terms of his dismay over the tragedy of the war in Vietnam and his desire to find a way to negotiate an end to it. Unmentioned in the historical documentary was the fact that he announced his decision not to run on the eve of the Wisconsin primary election, when political polls there predicted that Senator Eugene McCarthy would beat him by a large margin in that primary, and when newspaper articles spoke of the pending humiliation of an incumbent president of Johnson's stature being rejected by the voters of his own party. Was that omission due to overreliance on primary sources who were close to, and fond of, Lyndon Johnson? We can only surmise.

In conducting historical research, then, keep these cautions in mind. As we saw in the case of existing statistics, you cannot trust the accuracy of records—official or unofficial, primary or secondary. You need always be wary of bias in your data sources. If all of your data on a pioneer social worker are taken from people who worked for that social worker, you are unlikely to get a well-rounded view of that person. If all of your data on the development of a social movement are taken from activists in the movement itself, then you are unlikely to gain a well-rounded view of the movement. The diaries of affluent, friendly visitors of the Charity Organization Societies of a century ago may not give you an accurate view of life among the immigrant poor they visited during those times.

As a final illustration of this point, suppose you conduct historical research in an effort to understand the chief forces at play that led to massive discharges from state hospitals as part of the deinstitutionalization movement in mental health. If you rely only on the reports of the staff of state mental health bureaucracies, you may be led to believe that those discharges were primarily a humanitarian response to advances in psychopharmacology and concern for the civil liberties of the mentally ill. You might not discover that the greatest number of discharges occurred long after the discovery of psychotropic drugs in the mid-1950s. Instead, they came in the mid-1970s, when fiscal crises in state governments prompted state officials to recognize that by discharging patients from state hospitals to community facilities, the costs of caring for the mentally ill could be passed on from the state to the federal government (Morrissey and Goldman, 1984).

Your protection against these dangers in historical research lies in *corroboration.* If several sources point to the same set of "facts," your confidence in them might reasonably increase. Thus, when conducting historical research, you should try not to rely on a single source or on one type of source. Try to obtain data from every relevant source you can find, and be sure to seek sources that represent different vested interests and different points of view. The box titled "Reading and Evaluating Documents" provides additional suggestions on how to use historical documents and what to make of them.

The critical review that Aminzade and Laslett urge for the reading of historical documents can serve you more generally in life and not just in the pursuit of historical and comparative research. Consider applying some of the boxed questions with regard to presidential press conferences, advertising, or—gasp!—college textbooks. None of these offers a direct view of reality; all have human authors and human subjects.

Analytic Techniques

As a qualitative research method, **historical and comparative research** treats hypotheses differently from the way quantitative methods do when seeking to formulate explanations. Rather than sticking with a hypothesis throughout an entire study that has been rigidly designed in advance to test it, historical researchers are likely to revise and reformulate their hypotheses continually throughout the process of examining, analyzing, and synthesizing the historical documents they encounter.

Because historical and comparative research is a fluid qualitative method, there are no easily listed steps to follow in the analysis of historical data. Max Weber used the German term ***verstehen***—understanding—in reference to an essential quality of social research.

READING AND EVALUATING DOCUMENTS

by Ron Aminzade and Barbara Laslett, University of Minnesota

The purpose of the following comments is to give you some sense of the kind of interpretive work that historians do and the critical approach they take toward their sources. It should help you to appreciate some of the skills that historians develop in their efforts to reconstruct the past from residues, to assess the evidentiary status of different types of documents, and to determine the range of permissible inferences and interpretations.

Here are some of the questions historians ask about documents:

1. Who composed the documents? Why were they written? Why have they survived all these years? What methods were used to acquire the information contained in the documents?

2. What are some of the biases in the documents and how might you go about checking or correcting them? How inclusive or representative is the sample of individuals, events, etc. contained in the document? What were the institutional constraints and the general organizational routines under which the document was prepared? To what extent does the document provide more of an index of institutional activity than of the phenomenon being studied? What is the time lapse between the observation of the events documented and the witnesses' documentation of them? How confidential or public was the document meant to be? What role did etiquette, convention, and custom play in the presentation of the material contained within the document? If you relied solely upon the evidence contained in these documents, how might your vision of the past be distorted? What other kinds of documents might you look at for evidence on the same issues?

3. What are the key categories and concepts used by the writer of the document to organize the information presented? What are the selectivities or silences that result from these categories of thought?

4. What sort of theoretical issues and debates do these documents cast light upon? What kinds of historical or sociological questions do they help answer? What sorts of valid inferences can one make from the information contained in these documents? What sorts of generalizations can one make on the basis of the information contained in these documents?

Weber meant that the researcher must be able to take on, mentally, the circumstances, views, and feelings of those being studied to interpret their actions appropriately. More recently, social scientists have adopted the term **hermeneutics** for this aspect of social research. Originally a Christian theological term that referred to the interpretation of spiritual truth in the Bible, *hermeneutics* has been secularized to mean the art, science, or skill of interpretation.

Whereas the conclusions drawn from quantitative research methods can rest, in part, on numerical calculations—x is either greater than y or it isn't—hermeneutic conclusions are harder to pin down and more subject to debate. But hermeneutics involves more than mere opinions. Albert Einstein (1940) described the foundation of science this way:

> Science is the attempt to make the chaotic diversity of our sense-experience correspond to a logically uniform system of thought. In this system single experiences must be correlated with the theoretic structure in such a way that the resulting coordination is unique and convincing.
>
> (1940:487)

The historical and comparative researcher must find patterns among the voluminous details that describe the subject matter of study. Often the "theoretic structure" Einstein mentioned takes the form of what Weber called *ideal types:* conceptual models composed of the essential characteristics of social phenomena. Thus, for example, Weber himself did considerable research on bureaucracy. Having observed numerous actual bureaucracies, Weber (1925) detailed those qualities essential to bureaucracies in general: jurisdictional areas, hierarchically structured authority, written files, and so on. Weber did not merely list characteristics common to all the actual bureaucracies he observed. Rather, he needed to understand fully the essentials of bureaucratic operation to create a theoretical model of the "perfect" (ideal type) bureaucracy.

Often, historical and comparative research is informed by a particular theoretical paradigm. Thus, Marxist scholars may undertake historical analyses of particular situations—such as the history of Hispanic minorities in the United States—to determine whether they can be understood in terms of the Marxist version of conflict theory.

Although historical and comparative research is regarded as a qualitative rather than a quantitative technique, historians often make use of quantitative methods. For example, historical analysts often use time-series (see Chapter 11) data to monitor changing conditions over time, such as data on population, crime rates, unemployment, and infant mortality rates. When historical researchers rely on quantitative data, their reports will rely on numbers, graphs, statistical trends, and the like to support their conclusions. When they rely on qualitative methods, their reports will contain less quantitative data and instead cite narrative material in their sources to illustrate the recurring patterns that they think they have detected.

Main Points

- Unobtrusive measures are ways of studying social behavior without affecting it in the process.

- Secondary analysis is a form of research in which the data collected and processed in one study are reanalyzed in a subsequent study. Often, the subsequent study is conducted by a different researcher, and often for a different purpose. Sometimes, however, a different researcher will reanalyze the data for the same purpose, stemming perhaps from doubts about the conclusions derived from the original analysis in the first study.

- Some data sets are in the form of aggregated existing statistics in administrative and public records. When the data are in aggregate form, only, they cannot be reanalyzed using the individual as the unit of analysis, Instead, they can be analyzed only in the form of statistics that apply to the aggregate, such as the prevalence of child abuse in different geographic areas, the proportions of different types of services provided in different agencies, and so on.

- Common potential advantages of secondary analysis include cost savings, benefiting from the work of top-flight professionals, analyzing data generated by rigorous sampling approaches with large samples and high response rates, having a large number of variables that makes it possible to conduct a sophisticated multivariate statistical analysis, the likelihood that the original study was methodologically strong in general, facilitating IRB approval, accessing hard-to-identify populations, monitoring trends over time, facilitating cross-national comparisons, and obtaining technical support.

- Common potential limitations of secondary analysis include problems of validity and reliability, missing data, inadequate documentation, and unanticipated feasibility issues.

- A variety of government and nongovernment agencies provide aggregate data for social work research studies.

- Before investing a great deal of time in planning a secondary analysis, you should check the data source to see if the data you need are there at all. If they are there, you should check to see whether large chunks of the data on certain key variables are missing and whether the data contain sufficient variation on your intended variables.

- Content analysis is a social research method that is appropriate for studying human communications. Besides being used to study communication processes, it may be used to study other aspects of social behavior.

- Standard probability sampling techniques are appropriate in content analysis.

- Manifest content refers to the directly visible, objectively identifiable characteristics of a communication, such as the specific words in a book, the specific colors used in a painting, and so forth. That is one focus for content analysis.

- Latent content refers to the meanings contained within communications. The determination of latent content requires judgments on the part of the researcher.

• Coding is the process of transforming raw data—either manifest or latent content—into standardized, quantitative form.

• Both quantitative and qualitative techniques are appropriate for interpreting content analysis data.

• The advantages of content analysis include economy, ease of correcting mistakes, and the ability to study processes occurring over a long time. Its disadvantages are that it is limited to recorded communications and can raise issues of reliability and validity.

• Social work researchers also use historical and comparative methods to discover common patterns that recur in different times and places.

• Two broad types of source materials for historical research are primary sources and secondary sources.

• Primary sources provide firsthand accounts by someone who was present at an event—for example, diaries, letters, organizational bylaws, the minutes of a meeting, the orally reported memory of an eyewitness, and so on. Secondary sources describe past phenomena based on primary sources.

• A danger in working exclusively with secondary sources is that you may merely repeat the mistakes contained in those sources and fail to give yourself the opportunity to provide a new, independent perspective on past events. But primary sources can be flawed as well. For example, an eyewitness could have been biased or may experience faulty memory.

• When conducting historical research, you should try not to rely on a single source or on one type of source. Your protection against dangers in using primary and secondary sources lies in corroboration. If several sources point to the same set of "facts," then your confidence in them might reasonably increase.

• *Hermeneutics* refers to interpreting social life by mentally taking on the circumstances, views, and feelings of the participants.

• An *ideal type* is a conceptual model that is composed of the essential qualities of a social phenomenon.

Review Questions and Exercises

1. In two or three paragraphs, outline a content analysis design to determine whether the Republican Party or the Democratic Party is more supportive of public spending on social welfare. Be sure to specify sampling methods, and the relevant measurements.

2. In response to managed care pressures, five years ago your child and family services agency dramatically increased the amount of time practitioners had to spend filling out forms on each case, including the provision of details about diagnoses and other information bearing on whether and how long services for each case were eligible for reimbursement from managed care companies. Discuss the specific ways in which this development might create special problems in analyzing existing agency statistics regarding historical trends in the types of diagnoses of clients served by your agency, the nature and amount of services provided, and client background characteristics.

Internet Exercises

1. Using InfoTrac College Edition, find the following articles that utilized content analysis and were published in the October 2002 issue of the journal *Social Work*:

> "Among the Missing: Content on Lesbian and Gay People in Social Work Journals," by R. V. Voorhis and M. Wagner
>
> "Client's View of a Successful Helping Relationship," by D. S. Ribner and C. Knei-Paz

Identify each study's methodological strengths and weaknesses, indicate whether it used manifest or latent coding (or both), and indicate whether its methods were quantitative or qualitative. Finally, briefly explain why, in your view, each study's findings did or did not provide important implications for social policy or social work practice.

2. Go to the following "Content Analysis Resources" website: www.gsu.edu/~wwwcom/. Once there, find the following: (a) a list of software programs for conducting a qualitative content analysis, (b) lists of other sites and resources that might be helpful in conducting a content analysis, and (c) lists of publications and bibliographies on content analysis.

3. Using a search engine such as Google or Yahoo!, enter the search term *existing statistics*, then click on *search*. Your window will then display a list of various sources of existing statistics. Click on a source that piques your interest. Examine the types of data that are displayed and formulate a research question

of general interest that could be answered with the displayed data.

4. Go to the following U.S. Census Bureau website for its online Statistical Abstract of the United States: www.census.gov/compendia/statab/. For the 2006 edition, find the Guide to Sources of Statistics (Appendix I) and download it. How many sources do you find there that seem to be likely to have existing data related to social work? Write down at least five such sources.

5. Using the World Wide Web, find out how many countries have a higher "expected life expectancy" than the United States. (You might want to try the Population Reference Bureau at www.prb.org.)

Additional Readings

Baker, Vern, and Charles Lambert. 1990. "The National Collegiate Athletic Association and the Governance of Higher Education," *Sociological Quarterly*, *31*(3), 403–421. This article offers a historical analysis of the factors that have produced and shaped the NCAA.

Berg, Bruce L. 1998. *Qualitative Research Methods for the Social Sciences*. 3rd ed. Boston: Allyn & Bacon. Contains excellent materials on unobtrusive measures, including a chapter on content analysis. While focusing on qualitative research, Berg shows the logical links between qualitative and quantitative approaches.

Elder, Glen H., Jr., Eliza K. Pavalko, and Elizabeth C. Clipp. 1993. *Working with Archival Data: Studying Lives*. Newbury Park, CA: Sage. This book discusses the possibilities and techniques for using existing data archives in the United States, especially those providing longitudinal data.

Evans, William. 1996. "Computer-Supported Content Analysis: Trends, Tools, and Techniques," *Social Science Computer Review*, *14*(3): 269–279. Here's a review of current computer software for content analysis, such as CETA, DICTION, INTEXT, MCCA, MECA, TEXTPACK, VBPro, and WORDLINK.

Ginsberg, Leon. 1995. *Social Work Almanac*, 2nd ed. Washington, DC: NASW Press. Although somewhat dated, this illustrates a source of existing statistics for social workers. It contains more than 200 tables and figures selected for their relevance to social workers and social service delivery.

Øyen, Else (ed.). 1990. *Comparative Methodology: Theory and Practice in International Social Research*. Newbury Park, CA: Sage. Here are a variety of viewpoints on different aspects of comparative research. Appropriately, the contributors are from many different countries.

U.S. Bureau of the Census. 2006. *Statistical Abstract of the United States, 2006, National Data Book and Guide to Sources*. Washington, DC: U.S. Government Printing Office. This is absolutely the best book bargain available (present company excluded). Although the hundreds of pages of tables of statistics are not exciting bedtime reading—the plot is a little thin—it is an absolutely essential resource volume for every social scientist. Also available online at www.census.gov/compendia/statab/.

Webb, Eugene J., Donald T. Campbell, Richard Schwartz, and Lee Sechrest. 2000. *Unobtrusive Measures*. Thousand Oaks, CA: Sage.

Webb, Eugene J., Donald T. Campbell, Richard D. Schwartz, Lee Sechrest, and Janet Belew Grove. 1981. *Nonreactive Measures in the Social Sciences*. Boston: Houghton Mifflin. This compendium of unobtrusive measures includes discussion of physical traces, a variety of archival sources, and observation, as well as a good discussion of the ethics involved and the limitations of such measures.

Weber, Robert Philip. 1990. *Basic Content Analysis*. Newbury Park, CA: Sage. Here's an excellent beginner's book for the design and execution of content analysis. Both general issues and specific techniques are presented.

PART 6

Qualitative Research Methods

Throughout this text, we have been discussing ways to improve the quality of research data by using qualitative and unobtrusive methods of data collection. For the most part, however, we have examined these methods as a way to complement and strengthen primarily quantitative studies and in the context of other issues such as measurement, sampling, and evaluation. The chapters in Part 6 will be devoted exclusively to qualitative research methods, discussing them in more depth than in previous chapters.

Chapter 17 will focus on general principles in qualitative research, such as appropriate topics, qualitative research paradigms, qualitative sampling, strengths and weaknesses of qualitative research, and ethics in qualitative research. It will show how qualitative studies can sometimes provide deeper understandings and new insights that might escape quantitative studies. It will also address some strategies for strengthening the rigor of qualitative studies.

Chapter 18 will discuss specific types of qualitative research methods, such as participant observation, qualitative interviewing, recording observations, life history, and focus groups. As you read these chapters you will see how the distinction sometimes can be fuzzy between the general principles and paradigms of qualitative research and the specific methods of qualitative research.

Chapter 19 examines how to analyze the open-ended data generated by qualitative research studies. We'll look at some conceptual procedures used in searching for meaning among qualitative data and also examine the use of computer software designed for analyzing qualitative data.

CHAPTER 17

Qualitative Research: General Principles

What You'll Learn in This Chapter

This chapter discusses general principles for the use of qualitative techniques for conducting social work research in natural settings—where the action is. This type of research can produce a richer understanding of many social phenomena than can be achieved through other observational methods, provided that the researcher observes in a deliberate, well-planned, and active way.

INTRODUCTION

Many of the research methods discussed so far in this book are designed to produce data that are appropriate for *quantitative* (statistical) analysis. For example, surveys provide data from which to calculate the percentage unemployed in a population, mean incomes, and so forth. In contrast, qualitative research methods attempt to tap the deeper meanings of particular human experiences and are intended to generate *qualitative* data: theoretically richer observations that are not easily reduced to numbers. For example, a qualitative investigation of homelessness might note the "defiant dignity" of homeless people who refuse to use squalid shelters. Likewise, a qualitative investigation might describe the "fatalism" of chronically unemployed men who hang out together. In both cases, the qualitative investigations would not be able to express either the dignity or the fatalism as numerical quantities or degrees.

Qualitative research is not only a data-collecting activity, but also frequently, and perhaps typically, a theory-generating activity. As a qualitative researcher, you will seldom approach your task with precisely defined hypotheses to be tested. More typically, you will attempt to make sense of an ongoing process that cannot be predicted in advance—making initial observations, developing tentative general conclusions that suggest particular types of further observations, making those observations and thereby revising your conclusions, and so forth. The alternation of induction and deduction discussed in Chapter 3 of this book is perhaps nowhere more evident and essential than in good qualitative research.

TOPICS APPROPRIATE FOR QUALITATIVE RESEARCH

One of the key strengths of qualitative research is the comprehensiveness of perspective it gives the researcher. By going directly to the social phenomenon under study and observing it as completely as possible, you can develop a deeper understanding of it. This mode of observation, then, is especially, though not exclusively, appropriate to research topics that appear to defy simple quantification. The qualitative researcher may recognize several nuances of attitude and behavior that might escape researchers using other methods.

Somewhat differently, qualitative research is especially appropriate to the study of those topics for which attitudes and behaviors can best be understood within their natural setting. Experiments and surveys may be able to measure behaviors and attitudes in somewhat artificial settings, but not all behavior is best measured this way. For example, qualitative research provides a superior method for studying the experience of being homeless.

Finally, qualitative research is especially appropriate to the study of social processes over time. Thus, the qualitative researcher might be in a position to examine the rumblings and final explosion of a riot as events actually occur rather than try to reconstruct them afterward.

Other good uses of qualitative research methods would include protest demonstrations, agency board meetings, labor negotiations, public hearings, interactions between social workers and clients, and similar events that take place within a relatively limited area and time. Several such observations must be combined in a more comprehensive examination across time and space.

In *Analyzing Social Settings* (1995:101–113), John Lofland and Lyn Lofland discuss several elements of social life appropriate for qualitative research. They call them *thinking topics*.

1. *Practices*. This refers to various kinds of behavior.

2. *Episodes*. Here the Loflands include a variety of events such as divorce, crime, and illness.

3. *Encounters*. This involves two or more people meeting and interacting in immediate proximity with one another.

4. *Roles*. Qualitative research is also appropriate to the analysis of the positions people occupy and the behavior associated with those positions: occupations, family roles, and ethnic groups.

5. *Relationships*. Much social life can be examined in terms of the kinds of behavior that are appropriate to pairs or sets of roles: mother–son relationships, friendships, and the like.

6. *Groups*. Moving beyond relationships, qualitative research can also be used to study small groups such as friendship cliques, athletic teams, and work groups.

7. *Organizations*. Beyond small groups, qualitative researchers also study formal organizations such as hospitals and schools.

8. *Settlements.* It is difficult to study large societies such as nations, but qualitative researchers often study smaller-scale "societies" such as villages, ghettos, and neighborhoods.

9. *Social worlds.* There are also ambiguous social entities with vague boundaries and populations that are nonetheless proper participants for social scientific study: "the sports world," "Wall Street," and the like.

10. *Lifestyles or subcultures.* Finally, social scientists sometimes focus on ways that large numbers of people adjust to life: groups such as a "ruling class" or an "urban underclass." In all of these social settings, qualitative research can reveal things that would not otherwise be apparent. It does so by probing social life in its natural setting. Although some things can be studied adequately in questionnaires or in the laboratory, others cannot. And direct observation in the field lets you observe subtle communications and other events that might not be anticipated or measured otherwise.

PROMINENT QUALITATIVE RESEARCH PARADIGMS

There are many different approaches to qualitative research. This section examines four qualitative field research paradigms that are particularly applicable to social work: naturalism, grounded theory, participatory action research, and case studies. Although this survey won't exhaust the variations on the method, it should give you an appreciation of the possibilities. It's important to recognize that specific methods are not attached exclusively to any of these paradigms. The important distinctions of this section are epistemological, having to do with what data mean, regardless of how they were collected.

Naturalism

Naturalism is an old tradition in qualitative research. It emphasizes observing people in their everyday settings and reporting their stories as they tell them. The earliest field researchers operated on the positivist assumption that social reality was "out there," ready to be naturally observed and reported by the researcher as it "really is" (Gubrium and Holstein, 1997). This tradition started in the 1930s and 1940s at the University of Chicago's sociology department, whose faculty and students fanned out across the city to observe and understand local neighborhoods and communities. The researchers of that era and their research approach are now often referred to as the "Chicago School."

One of the earliest and best-known studies that illustrates this research tradition is William Foote Whyte's ethnography of Cornerville, an Italian American neighborhood, in his book *Street Corner Society* (1943). An **ethnography** is a study that focuses on detailed and accurate description rather than explanation. Like other naturalists, Whyte believed that to fully learn about social life on the streets, he needed to become more of an insider. He made contact with "Doc," his key informant, who appeared to be one of the streetgang leaders. Doc let Whyte enter his world, and Whyte got to participate in the activities of the people of Cornerville. His study offered something that surveys could not: a richly detailed picture of life among the Italian immigrants of Cornerville.

An important feature of Whyte's study is that he reported the reality of the people of Cornerville on their terms. The naturalist approach is based on telling "their" stories the way they "really are," not the way the ethnographer understands "them." The narratives collected by Whyte are taken at face value as the social "truth" of the Cornerville residents. The box "Two Illustrations of Naturalistic, Ethnographic Studies of Homelessness" provides a more detailed illustration of the application of the naturalism paradigm to a problem of great concern to social workers.

Grounded Theory

Grounded theory, a term coined by Barney Glaser and Anselm Strauss (1967), was mentioned earlier, in connection with the *inductive* approach to understanding. Grounded theory begins with observations and looks for patterns, themes, or common categories. This does not mean that researchers have no preconceived ideas or expectations. In fact, what has been previously learned will shape the new search for generalities. However, the analysis is not set up to confirm or disconfirm specific hypotheses. By the same token, the openness of the grounded theory approach allows a greater latitude for the discovery of the unexpected, some regularity (or disparity) totally unanticipated by the concepts that might make up a particular theory or hypothesis.

Although grounded theory emphasizes an inductive process, it can also incorporate deductive processes. It does this through the use of constant comparisons. As

TWO ILLUSTRATIONS OF NATURALISTIC, ETHNOGRAPHIC STUDIES OF HOMELESSNESS

As research associates of the Community Service Society of New York City, Ellen Baxter and Kim Hopper (1982) embarked in 1979 on an ethnographic investigation of the habitats of homeless individuals in New York City. They originally envisioned their research as part of a larger study of the living conditions of the chronically mentally disabled. Their early observations, however, revealed that the homeless population was far too heterogeneous and the origins of homelessness too diverse to limit their study to the mentally disabled. Displaying the flexibility of field researchers, they modified their focus to include more than the mentally disabled. Their chief concern was "to document how the homeless meet and resolve daily problems of survival in an often hostile environment" (1982:395). They conducted their observations wherever the homeless might sleep, stake out a domain, be fed, or receive services—at

> . . . park benches, street corners, doorways, subways, train stations, bus and ferry terminals, missions and flophouses, publicly and privately operated shelters, food programs, and emergency rooms. The terrain was initially mapped out through interviews with individuals and groups . . . serving, researching, or advocating on behalf of the homeless. In the course of our own field work, additional sites were periodically discovered and investigated, including hallways and stairwells in occupied buildings, abandoned buildings, the piers along the East and Hudson rivers, alleyways, and heating vents—often with the homeless serving as guides.
>
> (1982:395)

Baxter and Hopper also found some homeless individuals in such out-of-the-way refuges as the steam tunnels running under Park Avenue and loading docks in commercial districts that are unused at night. Had they not used a qualitative approach, they would not have been able to anticipate such locations, and consequently they would not have found as diverse a sample.

They typically began their observations by initiating conversation with the offer of food, coffee, cigarettes, or change, and they introduced themselves as researchers on homelessness. But after encountering resistance, they again displayed flexibility; they began delaying this information awhile and describing their work in simpler terms, such as that of writers doing a story on homelessness.

In addition to their direct observations and interviews with the homeless, Baxter and Hopper interviewed others who worked with or were connected with homeless people. And on some occasions, they posed as homeless individuals themselves, such as when they entered public shelters to stay overnight. This enabled them to gain insights that would have been difficult to gain from the outside. For example, they were able to discover that from the standpoint of the homeless, their refusal of service has a more rational meaning than it does to professionals or to the public. The latter groups view service refusal as a reflection of defects in character or judgment, a disinterest in being helped, or a preference to live on the street. But Baxter and Hopper's observations indicated that whenever services were offered, they were not adequate to accommodate the number of homeless individuals who sought to use them. Refusal of service seemed rational in light of the deplorable conditions they observed in the public shelters, conditions that sometimes made living in the streets and parks seem more attractive.

In the public shelters, Baxter and Hopper observed overcrowding, lack of sanitation, and inadequate security—conditions that "would not meet federal regulations for prison cells" (1982:398). Among other things, they noted the few toilets and showers, which were often filthy or out of order; louse-infested mattresses and linens; pilfering of clothing; threats of violence; and fears of catching some dread disease.

But despite observing how service refusal can have an element of rationality, Baxter and Hopper also observed the harshness and toll of life on

(continued)

the streets, where the homeless are hungry, cold, socially isolated, and deprived of sleep. They observed how this strain can disorient individuals who were not mentally ill before they became homeless, and they noted that clinicians generally do not understand this because they typically see the homeless only after their desperate straits have taken a toll on their mental health. Through their immersion with the homeless, they also gained insights about the deeper meanings of other aspects of homelessness. For example, they observed the protective function of appearing bizarre and filthy and of having a noxious odor, which can protect homeless women by repelling men on the prowl. (Baxter and Hopper added, however, that foulness of appearance is virtually unavoidable, given the scarcity of toilets and bathing and laundry facilities.)

In light of these insights—insights that have escaped others—Baxter and Hopper concluded that the presumption of incompetence on the part of the homeless was a self-fulfilling prophecy because the homeless are eager to receive decent and humane care in those rare instances when such care is available. Despite the great hardships of living on the streets, that decision can have the deeper meaning of salvaging a sense of defiant dignity and self-determination for the homeless in the face of the deplorable conditions of the shelters available to them. Baxter and Hopper ended their report with several proposals intended to make more and better services available to the homeless, to make it more rational for them to use those services, and to enhance the efforts of social workers to help the homeless.

Several years later, David A. Snow and Leon Anderson (1987) conducted exploratory field research into the lives of homeless people in Austin, Texas. Their major task was to understand how the homeless construct and negotiate their identity while knowing that the society they live in attaches a stigma to homelessness. Snow and Anderson believed that, to achieve this goal, the collection of data had to arise naturally. Like Whyte in *Street Corner Society,* they found key informants whom they followed in their everyday journeys, such as at their day-labor pickup sites or under bridges. Snow and Anderson chose to memorize the conversations they participated in or the "talks" that homeless people had with each other. At the end of the day, the two researchers debriefed and wrote detailed field notes about all the "talks" they encountered. They also taped in-depth interviews with their key informants.

Snow and Anderson reported "hanging out" with homeless people over the course of 12 months for a total of 405 hours in 24 different settings. Out of these rich data, they identified three related patterns in homeless people's conversations. First, the homeless showed an attempt to "distance" themselves from other homeless people, from the low-status job they currently had, or from the Salvation Army they depended on. Second, they "embraced" their street-life identity, their group membership, or a certain belief about why they are homeless. Third, they told "fictive stories" that always contrasted with their everyday life. For example, they would often say that they were making much more money than they really were or even that they were "going to be rich."

researchers detect patterns in their inductive observations, they develop concepts and working hypotheses based on those patterns. Then they seek out more cases and conduct more observations and compare those observations against the concepts and hypotheses developed from the earlier observations.

Their selection of new cases is guided by theoretical sampling concepts. Theoretical sampling begins by selecting new cases that seem to be similar to those that generated previously detected concepts and hypotheses. Once the researcher perceives that no new insights are being generated from the observation of similar cases, a different type of case is selected, and the same process is repeated: Additional cases similar to this new type of case are selected until no new insights are being generated. This cycle of exhausting similar cases and then seeking a different category of cases can be repeated until the researcher believes that further seeking of new types of cases will not alter the findings.

Grounded theorists use basically the same methods that are used by other qualitative researchers—

methods that we'll discuss in greater depth in Chapter 18, such as participant observation and open-ended interviewing.

To understand the use of constant comparisons in the grounded theory process, imagine that you are seeking to discover the key components of effective community-based social work intervention aimed at forestalling relapse among young adults who have had schizophrenia. You might begin with open-ended interviews of several practitioners who have excellent reputations for their clinical effectiveness in this area. Perhaps you'd ask those practitioners to recall their most successful cases and discuss the interventions they used with them.

Let's suppose that you perceive a common pattern across every interview—a pattern in which each practitioner mentions the use of social skills training in the rehabilitation of the young adults and communication skills training in helping their parents cope with them. You might therefore develop a working hypothesis that the use of such behavioral interventions distinguishes effective from ineffective practice in this area.

To better ground your hypothesis in the empirical world, you might interview several additional practitioners with good clinical reputations to see if the same patterns are generated. If those interviews fail to generate new insights, you might reinterview the practitioners but use a different case-sampling approach. This time you might ask them to discuss the interventions they employed with their least successful cases. Suppose a few of them mention the same behavioral interventions that they mentioned with their most successful cases—the same behavioral interventions to which your working hypothesis refers. This would force you to modify your hypothesis. You might probe to uncover other aspects of their practice with their least successful cases—aspects that might help explain why the same interventions that seemed to work well with other cases did not work with these cases.

Let's suppose that these probes generate another common pattern—a pattern in which each of the least successful clients failed or refused to take their prescribed medications. Based on this observation, your modified working hypothesis might combine medication-monitoring interventions with behavioral interventions in distinguishing effective practice.

Continuing the grounded theory process, you would interview additional practitioners and ask about different types of cases. For example, you might learn of parents who did not benefit from the communications skills training because the practitioner did not adequately develop a therapeutic alliance with them before introducing that training. This might lead you to modify your working hypothesis further, perhaps by adding the prerequisite that family intervention be delivered in the context of a supportive relationship with the practitioner, one in which the parents understand that they are not being blamed for their children's illness.

At this point, you might realize that all of your cases have involved clients who live with their parents. Therefore, you might conduct interviews in reference to successful and unsuccessful cases in which the clients did not live with their parents. You might learn that with clients who do not live with their parents, effective practice also requires a lot of attention to securing suitable living arrangements and does not involve family communication skills training. Further sampling might identify many cases that involve dual diagnoses of schizophrenia and substance abuse. You might have to modify your hypothesis to include substance abuse interventions geared for this target population.

By the time you have completed the grounded theory process, you will have interviewed many different practitioners (perhaps including some with poor clinical reputations) and asked about many other types of cases. This additional empirical grounding will probably have led you to add many more modifications to your hypothesis. Some of them might deal with practitioner attributes such as empathy, warmth, and diagnostic skill. Some modifications might deal with client attributes, such as the need for different types of interventions depending on client degree of impairment, social support resources, and so on. Other modifications might deal with the full gamut of case management functions.

Gilgun (1991) sees several parallels between the grounded theory method and what social workers do in direct practice—particularly regarding clinical assessment. Both methods start where the case is and focus on the informant's perceptions. Both try to understand the case in a wider environmental context. Both combine induction and deduction and the constant comparison method in formulating working hypotheses based on observations and then modifying those hypotheses in light of further observations. Both try to avoid imposing preconceived ideas or theories on cases. Both rely heavily on open-ended interviewing and use largely the same interviewing skills (as will be evident later in this chapter, when we discuss qualitative interviewing). The process of using notes and memos in grounded theory resembles the social worker's use of process recording and problem-oriented case record keeping. Both attempt "to keep a balance between being in tune with clients and maintaining an analytic stance" (1991:17). Both like to conduct observations in natural settings, such as in the home or community. The box "An Illustration of Using Grounded Theory in Studying Homelessness" provides an example of a social work investigation based on the grounded theory paradigm.

Participatory Action Research

In the **participatory action research (PAR)** paradigm, the researcher's function is to serve as a resource to those being studied—typically, disadvantaged groups—as an opportunity for them to act effectively in their own interest. The disadvantaged participants define their problems, define the remedies desired, and take the lead in designing the research that will help them realize their aims.

This approach began in Third World research development, but it spread quickly to Europe and North America (Gaventa, 1991). It comes from a vivid critique of classical social science research. According to the PAR paradigm, traditional research is perceived as an "elitist model" (Whyte, Greenwood, and Lazes, 1991) that reduces the "subjects" of research to "objects" of research. According to many advocates of this perspective, the distinction between the researcher and the researched should disappear. They argue that the subjects who will be affected by research should also be responsible for its design.

Implicit in this approach is the belief that research functions not only as a means of knowledge production but also as a "tool for the education and development of consciousness as well as mobilization for action" (Gaventa, 1991:121–122). Advocates of participatory action research equate access to information with power and argue that this power has been kept in the hands of the dominant class, sex, ethnicity, or nation. Once people see themselves as researchers, they automatically regain power over knowledge.

Examples of this approach include community power structure research, corporate research, and "right-to-know" movements (Whyte, Greenwood, and Lazes, 1991). Most germane to social work, participatory action research often involves poor people, because they are typically less able to influence the policies and actions that affect their lives. Bernita Quoss, Margaret Cooney, and Terri Longhurst (2000) report a research project involving welfare policy in Wyoming. University students, many of them welfare recipients, undertook research and lobbying efforts aimed at getting Wyoming to accept postsecondary education as "work" under the state's new welfare regulations.

This project began against the backdrop of the 1996 Personal Responsibility and Work Opportunity Reconciliation Act, which eliminated education waivers that had been available under the previous welfare law, the 1988 Family Support Act. These waivers had permitted eligible participants in the cash assistance Aid to Families with Dependent Children program to attend college as an alternative to work training requirements. Empirical studies of welfare participants who received these waivers have provided evidence that education, in general, is the most effective way to stay out of poverty and achieve self-sufficiency (Quoss, Cooney, and Longhurst, 2000:47).

The students began by establishing an organization, Empower, and making presentations on campus to enlist broad student and faculty support. They compiled existing research relevant to the issue and established relationships with members of the state legislature. By the time the 1997 legislative session opened, they were actively engaged in the process of modifying state welfare laws to take account of the shift in federal policy.

The students prepared and distributed fact sheets and other research reports that would be relevant to the legislators' deliberations. They attended committee meetings and lobbied legislators on a one-to-one basis. When erroneous or misleading data were introduced into the discussions, the student-researchers were on hand to point out the errors and offer corrections.

Ultimately, they were successful. Welfare recipients in Wyoming were allowed to pursue postsecondary education as an effective route out of poverty.

Case Studies

A **case study** is an idiographic examination of a single individual, family, group, organization, community, or society. Its chief purpose is description, although attempts at explanation are also acceptable. Examples would include an in-depth description of a client system and an intervention with it, a depiction of the daily life and folkways of a street gang, an analysis of the organizational dynamics of a social welfare agency and how those dynamics influence the way

AN ILLUSTRATION OF USING GROUNDED THEORY IN STUDYING HOMELESSNESS

Another qualitative study of homelessness was reported by John Belcher (1991). Belcher was interested in the pathways people travel as they drift from one stage of homelessness to another. Using the grounded theory method, Belcher and two colleagues conducted three rounds of informal conversational interviews over a three-month period with 40 Baltimore homeless men and women whom they identified using snowball sampling in facilities for the homeless. To gain the trust of respondents and to reduce their anxiety about the interviews, Belcher and his colleagues eschewed carrying paper and pencil, bringing interview guides, or arranging specific interview times. They did not, however, pose as homeless persons, and they told the respondents who they were.

Their interview process began with an initial orienting interview, after which the researchers recorded responses into a case file for the respondent. All the files were then reviewed in an attempt to identify common themes. A second interview was then conducted with the same respondents (after locating them), guided by a set of questions that the researchers developed and kept in mind based on the themes identified from the first set of interviews. After these interviews, responses were again recorded in the case files. Patterns that were detected from responses to both rounds of interviews enabled the researchers to formulate working hypotheses, which they checked out with respondents in the third round of interviews. These hypotheses were then revised in light of the responses to the third interview.

The researchers used triangulation in the study by verifying important interview responses with other sources. If, for example, a respondent reported being ejected from a particular shelter, the researchers cross-checked this information with the operator of that shelter.

The process just described led to the postulation that homeless individuals tend to drift downward through three stages of homelessness. In the first stage they are living below the poverty line and move in and out of intense poverty. Their living arrangements fluctuate episodically, in line with fluctuations in their economic plight—sometimes they reside in a tenuous home and at other times double up with friends or family. They are anxious and fearful, may abuse substances somewhat, have a network of informal supports, and are connected to service providers.

In the second stage, they have been homeless for an extended period, but less than a year. They abuse substances more commonly, experience deterioration in their social relationships, are beginning to lose hope, but still do not identify with the community of homeless individuals.

In the third stage, they have been homeless for about a year or more, see themselves as part of the homeless community, have lost hope, abuse substances, stay in shelters, have no social relationships, and are extremely suspicious of and shun members of mainstream society. All their limited energies are focused on surviving on the street; the rest of the world is meaningless to them.

If the preceding hypothesis is true, then homeless individuals drift downward through the stages as they lose income, relationships, and hope. When they drift into the lower two stages, Belcher suggests, it becomes harder to intervene effectively to help them escape homelessness. Consequently, Belcher recommends preventive strategies to deal with homelessness, including social change efforts for long-term prevention and expanding welfare benefits to prevent homelessness, at least temporarily.

social services are delivered, and a description of the emergence and experience of a grassroots community organization.

Although case studies are generally seen as a qualitative approach to research, the mode of observation used is not what distinguishes a case study. Instead, case studies are distinguished by their exclusive focus on a particular case (or several cases in a multiple-case study) and their use of a full variety of evidence regarding that case, including, perhaps, evidence gathered by quantitative research methods. Sources of evidence might include existing documents, observations, and interviews. Evidence might also be sought by surveying people about the case or perhaps manipulating some variables (such as when we employ single-case evaluation designs as described in Chapter 12).

For example, a case study might be conducted to understand why a state decided to close down several of its institutions for the mentally or developmentally disabled, how it implemented that decision, what unanticipated problems occurred in the aftermath of the closings, and so on. Or a case study might be on a particular client, perhaps employing a single-case evaluation of intervention with that client as part of the case study.

Although case study researchers typically seek an idiographic understanding of the particular case under examination, case studies can form the basis for the development of more general, nomothetic theories. The logical focus in case studies is not on statistical generalization to other cases (or external validity). Instead, the focus is on connecting case study findings to a particular theory. This is done by showing how the weight of the various sources of evidence gathered in the case study is consistent with a theory. This is not an adequate test of the theory, because it is only one case, but the accumulation of consistent results in the replication process can serve as a useful test of the theory in the same way that replications of single-case evaluations or group experiments are utilized.

The rationale for using the case study method typically is the availability of a special case that seems to merit intensive investigation. For example, suppose a particular state is the first to implement a massive program of deinstitutionalization. You might want to conduct a case study of that event and its impact as a way of informing similar policy considerations in other states. Another example might be the first effort to provide case management services in a rural area. A case study might identify implementational problems and the ways they were handled—information that could be of great value to program planners in other rural regions.

Here is one more example. Suppose you theorize that people who volunteer in social service agencies do so primarily to meet egoistic needs that are not being fulfilled in their other life roles, even though they might say they are doing it for altruistic reasons. You might decide to select an agency where your theory might get its stiffest test, with the rationale that if it seems to hold up in that agency, then it would probably hold up anywhere. Maybe, for example, you would study volunteers who work with terminally ill patients in a hospice program, believing that such a program offers the greatest likelihood of finding people whose real, underlying motives are truly as altruistic as they claim.

The application of the case study method that is perhaps of greatest interest to social workers is when the case being studied is an individual, group, or family engaged in social work treatment. In the past, much of our profession's "practice wisdom" was generated by clinical case studies of clients. That method fell out of favor in the 1960s and 1970s as skepticism grew about the objectivity and validity of qualitative case studies about one's own clients, accompanied by a demand for evidence generated from studies with experimental controls for internal validity.

Today, however, a new wave of enthusiasm has emerged for qualitative methods in general, as well as for the incorporation of qualitative methods into experimental research. Thus, an experiment evaluating the effectiveness of a program or intervention might use qualitative methods to assess problems in the implementation of the program or intervention—information that may help suggest ways to improve future outcomes or that may show that a program or intervention with a negative outcome was never implemented properly in the first place.

Of special interest to practitioners is the trend toward using a case study approach that combines qualitative and quantitative methods while using single-case designs to evaluate one's own practice effectiveness. When we discussed single-case evaluation designs in Chapter 12, for instance, we noted that it is often difficult to detect from the graphed quantitative results whether an improvement in the target behavior was caused by the intervention or by some extraneous event(s). Intensive qualitative (clinical) interviewing of the client, as well as the client's significant others, can help identify what other important changes in the client's social environment may have coincided with changes in the quantitative data on the target behavior. Also helpful in this regard is the use of *client logs*. If the qualitative information indicates that important extraneous events did indeed coincide with the quantitative changes, then the notion that the intervention is responsible for those changes will be less plausible. On the other hand, if intensive interviewing or client logs reveal no such extraneous coincidences, then it becomes more plausible to view changes in the target behavior as intervention effects.

We will take a closer look at qualitative methods involving interviewing in the next chapter. Let's now take a closer look at the use of client logs in case studies.

Client Logs **Client logs** are journals that clients keep of events that are relevant to their problems. The logs can be utilized to record quantitative data about target behaviors as well as qualitative information about critical incidents. Bloom, Fischer, and Orme (2006) illustrate the use of different logs for different purposes. For example, an exploratory log might be used to obtain beginning assessment information about a problem and therefore involve recording where and when a critical incident occurs, what happened, who was present, the situational context (that is, a staff meeting, over dinner, and so on), what the client wanted, and the client's cognitive and behavioral reaction to the incident. A slightly different type of log might be used later in assessment—one that refers to the occurrence of the specified target problem only and that seeks to identify the conditions under which the problem tends to be better or worse.

Client logs can also be useful in recording extraneous events that occur during the baseline and intervention phases of a single-case evaluation when quantitative outcome data are being collected. The information on these logs can help the practitioner determine whether some important extraneous change may have coincided with the improvement in the target problem during the intervention phase, and this determination will illuminate inferences about whether it was really the intervention or something else that produced the change. Although qualitative interviews can also provide this information, a log can help to avoid distortions of memory that might occur in an interview. This may be particularly important with regard to the exact dates when critical incidents occurred; for example, the client may not remember accurately whether an incident occurred during the baseline phase or early during the intervention phase. Likewise, for assessment purposes, knowing whether the improvement may have begun a day or so before the critical incident occurred would be crucial in drawing inferences about that incident's bearing on the target problem.

We refer you to the Bloom text if you would like to see detailed illustrations of several types of logs. All of these logs are easy to construct. You can head the first column as the date, the next column as the time of day, and then have subsequent column headings for the place, the activity, who was present, what happened, events that led up to or followed the problem, the client's cognitive and behavioral reaction, and so on. Alternatively, you can use a simplified version that has fewer columns. It's up to you to judge what best fits the client, the problem, and the log's purpose.

Whatever approach you use, however, make sure that there are lined rows in each column with plenty of open-ended space for the clients to record their qualitative observations. Also, be sure to explain the log carefully to the client, including the log's purpose and value, how it is to be used, the need to restrict entries to brief summaries of critical incidents only, and the importance of recording incidents as soon as possible after they occur (to reduce memory distortions). Bloom and his associates also suggest practicing making entries with the client using hypothetical situations.

QUALITATIVE SAMPLING METHODS

Chapter 14 of this book discussed the logic and techniques involved in both probability and nonprobability sampling in social research. This section will discuss the matter of sampling as it typically applies in qualitative research. In part, we'll see how the nonprobability sampling techniques discussed earlier would apply specifically to qualitative research. But first we should acknowledge that the use of probability sampling techniques in qualitative research is not unheard of. Allison Zippay (2002), for example, reports a longitudinal qualitative interviewing study in which she randomly selected displaced steelworkers, using a sampling frame listing all blue-collar steelworkers at two steel fabrication plants that had closed down.

Although probability sampling is sometimes used in qualitative research, nonprobability techniques are much more common. The reasons for this are many. To begin, the population and the units of analysis in the qualitative research project may be somewhat ambiguous. In studying a community group engaged in social action activities, for example, what exactly are you interested in studying—that group only? the members of the group? social action in general? If you are studying three juvenile gangs in a particular city, are the gangs, the individual juveniles, or the city your units of analysis? Are you interested only in describing the gangs, or does your interest extend to juvenile peer relations in general? It is important that you ask yourself what population you wish to make general assertions about when you are finished with your research. The answer to this question will not always be obvious to you, and it may change over the course of your research. A limited initial concern may be expanded later as you conclude that certain of the phenomena you are observing apply well beyond your specific study participants. Although this general issue may not be easy to resolve in practice, sensitivity to it should help clarify your goals and methods.

The concept of sampling in connection with qualitative research is more complicated than for the kinds of research dealt with in the earlier chapters. Many qualitative researchers attempt to observe everything within their field of study; thus, in a sense, they do not sample at all. In reality, of course, it is impossible to observe everything. To the extent that qualitative researchers observe only a portion of what happens, then, what they do observe is a de facto sample of all the possible observations that might have been made. If several people are shouting support for the speaker in a community meeting, those shouts the researcher hears and understands represent a sample of all such shouts. Or if a researcher observes acts of violence during a riot, the observed acts are a sample of all such acts of violence. You will seldom be able to select a controlled sample of such observations, but you should bear in mind the general principles of representativeness and interpret your observations accordingly.

Sometimes, however, you will be in a position to sample among possible observations. If you are studying the development of a grassroots community organization over time, for instance, you may choose to interview different members of that organization by listing all of the members and then selecting a probability sample. This might not be the best method of sampling for your purposes, however. Three types of nonprobability sampling methods that are specifically appropriate to qualitative research are the quota sample, the snowball sample, and deviant cases.

To begin, if the group or social process under study has clearly defined categories of participants, then some kind of **quota sample** might be used: persons representing all different participation categories should be studied. (Review Chapter 14 for a more detailed discussion of quota sampling as a general procedure.) In the study of a formal group, for instance, you might wish to interview both leaders and nonleaders. In studying a community organization, it might be useful to interview both radical and more moderate members of that group. In general, whenever representativeness is desired, you should use quota sampling and interview both men and women, young people and old people, and the like.

Second, the **snowball sample** is a technique that begins a sample with a few relevant participants you've identified and then expands through referrals. If you wish to learn the pattern of recruitment to a community organization over time, then you might begin by interviewing fairly recent recruits, asking them who introduced them to the group. You might then interview the persons named, asking them who introduced them to the group. You might interview those persons in turn, asking, in part, who introduced them. In studying a loosely structured group, you might ask one of the participants whom he or she believes to be the most influential members of the group. You might interview those people and, in the course of the interviews, ask whom they believe to be the most influential. In each example, your sample would "snowball" as each interviewee suggested others.

Third, there is **deviant case sampling**, which entails examining cases that do not fit into the regular pattern Often, our understanding of fairly regular patterns of attitudes and behaviors is further improved by such deviant cases. You might gain important insights into the nature of group morale as exhibited at a meeting by interviewing people who did not appear to be caught up in the emotions of the crowd or by interviewing people who did not attend the meeting at all.

Deviant cases are unusual in some respect. Suppose, for example, you are interested in conducting a case study of several case management programs to describe the diversity of case management practice and generate hypotheses about factors that influence the case management process. If you suspect that the nature of case management may vary considerably depending on the size of the case manager's caseload, you might want to select a couple of programs known for their extremely high caseloads and a couple known for their extremely low caseloads.

For another example, suppose you seek to generate hypotheses about the extent of family involvement in nursing home care. You might want to study intensively several families that are known by nursing home staff as being the most highly involved in the care of their relatives and several that are known to be the least involved.

Perhaps, however, you might suspect that extreme or deviant cases are so unusual that they provide a distorted portrayal of the phenomenon you want to study. If so, Patton (1990) suggests that you consider using *intensity sampling:* Select cases that are more or less intense than usual, but not so unusual that they would be called deviant. Thus, rather than selecting families that are most and least involved in nursing home care, you might select families known to be more or less involved than most families, but which are not so involved or uninvolved that they represent aberrations whose information might be misleading or not particularly useful.

Suppose, for example, that you are studying case management processes in a county mental health program where the case managers' average caseload size is 200 cases, and in a federally funded model mental health program in a different locality with an average caseload size of two cases. The former program may be in a state with no real commitment to case management, where funding is abysmally low, and where "case manager" may be a meaningless label used for the sake of appearing to comply with current trends without spending more money. "Case management" in that program would be a misnomer, and the "case managers" in that program would have so little time to spend on any case that studying what they do might not provide a particularly rich source of information about the case management process. The latter program, as well, might not be a rich source of information. It may be so well endowed as a model program that it bears no resemblance to case management programs elsewhere, programs whose caseload sizes tend to range between 20 and 40 cases. Case managers in the model program may have so much time to spend on each case that they perform functions that go far beyond what case managers normally do even in good case management programs. Consequently, rather than select these extreme programs for study, you might select an *intensity sample* of programs with average caseload sizes of approximately 20 and approximately 40.

Another strategy that can perhaps be viewed as a form of extreme case sampling is *critical incidents sampling.* The critical incidents technique is particularly useful for generating hypotheses about social work practice effectiveness. A critical incident is one in which something of special importance seemed to happen—something either positive or negative—that might offer valuable new insights about how we can improve practice.

One way you could apply this technique would be to ask direct-service practitioners to identify the cases that, in their judgment, turned out to be their best successes or worst failures. Then you could interview them intensively about each case they identify, seeking to detect commonalities in what different practitioners did with their most and least successful cases. From these patterns, you could suggest hypotheses for further study about the attributes that might distinguish successful and unsuccessful practice.

Maximum variation sampling is another option identified by Patton. This strategy aims to capture the diversity of a phenomenon within a small sample to be studied intensively. By observing a phenomenon under heterogeneous conditions, we are likely to generate more useful insights about it. Thus, if you want to study case management processes, you might select programs with high, medium, and low caseload sizes; some in urban, suburban, and rural areas; some that are old, some that are new; and so on.

On the other hand, you might opt for a *homogeneous sample.* Suppose you are interested in studying how case managers attempt to handle role overload. You probably would restrict your sample to programs in which the case managers' caseload sizes were unusually large.

Earlier in this chapter when we discussed grounded theory, we mentioned *theoretical sampling.* We indicated that theoretical sampling begins by selecting new cases that seem to be similar to those that generated previously detected concepts and hypotheses, but that once the researcher perceives that no new insights are being generated from observing similar cases, a different type of case is selected, and the same process is repeated until the observation of different types of cases seems to be generating no new insights. Theoretical sampling thus combines elements of homogeneous sampling and deviant case sampling. (In our earlier example of the grounded theory process, we actually combined theoretical sampling with the critical incidents technique.)

The types of nonprobability samples and sampling strategies that we've been discussing can all be called **purposive samples**, generated by *purposive sampling* (also discussed in Chapter 14). In purposive sampling—unlike probability sampling—you select a sample of observations that you believe will yield the most comprehensive understanding of your subject of study, based on the intuitive feel for the subject that comes from extended observation and reflection. You can use purposive sampling procedures to select deviant cases or critical cases, but you can also use them to try to obtain a fairly representative portrayal of the phenomenon you are studying.

In a study of homelessness, you might wish to observe many different locations in the city. You could pick the sample of locations through standard probability methods; or, more likely, you could use a rough quota system, observing busy areas and deserted ones, or including samples from different times of day. In a study of the way nursing home staff and residents interact, you would observe different kinds of nursing homes and different areas of each home, for example. You might even seek to study deviant cases within a representative sample of larger groupings, such as applying the critical incidents technique across a representative sample of agencies. Although controlled probability sampling is seldom used in qualitative research, understanding its principles and logic (as discussed in Chapter 14) is likely to produce more effective intuitive sampling in qualitative research.

In qualitative research, bear in mind two stages of sampling. First, to what extent are the total situations *available* for observation representative of the more *general class* of phenomena you wish to describe and explain? Are the three juvenile gangs you are observing representative of all gangs? Second, are your *actual* observations within those total situations representative of all *possible* observations? Have you observed a representative sample of the members of the three gangs? Have you observed a representative sample of the interactions that have taken place? Even when controlled probability sampling methods are impossible or inappropriate, the logical link between representativeness and generalizability still holds.

Having discussed specific techniques that may be used for sampling in qualitative research, we conclude with the injunction offered by Lofland and Lofland (1995:16):

> Your overall goal is to collect the *richest possible data*. Rich data mean, ideally, a wide and diverse range of information collected over a relatively prolonged period of time. Again, ideally, you achieve this through direct, face-to-face contact with, and prolonged immersion in, some social location or circumstance.

STRENGTHS AND WEAKNESSES OF QUALITATIVE RESEARCH

Like all research methods, qualitative research has distinctive strengths and weaknesses. Let's take a look at some of them now.

Depth of Understanding

Qualitative research is especially effective for studying subtle nuances in attitudes and behaviors and for examining social processes over time. As such, the chief strength of this method lies in the depth of understanding it permits. Whereas other research methods may be challenged as "superficial," this charge is seldom lodged against qualitative research. Let's review a couple of qualitative research examples to see why this is so.

"Being there" is a powerful technique for gaining insights into the nature of human affairs. Listen, for example, to what this nurse reports about the impediments to patients' coping with cancer:

> Common fears that may impede the coping process for the person with cancer can include the following:
>
> —Fear of death—for the patient, and the implications his or her death will have for significant others.
>
> —Fear of incapacitation—because cancer can be a chronic disease with acute episodes that may result in periodic stressful periods, the variability of the person's ability to cope and constantly adjust may require a dependency upon others for activities of daily living and may consequently become a burden.
>
> —Fear of alienation—from significant others and health care givers, thereby creating helplessness and hopelessness.
>
> —Fear of contagion—that cancer is transmissible and/or inherited.
>
> —Fear of losing one's dignity—losing control of all bodily functions and being totally vulnerable.
>
> (Garant, 1980:2167)

Observations and conceptualizations such as these are valuable in their own right. In addition, they can provide the basis for further research—both qualitative and quantitative.

Now listen to what Joseph Howell (1973) has to say about "toughness" as a fundamental ingredient of life on Clay Street, a white, working-class neighborhood in Washington, DC:

> Most of the people on Clay Street saw themselves as fighters in both the figurative and literal sense. They considered themselves strong, independent people who would not let themselves be pushed around. For Bobbi, being a fighter meant battling the welfare department and cussing out social workers and doctors upon occasion. It meant spiking Barry's beer with sleeping pills and bashing him over the head with a broom. For Barry it meant telling off his boss and refusing to hang the door, an act that led to his being fired. It meant going through the ritual of a duel with Al. It meant pushing Bubba around and at times getting rough with Bobbi. June and Sam had less to fight about, though if pressed they both hinted that they, too, would fight. Being a fighter led Ted into near conflict with Peg's brothers, Les into conflict with Lonnie, Arlene into conflict with Phyllis at the bowling alley, etc.
>
> (1973:292)

Even though you haven't heard the episodes Howell refers to in this passage, you have the distinct impression that Clay Street is a tough place to live. That "toughness" comes through far more powerfully than would a set of statistics on the median number of fistfights occurring during a specified period of time.

These examples point to the greater depth of meaning that qualitative methods can tap in describing concepts such as liberal and conservative that is generally unavailable to surveys and experiments. Instead of defining concepts, qualitative researchers will commonly give some detailed illustrations.

Flexibility

Flexibility is another advantage of qualitative research: You may modify your research design at any time, as discussed earlier. Moreover, you are always prepared to engage in qualitative research, whenever the occasion arises, whereas you could not as easily initiate a survey or an experiment.

Cost

Qualitative research can be relatively inexpensive. Other social scientific research methods may require expensive equipment or an expensive research staff, but qualitative research typically can be undertaken by one researcher with a notebook and pencil. This is not to say that qualitative research is never expensive. The nature of the research project, for example, may require a large number of trained observers. Expensive recording equipment may be needed. Or the researcher may wish to undertake participant observation of interactions in expensive Paris nightclubs.

Subjectivity and Generalizibility

Qualitative research also has several weaknesses. First, being qualitative rather than quantitative, it seldom yields precise statistical statements about a large population. Observing casual political discussions in laundromats, for instance, would not yield trustworthy estimates of the future voting behavior of the total electorate. Nevertheless, the study could provide important insights into the process of political attitude formation. Many of the strengths and weaknesses of qualitative research can be understood in terms of subjectivity and generalizability.

Subjectivity Suppose you were to characterize your best friend's political orientations based on everything you know about him or her. Clearly your assessment of that person's politics is not superficial. The measurement you arrived at would appear to have considerable validity. We can't be sure, however, that someone else would characterize your friend's politics the same way you did, even with the same amount of observation.

Qualitative research measurements—although in-depth—are also often very personal. How others judge your friend's political orientation depends very much on their own orientation, just as your judgment would depend on your political orientation. Conceivably, then, you would describe your friend as middle-of-the-road, although others might perceive him or her as a fire-breathing radical.

Be wary, therefore, of any purely descriptive measurements in qualitative research. If a researcher reports that the members of a club tend to be conservative, know that such a judgment is unavoidably linked to the researcher's own politics. You can be more trusting, however, of comparative evaluations: identifying who is more conservative than whom, for example. Even if we had different political orientations, we would probably agree pretty much in ranking the relative conservatism of the members of a group.

As we've suggested earlier, those researchers who use qualitative techniques are conscious of this issue and take pains to address it. Not only are individual researchers often able to sort out their own biases and points of view, but also the communal nature of science means that their colleagues will help them in that regard.

In a sense, we've been talking about the issue of generalizability. Let's look at that more directly now.

Generalizability One of the chief goals of science is generalization. Social scientists study particular situations and events to learn about social life in general. Usually, nobody would be interested in knowing about the specific participants observed by the researcher. Who cares, after all, how George Gallup's sample of 1,500 voters is going to vote? We are interested only if the voters' intentions can be generalized to the total electorate. (This was the key issue in Chapter 14, on sampling.)

Generalizability is a problem for qualitative research. It crops up in three forms. First, as we've already suggested, the personal nature of the observations and measurements made by the researcher can produce results that would not necessarily be replicated by another, independent researcher. If the observation depends in part on the particular observers, then it becomes more valuable as a source of insight than as proof or truth.

Second, because qualitative researchers get a full and in-depth view of their subject matter, they can reach an unusually comprehensive understanding. By its very comprehensiveness, however, this understanding is less generalizable than results based on rigorous sampling and standardized measurements. Let's say you set out to fully understand how your city council operates. You study each of the members in great depth, learning about their ideological positions, how they came to public life, how they got elected, who their friends and enemies are. You could learn about their family lives, seeing how personal feelings enter into their public acts. After such an in-depth study, you could probably understand the actions of the council really well. But would you be able to say much about city councils in general? Surely your study would have provided you with some general insights, but you wouldn't be able to carry over everything you learned from the specific to the general. Having mastered the operations of the Dayton City Council, you might not be able to say much about Cleveland's. You should, however, be in a position to organize a great study of the Cleveland City Council.

In reviewing reports of qualitative research projects, you should determine where and to what extent the researcher is generalizing beyond his or her specific observations to other settings. Such generalizations may be in order, but you need to judge that. Nothing in this research method guarantees it.

Finally, there is often a problem of generalizability even within the specific subject matter being observed. As an illustration, let's imagine you were interested in learning about Scientology. Suppose you were particularly interested in the church's recruitment practices: How does it attract new members, what kinds of people are attracted, and so on? One way to find the answers to such questions would be for you to express interest in the church yourself. Talk to members, attend meetings and retreats. In this fashion, you'd be able to get a firsthand experience of what you wanted to study. You could observe the way you were treated after expressing interest, and you could observe the treatment of other newcomers. By getting to know the other people who were considering joining the church, you would get an idea of the kinds of people who were joining.

Here's the problem of generalizability. Although you might talk to many church members, you couldn't be sure how "typical" they were. You might end up talking only to people assigned the job of talking to potential recruits. Or perhaps you make your contact through your English class and meet mostly members majoring in the humanities and none majoring in the sciences. The potentials for biased sampling are endless. The same would apply to the new recruits you got to know. They might not be typical of new recruits in general.

As we finish discussing the strengths and weaknesses of qualitative research, we should point out that although we did not have a section on the strengths and weaknesses of "quantitative" research per se in previous chapters, we did devote considerable attention throughout those chapters to the many strengths and weaknesses of quantitative research. With regard to weaknesses, for example, we discussed biases and other flaws in the wording of quantitative measurement instruments, quantitative scales that lack reliability and validity, unrepresentative surveys with inadequate response rates or biased sampling procedures, practice evaluations that lack internal validity or use biased measurement procedures, and so on. Moreover, even in this chapter we have discussed the strengths and limitations of qualitative research in the context of comparing them with the strengths and limitations of quantitative research. Thus, we hope you do not get the impression that qualitative methods are weaker or stronger than quantitative methods. Which line of inquiry is more appropriate will depend on the aim of our research and the nature of the research question we seek to answer.

STANDARDS FOR EVALUATING QUALITATIVE STUDIES

As can be seen in this chapter and the next, qualitative inquiry involves a variety of dissimilar research methods and paradigms. This diversity in methods and paradigms is accompanied by different perspectives on how to critically appraise the rigor of qualitative research. Regardless of one's perspective, however, there is general agreement that one key issue in evaluating the rigor of qualitative research is *trustworthiness*. However, one's epistemological paradigm will influence the criteria used to assess trustworthiness as well as whether some other key issues are just as important as trustworthiness.

For those whose epistemological paradigm is mainly oriented toward contemporary positivism (as discussed in Chapter 3), trustworthiness will be the prime focus in evaluating the rigor of a qualitative study. They will be primarily concerned with the extent to which a study can take steps to maximize objectivity and minimize bias. Those who view research through the lens of the critical social science or participatory action research paradigm, however, will additionally ask whether people were empowered by the research. Those with a postmodern or social constructivist paradigm will also use trustworthiness as a key criterion, but they will approach that criterion somewhat differently than contemporary positivists in keeping with a rejection of the notion of an objective reality and an emphasis on multiple subjective realities. Let's begin by examining the contemporary positivist perspective on critically appraising the trustworthiness of qualitative research. Then we'll examine the similarities and differences between that approach and those that emphasize alternative paradigms.

Contemporary Positivist Standards

As we mentioned above, for contemporary positivists the key issue in evaluating the rigor of qualitative research is *trustworthiness*. In her book *Qualitative Methods in Social Work Research,* Deborah Padgett (1998b) identifies three key threats to trustworthiness: reactivity, researcher biases, and respondent biases. *Reactivity* occurs when the researcher's presence in the field distorts the naturalism of the setting and consequently the things being observed there. As we discussed earlier, *researcher biases* can distort what researchers perceive or how they selectively observe. *Respondent bias* is another concept you may recall from earlier sections; it refers most typically to the need to appear socially desirable.

To minimize the distorting influence of these threats, Padgett recommends six commonly used strategies to enhance the rigor of qualitative studies. Not every strategy is feasible or applicable to every qualitative investigation. You can evaluate the rigor of the qualitative studies you read by asking yourself which of these strategies are applicable to a given study, and if applicable, were they used?

Padgett terms the first strategy **prolonged engagement.** It is used to reduce the impact of reactivity and respondent bias. It assumes that a long and trusting relationship with the researcher gives respondents less opportunity to deceive and makes them less inclined to withhold information or to lie. Padgett adds that lengthy interviews or a series of follow-up interviews with the same respondent makes it easier for the researcher to detect distortion or for the respondent ultimately to disclose socially undesirable truths.

Prolonged engagement also can have a drawback. A lengthy engagement can lead to bias if the researchers overidentify with their respondents and lose their objective, analytic stance or their own sense of identity. The term for this phenomenon is **going native.** Despite this risk, qualitative studies that lack prolonged engagement should be viewed with caution. Some authors, for example, seem to think that because qualitative inquiry emphasizes flexibility, the label "qualitative" means "anything goes." We have seen this in some manuscripts we've reviewed for publication in professional journals. The most common example occurs when an investigator thinks that one brief open-ended interview with each respondent is sufficient. (Conceivably that may be sufficient in some unusual qualitative studies, but if so, the author should provide a compelling justification of that as opposed to ignoring the issue.)

The second strategy is *triangulation,* a term we have used repeatedly throughout this book. Triangulation occurs when researchers seek corroboration between two or more sources for their data and interpretations. Padgett describes five types of triangulation in qualitative inquiry. One approach is to have the data analyzed by colleagues who hold contrasting theoretical orientations. Another is to use more than one qualitative method (and perhaps some quantitative methods, too) to collect and analyze data. A third approach is to use multiple observers to collect the data and multiple coders to classify the collected observations. A fourth approach is to use more than one data source (such as direct observations, interviews, and existing records). A fifth type is called *interdisciplinary triangulation,* in which a team of researchers from different fields collaborate. Padgett cautions us, however, not to overreact to inconsistencies in triangulated data. Sometimes disagreement between different data sources simply reveals different perspectives about a phenomenon, such as when two conflicting family members express different versions of family problems.

A third strategy, one that overlaps somewhat with triangulation, is called **peer debriefing and support.** This occurs when teams of investigators meet regularly to give each other feedback, emotional support, and ideas. They might exchange alternative perspectives and new ideas about how they are collecting data, about problems, and about meanings in the data already collected. The idea here is that the peer debriefing process increases the likelihood of spotting and correcting for biases and other problems in data collection and interpretation.

The next two strategies, negative case analysis and member checking, were discussed in Chapter 8, when we examined how the terms *reliability* and *validity* are sometimes used in qualitative research. **Negative case analysis**, for example, occurs when researchers show they have searched thoroughly for disconfirming evidence—looking for deviant cases that do not fit the researcher's interpretations. **Member checking** occurs when researchers ask the participants in their research to confirm or disconfirm the accuracy of the research observations and interpretations. Do the reported observations and interpretations ring true and have meaning to the participants?

The final strategy, **auditing**, occurs when the researcher leaves a paper trail of field notes, transcripts of interviews, journals, and memos documenting decisions made along the way, and so on. This enables an impartial and qualitatively adept investigator who is not part of the study to scrutinize what was done in order to determine if efforts to control for biases and reactivity were thorough, if the procedures used were justifiable, and if the interpretations fit the data that were collected. Thus, auditing encompasses each of the preceding five strategies, because part of the purpose of the audit is to ascertain whether those strategies were appropriately implemented.

Social Constructivist Standards

Social constructivists also emphasize trustworthiness in appraising qualitative research, and they recommend the preceding strategies for enhancing the rigor of qualitative studies. However, they view trustworthiness and these strategies more in terms of capturing multiple subjective realities than of ensuring the portrayal of an objective social reality, the objective of contemporary positivists. Thus, for example, minimizing respondent bias becomes less important than making sure that the research participants' multiple subjective realities are revealed as adequately as possible (Krefting, 1991). The point in member checking, then, becomes less concerned with whether the researcher's interpretations were objective and accurate, and more concerned with whether participants acknowledge that their subjective realities are being depicted as they see them.

Another criterion is whether the qualitative research report provides enough detail about the study contexts and participants to enable readers in other situations to judge whether the findings seem likely to apply to the context or population with which they are concerned. Guba (1981) referred to this criterion as *fittingness,* or *transferability.* Lincoln and Guba (1985) added that this criterion is unlike the external validity or generalizability criteria that we have discussed in connection to quantitative studies. The onus is not on the qualitative researchers to demonstrate that their studies have external validity or to say to whom their findings generalize. Instead, the onus is on the research consumers to make the judgment as to whether the findings seem applicable to their situation or population of concern. To enable the consumer to make that judgment, however, the onus is on the researcher to provide "thick" background information about the research context, setting, and participants.

The constructivist approach also uses triangulation somewhat differently than does the contemporary positivist approach. The contemporary positivist approach would see inconsistencies revealed in triangulation as a reflection of unreliability in the data. It might also reflect researcher bias if two investigators derived contradictory interpretations of the data. In contrast, the constructivist approach would see inconsistencies as a possible reflection of multiple realities.

They would want to see the inconsistencies explained; perhaps the explanations of inconsistency in triangulated data would produce a better understanding of the range of subjective realities—especially those that are atypical.

Empowerment Standards

As we mentioned above, those who take a critical social science or participatory action research approach to qualitative research would add empowerment standards to those mentioned above. Rodwell (1998) discusses empowerment standards for evaluating qualitative research in terms of what she calls *catalytic authenticity* and *tactical authenticity*. According to her paradigm, which actually combines constructivism with empowerment, creating new knowledge is not sufficient in constructivist research. In addition, the research must evoke action by participants to effect desired change and a redistribution of power. She adds that although it will be impossible to prove that the research caused the change, a follow-up should obtain and report participant testimonials suggesting a change in their views about the need for change and whether the research increased their optimism about the possibility for change.

RESEARCH ETHICS IN QUALITATIVE RESEARCH

We introduced the topic of research ethics in Chapter 4 and pointed out that a wide range of ethical issues must be faced in connection with any form of social research. Yet qualitative field research, by bringing researchers into direct and often intimate contact with their participants, seems to raise these concerns dramatically. Here are some of the issues mentioned by John and Lyn Lofland (1995:63):

- Is it ethical to talk to people when they do not know you will be recording their words?
- Is it ethical to get information for your own purposes from people you hate?
- Is it ethical to see a severe need for help and not respond to it directly?
- Is it ethical to be in a setting or situation but not commit yourself wholeheartedly to it?
- Is it ethical to develop a calculated stance toward other humans, that is, to be strategic in your relations?
- Is it ethical to take sides or to avoid taking sides in a factionalized situation?
- Is it ethical to "pay" people with trade-offs for access to their lives and minds?
- Is it ethical to "use" people as allies or informants in order to gain entree to other people or to elusive understandings?

In light of these issues, it bears stressing that qualitative research studies are required to be reviewed and approved by institutional review boards (see Chapter 4) just as quantitative studies are.

Although we have discussed qualitative inquiry throughout this book, this completes the first chapter that focused exclusively on this important type of research. The next chapter will examine specific types of qualitative research methods. As you read the next chapter you may notice a fuzzy distinction and considerable overlap between general principles and paradigms of qualitative research and specific methods of qualitative research. After that, Chapter 19 will deal exclusively with the data analysis phase of qualitative research.

Main Points

- Qualitative research can involve the direct observation of social phenomena in their natural settings.
- Appropriate topics for qualitative research include practices, episodes, encounters, roles, relationships, groups, organizations, settlements, social worlds, lifestyles, and subcultures.
- Qualitative research in social work can be guided by any one of several paradigms, such as naturalism or ethnography, grounded theory, case studies, and participatory action research.
- Ethnography involves naturalistic observations and holistic understandings of cultures or subcultures.
- Grounded theory refers to the attempt to derive theories from an analysis of the patterns, themes, and common categories discovered among observational data.
- A case study is an idiographic examination of a single individual, family, group, organization, community, or society.

- Some case studies combine qualitative methods with single-case experiments to evaluate practice effectiveness.

- Commonly used qualitative methods in these studies involve intensive interviews and client logs.

- Because controlled probability sampling techniques are usually impossible in qualitative research, a rough form of quota sampling may be used in the attempt to achieve better representativeness in observations.

- Snowball sampling is a method through which you develop an ever-increasing set of sample observations. You ask one participant in the event under study to recommend others for interviewing, and each subsequently interviewed participant is asked for further recommendations.

- Often, the careful examination of deviant cases in qualitative research can yield important insights into the "normal" patterns of social behavior.

- Compared with surveys and experiments, qualitative research measurements generally tap more depth of meaning but have less reliability, and field research results cannot be generalized as safely as those based on rigorous sampling and standardized questionnaires.

- Six strategies for evaluating the rigor of qualitative studies are (1) prolonged engagement, (2) triangulation, (3) peer debriefing and support, (4) negative case analysis, (5) member checking, and (6) auditing.

- Diversity in epistemological paradigms is accompanied by different perspectives on how to critically appraise the rigor of qualitative research.

- The contemporary positivist paradigm emphasizes three key threats to the trustworthiness of qualitative research: reactivity, researcher biases, and respondent biases.

- The social constructivist paradigm views trustworthiness and strategies to enhance rigor more in terms of capturing multiple subjective realities than of ensuring the portrayal of an objective social reality, the objective of contemporary positivists. Thus, minimizing respondent bias is less important than making sure that the research participants' multiple subjective realities are revealed as adequately as possible.

- Those who take a critical social science or participatory action research approach to qualitative research include empowerment standards in critically appraising qualitative research studies.

- Conducting qualitative research responsibly involves confronting several ethical issues that arise from the researcher's direct contact with participants.

Review Questions and Exercises

1. Choose any two of the paradigms discussed in this chapter. Then describe how a hypothetical qualitative study that you make up might be conducted differently if you followed each paradigm. Compare and contrast the way these paradigms might work in the context of your study.

2. To explore the different strengths and weaknesses of experiments, surveys, and qualitative research, give brief descriptions of two studies especially appropriate to each method. Be sure each study would be most appropriately studied by the method you would choose.

3. Write down the potential threats to the trustworthiness of the findings for each of the following hypothetical scenarios. Compare your answers with those of your classmates and discuss any differences you encounter.

a. A researcher draws conclusions about the main reasons clients prematurely terminate treatment based on 15-minute interviews with each of the 20 clients who most recently dropped out of treatment (one interview per client).

b. A researcher who had been a victim of a violent crime interviews other such victims to generate theory about the emotional impact of violent crimes on victims.

c. A young researcher seeking to understand why youths abuse drugs begins to see the world through the eyes of the youths being observed, and draws conclusions based exclusively on their outlook.

4. What strategies could be used to alleviate the threats you identified regarding the scenarios in Exercise 3? Discuss your rationale for each strategy. Compare your answers with those of your classmates and discuss any differences you encounter.

Internet Exercises

1. Use InfoTrac College Edition to find five articles in the journal *Social Work* that debate the goodness of fit between clinical social work practice and qualitative research. The article that sparked the debate, "Does the Glove Really Fit? Qualitative Research and Clinical Social Work Practice" by Deborah K. Padgett, appeared in the July 1998 issue. Three articles that responded to Padgett's article, as well as her response to them, appeared in the May 1999 issue. Briefly describe the main points of each article and discuss your position on this debate.

2. Use InfoTrac College Edition to find two articles that discuss methodological issues in qualitative research. Write down the bibliographic reference information for each article and identify the methodological issues it discusses.

3. Use InfoTrac College Edition to find one to three articles illustrating the use of ethnography, grounded theory, and participatory action research. (Some articles might report a study using more than one of these paradigms.) Write down the bibliographic reference information for each article and identify its methodological strengths and weaknesses.

Additional Readings

Denzin, Norman K., and Yvonna S. Lincoln. 1994. *Handbook of Qualitative Research.* Thousand Oaks, CA: Sage. This compendium of readings provides a wide range of papers about doing qualitative research primarily by using postmodern and naturalistic paradigms. This book will give you more information on various qualitative methods, interpreting qualitative data, and perspectives on positivist and alternative paradigms. This book also exists in three volumes: Vol. 1, *The Landscape of Qualitative Research: Theories and Issues;* Vol. 2, *Strategies of Qualitative Inquiry;* and Vol. 3, *Interpreting Qualitative Materials.*

Glaser, Barney G., and Anselm L. Strauss. 1967. *Discovery of Grounded Theory: Strategies for Qualitative Research.* Chicago: Aldine. This classic on grounded theory is perhaps one of the most commonly cited and most highly recommended books on the inductive philosophy of qualitative inquiry, strategies for conducting it, and analyzing qualitative data.

Gubrium, Jaber F., and James A. Holstein. 1997. *The New Language of Qualitative Method.* New York: Oxford University Press. This book provides the necessary foundations for understanding some of the main approaches or traditions in qualitative research.

Johnson, Jeffrey C. 1990. *Selecting Ethnographic Informants.* Newbury Park, CA: Sage. The author discusses the various strategies that apply to the task of sampling in qualitative research.

Lofland, John, and Lyn Lofland. 1995. *Analyzing Social Settings,* 3rd ed. Belmont, CA: Wadsworth. An unexcelled presentation of qualitative research methods from beginning to end, this eminently readable little book successfully manages to draw the links between the logic of scientific inquiry and the nitty-gritty practicalities of observing, communicating, recording, filing, reporting, and everything else involved in field research. In addition, the book contains a wealth of references to field research illustrations.

Padgett, Deborah K. 1998. *Qualitative Methods in Social Work Research.* Thousand Oaks, CA: Sage. This introductory text emphasizes the how-to of qualitative research methods for social workers. Two nice features of this book are its coverage of alternative epistemological perspectives and its coverage of assessing rigor in qualitative studies.

Patton, Michael Quinn. 1990. *Qualitative Evaluation and Research Methods,* 2nd ed. Newbury Park, CA: Sage. This text provides a comprehensive treatment of qualitative inquiry, with a special focus on its use in program evaluation. It covers conceptual issues in qualitative inquiry, the design of qualitative studies, and the analysis, interpretation, and reporting of qualitative data.

Reissman, Catherine (ed.). 1994. *Qualitative Studies in Social Work Research.* Thousand Oaks, CA: Sage, 1994. This is a useful compendium of qualitative research studies relevant to social welfare policy and social work practice. It illustrates the application of grounded theory to research on social work and health, narrative methods in studying traumatized target groups, and the benefits of subjectivity in qualitative research.

Strauss, Anselm, and Juliet Corbin. 1990. *Basics of Qualitative Research: Grounded Theory Procedures and Techniques.* Newbury Park, CA: Sage. This is a very important book to read before data collection and during data analysis if you choose to take a grounded theory approach.

CHAPTER **18**

Qualitative Research: Specific Methods

What You'll Learn in This Chapter

This chapter will continue our discussion of qualitative research, and will do so with a greater emphasis on specific types of qualitative research methods, such as participant observation, qualitative interviewing, recording observations, life history, feminist methods, and focus groups. Each method involves principles that were discussed in the previous chapter.

INTRODUCTION

In the previous chapter we considered the kinds of topics appropriate to qualitative research, some of the paradigms that direct different types of qualitative research efforts, qualitative sampling methods, the strengths and weaknesses of qualitative research, and ethical issues in qualitative research. Along the way we saw some examples that illustrate qualitative research in action. To round out the picture, we turn now to specific ideas and techniques for conducting qualitative research. In qualitative research the distinction between general principles, paradigms, and specific data-collection methods is sometimes fuzzy. For example, grounded theory and ethnography at times are discussed as methods. We hope that you will not let such semantic distinctions stymie you. The main objectives are to see the value in these methods, to recognize how to use these methods in your own research, and to critically appraise studies that report having used them. Let's begin by examining how qualitative researchers prepare for their contact with the people they plan to study.

PREPARING FOR THE FIELD

Suppose for the moment that you have decided to undertake qualitative research on a grassroots community organization. Let's assume further that you are not a member of that group, that you do not know much about it, and that you will identify yourself to the participants as a researcher. This section will discuss some of the ways in which you might prepare yourself before undertaking direct observation of the group.

As is true of all research methods, you would be well advised to begin with a search of the relevant literature, filling in your knowledge of the subject and learning what others have said about it. Because library research is discussed at length in Appendix A, we won't say anything further at this point.

In the next phase of your research, you may wish to make use of key informants. You might wish to discuss the community group with others who have already studied it or with anyone else who is likely to be familiar with it. In particular, you might find it useful to discuss the group with one of its members. Perhaps you already know a member or can meet one. This aspect of your preparation is likely to be more effective if your relationship with the informant extends beyond your research role. In dealing with members of the group as informants, you should take care that your initial discussions do not compromise or limit later aspects of your research. Realize that the impression you make on the member informant, the role you establish for yourself, may carry over into your later effort. For example, creating the initial impression that you may be a spy for an opposing group is unlikely to facilitate later observations of the group.

You should also be wary about the information you get from informants. Although they may have more direct, personal knowledge of the subject under study than you, what they "know" is probably a mixture of fact and point of view. Members of the community group in our example are unlikely to give you completely unbiased information (neither would members of opposing groups). Before making your first contact with the group, then, you should be already quite familiar with it, and you should understand the general, theoretical context within which it exists.

You can establish your initial contact with the people you plan to study in a variety of ways. How you do it will depend, in part, on the role you intend to play. Suppose, for example, you want to take on the role of *complete participant* in the organization, as opposed to conspicuously appearing as an outside researcher. (We'll discuss the complete participant and alternative observation roles shortly.) You'll have to find a way to develop an identity with the people to be studied. If you wish to study dishwashers in a restaurant, the most direct method would be to get a job as a dishwasher. In the case of the community organization, you might simply join the group. Many of the social processes that are appropriate to qualitative research are sufficiently open to make your contact with the people to be studied simple and straightforward. If you wish to observe a mass demonstration, just be there. If you wish to observe patterns in jaywalking, hang around busy streets.

Whenever you wish to make a more formal contact with the people and identify yourself as a researcher, you must be able to establish a certain rapport with them. You might contact a participant with whom you feel comfortable and gain that person's assistance. If you are studying a formal group, you might approach the group leaders. Or you may find that one of your informants who has studied the group can introduce you.

Although you will probably have many options in making your initial contact with the group, you should realize that your choice can influence your subsequent observations. Suppose, for example, that you are studying a community clinic and begin with high-level administrators. First, your initial impressions of the clinic are going to be shaped by the administrators' views, which will be quite different from those of patients or staff. This initial impression may influence the way you subsequently observe and interpret—even though you are unaware of the influence.

Second, if the administrators approve of your research project and encourage patients and staff to cooperate with you, then the latter groups will probably look on you as somehow aligned with the administration, which can affect what they say to you. Nurses might be reluctant to tell you about their plans to organize through the Teamsters Union, for example.

In making direct, formal contact with the people you want to study, you will be required to give them some explanation of the purpose of your study. Here again, you face an ethical dilemma. Telling them the complete purpose of your research might lose their cooperation altogether or have important effects on their behavior. On the other hand, giving only what you believe would be an acceptable explanation may involve outright deception. Realize in all this that your decisions—in practice—may be largely determined by the purpose of your study, the nature of what you are studying, observations you wish to use, and other such factors.

Previous qualitative research offers no fixed rule—methodological or ethical—to follow in this regard. Your appearance as a researcher, regardless of your stated purpose, may result in a warm welcome from people who are flattered that a scientist finds them important enough to study. Or you may end up being ostracized or worse. (Do not, for example, burst into a meeting of an organized crime syndicate and announce that you are writing a term paper on organized crime.)

THE VARIOUS ROLES OF THE OBSERVER

As we alluded to above, in qualitative research, observers can play any of several roles, including participating in what they want to observe. As Marshall and Rossman (1995:60) point out:

> . . . the researcher may plan a role that entails varying degrees of "participantness"—that is, the degree of actual participation in daily life. At one extreme is the full participant, who goes about ordinary life in a role or set of roles constructed in the setting.
>
> At the other extreme is the complete observer, who engages not at all in social interaction and may even shun involvement in the world being studied. And, of course, all possible complementary mixes along the continuum are available to the researcher.

In the classic work on this subject, Raymond Gold (1969:30–39) discussed four different positions on a continuum of roles that qualitative researchers may play in this regard: *complete participant, participant-as-observer, observer-as-participant,* and *complete observer.*

The *complete participant,* in this sense, may either be a genuine participant in what he or she is studying (for example, a participant in a protest demonstration) or pretend to be a genuine participant. In any event, if you are acting as the complete participant, you let people see you only as a participant, not as a researcher.

Clearly, if you are not a genuine participant in what you are studying, you must learn to behave as though you were. If you are studying a group of uneducated and inarticulate people, it would not be appropriate for you to talk and act like a university professor or student.

Here let us remind you of an ethical issue, one on which social researchers themselves are divided. Is it ethical to deceive the people you are studying in the hope that they will confide in you as they will not confide in an identified researcher? Will the humanitarian value of your study offset such ethical considerations? Although many professional associations have addressed this issue, the norms to be followed remain somewhat ambiguous when applied to specific situations.

Related to this ethical consideration is a scientific one. No researcher deceives his or her participants solely for the purpose of deception. Rather, it is done in the belief that the data will be more valid and reliable, that the participants will be more natural and honest if they do not know the researcher is doing a research project. If the people being studied know they are being studied, they might modify their behavior in a variety of ways. First, they might expel the researcher. Second, they might modify their speech and behavior to appear more respectable than they would otherwise be. Third, the social process itself might be radically changed. Students making plans to burn down the university administration building, for example, might give up the plan altogether once they learn that a member of their group is a social scientist conducting a research project.

On the other side of the coin, if you are a complete participant, you may affect what you are studying. To play the role of participant, you must *participate*. Yet your participation may have important effects on the social process you are studying. Suppose, for example, that you are asked for your ideas about what the group should do next. No matter what you say, you will affect the process in some fashion. If the group follows your suggestion, your influence on the process is obvious. If the group decides not to follow your suggestion, the process by which the suggestion is rejected may affect what happens next. Finally, if you indicate that you just don't know what should be done next, you may be adding to a general feeling of uncertainty and indecisiveness in the group.

Ultimately, *anything* the participant observer does or does not do will have some effect on what is being observed; it is simply inevitable. More seriously, what you do or do not do may have an *important* effect on what happens. There is no complete protection against this effect, though sensitivity to the issue may provide partial protection.

Because of these several considerations, ethical and scientific, the qualitative researcher frequently chooses a different role from that of complete participant. In Gold's terminology, you might choose the role of *participant-as-observer*. In this role, you would participate fully with the group under study, but you would make it clear that you were also undertaking research. If you were a member of the volleyball team, for example, you might use that position to launch a study in the sociology of sports, letting your teammates know what you were doing. There are dangers in this role also, however. The people being studied may shift much of their attention to the research project rather than focus on the natural social process, and the process being observed may no longer be typical. Or, conversely, you yourself may come to identify too much with the participants' interests and viewpoints. You may begin to "go native" and lose much of your scientific detachment.

The *observer-as-participant* is one who identifies himself or herself as a researcher and interacts with the participants in the social process but makes no pretense of actually being a participant. A good example of that would be a newspaper reporter learning about a social movement—for instance, the unionization of migrant farm workers. The reporter might interview leaders and also visit workers where they live, watch strawberry picking, go with an injured worker to the hospital, and so on.

The *complete observer*, at the other extreme, observes a social process without becoming a part of it in any way. The participants in a study might not realize they are being studied because of the researcher's unobtrusiveness. Sitting at a bus stop to observe jaywalking behavior at a nearby intersection would be an example. Although the complete observer is less likely to affect what is being studied and less likely to "go native" than the complete participant, he or she is also less likely to develop a full appreciation of what is being studied. Observations may be more sketchy and transitory.

Fred Davis (1973) characterized the extreme roles that observers might play as "the Martian" and "the Convert." The latter involves the observer delving deeper and deeper into the phenomenon under study, running the risk that anthropologists refer to as "going native." We'll examine this further in the next section.

On the other hand, you may be able to most fully grasp the "Martian" approach by imagining that you were sent to observe life on Mars (assuming life forms had been found there). Probably you would feel yourself inescapably separate from the Martians. Some social scientists adopt this degree of separation when observing cultures or social classes different from their own.

Ultimately, different situations require different roles for the researcher. Unfortunately, there are no clear guidelines for making this choice, and you must rely on your understanding of the situation and your own good judgment. In making your decision, however, you must be guided by both methodological and ethical considerations. Because these often conflict with one another, your decision will frequently be a difficult one, and you may find sometimes that your role limits your study.

RELATIONS TO PARTICIPANTS: EMIC AND ETIC PERSPECTIVES

Having introduced the different roles you might play in connection with your field research observations, we'll now focus more specifically on how you may relate to the participants in your study and to their points of view. In the previous section, we opened the possibility of pretending to occupy social statuses you don't really occupy. Now let's consider how you would think and feel in such a situation.

Let's suppose you have decided to study a religious cult that has enrolled many people in your own neighborhood or in one for which you have social work responsibilities. You might study the group by joining it or pretending to join it. Take a moment to ask yourself what the difference is between "really" joining and "pretending" to join. The main difference is one of whether you actually take on the beliefs, attitudes, and other points of view shared by the "real" members. If the cult members believe that Jesus will come next Thursday to destroy the world and save the members of the cult, do you believe that or do you simply pretend to believe it?

Traditionally, social scientists have tended to emphasize the importance of "objectivity" in such matters. In this example, that injunction would be to avoid getting swept up in the beliefs of the group. In qualitative research, the term for maintaining your objectivity as an outsider and thus being able to raise questions about the culture you are observing—questions that would not occur to members of that culture—is the **etic perspective.** Without denying the advantages associated with such objectivity, social scientists today also recognize the benefits to be gained by immersing themselves in the points of view they are studying, gaining what Lofland and Lofland (1995:61) refer to as *insider understanding.* Ultimately, you will not be able to understand the thoughts and actions of the cult members unless you are able to *adopt their points of view as true*—even if you only do so on a temporary basis. In a sense, you need to believe that Jesus is coming next Thursday night to fully appreciate the phenomenon you've set out to study. In contrast to the etic perspective, the **emic perspective** refers to trying to adopt the beliefs, attitudes, and other points of view shared by the culture being studied.

Adopting an alien point of view is an uncomfortable prospect for most people. It's one thing to learn about the strange views that others may hold, and sometimes you probably have difficulty even tolerating those views, but to take them on as your own is 10 times worse. Robert Bellah (1970, 1974) has offered the term *symbolic realism* in this regard, indicating the need for social researchers to treat the beliefs they study as worthy of respect rather than as objects of ridicule. If you seriously entertain this prospect, you may appreciate why William B. Shaffir and Robert A. Stebbins (1991:1) concluded that "fieldwork must certainly rank with the more disagreeable activities that humanity has fashioned for itself."

There is, of course, a danger in adopting the points of view of the people you are studying. When you abandon your objectivity in favor of the views you are studying, you lose the possibility of seeing and understanding the phenomenon within frames of reference that are unavailable to your participants. On the one hand, accepting the belief that the world will end Thursday night allows you to appreciate aspects of that belief that are available only to believers; stepping outside that view, however, makes it possible for you to consider some of the reasons why people might adopt such a view. You may discover that some reached that state as a consequence of personal traumas (such as unemployment or divorce), whereas others were brought into the fold through their participation in particular social networks (for instance, their whole bowling team joined the cult). Notice that the cult members might disagree with those "objective" explanations, and you might not come up with those explanations to the extent that you were operating legitimately within the group's views.

The apparent dilemma here is that although the emic and etic perspectives each offer important advantages, they also seem mutually exclusive. Yet it is possible, though challenging, to assume both postures. Sometimes you can simply shift viewpoints at will. When appropriate, you can fully assume the beliefs of the cult; later, you can step outside those beliefs (more accurately, you step inside the viewpoints associated with social science). As you become more adept at this kind of research, you may come to hold contradictory viewpoints simultaneously, rather than switch back and forth.

Social researchers often refer to the concerns just discussed as a matter of *reflexivity,* in the sense of things acting on themselves. Thus, your own characteristics can have an effect on what you see and how you interpret it. The issue is broader than that, however, and applies to the participants as well as to the researcher. Imagine yourself interviewing a homeless person (1) on the street, (2) in a homeless shelter, or (3) in a social welfare office. The research setting could affect the person's responses. In other words, you might get different results depending on where you conducted the interview. Moreover, you might act differently as a researcher in those different settings. If you reflect on this issue, you'll be able to identify other aspects of the research encounter that complicate the task of "simply observing what's so."

The problem we've just been discussing could be seen as psychological, occurring mostly inside the researchers' or participants' heads. There is a corresponding problem at a social level, however. When you become deeply involved in the lives of the people you're studying, you're likely to be moved by their personal problems and crises. Imagine, for example, that one of the cult members becomes ill and needs a ride to the hospital. Should you provide transportation? Sure. Suppose someone wants to borrow money to buy a stereo. Should you loan it? Probably not. Suppose they need the money for food?

There are no black-and-white rules for resolving situations such as these, but you should realize that you will need to deal with them regardless of whether or not you reveal you're a researcher. Such problems do not tend to arise in other types of research—surveys and experiments, for example—but they are part and parcel of qualitative research.

This discussion of the qualitative researcher's relations to participants flies in the face of the conventional view of "scientific objectivity." Before concluding this section, let's take the issue one step further.

In the conventional view of science, there are implicit differences of power and status separating the researcher from the participants in research. When we discussed experimental designs in Chapter 11, for example, it was obvious who was in charge: the experimenter. The experimenter organized things, assigned participants to groups, and determined whether each group would receive a particular form of intervention. Something similar might be said about survey research. The person running the survey designs the questions, decides who will be selected for questioning, and is responsible for making sense out of the data collected.

These sorts of relationships can be seen as power or status relationships. In experimental and survey designs, the researcher clearly has more power and a higher status than the people being studied. The researchers have a special knowledge that the participants don't enjoy. They're not so crude as to say they're superior to their participants, but there's a sense in which that's implicitly assumed.

In qualitative research, such assumptions can be problematic. When the early European anthropologists set out to study what were originally called "primitive" societies, there was no question but that the anthropologists knew best. Whereas the natives "believed" in witchcraft, for example, the anthropologists "knew" it wasn't really true. While the natives said some of their rituals would appease the gods, the anthropologists explained that the "real" functions of these rituals were the creation of social identity, the establishment of group solidarity, and so on. The more social researchers have gone into the field to study their fellow humans face-to-face, however, the more they have become conscious of these implicit assumptions about researcher superiority, and the more they have considered alternatives.

QUALITATIVE INTERVIEWING

In part, qualitative research is a matter of going where the action is and simply watching and listening. You can learn a lot merely by being attentive to what's going on. At the same time, as we've already indicated, field research can involve more active inquiry. Sometimes, it's appropriate to ask people questions and record their answers. Your on-the-spot observations of a full-blown riot will lack something if you don't know why people are rioting. Ask somebody.

We have already discussed interviewing in Chapter 15, on survey research. The interviewing you will do in connection with qualitative observation, however, is different enough to demand a separate treatment here. In surveys, questionnaires are always structured and commonly use many closed-ended questions, but in qualitative research interviews will be almost entirely open-ended and are likely to be unstructured.

Rubin and Rubin (1995:43) make this distinction: "Qualitative interviewing design is *flexible, iterative,* and *continuous,* rather than prepared in advance and locked in stone."

> Design in qualitative interviewing is iterative. That means that each time you repeat the basic process of gathering information, analyzing it, winnowing it, and testing it, you come closer to a clear and convincing model of the phenomenon you are studying. . . .
>
> The continuous nature of qualitative interviewing means that the questioning is redesigned throughout the project.
>
> (RUBIN AND RUBIN, 1995:46, 47)

A **qualitative interview** is an interaction between an interviewer and a respondent in which the interviewer has a general plan of inquiry but not a specific set of questions that must be asked in particular words and in a particular order. A qualitative interview is essentially a conversation in which the interviewer establishes a general direction for the conversation and pursues specific topics raised by the respondent. Ideally, the respondent does most of the talking. If you're talking more than 5 percent of the time, that's probably too much.

Steinar Kvale (1996:3–5) offers two metaphors for interviewing: the interviewer as a "miner" and the interviewer as a "traveler." The first model assumes that the subject possesses specific information and the interviewer's job is to dig it out. By contrast, in the second model, the interviewer

> . . . wanders through the landscape and enters into conversations with the people encountered. The traveler explores the many domains of the country, as unknown territory or with maps, roaming freely around the territory. . . .The interviewer wanders along with the local inhabitants, asks questions that lead the subjects to tell their own stories of their lived world. . . .

Patton (1990:280) identifies three forms of qualitative, open-ended interviewing:

1. Informal conversational interview
2. General interview guide approach
3. Standardized open-ended interview

Informal Conversational Interviews

An **informal conversational interview** is an unplanned and unanticipated interaction between an interviewer and a respondent that occurs naturally during the course of fieldwork observation. It is the most open-ended form of interviewing. When this type of interviewing occurs, the person with whom you are talking may not even think of the interaction as an interview.

When you conduct an informal conversational interview, you should be extremely flexible so that you can pursue relevant information in whatever direction seems appropriate. Your questions should be generated naturally and spontaneously from what you happen to observe at a particular point in a particular setting or from what individuals in that setting happen to say to you. In other words, this is the type of interviewing that will occur spontaneously when you are conducting fieldwork observations and want to maximize your understanding of what you are observing and what the people whom you are observing think about what is happening.

Because you cannot anticipate the situation beforehand, you conduct informal conversational interviews with no predetermined set of questions. Nonetheless, it is important for you to use your skills in asking questions and listening—skills that you probably learned as part of your social work practice training.

Lofland and Lofland (1995:56–57) suggest that investigators adopt the role of the "socially acceptable incompetent" when interviewing. You should offer yourself as someone who does not understand the situation in which you find yourself and so must be helped to grasp even the most basic and obvious aspects of that situation:

> A naturalistic investigator, almost by definition, is one who does not understand. She or he is "ignorant" and needs to be "taught." This role of watcher and asker of questions is the quintessential *student role*.
>
> (LOFLAND AND LOFLAND, 1995:56)

Asking questions and noting answers is a natural process for all of us, and it seems simple enough to add it to your bag of tricks as a qualitative researcher. Be cautious, however. There is a danger that what you ask is what you get.

As we've already discussed in Chapter 9, question wording is a tricky business. All too often, the way we ask questions subtly biases the answers we get. Sometimes, we put our respondent under pressure to look good. Sometimes we put the question in a particular context that completely precludes the most relevant answers.

Suppose you want to find out why a group of youths in a residential facility for emotionally distressed children is running amok. You might be tempted to focus your questioning on how the youths feel about the disciplinary style of their cottage parents. Although you may collect a great deal of information about their attitudes toward their cottage parents, they may be rioting for some other reason. Or perhaps most are simply joining in for the excitement. Properly done, informal conversational interviewing would enable you to find out.

One of the special strengths of this type of interviewing is its flexibility in the field. It allows you to respond to things you see or hear that you could not anticipate. The answers evoked by your initial questions should shape your subsequent ones. In this situation, merely asking pre-established questions and recording answers doesn't work. You need to ask a question, hear the answer, interpret its meaning for your general inquiry, frame another question either to dig into the earlier answer in more depth or to redirect the person's attention to an area more relevant to your inquiry. In short, you need to be able to listen, think, and talk almost at the same time.

The discussion of *probes* in Chapter 15 provides a useful guide to getting answers in more depth without biasing later answers. Learn the skills of being a good listener. Be more interested than interesting. Learn to ask such questions as "How is that?" "In what ways?" "How do you mean that?" "What would be an example of that?" Learn to look and listen expectantly, and let the person you are interviewing fill the silence.

At the same time, you can't afford to be a totally passive receiver in the interaction. You'll probably have some general (or specific) questions in mind based on what you are observing, and you will have to learn the skills of subtly directing the flow of conversation.

There's something you can learn here from Asian martial arts. The aikido master never resists an opponent's blow but rather accepts it, joins with it, and then subtly redirects it in a more appropriate direction. You should master a similar skill for interviewing. Don't try to halt your respondent's line of discussion, but learn to take what he or she has just said and branch that comment back in a direction that is appropriate to your purposes. Most people love to talk to anyone who's really interested. Stopping their line of conversation tells them you aren't interested; asking them to elaborate in a particular direction tells them you are.

Consider this hypothetical example in which you are interested in why college students chose their majors.

You: What are you majoring in?

Resp: Engineering.

You: I see. How did you come to choose engineering?

Resp: I have an uncle who was voted the best engineer in Arizona in 1981.

You: Gee, that's great.

Resp: Yeah. He was the engineer in charge of developing the new civic center in Tucson. It was written up in most of the engineering journals.

You: I see. Did you talk to him about your becoming an engineer?

Resp: Yeah. He said that he got into engineering by accident. He needed a job when he graduated from high school, so he went to work as a laborer on a construction job. He spent eight years working his way up from the bottom, until he decided to go to college and come back nearer the top.

You: So is your main interest in civil engineering, like your uncle, or are you more interested in some other branch of engineering?

Resp: Actually, I'm leaning more toward electrical engineering—computers in particular. I started messing around with microcomputers when I was in high school, and my long-term plan is. . . .

Notice how the interview first begins to wander off into a story about the respondent's uncle. The first attempt to focus things back on the student's own choice of major failed. The second attempt succeeded. Now the student is providing the kind of information you want. It's important for you to develop the ability to "control" conversations in that fashion.

Rubin and Rubin (1995) offer several guides to controlling a "guided conversation." For example:

> If you can limit the number of main topics, it is easier to maintain a conversational flow from one topic to another. Transitions should be smooth and logical. "We have been talking about mothers, now let's talk about fathers," sounds abrupt. A smoother transition might be, "You mentioned your mother did not care how you performed in school—was your father more involved?" The more abrupt the transition, the more it sounds like the interviewer has an agenda that he or she wants to get through, rather than wanting to hear what the interviewee has to say.
>
> (RUBIN AND RUBIN, 1995:123)

Because informal conversational interviewing is so much like normal conversations, it is essential that you keep reminding yourself that you are not having a normal conversation. In normal conversations, we want to come across as an interesting, worthwhile person. If you'll watch yourself the next time you are chatting with someone you don't know too well, you may find that much of your attention is spent on thinking up interesting things to say—contributions to the conversation that will make a good impression. Often, we don't really hear each other because we're too busy thinking of what we'll say next. As an interviewer, the desire to appear interesting is counterproductive to your job. You need to make the other person seem interesting—by being interested. (Do this in ordinary conversations, by the way, and people will actually regard you as a great conversationalist.)

Interviewing needs to be an integral part of your whole field research process. Later, we'll stress the need to review your notes every night—making sense out of what you've observed, getting a clearer feel for the situation you're studying, and finding out what you should pay more attention to in further observations.

In this same fashion, you need to review your notes on informal conversational interviews, detecting all of the things you should have asked but didn't. Start asking those things the next time an appropriate informal conversational interview emerges. As with all other aspects of field research, informal conversational interviewing improves with practice. Fortunately, it is something you can practice any time you want. Practice on your friends.

Interview Guide Approach

Besides including the unplanned interviews that emerge spontaneously in the conduct of field observations, qualitative inquiry can include the use of interviews that are planned in advance and that are therefore more structured than informal conversational interviews. Although all qualitative interviewing is open-ended and allows respondents to express their own perspectives in their own words, qualitative interviewing strategies can vary in the extent to which the sequencing and wording of the open-ended questions is predetermined.

Highly structured strategies attempt to ensure that all respondents are asked the same questions in the same sequence to maximize the comparability of responses and to ensure that complete data are gathered from each person on all relevant questions. Greater structure can also reduce interviewer biases and inconsistencies in the way different interviewers conduct their interviews. More structure also eases the researcher's task of organizing and analyzing interview data and helps readers of the research report judge the quality of the interviewing methods and instruments used.

The downside to the highly structured approach, however, is that it reduces the natural, conversational nature of the interview and the interviewer's flexibility to follow up on important unanticipated circumstances or responses. Patton (1990) suggests that one way to provide more structure than in the completely unstructured informal conversational interview, while maintaining a relatively high degree of flexibility, is to use the interview guide strategy.

An *interview guide* lists in outline form the topics and issues that the interviewer should cover in the interview, but it allows the interviewer to adapt the sequencing and wording of questions to each particular interview. Thus, the interview guide ensures that different interviewers will cover the same material and keep focused on the same predetermined topics and issues while remaining conversational and free to probe into unanticipated circumstances and responses. Interview guides will vary in the extent of detail they provide. How much detail you provide in your guide will depend on the extent to which you are able to anticipate the important topics and issues in advance and how much detail you think your interviewers need to ensure that they will all cover the same material in a thorough fashion (Patton, 1990).

Suppose, for example, that you want to use intensive interviews of social workers in a qualitative evaluation of an in-service training program aimed at improving their own interviewing skills in conducting clinical assessments. A relatively brief interview guide might list a handful or so of broad question areas to ask about, such as:

1. What interviewing training activities and assignments did the trainee do in the program?

2. In what areas of interviewing, if any, does the trainee feel more or less skillful as a result of the program?

3. What service functions, if any, does the trainee feel better (or worse) prepared to provide as a result of the training?

4. Has the program influenced the trainee's career plans, and if so, how?

5. What did the trainee like and dislike most about the program? What are its strengths and weaknesses, and what changes, if any, does the trainee suggest?

A more detailed interview guide for the same type of evaluation might look something like the following rough example:

I. Overall impression of program
  A. Likes? Dislikes?
  B. Strengths? Weaknesses?
  C. Suggested changes?
  D. Perceived influence of program on trainee?
    1. Service functions prepared to provide
    2. Career plans
    3. Interviewing skills, in general

II. Activities in program
   A. Readings?
   B. Written experiential assignments?
   C. Role plays?
   D. Peer or instructor feedback?
   E. Instructor modeling of interview skills?

III. Progress made or not made in specific areas of interviewing
   A. Beginning the interview
      1. Meeting and greeting clients
      2. Introductions
      3. Putting client at ease
      4. Explaining purpose of interview
      5. Obtaining client's reason for coming
   B. Physical attending
      1. Eye contact
      2. Posture
      3. Intermittent positive gestures
      4. Appropriately relaxed and professionally comfortable?
   C. Verbal attending
      1. Nonjudgmental prompts
      2. Brief pauses before responding
      3. Appropriate paraphrasing
      4. Encouraging client to talk
      5. Sensitivity to differences in culture or ethnicity
      6. Conveying empathy and warmth
      7. Speaking in a natural, spontaneous, genuine manner
   D. Exploring the problem
      1. Taking social histories
      2. Examining problem from different perspectives
      3. Assessing situational and systemic factors
   E. Questioning and probing
      1. Asking clear and succinct questions
      2. Asking questions in an unbiased manner
      3. Asking exploratory questions in an open-ended manner
      4. Interspersing closed- and open-ended questions
      5. Pursuing important details with neutral probes
      6. Knowing not to bombard with too many questions
      7. Logical sequencing of questions
      8. Sensitivity to privacy concerns

In addition to facilitating your learning about the use of detailed interview guides, we hope this illustrative guide will be useful to you as you think about developing your own skills as a qualitative interviewer and as an interviewer in your social work practice roles.

Regardless of how detailed you make your interview guide, you should make sure that your interviewers are completely familiar with its contents and purposes before they begin any interviews. If they are not, the interview will not flow smoothly, and your efforts to ensure that all of the material is covered in the context of a natural, conversational interview will be imperiled.

Interviewers also have to be prepared to decide when and when not to follow up in a neutral probing manner on unanticipated topics that emerge during the interview, depending on their importance to the respondent and to the purpose of the research. Thus, interviewers should be trained carefully before embarking on any interviews. (See our discussion of coordination and control in Chapter 15 for information on training interviewers.)

Standardized Open-Ended Interviews

As we just mentioned, sometimes you will want to ensure that all interviews are conducted in a consistent, thorough manner—with a minimum of interviewer effects and biases. When this is your aim, the most appropriate strategy is to conduct standardized open-ended interviews. This strategy may also be needed when resource limitations leave you with insufficient time to pursue less structured strategies in a comprehensive way with large numbers of respondents, or when you are tracking individuals over time and therefore want to reduce the chances that changes observed over time are being caused by changes in the way interviews are being conducted.

In light of these concerns, the **standardized open-ended interview** consists of questions that are "written out in advance exactly the way they are to be asked in the interview" (Patton, 1990:285). Great care goes into the wording of the questions and their sequencing. Probes are to be limited to where they are indicated on the interview schedule, although some studies that use highly skilled interviewers may permit more flexibility in probing than other studies that use this strategy. We presented excerpts from an exemplary standardized open-ended interview schedule in Figure 9-8, way back in Chapter 9, on constructing measurement instruments. You may want to take another look at those excerpts at this point to see how a standardized open-ended interview schedule compares to an interview guide.

Before leaving this topic, we should remind you that the social class issues mentioned in Chapter 15 regarding surveys, such as appearance and demeanor, apply to interviewing in qualitative research as well. So too do the cultural issues that we discussed in Chapter 5.

LIFE HISTORY

Another method of qualitative interviewing is called **life history** or **life story.** Using this method, researchers ask open-ended questions to discover how the participants in a study understand the significant events and meanings in their own lives. Another term sometimes used in connection with this method is *oral history interviews.*

Because life histories provide idiographic examinations of individuals' lives, they can be viewed within the case study paradigm. They are also in keeping with the *naturalist* tradition because their main purpose is to see how the individual subjectively remembers and understands the significant events of their lives—even if the remembrances and interpretations lack objective accuracy.

Robin Robinson's dissertation (1994) in social welfare at Brandeis University provides an illustration of the life history method. Robinson sought to give voice to her informants without questioning the veracity of their accounts. Her goal was to describe the significant events in the life stories of delinquent girls as told to her in oral history interviews. In particular, she was interested in life experiences that led to delinquent behaviors resulting in their referral for social services.

She interviewed 30 girls she randomly selected from purposively selected areas thought to be representative of Massachusetts. Robinson embarked on her study with the notion that a history of sexual abuse might be prevalent among this population of girls and that abuse might be a key factor in leading them to delinquent behaviors. Rather than operationally define *sexual abuse,* however, she relied on the girls' own subjective experiences and perceptions. Robinson looked for cues suggestive of possible incidents of sexual abuse, and when she felt there was a cue she encouraged the girls to elaborate on the nature of the abuse and how they experienced it.

She began each interview with an open-ended question: "Tell me about your family?" (1994:81). In addition to observing their verbal responses during the interviews, Robinson took note of the girls' facial expressions, body language, and overall affect. The interviews were unstructured and conversational, although Robinson slowly and gently probed when the girls mentioned or hinted at sensitive events that were difficult for them to talk about. The girls discussed many painful and traumatic life events—including betrayal by parents, miscarriages and abortions, suicide attempts, and others—but Robinson focused on sexual abuse as the key event, noting that 23 of the 30 girls reported having been sexually abused. Ten of the girls reported being victimized by more than one person. Robinson's report cites various excerpts from her interviews, giving readers a sense of the girls' experiences of the abuse in their own voices.

From this information, and guided by her theoretical framework and feminist perspective, Robinson concluded that correctional systems and social agencies should begin to view these girls not just as offenders, but as victims of horrendous experiences who need services specifically geared to sexual abuse.

FEMINIST METHODS

Robinson's study illustrates how the different types of qualitative studies we are discussing are not mutually exclusive. For example, her study combined life history interviews with a feminist perspective. We alluded to feminist studies back in Chapter 3, as an application of the critical social science paradigm. Many studies using feminist methods aim to generate findings that can be used to improve the well-being of women in a historically male-dominated society. Although feminist studies use both quantitative and qualitative methods, they most commonly use qualitative methods and are most commonly associated with qualitative research. Feminist studies typically employ features of ethnography and oral history in that they attempt to let the voices of women be heard from their own point of view. In this connection, feminist studies typically rest on the assumption that women are different from men in the ways they acquire knowledge and view the world.

FOCUS GROUPS

Our discussions of qualitative research so far have focused on studying or interviewing people in their natural settings. Sometimes, however, researchers bring people into the laboratory to be observed and interviewed as a group. The **focus group,** which is also called *group interviewing*, is usually considered a qualitative method (although it can also be used in a quantitative way, such as by merely counting how many times certain words are expressed). It is based on structured, semistructured, or unstructured interviews. It allows the researcher–interviewer to question several individuals systematically and simultaneously.

Focus groups are often used to assess whether a new social program or social service being considered is really needed in a community. In a focus group, a small group of people (some researchers recommend 12 to 15 people; others recommend no more than 8) are brought together in a room to engage in a guided discussion of a specified topic.

Participants in focus groups are not likely to be chosen using probability sampling techniques. They are more likely to be selected using purposive sampling—based on their relevancy to the topic being discussed. For example, if the topic pertains to prospective consumer utilization of a new service that an agency is considering, then the participants may be community leaders, service providers from other agencies, referral sources, current service consumers, or perhaps a sample of community residents in targeted neighborhoods. If the topic concerns consumer satisfaction with agency services, then the participants may be drawn from current consumers.

It's also common to convene more than one focus group; relying on only one group is generally considered too risky because any one particular group may be atypical.

Despite the risks inherent in generalizing from focus groups, they offer several advantages. They are inexpensive, generate speedy results, and offer flexibility for probing. The group dynamics that occur in focus groups can bring out aspects of the topic that researchers may not have anticipated and that may not have emerged in individual interviews.

Imagine, for example, that you, as a consumer in a social work education program, are being asked about your satisfaction with the program and how it might be improved to offer better services. Suppose you are responding to a structured questionnaire or a structured interview with closed-ended questions about your degree of satisfaction with the classroom course offerings, field practicums, audiovisual or computer resources, the quality of the teaching, advisement, instructor accessibility, and so forth. Your responses would be limited to checking off things like "moderately satisfied, slightly dissatisfied," and so on to program attributes anticipated by those who designed the survey.

Suppose the survey questionnaire also contains open-ended items that ask you to think of anything else you particularly liked or disliked about the program or recommendations you have for improvement. You may or may not give a great deal of thought to these open-ended items, and even if you give them considerable thought you may not think of some things that others may think of and with which you would agree.

Now suppose that you were being asked about these things not in a structured survey format but in a focus group. Instead of asking you to check off your degree of satisfaction with this or that, or to come up with your own new ideas for improvements, the focus group leader would ask you and some of your cohorts to engage in a sort of bull-session discussion about your satisfaction or dissatisfaction with the program and how it could be improved. Chances are, if one or more of your colleagues began expressing dissatisfaction with something with which you also were dissatisfied, then you might feel more comfortable in expressing the extent of your own dissatisfaction and its sources. As the members of the focus group interact about these issues, new ideas might be stimulated that would not have occurred to you in an individual interview or in completing a questionnaire.

For instance, someone might say, "Gee, I sure wish the program offered an elective course on interventions connected to death and dying." This might spark someone else to say, "Yeah, and I would have loved to take a course on play therapy." Neither of these ideas may have occurred to you as an individual survey respondent, but on hearing them in a focus group you might respond, "Wow, I had assumed that the faculty knew best what courses were and were not appropriate to offer in a school of social work, but if those two courses were offered I sure would have taken them both. They sound like they would have prepared me with specific practice intervention competencies more than a lot of the other electives offered!" This might spur other group participants who, like you, may not have thought of these courses in the context of an individual survey, and they might indicate that they also would love to take these two courses. And perhaps a few other prospective elective courses would be identified that students would find highly relevant to practice and that would be fully enrolled. At the same time, these comments might prompt the group members to focus more on preparation for practice competency as their chief source of dissatisfaction with the program, and a rich discussion might ensue identifying issues, potentially popular elective courses, and other ways to improve the program that would not have been anticipated or identified by many respondents in a survey.

Instead of only one or two prospective new elective courses being identified by one or two isolated individuals in a survey, the focus group might identify a larger number of new courses and show which ones would generate the most excitement and the largest potential enrollments.

That said, however, it's important to remember that focus groups also have disadvantages. As mentioned above, the representativeness of focus group members is questionable. Perhaps those who agree to participate or who are the most vocal are the ones with the biggest axes to grind about the program, the ones most satisfied with it, or those most eager to curry favor with program providers. Although the group dynamics can bring out information that would not have emerged in a survey, those dynamics can also create pressures for people to say things that may not accurately reflect their true feelings or prospective deeds. Whereas some individuals who feel dissatisfied with a program may feel more comfortable about expressing it if others do so first, the same individuals may be less likely to express their dissatisfaction if those who speak up first express great satisfaction with the program.

If a couple of members show enthusiasm for a prospective service, then others may feel group pressure to say that they, too, would utilize the service, even though, in reality, they would not. In light of these dynamics, special knowledge about group dynamics and special groupwork skills are needed to moderate focus groups. In a focus group interview, much more than in any other types of interviews, the interviewer has to develop the skills of a moderator. Controlling the dynamic within the group is a major challenge. Letting one interviewee dominate the focus group interview reduces the likelihood that the other participants will express themselves. This can generate the problem of group conformity or *groupthink*, which is the tendency for people in a group to conform with opinions and decisions of the most outspoken members of the group. Interviewers need to be aware of this phenomenon and try to get everyone to participate fully on all the issues brought in the interview. Adding to the challenge, of course, you must resist overdirecting the interview and the interviewees, thus bringing your own views into play.

Another disadvantage of focus groups is that the data that emerge are likely to be voluminous and less systematic than structured survey data. Analyzing focus group data, therefore, can be more difficult, tedious, and subject to the biases of the evaluator. The analysis becomes more difficult to the extent that multiple focus groups yield inconsistent open-ended data. Thus, focus groups, like any other qualitative or quantitative research method, have certain advantages and disadvantages and are best used in combination with other research methods.

Although focus group research differs from other forms of qualitative research, it further illustrates the possibilities for doing social research face-to-face with those we wish to understand. In addition, David Morgan (1993) suggests that focus groups are an excellent device for generating questionnaire items for a subsequent survey. The box "An Illustration of the Use of Focus Groups and Feminist Methods: The Voices of Battered Women in Japan" describes the use of focus groups in a study conducted by a social worker in the context of using feminist methods as well as the participatory action research paradigm that was discussed in Chapter 17.

RECORDING OBSERVATIONS

Because of the in-depth, open-ended nature of qualitative interviews, recording responses poses quite a challenge to the interviewer. The aims and philosophical roots of qualitative inquiry mandate that the respondent's answers should be recorded as fully as possible. Recording them verbatim is ideal. A tape re-

AN ILLUSTRATION OF THE USE OF FOCUS GROUPS AND FEMINIST METHODS: THE VOICES OF BATTERED WOMEN IN JAPAN

Mieko Yoshihama, a social work professor at the University of Michigan, was concerned about the dearth of research that examined the perspectives and experiences of battered women in Japan and the barriers to their seeking and using services. Consequently, she conducted "the first study in Japan to use face-to-face interviews with a community sample of battered women" (Yoshihama, 2002:391). She used focus groups to conduct the interviews because she believed that hearing the experiences and perspectives of other battered women would help alleviate a sense of shame and isolation among study participants, enhance their understanding of their own situation, and make it easier for them to discuss how they perceived and coped with it. She recruited as study participants battered women of various backgrounds by sending fliers to organizations and professionals in Tokyo who come into contact with battered women and by announcing the study in national and local newspapers.

To facilitate the ability of women with diverse backgrounds and time constraints to participate in the study, she scheduled four focus groups during different times of the day, including one weekend group. On-site child care was provided. Participants received small cash reimbursements to partially cover their transportation and other costs of attending. They also received written materials about domestic violence and a list of assistance programs. Sessions were held at convenient and safe sites and lasted two hours. To ensure anonymity, participants did not divulge their last names. Some used pseudonyms or nicknames. Each session was audiotaped. The tapes were transcribed, and the meanings or themes expressed by participants in the transcripts were coded. Using the grounded theory method, repeated reviews of the transcripts yielded repeated revisions and improvements of the conceptual and thematic codes. Yoshihama's findings can be best summarized by the following excerpt from the abstract of her article:

> Participants' narratives of their experience with their partners' violence suggest a web of entrapment, from which women saw little possibility of escape. The partners' physical violence, interference with the women's social participation, isolation from supportive networks, and degradation and debasement entrapped participants. The victim-blaming attitudes of family, friends, and professionals, as well as the lack of assistance programs and police protection often reinforced the web. When these women took the risk of exposing what was long considered private and shameful, isolation was broken.
>
> (2002:389)

In contrast with prevailing views, Yoshihama noted the similarities between the experiences of battered women in Japan and those in Western countries. Despite these similarities, Yoshihama pointed out that the victim-blaming reaction to this problem in Japanese society makes it harder for battered women there to obtain services and protection. Consequently, Yoshihama's study developed various implications for reforming social policy and social work practice in Japan to increase the amount of programs and services for battered women and to make them more sensitive and responsive to the safety needs and rights of battered women instead of blaming them and emphasizing preservation of the marriage. Her study also offered implications for social work practice with battered women immigrants from Japan in the United States, who may not be aware of their increased options in the United States and who may need several repeated explanations to understand how things are different than in Japan.

Yoshihama also identified some limitations of her focus group study, specifically its limited generalizability in light of its small sample of self-selected women residing in one city. One of the strengths of the study pertained to its participatory action research function. By participating in the focus groups, the women were able to overcome their sense of shame and isolation, develop a shared understanding of their mutual problem, and obtain information about their legal rights and available assistance programs. Consequently, the participants formed support groups for battered women.

corder, therefore, is a powerful tool for the qualitative interviewer. It not only ensures verbatim recording, but also frees interviewers to keep their full attention focused on respondents, to communicate that they are listening to what is being said, and to probe into important cues.

Noting these advantages of tape recording, Patton (1990) nevertheless urges interviewers who use tape recorders to take notes while they interview so they can refer back to something important said earlier in the interview or to occasionally jot down summary points or key phrases to facilitate later analysis of the tape. He also suggests that note taking (done in moderation) helps pace the interview and lets respondents know that you find what they are saying important.

Tape recorders, however, are not applicable for a great deal of the data gathering in field research, particularly data gathered as a result of observation outside the interview context. And even in interviews, tape recorders cannot capture all of the relevant aspects of social processes. Therefore, other basic tools of field research include a notebook—or field journal—and a pencil. The greatest advantage of the field research method is the presence of an observing, thinking researcher on the scene. If possible, take notes on your observations as you make them. When that's not possible, write down your notes as soon as possible afterward.

Your notes should include both your empirical observations and your interpretations of them. You should record what you "know" has happened and what you "think" has happened. It is important, however, that these different kinds of notes be identified for what they are. For example, you might note that Person X spoke in opposition to a proposal made by a group leader, that you think this represents an attempt by Person X to take over leadership of the group, and that you think you heard the leader comment to that effect in response to the opposition.

Just as you cannot hope to observe everything, neither can you record everything you do observe. Just as your observations represent a de facto sample of all possible observations, your notes represent a sample of your observations. Rather than record a random sample of your observations, you should, of course, record the most important ones. The box titled "Interview Transcript Annotated with Researcher Memos" provides an example given by Sandrine Zerbib from an in-depth interview with a woman film director.

Some of the most important observations can be anticipated before the study begins; others will become apparent as your observations progress. Sometimes, your note taking can be made easier if you prepare standardized recording forms in advance. In a study of the homeless, for instance, you might anticipate the characteristics of homeless individuals that are the most likely to be useful for analysis—age, gender, social class, ethnicity, psychiatric history, and so forth—and prepare a form in which actual observations can be recorded easily. Or you might develop a symbolic shorthand in advance to speed up recording. For studying citizen participation at a community meeting, you might want to construct a numbered grid to represent the different sections of the meeting room; then you would be able to record the location of participants easily, quickly, and accurately.

None of this advance preparation should limit your recording of unanticipated events and aspects of the situation. Quite the contrary, speedy handling of anticipated observations can give you more freedom to observe the unanticipated.

Every student is familiar with the process of taking notes. However, good note taking in qualitative research requires more careful and deliberate attention and involves specific skills. Some guidelines follow. You can learn more about this in John Lofland and Lyn Lofland's *Analyzing Social Settings* (1995:91–96), mentioned earlier in the chapter.

First, don't trust your memory any more than you have to; it's untrustworthy. If this sounds too unkind, try this experiment. Recall the last few movies you saw that you really liked. Now, name five of the actors or actresses. Who had the longest hair? Who was the most likely to start conversations? Who was the most likely to make suggestions that others followed? ("Quick! Bring the wagons into a circle!") Now, if you didn't have any trouble answering any of those questions (and think you outsmarted us), how sure are you of your answers? Would you be willing to bet $100 that a panel of impartial judges would observe what you recall? If you are absolutely certain of your answers, what color shoes was your methods instructor wearing three class meetings ago? Gotcha! Even if you pride yourself on having a photographic memory, it's a good idea to take notes either during the observation or as soon afterward as possible. If you are taking notes during observation, then do it unobtrusively, because people are likely to behave differently if they see you taking down everything they say or do.

Second, it's usually a good idea to take notes in stages. In the first stage, you may need to take sketchy

INTERVIEW TRANSCRIPT ANNOTATED WITH RESEARCHER MEMOS

Thursday August 26, 12:00–1:00

R: What is challenging for women directors on a daily experience, on a daily life?

J: Surviving.

R: OK. Could you develop a little bit on that? [I need to work on my interview schedule so that my interviewee answers with more elaboration without having to probe.]

J: Yeah, I mean it's all about trying to get, you know, in, trying to get the job, and try, you know, to do a great job so that you are invited back to the next thing. And particularly since they are so many, you know, difficulties in women directing. It makes it twice as hard to gain into this position where you do an incredible job, because . . . you can't just do an average job, you have to [347] do this job that just knocks your socks off all the time, and sometimes you don't get the opportunity to do that, because either you don't have a good producer or you have so many pressures that you can't see straight or your script is lousy, and you have to make a silk purse out of sow's hair. You know, you have a lot of extra strikes against you than the average guy who has similar problems, because you are a woman and they look at it, and women are more visible than men . . . in unique positions.

[It seems that Joy is talking about the particularities of the film industry. There are not that many opportunities and in order to keep working, she needs to build a certain reputation. It is only by continuing to direct that she can maintain or improve her reputation. She thinks that it is even harder for women but does not explain it.]

R: Hum . . . what about on the set did you experience, did it feel . . . did people make it clear that you were a woman, and you felt treated differently? [I am trying to get her to speak about more specific and more personal experiences without leading her answer.]

J: Yeah, oh yeah, I mean . . . a lot of women have commiserated about, you know when you have to walk on the set for the first time, they're all used to working like a well-oiled machine and they say, "Oh, here is the woman, something different" and sometimes they can be horrible, they can resist your directing and they can, they can sabotage you, by taking a long time to light, or to move sets, or to do something . . . and during that time you're wasting time, and that goes on a report, and the report goes to the front [368] office, and, you know, and so on and so on and so on and so forth. And people upstairs don't know what the circumstances are, and they are not about to fire a cinematographer that is on their show for ever and ever . . . nor do they want to know that this guy is a real bastard, and making your life a horror. They don't want to know that, so therefore, they go off, because she's a woman let's not hire any more women, since he has problems with women. You know, so, there is that aspect.

[I need to review the literature on institutional discrimination. It seems that the challenges that Joy is facing are not a matter of a particular individual. She is in a double bind situation where whether she complains or not, she will not be treated equal to men. Time seems to be one quantifiable measurement of how well she does her job and, as observed in other professions, the fact that she is a woman is perceived as a handicap. Review literature on women in high management position. I need to keep asking about the dynamics between my interviewees and the crewmembers on the set. The cinematographer has the highest status on the set under the director. Explore other interviews about reasons for conflict between them.]

[Methods (note to myself for the next interviews): try to avoid phone interviews unless specific request from the interviewee. It is difficult to assess how the interviewee feels with the questions. Need body language because I become more nervous about the interview process.]

Note: A number in brackets represents a word that was inaudible from the interview. It is the number that appeared on the transcribing machine, with each interview starting at count 0. The numbers help the researcher locate a passage quickly when he or she reviews the interview.

notes (words and phrases) to keep abreast of what's happening. Then remove yourself and rewrite your notes in more detail. If you do this soon after the events you've observed, the sketchy notes should allow you to recall most of the details. The longer you delay, the less likely it is you'll recall things accurately and fully.

We know this method sounds logical, and you've probably made a mental resolution to do it that way if you're ever involved in qualitative research. Let us warn you, however, that you'll need self-discipline to keep your resolution in practice. Careful observation and note taking can be tiring, especially if they involve excitement or tension and extend over a long period of time. If you've just spent eight hours straight observing and making notes on how people have been coping with a disastrous flood, then your first thought afterward is likely to be directed toward getting some sleep, dry clothes, or a drink. You may need to take some inspiration from newspaper reporters who undergo the same sorts of hardships, before writing their stories and meeting their deadlines.

Third, you will inevitably wonder how much you should record. Is it really worth the effort to write out all of the details you can recall right after the observation session? The general guideline here is yes. Generally, in qualitative research you can't be really sure of what is and is not important until you've had a chance to review and analyze a great volume of information, so you should even record things that don't seem important at the outset. They may turn out to be significant after all. Also, the act of recording the details of something "unimportant" may jog your memory on something that is important.

You should realize that most of your field notes will not be reflected in your final report on the project. Put more harshly, most of the notes you take will be "wasted." But take heart: Even the richest gold ore yields only about 30 grams of gold per metric ton, meaning that 99.997 percent of the ore is wasted. Yet that 30 grams of gold can be hammered out to cover an area 18 feet square—the equivalent of almost 700 book pages! So take a ton of notes, and plan to select and use only the gold.

Like other aspects of qualitative research (and all research for that matter), proficiency comes with practice. The nice thing about qualitative research is you can begin practicing now and can continue practicing in almost any situation. You don't have to be engaged in an organized research project to practice observation and recording. You might start by volunteering to take the minutes at committee meetings, for example.

Main Points

- You may or may not identify yourself as a researcher to the people you are observing. Identifying yourself as a researcher may have some effect on the nature of what you are observing, but concealing your identity may involve deceit.

- Because qualitative research takes you into close contact with participants, you must negotiate your relationship with them; there are several options.

- You may or may not participate in what you are observing. Participating in the events may make it easier for you to conceal your identity as a researcher, but participation is likely to affect what is being observed.

- Participant observation is a form of qualitative research in which the researcher participates as an actor in the events under study.

- Four different positions on a continuum of participant observation roles are: complete participant, participant-as-observer, observer-as-participant, and complete observer.

- Qualitative researchers using the method of participant observation should learn how to simultaneously hold two contradictory perspectives: (1) trying to adopt the beliefs, attitudes, and other points of view shared by the members of the culture being studied (the emic perspective), while (2) maintaining objectivity as an outsider and raising questions about the culture being observed that wouldn't occur to members of that culture (the etic perspective).

- Qualitative researchers often engage in in-depth interviews with the participants, interviews that are far less structured than the interviews conducted in survey research.

- Qualitative interviewing tends to be open-ended and unstructured. Three forms of qualitative, open-ended interviewing are (1) the informal conversational interview, (2) the general interview guide approach, and (3) the standardized open-ended interview.

- An informal conversational interview is an unplanned and unanticipated interaction between an interviewer and a respondent that occurs naturally during the course of fieldwork observation.

- With the interview guide approach to qualitative interviewing, an interview guide lists in outline form the topics and issues that the interviewer should cover in the interview, but it allows the interviewer to adapt the sequencing and wording of questions to each particular interview.

- The standardized open-ended interview consists of questions that are written out in advance exactly the way they are to be asked in the interview.

- Life histories involve asking open-ended questions to discover how the participants in a study understand the significant events and meanings in their own lives.

- To create a focus group, researchers bring participants together and observe their interactions as they explore a specific topic.

- Some key advantages of focus groups are as follows: they are inexpensive, they generate speedy results, and they offer flexibility for probing. The group dynamics that occur in focus groups can bring out aspects of the topic that researchers may not have anticipated and that may not have emerged in individual interviews.

- Among the disadvantages of focus groups are the questionable representativeness of participants, the influence of group dynamics to pressure people to say things that don't accurately reflect what they really believe or do, and the difficulty in analyzing the voluminous data generated.

- The field journal is the backbone of qualitative research, because that is where the researcher records his or her observations. Journal entries should be detailed, yet concise.

- Note taking in qualitative research should include both the investigator's empirical observations and the investigator's interpretations of them. You should record what you "know" has happened and what you "think" has happened.

- If possible, observations should be recorded as they are made; otherwise, they should be recorded in stages and as soon as possible (without detracting from your interviewing or observations). Don't trust your memory any more than you have to.

Review Questions and Exercises

1. Think of some group or activity in which you participate or that you know well. In two or three paragraphs, describe how an outsider might effectively go about studying that group or activity. What should he or she read, what contacts should be made, and so on?

2. Accompanied by one of your classmates, show up 10 minutes early for your next research class session. Each of you should independently observe and take notes on what other classmates say to each other before and after the instructor shows up. Repeat this at the end of class and as students chat outside the classroom. Later on, analyze and interpret your notes as to how communications may or may not differ depending on the instructor's presence or absence. Have your classmate do the same—but independent of your notes and conclusions. Compare your conclusions with those of your classmate. Write down any disagreements you had in your conclusions and what you think explains your differences.

3. Together with two other classmates prepare and carry out the three qualitative interview approaches discussed in this chapter. Each of you should utilize a different approach, and the focus of the interview should be on student attitudes about a topic of your choosing. At three different times you and your two classmates should separately interview the same student (or perhaps two or three of the same students). Each of you should independently analyze and interpret your own interview data. Compare the similarities and differences in your conclusions and write down why you think you agreed or disagreed.

Internet Exercises

1. Use InfoTrac College Edition to find the following articles in the October 2002 issue of the journal *Social Work* that illustrate the use of focus groups. Briefly identify the similarities and differences in the way these studies used focus groups methodology, and critically appraise the strengths and weaknesses of each study.

> "Deciding Who to See: Lesbians Discuss Their Preferences in Health and Mental Health Care Providers," by C. F. Saulnier
>
> "Work-Family Fit: Voices of Parents of Children with Emotional and Behavioral Disorders," by

J. M. Rosenzweig, E. M. Brennan, and A. M. Ogilvie

"Opportunities and Barriers to Empowering People with Severe Mental Illness through Participation in Treatment Planning," by D. M. Linhorst, G. Hamilton, E. Young, and A. Eckert

"The Functions of the Social Worker in Empowering: The Voices of Consumers and Professionals," by A. Boehm and L. H. Staples

"Voices of African American Families: Perspectives on Residential Treatment," by J. M. Kruzich, B. J. Friesen, T. Williams-Murphy, and M. J. Longley

2. Use InfoTrac College Edition to find one to three articles illustrating the use of participant observation, qualitative interviewing, life history, and feminist methods. (Some articles might report a study using more than one of these methods.) Write down the bibliographic reference information for each article and identify its methodological strengths and weaknesses.

Additional Readings

Alexander, Leslie B., and Phyllis Solomon (eds.). 2006. *The Research Process in the Human Services: Behind the Scenes.* Belmont, CA: Thomson Brooks/Cole. Once again we recommend this valuable book—this time for its section containing four chapters on qualitative methods. Each chapter presents a qualitative study followed by investigator comments on the practical and methodological challenges they dealt with in carrying out the study and the rationales for decisions made in the course of conducting each study.

Gilgun, Jane, Kerry Daly, and Gerald Handel (eds.). 1992. *Qualitative Methods in Family Research.* Thousand Oaks, CA: Sage. This useful compendium of qualitative studies on families with relevance to social work practice illustrates the use of qualitative interviewing, case studies, life history interviews, participant observation, and document analysis.

Kvale, Steinar. 1996. *InterViews: An Introduction to Qualitative Research Interviewing.* Thousand Oaks, CA: Sage. This is an in-depth presentation on in-depth interviewing. In addition to presenting techniques, Kvale places interviewing in the context of postmodernism and other philosophical systems.

Padgett, Deborah K. (ed.). 2004. *The Qualitative Research Experience.* Belmont, CA: Brooks/Cole. This text provides a valuable compendium of exemplary qualitative studies using many of the methods discussed in this chapter. The studies are followed by "behind the scenes" essays in which the authors describe their experiences while conducting the research.

Shaffir, William B., and Robert A. Stebbins (eds.). 1991. *Experiencing Fieldwork.* Newbury Park, CA: Sage. This fine collection of fieldworker accounts of the field research enterprise offers an especially strong treatment of researchers' relationships with their participants.

Silverman, David. 1999. *Doing Qualitative Research: A Practical Handbook.* Thousand Oaks, CA: Sage. This book focuses on the process of collecting and interpreting qualitative data.

CHAPTER 19

Qualitative Data Analysis

What You'll Learn in This Chapter

This chapter shows how you can analyze nonnumerical observations made through qualitative research techniques. Although qualitative analysis is an art as much as a science, it has its own logic and techniques, some of which are enhanced by special computer programs.

INTRODUCTION

As you may have surmised while reading the previous two chapters, data analysis, data collection, and theory are intimately intertwined in qualitative research. Therefore, it is difficult to learn the steps involved in qualitative data analysis in a rote manner. This is unlike the analysis of data generated by quantitative research methods, which we'll examine in the next section of this book. Because **qualitative analysis**—the nonnumerical examination and interpretation of observations for the purpose of discovering underlying meanings and patterns of relationships—involves a continuing interplay between data collection and theory, understanding must precede practice. In this chapter, we begin with the links between research and theory in qualitative analysis. Then we examine some procedures that have proven useful in pursuing the theoretical aims. After considering some simple manual techniques, we'll take some computer programs out for a spin.

LINKING THEORY AND ANALYSIS

Our discussion of qualitative data analysis will be based on the image of theory offered by Anselm Strauss and Juliet Corbin (1994:278) as consisting of "*plausible* relationships proposed among *concepts* and *sets of concepts*." They stress "plausible" to indicate that theories represent our best understanding of how life operates. The more our research confirms a particular set of relationships among particular concepts, however, the more confident we become that our understanding corresponds to social reality.

Although qualitative research is sometimes undertaken for purely descriptive purposes—such as the anthropologist's ethnography detailing ways of life in a previously unknown tribe—this chapter focuses primarily on the search for explanatory patterns. As we'll see, sometimes the patterns occur over time, and sometimes they take the form of causal relations among variables. Let's look at some of the ways qualitative researchers uncover such patterns.

Discovering Patterns

John and Lyn Lofland (1995:127–145) suggest six different ways of looking for patterns in a particular research topic. Let's suppose you're interested in analyzing child abuse in a certain neighborhood. Here are some questions you might ask yourself to make sense out of your data.

1. Frequencies: How often does child abuse occur among families in the neighborhood under study? (Realize that there may be a difference between the frequency and what people are willing to tell you.)

2. Magnitudes: What are the levels of abuse? How brutal are they?

3. Structures: What are the different types of abuse: physical, mental, sexual? Are they related in any particular manner?

4. Processes: Is there any order among the elements of structure? Do abusers begin with mental abuse and move on to physical and sexual abuse, or does the order of elements vary?

5. Causes: What are the causes of child abuse? Is it more common in particular social classes or among different religious or ethnic groups? Does it occur more often during good times or bad?

6. Consequences: How does child abuse affect the victims, in both the short and the long term? What changes does it cause in the abusers?

For the most part, in examining your data you'll look for patterns appearing across several observations that typically represent different cases under study. Matthew B. Miles and A. Michael Huberman (1994:435–436) offer two strategies for cross-case analysis: variable-oriented and case-oriented analyses. Variable-oriented analysis is similar to a model we've already discussed from time to time in this book. If we were trying to predict the decision to attend college, Miles and Huberman suggest, we might consider variables such as "gender, socioeconomic status, parental expectations, school performance, peer support, and decision to attend college" (1994:435). Thus, we would determine whether men or women were more likely to attend college. This is a **variable-oriented analysis**, in which the focus is on interrelations among variables, and the people observed are primarily the carriers of those variables.

Variable-oriented analysis may remind you of the discussion in Chapter 3 that introduced the idea of nomothetic explanation. The aim here is to achieve a partial, overall explanation using a relatively small number of variables. The political pollster who attempts to explain voting intentions on the basis of two or three key variables is using this approach. There is no pretense that the researcher can predict every individual's behavior or even explain any one person's motivations in full. Sometimes, though, it's useful to have even a partial explanation of overall orientations and actions.

You may also recall the Chapter 3 introduction of idiographic explanation, wherein we attempt to understand a particular case fully. This orientation lies at the base of what Miles and Huberman call a **case-oriented analysis.** In the voting example, we would attempt to learn everything we could about all the factors that came into play in determining one person's decision on how to vote.

> In a case-oriented analysis, we would look more closely into a particular case, say, Case 005, who is female, middle-class, has parents with high expectations, and so on. These are, however, "thin" measures. To do a genuine case analysis, we need to look at a full history of Case 005; Nynke van der Molen, whose mother trained as a social worker but is bitter over the fact that she never worked outside the home, and whose father wants Nynke to work in the family florist shop. Chronology is also important: two years ago, Nynke's closest friend decided to go to college, just before Nynke began work in a stable and just before Nynke's mother showed her a scrapbook from social work school. Nynke then decided to enroll in veterinary studies.
>
> (MILES AND HUBERMAN, 1994:436)

This abbreviated commentary should give some idea of the detail involved in this type of analysis. Of course, an entire analysis would be more extensive and pursue issues in greater depth. This full, idiographic examination, however, tells us nothing about people in general. It offers nothing in the way of a theory about why people choose to attend college.

Even so, in addition to understanding one person in great depth, the researcher sees the critical elements of the subject's experiences as instances of more general social concepts or variables. For example, Nynke's mother's social work training can also be seen as "mother's education." Her friend's decision can be seen as "peer influence." More specifically, these could be seen as independent variables having an impact on the dependent variable of attending college.

Of course, one case does not a theory make—hence Miles and Huberman's reference to **cross-case analysis,** in which the researcher turns to other subjects, looking into the full details of their lives as well but paying special note to the variables that seemed important in the first case. How much and what kind of education did other subjects' mothers have? Is there any evidence of close friends attending college?

Some subsequent cases will closely parallel the first one in the apparent impact of particular variables. Other cases will bear no resemblance to the first. These latter cases may require the identification of other important variables, which may invite the researcher to explore why some cases seem to reflect one pattern while others reflect another.

Grounded Theory Method

The cross-case method just described should sound somewhat familiar. In the discussion of grounded theory in Chapter 17, we saw how qualitative researchers sometimes attempt to establish theories on a purely inductive basis. This approach begins with observations rather than hypotheses and seeks to discover patterns and develop theories from the ground up, with no preconceptions, though some research may build and elaborate on earlier grounded theories.

Grounded theory was first developed by the sociologists Barney Glaser and Anselm Strauss (1967) in an attempt to come to grips with their clinical research in medical sociology. (You can hear Glaser discuss grounded theory on the web at www.groundedtheory.com/vidseries1.html.) Since then, it has evolved as a method, with the cofounders taking it in slightly different directions. The following discussion will deal with the basic concepts and procedures of the **grounded theory method (GTM).**

In addition to the fundamental, inductive tenet of building theory from data, GTM employs the **constant comparative method.** As Glaser and Strauss originally described this method, it involved four stages (1967:105–113):

1. "Comparing incidents applicable to each category." As Glaser and Strauss researched the reactions of nurses to the possible death of patients in their care, the researchers found that the nurses were assessing the "social loss" attendant upon a patient's death. Once this concept arose in the analysis of one case, they looked for evidence of the same phenomenon in other cases. When they found the concept arising in the cases of several nurses, they compared the different incidents. This process is similar to conceptualization as described in Chapter 7—specifying the nature and dimensions of the many concepts arising from the data.

2. "Integrating categories and their properties." Here the researcher begins to note relationships among concepts. In the assessment of social loss, for example, Glaser and Strauss found that nurses took special notice of a patient's age, education, and family responsibilities. For these relationships to emerge, however, it was necessary for the researchers to have noticed all these concepts.

3. "Delimiting the theory." Eventually, as the patterns of relationships among concepts become clearer, the researcher can ignore some of the concepts initially noted but evidently irrelevant to the inquiry. In addition to the number of categories being reduced, the theory itself may become simpler. In the examination of social loss, for example, Glaser and Strauss found that the assessment processes could be generalized beyond nurses and dying patients: They seemed to apply to the ways all staff dealt with all patients (dying or not).

4. "Writing theory." Finally, the researcher must put his or her findings into words to be shared with others. As you may have already experienced for yourself, the act of communicating your understanding of something actually modifies and even improves your own grasp of the topic. In GTM, the writing stage is regarded as a part of the research process. A later section of this chapter (on memoing) elaborates on this point.

This brief overview should give you an idea of how grounded theory proceeds. The many techniques associated with GTM can be found both in print and on the web. One of the key publications is Anselm Strauss and Juliet Corbin's *Basics of Qualitative Research* (1990), which elaborates on and extends many of the concepts and techniques found in the original Glaser and Strauss volume. On the web, you might want to explore Gaelle T. Morin's "Grounded Theory Methodology on the Web" at http://gtm.vlsm.org/gtm-12.en.html.

GTM is only one analytical approach to qualitative data. In the remainder of this section, we'll take a look at some other specialized techniques.

Semiotics

Semiotics is commonly defined as the "science of signs" and has to do with symbols and meanings. It's commonly associated with content analysis, which was discussed in Chapter 16, though it can be applied in a variety of research contexts.

Peter K. Manning and Betsy Cullum-Swan (1994: 466) offer some sense of the applicability of semiotics, as follows: "Although semiotics is based on language, language is but one of the many sign systems of varying degrees of unity, applicability, and complexity. Morse code, etiquette, mathematics, music, and even highway signs are examples of semiotic systems." There is no meaning inherent in any sign, however. Meanings reside in minds. So, a particular sign means something to a particular person.

However, the agreements we have about the meanings associated with particular signs make semiotics a *social* science. As Manning and Cullum-Swan point out:

> For example, a lily is an expression linked conventionally to death, Easter, and resurrection as a content. Smoke is linked to cigarettes and to cancer, and Marilyn Monroe to sex. Each of these connections is social and arbitrary, so that many kinds of links exist between expression and content.
>
> (1994:466)

To explore this contention, see if you can link the signs with their meanings in Figure 19-1. Most American readers probably know all the "correct" associations. For readers who don't know them, they are 1c, 2a, 3b, 4e, 5d. The point is this: What do any of these signs have to do with their "meanings"? Draft an e-mail message to a Martian social scientist explaining the logic at work here. (You might want to include some "emoticons" such as :)—which is another example of semiotics.)

Although there is no doubt a story behind each of the linkages in Figure 19-1, the meanings we "know" today are socially constructed. Semiotic analysis involves a search for the meanings intentionally or unintentionally attached to signs.

SIGN	MEANING
1. Poinsettia	a. Good luck
2. Horseshoe	b. First prize
3. Blue ribbon	c. Christmas
4. "Say cheese"	d. Acting
5. "Break a leg"	e. Smile for a picture

Figure 19-1 Matching Signs and Their Meanings

Figure 19-2 Mixed Signals?

Consider the sign shown in Figure 19-2, from a hotel lobby in Portland, Oregon. What's being communicated by the rather ambiguous sign? The first sentence seems to be saying that the hotel is up-to-date with the current move away from tobacco in the United States. Guests who want a smoke-free environment need look no further: This is a healthy place to stay. At the same time, says the second sentence, the hotel would not like to be seen as inhospitable to smokers. There's room for everyone under this roof. No one needs to feel excluded. This sign is more easily understood within a marketing paradigm than one of logic.

The "signs" examined in semiotics, of course, are not limited to this kind of sign. Most are quite different, in fact. *Signs* are any things that are assigned special meanings. They can include such things as logos, animals, people, and consumer products. Sometimes the symbolism is a bit subtle. A classic analysis can be found in Erving Goffman's *Gender Advertisements* (1979). Goffman focused on advertising pictures found in magazines and newspapers. The overt purpose of the ads, of course, was to sell specific products. But what else was communicated, Goffman asked. What in particular did the ads say about men and women?

Analyzing pictures containing both men and women, Goffman was struck by the fact that men were almost always bigger and taller than the women accompanying them. (In many cases, in fact, the picture managed to convey the distinct impression that the women were merely accompanying the men.) Although the most obvious explanation is that men are, on average, heavier and taller than women, Goffman suggested the pattern had a different meaning: that size and placement implied *status*. Those larger and taller presumably had higher social standing—more power and authority (1979:28). Goffman suggested that the ads communicated that men were more important than women.

In the spirit of Freud's comment that "sometimes a cigar is just a cigar" (he was a smoker), how would you decide whether the ads simply reflected the biological differences in the average sizes of men and women or whether they sent a message about social status? In part, Goffman's conclusion was based on an analysis of the exceptional cases: those in which the women appeared taller than the men. In these cases, the men were typically of a lower social status—the chef beside the society matron, for example. This confirmed Goffman's main point that size and height indicated social status.

The same conclusion was to be drawn from pictures with men of different heights. Those of higher status were taller, whether it was the gentleman speaking to a waiter or the boss guiding the work of his younger assistants. Where actual height was unclear, Goffman noted the placement of heads in the picture. The assistants were crouching down while the boss leaned over them. The servant's head was bowed so it was lower than that of the master.

The latent message conveyed by the ads, then, was that the higher a person's head appeared in the ad, the more important that person was. And in the great majority of ads containing men and women, the former were clearly portrayed as more important. The subliminal message in the ads, whether intended or not, was that men are more powerful and enjoy a higher status than do women.

Goffman examined several differences in the portrayal of men and women besides physical size. As another example, men were typically portrayed in active roles, women in passive ones. The (male) doctor examined the child while the (female) nurse or mother looked on, often admiringly. A man guided a woman's tennis stroke (all the while keeping his head higher than hers). A man gripped the reins of his galloping horse, while a woman rode behind him with her arms wrapped around his waist. A woman held the football, while a man kicked it. A man took a photo, which contained only women.

Goffman suggested that such pictorial patterns subtly perpetuated a host of gender stereotypes. Even as people spoke publicly about gender equality, these advertising photos established a quiet backdrop of men and women in the "proper roles."

Conversation Analysis

Conversation analysis (CA) seeks to uncover the implicit assumptions and structures in social life through an extremely close scrutiny of the way we converse with one another. David Silverman, reviewing the work of other CA theorists and researchers, speaks of three fundamental assumptions (1993:435–436). First, conversation is a socially structured activity. Like other social structures, it has established rules of behavior. For example, we're expected to take turns, with only one person speaking at a time. In telephone conversations, the person answering the call is expected to speak first (e.g., "Hello"). You can verify the existence of this rule, incidentally, by picking up the phone without speaking.

Second, Silverman points out that conversations must be understood contextually. The same utterance will have totally different meanings in different contexts. For example, notice how the meaning of "Same to you!" varies if preceded by "I don't like your looks" or by "Have a nice day." Third, CA aims to understand the structure and meaning of conversation through excruciatingly accurate transcripts of conversations. Not only are the exact words recorded, but all the *uh*s, *er*s, bad grammar, and pauses are also noted. Pauses, in fact, are recorded to the nearest tenth of a second.

The practical uses of this type of analysis are many. Ann Marie Kinnell and Douglas Maynard (1996), for example, analyzed conversations between staff and clients at an HIV testing clinic to examine how information about safe sex was communicated. Among other things, they found that the staff tended to provide standard information rather than try to speak directly to a client's specific circumstances. Moreover, they seemed reluctant to give direct advice about safe sex, settling for information alone.

These discussions should give you some sense of the variety of qualitative analysis methods available to researchers. Now let's look at some of the data-processing and data analysis techniques commonly used in qualitative research.

QUALITATIVE DATA PROCESSING

Let's begin this section with a warning. The activity we are about to examine is as much art as science. At the very least, there are no cut-and-dried steps that guarantee success.

It's a lot like learning how to paint with watercolors or compose a symphony. Education in such activities is certainly possible, and university courses are offered in both. Each has its own conventions and techniques as well as tips you may find useful as you set out to create art or music. However, instruction can carry you only so far. The final product must come from you. Much the same can be said of qualitative data processing.

This section presents some ideas relating to the coding of qualitative data, writing memos, and mapping concepts graphically. Although far from a "how-to" manual, these ideas give a useful starting point for finding order in qualitative data.

Coding

Whether you've engaged in participant observation, in-depth interviewing, collecting biographical narratives, doing content analysis, or some other form of qualitative research, you will now be in the possession of a growing mass of data—most typically in the form of textual materials. Now what do you do?

The key process in the analysis of qualitative social research data is **coding**—classifying or categorizing individual pieces of data—coupled with some kind of retrieval system. Together, these procedures allow you to retrieve materials you may later be interested in.

Let's say you're chronicling the growth of a social movement. You recall writing up some notes about the details of the movement's earliest beginnings. Now you need that information. If all your notes have been catalogued by topic, retrieving those you need should be straightforward. As a simple format for coding and retrieval, you might have created a set of file folders labeled with various topics, such as "History." Data retrieval in this case means pulling out the "History" folder and rifling through the notes contained therein until you find what you need.

As you'll see later in this chapter, there are now some very sophisticated computer programs that allow for a faster, more certain, and more precise retrieval process. Rather than looking through a "History" file, you can go directly to notes dealing with the "Earliest History" or the "Founding" of the movement.

Coding has another, even more important purpose. As discussed earlier, the aim of data analysis is the discovery of patterns among the data, patterns that point to theoretical understanding of social life. The coding and relating of concepts is key to this process and requires a more refined system than a set of manila folders. In this section, we'll assume that you'll be doing your coding manually. The concluding section of the chapter will illustrate the use of computer programs for qualitative data analysis.

Coding Units As you may recall from the earlier discussion of content analysis in Chapter 16, for statistical analysis it's important to identify a standardized unit of analysis prior to coding. If you were comparing American and French novels, for example, you might evaluate and code sentences, paragraphs, chapters, or whole books. It would be important, however, to code the same units for each novel analyzed. This uniformity is necessary in a quantitative analysis, as it allows us to report something like "23 percent of the paragraphs contained metaphors." This is only possible if we've coded the same unit—paragraphs—in each of the novels.

Coding data for a qualitative analysis, however, is quite different. The *concept* is the organizing principle for qualitative coding. Here the units of text appropriate for coding will vary within a given document. Thus, in a study of organizations, "Size" might require only a few words per coding unit, whereas "Mission" might take a few pages. Or, a lengthy description of a heated stockholders meeting might be coded as "Internal Dissent."

Realize also that a given code category may be applied to text materials of quite different lengths. For example, some references to the organization's mission may be brief, others lengthy. Whereas standardization is a key principle in quantitative analysis, this is not the case in qualitative analysis.

Coding as a Physical Act Before continuing with the logic of coding, let's take a moment to see what it actually looks like. John and Lyn Lofland (1995:188) offer this description of manual filing:

> Prior to the widespread availability of personal computers beginning in the late 1980s, coding frequently took the specific physical form of *filing*. The researcher established an expanding set of file folders with code names on the tabs and physically placed either the item of data itself or a note that located it in the appropriate file folder. . . . Before photocopying was easily available and cheap, some fieldworkers typed their fieldnotes with carbon paper, wrote codes in the margins of the copies of the notes, and cut them up with scissors. They then placed the resulting slips of paper in corresponding file folders.

As the Loflands point out, personal computers have greatly simplified this task. However, the image of slips of paper that contain text and are put in folders representing code categories is useful for understanding the process of coding. In the next section, when we suggest that we code a textual passage with a certain code, imagine that we have the passage typed on a slip of paper and that we place it in a file folder bearing the name of the code. Whenever we assign two codes to a passage, imagine placing duplicate copies of the passage in two different folders representing the two codes.

Creating Codes So, what should your code categories be? Glaser and Strauss (1967:101–102) allow for the possibility of coding data for the purpose of testing hypotheses that have been generated by prior theory. In that case, then, the codes would be suggested by the theory, in the form of variables.

In this section, however, we're going to focus on the more common process of **open coding.** Strauss and Corbin (1990:62) define it as follows:

> Open coding is the part of analysis that pertains specifically to the naming and categorizing of phenomena through close examination of data. Without this first basic analytical step, the rest of the analysis and communication that follows could not take place. During open coding the data are broken down into discrete parts, closely examined, compared for similarities and differences, and questions are asked about the phenomena as reflected in the data. Through this process, one's own and others' assumptions about phenomena are questioned or explored, leading to new discoveries.

Here's a concrete example to illustrate how you might proceed. Suppose you are concerned about the problem of homophobia and want to do something to alleviate it. To begin, you interview some people who are opposed to homosexuality, and they cite a religious basis for their feelings. Specifically, they refer you to these passages in the Book of Leviticus (Revised Standard Version):

> 18:22 You shall not lie with a male as with a woman; it is an abomination.
>
> 20:13 If a man lies with a male as with a woman, both of them have committed an abomination; they shall be put to death, their blood is upon them.

Although the point of view expressed here seems unambiguous, you might decide to examine it in more depth. Perhaps a qualitative analysis of Leviticus can yield a fuller understanding of where these injunctions against homosexuality fit into the larger context of Judeo-Christian morality. By gaining this understanding, you hope to be better prepared to develop a social change strategy for combating homophobia.

Let's start our analysis by examining the two passages just quoted. We might begin by coding each passage with the label "Homosexuality." This is clearly a key concept in our analysis. Whenever we focus on the issue of homosexuality in our analysis of Leviticus, we want to consider these two passages.

Because homosexuality is such a key concept, let's look more closely into what it means within the data under study. We first notice the way *homosexuality* is identified: a man lying with a man "as with a woman." Although we can imagine a lawyer seeking admission to heaven saying, "But here's my point; if we didn't actually lie down . . ." it seems safe to assume the passage refers to having sex, though it is not clear what specific acts might or might not be included.

Notice, however, that the injunctions appear to concern *male* homosexuality only; lesbianism is not mentioned. In our analysis, then, each of these passages might also be coded "Male Homosexuality." This illustrates two more aspects of coding: (1) Each unit can have more than one code and (2) hierarchical codes (one included within another) can be used. Now each passage has two codes assigned to it.

An even more general code might be introduced at this point: "Prohibited Behavior." This is important for two reasons. First, homosexuality is not inherently wrong, from an analytical standpoint. The purpose of the study is to examine the way it's made wrong by the religious texts in question. Second, our study of Leviticus may turn up other behaviors that are prohibited.

There are at least two more critical concepts in the passages: "Abomination" and "Put to Death." Notice that although these are clearly related to "Prohibited Behavior," they are hardly the same. Parking without putting money in the meter is prohibited, but few would call it an abomination and fewer still would demand the death penalty for that transgression. Let's assign these two new codes to our first two passages.

At this point, we want to branch out from the two key passages and examine the rest of Leviticus. We therefore examine and code each of the remaining chapters and verses. In our subsequent analyses, we'll use the codes we have already and add new ones as appropriate. When we do add new codes, it will be important to review the passages already coded to see whether the new codes apply to any of them.

Here are the passages we decide to code "Abomination." (We've boldfaced the abominations.)

7:18 If any of the flesh of the sacrifice of **his peace offering is eaten on the third day,** he who offers it shall not be accepted, neither shall it be credited to him; it shall be an abomination, and he who eats of it shall bear his iniquity.

7:21 And if any one **touches an unclean thing,** whether the uncleanness of man or an unclean beast or any unclean abomination, **and then eats of the flesh of the sacrifice** of the LORD's peace offerings, that person shall be cut off from his people.

11:10 But **anything in the seas or the rivers that has not fins and scales,** of the swarming creatures in the waters and of the living creatures that are in the waters, is an abomination to you.

11:11 They shall remain an abomination to you; of their flesh you shall not eat, and their carcasses you shall have in abomination.

11:12 **Everything in the waters that has not fins and scales** is an abomination to you.

11:13 And these you shall have in abomination among the birds, they **shall not be eaten,** they are an abomination: the **eagle,** the **vulture,** the **osprey,**

11:14 the **kite,** the **falcon** according to its kind,

11:15 every **raven** according to its kind,

11:16 the **ostrich,** the **nighthawk,** the **sea gull,** the **hawk** according to its kind,

11:17 the **owl,** the **cormorant,** the **ibis,**

11:18 the **water hen,** the **pelican,** the **carrion vulture,**

11:19 the **stork,** the **heron** according to its kind, the **hoopoe,** and the **bat.**

11:20 **All winged insects that go upon all fours** are an abomination to you.

11:41 **Every swarming thing** that swarms upon the earth is an abomination; it shall not be eaten.

11:42 Whatever goes on its belly, and whatever goes on all fours, or whatever has many feet, all the **swarming things** that swarm upon the earth, you shall not eat; for they are an abomination.

11:43 You shall not make yourselves abominable with **any swarming thing that swarms;** and you shall not defile yourselves with them, lest you become unclean.

18:22 You shall not **lie with a male as with a woman;** it is an abomination.

19:6 It shall be eaten the same day you offer it, or on the morrow; and anything left over until the third day shall be burned with fire.

19:7 **If it is eaten at all on the third day,** it is an abomination; it will not be accepted,

19:8 and every one who eats it shall bear his iniquity, because he has profaned a holy thing of the LORD; and that person shall be cut off from his people.

20:13 **If a man lies with a male as with a woman,** both of them have committed an abomination; they shall be put to death, their blood is upon them.

20:25 You shall therefore make a distinction between the clean beast and the unclean, and between the unclean bird and the clean; **you shall not make yourselves abominable by beast or by bird or by anything with which the ground** teems, which I have set apart for you to hold unclean.

Male homosexuality, then, isn't the only abomination identified in Leviticus. As you compare these passages, looking for similarities and differences, it will become apparent that most of the abominations have to do with dietary rules—specifically those potential foods deemed "unclean." Other abominations flow from the mishandling of ritual sacrifices. "Dietary Rules" and "Ritual Sacrifices" thus represent additional concepts and codes to be used in our analysis.

Earlier, we mentioned the death penalty as another concept to be explored in our analysis. When we take this avenue, we discover that many behaviors besides male homosexuality warrant the death penalty. Among them are these:

20:2 Giving your children to Molech (human sacrifice)

20:9 Cursing your father or mother

20:10 Adultery with your neighbor's wife

20:11 Adultery with your father's wife

20:12 Adultery with your daughter-in-law

20:14 Taking a wife and her mother also

20:15 Men having sex with animals (the animals are to be killed, also)

20:16 Women having sex with animals

20:27 Being a medium or wizard

24:16 Blaspheming the name of the Lord

24:17 Killing a man

As you can see, the death penalty is broadly applied in Leviticus: everything from swearing to murder, including male homosexuality somewhere in between.

An extended analysis of prohibited behavior, short of abomination and death, also turns up a lengthy list. Among them are slander, vengeance, grudges, cursing the deaf, and putting stumbling blocks in front of blind people. In chapter 19, verse 19, Leviticus quotes God as ordering, "You shall not let your cattle breed with a different kind; you shall not sow your field with two kinds of seed; nor shall there come upon you a garment of cloth made of two kinds of stuff." Shortly thereafter, he adds, "You shall not eat any flesh with the blood in it. You shall not practice augury or witchcraft. You shall not round off the hair on your temples or mar the edges of your beard." Tattoos were prohibited, though Leviticus is silent on body piercing. References to all of these practices would be coded "Prohibited Acts" and perhaps given additional codes as well (recall "Dietary Rules").

We hope this brief glimpse into a possible analysis will give you some idea of the process by which codes are generated and applied. You should also have begun to see how such coding would allow you to better understand the messages being put forward in a text and to retrieve data appropriately as you need them.

Memoing

In the grounded theory method, the coding process involves more than simply categorizing chunks of text. As you code data, you should also be using the technique of **memoing**—writing memos or notes to yourself and others involved in the project. Some of what you write during analysis may end up in your final report; much of it will at least stimulate what you write.

In GTM, these memos have a special significance. Strauss and Corbin (1990:197–198) distinguish three kinds of memos: *code notes, theoretical notes,* and *operational notes.*

Code notes identify the code labels and their meanings. This is particularly important because, as in all social science research, most of the terms we use with technical meanings also have meanings in everyday language. It's essential, therefore, to write down a clear account of what you mean by the codes used in your analysis. In the Leviticus analysis, for example, you would want a code note regarding the meaning of *abomination* and how you've used that code in your analysis of text.

Theoretical notes cover a variety of topics: reflections of the dimensions and deeper meanings of concepts, relationships among concepts, theoretical propositions, and so on. All of us have times of ruminating over the nature of something, trying to think it out, to make sense out of it. In qualitative data analysis, it's vital to write down these thoughts, even those you'll later discard as useless. They will vary greatly in length, though you should limit them to a single main thought so that you can sort and organize them later. In the Leviticus analysis, one theoretical note might discuss the way that most of the injunctions implicitly address the behavior of *men,* with women being mostly incidental.

Operational notes deal primarily with methodological issues. Some will draw attention to data-collection circumstances that may be relevant to understanding the data later on. Others will consist of notes directing future data collection.

Writing these memos occurs throughout the data-collection and analysis process. Thoughts demanding memos will come to you as you reread notes or transcripts, code chunks of text, or discuss the project with others. It's a good idea to get in the habit of writing out your memos as soon as possible after the thoughts come to you.

John and Lyn Lofland (1995:193–194) speak of memoing somewhat differently, describing memos that come closer to the final writing stage. The *elemental memo* is

> a detailed analytic rendering of some relatively specific matter. Depending on the scale of the project, the worker may write from one to several dozen or more of these. Built out of selective codes and codings, these are the most basic prose cannon fodder, as it were, of the project.
>
> (1995:194)

The *sorting memo* is based on several elemental memos and presents key themes in the analysis. Whereas we create elemental memos as they come to mind, with no particular rhyme nor reason, we write sorting memos as an attempt to discover or create reason among the data being analyzed. A sorting memo will bring together a set of related elemental memos. A given project may see the creation of several sorting memos dealing with different aspects of the project.

Finally, the *integrating memo* ties together the several sorting memos to bring order to the whole project. It tells a coherent and comprehensive story, casting it in a theoretical context. In any real project, however, there are many different ways of bringing about this kind of closure. Hence, the data analysis may result in several integrating memos.

Notice that whereas we often think of writing as a linear process, starting at the beginning and moving through to the conclusion, memoing is very different. It might be characterized as a process of creating chaos and then finding order within it.

To explore this process further, refer to the works cited in this discussion and at the end of the chapter. You'll also find a good deal of information on the web. For Barney Glaser's rules on memoing, for example, you might go to http://gtm.vlsm.org/gnm-gtm3.en.html. Ultimately, the best education in this process comes from practice. Even if you don't have a research project under way, you can practice now on class notes. Or start a journal and code it.

Concept Mapping

It should be clear by now that analysts of qualitative data spend a lot of time committing thoughts to paper (or to a computer file), but this process is not limited to text alone. Often, we can think out relationships among concepts more clearly by putting the concepts in a graphical format, a process called **concept mapping.** Some researchers find it useful to put all their major concepts on a single sheet of paper, whereas others spread their thoughts across several sheets of paper, blackboards, magnetic boards, computer pages, or other media. Figure 19-3 shows how we might think out some of the concepts of Goffman's examination of gender and advertising. (This image was created through the use of Inspiration, a concept-mapping computer program.)

Incidentally, many of the topics discussed in this section have useful applications in quantitative as well as qualitative analyses. Certainly, concept mapping is appropriate in both types of analysis. The several types of memos would also be useful in both. And the discussion of coding readily applies to the coding of open-ended questionnaire responses for the purpose of quantification and statistical analysis. (We'll look at coding again in the next chapter, on quantifying data.)

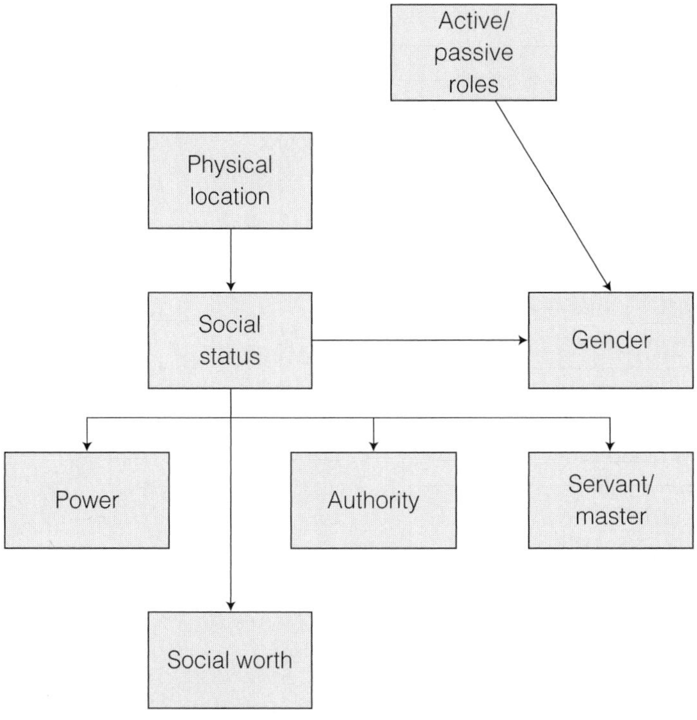

Figure 19-3 An Example of Concept Mapping

Having noted the overlap of qualitative and quantitative techniques, it seems fitting now to address an instrument that is primarily associated with quantitative research but that is proving very valuable for qualitative analysts as well—the personal computer.

COMPUTER PROGRAMS FOR QUALITATIVE DATA

The advent of computers has been a boon to quantitative research, allowing the rapid calculation of extremely complex statistics. The importance of the computer for qualitative research has been somewhat more slowly appreciated. Some qualitative researchers were quick to adapt the basic capacities of computers to nonnumerical tasks, but it took a bit longer for programmers to address the specific needs of qualitative research per se. Today, however, several powerful programs are available.

Let's start this section with a brief overview of some of the ways you can use basic computer tools in qualitative research. The computer can be a valuable note-taking device for all the observations to be recorded, as called for in Chapter 18. Perhaps only those who can recall hours spent with carbon paper and white-out can fully appreciate the glory of computers in this regard. "Easier editing" and "easier duplication" simply don't capture the scope of the advance.

Moving beyond the basic recording and storage of data, simple word-processing programs can be used for some data analysis. The "find" or "search" command will take you to passages containing key words. Or, going one step further, you can type code words alongside passages in your notes so that you can search for those keywords later.

Database and spreadsheet programs can also be used for processing and analyzing qualitative data. Figure 19-4 is a simple illustration of how some of the verses from Leviticus might be manipulated within a spreadsheet. The three columns to the left represent three of the concepts we've discussed. An "X" means that the passage to the right contains that concept. As shown, the passages are sorted in such a way as to gather all those dealing with punishment by death. Another simple "sort" command would gather all those dealing with sex, with homosexuality, or any of the other concepts coded.

This brief illustration should give you some idea of the possibilities for using readily available programs as tools in qualitative data analysis. Happily, there are now a large number of programs created specifically

Sex	Homosex	Death	Verse	Passage
X	X	X	20:13	If a man lies with a male as with a woman, both of them have committed an abomination; they shall be put to death, their blood is upon them.
X		X	20:12	If a man lies with his daughter-in-law, both of them shall be put to death; they have committed incest, their blood is upon them.
X		X	20:15	If a man lies with a beast, he shall be put to death; and you shall kill the beast.
		X	20:09	For every one who curses his father or his mother shall be put to death; he has cursed his father or his mother, his blood is upon him.
		X	20:02	Any man of the people of Israel, or of the strangers that sojourn in Israel, who gives any of his children to Molech shall be put to death.
X	X		18:22	You shall not lie with a male as with a woman; it is an abomination.

Figure 19-4 Using a Spreadsheet for Qualitative Analysis

for that purpose. Here's an excellent list prepared by sociologists at the University of Surrey, England (www.soc.surrey.ac.uk/sru/SRU1.html):

The Ethnograph

HyperQual

HyperResearch

NUD*IST

QUALPRO

QUALOG

Textbase Alpha

SONAR

ATLAS.ti

This website also provides a brief description of each of the programs listed, along with the price and contact, where available.

Leviticus as Seen through NUD*IST

Let's take a closer look at how qualitative data analysis programs operate by considering one of the programs just mentioned, **NUD*IST** (Nonnumeric Unstructured Data, Index Searching, and Theorizing). Although each of the programs has somewhat different features and different approaches to analysis, NUD*IST is one of the most popular programs, and it offers a fairly representative view of the genre. We'll begin with a brief examination of Leviticus, and then we'll examine a project focused on understanding the experiences of women film directors.

Although it is possible to type directly into NUD*IST the text materials to be coded, usually materials already in existence—such as field notes or, in this case, the verses of Leviticus—are *imported* into the program. Menu-based commands do this easily, though the text must be in a *plaintext* format (that is, without word-processing or other formatting).

Figure 19-5 shows how the text is displayed within NUD*IST. For the illustrations in this section, we have used the Macintosh version of NUD*IST. We'll use the Windows version in the film director illustration, so you can note the difference and similarities in the two platforms.

To see the document, select its name in the "Document Explorer" window and click "Browse." The text window can be resized and moved around the screen to suit your taste.

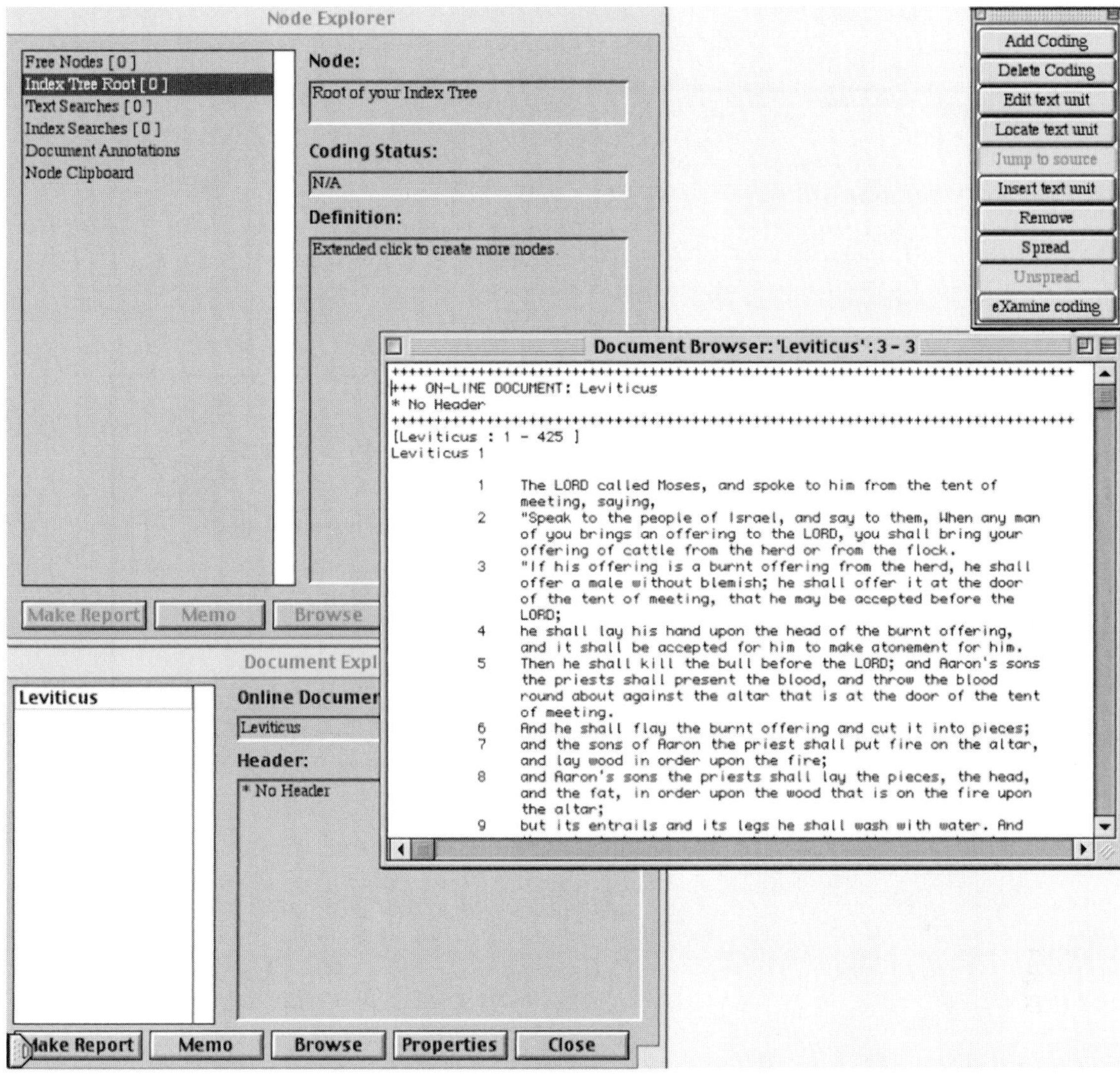

Figure 19-5 How Text Materials Are Displayed in NUD*IST

Note the set of buttons in the upper right corner of the illustration. These allow you to select portions of the text for purposes of editing, coding, and other operations.

Now let's create a concept code: "homosex." This will stand for references to male homosexuality. Figure 19-6 shows what the creation of a concept code looks like.

As we create codes for our concepts, we can use them to code the text materials. Figure 19-7 illustrates how this is done. In the text browser, you can see that verse 22:13 has been selected (indicated by the box outline around this verse). Having done that, we click the button labeled "Add Coding" (not shown in this illustration). This prompts the computer to ask us to identify the appropriate code. The easiest way to respond is to click the "Browse" button, which presents you with a list of the current codes. In this example, we selected "homosex" and entered the code ID (100).

As text materials are coded, the program can then be used for purposes of analysis. As a simple example, we might want to pull together all the passages coded "homosex." This would allow us to see them all at once, looking for similarities and differences.

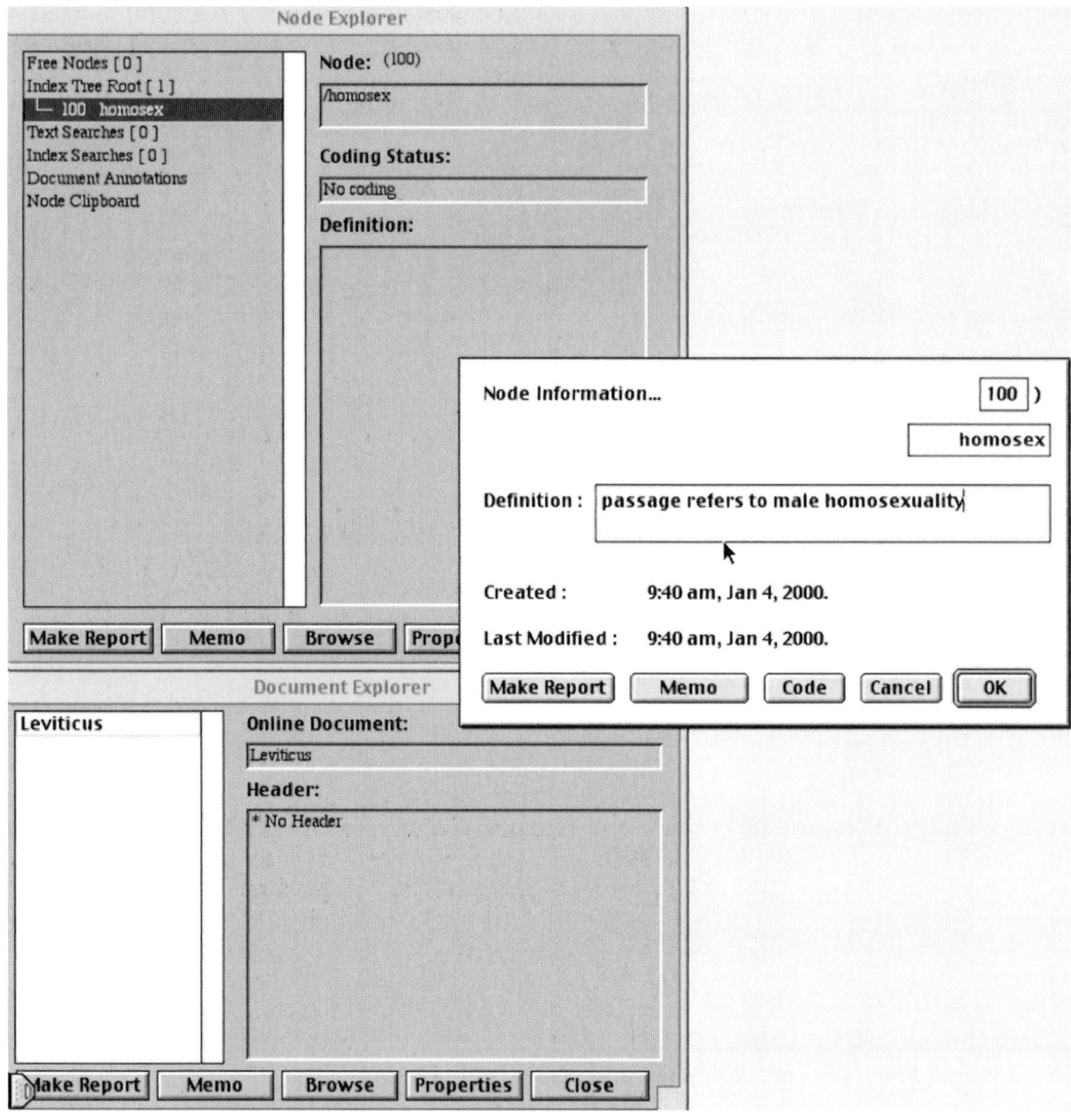

Figure 19-6 Creating the Code *homosex*

Figure 19-8 shows how NUD*IST would bring together the passages referring to male homosexuality. To do this, all you do is select the code name in the "Node Explorer" window and click the "Make Report" button.

This simple example illustrates the possibilities opened up by a program designed specifically for qualitative data analysis. To get a little deeper into its use, let's shift to a different research example.

Sandrine Zerbib: Understanding Women Film Directors

Sandrine Zerbib is a French sociologist interested in understanding the special difficulties faced by women breaking into the male-dominated world of film direction. To address this issue, she interviewed 30 women directors in depth. Having compiled hours of recorded interviews, she turned to NUD*IST as a ve-

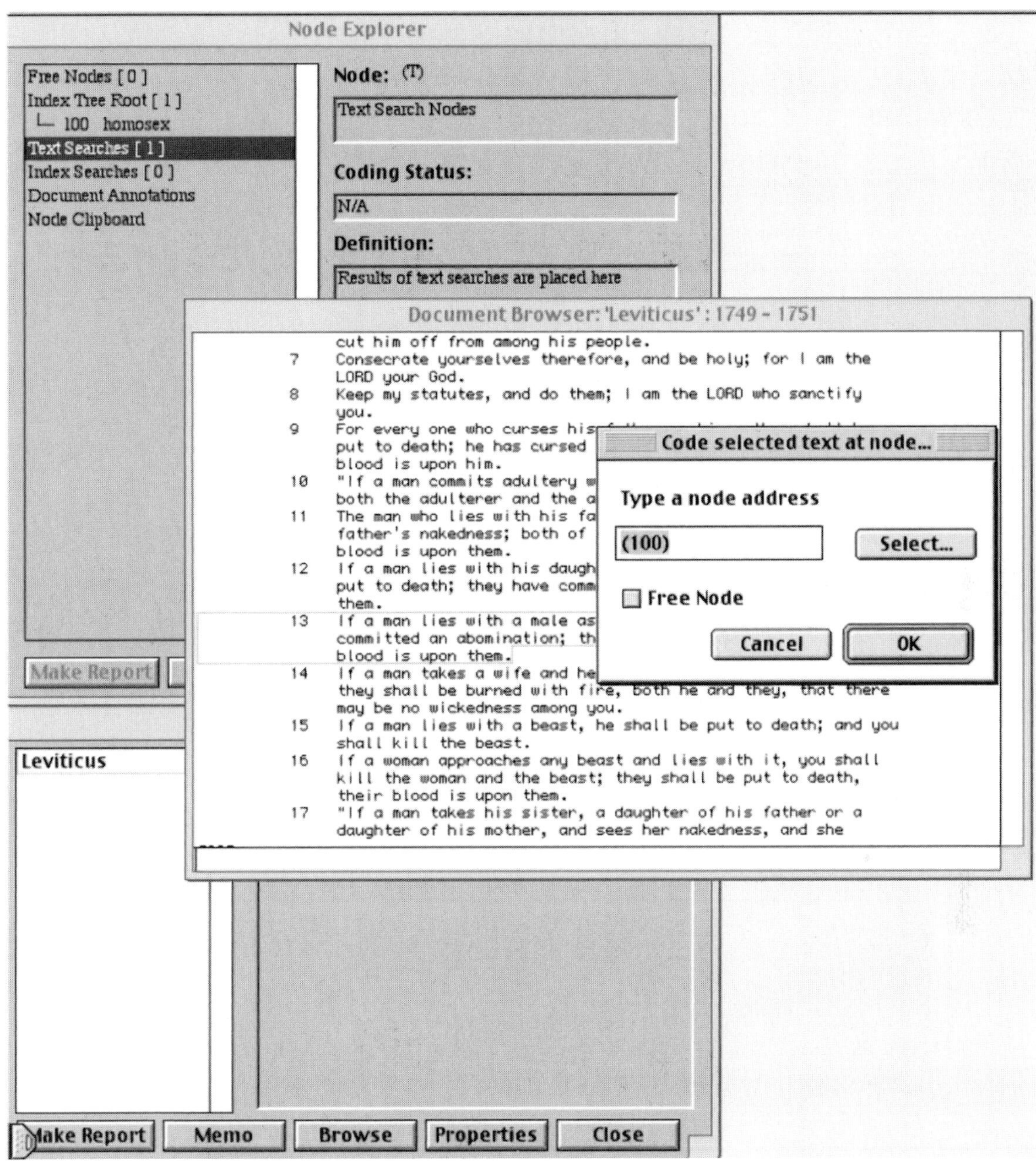

Figure 19-7 Coding a Text Passage

hicle for analysis. Let's have her describe the ongoing process in her own words.

> Most software for qualitative analysis allows researchers to simultaneously analyze several interviews from different interviewers. However, I find it more efficient to start by importing only one interview into NUD*IST. Because you will have transcribed or at least read your interviews beforehand, you may be able to select the interview you think will be most fruitful. You should trust yourself, because you are becoming an expert in what you are currently studying and also because comparing and contrasting interviews should help you get a sense of how accurate your analysis is.
>
> After having completed about 30 interviews with women filmmakers, I had a sense of what the main

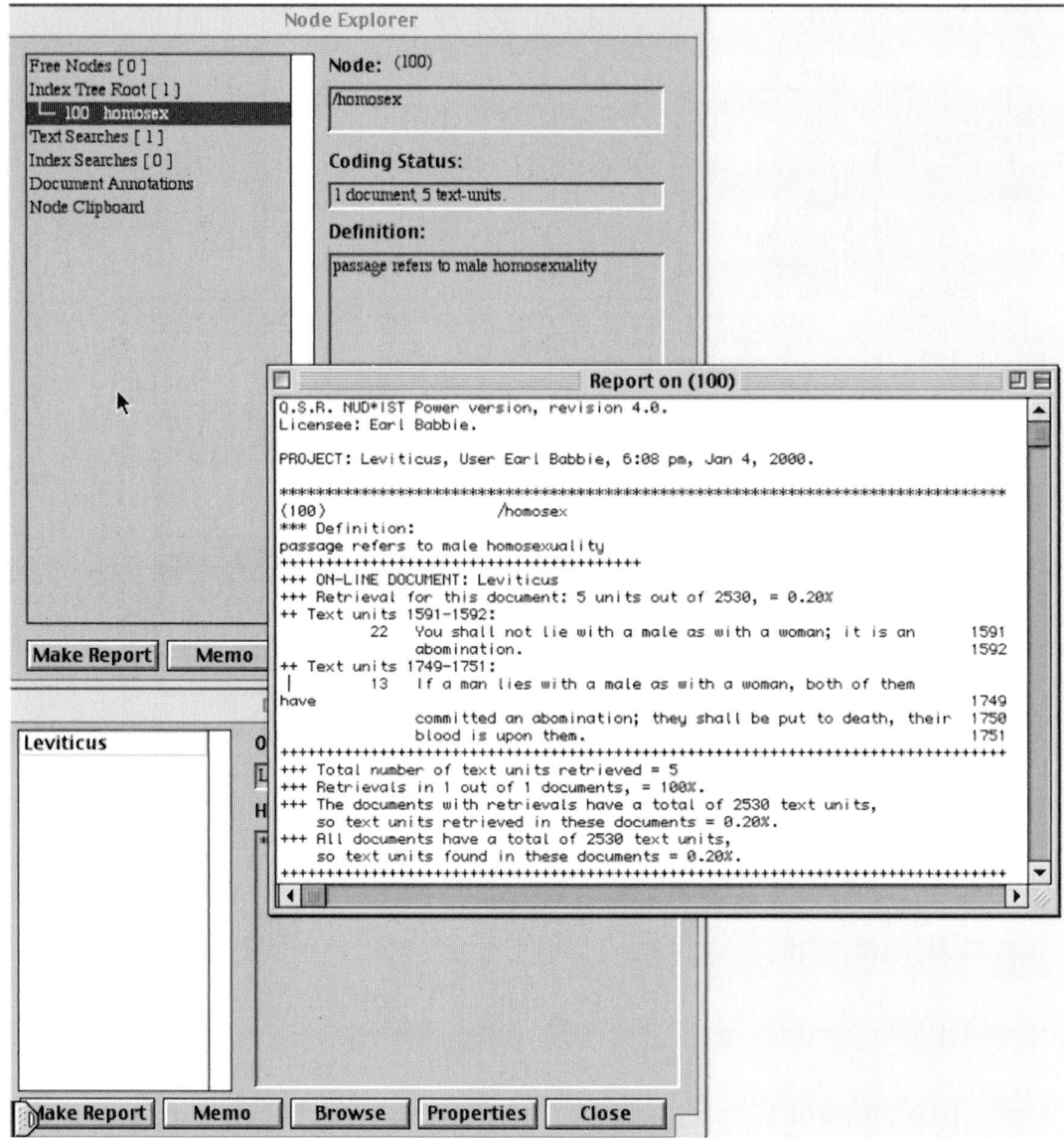

Figure 19-8 Reporting on *homosex*

themes were, because they kept coming up in each interview. Nevertheless, I needed a tool for synthesizing those pages and pages of interviews. I chose to start with my interview with Joy. I had made a note to myself to use her interview as a starting point. An older film director, she seemed to have strong points she wanted to get across.

In Figure 19-9, my interview with Joy has been imported as a "text only" file. (Only part of the file is visible in the window.)

In your own coding, remember that NUD*IST only reads text documents. There is no need to get fancy with your interview transcription; all formats are erased. At this point you are ready to enjoy the coding process. You can simply highlight words, sentences, or sections and add nodes (or codes) to it. The first step is to create "free nodes," that is, nodes independent of one another. How much text you should highlight per code is a decision you will have to make. However, keep in mind that you will have to use those quotes in the writing part

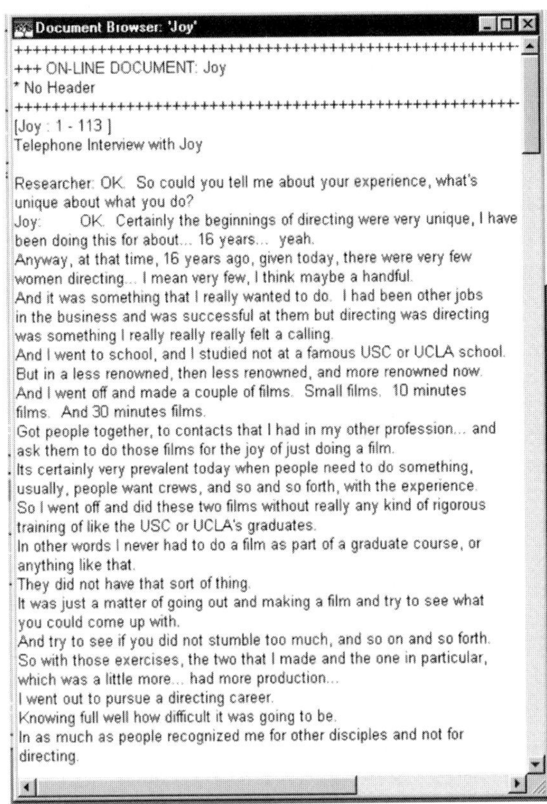

Document Browser: 'Joy'

++

+++ ON-LINE DOCUMENT: Joy

* No Header

++

[Joy : 1 - 113]

Telephone Interview with Joy

Researcher: OK. So could you tell me about your experience, what's unique about what you do?

Joy: OK. Certainly the beginnings of directing were very unique, I have been doing this for about... 16 years... yeah.

Anyway, at that time, 16 years ago, given today, there were very few women directing... I mean very few, I think maybe a handful.

And it was something that I really wanted to do. I had been other jobs in the business and was successful at them but directing was directing was something I really really really felt a calling.

And I went to school, and I studied not at a famous USC or UCLA school.

But in a less renowned, then less renowned, and more renowned now.

And I went off and made a couple of films. Small films. 10 minutes films. And 30 minutes films.

Got people together, to contacts that I had in my other profession... and ask them to do those films for the joy of just doing a film.

Its certainly very prevalent today when people need to do something, usually, people want crews, and so and so forth, with the experience.

So I went off and did these two films without really any kind of rigorous training of like the USC or UCLA's graduates.

In other words I never had to do a film as part of a graduate course, or anything like that.

They did not have that sort of thing.

It was just a matter of going out and making a film and try to see what you could come up with.

And try to see if you did not stumble too much, and so on and so forth.

So with those exercises, the two that I made and the one in particular, which was a little more... had more production...

I went out to pursue a directing career.

Knowing full well how difficult it was going to be.

In as much as people recognized me for other disciples and not for directing.

Figure 19-9 Text of Interview with "Joy"

of your research. You will need to be convincing. You also want to deconstruct the whole interview. Try to not leave anything out. It is easier to forgo using a quote because you have found a better one later than to have nothing to use because you were not consistent enough in your dissection of the interview.

When you create a node or code, you first want to use wide categories that would be more inclusive of other potential quotes. But you also want to be specific enough for your coding system to have validity. In Figure 19-10, for instance, I have created the free node "past" because my interviewee referred to the past as being extremely challenging for women who wanted to be film directors. There were very few women directors back then, many fewer than today. I decided to add a definition of this node so that I could remember why I used "past" as a node. I also anticipated having another free node called "today." Then I could move the "change" node to the index tree root and create "past" and "today" as subnodes under "change."

In Figure 19-11, I have highlighted a passage that deals with several things. Joy talks about the Directors Guild of America (DGA, or the directors' union), and more specifically about the efforts of its president. She also expresses her feelings toward gender inequalities. According to her, having talent is not enough in Hollywood if there is a bias against women. I decided to add two nodes to this quote, "DGA," which I needed to create, and "discrimination," which I had already created.

In Figure 19-12, I have attempted to transform some free nodes into index trees. The software is flexible enough for me to move nodes, rename them, or see what quotes are under each node. You can attach a different node to a quote you have wrongly coded. It is preferable to start with free nodes before you build a hierarchy of codes (or tree), because it takes time and patience to understand how categories are linked to one another. Coding other interviews should help you organize your coding system.

Figure 19-13 illustrates my decision to import two more interviews, Berta's and Queena's. I could browse all three interviews on the same screen. Because it was still early in the analysis process, I chose to analyze these two new interviews one by one. It was now starting to make sense; I was starting to see patterns. NUD*IST let me keep records of number of occurrences each node was attached to a quote, not only in Joy's interview but now also in Berta's and Queena's. With several nodes often attached to a single quote, the qualitative analysis allowed me to find out which nodes were more likely to overlap with one another.

One of my first observations was that the term sabotage was used fairly often by Joy and Queena. I decided to run a report that would synthesize all the quotes that I attached to the node "sabotage." Figure 19-14 shows the first page of the report created by NUD*IST. The program searched for all quotes under "sabotage," which is a subnode of "discrimination," for all online documents. It also provided the number assigned to each text unit, which allowed me to go back and see a quotation in the context of the whole document.

This procedure is only one of the many capabilities of this program. You may want to spend some time learning about this software before committing to it. What seems to be an efficient tool for me may not be for you. There are plenty [of] qualitative research analysis software [packages] in the market; try to find out what works for you.

Although it is important and appropriate to distinguish between qualitative and quantitative research and often to discuss them separately, they are not incompatible or competing. Unless you can operate in both modes, you will limit your potential as a

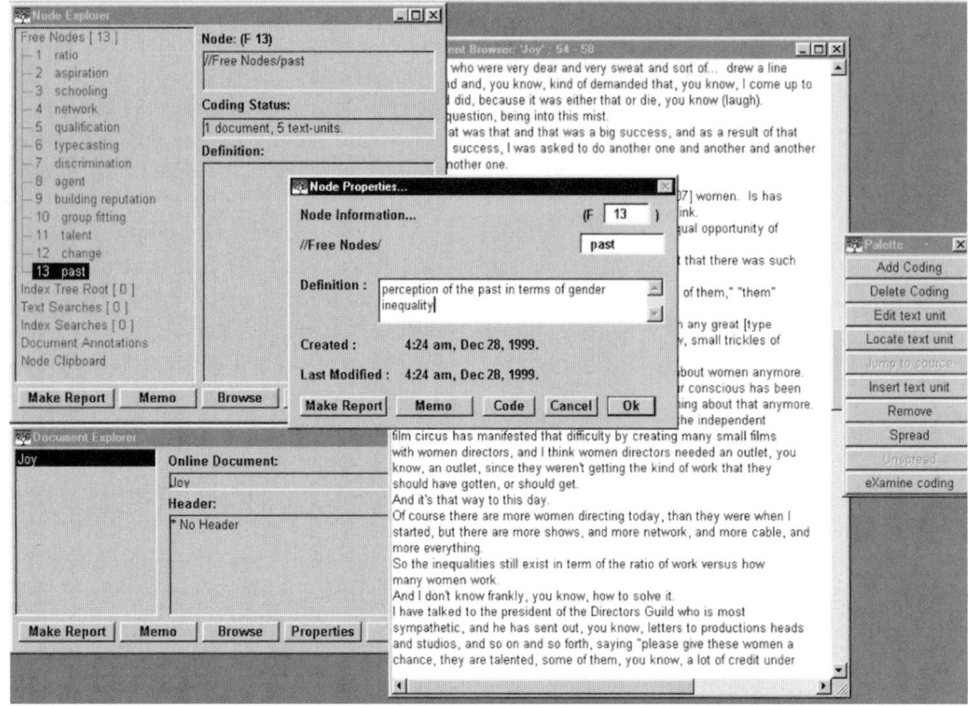

Figure 19-10 Creating the Code *past*

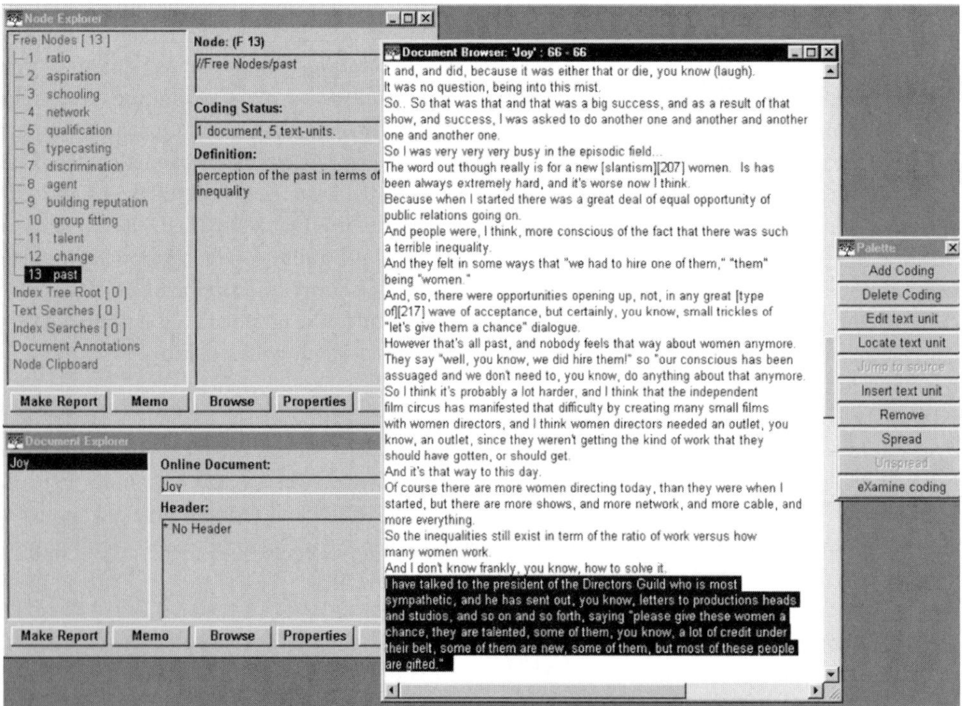

Figure 19-11 Coding a Passage in the Interview

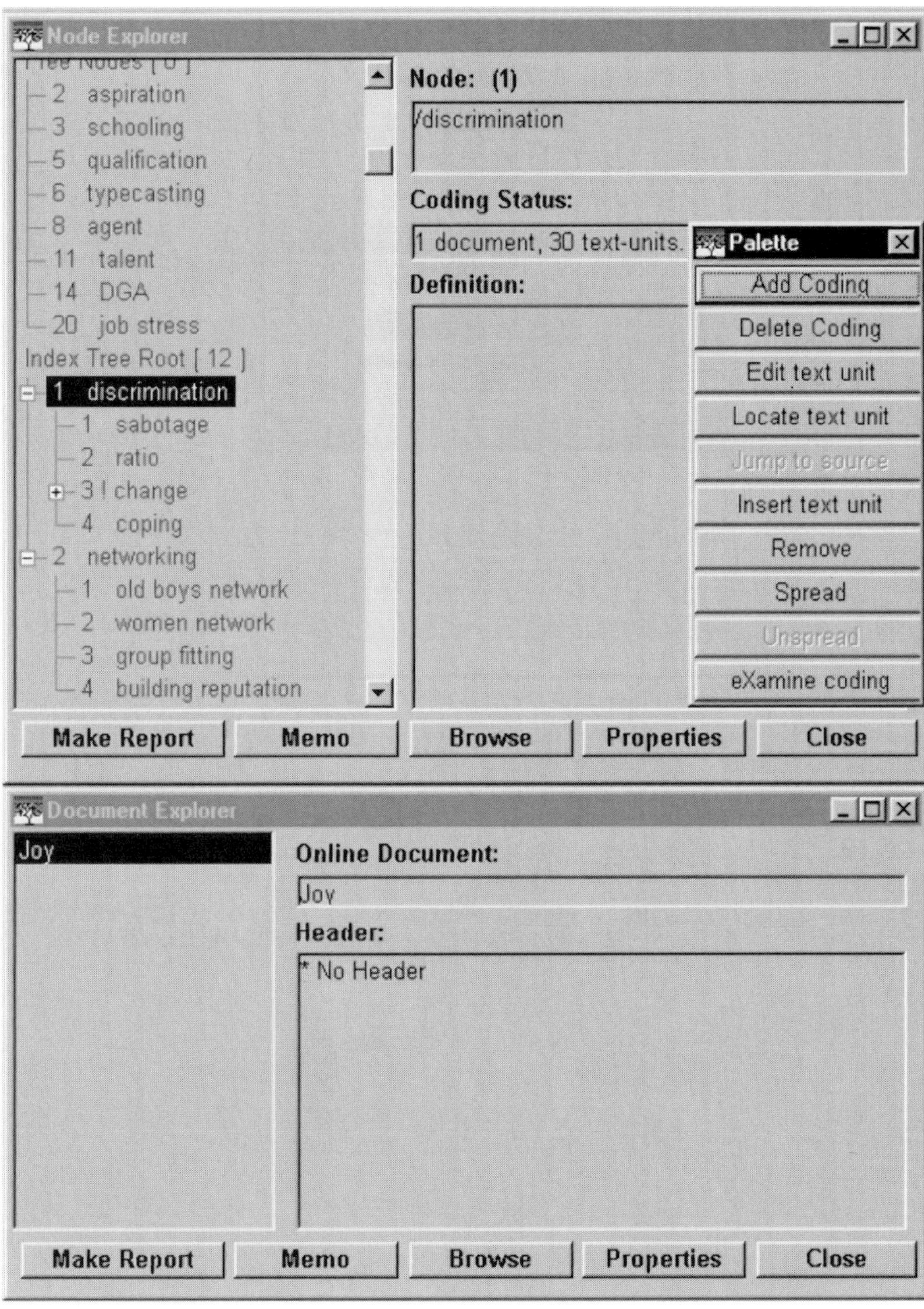

Figure 19-12 Creating an Index Tree

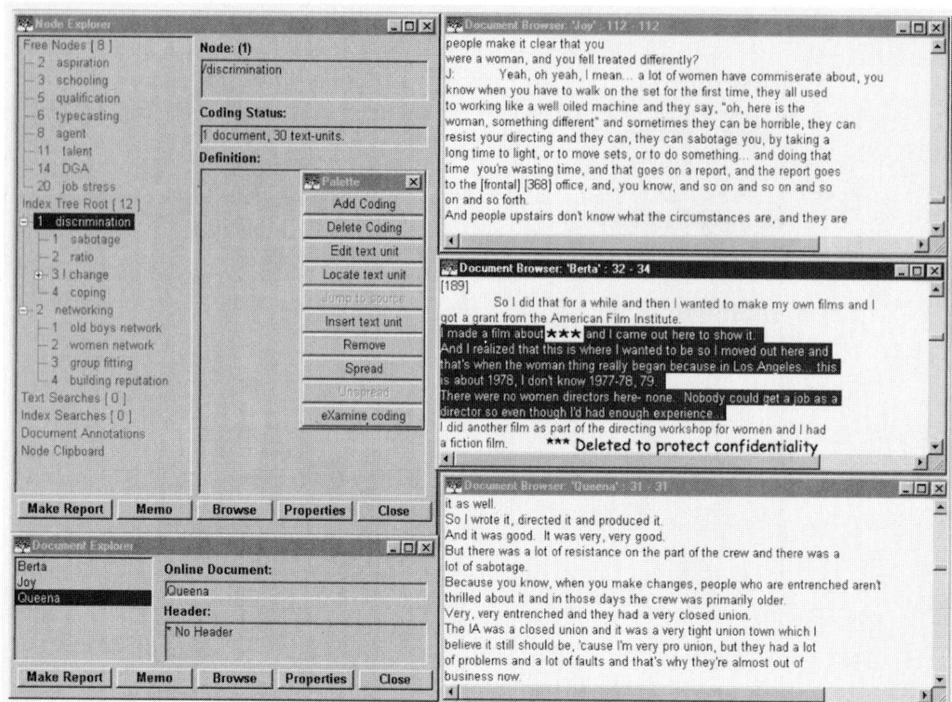

Figure 19-13 Adding Two More Cases to the Analysis

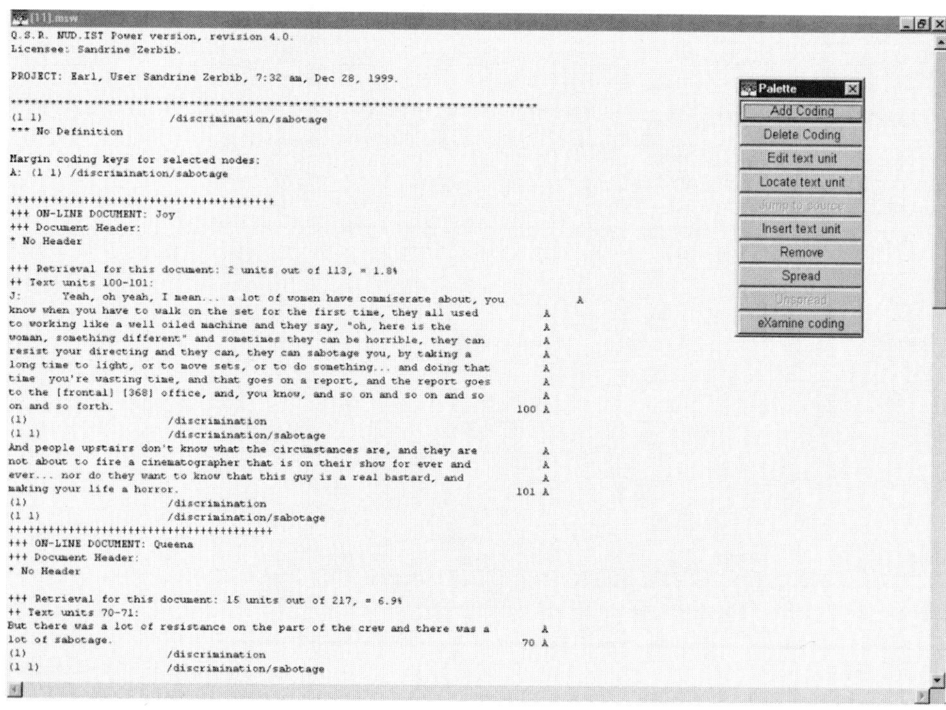

Figure 19-14 Analyzing the Node *sabotage*

social researcher. In Chapter 20, we'll indicate ways in which quantitative analyses can strengthen qualitative studies.

Main Points

- Qualitative analysis is the nonnumerical examination and interpretation of observations.
- Qualitative analysis involves a continual interplay between theory and analysis. In analyzing qualitative data, we seek to discover patterns such as changes over time or possible causal links between variables.
- Examples of approaches to the discovery and explanation of such patterns are grounded theory method (GTM), semiotics, and conversation analysis.
- The processing of qualitative data is as much art as science. Three key tools for preparing data for analysis are coding, memoing, and concept mapping.
- In contrast to the standardized units used in coding for statistical analyses, the units to be coded in qualitative analyses may vary within a document. Although codes may be derived from the theory being explored, more often researchers use open coding, in which codes are suggested by the researchers' examination and questioning of the data.
- Memoing is appropriate at several stages of data processing to capture code meanings, theoretical ideas, preliminary conclusions, and other thoughts that will be useful during analysis.
- Concept mapping uses diagrams to explore relationships in the data graphically.
- Several computer programs, such as NUD*IST, are specifically designed to assist researchers in the analysis of qualitative data. In addition, researchers can take advantage of the capabilities of common software tools such as word processors, database programs, and spreadsheets.

Review Questions and Exercises

1. Review Goffman's examination of gender advertising, and collect and analyze a set of advertising photos from magazines or newspapers that allow you to explore the relationship between gender and status.

2. Review the discussion of homosexuality in the Book of Leviticus and suggest ways that the examination might be structured as a cross-case analysis.

3. Imagine you were conducting a cross-case analysis of revolutionary documents such as the Declaration of Independence and the Declaration of the Rights of Man and of the Citizen (from the French Revolution). Identify the key concepts you might code in the following sentence: When in the Course of human events, it becomes necessary for one people to dissolve the political bands which have connected them with another, and to assume among the Powers of the earth, the separate and equal station to which the Laws of Nature and of Nature's God entitle them, a decent respect to the opinions of mankind requires that they should declare the causes which impel them to the separation.

4. Write one code note and one theoretical note for Exercise 3.

5. Using the library, InfoTrac, or the web, find a research report using conversation analysis. Summarize the main conclusions in your own words.

Internet Exercises

1. Using InfoTrac College Edition, conduct an electronic search using the keyword term *qualitative data analysis*. Briefly describe the data analytic approaches used in two qualitative research studies you find.

2. Using InfoTrac College Edition, conduct an electronic search using the keyword term *concept mapping*. Briefly describe a qualitative research study you find and how it used concept mapping.

3. Using InfoTrac College Edition, conduct an electronic search using the keyword term *grounded theory*. Briefly describe a qualitative research study you find that used the grounded theory method and summarize its data analysis approach.

4. You can become more familiar with the computer analysis of qualitative data by going to the Wadsworth Social Work Web site at http://info.wadsworth.com/rubbin_babbie/. At that site, first click on the "Companion site" prompt button. Then go to the "Select a chapter" button and choose this chapter (Qualitative Data Analysis). Then click on "Learning Guide to NViVO," which is a successor to NUD*IST.

Additional Readings

Glaser, Barney G., and Anselm L. Strauss. 1967. *The Discovery of Grounded Theory: Strategies for Qualitative Research.* Chicago: Aldine. This is the classic statement of grounded theory with practical suggestions that are still useful today.

Hutchby, Ian, and Robin Wooffitt. 1998. *Conversation Analysis: Principles, Practices and Applications.* Cambridge, England: Polity Press. An excellent overview of the conversation analysis method. The book examines the theory behind the technique, how to use it, and some possible applications.

Miles, Matthew B., and A. Michael Huberman. 1994. *Qualitative Data Analysis,* 2nd ed. Thousand Oaks, CA: Sage. If you ever do a qualitative study and find yourself overwhelmed with masses of unstructured data and at sea as to how to analyze or report the data, this sourcebook will come in handy. It provides many practical illustrations of alternative ways to reduce, display, and draw verifiable conclusions from qualitative data.

Silverman, David. 1993. *Interpreting Qualitative Data: Methods for Analyzing Talk, Text, and Interaction.* Newbury Park, CA: Sage, 1993. This book brings together theoretical concerns, data-collection techniques, and the process of making sense of what is observed.

Strauss, Anselm, and Juliet Corbin. 1990. *Basics of Qualitative Research: Grounded Theory Procedures and Techniques.* Newbury Park, CA: Sage. This updated statement of grounded theory offers special guidance on coding and memoing.

PART 7

Analysis of Quantitative Data

In this part of the book, we'll discuss the analysis and reportage of data in quantitative research studies. We'll begin by examining levels of measurement and how they influence data analysis. Then we'll see how data are prepared for analysis. After that we'll look at procedures for describing variables separately and then relationships between variables. Then we'll move on to some more challenging topics in the use of statistics to draw inferences about relationships among variables.

Chapter 20 addresses levels of measurement, converting observations into a form that is appropriate for computer analysis, the interpretation of some basic descriptive statistics for analyzing and presenting the data related to a single variable, and then how to construct and read bivariate and multivariate tables that display relationships between and among two or more variables.

Chapters 21 and 22 provide an introduction to statistical procedures that social work researchers commonly use to guide decisions concerning whether they can generalize beyond their own study about the relationships they observe in their findings, the causal processes that underlie the observed relationships, and the strengths of those relationships. The emphasis of these chapters is on understanding the logic of inferential statistics rather than on procedures for computing them. Chapter 22 also examines the criteria that are used to decide when to use each of the various statistical procedures, mistakes that are commonly made in using or interpreting them, and controversies about their use.

CHAPTER 20

Quantitative Data Analysis

What You'll Learn in This Chapter

Often, social work research data are converted to numerical form for statistical analyses. In this chapter, we'll begin with the process of quantifying data and then turn to analysis. Quantitative analysis may be descriptive or explanatory; it may involve one, two, or more variables. We begin our examination of how quantitative analyses are done with some simple but powerful ways of manipulating data in order to arrive at research conclusions.

INTRODUCTION

In Chapter 19, we saw some of the logic and techniques for analyzing qualitative data. This chapter will examine **quantitative analysis,** or the techniques by which researchers convert data to a numerical form and subject it to statistical analysis. To begin, we'll look at four different levels of measurement. The level of measurement of the variables we seek to analyze influences the quantitative statistical techniques we can use to analyze those variables. Then we'll look at *coding*—the process of converting data to a numerical format. Finally, we'll look at basic descriptive statistics and tables for analyzing and presenting data about variables.

LEVELS OF MEASUREMENT

An attribute, you'll recall, is a characteristic or quality of something. *Female* would be an example. So would *old*. Variables, on the other hand, are logical sets of attributes. Thus, *sex* or *gender* is a variable composed of the attributes *female* and *male*. In contrast, *age* is a variable that can be composed of different kinds of attributes. For example, we could use attributes such as *infant, toddler, child, adolescent, adult, elderly,* and so on. Or we could be more precise and specify age as how many years old a person is. Notice that with the variable *gender,* we are limited to discrete, nonmetric (categorical) attributes. A person is either male or female; we don't ask how much. Notice also that *age* is a metric variable; that is, its attributes involve quantities. Finally, notice that with the variable *age,* we can choose attributes that are relatively imprecise (such as child, adult, elderly) or relatively precise (such as 6 months, 6 years, and so on). These differences in the types of attributes represent different levels of measurement. We will examine four *levels of measurement* in this section: *nominal, ordinal, interval,* and *ratio*.

Nominal Measures

Variables with only discrete, nonmetric (categorical) attributes are **nominal measures.** Examples of these include gender, ethnicity, religious affiliation, political party affiliation, birthplace, college major, and hair color. Although the attributes that compose each variable—*male* and *female* for the variable gender—are distinct from one another and exhaust the possibilities of gender among people, they have none of the additional structures mentioned below.

It might be useful to imagine a group of people that is being characterized in terms of one such variable and then physically grouped by the applicable attributes. Imagine asking a large gathering of people to stand together in groups according to the states in which they were born: all those born in Vermont in one group, those born in California in another, and so forth. (The variable would be *place of birth;* the attributes would be *born in California, born in Vermont,* and so on.) All of the people standing in a given group would share at least one thing in common; the people in any one group would differ from the people in all other groups in that same regard. Where the individual groups formed, how close they were to one another, or how the groups were arranged in the room would be irrelevant. All that would matter would be that all of the members of a given group share the same state of birthplace and that each group has a different shared state of birthplace.

To facilitate the collection and processing of data, we assign different code numbers to the different categories, or attributes, of nominal variables. Thus, we might record a "1" to designate male and a "2" to designate female. But, unlike other levels of measurement, with nominal variables the code numbers have no quantitative meaning. They're only convenient devices to record *qualitative* differences.

The word *nominal* comes from the same Latin root used in words like *nominate* and *nomenclature*—words that have something to do with naming. No matter what code number we may assign to them, no matter how high or low that number may be, the code refers only to a name, not an amount. Thus, in coding ethnicity, if we assign a "1" to white, a "2" to African American, a "3" to Hispanic, a "4" to Asian American, a "5" to Native American, and a "6" to Other, we are not implying that someone with a higher code number has more of something than someone with a lower code number. An Asian American receiving a code 4 does not have more ethnicity than an African American receiving a code 2. Consequently, when we statistically analyze nominal data, we cannot calculate a mean or a median. It would make no sense, for example, to say that the mean (average) ethnicity of an agency with the above six categories of ethnicity was 2.7. Our analysis would be restricted to calculating how many people were in the various categories, such as when we say that 40 percent of the caseload is white, 30 percent is African American, 20 percent is Hispanic, and so on.

Ordinal Measures

Variables whose attributes may be logically *rank-ordered* are **ordinal measures.** The different attributes represent relatively more or less of the variable, but do not specify the degree of difference in precise terms. Variables of this type are social class, racism, sexism, client satisfaction, and the like. Thus, when we use attributes such as young and old to characterize *age,* we are treating age as an ordinal variable. That is, we would know that an old person is older than a young person, but we would not know *how much* older.

Likewise, we would have ordinal data if we ask clients how satisfied they are with the services they received or to rate the quality of those services. We might ask them whether they are very satisfied, satisfied, dissatisfied, or very dissatisfied. This would tell us the *rank order* of their level of satisfaction, but it would not provide a quantity that allowed us to say that clients at one level of satisfaction were exactly twice as satisfied or three times more dissatisfied than clients at another level of satisfaction. Similarly, if one client rated the quality of the services as excellent and a second client rated them as good, then we could say that the first client gave a higher rating to the services but not precisely how much higher the rating was. For example, we could not say that excellent is one-third better than good or two times better than good, and so on.

As with nominal measurement, we would assign code numbers to represent an individual's rank order. For instance, if clients are rating service quality on an ordinal scale with the categories excellent, good, fair, or poor, the codes might be excellent "4," good "3," fair "2," and poor "1." Unlike nominal measurement, these code numbers would have some quantitative meaning. That is, the code 4 would represent a higher rating than the code 3, and so on. But the quantitative meaning would be imprecise; it would not mean the same thing as having four children as opposed to three, two, one, or no children. Whereas we can say that a parent with four children has four times as many children as a parent with one child, we cannot say that a client who felt the services were excellent (code 4) found them four times better than the client who felt they were poor (code 1). The word *ordinal* is thus connected to the word *order,* and means that we know only the *order* of the categories, not their precise quantities or the precise differences between them.

Interval Measures

For the attributes that compose some variables, the actual distance separating those attributes does have meaning. Such variables are **interval measures.** For these, the logical distance between attributes can be expressed in meaningful standard intervals. A physical science example would be the Fahrenheit or Celsius temperature scale. The difference, or distance, between 80 degrees and 90 degrees is the same as that between 40 degrees and 50 degrees. However, 80 degrees Fahrenheit is not twice as hot as 40 degrees Celsius, because the zero point in the Fahrenheit and Celsius scales is arbitrary—zero degrees does not really mean lack of heat, nor does −30 degrees represent 30 degrees less than no heat. (The Kelvin scale is based on an *absolute zero,* which does mean a complete lack of heat.)

About the only interval measures commonly used in social scientific research are constructed measures, such as standardized intelligence tests that have been more or less accepted. The interval separating IQ scores of 100 and 110 may be regarded as the same as the interval separating scores of 110 and 120 by virtue of the distribution of observed scores obtained by many thousands of people who have taken the tests over the years. (A person who received a score of zero on a standard IQ test could not be regarded, strictly speaking, as having no intelligence, although we might feel he or she was unsuited to be a college professor or even a college student.)

Ratio Measures

Most of the social scientific variables that meet the minimal requirements for interval measures also meet the requirements for **ratio measures.** In ratio measures, the attributes that compose a variable, besides having all of the structural characteristics just discussed, are based on a true zero point. We have already mentioned the Kelvin temperature scale in contrast to the Fahrenheit and Celsius scales. Examples from social work research would include length of residence in a given place, number of children, number of service delivery contacts, number of days spent hospitalized, number of organizations belonged to, number of times

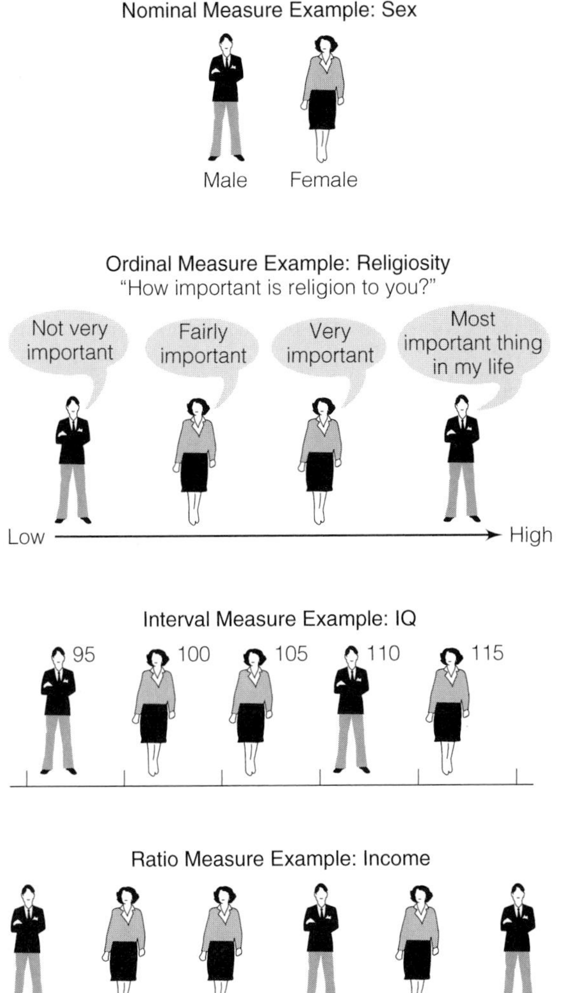

Figure 20-1 Levels of Measurement

married, number of arrests, and number of antisocial behaviors.

Age, too, can be a ratio-level variable when it is defined in precise time increments. But, as we noted above, it (like any ratio-level variable) could be defined imprecisely and thus become an ordinal-level variable. Suppose at a social gathering we ask people to stand in a line from youngest to oldest. That would give us an ordinal measure of age in that we could determine if one person is older than or younger than another. If we ask them to stand one foot apart for every month older or younger they are than the person next to them, then we satisfy the additional requirements of an interval measure and will be able to say *how much* older one person is than another. Finally, because one of the attributes included in age represents a true zero (babies carried by women about to give birth), knowing a person's precise age meets the requirements for a ratio measure, permitting us to say that one person is twice as old as another. To review this discussion, Figure 20-1 presents a graphic illustration of the four levels of measurement.

Implications of Levels of Measurement

Because it's unlikely you'll undertake the physical grouping of people just described (try it once at a party, and you won't be invited to many parties), we draw your attention to some of the statistical implications of the differences that have been distinguished. For example, if you want to compute the mean (average) age of your sample, you'll need to measure age as a ratio variable—just knowing categories such as adult versus child, or young versus old, won't do.

Because the ratio level of measurement offers the most statistical options, it is considered the highest level of measurement. As we noted above, for example, age could be treated as a ratio-level variable, an interval-level variable, or an ordinal-level variable. It could even be treated as a nominal-level variable, such as by grouping people by whether or not they are part of the baby boom generation born between 1945 and 1960. Thus, if we know age at the ratio level of measurement, we can convert it to a lower level. For example, people who are 60 years old are older than people who are 25 years old, and were born during the baby boom generation.

Variables at the ordinal level of measurement have fewer statistical options than those at the ratio level, but more than those at the nominal level. Thus, the ordinal level of measurement is lower than the ratio level, but higher than the nominal level. For example, suppose we ask new clients entering a substance abuse program how often they use alcohol, how often they use opiate drugs, and how often they use hallucinogenic drugs—with the response categories *often*, *rarely*, or *never*. At the ordinal level, we would know that the person answering *often* regarding any substance uses that substance more often than the person who answers *never*. At the nominal level, we would know that the person answering *never* to opiates and to hallucinogens, but often to alcohol, can be classified nominally into a group whose drug of choice is alcohol.

Although ratio measures can be reduced to ordinal ones, converting an ordinal measure to a ratio measure is not possible. More generally, you cannot convert a lower-level measure to a higher-level one. That's a one-way street worth remembering.

CODING

Today, quantitative analysis is almost always done by computer programs such as SPSS and MicroCase. For these programs to work their magic, they must be able to read the data you've collected in your research. If you've conducted a survey, for example, some of your data are inherently numerical: age or income, for example. Although the writing and check marks on a questionnaire are qualitative in nature, a scribbled age is easily converted to quantitative data. Thus, if a respondent reports her age as *sixty-five,* you can just enter *65* into the computer.

Other data are also easily quantified: Transforming *male* and *female* into "1" and "2" is hardly rocket science. Researchers can also easily assign numerical representations to such variables as *religious affiliation, ethnicity,* and *region of the country.*

Some data are more challenging, however. If a survey respondent tells you that he or she thinks the biggest problem facing social service delivery in California today is "immigration from Mexico," the computer can't process that response numerically. You must translate by *coding* the responses. We have already discussed coding in connection with content analysis (Chapter 16) and again in connection with qualitative data analysis (Chapter 19). Now we look at coding specifically for quantitative analysis.

To conduct a quantitative analysis, researchers often must engage in a coding process after the data have been collected. For example, open-ended questionnaire items result in nonnumerical responses that must be coded before analysis. As with content analysis, the task is to reduce a wide variety of idiosyncratic items of information to a more limited set of attributes that compose a variable. Suppose, for example, that a survey researcher asks respondents, "What is your occupation?" The responses to such a question will vary considerably. Although it will be possible to assign each reported occupation a separate numerical code, this procedure will not facilitate analysis, which typically depends on several subjects having the same attribute.

The occupation variable has many pre-established coding schemes. One such scheme distinguishes professional and managerial occupations, clerical occupations, semiskilled occupations, and so forth. Another scheme distinguishes among different sectors of the economy: manufacturing, health, education, commerce, and so on. Still other schemes combine both.

The chosen occupational coding scheme should be appropriate to the theoretical concepts being examined. For some studies, coding all occupations as either white-collar or blue-collar might be sufficient. For others, self-employed and not self-employed might be sufficient. Or a peace researcher might wish to know only whether or not an occupation depended on the defense establishment.

Although the coding scheme ought to be tailored to meet the analysis's particular requirements, keep one general guideline in mind: If the data are coded to maintain considerable detail, then code categories can always be combined during an analysis that does not require such detail. Appendix D describes how to do this in SPSS, using the "Transform/Recode" menu option. It is usually wise to create a new variable ("Into Different Variables") so you'll have the new set of categories without losing the original details. In this SPSS procedure, you (1) select the variable to recode, (2) give a name to the new variable, and (3) indicate which codes on the old variable will be included in each of the codes of the new variable. If the data are coded into relatively few, gross categories, however, there is no way to re-create the original detail during analysis, so be sure to code your data in somewhat more detail than you plan to use in the analysis.

Developing Code Categories

There are two basic approaches to the coding process. First, you may begin with a relatively well-developed coding scheme derived from your research purpose. Thus, as suggested previously, the peace researcher might code occupations in terms of their relationship to the defense establishment. Or you may want to use an existing coding scheme so that you can compare your findings with those of previous research.

The alternative method is to generate codes from your data as discussed in Chapter 19. Let's say we've conducted a self-administered survey of clients who

Table 20-1 Responses That Can Be Coded "Financial Concerns"

RESPONSE	FINANCIAL CONCERNS
Service fees are too high	X
Not enough parking spaces	
Services are not helpful	
Have to wait too long to be seen	
No appointment times during evenings or weekends	X
Receptionists are rude	
No child-care services provided during appointments	X
Cannot afford transportation	X
Did not like my social worker	
No bilingual staff	

prematurely terminated our agency's services, asking them why they terminated. Here are a few of the answers they might have written in:

Service fees are too high

Not enough parking spaces

Services are not helpful

Have to wait too long to be seen

No appointment times during evenings or weekends

Receptionists are rude

No child-care services provided during appointments

Cannot afford transportation

Did not like my social worker

No bilingual staff

Take a minute to review these responses and see whether you can identify some of the categories represented. There is no right answer, but several coding schemes might be generated from these answers.

Table 20-2 Responses Coded as "Staff" and "Nonstaff"

RESPONSE	STAFF	NONSTAFF
Service fees are too high		X
Not enough parking spaces		X
Services are not helpful		
Have to wait too long to be seen		
No appointment times during evenings or weekends		
Receptionists are rude	X	
No child-care services provided during appointments		X
Cannot afford transportation		X
Did not like my social worker	X	
No bilingual staff	X	

Let's start with the first response: "Service fees are too high." What general areas of concern does that response reflect? One obvious possibility is "Financial Concerns." Are there other responses that would fit that category? Table 20-1 shows which of the questionnaire responses could fit.

In more general terms, the first answer can also be seen as reflecting nonstaff concerns. This categorization would be relevant if your research interest included the distinction between staff and nonstaff concerns. If that were the case, then the responses might be coded as shown in Table 20-2.

Notice that we didn't code three of the responses in Table 20-2: (1) *Services are not helpful*, (2) *Have to wait too long to be seen*, and (3) *No appointment times during evenings or weekends*. We did not code them because they could be seen as representing both categories. Services may not be helpful because of ineffectual staff or because the agency doesn't offer the type of services clients feel they really need. Having to wait too long to be seen might be the result either of staff not being punctual or of agency procedures. Inability to get evening or weekend appointments might be the result of staff inflexibility or agency rules.

This signals the need to refine the coding scheme we are developing. Depending on our research purpose, we might be especially interested in identifying any problems that conceivably could have a staffing element; hence we'd code the above three responses "Staff." Just as reasonably, however, we might be more interested in identifying problems that conceivably were more administrative in nature and would code the responses accordingly. Or, as another alternative, we might create a separate category for responses that involved both staff and nonstaff matters.

As these examples illustrate, there are many possible schemes for coding a set of data. Your choices should match your research purposes and reflect the logic that emerges from the data themselves. Often, you'll find yourself modifying the code categories as the coding process proceeds. Whenever you change the list of categories, however, you must review the data already coded to see whether changes are in order.

Like the set of attributes composing a variable, and like the response categories in a closed-ended questionnaire item, code categories should be both exhaustive and mutually exclusive. Every piece of information being coded should fit into one and only one category. Problems arise whenever a given response appears to fit equally into more than one code category or whenever it fits into no category. Both signal a mismatch between your data and your coding scheme.

If you're fortunate enough to have assistance in the coding process, then you'll need to train your coders in the definitions of code categories and show them how to use those categories properly. To do so, explain the meaning of the code categories and give several examples of each. To make sure your coders fully understand what you have in mind, code several cases ahead of time. Then ask your coders to code the same cases without knowing how you coded them. Finally, compare your coders' work with your own. Any discrepancies will indicate an imperfect communication of your coding scheme to your coders. Even with perfect agreement between you and your coders, however, it's best to check the coding of at least a portion of the cases throughout the coding process.

If you're not fortunate enough to have assistance in coding, then you should still verify your own reliability as a coder. Nobody's perfect, especially a researcher hot on the trail of a finding. Suppose that you're coding the reasons given by runaway adolescents as to why they ran away. Suppose your hunch is that most have run away because they were abused at home. The danger is that you might unconsciously bias your coding to fit your hunch. For example, you might code as *abuse* responses that merely referred to parents being too harsh in their discipline. You might not consider that some adolescents might deem things such as being grounded as harsh discipline. If at all possible, then, get someone else to code some of your cases to see whether that person makes the same assignments you did. Ideally, that person should not have the same predilection you have and should not be aware of the hypothesis you are hoping to support.

Codebook Construction

The end product of the coding process is the conversion of data items into numerical codes. These codes represent attributes composing variables that, in turn, are assigned locations within a data file. A **codebook** is a document that describes the locations of variables and lists the assignments of codes to the attributes composing those variables.

A codebook serves two essential functions. First, it is the primary guide used in the coding process. Second, it is your guide for locating variables and interpreting codes in your data file during analysis. If you decide to correlate two variables as a part of your analysis of your data, the codebook tells you where to find the variables and what the codes represent.

Figure 20-2 is a partial codebook created from two variables from the General Social Survey. There is no one right format for a codebook, but we have presented some of the common elements in this example.

Several elements are worth noting in the partial codebook in Figure 20-2. First, each variable is identified by an abbreviated variable name: *POLVIEWS, ATTEND*. We can determine the church attendance of respondents, for example, by referencing *ATTEND*. In this example, we have used the format established by the General Social Survey, which has been carried over into SPSS. Realize that other data sets or other analysis programs might format variables differently. Some use numerical codes in place of abbreviated names, for example. You must, however, have some identifier that will allow you to locate and use the variable in question.

Next, every codebook should contain the full definition of the variable. In the case of a question-

POLVIEWS

We hear a lot of talk these days about liberals and conservatives. We're going to show you a seven-point scale on which the political views that people might hold are arranged from extremely liberal—point 1—to extremely conservative—point 7. Where would you place yourself on this scale?

_______ 1. Extremely liberal

_______ 2. Liberal

_______ 3. Slightly liberal

_______ 4. Moderate, middle of the road

_______ 5. Slightly conservative

_______ 6. Conservative

_______ 7. Extremely conservative

_______ 8. Don't know

_______ 9. No answer

ATTEND

How often do you attend religious services?

_______ 0. Never

_______ 1. Less than once a year

_______ 2. About once or twice a year

_______ 3. Several times a year

_______ 4. About once a month

_______ 5. 2–3 times a month

_______ 6. Nearly every week

_______ 7. Every week

_______ 8. Several times a week

_______ 9. Don't know, No answer

Figure 20-2 A Partial Codebook

naire, this would be the exact wording of the question asked; as we've seen earlier, the wording of questions has a strong influence on the answers returned. In the case of *POLVIEWS,* you know that respondents were handed a card containing the several political categories and asked to pick the one that best fit them.

Your codebook will also indicate the attributes composing each variable. Thus in *POLVIEWS,* respondents could characterize their political orientations as "Extremely liberal," "Liberal," "Slightly liberal," and so forth. Finally, notice that each attribute also has a numeric label: "Extremely liberal" in *POLVIEWS* is code category "1," for example. These numeric codes are used in various manipulations of the data: For example, you might decide to combine categories 1, 2, and 3 (combining all of the "liberal" responses). It's easier to do this using code numbers than lengthy names. (You can visit the GSS codebook online at www.icpsr.umich.edu/GSS99/codebook.htm. If you know the symbolic name, such as POLVIEWS, you can locate it in the Mnemonic index. Otherwise, you can browse the Subject index to find all the different questions that have been asked regarding a particular topic.)

DATA ENTRY

In addition to transforming data into quantitative form, researchers need to convert data into a machine-readable format so that computers can read and manipulate the data. There are many ways of accomplishing this step, depending on the original form of your data and also the computer program you will use for analyzing the data. We'll simply introduce you to the process here. If you find yourself undertaking this task, you should be able to tailor your work to the particular data source and program you are using.

If your data have been collected by questionnaire, you might do your coding on the questionnaire itself. Then data-entry specialists (including yourself) could enter the data into, say, an SPSS data matrix or an Excel spreadsheet and later import it into SPSS.

Sometimes, social researchers use optical scan sheets for data collection. These sheets can be fed into machines that will convert the black marks into data that can be imported into the analysis program. This procedure will only work with research participants who are comfortable using such sheets, and it will usually be limited to closed-ended questions.

Sometimes, data entry occurs in the process of data collection. In computer-assisted telephone interviewing (CATI), for example, the interviewer keys responses directly into the computer, where the data are compiled for analysis (see Chapter 15). Even more effortlessly, online surveys can be constructed so that the respondents enter their own answers directly into the accumulating database without the need for an intervening interviewer or data-entry person.

DATA CLEANING

Whichever data-processing method you have used, the next important step is the elimination of errors—that is, "cleaning" the data. No matter how or how carefully the data have been entered, errors are inevitable. Depending on the data-processing method, these errors may result from incorrect coding, incorrect reading of written codes, incorrect sensing of black marks, and so forth.

A simple form of data cleaning is called **possible-code cleaning.** For any given variable, a specified set of legitimate attributes translates into a set of possible codes. In the variable gender, for example, there will be perhaps three possible codes: 1 for *male,* 2 for *female,* and 0 for *no answer.* If a case has been coded 7, say, in the variable assigned to gender, then an error clearly has been made.

Possible-code cleaning can be accomplished in two different ways. First, some computer programs can check for errors as the data are entered. If you tried to enter a 7 for gender in such programs, for example, the computer might "beep" and refuse the erroneous code. Other computer programs are designed to test for illegitimate codes in data files that weren't checked during data entry.

If you don't have access to these kinds of computer programs, then you can achieve a possible-code cleaning by examining the distribution of responses to each item in your data set. Thus, if you find your data set contains 350 people coded 1 on gender (for female), 400 people coded 2 (for male), and one person coded 7, then you'll probably suspect the 7 is an error.

Whenever you discover errors, the next step is to locate the appropriate source document (for example, the questionnaire), determine what code should have been entered, and make the necessary correction.

Although data cleaning is an essential step in data processing, it may be safely avoided in certain cases. Perhaps you will feel you can safely exclude the very few errors that appear in a given item—if the exclusion of those cases will not significantly affect your results. Or some inappropriate contingency responses may be safely ignored. If some men have been given motherhood status, then you can limit your analysis of this variable to women. However, you should not use these comments as rationalizations for sloppy research. "Dirty" data will almost always produce misleading research findings.

Once data have been fully quantified and entered into the computer, researchers can begin quantitative analysis. Let's look now at some basic descriptive statistics for analyzing and presenting data about a single variable. This is called **univariate analysis.** Later we'll look at tables and statistics that portray relationships among variables. This is called *bivariate* or *multivariate analysis,* depending on how many variables are examined simultaneously.

UNIVARIATE ANALYSIS

Univariate analysis is the examination of the distribution of cases on only one variable at a time. For example, if *gender* was measured, we would look at how many of the subjects were men and how many were women. We'll begin with the logic and formats for the analysis of univariate data.

Distributions

The most basic format for presenting univariate data is to report all individual cases; that is, to list the attribute for each case under study in terms of the variable in question. Suppose you are interested in the ages of clients served by your agency, and suppose hundreds of clients have been served. (Your data might have come from agency records.) The most direct manner of reporting the ages of clients would be to list them: 63, 57, 49, 62, 80, 72, 55, and so forth. Such a report would provide your reader with the fullest details of the data, but it would be too cumbersome for most purposes. You could arrange your data in a somewhat more manageable form without losing any of the detail by reporting that 5 clients were 38 years old, 7 were 39, 18 were 40, and so forth. Such a format would avoid duplicating data on this variable. It provides a **frequency distribution,** which describes the number of times the various attributes of a variable are observed in a sample.

For an even more manageable format—with a certain loss of detail—you could report clients' ages as *marginals,* which are frequency distributions of *grouped data:* 246 clients under 45 years of age, 517 between 45 and 50 years of age, and so forth. In this case, your reader would have fewer data to examine and interpret, but he or she would not be able to reproduce fully the original ages of all the clients. Thus, for example, the reader would have no way of knowing how many clients were 41 years of age.

The preceding example presented marginals in the form of raw numbers. An alternative form would be the use of *percentages.* Thus, for example, you could report that *x* percent of the clients were under 45, *y* percent were between 45 and 50, and so forth. (See Table 20-3.) In computing percentages, you frequently must decide from what base to compute—that is, the number that represents 100 percent. In the most straightforward examples, the base is the total number of cases under study. A problem arises, however, whenever cases have missing data. Let's as-

Table 20-3 An Illustration of a Univariate Analysis

AGES OF AGENCY CLIENTS (HYPOTHETICAL)	PERCENTAGE
Under 35	9%
36–45	21
46–55	45
56–65	19
66 and older	6
	100% = (433)
No data =	(18)

sume, for example, that you have conducted a survey in which respondents were asked to report their ages. If some respondents failed to answer that question, then you have two alternatives. First, you might still base your percentages on the total number of respondents, reporting those who failed to give their ages as a percentage of the total. Second, you could use the number of persons giving an answer as the base from which to compute the percentages. You should still report the number who did not answer, but they would not figure in the percentages.

The choice of a base depends wholly on the purposes of the analysis. If you wish to compare the age distribution of your survey sample with comparable data that describe the population from which the sample was drawn, then you probably will want to omit the "no answers" from the computation. Your best estimate of the age distribution of all respondents is the distribution for those who answer the question. Because "no answer" is not a meaningful age category, its presence among the base categories would confuse the comparison of sample and population figures. (See Table 20-3 for an example.)

Central Tendency

Beyond simply reporting marginals, you may choose to present your data in the form of summary **averages,** or measures of *central tendency*. Your options in this regard are the **mode** (the most frequent attribute, either grouped or ungrouped), the arithmetic **mean,** and the **median** (the *middle* attribute in the ranked distribution of observed attributes). Here's how the three averages would be calculated from a set of data.

Suppose that you're analyzing the case records of an adolescent residential facility whose clients range in age from 13 to 19, as indicated in the accompanying table.

AGE	NUMBER
13	3
14	4
15	6
16	8
17	4
18	3
19	3

Now that you've seen the actual ages of the 31 clients, how old would you say they are in general, or on the average? Let's look at three different ways to answer that question.

The easiest average to calculate is the mode, or the most frequent value. As you can see, there were more 16-year-olds (8 of them) than any other age, so the modal age is 16, as indicated in Figure 20-3.

Figure 20-3 also demonstrates how to calculate the mean. There are three steps: (1) Multiply each age by the number of clients of that age, (2) total the results of all those multiplications, and (3) divide that total by the number of clients. As indicated in Figure 20-3, the mean age in this illustration is 15.87.

The median represents the "middle" value: Half are above it, half below. If we had the *precise ages* of each client (for example, 17 years and 124 days), we'd be able to arrange all 31 subjects in order by age, and the median for the whole group would be the age of the middle subject.

As you can see, however, we do not know precise ages; our data constitute "grouped data" in this regard: Three people who are not precisely the same age have been grouped in the category "13 years old," for example.

Figure 20-3 illustrates the logic of calculating a median for grouped data. Because there are 31 clients altogether, the "middle" client would be number 16, if they were arranged by age: 15 would be younger, and 15 would be older. Look at the bottom portion of Figure 20-3: The middle person is one of the 16-year-olds.

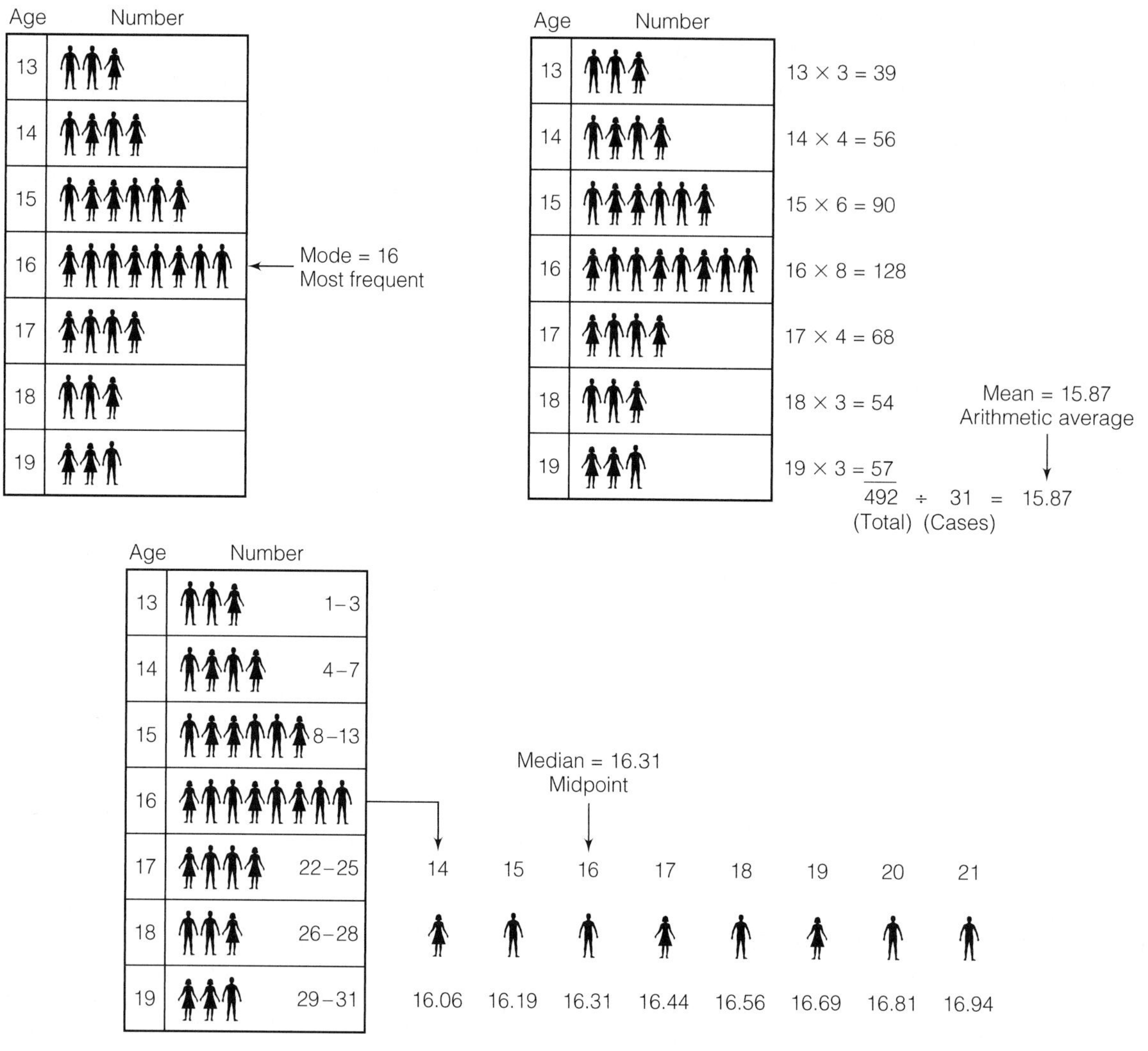

Figure 20-3 Three "Averages"

In the enlarged view of that group, we see that number 16 is the third from the left.

Because we do not know the precise ages of the clients in this group, the statistical convention here is to assume they are evenly spread along the width of the group. In this instance, the possible ages of the clients go from 16 years and no days to 16 years and 364 days. Strictly speaking, the range, then, is 364/365 days. As a practical matter, it's sufficient to call it one year.

If the eight clients in this group were evenly spread from one limit to the other, they would be one-eighth of a year apart from each other—a 0.125-year interval. Look at Figure 20-3 and you'll see that if we place the first client half the interval from the lower limit and add a full interval to the age of each successive client, the final one is half an interval from the upper limit.

What we have done, therefore, is to calculate, hypothetically, the precise ages of the eight clients—assuming their ages were spread out evenly. Having done that, we merely note the age of the middle client—16.31—and that is the median age for the group. Whenever the total number of clients is an even number, of course, there is no middle case. In that case, you merely calculate the mean of the two values it falls between. Suppose there were one more 19-year-old, for example. The midpoint in that case would fall between number 16 and number 17. The mean would then be calculated as (16.31 + 16.44)/2 = 16.38.

In the research literature, you'll find both means and medians presented. Whenever means are presented, you should be aware that they are susceptible to extreme values: a few very large or very small numbers. At one time, for example, the (mean) average person in Redmond, Washington, had a net worth in excess of a million dollars. If you had visited Redmond, however, you would have found that the "average" resident did not live up to your idea of a millionaire. The very high mean reflected the influence of one extreme case among Redmond's 40,000 residents—Bill Gates of Microsoft, who had a net worth in excess of tens of billions of dollars. Clearly, the median wealth would have given you a more accurate picture of the residents of Redmond as a whole.

Here's another example of how extreme values can make the mean misleading, as discussed in a February 10, 2003, editorial in the *New Republic* magazine (p. 9). In President George W. Bush's 2003 State of the Union address, he promoted his proposed tax cut of $674 billion as enabling 92 million Americans to "keep an average of almost $1,100 more of their own money." Hearing this, "average" taxpayers easily got the impression that the tax cut would save them nearly $1,100. But according to a study by the Urban–Brookings Tax Policy Center, this was not so. The mean tax cut would be $90,200 for taxpayers whose incomes exceed $1 million and $24,100 for taxpayers whose incomes are in the top 1 percent. The "average" taxpayer would receive a tax cut of only $256—much less than $1,100. Nevertheless, one mainstream newspaper, the *Christian Science Monitor,* described the president's tax proposal as making 92 million people eligible for a $1,000 per person tax cut. A well-known radio talk show host asserted, "Ninety-two million hardworking Americans are going to receive this year alone and then every year thereafter $1,083 because the president is reducing the amount of money they have to pay." Senate Majority Leader Bill Frist argued in favor of the president's proposed tax cut in an appearance on *Fox News Sunday* as follows, "When you say there are 92 million people who are going to be handed a check for $1,000 this year, your viewers right now, is that a tax cut for the rich?" (All of the above quotes are in the *New Republic,* February 10, 2003, p. 9.) This example illustrates the value to you of understanding basic statistical concepts even if you will never do any research yourself. One of those basic concepts, as we discussed above, is how extreme values can make the mean misleading. Let's now turn to another basic statistical concept related to this example, the concept of *dispersion.*

Dispersion

For the reader, averages have reduced the raw data to the most manageable form: a single number (or attribute) that represents all of the detailed data collected for the variable. This advantage comes at a cost, of course, because the reader cannot reconstruct the original data from an average. This disadvantage of averages can be somewhat alleviated by reporting summaries of the **dispersion** of responses, the distribution of values around some central value. The simplest measure of dispersion is the *range*: the distance separating the highest from the lowest value. Thus, besides reporting that our clients have a mean age of 15.87, we might also indicate that their ages ranged from 13 to 19.

There are many other measures of dispersion. In reporting intelligence test scores, for example, you might determine the *interquartile range,* the range of scores for the middle 50 percent of subjects. If the highest one-fourth had scores ranging from 120 to 150, and if the lowest one-fourth had scores ranging from 60 to 90, then you could report that the interquartile range was 90 to 120, or 30, with a mean score of, let's say, 102.

The **standard deviation** is a somewhat more sophisticated measure of dispersion, but one that is widely used. The utility of this measure is illustrated in Figure 20-4, which displays a normal curve. A *normal curve* is symmetrical and has a shape that resembles a bell. (It is sometimes called a *bell-shaped curve* or simply a *bell curve.*) When we can assume that our data have a normal distribution (that is, when they are distributed in the shape of a normal curve), then approximately 34 percent (.3413) of our sample data will fall within one standard deviation above the mean, and another 34 percent will fall within one standard deviation below the mean, as illustrated in Figure 20-4. That leaves almost one-third of the sample values falling more than one standard deviation away from the mean (approximately 16 percent are more than one standard deviation above the mean, and approximately 16 percent are more than one standard deviation below the mean). Knowing this, we can get a sense of how far away from the mean the values in our data are falling by calculating the standard deviation.

For example, suppose a large state mental health department's mean caseload size for its case managers working with people with long-term mental disorders is 28, and its standard deviation is 2. If we assume a normal distribution of caseload size, then we know that approximately 68 percent of case managers have

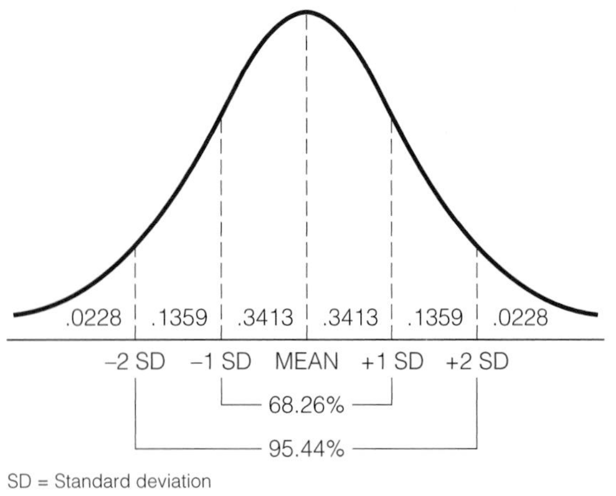

Figure 20-4 Standard Deviation Proportions of the Normal Curve

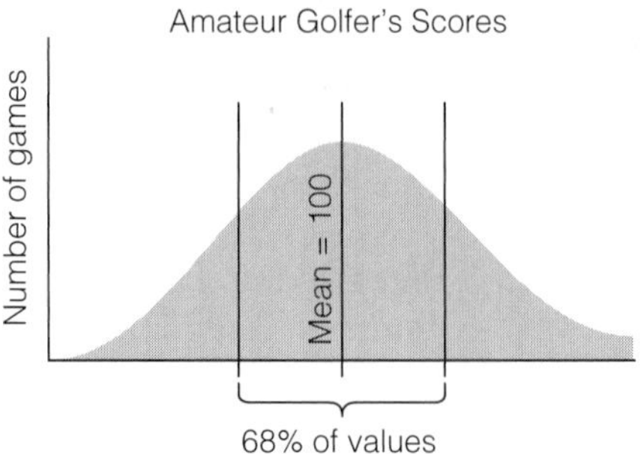

B. Low standard deviation = tightly clustered values

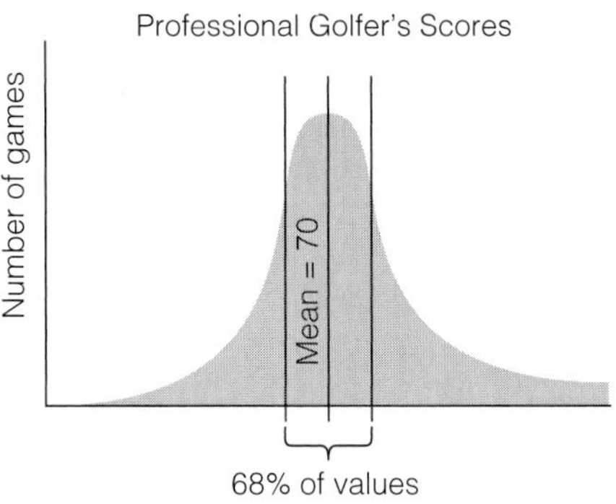

Figure 20-5 High and Low Standard Deviations

caseload sizes between 26 and 30 (with approximately 34 percent between 26 and 28, and 34 percent between 28 and 30). We would also know that approximately 16 percent had caseload sizes of less than 26, and some 16 percent had caseload sizes of more than 30. Because the case management research literature tends to recommend that caseload sizes should not much exceed 30 (Rubin, 1987), we might portray that state's caseload size as conforming reasonably well to what is recommended.

Suppose another state reports a mean caseload size of 25, but with a standard deviation of 15. Although that state's mean of 25 is lower than the first state's mean of 28, approximately 16 percent of its case managers have caseload sizes in excess of 40 (25 plus one standard deviation of 15), and approximately 34 percent have caseload sizes somewhere between 25 and 40 (as compared to 28 and 30 for the first state). Therefore, despite the lower mean in the second state, we might portray the first state's caseload sizes more favorably, because far fewer of its case managers were dispersed far above the mean (or far above the recommended caseload size).

Figure 20-5 further illustrates how a higher standard deviation means that data are more dispersed, whereas a lower standard deviation means they are more bunched together. Notice that the professional golfer not only has a lower mean score but also is more consistent—represented by the smaller standard deviation. The duffer, on the other hand, has a higher average and is also less consistent, often doing much better or much worse.

Now that we see the value in knowing the standard deviation (and do not just rely exclusively on statistics that portray central tendency), you may be wondering how to calculate it. If you'd like to find out, we recommend the book *Statistics for Evidence-Based Practice and Evaluation*. (The citation for that book appears in the Additional Readings section at the end of this chapter.) We won't go into the calculations here for two reasons: (1) You probably have access to computer software that can calculate it for you, and if you don't you can find websites that will do it, as indicated in the Internet Exercises at the end of this chapter. (2) We don't want you to lose focus on the meaning of the statistic, which is easy to do when confronted with the manual calculations.

Continuous and Discrete Variables

The calculations we've been discussing regarding central tendency and dispersion are not appropriate for all variables. In line with our earlier discussion in this chapter regarding levels of measurement, we can examine two types of variables: *continuous* and *discrete*. Age is a continuous, ratio variable; it increases steadily in tiny fractions instead of jumping from category to category as does a discrete variable such as gender or military rank. If discrete variables were being analyzed—a nominal or ordinal variable, for example—some of the techniques discussed here would not be applicable. Strictly speaking, medians, means, and standard deviations should be calculated only for interval and ratio data. If the variable in question were gender, for example, raw number or percentage marginals would be appropriate and useful analyses. Calculating the mode would be a legitimate, though not very revealing, analysis, but reports of mean, median, or dispersion summaries would be inappropriate. Although researchers can sometimes learn something of value by violating rules like these, you should only do so with caution.

There are, however, numerous "gray-area" situations in the calculation of averages. Suppose, for example, that you were assessing clients' satisfaction with the services they received by asking them to rate those services on a four-point scale: 4 = very satisfied, 3 = satisfied, 2 = dissatisfied, and 1 = very dissatisfied. You should note that this would be an ordinal-level measurement because you would have no reason to believe that the distance from rating 1 (very dissatisfied) to rating 2 (dissatisfied) is the same as the distance between rating 2 and rating 3 (satisfied), and so on. Consequently, calculating the mean rating or the standard deviation for a large number of clients would be technically questionable because such calculations would treat these ordinal-level ratings as if they were real values.

Yet such technical violations are commonly found and can still be useful. A mean score across all clients may not have a precise mathematical meaning in regard to client satisfaction, but it could be useful in comparing large numbers of ratings across client subgroups. For example, suppose the mean rating from ethnic minority clients was 1.4, as compared to a mean rating of 3.2 from white clients. Despite its imprecise meaning, this comparison would provide a clear and useful indication that the two groups do not express the same levels of satisfaction and that you ought to assess and deal with the reasons for the difference. (We make similar comparisons all the time, by the way, when we discuss students' grade point averages!)

The key here is *utility*. If you find that a researcher's statistical calculations are useful in guiding practice, then you should be somewhat lenient in the application of statistical techniques to data that do not warrant them. The other edge of this sword, however, is the danger of being lulled into thinking that the results represent something truly precise. In this case, for example, you might question the utility and appropriateness of carrying the means and standard deviations out to three decimal places.

Detail versus Manageability

In presenting univariate—and other—data, you will be constrained by two often-conflicting goals. You should attempt to provide your reader with the fullest degree of detail about those data but also present the data in a manageable form. These two goals often directly counter each other, so you'll find yourself continually seeking the best compromise between them. One useful solution is to report a given set of data in more than one form. In the case of age, for example, you might report the distribution of ungrouped ages *plus* the mean age and standard deviation.

"Collapsing" Response Categories

"Textbook examples" of tables are often simpler than you'll typically find in published research reports or in your own analyses of data, so this section and the next one address two common problems and suggest solutions.

Let's begin by turning to the data reported in Table 20-4, which reports data collected in a multinational poll conducted by the *New York Times*, CBS News, and the *Herald Tribune* in 1985 concerning attitudes about the United Nations. The question reported in Table 20-4 deals with general attitudes about the way the United Nations was handling its job.

Here's the question: How do people in the five nations reported in Table 20-4 compare in their support for the kind of job the United Nations was doing? As you review the table, you may find there are simply so many numbers that it's hard to see any meaningful pattern.

Part of the problem with Table 20-4 lies in the relatively small percentages of respondents selecting the two extreme response categories: The United Nations is doing a very good or a very poor job. Furthermore, although we might be tempted to read only the second line of the table—those saying "good job"—that would be improper. Looking at only the second row, we would conclude that West Germany and the United States were the most positive (46 percent) about the United Nations' performance, followed closely by

Table 20-4 Attitudes toward the United Nations: "How is the UN doing in solving the problems it has had to face?"

RESPONSE	WEST GERMANY	BRITAIN	FRANCE	JAPAN	UNITED STATES
Very good job	2%	7%	2%	1%	5%
Good job	46	39	45	11	46
Poor job	21	28	22	43	27
Very poor job	6	9	3	5	13
Don't know	26	17	28	41	10

Source: "5-Nation Survey Finds Hope for U.N.," *New York Times,* June 26, 1985, p. 6.

Table 20-5 Collapsing Extreme Categories

CATEGORY	WEST GERMANY	BRITAIN	FRANCE	JAPAN	UNITED STATES
Good job or better	48%	46%	47%	12%	51%
Poor job or worse	27	37	25	48	40
Don't know	26	17	28	41	10

France (45 percent), with Britain (39 percent) less positive than any of those three, and Japan (11 percent) the least positive of all.

This procedure is inappropriate in that it ignores all those respondents who gave the most positive answer of all: "very good job." In a situation such as this, you should combine or "collapse" the two ends of the range of variation. In this instance, combine "very good" with "good" and "very poor" with "poor." If you were to do this in the analysis of your own data, it would be wise to add the raw frequencies together and recompute percentages for the combined categories, but in analyzing a published table such as this one, you can simply add the percentages as illustrated by the results shown in Table 20-5.

With the collapsed categories illustrated in Table 20-5, we can now rather easily read across the several national percentages of people who said the United Nations was doing at least a good job. Now the United States appears the most positive; Germany, Britain, and France are only slightly less positive and nearly indistinguishable from one another; and Japan stands alone in its quite low assessment of the United Nations' performance. Although the conclusions to be drawn now do not differ radically from what we might have concluded from simply reading the second line of Table 20-4, we should note that Britain now appears relatively more supportive.

Here's the risk we'd like to spare you. Suppose you had hastily read the second row of Table 20-4 and noted that the British had a somewhat lower assessment of the job the United Nations was doing than was true of people in the United States, West Germany, and France. You might feel obliged to think up an explanation for why that was so—possibly creating an ingenious psychohistorical theory about the painful decline of the once powerful and dignified British Empire. Then, once you had touted your "theory," someone else might point out that a proper reading of the data would show the British were not actually less positive than the other three nations. This is not a hypothetical risk. Errors such as these happen frequently, but they can be avoided by collapsing answer categories where appropriate.

Table 20-6 Omitting the "Don't Knows"

CATEGORY	WEST GERMANY	BRITAIN	FRANCE	JAPAN	UNITED STATES
Good job or better	65%	55%	65%	20%	57%
Poor job or worse	35%	45%	35%	81%	44%

Handling "Don't Know"s

Tables 20-4 and 20-5 illustrate another common problem in the analysis of survey data. It's usually a good idea to give people the option of saying "Don't know" or "No opinion" when asking for their opinions on issues. But what do you do with those answers when you analyze the data?

Notice there is a good deal of variation in the national percentages saying "Don't know" in this instance, ranging from only 10 percent in the United States to 41 percent in Japan. The presence of substantial percentages saying they don't know can confuse the results of tables such as these. For example, were the Japanese so much less likely to say the United Nations was doing a good job simply because so many didn't express any opinion?

Here's an easy way to recalculate percentages with the "Don't know"s excluded. Look at the first column of percentages in Table 20-5: West Germany's answers to the question about the United Nations' performance. Notice that 26 percent of the respondents said they didn't know. This means that those who said "good" or "bad" job—taken together—represent only 74 percent (100 minus 26) of the whole. If we divide the 48 percent saying "good job or better" by .74 (the proportion giving any opinion), we can say that 65 percent "of those with an opinion" said the United Nations was doing a good or very good job (48%/.74 = 65%).

Table 20-6 presents the whole table with the "Don't know"s excluded. Notice that these new data offer a somewhat different interpretation than do the previous tables. Specifically, it would now appear that France and West Germany were the most positive in their assessments of the United Nations, with the United States and Britain a bit lower. Although Japan still stands out as lowest in this regard, it has moved from 12 percent to 20 percent positive.

At this point, having seen three versions of the data, you may be asking yourself, Which is the right one? The answer depends on your purpose in analyzing and interpreting the data. For example, if it is not essential to distinguish "very good" from "good," then it makes sense to combine them because it's easier to read the table.

Whether to include or exclude the "Don't know"s is harder to decide in the abstract. It may be a very important finding that such a large percentage of the Japanese had no opinion—if you wanted to find out whether people were familiar with the work of the United Nations, for example. On the other hand, if you wanted to know how people might vote on an issue, then it might be more appropriate to exclude the "Don't know"s on the assumption that they wouldn't vote or ultimately would be likely to divide their votes between the two sides of the issue.

In any event, the *truth* contained within your data is that a certain percentage said they didn't know and the remainder divided their opinions in whatever manner they did. Often, it's appropriate to report your data in both forms—with and without the "Don't know"s—so your readers can also draw their own conclusions.

BIVARIATE ANALYSIS

You may have noticed that in the previous three tables we moved from describing one variable at a time to two variables at a time. The two variables in those tables were *nation* and *attitude about the United Nations*. Thus, we moved from illustrations of univariate analysis, which looks at one variable at a time, to **bivariate analysis,** which examines *relationships* between two variables. By looking at relationships, bivariate analyses typically have explanatory purposes.

Notice, then, that Table 20-7 shows a relationship between gender attitudes toward sexual equality. It shows that the women under study are more support-

Table 20-7 "Do you approve or disapprove of the proposition that men and women should be treated equally in all regards?"

RESPONSE	MEN	WOMEN
Approve	63%	75%
Disapprove	37	25
	100%	100%
	(400)	(400)
No answer =	(12)	(5)

ive of equality than the men. Of the women, 75 percent approve of gender equality as compared to 63 percent of the men.

Percentaging a Table

One of the chief bugaboos for new data analysts is deciding on the appropriate "direction of percentaging" for any given table. In Table 20-7, for example, we have divided the group of subjects into two subgroups—men and women—and then described the attitudes of each subgroup. That is the correct method for constructing this table.

Notice, however, that it would have been possible—though inappropriate—to construct the table differently. We could have first divided the subjects into those who approve and those who disapprove of gender equality, and then we could have described each subgroup in terms of the percentages of men and women in each. This method would make no sense in terms of explanation, however.

Table 20-7 suggests that your gender will affect how you feel about gender equality. Had we used the other method of construction, the table would suggest that your attitude toward gender equality affects whether you are a man or a woman—which makes no sense; your attitude cannot determine your gender.

There is another, related problem that complicates the lives of new data analysts. How do you read a percentage table? There is a temptation to read Table 20-7 as follows: "Of the women, 75 percent approved and only 25 percent disapproved; therefore being a woman makes you more likely to approve." That is not the correct way to read the table, however. The conclusion that gender—as a variable—has an effect on attitudes must hinge on a comparison between men and women. Specifically, we note that *women are more likely than men* to approve of gender equality: comparing the 75 percent with the 63 percent. Suppose, for example, that 100 percent of the men approved. Regardless of the fact that women approved 3 to 1, it wouldn't make sense to say that being a woman increased the likelihood of approval. In fact, the opposite would be true in such a case. The comparison of subgroups, then, is essential in reading an explanatory bivariate table.

In constructing and presenting Table 20-7, we have used a convention called *percentage down*. This term means that you can add the percentages down each column to total 100 percent. You read this form of table across a row. For the row labeled "Approve," what percentage of the men approve? What percentage of the women approve?

The direction of percentaging in tables is arbitrary, and some researchers prefer to percentage across. They would organize Table 20-7 so that "men" and "women" were shown on the left side of the table, identifying the two rows, and "Approve" and "Disapprove" would appear at the top to identify the columns. The actual numbers in the table would be moved around accordingly, and each row of percentages would total 100 percent. In that case, you would read the table down a column, still asking what percentage of men and women approved. The logic and the conclusion would be the same in either case; only the form would be different.

In reading a table that someone else has constructed, therefore, you need to find out in which direction it has been percentaged. Usually, that will be apparent in the labeling of the table or in the logic of the variables being analyzed. As a last resort, however, you should add the percentages in each column and each row. If each column totals 100 percent, then the table has been percentaged down. If the rows total 100 percent each, then it has been percentaged across. The rule of thumb, then, is as follows:

1. If the table is percentaged down, read across.
2. If the table is percentaged across, read down.

Figure 20-6 reviews the logic by which we create percentage tables from two variables. We've used the same variables as in the previous example—gender and attitudes toward equality for men and women—but we have reduced the numbers to make the illustration more manageable.

A. Some men and women who either favor (=) sexual equality or don't (≠) favor it.

B. Separate the men and the women (the independent variable).

C. Within each gender group, separate those who favor equality from those who do not (the dependent variable).

D. Count the numbers in each cell of the table.

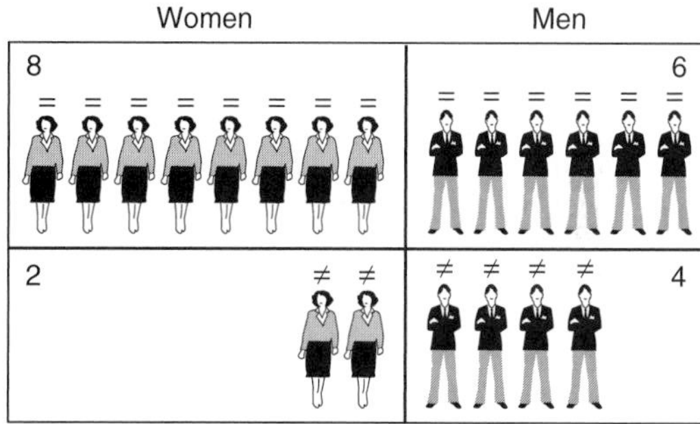

E. What percentage of the women favor equality?

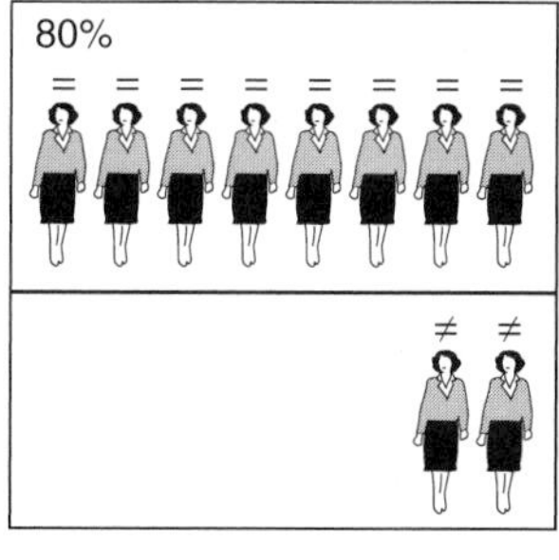

F. What percentage of the men favor equality?

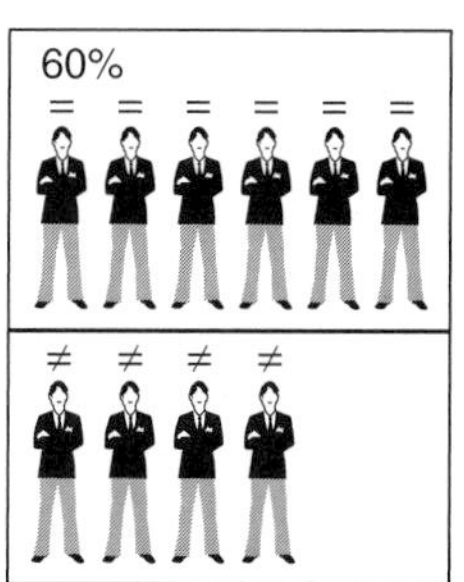

G. Conclusions

While a majority of both men and women favored sexual equality, women were more likely than men to do so.

Thus, gender appears to be one of the causes of attitudes toward sexual equality.

	Women	Men
Favor equality	80%	60%
Don't favor equality	20%	40%
Total	100%	100%

Figure 20-6 Percentaging a Table

Constructing and Reading Bivariate Tables

Let's now review the steps involved in the construction of explanatory bivariate tables:

1. The cases are divided into groups according to their attributes of the independent variable.

2. Each subgroup is then described in terms of attributes of the dependent variable.

3. Finally, the table is read by comparing the independent variable subgroups with one another in terms of a given attribute of the dependent variable.

Let's repeat the analysis of gender and attitudes toward gender equality following these steps. For the reasons just outlined, gender is the independent variable; attitudes toward gender equality constitute the dependent variable. Thus, we proceed as follows:

1. The cases are divided into men and women.

2. Each gender subgrouping is described in terms of approval or disapproval of gender equality.

3. Men and women are compared in terms of the percentages that approve of gender equality.

Bivariate Table Formats

Tables such as Table 20-7 are commonly called **contingency tables:** Values of the dependent variable are contingent on values of the independent variable. Although contingency tables are common in social work research, their format has never been standardized. As a result, a variety of formats will be found in research literature. As long as a table is easy to read and interpret, then there is probably no reason to strive for standardization. However, several guidelines should be followed in the presentation of most tabular data.

1. A table should have a heading or a title that succinctly describes what is contained in the table.

2. The original content of the variables should be clearly presented—in the table itself if at all possible, or in the text with a paraphrase in the table. This information is especially critical when a variable is derived from responses to an attitudinal question because the meaning of the responses will depend largely on the wording of the question.

3. The attributes of each variable should be clearly indicated. Complex categories will have to be abbreviated, but the meaning should be clear in the table and, of course, the full description should be reported in the text.

4. When percentages are reported in the table, the base on which they are computed should be indicated. It is redundant to present all of the raw numbers for each category; these could be reconstructed from the percentages and the bases. Moreover, the presentation of both numbers and percentages often makes a table confusing and more difficult to read.

5. If any cases are omitted from the table because of missing data ("no answer," for example), their numbers should be indicated in the table.

After following the above guidelines, you should examine your table and ask yourself, "Would readers be able to tell what each variable in this table is, and would they be able to interpret the overall meaning of this table, without having to read the narrative text of my report?" If the answer is no, then you'll probably need to make some improvements—perhaps changing the title of the table so that it more clearly portrays what the table contains, or perhaps more clearly labeling the table's variables or their attributes.

MULTIVARIATE ANALYSIS

A more complex form of explanation involves tables that include more than two variables. Typically this is done when we want to examine the relationship between an independent and a dependent variable while controlling for the effects of one or more extraneous (or moderating) variables. (Recall our discussion in Chapter 7 of extraneous, moderating, and control variables. Recall also our discussion of the elaboration model in Chapter 10.) Tables that include more than two variables are called *multivariate tables.* Likewise, when we interpret these tables, we engage in **multivariate analysis.**

Let's return to the example of attitudes toward gender equality. Suppose we believed age would also affect such attitudes, that young people would approve of gender equality more than older people. As the first step in table construction, we would divide the total sample into subgroups based on the various attributes of both independent variables simultaneously: young men, old men, young women, and old women. Then the several subgroups would be described in terms of the dependent variable, and comparisons would be made. Table 20-8 shows a hypothetical result.

Following the convention presented here, this table has also been percentaged down and thus should be read across. The interpretation of this table warrants several conclusions.

1. Among both men and women, younger people are more supportive of gender equality than older people. Among women, 90 percent of those younger than 30 and 60 percent of those 30 and older approve.

2. Within each age group, women are more supportive than men. Among those respondents younger than 30, 90 percent of the women approve, compared with 78 percent of the men. Among those 30 and older, 60 percent of the women and 48 percent of the men approve.

Table 20-8 Multivariate Relationship: Attitude, Sex, and Age: "Do you approve or disapprove of the proposition that men and women should be treated equally in all regards?"

	YOUNGER THAN 30		30 AND OLDER	
RESPONSE	WOMEN	MEN	WOMEN	MEN
Approve	90%	78%	60%	48%
Disapprove	10	22	40	52
	100%	100%	100%	100%
	(200)	(200)	(200)	(200)
No Answer =	(2)	(10)	(3)	(2)

Table 20-9 Simplification of Table 20-8, "Do you approve or disapprove of the proposition that men and women should be treated equally in all regards?"

	PERCENTAGE WHO APPROVE	
AGE	WOMEN	MEN
Less than 30	90	78
	(200)	(200)
30 and older	60	48
	(200)	(200)

3. As measured in the table, age appears to have a stronger effect on attitudes than gender. For both men and women, the effect of age may be summarized as a 30 percentage point difference. Within each age group, the percentage point difference between men and women is 12.

4. Age and gender have independent effects on attitudes. Within a given attribute of one independent variable, different attributes of the second still affect attitudes.

5. Similarly, the two independent variables have a cumulative effect on attitudes. Young women are most supportive, and older men are the least supportive. (Notice that we are treating age as a second independent variable instead of as a control variable, which is also possible in multivariate analysis.)

A more efficient way to show the same multivariate explanation as in Table 20-8 is displayed in Table 20-9. Table 20-9 is more efficient because if we know that 90 percent of the women under 30 approve of gender equality, then we know automatically that 10 percent disapprove. So reporting the percentages of those who disapprove is unnecessary. In Table 20-9, the percentages of those who approve of gender equality are reported in the cells that represent the intersections of the two independent variables. The numbers presented in parentheses below each percentage represent the number of cases on which the percentages are based. Thus, for example, the reader knows that there are 200 women under 30 years of age in the sample, and 90 percent of those approved of gender equality. This shows, moreover, that 180 of those 200 women approved, and that the other 20 (or 10 percent) disapproved. This new table is easier to read than the former one, and it does not sacrifice any detail.

DESCRIPTIVE STATISTICS AND QUALITATIVE RESEARCH

When statistics are reported to *describe* the characteristics of a sample or to *describe* the relationship among variables in a sample, they are called **descriptive statistics.** In contrast, when statistics go beyond just describing a set of sample observations and attempt to make *inferences* about causal processes or about a larger population, they are called **inferential statistics.** Both types of statistics apply more to quantitative than to qualitative research. The next two chapters will discuss inferential statistics. Before we go there, we'll end this chapter by illustrating the use of descriptive statistics in qualitative research.

The material you have been reading in this chapter clearly applies more to quantitative than to qualitative research, although it is not irrelevant to the latter. It is a mistake to believe that the distinction between qualitative and quantitative research is only about whether counting takes place or statistics are used. Researchers who interpret descriptive statistics often find that some of those statistics imply the need for a qualitative inquiry to understand their meaning better. Researchers who conduct qualitative studies rarely report elaborate statistical analyses, but they often find that counting some things is an inescapable part of detecting patterns or developing a deeper understanding of the phenomenon they are studying.

Suppose you are conducting a qualitative inquiry to gain a deeper understanding of what it is like to have a sleep disorder. Would your understanding of what it feels like to have the disorder be more or less superficial if, in addition to qualitative observations, you counted things such as the mean number of hours the people you observed slept and the proportion of nights they didn't sleep at all? You wouldn't want to rely on the numbers alone, and you certainly would want to emphasize how the individuals with the disorder subjectively and perhaps idiosyncratically felt about their lack of sleep. At the same time, though, knowing whether we are talking about someone who almost never sleeps versus someone who sleeps on average a handful of hours per night—perhaps with wild swings from night to night (that is, high dispersion)—gives us a more informed basis to consider their experience. If you tell us that such people's lack of sleep makes it hard for them to concentrate at work, for example, our ability to sense what that must be like for them might be enhanced if we know they are averaging only about one hour of sleep per night.

Here's an example that starts with a quantitative inquiry. Suppose you are administering a child welfare program that aims to improve parenting and preserve families. Your program's funding level is influenced by descriptive statistics about the number of days that children spend in out-of-home placements and scores on a scale that measure risk of child abuse. On both measures you find that the agency mean is mediocre and that the standard deviation is huge.

This prompts you to examine closely the univariate frequency distribution of each variable, and you find that in each distribution, most cases are not clustered near the mean. Instead, approximately one-third are way above the mean and one-third are way below the mean. You recognize the need to probe into the meaning of these findings to discover what is going on differently with the very successful and terribly unsuccessful cases, realizing that your mean is misleading and that what you find might imply ways to improve outcomes among cases such as those that currently have unsuccessful outcomes.

If you had solid hunches about what was accounting for the difference between the successful and unsuccessful cases, then you might examine additional variables quantitatively. However, you don't have a clue, so you decide to conduct a qualitative investigation, using a couple of social work doctoral students who are seeking hands-on practicum experience in doing qualitative research in an agency setting. They begin by interviewing practitioners qualitatively, probing into their ideas and recollections about what the practitioners did differently with their most and least successful cases. They also pore through case records in an unstructured, open-ended fashion looking for patterns that might distinguish the two sets of cases. Quickly they find that almost all of the cases with the very worst outcomes had been assigned to three particular practitioners, and almost all of the cases with the very best outcomes had been assigned to three other practitioners.

Nobody knows what might explain the differences in outcome between the two sets of practitioners, so the students decide to observe the six practitioners with extreme outcomes in a qualitative fashion in both their office sessions and home visits with clients. After collecting and analyzing a considerable amount of qualitative information, they begin to notice differences in the ways the two sets of practitioners work with parents. The practitioners with the more successful outcomes seem to be more prone toward providing services in the parents' homes, listening to parents empathically and helping them obtain needed resources, educating the parents about child development and child rearing, and teaching specific parenting skills. The ones with less successful outcomes seem to spend less time with parents, make fewer home visits, be less responsive to the concrete needs for resources parents express, and spend more time moralizing to them.

The students who are conducting the qualitative observations recognize that their insights and report will be more meaningful if they can describe the extent of the differences they so far have been observing qualitatively. For example, to just say one group did something more or less than another group is less meaningful in terms of the qualitative goal of developing a richer understanding of the phenomenon than saying that the successful practitioners averaged three home visits to each client per week as compared to the unsuccessful ones seeing clients only once a month and only in their offices.

So in their qualitative journal log of observational notes, the students begin including such quantitative information as the number and length of home visits versus office sessions, the number of times the practitioner obtains a resource, the number of empathic versus moralizing statements, and the amount of time spent teaching about parenting. We are not saying that these quantitative indicators are the only things or the main things the students will record. They will continue to record qualitative information, such as obtaining the clients' subjective perspectives on how they experience the practitioner's services. Moreover, the quantitative measures will have emerged from an analysis of the qualitative material collected earlier. Eventually, their report might stimulate others to conduct quantitative, hypothesis-testing studies to see if the patterns emerging from this qualitative study can be generalized beyond these six practitioners and their clients. As the never-ending process in the scientific search for understanding continues, those quantitative studies might stimulate future qualitative inquiries to discover the meanings of their findings. And so on.

Now let's consider a hypothetical example of a purely qualitative study. Perhaps you decide to pursue a Ph.D. degree in social work, for which you must produce a research dissertation. You decide to conduct a qualitative study like the one that Elliott Liebow (1993) conducted to portray the lives of homeless women. Your methodology relies on observation and informal conversational interviews with a small group of homeless women whom you come to know at a shelter and a soup kitchen where you volunteer to help and befriend them.

Perhaps you begin to find, as Liebow did, that what may seem irrational or aimless to most people might be rational and purposeful from the perspective of the homeless women. For example, perhaps you find that a reason they express for neglecting personal hygiene is to make oneself repulsive to men who are abusive and thus prevent victimization while sleeping in dangerous settings. If you begin to detect a pattern regarding this explanation for neglecting personal hygiene, then you might find yourself inescapably wondering how many of the homeless women you meet this explanation applies to. Was the first woman who expressed a rational explanation for neglecting personal hygiene the only one who felt this way? Indeed, it's hard to imagine how you could detect such a "pattern" in the first place without some awareness of the proportion of your observations that fit the pattern.

In this connection, reports of qualitative studies commonly comment about the proportion of observations that fit various qualitative categories. The researchers may not couch those comments in the context of formal tables of frequency distributions, particularly because they tend to deal with relatively small amounts of numbers. They may couch their quantitative allusions in imprecise terms such as most, or few, or often, but if you read many reports of qualitative research you are likely to find quite a few instances where the researcher obviously counted something. This point, and the more formal use of descriptive statistics in qualitative studies, is elaborated in the box "Numerical Descriptions in Qualitative Research."

NUMERICAL DESCRIPTIONS IN QUALITATIVE RESEARCH

Unfortunately, some people think in black and white or stereotypical ways about quantitative and qualitative studies and the investigators who conduct them. In their most extreme forms, these stereotypes may portray quantitative researchers as inchworms who can do nothing but count and qualitative researchers as never counting anything and perhaps having some kind of math phobia. Those who think qualitative researchers never count anything or never use statistics might find their stereotypes dispelled by reading two compendiums of qualitative studies edited or co-edited by social work professors. The two books are *Qualitative Studies in Social Work Research*, edited by Catherine Reissman (Sage, 1994), and *Qualitative Methods in Family Research*, edited by Jane Gilgun, Kerry Daly, and Gerald Handel (Sage, 1992). In the latter volume, we found that the researchers alluded to doing some counting in nine of the 16 studies. In four studies, the counting was mentioned only in imprecise terms (which we'll italicize), as exemplified by the following excerpts:

> Participants *often* prescribed to more than one personal theory . . . members of couples *frequently* shared the same . . . theories (p. 54).
>
> Caregivers were *often* optimistic. . . . Weight *loss* or *gain*, sleep disturbances, and *reduced* exercise were characteristic of this phase (p. 75).

(*continued*)

> Caregivers *often* spend *a great deal* of time at the bedside of the PWA [person with AIDS] (p. 77).
>
> . . . retirement—*with few exceptions*—has meant husbands' retirement (p. 274).

In five of the studies, the counting clearly involved descriptive statistics, reported in precise terms, usually in connection with describing study participants. Here are some excerpts:

> The average age of the elders was 65, with a range of 48 to 83 . . . one-quarter were unsure of their marital status (p. 90).
>
> The mean age of the sample was 31 for husbands and 30 for wives. The mean length of marriage was 6 years. The couples had experienced a fertility problem for a mean average of 5 years (p. 107).
>
> The mean age of daughters in the study was 55 years, although there was a range from 33 to 72. More than half (52%) were married, although 21% were widowed and 14% were divorced (p. 204).

In one study, Mark Rank (1992) used qualitative methods to explain quantitative data that indicated that women on welfare have a low fertility rate. The quantitative data are presented in two tables, one of which displays the number and proportion of births in relation to six separate time periods. The other shows the relationship between fertility rates and five demographic variables for different populations.

The Reissman volume contains 10 qualitative studies, four of which report some quantitative data, similarly to the Gilgun book. In one study, Denise Burnette (1994) used a multivariate frequency table to portray her sample of elderly people. Her narrative further described her sample in terms of means and proportions for various demographic characteristics. Later in her report she referred to a *median* of 13 years of long-term illness, the proportion of elderly who were cognitively intact, the amount of hours spent watching television, the proportion speaking with friends and relatives at least four times a week, and people in the lowest *quartile* or *quintile* of poor health.

The editors of these two volumes have made valuable contributions to the social work research literature. Their work illustrates the diversity in qualitative research, its complementarity with quantitative research, and the ways descriptive data are and can be used in qualitative studies.

Here is one more example that demonstrates the special power that can be gained from a combination of qualitative and quantitative approaches. When David Silverman wanted to compare the cancer treatments received by patients in private clinics with those in Britain's National Health Service, he primarily chose in-depth analyses of the interactions between doctors and patients:

> My method of analysis was largely qualitative and . . . I used extracts of what doctors and patients had said as well as offering a brief ethnography of the setting and of certain behavioural data. In addition, however, I constructed a coding form which enabled me to collate a number of crude measures of doctor and patient interactions.
>
> (SILVERMAN 1993:163)

Not only did the numerical data fine-tune Silverman's impressions based on his qualitative observations, but his in-depth understanding of the situation allowed him to craft an ever more appropriate quantitative analysis. Listen to the interaction between qualitative and quantitative approaches in this lengthy discussion:

> My overall impression was that private consultations lasted considerably longer than those held in the NHS clinics. When examined, the data indeed did show that the former were almost twice as long as the latter (20 minutes as against 11 minutes) and that the difference was statistically highly significant. However, I recalled that, for special reasons, one of the NHS clinics had abnormally short consultations. I felt a fairer comparison of consultations in the two sectors should exclude this clinic and should only compare consultations taken by a single doctor in both sectors. This subsample of cases revealed that the difference in length between NHS and private consultations was now reduced to an average of under 3 minutes.
>
> This was still statistically significant, although the significance was reduced. Finally, however, if I compared only *new* patients seen by the same doctor, NHS patients got 4 minutes more on the average—34 minutes as against 30 minutes in the private clinic.
>
> (SILVERMAN 1993:163–64)

Main Points

• Nominal measures refer to those variables whose attributes are simply different from one another. An example would be gender.

• Ordinal measures refer to those variables whose attributes may be rank-ordered along some progression from more to less. An example would be the variable *prejudice* as composed of the attributes "very prejudiced," "somewhat prejudiced," and "not at all prejudiced."

• Interval measures refer to those variables whose attributes are not only rank-ordered but also separated by a uniform distance between them. An example would be IQ.

• Ratio measures are the same as interval measures except that ratio measures are also based on a true zero point. Age would be an example of a ratio measure because that variable contains the attribute *zero years old.*

• A given variable can sometimes be measured at different levels of measurement. Thus, age, which is potentially a ratio measure, may also be treated as interval, ordinal, or even nominal.

• Quantifying data is necessary when statistical analyses are desired.

• The attributes of a given variable are represented by numerical codes.

• A codebook is the document that describes the identifiers assigned to different variables and the codes assigned to represent different attributes.

• Data entry can be accomplished in a variety of ways. Increasingly, data are keyed directly into computer disk files.

• *Possible-code cleaning* refers to the process of checking to see that only those codes assigned to particular attributes—possible codes—appear in the data files. This process guards against one kind of data-processing error.

• Descriptive statistics is a method for presenting quantitative descriptions in a manageable form.

• Univariate analysis is the analysis of a single variable.

• The full original data collected with regard to a single variable are, in that form, usually impossible to interpret. Data reduction is the process of summarizing the original data to make them more manageable, all the while maintaining as much of the original detail as possible.

• Several techniques allow researchers to summarize their original data to make them more manageable while maintaining as much of the original detail as possible. Frequency distributions, averages, grouped data, and measures of dispersion are all ways of summarizing data concerning a single variable.

• A frequency distribution shows the number of cases that have each attribute of a given variable.

• Grouped data are created through the combination of attributes of a variable.

• Averages (the mean, median, and mode) reduce data to an easily manageable form, but they do not convey the original data's detail.

• Means are susceptible to extreme values; when a small number of extreme values distort the mean, the median can more accurately portray the average.

• Measures of dispersion give a summary indication of the distribution of cases around an average value.

• The standard deviation is one commonly used measure of dispersion.

• When constructing tables for the purpose of making subgroup comparisons, attention should be given as to whether and how best to collapse response categories and handle "Don't know"s.

• In contrast to univariate analysis, bivariate analysis examines *relationships* between two variables, and it typically does so for *explanatory* purposes.

• Bivariate analysis (1) divides cases into subgroups in terms of their attributes on some independent variable, (2) describes each subgroup in terms of some dependent variable, (3) compares the dependent variable descriptions of the subgroups, and (4) interprets any observed differences as a statistical association between the independent and dependent variables.

• Guidelines to follow when constructing bivariate tables include (1) giving the table a succinct heading that describes its contents; (2) presenting the original content of the variables in the table itself, if at all possible, or in the text with a paraphrase in the table; (3) clearly indicating the attributes of each variable; (4) indicating the base numbers from which any percentages were computed; and (5) indicating the number of cases omitted from the table because of missing data.

- Readers should be able to tell what each variable in a table is, and they should be able to interpret the overall meaning of this table without having to read the narrative text of the report.
- As a rule of thumb in interpreting bivariate percentage tables: (1) If the table is "percentaged down" then "read across" in making the subgroup comparisons, or (2) if it is "percentaged across" then "read down" in making subgroup comparisons.
- Multivariate analysis is a method of analyzing the simultaneous relationships among several variables; it may be used to more fully understand the relationship between two variables.
- The use of descriptive statistics often can enrich a qualitative study, and it is not uncommon to find quantitative data included in reports of qualitative research.

Review Questions and Exercises

1. What level of measurement—nominal, ordinal, interval, or ratio—describes each of the following variables?

a. Agency auspices (public versus private)

b. Attitudes about increased social welfare spending (strongly approve, approve, disapprove, strongly disapprove)

c. Number of students with field placements in social action organizations

2. Create a codebook—with column and code assignments—for the following questions in a case record:

a. Does the client attend a sheltered workshop?

Yes — If yes, which one?
Workshop A Workshop B

No

b. Client's level of disability:

Mild

Moderate

Severe or profound

Other:

c. Most important target problem:

Social skills

Vocational

Social environmental support system

Personal hygiene

Housekeeping skills

Psychopathology

Self-esteem

Residential living arrangements

Family stress

Other:

3. Create another codebook—with column and code assignments—for the following questions in a community survey:

a. What do you feel is the most important problem facing this community today?

b. In the spaces provided below, please indicate the three community problems that most concern you by putting a 1 beside the one that most concerns you, a 2 beside your second choice, and a 3 beside your third choice.

Crime

Traffic

Drug abuse

Pollution

Prejudice and discrimination

Inflation

Unemployment

Housing shortage

4. You have provided a 15-session psychoeducational support group intervention for people who recently completed inpatient treatment for substance abuse. Of the 10 clients who were in the group, two attended all 15 sessions, two attended 14 sessions, two attended 13 sessions, two attended 12 sessions, and two attended just one session.

a. Calculate the mean and the median number of sessions attended.

b. Which measure of central tendency, the mean or the median, do you feel is more appropriate to use in portraying the average number of sessions attended for the above data? Why?

5. Using the hypothetical data in the following table, construct and interpret tables showing:

a. The bivariate relationship between age and attitude toward transracial adoption

b. The bivariate relationship between ethnicity and attitude toward transracial adoption

c. The multivariate relationship linking age, ethnicity, and attitude toward transracial adoption

AGE	ETHNICITY	ATTITUDE TOWARD TRANSRACIAL ADOPTION	FREQUENCY
Young	White	Favor	90
Young	White	Oppose	10
Young	Minority	Favor	60
Young	Minority	Oppose	40
Old	White	Favor	60
Old	White	Oppose	40
Old	Minority	Favor	20
Old	Minority	Oppose	80

6. Construct multivariate tables that use hypothetical data on a social work research question of interest to you.

Internet Exercises

1. Go to the Research Assistant website at www.theresearchassistant.com/. This site provides a wide range of resources, tools, and other website links related to various aspects of the research process. Once there, you can click on the prompt for Research Tools, then Statistical Support, and then on an array of prompts connected to descriptive statistics. Among the resources you'll find are explanations of descriptive statistical procedures and concepts as well as online computation tools.

2. Over the years, the General Social Survey (GSS) has tracked public opinion on the Equal Rights Amendment (ERA), reporting the percentages of those who are in favor and opposed. Your assignment is to discover some of the reasons respondents have given for their opinions. Begin by going to www.icpsr.umich.edu/GSS99/codebook.htm. Look through the appendixes, find the one dealing with the coding of opinions on ERA, and copy three reasons people gave for supporting and three reasons for opposing the ERA.

Additional Readings

Rubin, Allen. 2007. *Statistics for Evidence-Based Practice and Evaluation*. Belmont, CA: Thomson Brooks/Cole. This practitioner-friendly book provides a more detailed and in-depth introduction to the quantitative data analysis concepts discussed in this chapter. Throughout the text it discusses those concepts as an inescapable part of evidence-based practice, and in a manner that illustrates their utility to practitioners.

Ziesel, Hans. 1957. *Say It with Figures*. New York: Harper & Row. This is an excellent discussion of table construction and other elementary analyses. Although the book is old, it is still perhaps the best available presentation of that specific topic. It is eminently readable and understandable and has many concrete examples.

CHAPTER 21

Inferential Data Analysis: Part 1

What You'll Learn in This Chapter

Here you'll learn about statistical procedures that are frequently used in social work research to guide decisions about what can be generalized about the relationships we observe in our findings.

INTRODUCTION

When we analyze data for descriptive purposes, our focus is limited to the data we have collected on our study's sample. Descriptive analysis does not provide a basis for generalizing beyond our particular study or sample. Even the results of bivariate or multivariate analyses that show relationships between different variables in our study do not provide sufficient grounds for inferring that those relationships exist in general or have any theoretical meaning.

But we seldom conduct research just to describe our samples per se; in most instances, our purpose is to make assertions about the larger population from which our sample has been selected or about the causal processes in general that explain why we have observed a particular relationship in our data. This chapter will examine **inferential statistics:** the statistical measures used for making such inferences and their logical bases.

CHANCE AS A RIVAL HYPOTHESIS

In earlier chapters of this book, we considered in depth many potential sources of error that impinge on our ability to make inferences about the relationships we observe in our findings. For example, we discussed various sorts of bias, threats to internal validity, and the need to control for extraneous variables. If not adequately controlled, these sources of error represent rival hypotheses, or alternative explanations, to the interpretations we seek to draw from our data. Thus, if our data indicate the hypothesized relationship between our independent and dependent variables exists but we haven't controlled for a critical extraneous variable that might plausibly explain as spurious the relationship we think we observe, then a rival hypothesis that contains that extraneous variable represents a plausible alternative explanation of our findings.

Another rival hypothesis, one that we haven't yet discussed, is *chance*. Chance has to do with *sampling error,* a concept covered in Chapter 14 (on sampling theory). It also pertains to the so-called luck of the draw when subjects are randomly assigned to groups. No matter how rigorous our random assignment or sampling methods may be, there is always the possibility that, just due to chance, the data we obtain may be a fluke and are not representative of any broader population or causal processes.

For example, suppose we conduct the perfect experiment to evaluate the effectiveness of a social service, an experiment that is flawless in every conceivable way. When we randomly assign individuals to experimental and control groups, no matter how impeccable our random assignment procedures may be, there is always a chance that a large majority of the individuals who are going to improve with or without any treatment will get assigned to the experimental group and that a large majority of those whose problems are the most intransigent will get assigned to the control group. And it can work the other way around, too: The most difficult cases could be assigned to the treatment group and the others to the control group. Although random assignment minimizes the probability of such imbalances, it does not guarantee that they will never occur simply due to chance.

Flukes in random sampling or random assignment need not be dramatic, like an all-or-nothing occurrence, to threaten the validity of our inferences. Suppose you are conducting an experiment to evaluate the effectiveness of an intervention to prevent future incidents of child abuse or neglect by parents who have been referred for being abusive or neglectful. Let's assume that the intervention being evaluated is utterly ineffectual and worthless. Let's further assume that 26 parents will be randomly assigned to the treatment (experimental) group and another 26 to the control group. Thus, your sample size is 52.

Finally, let's assume that with or without receiving the worthless intervention, half of the 52 parents will recidivate and half will not—that is, half will be found to have been abusive or neglectful again during the test period. We will call that half the *recidivists*. What do you suppose the odds are that the 26 recidivists will be divided evenly between your experimental and control groups? Actually, the odds of that happening are less than 50:50. The chances are greater that the random assignment will have some other result; perhaps 14 or 15 recidivists will be assigned to one group and 12 or 11 to the other. Or maybe it will even be a split of 16:10, 17:9, and so on. It is even possible, albeit extremely unlikely, to have a 26:0 split.

This does not mean that the 13:13 even split is less likely to occur than any other particular split. To the contrary, no other singular split is as likely to occur as the 13:13 split. It just means that the odds are better than even that one of the other 26 possible splits will occur. In other words, if you add the odds of getting a 14:12 split, a 15:11 split, and so on until all possible splits other than 13:13 are included, then the sum of all those odds will be greater than the chances of getting a perfectly even 13:13 split.

You can demonstrate this to yourself quickly and easily without any mathematical gymnastics. All you need is a deck of cards. We'll designate each red card as a recidivist and each black one as a nonrecidivist. Begin by shuffling the deck so that the cards are randomly ordered. Next, deal (that is, randomly assign) the 52 cards alternately into two equal piles of 26, and see whether either pile has exactly 13 red cards and 13 black ones. Finally, repeat this little exercise a couple of times. Did you get a 13:13 split each time? It's possible, but not likely. (Of course, in a real study you wouldn't know who the recidivists would be or how many there would be before random assignment. You would learn that later, toward the end of the study. But in our hypothetical example, because we are assuming that the intervention has no effect whatsoever, we can just designate in advance those who will eventually recidivate for reasons having nothing to do with the intervention.)

Whenever we randomly assign people to groups or randomly select a sample, we use a process that is the same as putting each person's name on a card, shuffling the cards, and then dealing them into one or more piles. The point of this exercise is that when we subsequently collect data from the people (in each "pile"), the odds are that we are going to observe some relationships that are not generalizable or theoretically meaningful—relationships that inescapably result simply from the luck of the draw.

If, for example, you randomly dealt 12 red cards into one pile on your left and 14 into another pile on your right, then you would attribute the difference to luck: You would not infer that the position of the pile (left or right) in a general sense affects the likelihood of its getting red cards. Thus, if in a real study we find that our experimental group of 26 cases had a 46 percent rate of recidivism (or 12 of 26) and our control group had a 54 percent rate of recidivism (or 14 of 26), we must take into account the likelihood that the difference had more to do with the luck of the draw, or chance, than with the impact of the tested intervention.

This example illustrates that a study of an independent variable with absolutely no effect on the tested dependent variable has a good chance of obtaining findings that show some relationship—albeit perhaps quite weak—between the two variables. This point applies to all types of explanatory research designs, not just experimental ones. Every time we seek to infer whether the relationships we have observed have some theoretical meaning or can be generalized beyond our sample, we must take into account the role that chance, or sampling error, plays as a potential explanation of our findings.

Refuting Chance

In light of what we have said so far in this chapter, it may appear that we face a dilemma whenever we seek to infer whether relationships can be generalized in a theoretical sense or to a population. If any relationship, no matter how dramatic, conceivably could have resulted from the luck of the draw, then how can we decide where to draw the line between findings that can and cannot be generalized? In other words, how are we to decide whether the relationship we have observed verifies our hypothesis or, alternatively, whether it merely resulted from chance?

Suppose, for example, that the recidivism rate in our experimental group is lower than that for our control group. How much lower must it be for us to infer that the intervention, and not chance, is probably responsible for the difference? Would a difference of 1 percent be enough—say 49 percent of treated cases recidivate, as compared to 50 percent of control cases? No? Well, then how about a 2 percent difference—say 48 percent compared to 50 percent? Still not impressed? Where would *you* draw the line? When asked this question, students often look perplexed. Some say 5 percent. Others say 10 percent. Many shrug.

Fortunately, there is a solution to this dilemma, one that enables us to infer, for any particular relationship we observe in our sample, whether that relationship is strong enough to confirm our hypothesis and thus be generalized. That solution involves testing to see if the relationship we have observed is statistically significant.

STATISTICAL SIGNIFICANCE

Testing for statistical significance means calculating the probability, or odds, of finding due to chance a relationship that is at least as strong as the one we have observed in our findings. That probability will fall somewhere between zero and 1.0. For example, a probability of .05 means that 5 times out of 100, or 1 in 20, we can expect to obtain a relationship at least as strong as the observed one just due to the luck of the draw. If the probability is .10, then we can expect to obtain that strong a relationship 10 times out of 100, or 1 in 10, just due to the luck of the draw, and so on.

Statistical significance can be calculated in many alternative ways; the correct method for any given study depends on several considerations that we will address later. But the most important thing to understand here is that all of the methods for calculating statistical significance, no matter how different their mathematical assumptions and formulas, ultimately yield the same thing—a probability between zero and 1.0 that the observed relationship was obtained simply due to chance.

Theoretical Sampling Distributions

Tests of statistical significance ascertain the probability that observed relationships can be attributed to sampling error, or chance, by using theoretical sampling distributions. When you test your data for statistical significance, you will not have to confront a theoretical sampling distribution; your statistical software program (SPSS, for example) will already take that distribution into account and will calculate for you the probability that the relationship in question was obtained due to chance. Nevertheless, you should understand the underlying logic of theoretical sampling distributions in order to truly understand—and take the magic out of—statistical significance.

Just as there are different methods for calculating statistical significance, there are different types of sampling distributions that pertain to different types of data. For example, one type of sampling distribution pertains to sampling error that occurs when drawing a random sample from a population, and another type pertains to the chance variations that occur when using randomization to subdivide a given pool of subjects into subgroups. But the underlying logic of these distributions is similar. For the sake of simplicity, we'll focus our illustrations in this chapter on the latter type of sampling distribution that pertains to random assignment in experimental designs.

The logic of this type of theoretical sampling distribution can be illustrated in an uncomplicated fashion by returning to our hypothetical example of a deck of cards in which the red cards represent recidivists and the black cards represent nonrecidivists. Suppose we have just concluded a real experiment in which 12 (46 percent) of 26 treated cases recidivated, as compared to 14 (54 percent) of 26 untreated cases. We would want to know the odds that our lower recidivism rate for treated cases was due to the luck of the draw in randomly assigning cases to the two groups. Even though our experiment was real, one way to calculate those odds could involve using a deck of cards. We would begin by writing the name of each of the 26 recidivists, including both the treated and the untreated ones, on a separate red card. Then we would do the same on black cards for the nonrecidivists.

Next, we would shuffle the cards thoroughly, randomly assign (deal) them to two piles of 26 cards each, and record the red:black ratio in each pile. Then we would gather the cards, reshuffle thoroughly, and repeat the entire process, again recording the randomly obtained ratio at the end. We would continue to do this thousands of times, cumulatively tabulating the number of times that each red:black ratio occurred. At some point, perhaps after days of fanatical shuffling and dealing, we would see that continuing this merriment any further would be pointless; we already would have tabulated so many outcomes that any additional outcomes would not essentially alter the proportions we had already established for each possible outcome.

In other words, if a particular ratio had occurred 100 times after 1,000 deals, then we could say with confidence that the odds of that outcome occurring due to chance were 1 in 10, or .10. Even if we were to continue the process and get that particular ratio on the next two deals, its probability would remain essentially unchanged at 102 divided by 1,002, or .102 (which, with rounding off, would still be .10).

So at that point we would stop our shuffling and calculate the proportion of times that, just due to the luck of the draw, we obtained an outcome that signified a relationship at least as large as the one we observed in our real study; that is, we would add the proportion of 12:14 splits to that of 11:15 splits to that of 10:16 splits, and so on. The list of proportions that we calculated for the various outcomes would be our **theoretical sampling distribution.**

Table 21-1 displays the theoretical sampling distribution that we would obtain for this particular example.

Fortunately, the authors did not have to spend days shuffling and dealing cards to obtain this distribution; one of us did it in minutes on a computer using SPSS to calculate the chi-square significance test (corrected for small sample size).

To use Table 21-1, find the row that corresponds to the outcome we happened to obtain in our real exper-

Table 21-1 Theoretical Sampling Distribution for Randomly Assigning 26 Recidivists and 26 Nonrecidivists in Two Groups of 26 Cases per Group

	PROBABILITIES (ROUNDED OFF TO NEAREST ONE-THOUSANDTH)	
OUTCOME (DIVISION OF RECIDIVISTS BETWEEN THE TWO GROUPS)	PROBABILITY OF EACH PARTICULAR OUTCOME	CUMULATIVE PROBABILITY
26:0 or 0:26	.000	.000
1:25 or 25:1	.000	.000
2:24 or 24:2	.000	.000
3:23 or 23:3	.000	.000
4:22 or 22:4	.000	.000
5:21 or 21:5	.000	.000
6:20 or 20:6	.000	.000
7:19 or 19:7	.002	.002
8:18 or 18:8	.011	.013
9:17 or 17:9	.039	.052
10:16 or 16:10	.114	.166
11:15 or 15:11	.239	.405
12:14 or 14:12	.377	.782
13:13 or 13:13	.218	1.000

imental findings. We noted earlier that our hypothetical findings had 12 recidivists in the treated group and 14 in the untreated group. By locating that outcome in the theoretical sampling distribution, we can identify the probability associated with it. In Table 21-1, we find that the probability of obtaining that particular outcome due to chance is .377, and the cumulative probability of finding a difference between the two groups at least as large as the one we found in our experiment is .782. In other words, if we randomly assign 26 recidivists and 26 nonrecidivists into two equally sized groups an infinite number of times, then for every 1,000 assignments, 782 would produce differences between the two groups at least as large as the difference we found in our experiment, and 377 would produce the exact difference we found. Thus, mere chance produces relationships at least as large as the one we observed in our hypothetically real study 78.2 percent of the time. That means that we have a 78.2 percent likelihood of obtaining, just due to the luck of the draw, a difference between the two groups equal to or greater than 12 recidivists out of 26 cases in one group and 14 recidivists out of 26 cases in the other.

This would tell us that the relationship we observed in our actual findings is probably explained by chance and not by the effects of the tested intervention. This does not mean that we have "proven" that the relationship was due to the luck of the draw. Our hypothesis could still be true. Likewise, it is conceivable that if the entire population of abusive or neglectful parents were to receive the tested intervention, then 46 percent of them would recidivate, as compared to 54 percent if none received the tested intervention. All we can say at this point, based on our particular results with a sample of 52 people, is that we cannot reasonably rule out chance as a plausible rival hypothesis because findings at least as dramatic as ours occur 78.2 percent of the time when the only thing that affects the distribution of outcomes in the two groups is the luck of the draw.

As we mentioned before, fortunately we do not have to create a theoretical sampling distribution every time we seek to assess the probability that the relationships we observe in our findings were caused by chance. Statistical procedures called **tests of statistical significance** handle this for us. Indeed, once we have entered our data into a computer, we can hit a few keys and find out in the batting of an eye the probability that our observed relationship was caused by chance. But it's important to understand that statistical significance tests calculate that probability on the basis of the same theoretical sampling distribution logic that we have just described. Just why that understanding is important should become clearer as we continue our discussion of statistical significance testing.

Significance Levels

Up to now, we have addressed the logic underlying procedures to calculate the odds that a particular relationship we observed in our findings can be attributed to chance and not to the general veracity of our research hypothesis. But we still have not indicated where one draws the line between findings that should and should not be attributed to chance. Obviously, if the probability that chance explains the relationship is very high, say near or above .50 (that is, 50:50 odds), it would be unthinkable to rule out chance as a plausible rival explanation. But just how low must its probability be before we can risk ruling out its plausibility? Even if it were as low as .25, would we dare say that a rival hypothesis that is true as often as one out of every four times is not plausible?

No matter where we happen to draw the line between findings that will and will not be attributed to chance, we deem a finding to be of **statistical significance** when its probability of occurring due to chance is at or below a cutoff point that we select in advance—before we analyze our data. Thus, if we draw the line at .05, then we deem a relationship to be statistically significant if it occurs due to chance no more than 5 times out of 100 randomized trials (or 5 out of 100 deals of the deck). Drawing the line at .05 thus would mean that a relationship with, say, a .06 probability of being caused by chance would be deemed statistically not significant, whereas anything less than .05 would be deemed statistically significant. In short, we call a relationship statistically significant when the probability that it's explained by chance is at or below a point that we have identified in advance as so low that we are willing to risk refuting chance as a plausible rival hypothesis.

In other words, when we call a relationship statistically significant, we say that it can be generalized beyond our sample and that it reflects more than chance covariation. If we assess statistical significance by using a theoretical sampling distribution that pertains to random sampling from a population, then significance refers to generalizing from the sample to the population. On the other hand, if the sampling distribution is based on random assignment of cases, then significance pertains to generalizing about causal processes.

Traditionally, social scientists, including social work researchers, have settled on .05 as the most commonly used cutoff point to separate findings that are not deemed to be significant from those that are. Those findings that fall in the zone beyond the cutoff point, and which are therefore considered to be statistically significant, make up the **critical region** of the theoretical sampling distribution. The cutoff point is called the **level of significance** (or the **significance level**). When it's set at .05, it's signified by the expression $p \leq .05$. This means that any probability equal to or less than .05 will be deemed statistically significant. Researchers usually just report it as less than .05 ($p < .05$) because the probability rarely equals .05 exactly. A probability that is even a tiny bit above .05—say, at .051—would be considered to be greater than .05: outside of the critical region and therefore statistically not significant.

Returning to the theoretical sampling distribution in Table 21-1, how big a difference in recidivism between our experimental and control groups would we need to have statistical significance at the .05 level? To answer this question, we look at the column of cumulative probabilities until we find the cutoff point between values both above and below .05. Thus, we see that we would need to have no more than 8 recidivists in one group (and at least 18 in the other) for the difference to be statistically significant. Likewise, we see that any difference that is less extreme than an 8 to 18 split has a probability greater than .05 and would therefore be deemed not significant. Thus, even if our experimental group had a 35 percent recidivism rate (9 of 26) and our control group's recidivism rate was much higher, at 65 percent (17 of 26), using the .05 level of significance we would not be able to refute the plausibility of chance as a rival hypothesis. However, had we established in advance .10 as our level of significance, then a 9:17 split would be statistically significant because its cumulative probability of .052 is less than .10.

It is critical to bear in mind that the .05 level of significance is not dictated by mathematical theory. It is not sacred. Not all studies use that level; some use a lower level, perhaps at .01, although that almost never happens in social work research. A strong case can be made for using a higher level, perhaps around .10, under certain conditions, especially when our sample is small (for reasons to be discussed later).

Before moving on, we point out the importance of selecting your significance level (level of significance) before you conduct your data analysis. Doing so after your analysis would put you in the position of deciding the criterion of significance in light of the knowledge of which criteria would make your findings significant or not. Even if you have a great deal of integrity, it would be difficult to rule out the possibility that, perhaps unintentionally, your selection of a significance level was biased by your a priori knowledge of what each significance level would mean for the significance of your findings. Moreover, what if every researcher were in this position? We all may be confident of our own intellectual honesty and capacity to remain unbiased, but we would probably be uncomfortable if everyone else was selecting significance levels in light of whichever level would make their findings "significant."

One-Tailed and Two-Tailed Tests

In the preceding example, you may have wondered why the theoretical sampling distribution illustrated in Table 21-1 lumped together the probability of getting a split of either 12 recidivists in our experimental group and 14 in our control group or 14 recidivists in the experimental group and 12 in the control group. Because we were evaluating the effectiveness of an intervention aimed at preventing recidivism, why would we consider the probability of chance producing a 14:12 or worse split—in which the experimental group's recidivism would be greater (or worse) than the control group's? Why not just limit the probabilities of interest to those for relationships in which the experimental group's outcome (recidivism) is better (or lower) than the control group's?

The positive and negative outcomes were lumped together in our distribution because we did not say that our hypothetical study was interested in finding out only whether the effects of the evaluated intervention are beneficial. We stated that we were evaluating its effectiveness, but we did not foreclose the possibility of finding that it's harmful. And if our findings were to turn out in the harmful direction, we would want to know whether those findings allow us to generalize that the intervention is indeed harmful or whether the results were just a fluke caused by the luck of the draw. Consequently, we would be interested in the probabilities of finding either a positive or negative relationship due to chance.

Hypotheses that do not specify whether the predicted relationship will be positive or negative are called **nondirectional hypotheses.** When testing nondirectional hypotheses, we use **two-tailed tests of significance.** For any particular relationship that we find, regardless of whether it is positive or negative, two-tailed tests of significance add the probability of finding a relationship that strong in the positive direction to that of finding one in the negative direction. Using a two-tailed test in our example, we found that the probability of getting a relationship at least as large as a 12:14 or 14:12 split in either direction was .782. That figure adds the probability of getting 12 or fewer recidivists in one group to the probability of getting 12 or fewer recidivists in the other group. Thus, the probability of getting only 12 or fewer recidivists in the experimental group, and not including the probability of the reverse results, is one-half of .782, or .391.

We say a test has "two tails" because we are interested in extreme, unlikely values in the sampling distribution for both positive and negative relationships. To illustrate this point, we have modified the sampling distribution that appeared in Table 21-1. The revised version appears in Table 21-2. Instead of lumping positive and negative outcomes together, notice how Table 21-2 is symmetrical, with the positive outcomes and their probabilities in the left half and their negative counterparts in the right half. (This is a space-saving format; a computer-generated table would be a long, three-column table, with positive outcomes in the top half and negative ones in the bottom half.) Notice also that each probability is one-half the amount it was in Table 21-1.

The "two tails" in the distribution in Table 21-2 consist of those values at either end (top left or bottom right) of the table that are in our critical region for claiming statistical significance. Because we are using a two-tailed test of significance—that is, be-

Table 21-2 Theoretical Sampling Distribution (Showing Each Tail) for Randomly Assigning 26 Recidivists and 26 Nonrecidivists into Two Groups of 26 Cases per Group

OUTCOME (DIVISION OF RECIDIVISTS AND NONRECIDIVISTS BETWEEN THE TWO GROUPS)			OUTCOME (DIVISION OF RECIDIVISTS AND NONRECIDIVISTS BETWEEN THE TWO GROUPS)		
EXPERIMENTAL GROUP	CONTROL GROUP	CUMULATIVE PROBABILITY	EXPERIMENTAL GROUP	CONTROL GROUP	CUMULATIVE PROBABILITY
0:26	26:0	.0000	14:12	12:14	.3910
1:25	25:1	.0000	15:11	11:15	.2025
2:24	24:2	.0000	16:10	10:16	.0830
3:23	23:3	.0000	17:9	9:17	.0260
4:22	22:4	.0000	18:8	8:18	.0065
5:21	21:5	.0000	19:7	7:19	.0010
6:20	20:6	.0002	20:6	6:20	.0002
7:19	19:7	.0010	21:5	5:21	.0000
8:18	18:8	.0065	22:4	4:22	.0000
9:17	17:9	.0260	23:3	3:23	.0000
10:16	16:10	.0830	24:2	2:24	.0000
11:15	15:11	.2025	25:1	1:25	.0000
12:14	14:12	.3910	26:0	0:26	.0000
13:13	13:13	.5000			

cause we are interested in both positive and negative outcomes—we would have to add the probabilities we find in each tail to identify our cutoff points. In other words, we would add the two tails together.

Thus, although the probability in this distribution of having 9 or fewer recidivists in the experimental group is less than .05 (at .026), that finding would not be significant because, when added to the probability of having 9 or fewer recidivists in the control group, it exceeds .05 (that is, .026 plus .026 equals .052). The figures in Table 21-1, then, reflect the probabilities that pertain to a two-tailed test after adding the two tails together (as shown in Table 21-2). Our significance level in Table 21-2 would still be .05, but two cutoff points—points designating the two tails—would identify the critical region of results that would be deemed statistically significant. One "significant" tail would consist of outcomes with 8 or fewer recidivists in the experimental group, and the other "significant" tail would consist of outcomes with 8 or fewer recidivists in the control group. The probability for each tail would be .0065, but after adding the two tails, the probability becomes .013.

But suppose we had stipulated in advance that we were only interested in whether the intervention's effects were positive. Then we would have formulated a directional hypothesis. Directional hypotheses predict whether a relationship will be positive or negative. When we test a directional hypothesis, we can use a **one-tailed test of significance.** But this choice restricts our options; that is, we will be able to infer whether the relationship we find can be generalized in the predicted direction only. If our findings turn out to be in the opposite direction, then we cannot reverse gears and use a two-tailed test and then claim the same level of significance. Consequently, many social scientists recommend that two-tailed tests should usually be used even when the hypothesis is directional.

To illustrate the use of one-tailed tests, let's apply a one-tailed test of significance to the data in Table 21-2. Because we are only interested in generalizing about positive intervention effects—effects that are associated with lower recidivism in the experimental group—any finding in the opposite direction will simply be interpreted as not supporting the hypothesis and will not be generalized. Consequently, we would establish our cutoff point so we use the first, positive half of the distribution only; in essence, we would be assessing the probability of getting a certain result or better due to chance. Thus, still using the .05 level of significance, we would now be able to generalize outcomes in which the experimental group had 9 or fewer recidivists because the cumulative probability for that outcome in the one, preselected tail of the distribution is .026 (that is, $p < .05$).

Suppose, however, after having planned to use a one-tailed test with our directional hypothesis, we found 17 recidivists in the experimental group and only 9 in the control group. Wanting to alert others to the potentially harmful effects of the tested intervention, suppose we then reversed gears and used a two-tailed test. What would our significance level be if we were to claim this finding as statistically significant? It would not be .05, for we were prepared to call the other tail significant with its cumulative probability of .026. To deem this finding significant, then, our real significance level would have to be at .052 or higher. But if a significance level higher than .05 is acceptable, then why didn't we initially plan to use it in our anticipated one-tailed test? If we choose to use it now, aren't we deceiving ourselves and others and in effect merely manipulating the selection of a significance level to fit our findings?

One way to resolve this dilemma would be to report the two-tailed probability of the finding—calling it not significant—and informing readers that we used a one-tailed test in the other direction with a .05 significance level. If the tested intervention is in widespread use, we might want to alert readers of the unexpected and potentially worrisome direction of this finding and urge them to replicate our evaluation. Readers would then be informed adequately to make their own decision about how to respond to our findings. But it would be inappropriate to cite our findings as a basis for inferring that the tested intervention is indeed harmful.

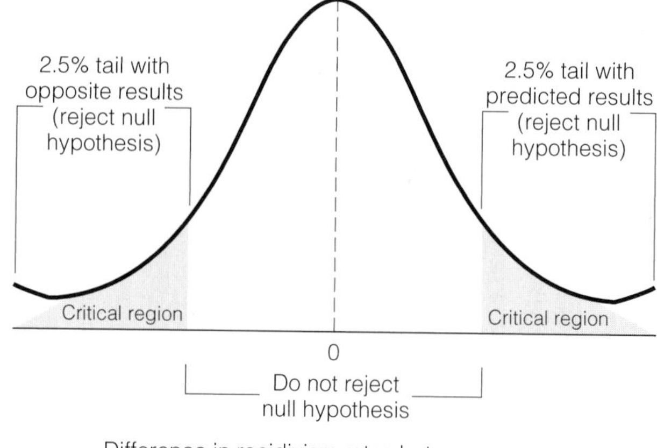

Figure 21-1 Theoretical Sampling Distribution Using a Two-Tailed Test of Statistical Significance

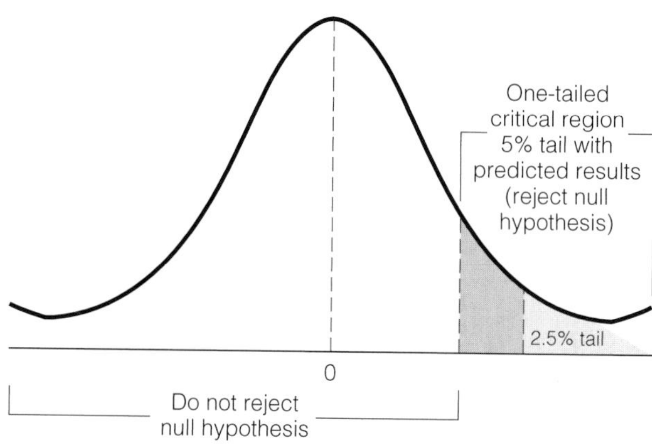

Figure 21-2 Theoretical Sampling Distribution Using a One-Tailed Test of Statistical Significance

Figures 21-1 and 21-2 illustrate theoretical sampling distributions with the use of two-tailed and one-tailed tests. Figure 21-1 illustrates a two-tailed test. In it the .05 level of significance is split between the two tails, forming two critical regions—one in the predicted direction and one in the opposite direction—with each containing 2.5% (half) of the randomly generated outcomes that have no more than a 5%

probability of occurring due to chance. Figure 21-2 depicts a one-tailed test, with the entire .05 critical region located in the predicted direction.

The Null Hypothesis

Now that you know what directional and nondirectional hypotheses are, let's consider another type of hypothesis called the *null hypothesis*—a term that you might understandably think was coined by impish statisticians out to make mischief. But you will encounter this term frequently as you produce, use, and participate in research studies, so it is important to understand.

Throughout this chapter, we have been referring to chance as a rival hypothesis. When we refer to that rival hypothesis, we call it the null hypothesis. Simply put, the **null hypothesis** postulates that the relationship being statistically tested is explained by chance—that it does not really exist in a population or in a theoretical sense—even though it may seem to be related in our particular findings. Thus, when our findings are shown to be statistically significant, we reject the null hypothesis because the probability that it is true—that our results were caused by chance—is less than our level of significance. So, if our results are statistically significant at the .05 level of significance, we would conclude that the null hypothesis has only a .05 probability of being true, and we would therefore reject it. (By reexamining Figures 21-1 and 21-2, you can see pictorial illustrations of when to reject and not reject the null hypothesis.)

What makes this term tricky is that whenever we are rejecting the null hypothesis, we are supporting the plausibility of our research hypothesis (assuming that we are predicting that two variables are related and that we are not seeking to show that they are unrelated). Conversely, whenever we fail to reject the null hypothesis, we are failing to support our research hypothesis.

So why bother having a null hypothesis? Weren't we managing just fine by referring to chance as a rival hypothesis? Although we could probably get along well enough without this term, it actually does serve one particularly important function: It reminds us that our level of statistical significance does not pertain to the probability that our research hypothesis is true. All it tells us is the probability that the observed relationship was caused by chance—that is, the probability that the null hypothesis is true. Suppose our results are significant at the .05 level. That would indicate that the null hypothesis has only a .05 probability of being true, but it absolutely would not tell us that our research hypothesis therefore has a .95 probability of being true.

Remember, chance is only one of many rival hypotheses that could account for our findings. We mentioned others at the beginning of this chapter: biases, threats to internal validity, extraneous variables, and so on. We need to remain vigilant about this, lest we allow low statistical probability levels to gull us into thinking that we can ignore the methodological strengths and weaknesses of a particular study. Indeed, there is no surer way to get statistically significant results than to introduce certain biases into the methodology—for example, rigging the measurement so that you get findings that will support your hypothesis. Thus, by using the term *null hypothesis*, we remind ourselves that the only hypothesis whose likely truth conforms to our significance level is a statistical hypothesis, not our research hypothesis.

The term *null hypothesis* also facilitates our consideration of other potential errors that are connected to statistical significance testing, errors that we will examine next.

Type I and Type II Errors

Every time we make a decision about the statistical significance of a tested relationship, we risk making an error. If we decide to reject the null hypothesis, then we risk making one type of error. If we do not reject the null hypothesis, then we risk making another type of error. This is true because we are dealing with probabilities, not certainties.

Remember that our significance level only tells us the probability that the null hypothesis is false. Although we may reject as implausible a null hypothesis with a probability of .05, we never reject it as impossible. There is always some chance, however slight, that a statistically significant relationship really was caused by chance. In other words, we may have gotten a rare and extremely lucky draw in the random assignment or in random sampling. With a .05 significance level, we can expect to get such a lucky draw once for every 20 tests of statistical significance that we perform.

The error that is risked when we have statistically significant results—and therefore reject the null hypothesis—is called a **Type I error.** A Type I error occurs if the null hypothesis we have rejected as implausible is really true. When we reject the null hypothesis, we have no way of knowing whether we are actually committing a Type I error; all we know is the probability that we are doing so. That probability is equivalent to our significance level. At the .05 level of significance, therefore, we take a .05 risk of committing a Type I error when we reject the null hypothesis.

The only way we can avoid risking a Type I error is by failing to reject the null hypothesis. However, whenever we do that, we automatically risk making a **Type II error.** A Type II error occurs if we fail to reject a false null hypothesis. Remember, just because the probability that the tested relationship can be attributed to chance is greater than our significance level, that does not guarantee that it was caused by chance. If our significance level is .05 and the probability that our result was due to chance is .06, then we fail to reject the null hypothesis—even though the probability that the null hypothesis is true is only .06!

Thus, findings that are not significant do not mean that our research hypothesis has been proven false. They just mean that we lack the level of probability we need to rule out chance as a plausible explanation for our findings. Consequently, if our probability level falls short of being statistically significant but is close to significant, then rather than claim to have disproven our hypothesis, we would probably alert readers to the low, albeit nonsignificant, probability level and encourage them to replicate our research in this area. It could be that our research hypothesis really is true but we had too small a sample or too unlucky a draw to verify it at a statistically significant level. (We will explain the role of sample size in this issue shortly.)

Table 21-3 summarizes the relationships between Type I errors and Type II errors. It is provided to help you visualize the impossibility of avoiding the risk of both a Type I and Type II error simultaneously. Whenever we lower our significance level to reduce the risk of committing a Type I error, we automatically increase the risk of making a Type II error. Conversely, whenever we raise our significance level to reduce the risk of committing a Type II error, we increase the risk of committing a Type I error.

Table 21-3 Type of Error Risked as Related to Decision about Null Hypothesis

	DECISION REGARDING NULL HYPOTHESIS	
TYPE OF ERROR	REJECT	NOT REJECT
Type I	Risked	Not risked
Type II	Not risked	Risked

Social scientists tend to accept a much lower risk of making a Type I error than a Type II error. This probably is connected to their desire to obtain statistically significant results and their consequent wish to offset any biases that might result from that desire. Thus, by taking a .05 or lower risk of incorrectly supporting their own hypotheses, they project an impressive image of scientific caution and objectivity.

But just because so many social scientists conform to this convention does not mean that Type I errors are necessarily more serious than Type II errors—especially when human suffering is at stake. Deciding which type of error is more serious requires making value judgments, and the choice will vary depending on the nature and context of the research question. To illustrate this point, let's return to our hypothetical example involving the prevention of recidivism among abusive parents, again using the theoretical sampling distribution illustrated in Table 21-2. Recall that a 9:17 split had a probability of .052 with a two-tailed test and therefore was not significant at the .05 level. Consequently, at that significance level we would decide to risk committing a Type II error and would be unwilling to take a .052 risk of committing a Type I error.

Would we be justified in that decision? Reasonable people might disagree about this issue, but what if we had little evidence that any alternative interventions effectively prevent child abuse? If nothing else works and there is no evidence that the intervention produces noxious side effects, which error has worse human consequences—recommending an intervention that really has no effect on child abuse or failing to recommend one that really does reduce the incidence of child abuse? As you think about this, realize that if our hypothetical 9:17 results could be generalized, it would mean that the intervention lowers the child abuse rate from 65 percent (17 out of 26 cases in the untreated control group) to 35 percent (9 out of 26 treated cases). That's prevention of a substantial amount of suffering and other damage. On the other hand, if the null hypothesis is true, then the use of this intervention by others would result in a lot of wasted resources that could have been spent seeking more effective ways to deal with this serious problem.

Of course, one way to resolve this dilemma is through replication. Another way is to increase our sample size. In fact, we would probably recommend that the preceding results warrant replicating our study with a larger sample. As we will see next, increasing our sample size provides a way to reduce the risk of committing a Type II error without having to increase the risk of committing a Type I error.

The Influence of Sample Size

As we discussed in Chapter 14 (on sampling), the larger our sample, the less sampling error we have. When we reduce sampling error, we reduce the probability that the relationships we observe in our findings can be attributed to it. Consequently, the same relationship that was too weak to be significant with a smaller sample can, without changing in magnitude, become statistically significant with a larger sample. In other words, it is safer to generalize findings from large samples than from small ones, and even a very weak relationship might warrant generalization if it was found in a very large sample.

For example, in a study of the salaries of social work faculty members in 1980, Rubin (1981) found that after controlling for several extraneous variables, the mean salary was $26,638 for men and $26,157 for women. With a very large sample size of 1,067 faculty members, he found that the $481 difference between the mean salaries of men and women was statistically significant at the .01 level.

To illustrate the effects of sample size further, let's return to our hypothetical example on evaluating an intervention to prevent child abuse, but this time we'll vary the sample size, relying in part on examples of hypothetical data presented by Blalock (1972). To begin, suppose that we assigned only five cases to each group, and found that 2 of the 5 treated parents recidivated as compared to 3 of the 5 untreated controls. Although 3:5 represents a 60 percent recidivism rate, and 2:5 is only 40 percent, with these small samples the role of chance is so great that it would be ludicrous to take such percentages seriously. If we were to double our sample size to 10 cases per group and found the same recidivism rates (that is, 4 out of 10 versus 6 out of 10), our results still would not be significant at the .05 level.

But if we found the same rates (that is, the same relationship) with 50 cases in each group (20 out of 50 versus 30 out of 50), then the probability of the null hypothesis being true would be less than .05, and we would reject it at that level of significance. And if we doubled the sample size to 100 per group, and still found the same 40 percent versus 60 percent rates, the probability of the null hypothesis being true would fall to below .01.

To help solidify your understanding of this point, let's compare one more pair of hypothetical results for the preceding example. Suppose we assigned 50 cases to each group and found 24 (48 percent) treated recidivists and 26 (52 percent) untreated recidivists. That outcome would not be significant at the .05 level. But suppose we found the exact same relationship with 5,000 cases in each group. That would entail 2,400 (48 percent) treated recidivists and 2,600 (52 percent) untreated recidivists. For that finding, the probability of the null hypothesis being true would be less than .001!

MEASURES OF ASSOCIATION

When we assess statistical significance, we ask only one question: "Can a relationship be inferred to exist in a theoretical sense or in a broader population?" We do not assess the relationship's strength. It is tempting to treat significance levels as indicators of the relative strength of different relationships—that is, to assume that a relationship that is significant at the .001 level is stronger than one that is significant at the .05 level—but such an assumption would be incorrect.

We just saw how sample size can influence statistical significance. We saw that a 40 percent recidivism rate among treated cases versus a 60 percent recidivism rate among controls would be significant at the .05 level for 50 cases per group, whereas a 48 percent versus a 52 percent recidivism rate would be significant at the .001 level for 5,000 cases per group. Therefore, the stronger relationship is not necessarily the one with the lower probability of a Type I error.

We may also be tempted to think that because significance testing doesn't tell us how strong a relationship is, it might be okay to bypass significance testing and just deal with measures of the strength of relationships. But that, too, would be inappropriate.

Some strong relationships can be caused by chance. If zero percent of two treated cases recidivate, as compared to 100 percent of two untreated cases, then generalizing that strong relationship would be no more appropriate than inferring that two coins were biased if you flipped two heads with one and two tails with the other. In short, significance testing is an essential first step in interpreting a relationship, but it only tells us the probability that a relationship was caused by chance. It does not tell us its strength.

Let's look now at how we measure relationship strength. We'll refer to the statistical procedures for doing so as *measures of association*. We can begin by recognizing that we have already been discussing measures of association when we cite differences in percentages between two dichotomous variables such as recidivism and the provision of treatment. It is intuitively obvious that a 40 percent versus a 60 percent recidivism rate signifies a stronger relationship than a 48 percent versus a 52 percent rate. But when we are dealing with variables that have more than two categories or those that are at ordinal or interval-ratio levels of measurement, then we need some other kind of summarizing statistic. (In our discussion of measures of association, we will commonly refer back to our recidivism example, which uses two dichotomous variables, just to simplify the discussion—that is, to illustrate strength of relationship concepts in intuitively obvious terms.)

Some commonly used measures of association yield values that range from zero, which signifies no relationship whatsoever, to 1.0, which signifies a perfect relationship. A value of −1.0 also would signify a perfect relationship. The minus sign in front of a relationship magnitude statistic does not mean the relationship is weaker than one with a plus sign. The minus sign only means that the variables are negatively (inversely) related: As one goes up, the other goes down. The closer the value is to zero, the less able we are to predict the relative value of one variable by knowing the other.

For example, if two groups had exactly the same recidivism rate, then knowing whether a particular case was in one group or the other would not affect our calculation of the odds that this case will recidivate. We might be able to predict the odds from the overall recidivism rate for cases in either group, but knowing what group the case was in would not influence our prediction one way or the other. Thus, the relationship magnitude would be zero.

Table 21-4 Illustrations of Relationship Magnitudes of Zero, 1.0, and −1.0

Example of a Relationship Magnitude of Zero

OUTCOME	EXPERIMENTAL GROUP	CONTROL GROUP
Recidivists	40	40
Nonrecidivists	60	60

Example of a Relationship Magnitude of 1.0

OUTCOME	EXPERIMENTAL GROUP	CONTROL GROUP
Recidivists	0	100
Nonrecidivists	100	0

Example of a Relationship Magnitude of −1.0

CASE NUMBER	NUMBER OF TREATMENT SESSIONS ATTENDED	NUMBER OF INCIDENTS OF VERBAL ABUSE OBSERVED
1	1	14
2	2	12
3	3	10
4	4	8
5	5	6
6	6	4
7	7	2
8	8	0

On the other hand, if one group had a zero percent recidivism rate and the other group had a 100 percent recidivism rate, then knowing which group a case was in would enable us to predict with 100 percent accuracy whether that case will recidivate. The relationship magnitude would be 1.0, a perfect relationship.

Table 21-4 illustrates two perfect relationships and one two-by-two table that shows a relationship magnitude of zero. The two-by-two table at the top shows no relationship, and the relationship magnitude therefore would be zero because the two groups have exactly the same recidivism rates. The fact that there are fewer recidivists than nonrecidivists (that is, the recidivism rate is 40 percent) may be an important descriptive finding. But because each group has the same 40 percent recidivism rate, knowing what group a case is in offers us nothing toward predicting whether that case will recidivate, and therefore the relationship magnitude is zero.

In the second two-by-two table, the relationship magnitude is 1.0 because none of the experimental group cases recidivated, whereas all of the control group cases did. Thus, knowing which group a case was in would be all we needed to know to predict with perfect accuracy whether or not the case will recidivate.

The same degree of predictability is evident in the third example, but this time there is a minus sign in front of the 1.0 because as one variable increases, the other decreases. The relationship magnitude is −1.0 because each additional session of treatment attended, without exception, reduces the number of incidents of verbal abuse observed by the same amount each time. It is a perfect relationship because knowing the number of sessions one attends is all we need to know to predict with perfect accuracy the number of incidents of verbal abuse observed. The minus sign is not pejorative and does not signify a weaker relationship; it simply means that an increase in one variable is associated with a decrease in the other.

So far we have contrasted a perfect relationship (with a magnitude of 1.0 or −1.0) with no relationship (zero magnitude). But what about something in between—for example, a 40 percent recidivism rate for treated cases versus a 60 percent one for controls? In that case, knowing that a case was in the treatment group would predispose us to predict nonrecidivism, and knowing the case was in the control group would predispose us to predict recidivism. But if we predicted recidivism for every control case and nonrecidivism for every treated case, then we would be wrong 40 percent of the time. That's a lot of errors. But with an overall recidivism rate of 50 percent (which would be the case with an equal number of cases in the 40 percent and 60 percent groups), we would be wrong 50 percent of the time if we tried to predict recidivism for each case without knowing which group each case was in. Thus, knowing which group a case was in would reduce our percentage of errors from 50 percent to 40 percent, or a proportional reduction in error of .20. (The .20 is derived from the fact that if we express the .10 reduction from .50 to .40 in proportional terms, then .10 is 20 percent, or .20, of .50.)

In short, if there is some relationship between our variables, it means that knowing the value for one variable will reduce the number of errors we make in predicting the value for the other. And the stronger the relationship is, the more our prediction errors will be reduced. The term for this process is **proportionate reduction of error (PRE).** Some measures are based on the PRE framework, and some are not. But each measure yields a statistic ranging from zero to 1.0 (or −1.0). The stronger the relationship, the closer the statistic will be to 1.0 (or −1.0), and the greater will be the reduction of uncertainty. The weaker the relationship, the closer the statistic will be to zero, and the less will be the reduction of uncertainty.

Which measure of association should be used depends primarily on the level of measurement of your variables. When two variables are at the *interval* or *ratio level of measurement,* for example, the most commonly used measure of association is *Pearson's product-moment correlation (r).* When both your independent and dependent variables are at the *nominal* level of measurement, common measures of association include *lambda, Yules' Q, phi,* and *Cramer's V.* When your independent variable is nominal (for example, whether a participant is in an experimental or a control group) and your dependent variable is interval or ratio (for example, how many times they did something), then two common statistics to use are *eta* and the *point-biserial correlation coefficient.* Most of these measures can be squared to determine what *proportion of variance in the dependent variable is explained by the independent variable.* Thus, if $r = .5$, then $r^2 = .25$, which means that one-fourth of the variation in the dependent variable has been explained. (For more information about these measures, we encourage you to examine the statistical text listed in the Additional Reading section at the end of this chapter.)

Effect Size

Statistics that portray the strength of association between variables are often referred to by the term **effect size.** This term is used especially in clinical outcome research. The relationship magnitude statistics we've been discussing so far—phi, *r*, point-biserial correlation coefficient, and so on—are all effect-size statistics. So are others that we haven't yet discussed but will address shortly. Effect-size statistics portray the strength of association found in any study, no matter what outcome measure is used, in terms that are comparable across studies. Thus, they enable us to compare the effects of different interventions across studies using different types of outcome measures.

To illustrate this function in clinical outcome research, suppose two different studies are conducted, each an experimental evaluation of the effectiveness of a different approach to treating male batterers. The first evaluates a cognitive-behavioral approach and finds that the experimental group subjects who receive the tested treatment averaged two physically abusive incidents per subject during a posttreatment follow-up period as compared to a mean of three physically abusive incidents for control subjects. The second study evaluates a psychosocial approach. Instead of using the ratio-level outcome measure of number of abusive incidents, it uses the nominal measure of whether or not any physical abuse occurred during the follow-up period. It finds that 40 percent of experimental subjects were abusive, as compared to 60 percent of control subjects. Suppose that the findings of each study are statistically significant.

How can we judge which of the two interventions had the stronger effects? Comparing their outcomes as just stated is a bit like comparing apples and oranges because they used different types of outcome indicators. Effect-size statistics help alleviate this problem. The point-biserial correlation coefficient for the first study can be compared to the phi statistic for the second study. Although their calculations are different, each has the same meaning. The intervention with the larger effect size is the one that explained more of the variation in its dependent variable. In other words, the intervention with the larger effect size had stronger effects on the particular outcome variable being assessed in connection with it (assuming that internally valid designs that permit causal inferences were used).

Not everyone who reports the foregoing measures of association (phi, *r*, and so on) refers to them as the "effect size." Some do, but many don't. For example, one author might say, "The effect size was substantial, because phi was .50," whereas another author might simply say, "The relationship was strong, because phi was .50."

But another type of effect-size statistic is usually referred to as the "effect size" (sometimes it is called Cohen's *d*). This statistic, abbreviated as ES (*E* for effect and *S* for size), is used when interval or ratio-level data permit dividing the difference between the means of the experimental and control groups by the standard deviation.

Different approaches to calculating ES vary as to whether the standard deviation that is used in the calculation is that of the control group, the pooled standard deviation of the two groups combined, or an estimate of the standard deviation of the population to which a study is attempting to generalize. To simplify our discussion, we'll just use the approach that involves the standard deviation of the control group, which is probably the most commonly used method (Fischer, 1990). In this approach, the effect-size formula is as follows:

$$\text{ES} = \frac{\begin{pmatrix}\text{experimental}\\ \text{group mean}\end{pmatrix} - \begin{pmatrix}\text{control}\\ \text{group mean}\end{pmatrix}}{(\text{control group standard deviation})}$$

To illustrate the use of the preceding formula, let's return to the hypothetical example of two studies, each of which evaluates the effectiveness of a different approach to treating male batterers. This time, however, assume that each uses a ratio-level measure of outcome. Let's say that the first study assesses the mean number of physically abusive incidents and finds an experimental group mean of 2, a control group mean of 3, and a standard deviation of 1. Its effect size would be as follows:

$$\text{ES} = \frac{2 - 3}{1} = -1.0 \rightarrow +1.0$$

When calculating ES this way, we interpret the plus or minus sign in the dividend according to whether a reduction in the outcome measure represents a desirable or undesirable effect. In the preceding example, it represents a desirable effect because we were seeking to reduce physical abuse. We would therefore report the ES as 1.0 (not −1.0), because the minus sign in reporting ES is used only to indicate undesirable effects (in the opposite direction of what was sought). We would interpret this ES of 1.0 by observing that the experimental group's mean was one standard deviation better than the control group's mean.

In a normal curve, as discussed in Chapter 20, only 16 percent of the cases have values at least one standard deviation better than the mean, and 84 percent of the cases have less desirable values. Therefore, if we assume a normal distribution of control group scores, then an ES of 1.0 indicates that the mean outcome for experimental subjects was better than 84 percent of the outcomes for control subjects. You can interpret any ES in this manner by using the Z-table commonly found in introductory texts on descriptive statistics. Z-tables show what proportion of a normal curve is found above and below z-scores. This ES formula produces a z-score, because z-scores tell how far a score is from a mean in standard deviation units. In Appendix C of this text, a Z-table displays ES values along with the corresponding proportion of outcomes for control subjects that is worse than the mean outcome for experimental subjects for each ES value.

Let's say that the second study in our hypothetical example assesses the mean number of verbally and physically abusive incidents combined (unlike the first study, which assessed only physical abuse) and has a longer posttreatment measurement period than did the first study. Suppose the second study finds an experimental group mean of 20, a control group mean of 26, and a standard deviation of 10. Its effect size would be as follows:

$$ES = \frac{20 - 26}{10} = -.60 \rightarrow +.60$$

Although the two studies quantified outcome in different ways—one dealing with much larger numbers than the other—dividing by the standard deviation makes the results of the two studies comparable. The preceding results indicate that the cognitive-behavioral intervention evaluated in the first study had stronger effects on its outcome measure than the psychosocial intervention evaluated in the second study had on its outcome measure.

At this point, you may be wondering whether the relative strength depicted in the preceding outcomes may have been different if, instead of reporting the ES statistic, our hypothetical authors had reported effect size in terms of the point-biserial correlation coefficient or some other measure of association. The answer is "no." Either approach would have shown the stronger effect size in the first study. In fact, some texts provide formulas and tables that enable us to translate one effect-size statistic into another.

For example, an ES of .60 always equals a correlation of .287, and an ES of 1.0 always equals a correlation of .447. Which to use depends primarily on whether you want to envision mean group differences in terms of standard deviation units on a normal curve. You should be familiar with both approaches to effect size so that you will not be mystified when you encounter studies that report effect sizes in different ways.

An important word of caution here: Notice that we have been careful not to say that effect-size statistics indicate which intervention had "better" outcomes. We have said that effect-size statistics indicate which intervention had stronger effects on its particular outcome variable and which explained more variation in its outcome variable. This is quite different from saying one intervention had a better outcome.

Suppose one intervention has an ES of 1.0 in respect to reducing less severe forms of verbal spouse abuse during a brief postintervention measurement period, and another has an ES of .6 with respect to extremely severe physical spouse abuse during a lengthy post-intervention measurement period. Conceivably, the latter intervention is more valuable than the former, despite its lower ES, because its ES was assessed in connection to a more severe form of spouse abuse and over a longer period. The process of deciding which intervention is preferable involves value judgments and other considerations that we will examine in the next two sections. Effect size is only one of several important issues to consider in that process.

Strong, Medium, and Weak Effect Sizes

It is often useful to interpret our effect sizes in terms such as *weak*, *medium*, or *strong* so that they take on added meaning relative to other research findings and other explanations. But interpreting some effect sizes can be a tricky business. For example, an r of .30 when squared equals .09, indicating that the independent variable is explaining 9 percent of the variation in the dependent variable.

We often have a reflexive tendency to attach the same meanings to these percentages as we attach to our exam scores, seeing percentages above 70 or 80 percent as strong and anything much lower as weak. Although these benchmarks may be applicable to studies of measurement reliability, using them as general guideposts to distinguish strong and weak relationships is incorrect.

As an illustration of this point, consider research on the causes of child abuse. A large, diverse array of factors can influence whether or not a parent becomes abusive. Whether or not a parent was abused as a child is one such factor, but there are many others. Many parents who were abused as children do not become abusive parents, and many other factors influence that outcome. Most studies of these factors show that each explains only a tiny percentage of the variation in whether the abused child becomes an abusive parent. If a study were to find that one such factor explained 20 percent of the variation in whether or not the abused child becomes an abusive parent, then there would probably be widespread agreement that this was a very "strong" relationship relative to other findings in this field of study. Indeed, it might be a major discovery.

For another example, suppose we conducted an experiment to evaluate the effectiveness of an intervention to prevent recidivism among parents referred for child abuse. Suppose our experiment found a 40 percent recidivism rate for 100 treated cases and a 60 percent recidivism rate for 100 untreated cases. We would find that the phi statistic for this relationship would equal .20. Squaring phi, we would conclude that 4 percent (.20 × .20 = .04) of the variation in recidivism is explained by whether or not the intervention was provided. Because we would have explained only 4 percent of the variation in recidivism, would we conclude that this was a weak relationship? Although we might not all give the same answer to that question, we probably would agree that there is no one mathematically correct answer to it. Four percent may seem small at first glance, but what about the fact that our intervention reduced the child abuse recidivism rate by 20 percent, which is a 33 percent reduction (20 percent is one-third of 60 percent)? Also, what if prior experimental research had found that alternative interventions had a weaker effect or even no impact on recidivism rates?

What if our hypothetical experiment were to find a 35 percent recidivism rate for treated cases versus a 65 percent recidivism rate for untreated cases? The phi statistic for that relationship would be .30. Squaring that would reveal that only 9 percent of the variation in recidivism rates is being explained. Yet the 65 percent recidivism rate for untreated cases would nearly double the 35 percent rate for treated cases. Clearly, then, a percentage such as 9 percent that may seem small in contexts such as a test grade or a reliability coefficient is not necessarily small in the context of explaining variation in some dependent variables.

In this connection, Cohen (1988) argues that an ES of approximately .5, in which about 6 percent of the dependent variable variance is explained, should be considered to be of medium strength, noting that .06 is the percentage of variation in height explained by age group if we compare 14- and 18-year-old girls. It also applies to the difference in mean IQ between clerical and semiskilled workers. Cohen also argues that an ES of .8, in which about 14 percent of variation is explained, should be considered strong, noting that this amount applies to the difference in the mean IQ between college graduates and persons with only a 50:50 chance of passing a high school academic curriculum.

Cohen deems as weak an ES of about .2, in which approximately 1 percent of dependent variable variance is explained. Yet Rosenthal and Rubin (1982) point out that a new intervention that improves a treatment success rate from 45 percent to 55 percent would have a correlation of only .10—when squared, this indicates that only 1 percent of the variance in outcome is explained by whether or not the new intervention was received. Noting that the increase from .45 to .55 might be very important when the increase is in such outcome indicators as survival rates or cure rates, they argue that the value of some interventions with "weak" effect sizes is often underestimated.

Some researchers have developed empirical guidelines for interpreting the relative magnitude of strength-of-relationship statistics. Smith and Glass (1977) calculated the mean ES of nearly 400 controlled evaluations of counseling and psychotherapy and found it to be .68, which is equivalent to an r of .32 and an r^2 of .10 (which means that on average 10 percent of dependent variable variance was explained). Haase, Waechter, and Solomon (1982) found that the median strength-of-association value for research reported during the 1970s in the *Journal of Counseling Psychology* was .08, meaning that on average 8 percent of dependent variable variance is explained by the independent variable. Hamblin (1971) estimated a comparable figure of .10 for sociological research. Rubin and Conway (1985) reported similar figures based on their survey of the social work research literature. Lipsey (1990) reported 102 mean effect sizes calculated in studies that reviewed psychological, educational, and behavioral treatment effectiveness research. The midpoint of these 102 mean effect sizes was .45, which corresponds to an r^2 of .05. This is lower than the figures found for psychotherapy, counseling, and clinical social work interventions and is closer to the figure for medium effects suggested by Cohen, as cited above.

The preceding findings on average effect sizes can provide approximate benchmarks that can be useful in interpreting effect sizes in future research. It seems reasonable to say that interventions whose effect sizes explain approximately 5 percent to 10 percent of outcome variance are about as effective as the average intervention reported in published evaluations.

Before squaring, the correlation coefficients of these "average" interventions would be in the neighborhood of .23 to .32. Their ES would be approximately .45 to .68.

We reiterate here that an intervention's effect size, alone, does not indicate its value. An intervention with a stronger effect size is not necessarily "better" than one with a weaker effect size. For example, an intervention that reduces the rate of child abuse or school dropout among high-risk individuals from 55 percent to 45 percent may be more valuable to society than an intervention that reduces the annual turnover rate among Big Brother or Big Sister volunteers from 60 percent to 40 percent. Or, returning to an example we used earlier, an intervention that reduces the rate of extreme physical abuse from 55 percent to 45 percent might be deemed more valuable than an intervention that reduces the rate of mild verbal abuse from 65 percent to 35 percent. Determining which intervention is "better" or more valuable involves considering the substantive significance of research findings, an issue we shall take up next.

Substantive Significance

Measures of the strength of a relationship do not automatically indicate the substantive significance of that relationship. In studies of the effectiveness of clinical interventions, the term **clinical significance** is likely to be used instead of the term *substantive significance*. Both terms mean the same thing. By the **substantive significance** of a relationship (or its clinical significance), we mean its importance from a practical standpoint. No matter how strong a relationship may be—no matter how well it compares to an average effect size or how close to 1.0 it may be in a measure of association—we still can ask whether it constitutes a substantively important or trivial finding.

Let's consider this issue in connection to the child abuse example we used earlier in this chapter. Suppose one intervention makes the difference between a 35 percent and a 65 percent recidivism rate. Assuming that the finding was statistically significant, how substantively significant is that finding? In other words, how much practical importance does it have for the field? Suppose another experiment finds that a different intervention with the same target population makes a statistically significant difference between a 20 percent recidivism rate and an 80 percent rate. Assuming that the two interventions were equal in terms of cost, time, and so on, determining which was the more substantively significant finding would seem to be a fairly straightforward process, and we would choose the one with the 20 percent recidivism rate. Because everything else but relationship magnitude was of equal importance, the stronger relationship would be the more substantively significant relationship.

But suppose a different experiment finds that after five years of daily psychoanalysis costing $500 per week, 80 percent of treated abusive parents as compared to 20 percent of untreated parents say they agree with Freud's ideas. Which intervention would you find to be more valuable if you were providing services to that target population: the one that made a 30 percent difference in child abuse recidivism, or the one that made a 60 percent difference in agreement with Freud's ideas? We hope you would deem the weaker relationship involving the intervention that reduced child abuse by 30 percent to have more substantive significance than the stronger relationship pertaining to attitudes about a theory. (Not that there is anything wrong with psychoanalysis per se; we would say the same thing about any theory in this practical context.)

The preceding admittedly extreme hypothetical comparison illustrates that no automatic correspondence exists between the strength of a relationship and that relationship's substantive significance. It's important to know how much variation in the dependent variable is explained by the independent variable and how that figure compares to the amount of variation previously explained in other, comparable studies that used comparable variables. But not all studies are comparable in practical importance.

Therefore, after we have ascertained the statistical significance of a relationship and measured the strength of the association, we must make subjective value judgments to gauge the substantive significance of that relationship—value judgments that might consider such intangibles as the importance of the variables and problem studied, whether the benefits of implementing the study's implications are worth the costs of that implementation, and what prior knowledge we have about the problem studied and how to alleviate it. If we judge that the study addresses a trivial problem, assesses trivial variables, reports results that imply actions whose costs far outweigh their benefits, or yields findings that add nothing to what is already known, then we might deem observed relationships to be trivial even if they explain a relatively large amount of variation in the dependent variable. To reiterate, we must consider all three issues: statistical significance, strength of relationship, and substantive significance.

Main Points

• Inferential statistics help rule out chance as a plausible explanation of our findings; thus, combined with our consideration of design issues, they help us decide whether we can generalize about populations or theoretical processes based on our findings.

• Statistical significance testing identifies the probability that our findings can be attributed to chance. Chance, or sampling error, represents a rival hypothesis for our findings—a purely statistical hypothesis called the *null hypothesis*.

• Tests of statistical significance use theoretical sampling distributions, which show what proportion of random distributions of data would produce relationships at least as strong as the one observed in our findings. The theoretical sampling distribution thus shows the probability that observing the relationship we observed was due to the luck of the draw when and if no such relationship really exists in a population or in a theoretical sense.

• The probability that the observed relationship could have been produced by chance is compared to a preselected level of significance. If the probability is equal to or less than that level of significance, then the finding is deemed statistically significant and the plausibility of the null hypothesis (chance) is refuted.

• Social researchers traditionally tend to use .05 as the level of significance, but that is merely a convention. A higher or lower level can be justified depending on the research context. When .05 is used, a finding that is significant at the .05 level is one that could not be expected to result from the luck of the draw, or sampling error, more than 5 times out of 100.

• When we test directional hypotheses, we can use one-tailed tests of significance. These locate the critical region of significant values at one predicted end of the theoretical sampling distribution.

• When testing nondirectional hypotheses, we must use two-tailed tests of significance. These place the critical regions at both ends of the theoretical sampling distribution.

• Type I errors occur when we reject a true null hypothesis. Type II errors occur when we accept a false null hypothesis. Every decision based on statistical significance testing will risk one error or the other.

• Increasing sample size reduces the risk of a Type II error, but the larger the sample, the greater the likelihood that weak relationships will be statistically significant.

• Measures of association such as correlation coefficients and analogous statistics (e.g., phi, Cramer's V, and eta) assess a relationship's strength. The stronger the relationship, the closer the measure-of-association statistic will be to 1.0 or −1.0. The weaker the relationship, the closer it will be to zero. Many measures of association are based on a proportionate reduction of error (PRE) model and tell us how much error in predicting attributes of a dependent variable is reduced by knowledge of the attribute of the independent variable. Many measure-of-association statistics can be squared to indicate the proportion of variation in the dependent variable that is explained by one or more independent variables.

• Statistics that portray the strength of association between variables are often referred to by the term *effect size*. Effect-size statistics might refer to proportion of variation in the dependent variable that can be explained or to the difference between the means of two groups divided by the standard deviation.

• Statistical significance, relationship strength, and substantive significance (also known as *clinical significance*) must not be confused with one another. Statistically significant relationships are not necessarily strong or substantively meaningful. Strong relationships are not necessarily substantively significant, and some seemingly weak relationships in which only a small percentage of dependent variable variance is explained can have great substantive (or clinical) significance. The substantive (or clinical) significance of a finding pertains to its practical or theoretical value or meaningfulness; it cannot be assessed without making value judgments about the importance of the variables or problem studied, what the finding adds to what is or is not already known about alleviating a problem, and so on.

Review Questions and Exercises

1. Here are some really silly hypotheses you can test at the beginning of class or while relaxing in the student lounge:

a. Firstborns are more likely to have an odd number of letters in their first name than are later-borns.

b. Firstborns are more likely to have an odd number of letters in their middle name than are later-borns.

c. Firstborns are more likely to have an odd number of letters in their last name than are later-borns.

d. Firstborns are more likely to be brunettes than are later-borns.

If you test these hypotheses among about 20 or 30 students and find that for one or more of the hypotheses the proportions are not exactly equal for firstborns and later-borns, then what does that signify? What would it mean if you tested the statistical significance of your results and found that the probability of getting the results due to chance, or sampling error, was .04?

Would you conclude that the hypothesis was really true and could be generalized? Or would you conclude that despite the significance it would be wrong to generalize? If the latter, what type of error would you be making if you generalized? Should you use a one- or two-tailed test of significance?

2. Deal a deck of cards into two piles of four cards per pile. Do this 20 times, subtracting the number of red cards in the left-hand pile from the number in the right-hand pile each time. After each deal, record the difference in the percentage of red cards between the two piles. Construct a theoretical sampling distribution based on those 20 differences in percentages. Repeat this process, but this time deal 20 cards in each pile. Compare the two sampling distributions. Which has the greater degree of dispersion—that is, the greater degree of sampling error? Suppose each red card represents a student who stayed in school and each black card represents a dropout. If the left-hand pile represents high-risk students who received school social work services, and the right-hand pile represents their control group counterparts, then what do these two theoretical sampling distributions illustrate about the influence of sample size on statistical significance? What do they illustrate about the importance of refuting the plausibility of chance?

Internet Exercises

1. Using InfoTrac College Edition, enter the search term *statistical significance* to find two articles on inferential data analysis issues discussed in this chapter. Write down the bibliographical reference information for each article and summarize its main points. Two articles worth looking for, both by Bruce Thompson, are as follows:

> "Improving Research Clarity and Usefulness with Effect Size Indices as Supplements to Statistical Significance Tests," *Exceptional Children,* Spring 1999.

> "Why Encouraging Effect Size Reporting Is Not Working: The Etiology of Researcher Resistance to Changing Practices," *Journal of Psychology,* March 1999.

2. Go to the following website: www.socialresearchmethods.net/OJtrial/ojhome.htm. Click on all of the prompts that appear on your screen, in order of appearance, to see how the O. J. Simpson trial illustrates the concepts of significance levels, null hypotheses, Type I and Type II errors, and effect size.

Additional Reading

Rubin, Allen. 2007. *Statistics for Evidence-Based Practice and Evaluation.* Belmont, CA: Thomson Brooks/Cole. As we mentioned in the previous chapter, this book is practitioner-friendly. Part 3, on inferential statistics, is particularly relevant to this chapter. It goes beyond the material presented in this chapter, but does so in an introductory manner and in a way that connects inferential statistics to evidence-based practice.

CHAPTER 22

Inferential Data Analysis: Part 2

What You'll Learn in This Chapter

Continuing our discussion of statistical analysis, we'll examine the probability of avoiding Type II errors, the use of meta-analysis, the functions of alternative statistical tests and what's involved in selecting them, and problems and issues in the use of inferential statistics.

INTRODUCTION

Now that you understand the concept of statistical significance and the need to consider relationship strength and substantive significance as well, let's cover some more advanced material on inferential statistics. We'll begin by looking at how you can assess the probability of avoiding Type II errors.

STATISTICAL POWER ANALYSIS

In Chapter 21, we defined Type I and Type II errors and discussed the importance of both types. We noted that tests of statistical significance assess the probability of making Type I errors. We also indicated that researchers can reduce the probability of making a Type II error by increasing their sample size, but we did not discuss how you can assess exactly how much they risk making a Type II error in any particular study. Assessing that risk is critical, but we saved that topic for this chapter because an understanding of measures of association and effect size is required to assess the risk of making Type II errors.

Such probability assessment is called *statistical power analysis*. Statistical power analysis is an often-neglected but terribly important area of inferential statistics. It can be an extremely complex topic from a mathematical standpoint, and most introductory research or statistics texts in the social sciences barely mention it. But recognition is growing of the topic's importance and the erroneous conclusions that are risked by its frequent neglect in social research studies. We think it's essential that you have a conceptual grasp of this topic so that you will be able to use available power tables to guide decision making about sample size and your interpretation of findings that are not statistically significant. For a more thorough treatment of this topic, including its mathematical underpinnings, we refer you to an outstanding book titled *Statistical Power Analysis for the Behavioral Sciences* by Jacob Cohen (1988).

Statistical power analysis deals with the probability of avoiding Type II errors. In other words, it assesses the probability of correctly rejecting a null hypothesis that is false. Recall that statistical significance testing tells us only the probability of incorrectly rejecting a null hypothesis that is true. In other words, significance testing tells us only the probability of committing a Type I error, whereas power analysis deals with the probability of committing a Type II error.

Historically, social scientists, including social work researchers, have virtually ignored the probability of committing Type II errors in reporting their studies. They routinely accept a .05 risk of a Type I error regardless of, and seemingly unaware of, the risk of committing a Type II error. Implicitly, they seem to assume that Type I errors are the only ones really worth worrying about. In a review of social work research, for example, Orme and Combs-Orme (1986) performed their own calculations on the results reported in the studies they reviewed and found that almost half of the studies took greater than a .20 risk of committing a Type II error for relationships equivalent to a correlation of .30—relationships of medium strength in which $r^2 = .09$. That magnitude of relationship would be found, for instance, if 35 percent of treated cases as compared to 65 percent of untreated cases recidivated. Thus, some studies that conclude that tested interventions or programs are ineffective might be incorrectly labeling as failures interventions or programs that actually have substantively important effects.

The neglect of this issue probably can be understood largely as a function of the neglect of statistical power analysis in the education of researchers, the self-perpetuating tradition of neglect of it in the literature, the mistaken notion that Type I errors are always many times more serious than Type II errors, and the incorrect perception that it is not feasible to estimate and reduce the risk of committing Type II errors. Assuming that we already have sufficiently illustrated the importance of Type II errors, let's look now at the feasibility of estimating and reducing the probability of committing them.

Mathematically calculating the risk of committing a Type II error is far too advanced a topic for this book, so we refer you to Cohen's text for that material. Fortunately, however, we can estimate that risk without performing calculations. We can do this simply by examining statistical power tables that Cohen constructed based on such calculations. What we find in statistical power tables is the power of statistical significance tests for varying levels of significance, sample sizes, and relationship magnitudes. Cohen's book provides such tables for various types of significance tests.

Drawing from the figures in Cohen's tables, Table 22-1 displays the power of testing the significance of correlation coefficients at the .05 and .10 levels of significance for small, medium, and large effect sizes. This table can be used to plan a research study even if your significance test does not involve correlation

Table 22-1 Power of Test of Significance of Correlation Coefficient by Level of Significance, Effect Size, and Sample Size[a]

	.05 SIGNIFICANCE LEVEL			.10 SIGNIFICANCE LEVEL[b]			
	EFFECT SIZE			EFFECT SIZE			
	SMALL	MEDIUM	LARGE	SMALL	MEDIUM	LARGE	
SAMPLE SIZE[a]	$r = .10$ $r^2 = .01$	$r = .30$ $r^2 = .09$	$r = .50$ $r^2 = .25$	$r = .10$ $r^2 = .01$	$r = .30$ $r^2 = .09$	$r = .50$ $r^2 = .25$	SAMPLE SIZE[a]
10	06	13	33	11	22	46	10
20	07	25	64	13	37	75	20
30	08	37	83	15	50	90	30
40	09	48	92	16	60	96	40
50	11	57	97	18	69	98	50
60	12	65	99	20	76	99	60
70	13	72	*	22	82	*	70
80	14	78		23	86		80
90	16	83		25	90		90
100	17	86		27	92		100
200	29	99		41	*		200
300	41	*		54			300
400	52			64			400
500	61			72			500
600	69			79			600
700	76			84			700
800	81			88			800
900	85			91			900
1000	89			94			1000

[a]The figures in this table are approximately the same as for tables on chi-square tests (with a 2-by-2 table) and *t*-tests. For *t*-tests, the number of cases in each group, added together, would approximate the sample size in this table.

[b]The figures at each level of significance are for a two-tailed test; however, the power figures at the .10 level approximate the power of one-tailed tests at the .05 level.

*Power values below this point exceed .995.

The figures for this table were derived from tables in Jacob Cohen, *Statistical Power Analysis for the Behavioral Sciences*, 2nd ed., New York: Lawrence Erlbaum Associates, Inc. 1988.

coefficients; the figures in Cohen's tables for other types of significance tests are approximately the same as in Table 22-1. If you desire more precision, examine Cohen's book and his more detailed tables.

When using Table 22-1 to plan a research study, we first choose a significance level. (If you choose the .01 level, you will need to examine the tables in Cohen's book.) The next step is to estimate the strength of the correlation (which is one form of effect size) between your independent and dependent variables that you expect exists in the population. The columns in the table pertain to small (r = .10; r^2 = .01), medium (r = .30; r^2 = .09), and large (r = .50; r^2 = .25) effect sizes. (If you want to assess the power for a different effect size—say, .20, .40, or larger than .50—you will need to consult Cohen's book. But you probably will be satisfied using Table 22-1, as you will see.)

Of course, you have no way of knowing before collecting your data the real effect size of the population or if a relationship exists at all, but you can identify a figure that approximates your expectations. For example, in Chapter 21 we noted that Rubin and Conway (1985) identified an r^2 of .10 as the average strength of significant relationships found in clinical social work outcome research. (You may recall that this effect size corresponds to the medium ES of .60 when using means and the standard deviation to calculate effect size.) Therefore, if that is your area of study and you expect that your hypothesis is true, then you might expect to find an r^2 of approximately .10. Thus, you would use one of the columns for medium effect size in Table 22-1.

Each figure in that column is the probability (imagine a decimal point before each figure) of correctly rejecting the null hypothesis for a population r value of .30 at different levels of sample size. The different sample sizes are listed in the "Sample Size" column.

Recall our earlier discussion of the effects of sample size on statistical significance. Note how the probability of rejecting the null hypothesis increases as sample size increases. For example, if your sample size is only 10 cases, and your significance level is .05, then your probability of correctly rejecting the null hypothesis is only .13; that is, your statistical power would be only .13. That would mean that you would have a probability of 1.00 minus .13, or .87, of incorrectly accepting a false null hypothesis. The latter probability of .87 would be your probability of committing a Type II error.

But if your sample size is 40 cases, then your power would be .48. Still, however, you would have a .52 probability (1.00 − .48 = .52) of committing a Type II error. To have a .20 probability of committing a Type II error (Cohen recommends .20 as a maximum), your power would have to be .80 (which we find by subtracting .20 from 1.00). To obtain at least that level of power, your sample size would have to be 90 cases. (More precisely, your power for 90 cases would be .83. If you consult Cohen's book, you will find that 84 cases will give you a power of exactly .80.) If you want your probability of committing a Type II error to equal your probability of committing a Type I error (that is, to be at .05), then your statistical power will have to be .95, and to obtain that level of power you will need a sample size of more than 100 cases (140 cases is the precise figure in Cohen's book).

In short, by using this table, you can select a sample size that will provide you with the level of risk of a Type II error that you desire. But what if it's impossible to obtain a sample that big? Suppose you plan to survey all of the social workers in a rural area where the population of social workers numbers only 50. Table 22-1 indicates that your statistical power is only .57 for n = 50, r = .30, and a significance level of .05. Thus, your probability of committing a Type II error would be .43 (1.00 − .57). It's probably not worth all the expense and effort to do a study when you know in advance that even if your research hypothesis is true you are taking almost a 50:50 risk of coming up with an incorrect conclusion, despite the fact that your risk of a Type I error is only .05. In that case, because you cannot increase your sample size, one reasonable alternative would be to lower your risk of committing a Type II error by increasing your risk of committing a Type I error.

For example, you might decide to raise your significance level from .05 to .10 and thus consult the column under the .10 significance level in Table 22-1. In the column for a medium effect size and a .10 significance level, you would find that your power would be .69 (as compared to .57 for the .05 significance level) for n = 50. Thus, by raising the risk of a Type I error to .10, you would reduce the probability of a Type II error to .31 (1.00 − .69). You might still conclude that the risk is too great to warrant doing the study. But if you did decide to pursue it, taking risks of .10 and .31 for the two types of errors might make more sense than taking risks of .05 and .43.

Ideally, of course, you would find some way to increase your sample size—perhaps by including another geographic area in the study—to have an acceptably low risk for both types of errors. Also, whatever you decided to do about your study and its sample size would be decided in light of the risks involved. It's mind-boggling to imagine that many researchers are implementing studies without taking statistical power analysis into account; consequently, they don't know the odds that they're spinning their wheels trying to confirm hypotheses that, even if true, have a low probability of being supported.

Imagine, for example, that you are evaluating the effectiveness of a school social work program in an inner-city high school. You think it will reduce dropout rates from 55 to 45 percent. As we indicated in Chapter 21, this reduction would correspond to a correlation of .10 (.01 when squared), which in Table 22-1 is found in the column for a small effect size. To have statistical power of .80 (and therefore a .20 probability of committing a Type II error), you would need a sample size of approximately 800 cases if you chose a .05 significance level, or about 600 cases if you chose a .10 significance level.

Although statistical power analysis has its greatest utility when conducted a priori—that is, while your study is still being designed—it also has value on a post hoc basis after you fail to reject the null hypothesis. When reporting null findings, it's important to inform readers of the probability that, in failing to reject the null hypothesis, you are committing a Type II error. This is true regardless of whether your power analysis was conducted before or after your study. Before readers dismiss your hypothesis as one that was not confirmed, they should be informed of the probability that the reason it could not be supported was a Type II error. The importance of this is perhaps most obvious when new interventions are being tested for problems for which we know of no other effective interventions.

Before leaving this topic, let's reiterate a point made earlier to clarify an aspect of statistical power analysis that may seem confusing. How can statistical power analysis tell us in advance the probability of incorrectly failing to reject a false null hypothesis when we have no way of determining ahead of time whether the null hypothesis is false or true? The answer: Statistical power analysis does not tell us in advance the odds that we will reject a false null hypothesis; the probability it gives us tells us only the odds that we will reject the null hypothesis if it really happens to be false. In other words, when using statistical power analysis, we begin by saying, "Suppose the null hypothesis really is false and that a relationship of a certain strength (we also specify the particular strength that we are assuming) really does exist in the population. If that is so, then what is the probability that we will obtain findings that are statistically significant were we to use a given sample size and significance level?"

META-ANALYSIS

In light of the preceding material on both Type I and II errors, you might correctly suppose that relying exclusively on the results of any one study to guide you in your practice can be precarious. Any one study might be making a Type I or II error. One study with a very small sample, for example, might obtain statistically insignificant results for an intervention with a moderate effect size. Another study of the same intervention, but with a much larger sample, might obtain statistically significant results with a smaller effect size.

If you've ever reviewed the research literature on a particular topic (perhaps when preparing a term paper), you know that different studies tend to arrive at different findings about the same topic or research question. One study, for example, might find that case management has strong effects, whereas a second study might find that it has weak effects. Several studies might find that case management has medium effects, and some might find that it has none. Another study might even find that it has harmful effects.

Different studies tend to come up with contrasting findings for a variety of reasons, not all of them statistical. Differences in research design and the ways data are collected constitute one common reason. In studies of intervention efficacy, different studies might come up with contrasting findings because they operationalize the intervention in different ways, differ with respect to the background characteristics of the client groups that make up their samples, or use different ways to measure outcome. Sometimes, studies that seem almost identical come up with different findings simply because of sampling error and chance fluctuations.

Drawing conclusions from a bewildering array of inconsistent findings across different studies on the same topic is not easy, yet it may be of great utility to figure out some way to make some general statement about how effective an intervention seems in light of all the studies taken as a whole. Suppose, for example, you are planning a new service delivery program and are torn between emphasizing case management services versus an alternative service delivery approach. You review the research literature evaluating the effectiveness of each approach, hoping to learn whether one by and large tends to be more effective than the other. If you were able to conclude that case management tended to have an effect size of ES = .70, and the alternate approach tended to have an ES of .25, then you might find that to be an important reason for favoring a case management approach in your planning deliberations.

A method for simplifying the process of drawing conclusions from a bewildering array of inconsistent findings across different studies on the same topic is called *meta-analysis*. Although the term sounds complicated, its underlying meaning is not. **Meta-analysis** simply involves calculating the mean effect size across previously completed research studies on a particular topic. Meta-analysis emerged in the late 1970s when Smith and Glass (1977) reported their classic meta-analysis (which we mentioned in Chapter 21) showing that the mean ES of nearly 400 controlled evaluations of counseling and psychotherapy was .68. In other words, Smith and Glass read the many studies, recorded the ES found in each study, added them up, and then divided the sum by the number of ES's they recorded to determine the average ES across all of the studies.

Meta-analyses need not be limited to the calculation of mean effect sizes; some statistically complex meta-analytic procedures can be used to calculate the statistical significance of an overall set of results aggregated across various studies. The latter procedures are less commonly used than those that just focus on aggregating effect sizes (Fischer, 1990).

Fischer (1990) found more than 300 meta-analyses conducted during the 1980s on such topics as psychotherapy in general, cognitive therapy, family therapy, and deinstitutionalization. Almost all of these meta-analyses were done in fields related to social work, but only two were found in social work per se: one on social work practice in mental health (Videka-Sherman, 1988) and one on adolescent drug prevention programs (Tobler, 1986).

In his excellent review of meta-analysis, Fischer identifies its benefits. One of the most important benefits is something we have already been discussing: By providing mean effect sizes, meta-analysis gives us benchmarks that are useful in considering the relative strengths of effectiveness of various interventions. A related benefit of meta-analysis is its ability to identify relationships across studies. For example, in addition to calculating overall mean effect sizes for broad intervention approaches, we can see how the mean effect size varies by various clinical or methodological factors.

Despite these benefits, meta-analysis has many critics and is highly controversial. One of the most serious criticisms is that researchers conducting meta-analyses might lump together studies that are methodologically strong with those that have serious methodological limitations and then treat their results equally in the analysis. Thus, if two studies with weak internal validity report effect sizes of 1.0 for a particular intervention, and one strong experiment reports an effect size of zero for the same intervention, then a mean effect size of .67 will be reported in the meta-analysis (1 + 1 + 0, divided by 3). Critics argue that this is misleading because the finding of the methodologically strong study may be the only one that is valid, and therefore the only one that should guide the selection of practice interventions.

An example of this controversy appeared in the social work literature in the late 1980s. In a meta-analysis of social work practice effects in treating chronic mentally ill clients, Lynn Videka-Sherman (1988) reported that shorter-term treatments produced better effect sizes than did longer-term treatments. This conclusion irked Gerard Hogarty, a social worker who had devoted his career to experimental research on the treatment of individuals with chronic mental illness. Hogarty had pointed out time and again in his research findings, and in reviewing the experimental research of his colleagues, that chronic mental illness tends to be a lifelong affliction that requires long-term care.

In his critique of Videka-Sherman's meta-analysis, Hogarty (1989) argued that her finding resulted largely from her inclusion of one study whose methodology did not apply to the comparison of short- versus long-term treatment effects. That study used a cross-sectional design and found that service users were much more likely to be rehospitalized than nonusers, with a very large negative effect size of −1.97. A negative ES indicates harmful effects. If one study finds a negative ES of −1.97, and another study finds a beneficial positive ES of +1.97, the mean ES of the two studies will be zero (no effects). Hogarty argued that this finding was due to a selectivity bias in which the treatment users were more impaired than the nonusers, and that Videka-Sherman was wrong to view the individuals who had no treatment as having had shorter-term treatment than the more severely impaired individuals who received some treatment.

Hogarty went on to show how Videka-Sherman's meta-analysis would have had the opposite conclusion if it had included only studies with strong experimental controls. In criticizing this and various other findings of the Videka-Sherman meta-analysis, Hogarty argued that "effect sizes from the better designed studies frequently were overwhelmed [in calculating mean effect sizes and correlations between effect size and treatment factors] by effect sizes from reports of lower quality that unduly influenced judgments of effective practice" (1989:363).

In attempting to handle the preceding criticism, some meta-analysts have rated the methodological quality of studies and then used that rating as a factor in their meta-analyses. The reliability and validity of those ratings, however, is open to question. Rather than include studies of varying methodological quality, and then rating their quality, some meta-analysts simply exclude studies with poor methodologies. However, there is no guarantee that their methodological judgment will be adequate in this regard (Fischer, 1990).

Another potential pitfall in meta-analysis involves sampling bias. Fischer (1990) explains how sampling bias can result from two problems: (1) The reviewer may have missed some important studies (as Hogarty claimed that Videka-Sherman did), and (2) much research is not published. The latter problem may make meta-analysis particularly vulnerable to biased findings because studies that do not support the effectiveness of tested interventions may be less likely to be submitted or accepted for publication than are studies with positive results. Therefore, studies with positive findings may be more likely to be identified by meta-analysts than are studies with negative findings.

In light of all these problems, therefore, perhaps the best advice to readers of meta-analyses, at least for the time being, is "Caveat emptor!" ("Let the buyer beware!").

SELECTING A TEST OF STATISTICAL SIGNIFICANCE

As we mentioned early in the previous chapter, statistical significance can be calculated in many different ways. In fact, new tests are continually being developed, and it is unrealistic to expect to have a deep understanding of all of them. In this section, we will focus on the criteria for selecting from among the tests that are commonly used in social work research. Our treatment of this topic will be kept to the conceptual level. We will not delve into the computational formulas or mathematical derivations of each statistical test.

Like measures of association, significance testing can be calculated by using computers. Our priority here will be knowing which test to run on the computer, not learning how to do the calculations yourself. But, again, we encourage you to pursue your studies in this area beyond this book and to examine the texts we recommend at the end of this chapter. The more you learn about the mathematical derivations and calculations associated with each test of significance, the richer will be your conceptual understanding of each test.

The prime criteria that influence the selection of a statistical significance test are: (1) the level of measurement of the variables, (2) the number of variables included in the analysis (bivariate or multivariate) and the number of categories in the nominal variables, (3) the type of sampling methods used in data collection, and (4) the way the variables are distributed in the population to which the study seeks to generalize. Depending on a study's attributes regarding these criteria, a selection will be made between two broad types of significance tests: parametric tests and nonparametric tests.

The term *parametric test* is derived from the word *parameter.* A parameter is a summary statistic that describes an entire population, such as the mean age of all abusive parents in the United States or the standard deviation in their income. **Parametric tests** assume that at least one variable being studied has an interval- or ratio-level of measurement, that the sampling distribution of the relevant parameters of those variables is normal, and that the different groups being compared have been randomly selected and are independent of one another. Commonly used parametric tests include the *t*-test, analysis of variance, and Pearson's product-moment correlation.

A Common Nonparametric Test: Chi-Square

Nonparametric tests, on the other hand, have been created for use when not all of the assumptions of parametric statistics can be met. Most do not require an interval or ratio level of measurement and can be used with nominal- or ordinal-level data that are not distributed normally. Some do not require independently selected samples. The most commonly used nonparametric test is chi-square.

The **chi-square** statistical test is used when we are treating both our independent and dependent variables as nominal level, such as in our hypothetical example in Chapter 21, which relates the provision of treatment (yes or no) to child abuse recidivism (yes or no). It was used to calculate the probabilities displayed in Tables 21-1 and 21-2. The chi-square test assesses the extent to which the frequencies you observe in your table of results differ from what you would expect to observe if the distribution was created by chance.

Thus, if 100 recidivists and 100 nonrecidivists were randomly divided between two groups, we would expect to observe 50 recidivists and 50 nonrecidivists in each group. The greater the deviation between that expected split and the observed split, the greater will be the value of the chi-square statistic. For example, if we observed a 40:60 split for treated cases and a 60:40 split for control cases for a sample size n of 200, the computer would calculate a chi-square value of 8.0 and would indicate that that value is significant at the .01 level.

Whether a particular chi-square value is statistically significant depends on something called degrees of freedom. The number of degrees of freedom we have depends on how many categories are in each variable. It's equal to one less than the number of categories in one variable times one less than the number of categories in the other variable and may be written as $(r - 1)(c - 1)$, where r is the number of categories in the row variable and c is the number of categories in the column variable. Once we know a particular chi-square value, we look it up in a table that shows what chi-square values are significant for what degrees of freedom. Standard tables of values permit us to determine whether a given association is statistically significant and at what level. Most standard statistics textbooks provide such tables and instructions on their use. They would show that for one degree of freedom (df), which we would have in our recidivism example (2 row categories minus 1, multiplied by 2 column categories minus 1), we would need a chi-square value of at least 6.6349 to be significant at the .01 level. Because our chi-square value of 8.0 exceeds that figure, our finding would be statistically significant at .01. If you have access to statistical software such as SPSS, then your computer will take everything into account and determine the significance for you, and you won't need to calculate chi-square or degrees of freedom or consult a table of chi-square values. Still, it's useful to know what steps the computer is taking for you, and we again encourage you to consult one of the statistics texts we recommend at the end of this chapter to develop a deeper understanding of these processes.

Additional Nonparametric Tests

As we said at the outset of our discussion of significance tests, so many statistical tests are available—and so many new ones are continually being developed—that it's unrealistic to try to be knowledgeable about all of them. Earlier, we discussed the most commonly used ones in social work research. Before leaving this topic, we'll just briefly identify some of the other types of tests that you might encounter. We again encourage you to consult the texts we'll recommend at the end of this chapter if you wish to become more knowledgeable about these tests.

Occasionally, we'll encounter situations or studies in which a nonparametric test other than chi-square is needed. For example, sometimes our sample size is too small to use the chi-square test. A test that is like chi-square but designed for use when the sample is too small for chi-square is called the *Fisher's exact test.*

Another example pertains to before-and-after designs in which the same sample is used for the "before" and "after" data on the same nominal variable, which means that the two groups of data being compared (that is, the "before" data and the "after" data) are related. This violates one of the assumptions of the chi-square test. In its place, therefore, we can use the *McNemar nonparametric test* because it was designed for such situations.

Other nonparametric tests have been designed for use with ordinal data. These include the *Mann–Whitney U test,* the *median test,* the *Kolmogorov–Smirnov two-sample test,* and the *Wilcoxon sign test.* Textbooks that cover nonparametric statistics, as well as some statistical software manuals for computers, will tell you more about when to use each test. As with all of the statistical tests we'll discuss, ultimately your computer can do all your calculations and provide you with the probability that the observed relationship was due to chance. No matter which test you use, however, its probability level will have the same meaning as the one we have been discussing throughout Chapters 21 and 22.

Common Bivariate Parametric Tests

Now let's review the commonly used parametric tests we mentioned above. We'll start with the ***t*-test.** The *t*-test is appropriate for use when we have a dichotomous nominal independent variable (that is, a variable with only two categories, such as when we compare treated and untreated cases) and an interval- or ratio-level dependent variable. Thus, if we were comparing treated and untreated cases in terms of the number of abusive incidents, then we would use the *t*-test instead of chi-square because the number of abusive incidents, unlike the nominal variable of recidivism (yes–no), is at the ratio level of measurement.

When you use the *t*-test, your computer will calculate a *t* value based on a complicated formula that divides the difference between the means of the two groups on the dependent variable by an estimate of the standard deviation of the theoretical sampling distribution, which itself must be calculated using a complicated formula that accounts for the sample size and standard deviation of each group in a sample. Despite the complexity of the formula, the function of the *t*-test ultimately is the same as that of any other significance test: to ascertain the probability that the observed relationship was the result of sampling error, or chance. And as for other significance tests, once we calculate the *t* value, we must take into account the degrees of freedom and then locate in a table of *t* values the probability that our finding was due to the luck of the draw. In a *t*-test, the degrees of freedom will equal our total sample size (summing across both groups) minus 2. Thus, for our example of two groups of 100 abusive parents each, our degrees of freedom would be 198 (200 − 2). Also, as for other significance tests, statistical software such as SPSS will account for all of this and determine the probability of a Type I error for us. Once we run our computer program, all we have to do is look at that probability figure to know whether or not the relationship is statistically significant.

Another parametric test is **analysis of variance,** which is abbreviated ANOVA. This test uses the same logic as the *t*-test and, if used when a *t*-test could have been used, will generate the same probability value. ANOVA can be used to test for the significance of bivariate and multivariate relationships. When testing bivariate relationships, the only difference between it and the *t*-test is that the *t*-test can be applied only when the nominal independent variable is dichotomous. ANOVA, on the other hand, can be used when the independent variable has more than two categories. (The dependent variable still must be interval or ratio level.)

Thus, if we wish to compare the outcomes of three or more different treated or untreated groups—instead of just comparing one treatment group to one control group—we would use ANOVA instead of the *t*-test. Its formula is even more complicated than the *t*-test's formula. It produces a statistic called the *F value,* which we compare to a table of significant *F* values, just as we do with other statistical tests. Ultimately, based on that *F* value, we want to know the probability that the differences between our groups (on an interval- or ratio-level dependent variable) result from chance. ANOVA will ascertain that by comparing the between-group differences to the variation within each group. Again, our computer will tell us the probability that the null hypothesis is true, just as it will when we use any other significance test.

Both of the preceding parametric tests, the *t*-test and ANOVA, apply when the independent variable is nominal. The other commonly used parametric test, the **Pearson product-moment correlation** (*r*), is used when both the independent and dependent variables are at the interval or ratio level of measurement. We discussed this statistic in Chapter 21 as a measure of association and stated that it can also be used to test for statistical significance.

When testing *r* for statistical significance we ask: Assuming there is no correlation between these two variables in the population (that is, $r = 0$), what is the probability of finding the correlation we found in a randomly drawn sample from that population as big as the sample we randomly selected? In other words, what is the probability that the null hypothesis ($r = 0$) is true for the entire population and that the correlation we found in our sample occurred just because of the luck of the draw, or sampling error? To find this probability, we look at a table showing what *r* values are statistically significant for different sample sizes and different levels of significance. (For positive relationships we would be interested in *r* values between 0.0 and 1.0. For negative, or inverse relationships, the *r* values would fall between 0.0 and −1.0. Chapter 7 discussed positive and negative relationships.) That table of significant values is constructed applying a complicated extension of the ANOVA formula for independent variables with indefinitely large numbers of categories. Again, our computer will not only calculate *r* for us, but also tell us the probability that the null hypothesis is true—that is, that $r = 0$ for the population. In other words, with the push of a few buttons, we will learn both the strength of the observed relationship and whether or not it is statistically significant.

Multivariate Analyses

So far, our discussion of statistical inference has been kept at the bivariate level. Inferential statistical tests have also been developed for **multivariate analyses,** which analyze the simultaneous relationships among more than two variables. A commonly used extension of correlational analysis for multivariate inferences is multiple regression analysis. **Multiple regression analysis** shows the overall correlation between each of a set of independent variables and an interval- or ratio-level dependent variable. That multiple correlation is symbolized by a capital R, which is the multiple correlation coefficient. As with bivariate correlational analysis, by squaring R we find the proportion of variance that is explained in the dependent variable. But whereas r^2 represents the proportion of variation explained by one independent variable, R^2 represents the proportion of variation that is explained by the entire set of independent variables.

For example, Rubin and Thorelli (1984) reported a multiple regression analysis that sought to explain variation in the duration of service among social service volunteers. Their analysis included 22 variables that might explain duration of service, including such factors as a volunteer's gender, age, ethnicity, socioeconomic status, family obligations, residential mobility, prior experiences, reasons for volunteering, and benefits expected from volunteering. The R value for the entire set of 22 variables was .56, which means that 31 percent (.56 squared equals .31) of the variation in duration of service was explained by all 22 variables acting in concert.

Multiple regression also calculates a statistic called the *standardized regression coefficient,* or *beta weight,* for each predictor variable. The higher the beta weight, the greater the relative effect of the particular predictor variable on the dependent variable when all other predictor variables are controlled. Multiple regression also tests the statistical significance of each beta weight, thus identifying which particular predictor variables are significantly related to the dependent variable after controlling for all other predictor variables.

In the Rubin and Thorelli study, the only significant predictor variable, and the one with the highest beta weight, was the extent of psychic benefits that volunteers expected to derive from their volunteer work—client gratitude, a sense that volunteers made a big difference in someone's life, and so on. The less they expected, the longer they lasted as volunteers. That variable alone—when the effects of all other 21 predictor variables were controlled—explained 18 percent of the variation in duration of service. Thus, its partial correlation coefficient was .43 (the square root of .18). The proportion of variation in duration of service attributable to all the other 21 variables combined was only 13 percent.

Partial correlation coefficients have the same meaning and uses as their bivariate counterparts, with one prime difference: They measure the association between two variables after other, extraneous variables have been controlled. In other words, they express the degree of a relationship at constant levels of the extraneous variables that are controlled. Their significance can be assessed as well, just as with bivariate correlations.

Discriminant function analysis is a multivariate statistic that is analogous to multiple regression analysis but which has been designed for use when the dependent variable is dichotomous. Discriminant function analysis produces the same sorts of statistics as does multiple regression analysis. The statistics have different names from the ones used in multiple regression analysis, but their inferential uses are essentially the same.

In their 1988 article in the *Schizophrenia Bulletin,* Bartko, Carpenter, and McGlashan provide an excellent discussion of the functions of multiple regression analysis and related multivariate statistics—a discussion that is geared to mental health practitioners who are consumers of research but who lack a strong background in statistics. The authors use Venn diagrams, reproduced here in Figures 22-1 and 22-2, to illustrate the logic of multiple regression analysis.

In Figure 22-1, we see three overlapping circles. The middle circle represents the variance of a dependent variable, which we'll call variable *Y*. The other two circles represent two independent variables, X_1 and X_2, which are each associated with the dependent variable, *Y*, but not with each other. Each of the circles for the two independent variables shares a relatively large area of variance with circle *Y*. For the purpose of simplicity, each has been made to share 25 percent of the variance of *Y*. Thus, X_1 and X_2 both have a correlation (r) of .50 with *Y*; when squared (r^2), this indicates that each accounts for 25 percent of the variance in *Y*. Together, the two independent

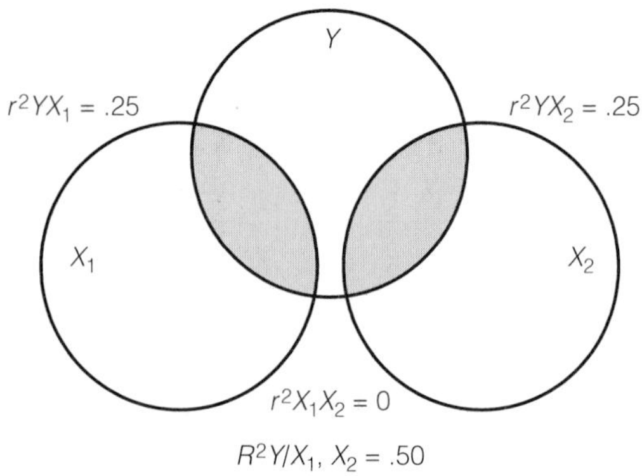

Figure 22-1 Two Predictor Variables X_1 and X_2 Correlate with Dependent Variable Y but Not Each Other, Resulting in a Larger R^2

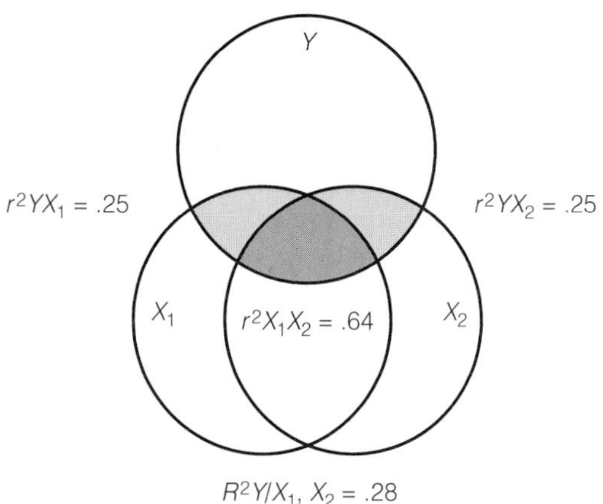

SOURCE: Fig. 17-1, 17-2: J. J. Bartko et al., "Statistical Issues in Long-Term Follow-up Studies," *Schizophrenia Bulletin, 14*(4), 1988, pp. 575–587. Used by permission of the National Institute of Mental Health.

Figure 22-2 Two Predictor Variables X_1 and X_2 Correlate with Dependent Variable Y and Each Other, Resulting in a Lower R^2

variables cumulatively account for 50 percent of the variance in Y, which we get by adding the two shaded areas of Y, each of which is 25 percent of Y. In other words, we are saying that the two independent variables combined have a multiple R^2 of .50, meaning that they explain half of the variation in Y and that the other half is unaccounted for (that is, it results from other factors not studied).

Figure 22-2 resembles Figure 22-1, but with an important difference: This time, the circles for the independent variables overlap each other in addition to overlapping Y. In this example, therefore, there is a relationship between the two independent variables. Both X_1 and X_2 have a .50 correlation with Y, and they have a .64 correlation with each other. If we look only at the bivariate correlation of X_1 with Y or X_2 with Y, we would say that either variable, when examined alone in relation to Y, explains 25 percent of the variation in Y. But because X_1 and X_2 in this case also overlap with each other, the multiple R^2 of Y with the two independent variables is not simply a sum of the r^2 of X_1 with Y and the r^2 of X_2 with Y. We must subtract the area of three-way overlap among X_1, X_2, and Y, which is represented by the darkest shading. Using multiple regression calculations, we would find that when the darkest area of three-way overlap is subtracted, the multiple R^2 of Y with X_1 and X_2 drops to .28. Because of the large overlap (correlation) between X_1 and X_2, in other words, those two variables together account for only an additional 3 percent of the variation in Y beyond the 25 percent that is accounted for by each alone.

Suppose our multiple regression analysis added a third variable, one that overlapped with the lighter shaded area of X_2 and Y. To the extent that this new variable had three-way overlap with X_2 and Y, it would further reduce the importance of X_2 as a factor in explaining Y. In other words, the importance of X_2 in explaining Y—which seemed quite important with a bivariate r of .50—would diminish as the other variables were controlled.

Two additional multivariate statistical procedures that you may encounter are called *path analysis* and *structural equation modeling*. Focusing on path analysis will suffice for our purposes because it represents a subset of structural equation models that is not too complex for a text such as this. (You can examine advanced statistical textbooks for a full treatment of either of these procedures.)

Path analysis is a *causal* model for understanding relationships between variables. Though based on regression analysis, it can provide a more useful graphic picture of relationships among several variables than other means can. Path analysis assumes that the values of one variable are caused by the values of another, so it is essential to distinguish independent and dependent variables. This requirement is not unique to path analysis, of course, but path analysis provides a unique way of displaying explanatory results for interpretation.

Recall for a moment, from our discussion of the elaboration model in Chapter 10, that an independent variable might have an impact on an intervening variable that, in turn, might have an impact on a depen-

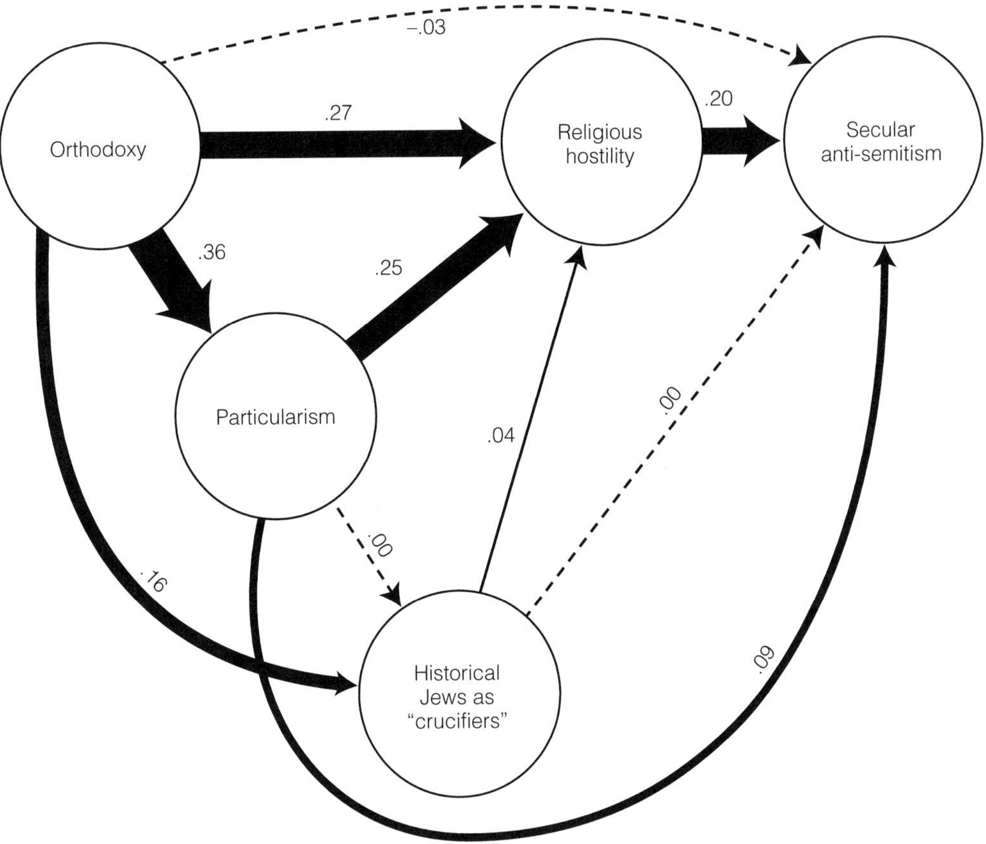

SOURCE: Figure based on information on the religious sources of anti-Semitism from *Wayward Shepherds: Prejudice and the Protestant Clergy* by Rodney Stark, Bruce D. Foster, Charles Y. Glock, and Harold E. Quinley. Copyright © 1971 by the Anti-Defamation League of B'nai B'rith. Reprinted by permission of HarperCollins Publishers, Inc. Patterns of American Prejudice Series.

Figure 22-3 Diagramming the Religious Sources of Anti-Semitism

dent variable. Here's how we might diagram the logic of interpretation:

Independent variable → Intervening variable → Dependent variable

The path analyst constructs similar patterns of relationships among variables, but the typical path diagram contains many more variables than shown in this diagram. Besides diagramming a network of relationships among variables, path analysis also shows the strengths of those several relationships. The strengths of relationships are calculated from a regression analysis that produces numbers analogous to the partial relationships in the elaboration model. These *path coefficients,* as they are called, represent the strengths of the relationships between pairs of variables, with the effects of all other variables in the model held constant.

The analysis in Figure 22-3, for example, focuses on the religious causes of anti-Semitism among Christian church members. The variables in the diagram are, from left to right, (1) orthodoxy, or the extent to which the subjects accept conventional beliefs about God, Jesus, biblical miracles, and so forth; (2) particularism, the belief that one's religion is the "only true faith"; (3) acceptance of the view that the Jews crucified Jesus; (4) religious hostility toward contemporary Jews, such as believing that God is punishing them or that they will suffer damnation unless they convert to Christianity; and (5) secular anti-Semitism, such as believing that Jews cheat in business, are disloyal to their country, and so forth.

To start with, the researchers who conducted this analysis proposed that secular anti-Semitism was produced by moving through the five variables: Orthodoxy caused particularism, which caused the view of the historical Jews as crucifiers, which caused religious hostility toward contemporary Jews, which resulted, finally, in secular anti-Semitism.

The path diagram tells a different story. The researchers found, for example, that belief in the historical role of Jews as the crucifiers of Jesus doesn't seem to matter in the process that generates anti-Semitism. And, although particularism is a part of one process that results in secular anti-Semitism, the diagram also shows that anti-Semitism is created more directly by orthodoxy and religious hostility. Orthodoxy produces religious hostility even without particularism, and religious hostility generates secular hostility in any event.

One last comment on path analysis is in order. Although it is an excellent way of handling complex causal chains and networks of variables, path analysis itself does not tell the causal order of the variables. Nor was the path diagram generated by computer. The researcher decided the structure of relationships among the variables and used computer analysis merely to calculate the path coefficients that apply to such a structure.

COMMON MISUSES AND MISINTERPRETATIONS OF INFERENTIAL STATISTICS

Inferential statistics are commonly misused and misinterpreted by the producers and consumers of social research. These errors are common across social science disciplines, not just in social work research. In this section, we'll summarize those errors, most of which we have already alluded to in the earlier sections of this chapter and the previous chapter.

Our discussion of statistical power analysis identified one common mistake in the use and interpretation of inferential statistics: the failure to consider statistical power. This error can have one or more of the following unfortunate consequences:

1. A study is conducted with a sample size so small that the probability of obtaining statistically significant results, even if the null hypothesis is false, is so small that the study is not worth doing.

2. Resources are wasted by selecting a sample size that is much larger than needed to have an adequate level of statistical power.

3. Null findings (insignificant findings) are not interpreted in light of statistical power, and the probability that a Type II error accounts for the lack of support for the research hypothesis is thus overlooked.

A related error is the mistaken notion that failure to reject the null hypothesis means the same thing as verifying it. Results that fall short of statistical significance may still have a relatively low probability of having been caused by chance or by sampling error. This is especially problematic with near-significant results and low statistical power.

Conversely, it is incorrect to interpret a rejection of the null hypothesis (that is, when results are statistically significant) as a confirmation of the research hypothesis. The null hypothesis is a statistical hypothesis only. As such, it deals only with chance as a rival hypothesis, not with alternate explanations such as measurement error or errors in the research design. In this connection, do not be so impressed by the sophistication of a study's statistical analysis or the significance and strength of its findings that you become less vigilant about nonstatistical sources of methodological error and bias. Do not let fancy-schmancy statistical procedures camouflage serious nonstatistical methodological limitations. To draw appropriate inferences from a study, we must consider how all facets of its methodology bear on our ability to generalize from its findings, not just the role of chance.

Even when a relationship is statistically significant and a study's methodology is relatively flawless, we must remember to distinguish between statistical significance and relationship strength. Failing to make this distinction is an error common to both the producers and consumers of research. A statistically significant relationship is not necessarily a strong one, and weak relationships can be statistically significant given a large enough sample size.

A related error commonly made by both producers and consumers of research is the failure to distinguish substantive significance from either statistical significance or relationship strength. Statistically significant relationships may or may not be meaningful from a substantive, or practical, standpoint. Even when statistically significant relationships are strong, they may contain variables that are substantively trivial.

Let's look now at an error that we haven't yet mentioned in this or the previous chapter, but one that has become quite worrisome in this high-tech computer age. Now that researchers can complete many different inferential analyses of their data just by pressing a few buttons on a computer keyboard, they have become increasingly vulnerable to unwittingly inflating the probability of committing a Type I error by conducting multiple bivariate tests of significance. Suppose, for example, that a research team separately tests 20 different bivariate relationships using the .05 level of significance each time. Suppose further that they find that only one of the relationships is statistically significant at the .05 level. Should they reject the null hypothesis? No, they shouldn't. Here's why.

When we set our significance level at .05, we are recognizing that for every 100 statistically significant relationships observed, 5 are produced by chance. It also means that for every 100 tests of hypothesized relationships that do not really exist in a population or in a theoretical sense, 5 will turn out to be statistically significant in our findings just due to the luck of the draw. As explained earlier, that's what we mean when we recognize that with statistically significant findings we take a .05 risk of committing a Type I error. Five out of 100 equals 1 out of 20. Thus, if we run 20 separate significance tests, we can expect to find approximately 1 that will be "significant" due just to chance.

To illustrate the preceding point, imagine that a voluntary social welfare organization where you work sponsors a "Las Vegas Night" to raise funds, and you volunteer to operate a roulette wheel with 20 numbers on it. Suppose the payoff odds for betting on the correct number are 15 to 1. (The odds favor the "house" so it can raise funds!) Suppose some jokers come along and insist that they be able to spin the wheel 20 times instead of once to try to win a 15-to-1 payoff on their one bet. You wouldn't let them because you intuitively recognize that the odds apply to one spin of the wheel only. The odds that their number will come up get better the more spins they take, and after 20 spins you would expect that their number probably will come up at least once. The precise probability that their number would come up once in 20 spins is .64 (better than 50:50).

For exactly the same reason, researchers take more than a .05 risk of committing a Type I error if they run multiple, separate significance tests of bivariate relationships. For every 20 separate tests they run at the .05 level of significance, the probability of committing a Type I error with just one "significant" finding is really .64, not .05. The more separate bivariate tests they run, the greater their real probability of committing a Type I error. The .05 level applies only to the case in which only one test is run.

This does not mean that researchers should never test more than one relationship per study. It just means that if they wish to test more than one, they must recognize and deal with the potential this has for inflating their real risk of committing a Type I error. Perhaps the simplest way to resolve this problem is to use what is termed the *Bonferroni adjustment*. This involves reducing our significance level by dividing it by the number of separate bivariate tests of significance being run. Thus, if our initial significance level is .05, and we want to run 20 bivariate tests, we divide .05 by 20 and then use the dividend of .0025 as our significance level for each test.

Another way to overcome this problem is by selecting one of the appropriate advanced, multivariate tests of significance that tests various hypotheses simultaneously and adjusts for the multiple comparisons in calculating the probability of committing a Type I error. Earlier, we mentioned two such tests: multiple regression analysis and discriminant function analysis. (Other advanced tests, such as multivariate analysis of variance, are beyond the scope of this book, but research reports will usually inform the reader if any were used to avoid inflating the probability of a Type I error.)

A risky alternative would be to conduct the multiple bivariate tests and hope that so many of them are statistically significant that the probability of that happening by chance is still quite slim (like seeing our number come up in the majority of spins of the roulette wheel). A less risky alternative would be to interpret the "significant" bivariate findings, not as verification of the tested relationships, but rather as a basis for hypothesizing that the "significant" relationships exist. Then we could see if the significance of that reduced number of relationships is indeed replicated in a subsequent study. In other words, we could conduct multiple significance testing with an exploratory purpose: to generate those hypotheses that merit further testing.

But one of the worst sins that can be committed after conducting an analysis of many different variables in order to discover which variables are significantly related is to turn around after completing such a "fishing expedition" and claim that the "significant" relationships were the hypotheses that were really being tested in the first place and then to interpret the findings as a verification of those hypotheses.

The various errors that can be made in the use and interpretation of inferential statistics offer another reason to consider the complementarity of quantitative and qualitative methods (we have been discussing this at the end of most of the previous chapters). This point is illustrated in the box "Type III Errors and the Role of Qualitative Inquiry."

TYPE III ERRORS AND THE ROLE OF QUALITATIVE INQUIRY

In this and the previous chapter, you've been reading a lot about Type I and Type II errors, and you may have trouble keeping them straight. Here's a simple mnemonic device for remembering the difference.

Associate the issue with the words *gullible* and *skeptical* in alphabetical order.

> *Type I:* You gullibly conclude that the statistically significant relationship in your data is genuine, when it really resulted from chance. Thus, you might gullibly conclude that listening to Barry Manilow music causes delinquency when a weird sampling fluke (that is, chance) produces a significant difference in which most of the particular delinquents you happen to study say they listen to his music regularly while most of the nondelinquents respond, "Barry who?" (You mistakenly reject a true null hypothesis.)
>
> *Type II:* You skeptically conclude that there is no genuine relationship, when there really is one. Thus, you might skeptically conclude that teenagers are not more likely to listen to rap music than are senior citizens because the probability that your results were due to chance was slightly above the .05 level. (You therefore fail to reject a false null hypothesis.)

Now that you can keep Type I and Type II errors straight, we want to add a third: *Type III errors.* A Type III error means asking the wrong research question, or solving the wrong research problem, in the first place (Miller and Crabtree, 1994). One common way quantitative studies commit Type III errors—a way particularly germane to inferential statistics—is by testing the wrong hypothesis or by operationally defining a variable in the hypothesis in the wrong way. Here's a hypothetical example to illustrate Type III errors and the role of qualitative inquiry in dealing with or avoiding them. Suppose you're studying *caregiver burden,* a term that refers to the toll taken on people who care for loved ones who suffer from chronic, debilitating illnesses such as Alzheimer's disease (AD), AIDS, or profound mental illness. Suppose you postulate that the weaker the informal support systems (close relatives, close friends, and so on) nearby to give caregivers emotional encouragement and respite, the greater the degree of caregiver burden that will be experienced.

You conduct a cross-sectional study and find that a moderate and statistically significant relationship exists between your two variables. Because your findings are statistically significant, you are risking a Type I but not a Type II error. Then a colleague points out that the caregiver burden scale you used to operationally define your dependent variable includes items that quantify the strength of the informal support system. In other words, the operational definitions of the two variables overlapped, and your hypothesis therefore was really a tautology, a foregone and irrelevant conclusion, because the strength of the informal support system was quantified in both your independent and dependent variables. You have committed what some call a Type III error, and your statistically significant finding has little value to the field.

Some qualitative methodologists argue that you would have been less likely to complete an entire study on the wrong variables had your study been more open-ended, flexible, and inductive. A qualitative approach, they argue, would enable you to learn incrementally about the most relevant variables and their deeper meanings and would enable you to adjust your inquiry as you go along rather than be stuck throughout the entire study with the operational definition you selected in advance.

Suppose you are planning to develop a support group intervention in which caregivers can meet weekly to receive information you provide, discuss their situation, and give each other suggestions and emotional support. You are wondering whether the nature of the intervention needs to vary depending on the loved one's type of illness. Relatedly, you are wondering whether each group should consist exclusively of caregivers whose loved ones have the same type of illness. You conduct a cross-sectional survey and find no statistically significant differences across illness types in the degree of caregiver burden (using the same caregiver burden scale as above). Based on these findings, you decide not to individually tailor the intervention to specific illness types. You wonder whether, in failing to reject the null hypothesis, you might be committing a Type II error. You discuss this with your colleague (an insomniac who lately has been reading up on qualitative inquiry at bedtime), and she suggests that you need to worry more about a Type III error than a Type II error. "Just because the different groups have the same amount of burden," she says, "doesn't imply that the nature of the burden or its deeper meaning is the same across different illness types."

You decide to follow her suggestion and conduct an in-depth qualitative inquiry, relying on open-ended interviews, with a handful of caregivers in each illness type. You find that your colleague was right; although each group seems to be experiencing comparable *levels* of burden, its deeper *meanings* are different for each group. The caregivers of people with AD, for example, are more likely to be burdened by the physical demands of caregiving and by the conflicting emotions they experience in having to care for someone who can't remember who they are or who can't appreciate the caregiver's sacrifice. The caregivers of people with mental illness are more likely to be emotionally burdened by the blame they feel implicit in some mental health professionals' views that family dysfunction is in part responsible for the illness. The caregivers of people with AIDS are more likely to be burdened by the shame they irrationally feel about their loved one's illness and the need to keep the illness a secret from friends and relatives because of society's unjustified stigmatization of people with AIDS and those who are in close contact with them. These findings convince you to tailor the intervention individually to specific illness types, the opposite implication of your quantitative findings.

Suppose you evaluate the effectiveness of your support group intervention for people with AIDS, assessing whether their burden scale score decreases after intervention more than for a comparison group. Suppose the difference in the decrease between the two groups is in the predicted direction and seems to be of a meaningful magnitude, but it's not statistically significant. Again you wonder about a Type II error, especially since you had a small sample, and again your colleague reminds you of Type III errors. In this instance, the Type III concern has to do with the fact that the burden scale you used was developed for caregivers in general and has nothing in it about stigma.

A qualitative inquiry with participants in both groups, again relying on open-ended interviews, might help you resolve your doubt about both Type II and III errors. Suppose, for example, that the participants in the comparison group discussed experiencing the same high levels of stigma throughout the study period, whereas virtually all of the participants who had received your intervention talked about how the support group empowered them to no longer hide the nature of their loved one's illness from friends and relatives. Suppose they said that although the physical burden of caregiving was still the same, and although the tragic impending loss of their loved one at such a young age continued its serious emotional toll on them, they experienced the support group as immensely helpful in lifting an extremely burdensome stigma from them.

Qualitative data like these would tell you that perhaps the support group intervention was more effective than depicted by your quantitative data, because the quantitative measure did not address stigma. Thus, you might strongly suspect that a Type III error would be made by relying exclusively on the quantitative data. Moreover, the qualitative evidence in which support group recipients reported feeling immensely helped in overcoming social stigma might give you further reason to suppose that your intervention really was effective, and that a serious Type II error would be committed were you to dismiss or ignore its potential effectiveness. Of course, a better scenario would have been to conduct your qualitative interviews in a pilot study before designing your quantitative analysis. Had you done so, you might have anticipated the need to include a measure of stigma in your quantitative evaluation; consequently, you would have come up with more meaningful and conclusive quantitative findings.

CONTROVERSIES IN THE USE OF INFERENTIAL STATISTICS

When we think of statistics, we tend to think of mathematics and logic—topics that we tend to associate with right and wrong answers. Consequently, neophyte researchers are often surprised to learn that even the foremost authorities disagree about some basic issues in the use of inferential statistics. As you read professional journals, you'll occasionally notice a study that used a statistical procedure that seems to violate certain statistical assumptions—perhaps applying a parametric test when the data seem to warrant a nonparametric test. Sometimes, you will notice intense debates among authors about the appropriateness of the statistical procedure that one of them has used.

A thorough treatment of unresolved statistical issues that continue to be debated by statistics luminaries would require material far too advanced and lengthy for the purposes of this text. But in this concluding section of the chapter, we do want to introduce you to the chief issues being debated in a way that will help you avoid feeling overwhelmed by these debates and immobilized from using inferential analyses.

A common theme that cuts across various ongoing controversies in inferential analysis involves the violation of assumptions that underlie some or all of the tests of statistical significance. Where one stands in these controversies seems to be connected to whether one thinks statistical significance is supposed to provide a sufficient and precise proof of the probability of error in generalizing from a sample to a population or whether it is viewed less rigidly as merely a first step—just one approximate guideline—in considering what can and cannot be inferred.

At one extreme are those statisticians who believe that statistical significance is irrelevant and misleading unless all of the assumptions of the chosen significance test have been met, including the assumption of perfectly random sampling or random assignment. For example, if a study that either did not use random sampling or had missing data for one of the variables being tested were to report statistically significant findings at the .05 level, then members of this camp would argue that because the sampling was not strictly random, we really have no basis for saying that there is a .05 probability that the findings are generalizable to the population.

If we agree that the point of significance testing is to provide sufficient grounds for making precise inferences about the probability of correctly generalizing from a sample to a population, then it's difficult to dispute the preceding argument. But another camp of statisticians makes the distinction between inference based on statistical tests of significance and inference based on design issues. Members of this camp see testing for statistical significance as a first but not sufficient step in the inferential process. Design issues regarding sampling techniques, measurement error, and so on also must be considered. Those with this point of view do not expect significance tests to "prove" that the precise probability that the research hypothesis is true is the significance level. Rather, the significance level is interpreted only as the probability that the null hypothesis is true—that the result can be attributed to chance. Having ruled out chance, our inferential analysis is far from over. We must then use our informed judgment about other obstacles to the generalizability of our findings—obstacles that are connected to flaws in the overall research design.

If we have the more rigid and ambitious expectations—that statistical inference is considered sufficient and that significance level must reflect the exact probability that our research hypothesis can be correctly generalized to a population—then any violation of statistical assumptions may be unacceptable. But if we view the significance level as merely a useful guideline for an appropriate cutoff point for dismissing the plausibility of chance, recognize that a host of design issues must also be considered, and consider that even the best significance level is no more than a judgment call, then it's easier to live with violations of the statistical assumptions of significance tests.

Ironically, those who have the more ambitious expectations of statistical significance tests may be the ones least likely to use them and most likely to fault others for using them. This is because feasibility constraints in social work research make it so difficult to meet all of the assumptions of statistical significance tests, especially those regarding perfectly random sampling with no missing data whatsoever on tested variables. In light of this reality, other statisticians argue that there is no reasonable alternative to combining inference based on statistical significance and inference based on design.

Another issue over which statisticians disagree has to do with applying tests of significance when data have been gathered from an entire population rather than from a sample. Some argue that significance testing applies only to generalizations about a population based on statistics gained from a sample. Their central point is that with an entire population, unlike a sample, we have no sampling error. Therefore, testing to see if our findings can be attributed to sampling error is both inappropriate and unnecessary. Any relationships we observe in our findings, no matter how weak, can be generalized to the population because our data came from the entire population. The relationships observed in population data may vary with regard to their strength and substantive significance, but they are automatically significant in the statistical sense and thus can be generalized: Without sampling error, there is no probability of a Type I error.

Other statisticians, however, argue that there are some instances when significance testing with population data is both necessary and appropriate. Those who advance this point of view do not deny the essential logic of the preceding point of view but instead cite an exception to it. That exception occurs when we seek to go beyond learning whether two variables are related in a population in a descriptive sense and wish to infer the likelihood that the independent variable really helps us explain the variation in the dependent variable. When the latter is the case, then significance testing might be done with population data to form inferences that one seeks to make about the causal processes that explain the dependent variable.

The function of significance testing with population data is not to see whether the observed relationship really exists in the population as a whole, but to determine the likelihood that its existence in the population is merely a function of random processes (as opposed to being evidence of some theoretical process). Blalock (1972) uses an example involving all 50 of the United States to illustrate this point. We'll borrow from his example and modify it somewhat to make it more relevant to social work.

Suppose a study of all 50 states found that welfare payments were higher in states with an even number of letters in their names than in states with odd numbers of letters in their names. If so, we wouldn't need significance testing to generalize this finding to the population of states. But who would argue that having an even number of letters in a state's name plausibly played a causal role in increasing welfare payments and should be considered in developing theory about social welfare policy? Any time we look for a relationship in population data, we are subdividing the population into various subsets according to the categories of our independent variable—a process not unlike dealing a population (deck) of 52 cards into two or more piles. The odds are that we will find some differences on a dependent variable between some subsets, no matter how inane our independent variable may be. For example, after we randomly subdivide a deck of cards, there may be no theoretical reason to suppose that one pile of cards will have, say, more hearts or diamonds or kings or queens than another pile. Nevertheless, it's extremely unlikely that we would find no differences between the two piles. In the same sense, if we look for relationships in a population, the odds are that we will find some covariation among some of the variables just from chance. Significance testing identifies the probability that relationships observed in a population could have been generated by random processes (like shuffling and dealing a deck of cards), and therefore it enhances our consideration of the plausibility of the notion that the relationships we find reflect causal processes and thus have potential theoretical value.

Our expectations about the role of statistical tests of significance and the precise meaning of the level of significance will also influence our stances about other statistical issues. For example, some statisticians prefer parametric tests of significance over nonparametric tests even when the characteristics of the variables being tested call for the use of nonparametric tests. They may justify their preference based on the greater statistical power associated with parametric tests. Realizing that there is nothing sacred about the .05 level of significance—or any other level that might be chosen—they would prefer to trade precision in the probability of committing a Type I error for a reduced probability of committing a Type II error. Thus, if their findings are significant at the .05 level, they would recognize that their probability of making a Type I error is not exactly .05 because their data did not meet all of the assumptions of parametric tests.

Whatever course of action researchers choose, the best statistical option would be debatable, and no mathematical formula will resolve the debate. When analyzing your own data—so long as you understand the meaning and limitations of statistical inference as explained in these last two chapters—we encourage you to use whatever procedure you judge to be best in light of what you have learned and not to let these controversies immobilize you. Likewise, when you encounter research done by others that seems to be methodologically rigorous, we encourage you not to disregard it just because its inferential statistics violate certain assumptions. Just as a sophisticated statistical analysis should not cause us to overlook design flaws, a debatable statistical analysis alone should not be sufficient grounds for disregarding the potential utility of an otherwise well-designed study.

Remember, the replication process ultimately should be used to verify the generalizations made in any particular study. Some researchers would even argue that if the same finding is consistently replicated in study after study, then whether or not it is statistically significant in any or all of those studies is beside the point. Significant or not, it is unlikely that we would make a Type I or a Type II error in generalizing about the same finding replicated again and again. It might be the case that a persistent design flaw explains the result, but we would have a pretty good idea about the plausibility of chance as an explanation.

For example, suppose four studies all fail to get significant results at the .05 level, but for each one the probability of making a Type I error is .10. The probability of that happening due to chance four consecutive times is (.10) (.10) (.10) (.10), or .0001. Although each result by itself is not significant, the consistent replication of the same finding might reasonably predispose us to rule out chance as the explanation.

In fact, those statisticians who argue against using statistical significance tests unless all assumptions are met might also argue that the preceding type of replication would yield the same inferences even if none of the studies bothered to test the significance of their findings or to report the probability of committing a Type I error. For example, if every study of a particular intervention finds that treated cases have a recidivism rate that is approximately 30 percent less than the recidivism rate of untreated cases, then after a large number of replications with the same result (assuming that we can rule out flaws in the research designs) we don't need to know whether any of the findings were statistically significant to infer that the particular intervention seems to reduce the recidivism rate by some 30 percent.

This concludes our chapters on data analysis. If some of our points in these chapters seemed too technical, don't be discouraged; you probably have a lot of company. You don't need to understand all of this material completely to contribute significantly to the research process or to use research intelligently. But if you want to pursue some of these topics further, we encourage you to study the additional readings below. And if you wish to peruse illustrations of how social workers have debated the statistical controversies we've been discussing these last few pages, we refer you to articles in the *Social Service Review* by Cowger (1984, 1985, 1987), by Rubin (1985b), and by Glisson (1987).

Main Points

- Statistical power analysis calculates the probability of avoiding a Type II error. It does so by calculating the probability of committing a Type II error and subtracting that probability from 1.0. The remainder is the statistical power. By consulting statistical power tables (in which the calculations have already been done for us) in planning our study, we can learn which sample size or significance level will be ideal to effect the level of statistical power we desire. When we test hypotheses without first consulting statistical power tables, we risk having a low likelihood of obtaining findings that would support those hypotheses even if they are true.

- Meta-analysis is a procedure for calculating the mean effect size across previously completed research studies in a particular field.

- There are many different tests of statistical significance, and the most appropriate one to use will depend primarily on the level of measurement of your variables, the number of variables in the analysis, sampling procedures, and the way the variables are distributed in the population. All of these tests ultimately will tell you the probability of committing a Type I error.

- Unresolved debates among authorities on inferential statistics pertain to the conditions under which significance tests can be used justifiably in light of the fact that some of their underlying assumptions are not being met.

Review Questions and Exercises

1. Find several explanatory research articles on a problem area that concerns you in a social work or interdisciplinary journal. Bring them to class and critique them from the following standpoints:

a. If the null hypothesis was not rejected, did the author adequately address statistical power issues and the probability of committing a Type II error? If correlations are reported, locate in Table 22-1 the closest column heading to each correlation. Then locate the row that corresponds to the sample size used in the study. Then locate the row–column intercept to identify the statistical power for a two-tailed test at the .05 significance level. Was that level of power adequate, in your judgment?

b. If the null hypothesis was rejected, did the author seem to confuse statistical significance with relationship strength or substantive significance? Was any measure of association used? Or did the author stop the analysis once statistical significance was assessed? How would you interpret the substantive significance of the findings?

2. Examine one of the articles that reviewed practice effectiveness research as discussed in Chapter 1 (Fischer, 1973; Wood, 1978; Reid and Hanrahan, 1982; Rubin, 1985a). Consider the sample size (combining all experimental and control groups) of each reviewed study that failed to reject the null hypothesis (that is, each study that failed to support the effectiveness of the evaluated program or intervention). If the evaluated program or intervention really was correlated at the .30 level with the outcome variable, then what probability would each of the studies have had of accepting the false null hypothesis (that is, of committing a Type II error)? This can be answered by using Table 22-1, as described in Exercise 1a above. Discuss the implications of this for social work practice.

Internet Exercises

1. Using InfoTrac College Edition, enter the key words *statistical power* to find an article on that concept. Write down the bibliographical reference information for each article and summarize its main points.

2. Using InfoTrac College Edition, enter the search term *meta-analysis* to find two articles on that concept. Try to find one article that reports a meta-analytic study on a topic that interests you. Write down the bibliographical reference information for that article and briefly identify its methodological strengths and weakness. Try to find another article that discusses methodological issues in meta-analysis. Write down the bibliographical reference information for that article and summarize its main points.

3. Go to the Power Analysis website at http://hedwig.mgh.harvard.edu/size.html. Once there, click on "Quantitative Measurement" in the first row headed "Parallel Study."

a. Suppose you want to find the power for an outcome evaluation that involves 100 subjects and an assumed effect size (the difference in means in standard deviation terms) of .6. Enter 100 in Box 2 and .6 in Box 3-1. Click on "Calculate" and find your power.

b. Suppose you want to have .95 power in the above study. Enter .95 in Box 1 and .6 in Box 3-1. Click on "Calculate" and find how many subjects you will need.

4. Go to the Center for Social Research Methods website: www.socialresearchmethods.net/. Once there, click on the prompt for selecting a statistical test. You will then encounter a series of interactive questions about your variables.

a. Answer the questions in ways that lead to a *t*-test as the proper selection.

b. Answer the questions in ways that lead to a chi-square test as the proper selection.

c. Answer the questions in ways that lead to a multiple regression analysis as the proper selection.

Additional Readings

Bloom, Martin, Joel Fischer, and John G. Orme. 2006. *Evaluating Practice: Guidelines for the Accountable Professional*, 5th ed. Boston: Allyn & Bacon. At the end of Chapter 12, we originally recommended this excellent, comprehensive text on the use of single-case evaluation designs in evaluating one's own practice. We mention it again because it has several helpful chapters on statistical approaches to the analysis of single-case evaluation design data.

Cohen, Jacob. 1988. *Statistical Power Analysis for the Behavioral Sciences*, 2nd ed. New York: Lawrence Erlbaum Associates. This is the most thorough and clear explanation of statistical power analysis we know of, filled with tables that simplify the determination of statistical power to guide decisions about sample size and significance levels in planning research. Cohen offers guidelines on relationship strength and elaborates on distinctions among statistical significance, relationship strength, and substantive significance. Mathematical formulas and derivations are also provided, along with excellent illustrative examples. This highly readable book is a must reference for serious researchers. Consumers of research, too, will find value in Cohen's simple formulas for calculating relationship strength when authors report only statistical significance.

Lipsey, Mark W. 1990. *Design Sensitivity: Statistical Power for Experimental Research.* Newbury Park, CA: Sage. Here is another excellent book on statistical power analysis. It also discusses meta-analysis and the impact of research design attributes on statistical power. Some of the material in this book is a bit advanced for students who do not yet have a strong background in statistics, but we recommend it highly anyway.

Morrison, Denton, and Ramon Henkel (eds.). 1970. *The Significance Test Controversy: A Reader.* Chicago: Aldine-Atherton. This is a good representation of perspectives—pro and con—on tests of statistical significance. The question of the validity or utility of tests of statistical significance reappears periodically in social science journals. Each reappearance is marked by an extended exchange between different points of view. This collection of such articles offers an excellent picture of the persistent debate.

PART 8

Writing Research Proposals and Reports

This section contains the final chapter of this text. We'll discuss how to communicate the findings of your study as well as all the other aspects of it covered in the previous chapters of the book. We'll begin with the writing of research proposals. You'll see how writing a good proposal is enhanced by comprehension of the material in each of the earlier sections of this text.

CHAPTER 23

Writing Research Proposals and Reports

What You'll Learn in This Chapter

As the title of this chapter implies, here you'll learn how to write proposals to obtain funding for your research and how to report your research once it is completed. We'll also suggest some tips for finding a funding source and some preliminary steps worth taking before you begin writing your proposal. As to the writing of proposals and reports, we'll look at the components of each as well as some general guidelines for how best to communicate with your intended audience.

INTRODUCTION

You've come a long way. Among other things, you've learned about the value of social work research, the scientific method, research ethics and politics, how to formulate and design a useful and valid research study, alternative ways to measure things and collect data, how to conduct culturally competent research, and how to analyze and interpret your data. Now it's time to take a closer look at how to communicate your work. We'll begin with communicating what you propose to study, as you seek approval of your study and perhaps funding for it. Then we'll discuss how to write a report of your completed study. You'll see in both of these endeavors how comprehending the material in the previous chapters of this book will enhance the quality of your research proposal or your research report.

WRITING RESEARCH PROPOSALS

Quite often, in the design of a research project, you will have to lay out the details of your plan for someone else's review or approval or both. In the case of a course project, for example, your instructor might very well want to see a "proposal" before you set off to work. Later in your career, if you wanted to undertake a major project, you might need to obtain funding from a foundation or government agency, which would most definitely want a detailed proposal that described how you were going to spend its money.

The guidelines for writing a research proposal will vary depending on its purpose. At one extreme, a relatively lengthy and detailed proposal will be expected when you seek grants to fund your research from federal government agencies, such as the National Institute of Mental Health (NIMH) or the National Institute of Drug Abuse (NIDA). Research grants from such agencies range from less than $50,000 for a new investigator to conduct a modest study to as high as several hundred thousand dollars per year over several years for more experienced investigators to conduct more ambitious studies. These agencies will evaluate your proposal not only according to how well you write it, but also according to the degree of methodological rigor in the proposed design. Do not expect to be funded, for example, if you seek $250,000 to fund a pre-experiment or quasi-experiment with weak internal validity or a survey that does not include probability sampling.

At the other extreme are sources that fund much smaller grants, typically well under $10,000. These might include state or local government agencies seeking a limited evaluation of a program they fund, private foundations, or universities that offer small grants to encourage and facilitate research by faculty members. Although the proposal demands from these sources are likely to be less rigorous than from federal agencies, you should not underestimate them. Your best bet is to learn about the expectations of the funding source before you prepare your proposal and then develop your proposal according to those expectations.

FINDING A FUNDING SOURCE

The process of finding a funding source will vary, depending on your degree of flexibility in what you are willing to research. If you are already committed to a specific research question and design and seek to find funding for that specific study, you will need to find a funding source for which that research question and type of study is a priority. On the other hand, perhaps you are not wedded to any specific line of research and instead want to adapt to the priorities that funding sources have regarding what sorts of research questions and designs *they* seek to fund. In that case, your task will be to stay current in reading various publications and announcements from a wide range of funding sources, looking for a **request for proposals (RFP)** that piques your interest and fits your area of expertise. An RFP will identify the research questions and types of designs the funding source has in mind, encourage researchers to submit proposals to carry out such research, specify the maximum size of the grants, and provide other information about the source's expectations and funding process.

The most efficient way to find potential funding sources or to be notified of recently issued RFPs is by using the Internet. For example, you might go to www.nih.gov to learn about federal funding opportunities. A particularly expedient way to learn about new RFPs and other funding opportunities relevant to social work researchers is to subscribe to the e-mail list server of the Institute for the Advancement of Social Work Research (IASWR). To subscribe, send an e-mail message (no text on subject line) to: LISTSERV@LISTSERV.SC.EDU and type a one-line message as follows: Subscribe iaswrlst <your first name> <your last name> at <www.> (don't type the symbols < and >).

The IASWR website at www.iaswresearch.org/ provides links to a wide range of federal agencies, foundations, and research organizations that are potential funding sources for social work research or that provide information on finding funding sources. The SSWR website also provides links to sites providing information on funding sources, such as the National Institutes of Health Guide for Grants and Contracts (http://grants2.nih.gov/grants/guide/) and the Grantsmanship Center (www.tgci.com/). At the National Institutes of Health site, for example, you will find useful sections on RFPs, how to apply for a grant, and other helpful topics. A useful resource for identifying foundations that might be interested in the sort of research you have in mind is the Foundation Center. Its website (http://foundationcenter.org/) includes a link to the Foundation Directory (http://fconline.fdncenter.org), which provides information on a comprehensive list of foundations—information on the areas of research the foundation is interested in funding, the average range of dollar amounts it typically funds, application procedures, and so on.

You might also be able to obtain e-mail notifications of RFPs and other funding opportunities by joining a professional association connected to your particular research interests. For example, the Research Committee of the Eye Movement Desensitization and Reprocessing International Association (EMDRIA) regularly e-mails its members about recently issued RFPs that seem potentially related to EMDR research. If your school of social work has a research center, then it too might be able to provide you with continually updated listings of recently issued RFPs relevant to social work.

You can also enter search terms such as *research grants* on a search engine such as Google (www.google.com) or Yahoo! (www.yahoo.com) to find funding sources and their RFPs. If you are interested in research grants in a particular area, such as child abuse, you might enter *research grants child abuse*. The search engine will then list various sites to click on that might provide what you are looking for. Or you might just enter a particular governmental agency such as the *National Institutes of Health* (mentioned above). Websites associated with that agency will then be listed. You can then click on the site or sites that mention funding opportunities.

Because time may elapse between the issuing of an RFP and its posting on some of the above sites or your notification of it via an e-mail list, you may want to regularly examine the *Federal Register*, which is issued daily. Most of its contents deal with government activities and announcements unrelated to social work research. However, because it is the first place in which new RFPs for federal funding will be announced, you may want to wade through it looking for a relevant RFP so that you will have more time to prepare your proposal before the proposal submission deadline. You can access the *Federal Register* at www.gpoaccess.gov/nara/.

GRANTS AND CONTRACTS

The foregoing section on finding a funding source pertains mainly to **research grants.** Although a funding source will usually identify some broad priority areas as its funding interests, researchers typically have considerable leeway in the specifics of what they want to investigate within that area and how they want to investigate it. The funding source may not approve the researchers' proposal, but the proposals it does approve can vary significantly. For example, suppose a federal agency issues an RFP in the area of research on the treatment of substance abuse among ethnic minorities in the United States. It might fund one proposal to conduct an experimental evaluation of the effectiveness of a new therapeutic community approach to treating Mexican American cocaine users. At the same time, it might fund another proposal to assess the factors associated with completing versus dropping out of treatment among African American heroin users. A third proposal might be funded to conduct a qualitative investigation on how parental substance abuse impacts the lives of Native American children, how they attempt to cope, and their treatment needs.

Unlike research grants, **research contracts** provide much greater specificity regarding what the funding source wants to have researched and how the research is to be conducted. The research proposal for a research contract will have to conform precisely with those specifications. If a state agency wants to contract for a mailed survey of how satisfied its service consumers are with a new way to provide services that is being pilot tested, you won't get funded if you propose an experiment or a qualitative investigation utilizing participant observation and unstructured interviews—no matter how methodologically rigorous or theoretically profound your proposal might be.

This does not mean that you have no leeway whatsoever in writing proposals for contracts. After all, the funding source will not have written the proposal for you. If the source wants a mailed survey on consumer satisfaction, then it probably won't stipulate the exact sampling procedures or questionnaire format and contents. You will have to propose many of those technical details. But the degree of leeway you will have in a contract proposal will be much less than in a grant proposal. Also, with governmental research contracts, the size of the proposed budget may be a chief criterion in selecting which proposal to fund.

The process of finding a funding source for research contracts also may differ from the process for research grants. The funding source might seek out a specific researcher or research center and work closely with it in preparing the proposal. Your chances of being awarded a research contract might be greatly influenced by the rapport and credibility you have previously established with key people who are administering or are otherwise connected with the funding source. This also applies to securing grants funded by state governmental agencies.

BEFORE YOU START WRITING THE PROPOSAL

Although research proposals are often conceived and written in response to a specific RFP, your chances of having your proposal funded will be enhanced if you take some preliminary steps before you start to write it. One such step, as we noted above, is to learn about the expectations of the funding source before you prepare your proposal and then develop your proposal according to those expectations. You can learn about those expectations from the funding source's website or by obtaining its written materials.

In addition, you should try to develop a relationship with a staff member at the funding source whose role includes acting as a liaison to prospective grant applicants. Through that relationship you can better learn of the funding source's potential interest in your research idea. If it is interested, the liaison can suggest how to develop or modify your idea and your proposal to fit the funding source's priorities and funding criteria. With some funding sources, it might be necessary to write a brief, preliminary letter summarizing your research idea before you can begin to relate to any of their staff members. If possible, however, it is best to develop a relationship before writing such a letter. Sometimes a liaison can guide you in writing even a preliminary letter and may perhaps advise you regarding the preparation of a brief concept paper (no more than a few pages) that summarizes your preliminary idea. In some instances, the concept paper might be enclosed with the preliminary letter; in others, it should be submitted only after the funding source expresses a preliminary interest in your idea and encourages you to submit a concept paper. By developing and nurturing a relationship with a liaison from the funding source and following the liaison's advice, you not only increase the degree of fit between your proposal and the source's funding criteria but also increase the chances that the liaison will act as an advocate for your proposal.

Another potentially helpful preliminary step is to examine proposals that have previously been funded by the source you are considering. Doing so might provide additional insights as to the funding source's expectations. Suppose, for example, that every successful proposal included a lengthy section on data analysis plans—not only identifying each statistical procedure that will be used but also providing a rationale for its selection and explaining how the assumptions of each procedure will be checked and what will be done if those assumptions are not met after the actual data are collected. Seeing such a section in every successful proposal will prompt you to emphasize it in your own proposal. It might even prompt you to engage a statistician as a collaborator in your research and in developing your proposal. Some funding sources will provide access to previously funded proposals, perhaps via a website. If a funding source does not, then you can request a list of previous grant recipients whom you can contact. Some of them might be willing to show you their successful proposals. Some might also be willing to give you helpful tips. You might even want to engage one as a collaborator on your project. Your prospects for being funded might be enhanced significantly if the funding source sees that someone with a good "track record" is collaborating on your project.

By the same token, if you have already established a good track record by having successfully completed previously funded research projects, your chances of being funded will be better, and you may have less need for collaborators with good track records. But if you have not yet established a track record, then you should realize that the process of getting your proposal funded might be a long one. You should not get too discouraged if your first proposal is not funded. Learn from the process. If the funding source provides feedback as to the reasons your proposal was not funded, try not to be defensive in examining those reasons. Based on what you learn, revise the proposal and resubmit it, perhaps to the same funding source. With some federal funding sources, for example, researchers often resubmit improved versions of their proposals several times before eventually being funded.

Finally, you should keep in mind that improving your prospects for getting funded for research involves many of the same grantsmanship principles and strategies that pertain to getting funded for other kinds of projects. Before you write your proposal, it will behoove you to learn about those principles and strategies and begin implementing them. Generic grantsmanship is a large topic that goes beyond the scope of this text. However, if you enter the search term *grantsmanship* on a search engine such as Google (www.google.com) or Yahoo! (www.yahoo.com), you will find links to useful websites on that topic. That said, let's now examine common components of a good research proposal.

RESEARCH PROPOSAL COMPONENTS

As we implied earlier, the specific components of your proposal and the guidelines for writing those components will vary depending on the purpose of your research and the expectations of your funding source. Proposals for primarily qualitative investigations, for example, will differ from primarily quantitative proposals. Proposals for small, preliminary pilot projects, for example, may not need to cover the following components as extensively or as rigorously as do more ambitious proposals. We present the following components on the assumption that you need to learn how to prepare an ideal proposal for a major piece of research. Learning how to do that should also prepare you to write less ambitious proposals. In large part, these components will apply to qualitative as well as quantitative research proposals. However, some of the material you are about to read will apply more to quantitative proposals than to qualitative ones. Moreover, preparing a proposal for a qualitative study can be more challenging than preparing one for a quantitative study. Therefore, after describing the following components we will discuss similarities and differences between quantitative and qualitative research proposals.

Cover Materials

Before reading your actual proposal, many funding sources will want to see some preliminary materials. A cover letter adapted to the source's expectations regarding cover letters is one rather obvious need. The source might also require a cover page that identifies the title of the proposal, the names and addresses of the people and organization submitting the proposal, and other information such as the amount of money being requested and the duration of the project. An executive summary statement might also be required. The length of the executive summary will vary. Some sources might expect it to be no more than a paragraph that can fit on the cover page. Others might expect a longer summary that requires a separate page. The preliminary steps that we've discussed above will guide you in determining just how brief the summary should be. Typically, it will supply a sentence or two on each of the proposal's components, highlighting the major features of each component.

Problem and Objectives

What exactly do you want to study? Why is it worth studying? Specify in precise terms the objectives of your proposed study. The objectives should be in the form of a brief list; for example, if you have two objectives, simply indent and number each of them, with a sentence or two after each number. Your objectives likely will be in the form of seeking answers to the research questions of your study, and they should reflect the attributes of good research questions as discussed in Chapter 6. They need to be narrow and specific, answerable by observable evidence, and feasible to investigate and answer. Most important, you need to explain how their answers have significance for practice and policy.

When discussing the importance of the study, cite facts. For instance, if you are proposing to study homelessness, then you might want to cite figures from prior studies that assessed the number of homeless individuals in the nation or in a particular city or state. Or you might describe concrete examples taken from previous case studies so that the subject of your study and its purpose are not vague abstractions. When discussing significant implications for policy or practice, be specific. For example, if you are proposing to study factors that influence school dropout, don't just make vague statements such as, "By identifying why some children drop out of school and others do not, we can develop new policies and programs to deal with this problem." Spell out in detail what kinds of findings might imply which specific possible policy or program alternatives. Thus, you might say something like: "If we find that the absence of positive male role models is an important factor that contributes to the dropout problem among males of a particular ethnic group, then this may imply the need to hire more male teachers of that ethnicity or to create a special alternative program where such male role models work exclusively with boys on academic material as well as on issues such as what it means to be a man. . . ."

As we noted earlier, you should know the funding source's priorities before you prepare or submit your proposal. Try to find a funding source whose priorities come closest to the problem you want to study and to your study's potential significant implications, then word your problem statement in a manner that emphasizes the degree of fit between your proposed study and the funding source's priorities.

Literature Review

What have others said about this topic? What theories address it and what do they say? What research has been done previously? Are there consistent findings or do past studies disagree? Are there flaws in the body of existing research that you feel you can remedy? How will your study relate to, yet go beyond, the previous studies? How has the prior work influenced your proposed study? For example, has it implied the need to examine certain variables or to assess them in new ways? Do not cite monotonous, minute details about every relevant study that has ever been done, especially if the body of existing literature is extensive. If the literature is extensive, concentrate on the most recent findings, while also including "classic" studies. Moss (1988:434) recommends that the literature review be "brief enough not to become tedious but extensive enough to inform proposal reviewers about the study's topic."

You might try to resolve this conflict by sticking to major themes and succinctly summing up groups of related studies, connecting them to a major theme. For instance, you might say something like this (we'll use fictitious references): "Prior studies on the effectiveness of case management with the severely mentally ill have had inconsistent findings. Four studies (Rubin, 1998; Babbie, 1999; Rubin and Babbie, 2000; Babbie, Rubin, and Freud, 2001) found that it is effective. Three studies (Nietzsche, 1998; Scrooge, 1999; Fischer, 2000) found that it is ineffective. The four studies with positive outcomes all used days hospitalized as the dependent variable, whereas the three studies with negative outcomes all used quality of life as the dependent variable. . . ." However, if you have difficulty finding prior studies that are directly relevant to your proposed research, then you should cite studies that are relevant in an indirect way. Thus, if you find no studies on the effectiveness of case management with the mentally ill, then you might look for studies that evaluate its effectiveness with other populations such as the physically or developmentally disabled.

The importance of avoiding excessive detail in your literature review does not mean that you can safely skip mentioning some relevant studies, especially if the literature is not extensive. Funding source review committees are likely to evaluate your expertise in the topic and your competence as an investigator based on the thoroughness and adequacy of your literature review. They may, for example, ask an expert in your topic to provide an external review of your proposal. That expert might know the literature on your topic as well as or better than you do. If your review has omitted any relevant studies, then your chances of being funded can be significantly diminished, particularly if the reviewer thinks the omitted studies are important. Although you don't want to be tedious in reporting the details of each study, you should cite all the relevant ones and be sure to give adequate attention to those that are most relevant to your line of inquiry.

Also, try to avoid bias in deciding which prior studies to emphasize. Suppose, for example, you propose to evaluate the effectiveness of a promising new intervention to prevent child abuse among Mexican American teenage parents. Suppose there have been five previous evaluations of the intervention, none with Mexican American parents, and that four of the five studies concluded that the intervention was effective, with the fifth study concluding the opposite. In your eagerness to impress the funding source with the promise of this new intervention, you may be tempted to emphasize the four studies with positive findings and deemphasize or even omit the fifth study. You should resist this temptation. If you do not resist it, reviewers who are aware of that fifth study are likely to interpret your omission or deemphasis of it as an indication that you may lack sufficient competence or objectivity to merit being funded.

You should also avoid writing your literature review in a perfunctory manner—that is, as if it were just a ritualistic list of studies that you are required to provide in a superficial manner without thoughtful organization. Rather than merely provide a summary listing of what other studies have reported, your literature review should show why you chose your particular line of inquiry and why you conceptualized it the way you did. When reviewers read your research questions and hypotheses, they should not perceive them as coming out of thin air. Having read your literature review, they should see where your hypotheses and variables came from. For example, a common mistake students make when proposing studies to evaluate an intervention is to review the literature on the problem the intervention is aimed at alleviating without showing how the literature led them to choose the particular intervention they want to evaluate instead of alternative possibilities.

The box titled "Improving a Weak Literature Review" illustrates some of the points we've been making.

Conceptual Framework

In this section of your proposal, you clearly specify and provide rationales for your research questions, hypotheses, variables, and operational definitions. You should justify why and how you chose to study each item. Your explanation should flow in part from your literature review. It should also show the logic of your own thinking about the inquiry, as well as how your study goes beyond and builds upon the prior literature. For example, if none of the previous studies supporting an intervention to prevent child abuse included Mexican Americans in their samples, then you could refer to those studies (which should be in your literature review), and the absence of Mexican Americans in their samples as the rationale for your point of departure. Suppose all of the previous studies only looked at the reduction of out-of-home placement of children as the sole indicator of success and none assessed whether the children who were kept in their homes were actually better off than those placed elsewhere. Even if this issue has not been raised in the previous literature, you can raise it yourself in your conceptual framework, explaining your reasoning. You would thus show how your study improves on the methods of prior studies in this regard, as well as explaining to readers why you chose your particular variables and why you chose to operationally define them the way you did.

Measurement

In this section, you elaborate on how you will measure the variables that you identified and operationally defined in your conceptual framework. This section should flow smoothly from the operational definitions in your conceptual framework, and you should make sure that you are not too redundant and repetitive regarding the specifying of your operational definitions and your measurement procedures. For example, if you plan to operationally define child well-being as a score on a validated instrument for assessing the well-being of children in families at risk for abuse, avoid repeating the detail about that scale in both the conceptual framework and measurement sections of your proposal. Instead, you might simply mention that scores on the scale will be your operational definition; later, in your measurement section, go into detail about the nature of the scale, how it is scored, what subscales it contains, and its reliability and validity.

Regardless of whether you are using existing scales or measurement instruments you may have developed yourself, you should include a copy of each in an appendix to your proposal. If you are using an instrument that has had its reliability and validity tested, then you should not just cite studies that have tested them but should report specific reliability and validity data. For example, you might say that the five studies that have tested the internal consistency reliability of a scale have found coefficient alphas ranging from .87 to .94, all indicating good to excellent internal consistency reliability. In many studies, the investigator can choose from more than one validated instrument to measure a particular construct. There are various validated scales, for example, to measure constructs such as depression and self-esteem. If this is true for your study, then provide a rationale for your choice of scale.

For example, some scales to measure self-esteem are quite valid in distinguishing between people with very low and very high self-esteem but are not sensitive to detecting subtle improvements in self-esteem among people who had very low self-esteem before an intervention and not quite so low self-esteem after the intervention. If you are proposing to evaluate

IMPROVING A WEAK LITERATURE REVIEW

Below are two literature review sections for a hypothetical proposal seeking funding to evaluate the effectiveness of a cognitive-behavioral therapy in alleviating the behavioral problems of girls residing in a residential treatment center. The girls had been victims of multiple incidents of child abuse before being admitted to the residential treatment center. We suggest that you write down the weaknesses you notice in the first review and how they were improved in the second review. Then you can compare your notes to the points we make at the end of this box in our "Critical Comparison of the Two Reviews."

Example of a Weak Literature Review Section

Child abuse is a tragic problem that can cause many horrific problems for its victims. According to many news media reports, it is a growing epidemic. Its victims commonly experience PTSD. EMDR is an exciting new therapy that has been developed to treat PTSD symptoms and other problems resulting from trauma. Francine Shapiro described this innovative and promising therapy in her excellent book, *Eye movement desensitization and reprocessing: Basic principles, protocols, and procedures* (New York: Guilford Press, 1995). Shapiro shows how this cognitive-behavioral therapy that was developed in 1987 is virtually a miracle cure in desensitizing clients to distressing memories, feelings, and cognitions and in replacing negative cognitions with positive ones. The key component in EMDR is the use of bilateral stimulation. The therapist typically stimulates rapid back-and-forth eye movements or alternates right and left hand taps or sounds in the right and left ear while the client visualizes the distressful scene and keeps in mind the related cognitions and feelings.

The optimism about the effectiveness of EMDR is understandable in light of the original experiment by Francine Shapiro (1989), which found that EMDR had very powerful effects in resolving trauma symptoms. Shapiro randomly assigned 22 clients to an experimental group that received EMDR and a control group that received an alternative form of treatment. The clients ranged in age from 11 to 55. They had experienced various types of trauma. She measured outcome with the Subjective Units of Distress Scale and the Validity of Cognitions Scale. On each measure the EMDR clients' scores were significantly better than those of the control group clients. The effect sizes were very large. Many mental health therapists who learned of Shapiro's results sought training in EMDR. An intriguing article by Kadet (2002), titled "Good Grief," appeared in *Smart Money* magazine in June 2002. In it, we learn that more than 40,000 mental health practitioners have been trained in EMDR, indicating the promise of this new therapy and how well received it has been among mental health experts.

The research literature evaluating the effectiveness of EMDR with children provides significant additional grounds for optimism about using EMDR to eradicate the devastating effects child abuse has on its victims. For example, Pellicer (1993) used a case study technique in evaluating the effectiveness of one session of EMDR for a 10-year-old girl who had been experiencing nightmares. Pellicer found that that one session of EMDR ended the girl's nightmares. Greenwald (1994) reported five case studies evaluating the effectiveness of EMDR in alleviating trauma symptoms among children who had survived a hurricane. The case studies showed EMDR to be effective. In a quasi-experiment, Puffer, Greenwald, and Elrod (1998) concluded that a single session of EMDR reduced trauma symptoms among children and adolescents who had experienced a single trauma or loss.

Chemtob et al. (2002) used a randomized lagged-groups design in examining pre- to post-change among two groups of elementary school children who had experienced a hurricane. There were 32 children in their sample. Most of the children met the criteria for disaster-related PTSD. Their ages were 6 to 12. One group received three EMDR sessions. The other group did not. Various standardized psychological measures were

(continued)

used. The study concluded that EMDR was effective in alleviating PTSD symptoms.

Another experiment, this one by Muris et al. (1997), evaluated the effectiveness of EMDR in reducing avoidance behaviors among spider-phobic children. The sample size was 26. One group of the children received one session of EMDR. The other group received an exposure in vivo treatment. Different therapists were used for each group. Outcome was measured by direct observation of behavior as well as by self reports of spider fear by the children. Muris et al. (1997) found positive effects for EMDR.

In another experiment, this one by Muris et al. (1998), the effectiveness of EMDR in reducing avoidance behaviors among spider-phobic children was again evaluated. The sample size was 22. One group of the children received EMDR. The other group received an exposure in vivo treatment. Different therapists were used for each group. Muris et al. (1998) found that EMDR produced significant improvement on self-reported spider fear.

The foregoing studies suggest that the prospects are indeed excellent regarding the effectiveness of EMDR in treating children who have been abused and thus underscore the importance of the proposed study, which seeks to evaluate the effectiveness of EMDR in treating children who have been abused.

Example of an Improved Literature Review Section

Eye Movement Desensitization Reprocessing (EMDR) is a cognitive-behavioral therapy that was developed in 1987 to desensitize clients to distressing memories, feelings, and cognitions and to replace negative cognitions with positive ones (Rubin, 2002a). The key component in EMDR is the use of bilateral stimulation. The therapist typically stimulates rapid back-and-forth eye movements or alternates right and left hand taps or sounds in the right and left ear while the client visualizes the distressful scene and keeps in mind the related cognitions and feelings. A full description of the eight-phase EMDR protocol can be found in a text written by Shapiro (1995).

Soon after its inception, the popular media depicted EMDR as almost a miracle cure for a wide range of problems, spurring more than 40,000 mental health practitioners to obtain EMDR training (Kadet, 2002). That depiction was fostered by Shapiro's (1989) original study, which found very large effect sizes supporting EMDR's effectiveness. Despite being a randomized experiment, however, Shapiro's study was widely criticized for using measurement procedures that were highly vulnerable to bias and experimenter demand (Herbert et al., 2000; Rosen, 1999). Subsequent studies used less biased measures, and several reviews have indicated that more controlled studies have been done supporting the effectiveness of EMDR in treating adults with single-trauma post-traumatic stress disorder (PTSD) than has been the case for any other psychotherapy for PTSD (Spector & Read, 1999; Chambless et al., 1998; Chemtob, Tolin, van der Kolk & Pitman, 2000; Van Etten & Taylor, 1998; Davidson & Parker, 2001).

However, we still do not know whether EMDR is effective with children and adolescents, especially those who have experienced multiple traumas. Moreover, we do not know if it is more effective than alternative exposure treatments. Three pilot studies, which lacked randomized experimental control, supported the effectiveness of EMDR with children who had experienced only a single trauma or loss (Pellicer, 1993; Greenwald, 1994; Puffer, Greenwald, & Elrod, 1998). Only four randomized experiments have assessed EMDR's effectiveness with a sample comprised exclusively of children. Chemtob et al. (2002) used a randomized lagged-groups design and concluded that EMDR was effective in alleviating PTSD symptoms (using standardized measures) with 32 elementary school children (aged 6 to 12) who had experienced a hurricane. Two experiments by Muris and his associates compared EMDR with an exposure treatment for reducing avoidance behaviors among spider-phobic children. In one, Muris et al. (1997) found positive effects for EMDR, but superior effects for the exposure treatment. They concluded that EMDR adds nothing of value to the exposure treatment.

In the other experiment, the exposure treatment produced significant improvement on behavioral as well as self-report measures, but EMDR produced significant improvement only on self-reported spider fear (Muris et al., 1998). In another randomized experiment, Rubin et al. (2001) found no significant differences in parental reports of emotional and behavioral problems between children in a child guidance center who were treated with EMDR plus routine treatment and children who received routine treatment only. The children had mixed diagnoses. Although some of the children had experienced a single trauma, others had problems connected to multiple traumas or unconnected to any trauma.

Among the studies on children, only those that focused exclusively on PTSD symptoms connected to a single trauma obtained results supporting the efficacy of EMDR. And only one of those studies was a randomized experiment. Nevertheless, EMDR continues to be used by therapists working with children whose problems are not trauma based or whose problems are connected to multiple traumas. And proponents of EMDR continue to tout its effectiveness across a wide array of emotional and behavioral problems among children, including children younger than two years old (Tinker & Wilson, 1999). More experimental research is needed to test such claims, particularly regarding the effectiveness of EMDR in treating problems other than single-trauma PTSD symptoms. The proposed study will help meet this need by testing the hypothesis that EMDR will be more effective than an alternative exposure therapy in reducing the frequency of serious incident reports of behavioral problems among girls residing in a residential treatment center.

Critical Comparison of the Two Reviews

Notice how the second review, despite containing some 50 fewer words than the first review, provides more objective information and does so in a more objective manner. The first paragraph of the first review, for example, begins with several sentences of unsubstantiated hyperbole. The acronym *PTSD* is not spelled out. The citation for Shapiro's book is excessive. Notice how the second review merely refers to it as *Shapiro (1995)* and does so without the hyperbole.

The second paragraph of the first review continues the hype and uses excessive detail in reporting Shapiro's study. Moreover, it reports that study in a biased manner, not mentioning a critical methodological flaw in it. The final two sentences of the paragraph continue the hype and the excessive detail in the Kadet citation. Notice how the second paragraph of the second review comes across as more informed and objective, while providing more information in fewer words.

The third paragraph of the first review is less efficient than the second review in describing the pilot studies, and it reports them in a biased fashion, not pointing out the design limitation in these studies that the second review points out. Similar problems can be seen in the remaining paragraphs of the first review, which give excessive detail about the experiments and report their mixed findings in a biased fashion conveying a more favorable impression of EMDR's effectiveness than is warranted. Moreover, the first review completely omits the Rubin et al. (2001) study, which is mentioned in the second review and which had results questioning the effectiveness of EMDR in treating children with mixed diagnoses who had experienced multiple traumas. Notice also how the second review identifies unresolved issues regarding multiple traumas and comparisons to exposure therapy that are absent in the first review. In that connection, notice how the second review, despite containing fewer words, builds a better foundation for testing the hypothesis in the proposed study than does the first review. If you were on a funding source's review panel, which of these two reviews would make you more predisposed to want to fund the proposed study?

an intervention for people with very low self-esteem, then you might justify choosing an instrument with good reliability and validity and good sensitivity over an alternative instrument with excellent reliability and validity but very low sensitivity. You might also choose to measure a particular variable in more than one way. In previous chapters, we discussed the value of doing this in connection with the principle of *triangulation*. Review committees are likely to be favorably impressed by proposals that incorporate triangulation in their measurement procedures.

Study Participants (Sampling)

Who or what will you study to collect data? First, identify them in general, theoretical terms, and then ascertain more concretely who is available for study and how you will reach them. Identify any inclusion or exclusion criteria you will use. Will it be appropriate to select a sample? If so, how will you do that? If you will be conducting an exploratory, qualitative study, you will need to use your judgment in identifying and observing variations (such as age, ethnicity, class) among participants as you go along—ensuring that you have tapped into the range of those variations. If your aim is to conduct a survey for purposes of estimating frequencies of characteristics in the population (for instance, determining the unemployment rate), then you will need to select a probability sample. Is there any possibility that your research will significantly affect those you study? If so, how will you ensure that they will not be harmed by the research? That, too, should be addressed in your proposal.

If you must use nonprobability sampling procedures, then you will need to justify that, including attention to the chances that your sample will be biased and unrepresentative of your target population. What efforts will you make to offset or avoid those potential biases? Regardless of whether you use probability or nonprobability sampling procedures, you will need to address issues associated with sample attrition and refusal to participate. What special efforts will you make to enhance recruitment and retention of participants? (We discussed such efforts in Chapter 5 in reference to minority and oppressed populations and in Chapter 11 in reference to experiments.)

You will also need to justify the projected size of your sample. We discussed sample size issues in Chapter 14 on sampling and in Chapter 22. As we mentioned in the latter chapter, a *statistical power analysis* shows whether your sample size is large enough to give you a good chance of supporting your hypothesis if it is indeed true. You should include a statistical power analysis in the sampling section (and perhaps also in the data analysis plans section) of your proposal. You should also tell reviewers why you think it will be feasible for you to obtain the needed sample size. For example, if you are proposing to evaluate an intervention to prevent child abuse among Mexican Americans, provide evidence that child welfare agencies will supply participants for your study in sufficiently large numbers. Such evidence might be letters of support from the agencies as well as data showing how many Mexican American clients who would be eligible for your study have been served by those agencies in recent years.

Design and Data-Collection Methods

How will you actually collect the data for your study? Will you conduct an experiment or a survey? Will you undertake field research, conduct a historical study, or focus on reanalyzing statistics already created by others? Regardless of which design you employ, be sure to address the key methodological issues that we discussed previously in the chapter on the design you plan to use.

For example, if you are conducting an experiment or a quasi-experiment, describe the logic of your design. Be sure to cover all the important issues discussed in Chapter 11, such as controlling for internal validity and assessing treatment fidelity. Regardless of which design you use, describe when, where, and by whom your data will be collected with each instrument. What expertise and experience qualifications will you seek in your data collectors? How will you recruit and train them? What will be done to avoid or minimize bias among them? Will they, for example, be blind as to the hypotheses of your study or the experimental group membership status of the individuals to whom they are administering pretests and posttests? If they are not blind, then will they have vested interests in the outcome of the study? (Hopefully not!) Will you assess their interrater reliability? Will you triangulate data-collection methods? (Hopefully, yes!) What is your rationale for collecting your data at the time points and places you specify? What about feasibility issues, such as agency cooperation with your proposed procedures or the amount of time it will take for respondents to complete your instruments or interviews? Are any of your data-collection procedures particularly vulnerable to research reactivity (see Chapter 11)?

Data Analysis

Spell out the kind of analysis you plan to conduct. If you anticipate the use of specific statistical analytic techniques—multiple regression, analysis of variance, and so on—identify, describe, and justify your choice. Perhaps your intention is to construct ethnographic ideal types that represent variations in the phenomenon under study. Describe how you will do that. More important, however, is that you spell out the purpose and logic of your analysis. Are you interested in precise description? Do you intend to explain why things are the way they are? Do you plan to account for variations in some quality—for example, why some children are harder to treat than others? What possible explanatory variables will your analysis consider, and how will you know if you've explained variations adequately?

As we noted earlier, different funding sources will have different expectations regarding the length and detail of this section of your proposal. If you are not sure of those expectations, the safe thing to do is to develop this section in detail—providing a detailed rationale for the selection of each data analysis procedure. When using statistical procedures, for example, explain how the assumptions of each procedure will be checked and what will be done if those assumptions are not met after the actual data are collected. Also discuss the statistical power of each procedure in light of your projected sample size. If you must use procedures in which you lack sufficient expertise, then it is advisable to engage a statistician as a collaborator in your research and in writing this section of your proposal.

Schedule

It is often appropriate to provide a schedule for the various stages of research. Even if you don't do this for the proposal, do it for yourself. Unless you have a time line for accomplishing the several stages of research—and keep in touch with how you're doing—you may end up in trouble. Your proposed time line in your proposal should be reasonable. If you project too little or too much time for specific stages of the research, reviewers might question how well prepared you are to carry out the research successfully.

Budget

If you are asking someone to give you money to pay the costs of your research, then you will need to provide a budget that specifies where the money will go. Large, expensive projects include budgetary categories such as personnel, equipment, supplies, and expenses such as telephones and postage. Even for a more modest project that you will pay for yourself, it is a good idea to spend time anticipating expenses: office supplies, photocopying, computer disks, telephone calls, transportation, and so on. The costs you specify in your budget should be reasonable, and you should justify each. You can hurt your chances of being funded by overestimating the costs or by underestimating them. If you overestimate them, funders may fear being "ripped off" or may deem the benefits of the study to be not worth the costs. If you underestimate the costs, you may convey the impression of an inexperienced investigator who does not yet "know the ropes." You may need technical assistance to calculate some expenses such as pay rates and fringe benefits for personnel. You should inquire as to whether there is a staff member at your school or agency who provides such technical assistance in the preparation of grant applications.

Additional Components

Most funding sources will require additional proposal components, perhaps attached as appendices. For example, you'll probably have to supply materials showing that your proposed study has been approved by an institutional review board (IRB) regarding its ethics and protection of human subjects. Chapter 4 discussed this process. You may also need to supply attachments that provide evidence of the proposed project's feasibility and your preparedness to carry it out successfully. These attachments might include: (1) your resume or a biographical sketch and perhaps the resumes and biographical sketches of your co-investigators showing how your prior experiences have prepared you to carry out the research successfully; (2) letters of support from administrators of the agencies that will supply you with data or research participants; (3) statements supplying additional evidence as to the potential feasibility of the study regarding recruiting and retaining a sufficient sample and collecting sufficient data in an appropriate manner; and (4) plans for disseminating the results of your research, such as through publication in professional journals and newsletters and through presentations at professional conferences or agency meetings attended by those whose practice or research can be guided by your findings.

As you can see, if you were interested in conducting a social work research project, then it would be a good idea to prepare a research proposal for your own purposes, even if you weren't required to do so by your instructor or a funding agency. If you are going to invest your time and energy in such a project, then you should do what you can to ensure a return on that investment. The degree of difficulty you will encounter in preparing a proposal is likely to vary depending on the type of study you plan to conduct. Preparing a proposal for a qualitative study that you will submit for funding is likely to be particularly challenging, as discussed in the box titled "Similarities and Differences between Quantitative and Qualitative Research Proposals."

SIMILARITIES AND DIFFERENCES BETWEEN QUANTITATIVE AND QUALITATIVE RESEARCH PROPOSALS

The elements of research proposals that we've identified in this book are fairly common, irrespective of the type of research being proposed. Whether you are proposing a quantitative or qualitative study (or perhaps a blending of the two), you will probably need to begin with a statement of the problem or objective and follow that with a literature review, a description of your research methods, and so on. Regardless of which type of study you propose to do, you will have to make a persuasive case as to the importance of the research question and the value of the study. The criteria for a good literature review will also be similar in both types of proposals. Other similarities include the need for a schedule with a realistic time line, a section covering human subjects review approval, a reasonable budget that anticipates all of the various costs you will encounter, clear and interesting writing, and a neat, professional appearance with laser printing.

Although certain criteria for proposal preparation such as those mentioned above commonly apply to all research proposals, qualitative methodologists have been identifying ways in which proposals for qualitative studies differ from those for quantitative studies. Qualitative proposals are generally agreed to be more difficult to write than quantitative proposals, mainly because of the greater degree of structure and preplanning involved in designing quantitative research. Sandelowski, Davis, and Harris (1989:77), for example, see the preparation of the proposal for a qualitative study as requiring the negotiation of "the paradox of planning what should not be planned in advance." Likewise, Morse (1994) notes the relatively unstructured, unpredictable nature of qualitative research and the difficulty this presents for writing a proposal that promises exciting results or is even specific about the types of alternative conclusions the study is likely to generate. These authors point out that the design of qualitative research tends to be in the form of an open-ended starting point from which methods and truth will emerge through encountering subjects in their natural environment. This is unlike quantitative research, in which the methods and specific alternative findings can be planned and spelled out in detail in advance.

The dilemma for the qualitative researcher, then, is figuring out how to put enough detail about the plan in the proposal to enable potential funders to evaluate the proposal's merits, while remaining true to the unstructured, flexible, inductive qualitative approach. In the words of Sandelowski and her colleagues, "The most difficult task in preparing the proposal . . . is delineating the method when the investigator can have no definitive method prior to initiating inquiry" (1989:78). This task is even more challenging to the extent that the merits of the proposal will be judged by reviewers who are likely to be more oriented to quantitative research and who expect the precise planning that goes into proposals for quantitative research studies.

One suggestion for those preparing proposals for qualitative studies is to go ahead and describe a plan for sampling and data collection and analysis, but indicate that it is only a tentative and initial direction that is open to change as the study proceeds and new insights emerge. Also, the proposal can specify the type of qualitative approach being employed and then describe the general ideas underlying that approach. (Some of the more common qualitative approaches, and their orienting guidelines, are discussed in Chapters 17 and 18 of this book.) Although you will not be able to say in advance exactly what you will do or find, you can convey to reviewers the general principles you will follow in conducting your flexible, emergent inquiry.

The same general idea applies to other qualitative proposal sections that, in a quantitative proposal, would contain a much greater degree of operational specificity. For example, when you discuss sampling, you may not be able to anticipate with the precision of a quantitative proposal the exact number of subjects who will participate in the study and their characteristics. But you can discuss the variety of types of subjects you tentatively think are likely to participate and who you think are likely to supply the most relevant data. You can also describe the general ideas and rationale that underlie the qualitative sampling methods you expect to employ. (These methods were discussed in Chapters 14 and 17 of this book.)

Although you may find these suggestions helpful, they won't change the fact that qualitative proposals are more difficult to write and may be reviewed by people who are more accustomed to reading proposals for quantitative research and to judging proposals according to the canons of quantitative research design. Because they may be apt to react to your qualitative proposal with puzzlement, it is particularly important that your proposal demonstrate your expertise about qualitative research and your ability to carry it out. Make sure that every section of your proposal is well written and that your literature review is adequate. (The literature review in qualitative proposals should perhaps be more extensive than in quantitative proposals to demonstrate the investigator's expertise, because it may appear as though the funders are being told "Trust me" in qualitative studies more than in quantitative ones.)

Along these lines, it may be helpful to conduct a pilot study on the topic addressed in your proposal and then describe that pilot study in your proposal and submit it as an appendix to the proposal. This will show your commitment and competence. It can also demonstrate how you might go about analyzing the data that might emerge in the proposed study. Of course, being able to refer to previously completed pilot studies will also help your prospects for funding in submitting a proposal for quantitative research, and the two types of proposals are similar in this respect.

Although we do not want to understate the similarities between the two types of proposals, or overstate their differences, anyone planning to prepare a proposal for qualitative research should be aware of the special dilemma they face. Reviewers and board members of funding sources should also understand this dilemma and apply different criteria when reviewing the two types of proposals.

WRITING SOCIAL WORK RESEARCH REPORTS

Let's leap forward in time now, from writing your research proposal to writing the report of your completed study. By the time you are ready to write your report, you will have invested a great deal in your research. But, unless your research is properly communicated, all the efforts devoted to the various procedures discussed throughout this book will go for naught. This means, first and foremost, that good research reporting requires good English (or Spanish or whatever language you use). Whenever we ask the figures "to speak for themselves," they tend to remain mute. Whenever we use unduly complex terminology or construction, communication is reduced.

Our first advice to you is to read and reread (at approximately three-month intervals) an excellent small book by William Strunk, Jr., and E. B. White, *The Elements of Style*.* If you do this faithfully, and if even 10 percent of the contents rub off, you stand a good chance of making yourself understood and your findings appreciated.

Scientific reporting has several functions. First, your report should communicate a body of specific data and ideas. You should provide those specifics clearly and with sufficient detail to permit an informed evaluation by others. Second, you should view your report as a contribution to the general body of scientific knowledge. While remaining appropriately humble, you should always regard your research report as an addition to what we know about social practice or policy. Finally, the report should stimulate and direct further inquiry.

SOME BASIC CONSIDERATIONS

Despite these general guidelines, different reports serve different purposes. A report appropriate for one purpose might be wholly inappropriate for another. This section deals with some of the basic considerations in this regard.

Audience

Before drafting your report, ask yourself who you hope will read it. Normally you should make a distinction between professional colleagues and general readers. If the report is written for the former, you may make certain assumptions about their existing knowledge and therefore summarize certain points rather than explain them in detail. Similarly, you may use more technical language than would be appropriate for a general audience.

At the same time, remain aware that social work, like other professions, is diverse. Terms, assumptions, and special techniques familiar to some of your colleagues may only confuse others. If you report a study on cognitive-behavioral interventions to an audience of colleagues who are not familiar with those interventions, for example, you should explain previous findings in more detail than would be necessary if you were addressing an audience of social workers who specialize in cognitive-behavioral interventions.

Likewise, you should communicate differently depending on the research expertise and professional roles of the colleagues in your intended audience. For example, how you describe the logic of your research design or your data analysis procedures should vary depending on whether your intended audience consists primarily of researchers, administrators, or direct-service practitioners. If your target audience consists primarily of researchers you'll have less need to explain or avoid using technical research terminology. If your target audience consists primarily of administrators or other practitioners with relatively little advanced technical experience in research, you should keep the terminology as simple as possible and be sure to explain any unavoidable technical terms that they may not yet understand. Also keep in mind that administrators and other practitioners will be far more attentive to executive summaries, visual representations via simple charts and graphs, and implications for practice than to the technical details of your research methodology. (For more tips on writing for an audience made up of administrators or other practitioners, you may want to reexamine our comments in Chapter 13, which appear toward the end of the section "Planning an Evaluation and Fostering Its Utilization.")

Even if you are writing your report for submission to a professional journal, you'll need to keep in mind the varying expectations and types of readerships of different professional journals. With some social work journals, such as those with the term *research* in their title, your audience will consist largely of researchers who will understand and value your discussion of methodological issues and who will need less explanation of technical terms. Some other journals might be at the opposite end of the spectrum—with a greater emphasis on practice implications—and still others somewhere in between. Before you write your report for submission to a journal, you should do two things: (1) Carefully select a journal whose expectations and audience best match your topic and the type of report you'd like to write; and (2) examine the page in that journal where its editor describes the types of articles it is interested in as well as its article format and style expectations. The National Association of Social Workers publishes *An Author's Guide to Social Work Journals* (NASW, 1997) that might help you in selecting a journal that appears to be the best fit for your report.

*Fourth ed. (New York: Macmillan, 1999). Here's another useful reference on writing: R. W. Birchfield, *The New Fowler's Modern English Usage*, 3rd ed. (New York: Oxford University Press, 1998).

Form and Length of the Report

Our comments here apply to both written and oral reports. Each form, however, affects the nature of the report.

It's useful to think about the variety of reports that might result from a research project. To begin, you may wish to prepare a short *research note* for publication in a professional journal. Such reports are approximately one to five pages long (typed, double-spaced) and should be concise and direct. In a small amount of space, you can't present the state of the field in any detail, so your methodological notes must be abbreviated. Basically, you should tell the reader why you feel a brief note is justified by your findings, then tell what those findings are.

Often researchers must prepare reports for the sponsors of their research. These reports may vary greatly in length. In preparing such a report, you should bear in mind its audience—professional or lay—and their reasons for sponsoring the project in the first place. It is both bad politics and bad manners to bore the sponsors with research findings that are of no interest or value to them. At the same time, it may be useful to summarize how the research has advanced social work knowledge (if it has).

Working papers are another form of research reporting. In a large and complex project especially, you'll find comments on your analysis and the interpretation of your data useful. A working paper constitutes a tentative presentation with an implicit request for comments. Working papers can also vary in length, and they may present all of the research findings of the project or only a portion of them. Because your professional reputation is not at stake in a working paper, feel free to present tentative interpretations that you can't altogether justify—identifying them as such and asking for evaluations.

Many research projects result in papers delivered at professional meetings. Often, these serve the same purpose as working papers. You can present findings and ideas of possible interest to your colleagues and ask for their comments. Although the length of *professional papers* may vary depending on the organization of the meetings, it's best to say too little rather than too much. Although a working paper may ramble somewhat through tentative conclusions, conference participants should not be forced to sit through an oral unveiling of the same. Interested listeners can always ask for more details later, and uninterested ones can gratefully escape.

Probably the most popular research report is the *article* published in a professional journal. Again, lengths vary, and you should examine the lengths of articles previously published by the journal in question. As a rough guide, however, 20 to 25 typed pages is a good length. A subsequent section on the organization of the report is primarily based on the structure of a journal article, so we shall say no more at this point except to indicate that student term papers should follow this model. As a general rule, a term paper that would make a good journal article also makes a good term paper.

A *book*, of course, is the lengthiest and most detailed form of research report. If your book is published by a prestigious publishing company, some readers may be led to accept your findings uncritically. Consequently, you have a special obligation to your audience.

Aim of the Report

Earlier in this book, we considered the different purposes of social work research projects. In preparing your report, you should keep these different purposes in mind.

Some reports may focus primarily on the *exploration* of a topic. As such, their conclusions are tentative and incomplete. You should clearly indicate to your audience the exploratory aim of the study and point to the shortcomings of the particular project. An exploratory report serves to point the way to more-refined research on the topic.

Most research reports have a descriptive element reflecting the descriptive purpose of the studies they document. Carefully distinguish those descriptions that apply only to the sample and those that apply to the population. Give your audience some indication of the probable range of error in any inferential descriptions you make.

Many reports have an explanatory aim: pointing to causal relationships among variables. Depending on your probable audience, carefully delineate the rules of explanation that lie behind your computations and conclusions. Also, as in the case of description, give your readers some guide to the relative certainty of your conclusions.

Regardless of your research purpose, all social work research projects should have the overarching aim of providing information that will be useful in guiding practice or policy. Thus, your report probably will propose implications for action. Be sure that the recommendations you propose are warranted by your data. Thus, you should be especially careful to spell out the logic by which you move from empirical data to proposed action.

Avoiding Plagiarism

Whenever you're reporting on the work of others, you must be clear about who said what. That is, you must avoid plagiarism: the theft of another's words or ideas—whether intentional or accidental—and the presentation of those words and ideas as your own. Because this is a common and sometimes unclear problem for students, let's examine it. Here are the ground rules regarding plagiarism:

- You cannot use another writer's exact words without using quotation marks and giving a complete citation, which indicates the source of the quotation such that your reader could locate that quotation in its original context. As a general rule, taking a passage of eight or more words without citation is a violation of federal copyright laws.
- It's also not acceptable to edit or paraphrase another's words and present the revised version as your own work.
- Finally, it's not even acceptable to present another's ideas as your own—even if you use totally different words to express those ideas.

The following examples should clarify what is or is not acceptable in the use of another's work.

The Original Work:

Laws of Growth

Systems are like babies: once you get one, you have it. They don't go away. On the contrary, they display the most remarkable persistence. They not only persist; they grow. And as they grow, they encroach. The growth potential of systems was explored in a tentative, preliminary way by Parkinson, who concluded that administrative systems maintain an average growth of 5 to 6 percent per annum regardless of the work to be done. Parkinson was right so far as he goes, and we must give him full honors for initiating the serious study of this important topic. But what Parkinson failed to perceive, we now enunciate—the general systems analogue of Parkinson's Law.

The System Itself Tends to Grow At 5 To 6 Percent Per Annum

Again, this Law is but the preliminary to the most general possible formulation, the Big-Bang Theorem of Systems Cosmology.

Systems Tend to Expand to Fill the Known Universe

(GALL, 1975:12–14)

Now let's look at some of the *acceptable* ways you might make use of Gall's work in a term paper.

Acceptable: John Gall, in his work *Systemantics,* draws a humorous parallel between systems and infants: "Systems are like babies: once you get one, you have it. They don't go away. On the contrary, they display the most remarkable persistence. They not only persist; they grow."*

Acceptable: John Gall warns that systems are like babies. Create a system and it sticks around. Worse yet, Gall notes, systems keep growing larger and larger.**

Acceptable: It has also been suggested that systems have a natural tendency to persist, even grow and encroach (Gall, 1975:12).

Note that the last format requires that you give a complete citation in your bibliography, as we do in this book. Complete footnotes, as shown for the first two examples, or endnotes work as well. See the publication manuals of various organizations such as the American Psychological Association or the American Sociological Association, as well as the *Chicago Manual of Style,* for appropriate citation formats.

Here now are some *unacceptable* uses of the same material, reflecting some common errors.

Unacceptable: In this paper, I want to look at some of the characteristics of the social systems we create in our organizations. First, systems are like babies: once you get one, you have it. They don't go away. On the contrary, they display the most remarkable persistence. They not only persist; they grow. [It is unacceptable to directly quote someone else's materials without using quotation marks and giving a full citation.]

Unacceptable: In this paper, I want to look at some of the characteristics of the social systems we create in our organizations. First, systems are a lot like children: once you get one, it's yours. They

*John Gall, *Systemantics: How Systems Work and Especially How They Fail* (New York: Quadrangle, 1975), 12–14.
**John Gall, *Systemantics: How Systems Work and Especially How They Fail* (New York: Quadrangle, 1975), 12.

don't go away; they persist. They not only persist, in fact: they grow. [It is unacceptable to edit another's work and present it as your own.]

Unacceptable: In this paper, I want to look at some of the characteristics of the social systems we create in our organizations. One thing I've noticed is that once you create a system, it never seems to go away. Just the opposite, in fact: they have a tendency to grow. You might say systems are a lot like children in that respect. [It is unacceptable to paraphrase someone else's ideas and present them as your own.]

Each of the preceding unacceptable examples is an example of plagiarism and represents a serious offense. Admittedly, there are some "gray areas." Some ideas are more or less in the public domain, not "belonging" to any one person. Or you may reach an idea on your own that someone else has already put in writing. If you have a question about a specific situation, discuss it with your instructor in advance.

We've discussed this topic in some detail because, although you must place your research in the context of what others have done and said, the improper use of their materials is a serious offense. Learning to avoid plagiarism is a part of your "coming of age" as a scholar.

ORGANIZATION OF THE REPORT

Although the organization of reports differs somewhat in terms of form and purpose, a general format for presenting research data can be helpful. The following comments apply most directly to a journal article, but with some modification they apply to most forms of research reports as well.

Title

At this point in your education you probably don't need to be reminded that your report should have a title. You also probably don't need to be told that your title should closely reflect the main point of your research. Deciding on the best title, however, is not always easy. You should try to give readers enough information without making it too wordy. If it is more than about a dozen words, it probably needs to be shortened. If it has a subtitle, however, it can be a bit longer. Still, it should be as terse as possible.

If possible, you may want to devise a title that is likely to pique the interest of potential readers. A catchy title may be a good idea, but be careful not to go overboard. You don't want your audience to think you are being unscholarly in hyping your report in a misleading manner. This is a judgment call. Certainly, however, the nature of the journal to which you are submitting your report should influence your choice of a title. To be on the safe side, you may want to devise several alternative tentative titles and then seek feedback from your colleagues or any coauthors you have as to their reactions to the various titles. Based on their feedback, you might use one of the titles as currently worded or modify the wording somewhat.

Abstract

Immediately after the title page (which will also list all authors, their degrees, organizational affiliations, and so on), reports will include a separate page containing an **abstract** that briefly summarizes the study. Different journals vary regarding the maximum length of abstracts, with most maximums falling somewhere between 75 and 150 words. Abstracts typically begin with a sentence identifying the purpose of the research. Next, there is usually a sentence or two that summarizes the main features of the research design and methodology. The main findings are then highlighted in one or two sentences, followed by a brief mention of any major implications. Here is an illustrative abstract:

> A randomized experiment tested the effectiveness of adding a psychoeducational group therapy intervention to standard inpatient chemical dependency services for clients dually diagnosed with mental and substance dependence disorders. One hundred clients were randomly assigned to an experimental group and a control group. Outcome variables included drug and alcohol use, incarceration days, psychiatric symptoms, and psychiatric inpatient admissions. No significant treatment effects were found on any of the outcome variables. The tested intervention did not add to the effects of standard treatments for dually diagnosed clients. Practitioners should continue to develop and evaluate alternative treatment approaches that might prove to be more effective than the one tested in this study.

An old forensic dictum says, "Tell them what you're going to tell them; tell them; and tell them what you told them." You would do well to follow this dictum. Your abstract will tell your readers what you are going to tell them. Now let's examine the sections where you go ahead and tell them.

Introduction and Literature Review

The main narrative of your report should begin with an introduction that provides a background to the problem you have investigated. This section of your report should share some of the same features as the problems and objectives and literature review sections of your research proposal. It should, for example, convey the scope of the problem, the objectives and rationale for the study, and the study's importance. It should summarize the previous research as briefly as possible, yet provide enough detail to give readers an adequate overview of the topic and to show them how your study is connected to and builds on the prior literature. The entire introductory part of your report—including your problem statement, literature review, objectives, and hypotheses—might appear under one subheading called "Introduction." Or it might be broken up under one or more additional subheadings such as "Literature Review," "Hypotheses," and so on. More important than how many subheadings you use is whether your introductory material clearly shows the reader the objectives of your research and their rationale, why your study is timely and important, and how your study connects to and builds upon the prior literature.

Your review of the literature should bring the reader up to date on the previous research in the area, and should point out any general agreements or disagreements among the previous researchers. If you wish to challenge previously accepted ideas, carefully review the studies that have led to the acceptance of those ideas, then indicate the factors that have not been previously considered or the logical fallacies present in the previous research. When you're concerned with resolving a disagreement among previous researchers, you should summarize the research supporting one view, then summarize the research supporting the other, and finally suggest the reasons for the disagreement.

Your review of the literature serves a bibliographical function for readers, indexing the previous research on a given topic. This can be overdone, however, and you should avoid an opening paragraph that runs three pages, mentioning every previous study in the field. The comprehensive bibliographical function can best be served by a bibliography at the end of the report, and the review of the literature should focus only on those studies that have direct relevance to your study. Furthermore, as you focus on the most relevant studies, you should report only the most relevant aspects of those studies. Finally, if multiple studies have had similar findings, rather than discuss each study separately you might simply identify the general finding that they agreed upon followed by a citation of the authorship and date of each study in parentheses.

Earlier in this chapter, we presented a box titled "Improving a Weak Literature Review" that illustrated the points we had made about writing the literature review section of a research proposal. That box also applies to reviewing the literature as part of the introductory material in a report of completed research.

Methods

As we've discussed throughout most of the previous chapters of this book, the worth of the findings of a study depends on the validity of the study's design and data-collection procedures. Informed readers will want to read the details of your study's methodological design and execution so they can judge the value of your findings and decide whether to be guided by them. Readers need to be provided with sufficient detail to enable them to know precisely what was done and to replicate your study.

For some studies this section will begin with a specification of your hypotheses and variables. For other studies you might provide that information in the preceding section, showing how your conceptual framework flows from the prior literature. In either case, your methods section should describe in detail how you measured each variable, and should give readers enough information to ascertain whether your measurement procedures were reliable and valid. The same sort of detail is needed regarding your data-collection procedures, the logical arrangements for drawing causal inferences (if that was your study's purpose), and your sampling procedures.

In reporting the design and execution of a survey, for example, always include the following: the population, the sampling frame, the sampling method, the sample size, the data-collection method, the completion rate, and the methods of data processing and analysis. Comparable details should be given if other methods are used. The experienced researcher can report these details in a rather short space, without omitting anything required for the reader's evaluation of the study.

Results

Having set the study in the perspective of previous research and having described the design and execution of it, you should then present your data. The presentation of data analyses should provide a maximum of detail without being cluttered. You can accomplish this best by continually examining your report to see whether it achieves the following aims.

If you're using quantitative data, present them so the reader can recompute them. In the case of percentage tables, for example, the reader should be able to collapse categories and recompute the percentages. Readers should receive sufficient information to permit them to compute percentages in the table in the opposite direction from that of your own presentation.

Describe all aspects of a quantitative analysis in sufficient detail to permit a secondary analyst to replicate the analysis from the same body of data. This means that he or she should be able to create the same indexes and scales, produce the same tables, arrive at the same regression equations, obtain the same factors and factor loadings, and so forth. This will seldom be done, of course, but if the report allows for it, the reader will be far better equipped to evaluate the report than if it does not.

Provide details. If you're doing a qualitative analysis, you must provide enough detail that your reader has a sense of having made the observations with you. Presenting only those data that support your interpretations is not sufficient; you must also share those data that conflict with the way you've made sense of things. Ultimately, you should provide enough information that the reader might reach a different conclusion than you did—though you can hope your interpretation will make the most sense. The reader, in fact, should be in a position to replicate the entire study independently, whether it involves participant observation of people who are homeless, an experiment evaluating the effectiveness of an intervention for abused children, or any other kind of study. Recall that replicability is an essential norm of science. A single study does not prove a point; only a series of studies can begin to do so. And unless studies can be replicated, there can be no meaningful series of studies.

Integrate supporting materials. We have previously mentioned the importance of integrating data and interpretations in the report. Here is a more specific guideline for doing this. Tables, charts, and figures, if any, should be integrated into the text of the report—appearing near that portion of the text discussing them. Sometimes students (as well as authors of manuscripts submitted for publication in journals) describe their analyses in the body of the report and place all the tables in an appendix. This procedure can impede the reader, however. As a general rule, it is best to (1) describe the purpose for presenting the table, (2) present it, and (3) review and interpret it.

In published research reports it is often best to wait until you reach your *Discussion* section, which follows the *Results* section, to present your interpretations of the implications of your results. Interpretations in the *Results* section are usually limited to explaining what the data mean in a technical, factual sense. For example, suppose you have used a relatively new and complex statistical procedure. You'd probably want to briefly explain how to interpret that statistic in your *Results* section. Suppose further that your study finds that an intervention for spouse abusers appears to be effective according to the self-reports of the perpetrators, but ineffective according to the reports of their spouses. You would factually report each of those findings in your *Results,* but might want to delay trying to explain the discrepancy until your *Discussion* section. On the other hand, your report might be more readable if you integrated the presentation of data, the manipulations of those data, and your interpretations into a logical whole. That is, you would do that all in one section, called *Findings,* instead of having separate *Results* and *Discussion* sections. It can frustrate readers to discover a collection of seemingly unrelated analyses and findings in a *Results* section with a promise that all the loose ends will be tied together later in the report. You could prevent such frustration by explaining every step in the analysis at the time it is initially reported. In your *Findings* section, you could present your rationale for each particular analysis, present the data relevant to it, interpret the results, and then indicate where that result leads next.

Discussion and Conclusions

The narrative part of your report should conclude with a section that develops explicit conclusions, draws practical implications based on those conclusions, discusses the methodological limitations of your study, and draws implications for future research.

Many studies have findings that can be interpreted in alternative ways. Reasonable people may disagree about the most appropriate interpretations and conclusions to be drawn. You should acknowledge all of the alternative interpretations that may reasonably be made of your data. Then you should identify which interpretations seem the most warranted and explain why. This is not to imply, however, that you should merely editorialize. The conclusions you draw should be warranted by your data. You should carefully note the specific basis for each conclusion. Otherwise you may lead your reader into accepting unwarranted conclusions. Point to any qualifications or conditions warranted in the evaluation of conclusions, including the methodological limitations bearing on each conclusion. Typically, you know best the shortcomings and tentativeness of your conclusions, and you should give the reader the advantage of that knowledge.

Based on your conclusions, you should draw implications for social work practice or social welfare policy. Some studies may yield implications for social work education. You should also develop implications for future research, based on new questions emerging from your findings and perhaps also based on any unanticipated practical or methodological pitfalls you encountered in conducting your study. Many journal articles end with the statement, "It is clear that much more research is needed." This conclusion is probably always true, but it has little value unless you can offer pertinent suggestions about the nature of that future research. You should review the particular shortcomings of your own study and suggest ways those shortcomings might be avoided.

Following the forensic dictum mentioned earlier, at the end of your report you may want to tell your readers what you told them. In summarizing your research report you should avoid reviewing every specific finding, but you should review all the significant ones, pointing once more to their general significance.

References and Appendices

Immediately following the conclusion of the narrative portion of your report should be a list of all the references you cited in the report. Typically, each reference will be indicated in the narrative by putting the authors' last names and the year of publication in parentheses. For example, if we are citing the previous edition of the book you are reading we would do this as follows: (Rubin and Babbie, 2005). We could also cite ourselves as follows: Rubin and Babbie (2005) suggest that when the author's names that you are citing are a normal part of the sentence, you should just put the date in parentheses. Your list of references at the end of your report will then display each full citation in the alphabetical order of the first author's last name.

An alternative method is to just number each reference as follows,[1] and then list each full citation in your reference list by number, in the order that they appear in the text. Your decision as to which reference format to use should be based on the expectations of those to whom you will be submitting your report. In lieu of such expectations, it's probably best to use the former method because it is used more widely.

If you have any tables, figures, or graphs that you opted not to integrate into the text of your report, these should be placed immediately after your list of references, followed by any other appendices you may have.

ADDITIONAL CONSIDERATIONS WHEN WRITING QUALITATIVE REPORTS

Most of our foregoing comments about writing research reports apply to both quantitative and qualitative studies. We have, however, cited some of the ways in which reports of qualitative research may differ from reports of quantitative research. Let's now look at some additional considerations that apply only to qualitative reports—considerations suggested by Neuman (2000).

Because qualitative studies collect data that are harder to condense than the statistics in quantitative studies, and because qualitative studies often seek to provide a deeper, empathic understanding of phenomena, qualitative reports tend to be lengthier than quantitative reports. For example, instead of providing summary statistics, qualitative reports may need to present lengthy quotes. They may need to present photographs and very detailed descriptions of the people and circumstances that have been observed. Descriptions of and justifications for less structured, less standardized, and sometimes idiosyncratic data-collection methods often need to be longer in qualitative reports than in quantitative ones. More space might also be needed to explain the development of new concepts and new theory that may emerge from a qualitative study. In historical and comparative studies, many detailed footnotes may be needed to describe the sources and evidence for each conclusion. In light of all these factors, it may be difficult to meet the page limitations of many journals that are more accustomed to publishing reports of quantitative studies. Authors of lengthy qualitative reports may need to submit their studies to journals that specialize in qualitative research, such as those with the term *qualitative* in the journal title. Such authors also commonly report their research in book-length form.

Whereas quantitative reports typically are written in a formal and succinct style, qualitative reports are more likely to use more creative and varied literary styles in order to convey to readers a deeper, more empathic, more subjective understanding of what it is like to walk in the shoes of the people being portrayed in the report. This is not to imply that anything goes. As we noted earlier, the conclusions being drawn in a qualitative report should be well supported by a wealth of data. Although qualitative researchers have more leeway regarding the style and organization of their reports, each conclusion they draw should be accompanied by sufficient supportive evidence collected in a plausible manner.

We will conclude with a point we mentioned earlier. Research reports should be written in the best possible style. Writing lucidly is easier for some people than for others, and it is always harder than writing poorly. You are again referred to the Strunk and White book. Every researcher would do well to follow this procedure: Write. Read Strunk and White. Revise. Reread Strunk and White. Revise again. After you are satisfied with your report, ask your colleagues to read and criticize it. Based on their criticism, revise yet again. This will be a difficult and time-consuming endeavor, but so is science.

A perfectly designed, carefully executed, and brilliantly analyzed study will be altogether worthless unless you can communicate your findings to others. We have attempted to provide some guidelines toward that end. The best guides are logic, clarity, and honesty. Ultimately, there is no substitute for practice.

Main Points

- Learn about the expectations of a funding source before preparing a research proposal to it.

- Requests for proposals provide information about the expectations and funding processes of potential research grant funding sources.

- Various websites on the Internet provide the most efficient way to find potential funding sources for research grants.

- Research grants provide much greater leeway to investigators than do research contracts.

- Before writing your research proposal you should develop a relationship with a liaison from the funding source and examine proposals that have been funded by that source.

- Proposal components and guidelines will differ depending on the purpose of the research and the expectations of the funding source.

- Preparing a proposal for a qualitative study can be more challenging than preparing one for a quantitative study.

- Research proposals are often prefaced with a cover letter, a cover page, and an executive summary.

- Research proposals should begin with a problem and objectives section specifying exactly what is to be studied and why it is worth studying.

- An important early section of the research proposal is the literature review, which should be both thorough and terse.

- The conceptual framework section of the research proposal specifies and provides rationales for your research questions, hypotheses, variables, and operational definitions.

- The research proposal should contain methodological sections on measurement procedures, sampling procedures, design, and data-collection methods.

- Additional components of research proposals often include a schedule for the various stages of the research, a budget, materials showing IRB approval, evidence of feasibility, and plans for dissemination of findings.

- Good social research writing begins with good writing. Write to communicate rather than to impress.

- Be mindful of your audience and your purpose in writing the report of your completed research study.

- Avoid plagiarism, that is, presenting someone else's words or thoughts as though they were your own.

- If you use someone else's exact words, be sure to use quotation marks or some other indication that you are quoting.

- If you paraphrase someone else's ideas, be sure to cite them, providing a full bibliographic citation.

- The title of your research report should be as terse as possible, yet give readers enough information about the main point of your study.

- Most research reports are prefaced by an abstract summarizing the main purpose of the study, the main features of its design and methods, and the main findings and implications.
- Research reports commonly include the following sections: introduction and literature review, methods, results, discussion and conclusions, references and appendices.
- Compared to reports of quantitative research, reports of qualitative research often have more leeway as to organization and style and require more length in order to provide a deeper understanding of phenomena and to accompany each conclusion with sufficient plausible and supportive evidence.

Review Questions and Exercises

1. Try to obtain a copy of a funded research grant proposal and a funded research contract proposal in social work or an allied human service field. Begin by asking your instructor whether your school has a center for social work research. If they do not, perhaps individual faculty members have had funded grants or contracts that they can show you. There might also be a university-wide research center that can help you. Local or state social service agencies might also have some funded grants or contracts they can share.

a. Describe the contrasting degrees of leeway the grant and the contract provide to the investigators.

b. Describe the ways in which each funded proposal conforms to or deviates from the guidelines for writing research proposals, and the components of research proposals, discussed in this chapter.

2. Inquiring with the same resources as in Exercise 1, try to obtain a copy of a research grant proposal in social work or an allied human service field that was not funded.

a. Describe the ways in which the nonfunded proposal conforms to or deviates from the guidelines for writing research proposals, and the components of research proposals, discussed in this chapter.

b. Describe how the nonfunded proposal does or does not contain more weaknesses than the funded proposals, from the standpoint of the guidelines for writing research proposals and the components of research proposals discussed in this chapter.

3. Try to obtain interviews with authors of one of the nonfunded and one of the funded proposals discussed in Exercises 1 and 2. Ask them to describe their experiences in seeking funding for those proposals. Using notes from your interviews, discuss the ways in which their experiences reflect or diverge from the guidelines for writing research proposals and the components of research proposals discussed in this chapter.

Internet Exercises

1. Using one or more of the websites described in the "Finding a Funding Source" section of this chapter, find a request for proposals (RFP) related to a social work research question. After you find the RFP, write down the research question, the funding source, the maximum size of the grants, and the types of designs the funding source has in mind.

2. Use InfoTrac College Edition to find an article that discusses proposal writing. Select the "Subject Guide" icon and enter the term *proposal writing.* Then click on "Submit Search." Read an article whose title or abstract seems to indicate that it contains useful tips for proposal writing. Write down the bibliographical reference information for the article and summarize the article in a few sentences. Identify any tips for proposal writing that are suggested in the article that you think are particularly helpful or that you question.

3. Use InfoTrac College Edition to find two quantitative research articles related to social work. Compare and critique each from the standpoint of the guidelines for writing research reports and components of research reports described in this chapter.

4. Go to www.nova.edu/ssss/QR/index.html to find *The Qualitative Report,* an online journal published by Nova Southeastern University. There you can find online copies of articles reporting qualitative research studies. Read an article with a topic related to social work research. Discuss the similarities and differences between that article and the quantitative studies you found in Internet Exercise 3 in regard to the guidelines for writing research reports and components of research reports described in this chapter.

5. Go to www.ucalgary.ca/md/CAH/research/res_prop.htm. This site will walk you through the process of preparing a research proposal. Click on "Common Pitfalls." Briefly describe what you find there.

6. Go to www.nova.edu/ssss/QR/QR3-1/heath.html to find: Anthony W. Heath, "The Proposal in Qualitative Research." This article, which is in the online journal *The Qualitative Report* (vol. 3, no. 1, March 1997) provides another guide to proposal writing, this time specifically for qualitative research projects. Briefly summarize how it contrasts with guidelines for writing quantitative research proposals.

7. Go to the InfoTrac College Edition website and click on the "InfoWrite" bar at the left. At InfoWrite you will find various prompts relevant to writing a research paper. Explore the various topics and briefly describe one or more guidelines you find that you feel might be most helpful to you if and when you prepare to write a research paper.

Additional Readings

Beebe, Linda. 1993. *Professional Writing for the Human Services*. Washington, DC: NASW Press. If you want to write an article for publication in a professional social work journal, this handbook may help.

Birchfield, R. W. 1998. *The New Fowler's Modern English Usage*, 3rd ed. New York: Oxford University Press. H. W. Fowler's concise and witty *Modern English Usage* has been the chief resource and final word on "proper" English since it was first published in 1926. The third edition ensures the advice is "modern."

Strunk, William, Jr., and E. B. White. 1999. *The Elements of Style*, 4th ed. New York: Macmillan. This marvelous little book provides specific guidance as to grammar and spelling, but its primary power is its ability to *inspire* good writing.

Walker, Janice R., and Todd Taylor. 1998. *The Columbia Guide to Online Style*. New York: Columbia University Press. A guide to citing web materials in a scholarly report.

Using the Library

INTRODUCTION

We live in a world filled with social science research reports. Our daily newspapers, magazines, professional journals, alumni bulletins, and club newsletters—virtually everything you pick up to read—can carry reports that deal with a particular topic. For formal explorations of a topic, of course, the best place to start is still a good college or university library. Today, there are two major approaches to finding library materials: the traditional paper system and the electronic route. Let's begin with the traditional method and then examine the electronic option.

GETTING HELP

When you want to find something in the library, your best friends are the reference librarians, who are specially trained to find things in the library. Some libraries have specialized reference librarians—for the social sciences, humanities, government documents, and so forth. Find the librarian who specializes in your field. Make an appointment. Tell the librarian what you're interested in. He or she will probably put you in touch with some of the many available reference sources.

REFERENCE SOURCES

You've probably heard the expression "information explosion." Your library is one of the main battlefields. Fortunately, a large number of reference volumes offer a guide to the information that's available.

- *Books in Print:* This volume lists all of the books currently in print in the United States, listed separately by author and by title. Out-of-print books often can be found in older editions of *Books in Print*.

- *Readers' Guide to Periodical Literature:* This annual volume with monthly updates lists articles published in many journals and magazines. Because the entries are organized by subject matter, this is an excellent source for organizing your reading on a particular topic.

In addition to these general reference volumes, you'll find a great variety of specialized references. Here are a few examples:

- *Social Work Abstracts*
- *Sociological Abstracts*
- *Psychological Abstracts*
- *Social Science Index*
- *Social Science Citation Index*
- *Popular Guide to Government Publications*
- *New York Times Index*
- *Facts on File*
- *Editorial Research Reports*
- *Monthly Catalog of Government Publications*
- *Public Affairs Information Service Bulletin*
- *Biography Index*
- *Congressional Quarterly Weekly Report*
- *Library Literature*
- *Bibliographic Index*

USING THE STACKS

Serious research usually involves using the stacks, where most of the library's books are stored. This section provides information about finding books there.

The Card Catalog

In the traditional paper system, the card catalog is the main reference system for finding out where books are stored. Each book is described on three separate 3 × 5 cards. The cards are then filed in three alphabetic sets: one by author, another by title, and the third by subject matter.

If you want to find a particular book, you can look it up in either the author file or the title file. If you only have a general subject area of interest, thumb through the subject catalog. Subject catalog cards typically have the following elements:

1. Subject heading (always in capital letters)
2. Author's name (last name, first name)
3. Title of the book
4. Publisher
5. Date of publication
6. Number of pages in the book plus other information.
7. Call number. (This is needed to find a nonfiction book on the library shelves. A book of fiction generally carries no number and is found in alphabetical order by the author's name.)

Library of Congress Classification

Here's a useful strategy to use when you're researching a topic. Once you've identified the call number for a particular book in your subject area, go to the stacks, find that book, and look over the other books on the shelves near it. Because the books are arranged by subject matter, this method will help you locate relevant books you didn't know about.

Alternatively, you may want to go directly to the stacks and look at books in your subject area. In most libraries, books are arranged and numbered according to a subject matter classification system developed by the Library of Congress. (Some follow the Dewey decimal system.) The following is a shortened list of some Library of Congress categories.

Library of Congress Classifications (partial)

A GENERAL WORKS

B PHILOSOPHY, PSYCHOLOGY, RELIGION
- *B–BD* *Philosophy*
- *BF* *Psychology*
- *BL–BX* *Religion*

C HISTORY–AUXILIARY SCIENCES

D HISTORY (EXCEPT AMERICA)

E–F HISTORY (AMERICA)
- *E* *United States*
- *E51–99* *Indians of North America*

G GEOGRAPHY–ANTHROPOLOGY
- *GN* *Anthropology*

H SOCIAL SCIENCES
- *HB–HJ* *Economics and Business*
- *HM–HX* *Sociology*

J POLITICAL SCIENCE

K LAW

L EDUCATION

M MUSIC

N FINE ARTS

P LANGUAGE AND LITERATURE

Q SCIENCE

R MEDICINE
- *RT* *Nursing*

S AGRICULTURE—PLANT AND ANIMAL INDUSTRY

T TECHNOLOGY

U MILITARY SCIENCE

V NAVAL SCIENCE

Z BIBLIOGRAPHY AND LIBRARY SCIENCE

ABSTRACTS

Some publications present summaries of books and articles that help you locate a great many references easily and effectively. These summaries, called *abstracts,* are often prepared by the original authors. As you find relevant references, you can track down the original works and see the full details. In social work, the most relevant publication of these abstracts is *Social Work Abstracts* (formerly *Social Work Research & Abstracts*).

The first step in using *Social Work Abstracts* is to look at the subject index to find general subject headings related to your specific topic of interest. Examine the subtopics listed under the relevant general headings and look for topics that appear to be most directly related to your specific topic of interest. Beside each will be one or more numbers. Because the abstracts are presented in numerical order, you can use the listed numbers to locate the abstracts of potential interest to you. When you read the abstract, you will learn whether the study it summarizes is of sufficient likely relevance to warrant finding and reading the report in its entirety. If it is worth reading, then the abstract will provide the reference information you'll need to find the full report, as well as where you can contact its author.

Let's walk through this process. Suppose you are searching the literature for a valid scale to assess the degree of acculturation of foreign-born Chinese Americans. In using *Social Work Abstracts,* your first step would be to find a subject heading in the Subject Index that fits the focus of your search. If you looked for the heading "acculturation of foreign-born Chinese Americans," you wouldn't find it. It's too specific. But if you looked for the broader heading "Acculturation," you would find it in the alphabetized Subject Index between the two headings "Accountability" and "Activism," as follows:

Accountability

 and Joint Reviews in England, 1083
 and school choice, 1243

Acculturation

 of Chinese Americans, 1081
 of Hispanic middle school students, 1231
 of Russian immigrants, 1430
 of West Indians, 1387

Activism

 judicial, 1366

Under the heading "Acculturation," you would find four subheadings. The first, "of Chinese Americans," is the one you'd want. The number beside it refers to the number of the abstract you'd want to examine. Because each issue of *Social Work Abstracts* lists the abstracts it contains in numerical order, you could just flip pages until you found the page that contains abstract number 1081.

Many of the abstracts in *Social Work Abstracts* are referenced under multiple subject headings. Suppose instead of the heading "Acculturation" you looked for the heading "Chinese Americans." You would find it in the Subject Index between the headings: "Children's services" and "Citizen participation," as follows:

Children's services

 vouchers for, 1003

Chinese Americans

 and acculturation, 1081
 psychosocial issues in working with, 1426

Citizen participation

 in advocacy for persons with disabilities, 1219

Under the heading "Chinese Americans," you would find two subheadings. The first subheading, "and acculturation," is the one you'd want, and again you would be referred to abstract number 1081.

You can see the names of the article's coauthors, the title of the article, the journal in which it appeared, the volume and issue numbers of that journal, what pages the article appeared on, the date the article was published, a publication code number for that journal, an address for contacting the article's lead author, and a summary of the article.

Social Work Abstracts also provides an Author Index. Suppose you learn the name of an author who had studied the assessment of acculturation of foreign-born Chinese Americans. You could look up her name in the alphabetized Author Index and find the numbers of the abstracts of works written by that author appearing in the volume of *Social Work Abstracts* you happen to be examining. For example, if the author's name was R. Gupta, you would find abstract 1081 by examining the following section of the Author Index of the September 2002 issue of *Social Work Abstracts:*

Gumport, P. J., 1231

Gunther-Kellar, Y., 1003

Gupta, R., 1081

Gupta, R., 1398

Gurnack, A. M., 1122

Guzley, R. M. 1080

H

Hackworth, J., 1359

Gupta's name is listed twice. That's because Gupta authored two of the works abstracted in that issue of *Social Work Abstracts*. You'd want to look at all of the abstracts listed for the person you look up in the *Authors Index;* perhaps all of them would be of interest to you.

ELECTRONICALLY ACCESSING LIBRARY MATERIALS

In Chapter 2 we discussed how to use your computer to search online for literature that can guide evidence-based practice. Instead of repeating that material here, we'll just briefly remind you that library materials often can be accessed electronically. Although there are different types of computerized library systems, here's a typical example of how they work.

As you sit at a computer terminal in the library, at a computer lab, or at home, you can type the title of a book and in seconds see a video display of a catalog card. If you want to explore the book further, you can type an instruction at the terminal and see an abstract of the book. Alternatively, you might type a subject name and see a listing of all the books and articles written on that topic. You could skim through the list and indicate which ones you want to see.

Most college libraries today provide online access to periodicals, books, and other library materials. Your library's computerized system should allow you to see which materials are available online and whether paper copies of the materials you seek are available in your library. If your library holds those materials, the system may indicate their call numbers, whether the books you seek have been checked out and, if so, the due date for their return. As discussed in Chapter 2, your library may also provide a variety of Internet professional literature database services to help you search for literature online. (How to use them was discussed in Chapter 2.)

PROFESSIONAL JOURNALS

Despite the exciting advances occurring in computer-based systems and the great practical value of online database services and publications containing abstracts, you should not rely exclusively on them to locate journal articles that are pertinent to your interests. There is no guarantee that every reference of value to you will be identified in a computer search or a publication of abstracts. You should therefore augment your search by examining the tables of contents in recent issues of professional journals that are the most relevant to your particular interest. For example, if you are searching for studies on interventions for abused children, two of the various journals you may want to examine are *Child Welfare* and *Children and Youth Services Review.*

Examining recent issues of journals is less time-consuming than you might imagine. These issues ought to be available in the section of your library that contains unbound current periodicals. Once you locate the recent issues of the relevant journals (the last two years or so ought to suffice), it should take only a few minutes to thumb through the tables of contents looking for titles that have some potential bearing on your topic. Once you spot a relevant title, turn to the page on which the article begins. There you will find an abstract of the article; just like the abstracts that appear in publications of abstracts, this one should take only seconds to read and will help you determine if the article is pertinent enough to warrant reading in greater detail.

Your examination of relevant journals can be expedited if your library's computerized system offers an online service listing the tables of contents of thousands of journals. It might also provide a list of *online journals*—journals whose entire contents can be downloaded and read online.

If you are uncertain about the professional journals that are pertinent to your topic, you might want to examine the list of journals reviewed in several issues of *Social Work Abstracts.* Each issue contains a list of the journals that have been reviewed for that issue. You might also want to get help with this from your reference librarian. Just to start you thinking about some of the journals you might review, here's a beginning list of some of the major journals related to social work, by subject area:

Aging and the Aged
- *Abstracts in Social Gerontology*
- *Clinical Gerontologist*
- *International Journal of Aging and Human Development*
- *Journal of Gerontological Social Work*
- *Journal of Gerontology*
- *Journal of Women and Aging*
- *The Gerontologist*

Children and Adolescents
- *Adolescence*
- *Child & Adolescent Social Work Journal*
- *Children and Youth Services Review*

Children Today
Journal of Adolescence
Journal of Adolescent & Interpersonal Violence & Trauma

Child Welfare
Adoption and Fostering
Child Care Quarterly
Child Maltreatment
Child Survivor of Traumatic Stress
Child Welfare
Journal of Child Sexual Abuse

Cognitive or Behavioral Interventions
Behavior Modification
Behavior Research & Therapy
Behavior Therapy
Behavioural & Cognitive Psychotherapy
Cognitive Therapy and Research
Journal of Applied Behavior Analysis

Crime and Delinquency
Canadian Journal of Criminology
Crime and Delinquency
Journal of Research in Crime and Delinquency
Youth and Society

Domestic Violence
Journal of Emotional Abuse
Journal of Family Violence
Journal of Traumatic Stress
Trauma, Violence & Abuse
Traumatology

Families
Families in Society
Family Process
Family Therapy
Journal of Family Issues
Journal of Family Social Work
Journal of Marital and Family Therapy

Gay and Lesbian Services
Journal of Gay & Lesbian Psychotherapy
Journal of Gay & Lesbian Social Services

Group Work
Group Dynamics—Theory, Research, and Practice
Social Work with Groups

Health
Health and Social Work
Journal of Health and Social Behavior
Social Work in Health Care

Mental Health
American Journal of Orthopsychiatry
Archives of General Psychiatry
Clinical Social Work Journal
Community Mental Health Journal
Evidence-Based Mental Health
Journal of Psychotherapy Practice and Research
Mental Health Services Research
Psychiatric Rehabilitation Journal
Psychotherapy Research
Schizophrenia Bulletin
Social Work in Mental Health

Mental Retardation
American Journal of Mental Deficiency
Journal of Mental Deficiency Research
Mental Retardation & Developmental Disabilities Research Reviews
Retardation

Program Evaluation
Canadian Journal of Program Evaluation
Evaluation
Evaluation Review
New Directions for Evaluation
The American Journal of Evaluation

Qualitative Research
Grounded Theory Review
Qualitative Health Research
Qualitative Inquiry
Qualitative Research
Qualitative Social Work: Research and Practice
Qualitative Sociology

School Social Work
School Social Work Journal
Social Work in Education

Social Policy
Australian Social Policy
Global Social Policy
Journal of Aging & Social Policy
Journal of Children and Poverty
Journal of Mental Health Policy and Economics
Journal of Poverty
Journal of Sociology and Social Welfare
Public Welfare
Social Policy
Social Policy and Social Work
Social Policy Review
Urban Policy and Research

Social Work (General)
Australian Social Work
British Journal of Social Work
Canadian Social Work Review
International Social Work
Irish Social Work
Smith College Studies in Social Work
Social Service Review
Social Work
Social Work Abstracts

Social Work Research
Journal of Social Service Research
Journal of Social Work Research and Evaluation
Research on Social Work Practice
Social Work Research

Substance Abuse
Advances in Alcohol and Substance Abuse
American Journal or Drug and Alcohol Abuse
International Journal of the Addictions
Journal of Addictions & Offender Counseling
Journal of Chemical Dependency Treatment
Journal of Child & Adolescent Substance Abuse
Journal of Drug Issues
Journal of Ethnicity in Substance Abuse
Journal of Psychoactive Drugs
Journal of Social Work Practice in the Addictions
Journal of Studies on Alcohol
Journal of Substance Abuse Treatment
Substance Abuse

Women's Issues
Affilia
Archives of Women's Mental Health
Australian Feminist Studies
Feminism & Psychology
Feminist Theory
Journal of Feminist Family Therapy
Violence Against Women
Women & Trauma

Other
Administration in Social Work
Community Development Journal
Hispanic Journal of the Behavioral Sciences
Journal of Applied Behavioral Science
Journal of Jewish Communal Service
Rural Social Work

No matter what approach you take to finding library materials, chances are there will be some documents you miss or that are not available in your library or online. If a document is not available at your particular library or via the web, then you can request an interlibrary loan, which is often free. Many libraries have loan agreements, but it might take some time before the document you need arrives at your library. If the document is located at another library nearby, then you may want to go there yourself to get it directly. The key to a good library search is to become well informed; so remember what we said earlier: *When you want to find something in the library, your best friends are the reference librarians.* Don't be shy about seeking their assistance at various points in your search.

Statistics for Estimating Sampling Error

In Chapter 14 we noted that probability theory provides a statistical basis for estimating sampling error and selecting a sample size with an acceptable amount of likely sampling error. We also referred you to this appendix if you wished to examine the more mathematical aspects of how probability theory works. Probability theory enables us to estimate sampling error by way of the concept of sampling distributions. A single sample selected from a population will give an estimate of the population parameter. Other samples would give the same or slightly different estimates. Probability theory tells us about the distribution of estimates that would be produced by a large number of such samples. To see how this works, we'll look at two examples of sampling distributions, beginning with a simple example in which our population consists of just 10 cases.

THE SAMPLING DISTRIBUTION OF 10 CASES

Suppose 10 people are in a group, and each person has a certain amount of money in his or her pocket. To simplify, let's assume that one person has no money, another has one dollar, another has two dollars, and so forth up to the person with nine dollars. Figure B-1 presents the population of 10 people.

Our task is to determine the average amount of money one person has—specifically, the mean number of dollars. If you simply add the money in Figure B-1, you'll find that the total is $45, so the mean is $4.50. Our purpose in the rest of this exercise is to estimate that mean without actually observing all 10 individuals. We'll do that by selecting random samples from the population and using the means of those samples to estimate the mean of the whole population.

To start, suppose we were to select—at random—a sample of only one person from the 10. Depending on which person we selected, we'd estimate the group's mean as anywhere from $0 to $9. Figure B-2 displays those 10 possible samples. The 10 dots shown on the graph represent the 10 "sample" means we would get as estimates of the population. The dots' distribution on the graph is called the *sampling distribution*. Obviously, selecting a sample of only one would not be a good idea, because we stand a strong chance of missing the true mean of $4.50 by quite a bit.

Figure B-1 A Population of 10 People with $0–$9

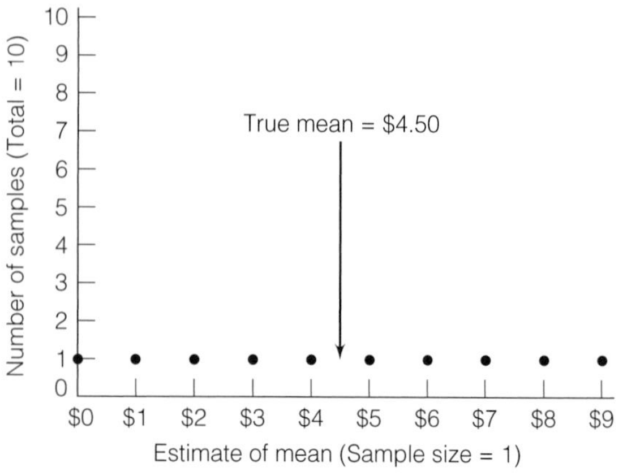

Figure B-2 The Sampling Distribution of Samples of 1

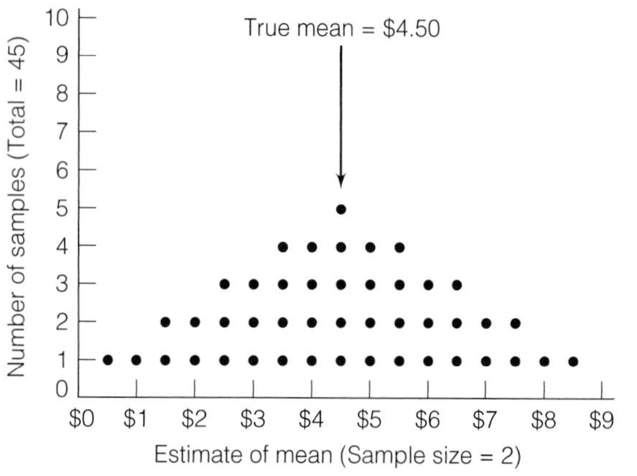

Figure B-3 The Sampling Distribution of Samples of 2

But what if we take samples of two each? As you can see from Figure B-3, increasing the sample size improves our estimations. We now have 45 possible samples: [$0 $1], [$0 $2], . . . [$7 $8], [$8 $9]. Moreover, some of those samples produce the same means. For example, [$0 $6], [$1 $5], and [$2 $4] all produce means of $3. In Figure B-3, the three dots shown above the $3 mean represent those three samples.

The 45 sample means are not evenly distributed, as you can see. Rather, they are somewhat clustered around the true value of $4.50. Only two samples deviate by as much as four dollars from the true value ([$0 $1] and [$8 $9]), whereas five of the samples would give the true estimate of $4.50; another eight samples miss the mark by only 50 cents (plus or minus).

Now suppose we select even larger samples. What do you suppose that will do to our estimates of the mean? Figure B-4 presents the sampling distributions of samples of 3, 4, 5, and 6.

The progression of sampling distributions is clear. Every increase in sample size improves the distribution of estimates of the mean. The limiting case in this procedure, of course, is to select a sample of 10: Only one sample of that size is possible—everyone—and it would give us the true mean of $4.50. As we will see shortly, this principle applies to actual sampling of meaningful populations. The larger the sample selected, the more accurate it is as an estimation of the population from which it was drawn.

SAMPLING DISTRIBUTION AND ESTIMATES OF SAMPLING ERROR

Let's turn now to a more realistic sampling situation and see how the notion of sampling distribution applies, using a simple example that involves a population much larger than 10. Let's assume for the moment that we wish to study the adult population of a small town in a rural region. We want to determine whether residents would approve or disapprove of the establishment there of a community-based residential facility for formerly institutionalized, chronically mentally disabled individuals. The study population will be that aggregation of, say, 20,000 adults as identified in the city directory: the sampling frame. (As we discuss in Chapter 14, sampling frames are the lists of elements from which a sample is selected.) The elements will be the town's adult residents. The variable under consideration will be attitudes toward the facility; it is a binomial variable—*approve* and *disapprove.* (The logic of probability sampling applies to the examination of other types of variables, such as mean income, but the computations are somewhat more complicated. Consequently, this introduction focuses on binomials.) We'll select a random sample of, say, 100 residents to estimate the entire population of the town.

The horizontal axis of Figure B-5 presents all possible values of this parameter in the population—from zero percent approval to 100 percent approval. The midpoint of the axis—50 percent—represents one-half the residents approving the facility and the other half disapproving.

To choose our sample, we give each resident in the directory a number and select 100 random numbers from a table of random numbers. (How to use a table of random numbers, such as the one in Table B-1, is explained in the box "Using a Table of Random Num-

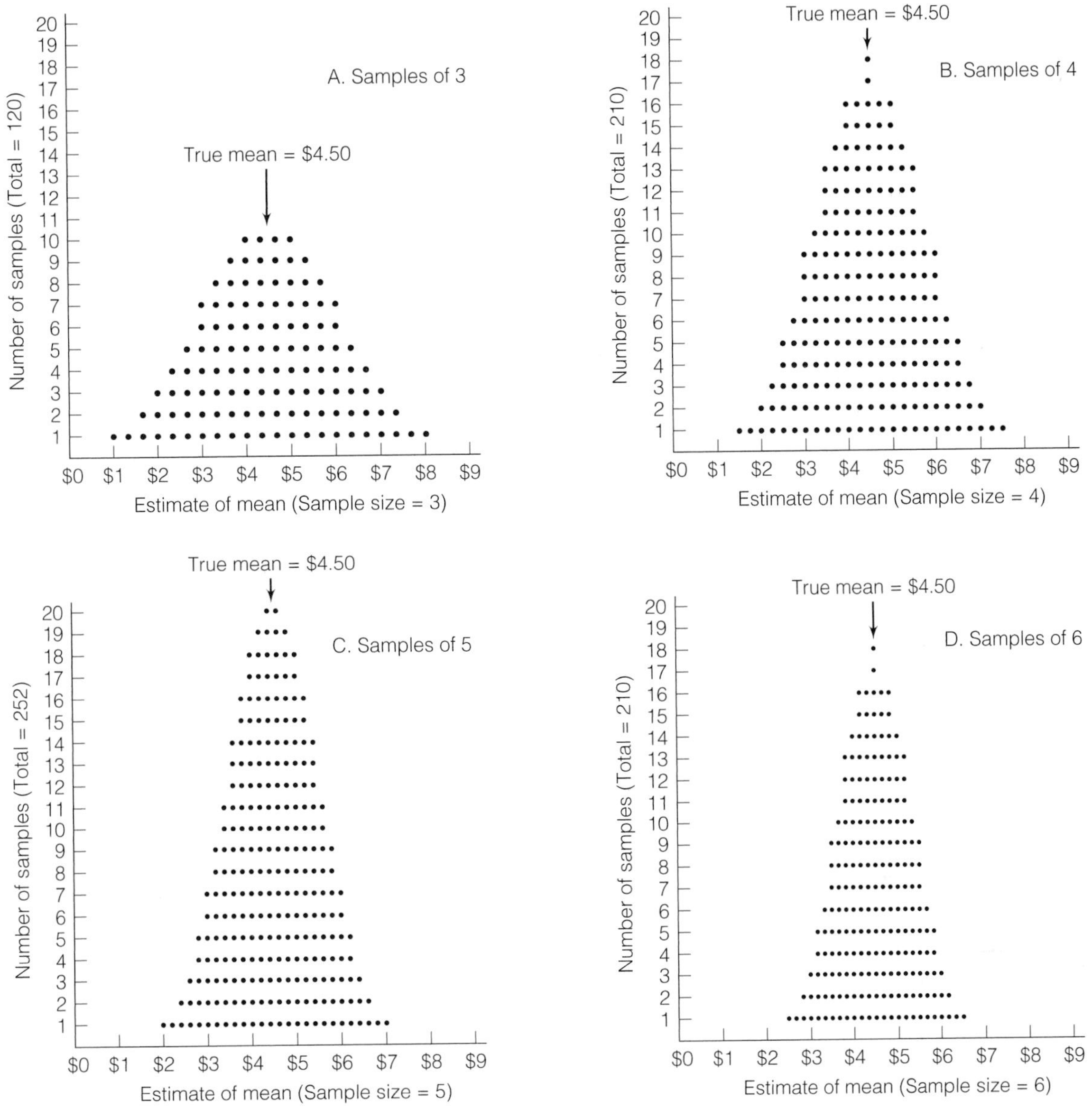

Figure B-4 The Sampling Distributions of Samples of 3, 4, 5, and 6

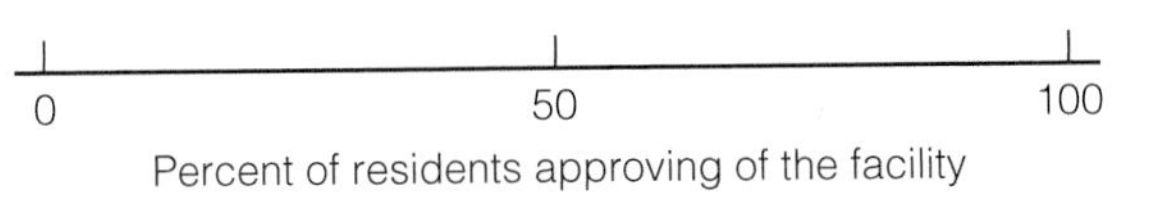

Figure B-5 Range of Possible Sample Study Results

bers.") A speedier alternative is to use a computer software program that can select cases randomly.)

Then we interview the 100 residents whose numbers have been selected and ask for their attitudes toward the facility: whether they approve or disapprove. Suppose this operation gives us 48 residents who approve of the facility and 52 who disapprove. This summary description of a variable in a sample is called a **statistic.** We present this statistic by placing a dot on the x-axis at the point that represents 48 percent.

Now let's suppose we select another sample of 100 residents in exactly the same fashion and measure their approval or disapproval of the facility. Perhaps 51 residents in the second sample approve of the facility. We place another dot in the appropriate place on the x-axis. Repeating this process once more, we may

USING A TABLE OF RANDOM NUMBERS

Suppose you want to select a simple random sample of 100 people (or other units) out of a population totaling 980.

1. To begin, number the members of the population in this case, from 1 to 980. Now the problem is to select 100 random numbers. Once you've done that, your sample will consist of the people having the numbers you've selected. (*Note:* It's not essential to actually number them, as long as you're sure of the total. If you have them in a list, for example, you can always count through the list after you've selected the numbers.)

2. The next step is to determine the number of digits you will need in the random numbers you select. In our example, there are 980 members of the population, so you will need three-digit numbers to give everyone a chance of selection. (If there were 11,825 members of the population, you'd need to select five-digit numbers.) Thus, we want to select 100 random numbers in the range from 001 to 980.

3. Now turn to the first page of Table B-1, the table of random numbers. Notice there are several rows and columns of five-digit numbers, and there are two pages. The table represents a series of random numbers in the range from 00001 to 99999. To use the table for your hypothetical sample, you have to answer these questions:

a. How will you create three-digit numbers out of five-digit numbers?

b. What pattern will you follow in moving through the table to select your numbers?

c. Where will you start?

Each of these questions has several satisfactory answers. The key is to create a plan and follow it. Here's an example.

4. To create three-digit numbers from five-digit numbers, let's agree to select five-digit numbers from the table but consider only the left-most three digits in each case. If we picked the first number on the first page—10480—we would only consider the 104. (We could agree to take the digits furthest to the right, 480, or the middle three digits, 048, and any of these plans would work.) The key is to make a plan and stick with it. For convenience, let's use the left-most three digits.

5. We can also choose to progress through the table any way we want: down the columns, up them, across to the right or to the left, or diagonally. Again, any of these plans will work just fine so long as we stick to it. For convenience, let's agree to move down the columns. When we get to the bottom of one column, we'll go to the top of the next; when we exhaust a given page, we'll start at the top of the first column of the next page.

6. Now, where do we start? You can close your eyes and stick a pencil into the table and start wherever the pencil point lands. (We know it doesn't sound scientific, but it works.) Or, if you're afraid you'll hurt the book or miss it altogether, close your eyes and make up a column number and a row number. ("I'll pick the number in the fifth row of column 2.") Start with that number. If you prefer more methodological purity, you might use the first two numbers on a dollar bill, which are randomly distributed, to determine the row and column on which to start.

7. Let's suppose we decide to start with the fifth number in column 2. If you look on the first page of the table, you'll see that the starting number is 39975. We have selected 399 as our first random number, and we have 99 more to go. Moving down the second column, we select 069, 729, 919, 143, 368, 695, 409, 939, and so forth. At the bottom of column 2, we select number 649 and continue to the top of column 3: 015, 255, and so on.

8. See how easy it is? But trouble lies ahead. When we reach column 5, we are speeding along, selecting 816, 309, 763, 078, 061, 277, 988. . . . Wait a minute! There are only 980 students in the senior class. How can we pick number 988? The solution is simple: Ignore it. Any time you come across a number that lies outside your range, skip it and continue on your way: 188, 174, and so forth. The same solution applies if the same number comes up more than once. If you select 399 again, for example, just ignore it the second time.

9. That's it. You keep up the procedure until you've selected 100 random numbers. Returning to your list, your sample consists of person number 399, person number 69, person number 729, and so forth.

Table B-1 Random Numbers

10480	15011	01536	02011	81647	91646	69179	14194	62590	36207	20969	99570	91291	90700
22368	46573	25595	85393	30995	89198	27982	53402	93965	34095	52666	19174	39615	99505
24130	48360	22527	97265	76393	64809	15179	24830	49340	32081	30680	19655	63348	58629
42167	93093	06243	61680	07856	16376	39440	53537	71341	57004	00849	74917	97758	16379
37570	39975	81837	16656	06121	91782	60468	81305	49684	60672	14110	06927	01263	54613
77921	06907	11008	42751	27756	53498	18602	70659	90655	15053	21916	81825	44394	42880
99562	72905	56420	69994	98872	31016	71194	18738	44013	48840	63213	21069	10634	12952
96301	91977	05463	07972	18876	20922	94595	56869	69014	60045	18425	84903	42508	32307
89579	14342	63661	10281	17453	18103	57740	84378	25331	12566	58678	44947	05585	56941
85475	36857	53342	53988	53060	59533	38867	62300	08158	17983	16439	11458	18593	64952
28918	69578	88231	33276	70997	79936	56865	05859	90106	31595	01547	85590	91610	78188
63553	40961	48235	03427	49626	69445	18663	72695	52180	20847	12234	90511	33703	90322
09429	93969	52636	92737	88974	33488	36320	17617	30015	08272	84115	27156	30613	74952
10365	61129	87529	85689	48237	52267	67689	93394	01511	26358	85104	20285	29975	89868
07119	97336	71048	08178	77233	13916	47564	81056	97735	85977	29372	74461	28551	90707
51085	12765	51821	51259	77452	16308	60756	92144	49442	53900	70960	63990	75601	40719
02368	21382	52404	60268	89368	19885	55322	44819	01188	65255	64835	44919	05944	55157
01011	54092	33362	94904	31273	04146	18594	29852	71585	85030	51132	01915	92747	64951
52162	53916	46369	58586	23216	14513	83149	98736	23495	64350	94738	17752	35156	35749
07056	97628	33787	09998	42698	06691	76988	13602	51851	46104	88916	19509	25625	58104
48663	91245	85828	14346	09172	30168	90229	04734	59193	22178	30421	61666	99904	32812
54164	58492	22421	74103	47070	25306	76468	26384	58151	06646	21524	15227	96909	44592
32639	32363	05597	24200	13363	38005	94342	28728	35806	06912	17012	64161	18296	22851
29334	27001	87637	87308	58731	00256	45834	15398	46557	41135	10367	07684	36188	18510
02488	33062	28834	07351	19731	92420	60952	61280	50001	67658	32586	86679	50720	94953
81525	72295	04839	96423	24878	82651	66566	14778	76797	14780	13300	87074	79666	95725
29676	20591	68086	26432	46901	20849	89768	81536	86645	12659	92259	57102	80428	25280
00742	57392	39064	66432	84673	40027	32832	61362	98947	96067	64760	64584	96096	98253
05366	04213	25669	26422	44407	44048	37937	63904	45766	66134	75470	66520	34693	90449
91921	26418	64117	94305	26766	25940	39972	22209	71500	64568	91402	42416	07844	69618
00582	04711	87917	77341	42206	35126	74087	99547	81817	42607	43808	76655	62028	76630
00725	69884	62797	56170	86324	88072	76222	36086	84637	93161	76038	65855	77919	88006
69011	65795	95876	55293	18988	27354	26575	08625	40801	59920	29841	80150	12777	48501
25976	57948	29888	88604	67917	48708	18912	82271	65424	69774	33611	54262	85963	03547
09763	83473	73577	12908	30883	18317	28290	35797	05998	41688	34952	37888	38917	88050
91567	42595	27958	30134	04024	86385	29880	99730	55536	84855	29080	09250	79656	73211
17955	56349	90999	49127	20044	59931	06115	20542	18059	02008	73708	83517	36103	42791
46503	18584	18845	49618	02304	51038	20655	58727	28168	15475	56942	53389	20562	87338
92157	89634	94824	78171	84610	82834	09922	25417	44137	48413	25555	21246	35509	20468
14577	62765	35605	81263	39667	47358	56873	56307	61607	49518	89656	20103	77490	18062
98427	07523	33362	64270	01638	92477	66969	98420	04880	45585	46565	04102	46880	45709
34914	63976	88720	82765	34476	17032	87589	40836	32427	70002	70663	88863	77775	69348
70060	28277	39475	46473	23219	53416	94970	25832	69975	94884	19661	72828	00102	66794
53976	54914	06990	67245	68350	82948	11398	42878	80287	88267	47363	46634	06541	97809
76072	29515	40980	07391	58745	25774	22987	80059	39911	96189	41151	14222	60697	59583
90725	52210	83974	29992	65831	38857	50490	83765	55657	14361	31720	57375	56228	41546
64364	67412	33339	31926	14883	24413	59744	92351	97473	89286	35931	04110	23726	51900
08962	00358	31662	25388	61642	34072	81249	35648	56891	69352	48373	45578	78547	81788
95012	68379	93526	70765	10592	04542	76463	54328	02349	17247	28865	14777	62730	92277
15664	10493	20492	38391	91132	21999	59516	81652	27195	48223	46751	22923	32261	85653
16408	81899	04153	53381	79401	21438	83035	92350	36693	31238	59649	91754	72772	02338
18629	81953	05520	91962	04739	13092	97662	24822	94730	06496	35090	04822	86774	98289
73115	35101	47498	87637	99016	71060	88824	71013	18735	20286	23153	72924	35165	43040
57491	16703	23167	49323	45021	33132	12544	41035	80780	45393	44812	12515	98931	91202
30405	83946	23792	14422	15059	45799	22716	19792	09983	74353	68668	30429	70735	25499
16631	35006	85900	98275	32388	52390	16815	69298	82732	38480	73817	32523	41961	44437
96773	20206	42559	78985	05300	22164	24369	54224	35083	19687	11052	91491	60383	19746
38935	64202	14349	82674	66523	44133	00697	35552	35970	19124	63318	29686	03387	59846
31624	76384	17403	53363	44167	64486	64758	75366	76554	31601	12614	33072	60332	92325
78919	19474	23632	27889	47914	02584	37680	20801	72152	39339	34806	08930	85001	87820
03931	33309	57047	74211	63445	17361	62825	39908	05607	91284	68833	25570	38818	46920
74426	33278	43972	10119	89917	15665	52872	73823	73144	88662	88970	74492	51805	99378
09066	00903	20795	95452	92648	45454	09552	88815	16553	51125	79375	97596	16296	66092
42238	12426	87025	14267	20979	04508	64535	31355	86064	29472	47689	05974	52468	16834
16153	08002	26504	41744	81959	65642	74240	56302	00033	67107	77510	70625	28725	34191
21457	40742	29820	96783	29400	21840	15035	34537	33310	06116	95240	15957	16572	06004
21581	57802	02050	89728	17937	37621	47075	42080	97403	48626	68995	43805	33386	21597
55612	78095	83197	33732	05810	24813	86902	60397	16489	03264	88525	42786	05269	92532
44657	66999	99324	51281	84463	60563	79312	93454	68876	25471	93911	25650	12682	73572
91340	84979	46949	81973	37949	61023	43997	15263	80644	43942	89203	71795	99533	50501
91227	21199	31935	27022	84067	05462	35216	14486	29891	68607	41867	14951	91696	85065
50001	38140	66321	19924	72163	09538	12151	06878	91903	18749	34405	56087	82790	70925
65390	05224	72958	28609	81406	39147	25549	48542	42627	45233	57202	94617	23772	07896
27504	96131	83944	41575	10573	08619	64482	73923	36152	05184	94142	25299	84387	34925
37169	94851	39117	89632	00959	16487	65536	49071	39782	17095	02330	74301	00275	48280
11508	70225	51111	38351	19444	66499	71945	05422	13442	78675	84081	66938	93654	59894
37449	30362	06694	54690	04052	53115	62757	95348	78662	11163	81651	50245	34971	52924
46515	70331	85922	38329	57015	15765	97161	17869	45349	61796	66345	81073	49106	79860
30986	81223	42416	58353	21532	30502	32305	86482	05174	07901	54339	58861	74818	46942
63798	64995	46583	09785	44160	78128	83991	42865	92520	83531	80377	35909	81250	54238

(continued)

Table B-1 *(continued)*

82486	84846	99254	67632	43218	50076	21361	64816	51202	88124	41870	52689	51275	83556
21885	32906	92431	09060	64297	51674	64126	62570	26123	05155	59194	52799	28225	85762
60336	98782	07408	53458	13564	59089	26445	29789	85205	41001	12535	12133	14645	23541
43937	46891	24010	25560	86355	33941	25786	54990	71899	15475	95434	98227	21824	19585
97656	63175	89303	16275	07100	92063	21942	18611	47348	20203	18534	03862	78095	50136
03299	01221	05418	38982	55758	92237	26759	86367	21216	98442	08303	56613	91511	75928
79626	06486	03574	17668	07785	76020	79924	25651	83325	88428	85076	72811	22717	50585
85636	68335	47539	03129	65651	11977	02510	26113	99447	68645	34327	15152	55230	93448
18039	14367	61337	06177	12143	46609	32989	74014	64708	00533	35398	58408	13261	47908
08362	15656	60627	36478	65648	16764	53412	09013	07832	41574	17639	82163	60859	75567
79556	29068	04142	16268	15387	12856	66227	38358	22478	73373	88732	09443	82558	05250
92608	82674	27072	32534	17075	27698	98204	63863	11951	34648	88022	56148	34925	57031
23982	25835	40055	67006	12293	02753	14827	23235	35071	99704	37543	11601	35503	85171
09915	96306	05908	97901	28395	14186	00821	80703	70426	75647	76310	88717	37890	40129
59037	33300	26695	62247	69927	76123	50842	43834	86654	70959	79725	93872	28117	19233
42488	78077	69882	61657	34136	79180	97526	43092	04098	73571	80799	76536	71255	64239
46764	86273	63003	93017	31204	36692	40202	35275	57306	55543	53203	18098	47625	88684
03237	45430	55417	63282	90816	17349	88298	90183	36600	78406	06216	95787	42579	90730
86591	81482	52667	61582	14972	90053	89534	76036	49199	43716	97548	04379	46370	28672
38534	01715	94964	87288	65680	43772	39560	12918	86537	62738	19636	51132	25739	56947

Abridged from *Handbook of Tables for Probability and Statistics*, Second Edition, edited by William H. Beyer (Cleveland: The Chemical Rubber Company, 1968). Used by permission of The Chemical Rubber Company.

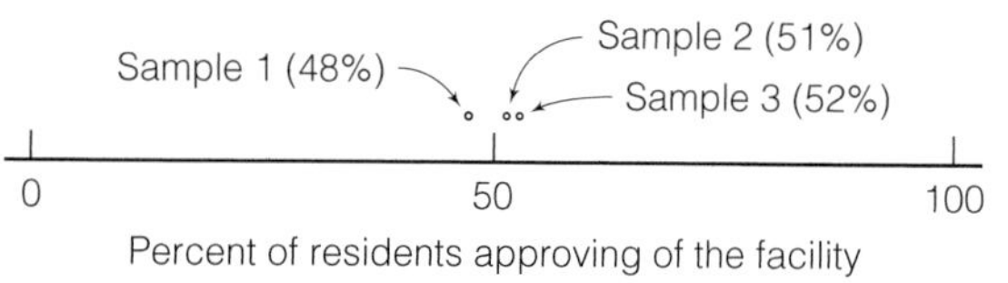

Figure B-6 Results Produced by Three Hypothetical Studies

discover that 52 residents in the third sample approve of the facility.

Figure B-6 presents the three different sample statistics that represent the percentages of residents in each of the three random samples who approved of the facility. The basic rule of random sampling is that such samples drawn from a population give estimates of the parameter that pertains in the total population. Each random sample, then, gives us an estimate of the percentage of residents in the town population who approve of the facility. Unhappily, however, we have selected three samples and now have three separate estimates.

To resolve this dilemma, let's draw more and more samples of 100 residents each, question each sample about its approval or disapproval of the facility, and plot the new sample statistics on our summary graph. In drawing many such samples, we discover that some of the new samples provide duplicate estimates, as in Figures B-3 and B-4 for the previous example with a population of 10 cases. Figure B-7 shows the sampling distribution of, say, hundreds of samples. This is often referred to as a *normal curve*.

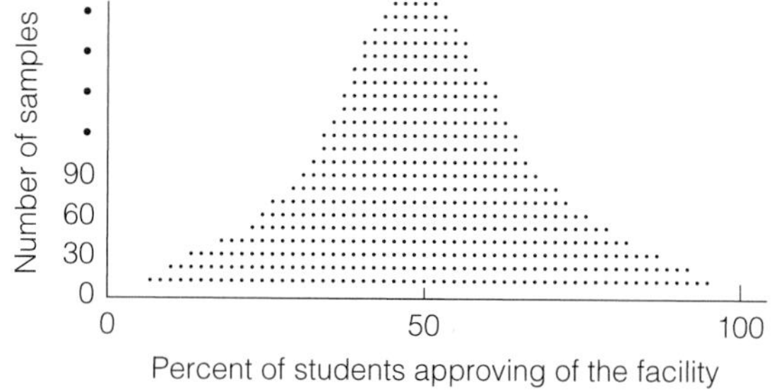

Figure B-7 The Sampling Distribution

Note that by increasing the number of samples selected and interviewed, we have also increased the range of estimates that are provided by the sampling operation. In one sense, we have increased our dilemma in attempting to guess the parameter in the population. Probability theory, however, provides certain important rules about the sampling distribution in Figure B-7.

First, if many independent random samples are selected from a population, then the sample statistics provided by those samples will be distributed around the population parameter in a known way. Thus, although Figure B-7 shows a wide range of estimates, more of them are in the vicinity of 50 percent than elsewhere in the graph. Probability theory tells us, then, that the true value is in the vicinity of 50 percent.

Second, probability theory gives us a formula for estimating how closely the sample statistics are clustered around the true value. To put it another way, probability theory enables us to estimate the **sampling error**—the degree of error to be expected for a given sample design. This formula contains three factors: the parameter, the sample size, and the standard error (a measure of sampling error):

$$s = \sqrt{\frac{P \times Q}{n}}$$

The symbols P and Q in the formula equal the population parameters for the binomial: If 60 percent of the residents approve of the facility and 40 percent disapprove, then P and Q are 60 percent and 40 percent, respectively, or .6 and .4. Note that $Q = 1 - P$ and $P = 1 - Q$. The symbol n equals the number of cases in each sample, and s is the standard error.

Let's assume that the population parameter in the hypothetical small town is 50 percent approving of the facility and 50 percent disapproving. Recall that we have been selecting samples of 100 cases each. When these numbers are put into the formula, we find that the standard error equals .05, or 5 percent. In probability theory, the standard error is a valuable piece of information because it indicates the extent to which the sample estimates will be distributed around the population parameter. If you are familiar with the standard deviation in statistics, you may recognize that the standard error in this case is the standard deviation of the sampling distribution. (We discuss the meaning of the standard deviation in Chapter 20.)

Specifically, probability theory indicates that certain proportions of the sample estimates will fall within specified increments—each equal to one standard error—from the population parameter. Approximately 34 percent (.3413) of the sample estimates will fall within one standard error increment above the population parameter, and another 34 percent will fall within one standard error below the parameter. In our example, the standard error increment is 5 percent, so we know that 34 percent of our samples will give estimates of resident approval between 50 percent (the parameter) and 55 percent (one standard error above); another 34 percent of the samples will give estimates between 50 percent and 45 percent (one standard error below the parameter). Taken together, then, we know that roughly two-thirds (68 percent) of the samples will give estimates within ±5 percent of the parameter.

Moreover, probability theory dictates that roughly 95 percent of the samples will fall within plus or minus two standard errors of the true value, and

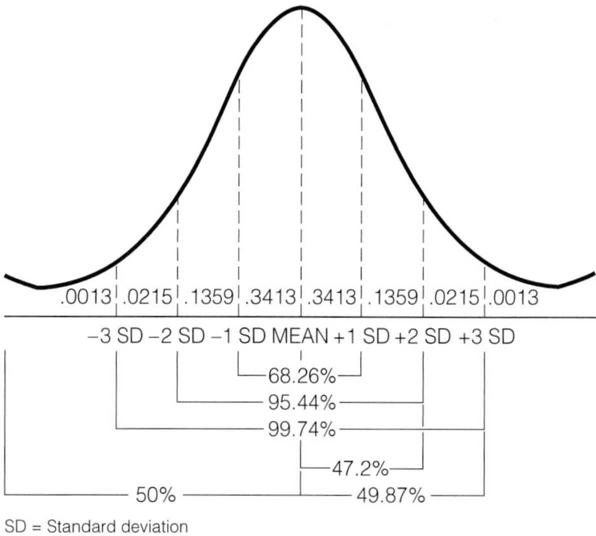

Figure B-8 Standard Deviation Proportions of the Normal Curve

99.9 percent of the samples will fall within plus or minus three standard errors. In our current example, then, we know that only one sample out of a thousand would give an estimate lower than 35 percent approval or higher than 65 percent. Figure B-8 graphically illustrates a normal (bell-shaped) curve with the standard deviation proportions that apply to any normal curve. The normal curve represents the sampling distribution—how an infinite number of randomly drawn samples would be distributed. The mean of the curve is the true population parameter.

The proportion of samples that fall within one, two, or three standard errors of the population parameter is constant for any random sampling procedure such as the one just described—if a large number of samples are selected. The size of the standard error in any given case, however, is a function of the population parameter and the sample size. If we return to the formula for a moment, we note that the standard error will increase as a function of an increase in the quantity P times Q. Note further that this quantity reaches its maximum in the situation of an even split in the population:

If $P = .5$, $PQ = .25$

If $P = .6$, $PQ = .24$

If $P = .8$, $PQ = .16$

If $P = .99$, $PQ = .0099$

By extension, if P is either 0.0 or 1.0 (either zero percent or 100 percent approve of the facility), then the standard error will be zero. If everyone in the population has the same attitude (no variation), then every sample will give exactly that estimate.

The standard error is also a function of the sample size—and an inverse function. As the sample size increases, the standard error decreases. As the sample size increases, the several samples will cluster closer to the true value. Another rule of thumb is evident in the formula: Because of the square root formula, the standard error is reduced by half if the sample size quadruples. In our current example, samples of 100 produce a standard error of 5 percent; to reduce the standard error to 2.5 percent, we must increase the sample size to 400.

All of this information is provided by established probability theory as it relates to the selection of large numbers of random samples. (If you've taken a statistics course, you may know this as the "central tendency theorem.") If the population parameter is known and a large number of random samples are selected, then we can predict how many of the sample estimates will fall within specified intervals from the parameter. Be clear that this discussion only illustrates the logic of probability sampling and does not describe the way research is actually conducted. Usually, we do not know the parameter: We conduct a sample survey to estimate that value. Moreover, we don't actually select large numbers of samples: We select only one sample. Nevertheless, the preceding discussion of probability theory provides the basis for inferences about the typical social research situation. Knowing what it would be like to select thousands of samples allows us to make assumptions about the one sample we do select and study.

CONFIDENCE LEVELS AND CONFIDENCE INTERVALS

Whereas probability theory specifies that 68 percent of that fictitious large number of samples would produce estimates that fall within one standard error of the parameter, we turn the logic around and infer that any single random sample estimate has a 68 percent chance of falling within that range. This observation leads us to the two key components of sampling error estimates: **confidence level** and **confidence interval.** We express the accuracy of our sample statistics in terms of a *level of confidence* that the statistics fall within a specified *interval* from the parameter. For example, we are 68 percent confident that our sample estimate is within one standard error of the parameter. Or we may say that we are 95 percent confident that the sample statistic is within two standard errors of the parameter, and so forth. Quite reasonably, our confidence increases as the margin for error is extended. We are virtually positive (99.74 percent) that we are within three standard errors of the true value.

Although we may be confident (at some level) of being within a certain range of the parameter, we have already noted that we seldom know what the parameter is. To resolve this dilemma, we substitute our sample estimate for the parameter in the formula; lacking the true value, we substitute the best available guess.

The result of these inferences and estimations is that we are able to estimate a population parameter as well as the expected degree of error on the basis of one sample drawn from a population. Beginning with the question "What percentage of the town population approves of the facility?" we could select a random sample of 100 residents and interview them. We might then report that our best estimate is that 50 percent of the population approves of the facility and that we are 95 percent confident that between 40 and 60 percent (plus or minus two standard errors) approves. The range from 40 to 60 percent is called the confidence interval. (At the 68 percent confidence level, the confidence interval would be 45 percent to 55 percent.)

The logic of confidence levels and confidence intervals also provides the basis for determining the appropriate sample size for a study. Once you have decided on the degree of sampling error you can tolerate, you'll be able to calculate the number of cases needed in your sample. Thus, for example, if you want to be 95 percent confident that your study findings are accurate within plus or minus 5 percentage points of the population parameters, then you should select a sample of at least 400.

The foregoing discussion has considered only one type of statistic: the percentages produced by a binomial or dichotomous variable. The same logic, however, would apply to the examination of other statistics, such as mean income.

Two cautions are in order here. First, the survey uses of probability theory as discussed here are not wholly justified technically. The theory of sampling distribution makes assumptions that almost never apply in survey conditions. The exact proportion of samples contained within specified increments of standard errors, for example, mathematically assumes an infinitely large population, an infinite number of samples, and sampling with replacement—that is, every sampling unit selected is "thrown back into the pot" and could be selected again. Second, our discussion has greatly oversimplified the inferential jump from the distribution of several samples to the probable characteristics of one sample.

These cautions are offered as perspective. Researchers often appear to overestimate the precision of estimates produced by using probability theory. As has been mentioned elsewhere in this appendix and throughout the book, variations in sampling techniques and nonsampling factors may further reduce the legitimacy of such estimates. For example, those selected in a sample who fail or refuse to participate further detract from the representativeness of the sample.

Nevertheless, the calculations discussed in this appendix can be extremely valuable to you in understanding and evaluating your data. Although the calculations do not provide estimates that are as precise as some researchers might assume, they can be quite valid for practical purposes. They are unquestionably more valid than less rigorously derived estimates based on less rigorous sampling methods. Most important, you should be familiar with the basic logic underlying the calculations. If you are so informed, then you will be able to react sensibly to your own data and those reported by others.

APPENDIX **C**

Proportion under Normal Curve Exceeded by Effect-Size Values

Assuming a normal distribution of control group scores, the figures in the table in this appendix display the proportion of outcomes for control subjects that is worse than the mean outcome for experimental subjects for each specified effect-size (ES) value. (See Chapter 21 for a discussion of effect size.) For example, an ES of 1.0 signifies that the mean outcome for experimental subjects is one standard deviation better than the mean outcome for control subjects. In this table, you can see that that particular ES (that is, 1.0, or one standard deviation) means that the average experimental subject's outcome was better than 84 percent of the outcomes for control subjects.

To simplify this table, we have not listed every possible ES value. To find precise normal curve figures for exact ES values not listed in the table, consult the *Z*-table commonly found in introductory texts on descriptive statistics. *Z*-tables show what proportion of a normal curve is found above and below *z* scores. The ES values in this table are the same as *z* scores.

The two normal curves below illustrate the meaning of the values in the table. Each normal curve represents the theoretical sampling distribution of outcomes for the population of people who do not receive the experimental intervention. The shaded area under the curve represents the proportion of outcomes that is exceeded in the desired direction by (worse than) the experimental group mean. The unshaded area is the proportion of outcomes that is better than the experimental group mean. For negative effect sizes, the unshaded portion will be greater than the shaded portion, meaning that the experimental group did worse than the control group (indicating harmful intervention effects). For positive effect sizes, the shaded portion will be greater than the unshaded portion, indicating beneficial treatment effects.

(a) Positive ES

(b) Negative ES

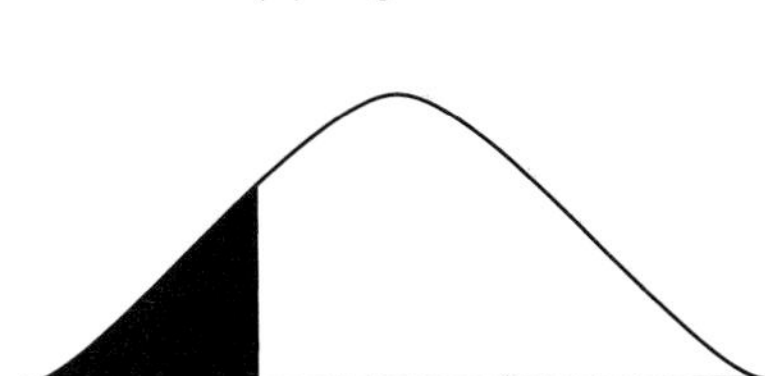

POSITIVE ES VALUES		NEGATIVE ES VALUES	
ES	PROPORTION UNDER NORMAL CURVE EXCEEDED	ES	PROPORTION UNDER NORMAL CURVE EXCEEDED
3.0	.9987	−3.0	.0013
2.8	.9974	−2.8	.0026
2.6	.9953	−2.6	.0047
2.4	.9918	−2.4	.0082
2.2	.9861	−2.2	.0139
2.0	.9772	−2.0	.0228
1.8	.9641	−1.8	.0359
1.6	.9452	−1.6	.0548
1.5	.9332	−1.5	.0668
1.4	.9192	−1.4	.0808
1.3	.9032	−1.3	.0968
1.2	.8849	−1.2	.1151
1.1	.8643	−1.1	.1357
1.0	.8413	−1.0	.1587
0.9	.8159	−0.9	.1841
0.8	.7881	−0.8	.2119
0.7	.7580	−0.7	.2420
0.6	.7257	−0.6	.2743
0.5	.6915	−0.5	.3085
0.4	.6554	−0.4	.3446
0.3	.6179	−0.3	.3821
0.2	.5793	−0.2	.4207
0.1	.5398	−0.1	.4602
0.0	.5000		

APPENDIX **D**

Learner's Guide to SPSS 11.0 for Windows

What You'll Learn in This Appendix

This appendix will provide you with a brief overview of the Statistical Package for the Social Sciences™ (SPSS). For many years, SPSS has been the most commonly used program for quantitative data analysis in the social sciences. It has gone through many versions for both the Windows and Macintosh platforms. This appendix will use SPSS 11.0 along with data from the 2000 General Social Survey (GSS). If you're using a different version of SPSS or a different data set, then you'll need to make adjustments, but this guide will still serve to introduce you to the overall logic and application of SPSS. Whatever version you have, consult the user manual for assistance. You can access the GSS data through our Book Companion website at http://socialwork.wadsworth.com/.

In addition, several books have recently been written to introduce social researchers to SPSS. One is by Allen Rubin: *Statistics for Evidence-Based Practice,* Belmont, CA: Thomson Brooks/Cole, 2007. Another is by Earl Babbie, Fred Halley, and Jeanne Zaino: *Adventures in Social Research,* Newbury Park, CA: Pine Forge Press, 2000.

GETTING STARTED*

When you first open SPSS 11.0 for Windows on your computer, Figure D-1 will appear. You have several options to start with. You can click on **Run Tutorial** and click **OK.** This is a good step for becoming familiar with some of the basic features of SPSS. You also have the option to create your own data. You would choose this option if you had collected your own survey and were ready to transpose your respondents' answers into an SPSS data spreadsheet. If you are using the GSS data, then you will need to ask SPSS to import a data file that has already been formatted and is ready for analysis. GSS files will often come as SPSS files (they are recognizable by their *.sav* extension) or as SPSS portable files (saved as *.por* files).

The next step is to load data into the program.

Opening a Data File

When "Open an existing data source" is selected, click **OK.** You will have to browse your computer and select the location in which your GSS file is saved. Notice that at the bottom of this window, you can opt not to use this dialog window in the future. Then when you start SPSS, the window in the background will appear and you can simply click on **File** and then **Open**, and select the GSS data file you want to analyze. The advantage of the dialog box we started with is that after your first opening of the

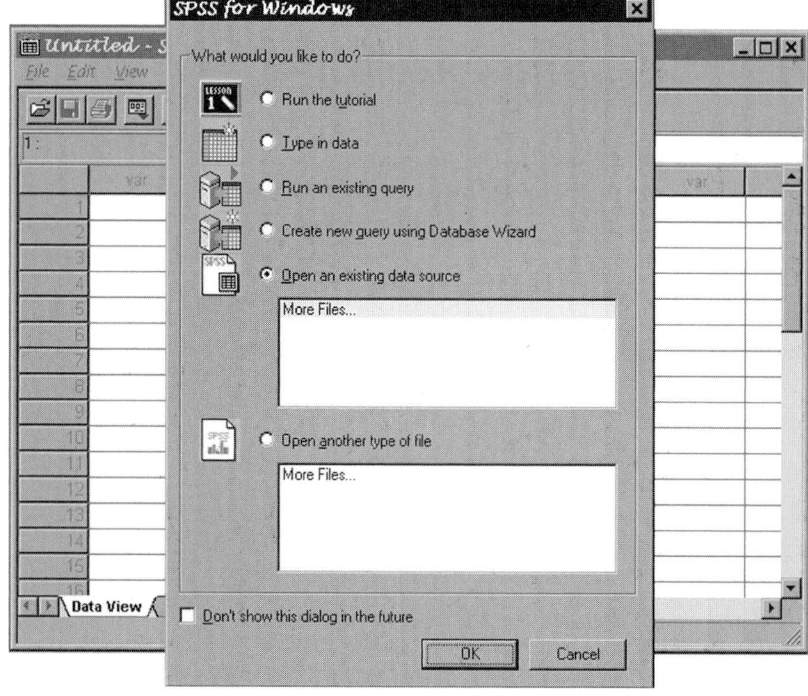

Figure D-1 Opening SPSS

*The SPSS screen captures in this appendix are copyrighted by SPSS.

GSS file, SPSS will list your file in place where "More files . . ." is highlighted. In other words, if you need to work on this file again, you can simply select it with your mouse and click **OK.** SPSS will open your file in one step.

Let us guide you through the process of opening the GSS file. (Recall that you can download the GSS data through our Book Companion website at http://socialwork.wadsworth.com/.) Simply close the window in Figure D-1. Look at the top row in Figure D-2. It contains several menus: File, Edit, View, Data, Transform, Analyze, Graphs, Utilities, Window, and Help. We'll use these menus throughout this guide. You can activate the menu you want by simply clicking the menu name. For example, clicking on the word **File** will bring up the File menu shown in Figure D-2.

As you can see, the File menu offers several possible actions, but right now we're only interested in opening a file. Click **Open** to indicate that you want to load a data file into the program. Next you'll see a dialog box that asks you to select among several options. Click **Data** to open the Data menu. Your steps in browsing your computer to open the data file are illustrated in Figures D-3, D-4, and D-5.

Select the data set you want by double-clicking it, or by single-clicking it and then clicking **Open.** We've selected the 2000 General Social Survey (GSS) data set, which contains hundreds of variables collected from 2,817 respondents. The research was conducted by the National Opinion Research Center at the University of Chicago to establish a representative sample of U.S. residents 18 and older.

It is important to note that SPSS is set to open *.sav* files by default. Here the GSS 2000 data file was created as a *.por* file. We changed the file type to SPSS Portable (*.por) as illustrated in Figure D-4. When the *GSS2000.por* file appeared, we made sure it was highlighted and clicked **Open.** See Figure D-5.

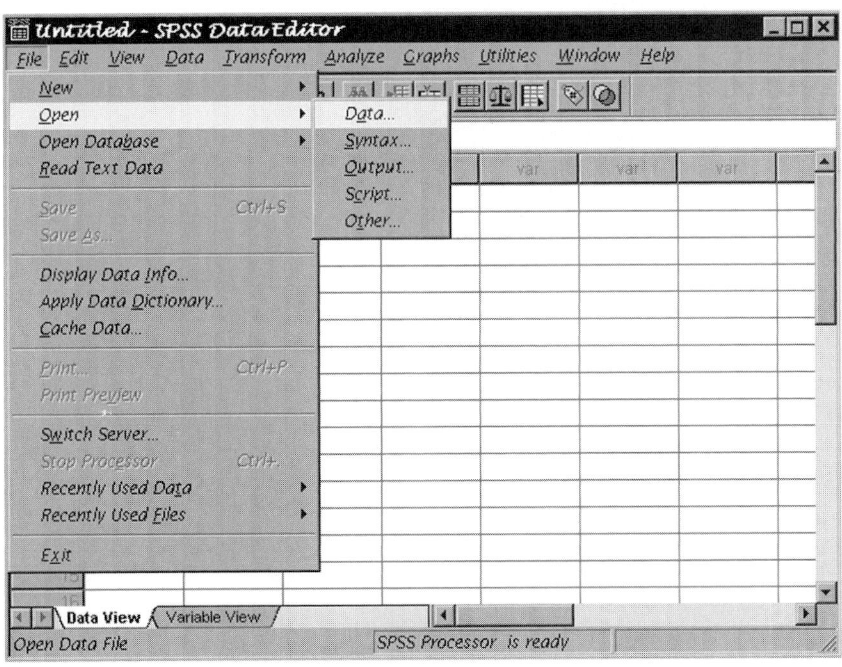

Figure D-2 Opening the File Menu

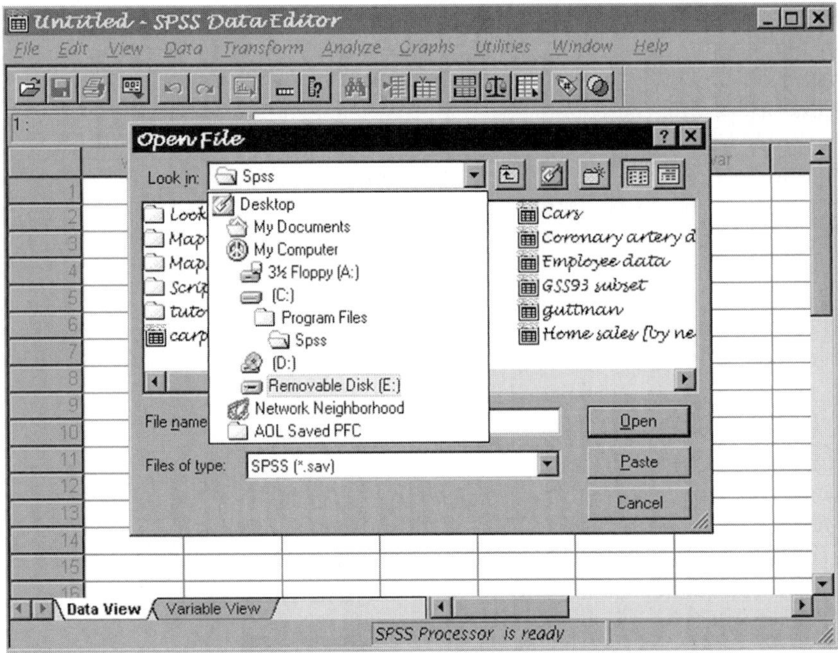

Figure D-3 Picking a Data Set

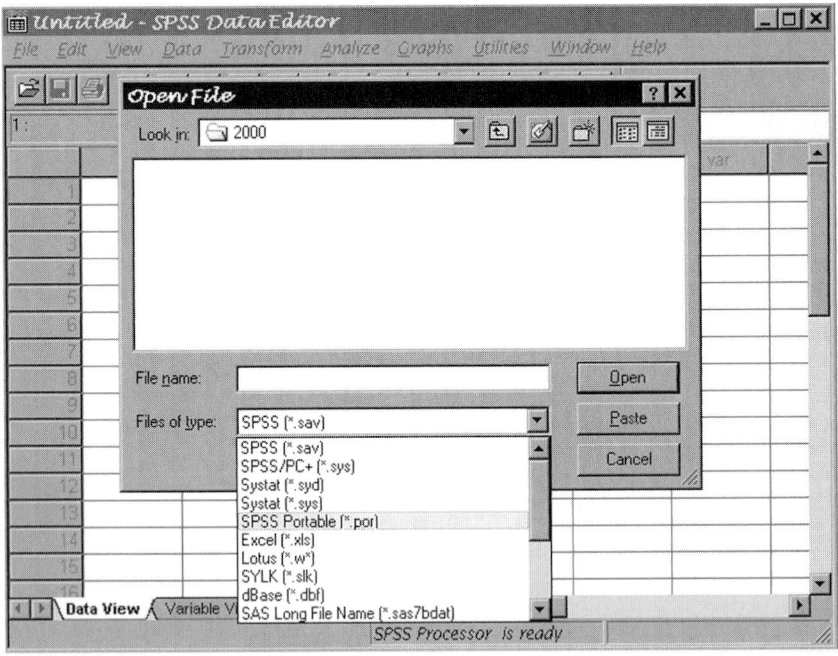

Figure D-4 Changing the File Type

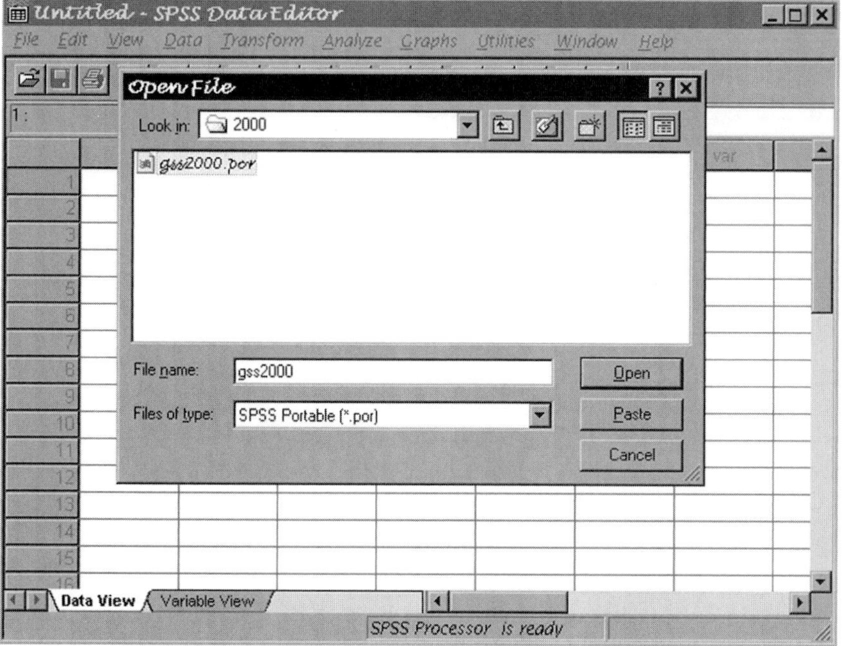

Figure D-5 Choosing an SPSS Portable Data Set

Saving Changes

When you modify your data set—creating recoded variables, for example—you'll probably want to save those changes for later use. Realize that any such changes will stay in effect throughout this SPSS session, but when you exit the program (see the last section of these SPSS Guidelines), you can lose all your changes. It's wise to save changes as soon as you're sure you want them.

Saving an altered file is hardly rocket science. First, select the **Data View** window or the **Variable View** window (not the Output window, which contains all statistical jobs you asked SPSS to perform on your data). Then, under the **File** menu, select **Save.** Realize that when you save the file in this fashion, the changed file replaces the original one. So if you madly deleted data or altered variables using their original names, you'll have put the original file forever out of reach.

If you wish to save the original file as well as your changes, choose **Save As** under the **File** menu (see Figure D-6). This time, SPSS will ask you to supply a name for the data set about to be saved. Use some name other than that of the original data set. Also, pay attention to where on your disk it is saved so you can find it later on.

You may also want to save your data file as an SPSS file if it is a portable file or other type of data spreadsheet. In Figure D-7, we saved *GSS2000.por* as a *GSS2000.sav,* which will help us process this file more quickly later. There won't be a need to wait for conversion time.

GETTING AROUND WITH SPSS WINDOWS

By default, the window that appears is the **Data Editor** window. No matter what data file you open, the setting of this spreadsheet is always the same. Each column represents a variable such as the respondent's gender, age, or attitude about abortion. Each

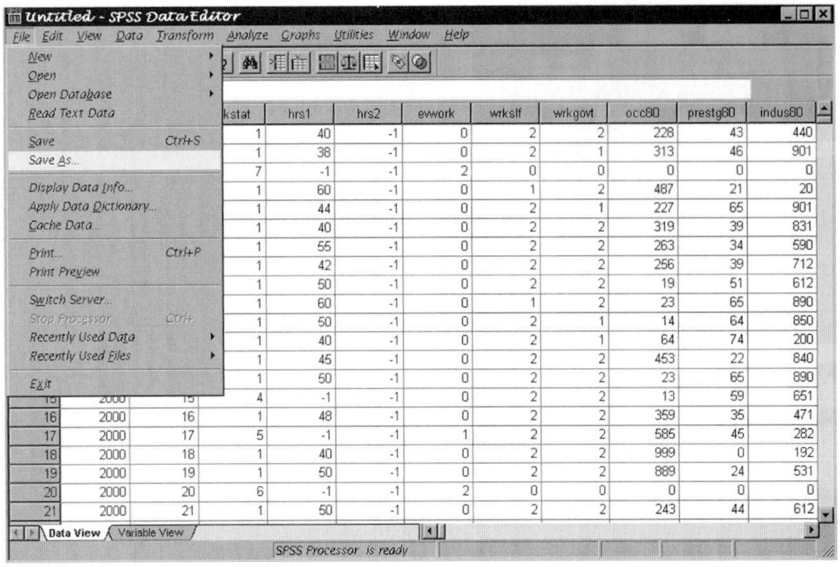

Figure D-6 Saving an SPSS Portable Data Set

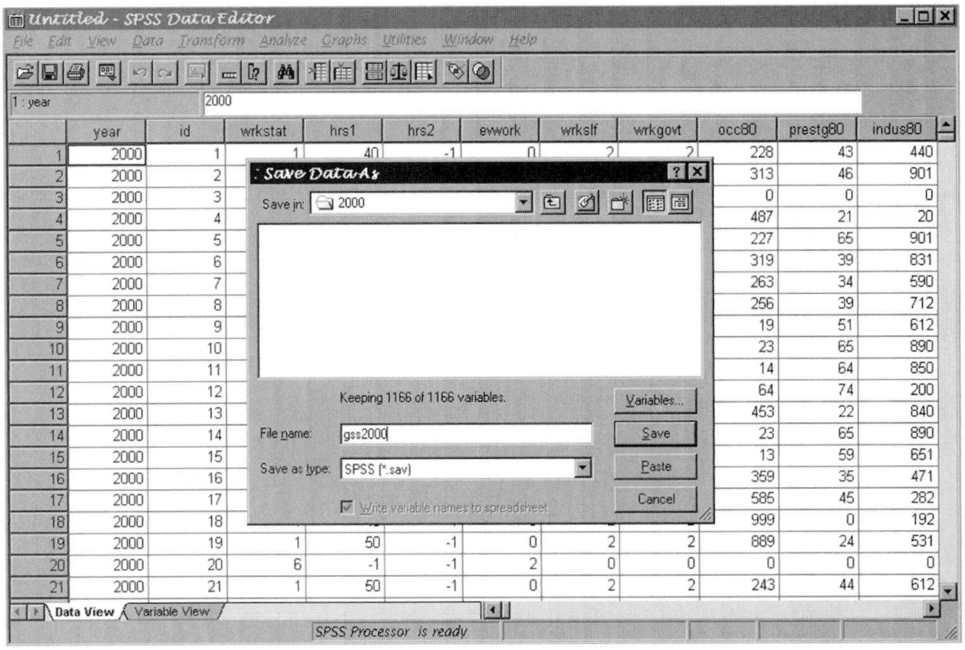

Figure D-7 Saving as a *.sav* File

row represents a particular respondent. Thus, each cell of the matrix stores some item of information about a person. In Figure D-2, all the cells are empty.

Once you've instructed SPSS to open your data set, the original matrix will be filled with data, the way it is in Figure D-8. Notice that the row just above the matrix now contains the names of the variables that constitute the data set: hrs1, wrkgovt, and so forth. SPSS uses abbreviated labels, each no more than eight characters long.

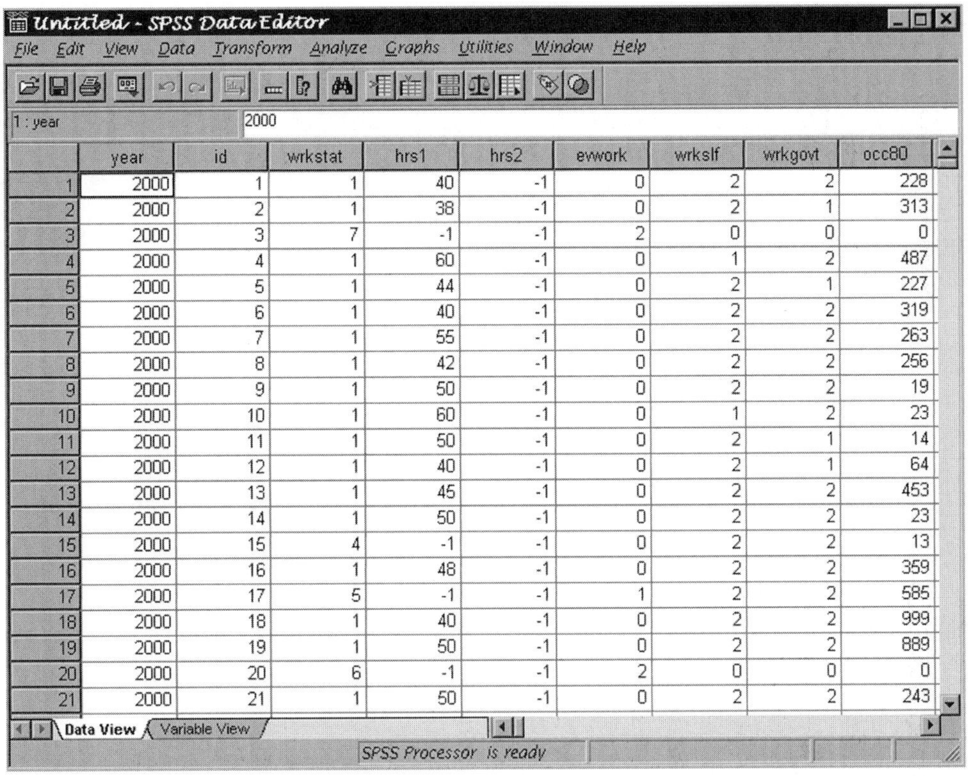

Untitled - SPSS Data Editor

File Edit View Data Transform Analyze Graphs Utilities Window Help

1 : year 2000

	year	id	wrkstat	hrs1	hrs2	evwork	wrkslf	wrkgovt	occ80
1	2000	1	1	40	-1	0	2	2	228
2	2000	2	1	38	-1	0	2	1	313
3	2000	3	7	-1	-1	2	0	0	0
4	2000	4	1	60	-1	0	1	2	487
5	2000	5	1	44	-1	0	2	1	227
6	2000	6	1	40	-1	0	2	2	319
7	2000	7	1	55	-1	0	2	2	263
8	2000	8	1	42	-1	0	2	2	256
9	2000	9	1	50	-1	0	2	2	19
10	2000	10	1	60	-1	0	1	2	23
11	2000	11	1	50	-1	0	2	1	14
12	2000	12	1	40	-1	0	2	1	64
13	2000	13	1	45	-1	0	2	2	453
14	2000	14	1	50	-1	0	2	2	23
15	2000	15	4	-1	-1	0	2	2	13
16	2000	16	1	48	-1	0	2	2	359
17	2000	17	5	-1	-1	1	2	2	585
18	2000	18	1	40	-1	0	2	2	999
19	2000	19	1	50	-1	0	2	2	889
20	2000	20	6	-1	-1	2	0	0	0
21	2000	21	1	50	-1	0	2	2	243

Data View / Variable View

SPSS Processor is ready

Figure D-8 A Full Data Matrix

In Figure D-8, notice that the cell at the top right, in the next-to-last column in the figure, links together case number one (respondent number 1) and the variable labeled wrkgovt. The first respondent has a value of 2 on the variable wrkgovt. But what on Earth does that mean?

This is where SPSS 11.0 is different from earlier versions. In addition to the **Data View** subwindow, the **Data Editor** window has a **Variable View** subwindow. You can simply click on **Variable View** at the bottom of the Data Editor window. In Figure D-9, you can see how this window is organized. This time, the rows represent the variables and the columns are the various categorizations associated with each variable. The columns are as follows: Name, Type, Width, Decimals, Label, Values, Missing, Columns, Align, and Measure. The **Name** is the abbreviated name of the variable (never more than eight characters). The **Type** of the variable is often "numeric" but could be "string" if you wanted to input words as data instead of numbers. **Label** is the description of the variable and indicates more clearly what the question on the questionnaire was about. In the column **Values**, you can find the values associated with each possible answer for each variable. Notice also that you can increase the width of any of these columns on the **Variable View** of the **Data Editor.** This feature is particularly useful if you want to read the variable label in its totality.

You can find the meaning of a particular variable label in several ways. The first and easiest is to find the variable name on the **Variable View.** If you were on the **Data View,** you could double-click the variable name in the column heading, and the **Variable View** would open automatically and highlight the row of the variable you just

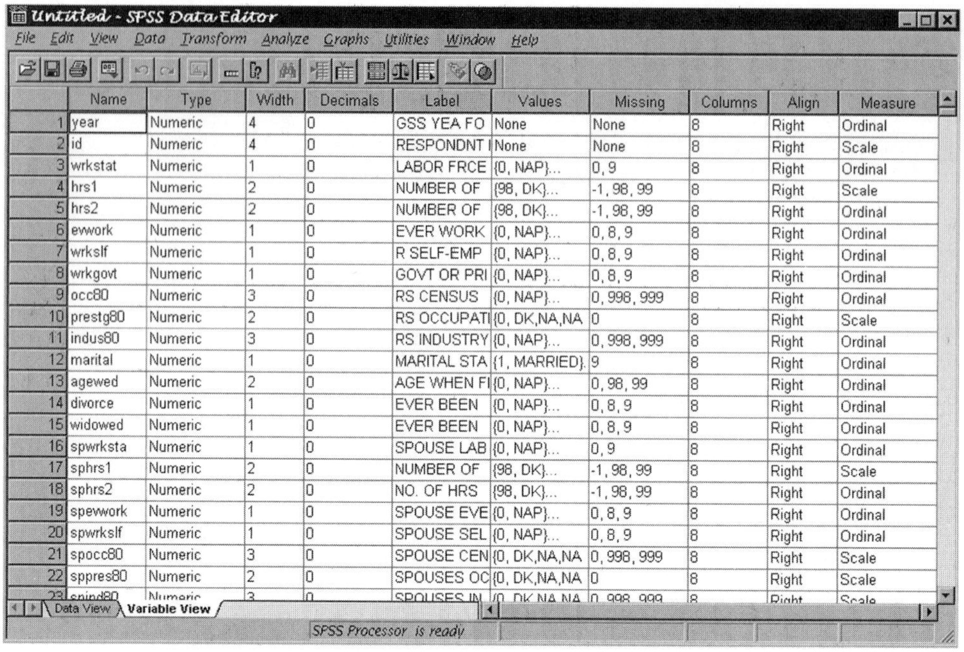

Untitled - SPSS Data Editor

File Edit View Data Transform Analyze Graphs Utilities Window Help

	Name	Type	Width	Decimals	Label	Values	Missing	Columns	Align	Measure
1	year	Numeric	4	0	GSS YEA FO	None	None	8	Right	Ordinal
2	id	Numeric	4	0	RESPONDNT I	None	None	8	Right	Scale
3	wrkstat	Numeric	1	0	LABOR FRCE	{0, NAP}...	0, 9	8	Right	Ordinal
4	hrs1	Numeric	2	0	NUMBER OF	{98, DK}...	-1, 98, 99	8	Right	Scale
5	hrs2	Numeric	2	0	NUMBER OF	{98, DK}...	-1, 98, 99	8	Right	Ordinal
6	evwork	Numeric	1	0	EVER WORK	{0, NAP}...	0, 8, 9	8	Right	Ordinal
7	wrkslf	Numeric	1	0	R SELF-EMP	{0, NAP}...	0, 8, 9	8	Right	Ordinal
8	wrkgovt	Numeric	1	0	GOVT OR PRI	{0, NAP}...	0, 8, 9	8	Right	Ordinal
9	occ80	Numeric	3	0	RS CENSUS	{0, NAP}...	0, 998, 999	8	Right	Ordinal
10	prestg80	Numeric	2	0	RS OCCUPATI	{0, DK,NA,NA	0	8	Right	Scale
11	indus80	Numeric	3	0	RS INDUSTRY	{0, NAP}...	0, 998, 999	8	Right	Ordinal
12	marital	Numeric	1	0	MARITAL STA	{1, MARRIED}.	9	8	Right	Ordinal
13	agewed	Numeric	2	0	AGE WHEN FI	{0, NAP}...	0, 98, 99	8	Right	Ordinal
14	divorce	Numeric	1	0	EVER BEEN	{0, NAP}...	0, 8, 9	8	Right	Ordinal
15	widowed	Numeric	1	0	EVER BEEN	{0, NAP}...	0, 8, 9	8	Right	Ordinal
16	spwrksta	Numeric	1	0	SPOUSE LAB	{0, NAP}...	0, 9	8	Right	Ordinal
17	sphrs1	Numeric	2	0	NUMBER OF	{98, DK}...	-1, 98, 99	8	Right	Scale
18	sphrs2	Numeric	2	0	NO. OF HRS	{98, DK}...	-1, 98, 99	8	Right	Ordinal
19	spevwork	Numeric	1	0	SPOUSE EVE	{0, NAP}...	0, 8, 9	8	Right	Ordinal
20	spwrkslf	Numeric	1	0	SPOUSE SEL	{0, NAP}...	0, 8, 9	8	Right	Ordinal
21	spocc80	Numeric	3	0	SPOUSE CEN	{0, DK,NA,NA	0, 998, 999	8	Right	Scale
22	sppres80	Numeric	2	0	SPOUSES OC	{0, DK,NA,NA	0	8	Right	Scale
23	spind80	Numeric	3	0	SPOUSES IN	{0, DK,NA,NA	0, 998, 999	8	Right	Scale

Data View / **Variable View**

SPSS Processor is ready

Figure D-9 A Full Variable Matrix

double-clicked on. Here's another way to learn about variables in the data set: Go to the **Utilities** menu above the data matrix and select the first option, **Variables.** See Figure D-10 for an illustration. A list of all the variables will appear, and to see how one was formatted you can simply select the variable of your choice from this window by clicking on it. Here we selected the *divorce* variable.

Variables are listed in the order they were imported from the GSS site. However, if you want to see them listed alphabetically, open the **Edit** menu and select the **Option** submenu. Then, as in Figure D-11, select **Alphabetical** from the **Variable Lists** option in the **General** subwindow and click **OK** twice. Note that the list in the left column may consist of the variable names instead of the abbreviated labels, but you can change this easily. In the **Edit** menu, select **Options.** In the **General** tab, find the section on **Variable Lists** in the right-hand column. Click **Display Labels.** You'll have to reload the data set, but it will be worth the effort because you'll be able to track down the abbreviated name you're looking for.

Having made these changes, reopen the variable information window from the **Utilities** menu. All variables are listed alphabetically. Notice the words next to **Variable Label:** "EVER BEEN DIVORCED OR SEPARATED." Although this is still abbreviated, you may figure out that it represents whether this person has been divorced or separated.

If you would like to view the value labels instead of the numeric codes they have been given, simply make sure you are on the **Data View**, select **View** from the menu, and click on **Value Label.** A check mark will appear next to this menu selection, and you will be able to read directly what your respondents' answers were for each variable. For instance, in Figure D-12 we now can see that respondent number 1623 is female, 50 years old, and married to a man who is 51 years old. In Figure D-13, the numeric values "1" and "2" for *divorce* have been replaced by "Yes" and "No," respectively.

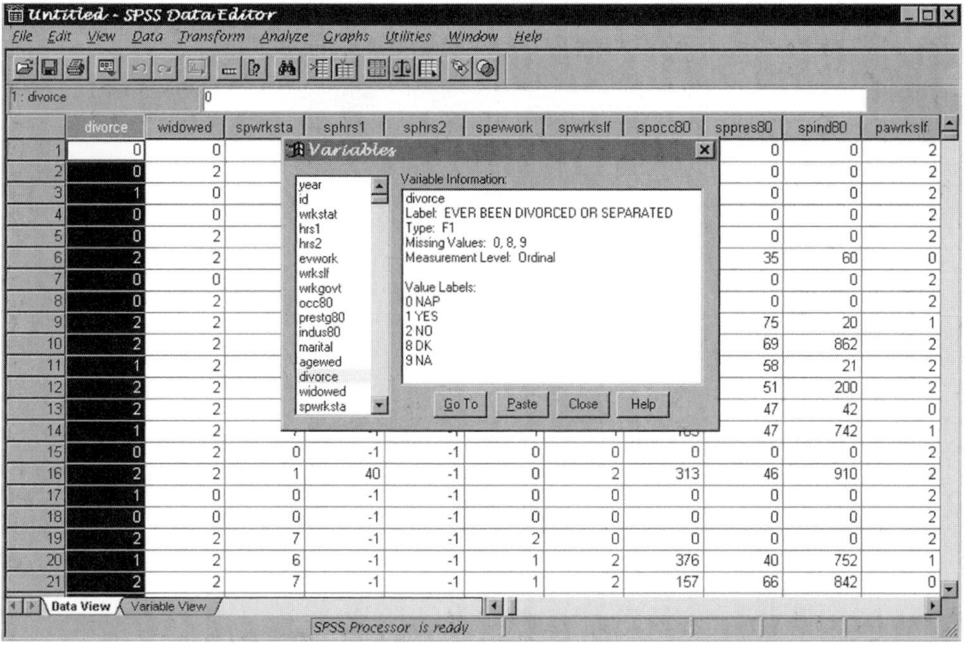

Figure D-10 Decoding the Variable *divorce*

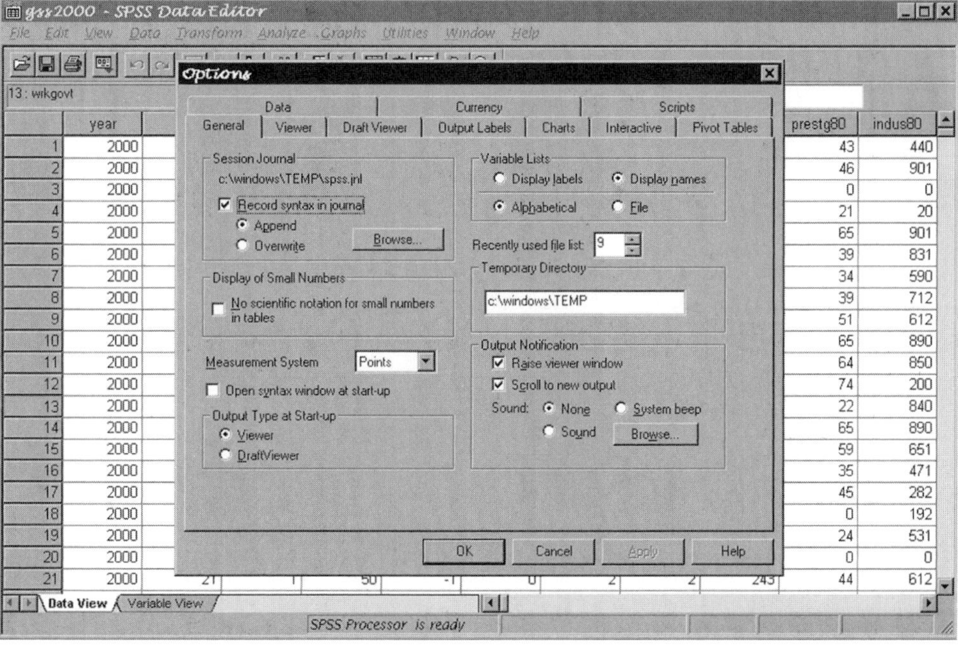

Figure D-11 Sorting the Variable List

Untitled - SPSS Data Editor

File Edit View Data Transform Analyze Graphs Utilities Window Help

6 : evwork 0

	gender1	old1	mar1	away1	where1	relate2	gender2	old2	mar2	away2	where2
1623	FEMAL	50	MARRIE	NAP	NAP	SPOUS	MALE	51	MARRIE	NAP	NAP
1624	MALE	18	NEVER	NAP	NAP	NON-RE	FEMAL	18	NEVER	NAP	NAP
1625	MALE	61	MARRIE	NAP	NAP	SPOUS	FEMAL	60	MARRIE	NAP	NAP
1626	FEMAL	31	NEVER	NAP	NAP	CHILD	NA	6	NAP	NAP	NAP
1627	FEMAL	50	DIVORC	NAP	NAP	NAP	NAP	NAP	NAP	NAP	NAP
1628	MALE	57	MARRIE	NAP	NAP	SPOUS	FEMAL	53	MARRIE	NAP	NAP
1629	FEMAL	51	MARRIE	NAP	NAP	SPOUS	MALE	51	MARRIE	NAP	NAP
1630	FEMAL	85	WIDOW	NAP	NAP	CHILD	FEMAL	51	DIVORC	NAP	NAP
1631	FEMAL	42	MARRIE	NAP	NAP	SPOUS	MALE	47	MARRIE	NAP	NAP
1632	MALE	33	MARRIE	NAP	NAP	SPOUS	MALE	31	MARRIE	NAP	NAP
1633	FEMAL	47	MARRIE	NAP	NAP	SPOUS	MALE	49	MARRIE	NAP	NAP
1634	MALE	55	MARRIE	NAP	NAP	SPOUS	FEMAL	54	MARRIE	NAP	NAP
1635	MALE	31	NEVER	NAP	NAP	NAP	NAP	NAP	NAP	NAP	NAP
1636	MALE	52	MARRIE	NAP	NAP	SPOUS	FEMAL	49	MARRIE	NAP	NAP
1637	MALE	58	MARRIE	NAP	NAP	SPOUS	FEMAL	57	MARRIE	NAP	NAP
1638	MALE	59	MARRIE	NAP	NAP	SPOUS	FEMAL	59	MARRIE	NAP	NAP
1639	MALE	38	MARRIE	NAP	NAP	SPOUS	FEMAL	38	MARRIE	NAP	NAP
1640	MALE	46	MARRIE	NAP	NAP	SPOUS	FEMAL	46	MARRIE	NAP	NAP
1641	FEMAL	31	NEVER	NAP	NAP	NON-RE	MALE	33	NEVER	NAP	NAP
1642	FEMAL	42	NEVER	NAP	NAP	CHILD	FEMAL	25	NA	NAP	NAP
1643	FEMAL	73	WIDOW	NAP	NAP	CHILD	MALE	43	DIVORC	NAP	NAP

Data View / Variable View

SPSS Processor is ready

Figure D-12 Viewing Variable Value Labels

Untitled - SPSS Data Editor

File Edit View Data Transform Analyze Graphs Utilities Window Help

1 : divorce 0

	divorce	widowed	spwrksta	sphrs1	sphrs2	spevwork	spwrkslf	spocc80	sppres80	spind80	pawrkslf
1	NAP	NAP	NAP	NAP	NAP	NAP	NAP	DK,NA,	DK,NA,	DK,NA,	SOMEO
2	NAP	NO	NAP	NAP	NAP	NAP	NAP	DK,NA,	DK,NA,	DK,NA,	SOMEO
3	YES	NAP	NAP	NAP	NAP	NAP	NAP	DK,NA,	DK,NA,	DK,NA,	SOMEO
4	NAP	NAP	NAP	NAP	NAP	NAP	NAP	DK,NA,	DK,NA,	DK,NA,	SOMEO
5	NAP	NO	NAP	NAP	NAP	NAP	NAP	DK,NA,	DK,NA,	DK,NA,	SOMEO
6	NO	NO	WORKI	40	NAP	NAP	SOMEO	587	35	60	NAP
7	NAP	NAP	NAP	NAP	NAP	NAP	NAP	DK,NA,	DK,NA,	DK,NA,	SOMEO
8	NAP	NO	NAP	NAP	NAP	NAP	NAP	DK,NA,	DK,NA,	DK,NA,	SOMEO
9	NO	NO	WORKI	40	NAP	NAP	SELF-E	178	75	20	SELF-E
10	NO	NO	WORKI	40	NAP	NAP	SOMEO	176	69	862	SOMEO
11	YES	NO	WORKI	45	NAP	NAP	SOMEO	77	58	21	SOMEO
12	NO	NO	WORKI	50	NAP	NAP	SOMEO	19	51	200	SOMEO
13	NO	NO	WORKI	40	NAP	NAP	SOMEO	337	47	42	NAP
14	YES	NO	KEEPIN	NAP	NAP	YES	SELF-E	185	47	742	SELF-E
15	NAP	NO	NAP	NAP	NAP	NAP	NAP	DK,NA,	DK,NA,	DK,NA,	SOMEO
16	NO	NO	WORKI	40	NAP	NAP	SOMEO	313	46	910	SOMEO
17	YES	NAP	NAP	NAP	NAP	NAP	NAP	DK,NA,	DK,NA,	DK,NA,	SOMEO
18	NAP	NAP	NAP	NAP	NAP	NAP	NAP	DK,NA,	DK,NA,	DK,NA,	SOMEO
19	NO	NO	KEEPIN	NAP	NAP	NO	NAP	DK,NA,	DK,NA,	DK,NA,	SOMEO
20	YES	NO	SCHOO	NAP	NAP	YES	SOMEO	376	40	752	SELF-E
21	NO	NO	KEEPIN	NAP	NAP	YES	SOMEO	157	66	842	NAP

Data View / Variable View

Value Labels SPSS Processor is ready

Figure D-13 Viewing Variable Value Labels on Data View

gss2000 - SPSS Data Editor

File Edit View Data Transform Analyze Graphs Utilities Window Help

	Name	Type	Width	Decimals	Label	Values	Missing	Columns	Align	Measure
193	wksubs	Numeric	1	0	DOES SUPER	{0, NAP}...	0, 8, 9	8	Right	Ordinal
194	wksup	Numeric	1	0	DOES R OR S	{0, NAP}...	0, 8, 9	8	Right	Ordinal
195	wksups	Numeric	1	0	DOES SUBOR	{0, NAP}...	0, 8, 9	8	Right	Ordinal
196	unemp	Numeric	1	0	EVER UNEMP	{0, NAP}...	0, 8, 9	8	Right	Ordinal
197	union	Numeric	1	0	DOES R OR S	{0, NAP}...	0, 8, 9	8	Right	Ordinal
198	getahead	Numeric	1	0	OPINION OF	{0, NAP}...	0, 8, 9	8	Right	Ordinal
199	parsol	Numeric	1	0	RS LIVING ST	{0, NAP}...	0, 8, 9	8	Right	Ordinal
200	kidssol	Numeric	1	0	RS KIDS LIVIN	{0, NAP}...	0, 8, 9	8	Right	Ordinal
201	fepol	Numeric	1	0	WOMEN NOT	{0, NAP}...	0, 8, 9	8	Right	Ordinal
202	abdefect	Numeric	1	0	STRONG CHA	{0, NAP}...	0, 8, 9	8	Right	Ordinal
203	abnomore	Numeric	1	0	MARRIED--W	{0, NAP}...	0, 8, 9	8	Right	Ordinal
204	abhlth	Numeric	1	0	WOMANS HE	{0, NAP}...	0, 8, 9	8	Right	Ordinal
205	abpoor	Numeric	1	0	LOW INCOME	{0, NAP}...	0, 8, 9	8	Right	Ordinal
206	abrape	Numeric	1	0	PREGNANT A	{0, NAP}...	0, 8, 9	8	Right	Ordinal
207	absingle	Numeric	1	0	NOT MARRIE	{0, NAP}...	0, 8, 9	8	Right	Ordinal
208	abany	Numeric	1	0	ABORTION IF	{0, NAP}...	0, 8, 9	8	Right	Ordinal
209	chldidel	Numeric	1	0	IDEAL NUMB	{7, SEVEN+}...	-1, 9	8	Right	Ordinal
210	pillok	Numeric	1	0	BIRTH CONTR	{0, NAP}...	0, 8, 9	8	Right	Ordinal
211	sexeduc	Numeric	1	0	SEX EDUCATI	{0, NAP}...	0, 8, 9	8	Right	Ordinal
212	divlaw	Numeric	1	0	DIVORCE LA	{0, NAP}...	0, 8, 9	8	Right	Ordinal
213	premarsx	Numeric	1	0	SEX BEFORE	{0, NAP}...	0, 8, 9	8	Right	Ordinal
214	teensex	Numeric	1	0	SEX BEFORE	{0, NAP}...	0, 8, 9	8	Right	Ordinal
215	xmarsex	Numeric	1	0	SEX WITH PE	{0, NAP}	0, 8, 9	8	Right	Ordinal

Data View / Variable View

SPSS Processor is ready

Figure D-14 Starting to Decode Value Labels on Variable View

To turn off value labels, by the way, simply open **View** and click **Value Labels** again. Notice that the check mark indicates whether the feature is on or off.

You can obtain the full wording of variables most easily from the GSS website. The codebook index (by variable name) is located at www.icpsr.umich.edu/GSS. On that website, click on **Mnemonic** to go to a list of variables beginning with "A." You can see any other variable by simply clicking on the first letter of the variable you are looking for.

Let's take a close look at the variable *abany,* which we will use in our analysis further on. Now you can see more clearly what this variable represents. Respondents were asked a battery of questions concerning their attitudes toward abortion—specifically, the conditions under which they felt a woman should be able to obtain one legally (such as rape or danger of birth defects). In this case, respondents were asked if they would support a woman's right to a legal abortion as a purely personal choice: "for any reason."

Besides presenting the actual wording of the question, this web page also reports the answer categories and the results of several surveys that asked the question over the years. Notice that a numeric code of 1 stands for saying "Yes." Now we know that the first person in the data set feels that a woman should be able to choose an abortion for any reason.

Let's go back to variable *abany*. To find out what "0" means, let's learn how to examine variable codes within SPSS. Double-click *abany* in the column heading. The **Variable View** window opens and the variable *divorce* is automatically highlighted. Now click on the little square in the value label cell for *abany* as shown in Figure D-14.

As you can see in Figure D-15, "0" stands for "NAP," which means "not applicable." In other words, this particular question was not asked of some respondents.

Another method for decoding the value labels of a particular variable begins by selecting **Variables** from the **Utilities** menu. Figure D-16 presents the result of this

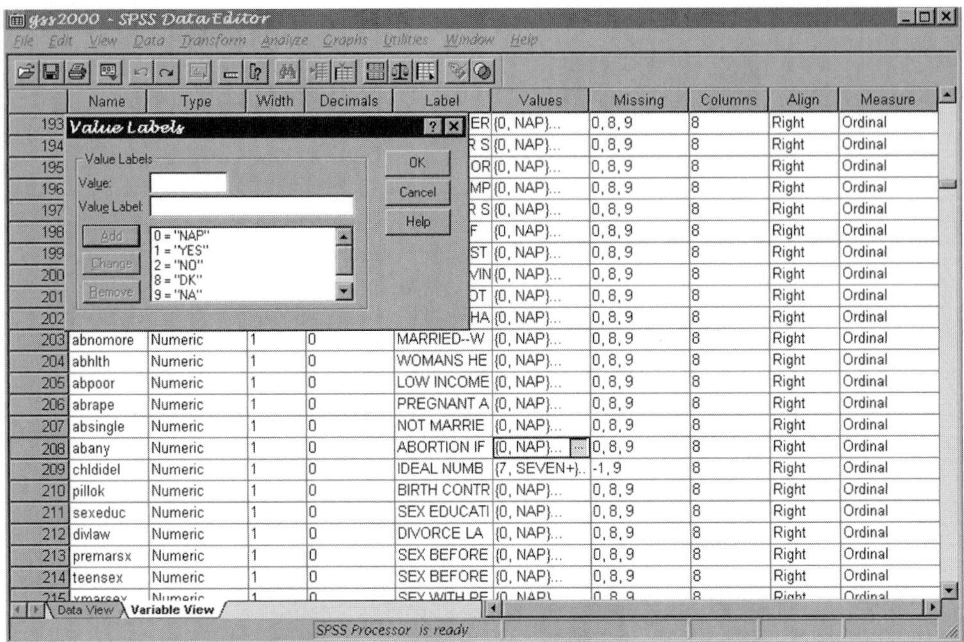

Figure D-15 Decoding Value Labels for *abany*

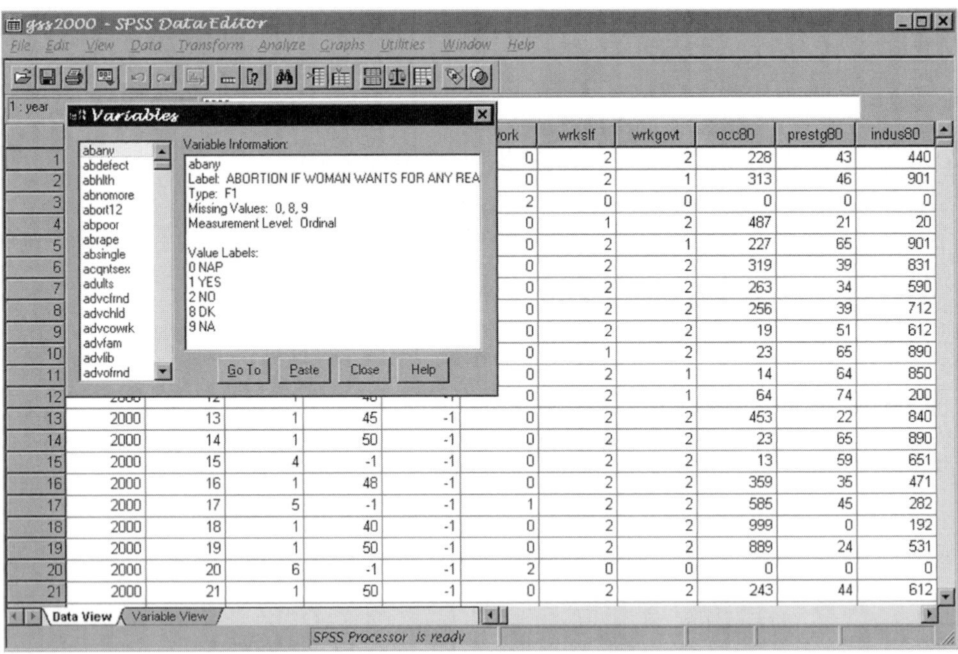

Figure D-16 Alternative for Decoding Value Labels for *abany*

action. First you'll see that we have pretty much the same information we obtained before. Notice the column to the left, however. It's the beginning of a list of all the variables in the data set. (You can use the scroll bar to see the rest of the list.) Find the name of a variable you're interested in and click it. You'll instantly get the variable and value labels.

Again, you can view all value labels for *abany* by simply selecting this variable. The advantage of the **Variables** dialog box is that you also have the option to find the variable *abany* quickly on your SPSS data editor by clicking on **GoTo.** The *abany* column will be selected and highlighted instantly on your **Data View** window.

Person 3, for example, was not asked this question. By asking different sets of questions of different people in the sample, the researchers can collect data for hundreds of variables without driving any of the respondents to suicide or homicide.

FREQUENCY DISTRIBUTIONS

Now that we've seen what the abbreviated variable labels and numerical code categories stand for, we're ready to examine some public opinion. Think about the question we've looked at so far. How do you suppose people in the United States feel about a woman's right to an abortion? That is, what percentage do you suppose said "Yes" and what percentage said "No"? To start finding out, select **Frequencies . . .** from the **Descriptive Statistics** menu in the **Analyze** general menu (see Figure D-17).

This command will get you a list of variables to choose from as illustrated in Figure D-18.

Now you can double-click a variable label, or single-click it and then click the right-pointing triangular arrow. Either action will move labels from the left-hand to the right-hand column. Figure D-19 shows the results of three variables being selected this way.

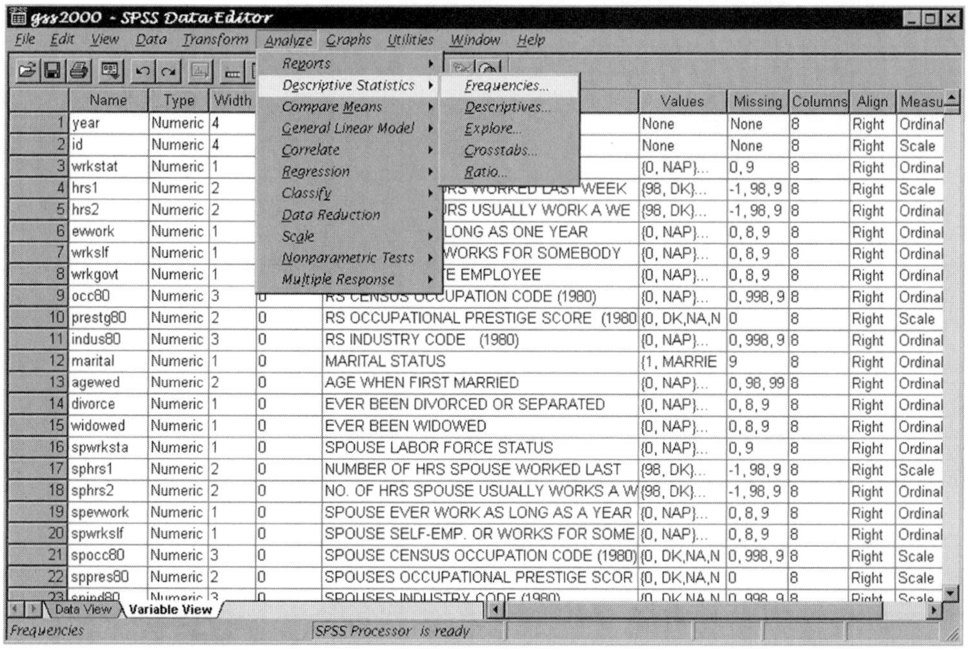

Figure D-17 Getting Frequency Distributions

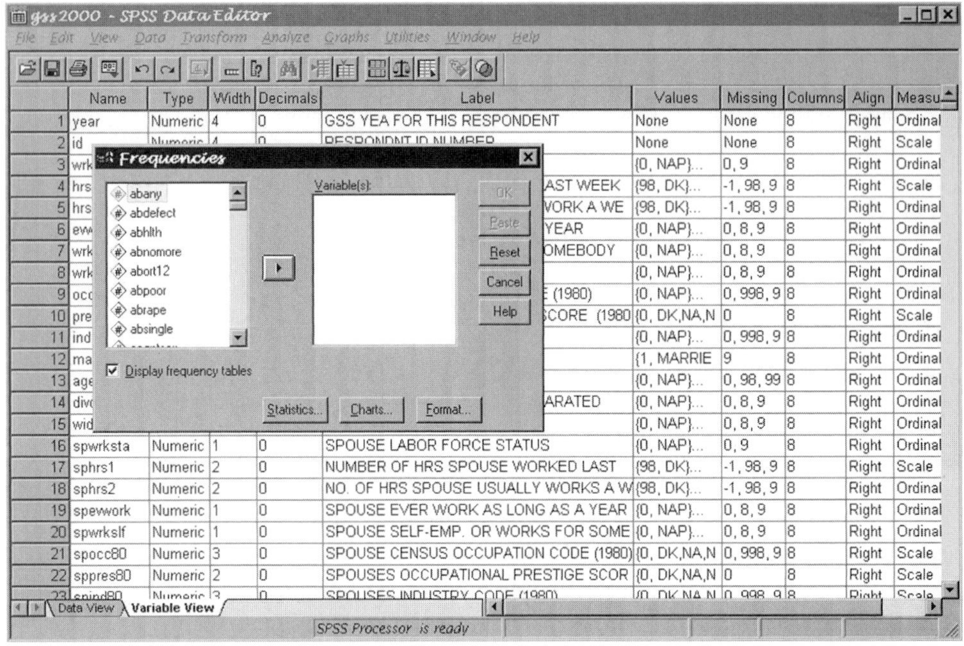

Figure D-18 Choosing a Variable for Frequencies

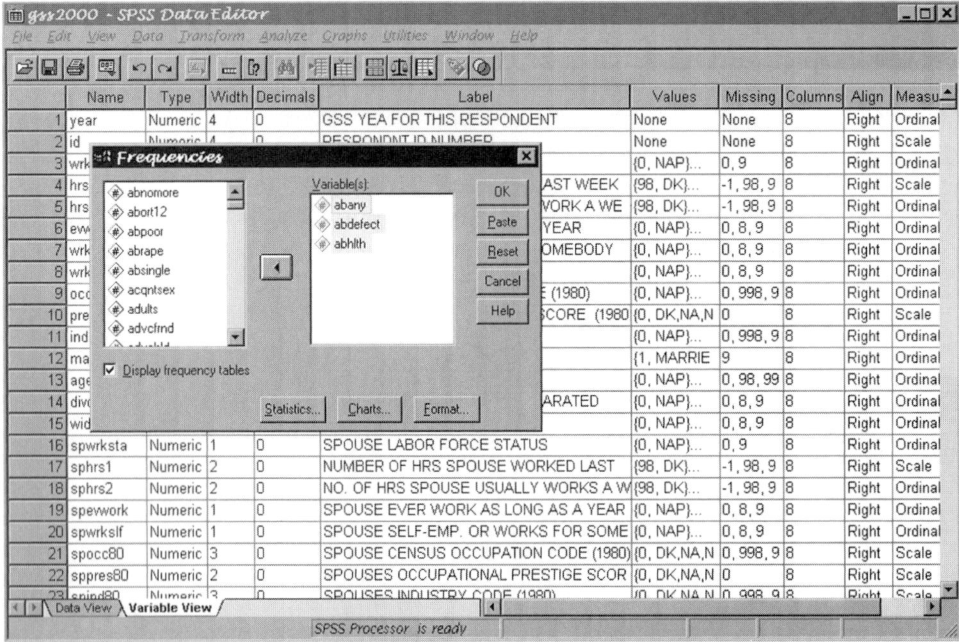

Figure D-19 Selecting Frequency Variables

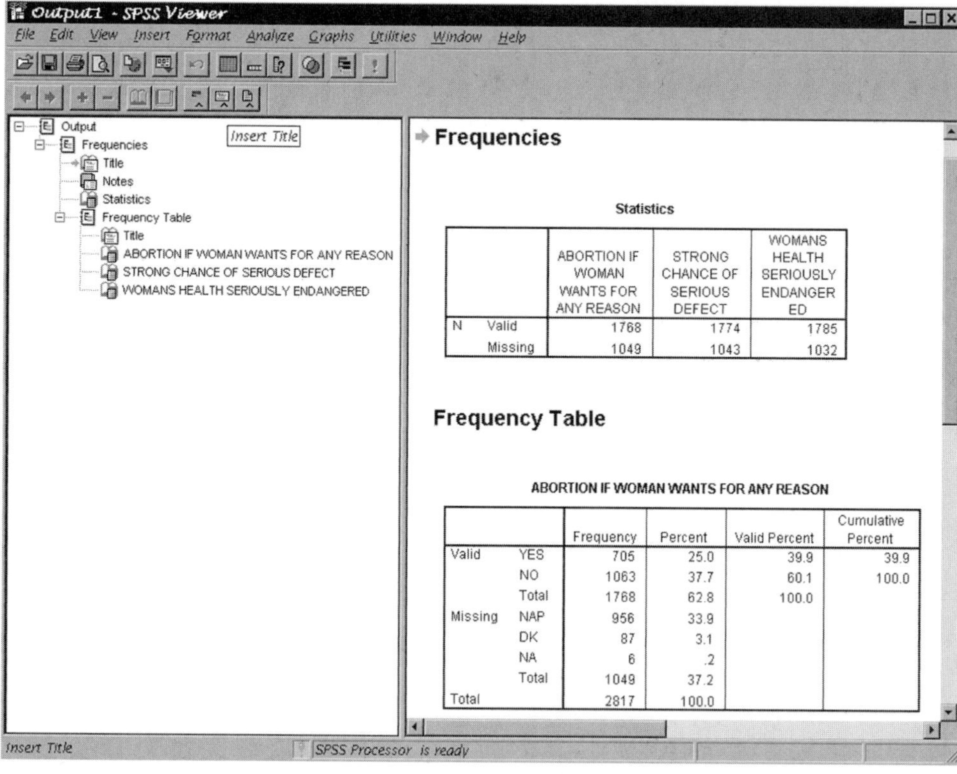

Statistics

		ABORTION IF WOMAN WANTS FOR ANY REASON	STRONG CHANCE OF SERIOUS DEFECT	WOMANS HEALTH SERIOUSLY ENDANGERED
N	Valid	1768	1774	1785
	Missing	1049	1043	1032

ABORTION IF WOMAN WANTS FOR ANY REASON

		Frequency	Percent	Valid Percent	Cumulative Percent
Valid	YES	705	25.0	39.9	39.9
	NO	1063	37.7	60.1	100.0
	Total	1768	62.8	100.0	
Missing	NAP	956	33.9		
	DK	87	3.1		
	NA	6	.2		
	Total	1049	37.2		
Total		2817	100.0		

Figure D-20 Frequency Distribution Tables

Next we click the **OK** button. SPSS will then determine the distributions of responses to each of the three variables in our example and produce the frequency tables shown in Figure D-20.

Notice that SPSS has now opened a new window, labeled **Output.** As you continue with SPSS, you'll often work back and forth between the Data and Output windows; often the program alternates them automatically.

The left-hand frame in Figure D-20 presents an outline of the results. Click on any item in the outline to fill the right-hand frame with the data you've requested. Here is where you can easily cut and paste from SPSS to a Microsoft Word document. Click on the outline **Frequency Table** in the left-hand side. All of the frequency tables are now selected. Select **Copy Objects** from the **Edit** menu. Figures D-21 and D-22 illustrate this process. In this case, we were only interested in copying and pasting the frequency table for *abany*. Now open your **Word** document and select **Paste** from the **Edit** menu.

In Figure D-20, the right-hand side presents two tables. The first one summarizes the three variables we chose originally. All we are told here, however, is the number of respondents with and without valid responses. The second table gives the distribution of data for the question of whether a woman should have the right to an abortion for any reason. In addition to "Yes" and "No," the table reports three other possibilities:

NAP: "Not applicable" (the question was not asked)

DK: Respondents who said they "Don't know"

NA: Respondents who were asked but gave "No answer"

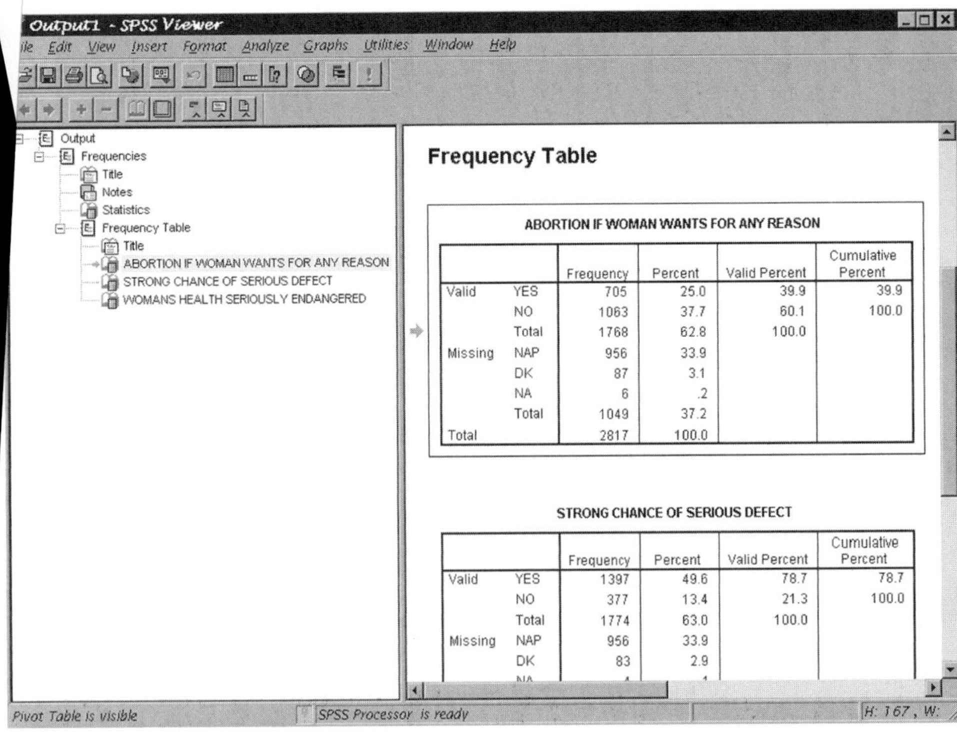

Figure D-21 Selecting Frequency Distribution Tables

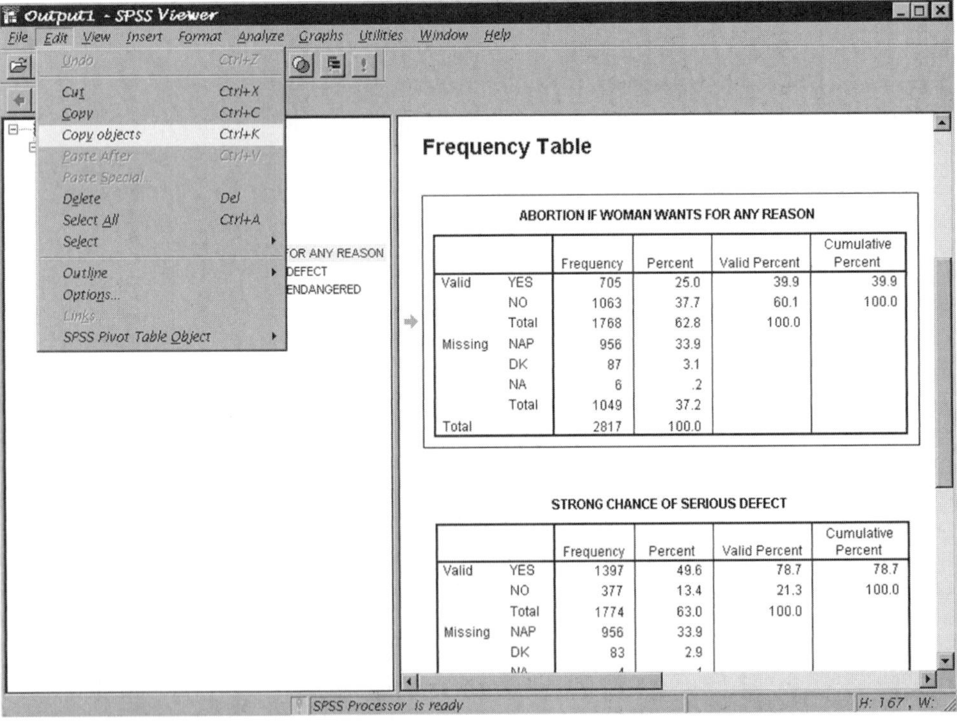

Figure D-22 Copying Frequency Distribution Tables

In the second table's **Frequency** column, you can learn how many respondents fall under each category. The **Percent** column puts the information into a more useful form by showing the percentage represented by each category. The most useful column is **Valid Percent.** This column tells us that of the 1,768 respondents who gave a valid response, 39.9 percent said "Yes" and 60.1 percent said "No."

By scrolling down the window or using the outline in the left-hand frame, you can check the results for the other variables. For now, let's move along to more complex analyses.

CROSS-TABULATIONS

The frequency distributions we've just undertaken are called *univariate* analyses (analyzing one variable at a time). Now we'll turn to *bivariate* analyses (two variables at a time).

Let's stay with the issue of "abortion for any reason." We've seen that U.S. residents are almost evenly divided on the issue. What do you suppose accounts for this difference? People often guess that women would be more likely than men to support abortion as a woman's right. Let's see how to determine the accuracy of that guess.

Return to the **Descriptive Statistics** menu from the **Analyze** menu, but check **Crosstabs** this time. This brings you a somewhat different dialog box, as indicated in Figure D-23.

We are now going to set up a percentage table involving two variables: *abany* and *sex*. The table will have both columns and rows. Although there are many ways to construct such a table, we're going to assign the categories of sex (male and female)

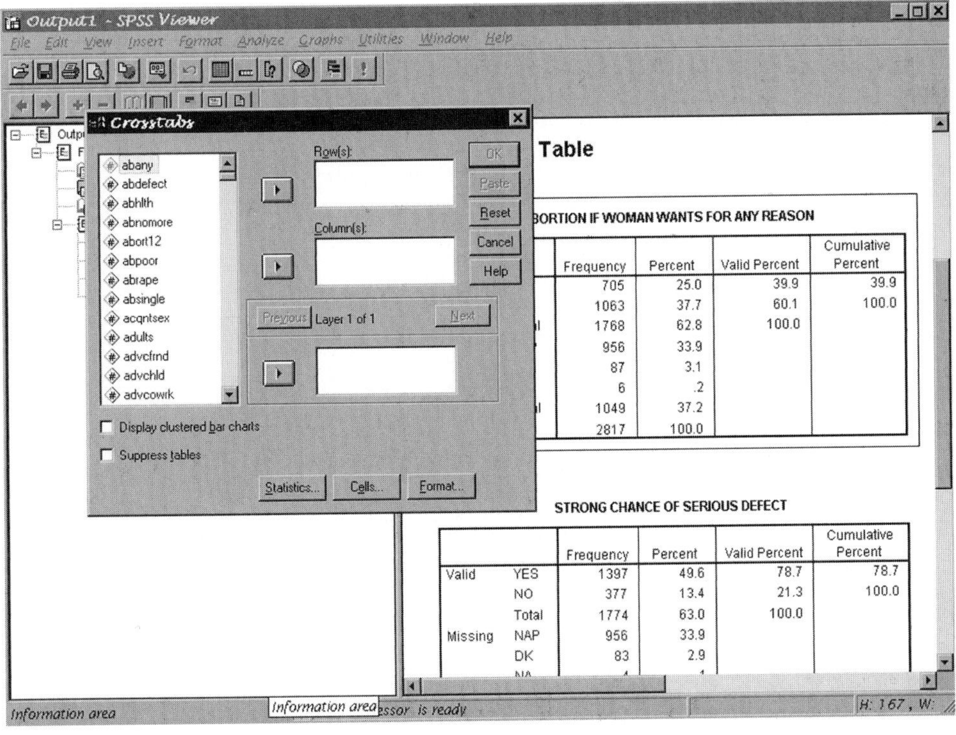

Figure D-23 Crosstabs Dialog Box

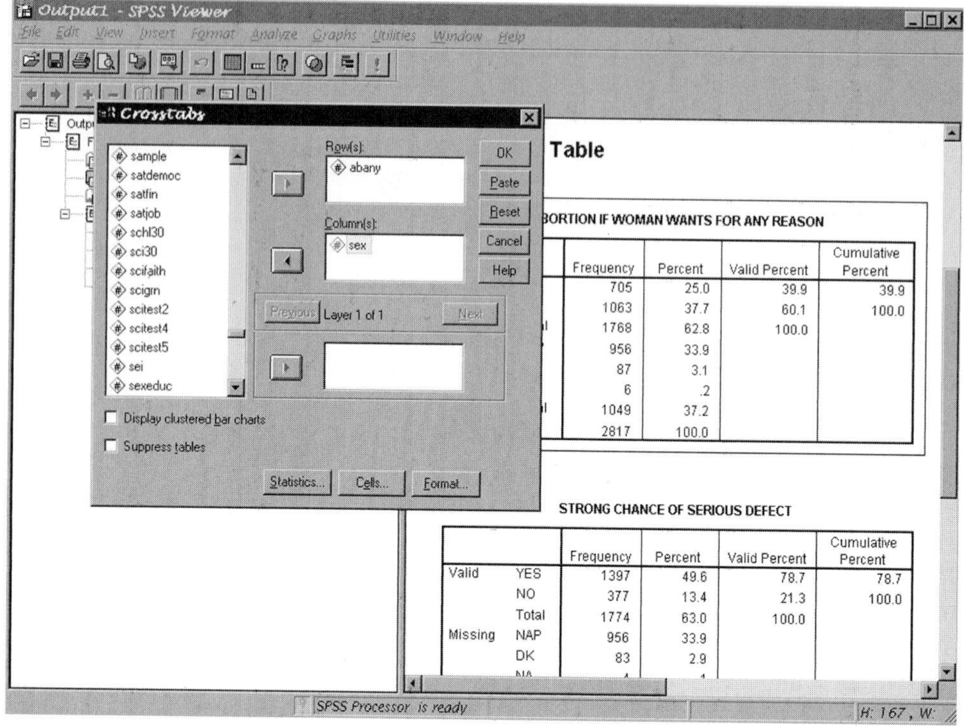

Figure D-24 Selecting Variables for the Cross-Tabulation

to the columns and then look at the opinions on *abany* within each category. In the logic and language of SPSS, that makes *abany* the "row variable" and *sex* the "column variable." To assign categories, select variable labels from the list and drag them to the appropriate windows on the right. Figure D-24 shows this step.

To find a variable label in the list, you can either scroll through the list or click any label in the list and then type the variable you want. It may take a little experimentation to discover how quickly you must type to have it work.

Thus far, we've told SPSS to organize the table like this:

	Men	**Women**
Approve		
Disapprove		

To complete our request, we have to tell SPSS how to percentage the data. In this case, we'll ask for the percentage of men who approve of abortion and the percentage who disapprove, with the two percentages totaling 100 percent. Then we'll ask for the corresponding percentages of women. In other words, we'll ask SPSS to "percentage down" the columns (using the terminology of Chapter 20). The **Crosstab** option provides a means for us to indicate that preference. Click the **Cells** button in the dialog box (the result is shown in Figure D-25).

When the dialog box opens, the **Observed** box will already be checked. Leave it that way. In the section on **Percentages**, click the **Column** box. That instructs SPSS to percentage down the columns. Click **Continue** to complete this dialog, and then click **OK** to launch the request for a crosstab. Once SPSS has completed the table, we'll be returned to the **Output** window shown in Figure D-26.

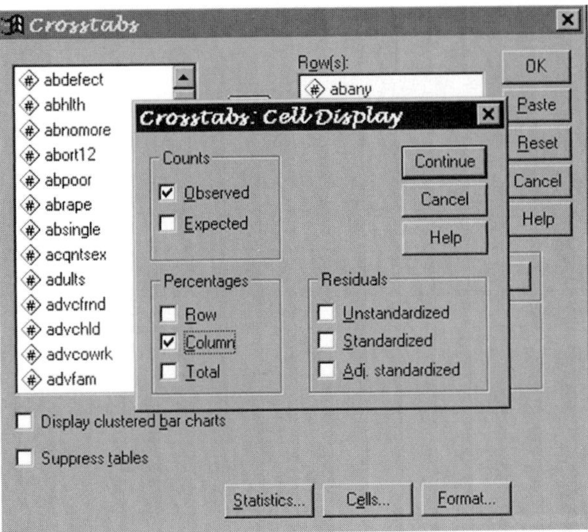

Figure D-25 Specifying the Percentaging Method

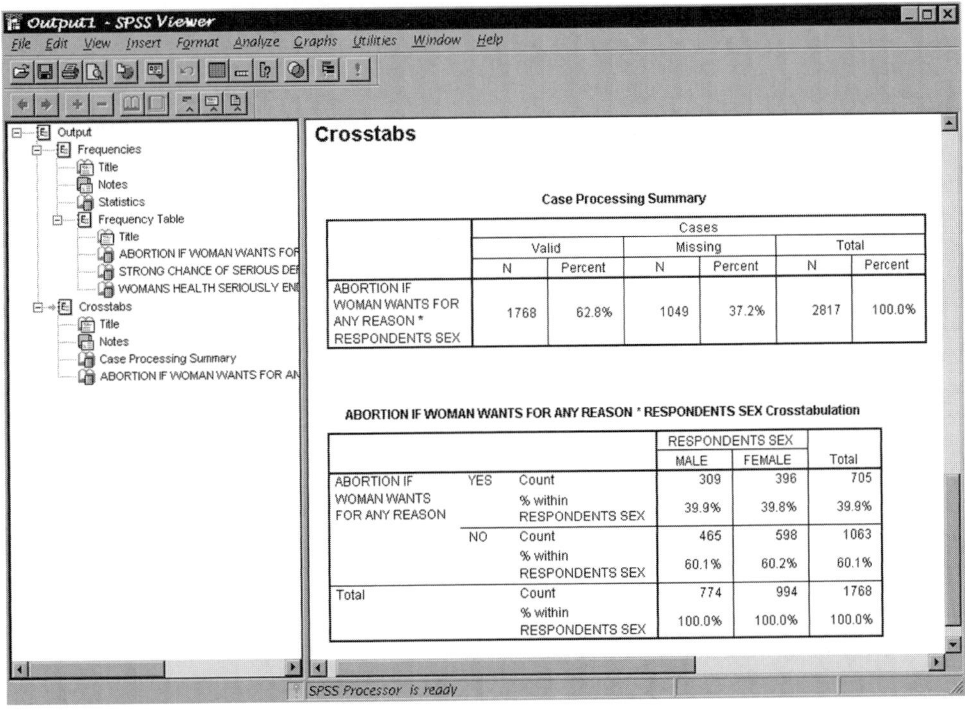

Crosstabs

Case Processing Summary

	Cases					
	Valid		Missing		Total	
	N	Percent	N	Percent	N	Percent
ABORTION IF WOMAN WANTS FOR ANY REASON * RESPONDENTS SEX	1768	62.8%	1049	37.2%	2817	100.0%

ABORTION IF WOMAN WANTS FOR ANY REASON * RESPONDENTS SEX Crosstabulation

			RESPONDENTS SEX		
			MALE	FEMALE	Total
ABORTION IF WOMAN WANTS FOR ANY REASON	YES	Count	309	396	705
		% within RESPONDENTS SEX	39.9%	39.8%	39.9%
	NO	Count	465	598	1063
		% within RESPONDENTS SEX	60.1%	60.2%	60.1%
Total		Count	774	994	1768
		% within RESPONDENTS SEX	100.0%	100.0%	100.0%

Figure D-26 Cross-Tabulation of *abany* and *sex*

Let's see what the table tells us. We wanted to find out if men and women differed in their attitudes about whether a woman should be able to choose an abortion just because she wanted one. The table suggests that there's no appreciable difference. The same proportion of men (39.9%) and women (39.8%) say a woman should have the right to an abortion for any reason.

Output1 - SPSS Viewer

File Edit View Insert Format Analyze Graphs Utilities Window Help

ABORTION IF WOMAN WANTS FOR ANY REASON * THINK OF SELF AS LIBERAL OR CONSERVATIVE Crosstabulation

			THINK OF SELF AS LIBERAL OR CONSERVATIVE							
			EXTREMELY LIBERAL	LIBERAL	SLIGHTLY LIBERAL	MODERATE	SLGHTLY CONSER VATIVE	CONSER VATIVE	EXTRMLY CONSER VATIVE	Total
ABORTION IF WOMAN WANTS FOR ANY REASON	YES	Count	42	110	95	280	81	59	12	679
		% within THINK OF SELF AS LIBERAL OR CONSERVATIVE	67.7%	54.2%	52.2%	41.7%	32.8%	23.6%	21.4%	40.6%
	NO	Count	20	93	87	391	166	191	44	992
		% within THINK OF SELF AS LIBERAL OR CONSERVATIVE	32.3%	45.8%	47.8%	58.3%	67.2%	76.4%	78.6%	59.4%
Total		Count	62	203	182	671	247	250	56	1671
		% within THINK OF SELF AS LIBERAL OR CONSERVATIVE	100.0%	100.0%	100.0%	100.0%	100.0%	100.0%	100.0%	100.0%

Figure D-27 Cross-Tabulation of *abany* and *polviews*

Let's try another variable that could affect people's attitudes toward abortion: political orientation. In the GSS, *polviews* represents a standard item that asks respondents to characterize their political views as something between "Extremely Liberal" and "Extremely Conservative." Figure D-27 shows the impact of this variable on attitudes toward abortion.

Because there are so many categories for political views, you may have to use the scroll bar at the bottom of the window to move back and forth across the table. Notice that we've scrolled all the way to the right in Figure D-27.

The impact of political views on abortion attitudes is fairly clear. Overall, liberals support abortion more than do conservatives.

RECODING VARIABLES

It's often useful to recode variables with many categories, reducing the number to something more manageable. In the present case, we might want to combine the categories in *polviews* to make three: Liberal, Moderate, and Conservative.

We can combine categories by hand from the kind of table presented in Figure D-27. For example, we can easily calculate that 447 of the respondents in the table considered themselves liberals (62 + 203 + 182). Of those, 247 supported a woman's right to an abortion for any reason (42 + 110 + 95). Dividing these two numbers tells us that 55 percent of the liberals supported abortion. A similar calculation tells us that 152 of the 553 conservatives—27 percent—were supportive. The 42-percent support among moderates fits neatly between the liberals and conservatives.

Combining categories like this makes it easier to use the variable in further analyses. However, we should have SPSS create a new, recoded variable so that we don't have to undertake the job by hand each time. To do this, we must first return to the **Data** window. If you're in the **Output** window, you can simply click the **Data View tab** at the bottom of your screen or select the SPSS **Data Editor** item from the **Window** menu (see Figure D-28).

Once you've returned to the **Data** window, click the **Transform** menu and move your pointer to the **Recode** option. When you do that, you'll be presented with another choice, as Figure D-29 shows.

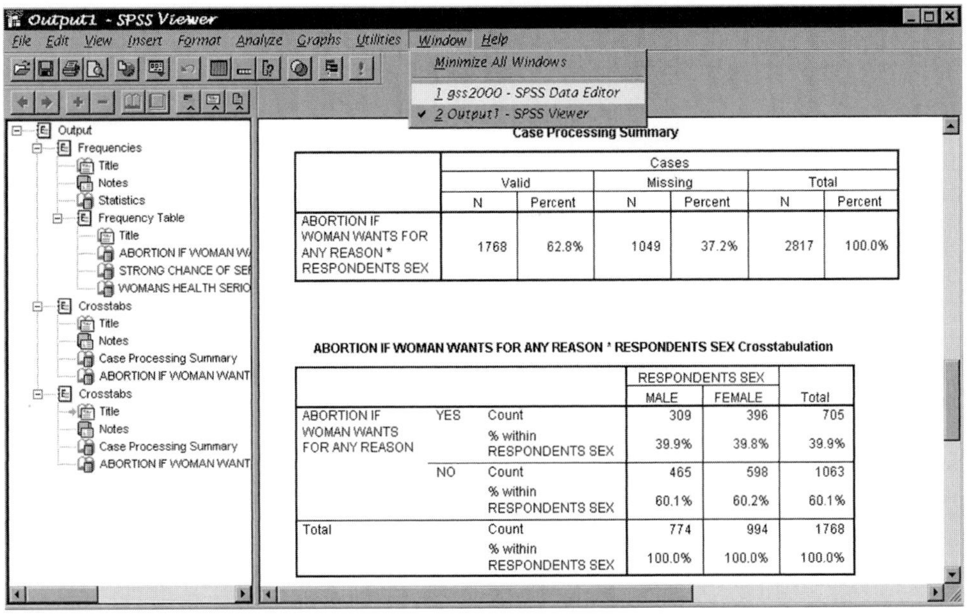
Output1 - SPSS Viewer
File Edit View Insert Format Analyze Graphs Utilities Window Help
Minimize All Windows
1 gss2000 - SPSS Data Editor
2 Output1 - SPSS Viewer
Output
Frequencies
Title
Notes
Statistics
Frequency Table
ABORTION IF WOMAN W
STRONG CHANCE OF SE
WOMANS HEALTH SERI
Crosstabs
Case Processing Summary
ABORTION IF WOMAN WANT
Case Processing Summary
Cases
Valid
Missing
Total
N
Percent
ABORTION IF WOMAN WANTS FOR ANY REASON * RESPONDENTS SEX
1768
62.8%
1049
37.2%
2817
100.0%
ABORTION IF WOMAN WANTS FOR ANY REASON * RESPONDENTS SEX Crosstabulation
RESPONDENTS SEX
MALE
FEMALE
Total
ABORTION IF WOMAN WANTS FOR ANY REASON
YES
Count
309
396
705
% within RESPONDENTS SEX
39.9%
39.8%
39.9%
NO
Count
465
598
1063
% within RESPONDENTS SEX
60.1%
60.2%
60.1%
Total
Count
774
994
1768
% within RESPONDENTS SEX
100.0%
100.0%
100.0%

Figure D-28 Switching to Data View

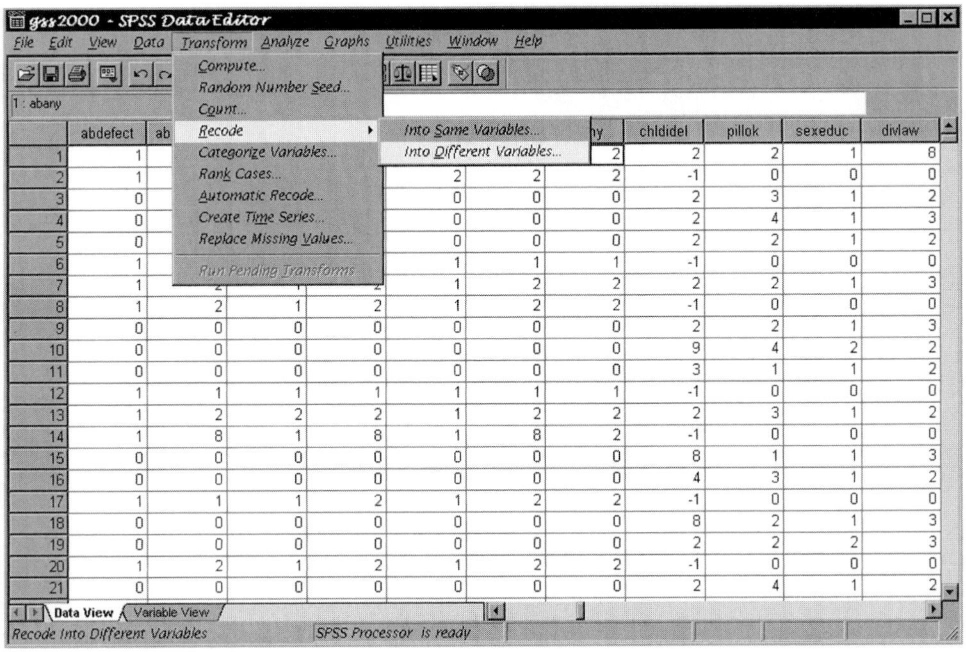
gss2000 - SPSS Data Editor
File Edit View Data Transform Analyze Graphs Utilities Window Help
Compute...
Random Number Seed...
Count...
Recode
Categorize Variables...
Rank Cases...
Automatic Recode...
Create Time Series...
Replace Missing Values...
Run Pending Transforms
Into Same Variables...
Into Different Variables...
1 : abany
abdefect
chldidel
pillok
sexeduc
divlaw
Data View
Variable View
Recode Into Different Variables
SPSS Processor is ready

Figure D-29 Opening the Recode Dialog Box

SPSS offers two options for recoding: It will either modify the data contained under the existing variable label (Same Variables) or create a new variable for the modified results (Different Variables). Choose **Different Variables** because the first option will destroy the original data.

Next you'll see a large dialog box like the one in Figure D-30.

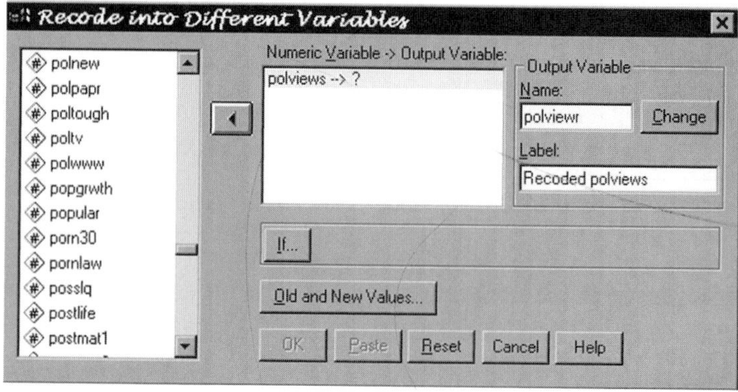

Figure D-30 The Recode Dialog Box

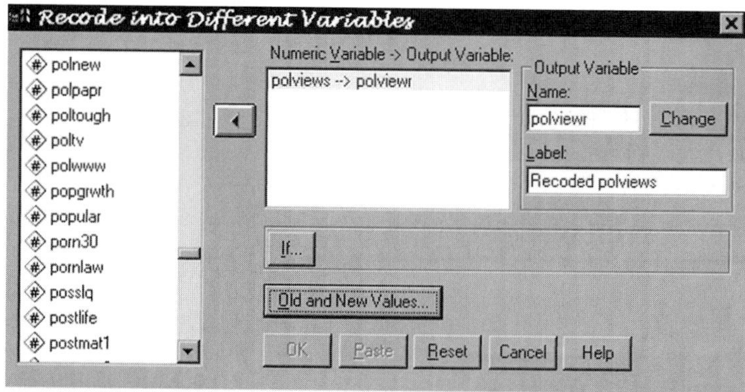

Figure D-31 The Completed Recode Dialog Box

Initially, the right-hand frame will have nothing in it. To create the situation shown in Figure D-31:

1. Select *polviews* in the variable list and move it to the center frame by double-clicking it or using the triangular arrow.
2. Type "polviewr" in the space under **Output Variable Name** and click **Change.**
3. Type in a descriptive label to identify what *polviewr* stands for.

To continue the process, click **Old and New Values.** This will bring you the dialog box shown in Figure D-32.

To tell SPSS how to create *polviewr* from *polviews,* we identify values of *polviews* and indicate what values they should get in *polviewr.* Let's start by creating a "Liberals" category that includes everyone with a "1," "2," or "3" on *polviews.* We'll give the new category the value "1." In Figure D-33, we've chosen the Range option and indicated that anyone with a value of "1" through "3" on *polviews* should be assigned a "1" on *polviewr.* Make sure you see where those instructions are entered in the dialog box.

When you click the **Add** button, the transformation instruction is transferred to the field on the right-hand side of the dialog box, as you can see in Figure D-34.

We'll use a different option to create a new "Moderate" category. As you recall, they were scored "4" on *polviews.* We'll give them a "2" in *polviewr* by entering the old

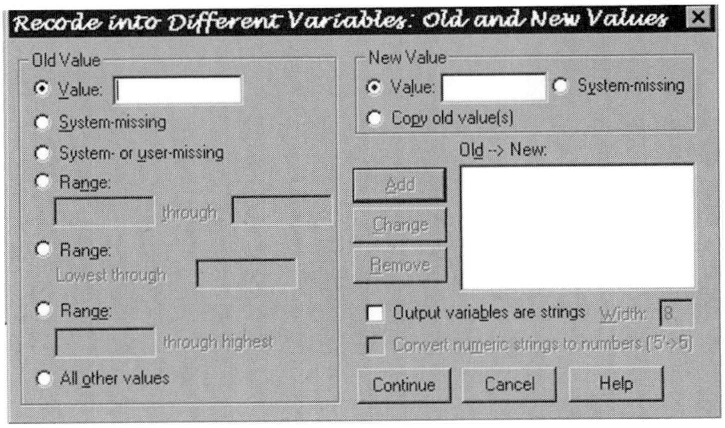

Figure D-32 Specifying How to Recode Categories

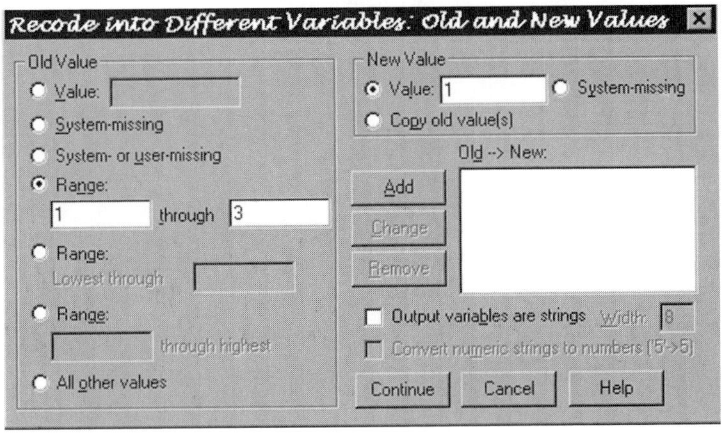

Figure D-33 Creating "Liberals" as a Single Category

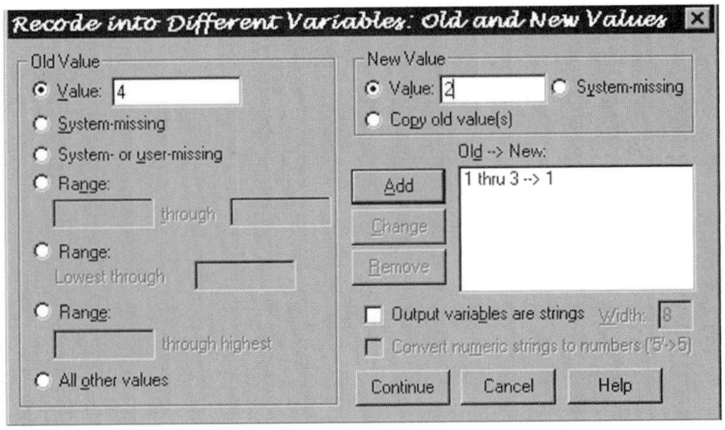

Figure D-34 Renumbering the "Moderate" Category

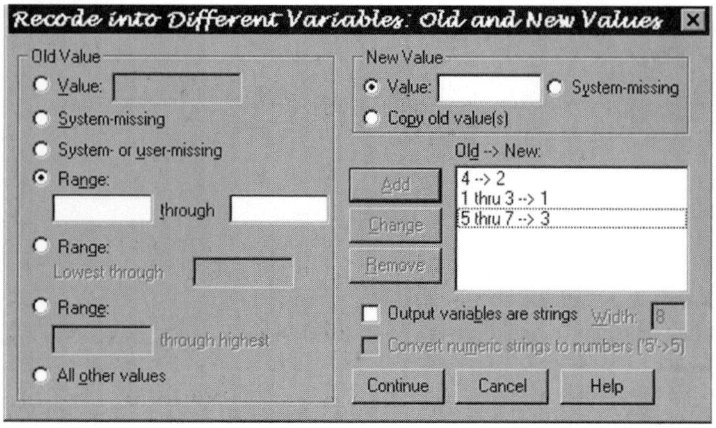

Figure D-35 The Recoding Instructions Completed

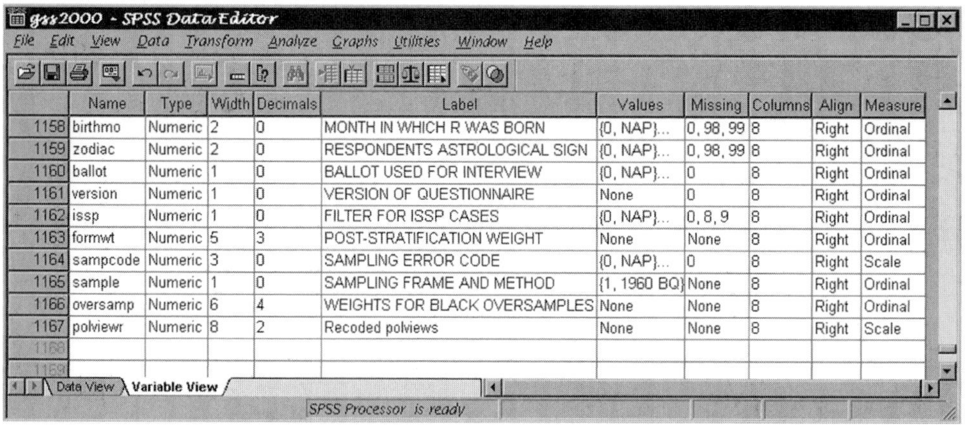

	Name	Type	Width	Decimals	Label	Values	Missing	Columns	Align	Measure
1158	birthmo	Numeric	2	0	MONTH IN WHICH R WAS BORN	{0, NAP}...	0, 98, 99	8	Right	Ordinal
1159	zodiac	Numeric	2	0	RESPONDENTS ASTROLOGICAL SIGN	{0, NAP}...	0, 98, 99	8	Right	Ordinal
1160	ballot	Numeric	1	0	BALLOT USED FOR INTERVIEW	{0, NAP}...	0	8	Right	Ordinal
1161	version	Numeric	1	0	VERSION OF QUESTIONNAIRE	None	0	8	Right	Ordinal
1162	issp	Numeric	1	0	FILTER FOR ISSP CASES	{0, NAP}...	0, 8, 9	8	Right	Ordinal
1163	formwt	Numeric	5	3	POST-STRATIFICATION WEIGHT	None	None	8	Right	Ordinal
1164	sampcode	Numeric	3	0	SAMPLING ERROR CODE	{0, NAP}...	0	8	Right	Scale
1165	sample	Numeric	1	0	SAMPLING FRAME AND METHOD	{1, 1960 BQ}	None	8	Right	Ordinal
1166	oversamp	Numeric	6	4	WEIGHTS FOR BLACK OVERSAMPLES	None	None	8	Right	Ordinal
1167	polviewr	Numeric	8	2	Recoded polviews	None	None	8	Right	Scale

Figure D-36 Finding *polviewr* in Variable View

and new values in the **Old Value** and **New Value** fields. When we click **Add** again, the new instruction is added to the field. Now take a moment to figure out how you would create a "Conservative" category, transforming scores of 5, 6, and 7 on *polviews* into a score of 3 on *polviewr.* Once you've done that, you should have the dialog box shown in Figure D-35. All that remains now is to click **Continue**, which will return you to the earlier dialog box, and then click **OK.**

Let's tidy up our new variable. First, return to the **Data View** window. Next, scroll across the list of variables to the far-right end. SPSS places each new variable at the end of all the other variables. Because you just created a new variable called *polviewr,* SPSS created a new column located last on your spreadsheet. When you find *polviewr,* double-click the variable label at the head of the column. This will open up the **Variable View** window and *polviewr* will be automatically selected at the bottom of your variable list. See Figure D-36.

Click on the right-hand side of the cell located in the **Decimals** column and *polviewr* row. A little square with up–down arrows will appear in the cell as shown in Figure D-37. You can then use the down arrow to reduce to 0 the number of decimals for each value of *polviewr.* In other words, you can convert each 1.00 score to simply 1.

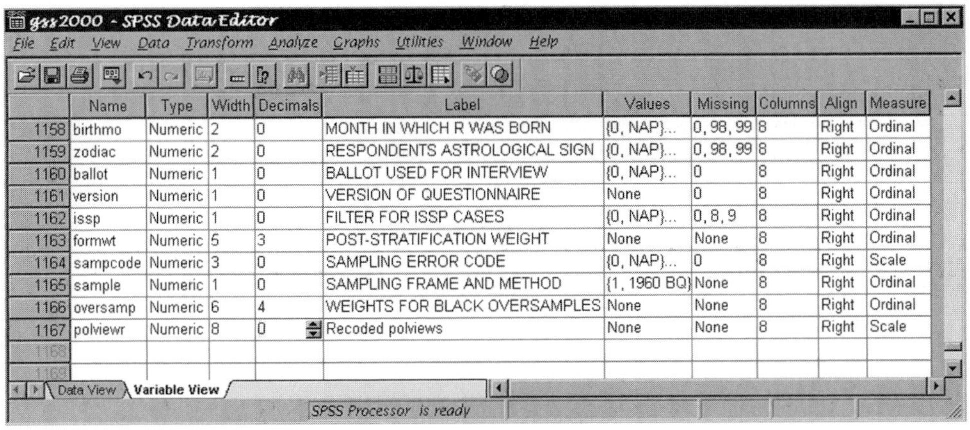

Figure D-37 Changing Decimals Format for *polviewr* in Variable View

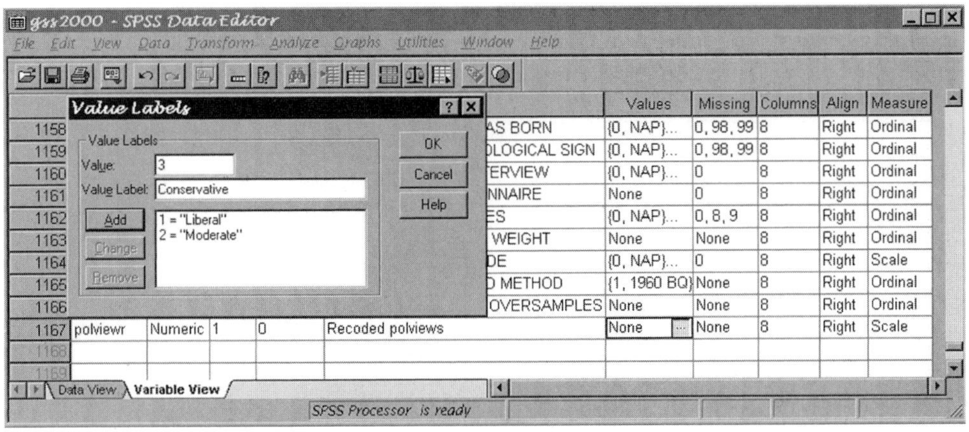

Figure D-38 Assigning Value Labels to *polviewr*

Now click on the right-hand side of the cell in the **Values** column and the *polviewr* row. A **Value Labels** dialog box will appear as shown in Figure D-38. Give the names to the new category values:

1. Type "1" in the **Value** field.
2. Type "Liberal" in the **Value Label** field.
3. Click the **Add** button.

Repeat the process to assign "Moderate" to the value of "2" and "Conservative" to "3," being sure to click **Add** each time. Just before you click **Add** the last time, the dialog box should look like Figure D-38. Click **Continue**, then **OK.**

Click then on the right-hand side of the cell in the **Missing** column and the *polviewr* row. The dialog box is shown in Figure D-39. Type 9 in the first space available under **Discrete Missing Values.** You have just indicated to SPSS that any value 9 in the data set for *polviewr* should be considered "missing answer" and removed from statistical computation.

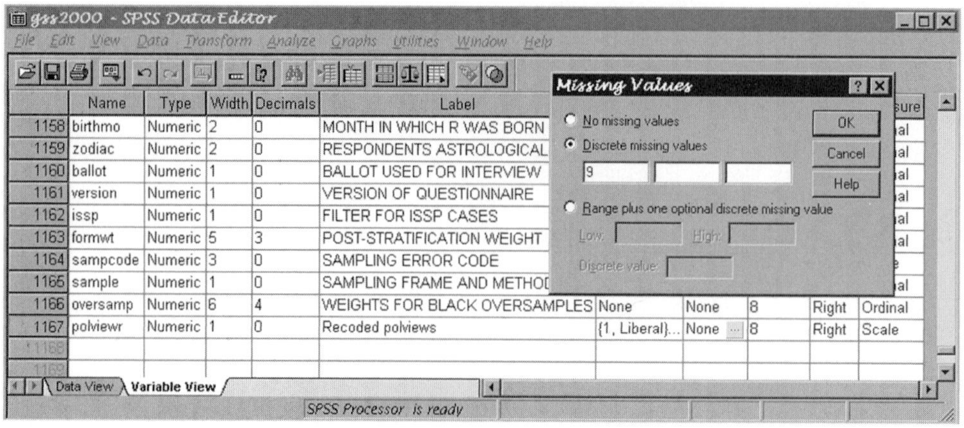

Figure D-39 Assigning Missing Values to *polviewr*

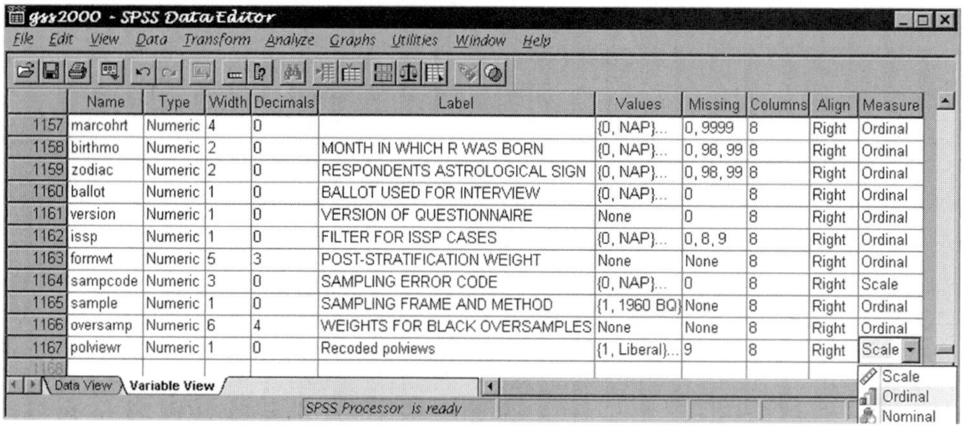

Figure D-40 Assigning Measurement Type to *polviewr*

Finally, you can change the measurement type for *polviewr* as shown in Figure D-40. We selected **Ordinal** for *polviewr* because the values can be ranked from low to high level of conservatism.

Now when you select **Analyze/Descriptive Statistics/Frequencies** and scroll through the list of variables, you'll find a new entry in the list: *polviewr*. Choose it to see the frequency distribution generated by our new categories (see Figure D-41).

Because we have gone to all this trouble to make our analysis simpler, let's see if it worked. Let's use *polviewr* to reexamine the relationship between political orientations and attitudes toward abortion. Use **Analyze/Descriptive Statistics /Crosstabs** to create a table with *abany* and *polviewr*. Figure D-42 illustrates what you should get.

Notice how much easier it is to read this table compared with the one in Figure D-27. We see that 55 percent of the liberals, 42 percent of the moderates, and 28 percent of the conservatives support a woman's right to an abortion for any reason. (It's good to round off the decimal points in percentages such as these because they're based on samples, which only provide estimates of populations in the first place.)

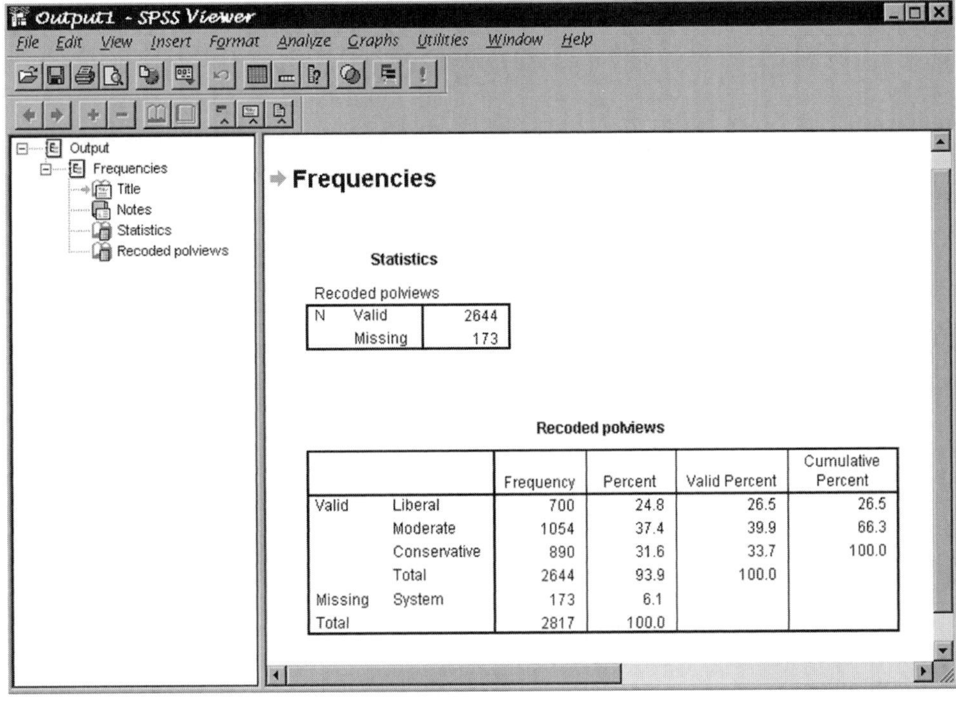

Figure D-41 Frequency Distribution for *polviewr*

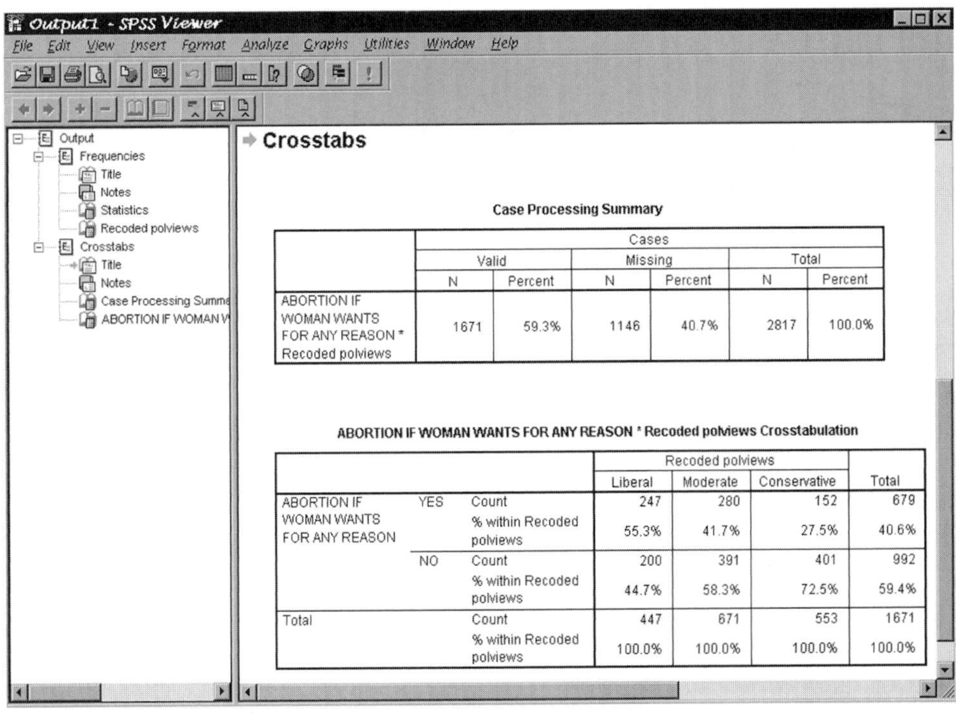

Figure D-42 Cross-Tabulation of *abany* and *polviewr*

MULTIVARIATE TABLES

Bivariate tables are typically only the beginning of quantitative data analysis. For example, you might want to see if the observed relationship between politics and abortion holds equally for men and women. SPSS makes it a simple matter to satisfy your curiosity about such matters.

Return to **Analyze/Descriptive Statistics/Crosstabs** and specify a third variable as shown in Figure D-43.

Notice that we've simply transferred the third variable, *sex,* into the bottom field in the dialog box. Press **OK** to see the result as illustrated in Figure D-44.

In a sense, this new table splits the one shown in Figure D-42 into two parts. The top half shows the relationship between *polviewr* and *abany* for men; the bottom half shows the same relationship for women. We can see immediately that the original relationship is replicated for each gender category.

In the far-right column, the summary statistics show the relationship between gender and support for abortion. Overall (i.e., forgetting about political orientations), an equal 41 percent for men and women support a woman's right to an abortion for any reason—an interesting similarity. (Notice that we've rounded off the figures, 40.5% and 40.8%, presented in the table.) It seems that there is no sex effect on *abany*. The sex of the respondent does not matter for this GSS question.

Comparing men and women in the other columns of the table tells us that sex has little impact regardless of a person's political orientation. Women are more supportive among liberals, men are slightly more supportive among moderates and among conservatives. None of the differences are very large, however.

SPSS allows you to go beyond trivariate tables, though they grow increasingly difficult to read and analyze. To experiment with this possibility, click the **Next** button near the bottom of the **Crosstabs** dialog box to add new **Layers** of variables to the table.

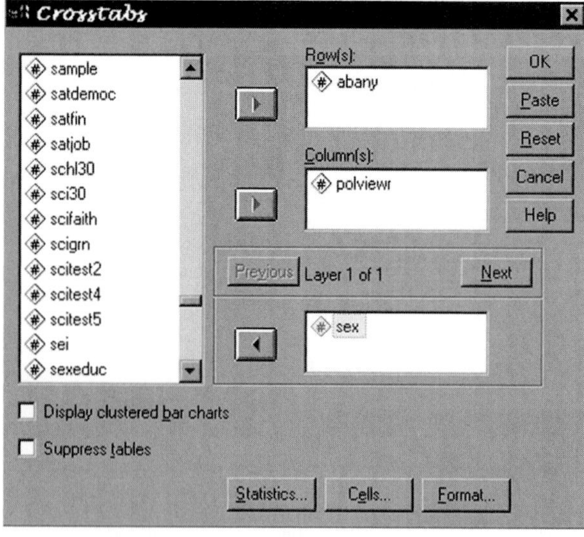

Figure D-43 Trivariate Table Request

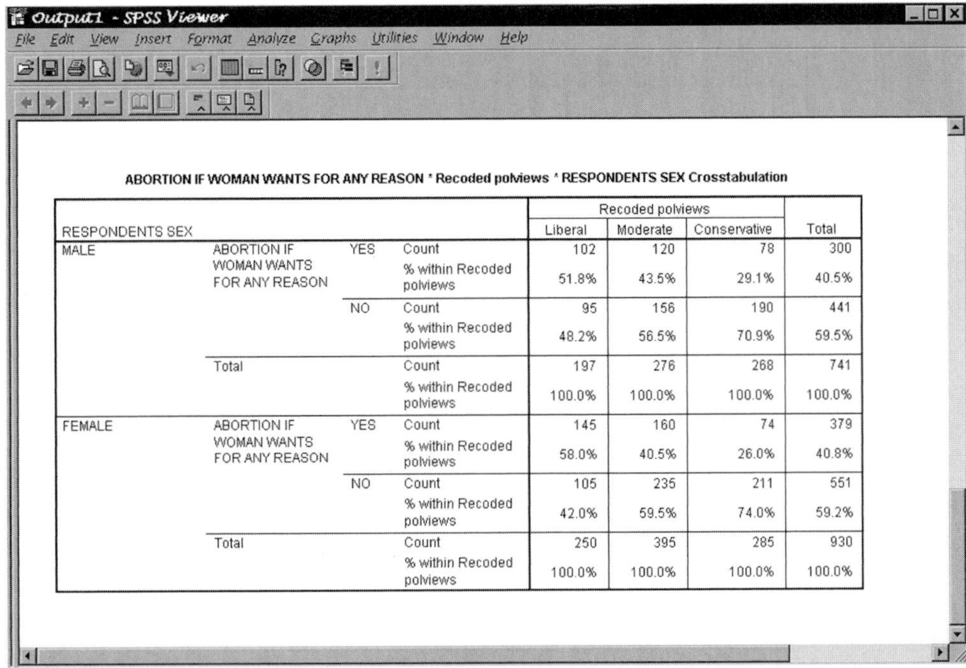

ABORTION IF WOMAN WANTS FOR ANY REASON * Recoded polviews * RESPONDENTS SEX Crosstabulation

RESPONDENTS SEX				Recoded polviews Liberal	Moderate	Conservative	Total
MALE	ABORTION IF WOMAN WANTS FOR ANY REASON	YES	Count	102	120	78	300
			% within Recoded polviews	51.8%	43.5%	29.1%	40.5%
		NO	Count	95	156	190	441
			% within Recoded polviews	48.2%	56.5%	70.9%	59.5%
	Total		Count	197	276	268	741
			% within Recoded polviews	100.0%	100.0%	100.0%	100.0%
FEMALE	ABORTION IF WOMAN WANTS FOR ANY REASON	YES	Count	145	160	74	379
			% within Recoded polviews	58.0%	40.5%	26.0%	40.8%
		NO	Count	105	235	211	551
			% within Recoded polviews	42.0%	59.5%	74.0%	59.2%
	Total		Count	250	395	285	930
			% within Recoded polviews	100.0%	100.0%	100.0%	100.0%

Figure D-44 Table of *abany* by *polviewr* by *sex*

TESTS OF STATISTICAL SIGNIFICANCE

In the previous example, we noted that the percentage differences were not very large. This was a subjective assessment of the substantive significance of the differences.

As you know from Chapter 21, tests of statistical significance can determine the likelihood that relationships observed in a sample are merely an artifact of sampling error rather than a reflection of a real difference in the population from which the sample was drawn. Let's take a look at how SPSS offers us the use of those tests.

Return to the **Crosstabs** dialog box via **Analyze/Descriptive Statistics.** At the bottom of the box, click a button marked **Statistics.** Figure D-45 illustrates the results.

As you can see, SPSS offers several summary statistics, several of which you may recognize from this textbook, especially chi-square, discussed in Chapter 22. Recall that chi-square is appropriate to nominal variables such as *abany* and *sex,* so let's use those variables to see how we can use SPSS to work with chi-square.

Click the **Chi-square** box. Then click **Continue** and enter *abany* and *sex* in the appropriate places in the **Crosstabs** dialog box. In addition to the regular percentage table, SPSS now provides an additional table, shown in Figure D-46.

If you've had a statistics course, you'll recognize many of the tests presented in this table. For our purposes, let's focus on the first row of the results, the Pearson Chi-Square. The third column tells us the probability that sampling error alone could have generated a relationship as strong as the one we've observed, if men and women in the whole population were exactly the same in their attitudes toward abortion. Specifically, it tells us that the probability is .972, or 97 chances in 100. This probability level is extremely high. Thus, the chi-square test confirms what we had concluded subjec-

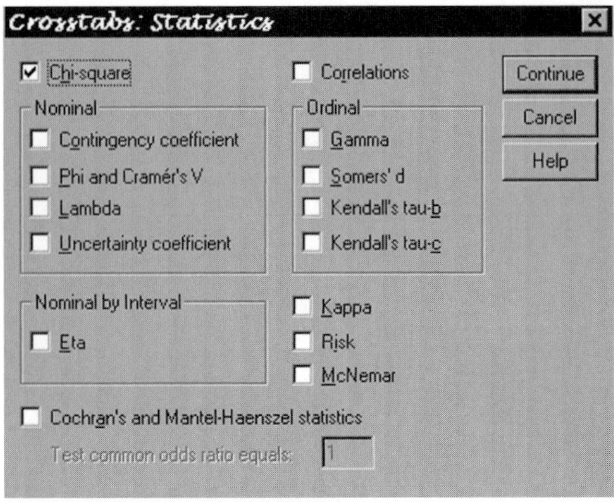

Figure D-45 Choice of Statistics in a Crosstabs Dialog Box

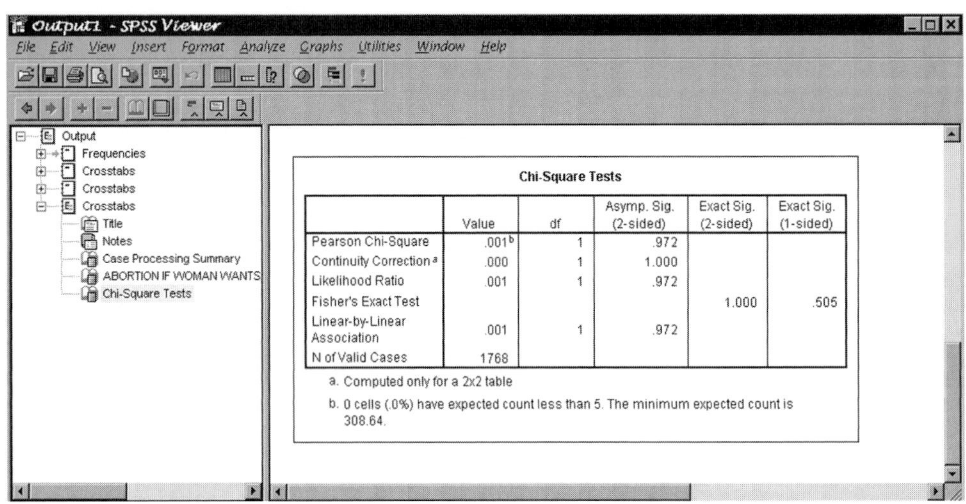

Chi-Square Tests

	Value	df	Asymp. Sig. (2-sided)	Exact Sig. (2-sided)	Exact Sig. (1-sided)
Pearson Chi-Square	.001[b]	1	.972		
Continuity Correction[a]	.000	1	1.000		
Likelihood Ratio	.001	1	.972		
Fisher's Exact Test				1.000	.505
Linear-by-Linear Association	.001	1	.972		
N of Valid Cases	1768				

a. Computed only for a 2x2 table

b. 0 cells (.0%) have expected count less than 5. The minimum expected count is 308.64.

Figure D-46 Chi-Square for *abany* and *sex*

tively from our cross-tabulations: Men and women do not differ at all in their support for a woman's right to an abortion.

The relationship between *abany* and *polviewr* was much stronger. Let's see how chi-square evaluates that relationship. Repeat the above procedure, changing *sex* to *polviewr.* Notice that you don't have to select **Chi-square** again, any more than you have to select **Columns.** SPSS maintains those specifications until you shut down the program. When you start it up again, you'll have to specify such preferences again. Of course, you can turn them off any time you no longer desire them.

See Figure D-47 for the chi-square evaluation of *abany* and *polviewr.* Notice that the significance in this case is calculated at .000. SPSS only presents the first three decimal points in this calculation. Hence, the likelihood of the observed relationship

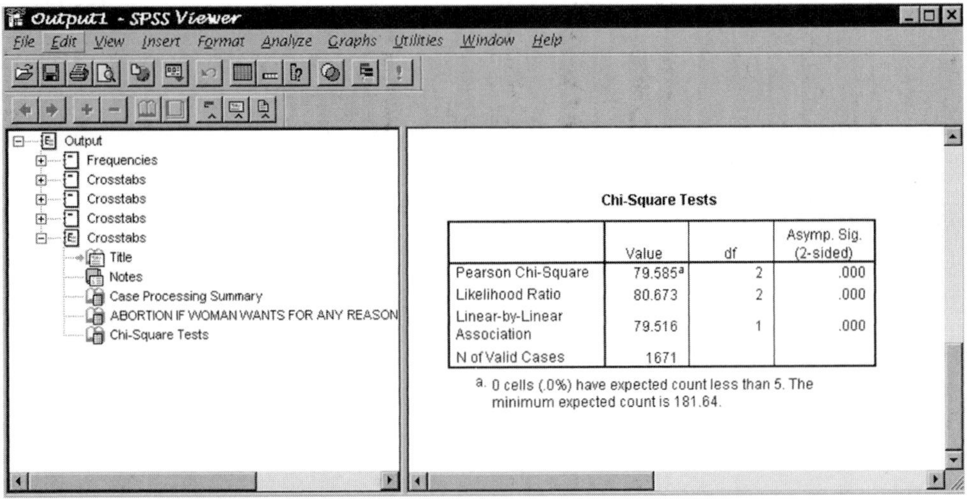

Chi-Square Tests

	Value	df	Asymp. Sig. (2-sided)
Pearson Chi-Square	79.585[a]	2	.000
Likelihood Ratio	80.673	2	.000
Linear-by-Linear Association	79.516	1	.000
N of Valid Cases	1671		

a. 0 cells (.0%) have expected count less than 5. The minimum expected count is 181.64.

Figure D-47 Chi-Square for *abany* and *polviewr*

being simply a product of sampling error isn't exactly zero—it could happen, but the chances are not very high that it did. Specifically, the probability is less than .001, or less than one chance in a thousand, which commonly indicates statistical significance. Thus, we conclude that the relationship we've observed in this carefully selected sample very likely represents something that exists in the larger population.

CORRELATION AND REGRESSION

Thus far we've been examining nominal and ordinal data. SPSS can also help you work with interval and ratio data.

For example, you may have heard that highly educated people tend to have fewer children than do those with less education. Let's use SPSS to see if it's so. In the GSS, these variables are *educ* and *childs*. Under **Analyze**, select **Correlate** and, when asked, **Bivariate.** (SPSS can undertake more complex correlational analyses, but we'll keep it simple for this introduction.) In the **Correlations** dialog box, select *educ* and *childs* and click **OK.** That will produce a correlation of −.210 (or a "negative correlation of .210") between the two variables. The negative correlation means that as the years of education increase, the number of children decreases.

Of course, this analysis cannot determine the causal direction, so we could also say that as the number of children increases, the amount of education completed decreases. Both interpretations make sense and probably apply in some cases. Some young people have to cut their educations short to accommodate the demands of parenthood, and those who keep going to school may have to delay parenthood and have fewer children once they get started.

Whatever the explanation for the relationship, SPSS informs us that the correlation is significant at the 0.01 level. In other words, sampling error could account for a correlation like this one less than once in a hundred times.

Although we entered only two variables in this analysis, SPSS will accept as many at a time as you want and will create a correlation matrix in which every variable is correlated with every other variable. Experiment with this possibility.

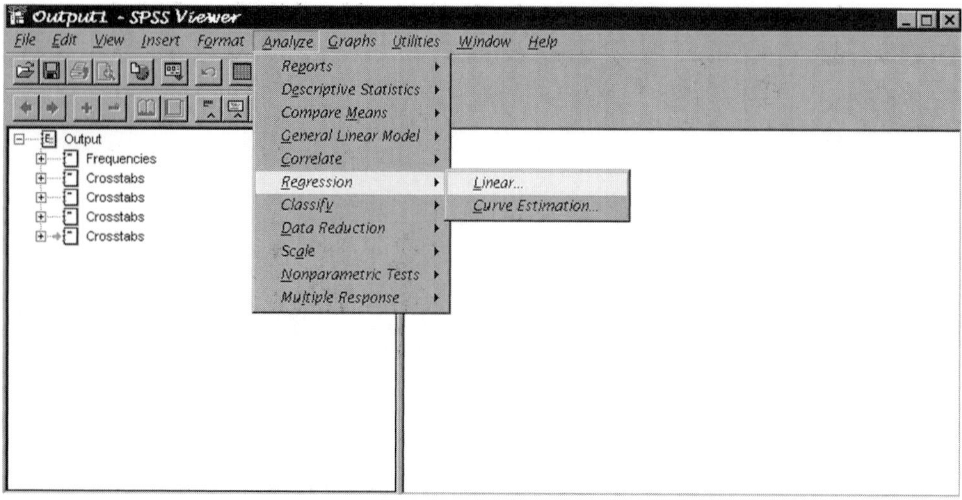

Figure D-48 Pearson's Product-Moment Correlation

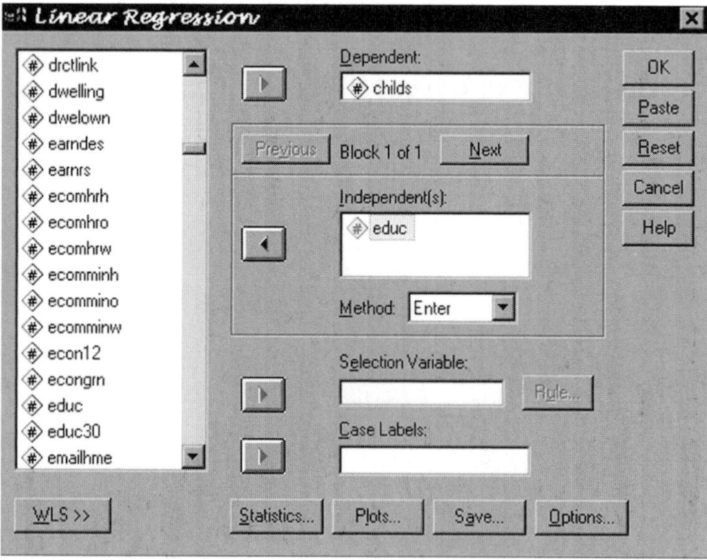

Figure D-49 Linear Regression Dialog Box

Regression analysis builds on the logic of correlation and creates equations that predict values of one variable based on values of others. Here's how we could represent the relationship between *childs* and *educ* as a regression equation. Under **Analyze,** select **Regression,** choosing **Linear** from among the alternatives offered, as illustrated in Figure D-48. This will present you with the dialog box presented in Figure D-49.

Let's use the logic of accounting for the number of children people have; thus, *childs* is our dependent variable, and *educ* is the independent variable we'll use to account for differences in numbers of children. Enter the two variables into the dialog box as shown in Figure D-49. Click **OK** to get the result shown in Figure D-50.

SPSS will present you with three tables of calculations, but we are only interested here in the third one, **Coefficients.** In fact, we're only interested in the first column of

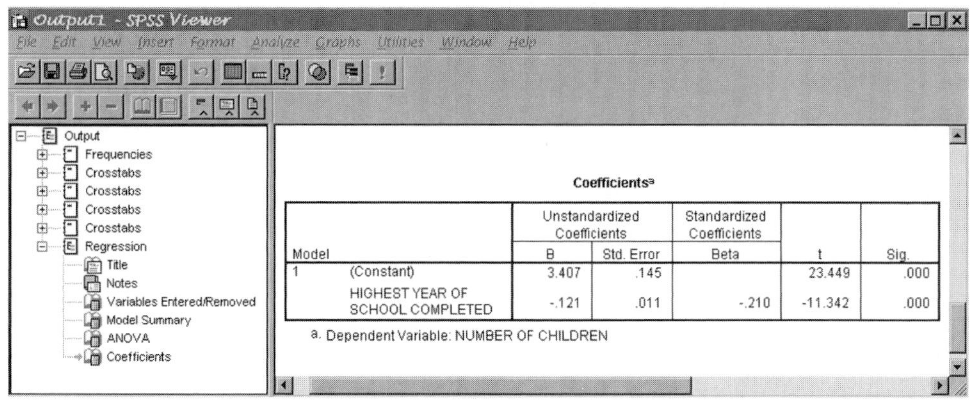

Coefficients[a]

Model		Unstandardized Coefficients		Standardized Coefficients	t	Sig.
		B	Std. Error	Beta		
1	(Constant)	3.407	.145		23.449	.000
	HIGHEST YEAR OF SCHOOL COMPLETED	-.121	.011	-.210	-11.342	.000

a. Dependent Variable: NUMBER OF CHILDREN

Figure D-50 Linear Regression Predicting *childs* with *educ*

this table, **Unstandardized Coefficients.** The first of these, the **Constant**, represents the value of the dependent variable (number of children) when the value of the independent variable (years of education) is zero. Statisticians sometimes refer to this as the *y*-intercept or the point where the line crosses the *y*-axis when the regression line is plotted on a graph.

The B value associated with the independent variable (−.121) indicates how much the dependent variable changes with each added unit of the independent variable. In our example, this means what change we should expect in the number of children for each added year of education. Stated as an equation, the regression looks like this:

$$childs = 3.407 - (.121 \times educ)$$

Suppose a person has 10 years of education. We would predict she or he has

$$3.407 - 1.21 = 2.197 \text{ children}$$

For college graduates with 16 years of education, we'd predict they have

$$3.407 - 1.936 = 1.471 \text{ children}$$

Clearly, these estimates represent statistical averages, because no one can have 2.197 or 1.471 children. Still, if you were to bet on the number of children people had and knew only their education, then this equation would be your best guide for betting. If you could make a lot of even-money bets on this basis, you'd be a winner overall.

To explore regression further, try adding another independent variable. SPSS will provide you with a new *y*-intercept and coefficients for each of the independent variables. Be sure to interpret positive and negative signs correctly.

CREATING INDEXES

Chapter 8 discussed the creation of composite measures such as indexes and scales. This section looks briefly at how to use SPSS to create a simple index.

Without reviewing the logic of index construction, let's create an index of sexual permissiveness including the following GSS variables:

premarsx: sex before marriage

xmarsex: sex with person other than spouse

homosex: homosexual relations

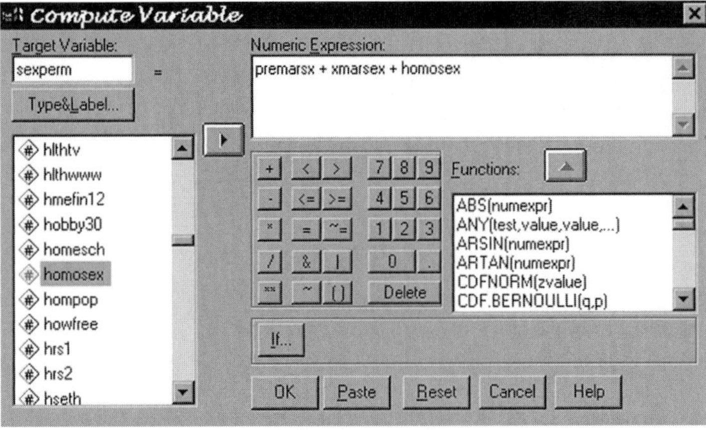

Figure D-51 Adding the Values of *premarsx*, *xmarsex*, and *homosex*

In each of these items, respondents were asked whether the action was:

1. Always wrong
2. Almost always wrong
3. Sometimes wrong
4. Not wrong at all

Given the format of these three items, we can create a composite index quite simply. Although the values 1–4 used to represent the answers to these questions are merely labels—just as we used "1" for male and "2" for female—we can in this case take advantage of their numerical quality. In each of these items, the higher the numerical code, the higher the level of sexual permissiveness. If we add the values respondents received on the three items, the possible totals range from 3 to 12, with 12 representing the highest and 3 the lowest degree of sexual permissiveness.

We can now use the **Transform/Compute** menu option to generate the index as illustrated in Figure D-51. Enter the information by typing or by selecting the variable names from the list and clicking the plus sign in the keypad provided in the dialog box (see Figure D-51).

When you're through, click **OK** in the dialog box. SPSS will create a new variable, *sexperm*, in your data set and will assign the appropriate values to each of the respondents. In the **Data** window, scroll to the far right and find the new variable in the last column. Scroll up and down to see the values assigned to respondents. Those with no values in the new column were missing data on the three items used to construct it.

For a more comprehensive view of the new variable, run the frequency distribution for *sexperm* (Figure D-52).

Having created a composite measure such as this one, it's always good to validate the scores if possible—that is, if the index scores truly distinguish levels of sexual permissiveness, then those scores should predict the answers people gave to other questions. For example, we might wonder if attitudes toward abortion are related to sexual permissiveness. We can find out by running a cross-tabulation of the index and, say, *abany*.

The result of this validation effort is presented in Figure D-53. Notice that this table uses a somewhat different format than those we've created earlier. Given the large num-

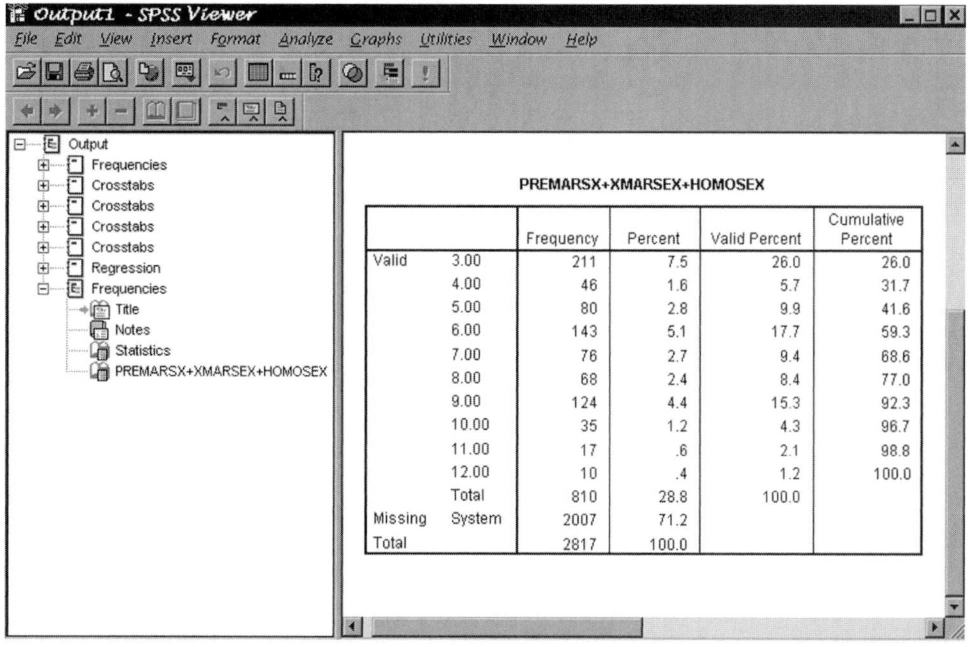

PREMARSX+XMARSEX+HOMOSEX

		Frequency	Percent	Valid Percent	Cumulative Percent
Valid	3.00	211	7.5	26.0	26.0
	4.00	46	1.6	5.7	31.7
	5.00	80	2.8	9.9	41.6
	6.00	143	5.1	17.7	59.3
	7.00	76	2.7	9.4	68.6
	8.00	68	2.4	8.4	77.0
	9.00	124	4.4	15.3	92.3
	10.00	35	1.2	4.3	96.7
	11.00	17	.6	2.1	98.8
	12.00	10	.4	1.2	100.0
	Total	810	28.8	100.0	
Missing	System	2007	71.2		
Total		2817	100.0		

Figure D-52 Frequency Distribution for *sexperm*

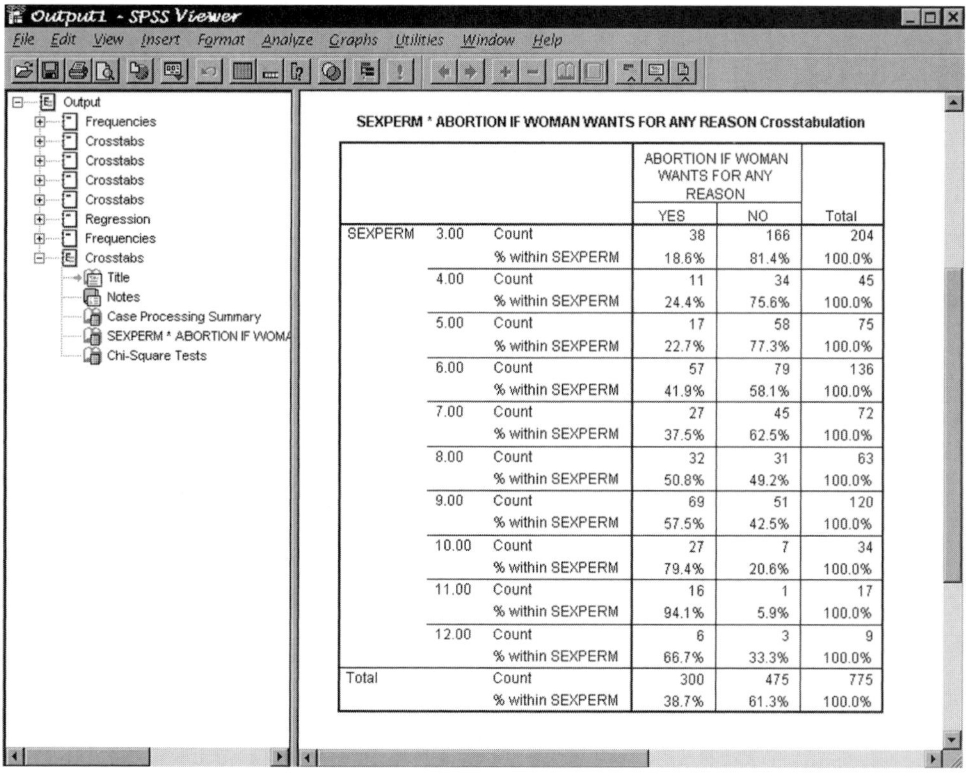

SEXPERM * ABORTION IF WOMAN WANTS FOR ANY REASON Crosstabulation

			ABORTION IF WOMAN WANTS FOR ANY REASON		
			YES	NO	Total
SEXPERM	3.00	Count	38	166	204
		% within SEXPERM	18.6%	81.4%	100.0%
	4.00	Count	11	34	45
		% within SEXPERM	24.4%	75.6%	100.0%
	5.00	Count	17	58	75
		% within SEXPERM	22.7%	77.3%	100.0%
	6.00	Count	57	79	136
		% within SEXPERM	41.9%	58.1%	100.0%
	7.00	Count	27	45	72
		% within SEXPERM	37.5%	62.5%	100.0%
	8.00	Count	32	31	63
		% within SEXPERM	50.8%	49.2%	100.0%
	9.00	Count	69	51	120
		% within SEXPERM	57.5%	42.5%	100.0%
	10.00	Count	27	7	34
		% within SEXPERM	79.4%	20.6%	100.0%
	11.00	Count	16	1	17
		% within SEXPERM	94.1%	5.9%	100.0%
	12.00	Count	6	3	9
		% within SEXPERM	66.7%	33.3%	100.0%
Total		Count	300	475	775
		% within SEXPERM	38.7%	61.3%	100.0%

Figure D-53 Validating the *sexperm* Index

ber of categories that constitute *sexperm*, it's difficult to fit the table on the computer screen (and in this book). Thus, we have made *sexperm* the row variable and *abany* the column variable and requested that the table be percentaged by row rather than column. Thus, we read this table "down" instead of "across" as in the earlier ones.

The relationship between these two variables is extremely strong and consistent. Of those with a score of 3 on the index (representing the lowest level of sexual permissiveness), only 19 percent support a woman's right to an abortion for any reason. This percentage increases steadily as index scores increase, reaching 67 percent among those with a score of 12 on the index.

Creating an index from variables that do not permit such a simple addition of code values is a little more involved. To illustrate, let's create an index of where respondents stand on the issue of guns. Two items in the GSS are relevant:

gunlaw: favor or oppose gun permits

1. Favor
2. Oppose

owngun: have gun in home

1. Yes
2. No

It makes sense that those who have a gun and oppose requiring permits for owning guns are the most progun, whereas those without a gun of their own and who favor gun permits would be the most antigun. Notice, however, that the progun position is represented by a "2" on *gunlaw* and a "1" on *owngun*. Thus, we can't simply add the values. Here's how to generate a simple index from these two items.

Let's create a new variable, *progun*, for which higher scores indicate greater support for guns. To start this process, return to **Transform/Compute.** Type in the **Target Variable** and give everyone a starting score of "0" as in Figure D-54. Click **OK** to create the variable. Then return to **Transform/Compute** and change the "0" to "progun + 1" as indicated in Figure D-55.

We're not going to add a point to everyone's index score, however. Click the **If** button near the bottom of the dialog box so we can specify the conditions under which we want to add a point. Next, click the button beside the phrase "Include if case satisfies condition." Then create the condition shown in Figure D-56. By doing this, we're

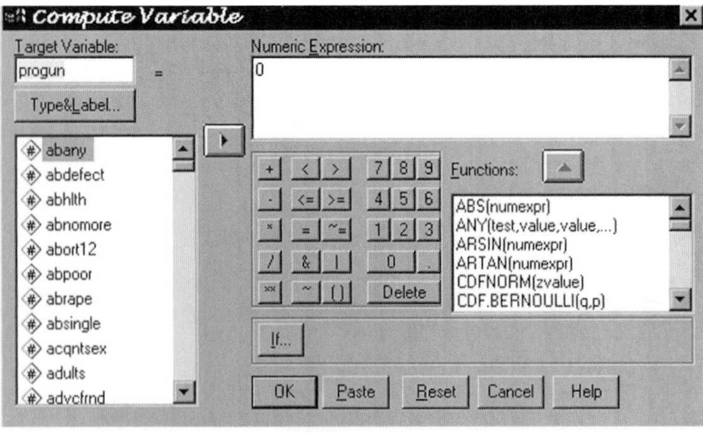

Figure D-54 Initializing *progun*

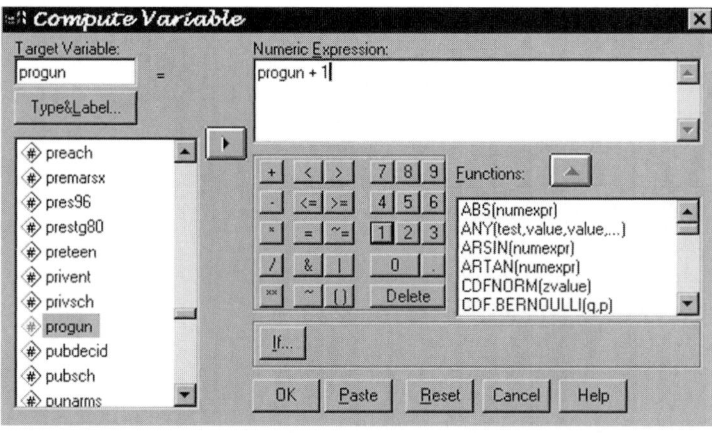

Figure D-55 Adding a Point to *progun*

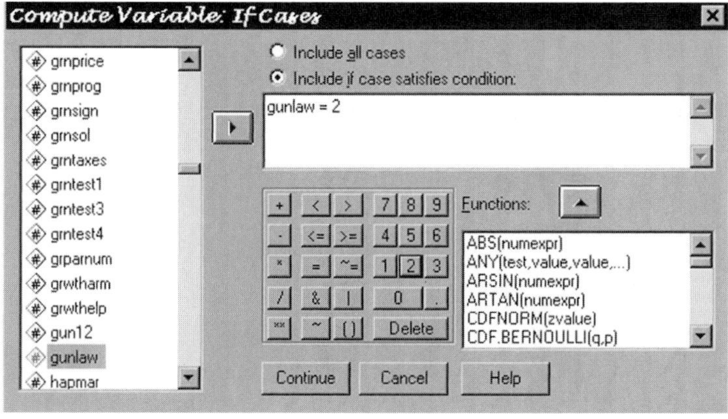

Figure D-56 Adding a Point for Opposing Gun Permits

telling SPSS to give an additional point to anyone who said they oppose gun permits (i.e., a "2" on *gunlaw*).

Click **Continue** to return to the earlier dialog box. Then click **OK** to instruct SPSS to take the action specified. When SPSS tells you that you're about to change an existing variable, say "Yes."

Select **Transform/Compute** again. Notice that the earlier instruction to add a point is still there. Leave it but click **If** to modify the condition. Change it to specify those who said they owned a gun ("1" on *owngun*) by indicating "*owngun* = 1" as the condition. Click **Continue**, then **OK**, and then "Yes" as before. Now those who had a score of 0 for favoring gun permits will get 1 point (for a total of "1") if they own a gun; they still have 0 points if they don't have a gun. Those who scored a point for opposing gun permits will get another point if they own a gun (a total of "2") but will stay at 1 point if they don't have a gun. The resulting index is made up of the scores "0," "1," and "2." There's only one problem with the index as it stands. Because everyone started with 0 points, those who didn't answer one or both of these questions will end up with a score of zero, thus seeming to oppose guns. The final step in creating this index involves culling out those with missing data.

First, let's create a "missing data" code. We'll use "99." Return to **Transform/Compute.** In the first dialog box, type "progun = 99." Click **If** to specify the condition: "MISSING(*gunlaw*)" as shown in Figure D-57. You need to first select the "MISSING (variable)" function and select gunlaw and click on the arrow. Click **Continue** and **OK**, then repeat the procedure for "MISSING(*owngun*)."

If you examine the response possibilities for *owngun,* however, you'll find that 23 people refused to answer and were coded "3." Return to **Transform/Compute** and assign an index value of 99 for anyone with "*owngun* = 3."

As a final step, we're going to recode the 99. Select **Transform/Recode,** but this time choose **Same Variables.** Once you reach the dialog box, convert the 99 to a **SYSMIS** as illustrated in Figure D-58. Enter 99 as the old value, click "System-missing," and then click the **Add** button.

To complete the action, click **Continue** and **OK.** The index is now complete. You can check it out by running **Analyze/Descriptive Statistics/Frequencies.** To reassure yourself further, run a cross-tabulation between the two items (*owngun* and *gunlaw*) to verify that the correct number of people received each of the scores on the *progun* index.

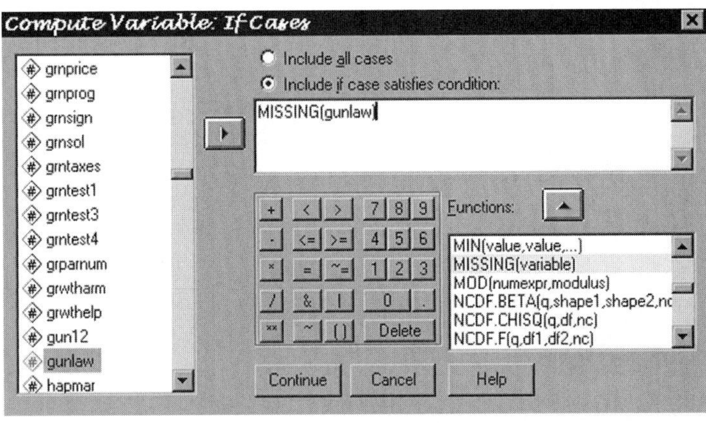

Figure D-57 Missing Data as a Condition

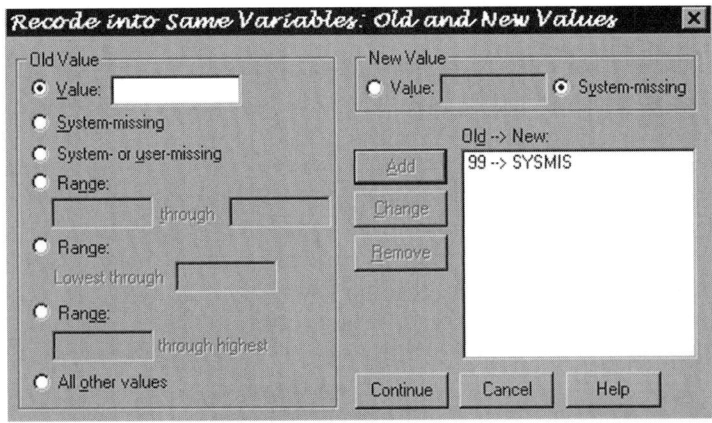

Figure D-58 Converting 99 to SYSMIS

GRAPHICS

With the improvement of computer graphics, SPSS now offers many options for presenting data in nontabular formats. Let's explore a few of these, beginning with simple frequency distributions.

Figure D-59 shows the dialog box for presenting the distribution of GSS data on religious affiliation (relig) as a pie chart. You can open this box by (1) selecting **Pie** under **Graphs**, (2) choosing **Summaries for Groups of Cases**, then (3) specifying *relig* as the variable to portray. Select "% of cases." Before clicking **OK**, click on the **Titles** button and type the title of your graph in the dialog box. Here we typed "Pie Chart of Religious Affiliation."

Figure D-60 shows the results of this operation. As you can see, the pie chart is small and refers to all religious categories. This pie chart is not very useful and requires some simple formatting. We need to collapse into one larger label all these slices that are too small to allow us to make sense of the graph.

Double-click on the graph in your Output window and a graph dialog box will appear. Select **Option** from the **Chart** menu. A **Pie Options** dialog box appears, as shown in Figure D-61. Select "Collapse (sum) slices less than 5%" (note that you can change this percentage if you want to include more categories under this new collapsed one). Under this same dialog box, select **Percents** so that the percentage of each slice is indicated on the graph. Click **OK** and close the **Chart Editor** window.

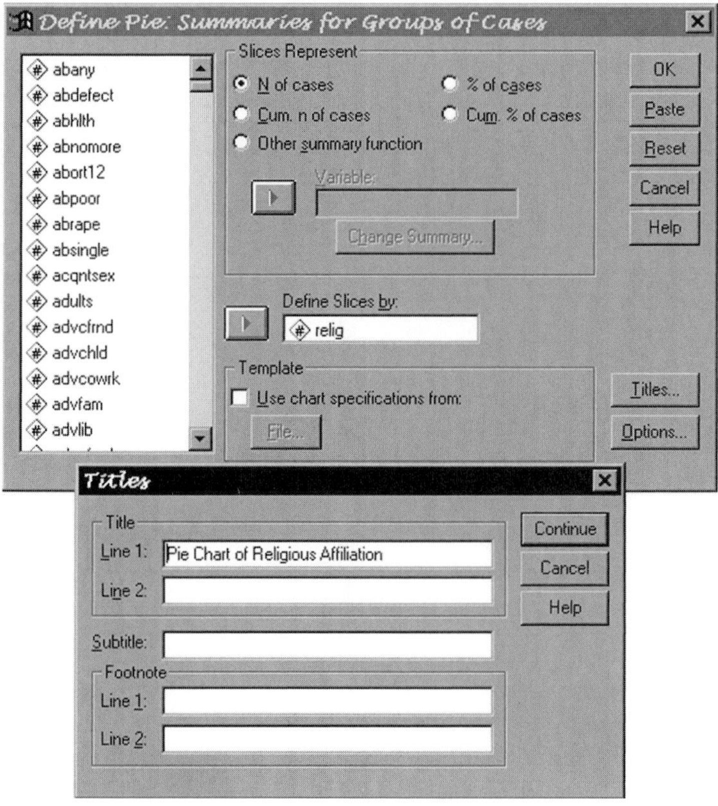

Figure D-59 Defining the Pie Chart of Religious Affiliation

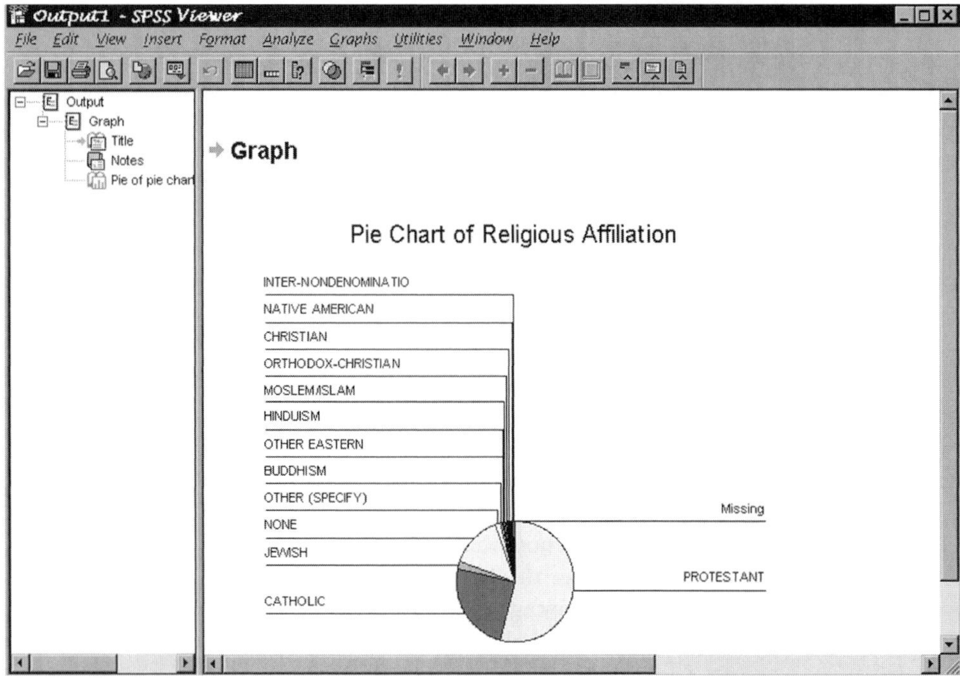

Figure D-60 Pie Chart of Religious Affiliation in Output Window

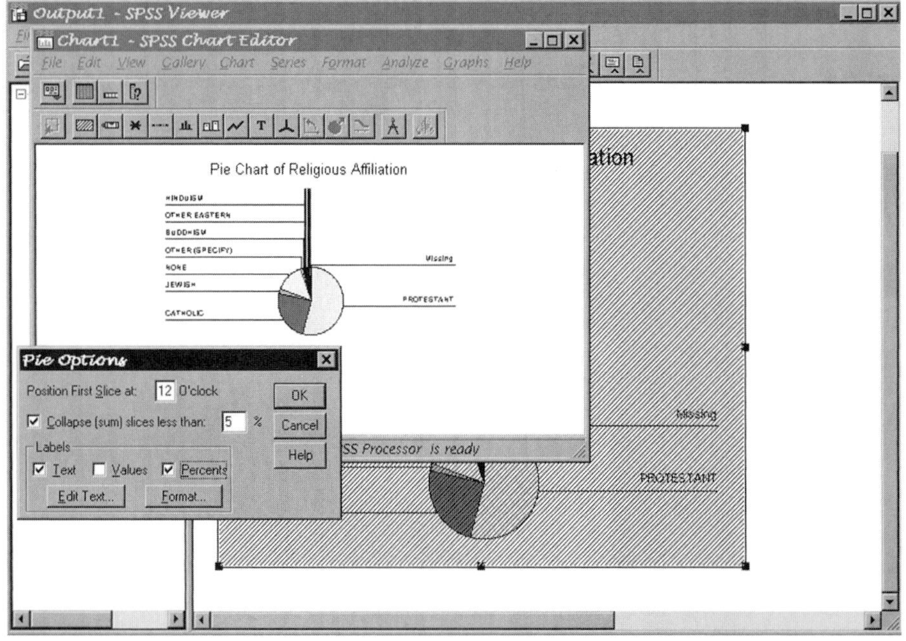

Figure D-61 Formatting the Pie Chart of Religious Affiliation

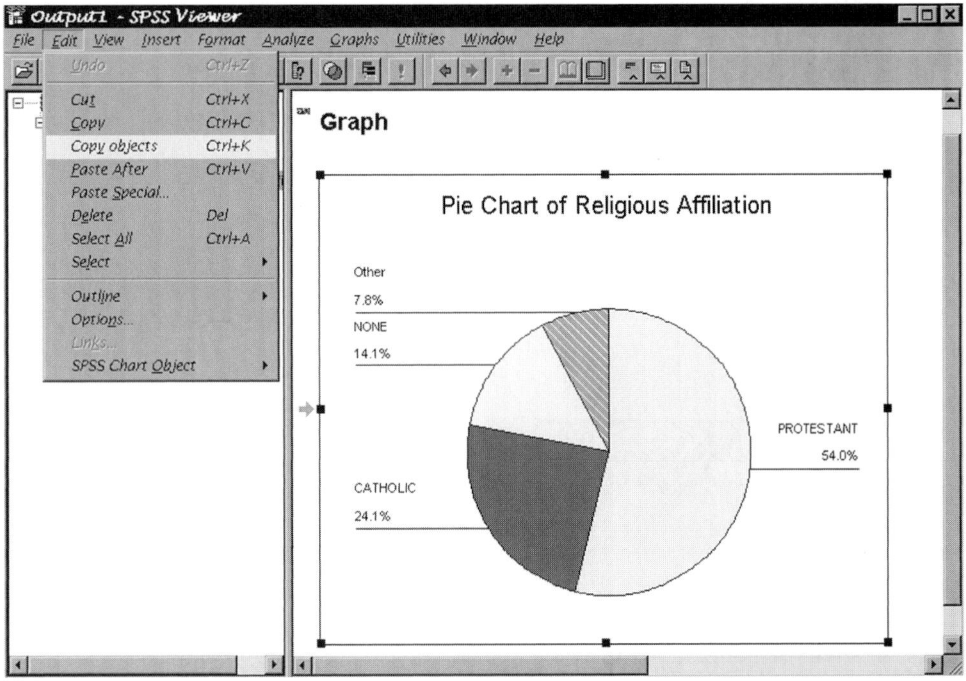

Figure D-62 Copying the Pie Chart of Religious Affiliation

Figure D-62 shows the result of this formatting procedure. Only the "Catholic," "None," and "Protestant" slices remain unchanged. All other categories are collapsed under the "Other" pie slice. There are many options to explore. Experiment on your own in order to polish statistical visual representations in your papers. When you are ready to import an SPSS graph to your paper, simply select this graph from the outline menu on the left side of the Output window. A frame around the graph will indicate that you have selected it. Then choose **Copy Objects** from the **Edit** menu. Open your Word document and paste the graph wherever you want.

If you're on a diet that rules out pies, see Figure D-63 for a bar graph of *relig*.

Ratio variables, such as the number of years of education, might be presented as line graphs. See Figure D-64.

These are just a few of the graphic options available to you in SPSS. Experiment with them to find the form of presentation most appropriate to your purposes.

MAKING COPIES OF RESULTS FOR A PAPER

Often, you will use SPSS to undertake quantitative analyses for a term paper, thesis, or other project. Although you can retype the results of SPSS into your paper, you can also take advantage of some energy-saving options. Depending on your word-processing system, you may have to experiment a bit.

As shown earlier, it is easy to copy and paste from SPSS outputs to Word documents. Simply make sure you have selected the objects you want to copy (a frame appears around them) and use the **Edit/Copy objects** command from SPSS and then **Paste** in the Word document of your choice.

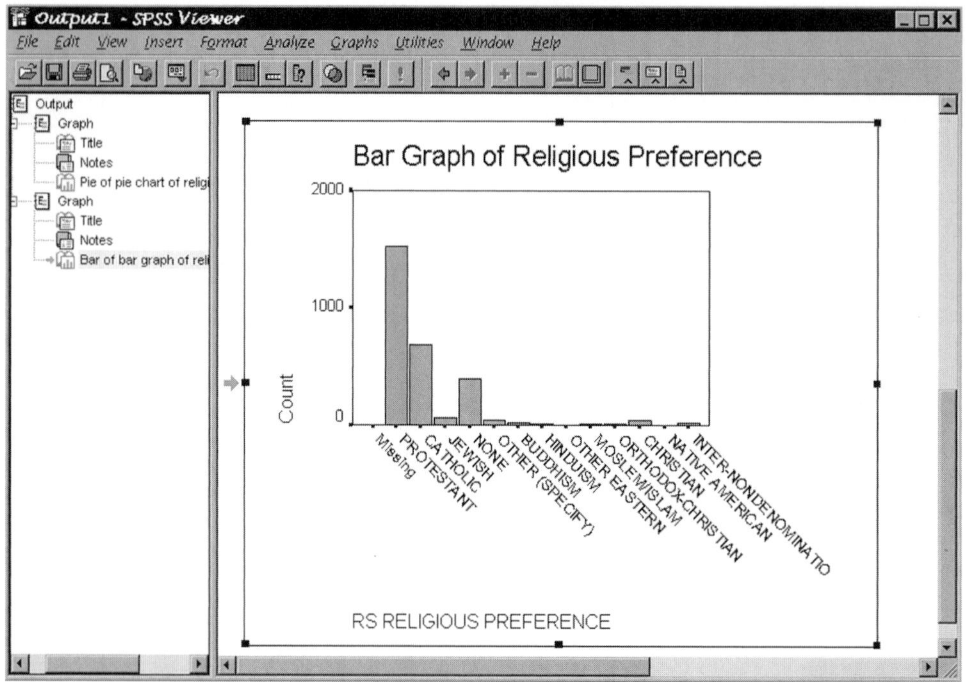

Figure D-63 Bar Graph of *relig*

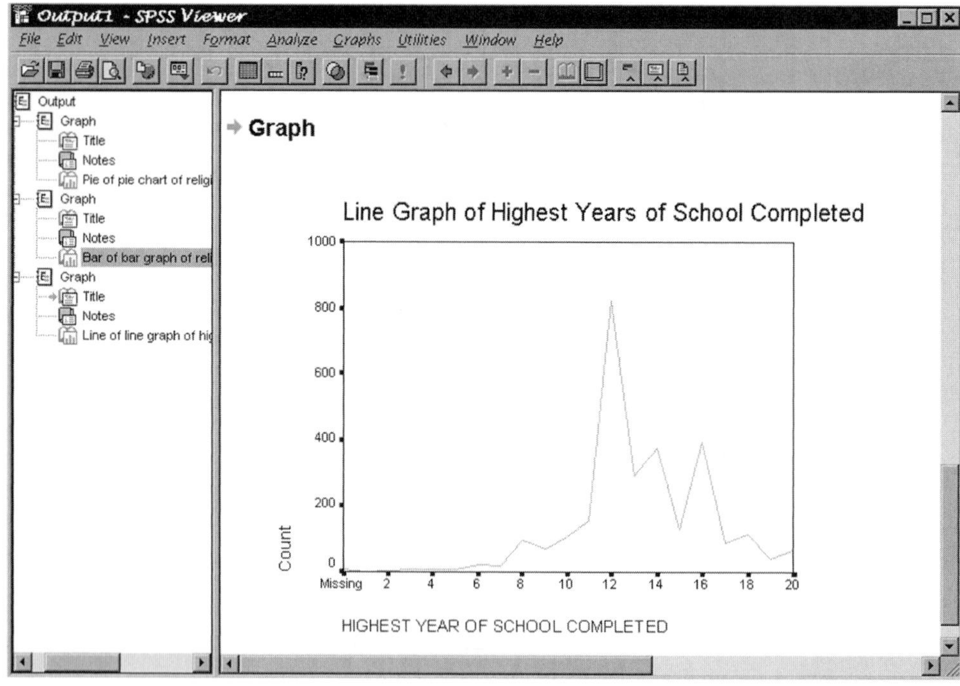

Figure D-64 Line Graph of *educ*

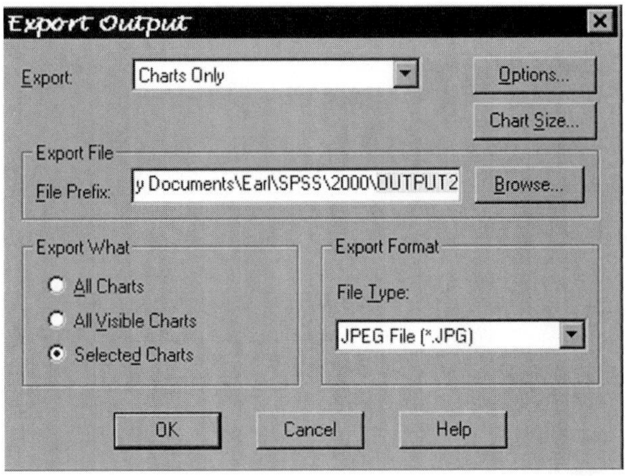

Figure D-65 Export Dialog Box

Though the easiest strategy is to copy and paste from SPSS to Word, you can also export your statistical results. To try making a hard copy of a graph, create the pie chart for *polviewr.* Click the resulting graph. As explained above, you'll see a box appear around it, indicating that it has been selected by the computer. Then in the **File** menu select **Export.** Figure D-65 illustrates the resulting dialog box.

You have several options here. You can export your output document with charts, without charts, or exclusively as the charts of your Output window. For our purposes, export the **Chart Only.** You can then either change the name of the export file you are going to create or accept (and remember) the name and location SPSS has proposed. Again, for present purposes, choose to export the **Selected Objects** and choose **JPEG File** (*.**JPG**) as the export format. Once you've done all this, click **OK.**

Run your word-processing system and open the document that desperately needs this table. Click where you want the graph and select **Picture** and then **From File** from the **Insert** menu (this procedure may be different if you are using another word processor than Microsoft Word). Browse your computer until you find your JPEG file. Remember to change the **Files of Type** option to **All Files** to view all documents and not exclusively Word documents.

To try making a hard copy of a table, create a frequency distribution for *gunlaw.* The same procedure you used to export graphs is possible if you choose to export tables. However, you will lose the formatting of the tables you export. We suggest that you choose the **Export Format HTML File** (*.**htm**) option. This format preserves the best layout of your tables with SPSS. Open your Word document and select **File** from the **Insert** menu and browse until you find your output file. You should be rewarded with something like the table in Figure D-66.

In all this, you may also want to take advantage of SPSS's multitude of table formats. To explore these, choose **Edit/Options** in SPSS and click on the **Pivot Tables** tab. Once there, click the various options under **TableLook** and SPSS will give you a sample layout in the field to the right of the list. If you find a format that interests you, leave it highlighted when you close the dialog box and then create a new table. It will be done in the format you've specified.

FAVOR OR OPPOSE GUN PERMITS					
		Frequency	Percent	Valid Percent	Cumulative Percent
Valid	FAVOR	1479	52.5	81.7	81.7
	OPPOSE	332	11.8	18.3	100.0
	Total	1811	64.3	100.0	
Missing	NAP	956	33.9		
	DK	46	1.6		
	NA	4	.1		
	Total	1006	35.7		
Total		2817	100.0		

Figure D-66 Text Version of *gunlaw* Frequency Distribution

SHUTTING DOWN

As much as you may come to love SPSS, you'll have to quit the program eventually. Go to the **File** menu and select **Exit.** SPSS will respond with a question that asks whether you want to save the **Output** file you've created. If you give it a name and a disk location for saving it, you'll be able to open it later on and retrieve any data created in your analyses. If you've just been practicing SPSS, then you'll probably want to say "No." If you've changed the data set—by creating a recoded variable, for example—SPSS will ask if you want to save the changes. Unless you want to get rid of the changes, say "Yes." However, you should only alter the data file if you have permission to do that.

If you're sharing a file with others in your class, for example, it may not be appropriate for you to save your changes. Discuss this with your instructor if in doubt.

SPSS will now close. And so this appendix ends. Have fun.

Glossary

AB design The simplest single-case evaluation design that includes one baseline phase (A) and one intervention phase (B). This is a popular design among practitioners and researchers because it involves only one baseline phase and therefore poses the least conflict with service delivery priorities. It has less control for history, however, than most alternative single-case evaluation designs. See Chapter 12.

ABAB withdrawal/reversal design A single-case evaluation design that adds a second baseline phase (A) and a second intervention phase (B). This design assumes that if the intervention caused the improvement in the target problem during the first intervention period, then the target problem will reverse toward its original baseline level during the second baseline. When the intervention is reintroduced, the target problem should start improving again. The basic inferential principle here is that if shifts in the trend or level of the target problem occur successively each time the intervention is introduced or withdrawn, then it is not plausible that history explains the change. See Chapter 12.

abstract A separate page at the beginning of a research proposal or report that briefly summarizes the proposed or completed study. See Chapter 23.

accidental sampling See *availability sampling.*

acculturation The process in which a group or individual changes after coming into contact with a majority culture, taking on its language, values, attitudes, and lifestyle preferences. See Chapter 5.

acquiescent response set A source of measurement error in which people agree or disagree with most or all statements regardless of their content. See Chapter 8.

agency tracking Asking service providers or other community agencies whether they have been in recent contact with research participants—particularly those who are transient or homeless—whom you are unable to locate and whom you need to contact for further sessions or interviews. See Chapter 5.

alternative treatment design with pretest An experiment that compares the effectiveness of two alternative treatments. Participants are assigned randomly to two experimental groups, each of which receives a different intervention being evaluated, and to a control group that does not receive any intervention. Each group is tested on the dependent variable before and after the experimental groups receive the intervention. See Chapter 11.

analysis of variance A form of data analysis in which the variance of a *dependent variable* is examined for the whole sample and for separate subgroups created on the basis of one or more independent variables. See Chapter 22.

anchor points Pieces of information about the various places you may be able to find particular research participants—particularly transient or homeless participants—for future follow-up sessions or interviews. See Chapter 5.

anonymity An arrangement that makes it impossible for a researcher to link any research data with a given research participant. Distinguished from *confidentiality,* in which the researcher is able to identify a given person's responses but essentially promises not to do so publicly. See Chapter 4.

anonymous enrollment A method of recruiting members of hidden and oppressed populations to participate in research studies; the method emphasizes techniques that enable prospective participants to feel safer in responding to recruitment efforts and participating in studies. See Chapter 5.

area probability sample A form of multistage *cluster sample* in which geographic areas such as census blocks or tracts serve as the first-stage sampling unit. Units selected in the first stage of sampling are then listed—all the households on each selected block would be written down after a trip to the block—and such lists would be subsampled. See Chapter 14.

assent form A brief *consent form* that a child can understand and sign before participating in a study; it uses simpler language than consent forms for adults about the features of the study that might affect their decision about whether they want to participate in it. See *consent form* and Chapter 4.

attributes Characteristics of persons or things. See *variables* and Chapters 3 and 7.

attrition A threat to the validity of an experiment that occurs when participants drop out of an experiment before it is completed. Also called *experimental mortality.* See Chapter 11.

auditing A strategy for improving the trustworthiness of qualitative research findings in which the researcher leaves a paper trail of field notes, transcripts of interviews, journals, and memos documenting decisions made along the way, and so on. This enables an impartial and qualitatively adept investigator who is not part of the study to scrutinize what was done in order to determine if efforts to control for biases and reactivity were thorough, if the procedures used were justifiable, and if the interpretations fit the data that were collected. See Chapter 17.

availability sampling A sampling method that selects elements simply because of their ready availability and convenience. Frequently used in social work because it is usually less expensive than other methods and because other methods may not be feasible for a particular type of study or population. See Chapter 14.

available records A source of data for a study, in which the information of concern already has been gathered by others. For example, an evaluation of a statewide dropout prevention program may use available school records on dropout rates. See Chapter 16.

average An ambiguous term that generally suggests typical or normal. *Mean, median,* and *mode* are specific examples of mathematical averages, or measures of central tendency. See Chapter 20.

back-translation A method used when translating instruments from one language into another. The steps are: (1) a bilingual person translates the instrument and its instructions to a target language, (2) another bilingual person translates from the target language back to the original language (not seeing the original version of the instrument), (3) the original instrument is compared to the back-translated version, and (4) items with discrepancies are further modified. See Chapter 5.

baseline The phase of a *single-case evaluation design* that consists of repeated measures before a new intervention or policy is introduced. See Chapter 12.

bias (1) That quality of a measurement device that tends to result in a misrepresentation of what is being measured in a particular direction. For example, the questionnaire item "Don't you agree that the president is doing a good job?" would be *biased* because it would generally encourage more favorable responses. See Chapters 8 and 9 for more on this topic. (2) The thing inside a person that makes other people or groups seem consistently better or worse than they really are.

binomial variable A variable that has only two attributes is binomial. "Gender" would be an example, having the attributes "male" and "female."

bivariate analysis The analysis of two variables simultaneously to determine the empirical relationship between them. The construction of a simple percentage table or the computation of a simple correlation coefficient would be examples of *bivariate analyses*. See Chapter 20.

CA See *conversation analysis.*

case-control design A design for evaluating interventions that compares groups of cases that have had contrasting outcomes and then collects retrospective data about past differences that might explain the difference in outcomes. It relies on multivariate statistical procedures. See Chapter 10.

case-oriented analysis An idiographic qualitative data analysis method that focuses on attempting to understand a particular case fully. See Chapter 19.

case study An idiographic examination of a single individual, family, group, organization, community, or society using a full variety of evidence regarding that case. See Chapter 17.

causal inference An inference derived from a research design and findings that logically imply that the independent variable really has a *causal* impact on the dependent variable. See Chapter 10.

census An enumeration of the characteristics of some population. A census is often similar to a survey, with the difference that the *census* collects data from *all* members of the population and the survey is limited to a sample. See Chapter 15.

chi-square A statistical significance test used when both the independent and dependent variables are nominal level. See Chapter 22.

client logs A qualitative or quantitative method that can be used as part of case studies or single-case evaluations in which clients keep journals of events that are relevant to their problems. See Chapter 17.

clinical significance The term used for substantive significance in clinical outcome studies. See also *substantive significance* and Chapter 21.

closed-ended questions Unlike in *open-ended questions,* the respondent is asked to select an answer from among a list provided by the researcher. See Chapter 9.

cluster sample A sample drawn using *cluster sampling* procedures. See Chapter 14.

cluster sampling A multistage sampling procedure in which natural groups (clusters) are sampled initially, with the members of each selected group being subsampled afterward. For example, we might select a sample of U.S. colleges and universities from a directory, get lists of the students at all the selected schools, and then draw samples of students from each. This procedure is discussed in Chapter 14.

codebook The document used in data processing and analysis that tells the location of different data items in a data file. Typically, the *codebook* identifies the locations of data items and the meaning of the codes used to represent different attributes of variables. See Chapter 20.

coding The process whereby raw data are transformed into a standardized form that is suitable for machine processing and analysis. See Chapters 19 and 20.

coefficient alpha A statistic for depicting the *internal consistency reliability* of an instrument; it represents the average of the correlations between the subscores of all possible subsets of half of the items on the instrument. See Chapter 8.

cohort study A study in which some specific group is studied over time, although data may be collected from different members in each set of observations. For example, a study of the professional careers of students earning their social work degrees in 1990, in which questionnaires were sent every five years, would be a cohort study. See Chapter 6.

community forum An approach to *needs assessment* that involves holding a meeting where concerned members of the community can express their views and interact freely about their needs. See Chapter 13.

compensatory equalization A threat to the validity of an evaluation of an intervention's effectiveness that occurs when practitioners in the comparison routine-treatment condition compensate for the differences in treatment between their group and the experimental group by providing enhanced services that go beyond the routine-treatment regimen for their clients, thus potentially blurring the true effects of the tested intervention. See Chapter 11.

compensatory rivalry A threat to the validity of an evaluation of an intervention's effectiveness that occurs when practitioners in the comparison routine-treatment condition decide to compete with the therapists in the other unit. They may start reading more, attending more continuing education workshops, and increasing their therapeutic contact with clients. Their extra efforts might improve their effectiveness and thus blur the true effects of the tested intervention. See Chapter 11.

computer-assisted personal interviewing (CAPI) Interviewing face-to-face by reading questions from a computer screen and immediately entering responses into the computer. See Chapter 15.

computer-assisted self-interviewing (CASI) A research worker brings a computer to the respondent's home, and the respondent reads questions on the computer screen and enters his or her own answers. See Chapter 15.

computer-assisted telephone interviewing (CATI) Interviewing over the phone by reading questions from a computer screen and immediately entering responses into the computer. See Chapter 15.

computerized self-administered questionnaire (CSAQ) The respondent receives the questionnaire via floppy disk, bulletin board, or other means and runs the software, which asks questions and accepts the respondent's answers. The respondent then returns the data file. See Chapter 15.

concept A mental image that symbolizes an idea, an object, an event, or a person. See Chapter 3.

concept mapping A qualitative data analysis method in which relationships among concepts are examined and diagrammed in a graphical format. See Chapter 19.

conceptual equivalence Instruments and observed behaviors having the same meanings across cultures. See Chapter 5.

conceptualization The mental process whereby fuzzy and imprecise notions (*concepts*) are made more specific and precise. So you want to study prejudice. What do you mean by "prejudice"? Are there different kinds? What are they? See Chapter 7.

concurrent validity A form of *criterion-related validity* examining a measure's correspondence to a criterion that is known concurrently. See Chapter 8.

confidence interval The range of values within which a population parameter is estimated to lie. A survey, for example, may show 40 percent of a sample favoring candidate A (poor devil). Although the best estimate of the support existing among all voters would also be 40 percent, we would not expect it to be exactly that. We might, therefore, compute a *confidence interval* (for example, from 35 to 45 percent) within which the actual percentage of the population probably lies. Note that it's necessary to specify a *confidence level* in connection with every *confidence interval*. See Appendix B.

confidence level The estimated probability that a population parameter lies within a given *confidence interval*. Thus, we might be 95 percent confident that between 35 and 45 percent of all voters favor candidate A. See Appendix B.

confidentiality A promise by the researcher not to publicly identify a given research participant's data. Distinguished from *anonymity*, which makes it impossible for a researcher to link any research data with a given research participant. See Chapter 4.

consent form A form that human subjects sign before participating in a study that provides full information about the features of the study that might affect their decision about whether to participate—particularly regarding its procedures, potential harm, and *anonymity* and *confidentiality*. See Chapter 4.

constant comparative method A qualitative data analysis method in which the researcher looks for patterns in inductive observations, develops concepts and working hypotheses based on those patterns, seeks out more cases and conducts more observations, and then compares those observations against the concepts and hypotheses developed from the earlier observations. The selection of new cases is guided by theoretical sampling concepts in which new cases are selected that seem to be similar to those generated by previously detected concepts and hypotheses. Once the researcher perceives that no new insights are being generated from the observation of similar cases, a different type of case is selected and the same process is repeated. Additional cases similar to this new type of case are selected until no new insights are being generated. This cycle of exhausting similar cases and then seeking a different category of cases is repeated until the researcher believes that further seeking of new types of cases will not alter the findings. See Chapter 19.

construct validity The degree to which a measure relates to other variables as expected within a system of theoretical relationships and as reflected by the degree of its convergent validity and discriminant validity. See also *convergent validity, discriminant validity*, and Chapter 8.

content analysis A research method for studying virtually any form of communication, consisting primarily of coding and tabulating the occurrences of certain forms of content that are being communicated. See Chapter 16.

content validity The degree to which a measure covers the range of meanings included within the concept. See Chapter 8.

contingency question A survey question that is to be asked of only some of the respondents, depending on their responses to some other question. For example, all respondents might be asked whether they belong to the Cosa Nostra, and only those who said yes would be asked how often they go to company meetings and picnics. The latter would be a *contingency question*. See Chapter 9 for illustrations of this topic.

contingency table Any table format for presenting the *relationships* among variables in the form of percentage distributions. See Chapter 20.

control group In experimentation, a group of participants who do *not* receive the intervention being evaluated and who should resemble the *experimental group* in all other respects. The comparison of the control and experimental groups at the end of the experiment points to the effect of the tested intervention. See Chapter 11.

control variable A variable that is held constant in an attempt to further clarify the relationship between two other variables. Having discovered a relationship between education and prejudice, for example, we might hold gender constant by examining the relationship between education and prejudice among men only and then among women only. In this example, "gender" would be the *control variable*. See Chapter 10 to see the importance of the proper use of control variables in analysis.

convenience sampling See *availability sampling*.

convergent validity The degree to which scores on a measure correspond to scores of other measures of the same construct. See also *construct validity, discriminant validity*, and Chapter 8.

conversation analysis (CA) A qualitative data analysis approach that aims to uncover the implicit assumptions and structures in social life through an extremely close scrutiny of the way we converse with one another. See Chapter 19.

cost–benefit analysis An assessment of program efficiency in which an attempt is made to monetize the benefits associated with a program's outcome and thus see if those monetary benefits exceed program costs. See Chapter 13.

cost-effectiveness analysis An assessment of program efficiency in which the only monetary considerations are the costs of the program; the monetary benefits of the program's effects are not assessed. Cost-effectiveness analysis looks at the cost per unit of outcome without monetizing the outcome. See Chapter 13.

criterion-related validity The degree to which a measure relates with some external criterion. For example, the validity of the college board exam is shown in its ability to predict the college success of students. See *known groups validity, concurrent validity, predictive validity,* and Chapter 8.

critical region Those values in the statistically significant zone of a theoretical sampling distribution. See Chapter 21.

critical social science A *paradigm* distinguished by its focus on oppression and its commitment to use research procedures to empower oppressed groups. See Chapter 3.

cross-case analysis A qualitative data analysis method that is an extension of *case-oriented analysis,* in which the researcher turns to other subjects, looking into the full details of their lives as well but paying special note to the variables that seemed important in the first case. Some subsequent cases will closely parallel the first one in the apparent impact of particular variables. Other cases will bear no resemblance to the first. These latter cases may require the identification of other important variables, which may invite the researcher to explore why some cases seem to reflect one pattern whereas others reflect another. See *case-oriented analysis* and Chapter 19.

cross-sectional study A study based on observations that represent a single point in time. Contrasted with a *longitudinal study.* See Chapter 10.

cultural bias A source of measurement error or *sampling error* stemming from researcher ignorance or insensitivity regarding how cultural differences can influence measurement or generalizations made to the entire population when certain minority groups are inadequately represented in the sample. A measurement procedure is culturally biased when it is administered to a minority culture without adjusting for the ways in which the minority culture's unique values, attitudes, lifestyles, or limited opportunities alter the accuracy or meaning of what is really being measured. See Chapters 5 and 8.

cultural competence A researcher's ability to obtain and provide information that is relevant, useful, and valid for minority and oppressed populations. Cultural competence involves knowledge about the minority culture's historical experiences, traditions, values, family systems, socioeconomic issues, and attitudes about social services and social policies; awareness of how one's own attitudes are connected to one's own cultural background and how they may differ from the worldview of members of the minority culture; and skills in communicating effectively both verbally and nonverbally with members of the minority culture and establishing rapport with them. See Chapter 5.

culturally competent research Being aware of and appropriately responding to the ways in which cultural factors and cultural differences should influence what we investigate, how we investigate, and how we interpret our findings—thus resulting in studies that are useful and valid for minority and oppressed populations. See Chapter 5.

curvilinear relationship A relationship between two variables that changes in nature at different values of the variables. For example, a curvilinear relationship might exist between amount of social work practice experience and practice effectiveness, particularly if we assume that practitioners with a moderate amount of experience are more effective than those with none and at least as effective as those nearing retirement. See Chapter 7.

deduction The logical model in which specific expectations of *hypotheses* are developed on the basis of general principles. Starting from the general principle that all deans are meanies, you might anticipate that Dean Moe won't let you change courses. That anticipation would be the result of *deduction.* See also *induction* and Chapter 3.

dependent variable That variable that is assumed to depend on, or be caused by, another (called the *independent variable*). If you find that income is partly a function of amount of formal education, then income is being treated as a *dependent variable.* See Chapter 3.

descriptive statistics Statistical computations that describe either the characteristics of a sample or the relationship among variables in a sample. *Descriptive statistics* merely summarize a set of sample observations, whereas *inferential statistics* move beyond the description of specific observations to make inferences about the larger population from which the sample observations were drawn. See Chapter 20.

deviant case sampling A type of *nonprobability sampling* in which cases selected for observation are those that are not thought to fit the regular pattern. For example, the deviant cases might exhibit a much greater or lesser extent of something. See Chapters 14 and 17.

dichotomous variable A variable that has only two categories. See also *binomial variable.*

diffusion (or imitation) of treatments A threat to the validity of an evaluation of an intervention's effectiveness that occurs when practitioners who are supposed to provide routine services to a comparison group implement aspects of the experimental group's intervention in ways that tend to diminish the planned differences in the interventions received by the groups being compared. See Chapter 11.

dimension A specifiable aspect or facet of a concept.

direct behavioral observation A source of data, or type of data collection, in which researchers watch what people do rather than rely on what they say about themselves or what others say about them. See Chapters 7 and 8.

direct observation A way to operationally define variables based on observing actual behavior. See also *direct behavioral observation* and Chapters 7 and 8.

discriminant validity The degree to which scores on an instrument correspond more highly to measures of the same construct than they do to scores on measures of other constructs. See also *convergent validity, construct validity,* and Chapter 8.

dismantling studies Experiments designed to test not only whether an intervention is effective, but also which components of the intervention may or may not be necessary to achieve its effects. Participants are assigned randomly to groups that either receive the entire intervention package, separate components of it, or a control condition, and are tested on a *dependent variable* before and after the intervention components are provided. See Chapter 11.

dispersion The distribution of values around some central value such as an *average.* The *range* is a simple example of a measure of *dispersion.* Thus, we may report that the *mean* age of a group is 37.9, and the range is from 12 to 89. See Chapter 20.

disproportionate stratified sampling A sampling method aimed at ensuring that enough cases of certain minority groups are selected to allow for subgroup comparisons within each of those minority groups. See Chapters 5 and 14.

distorter variable A variable that, when controlled in a multivariate analysis, shows that the direction of a bivariate relationship reverses. For example, a relationship that originally was negative might become positive or vice versa. See Chapter 10.

double-barreled question Asking for a single answer to a question that really contains multiple questions; for example, "Should taxes be raised so welfare funding can be increased? See Chapter 9.

ecological fallacy Erroneously drawing conclusions about individuals based solely on the observation of groups. See Chapter 6.

effect size A statistic that portrays the strength of association between variables. Effect-size statistics might refer to various measures of proportion of dependent variable variation explained or specifically to the difference between the means of two groups divided by the standard deviation. The latter is usually called the effect size, ES, or Cohen's *d*. See Chapter 21 and Appendix C.

elaboration model A way to better understand the meaning of a relationship (or lack of a relationship) between two variables; done by examining multivariate frequency tables to study the effects on the original bivariate relationship that are produced by introducing additional variables into the tables. See Chapter 10.

element That unit in a sample about which information is collected and that provides the basis of analysis. Typically, in survey research, elements are people or certain types of people. See Chapter 14.

emic perspective Trying to adopt the beliefs, attitudes, and other points of view shared by the members of the culture being studied. See Chapter 18.

empirical support Observations that are consistent with what we would expect to experience if a theory is correct or an intervention is effective. See Chapters 1, 2, and 3.

EPSEM See *equal probability of selection method.*

equal probability of selection method (EPSEM) A sample design in which each member of a population has the same chance of being selected into the sample. See Chapter 14.

ES See *effect size.*

ethnocentrism The belief in the superiority of one's own culture. See Chapter 5.

ethnography A qualitative research approach that focuses on providing a detailed and accurate description of a culture from the viewpoint of an insider rather than the way the researcher understands things. See Chapter 17.

etic perspective Maintaining objectivity as an outsider and raising questions about the culture being observed that wouldn't occur to members of that culture. See Chapter 18.

evidence-based practice Using the best scientific evidence available in deciding how to intervene with individuals, families, groups, or communities. See Chapter 2.

existing statistics analysis Research involving the analysis of statistical information in official government or agency documents and reports. See Chapter 16.

experimental demand characteristics Research participants learn what experimenters want them to say or do, and then they cooperate with those "demands" or expectations. See Chapter 11.

experimental design A research method that attempts to provide maximum control for threats to *internal validity* by: (1) randomly assigning individuals to experimental and control groups, (2) introducing the *independent variable* (which typically is a program or intervention method) to the experimental group while withholding it from the control group, and (3) comparing the amount of experimental and control group change on the *dependent variable.* See Chapter 11.

experimental group In experiments, a group of participants who receive the intervention being evaluated and who should resemble the control group in all other respects. The comparison of the experimental group and the control group at the end of the experiment points to the effect of the tested intervention. See Chapter 11.

experimental mortality A threat to the validity of an experiment that occurs when participants drop out of an experiment before it is completed. Also called *attrition.* See Chapter 11.

experimenter expectancies Research participants learn what experimenters want them to say or do, and then they cooperate with those "demands" or expectations. See Chapter 11.

explanation (in the *elaboration model*) One possible result in the elaboration model that occurs when an original bivariate relationship is explained away as *spurious*—that is, two variables that were related in a *bivariate analysis* are no longer related when one or more *extraneous variables* are controlled for in a multivariate analysis. See *elaboration model* and Chapter 10.

external evaluators Program evaluators who do not work for the agency being evaluated but instead work for external agencies such as government or regulating agencies, private research consultation firms, or universities. See Chapter 13.

external validity Refers to the extent to which we can generalize the findings of a study to settings and populations beyond the study conditions. See Chapter 10.

extraneous variable See *control variable.*

face validity That quality of an indicator that makes it seem a reasonable measure of some variable. That the frequency of church attendance is some indication of a person's religiosity seems to make sense without a lot of explanation: It has *face validity.* See Chapter 8.

factor analysis A statistical procedure that identifies which subsets of variables or items on a scale correlate with each other more than with other subsets. In so doing, it identifies how many dimensions a scale contains and which items cluster on which dimensions. See Chapter 8.

factorial validity Whether the number of constructs and the items that make up those constructs on a measurement scale are what the researcher intends. See Chapter 8.

field tracking Talking with people on the streets about where to find research participants—particularly those who are homeless—to secure their participation in future sessions or interviews. See Chapter 5.

focus groups An approach to needs assessment in which a small group of people are brought together to engage in a guided discussion of a specified topic. See Chapters 13 and 18.

formative evaluation A type of program evaluation not concerned with testing the success of a program, but focusing instead on obtaining information that is helpful in planning the program and improving its implementation and performance. See Chapter 13.

frequency distribution A description of the number of times the various attributes of a variable are observed in a sample. The report that 53 percent of a sample were men and 47 percent were women would be a simple example of a *frequency distribution*. Another example would be the report that 15 of the cities studied had populations under 10,000, 23 had populations between 10,000 and 25,000, and so forth. See Chapter 20.

gender bias The unwarranted generalization of research findings to the population as a whole when one gender is not adequately represented in the research sample. See Chapter 14.

generalizability That quality of a research finding that justifies the inference that it represents something more than the specific observations on which it was based. Sometimes, this involves the *generalization* of findings from a sample to a population. Other times it is a matter of concepts: If you are able to discover why people commit burglaries, can you *generalize* that discovery to other crimes as well? See Chapter 17.

generalization of effects A rival explanation in a *multiple-baseline design* that occurs when an intervention that is intended to apply to only one behavior or setting affects other behaviors or settings that are still in baseline. See Chapter 12.

generalize To infer that the findings of a particular study represent causal processes or apply to settings or populations beyond the study conditions. See Chapter 17.

going native A risk in qualitative field research that occurs when researchers overidentify with their respondents and lose their objective, analytic stance or their own sense of identity. See Chapters 17 and 18.

grounded theory A qualitative research approach that begins with observations and looks for patterns, themes, or common categories. See Chapters 17, 18, and 19.

grounded theory method (GTM) A qualitative methodology for building theory from data by beginning with observations and looking for patterns, themes, or common categories in those observations. See Chapters 17 and 19.

GTM See *grounded theory method.*

hermeneutics A qualitative research approach in which the researcher mentally tries to take on the circumstances, views, and feelings of those being studied in order to interpret their actions appropriately. See Chapter 16.

historical and comparative research A research method that traces the development of social forms over time and compares those developmental processes across cultures, seeking to discover common patterns that recur in different times and places. See Chapter 16.

history A threat to *internal validity* referring to extraneous events that coincide in time with the manipulation of the *independent variable.* See Chapter 10.

hypothesis A tentative and testable prediction about how changes in one thing are expected to explain and be accompanied by changes in something else. It's a statement of something that ought to be observed in the real world if a theory is correct. See *deduction* and also Chapters 3, 6, and 7.

hypothesis testing The determination of whether the expectations that a hypothesis represents are actually found to exist in the real world. See Chapters 3 and 6.

ideology A closed system of beliefs and values that shapes the understanding and behavior of those who believe in it. See Chapter 3.

idiographic An approach to explanation in which we attempt to explain a single case fully, using as many idiosyncratic, explanatory factors as may be necessary. We might explain why Uncle Ed is such a bigot by talking about what happened to him that summer at the beach, what his college roommate did to him, and so on. This kind of explanation won't necessarily help us understand bigotry in general, but we'd feel we really understood Uncle Ed. By contrast, see *nomothetic*. See Chapter 3.

independent variable A variable whose values are not problematical in an analysis but are taken as simply given. An *independent variable* is presumed to cause or explain a *dependent variable.* If we discover that religiosity is partly a function of gender—women are more religious than men—gender is the *independent variable* and religiosity is the *dependent variable.* Note that any given variable might be treated as independent in one part of an analysis and dependent in another part of the analysis. Religiosity might become an *independent variable* in the explanation of crime. See Chapter 3.

index A type of composite measure that summarizes several specific observations and represents some more general dimension. See Chapter 9.

induction The logical model in which general principles are developed from specific observations. Having noted that Jews and Catholics are more likely to vote Democratic than are Protestants, you might conclude that religious minorities in the United States are more affiliated with the Democratic Party and explain why. That would be an example of *induction.* See also *deduction* and Chapter 3.

inference A conclusion that can be logically drawn in light of our research design and our findings. See Chapter 10.

inferential statistics The body of statistical computations that is relevant to making inferences from findings based on sample observations to some larger population. See also *descriptive statistics* and Chapters 21 and 22.

informal conversational interview An unplanned and unanticipated interaction between an interviewer and a respondent that occurs naturally during the course of fieldwork observation. It is the most open-ended form of interviewing, and the interviewee might not think of the interaction as an interview. Flexibility to pursue relevant information in whatever direction seems appropriate is emphasized, and questions should be generated naturally and spontaneously from what is observed at a particular point in a particular setting or from what individuals in that setting happen to say. See Chapter 18.

informant Someone who is well versed in the social phenomenon that you wish to study and willing to tell you what he or she knows. If you were planning participant observation among the members of a religious sect, then you would do well to make friends with someone who already knows about the members—

possibly even a sect member—who could give you background information about them. Not to be confused with a *respondent.* See Chapters 14 and 18.

in-house evaluators Program evaluators who work for the agency being evaluated and therefore may be under pressure to produce biased studies or results that portray the agency favorably. See Chapter 13.

institutional review board (IRB) An independent panel of professionals that is required to approve the ethics of research involving human subjects. See Chapter 4.

internal consistency reliability A practical and commonly used approach to assessing reliability that examines the homogeneity of a measurement instrument by dividing the instrument into equivalent halves and then calculating the correlation of the scores of the two halves. See Chapter 8.

internal invalidity Refers to the possibility that the conclusions drawn from experimental results may not accurately reflect what went on in the experiment itself. See Chapter 10 and also *external invalidity.*

internal validity The degree to which an effect observed in an experiment was actually produced by the experimental stimulus and not the result of other factors. See Chapter 10 and *external validity.*

interobserver reliability See *interrater reliability.*

interpretation A technical term used in connection with the *elaboration model.* It represents the research outcome in which a *control variable* is discovered to be the mediating factor through which an *independent variable* affects a *dependent variable.* See Chapter 10.

interpretivism An approach to social research that focuses on gaining an empathic understanding of how people feel inside, seeking to interpret individuals' everyday experiences, deeper meanings and feelings, and idiosyncratic reasons for their behaviors. See Chapter 3.

interrater reliability The extent of consistency among different observers in their judgments, as reflected in the percentage of agreement or degree of correlation in their independent ratings. See Chapter 8.

interrupted time-series with a nonequivalent comparison group time-series design The most common form of multiple time-series design, in which an experimental group and a control group are measured at multiple points in time before and after an intervention is introduced to the control group. See Chapter 11.

interval measure A level of measurement that describes a variable whose attributes are rank-ordered and have equal distances between adjacent attributes. The Fahrenheit temperature scale is an example of this, because the distance between 17° and 18° is the same as that between 89° and 90°. See also nominal measure, ordinal measure, ratio measure, and Chapter 20.

intervening variable See *mediating variable.*

intervention fidelity The degree to which an intervention being evaluated is actually delivered to clients as intended. See Chapter 11.

interview A data-collection encounter in which one person (an interviewer) asks questions of another (a *respondent*). *Interviews* may be conducted face-to-face or by telephone. See Chapters 15 and 18 for more information on interviewing.

interview guide approach A semistructured form of qualitative interviewing that lists in outline form the topics and issues that the interviewer should cover in the interview, but allows the interviewer to adapt the sequencing and wording of questions to each particular interview. See Chapter 18.

inverse relationship See *negative relationship.*

IRB See *institutional review board.*

judgmental sample A type of *nonprobability sample* in which we select the units to be observed on the basis of our own judgment about which ones will be the most useful or representative. Another name for this is *purposive sample.* See Chapter 14 for more details.

key informants An approach to needs assessment that is based on expert opinions of individuals who are presumed to have special knowledge about a target population's problems or needs. See Chapter 13.

known groups validity A form of *criterion-related validity* that pertains to the degree to which an instrument accurately differentiates between groups that are known to differ in respect to the variable being measured. See Chapter 8.

latent content As used in connection with content analysis, the underlying meaning of communications as distinguished from their *manifest content.* See Chapter 16.

level of significance See *significance level.*

life history (or **life story** or **oral history interviews**) A qualitative research method in which researchers ask open-ended questions to discover how the participants in a study understand the significant events and meanings in their own lives. See Chapter 18.

life story See *life history.*

Likert scale A type of composite measure developed by Rensis Likert in an attempt to improve the levels of measurement in social research through the use of standardized response categories in survey *questionnaires.* "Likert items" use such response categories as strongly agree, agree, disagree, and strongly disagree. Such items may be used in the construction of true *Likert scales* and also be used in the construction of other types of composite measures. See Chapter 9.

linguistic equivalence (or **translation equivalence**) The result of a successful translation and *back-translation* of an instrument originally developed for the majority language, but which will be used with research participants who don't speak the majority language. See Chapter 5.

logic model A graphic portrayal that depicts the essential components of a program, shows how those components are linked to short-term process objectives, specifies measurable indicators of success in achieving short-term objectives, conveys how those short-term objectives lead to long-term program outcomes, and identifies measurable indicators of success in achieving long-term outcomes. See Chapter 13.

longitudinal study A study design that involves the collection of data at different points in time, as contrasted with a *cross-sectional study.* See Chapter 6.

mail tracking A method of locating and contacting research participants by mailing reminder notices about impending interviews or about the need to call in to update any changes in how they can be contacted. It might also include sending birthday cards, holiday greetings, and certificates of appreciation for participation. See Chapter 5.

managed care A variety of arrangements that try to control the costs of health and human services by having a large organization that pays for the cost of services for many people contract with care providers who agree to provide that care at reduced costs. *Managed care* is thought to have contributed to the growth of program evaluation. See Chapter 13.

manifest content In connection with content analysis, the concrete terms contained in a communication, as distinguished from *latent content.* See Chapter 16.

matching In connection with experiments, the procedure whereby pairs of subjects are *matched* on the basis of their similarities on one or more variables, and one member of the pair is assigned to the *experimental group* and the other to the *control group.* See Chapter 11.

maturation A threat to internal validity referring to aging effects or developmental changes that influence the *dependent variable.* See Chapters 10 and 11.

mean An *average,* computed by summing the values of several observations and dividing by the number of observations. If you now have a grade point average of 4.0 based on 10 courses and you get an F in this course, then your new grade point average (the *mean*) will be 3.6. See Chapter 20.

measurement equivalence The degree to which instruments or observed behaviors have the same meaning across cultures, relate to referent theoretical constructs in the same way across cultures, and have the same causal linkages across cultures. See Chapter 5.

median Another *average;* it represents the value of the "middle" case in a rank-ordered set of observations. If the ages of five men are 16, 17, 20, 54, and 88, then the *median* would be 20 (the *mean* would be 39). See Chapter 20.

mediating variable (or **intervening variable**) The mechanism by which an independent variable affects a dependent variable. See Chapter 7.

member checking A strategy for improving the trustworthiness of qualitative research findings in which researchers ask the participants in their research to confirm or disconfirm the accuracy of the research observations and interpretations. Do the reported observations and interpretations ring true and have meaning to the participants? See Chapter 17.

memoing A qualitative data analysis technique used at several stages of data processing to capture code meanings, theoretical ideas, preliminary conclusions, and other thoughts that will be useful during analysis. See Chapter 19.

meta-analysis A procedure for calculating the average strength of association between variables (that is, the mean *effect size*) across previously completed research studies in a particular field. See Chapter 22.

metric equivalence (or **psychometric equivalence** or **scalar equivalence**) Scores on a measure being comparable across cultures. See Chapter 5.

mode The most frequently observed value or attribute. If a sample contains 1,000 Protestants, 275 Catholics, and 33 Jews, then *Protestant* is the *modal* category. See Chapter 20.

moderating variable A variable that influences the strength or direction of a relationship between independent and dependent variables. See Chapter 7.

multiple-baseline design A type of *single-case evaluation* design that attempts to control for extraneous variables by having more than one *baseline* and intervention phase. See Chapter 12.

multiple-component design A type of *single-case evaluation design* that attempts to determine which parts of an intervention package really account for the change in the target problem. See Chapter 12.

multiple regression analysis A multivariate statistical procedure that shows the overall correlation between a set (or sets) of independent variables and an interval- or ratio-level dependent variable. See Chapter 22.

multiple time-series designs A form of time-series analysis in which both an *experimental group* and a *nonequivalent comparison group* are measured at multiple points in time before and after an intervention is introduced to the experimental group. See Chapter 11.

multivariate analysis The analysis of the simultaneous relationships among several variables. Examining simultaneously the effects of age, sex, and social class on religiosity would be an example of *multivariate analysis.* See Chapters 10, 20, and 22.

naturalism A qualitative research paradigm that emphasizes observing people in their natural, everyday social settings and on reporting their stories the way they tell them. See Chapter 17.

needs assessment Systematically researching diagnostic questions for program planning purposes. For example, community residents might be surveyed to assess their need for new child-care services. See Chapter 13.

negative case analysis A strategy for improving the trustworthiness of qualitative research findings in which researchers show they have searched thoroughly for disconfirming evidence—looking for deviant cases that do not fit the researcher's interpretations. See Chapter 17.

negative relationship A relationship between two variables in which one variable increases in value as the other variable decreases. For example, we might expect to find a negative relationship between the level of utilization of community-based aftercare services and rehospitalization rates. See Chapter 7.

nominal measure A level of measurement that describes a variable whose different attributes differ only categorically and not metrically, as distinguished from *ordinal, interval,* or *ratio* measures. Gender would be an example of a nominal measure. See Chapter 20.

nomothetic An approach to explanation in which we attempt to discover factors that can offer a general, though imperfect, explanation of some phenomenon. For example, we might note that education seems to reduce prejudice in general. Even though we recognize that some educated people are prejudiced and some uneducated people are not, we have learned some of what causes prejudice or tolerance in general. By contrast, see *idiographic.* See Chapter 3.

nondirectional hypotheses Predicted relationships between variables that do not specify whether the predicted relationship will be positive or negative. See Chapter 21.

nonequivalent comparison groups design A quasi-experimental design in which the researcher finds two existing groups that appear to be similar and measures change on a dependent variable before and after an intervention is introduced to one of the groups. See Chapter 11.

nonparametric tests Tests of statistical significance that have been created for use when not all of the assumptions of parametric statistics can be met. Chi-square is the most commonly used nonparametric test. See Chapter 22.

nonprobability sample A sample selected in some fashion other than those suggested by probability theory. Examples include *judgmental (purposive), quota,* and *snowball samples.* See Chapters 14 and 17.

novelty and disruption effects A form of *research reactivity* in experiments in which the sense of excitement, energy, and enthusiasm among recipients of an evaluated intervention—and not the intervention itself—causes the desired change in their behavior. See Chapter 11.

NUD*IST A computer program designed to assist researchers in the analysis of qualitative data. See Chapter 19.

null hypothesis In connection with *hypothesis testing* and *tests of statistical significance,* the *hypothesis* that suggests there is no relationship between the variables under study. You may conclude that the two variables are related after having statistically rejected the *null hypothesis.* See Chapters 21 and 22.

observations Information we gather by experience in the real world that helps us build a theory or verify whether it is correct when testing hypotheses. See Chapter 3.

obtrusive observation This occurs when the participant is keenly aware of being observed and thus may be predisposed to behave in socially desirable ways and in ways that meet *experimenter expectancies.* See Chapters 11, 12, and 16.

one-group pretest–posttest design A pre-experimental design, with low internal validity, that assesses a dependent variable before and after a stimulus is introduced but does not attempt to control for alternative explanations of any changes in scores that are observed. See Chapter 11.

one-shot case study A pre-experimental research design, with low internal validity, that simply measures a single group of subjects on a dependent variable at one point in time after they have been exposed to a stimulus. See Chapter 11.

one-tailed tests of significance *Statistical significance tests* that place the entire *critical region* at the predicted end of the *theoretical sampling distribution* and thus limit the inference of statistical significance to findings that are only in the critical region of the predicted direction. See Chapter 21.

online surveys Surveys conducted via the Internet—either by e-mail or through a website. See Chapter 15.

open coding A qualitative data-processing method in which, instead of starting out with a list of code categories derived from theory, one develops code categories through close examination of qualitative data. During *open coding,* the data are broken down into discrete parts, closely examined, and compared for similarities and differences. Questions are asked about the phenomena as reflected in the data. Through this process, one's own and others' assumptions about phenomena are questioned or explored, leading to new discoveries. See Chapter 19.

open-ended questions Questions for which respondents are asked to provide their own answer, rather than selecting from among a list of possible responses provided by the researcher as for *closed-ended questions.* See Chapter 9.

operational definition The concrete and specific *definition* of something in terms of the *operations* by which observations are to be categorized. The *operational definition* of "earning an A in this course" might be "correctly answering at least 90 percent of the final exam questions." See Chapters 7 and 12.

operationalization One step beyond *conceptualization.* Operationalization is the process of developing *operational definitions.* See Chapter 7.

oral history interviews See *life history.*

ordinal measure A level of measurement describing a variable whose attributes may be rank-ordered along some dimension. An example would be measuring "socioeconomic status" by the *attributes* high, medium, and low. See also *nominal measure, interval measure,* and *ratio measure* and Chapter 20.

panel studies Longitudinal studies in which data are collected from the same sample (the panel) at several points in time. See Chapter 6.

PAR See *participatory action research.*

paradigm (1) A model or frame of reference that shapes our observations and understandings. For example, "functionalism" leads us to examine society in terms of the functions served by its constituent parts, whereas "interactionism" leads us to focus attention on the ways people deal with each other face-to-face and arrive at shared meanings for things. (2) Almost a quarter. See Chapter 3.

parallel-forms reliability Consistency of measurement between two equivalent measurement instruments. See Chapter 8.

parameter A summary statistic describing a given variable in a population, such as the mean income of all families in a city or the age distribution of the city's population. See Chapter 14 and Appendix B.

parametric tests Tests of statistical significance that assume that at least one variable being studied has an interval or ratio level of measurement, that the sample distribution of the relevant parameters of those variables is normal, and that the different groups being compared have been randomly selected and are independent of one another. Commonly used parametric tests are the *t-test, analysis of variance,* and *Pearson product-moment correlation.* See Chapter 22.

participatory action research (PAR) A qualitative research paradigm in which the researcher's function is to serve as a resource to those being studied—typically, disadvantaged groups—as an opportunity for them to act effectively in their own interest. The disadvantaged participants define their problems, define the remedies desired, and take the lead in designing the research that will help them realize their aims. See Chapter 17.

passage of time A threat to *internal validity* referring to changes in a *dependent variable* that occur naturally as time passes and not because of the *independent variable.* See Chapters 10 and 11.

path analysis A statistical procedure, based on regression analysis, that provides a graphic picture of a causal model for understanding relationships between variables. See Chapter 22.

Pearson product-moment correlation (*r*) A parametric measure of association, ranging from −1.0 to +1.0, used when both the independent and dependent variables are at the interval or ratio level of measurement. See Chapter 22.

peer debriefing and support A strategy for improving the trustworthiness of qualitative research findings in which teams of investigators meet regularly to give each other feedback, emotional support, alternative perspectives, and new ideas about how they are collecting data or about problems, and about meanings in the data already collected. See Chapter 17.

phone tracking A method of locating and contacting research participants—particularly those who are transient or homeless—to secure their participation in future sessions or interviews. This method involves repeated telephoning of *anchor points* in advance to schedule an interview and providing participants a toll-free number where they can leave messages about appointment changes or changes in how to locate them, incentives for leaving such messages, and a card that lists appointment times and the research project's address and telephone number. See Chapter 5.

placebo control group design An experimental design that controls for *placebo effects* by randomly assigning subjects to an experimental group and two control groups and exposing one of the control groups to a stimulus that is designed to resemble the special attention received by subjects in the experimental group. See *placebo effects* and Chapter 11.

placebo effects Changes in a dependent variable that are caused by the power of suggestion among participants in an experimental group that they are receiving something special that is expected to help them. These changes would not occur if they received the experimental intervention without that awareness. See Chapter 11.

plagiarism Presenting someone else's words or thoughts as though they were your own; constitutes intellectual theft. See Chapter 23.

population The group or collection that a researcher is interested in generalizing about. More formally, it is the theoretically specified aggregation of study elements. See Chapter 14.

positive relationship A relationship between two variables in which one variable increases in value as the other variable also increases in value (or one decreases as the other decreases). For example, we might expect to find a positive relationship between rate of unemployment and extent of homelessness. See Chapter 7.

positivism A paradigm introduced by August Comte that held that social behavior could be studied and understood in a rational, scientific manner—in contrast to explanations based in religion or superstition. See Chapter 3.

possible-code cleaning Examining the distribution of responses to each item in a data set to check for errors in data entered into a computer by looking for impossible code categories that have some responses and then correcting the errors. See Chapter 20.

postmodernism A paradigm that rejects the notion of a knowable objective social reality. See Chapter 3.

posttest-only control group design A variation of the classical experimental design that avoids the possible testing effects associated with pretesting by testing only after the experimental group receives the intervention, based on the assumption that the process of random assignment provides for equivalence between the experimental and control groups on the dependent variable before the exposure to the intervention. See also *pretest–posttest control group design*. See Chapter 11.

posttest-only design with nonequivalent groups A pre-experimental design that involves two groups that may not be comparable, in which the dependent variable is assessed after the independent variable is introduced for one of the groups. See Chapter 11.

PPS See *probability proportionate to size.*

practice models Guides to help us organize our views about social work practice that may reflect a synthesis of existing theories. See Chapter 3.

PRE See *proportionate reduction of error.*

predictive validity A form of *criterion-related validity* involving a measure's ability to predict a criterion that will occur in the future. See Chapter 8.

pre-experimental designs Pilot study designs for evaluating the effectiveness of interventions; they do not control for threats to *internal validity.* See Chapter 11.

pretesting Testing out a scale or questionnaire in a dry run to see if the target population will understand it and not find it too unwieldy, as well as to identify any needed modifications. See Chapters 5 and 9.

pretest–posttest control group design The classical experimental design in which subjects are assigned randomly to an experimental group that receives an intervention being evaluated and to a control group that does not receive it. Each group is tested on the dependent variable before and after the experimental group receives the intervention. See Chapter 11.

probabilistic knowledge Knowledge based on probability that enables us to say that if A occurs, then B is more likely to occur. It does not enable us to say that B will occur, or even that B will probably occur. See Chapter 3.

probability proportionate to size (PPS) This refers to a type of multistage *cluster sample* in which clusters are selected, not with equal probabilities (see *equal probability of selection method*) but with probabilities proportionate to their sizes—as measured by the number of units to be subsampled. See Chapter 14.

probability sample The general term for a sample selected in accord with probability theory, typically involving some *random selection* mechanism. Specific types of *probability samples* include *area probability sample, EPSEM, PPS, simple random sample,* and *systematic sample.* See Chapter 14.

probability sampling The use of random sampling techniques that allow a researcher to make relatively few observations and generalize from those observations to a much wider population. See Chapter 14.

probe A technique employed in interviewing to solicit a more complete answer to a question, this nondirective phrase or question is used to encourage a respondent to elaborate on an answer. Examples include "Anything more?" and "How is that?" See Chapters 15 and 18 discussions of interviewing.

prolonged engagement A strategy for improving the trustworthiness of qualitative research findings that attempts to reduce the impact of *reactivity* and respondent bias by forming a long and trusting relationship with respondents and by conducting lengthy interviews or a series of follow-up interviews with the same respondent. This improves the likelihood that the respondent ultimately will disclose socially undesirable truths, and improves the researcher's ability to detect distortion. See Chapter 17.

proportionate reduction of error (PRE) The proportion of errors reduced in predicting the value for one variable based on knowing the value for the other. The stronger the relationship is, the more our prediction errors will be reduced. See Chapter 21.

psychometric equivalence See *metric equivalence* and Chapter 5.

purposive sample See *judgmental sample* and Chapters 14 and 17.

purposive sampling Selecting a sample of observations that the researcher believes will yield the most comprehensive understanding of the subject of study, based on the researcher's intuitive feel for the subject that comes from extended observation and reflection. See Chapters 14 and 17.

qualitative analysis The nonnumerical examination and interpretation of observations for the purpose of discovering underlying meanings and patterns of relationships. This is most typical of field research and historical research. See Chapter 19.

qualitative interview An interaction between an interviewer and a respondent in which the interviewer usually has a general plan of inquiry but not a specific set of questions that must be asked in particular words and in a particular order. Ideally, the respondent does most of the talking. See Chapter 18.

qualitative research methods Research methods that emphasize depth of understanding and the deeper meanings of human experience, and that aim to generate theoretically richer, albeit more tentative, observations. Commonly used qualitative methods include participant observation, direct observation, and unstructured or intensive interviewing. See Chapters 3, 17, 18, and 19.

quantitative analysis The numerical representation and manipulation of observations for the purpose of describing and explaining the phenomena that those observations reflect. See especially Chapter 20 and also the remainder of Part 7.

quantitative methods Research methods that emphasize precise, objective, and generalizable findings. See Chapter 3.

quasi-experimental design Design that attempts to control for threats to internal validity and thus permits causal inferences but is distinguished from true experiments primarily by the lack of random assignment of subjects. See Chapter 11.

questionnaire A document that contains questions and other types of items that are designed to solicit information appropriate to analysis. *Questionnaires* are used primarily in survey research and also in experiments, field research, and other modes of observation. See Chapters 9 and 15.

quota sampling A type of *nonprobability sample* in which units are selected into the sample on the basis of prespecified characteristics so that the total sample will have the same distribution of characteristics as are assumed to exist in the population being studied. See Chapters 14 and 17.

r^2 The proportion of variation in the dependent variable that is explained by the independent variable. See Chapter 21.

random error A measurement error that has no consistent pattern of effects and that reduces the reliability of measurement. For example, asking questions that respondents do not understand will yield inconsistent (random) answers. See Chapter 8.

randomization A technique for assigning experimental participants to *experimental groups* and *control groups* at random. See Chapter 11 and Appendix B.

randomized clinical trials (RCTs) Experiments that use random means (such as a coin toss) to assign clients who share similar problems or diagnoses into groups that receive different interventions. If the predicted difference in outcome is found between the groups, it is not plausible to attribute the difference to a priori differences between two incomparable groups. See Chapters 2 and 11.

random selection A probability sampling procedure in which each element has an equal chance of selection independent of any other event in the selection process. See Chapter 14.

range A measure of *dispersion* that is composed of the highest and lowest values of a variable in some set of observations. In your class, for example, the *range* of ages might be from 20 to 37. See Chapter 20.

rates under treatment An approach to *needs assessment* based on the number and characteristics of clients already using a service in a similar community. See Chapter 13.

ratio measure A level of measurement that describes a variable whose attributes have all the qualities of *nominal, ordinal,* and *interval measures* and also are based on a "true zero" point. Age would be an example of a *ratio measure.* See Chapter 20.

reactivity A process in which change in a dependent variable is induced by research procedures. See Chapters 11 and 12.

recall bias A common limitation in case-control designs that occurs when a person's current recollections of the quality and value of past experiences are tainted by knowing that things didn't work out for them later in life. See Chapter 10.

reductionism A fault of some researchers: a strict limitation (reduction) of the kinds of concepts to be considered relevant to the phenomenon under study. See Chapter 6.

reification The process of regarding as real things that are not real. See Chapter 7.

relationship Variables that change together in a consistent, predictable fashion. See Chapters 3 and 7.

reliability That quality of measurement method that suggests that the same data would have been collected each time in repeated observations of the same phenomenon. In the context of a survey, we would expect that the question "Did you attend church last week?" would have higher reliability than the question "About how many times have you attended church in your life?" This is not to be confused with *validity.* See Chapter 8.

reminder calls Telephoning research participants to remind them of their scheduled treatment or assessment sessions in a study. See Chapter 5.

replication (1) Generally, the duplication of a study to expose or reduce error or the reintroduction or withdrawal of an intervention to increase the internal validity of a quasi-experiment or single-case design evaluation. See Chapters 1, 3, 11, and 12. (2) One possible result in the *elaboration model* that occurs when an original bivariate relationship appears to be essentially the same in the multivariate analysis as it was in the bivariate analysis. See *elaboration model* and Chapter 10.

representativeness That quality of a sample of having the same distribution of characteristics as the population from which it was selected. By implication, descriptions and explanations derived from an analysis of the sample may be assumed to represent similar ones in the population. *Representativeness* is enhanced by *probability sampling* and provides for *generalizability* and the use of *inferential statistics*. See Chapter 14.

request for proposals (RFP) An announcement put out by funding sources that identifies the research questions and types of designs the funding source would like to fund, encourages researchers to submit proposals to carry out such research, specifies the maximum size of the *research grant,* and provides other information about the source's expectations and funding process. See Chapter 23.

research contract Type of funding that provides great specificity regarding what the funding source wants to have researched and how the research is to be conducted. Unlike a *research grant,* a *research contract* requires that the research proposal conform precisely with the funding source's specifications. See Chapter 23.

research design A term often used in connection with whether logical arrangements permit causal inferences; also refers to all the decisions made in planning and conducting research. See Chapter 10.

research grant Type of funding that usually identifies some broad priority areas the funding source has and provides researchers considerable leeway in the specifics of what they want to investigate within that area and how they want to investigate it. See Chapter 23.

research reactivity A process in which change in a dependent variable is induced by research procedures. See Chapters 11 and 12.

resentful demoralization A threat to the validity of an evaluation of an intervention's effectiveness that occurs when practitioners or clients in the comparison routine-treatment condition become resentful and demoralized because they did not receive the special training or the special treatment. Consequently, their confidence or motivation may decline and may explain their inferior performance on outcome measures. See Chapter 11.

respondent A person who provides data for analysis by responding to a survey *questionnaire* or to an interview. See Chapters 15 and 18.

response rate The number of persons who participate in a survey divided by the number selected in the sample, in the form of a percentage. This is also called the "completion rate" or, in self-administered surveys, the "return rate"—the percentage of *questionnaires* sent out that are returned. See Chapter 15.

sampling error The degree of error to be expected for a given sample design, as estimated according to probability theory. See Chapter 14 and Appendix B.

sampling frame That list or quasi-list of units that compose a population from which a sample is selected. If the sample is to be *representative* of the population, then it's essential that the *sampling frame* include all (or nearly all) members of the population. See Chapter 14.

sampling interval The standard distance between elements selected from a population for a sample. See Chapter 14.

sampling ratio The proportion of elements in the population that are selected to be in a sample. See Chapter 14.

sampling unit That element or set of elements considered for selection in some stage of sampling. See Chapter 14.

scalar equivalence See *metric equivalence* and Chapter 5.

scale A type of composite measure composed of several items that have a logical or empirical structure among them. See Chapter 9.

scientific method An approach to inquiry that attempts to safeguard against errors commonly made in casual human inquiry. Chief features include viewing all knowledge as provisional and subject to refutation, searching for evidence based on systematic and comprehensive observation, pursuing objectivity in observation, and replication. See Chapter 1.

secondary analysis A form of research in which the data collected and processed by one researcher are reanalyzed—often for a different purpose—by another. This is especially appropriate in the case of survey data. Data archives are repositories or libraries for the storage and distribution of data for *secondary analysis*. See Chapter 16.

selection bias A threat to *internal validity* referring to the assignment of research participants to groups in a way that does not maximize their comparability regarding the dependent variable. See Chapters 10 and 11.

self-mailing questionnaire A mailed *questionnaire* that requires no return envelope: When the questionnaire is folded a particular way, the return address appears on the outside. The respondent therefore doesn't have to worry about losing the envelope. See Chapter 15.

self-reports A way to operationally define variables according to what people say about their own thoughts, views, or behaviors. See Chapters 7 and 8.

self-report scales A source of data in which research subjects all respond in writing to the same list of written questions or statements that has been devised to measure a particular construct. For example, a self-report scale to measure marital satisfaction might ask how often one is annoyed with one's spouse, is proud of the spouse, has fun with the spouse, and so on. See Chapters 7, 8, and 12.

semantic differential A scaling format that asks respondents to choose between two opposite positions. See Chapter 9.

semiotics The science of symbols and meanings, commonly associated with *content analysis* and based on language, that examines the agreements we have about the meanings associated with particular signs. See Chapter 19.

sensitivity The ability of an instrument to detect subtle differences. See Chapter 8.

significance level The probability level that is selected in advance to serve as a cutoff point to separate findings that will and will not be attributed to chance. Findings at or below the selected probability level are deemed to be statistically significant. See Chapter 21.

simple interrupted time-series design A quasi-experimental design in which no comparison group is utilized and that attempts to develop causal inferences based on a comparison of trends over multiple measurements before and after an intervention is introduced. See Chapter 11.

simple random sample (SRS) A type of *probability sample* in which the units that compose a population are assigned numbers.

A set of *random* numbers is then generated, and the units having those numbers are included in the sample. Although probability theory and the calculations it provides assume this basic sampling method, it's seldom used for practical reasons. An equivalent alternative is the *systematic sample* (with a random start). See Chapter 14.

single-case evaluation design A *time-series design* used to evaluate the impact of an intervention or a policy change on individual cases or systems. See Chapter 12.

snowball sample A *nonprobability sample* that is obtained by asking each person interviewed to suggest additional people for interviewing. See Chapters 14 and 17.

snowball sampling A *nonprobability sampling* method often employed in qualitative research. Each person interviewed may be asked to suggest additional people for interviewing. See Chapters 5, 14, and 17.

social desirability bias A source of systematic measurement error involving the tendency of people to say or do things that will make them or their reference group look good. See Chapter 8.

social indicators An approach to needs assessment based on aggregated statistics that reflect conditions of an entire population. See Chapter 13.

Solomon four-group design An experimental design that assesses testing effects by randomly assigning subjects to four groups, introducing the intervention being evaluated to two of them, conducting both pretesting and posttesting on one group that receives the intervention and one group that does not, and conducting posttesting only on the other two groups. See Chapter 11.

specification (1) Generally, the process through which concepts are made more specific. (2) A technical term used in connection with the *elaboration model,* representing the elaboration outcome in which an initially observed relationship between two variables is replicated among some subgroups created by the *control variable* and not among others. In such a situation, you will have *specified* the conditions under which the original relationship exists—for example, among men but not among women. See Chapter 10. (3) In preparing an interview questionnaire for interviewers, *specifications* are the explanatory and clarifying comments about how to handle difficult or confusing situations that may occur with specific questions. See Chapter 15.

spurious relationship A relationship between two variables that are no longer related when a third variable is controlled; the third variable explains away the original relationship. Thus, the relationship between number of storks and number of human births in geographic areas is spurious because it is explained away by the fact that areas with more humans are more likely to have a zoo or a larger zoo. See Chapters 7 and 10.

standard deviation A descriptive statistic that portrays the dispersion of values around the mean. It's the square root of the averaged squared differences between each value and the mean. See Chapter 20.

standardized open-ended interviews The most highly structured form of qualitative interviews, which are conducted in a consistent, thorough manner. Questions are written out in advance exactly the way they are to be asked in the interview, reducing the chances that variations in responses are being caused by changes in the way interviews are being conducted. See Chapter 18.

static-group comparison design A cross-sectional design for comparing different groups on a dependent variable at one point in time. The validity of this design will be influenced by the extent to which it contains multivariate controls for alternative explanations for differences among the groups. See Chapter 11.

statistic A summary description of a variable in a sample. See Appendix B.

statistical power analysis Assessment of the probability of avoiding *Type II errors.* See Chapter 22.

statistical regression A threat to *internal validity* referring to the tendency for extreme scores at pretest to become less extreme at posttest. See Chapter 10.

statistical significance A general term that refers to the unlikelihood that relationships observed in a sample could be attributed to sampling error alone. See *tests of statistical significance* and Chapter 21.

stratification The grouping of the units that compose a population into homogeneous groups (or "strata") before sampling. This procedure, which may be used in conjunction with *simple random, systematic,* or *cluster sampling,* improves the *representativeness* of a sample, at least in terms of the *stratification* variables. See Chapter 14.

stratified sampling A probability sampling procedure that uses *stratification* to ensure that appropriate numbers of elements are drawn from homogeneous subsets of that population. See *stratification* and Chapter 14.

study population The aggregation of elements from which the sample is actually selected. See Chapter 14.

substantive significance The importance, or meaningfulness, of a finding from a practical standpoint. See Chapter 21.

summative evaluation A type of program evaluation focusing on the ultimate success of a program and decisions about whether it should be continued or chosen from among alternative options. See Chapter 13.

suppressor variable A variable that, when controlled in a multivariate analysis, shows that two variables that appear unrelated or weakly related in the bivariate analysis are actually more strongly related than they appeared. See Chapter 10.

systematic error An error in measurement with a consistent pattern of effects. For example, when child welfare workers ask abusive parents whether they have been abusing their children, they may get biased answers that are consistently untrue because parents do not want to admit to abusive behavior. Contrast this to *random error,* which has no consistent pattern of effects. See Chapter 8.

systematic sample A type of *probability sample* in which every *k*th unit in a list is selected for inclusion in the sample—for example, every 25th student in the college directory of students. We compute *k* by dividing the size of the population by the desired sample size; the result is called the sampling interval. Within certain constraints, *systematic sampling* is a functional equivalent of *simple random sampling* and usually easier to do. Typically, the first unit is selected at random. See Chapter 14.

test–retest reliability Consistency, or stability, of measurement over time. See Chapter 8.

tests of statistical significance A class of statistical computations that indicate the likelihood that the relationship observed between variables in a sample can be attributed to sampling error only. See *inferential statistics* and Chapter 21.

theoretical sampling distribution The distribution of outcomes produced by an infinite number of randomly drawn samples or random subdivisions of a sample. This distribution identifies the proportion of times that each outcome of a study could be expected to occur as a result of chance. See Chapter 21.

theory A systematic set of interrelated statements intended to explain some aspect of social life or enrich our sense of how people conduct and find meaning in their daily lives. See Chapter 3.

time-series designs A set of quasi-experimental designs in which multiple observations of a dependent variable are conducted before and after an intervention is introduced. See Chapter 11.

touch-tone data entry (TDE) A method for self-administered questionnaires in which the respondent initiates the process by calling a number at the research organization. This prompts a series of computerized questions, which the respondent answers by pressing keys on the telephone keypad. See Chapter 15.

translation equivalence See *linguistic equivalence, translation validity,* and Chapter 5.

translation validity Successful translation of a measure into the language of respondents who are not fluent in the majority language, thus attaining *linguistic equivalence.* See Chapter 5.

trend studies Longitudinal studies that monitor a given characteristic of some population over time. An example would be annual canvasses of schools of social work to identify trends over time in the number of students who specialize in direct practice, generalist practice, and administration and planning. See Chapter 6.

triangulation The use of more than one imperfect data-collection alternative in which each option is vulnerable to different potential sources of error. For example, instead of relying exclusively on a client's self-report of how often a particular target behavior occurred during a specified period, a significant other (teacher, cottage parent, and so on) is asked to monitor the behavior as well. See Chapters 8, 12, and 17.

***t*-test** A test of the statistical significance of the difference between the means of two groups. See Chapter 22.

two-tailed tests of significance Statistical significance tests that divide the *critical region* at both ends of the *theoretical sampling distribution* and add the probability at both ends when calculating the level of significance. See Chapter 21.

Type I error An error we risk committing whenever we reject the *null hypothesis.* It occurs when we reject a true null hypothesis. See Chapter 21.

Type II error An error we risk committing whenever we fail to reject the *null hypothesis.* It occurs when we fail to reject a false null hypothesis. See Chapters 21 and 22.

units of analysis The "what" or "whom" being studied. In social science research, the most typical units of analysis are individual people. See Chapter 6.

univariate analysis The analysis of a single variable for purposes of description. *Frequency distributions, averages,* and measures of *dispersion* would be examples of *univariate analysis,* as distinguished from *bivariate* and *multivariate analysis.* See Chapter 20.

unobtrusive observation Unlike in *obtrusive observation,* the participant does not notice the observation and is therefore less influenced to behave in socially desirable ways and ways that meet *experimenter expectancies.* See Chapters 11, 12, and 16.

validity A descriptive term used of a measure that accurately reflects the concept that it's intended to measure. For example, your IQ would seem a more *valid* measure of your intelligence than would the number of hours you spend in the library. Realize that the ultimate *validity* of a measure can never be proven, but we may still agree to its relative *validity, content validity, construct validity, internal validation,* and *external validation.* This must not be confused with *reliability.* See Chapter 8.

variable-oriented analysis A qualitative data analysis method that focuses on interrelations among variables, with the people observed being the primary carriers of those variables. See Chapter 19.

variables Logical groupings of *attributes.* The variable "gender" contains the attributes "male" and "female." See Chapters 3 and 7.

verstehen The German word meaning "understanding," used in qualitative research in connection to *hermeneutics,* in which the researcher tries mentally to take on the circumstances, views, and feelings of those being studied to interpret their actions appropriately. See Chapter 16.

voice recognition (VR) A method for self-administered questionnaires in which the respondent initiates the process by calling a number at the research organization. This prompts a series of computerized questions by the system, which accepts spoken responses. See Chapter 15.

weighting A procedure employed in connection with sampling whereby units selected with unequal probabilities are assigned weights in such a manner as to make the sample *representative* of the population from which it was selected. See Chapter 14.

withdrawal/reversal design See *ABAB withdrawal/reversal design.*

Bibliography

Abramovitz, Robert, Andre Ivanoff, Rami Mosseri, and Anne O'Sullivan. 1997. "Comments on Outcomes Measurement in Mental and Behavioral Health," pp. 293–296 in Edward J. Mullen and Jennifer L. Magnabosco (eds.), *Outcomes Measurement in the Human Services: Cross-Cutting Issues and Methods.* Washington, DC: NASW Press.

Acker, J., K. Barry, and J. Esseveld. 1983. "Objectivity and Truth: Problems in Doing Feminist Research," *Women's Studies International Forum, 6,* 423–435.

Adler, Patricia A., and Peter Adler. 1994. "Observational Techniques," pp. 377–392 in Norman K. Denzin and Yvonna S. Lincoln (eds.), *Handbook of Qualitative Research.* Thousand Oaks, CA: Sage.

Aiken, L. R. 1985. *Psychological Testing and Assessment.* Rockleigh, NJ: Allyn & Bacon.

Alexander, Leslie B., and Phyllis Solomon (eds.). 2006. *The Research Process in the Human Services: Behind the Scenes.* Belmont, CA: Thomson Brooks/Cole.

Allen, James, and James A. Walsh. 2000. "A Construct-Based Approach to Equivalence: Methodologies for Cross-Cultural/ Multicultural Personality Assessment Research," pp. 63–85 in Richard Dana (ed.), *Handbook of Cross-Cultural Personality Assessment.* Mahwah, NJ: Lawrence Erlbaum Associates.

Allen, Katherine R., and Alexis J. Walker. 1992. "A Feminist Analysis of Interviews with Elderly Mothers and Their Daughters," pp. 198–214 in Jane Gilgun, Kerry Daly, and Gerald Handel (eds.), *Qualitative Methods in Family Research.* Thousand Oaks, CA: Sage.

Altheide, David L., and John M. Johnson. 1994. "Criteria for Assessing Interpretive Validity in Qualitative Research," pp. 485–499 in Norman K. Denzin and Yvonna S. Lincoln (eds.), *Handbook of Qualitative Research.* Thousand Oaks, CA: Sage.

Alvidrez, Jennifer, Francisca Azocar, and Jeanne Miranda. 1996. "Demystifying the Concept of Ethnicity for Psychotherapy Researchers," *Journal of Consulting and Clinical Psychology, 64*(5), 903–908.

American Psychiatric Association. 2000. *Handbook of Psychiatric Measures.* Washington, DC: Author.

Anastasi, A. 1988. *Psychological Testing.* New York: Macmillan.

Andrulis, R. S. 1977. *Adult Assessment: A Source Book of Tests and Measures of Human Behavior.* Springfield, IL: Thomas.

Aneshenshel, Carol S., Rosina M. Becerra, Eve P. Fiedler, and Roberleigh A. Schuler. 1989. "Participation of Mexican American Female Adolescents in a Longitudinal Panel Survey," *Public Opinion Quarterly, 53* (Winter), 548–562.

Areán, Patricia A., and Dolores Gallagher-Thompson. 1996. "Issues and Recommendations for the Recruitment and Retention of Older Ethnic Minority Adults into Clinical Research," *Journal of Consulting and Clinical Psychology, 64*(5), 875–880.

Arnold, Bill R., and Yolanda E. Matus. 2000. "Test Translation and Cultural Equivalence Methodologies for Use with Diverse Populations," pp. 121–135 in Israel Cuéllar and Freddy A. Paniagua (eds.), *Handbook of Multicultural Mental Health: Assessment and Treatment of Diverse Populations.* San Diego, CA: Academic Press.

Asch, Solomon E. 1958. "Effects of Group Pressure upon the Modification and Distortion of Judgments," pp. 174–183 in Eleanor E. Maccoby, Theodore M. Newcomb, and Eugene L. Hartley (eds.), *Readings in Social Psychology,* 3rd ed. New York: Holt, Rinehart and Winston.

Asher, Ramona M., and Gary Alan Fine. 1991. "Fragile Ties: Sharing Research Relationships with Women Married to Alcoholics," pp. 196–205 in William B. Shaffir and Roberta A. Stebbins (eds.), *Experiencing Fieldwork: An Inside View of Qualitative Research.* Newbury Park, CA: Sage.

Babbie, Earl R. 1966. "The Third Civilization," *Review of Religious Research* (Winter), 101–102.

———. 1985. *You Can Make a Difference.* New York: St. Martin's Press.

———. 1986. *Observing Ourselves: Essays in Social Research.* Belmont, CA: Wadsworth.

———. 1990. *Survey Research Methods.* Belmont, CA: Wadsworth.

———, Fred Halley, and Jeanne Zaino. 2000. *Adventures in Social Research.* Newbury Park, CA: Pine Forge Press.

Baker, Vern, and Charles Lambert. 1990. "The National Collegiate Athletic Association and the Governance of Higher Education," *Sociological Quarterly, 31*(3), 403–421.

Banfield, Edward. 1968. *The Unheavenly City: The Nature and Future of Our Urban Crisis.* Boston: Little, Brown.

Barlow, David H., and Michel Hersen. 1984. *Single Case Experimental Designs: Strategies for Studying Behavior Change,* 2nd ed. New York: Pergamon Press.

Bartko, John J., William T. Carpenter, and Thomas H. McGlashan. 1988. "Statistical Issues in Long-Term Follow-Up Studies," *Schizophrenia Bulletin, 14*(4), 575–587.

Baxter, Ellen, and Kim Hopper. 1982. "The New Mendicancy: Homeless in New York City," *American Journal of Orthopsychiatry, 52*(3), 393–407.

Bednarz, Marlene. 1996. "Push polls statement." Report to the AAPORnet listserv, April 5 @Online. Available: mbednarz@umich.edu.

Beebe, Linda. 1993. *Professional Writing for the Human Services.* Washington, DC: NASW Press.

Beere, C. A. 1979. *Women and Women's Issues: A Handbook of Tests and Measures.* San Francisco: Jossey-Bass.

———. 1990. *Sex and Gender Issues: A Handbook of Tests and Measures.* New York: Greenwood Press.

Belcher, John. 1991. "Understanding the Process of Social Drift Among the Homeless: A Qualitative Analysis." Paper presented at the Research Conference on Qualitative Methods in Social Work Practice Research, Nelson A. Rockefeller Institute of Government, State University of New York at Albany, August 24.

Bellah, Robert N. 1970. "Christianity and Symbolic Realism," *Journal for the Scientific Study of Religion, 9,* 89–96.

———. 1974. "Comment on the Limits of Symbolic Realism," *Journal for the Scientific Study of Religion, 13,* 487–489.

Bennet, Carl A., and Arthur A. Lumsdaine (eds.). 1975. *Evaluation and Experiment.* New York: Academic Press, 1975.

Benton, J. Edwin, and John Daly. 1991. "A Question Order Effect in a Local Government Survey," *Public Opinion Quarterly, 55,* 640–642.

Berg, Bruce L. 1989. *Qualitative Research Methods for the Social Sciences,* 1st ed. Boston: Allyn & Bacon.

———. 1998. *Qualitative Research Methods for the Social Sciences,* 3rd ed. Boston: Allyn & Bacon.

Bernstein, Ira H., and Paul Havig. 1999. *Computer Literacy: Getting the Most from Your PC.* Thousand Oaks, CA: Sage.

Beutler, Larry E., Michael T. Brown, Linda Crothers, Kevin Booker, and Mary Katherine Seabrook. 1996. "The Dilemma of Factitious Demographic Distinctions in Psychological Research," *Journal of Consulting and Clinical Psychology, 64*(5), 892–902.

Beveridge, W. I. B. 1950. *The Art of Scientific Investigation.* New York: Vintage Books.

Bian, Yanjie. 1994. *Work and Inequality in Urban China.* Albany: State University of New York Press.

Biggerstaff, M. A., P. M. Morris, and A. Nichols-Casebolt. 2002. "Living on the Edge: Examination of People Attending Food Pantries and Soup Kitchens," *Social Work, 47*(3), 267–277.

Billups, James O., and Maria C. Julia. 1987. "Changing Profile of Social Work Practice: A Content Analysis," *Social Work Research and Abstracts, 23*(4), 17–22.

Black, Donald. 1970. "Production of Crime Rates," *American Sociological Review, 35* (August), 733–748.

Blair, Johnny, Shanyang Zhao, Barbara Bickart, and Ralph Kuhn. 1995. *Sample Design for Household Telephone Surveys: A Bibliography 1949–1995.* College Park: Survey Research Center, University of Maryland.

Blalock, Hubert M. 1972. *Social Statistics.* New York: McGraw-Hill.

Blaunstein, Albert, and Robert Zangrando (eds.). 1970. *Civil Rights and the Black American.* New York: Washington Square Press.

Blood, R. O., and W. Wolfe. 1960. *Husbands and Wives: The Dynamics of Married Living.* New York: The Free Press.

Bloom, Martin, Joel Fischer, and John G. Orme. 2006. *Evaluating Practice: Guidelines for the Accountable Professional,* 5th ed. Boston: Allyn & Bacon.

Blythe, Betty J., and Scott Briar. 1987. "Direct Practice Effectiveness," *Encyclopedia of Social Work,* 18th ed., vol. 1, pp. 399–408. Silver Spring, MD: National Association of Social Workers.

Bogdan, Robert, and Steven J. Taylor. 1990. "Looking at the Bright Side: A Positive Approach to Qualitative Policy and Evaluation Research," *Qualitative Sociology, 13*(2), 183–192.

Bohrnstedt, George W. 1983. "Measurement," pp. 70–121 in Peter H. Rossi, James D. Wright, and Andy B. Anderson (eds.), *Handbook of Survey Research.* New York: Academic Press.

Boone, Charlotte R., Claudia J. Coulton, Shirley M. Keller. 1981. "The Impact of Early and Comprehensive Social Work Services on Length of Stay," *Social Work in Health Care* (Fall), 1–9.

Booth, C. 1970. *The Life and Labour of the People of London.* New York: AMS Press. (Original work published 1891–1903.)

Botein, B. 1965. "The Manhattan Bail Project: Its Impact in Criminology and the Criminal Law Process," *Texas Law Review, 43,* 319–331.

Boyd, L., J. Hylton, and S. Price. 1978. "Computers in Social Work Practice: A Review," *Social Work, 23*(5), 368–371.

Bradburn, Norman M., and Seymour Sudman. 1988. *Polls and Surveys: Understanding What They Tell Us.* San Francisco: Jossey-Bass.

Briar, Scott. 1973. "Effective Social Work Intervention in Direct Practice: Implications for Education," pp. 17–30 in *Facing the Challenge: Plenary Session Papers from the 19th Annual Program Meeting.* Alexandria, VA: Council on Social Work Education.

———. 1987. "Direct Practice: Trends and Issues," *Encyclopedia of Social Work,* 18th ed., vol. 1, pp. 393–398. Silver Spring, MD: National Association of Social Workers.

Briggs, H. E., and T. L. Rzepnicki (eds.). 2004. *Using Evidence in Social Work Practice: Behavioral Perspectives.* Chicago: Lyceum Books.

Brodsky, S. L., and H. O. Smitherman. 1983. *Handbook of Scales for Research in Crime and Delinquency.* New York: Plenum Press.

Brownlee, K. A. 1975. "A Note on the Effects of Nonresponse on Surveys," *Journal of the American Statistical Association, 52*(227), 29–32.

Buckingham, R., S. Lack, B. Mount, L. MacLean, and J. Collins. 1976. "Living with the Dying," *Canadian Medical Association Journal, 115,* 1211–1215.

Burnette, Denise. 1994. "Managing Chronic Illness Alone in Late Life: Sisyphus at Work," pp. 5–27 in Catherine Reissman (ed.), *Qualitative Studies in Social Work Research.* Thousand Oaks, CA: Sage.

———. 1998. "Conceptual and Methodological Considerations in Research with Non-White Ethnic Elders," pp. 71–91 in Miriam Potocky and Antoinette Y. Rodgers-Farmer (eds.), *Social Work Research with Minority and Oppressed Populations: Methodological Issues and Innovations.* New York: Haworth Press.

Buros, O. 1978. *Eighth Mental Measurements Yearbook.* Highland Park, NJ: Gryphon Press.

Campbell, Donald T. 1971. "Methods for the Experimenting Society." Paper presented at the meeting of the Eastern Psychological Association, New York, and at the meeting of the American Psychological Association, Washington, DC.

———, and Julian Stanley. 1963. *Experimental and Quasi-experimental Designs for Research.* Chicago: Rand McNally.

Campbell, Patricia B. 1983. "The Impact of Societal Biases on Research Methods," pp. 197–213 in Barbara L. Richardson and Jeana Wirtenberg (eds.), *Sex Role Research.* New York: Praeger.

Carmines, Edward G., and Richard A. Zeller. 1979. *Reliability and Validity Assessment.* Beverly Hills, CA: Sage.

Cauce, Ana Mari, Nora Coronado, and Jennifer Watson. 1998. "Conceptual, Methodological, and Statistical Issues in Culturally Competent Research," pp. 305–329 in Mario Hernandez and Mareasa R. Isaacs, *Promoting Cultural Competence in Children's Mental Health Services.* Baltimore: Paul H. Brookes.

Cautela, J. R. 1981. *Behavior Analysis Forms for Clinical Intervention* (Vol. 2). Champaign, IL: Research Press.

Census Bureau. *See* U.S. Bureau of the Census.

Chaffee, Steven, and Sun Yuel Choe. 1980. "Time of Decision and Media Use During the Ford-Carter Campaign," *Public Opinion Quarterly* (Spring), 53–69.

Chambless, C. M., M. J. Baker, D. H. Baucom, L. E. Beutler, K. S. Calhoun, P. Crits-Christoph, A. Daiuto, R. DeRubeis, J. Detweiler, D. A. F. Haaga, S. B. Johnson, S. McCurry, K. T. Mueser, K. S. Pope, W. C. Sanderson, V. Shham, T. Stickle, D. A. Williams, and S. R. Woody. 1998. "Update on Empirically Validated Therapies II," *Clinical Psychologist, 51,* 3–16.

Chambless, D. L., W. C. Sanderson, V. Shoham, S. B. Johnson, K. S. Pope, P. Crits-Christoph, et al. 1996. "An Update on Empirically Validated Therapies," *Clinical Psychologist, 49,* 5–18.

Chronicle of Higher Education. 1988. "Scholar Who Submitted Bogus Article to Journals May Be Disciplined," Nov. 2, pp. A1, A7.

Chun, Ki-Taek, S. Cobb, and J. R. French. 1975. *Measures for Psychological Assessment: A Guide to 3,000 Original Sources and Their Applications.* Ann Arbor, MI: Institute for Social Research.

Ciarlo, J. A., T. R. Brown, D. W. Edwards, T. J. Kiresuk, and F. L. Newman. 1986. *Assessing Mental Health Treatment Outcome Measurement Techniques.* Rockville, MD: National Institute of Mental Health [DHHS Publication No. (ADM) 86–1301].

Cohen, Jacob. 1977. *Statistical Power Analysis for the Behavioral Sciences.* New York: Academic Press.

———. 1988. *Statistical Power Analysis for the Behavioral Sciences,* 2nd ed. New York: Lawrence Erlbaum Associates.

Coleman, James. 1966. *Equality of Educational Opportunity.* Washington, DC: U.S. Government Printing Office.

Compton, Beulah R., and Burt Galaway. 1994. *Social Work Processes.* Homewood, IL: Dorsey Press.

Comrey, A., T. Barker, and E. Glaser. 1975. *A Sourcebook for Mental Health Measures.* Los Angeles: Human Interaction Research Institute.

Comstock, Donald. 1980. "Dimensions of Influence in Organizations," *Pacific Sociological Review* (January), 67–84.

Conoley, J. C., and J. J. Kramer. 1995. *The 12th Mental Measurements Yearbook.* Lincoln, NE: Buros Institute of Mental Measurements.

Conrad, Kendon J., Frances L. Randolph, Michael W. Kirby, and Richard R. Bebout. 1999. "Creating and Using Logic Models: Four Perspectives," *Alcoholism Treatment Quarterly, 17*(1/2), 17–31.

Cook, Elizabeth. 1995. Communication to the METHODS listserv, April 25, from Michel de Seve (T120@music.ulaval.ca) to Cook (EC1645A@american.edu)@Online.

Cook, Thomas D., and Donald T. Campbell. 1979. *Quasi-experimentation: Design and Analysis Issues for Field Settings.* Chicago: Rand McNally.

Cooper, Harris M. 1989. *Integrating Research: A Guide for Literature Reviews.* Newbury Park, CA: Sage.

Cooper-Stephenson, Cynthia, and Athanasios Theologides. 1981. "Nutrition in Cancer: Physicians' Knowledge, Opinions, and Educational Needs," *Journal of the American Dietetic Association* (May), 472–476.

Corcoran, Jacqueline. 2000. *Evidence-Based Social Work Practice with Families: A Lifespan Approach.* New York: Springer.

———. 2003. *Clinical Applications of Evidence-Based Family Interventions.* Oxford: Oxford University Press.

Corcoran, K. J., and J. Fischer. 2000a. *Measures for Clinical Practice: Vol. 1. Couples, Families, Children.* (3rd ed). New York: The Free Press.

———. 2000b. *Measures for Clinical Practice: Vol. 2. Adults,* 3rd ed. New York: The Free Press.

Corcoran, Kevin, and Wallace J. Gingerich. 1994. "Practice Evaluation in the Context of Managed Care: Case-Recording Methods for Quality Assurance Reviews," *Research on Social Work Practice, 4*(3), 326–337.

Coulton, Claudia, Shanta Pandey, and Julia Chow. 1990. "Concentration of Poverty and the Changing Ecology of Low-Income, Urban Neighborhoods: An Analysis of the Cleveland Area," *Social Work Research and Abstracts, 26*(4), 5–16.

Couper, Mick P. 2001. "Web Surveys: A Review of Issues and Approaches." *Public Opinion Quarterly, 64*(4), 464–494.

Cournoyer, B., and G. T. Powers. 2002. "Evidence-Based Social Work: The Quiet Revolution Continues," pp. 798–807 in Albert R. Roberts and Gilbert J. Greene (eds.), *Social Workers' Desk Reference.* New York: Oxford University Press.

Cowger, Charles D. 1984. "Statistical Significance Tests: Scientific Ritualism or Scientific Method?" *Social Service Review, 58*(3), 358–372.

———. 1985. "Author's Reply," *Social Service Review, 59*(3), 520–522.

———. 1987. "Correcting Misuse Is the Best Defense of Statistical Tests of Significance," *Social Service Review, 61*(1), 170–172.

Crawford, Kent S., Edmund D. Thomas, and Jeffrey J. Fink. 1980. "Pygmalion at Sea: Improving the Work Effectiveness of Low Performers," *Journal of Applied Behavioral Science* (October–December), 482–505.

Crowe, Teresa V. 2002. "Translation of the Rosenberg Self-Esteem Scale into American Sign Language: A Principal Components Analysis," *Social Work Research, 26*(1), 57–63.

Cuéllar, Israel, and Freddy A. Paniagua (eds.). 2000. *Handbook of Multicultural Mental Health: Assessment and Treatment of Diverse Populations.* San Diego, CA: Academic Press.

Cummerton, J. 1983. "A Feminist Perspective on Research: What Does It Help Us to See?" Paper presented at the Annual Program Meeting of the Council on Social Work Education, Fort Worth, Texas.

Dahlstrom, W. Grant, and George S. Welsh. 1960. *An MMPI Handbook.* Minneapolis: University of Minnesota Press.

Dallas Morning News. 1990. "Welfare Study Withholds Benefits from 800 Texans," Feb. 11, p. 1.

Daly, Kerry. 1992. "The Fit Between Qualitative Research and Characteristics of Families," pp. 3–11 in Jane Gilgun, Kerry Daly, and Gerald Handel (eds.), *Qualitative Methods in Family Research.* Thousand Oaks, CA: Sage.

Dana, Richard (ed.). 2000. *Handbook of Cross-Cultural Personality Assessment.* Mahwah, NJ: Lawrence Erlbaum Associates.

Davis, Fred. 1973. "The Martian and the Convert: Ontological Polarities in Social Research," *Urban Life, 2*(3), 333–343.

DeFleur, Lois. 1975. "Biasing Influences on Drug Arrest Records: Implications for Deviance Research," *American Sociological Review* (February), 88–103.

De Maria, W. 1981. "Empiricism: An Impoverished Philosophy for Social Work Research," *Australian Social Work, 34,* 3–8.

Denzin, Norman K., and Yvonna S. Lincoln. 1994. *Handbook of Qualitative Research.* Thousand Oaks, CA: Sage, 1994.

DePanfilis, Diane, and Susan J. Zuravin. 2002. "The Effect of Services on the Recurrence of Child Maltreatment," *Child Abuse & Neglect, 26,* 187–205.

Dillman, Don A. 1978. *Mail and Telephone Surveys: The Total Design Method.* New York: Wiley.

———. 2000. *Mail and Internet Surveys: The Tailored Design Method,* 2nd ed. New York: Wiley.

Donald, Marjorie N. 1960. "Implications of Nonresponse for the Interpretation of Mail Questionnaire Data," *Public Opinion Quarterly, 24*(1), 99–114.

Draguns, Juris G. 2000. "Multicultural and Cross-Cultural Assessment: Dilemmas and Decisions," pp. 37–84 in Gargi Roysircar Sodowsky and James C. Impara (eds.), *Multicultural Assessment in Counseling and Clinical Psychology.* Lincoln, NE: Buros Institute of Mental Measurements.

DuBois, B. 1983. "Passionate Scholarship: Notes on Values, Knowing and Method in Feminist Social Science," pp. 105–116 in G. Bowles and R. Duelli-Klein (eds.), *Theories of Women's Studies.* London: Routledge & Kegan Paul.

Duelli-Klein, R. 1983. "How to Do What We Want to Do: Thoughts about Feminist Methodology," pp. 88–104 in G. Bowles and R. Duelli-Klein (eds.), *Theories in Women's Studies.* London: Routledge & Kegan Paul.

Eichler, Margrit. 1988. *Nonsexist Research Methods.* Boston: Allen & Unwin.

Einstein, Albert. 1940. "The Fundamentals of Theoretical Physics," *Science* (May 24), 487.

Elder, Glen H., Jr., Eliza K. Pavalko, and Elizabeth C. Clipp. 1993. *Working with Archival Data: Studying Lives.* Newbury Park, CA: Sage.

Emerson, Robert M. (ed.). 1988. *Contemporary Field Research.* Boston: Little, Brown.

England, Suzanne E. 1994. "Modeling Theory from Fiction and Autobiography," pp. 190–213 in Catherine K. Reissman (ed.), *Qualitative Studies in Social Work Research.* Thousand Oaks, CA: Sage.

Epstein, Irwin. 1985. "Quantitative and Qualitative Methods," pp. 263–274 in Richard M. Grinnell (ed.), *Social Work Research and Evaluation.* Itasca, IL: Peacock.

Epstein, W. M. 2004. "Confirmational Response Bias and the Quality of the Editorial Processes among American Social Work Journals," *Research on Social Work Practice, 14*(6), 450–458.

Evans, William. 1996. "Computer-Supported Content Analysis: Trends, Tools, and Techniques," *Social Science Computer Review, 14*(3), 269–279.

Feick, Lawrence F. 1989. "Latent Class Analysis of Survey Questions That Include Don't Know Responses," *Public Opinion Quarterly 53,* 525–47.

Festinger, L., H. W. Reicker, and S. Schachter. 1956. *When Prophecy Fails.* Minneapolis: University of Minnesota Press.

Fischer, Joel. 1973. "Is Social Work Effective: A Review," *Social Work, 18*(1), 5–20.

———. 1978. *Effective Casework Practice: An Eclectic Approach.* New York: McGraw-Hill.

———. 1990. "Problems and Issues in Meta-analysis," pp. 297–325 in Lynn Videka-Sherman and William J. Reid (eds.), *Advances in Clinical Social Work Research.* Silver Spring, MD: NASW Press.

Foa, E. B., T. M. Keane, and M. J. Friedman. 2000. *Effective Treatments for PTSD.* New York: Guilford Press.

Fong, Rowena, and Sharlene Furuto (eds.). 2001. *Culturally Competent Practice: Skills, Interventions, and Evaluations.* Boston: Allyn & Bacon.

Fowler, Floyd J., Jr. 1995. *Improving Survey Questions: Design and Evaluation.* Thousand Oaks, CA: Sage.

Frankfort-Nachmias, Chava, and Anna Leon-Guerrero. 1997. *Social Statistics for a Diverse Society.* Thousand Oaks, CA: Pine Forge Press.

Franklin, Cynthia, and Paula Nurius. 1998. *Constructivism in Practice: Methods and Challenges.* Milwaukee, WI: Families International.

Fredman, N., and R. Sherman. 1987. *Handbook of Measurements for Marriage and Family Therapy.* New York: Brunner/Mazel.

Gage, N. 1989. "The Paradigm Wars and Their Aftermath: A 'Historical' Sketch of Research and Teaching Since 1989," *Educational Research, 18,* 4–10.

Gall, John. 1975. *Systemantics: How Systems Work and Especially How They Fail.* New York: Quadrangle.

Gallup, George. 1984. "Where Parents Go Wrong," *San Francisco Chronicle* (Dec. 13), p. 7.

Gambrill, E. 1999. "Evidence-Based Practice: An Alternative to Authority-Based Practice," *Families in Society, 80,* 341–350.

———. 2001. "Educational Policy and Accreditation Standards: Do They Work for Clients?" *Journal of Social Work Education, 37,* 226–239.

Garant, Carol. 1980. "Stalls in the Therapeutic Process," *American Journal of Nursing* (December), 2166–2167.

Gaventa, J. 1991. "Towards a Knowledge Democracy: Viewpoints on Participatory Research in North America," pp. 121–131 in O. Fals-Borda and M. A. Rahman (eds.), *Action and Knowledge: Breaking the Monopoly with Participatory Action-Research.* New York: Apex Press.

Gibbs, Leonard, and Eileen Gambrill. 1999. *Critical Thinking for Social Workers: Exercises for the Helping Professions.* Thousand Oaks, CA: Pine Forge Press.

———. 2002. "Evidence-Based Practice: Counterarguments to Objections." *Research on Social Work Practice, 12,* 452–476.

Gilgun, Jane. 1991. "Hand into Glove: The Grounded Theory Approach and Social Work Practice Research." Paper presented at the Research Conference on Qualitative Methods in Social Work Practice Research, Nelson A. Rockefeller Institute of Government, State University of New York at Albany, August 24.

———, Kerry Daly, and Gerald Handel (eds.). 1992. *Qualitative Methods in Family Research.* Thousand Oaks, CA: Sage.

Ginsberg, Leon. 1995. *Social Work Almanac,* 2nd ed. Washington, DC: NASW Press.

Giuli, Charles A., and Walter W. Hudson. 1977. "Assessing Parent–Child Relationship Disorders in Clinical Practice: The Child's Point of View," *Journal of Social Service Research, 1*(1), 77–92.

Glaser, Barney, and Anselm Strauss. 1967. *The Discovery of Grounded Theory: Strategies for Qualitative Research.* Chicago: Aldine.

Glisson, Charles. 1987. "Author's Reply," *Social Service Review, 61*(1), 172–176.

Glock, Charles Y., Benjamin B. Ringer, and Earl R. Babbie. 1967. *To Comfort and to Challenge.* Berkeley: University of California Press.

Goffman, Erving. 1961. *Asylums: Essays on the Social Situation of Mental Patients and Other Inmates.* Chicago: Aldine.

———. 1963. *Stigma: Notes on the Management of a Spoiled Identity.* Englewood Cliffs, NJ: Prentice Hall.

———. 1974. *Frame Analysis.* Cambridge, MA: Harvard University Press.

———. 1979. *Gender Advertisements.* New York: Harper & Row.

Gold, Raymond L. 1969. "Roles in Sociological Field Observation," pp. 30–39 in George J. McCall and J. L. Simmons (eds.), *Issues in Participant Observation.* Reading, MA: Addison-Wesley.

Goldberg, W., and M. Tomlanovich. 1984. "Domestic Violence Victims in the Emergency Department," *Journal of the American Medical Association, 32* (June 22–29), 59–64.

Goldman, B. A., and J. C. Busch. 1982. *Directory of Unpublished Experimental Measures* (Vol. 3). New York: Human Sciences Press.

Goldstein, Eda G. 1995. "Psychosocial Approach," *Encyclopedia of Social Work,* 19th ed., vol. 3, pp. 1948–1954. Washington, DC: National Association of Social Workers.

Gorey, K. M. 1996. "Effectiveness of Social Work Intervention Research: Internal Versus External Evaluations," *Social Work Research, 20,* 119–128.

Gottlieb, Naomi, and M. Bombyk. 1987. "Strategies for Strengthening Feminist Research," *Affilia* (Summer), 23–35.

Goyder, John. 1985. "Face-to-Face Interviews and Mailed Questionnaires: The Net Difference in Response Rate," *Public Opinion Quarterly, 49,* 234–252.

Graham, Laurie, and Richard Hogan. 1990. "Social Class and Tactics: Neighborhood Opposition to Group Homes," *Sociological Quarterly, 31*(4), 513–529.

Graham, Mary. 1989. "One Toke over the Line," *New Republic, 200*(16), 20–21.

Greene, Robert, Katrina Murphy, and Shelita Snyder. 2000. "Should Demographics be Placed at the End or at the Beginning of Mailed Questionnaires? An Empirical Answer to a Persistent Methodological Question," *Social Work Research, 24*(4), 237–241.

Grinnell, R. M., Jr. 1997. *Social Work Research & Evaluation: Quantitative and Qualitative Approaches*. Itasca, IL: Peacock.

Grob, Gerald N. 1973. *Mental Institutions in America*. New York: The Free Press.

Grotevant, H. D., and D. I. Carlson (eds.). 1989. *Family Assessment: A Guide to Methods and Measures*. New York: Guilford Press.

Groves, Robert M. 1990. "Theories and Methods of Telephone Surveys," pp. 221–240 in W. Richard Scott and Judith Blake (eds.), *Annual Review of Sociology* (vol. 16). Palo Alto, CA: Annual Reviews.

Guba, E. G. 1981. "Criteria for Assessing the Trustworthiness of Naturalistic Inquiries," *Educational Resources Information Center Annual Review Paper, 29*, 75–91.

Gubrium, Jaber F., and James A. Holstein. 1997. *The New Language of Qualitative Method*. New York: Oxford University Press.

Haase, Richard F., Donna M. Waechter, and Gary S. Solomon. 1982. "How Significant Is a Significant Difference? Average Effect Size of Research in Counseling Psychology," *Journal of Counseling Psychology, 29*(2), 59–63.

Habermas, Jurgen. 1971. *Knowledge and Human Interests*. Boston: Beacon Press.

Hamblin, Robert L. 1971. "Mathematical Experimentation and Sociological Theory: A Critical Analysis," *Sociometry, 34*, 4.

Harrington, R. G. (ed.). 1986. *Testing Adolescents: A Reference Guide for Comprehensive Psychological Assessment Techniques*. Elmsford, NY: Pergamon Press.

Healey, Joseph F. 1999. *Statistics: A Tool for Social Research*. Belmont, CA: Wadsworth.

Heath, Anthony W. 1997. "The Proposal in Qualitative Research," *Qualitative Report, 3*(1) (March).

Heineman, M. B. 1981. "The Obsolete Scientific Imperative in Social Work Research," *Social Service Review, 55*, 371–397.

Hempel, Carl G. 1952. "Fundamentals of Concept Formation in Empirical Science," *International Encyclopedia of United Science*, vol. 2, no 7. Chicago: University of Chicago.

Hepworth, D. H., R. Rooney, and J. A. Larsen. 2002. *Direct Social Work Practice: Theory and Skills*, 6th ed. Belmont, CA: Wadsworth.

Herman, Daniel B., Ezra S. Susser, Elmer L. Struening, and Bruce L. Link. 1997. "Adverse Childhood Experiences: Are They Risk Factors for Adult Homelessness?" *American Journal of Public Health, 87*, 249–255.

Hernandez, Mario, and Mareesa R. Isaacs (eds.). 1998. *Promoting Cultural Competence in Children's Mental Health Services*. Baltimore: Paul H. Brookes.

Hersen, M., and A. S. Bellack (eds.). 1988. *Dictionary of Behavioral Assessment Techniques*. Elmsford, NY: Pergamon Press.

Higginbotham, A. Leon, Jr. 1978. *In the Matter of Color: Race and the American Legal Process*. New York: Oxford University Press.

Hill, R. R. 1978. "Social Work Research on Minorities: Impediments and Opportunities." Paper presented at the National Conference on the Future of Social Work Research, San Antonio, Texas; October.

Hirschi, Travis, and Hanan Selvin. 1973. *Principles of Survey Analysis*. New York: The Free Press.

Hogarty, Gerard. 1979. "Aftercare Treatment of Schizophrenia: Current Status and Future Direction," pp. 19–36 in H. M. Pragg (ed.), *Management of Schizophrenia*. Assen, Netherlands: Van Gorcum.

———. 1989. "Meta-analysis of the Effects of Practice with the Chronically Mentally Ill: A Critique and Reappraisal of the Literature," *Social Work, 34*(4), 363–373.

Hohmann, Ann A., and Delores L. Parron. 1996. "How the NIH Guidelines on Inclusion of Women and Minorities Apply: Efficacy Trials, Effectiveness Trials, and Validity," *Journal of Consulting and Clinical Psychology, 64*(5), 851–855.

Homans, George C. 1971. "Reply to Blain," *Sociological Inquiry, 41* (Winter), 23.

Hough, Richard L., Henry Tarke, Virginia Renker, Patricia Shields, and Jeff Glatstein. 1996. "Recruitment and Retention of Homeless Mentally Ill Participants in Research," *Journal of Consulting and Clinical Psychology, 64*(5), 881–891.

Howell, Joseph T. 1973. *Hard Living on Clay Street*. Garden City, NY: Doubleday Anchor.

Hudson, W. W. 1982. *The Clinical Measurement Package: A Field Manual*. Homewood, IL: Dorsey Press.

———. 1992. *The WALMYR Assessment Scales Scoring Manual*. Tempe, AZ: WALMYR.

———. 1997. "Assessment Tools as Outcomes Measures in Social Work," pp. 68–80 in Edward J. Mullen and Jennifer L. Magnabosco (eds.), *Outcomes Measurement in the Human Services: Cross-Cutting Issues and Methods*. Washington, DC: NASW Press.

Hughes, Michael. 1980. "The Fruits of Cultivation Analysis: A Reexamination of Some Effects of Television Watching," *Public Opinion Quarterly* (Fall), 287–302.

Humphreys, Laud. 1970. *Tearoom Trade: Impersonal Sex in Public Places*. Chicago: Aldine.

Hutchby, Ian, and Robin Wooffitt. 1998. *Conversation Analysis: Principles, Practices and Applications*. Cambridge, England: Polity Press.

Hyun, Sung Lim, and Miriam McNown Johnson. 2001. "Korean Social Work Students' Attitudes Toward Homosexuals," *Journal of Social Work Education, 37*(3), 545–554.

Jackman, Mary R., and Mary Scheuer Senter. 1980. "Images of Social Groups: Categorical or Qualified?" *Public Opinion Quarterly, 44*, 340–361.

Jackson, Aurora P., and Andre Ivanoff. 1999. "Reduction of Low Response Rates in Interview Surveys of Poor African-American Families," *Journal of Social Service Research, 25*(1–2), 41–60.

Jacob, T., and D. L. Tennebaum. 1988. *Family Assessment: Rationale, Methods, and Future Directions*. New York: Plenum Press.

Jayaratne, Srinika, and Rona L. Levy. 1979. *Empirical Clinical Practice*. New York: Columbia University Press.

Jayaratne, Srinika, Tony Tripodi, and Eugene Talsma. 1988. "The Comparative Analysis and Aggregation of Single Case Data," *Journal of Applied Behavioral Science, 1*(24), 119–128.

Jensen, Arthur. 1969. "How Much Can We Boost IQ and Scholastic Achievement?" *Harvard Educational Review, 39*, 273–274.

Johnson, Jeffrey C. 1990. *Selecting Ethnographic Informants*. Newbury Park, CA: Sage Publications.

Johnston, Hank. 1980. "The Marketed Social Movement: A Case Study of the Rapid Growth of TM," *Pacific Sociological Review* (July), 333–354.

Jones, James H. 1981. *Bad Blood: The Tuskegee Syphilis Experiment*. New York: The Free Press.

Jones, Lovell. 1991. "The Impact of Cancer on the Health Status of Minorities in Texas." Paper presented to the Texas Minority Health Strategic Planning Conference, July.

Kahane, Howard. 1992. *Logic and Contemporary Rhetoric*, 2nd ed. Belmont, CA: Wadsworth.

Kalton, Graham. 1983. *Introduction to Survey Sampling*. Newbury Park, CA: Sage.

Kaplan, Abraham. 1964. *The Conduct of Inquiry*. San Francisco: Chandler.

Keeter, Scott. 2006. "The Impact of Cell Phone Noncoverage Bias on Polling in the 2004 Presidential Election," *Public Opinion Quarterly, 70*(1), 88–98.

Keitel, Merle A., Mary Kopala, and Warren Stanley Adamson. 1996. "Ethical Issues in Multicultural Assessment," pp. 29–50 in Lisa Suzuki, Paul J. Meller, and Joseph G. Ponterotto (eds.), *Handbook of Multicultural Assessment.* San Francisco: Jossey-Bass.

Kellogg Foundation. 2004. *W. K. Kellogg Foundation Logic Model Development Guide.* Battle Creek, MI: Author.

Kelly, A. 1978. "Feminism and Research," *Women's Studies International Quarterly, 1,* 226.

Kendall, Patricia L., and Paul F. Lazarsfeld. 1950. "Problems of Survey Analysis," in Robert K. Merton and Paul F. Lazarsfeld (eds.), *Continuities in Social Research: Studies in the Scope and Method of "The American Soldier."* New York: The Free Press.

Kestenbaum, C. J., and D. T. Williams (eds.). 1988. *Handbook of Clinical Assessment of Children and Adolescents.* Austin, TX: Pro-Ed.

Kinnell, Ann Marie, and Douglas W. Maynard. 1996. "The Delivery and Receipt of Safer Sex Advice in Pretest Counseling Sessions for HIV and AIDS," *Journal of Contemporary Ethnography, 24,* 405–437.

Kirk, Stuart A., and William J. Reid. 2002. *Science and Social Work.* New York: Columbia University Press.

Kish, Leslie. 1965. *Survey Sampling.* New York: Wiley.

Knoff, H. M. 1986. *The Assessment of Child and Adolescent Personality.* New York: Guilford Press.

Krefting, Laura. 1991. "Rigor in Qualitative Research: The Assessment of Trustworthiness," *American Journal of Occupational Therapy, 45*(3), 214–222.

Kronick, Jane C. 1989. "Toward a Formal Methodology of Document Analysis in the Interpretive Tradition." Paper presented at the meeting of the Eastern Sociological Society, Baltimore, MD.

Kuhn, Thomas. 1970. *The Structure of Scientific Revolutions,* 2nd ed. Chicago: University of Chicago Press.

Kulis, Stephen, Maria Napoli, and Flavio Francisco Marsiglia. 2002. "Ethnic Pride, Biculturalism, and Drug Use Norms of Urban American Indian Adolescents," *Social Work Research,* June.

Kvale, Steinar. 1996. *InterViews: An Introduction to Qualitative Research Interviewing.* Thousand Oaks, CA: Sage.

Ladd, Everett C., and G. Donald Ferree. 1981. "Were the Pollsters Really Wrong?" *Public Opinion* (Dec.–Jan.), 13–20.

LaGreca, A. M. 1990. *Through the Eyes of the Child: Obtaining Self-Reports from Children and Adolescents.* Boston: Allyn & Bacon.

Lake, D. G., M. B. Miles, and R. B. Earle, Jr. 1973. *Measuring Human Behavior: Tools for the Assessment of Social Functioning.* New York: Teachers College Press.

Lasch, Christopher. 1977. *Haven in a Heartless World.* New York: Basic Books.

Lazarsfeld, Paul. 1959. "Problems in Methodology," in Robert K. Merton (ed.), *Sociology Today.* New York: Basic Books.

———, Ann Pasanella, and Morris Rosenberg (eds.). 1972. *Continuities in the Language of Social Research.* New York: The Free Press.

Lee, Raymond. 1993. *Doing Research on Sensitive Topics.* Newbury Park, CA: Sage.

Lewis-Beck, Michael. 1995. *Data Analysis: An Introduction* (vol. 103 in Quantitative Application in the Social Sciences series). Thousand Oaks, CA: Sage.

Liebow, Elliot. 1967. *Tally's Corner.* Boston: Little, Brown.

———. 1993. *Tell Them Who I Am: The Lives of Homeless Women.* New York: The Free Press.

Lincoln, Y. S., and E. A. Guba. 1985. *Naturalistic Inquiry.* Beverly Hills, CA: Sage.

Lipsey, Mark W. 1990. *Design Sensitivity: Statistical Power for Experimental Research.* Newbury Park, CA: Sage.

Literary Digest. 1936a. "Landon, 1,293,669: Roosevelt, 972,897," Oct. 31, 5–6.

———. 1936b. "What Went Wrong with the Polls?" Nov. 14, 7–8.

Lofland, John. 1995. "Analytic Ethnography: Features, Failings, and Futures," *Journal of Contemporary Ethnography, 24*(1), 30–67.

———, and Lyn H. Lofland. 1995. *Analyzing Social Settings,* 3rd ed. Belmont, CA: Wadsworth.

Longres, John F., and Edward Scanlon. 2001. "Social Justice and the Research Curriculum," *Health and Social Work, 37*(3), 447–463.

Luker, K. 1984. *Abortion and the Politics of Motherhood.* Berkeley: University of California Press.

Magura, S., and B. S. Moses. 1987. *Outcome Measures for Child Welfare Services.* Washington, DC: Child Welfare League of America.

Manning, Peter K., and Betsy Cullum-Swan. 1994. "Narrative, Content, and Semiotic Analysis," pp. 463–477 in Norman K. Denzin and Yvonna S. Lincoln (eds.), *Handbook of Qualitative Research.* Thousand Oaks, CA: Sage.

Marsden, Gerald. 1971. "Content Analysis Studies of Psychotherapy: 1954 through 1968," in Allen E. Bergin and Sol L. Garfield (eds.), *Handbook of Psychotherapy and Behavior Change: An Empirical Analysis.* New York: Wiley.

Marshall, Catherine, and Gretchen B. Rossman. 1995. *Designing Qualitative Research.* Thousand Oaks, CA: Sage.

Martin, R. P. 1988. *Assessment of Personality and Behavior Problems: Infancy through Adolescence.* New York: Guilford Press.

Maruish, M. E. (ed.). 2000. *Handbook of Psychological Assessment in Primary Care Settings.* Mahwah, NJ: Lawrence Erlbaum Associates.

———. 2002. *Psychological Testing in the Age of Managed Behavioral Health Care.* Mahwah, NJ: Lawrence Erlbaum Associates.

Marx, Karl. 1867. *Capital.* New York: International Publishers. (Reprinted 1967.)

———. 1880. *Revue Socialist* (July 5). Reprinted in T. B. Bottomore and Maximilien Rubel (eds.), *Karl Marx: Selected Writings in Sociology and Social Philosophy.* New York: McGraw-Hill, 1956.

Mash, E. J., and L. G. Terdal. 1988. *Behavioral Assessment of Childhood Disorders.* New York: Guilford Press.

Matocha, Linda K. 1992. "Case Study Interviews: Caring for Persons with AIDS," pp. 66–84 in Jane Gilgun, Kerry Daly, and Gerald Handel (eds.), *Qualitative Methods in Family Research.* Thousand Oaks, CA: Sage.

Maxwell, Joseph A. 1996. *Qualitative Research Design: An Interactive Approach.* Thousand Oaks, CA: Sage.

McAlister, Alfred, Cheryl Perry, Joel Killen, Lee Ann Slinkard, and Nathan Maccoby. 1980. "Pilot Study of Smoking, Alcohol, and Drug Abuse Prevention," *American Journal of Public Health* (July), 719–721.

McCall, George J., and J. L. Simmons (eds.). 1969. *Issues in Participant Observation.* Reading, MA: Addison-Wesley.

McCubbin, H. I., and A. I. Thompson (eds.). 1987. *Family Assessment Inventories for Research and Practice.* Madison: University of Wisconsin–Madison.

McRoy, Ruth G. 1981. *A Comparative Study of the Self-Concept of Transracially and Inracially Adopted Black Children.* Dissertation, University of Texas at Austin.

———, Harold D. Grotevant, Susan Ayers Lopez, and Ann Furuta. 1990. "Adoption Revelation and Communication Issues: Implications for Practice," *Families in Society, 71*(9), 550–557.

McWirter, Norris. 1980. *The Guinness Book of Records.* New York: Bantam.

Menard, Scott. 1991. *Longitudinal Research.* Newbury Park, CA: Sage.

Mercer, Susan, and Rosalie A. Kane. 1979. "Helplessness and Hopelessness among the Institutionalized Aged," *Health and Social Work, 4*(1), 91–116.

Messer, S. B. 2006. "What Qualifies as Evidence in Effective Practice? Patient Values and Preferences," pp. 31–40 in J. C. Norcross, L. E. Beutler, and R. F. Levant (eds.), *Evidence-Based Practices in Mental Health: Debate and Dialogue on the Fundamental Questions.* Washington, DC: American Psychological Association.

Mies, M. 1983. "Toward a Methodology for Feminist Research," pp. 117–139 in G. Bowles and R. Duelli-Klein (eds.), *Theories of Women's Studies.* London: Routledge & Kegan Paul.

Miles, Matthew B., and A. Michael Huberman. 1994. *Qualitative Data Analysis,* 2nd ed. Thousand Oaks, CA: Sage.

Milgram, Stanley. 1963. "Behavioral Study of Obedience," *Journal of Abnormal and Social Psychology, 67,* 371–378.

———. 1965. "Some Conditions of Obedience and Disobedience to Authority," *Human Relations, 18,* 57–76.

Miller, Delbert C. 1983. *Handbook of Research Design and Social Measurement,* 4th ed. New York: Longman.

———. 1991. *Handbook of Research Design and Social Measurement,* 5th ed. New York: Longman.

Miller, William L., and Benjamin F. Crabtree. 1994. "Clinical Research," pp. 340–352 in Norman K. Denzin and Yvonna S. Lincoln (eds.), *Handbook of Qualitative Research.* Thousand Oaks, CA: Sage.

Miranda, Jeanne. 1996. "Introduction to the Special Section of Recruiting and Retaining Minorities in Psychotherapy Research," *Journal of Consulting and Clinical Psychology, 64*(5), 848–850.

Mitchell, J. V. 1983. *Tests in Print III.* Lincoln, NE: Buros Institute of Mental Measurements.

——— (ed.). 1985. *The Ninth Mental Measurements Yearbook.* Lincoln: University of Nebraska Press.

Mitchell, Richard G., Jr. 1991. "Secrecy and Disclosure in Field Work," pp. 97–108 in William B. Shaffir and Robert A. Stebbins (eds.), *Experiencing Fieldwork: An Inside View of Qualitative Research.* Newbury Park, CA: Sage.

Mitofsky, Warren J. 1999. "Miscalls Likely in 2000," *Public Perspective, 10*(5), 42–43.

Monette, Duane R., Thomas J. Sullivan, and Cornell R. DeJong. 1994. *Applied Social Research: Tool for the Human Services,* 3rd ed. Fort Worth, TX: Harcourt Brace.

———. 2002. *Applied Social Research: Tool for the Human Services,* 5th ed. Fort Worth, TX: Harcourt Brace.

Moore, David W. 2002. "Measuring New Types of Question-Order Effects: Additive and Subtractive," *Public Opinion Quarterly, 66,* 80–91.

Moreland, Kevin L. 1996. "Persistent Issues in Multicultural Assessment of Social and Emotional Functioning," pp. 51–76 in Lisa Suzuki, Paul J. Meller, and Joseph G. Ponterotto (eds.), *Handbook of Multicultural Assessment.* San Francisco: Jossey-Bass.

Morgan, David L. 1993. *Successful Focus Groups: Advancing the State of the Art.* Newbury Park, CA: Sage.

Morgan, Lewis H. 1870. *Systems of Consanguinity and Affinity.* Washington, DC: Smithsonian Institution.

Morrison, Denton, and Ramon Henkel (eds.). 1970. *The Significance Test Controversy: A Reader.* Chicago: Aldine-Atherton.

Morrissey, J., and H. Goldman. 1984. "Cycles of Reform in the Care of the Chronically Mentally Ill," *Hospital and Community Psychiatry, 35*(8), 785–793.

Morse, Janice M. 1994. "Designing Funded Qualitative Research," in Norman K. Denzin and Yvonna S. Lincoln (eds.), *Handbook of Qualitative Research.* Thousand Oaks, CA: Sage.

Moskowitz, Milt. 1981. "The Drugs That Doctors Order," *San Francisco Chronicle* (May 23), 33.

Moss, Kathryn E. 1988. "Writing Research Proposals," pp. 429–445 in Richard M. Grinnell, Jr. (ed.), *Social Work Research and Evaluation,* 3rd ed. Itasca, IL: Peacock.

Mowbray, Carol T., Lisa C. Jordan, Kurt M. Ribisl, Angelina Kewalramani, Douglas Luke, Sandra Herman, and Deborah Bybee. 1999. "Analysis of Postdischarge Change in a Dual Diagnosis Population," *Health & Social Work, 4*(2), 91–101.

Moynihan, Daniel. 1965. *The Negro Family: The Case for National Action.* Washington, DC: U.S. Government Printing Office.

Mullen, Edward J. 2006. "Facilitating Practitioner Use of Evidence-Based Practice," pp. 152–159 in Albert R. Roberts and Kenneth R. Yeager (eds.), *Foundations of Evidence-Based Social Work Practice.* New York: Oxford University Press.

———, and Jennifer L. Magnabosco (eds.). 1997. *Outcomes Measurement in the Human Services: Cross-Cutting Issues and Methods.* Washington, DC: NASW Press.

———, and W. B. Bacon. 2004. "Implementation of Practice Guidelines and Evidence-Based Treatment: A Survey of Psychiatrists, Psychologists, and Social Workers," pp. 210–218 in A. R. Roberts and K. Yeager (eds.), *Evidence-Based Practice Manual: Research and Outcome Measures in Health and Human Services.* New York: Oxford University Press.

———, and J. R. Dumpson (eds.). 1972. *Evaluation of Social Intervention.* San Francisco: Jossey-Bass.

———, and D. L. Streiner. 2004. "The Evidence For and Against Evidence-Based Practice," *Brief Treatment and Crisis Intervention, 4,* 111–121.

Murray, Charles. 1984. *Losing Ground.* New York: Basic Books.

———, and Richard J. Herrnstein. 1994. *The Bell Curve.* New York: The Free Press.

Myrdal, Gunnar. 1944. *An American Dilemma.* New York: Harper & Row.

National Association of Social Workers. 1997. *An Author's Guide to Social Work Journals,* 4th ed. Washington, DC: NASW Press.

Neuman, W. Lawrence. 1994. *Social Research Methods: Qualitative and Quantitative Approaches.* Needham Heights, MA: Allyn & Bacon.

———. 2000. *Social Research Methods: Qualitative and Quantitative Approaches,* 4th ed., Boston: Allyn & Bacon.

Newton, Rae R., and Kjell Erik Rudestam. 1999. *Your Statistical Consultant: Answers to Your Data Analysis Questions.* Thousand Oaks, CA: Sage.

New York Times,. 1984. "Method of Polls in Two States," June 6, p. 12.

———. 1988. "Test of Journals Is Criticized as Unethical," Sept. 27, pp. 21, 25.

———. 1989. "Charges Dropped on Bogus Work," April 4, p. 21.

Nicholls, William L., II, Reginald P. Baker, and Jean Martin. 1996. "The Effect of New Data Collection Technology on Survey Data Quality," in *Survey Measurement and Process Quality,* L. Lyberg, P. Biemer, M. Collins, C. Dippo, N. Schwartz, and D. Trewin (eds.). New York: Wiley.

Nichols, David S., Jesus Padilla, and Emilia Lucio Gomez-Maqueo. 2000. "Issues in the Cross-Cultural Adaptation and Use of the MMPI-2," pp. 247–266 in Richard Dana (ed.), *Handbook of Cross-Cultural Personality Assessment.* Mahwah, NJ: Lawrence Erlbaum Associates.

Nie, Norman H., C. Hadlai Hull, Jean G. Jenkins, Karing Steinbrenner, and Dale H. Bent. 1975. *Statistical Package for the Social Sciences.* New York: McGraw-Hill.

Norton, Ilena M., and Spero M. Manson. 1996. "Research in American Indian and Alaska Native Communities: Navigating the Cultural Universe of Values and Process," *Journal of Consulting and Clinical Psychology, 64*(5), 856–860.

Nugent, William R. 1991. "An Experimental and Qualitative Analysis of a Cognitive-Behavioral Intervention for Anger," *Social Work Research and Abstracts, 27*(3), 3–8.

Nurius, P. S., and W. W. Hudson. 1988. "Computer-Based Practice: Future Dream or Current Technology?" *Social Work, 33*(4), 357–362.

Oakley, A. 1981. "Interviewing Women: A Contradiction in Terms," in H. Roberts (ed.), *Doing Feminist Research.* London: Routledge & Kegan Paul.

Ogles, B. M., and K. S. Masters. 1996. *Assessing Outcome in Clinical Practice.* Boston: Allyn & Bacon.

O'Hare, T. 2005. *Evidence-Based Practices for Social Workers: An Interdisciplinary Approach.* Chicago, IL: Lyceum Books.

Ollendick, T. H., and M. Hersen. 1992. *Handbook of Child and Adolescent Assessment.* Des Moines, IA: Allyn & Bacon.

Orme, John G., and Terri D. Combs-Orme. 1986. "Statistical Power and Type II Errors in Social Work Research," *Social Work Research & Abstracts, 22*(3), 3–10.

Ortega, Debora M., and Cheryl A. Richey. 1998. "Methodological Issues in Social Work Research with Depressed Women of Color," pp. 47–70 in Miriam Potocky and Antoinette Y. Rodgers-Farmer (eds.), *Social Work Research with Minority and Oppressed Populations: Methodological Issues and Innovations.* New York: Haworth Press.

Øyen, Else (ed.). 1990. *Comparative Methodology: Theory and Practice in International Social Research.* Newbury Park, CA: Sage.

Ozawa, Martha N. 1989. "Welfare Policies and Illegitimate Birth Rates among Adolescents: Analysis of State-by-State Data," *Social Work Research and Abstracts, 24*(2), 5–11.

Padgett, Deborah K. 1998a. "Does the Glove Really Fit? Qualitative Research and Clinical Social Work Practice," *Social Work, 43*(4), 373–381.

———. 1998b. *Qualitative Methods in Social Work Research.* Thousand Oaks, CA: Sage.

Padilla, Amado M., and Antonio Medina. 1996. "Cross-Cultural Sensitivity in Assessment," pp. 3–28 in Lisa Suzuki, Paul J. Meller, and Joseph G. Ponterotto (eds.), *Handbook of Multicultural Assessment.* San Francisco: Jossey-Bass.

Parsons, Talcott, and Edward A. Shils. 1951. *Toward a General Theory of Action.* Cambridge, MA: Harvard University Press.

Patton, Michael Quinn. 1990. *Qualitative Evaluation and Research Methods,* 2nd ed. Newbury Park, CA: Sage.

Payne, Charles M. 1995. *I've Got the Light of Freedom: The Organizing Tradition and the Mississippi Freedom Struggle.* Berkeley: University of California Press.

Perinelli, Phillip J. 1986. "No Unsuspecting Public in TV Call-In Polls," *New York Times,* February 14, letter to the editor.

Perlman, David. 1982. "Fluoride, AIDS Experts Scoff at Nelder's Idea," *San Francisco Chronicle,* Sept. 6, p. 1.

Petersen, Larry R., and Judy L. Maynard. 1981. "Income, Equity, and Wives' Housekeeping Role Expectations," *Pacific Sociological Review* (January), 87–105.

Polansky, Norman A. 1975. *Social Work Research.* Chicago: University of Chicago Press.

———, Ronald Lippitt, and Fritz Redl. 1950. "An Investigation of Behavioral Contagion in Groups," *Human Relations, 3,* 319–348.

Polster, Richard A., and Mary A. Lynch. 1985. "Single-Subject Designs," pp. 381–431 in Richard M. Grinnell (ed.), *Social Work Research and Evaluation.* Itasca, IL: Peacock.

Population Reference Bureau. 1980. "1980 World Population Data Sheet." Poster prepared by Carl Haub and Douglas W. Heisler. Washington, DC: Population Reference Bureau.

Posavac, Emil J., and Raymond G. Carey. 1985. *Program Evaluation: Methods and Case Studies.* Englewood Cliffs, NJ: Prentice-Hall.

Potocky, Miriam, and Antoinette Y. Rodgers-Farmer (eds.). 1998. *Social Work Research with Minority and Oppressed Populations.* New York: Haworth Press.

Presser, Stanley, and Johnny Blair. 1994. "Survey Pretesting: Do Different Methods Produce Different Results?" pp. 73–104 in Peter Marsden (ed.), *Sociological Methodology.* San Francisco: Jossey-Bass.

Public Opinion. 1984. "See How They Ran" (Oct.–Nov.), 38–40.

Quay, H. C., and J. S. Werry. 1972. *Psychopathological Disorders of Childhood.* New York: Wiley.

Quoss, Bernita, Margaret Cooney, and Terri Longhurst. 2000. "Academics and Advocates: Using Participatory Action Research to Influence Welfare Policy," *Journal of Consumer Affairs, 34*(1), 47.

Rank, Mark. 1992. "The Blending of Qualitative and Quantitative Methods in Understanding Childbearing Among Welfare Recipients," pp. 281–300 in Jane Gilgun, Kerry Daly, and Gerald Handel (eds.), *Qualitative Methods in Family Research.* Thousand Oaks, CA: Sage.

———, and T. A. Hirschl. 2002. "Welfare Use as a Life Course Event: Toward a New Understanding of the U.S. Safety Net," *Social Work, 47*(3), 237–248.

Ransford, H. Edward. 1968. "Isolation, Powerlessness, and Violence: A Study of Attitudes and Participants in the Watts Riots," *American Journal of Sociology, 73,* 581–591.

Rasinski, Kenneth A. 1989. "The Effect of Question Wording on Public Support for Government Spending," *Public Opinion Quarterly, 53,* 388–394.

Ray, William, and Ravizza, Richard. 1993. *Methods Toward a Science of Behavior and Experience.* Belmont, CA: Wadsworth,

Reed, G.M. 2006. "What Qualifies as Evidence of Effective Practice? Clinical Expertise," pp. 13–23 in J. C. Norcross, L. E. Beutler, and R. F. Levant (eds.), *Evidence-Based Practices in Mental Health: Debate and Dialogue on the Fundamental Questions.* Washington, DC: American Psychological Association.

Reid, William J. 1997. "Evaluating the Dodo's Verdict: Do All Evaluations Have Equivalent Outcomes?" *Social Work Research, 21,* 5–18.

———, and Laura Epstein. 1972. *Task-Centered Casework.* New York: Columbia University Press.

———, and Patricia Hanrahan. 1982. "Recent Evaluations of Social Work: Grounds for Optimism," *Social Work,* 27(4), 328–340.

Reinharz, Shulamit. 1992. *Feminist Methods in Social Research.* New York: Oxford University Press.

Reissman, Catherine (ed.). 1994. *Qualitative Studies in Social Work Research.* Thousand Oaks, CA: Sage.

Reynolds, C. R., and R. W. Kamphaus (eds.). 1990. *Handbook of Psychological and Educational Assessment of Children.* New York: Guilford Press.

Richmond, Mary. 1917. *Social Diagnosis.* New York: Russell Sage Foundation.

Roberts, Albert R., and Gilbert J. Greene (eds.). 2002. *Social Workers' Desk Reference*. New York: Oxford University Press.

Roberts, Albert R., and K. R. Yeager (eds.). 2004. *Evidence-Based Practice Manual: Research and Outcome Measures in Health and Human Services*. New York: Oxford University Press.

——— (eds.). 2006. *Foundations of Evidence-Based Social Work Practice*. New York: Oxford University Press.

Roberts, Michael C., and Linda K. Hurley. 1997. *Managing Managed Care*. New York: Plenum Press.

Robinson, Robin A. 1994. "Private Pain and Public Behaviors: Sexual Abuse and Delinquent Girls," pp. 73–94 in Catherine Reissman (ed.), *Qualitative Studies in Social Work Research*. Thousand Oaks, CA: Sage.

Rodwell, Mary K. 1987. "Naturalistic Inquiry: An Alternative Model for Social Work Assessment," *Social Service Review, 61*(2), 232–246.

———. 1998. *Social Work Constructivist Research*. New York: Garland.

Roethlisberger, F. J., and W. J. Dickson. 1939. *Management and the Worker*. Cambridge, MA: Harvard University Press.

Roffman, R. A., L. Downey, B. Beadnell, J. R. Gordon, J. N. Craver, and R. S. Stephens. 1997. "Cognitive-Behavioral Group Counseling to Prevent HIV Transmission in Gay and Bisexual Men: Factors Contributing to Successful Risk Reduction," *Research on Social Work Practice, 7*, 165–186.

Roffman, Roger A., Joseph Picciano, Lauren Wickizer, Marc Bolan, and Rosemary Ryan. 1998. "Anonymous Enrollment in AIDS Prevention Telephone Group Counseling: Facilitating the Participation of Gay and Bisexual Men in Intervention and Research," pp. 5–22 in Miriam Potocky and Antoinette Y. Rodgers-Farmer (eds.), *Social Work Research with Minority and Oppressed Populations: Methodological Issues and Innovations*. New York: Haworth Press.

Rogler, Lloyd H. 1989. "The Meaning of Culturally Sensitive Research in Mental Health," *American Journal of Psychiatry, 146*(3), 296–303.

———, and A. B. Hollingshead. 1985. *Trapped: Puerto Rican Families and Schizophrenia*. Maplewood, NJ: Waterfront Press.

Rosenberg, Morris. 1965. *Society and the Adolescent Self-Image*. Princeton, NJ: Princeton University Press.

———. 1968. *The Logic of Survey Analysis*. New York: Basic Books.

Rosenhan, D. L. 1973. "On Being Sane in Insane Places," *Science*, 179, 240–248.

Rosenthal, Richard N. 2006. "Overview of Evidence-Based Practice," in A. R. Roberts and K. Yeager (eds.), *Foundations of Evidence-Based Social Work Practice*. New York: Oxford University Press, 67–80.

Rosenthal, Robert, and Donald Rubin. 1982. "A Simple, General Purpose Display of Magnitude of Experimental Effect," *Journal of Educational Psychology, 74*(2), 166–169.

Rossi, Peter H., and Howard E. Freeman. 1982. *Evaluation: A Systematic Approach*. Beverly Hills, CA: Sage.

———. 1993. *Evaluation: A Systematic Approach*, 5th ed. Newbury Park, CA: Sage Publications.

Rothman, Ellen K. 1981. "The Written Record," *Journal of Family History* (Spring), 47–56.

Rowntree, Derek. 1981. *Statistics Without Tears: A Primer for Non-Mathematicians*. New York: Charles Scribner's Sons.

Royse, David. 1988. "Voter Support for Human Services," *ARETE, 13*(2), 26–34.

———. 1991. *Research Methods in Social Work*. Chicago: Nelson-Hall.

Rubin, Allen. 1979. *Community Mental Health in the Social Work Curriculum*. New York: Council on Social Work Education.

———. 1981. "Reexamining the Impact of Sex on Salary: The Limits of Statistical Significance," *Social Work Research & Abstracts, 17*(3), 19–24.

———. 1983. "Engaging Families as Support Resources in Nursing Home Care: Ambiguity in the Subdivision of Tasks," *Gerontologist, 23*(6), 632–636.

———. 1985a. "Practice Effectiveness: More Grounds for Optimism," *Social Work, 30*(6), 469–476.

———. 1985b. "Significance Testing with Population Data," *Social Service Review, 59*(3), 518–520.

———. 1987. "Case Management," *Encyclopedia of Social Work*, 18th ed. Silver Spring, MD: National Association of Social Work, vol. 1, pp. 212–222.

———. 1990. "Cable TV as a Resource in Preventive Mental Health Programming for Children: An Illustration of the Importance of Coupling Implementation and Outcome Evaluation," *ARETE, 15*(2), 26–31.

———. 1991. "The Effectiveness of Outreach Counseling and Support Groups for Battered Women: A Preliminary Evaluation," *Research on Social Work Practice, 1*(4), 332–357.

———. 1992. "Is Case Management Effective for People with Serious Mental Illness? A Research Review," *Health and Social Work, 17*(2), 138–150.

———. 1997. "The Family Preservation Evaluation from Hell: Implications for Program Evaluation Fidelity," *Children and Youth Services Review, 19*(1–2), 77–99.

———. 2002. "Is EMDR an Evidence-based Practice for Treating PTSD? Unanswered Questions," Paper presented at the annual conference of the Society for Social Work and Research, San Diego, January 18.

———. 2007. *Statistics for Evidence-Based Practice and Evaluation*. Belmont, CA: Thomson Brooks/Cole.

———, S. Bischofshausen, K. Conroy-Moore, B. Dennis, M. Hastie, L. Melnick, D. Reeves, and T. Smith. 2001. "The Effectiveness of EMDR in a Child Guidance Center," *Research on Social Work Practice, 11*(4), 435–457.

———, Jose Cardenas, Keith Warren, Cathy King Pike, and Kathryn Wambach. 1998. "Outdated Practitioner Views about Family Culpability and Severe Mental Disorders," *Social Work*, September, 412–422.

———, and Patricia G. Conway. 1985. "Standards for Determining the Magnitude of Relationships in Social Work Research," *Social Work Research & Abstracts, 21*(1), 34–39.

———, Patricia G. Conway, Judith K. Patterson, and Richard T. Spence. 1983. "Sources of Variation in Rate of Decline to MSW Programs," *Journal of Education for Social Work, 19*(3), 48–58.

———, and Peter J. Johnson. 1982. "Practitioner Orientations Toward the Chronically Disabled: Prospects for Policy Implementation," *Administration in Mental Health, 10*, 3–12.

———, and Peter J. Johnson. 1984. "Direct Practice Interests of Entering MSW Students," *Journal of Education for Social Work, 20*(2), 5–16.

———, and Guy E. Shuttlesworth. 1982. "Assessing Role Expectations in Nursing Home Care," *ARETE, 7*(2), 37–48.

———, and Irene Thorelli. 1984. "Egoistic Motives and Longevity of Participation by Social Service Volunteers," *Journal of Applied Behavioral Science, 20*(3), 223–235.

Rubin, Herbert J., and Riene S. Rubin. 1995. *Qualitative Interviewing: The Art of Hearing Data*. Thousand Oaks, CA: Sage.

Ruckdeschel, Roy A., and B. E. Faris. 1981. "Assessing Practice: A Critical Look at the Single-Case Design," *Social Casework, 62,* 413–419.

Rutter, M., H. H. Tuma, and I. S. Lann (eds.). 1988. *Assessment and Diagnosis in Child Psychopathology.* New York: Guilford Press.

Sackett, D. L., W. S. Richardson, W. Rosenberg, and R. B. Haynes. 1997. *Evidence-Based Medicine: How to Practice and Teach EBM.* New York: Churchill Livingstone.

———. 2000. *Evidence-Based Medicine: How to Practice and Teach EBM* (2nd ed.). New York: Churchill Livingstone.

Sacks, Jeffrey J., W. Mark Krushat, and Jeffrey Newman. 1980. "Reliability of the Health Hazard Appraisal," *American Journal of Public Health* (July): 730–732.

Sales, Esther, Sara Lichtenwalter, and Antonio Fevola. 2006. "Secondary Analysis in Social Work Research Education: Past, Present, and Future Promise," *Journal of Social Work Education, 42*(3), 543–558.

Saletan, William, and Nancy Watzman. 1989. "Marcus Welby, J. D." *New Republic, 200*(16), 22.

Sandelowski, M., D. H. Holditch-Davis, and B. G. Harris. 1989. "Artful Design: Writing the Proposal for Research in the Naturalistic Paradigm," *Research in Nursing and Health, 12,* 77–84.

Sarnoff, S. K. 1999. "'Sanctified Snake Oil': Ideology, Junk Science, and Social Work Practice," *Families in Society, 80,* 396–408.

Sattler, J. M. 1988. *Assessment of Children* (3rd ed.). Brandon, VT: Clinical Psychology Publishing.

Sawin, K. J., M. P. Harrigan, and P. Woog (eds.). 1995. *Measures of Family Functioning for Research and Practice.* New York: Springer.

Scholl, G., and R. Schnur. 1976. *Measures of Psychological, Vocational, and Educational Functioning in the Blind and Visually Handicapped.* New York: American Foundation for the Blind.

Schuerman, John. 1989. "Editorial," *Social Service Review, 63*(1), 3.

Selltiz, Claire, Lawrence S. Wrightsman, and Stuart W. Cook. 1976. *Research Methods in Social Relations.* New York: Holt, Rinehart and Winston.

Shadish, William R., Thomas D. Cook, and Donald T. Campbell. 2001. *Experimental and Quasi-experimental Designs for Generalized Causal Inference.* New York: Houghton Mifflin.

Shadish, William R., Thomas D. Cook, and Laura C. Leviton. 1991. *Foundations of Program Evaluation.* Newbury Park, CA: Sage.

Shaffir, William B., and Robert A. Stebbins (eds.). 1991. *Experiencing Fieldwork: An Inside View of Qualitative Research.* Newbury Park, CA: Sage.

Shanks, J. Merrill, and Robert D. Tortora. 1985. "Beyond CATI: Generalized and Distributed Systems for Computer-Assisted Surveys." Prepared for the Bureau of the Census, First Annual Research Conference, Reston, VA, March 20–23.

Silverman, David. 1993. *Interpreting Qualitative Data: Methods for Analyzing Talk, Text, and Interaction.* Newbury Park, CA: Sage.

———. 1999. *Doing Qualitative Research: A Practical Handbook.* Thousand Oaks, CA: Sage.

Simon, Cassandra E., John S. McNeil, Cynthia Franklin, and Abby Cooperman. 1991. "The Family and Schizophrenia: Toward a Psychoeducational Approach." *Families in Society, 72*(6), 323–333.

Smith, Andrew E., and G. F. Bishop. 1992. "The Gallup Secret Ballot Experiments: 1944–1988." Paper presented at the annual conference of the American Association for Public Opinion Research, St. Petersburg, FL, May.

Smith, Eric R.A.N., and Peverill Squire. 1990. "The Effects of Prestige Names in Question Wording," *Public Opinion Quarterly 54,* 97–116.

Smith, Joel. 1991. "A Methodology for Twenty-First Century Sociology," *Social Forces, 70*(1), 117.

Smith, Mary Lee, and Gene V. Glass. 1977. "Meta-analysis of Psychotherapy Outcome Studies," *American Psychologist, 32*(9), 752–760.

Smith, Tom W. 1988. "The First Straw? A Study of the Origins of Election Polls," *Public Opinion Quarterly, 54* (Spring), 21–36.

Snow, David A., and Leon Anderson. 1987. "Identity Work among the Homeless: The Verbal Construction and Avowal of Personal Identities," *Journal of Sociology, 92*(6), 1336–1371.

Sodowsky, Gargi Roysircar, and James C. Impara (eds.). 1996. *Multicultural Assessment in Counseling and Clinical Psychology.* Lincoln, NE: Buros Institute of Mental Measurements.

Solomon, Phyllis, and Robert I. Paulson. 1995. "Issues in Designing and Conducting Randomized Human Service Trials." Paper presented at the National Conference of the Society for Social Work and Research, Washington, DC.

Srole, Leo. 1956. "Social Integration and Certain Corollaries: An Exploratory Study," *American Sociological Review, 21,* 709–716.

Stouffer, Samuel. 1962. *Social Research to Test Ideas.* New York: Free Press of Glencoe.

Strachan, Angus M. 1986. "Family Intervention for the Rehabilitation of Schizophrenia: Toward Protection and Coping," *Schizophrenia Bulletin, 12*(4), 678–698.

Straus, M., and B. Brown. 1978. *Family Measurement Techniques: Abstracts of Published Instruments.* Minneapolis: University of Minnesota Press.

Strauss, Anselm, and Juliet Corbin. 1990. *Basics of Qualitative Research: Grounded Theory Procedures and Techniques.* Newbury Park, CA: Sage.

———. 1994. "Grounded Theory Methodology: An Overview," pp. 273–285 in *Handbook of Qualitative Research,* Norman K. Denzin and Yvonna S. Lincoln (eds.). Thousand Oaks, CA: Sage.

Stuart, Paul. 1981. "Historical Research," pp. 316–332 in Richard M. Grinnell, *Social Work Research and Evaluation.* Itasca, IL: Peacock.

Sudman, Seymour. 1983. "Applied Sampling," pp. 145–194 in Peter H. Rossi, James D. Wright, and Andy B. Anderson (eds.), *Handbook of Survey Research.* New York: Academic Press.

Sue, Stanley. 1996. "Measurement, Testing, and Ethnic Bias: Can Solutions be Found?" pp. 7–36 in Gargi Roysircar Sodowsky and James C. Impara (eds.), *Multicultural Assessment in Counseling and Clinical Psychology.* Lincoln, NE: Buros Institute of Mental Measurements.

Suzuki, Lisa A., Paul J. Meller, and Joseph G. Ponterotto (eds.). 1996. *Handbook of Multicultural Assessment.* San Francisco: Jossey-Bass.

Sweet, Stephen. 1999. "Using a Mock Institutional Review Board to Teach Ethics in Sociological Research," *Teaching Sociology, 27* (January): 55–59.

Taber, Sara M. 1981. "Cognitive-Behavior Modification Treatment of an Aggressive 11-Year-Old Boy," *Social Work Research & Abstracts, 17*(2), 13–23.

Takeuchi, David. 1974. *Grass in Hawaii: A Structural Constraints Approach.* M.A. thesis, University of Hawaii.

Tan, Alexis S. 1980. "Mass Media Use, Issue Knowledge and Political Involvement," *Public Opinion Quarterly, 44,* 241–248.

Tandon, Rajesh, and L. Dave Brown. 1981. "Organization-Building for Rural Development: An Experiment in India," *Journal of Applied Behavioral Science* (April–June), 172–189.

Task Force on the Promotion and Dissemination of Psychological Procedures. 1995. "Training in and Dissemination of Empirically-Validated Psychosocial Treatments: Report and Recommendations." *Clinical Psychologist,* 48, 3–23.

Taylor, Humphrey, and George Terhanian, 1999. "Heady Days Are Here Again: Online Polling Is Rapidly Coming of Age," *Public Perspective, 10*(4), 20–23.

Taylor, James B. 1977. "Toward Alternative Forms of Social Work Research: The Case for Naturalistic Methods," *Journal of Social Welfare, 4,* 119–126.

Thomas, W. I., and Florian Znaniecki. 1918. *The Polish Peasant in Europe and America.* Chicago: University of Chicago Press.

Thompson, Bruce. 1999a. "Improving Research Clarity and Usefulness with Effect Size Indices as Supplements to Statistical Significance Tests," *Exceptional Children, 65*(3), 329–337.

———. 1999b. "Why Encouraging Effect Size Reporting Is Not Working: The Etiology of Researcher Resistance to Changing Practices," *Journal of Psychology, 133*(2), 133–140.

Thompson, Estina E., Harold W. Neighbors, Cheryl Munday, and James S. Jackson. 1996. "Recruitment and Retention of African American Patients for Clinical Research: An Exploration of Response Rates in an Urban Psychiatric Hospital," *Journal of Consulting and Clinical Psychology, 64*(5), 861–867.

Thomson, Bill. 1996. Letter on Push Polling. Letter posted May 29 to the AAPORnet listserv [Online]. Available: billt@pos.org.

Thyer, Bruce. 2001. "Evidence-Based Approaches to Community Practice," pp. 54–65 in Harold E. Briggs and Kevin Corcoran (eds.), *Social Work Practice: Treating Common Client Problems.* Chicago: Lyceum Books.

———. 2002. "Principles of Evidence-Based Practice and Treatment Development," pp. 738–742 in Albert R. Roberts and Gilbert J. Greene (eds.), *Social Workers' Desk Reference.* New York: Oxford University Press.

Tobler, N. S. 1986. "Meta-analysis of 143 Adolescent Drug Prevention Programs: Quantitative Outcome Results of Program Participants Compared to a Control or Comparison Group," *Journal of Drug Issues, 4,* 537–567.

Todd, Tracy. 1998. "Co-constructing Your Business Relationship," pp. 323–347 in Cynthia Franklin and Paula Nurius, *Constructivism in Practice: Methods and Challenges.* Milwaukee, WI: Families International.

Touliatos, J., B. F. Perlmutter, and M. A. Straus (eds.). 1990. *Handbook of Family Measurement Techniques.* Newbury Park, CA: Sage.

Tuckel, Peter S., and Barry M. Feinberg. 1991. "The Answering Machine Poses Many Questions for Telephone Survey Researchers," *Public Opinion Quarterly, 55,* 200–217.

Turk, Theresa Guminski. 1980. "Hospital Support: Urban Correlates of Allocation Based on Organizational Prestige," *Pacific Sociological Review* (July), 315–332.

Turner, Jonathan. 1974. *The Structure of Sociological Theory.* Homewood, IL: Dorsey Press.

U.S. Bureau of the Census. 1979. *Statistical Abstract of the United States.* Washington, DC: U.S. Government Printing Office.

———. 1992. *Statistical Abstract of the United States.* Washington, DC: U.S. Government Printing Office.

———. 1995. *Statistical Abstract of the United States.* Washington, DC: U.S. Government Printing Office.

———. 1996. *Statistical Abstract of the United States, 1996, National Data Book and Guide to Sources.* Washington, DC: U.S. Government Printing Office.

———. 2006. *Statistical Abstract of the United States, 2006, National Data Book and Guide to Sources.* Washington, DC: U.S. Government Printing Office.

U.S. Department of Health and Human Services. 1992. *Survey Measurement of Drug Use.* Washington, DC: U.S. Government Printing Office.

U.S. Department of Labor (Bureau of Labor Statistics). 1978. *The Consumer Price Index: Concepts and Content Over the Years.* Report 517. Washington, DC: U.S. Government Printing Office.

Videka-Sherman, Lynn. 1988. "Meta-analysis of Research on Social Work Practice in Mental Health," *Social Work, 33*(4), 325–338.

Vonk, M. Elizabeth. 2001. "Cultural Competence for Transracial Adoptive Parents," *Social Work, 46*(3), 246–255.

Votaw, Carmen Delgado. 1979. *Women's Rights in the United States.* United States Commission of Civil Rights, Inter-American Commission on Women. Washington, DC: Clearinghouse Publications.

Wagner-Pacifici, Robin. 1995. *Discourse and Destruction: The City of Philadelphia versus MOVE.* Chicago: University of Chicago Press.

Walker, D. K. 1973. *Socioemotional Measure for Preschool and Kindergarten Children.* San Francisco: Jossey-Bass.

Walker, Janice R., and Todd Taylor. 1998. *The Columbia Guide to Online Style.* New York: Columbia University Press.

Walker, Jeffery T. 1994. "Fax Machines and Social Surveys: Teaching an Old Dog New Tricks," *Journal of Quantitative Criminology, 10*(2), 181–188.

Walker Research. 1988. *Industry Image Study,* 8th ed. Indianapolis: Walker Research.

Wallace, Walter. 1971. *The Logic of Science in Sociology.* Chicago: Aldine-Atherton.

Walster, Elaine, Jane Piliavian, and G. William Walster. 1973. "The Hard-to-Get Woman," *Psychology Today* (September), 80–83.

Webb, Eugene, Donald T. Campbell, Richard D. Schwartz, and Lee Sechrest. 1981. *Nonreactive Research in the Social Sciences.* Chicago: Rand McNally.

———. 2000. *Unobtrusive Measures.* Thousand Oaks, CA: Sage.

Weber, Max. 1925. "Science as a Vocation," in Hans Gerth and C. Wright Mills (trans., eds.) (1946), *From Max Weber: Essays in Sociology.* New York: Oxford University Press.

Weber, Robert Philip. 1990. *Basic Content Analysis.* Newbury Park, CA: Sage.

Weinbach, Robert, and Richard Grinnell. 1998. *Statistics for Social Workers,* 4th ed. New York: Longman.

Weisbrod, Burton A., Mary Ann Test, and Leonard I. Stein. 1980. "Alternative to Mental Hospital Treatment: II. Economic Benefit-Cost Analysis," *Archives of General Psychiatry, 37*(4), 400–408.

Weiss, Carol H. 1972. *Evaluation Research.* Englewood Cliffs, NJ: Prentice Hall.

Westen, D. I. 2006. "Patients and treatments in clinical trials are not adequately representative of clinical practice," pp. 161–171 in J. C. Norcross, L. E. Beutler, and R. F. Levant (eds.), *Evidence-Based Practices in Mental Health: Debate and Dialogue on the Fundamental Questions*. Washington, DC: American Psychological Association.

Wetzler, S. (ed.). 1989. *Measuring Mental Illness: Psychometric Assessment for Clinicians*. Washington, DC: American Psychiatric Press.

White, Karl R. 1988. "Cost Analyses in Family Support Programs," pp. 429–443 in Heather B. Weiss and Francine H. Jacobs (eds.), *Evaluating Family Programs*. New York: Aldine de Gruyter.

White, Ralph. 1951. *Value-Analysis: The Nature and Use of the Method*. New York: Society for the Psychological Study of Social Issues.

Whiteman, Martin, David Fanshel, and John F. Grundy. 1987. "Cognitive-Behavioral Interventions Aimed at Anger of Parents at Risk of Child Abuse," *Social Work, 32*(6), 469–474.

Whittaker, James K. 1987. "Group Care for Children," *Encyclopedia of Social Work,* 18th ed., vol. 1, pp. 672–682. Silver Spring, MD: National Association of Social Workers.

Whyte, William Foote. 1943. *Street Corner Society*. Chicago: University of Chicago Press.

———, D. J. Greenwood, and P. Lazes. 1991. "Participatory Action Research: Through Practice to Science in Social Research," pp. 19–55 in W. F. Whyte (ed.), *Participatory Action Research*. New York: Sage.

Williams, Janet, and Kathleen Ell. 1998. *Advances in Mental Health Research: Implications for Practice*. Washington, DC: NASW Press.

Wilson, Camilo, 1999. Private e-mail, September 8.

Wilson, Jerome. 1989. "Cancer Incidence and Mortality Differences of Black and White Americans: A Role for Biomarkers," in Lovell Jones (ed.), *Minorities and Cancer*. New York: Springer-Verlag.

Wood, Katherine M. 1978. "Casework Effectiveness: A New Look at the Research Evidence," *Social Work, 23*(6), 437–458.

Yin, Robert K. 1984. *Case Study Research: Design and Methods*. Beverly Hills, CA: Sage.

Yinger, J. Milton, Kiyoshi Ikeda, Frank Laycock, and Stephen J. Cutler. 1977. *Middle Start: An Experiment in the Educational Enrichment of Young Adolescents*. London: Cambridge University Press.

York, James, and Elmer Persigehl. 1981. "Productivity Trends in the Ball and Roller Bearing Industry," *Monthly Labor Review* (January), 40–43.

Yoshihama, Mieko. 2002. "Breaking the Web of Abuse and Silence: Voices of Battered Women in Japan," *Social Work, 47*(4), 389–400.

Yu, Elena S. H., Zhang Ming-Yuan, et al. 1987. "Translation of Instruments: Procedures, Issues, and Dilemmas," pp. 75–83 in W. T. Liu (ed.), *A Decade Review of Mental Health Research, Training, and Services*. Pacific/Asian American Mental Health Research Center.

Ziesel, Hans. 1957. *Say It with Figures*. New York: Harper & Row.

Zimbalist, Sidney E. 1977. *Historic Themes and Landmarks in Social Welfare Research*. New York: Harper & Row.

Zippay, Allison. 2002. "Dynamics of Income Packaging: A 10-Year Longitudinal Study," *Social Work, 47,* 291–300.

Zlotnik, J. L., and C. Galambos. 2004. "Evidence-Based Practices in Health Care: Social Work Possibilities," *Health and Social Work, 29,* 259–261.

Index

Note: Page numbers in italics indicate figures or tables.